◆ PROPERTY AND LAW

ATTENTION!
ANTI-RENTERS!
AWAKE! AROUSE!

A Meeting of the friends of Equal Rights will be held on *Second Tuesday – February at Court House*

in the Town of *Rensse —* at / O'clock.

Let the opponents of Patroonry rally in their strength. A great crisis is approaching. Now is the time to strike. The minions of Patroonry are at work. No time is to be lost. Awake! Arouse! and

Strike 'till the last armed foe expires,
Strike for your altars and your fires—
Strike for the green graves of your sires,
God and your happy homes!

☞ **The Meeting will be addressed by PETER FINKLE and other Speakers.**

Poster in New York State Library, Albany

◆ PROPERTY AND LAW

Second Edition

CHARLES M. HAAR
Louis D. Brandeis Professor of Law, Harvard University

LANCE LIEBMAN
Professor of Law, Harvard University

Little, Brown and Company   *Boston and Toronto*

Library of Congress Catalog Card No. 84-81025

ISBN 0-316-336823

Second Printing

HAM

Published simultaneously in Canada
by Little, Brown & Company (Canada) Limited

Printed in the United States of America

♦ SUMMARY OF CONTENTS

◆ TABLE OF CONTENTS

◆ PREFACE TO SECOND EDITION

This book now has the benefit of advice from many property teaching colleagues around the country, and also from a great many law students. We appreciate the feedback because on the whole it told us that students enjoyed the book, or at least the pictures. But we also heard about errors, omissions, confusions, and imprecisions. For this edition, we tried to correct and improve the original. We of course updated material; however, we also moved in new directions based on our observation of developments in this most fascinating field of doctrinal and institutional controversy.

Again, we had a great deal of help. Eve G. Penoyer, Louis Treiger, Craig Tyle, and Luci Daley Vincent assisted with imaginative research and editing. Enice Matera and Marilyn McLeod supported both the manuscript and the authors. At Little, Brown & Company, John Bergin, Nancy Campbell, Maureen Kaplan, Mary Ann Lane, and Bonnie Wood worked hard to make a book that would help students learn.

Charles M. Haar
Lance Liebman

February, 1985

◆ PREFACE TO FIRST EDITION

For many decades and at many law schools, the course in property law has been regarded as the most interesting and the most challenging of the basic subjects. An important reason is that the law of property is directly concerned with the nerve centers of society — with the acquisition, maintenance, and disposition of wealth, and so of power and status. As a result, its elegant conceptual structures are routinely invaded by an inelegant reality, and the resulting tension between theory and practice, between past and future, and between ideal and real assures property courses that are fascinating and difficult.

Property is created by scarcity. Thus property law is concerned with socially acknowledged claims to limited resources. Occasionally, this concern involves institutional arrangements for permitting property shares to be transferred efficiently. To that extent, Property is merely an instance of contract law. Usually, however, property rules perform a different function. They define and announce sanctioned arrangements for conducting human relationships affecting things. For example, the mortgage — the sophisticated arrangement by which money is borrowed against land — is not principally a negotiated secured loan. Rather, it is a transaction that is highly regularized — and has been so for more than 500 years because society has recognized the weakness of borrowers and the power of lenders and has said that this transaction should go forward only under prescribed terms. In most jurisdictions today, the lease from an urban landlord to a poor residential tenant is similarly regulated. Such standardized and directed relationships pose questions of social theory: of what sorts of relationships are proper, based on what deeper ideas of social claim and social obligation. They pose questions of economic doctrine: of limits, grounded in economic reality, upon the capacity of legislation to redistribute (or even control) power by such rules. They ask questions about politics: of institutional arrangements for deciding when public intervention should restrict the arrangements that individuals and groups can make. And they raise issues of social change, as new ideas develop, and as deference to prior truth, grounded in the underlying commitment to property, comes into conflict with new ideas.

Property law shows us ourselves. Its doctrines manifest the needs, aspirations, and expectations of groups and of individuals, meanwhile exerting pressure for change in social practice. Property law shapes society, its dominion extending to the most intimate relations: to parent and child, husband and wife, landlord and tenant, neighbor and neighborhood, as well as to the core structures of national and local government. At the same time, its doctrines have always been modified for society's collective ends. English property rules underwent dramatic changes when they were applied in Colonial America. The laws were further transformed as they were extended to the different physical and social circumstances in the West. Today, new changes are in process, as — for example — doctrines adopted in an age that perceived the need to build, develop, and consume are being modified in a historical period requiring preservation and conservation. Property's interplay between continuity and change is illustrated too in its traditional concern with interests more important than money. Property defines one's place in society, whether the place identified by relations to the land in feudal England or the place signified by job and pension in urban America. Also, property represents position in government. In England, freeholders could vote; today, residents of suburban America vote on zoning rules that affect inner-city residents who have no voice in the suburban decision. Property means the power to say who can be one's neighbor.

Thus, Property, more than the other introductory courses in law, manifests the law's interconnectedness with economic structures and political conflict. It deals with the questions of who keeps the fox hunted on a wild wasteland and of who gets the electric power dependent upon the fall of the Mississippi. Moreover, it deals with the ownership of Blackstone's "Blackacre," now turned into a low-income housing project, syndicated among doctors and dentists, financed by a state housing agency, underwritten by Wall Street, subsidized by the general taxpayer, serviced by a local government, appropriated for by a congressional subcommittee, supervised by a public corporation, and packaged by a developer. These new combinations of use, ownership, and reward raise fundamental questions concerning the relationship of law to society. Who gets what, and with what degree of legitimacy? The words of Holmes haunt us: "A man cannot create a new kind of inheritance." True, the basic estates remain fixed at common law, but what society does with them changes, and has far-reaching effects, identifying those who become enriched and those who are ultimately impoverished, and thereby shaping the very nature of the society. Property is a fundamental category of man's being and thought, and property law is the law of consequences, capable of being tested and recreated in the struggle for more appropriate consequences.

This book seeks to capture some of the vitality of its subject. Standard cases, statutes, and devices appear, as landmarks from which students and instructors can reach out. The materials are historical, seeking to convey the substance of earlier clashes over wealth and status not unlike those in which lawyers participate today. And even first-year students can begin to *use* doctrine: to plan the "new town" of Columbia, Maryland; and to work out the income tax consequences of investing in Manhattan's Sutton Townhouse or Buffalo's Harborview; to struggle with the alteration of landlord-tenant law in the District of Columbia. Property law is exciting to practice, and witnessing even a bit of that excitement can make it more interesting to learn.

Learning the law of property is a step toward professional participation in some of the most challenging public issues that will arise during the remainder of the twentieth century. Inevitably the materials and combinations of property law will continue the process of change and synthesis over time. The vessel of property law remains to be filled with the needs and desires of each succeeding age. This is the challenge raised by these materials — as it was raised in 1765 when property law was conceptualized for that century by William Blackstone: "We inherit an old Gothic castle, erected in the days of chivalry, but fitted up for a modern inhabitant. The moated ramparts, the embattled towers, and the trophied halls, are magnificent and venerable, but useless. The interior apartments, now converted into rooms of convenience, are chearful and commodious, though their approaches are winding and difficult."

No casebook authors have ever had such imaginative and diligent help from others. Nearly 1,000 first-year students have struggled with drafts of these materials and have not been reticent in demanding improvement. Mark Greenberg, Frank Gruber, Jim Kahn, Natalie Lichtenstein, and Ed Tuddenham accepted the challenge to do more than criticize, undertaking significant efforts of research and editing. At an early stage, Michael Spencer prepared the income tax note in Chapter 15. Photos were taken by Stephanie Smith and Rich Johnston. Typing, coordination, and solace came from Karen Dilts, Sally Fitzgerald, Pamela Huling, and Linda Ciano Mirabella. At Little, Brown & Company, Nancy Campbell, Cathy Corey, Stephen St. Clair, and Janet Bryan helped immensely. As usual, the authors made all the mistakes.

◆ DEFINITIONS

Blackstone, *Commentaries on the Laws of England,* book II, Chap. 1, p.2 (1765): "There is nothing which so generally strikes the imagination, and engages the affections of mankind, as the right of property or that sole and despotic dominion which one man claims and exercises over the external things of the world, in total exclusion of the right of any other individual in the universe."

French Civil Code, Article 544 (1804): "Ownership is the right to enjoy and dispose of things in the most absolute manner, provided they are not used in a way contrary to law or regulations."

P. J. Proudhon, What is Property? p.15 (1840): "Yes: all men believe and repeat that equality of conditions is identical with equality of rights; that property and robbery are synonymous terms; that every social advantage accorded, or rather usurped, in the name of superior talent or service, is iniquity and extortion."

German Civil Code, Article 903 (1900): "The owner of a thing may, insofar as neither the law nor the rights of third parties prevent it, dispose of the thing at his pleasure and exclude others from any influence."

Restatement of Property, Chap. 1, Introductory Note (1936): "The word 'property' is used in this Restatement to denote legal relations between persons with respect to a thing."

Walton Hamilton, "Property," Encyclopedia of Social Sciences, vol. 11, p.528 (1937 ed.): "Property is a euphonious collection of letters which serves as a general term for the miscellany of equities that persons hold in the commonwealth."

New York Times, September 17, 1959, p.18, col. 6 (at the National Press Club):
Question: "Does the sending of the emblem indicate any desire to claim possession of the moon?"
Khrushchev: "I do not want to offend anybody, but we represent different continents and different psychologies, and I would say this question reflects capitalist psychology, of a person thinking in terms of private ownership.

"But I represent a Socialist country, where the word 'mine' has long receded in the past and the word 'our' has taken its place, and therefore when we launched this rocket and achieved this great thing, we look upon this as our victory, meaning the victory not only of our country but of all countries, of all mankind."

Margaret Jane Radin, Property and Personhood, 34 Stan. L. Rev. 957 (1982): "[T]o achieve proper self-development — to be a *person* — an individual needs some control over resources in the external environment. The necessary assurances of control take the form of property rights. Although explicit elaboration of this perspective is wanting in modern writing on property, the personhood perspective is often implicit in the connections that courts and commentators find between property and privacy or between property and liberty. In addition to its power to explain certain aspects of existing schemes of property entitlement, the personhood perspective can also serve as an explicit source of values for making moral distinctions in property disputes, and hence for either justifying or criticizing current law."

◆ PROPERTY AND LAW

I ◆ PRIVATE PROPERTY

What is property?

Property law, according to one modern definition, is concerned with relations among persons with respect to things. Thus the rules and doctrines surrounding property are part of the process by which people subjugate, divide, use, improve, enjoy, consume, and alter the planet on which they live. Persons inevitably relate to each other in competing for resources, distributing the fruits of labor, staking claims and disputing their extent. Property law is thus a mechanism for bringing a degree of order to these relations, a mechanism whose rules change with alterations in economic practices and in the ideas that govern economic life. A society's shared thoughts about the relation between individual effort and its rewards, about an individual's legitimate claims to the social product, about appropriate relations within a family, and about the duty of the present generation to the future all interact with the society's legal system in the formation of property law.

In analyzing complex contemporary systems of allocating rights in things, it has often proved useful to imagine the primitive inception of property rights. Rousseau's "state of nature" and Rawls's "original position" are examples. Similarly, a traditional way to begin the study of property law is to consider the early steps by which individuals establish claims in the earth's bounty. There is, for example, a relation between the steps required to gain recognized ownership of a wild animal, and the steps that were necessary for a European country to take rights in part of the "new world." Similar issues are present in disputes between claimants to particular parcels of land or among users of a common source of water. In each situation, the rules, doctrines, and conceptions of property only have meaning within a social order — among individuals who share certain premises, and find it useful or correct to participate in certain institutions. Europe could divide America, but its division could bind only those who lived by Europe's rules.

1

If property starts with the first establishment of socially approved physical domination over some part of the natural world, then the nature of that domination — often called "occupancy" or "possession" — is important. Is possession different from ownership? Is ownership more sophisticated? Better? All of these subjects are considered in Part I, which explores basic concepts of property law and asks you to create an intellectual context for examining our society's present system of property rules.

1 ◆ SOVEREIGNTY

A. CHAIN OF TITLE: EUROPEAN VERSUS NATIVE AMERICAN

◆ JOHNSON v. M'INTOSH
21 U.S. (8 Wheat.) 543 (1823)

This was an action of ejectment for lands in the State and District of Illinois, claimed by the plaintiffs under a purchase and conveyance from the Piankeshaw Indians, and by the defendant, under a grant from the United States. . . . The case stated set out the following facts:

1st. That on the 23d of May, 1609, James I., King of England, by his letters patent of that date, under the great seal of England, did erect, form, and establish Robert, Earl of Salisbury, and others, his associates, in the letters patent named, and their successors, into a body corporate and politic, by the name and style of "The Treasurer and Company of Adventurers and Planters of the City of London, for the first Colony in Virginia," with perpetual succession, and power to make, have, and use a common seal; and did give, grant, and confirm unto this company, and their successors, under certain reservations and limitations in the letters patent expressed, "All the lands, countries, and territories, situate, lying, and being in that part of North America called Virginia, from the point of land called Cape or Point Comfort, all along the seacoast to the northward two hundred miles; and from the said Cape or Point Comfort, all along the seacoast to the southward, two hundred miles; and all that space and circuit of land lying from the seacoast of the precinct aforesaid, up into the land throughout from the sea, west and northwest; and also all the islands lying within one hundred miles, along the coast of both seas of the precinct aforesaid; with all the soil, grounds, rights, privileges, and appurtenances to these territories belonging, and in the letters patent particularly enumerated:" and did grant to this corporation, and their successors, various powers of government, in the letters patent particularly expressed. . . .

3d. That at the time of granting these letters patent, and of the discovery of the continent of North America by the Europeans, and during the whole intermediate time, the whole of the territory, in the letters patent described, except a small district on James River, where a settlement of Europeans had previously been made, was held, occupied, and possessed, in full sovereignty, by various independent tribes or nations of Indians, who were the sovereigns of their respective portions of the territory, and the absolute owners and proprietors of the soil; and who neither acknowledged nor owed any allegiance of obedience to any European sovereign or state whatever; and that in making settlements within this territory, and in all the other parts of North America, where settlements were made, under the authority of the English government, or by its subjects, the right of soil was previously obtained by purchase or conquest, from the particular Indian tribe or nation by which the soil was claimed and held; or the consent of such tribe or nation was secured.

4th. That in the year 1624, this corporation was dissolved by due course of law, and all its powers, together with its rights of soil and jurisdiction, under the letters patent in question, were revested in the crown of England; whereupon the colony became a royal government, with the same territorial limits and extent which had been established by the letters patent, and so continued until it became a free and independent State; except so far as its limits and extent were altered and curtailed by the treaty of February 10th, 1763, between Great Britain and France, and by the letters patent granted by the King of England for establishing the colonies of Carolina, Maryland, and Pennsylvania.

5th. That some time previous to the year 1756, the French government, laying a claim to the country west of the Allegheny or Appalachian mountains, on the Ohio and Mississippi rivers, and their branches, took possession of certain parts of it, with the consent of the several tribes or nations of Indians possessing and owning them; . . . and that the government of Great Britain, after complaining of these establishments as encroachments, and remonstrating against them at length, in the year 1756, took up arms to resist and repel them; which produced a war between those two nations, . . . and that on the 10th of February, 1763, this war was terminated by a definitive treaty of peace between Great Britain and France, and their allies, by which it was stipulated and agreed, that the river Mississippi, from its source to the Iberville, should forever after form the boundary between the dominions of Great Britain and those of France, in that part of North America, and between their respective allies there. . . .

10th. That on the 7th of October, 1763, the King of Great Britain made and published a proclamation, for the better regulation of the countries ceded to Great Britain by that treaty, [reserving, for the use of the Indians, "all the land and territories lying to the westward of the sources of the rivers which fall into the sea from the west and north-west," and forbidding all British subjects from making any purchases or settlements whatever, or taking possession of the reserved lands]. . . .

12th. That on the 5th of July, 1773, certain chiefs of the Illinois Indians, then jointly representing, acting for, and being duly authorized by that tribe . . . did, by their deed poll, duly executed and delivered, and bearing date on that day, at the post of Kaskaskias, then being a British military post, and at a public council there held by them, for and on behalf of the said Illinois nation of Indians, with William Murray, of the Illinois country, merchant, acting for himself and for Moses Franks and Jacob Franks, of London, in Great Britain, David Franks, John In-glis, Bernard Gratz, Michael Gratz, Alexander Ross, David Sproat, and James Milligan, all of Philadelphia, in the province of Pennsylvania; Moses Franks, Andrew Hamilton, William Hamilton, and Edmund Milne, of the same place; Joseph Simons, otherwise called Joseph Si-mon, and Levi Andrew Levi, of the town of Lancaster in Pennsylvania; Thomas Minshall, of York county, in the same province; Robert Callen-der and William Thompson, of Cumberland county, in the same prov-ince; John Campbell, of Pittsburgh, in the same province; and George Castles and James Ramsay of the Illinois country; and for a good and valuable consideration in the said deed stated, grant, bargain, sell, alien, lease, enfeoff, and confirm, to the said . . . their heirs and assigns forever, in severalty, or to George the Third, then king of Great Britain and Ireland, his heirs and successors, for the use, benefit, and behoof of the grantees, their heirs and assigns, in severalty, by whichever of those tenures they might most legally hold, all those two several tracts or parcels of land, situated, lying, and being within the limits of Virginia, on the east of the Mississippi, northwest of the Ohio, and west of the Great Miami, and thus butted. . . .

13th. That the consideration in this deed expressed, was of the value of 24,000 dollars, current money of the United States, and up-wards, and was paid and delivered, at the time of the execution of the deed, by William Murray, one of the grantees, in behalf of himself and the other grantees, to the Illinois Indians, who freely accepted it, and divided it among themselves. . . .

14th. That all the persons named as grantees in this deed, were, at the time of its execution, and long before, subjects of the crown of Great Britain, and residents of the several places named in the deed as their places of residence; and that they entered into the land, under and by virtue of the deed, and became seized as the law requires.

15th. That on the 18th of October, 1775, Tabac, and certain other Indians, all being chiefs of the Piankeshaws, and jointly representing, acting for, and duly authorized by that nation, in the manner stated above, did, by their deed poll, duly executed, and bearing date on the day last mentioned, at the post of Vincennes, otherwise called Post St. Vincent, then being a British military post, and at a public council there held by them, for and on behalf of the Piankeshaw Indians, with Louis Viviat, of the Illinois country, acting for himself, and for [others]; . . . and for good and valuable considerations, in the deed poll mentioned and enumerated, grant, bargain, sell, alien, enfeoff, release, ratify, and confirm to the said Louis Viviat, and the other persons last mentioned, their heirs and assigns, equally to be divided, or to George the Third, then king of Great Britain and Ireland, his heirs and successors, for the use, benefit, and behoof of all the above mentioned grantees, their heirs and assigns, in severalty, by whichever of those tenures they might most legally hold, all those two several tracts of land in the deed particularly described, situate, lying and being northwest of the Ohio, east of the Mississippi, and west of the Great Miami, within the limits of Virginia, and on both sides of the Ouabache, otherwise called the Wabash; . . .

16th. That the consideration in this deed expressed, was of the value of 31,000 dollars, current money of the United States, and upwards, and was paid and delivered at the time of the execution of the deed, by the grantee, Louis Viviat, in behalf of himself and the other grantees, to the Piankeshaw Indians, who freely accepted it, and divided it among themselves; . . . .

17th. That on the 6th of May, 1776, the colony of Virginia threw off its dependence on the crown and government of Great Britain, and declared itself an independent State and government, ...

18th. That on the 5th of October, 1778, the General Assembly of Virginia . . . did, by an act of Assembly of that date, entitled, "An act for establishing the county of Illinois, and for the more effectual protection and defense thereof," erect that country, with certain other portions of territory within the limits of the State, and northwest of the Ohio, into a county, by the name of the county of Illinois.

19th. That on the 20th of December, 1783, the State of Virginia, by an act of Assembly of that date, authorized their Delegates in the Congress of the United States, or such of them, to the number of three at least, as should be assembled in Congress, on behalf of the State, and by proper deeds or instruments in writing under their hands and seals, to convey, transfer, assign, and make over to the United States, in Congress assembled, for the benefit of the said States, all right, title, and claim, as well of soil as jurisdiction, which Virginia had to the territory or tract of country within her limits, as defined and prescribed by the letters patent of May 23d, 1609, and lying to the northwest of the Ohio; subject to certain limitations and conditions in the act prescribed and specified; and that on the 1st of March, 1784, Thomas Jefferson, Samuel

Hardy, Arthur Lee and James Monroe, then being four of the Delegates of Virginia to the Congress of the United States, did, by their deed poll, under their hands and seals, in pursuance and execution of the authority to them given by this act of Assembly, convey, transfer, assign, and make over to the United States, in Congress assembled, for the benefit of the said States, all right, title, and claim, as well of soil as jurisdiction, which that state had to the territory northwest of the Ohio, with the reservations, limitations, and conditions, in the act of Assembly prescribed; which cession the United States accepted.

20th. That on the twentieth day of July, in the year of our Lord one thousand eight hundred and eighteen, the United States, by their officers duly authorized for that purpose, did sell, grant, and convey to the defendant in this action, William M'Intosh, all those several tracts or parcels of land, containing 11,560 acres, and butted, bounded, and described, as will fully appear in and by the patent for the said lands, duly executed, which was set out at length.

21st. That the lands described and granted in and by this patent, are situated within the State of Illinois, and are contained within the lines of the last, or second of the two tracts, described and purporting to be granted and conveyed to Louis Viviat and others, by the deed of October 18th, 1775; and that William M'Intosh, the defendant, entered upon these lands under and by virtue of his patent, and became possessed thereof before the institution of this suit.

22d. That Thomas Johnson, one of the grantees, in and under the deed of October 18th, 1775, departed this life on or about the 1st of October, 1819, seized of all his undivided part or share of, and in the two several tracts of land, described and purporting to be granted and conveyed to him and others by that deed, having first duly made and published his last will and testament in writing, attested by three credible witnesses, which he left in full force, and by which he devised all his undivided share and part of those two tracts of land, to his son, Joshua Johnson, and his heirs, and his grandson, Thomas J. Graham, and his heirs, the lessors of the plaintiff in this action, as tenants in common.

23d. That Joshua Johnson, and Thomas J. Graham, the devisees, entered into the two tracts of land last above mentioned, under and by virtue of the will, and became thereof seized as the law requires. That Thomas Johnson, the grantee and devisor, during his whole life, and at the time of his death, was an inhabitant and citizen of the State of Maryland; that Joshua Johnson, and Thomas J. Graham, the lessors of the plaintiff, now are, and always have been, citizens of the same State; that the defendant, William M'Intosh, now is, and at and before the time of bringing this action was, a citizen of the State of Illinois; and that the matter in dispute in this action is of the value of 2,000 dollars, current money of the United States, and upwards.

24th. And that neither William Murray, nor any other of the grantees under the deed of July the 5th, 1773, nor Louis Viviat, nor any other of the grantees under the deed of October the 8th, 1775, nor any person for them, or any of them, ever obtained, or had the actual possession, under and by virtue of those deeds, or either of them, of any part of the lands in them, or either of them, described and purporting to be granted; but were prevented by the war of the American revolution, which soon after commenced, and by the disputes and troubles which preceded it, from obtaining such possession; and that since the termination of the war, and before it, they have repeatedly, and at various times, from the year 1781, till the year 1816, petitioned the Congress of the United States to acknowledge and confirm their title to those lands, under the purchases and deeds in question, but without success.

Judgment being given for the defendant on the case stated, the plaintiffs brought this writ of error.

The cause was argued by Mr. *Harper* and Mr. *Webster* for the plaintiffs, and by Mr. *Winder* and Mr. *Murray* for the defendants.

On the part of the plaintiffs, it was contended . . .

2. That the British King's proclamation of October 7th, 1763, could not affect this right of the Indians to sell, because they were not British subjects, nor in any manner bound by the authority of the British government, legislative or executive. And, because, even admitting them to be British subjects, absolutely, or *sub modo*, they were still proprietors of the soil, and could not be devested of their rights of property, or any of its incidents, by a mere act of the executive government, such as this proclamation.

3. That the proclamation of 1763 could not restrain the purchasers under these deeds from purchasing; because the lands lay within the limits of the colony of Virginia, of which, or of some other British colony, the purchasers, all being British subjects, were inhabitants. And because the king had not, within the limits of that colonial government, or any other, any power of prerogative legislation; which is confined to countries newly conquered, and remaining in the military possession of the monarch, as supreme chief of the military forces of the nation. . . . A proclamation that no person should purchase land in England or Canada, would be clearly void.

4. That the act of Assembly of Virginia, passed in May, 1779, cannot affect the right of the plaintiffs, and others claiming under these deeds; because on general principles, and by the constitution of Virginia, the legislature was not competent to take away private, vested rights, or appropriate private property to public use, under the circumstances of this case. . . .

On the part of the defendants, it was insisted, that . . . [e]ven if it should be admitted that the Indians were originally an independent people, they have ceased to be so. A nation that has passed under the dominion of another, is no longer a sovereign state. The same treaties and negotiations, before referred to, show their dependent condition. Or, if it be admitted that they are now independent and foreign states, the title of the plaintiffs would still be invalid: as grantees from the *Indians,* they must take according to *their* laws of property, and as Indian subjects. The law of every dominion affects all persons and property situate within it; and the Indians never had any idea of individual property in lands. It cannot be said that the lands conveyed were disjoined from their dominion; because the grantees could not take the sovereignty and eminent domain to themselves.

. . . It is unnecessary to show that [the Indians] are not *citizens* in the ordinary sense of that term, since they are destitute of the most essential rights which belong to that character. They are of that class who are said by jurists not to be citizens, but perpetual inhabitants with diminutive rights. . . . The measure of property acquired by occupancy is determined, according to the law of nature, by the extent of men's wants, and their capacity of using it to supply them. It is a violation of the rights of others to exclude them from the use of what we do not want, and they have an occasion for. Upon this principle the North American Indians could have acquired no proprietary interest in the vast tracts of territory which they wandered over; and their right to the lands on which they hunted, could not be considered as superior to that which is acquired to the sea by fishing in it. The use in the one case, as well as the other, is not exclusive. According to every theory of property, the Indians had no individual rights to land; nor had they any collectively, or in their national capacity; for the lands occupied by each tribe were not used by them in such a manner as to prevent their being appropriated by a people of cultivators. . . .

MR. CHIEF JUSTICE MARSHALL delivered the opinion of the Court. The plaintiffs in this cause claim the land, in their declaration mentioned, under two grants, purporting to be made, the first in 1773, and the last in 1775, by the chiefs of certain Indian tribes, constituting the Illinois and the Piankeshaw nations; and the question is, whether this title can be recognised in the Courts of the United States?

The facts, as stated in the case agreed, show the authority of the chiefs who executed this conveyance, so far as it could be given by their own people; and likewise show, that the particular tribes for whom these chiefs acted were in rightful possession of the land they sold. The inquiry, therefore, is, in a great measure, confined to the power of Indians to give, and of private individuals to receive, a title which can be sustained in the Courts of this country.

As the right of society, to prescribe those rules by which property may be acquired and preserved is not, and cannot be drawn into question; as the title to lands, especially, is and must be admitted to depend entirely on the law of the nation in which they lie; it will be necessary, in pursuing this inquiry, to examine, not singly those principles of abstract justice, which the Creator of all things has impressed on the mind of his creature man, and which are admitted to regulate, in a great degree, the rights of civilized nations, whose perfect independence is acknowledged; but those principles also which our own government has adopted in the particular case, and given us as the rule for our decision.

On the discovery of this immense continent, the great nations of Europe were eager to appropriate to themselves so much of it as they could respectively acquire. Its vast extent offered an ample field to the ambition and enterprise of all; and the character and religion of its inhabitants afforded an apology for considering them as a people over whom the superior genius of Europe might claim an ascendency. The potentates of the old world found no difficulty in convincing themselves that they made ample compensation to the inhabitants of the new, by bestowing on them civilization and Christianity, in exchange for unlimited independence. But, as they were all in pursuit of nearly the same object, it was necessary, in order to avoid conflicting settlements, and consequent war with each other, to establish a principle, which all should acknowledge as the law by which the right of acquisition, which they all asserted, should be regulated as between themselves. This principle was, that discovery gave title to the government by whose subjects, or by whose authority, it was made, against all other European governments, which title might be consummated by possession.

The exclusion of all other Europeans, necessarily gave to the nation making the discovery the sole right of acquiring the soil from the natives, and establishing settlements upon it. It was a right with which no Europeans could interfere. It was a right which all asserted for themselves, and to the assertion of which, by others, all assented.

Those relations which were to exist between the discoverer and the natives, were to be regulated by themselves. The rights thus acquired being exclusive, no other power could interpose between them.

In the establishment of these relations, the rights of the original inhabitants were, in no instance, entirely disregarded; but were necessarily, to a considerable extent, impaired. They were admitted to be the rightful occupants of the soil, with a legal as well as just claim to retain possession of it, and to use it according to their own discretion; but their rights to complete sovereignty, as independent nations, were necessarily diminished, and their power to dispose of the soil at their own will, to whomsoever they pleased, was denied by the original fundamental principle, that discovery gave exclusive title to those who made it.

While the different nations of Europe respected the right of the natives, as occupants, they asserted the ultimate dominion to be in themselves; and claimed and exercised, as a consequence of this ultimate dominion, a power to grant the soil, while yet in possession of the natives. These grants have been understood by all, to convey a title to the grantees, subject only to the Indian right of occupancy.

The history of America, from its discovery to the present day, proves, we think, the universal recognition of these principles. . . .

No one of the powers of Europe gave its full assent to this principle, more unequivocally than England. The documents upon this subject are ample and complete. So early as the year 1496, her monarch granted a commission to the Cabots, to discover countries then unknown to *Christian people,* and to take possession of them in the name of the king of England. Two years afterwards, Cabot proceeded on this voyage, and discovered the continent of North America, along which he sailed as far south as Virginia. To this discovery the English trace their title. . . .

Thus, all the nations of Europe, who have acquired territory on this continent, have asserted in themselves, and have recognised in others, the exclusive right of the discoverer to appropriate the lands occupied by the Indians. Have the American States rejected or adopted this principle?

By the treaty which concluded the war of our revolution, Great Britain relinquished all claim, not only to the government, but to the "propriety and territorial rights of the United States," whose boundaries were fixed in the second article. By this treaty, the powers of government, and the right to soil, which had previously been in Great Britain, passed definitively to these States. We had before taken possession of them, by declaring independence; but neither the declaration of independence, nor the treaty confirming it, could give us more than that which we before possessed, or to which Great Britain was before entitled. It has never been doubted, that either the United States, or the several States, had a clear title to all the lands within the boundary lines described in the treaty, subject only to the Indian right of occupancy, and that the exclusive power to extinguish that right, was vested in that government which might constitutionally exercise it.

Virginia, particularly, within whose chartered limits the land in controversy lay, passed an act, in the year 1779, declaring her "exclusive right of preemption from the Indians, of all the lands within the limits of her own chartered territory, and that no person or persons whatsoever, have, or ever had, a right to purchase any lands within the same, from any Indian nation, except only persons duly authorized to make such purchase; formerly for the use and benefit of the colony, and lately for the Commonwealth." The act then proceeds to annul all deeds made by Indians to individuals, for the private use of the purchasers.

Without ascribing to this act the power of annulling vested rights, . . . it may safely be considered as an unequivocal affirmance, on the part of Virginia, of the broad principle which had always been maintained, that the exclusive right to purchase from the Indians resided in the government.

In pursuance of the same idea, Virginia proceeded, at the same session, to open her land office, for the sale of that country which now constitutes Kentucky, a country, every acre of which was then claimed and possessed by Indians, who maintained their title with as much persevering courage as was ever manifested by any people.

The States, having within their chartered limits different portions of territory covered by Indians, ceded that territory, generally, to the United States, on conditions expressed in their deeds of cession, which demonstrate the opinion, that they ceded the soil as well as jurisdiction, and that in doing so, they granted a productive fund to the government of the Union. The lands in controversy lay within the chartered limits of Virginia, and were ceded with the whole country northwest of the river Ohio. This grant contained reservations and stipulations, which could only be made by the owners of the soil; and concluded with a stipulation, that "all the lands in the ceded territory, not reserved, should be considered as a common fund, for the use and benefit of such of the United States as have become, or shall become, members of the confederation," &c. "according to their usual respective proportions in the general charge and expenditure, and shall be faithfully and *bona fide* disposed of for that purpose, and for no other use or purpose whatsoever."

The ceded territory was occupied by numerous and warlike tribes of Indians; but the exclusive right of the United States to extinguish their title, and to grant the soil, has never, we believe, been doubted. . . .

The magnificent purchase of Louisiana, was the purchase from France of a country almost entirely occupied by numerous tribes of Indians, who are in fact independent. Yet, any attempt of others to intrude into that country, would be considered as an aggression which would justify war. . . .

The United States, then, have unequivocally acceded to that great and broad rule by which its civilized inhabitants now hold this country. They hold, and assert in themselves, the title by which it was acquired. They maintain, as all others have maintained, that discovery gave an exclusive right to extinguish the Indian title of occupancy, either by purchase or by conquest; and gave also a right to such a degree of sovereignty, as the circumstances of the people would allow them to exercise. . . .

We will not enter into the controversy, whether agriculturists, merchants, and manufacturers, have a right, on abstract principles, to expel hunters from the territory they possess, or to contract their limits. Conquest gives a title which the Courts of the conqueror cannot deny, whatever the private and speculative opinions of individuals may be, respecting the original justice of the claim which has been successfully asserted. The British government, which was then our government, and whose rights have passed to the United States, asserted a title to all the lands occupied by Indians, within the chartered limits of the British colonies. It asserted also a limited sovereignty over them, and the exclusive right of extinguishing the title which occupancy gave to them. These claims have been maintained and established as far west as the river Mississippi, by the sword. The title to a vast portion of the lands we now hold, originates in them. It is not for the Courts of this country to question the validity of this title, or to sustain one which is incompatible with it.

Although we do not mean to engage in the defence of those principles which Europeans have applied to Indian title, they may, we think, find some excuse, if not justification, in the character and habits of the people whose rights have been wrested from them.

The title by conquest is acquired and maintained by force. The conqueror prescribes its limits. Humanity, however, acting on public opinion, has established, as a general rule, that the conquered shall not be wantonly oppressed, and that their condition shall remain as eligible as is compatible with the objects of the conquest. Most usually, they are incorporated with the victorious nation, and become subjects or citizens of the government with which they are connected. The new and old members of the society mingle with each other; the distinction between them is gradually lost, and they make one people. Where this incorporation is practicable, humanity demands, and a wise policy requires, that the rights of the conquered to property should remain unimpaired; that the new subjects should be governed as equitably as the old, and that confidence in their security should gradually banish the painful sense of being separated from their ancient connexions, and united by force to strangers.

When the conquest is complete, and the conquered inhabitants can be blended with the conquerors, or safely governed as a distinct people, public opinion, which not even the conqueror can disregard, imposes these restraints upon him; and he cannot neglect them without injury to his fame, and hazard to his power.

But the tribes of Indians inhabiting this country were fierce savages, whose occupation was war, and whose subsistence was drawn chiefly from the forest. To leave them in possession of their country, was to leave the country a wilderness; to govern them as a distinct people, was impossible, because they were as brave and as high spirited as they were fierce, and were ready to repel by arms every attempt on their independence.

What was the inevitable consequence of this state of things? The Europeans were under the necessity either of abandoning the country, and relinquishing their pompous claims to it, or of enforcing those claims by the sword, and by the adoption of principles adapted to the condition of a people with whom it was impossible to mix, and who could not be governed as a distinct society, or of remaining in their neighbourhood, and exposing themselves and their families to the perpetual hazard of being massacred.

Frequent and bloody wars, in which the whites were not always the aggressors, unavoidably ensued. European policy, numbers, and skill, prevailed. As the white population advanced, that of the Indians neces- sarily receded. The country in the immediate neighbourhood of agricul- turists became unfit for them. The game fled into thicker and more unbroken forests, and the Indians followed. The soil, to which the crown originally claimed title, being no longer occupied by its ancient inhabitants, was parcelled out according to the will of the sovereign power, and taken possession of by persons who claimed immediately from the crown, or mediately, through its grantees or deputies.

That law which regulates, and ought to regulate in general, the relations between the conqueror and conquered, was incapable of appli- cation to a people under such circumstances. The resort to some new and different rule, better adapted to the actual state of things, was unavoidable. Every rule which can be suggested will be found to be attended with great difficulty.

However extravagant the pretension of converting the discovery of an inhabited country into conquest may appear; if the principle has been asserted in the first instance, and afterwards sustained; if a country has been acquired and held under it; if the property of the great mass of the community originates in it, it becomes the law of the land, and cannot be questioned. So, too, with respect to the concomitant principle, that the Indian inhabitants are to be considered merely as occupants, to be pro- tected, indeed, while in peace, in the possession of their lands, but to be deemed incapable of transferring the absolute title to others. However this restriction may be opposed to natural right, and to the usages of civilized nations, yet, if it be indispensable to that system under which the country has been settled, and be adapted to the actual condition of the two people, it may, perhaps, be supported by reason, and certainly cannot be rejected by Courts of justice. . . .

After bestowing on this subject a degree of attention which was more required by the magnitude of the interest in litigation, and the able and elaborate arguments of the bar, than by its intrinsic difficulty, the Court is decidedly of opinion, that the plaintiffs do not exhibit a title which can be sustained in the Courts of the United States; and that there is no error in the judgment which was rendered against them in the District Court of Illinois.

Judgment, affirmed with costs.

F. P. PRUCHA, AMERICAN INDIAN POLICY IN THE FORMATIVE YEARS: 1790-1834, 5-6, 13, 140-143 (1962): The United States in 1776 did not have a *tabula rasa* on which to sketch out its Indian policy. Heavy lines were already etched in, to be further deepened in some cases by American decisions or rubbed out when changes seemed imperative. All the English colonies had an Indian problem and had adopted measures

PHOTOGRAPH 1-1
Benjamin West, "Penn's Treaty With the Indians (1771)"
Courtesy Pennsylvania Academy of the Fine Arts

15

for regulating the relations between the Indians and the whites. Although there was no uniform policy, as decade after decade each colony was left to manage its own Indian affairs, certain basic procedures became fixed in all the colonies. The Indians, after all, were a class apart, distinguished by their primitive culture, their savagery, and their color. The English, like the French and the Spanish, were forced to develop some rationale on which to base their relations with these strange aborigines, but, whatever the theological and philosophical theories that evolved, it was soon apparent that the two races were not going to live in peace easily. The peace, rather, had to be maintained and safeguarded by public authority, and gradually a body of restrictions developed, designed to prevent or regulate contact between the whites and the Indians at crucial and dangerous points, which foreshadowed in some degree the later action of the United States. . . .

From the very beginning abuses marred the transfer of land titles from the Indians to individuals among the English colonists, and colonial laws struck at the difficulty by declaring null and void all bargains made with the Indians that did not have governmental approval. Not only did such laws seek to remove causes of resentment among the Indians by preventing unjust and fraudulent purchases, but they aimed as well at preserving the rights of the crown or the proprietor to the land, which would be seriously impaired by extinguishment of Indian titles in favor of just anybody. The preamble of the South Carolina act of December 18, 1739, called attention to this double motivation behind the restrictive legislation of the colonial governments, for it noted that "the practice of purchasing lands from the Indians may prove of very dangerous consequence to the peace and safety of this Province, such purchases being generally obtained from Indians by unfair representation, fraud and circumvention, or by making them gifts or presents of little value, by which practices, great resentments and animosities have been created amongst the Indians towards the inhabitants of this Province," and that "such practices tend to the manifest prejudice of his Majesty's just right and title to the soil of this Province, vested in his Majesty by the surrender of the late Lords Proprietors." . . .

[T]he famous Proclamation of 1763 . . . proclaimed three things: it established the boundaries and the government for the new colonies, offered specific encouragement to settlement in the newly acquired areas, and established a new policy in Indian affairs. The last of these was foremost in the minds of the Lords of Trade in the summer months of 1763.

The great departure from the past, the new turn in Indian policy found in the Proclamation of 1763, was the boundary line drawn between the lands of the Indians and those of the whites. In earlier colonial days there had been no distinct "Indian Country." Indian ownership of land was recognized — Massachusetts quoted Scripture in support of that principle — and care was taken to regularize the purchase of lands from the natives. . . . It was in the Proclamation of 1763 that the first official delineation and definition of the Indian Country was made. . . .

Although it required many years of actual contact between the groups before settled relations were agreed upon, as European exploration and colonization increased, a theory in regard to the territory in America gained general acceptance. It was a theory developed by the European nations without consultation with the natives, but it did not totally disregard the Indians' rights. According to the theory, the European discoverer acquired the right of pre-emption, the right to acquire title to the soil from the natives in the area, by purchase if the Indians were willing to sell, or by conquest, and to succeed the natives in occupancy of the soil if they should voluntarily leave the country or become extinct. Discovery gave this right against later discoverers; it could hardly make claim against the original possessors of the soil, the native Indians. In practice, nevertheless, and eventually in theory, the absolute dominion or sovereignty over the land rested in the European nations or their successors, leaving to the aborigines the right of occupancy.

Thomas Jefferson relied upon this accepted view when the British minister asked him in 1792 what he understood to be the American right in the Indian soil. The secretary of state replied: "A right of preëmption of their lands; that is to say, the sole and exclusive right of purchasing from them whenever they should be willing to sell. . . . We consider it as established by the usage of different nations into a kind of *Jus gentium* for America, that a white nation settling down and declaring that such and such are their limits, makes an invasion of those limits by any other white nation an act of war, but gives no right of soil against the native possessors." The following year he was even more emphatic in replying to queries posed by Washington to his cabinet. "I considered our right of pre-emption of the Indian lands," Jefferson remarked, "not as amounting to any dominion, or jurisdiction, or paramountship whatever, but merely in the nature of a remainder after the extinguishment of a present right, which gave us no present right whatever, but of preventing other nations from taking possession, and so defeating our expectancy; that the Indians had the full, undivided and independent sovereignty as long as they choose to keep it, and that this might be forever." . . .

In treaty after treaty, both under the Articles of Confederation and under the Constitution, the traditional principles were followed. A formal meeting between the plenipotentiary commissioners of the United States and the leading chiefs and headsmen of the tribes, a solemn document detailing the compensations, grants, and guarantee, then the approval or ratification by the Senate — this was the established procedure.

Although the accepted policy of the American government recognized the Indian rights to the land and made repeated provision by law and treaty and special proclamation to ensure justice to the aborigines, the views of the frontiersmen, the settlers who were the ones to come into contact with the Indians, were of a different nature altogether. Theorizing about *jus gentium* and rights or pre-emption played little part in the thinking of the settler on the frontier or of the eastern speculator in western lands. Their doctrine was simpler and earthier, and they had their own ideas about *jus gentium*. They saw the rich lands of the Indians and they wanted them.

A. DE TOCQUEVILLE, DEMOCRACY IN AMERICA 366-367, 369 (1835): The Union treats the Indians with less cupidity and violence than the several states, but the two governments are alike deficient in good faith. The states extend what they call the benefits of their laws to the Indians, believing that the tribes will recede rather than submit to them; and the central government, which promises a permanent refuge to these unhappy beings in the West, is well aware of its inability to secure it to them. Thus the tyranny of the states obliges the savages to retire; the Union, by its promises and resources, facilitates their retreat; and these measures tend to precisely the same end. . . .

The Spaniards were unable to exterminate the Indian race by those unparalleled atrocities which brand them with indelible shame, nor did they succeed even in wholly depriving it of its rights; but the Americans of the United States have accomplished this twofold purpose with singular felicity, tranquilly, legally, philanthropically, without shedding blood, and without violating a single great principle of morality in the eyes of the world. It is impossible to destroy men with more respect for the laws of humanity.

Notes

1. One of Webster's arguments in Johnson v. M'Intosh was that the English King, constrained by the Magna Carta, could not validly have barred purchases from the Indians without action by the British Parliament or the Virginia legislature.

In a 1983 case, the Commonwealth of Virginia made a similar argument. The dispute concerned title to submerged land, valuable because of its oyster grounds under a tributary of the Rappahannock River. Virginia said that private titles to the underwater land were invalid even though they could be traced in in an unbroken chain of record title back to a patent from Sir William Berkeley, Knight Governor of Virginia, in 1642. Virginia contended that the crown, without consent of Parliament, had "no power to grant the bottoms of navigable waters to private individuals thus interfering with the public right of fishing or oystering."

The Virginia Supreme Court disagreed with the state. Recognizing that the question has been debated seriously, the court relied heavily on the Treatise De Jure Maris of Lord Chief Justice Hale, published in 1787, that said: "Although the king hath *prima facie* this right in the armes and creeks of the sea *communi jure*, and in common presumption, yet a subject may have such a right . . . by the king's charter or grants. . . ." Commonwealth v. Morgan, 225 Va. 517, 303 S.E.2d 899 (1983).

2. In Tee-Hit-Ton Indians v. United States, 348 U.S. 272 (1955), "an identifiable group of American Indians of between 60 and 70 individuals residing in Alaska" alleged that the Secretary of Agriculture took their property without compensation when he sold timber on land they claimed. The Indians had been on the land "from time immemorial"; their use of the land did not change when Russia conveyed Alaska to the U.S. in 1867. The Court, per Justice Reed, said: "[O]riginal Indian title . . . means mere possession not specifically recognized as ownership by Congress. . . . This is not a property right but amounts to a right of occupancy which the sovereign grants and protects against intrusion by third parties but which right of occupancy may be terminated . . . by the sovereign itself without any legally enforceable obligation to compensate the Indians." Justice Reed quoted from Justice Jackson in an earlier case: "We agree . . . that no legal rights are today to be recognized in the Shoshones by reason of this treaty. We agree . . . as to their moral deserts. We do not mean to leave the impression that the two have any relation to each other." Northwestern Bands of Shoshone Indians v. United States, 324 U.S. 335, 358 (1944) (Jackson, J., concurring).

3. Of course neither Johnson v. M'Intosh nor Tee-Hit-Ton prevents Congress from choosing to confirm Indian claims, or to compensate for their denial. The largest instance is the Alaska Native Claims Settlement Act of 1971, 43 U.S.C. §1601, which attempted "a fair and just settlement of all claims by Natives and Native groups of Alaska, based on aboriginal land claims." The Act, which was stimulated in part by the discovery of vast oil reserves on the northern slope, granted 40 million acres and $925 million, the money to be paid over a period of years, to native villages, regional corporations, and certain individuals. The Settlement Act is an attempt to structure the political and social institutions of native populations, and also to guide the process by which they come to terms with the outside culture.

4. Issues similar to those posed by Johnson v. M'Intosh have been a staple of political and legal life in the southwestern United States since the conclusion of the Mexican War. In the Treaty of Guadalupe Hidalgo, the U.S. promised to its new residents "the choice of retaining the property which they possessed . . . or disposing thereof and removing the proceeds wherever they please." These were to be "guarantees equally ample as if the same belonged to citizens of the United States." Problems arose because the arrangements for holding property under

Spanish law, and the system of land titles, could not easily be assimilated to American practice. The most interesting litigation concerned communal lands, which Spanish governors had awarded, in the name of the King, to residents of particular towns. These residents had no title that individualistic Anglo-American law could comprehend. The courts eventually decided, echoing Johnson v. M'Intosh, that "as to the common lands the title remained in the sovereign and the settlers on a community grant had only the right to common use of the lands; when such lands became a part of the United States, the latter was free to issue a patent thereto to whomsoever it pleased and with such restrictions as it saw fit." Armijo v. Town of Atrisco, 56 N.M. 2, 10, 239 P.2d 535, 539 (1952), citing, inter alia, United States v. Santa Fe, 165 U.S. 657 (1897), and Rio Arriba Land & Cattle Co. v. United States, 167 U.S. 298 (1897). At least sometimes, these communal holdings did become assimilated into town land, like that held by other American municipalities, but quite unlike the arrangements anticipated by the seventeenth and early eighteenth century Spanish officials and settlers. Armijo v. Town of Atrisco, supra.

5. On January 9, 1978, the New York Times reported the first human birth on the continent of Antarctica, to the wife of an Argentine army captain.

Two weeks later, a letter to the *Times* pointed out the significance of the birth: "For the first time a nation claiming territorial sovereignty in Antarctica is attempting to support its claim natally. If this seems far-fetched legally it can be matched by the same nation's insistence that geologic affinity (the fact that the Transantarctic Range is a continuation of the Andes even though it is invisible in the 600 miles of the Drake Passage) supports its position as a claimant." Letter from Charles Neier, in N. Y. Times, Jan. 26, 1978.

6. In 1499, Albrecht Dürer painted portraits of Hans and Felicitas Tücher. For more than a century before 1945, they hung in the State Museum of Weimar, a city now in the German Democratic Republic. The paintings once belonged to the Grand Duke of Saxe-Weimar-Eisenach, but at least since 1927 they belonged to the Land (State) of Thuringia.

During World War II, the paintings were removed for safekeeping to Schwarzburg Castle, 25 miles from Weimar and now in the Federal Republic of Germany. American troops occupied Schwarzburg from April to July in 1945. During that time the paintings disappeared.

In 1966, Edward Elicofon, a New York lawyer, said he had the paintings on a wall in his Brooklyn home, and that he had bought them in 1946 for $450 from an ex-soldier who appeared on his doorstep.

In 1969, the F.R.G. sued, seeking "possession . . . in order ultimately to restore them to the person . . . truly and rightfully entitled." So did the hereditary Grand Duchess of Saxony-Weimar. The Kunstammlungen, the Weimar museum, sought to intervene, but leave was denied because the U.S. did not recognize the G.D.R. That incapacity was reversed with U.S. recognition in 1974. The Kunstammlungen was then allowed to intervene, and in 1975 the F.R.G. discontinued its claims with prejudice. In 1978, the U.S. District Court granted summary judgment for the Kunstammlungen.

The Grand Duchess lost because the court held that the paintings passed to the Land in the 1920s under an arbitral settlement after the Grand Duke abdicated. The court gave the following reasons for ruling against Elicofon:

(a) The paintings were stolen, so Elicofon could not get good title.

(b) Ownership of the paintings moved from Land Thuringia to the G.D.R.'s museum, not (as Elicofon contended) through Hitler's regime to the F.R.G.

(c) The statute of limitations did not run against the G.D.R. because the U.S. did not recognize it. It is irrelevant that during this period the U.S. recognized the F.R.G. in certain ways as the representative of the entire German nation. Also, although perhaps the Allied Powers could have asserted a claim for the paintings between 1946 and 1949, this could not exhaust the ten-year statute of limitations.

(d) In any case, under New York law, the statute of limitations does not run as to stolen property until the bona fide purchaser's refusal, upon demand, to return the property.

New York law applies, making irrelevant the German doctrine of *Ersitzung:* "A person who has a movable thing in his proprietary possession for ten years acquires ownership" unless he was "not in good faith in obtaining possession" or "subsequently . . . [learned] that he is not entitled to ownership." German Civil Code §932 (1975). If G.D.R. law applied, there might be relevance to the proposition that "people's owned property" cannot be acquired by *Ersitzung.*

As a result of the Second Circuit's opinion in Kunstammlungen Zu Weimar v. Elicofon, 678 F.2d 1150 (1982), affirming a federal district court judgment in favor of the State Museum (536 F. Supp. 813), the portraits were returned to Weimar in September 1982. According to an Associated Press account, "East German officials said they were 'moved' and 'overwhelmed' by the return of the paintings. 'I am a bit surprised they are so small,' one added."

7. N. Y. Times, Dec. 19, 1973:

"Discussions are taking place, but no firm proposals have been formulated," said the Duke of Wellington, about the Belgian Government's request that he "negotiate a settlement" on the annual $48,000 he receives from an estate in Belgium given to his famous ancestor after Napoleon's defeat at Waterloo. The money comes from taxes and hunting and property rights on the 2,500-acre estate near the site of the Waterloo battlefield.

PHOTOGRAPH 1-2
Albrecht Dürer, "Hans Tücher"

22

PHOTOGRAPH 1-3
Albrecht Dürer, "Felicitas Tücher"

Given to the "Iron Duke" by King William of the Netherlands in 1815, it was stipulated that income from the land should be paid to all of the Duke's male descendants. The Belgians took over the debt of gratitude when their nation became independent of the Netherlands in 1830.

But now that the Belgians want to end the arrangement, the current Duke must be worrying about the Spanish. He also owns a 2,500-acre estate near Granada, given to his illustrious ancestor after his rout of the French on the Iberian Peninsula.

B.   AMERICAN ACKNOWLEDGMENT OF NATIVE AMERICAN CLAIMS

◆ JOINT TRIBAL COUNCIL OF THE PASSAMAQUODDY TRIBE v. MORTON
388 F. Supp. 649 (D. Me. 1975), aff'd., 528 F.2d 370 (1st Cir. 1975)

GIGNOUX, District Judge. . . . Plaintiffs in this action are the Joint Tribal Council of the Passamaquoddy Indian Tribe and the Tribe's two governors, who are suing in their individual and official capacities and as representatives of all members of the Tribe. Defendants are the Secretary of the Interior, the Attorney General of the United States, and the United States Attorney for the District of Maine. The State of Maine has been permitted to intervene as a party defendant. Plaintiffs seek a declaratory judgment that the Indian Nonintercourse Act, 1 Stat. 137 (1790), now 25 U.S.C. §177, forbidding the conveyance of Indian land without the consent of the United States, is applicable to the Passamaquoddy Tribe and establishes a trust relationship between the United States and the Tribe. . . .

The Joint Tribal Council of the Passamaquoddy Tribe is the official governing body of the Passamaquoddy Tribe, a tribe of Indians residing on two reservations in the State of Maine. It is stipulated that since at least 1776 the present members of the Tribe and their ancestors have constituted and continue to constitute a tribe of Indians in the racial and cultural sense.

Plaintiffs allege that until 1794 the Passamaquoddy Tribe occupied as its aboriginal territory all of what is now Washington County together with other land in the State of Maine. During the Revolutionary War, the Tribe fought with the American colonies against Great Britain. In 1790, in recognition of the primary responsibility of the newly-formed Federal Government to the Indians in the United States, the First Congress adopted the Indian Nonintercourse Act which as presently codified, 25 U.S.C. §177, provides in pertinent part:

"No purchase, grant, lease, or other conveyance of lands, or of any title or claim thereto, from any Indian nation or tribe of Indians, shall be of any validity in law or equity, unless the same be made by treaty or convention entered into pursuant to the Constitution."[1]

Plaintiffs allege that in 1794, four years after passage of the 1790 Nonintercourse Act, the Commonwealth of Massachusetts, Maine's predecessor in interest,[2] negotiated a treaty with the Passamaquoddies, by which the Tribe ceded to Massachusetts practically all of its aboriginal territory. It is further alleged that out of the 23,000 acres which the 1794 treaty reserved to the Tribe, Maine and Massachusetts have sold, leased for 999 years, given easements on, or permitted flooding of approximately 6,000 acres. The complaint asserts that the United States has not consented to these transactions and therefore that they violated the express terms of the Nonintercourse Act.

Since the United States was organized and the Constitution adopted in 1789, the Federal Government has never entered into a treaty with the Passamaquoddy Tribe, and the Congress has never enacted legislation which specifically mentions the Passamaquoddies. Furthermore, since 1789, the contacts between the Federal Government and the Tribe have been sporadic and infrequent. In contrast, the State of Maine has enacted comprehensive legislation which has had a pervasive effect upon all aspects of Passamaquoddy tribal life. The stipulated record clearly shows that the Commonwealth of Massachusetts and the State of Maine, rather than the Federal Government, have assumed almost exclusive responsibility for the protection and welfare of the Passamaquoddies.

On February 22, 1972 representatives of the Passamaquoddy Tribe wrote to the Commissioner of the Bureau of Indian Affairs, Department of the Interior, and requested that the United States Government, on behalf of the Tribe, institute a suit against the State of Maine, as a means

1. The first Nonintercourse Act passed in 1790, 1 Stat. 137, 138, provided that "no sale of lands made by any Indians, or any nation or tribe of Indians within the United States, shall be valid to any person or persons, or to any state . . . unless the same shall be made and duly executed at some public treaty, held under the authority of the United States." By the second Nonintercourse Act passed in 1793, this language was amended to read as follows: "No purchase or grant of lands, or of any title or claim thereto, from any Indians or nation or tribe of Indians, within the bounds of the United States, shall be of any validity in law or equity, unless the same be made by a treaty or convention entered into pursuant to the Constitution." 1 Stat. 329, 330.

2. Maine was formerly a District of Massachusetts. In 1819 Massachusetts passed legislation, commonly known as the Articles of Separation, which permitted, subject to the consent of Congress, the separation of the District of Maine from Massachusetts, and the establishment of Maine as an independent state. Act of June 19, 1819, Mass. Laws, ch. 61, p.248. The Articles of Separation provided that Maine would "assume and perform all the duties and obligations of this Commonwealth towards the Indians within said District of Maine, whether the same arise from treaties or otherwise; . . ." Shortly thereafter, Congress approved of Maine's admission to the Union. Act of March 3, 1820, ch. 19, 3 Stat. 544. The Articles of Separation were incorporated into the Maine Constitution as Article X, Section 5.

of redressing the wrongs which arose out of the alleged unconscionable land transactions in violation of the Nonintercourse Act. The letter urged that the requested action be filed by July 18, 1972, the date as of which such an action would be barred by 28 U.S.C. §2415(b), a special statute of limitations for actions seeking damages resulting from trespass upon restricted Indian lands. On March 24, 1972 the Commissioner recommended to the Solicitor of the Department of the Interior that the litigation be instituted and advised the Solicitor that 28 U.S.C. §2415(b) might bar a suit after July 18, 1972. Defendants, however, despite repeated urgings by representatives of the Tribe, failed to take any action upon their request.

On June 2, 1972 plaintiffs filed the present action seeking a declaratory judgment that the Passamaquoddy Tribe is entitled to the protection of the Nonintercourse Act and requesting a preliminary injunction ordering the defendants to file a protective action on their behalf against the State of Maine before July 18, 1972. Following a hearing on June 16, 1972 the Court ordered defendants to decide by June 22, 1972 whether they would voluntarily file the protective action sought by plaintiffs. In addition, the Court directed defendants, in the event their decision was in the negative, to state their reasons for so deciding and to show cause on June 23, 1972 why they should not be ordered to bring suit. On June 20, 1972 the Acting Solicitor of the Department of the Interior advised the Assistant Attorney General, Land and Natural Resources Division, Department of Justice, by letter, that no request for litigation would be made. The reasons, as stated in the letter, were as follows:

> As you are aware, no treaty exists between the United States and the Tribe and, except for isolated and inexplicable instances in the past, this Department, in its trust capacity, has had no dealings with the Tribe. On the contrary, it is the States of Massachusetts and Maine which have acted as trustees for the tribal property for almost 200 years. This relationship between the Tribe and the States has apparently never been questioned by the Tribe until recently. . . .
>
> In view of the Court's Order of June 16, 1972, requesting it be advised of the Secretary's decision on the Tribe's request by June 22, 1972, this Department has again reviewed its position and has again determined that no request for litigation should be made.
>
> The Department does not reach its decision lightly. On the one hand, we are aware that the Tribe may thus be foreclosed from pursuing its claims against the State in the federal courts. However, *as there is no trust relationship between the United States and this tribe*, we are led inescapably to conclude that the Tribe's proper legal remedy should be sought elsewhere. . . . (emphasis supplied).

In their second amended and supplemental complaint, plaintiffs have dropped their original request for injunctive relief and seek only a

declaratory judgment. Their basic position is that the Nonintercourse
Act applies to all Indian tribes in the United States, including the Passamaquoddies, and that the Act establishes a trust relationship between
the United States and the Indian tribes to which it applies, including the
Passamaquoddies. Therefore, they say, defendants may not deny plaintiffs' request for litigation on the sole ground that there is no trust
relationship between the United States and the Tribe. In opposition,
defendants and intervenor contend that only those Indian tribes which
have been "recognized" by the Federal Government by treaty, statute or
a consistent course of conduct are entitled to the protection of the
Nonintercourse Act and, since the Passamaquoddies have not been
"federally recognized," the Act is not applicable to them. Defendants
and intervenor also deny that the Nonintercourse Act creates any trust
relationship between the United States and the Indian tribes to which it
applies. . . .

. . . [The] conclusion is inescapable that, as a matter of simple
statutory interpretation, the Nonintercourse Act applies to the Passamaquoddies. The literal meaning of the words employed in the statute,
used in their ordinary sense, clearly and unambiguously encompasses
all tribes of Indians, including the Passamaquoddies; the plain language
of the statute is consistent with the Congressional intent; and there is no
legislative history or administrative interpretation which conflicts with
the words of the Act. . . .

. . . The Court is aware of no legislative history of the Nonintercourse Act, which might reveal whether the First Congress had in mind
the Passamaquoddies when it enacted the 1790 Act. Nor have defendants been able to call to the Court's attention any administrative interpretation prior to the filing of the instant litigation as to the applicability
of the Act to the Passamaquoddies or any similarly situated Indian tribe.
Every court, however, which has considered the purposes of the Act has
agreed that the intent of Congress was to protect the lands of the Indian
tribes in order to prevent fraud and unfairness. As the Supreme Court
noted in Federal Power Commission v. Tuscarora Indian Nation, 362
U.S. 99, 119 (1960):

> The obvious purpose of that [the Nonintercourse] statute is to prevent
> the unfair, improvident or improper disposition by Indians of lands
> owned or possessed by them to other parties, except the United States,
> without the consent of Congress, and to enable the Government, acting as
> *parens patriae* for the Indians, to vacate any disposition of their lands made
> without its consent. . . .

A plain meaning interpretation of the phrase "any . . . tribe of
Indians" is also the only construction of the Nonintercourse Act which
comports with the basic policy of the United States, as reflected in

the Act, to protect the Indian right of occupancy of their aboriginal lands. . . .

In Oneida Indian Nation v. County of Oneida, 414 U.S. 664, 667-68 (1974), . . . the Supreme Court reaffirmed these fundamental propositions. . . . In *Oneida*, the Supreme Court also again summarized the policy of the United States to protect the rights of Indian tribes to their aboriginal lands:

> It very early became accepted doctrine in this Court that although fee title to the lands occupied by Indians when the colonists arrived became vested in the sovereign — first the discovering European nation and later the original States and the United States — a right of occupancy in the Indian tribes was nevertheless recognized. That right, sometimes called Indian title and good against all but the sovereign, could be terminated only by sovereign act. Once the United States was organized and the Constitution adopted, these tribal rights to Indian lands became the exclusive province of the federal law. Indian title, recognized to be only a right of occupancy, was extinguishable only by the United States. The Federal Government took early steps to deal with the Indians through treaty, the principal purpose often being to recognize and guarantee the rights of Indians to specified areas of land. This the United States did with respect to the various New York Indian tribes, including the Oneidas. The United States also asserted the primacy of federal law in the first Nonintercourse Act passed in 1790. . . .

It is thus clear that the policy embodied in the Nonintercourse Act is to protect Indian tribes against loss of their aboriginal lands by improvident disposition to members of other races. The Passamaquoddies, an Indian tribe, fall within the plain meaning of the statutory language, and there is no reason why they should be excluded from the protection which the Act affords. . . .

Defendants have rejected plaintiffs' request for assistance on the ground that no trust relationship exists between the United States and the Passamaquoddies. The Court disagrees. In the only decided cases to treat this issue, the Court of Claims has, in a series of decisions during the last ten years, definitively held that the Nonintercourse Act imposes a trust or fiduciary obligation on the United States to protect land owned by all Indian tribes covered by the statute. . . .

[See] President Washington's speech to the Senecas in December 1790, shortly after the passage of the Act:

> Here, then, is the security for the remainder of your lands. No State, no person, can purchase your lands, unless at some public treaty, held under the authority of the United States. *The General Government will never consent to your being defrauded, but it will protect you in all your just rights.* . . . But your great object seems to be, the security of your remaining lands;

and I have, therefore, upon this point, meant to be sufficiently strong and clear, that, in future, you cannot be defrauded of your lands; that you possess the right to sell, and the right of refusing to sell, your lands; that, therefore, the sale of your lands, in future, will depend entirely upon yourselves. But that, when you may find it for your interest to sell any part of your lands, the United States must be present, by their agent, *and will be your security that you shall not be defrauded in the bargain you may make.* . . . That, besides the before mentioned security for your land, you will perceive, *by the law of Congress for regulating trade and intercourse with the Indian tribes, the fatherly care the United States intend to take of the Indians.* . . .

American State Papers (Indian Affairs, Vol. I, 1832), p.142. Id. at 923-24 (emphasis in original). . . .

In view of the foregoing, the conclusion must be that the Nonintercourse Act establishes a trust relationship between the United States and the Indian tribes, including the Passamaquoddies, to which it applies. The Court holds that defendants erred in denying plaintiffs' request for litigation on the sole ground that no trust relationship exists between the United States and the Passamaquoddy Indian Tribe. . . .

Before and after the Passamaquoddy Litigation

The *Passamaquoddy* litigation began with a relatively minor incident that escalated into a claim for the return of nearly two-thirds of the land area of Maine. At Indian Township, a Passamaquoddy reservation in eastern Maine, a white man named Plaisted acquired several acres of land on Lewey's Lake in a poker game with another white man. In February 1964, Plaisted began clearing the land in order to build a road and tourist cabins.

Although the local Passamaquoddies had long accepted Plaisted as a neighboring landowner, they resented the way the state had sold much of their land, timber, and grass rights and had mismanaged the tribal trust fund resulting from those sales. For years, the tribal governor, John Stevens, had tried to find a lawyer willing to press the Indians' land claim based on a 1794 treaty between Massachusetts and the Passamaquoddy Tribe.

On discovering Plaisted's intentions, Stevens called a meeting of the Indian community. After discussing how Plaisted had acquired the lakeside property and other land, the Tribal Council voted to request a meeting with the Maine attorney general and to seek an audience with Governor Reed. The Governor kept the six-man delegation waiting for five hours to tell them he could not intervene personally. The attorney general, who by law represents the Indians in land disputes, wished them luck if they ever took the claim to court.

Bitter over their shabby treatment, members of the Tribal Council held another community meeting on their return to the reservation. This meeting ended with a vote to block Plaisted's construction. Ten peaceful demonstrators were arrested; five of them were charged with disorderly conduct and trespass, the others were released. Stevens hired a local attorney, Don Gellers, to represent them. Gellers reached an agreement with the prosecutor that neither Plaisted nor the Indians would enter the contested land until the ownership question was decided, and the prosecutor dropped the trespass charges. When Gellers began preparation of the claim for restoration of 6,000 acres of land alienated in violation of the 1794 treaty, he had no notion that the action would evolve into a claim for 12.5 million acres. See Brodeur, Annals of Law (Indian Land Claims), The New Yorker, Oct. 11, 1982, at 76.

The lawsuit even made it more difficult for Massachusetts to borrow money. See official statement of Commonwealth of Massachusetts attached to its offering of $125,000,000 in general obligation bonds at 38 (Jan. 1, 1977):

> The United States of America v. The State of Maine, (U.S. District Court for the District of Maine, Northern Division, Civil Action No. 1966-N.D.) is an action brought by the United States on behalf of the Passama-quoddy Tribe seeking an award of $150 million in damages for wrongs done to the Tribe by the defendant State of Maine in violation of the Indian Nonintercourse Act, 25 U.S.C. §177. A similar action (Civil Action No. 1969-N.D.) bearing the same caption has been brought by the United States on behalf of the Penobscot Nation seeking an award of $150 million in damages. The Attorney General of the State of Maine has advised the Attorney General of the Commonwealth that, if the United States decides to proceed with these claims, the State of Maine intends to implead the Commonwealth as a third party defendant. If the United States proceeds, it is possible that the complaints may be amended to seek damages in the billions of dollars or to assert claims with respect to the land itself. Potentially, 60% of the land area of Maine may be involved. The actions are at an early stage, and it is impossible to predict their course or outcome, or whether the Commonwealth will be made a party.

The *Passamaquoddy* case only held that the U.S. was obliged to bring a lawsuit on behalf of the tribe. (If the Nonintercourse Act was violated in the early nineteenth century, was not the U.S. a principal violator? If so, was it now to be both plaintiff and defendant in the lawsuit?) What defenses would be available to current possessors of land? Reconsider after you study Chapter 3.

But whatever the chances of eventual Indian victory in the case, the existence of the lawsuit, and then the holding and rhetoric of Judge Gignoux's opinion, clouded titles in a substantial part of Maine. Mortgages were hard to get, and even home improvement loans were affected. These developments, and the likelihood the matter would be in the courts for many years, created pressure for two kinds of resolution: first, for an agreed settlement by which the Indians would trade their claims for compensation; and second, for a federal statute extinguishing the Indian claims.

The Carter Administration pursued the first course, with ultimate success. Former Georgia Supreme Court Justice William Gunter was appointed as mediator. After many rounds of negotiation, the Indians agreed to accept more than 12 million acres of undeveloped Maine land and $27 million in cash. Congress voted to pay the cash settlement and to pay compensation of $54.5 million to landowners, chiefly paper companies, whose land was turned over to the Indians. 94 Stat. 1785, 25 U.S.C. §1721 (1980). Issues remain about who is a member of the Passamaquoddy Tribe, and about how the tribe will organize itself to manage its new resources.

While much of the land obtained by the Indians is excellent for logging, few members of the tribe are making a living off the land, and the unemployment rate among the Indians is high. Obstacles confronting the Indians in making use of their land include long distances between potential logging sites and the reservation, the high cost of necessary equipment, and inexperience in logging.

The only direct benefit the tribe members have seen from the settlement is the interest on the $27 million trust fund, amounting to about $1,000 per year for each person. N.Y. Times, Sept. 12, 1982, at 77.

The second approach, urged by some Maine political leaders, would have drawn upon the language of *Tee-Hit-Ton* to "extinguish" the Indian claim of occupancy. When that approach was under discussion, Professor Archibald Cox of Harvard Law School, a special counsel to the Indians, wrote a letter to Justice Gunter that included the following paragraphs:

> The Constitution, we submit, does not permit such injustice; and, if necessary, we will press the point through the courts. Tee-Hit-Ton Indians v. United States, 348 U.S. 272 (1955), may stand for the proposition that every extinguishment of aboriginal title is not a taking which gives rise to an immediate claim for just compensation. Congress has power, under *Tee-Hit-Ton*, to legislate concerning the property of Indian tribes but that regulatory power, like all other regulatory powers, must be exercised in conformity with the Bill of Rights, including the Due Process Clause of the Fifth Amendment. An exercise of Congressional power over Indian affairs which would simply confiscate the interest of the Indians would violate the guarantees of fundamental fairness embodied in the Due Process Clause. . . .
>
> While the facts and holdings of [*Tee-Hit-Ton*] and other cases are consistent with our constitutional position, some of the language can be read more broadly. We would point out, however, that none of these cases

involved total congressional disregard of the property interest of the Indians on the scale suggested by this question. Even if they had, the statements are mere dicta, inconsistent with current constitutional ideas of substantive due process. . . .

Our position is supported by Congress' traditional posture, which is one of respecting Indian claims. Indeed, there is a clearly discernible pattern to Congress' treatment of Indian lands from 1789 to the present. As a House Committee Report stated in explaining the Alaska Native Claims Settlement Legislation:

"The consistent policy of the United States in its dealings with Indian Tribes [has been] to grant to them title to a portion of the lands which they occupied, to extinguish the aboriginal title to the remainder of the land by placing such land in the public domain, and to pay the fair value of the title extinguished." (H. Rep. No. 92-523 at 4, 92nd Cong., 1st Sess. (1971).)

In *Passamaquoddy*, the parties proceeded on an assumption that the tribe had existed continuously from before the Nonintercourse Act until today. When similar Indian claims were asserted on Cape Cod, present non-Indian landowners decided to contest the continuous existence of the tribe, and they prevailed.

Mashpee Tribe v. New Seabury Corp., 592 F.2d 575 (1st Cir. 1979), *cert. denied*, 444 U.S. 866 (1979), affirmed a jury verdict that Indian plaintiffs could not recover for Nonintercourse Act violations because they have not been a tribe continuously from the date of violation to the present. The jury had given a special verdict that the Mashpees were not a tribe in 1790 (when the act was passed), were one in 1834 (when the District of Mashpee was established) and 1842 (when the land was partitioned), but were not in 1870 (when the town was incorporated) or 1976 (when the suit was brought). The jury had heard a variety of social scientists testifying on the definition of a tribe.

Numerous eastern Indian tribes have followed the lead of the Passamaquoddies. The Pequot tribe in Connecticut claimed 800 acres sold illegally in 1856. In April 1983, Congress approved a settlement of $900,000. President Reagan, however, arguing fiscal austerity and limited federal power, vetoed the settlement. He suggested paying the value of the land at the time of the sale — about $8,100 — plus interest. The President's advisers must not have told him that at an interest rate as low as 4 percent, the 1983 value of the settlement would be in excess of $900,000. (An interest rate of 3 percent, however, which could be defended given the long-term inflation record and real returns to various investments, would lead to a figure of about $350,000.)

2 ◆ PROPERTY IN ANIMALS

A. ACHIEVING OWNERSHIP THROUGH POSSESSION

◆ PIERSON v. POST
3 Caines 175 (N.Y. Sup. Ct. 1805)

This was an action of trespass on the case commenced in a justice's court, by the present defendant against the now plaintiff. The declaration stated that Post, being in possession of certain dogs and hounds under his command, did, "upon a certain wild and uninhabited, unpossessed and waste land, called the beach, find and start one of those noxious beasts called a fox," and whilst there hunting, chasing and pursuing the same with his dogs and hounds, and when in view thereof, Pierson, well knowing the fox was so hunted and pursued, did, in the sight of Post, to prevent his catching the same, kill and carry it off. A verdict having been rendered for the plaintiff below, the defendant there sued out a certiorari, and now assigned for error, that the declaration and the matters therein contained were not sufficient in law to maintain an action. . . .

PER CURIAM, delivered by TOMPKINS, J. This cause comes before us on a return to a certiorari directed to one of the justices of Queens county.

The question submitted by the counsel in this cause for our determination is, whether Lodowick Post, by the pursuit with his hounds in the manner alleged in his declaration, acquired such a right to, or property in, the fox, as will sustain an action against Pierson for killing and taking him away?

The cause was argued with much ability by the counsel on both sides, and presents for our decision a novel and nice question. It is admitted, that a fox is an animal *ferae naturae* and that property in such animals is acquired by occupancy only. These admissions narrow the discussion to the simple question of what acts amount to occupancy, applied to acquiring right to wild animals?

If we have recourse to the ancient writers upon general principles of law, the judgment below is obviously erroneous. Justinian's Institutes, lib. 2. tit. 1. sect. 13, and Fleta, lib. iii. c. ii. page 175, adopt the principle, that pursuit alone vests no property or right in the huntsman; and that even pursuit, accompanied with wounding, is equally ineffectual for that purpose, unless the animal be actually taken. The same principle is recognized by Bracton, lib. ii. c. i. page 8.

Puffendorf, lib. iv. c. 6 sec. 2. & 10. defines occupancy of beasts *ferae naturae,* to be the actual corporal possession of them, and Bynkers-hoek is cited as coinciding in this definition. It is indeed with hesitation that Puffendorf affirms that a wild beast mortally wounded, or greatly maimed, cannot be fairly intercepted by another, whilst the pursuit of the person inflicting the wound continues. The foregoing authorities are decisive to shew, that mere pursuit gave Post no legal right to the fox, but that he became the property of Pierson, who intercepted and killed him.

It therefore only remains to inquire whether there are any contrary principles, or authorities, to be found in other books, which ought to induce a different decision. Most of the cases which have occurred in England, relating to property in wild animals, have either been discussed and decided upon the principles of their positive statute regulations, or have arisen between the huntsman and the owner of the land upon which beasts *ferae naturae* have been apprehended; the former claiming them by title of occupancy, and the latter *ratione soli.* Little satisfactory aid can, therefore, be derived from the English reporters.

Barbeyrac, in his notes on Puffendorf, does not accede to the definition of occupancy by the latter, but, on the contrary, affirms, that actual bodily seizure is not, in all cases, necessary to constitute possession of wild animals. He does not, however, describe the acts which, according to his ideas, will amount to an appropriation of such animals to private use, so as to exclude the claims of all other persons, by title of occupancy, to the same animals; and he is far from averring that pursuit alone is sufficient for that purpose. To a certain extent, and as far as Barbeyrac appears to me to go, his objections to Puffendorf's definition of occupancy are reasonable and correct. That is to say, that actual bodily seizure is not indispensible to acquire right to, or possession of, wild beasts; but that, on the contrary, the mortal wounding of such beasts, by one not abandoning his pursuit, may, with the utmost propriety, be deemed possession of him; since, thereby, the pursuer manifests an unequivocal intention of appropriating the animal to his individual use, has deprived him of his natural liberty, and brought him within his certain control. So also, encompassing and securing such animals with nets and toils, or otherwise intercepting them, in such a manner as to deprive them of their natural liberty, and render escape impossible, may justly be deemed to give possession of them to those persons who, by their industry and labour, have used such means of apprehending them. . . . The case now under consideration is one of mere pursuit, and presents no circumstances or acts which can bring it within the definition of occupancy by Puffendorf, or Grotius, or the ideas of Barbeyrac upon that subject.

The case cited from 11 Mod. 74-130, I think clearly distinguishable from the present; inasmuch as there the action was for maliciously hindering and disturbing the plaintiff in the exercise and enjoyment of a private franchise; and in the report of the same case, 3 Salk. 9. Holt, Chief Justice, states, that the ducks were in the plaintiff's decoy pond and *so in his possession*, from which it is obvious the court laid much stress in their opinion upon the plaintiff's possession of the ducks, *ratione soli*.

We are the more readily inclined to confine possession or occupancy of beasts *ferae naturae*, within the limits prescribed by the learned authors above cited, for the sake of certainty, and preserving peace and order in society. If the first seeing, starting, or pursuing such animals, without having so wounded, circumvented or ensnared them, so as to deprive them of their natural liberty, and subject them to the control of their pursuer, should afford the basis of actions against others for intercepting and killing them, it would prove a fertile source of quarrels and litigation.

However uncourteous or unkind the conduct of Pierson towards Post, in this instance, may have been, yet his act was productive of no injury or damage for which a legal remedy can be applied. I am of opinion the judgment below was erroneous, and ought to be reversed.

LIVINGSTON, J. Whether a person who, with his own hounds, starts and hunts a fox, on waste and uninhabited ground, and is on the point of seizing his prey, acquires such an interest in the animal, as to have a right of action against another, who in view of the huntsman and his dogs in full pursuit, and with knowledge of the chase, shall kill and carry him away?

This is a knotty point, and should have been submitted to the arbitration of sportsmen, without poring over Justinian, Fleta, Bracton, Puffendorf, Locke, Barbeyrac, or Blackstone, all of whom have been cited; they would have had no difficulty in coming to a prompt and correct conclusion. In a court, thus constituted, the skin and carcass of poor Renard would have been properly disposed of, and a precedent set, interfering with no usage or custom which the experience of ages has sanctioned, and which must be so well known to every votary of Diana. But the parties have referred the question to our judgment, and we must dispose of it as well as we can, from the partial lights we possess, leaving to a higher tribunal, the correction of any mistake which we may be so unfortunate as to make. By the pleadings it is admitted that a fox is a "wild and noxious beast." Both parties have regarded him, as the law of nations does a pirate, *hostem humani generis*, and although *de mortuis nil nisi bonum*, be a maxim of our profession, the memory of the deceased has not been spared. His depredations on farmers and on barn-yards, have not been forgotten; and to put him to death wherever found, is allowed to be meritorious, and of public benefit. Hence it follows, that our decision should have in view the greatest possible encouragement to the destruction of an animal, so cunning and ruthless in his career. But who would keep a pack of hounds; or what gentleman, at the sound of the horn, and at peep of day, would mount his steed, and for hours together, *sub jove frigido* or a vertical sun, pursue the windings of this wily quadruped, if, just as night came on, and his stratagems and strength were nearly exhausted, a saucy intruder, who had not shared in the honours or labours of the chase, were permitted to come in at the death, and bear away in triumph the object of pursuit? Whatever Justinian may have thought of the matter, it must be recollected that his code was compiled many hundred years ago, and it would be very hard indeed, at the distance of so many centuries, not to have a right to establish a rule for ourselves. In his day, we read of no order of men who made it a business, in the language of the declaration in this cause, "with hounds and dogs to find, start, pursue, hunt, and chase," these animals, and that, too without any other motive than the preservation of Roman poultry; if this diversion had been then in fashion, the lawyers who composed his institutes, would have taken care not to pass it by, without suitable encouragement. If any thing, therefore, in the digests or pandects shall appear to militate against the defendant in error, who, on this occasion, was the foxhunter, we have only to say *tempora mutantur*; and if men themselves change with the times, why should not laws also undergo an alteration?

It may be expected, however, by the learned counsel, that more particular notice be taken of their authorities. I have examined them all, and feel great difficulty in determining, whether to acquire dominion over a thing, before in common, it be sufficient that we barely see it; or know where it is, or wish for it, or make a declaration of our will respecting it; or whether, in the case of wild beasts, setting a trap, or lying in wait, or starting, or pursuing, be enough; or if an actual wounding, or killing, or bodily tact and occupation be necessary. Writers on general law, who have favored us with their speculations on these points, differ on them all; but, great as is the diversity of sentiment among them, some conclusion must be adopted on the question immediately before us. After mature deliberation, I embrace that of Barbeyrac, as the most rational, and least liable to objection. If at liberty, we might imitate the courtesy of a certain emperor, who, to avoid giving offence to the advocates of any of these different doctrines, adopted a middle course, and by ingenious distinctions, rendered it difficult to say (as often happens after a fierce and angry contest) to whom the palm of victory belonged. He ordained, that if a beast be followed with *large dogs and hounds*, he shall belong to the hunter, not to the chance occupant; and in like manner, if he be killed or wounded with a lance or sword; but if chased with *beagles only*, then he passed to the captor, not to the first pursuer. If slain with a dart, a sling, or a bow, he fell to the hunter, if still in chase, and not to him who might afterwards find and seize him.

Now, as we are without any municipal regulations of our own, and the pursuit here, for aught that appears on the case, being with dogs and hounds of imperial stature, we are at liberty to adopt one of the provisions just cited, which comports also with the learned conclusion of Barbeyrac, that property in animals *ferae naturae*, may be acquired without bodily touch or manucaption, provided the pursuer be within reach, or have a reasonable prospect (which certainly existed here) of taking, what he has thus discovered an intention of converting to his own use.

When we reflect also that the interest of our husbandmen, the most useful of men in any community, will be advanced by the destruction of a beast so pernicious and incorrigible, we cannot greatly err, in saying, that a pursuit like the present, through waste and unoccupied lands, and which must inevitably and speedily have terminated in corporal possession, or bodily seisin, confers such a right to the object of it, as to make any one a wrongdoer, who shall interfere and shoulder the spoil. The justice's judgment ought, therefore, in my opinion, to be affirmed.

Notes

1. Concerning trespass on the case see Devereux v. Tuchet, Y.B. Hil. 3 Edw. II (S.S.) 16, 19 (1310):

> Bardelby, Master in Chancery: The Statute of Gloucester wills that, if women holding in dower alienate, the reversioner shall at once have his recovery; and Westminster the Second wills that *in consimili casu* etc.
>
> Bereford, C.J. Blessed be he who made that statute! Make the writ and we will maintain it.

Over time, trespass came to be an action alleging intentional infringement of possession. "Case" (trespass in a similar situation) then applied to allegations of unintentional but negligent violation, and of intentional infringement of nonpossessory ownership rights. It was, Plucknett wrote, "the name of the action which gave a remedy for damages from an indirect injury of some sort." But certain blasting cases held that recovery for injuries due to vibrations depended on proof of carelessness and actual harm while recovery for injuries due to thrown rocks did not. See Smith, Liability for Substantial Physical Damage to Land by Blasting, 33 Harv. L. Rev. 542, 667 (1920).

2. The unnamed case discussed by Justice Tompkins is Keeble v. Hickeringill, available (in different forms) in several common law reports including 11 Mod. 74, 88 Eng. Rep. 898 (K.B. 1707). Keeble had a duck pond on his own land. Hickeringill did not go upon Keeble's land, and did not seek to kill ducks himself, but maliciously made loud noises, frightening ducks away from Keeble's pond. Chief Justice Holt ruled for the plaintiff: "But suppose the defendant had shot in his own ground, if he had had occasion to shoot, it would have been one thing; but to shoot on purpose to damage the plaintiff is another thing, and a wrong."

3. Why were property claims in the fox fought to appellate courts? Surely not on the basis of purely economic calculations by the parties. Compare an incident that supposedly occurred in Sandisfield, Massachusetts, at about the same time as Pierson v. Post, as reported in the Federal Guide for the Berkshire Hills:

> Lawyer Ephraim Judson was engaged by Eliakian Hull as a Counsel in a Law Suit in 1807. Hull's dispute was with Squire Canfield, who also sought Judson's services. Unable to serve both parties, Judson recommended a colleague in Lenox and gave the Squire an introductory letter. As Canfield rode to Lenox he wondered about the letter. Finally, he opened it. He got very red, turned his horse around, went back to Sandisfield, and put the letter down on the desk of Hull. It said, "Two fat geese. You pluck one. I'll pluck the other."

4. Justinian was emperor of the Roman Empire at Constantinople from 527 to 565 A.D. We know a great deal about him because a brilliant observer named Procopius wrote, according to the vicissitudes of personal fame and disgrace, the history, the panegyric, and the satire of Justinian's time. Justinian built Hagia Sophia, and he was responsible for the gigantic bureaucratic ventures that compiled Roman Law and issued it as Pandects, Codes, and Institutes.

John Adams read Justinian in 1760. But civil law sources began to receive extensive attention from American judges and writers after the Revolution, as part of the process of modifying the common law system to what were seen as peculiarly new-world needs.

> Here we are obliged to ask: what were they trying to gain by ruggedly defending the Common Law on the one hand and on the other seeming to rank it lower than the Civil? I think we find the answer in Hoffman's urging that students of this country "will perceive the propriety of seeking . . . knowledge in the abundant wisdom of the corpus juris civilis." While the lawyers had indeed to resort to it because there were whole areas of

practice for which their inherited Common Law was inadequate, they also took pleasure in so doing because a knowledge of it became a badge of cultivation. They could dazzle clients and juries merely by reciting the exoteric names of Domat, Valin, Pothier, Emérigon, Straccha, Roccus, Huberus, et cetera, et cetera. Thus they could further express their contempt for those who did not follow the law "as a liberal and scientific study." . . . In practice the courts and the writers of textbooks did not make such extensive use of the Civil Law as the learned advocates pretended. [P. Miller, The Life of the Mind in America from the Revolution to the Civil War 169 (1965).]

HAY, POACHING AND THE GAME LAWS ON CANNOCK CHASE, in ALBION'S FATAL TREE: CRIME AND SOCIETY IN EIGHTEENTH CENTURY ENGLAND 189-191 (1975): By an act of 1670 a man had to be lord of a manor, or have a substantial income from landed property, even to kill a hare on his own land. The basic game qualification was an income of £100 yearly from a freehold estate, which in 1750 was between five and ten times the annual income of a labourer, and fifty times the property qualification to vote for a knight of the shire. From the beginning of the century a mass of other statutes re-enacted and stiffened the penalties for unqualified hunting: a £5 fine [half the annual wages for a labourer] or three months in gaol for keeping dogs or snares, the same for killing rabbits in warrens, £30 or a year's imprisonment for killing deer. . . . Deer were very heavily protected, and transportation, or death under the Black Act, could be invoked at the pleasure of the prosecutor if they had been killed within his park. Beyond these powers many great landlords held rights of free chase and free warren, which gave them sole privileges of game over large areas of land. . . .

The lawyers argued about the legal status of game, but usually agreed on the practical reasons for the code: the laws were "to prevent persons of inferior rank, from squandering that time, which their station in life requireth to be more profitably employed." . . . Meanwhile the poor ignored the war of words, reminded themselves that Genesis said the animals were made for man, and poached with passionate determination and courage.

___

Hay tells the story of a long dispute between tenants and cottagers, with ancient rights to graze cattle and sheep on "commons" land, and the Earl of Uxbridge, whose "free warren" rights to "game" let him protect and hunt 15,000 rabbits on the 3,500 acres of Cannock Chase, in Staffordshire. There was not enough food for the livestock and the rabbits. After self-help, violence, riot, and six years of litigation, the King's Bench decided for the Earl. If there were too many rabbits, the commoner could not destroy them as a nuisance, for he would be acting as his own judge "in a complicated question, which may admit of nicety to determine." Mr. Justice Dennison agreed: The commoner could not be allowed "to destroy the estate of the lord, in order to preserve his own small right of common."

The cases are Cooper v. Marshall and Cope v. Marshall, reported together in 1 Burrow 259, 2 Wilson 51, Sayer 234 & 285, 2 Kenyon 1, 97 Eng. Rep. 303 & 308 (K.B. 1757).

Hay argues that

> game could not legally be bought or sold because it was meant to symbolize [social] prerogatives: to show that its owner held power and position in landed society. . . . Legalized sale "would deprive the sportsman of his highest gratification," observed Lord Londonderry in 1827, ". . . the pleasure of furnishing his friends with presents of game: nobody would care for a present which everybody could give."

When Lord Chief Justice Mansfield came on circuit several years after having given the Earl of Uxbridge victory in the King's Bench litigation, "he was pleased to receive . . . two brace of carp, twenty dozen crawfish, a brace and a half of hares, a couple of wild ducks and a buck from the Park, in addition to the doe traditionally sent. . . ."

COHEN, DIALOGUE ON PRIVATE PROPERTY, 9 Rutgers L. Rev. 357, 366 (1954):

C: . . . Suppose it turns out that the mule's father was your jackass. Would that make you the owner of the mule?
F: I don't think it would.
C: Suppose you owned the land on which the mule was born. Would that make you the owner of the mule?
F: No
C: Suppose you owned a piece of unfenced prairie in Montana and the mule's mother during her pregnancy ate some of your grass. Would that make you the owner of the mule?
F: No, I don't think it would.
C: . . . Now tell us who really owns the mule.
F: I suppose the owner of the mare owns the mule.
C: Exactly. But tell us how you come to that conclusion.
F: Well, I think that is the law of Montana.
C: Yes, and of all other states and countries, as far as I know. For example, the Laws of Manu, which are supposed to be the oldest legal code in the world, declare: "50. Should a bull beget a hundred calves on cows not owned by his master, those calves belong solely to the proprietors of the cows; and the strength of the bull was wasted. (Institutes of Hindu Law or the Ordinances of Manu [trans. and ed. by S. G. Grady, c.10].)"

Now how does it happen, do you suppose, that the law of Montana in the twentieth century A.D. corresponds to the law of India of 4000 years or so ago? Is this an example of what Aristotle calls natural justice, which is everywhere the same, as distinguished from conventional justice which varies from place to place and from time to time?

F: Well, it does seem to be in accordance with the laws of nature that the progeny of the mother belong to the owner of the mother.

C: Wouldn't it be just as much in accordance with the laws of nature to say that the progeny of the father belong to the owner of the father?

F: I suppose that might be so, as a matter of simple biology, but as a practical matter it might be pretty hard to determine just which jackass was the mule's father.

C: Then, as a practical matter we are dealing with something more than biology. We are dealing with the human need for certainty in property distribution. If you plant seed in your neighbor's field the biological connection between your seed and the resulting plants is perfectly natural, but under the laws of Montana and all other states the crop belong to the landowner. And the Laws of Manu say the same thing: "49. They, who have no property in the field, but having grain in their possession, sow it in soil owned by another, can receive no advantage whatever from the corn, which may be produced. (Institutes of Hindu Law or the Ordinances of Manu [trans. and ed. by S. G. Grady, c.10].)"

Notes on Contemporary *Ferae Naturae* Litigation

1. "With more and more frequent reports of clashes between hunters and their opponents, New Hampshire may be the first New England state to enact legislation making it illegal to interfere with a sportsman's pursuit of hunting, trapping, or fishing." Hunters in New Hampshire spend $3 million annually on licenses and $220 million for gas, housing, guides, and supplies. Boston Globe, Jan. 27, 1983.

Arizona already has such a law, enacted in 1981. See Ariz. Rev. Stat. Ann. §17-316: "It is a class 2 misdemeanor for a person while in a designated hunting area to intentionally interfere with the lawful taking of wildlife by another or to intentionally harass, drive or disturb any game animal for the purpose of disrupting a lawful hunt." The statute authorizes persons licensed to take wildlife to "bring an action to restrain conduct declared unlawful in this section and to recover damages."

As reported in the Boston Globe, February 13, 1983, the director of the New England chapter of Friends of Animals, Priscilla Feral, said of the proposed New Hampshire law: "Passage of that stupid bill in no way would stop us from our legal hunt sabotage." Feral suggested that people enter the woods several days before the deer season, "strew human hair along paths and hang stuffed animals of biodegradable material in trees so hunters who don't see well or who are inebriated get a shot at them and the gun blasts scare off live animals. We're not foolish enough to want to be in the forest at the same time as the hunters."

2. See Conti v. ASPCA, 77 Misc. 2d 61, 353 N.Y.S.2d 288 (Sup. Ct. 1974):

> . . . Chester is a show parrot, used by the defendant ASPCA in various educational exhibitions presented to groups of children.
>
> On June 28, 1973 . . . Chester flew the coop. . . .
>
> On July 5, 1973 the plaintiff['s] . . . offer of food was eagerly accepted by the bird, [and plaintiff] was rewarded by the parrot's finally entering the plaintiff's home, where he was placed in a cage.
>
> The next day, the plaintiff phoned the defendant ASPCA and requested advice as to the care of a parrot he had found. Thereupon the defendant sent two representatives to the plaintiff's home. Upon examination, they claimed that it was the missing parrot, Chester, and removed it from the plaintiff's home.
>
> Upon refusal of the defendant ASPCA to return the bird, the plaintiff now brings this action in replevin. . . .
>
> . . . The Court called upon the parrot to indicate by name or other mannerism an affinity to either of the claimed owners. Alas, the parrot stood mute.
>
> Upon all the credible evidence the Court does find as a fact that the parrot in question is indeed Chester. . . .
>
> Where an animal is wild, its owner can only acquire a qualified right of property which is wholly lost when it escapes from its captor with no intention of returning. . . .
>
> The Court finds that Chester was a domesticated animal, subject to training and discipline. Thus the rule of ferae naturae does not prevail and the defendant as true owner is entitled to regain possession.

3. An experimental theater company in Cardiff, Wales, presented a play in which an apple was dropped into a goldfish bowl to illustrate cruelty to animals. The bowl broke, and the goldfish was catapulted onto the stage. "If we used a substitute, and not a living goldfish, we would not get the same reaction," one of the actors said. A Royal Society for the Prevention of Cruelty to Animals inspector, Roy Gee, leapt to the stage with a plastic bag full of water, saved the fish, and instituted legal proceedings under the 1911 Protection of Animals Act. Sir Lincoln Hallinan, stipendiary magistrate, dismissed the case, ruling that a goldfish is not a domestic animal and there was no evidence to show pain. The High Court reversed, Justice Donaldson concluding that the fish was a "captive animal" that had been "treated cruelly" under §15 of the act and thus that a violation of the act had been shown. The Guardian, June 26, 1980.

4. Mrs. Linscomb borrowed a trap from the Calcasieu Parish Animal Control Center, placed it in her yard, and trapped a cat known as "George." She returned the trap and George to the center where George was destroyed. Mrs. Peloquin sued the center for the value of George and also for mental anguish. She admitted she had not purchased George, nor received him as a gift, but had found him "while putting the children on a school bus," kept and fed him for several years, but never advertised the finding nor attempted to locate a prior owner.

Relevant Louisiana statutes:

Art. 3412: "Occupancy is a mode of acquiring property by which a thing which belongs to nobody, becomes the property of the person who took possession of it, with the intention of acquiring a right of ownership upon it."

Art. 3506. "If a person has possessed in good faith and by a just title, as owner, a movable thing, during three successive years without interruption, he shall acquire the ownership of it by prescription unless the thing was stolen or lost."

Art. 3454: "Rights, which are common to all possessors in good or bad faith, are . . . [t]hat they are considered provisionally as owners of the things which they possessed, so long as it is not reclaimed by the true owner. . . ."

Held: "Finding" is insufficient to constitute "just title," but possession alone is sufficient for an action against the disturber. Damages may include mental anguish or humiliation. Peloquin v. Calcasieu Parish Police Jury, 367 So. 2d 1246 (La. App. 1979). But a jury verdict that the dead cat was not George was affirmed. 378 So. 2d 560 (La. App. 1979).

5. Under the Wild Free-Roaming Horses and Burros Act of 1971, 16 U.S.C. §§1331-1340 (Supp. IV), the Secretaries of Agriculture and the Interior were directed to protect "all unbranded and unclaimed horses and burros on public land of the United States" from "capture, branding, harassment, or death." They were further "directed to protect and manage [the animals] as components of public lands . . . in a manner that is designed to achieve and maintain a thriving natural ecological balance on the public lands." Their responsibilities also include arranging for the removal of horses and burros that stray onto private lands. The New Mexico Livestock Board contested the power of the secretaries over wild horses and burros, and used its own authority to round up and then auction 19 burros found on federal land. Leaving open the issue as to whether the act protects burros that stray from federal lands, the Supreme Court held:

In brief, . . . appellees have presented no support for their position that the [Property] Clause [of the Constitution] grants Congress only the power to dispose of, to make incidental rules regarding the use of, and to protect federal property. This failure is hardly surprising, for the Clause, in broad terms, gives Congress the power to determine what are "needful" rules "respecting" the public lands. . . . In our view, the "complete power" that Congress has over public lands necessarily includes the power to regulate and protect the wildlife living there. . . . [Kleppe v. New Mexico, 426 U.S. 529 (1976).]

The lower court had held for the state:

Wild horses and burros do not become "property" of the United States simply by being physically present on the "territory" or land of the United States. The doctrine of the common law, dating back to the Roman law, has been that wild animals are owned by the state in its sovereign capacity, in trust for the benefit of the people. This sovereign ownership vested in the colonial government and was passed to the states. . . . The Government argues in its brief that the Act may be sustained as an exercise of the power granted in the Commerce Clause. No evidence was presented to support this theory; in fact, all the evidence establishes that the wild burros in question here do not migrate across state lines. [New Mexico v. Morton, 406 F. Supp. 1237 (D.N.M. 1975).]

6. Alex Leger sued the Louisiana Wildlife and Fisheries Commission for loss of his sweet potato crop to deer, who entered his land to avoid the flooding Red River. A commission employee had told Leger he would be prosecuted if he killed the deer to save his crop. Leger lost because "wild quadrupeds found in the state are owned by the State of Louisiana in its sovereign capacity, as distinguished from its proprietary capacity, and . . . solely as trustee for the use and common benefit of the people of the state." Leger v. Louisiana Dept. of Wildlife and Fisheries, 306 So. 2d 391 (La. App. 1975).

7. An Alabama statute that permitted Humane Society employees to seize an animal that they had decided was abused or neglected and to make the owner responsible for expenses was held to be a taking of the owner's property without adequate due process. Humane Society of Marshall County v. Adams, 439 So. 2d 150 (Ala. 1983).

8. For the English approach, see Wild Creatures and Forest Laws Act, Public General Acts & Measures 1971, c.47:

BE IT ENACTED by the Queen's most Excellent Majesty, by and with the advice and consent of the Lords Spiritual and Temporal, and Commons, in this present Parliament assembled, and by the authority of the same, as follows: —

1. — (1) There are hereby abolished —

(a) any prerogative right of Her Majesty to wild creatures (except royal fish and swans), together with any prerogative right to set aside land or water for the breeding, support or taking of wild creatures; and

(b) any franchises of forest, free chase, park or free warren.

(2) The forest law is hereby abrogated, _revoked_ except in so far as it relates to the appointment and functions of verderers.

(3) Any right of common originating in the forest law shall be free of restriction by reason of the fence month or the winter heyning or any payment in place of it, but the foregoing provision shall not affect the suspension or exclusion of any such right for the time being effected by or under any enactment or any limitations or restrictions for the time being imposed by or under any enactment on the exercise of any such right, . . . (being enactments which, or parts of which, are made unnecessary). . . .

(7) — (2) The partial repeal by this Act of section 2 of the Night Poaching Act 1828 extends to Scotland, but except as aforesaid this Act does not extend to Scotland. . . .

B.   DOCTRINES OF POSSESSION AND REALITIES OF COMMERCE

◆ GHEN v. RICH
8 Fed. 159 (D. Mass. 1881)

NELSON, D. J. This is a libel to recover the value of a fin-back whale. The libellant lives in Provincetown and the respondent in Wellfleet. The facts, as they appeared at the hearing, are as follows:

In the early spring months the easterly part of Massachusetts bay is frequented by the species of whale known as the fin-back whale. Fishermen from Provincetown pursue them in open boats from the shore, and shoot them with bomb-lances fired from guns made expressly for the purpose. When killed they sink at once to the bottom, but in the course of from one to three days they rise and float on the surface. Some of them are picked up by vessels and towed into Provincetown. Some float ashore at high water and are left stranded on the beach as the tide recedes. Others float out to sea and are never recovered. The person who happens to find them on the beach usually sends word to Provincetown, and the owner comes to the spot and removes the blubber. The finder usually receives a small salvage for his services. Try-works are established in Provincetown for trying out the oil. The business is of considerable extent, but, since it requires skill and experience, as well as some outlay of capital, and is attended with great exposure and hardship, few persons engage in it. The average yield of oil is about 20 barrels to a whale. It swims with great swiftness, and for that reason cannot be taken by the harpoon and line. Each boat's crew engaged in the business has its peculiar mark or device on its lances, and in this way it is known by whom a whale is killed. The usage on Cape Cod, for many years, has been that the person who kills a whale in the manner and under the circumstances described, owns it, and this right has never been disputed until this case. The libellant has been engaged in this business for ten years past. On the morning of April 9, 1880, in Massachusetts bay, near the end of Cape Cod, he shot and instantly killed with a bomb-lance the whale in question. It sunk immediately, and on the morning of the 12th was found stranded on the beach in Brewster, within the ebb and flow of the tide, by one Ellis, 17 miles from the spot where it was killed. Instead of sending word to [Provincetown], as is customary, Ellis advertised the whale for sale at auction, and sold it to the respondent, who shipped off the blubber and tried out the oil. The libellant heard of the finding of the whale on the morning of the 15th, and immediately sent one of his boat's crew to the place and claimed it. Neither the respondent nor Ellis knew the whale had been killed by the libellant, but they knew or might have known, if they had wished, that it had been shot and killed with a bomb-lance, by some person engaged in this species of business.

The libellant claims title to the whale under this usage. The respondent insists that this usage is invalid. It was decided by Judge Sprague, in Taber v. Jenny, 1 Sprague 315, that when a whale has been killed, and is anchored and left with marks of appropriation, it is the property of the captors; and if it is afterwards found, still anchored, by another ship, there is no usage or principle of law by which the property of the original captors is diverted, even though the whale may have dragged from its anchorage. The learned judge says:

> When the whale had been killed and taken possession of by the boat of the Hillman, (the first taker,) it became the property of the owners of that ship, and all was done which was then practicable in order to secure it. They left it anchored, with unequivocal marks of appropriation.

In Bartlett v. Budd, 1 Low. 223, the facts were these: The first officer of the libellant's ship killed a whale in the Okhotsk sea, anchored it, attached a waif to the body, and then left it and went ashore at some distance for the night. The next morning the boats of the respondent's ship found the whale adrift, the anchor not holding, the cable coiled round the body, and no waif or irons attached to it. Judge Lowell held that, as the libellants had killed and taken actual possession of the whale, the ownership vested in them. In his opinion the learned judge says: "A whale, being *ferae naturae*, does not become property until a firm possession has been established by the taker. But when such possession has become firm and complete, the right of property is clear, and has all the characteristics of property." . . .

In Swift v. Gifford, 2 Low. 110, Judge Lowell decided that a custom among whalemen in the Arctic seas, that the iron holds the whale, was reasonable and valid. In that case a boat's crew from the respondent's ship pursued and struck a whale in the Arctic ocean, and the harpoon and the line attached to it remained in the whale, but did not remain fast to the boat. A boat's crew from the libellant's ship continued the pursuit and captured the whale, and the master of the respondent's ship claimed it on the spot. It was held by the learned judge that the whale belonged to the respondents. It was said by Judge Sprague, in Bourne v. Ashley, an unprinted case referred to by Judge Lowell in Swift v. Gifford, that the usage for the first iron, whether attached to the boat or not, to hold the whale was fully established; and he added that, although local usages of a particular port ought not to be allowed to set aside the general maritime law, this objection did not apply to a custom which embraced an entire business, and had been concurred in for a long time by every one engaged in the trade.

In Swift v. Gifford, Judge Lowell also said:

> The rule of law invoked in this case is one of very limited application. The whale fishery is the only branch of industry of any importance in which it is likely to be much used, and if a usage is found to prevail generally in that business, it will not be open to the objection that it is likely to disturb the general understanding of mankind by the interposition of an arbitrary exception.

I see no reason why the usage proved in this case is not as reasonable as that sustained in the cases cited. Its application must necessarily be extremely limited, and can affect but a few persons. It has been recognized and acquiesced in for many years. It requires in the first taker the only act of appropriation that is possible in the nature of the case. Unless it is sustained, this branch of industry must necessarily cease, for no person would engage in it if the fruits of his labor could be appropriated by any chance finder. It gives reasonable salvage for securing or reporting the property. That the rule works well in practice is shown by the extent of the industry which has grown up under it, and the general acquiescence of a whole community interested to dispute it. It is by no means clear that without regard to usage the common law would not reach the same result. That seems to be the effect of the decisions in Taber v. Jenny and Bartlett v. Budd. If the fisherman does all that it is possible to do to make the animal his own, that would seem to be sufficient. Such a rule might well be applied in the interest of trade, there being no usage or custom to the contrary. Holmes, Com. Law, 217. But be that as it may, I hold the usage to be valid, and that the property in the whale was in the libellant.

The rule of damages is the market value of the oil obtained from the whale, less the cost of trying it out and preparing it for the market, with interest on the amount so ascertained from the date of conversion. As the question is new and important, and the suit is contested on both sides, more for the purpose of having it settled than for the amount involved, I shall give no costs.

Decree for libellant for $71.05, without costs.

Notes

1. Kilts's bees left his hive and flew off to a tree on the property of Lenox Iron Company. The plaintiff followed the swarm and marked the tree in which they settled. Two months later, Goff and others cut down the tree, killed the bees, and took the honey. Kilts recovered in trespass. The court held that if a swarm flies to another's land, ownership continues as long as the first owner keeps them in sight and "possesses the power to pursue them." That the owner must commit trespass to recover them does not destroy his ownership of the bees. Goff v. Kilts, 15 Wend. 550 (N.Y. Sup. Ct. 1836).

2. Egerton v. Harding, [1974] 3 W.L.R. 437 (C.A.):

> The plaintiff rested her case on the common law duty to prevent one's cattle from straying on to another's land. The defendant's case was that the plaintiff was under a duty to fence her land against the common. . . . The lord of the manor . . . invariably required that the land enclosed be fenced against the common, thus relieving himself and the commoners of the duty of keeping their cattle off the enclosed land over which they had enjoyed common rights prior to the enclosure. Evidence of ancient enclosures is often difficult to find. They were seldom the subject of any deed of grant: for seisin had not yet been displaced by deed and, while a copyholder's title would be recorded in the rolls of the manorial court, not all these rolls have survived. . . . [The judge below] recognised that a custom, to be upheld as local law, has to be shown to be of immemorial origin, reasonable, continued without interruption, and certain.

H. MELVILLE, MOBY DICK, CH. 89, "FAST-FISH AND LOOSE-FISH" (1851): Perhaps the only formal whaling code authorized by legislative enactment, was that of Holland. It was decreed by the States-General in A.D. 1695. But though no other nation has ever had any written whaling law, yet the American fishermen have been their own legislators and lawyers in this matter. They have provided a system which for terse comprehensiveness surpasses Justinian's Pandects and the By-laws of the Chinese Society for the Suppression of Meddling with other People's Business. Yes; these laws might be engraven on a Queen Anne's farthing, or the barb of a harpoon, and worn round the neck, so small are they.

I. A Fast-Fish belongs to the party fast to it.

II. A Loose-Fish is fair game for anybody who can soonest catch it. . . .

Some fifty years ago there was a curious case of whale-trover litigated in England, wherein the plaintiffs set forth that after a hard chase of a whale in the Northern seas; and when indeed they (the plaintiffs) had succeeded in harpooning the fish; they were at last, through peril of their lives, obliged to forsake not only their lines, but their boat itself. Ultimately the defendants (the crew of another ship) came up with the whale, struck, killed, seized, and finally appropriated it before the very eyes of the plaintiffs. And when those defendants were remonstrated with, their captain snapped his fingers in the plaintiffs' teeth, and assured them that by way of doxology to the deed he had done, he would now retain their line, harpoons, and boat, which had remained attached to the whale at the time of the seizure. Wherefore the plaintiffs now sued for the recovery of the value of their whale, line, harpoons, and boat. . . .

These pleadings, and the counter pleadings, being duly heard, the very learned judge in set terms decided, to wit, — That as for the boat, he awarded it to the plaintiffs, because they had merely abandoned it to save their lives; but that with regard to the controverted whale, harpoons, and line, they belonged to the defendants; the whale, because it was a Loose-Fish at the time of the final capture; and the harpoons and line because when the fish made off with them, it (the fish) acquired a property in those articles; and hence anybody who afterwards took the fish had a right to them. Now the defendants afterwards took the fish; ergo, the aforesaid articles were theirs.

A common man looking at this decision of the very learned Judge, might possibly object to it. But ploughed up to the primary rock of the matter, the two great principles laid down in the twin whaling laws previously quoted, and applied and elucidated by Lord Ellenborough in the above cited case; these two laws touching Fast-Fish and Loose-Fish, I say, will, on reflection, be found the fundamentals of all human jurisprudence; for notwithstanding its complicated tracery of sculpture, the Temple of the Law, like the Temple of the Philistines, has but two props to stand on.

Is it not a saying in every one's mouth, Possession is half of the law: that is, regardless of how the thing came into possession? But often possession is the whole of the law. What are the sinews and souls of Russian serfs and Republican slaves but Fast-Fish, whereof possession is the whole of the law? What to the rapacious landlord is the widow's last mite but a Fast-Fish? What is yonder undetected villain's marble mansion with a door-plate for a waif; what is that but a Fast-Fish? What is the ruinous discount which Mordecai, the broker, gets from poor Woebegone, the bankrupt, on a loan to keep Woebegone's family from starvation; what is that ruinous discount but a Fast-Fish? What is the Archbishop of Savesoul's income of £100,000 seized from the scant bread and cheese of hundreds of thousands of broken-backed laborers (all sure of heaven without any of Savesoul's help) what is that globular 100,000 but a Fast-Fish? What are the Duke of Dunder's hereditary towns and hamlets but Fast-Fish? What to that redoubted harpooner, John Bull, is poor Ireland, but a Fast-Fish? What to that apostolic lancer, Brother Jonathan, is Texas but a Fast-Fish? And concerning all these, is not Possession the whole of the law?

But if the doctrine of Fast-Fish be pretty generally applicable, the kindred doctrine of Loose-Fish is still more widely so. That is internationally and universally applicable.

What was America in 1492 but a Loose-Fish, in which Columbus struck the Spanish standard by way of waifing it for his royal master and mistress? What was Poland to the Czar? What Greece to the Turk? What India to England? What at last will Mexico be to the United States? All Loose-Fish.

What are the Rights of Man and the Liberties of the World but Loose-Fish? What all men's minds and opinions but Loose-Fish? What is the principle of religious belief in them but a Loose-Fish? What to the ostentatious smuggling verbalists are the thoughts of thinkers but Loose-Fish? What is the great globe itself but a Loose-Fish? And what are you, reader, but a Loose-Fish and a Fast-Fish, too?

K. LLEWELLYN & E. HOEBEL, THE CHEYENNE WAY 224-226 (1953): A nice distinction in the claiming of enemy horses existed, too. When a group was traveling, but not on a horse-taking raid, the person first to sight the tracks of a stray horse laid claim to the animal. He stopped his companions and called their attention to the tracks. This rule seems to have been socially recognized, but was perhaps not fully established as law. At least, there was dispute over its validity when challenged by a forceful man such as Bull Kills Him.

. . . Somebody, I have forgotten the name, found the tracks of some horses. But when he got to them, Bull Kills Him had come upon the horses from another way and had claimed them.

There were five horses, and that other man thought they should be his. He kept insisting that he saw the tracks before Bull Kills Him saw the horses. "You saw me trailing them down," he complained. "If you had left them alone, I would have come on them myself."

"Well, I don't see where you think you got any horses," was Bull Kills Him's logic. "You just got the tracks. The horses are better than the tracks."

"No," the other countered. "The tracks come first. And I am going to have those five horses."

"Oh no you don't. You think you'll get them. You shall have none of them." So saying, Bull Kills Him mounted his horse. Drawing five arrows from his quiver, he rode over and shot the horses dead. . . .

Bull Kills Him excused himself saying, "Well, if he hadn't been so selfish, it would not have turned out that way. If he had wanted to divide up on them, I would not have done that thing. But he could not have them all." . . .

What happened here was that two rules of property rights crossed. From Bull Kills Him's last statement . . . it was clear that the trackfinder's claim was recognized. . . .

. . . But Bull Kills Him set up a claim in another orbit, independent and supervening, as first horse-finder, and impishly announced that a horse in hand is worth two on the prairie. Possession may have borne legal weight. Nevertheless, the track-finder's claim would seem to have been the stronger — though it may have had need of modification for this unusual case — for Bull Kills Him maintained it was up to the other man to divide the finds; and when he was unwilling to share, Bull Kills Him as a willful and important warrior deprived him of all his game, daring him to complain at the violence. . . .

Another interesting point is found in the question of what happened to an owner's title to his horse when it had been stolen by enemy raiders and later recovered. The law was simple. If horses were recovered in pursuit, before the enemy getaway was complete, they went back to their owners. However, the owner of many horses, if generous, gave at least one horse to the recoverer for his pains. If the theft was successful, the title passed to the enemy, so that whosoever recovered a stolen horse became its full owner. But a personal bond lending a moral right was recognized. The former owner of a recaptured horse, if it was a favorite, went to its new-captor with a good blanket or other bundle. Placing the bundle on the ground before him he said, "Friend, I love that horse. Pray, will you give him to me again?" Stump Horn and High Forehead say they have never known a man to refuse such a request. Since the blanket or goods were not usually so valuable as the horse, a residue of proprietary right where sentimental attachment existed was recognized. There was no seizing a bargaining advantage in the former owner's desire to recover.

The desire for social approval and the self-regarding pleasures of altruism led some men to return horses beyond the demands of strict legality. Hairy Hand, who was a great taker of horses, used to give back recaptured horses to their former owners "to make them pleased."

AGNELLO & DONNELLY, PROPERTY RIGHTS AND EFFICIENCY IN THE OYSTER INDUSTRY, 18 J. Law & Econ. 521, 522-523 (1975): The American Eastern oyster represents the resource base of both the Gulf and Atlantic coast oyster industries. Following a brief larva stage (spat), the oyster connects permanently to a firm subaqueous material such as rock or shell deposits (cultch). Its habitat is the intermediate salinity waters of the seacoast's intertidal zone and of inland rivers and bays. Water current, temperature and biological productivity, in addition to salinity, are determinants of the resource productivity of a given parcel of subaqueous land.

Two property right structures characterizing the oyster industry in each of the Atlantic and Gulf states can be identified, a private right structure based mainly on leaseholds and a common right system. The courts have long recognized rights to subaqueous land for the people of each state for their common use. State legislatures have confirmed and modified these rights. Although the federal government claims jurisdiction over a three mile coastal zone, Congress has ceded jurisdiction over land and resource use rights within this zone back to the states.[5] The states have exercised their jurisdiction over the oyster resource in similar ways. In general, natural oyster beds have been set aside as a common fishery for state residents whereas other submerged land parcels are available for private leasing.

The distinction made by each state between natural oyster beds and other land permits the development of an empirical measure of a state's property right variable used in subsequent sections of this paper. Oysters found on subaqueous land classified as a "natural oyster bed" are in general an open access (common property) fishery for state residents. Other areas may be leased and used exclusively by the lessee for the cultivation of oysters. Regardless of how a state arrives at the determination of which lands are natural oyster beds and which are available for leasing, each state makes a clear demarcation of its common from leasable land. However, great variation among the states exists in the proportion of area and quality of land set aside for public or common use versus private use depending on how broadly administrators define the term "natural oyster bed." An examination of the proportion of oyster catch by weight on private grounds to total catch by state reveals ratios ranging from a maximum of 1 to almost zero during the 1950's and 1960's. . . .

In a world where transactions costs are significant and resources are scarce common property right systems result in less efficient resource allocation than private right systems. This occurs because communal rights do not ensure that the costs of an individual harvester's actions in exploiting the resource are borne fully by him. In attempting to maximize the value of his common right, the individual can be expected to over-exploit the resource leading to depletion of the stock, and in the extreme case to extinction of even replenishable resources. Private property internalizes the costs of the harvester's actions. In a similar way, a private right enables the producer to capture a greater proportion of the benefit of his activity in comparison to a communal right.

The type of externality manifested by communal rights to oysters depends on the stage at which the production process is being examined. In general, an oysterman can separate production into two stages: establishment of suitable conditions for oysters to mature, and second, the act of harvesting oysters for market.

The most important requirement under the control of an individual oysterman for ensuring maturation of oysters is that a cultch be estab-

5. See G. Power, More About Oysters Than You Wanted to Know, 30 Md. L. Rev. 199, 216-223 (1970) for a detailed review of court decisions involving rights to submerged land.

lished. Other things equal, an individual could transform barren sub-aqueous land into productive grounds by depositing rock or shells on to it. He could then plant seed oysters on the material to hasten maturity. It should be obvious, however, that this kind of activity is minimal unless the planter is given the exclusive right of harvesting oysters from that land parcel. Under a communal right system, such a guarantee is nonexistent.

Three problems arise at the harvesting stage. First, the harvesting process typically removes cultch. Unless replaced, cultch removal implies disinvestment. On communal property once again, incentive to replenish this material is minimal. In practice, most states stipulate that some proportion of shells be redeposited on communal oyster grounds. In many states, however, processors rather than harvesters bear this cost. Frequently, states also subsidize the communal system by undertaking cultch rehabilitation programs. Second, overcrowding of vessels on particularly rich water areas leads to congestion. Finally, immature oysters are caught indiscriminately with the mature. Consequently, the growth behavior of the stock is affected. Most states set a minimum size restriction and require that culling of undersized oysters be done immediately upon being caught. Culling restrictions are also accompanied by stipulations that any cultch that was removed by the act of harvesting also be replaced immediately. . . .

The empirical findings suggest that private property rights do in general make a significant difference in a state's average labor productivity in oyster harvesting. Common property rights are associated with low labor productivity resulting from disinvestment, congestion, over-exploitation and government restrictions. Regulation in common property rights states aims at conserving the oyster resource by mandating labor intensive technologies. If labor opportunity costs are roughly equal across states, it is likely that labor intensive methods in common property states are inefficient, and that social benefit could be increased by encouraging private leasing of oyster beds as an alternative to the common property structure utilized by many states.

The regression results provide an indication of the magnitude of the welfare loss due to common property rights. Based on R's coefficient of $5790 in Model I, the point elasticity of labor productivity with respect to private property rights evaluated at the sample mean is .608. Thus a 10 per cent increase in private property rights across states could be expected to increase average physical product of labor by 6.08 per cent. Using 1969 average product and exvessel prices across states, a 10 per cent increase in private property rights would increase average physical product by 338 pounds per man and average income by $179. Furthermore if all coastal states had relied entirely on private property in oyster harvesting in 1969, R would have increased by over 70 per cent implying an increase in average oystermen's incomes of around $1300 or almost fifty per cent of 1969 average income. Since costs of enforcing private rights do not seem to be a serious problem for sessile species in intertidal coastal waters, one can conclude that considerations other than economic efficiency are used by states relying on common property for the oyster industry.

Notes

1. Over-harvesting and invasion of the oyster beds by parasites threaten the oyster industry off the Maryland coast. The 1983 harvest was half of the 1980 harvest, which had netted 3.5 million bushels of oysters and brought $70 million into Maryland's economy. The over-harvesting is the result of new technology: divers, attached by air-hoses to an air compressor aboard ship, handpick the largest oysters from the mud and send the prizes to the surface in wire baskets. Traditional oystermen, who dig for oysters using long tongs from the decks of their fishing boats, resent the divers who clean out the more valuable oysters.

Along with the effects of new harvesting techniques, increasing salinity in the Chesapeake Bay has provided a hospitable environment for the parasite MSX that consumes oysters leaving behind empty shells. Because of the reduced harvest, some local packers have been forced to ship in oysters from the Gulf of Mexico to fill their orders; others have gone out of business. See N.Y. Times, Mar. 12, 1983.

2. In a Wall Street Journal column, Professor Steve H. Hanke of Johns Hopkins University opposed the Reagan Administration's efforts to clean up the shoreline of Chesapeake Bay. Professor Hanke wrote that "the Bay, with the exception of the private oyster culture in Virginia, is a publicly owned, open-access, common-property resource. Consequently, the history of the Chesapeake is the story of a 'tragedy of the commons,' in which a once pristine resource has become overused, depleted and politicized." What President Reagan should do, the column argued, is "observe the productive, private oyster regime in Virginia . . . It is private-property rights and not tax dollars that will save the Chesapeake." Wall Street Journal, Feb. 22, 1984.

But imagine the Chesapeake shore owned by unregulated individuals. Wouldn't each owner have an incentive to produce and pollute? Wouldn't those owners immediately look for legal mechanisms, private contracts, and official regulation to limit the external effects of individual decisions? Much of this book shows lawyers and the legal system grappling with essentially this problem.

3 ◆ PROPERTY IN LAND

The three principal cases that begin this chapter have been used to introduce first-year students to basic issues of property law since the property casebook by Edward H. ("Bull") Warren was first published in 1926.

A. ACQUIRING OWNERSHIP

1. *Withdrawing Land from the Common by Possession*

Johnson v. M'Intosh (see Chapter 1) says that the sovereign determines the validity of an ownership claim. The United States government encouraged settlement on the frontier by rewarding possession and use with ownership. But how much possession is required to achieve ownership rights against whom?

◆ BRUMAGIM v. BRADSHAW
  39 Cal. 24 (1870)

CROCKETT, J., delivered the opinion of the Court:
  The defendants asked for three instructions, the first of which was given, with a qualification added by the Court, and the two last were properly refused. They do not correctly define the presumptions arising from prior possession, as against a mere intruder without title, or color of title.
  At the instance of the plaintiff, [administrator of the estate of Dyson,] the Court gave twelve instructions to the jury, the second of which is in the following words:

If the jury are satisfied from the evidence given in this cause, that George Treat entered upon and inclosed the Potrero in the year 1850, and are further satisfied that he then made a complete inclosure of the same, and that such inclosure was sufficient to turn and protect stock, and that he actually used such inclosure for that purpose up to the time of the alleged conveyance to Dyson, and that he deeded the same to Dyson, and that the land was used by Dyson subsequent thereto, for the purpose of pasturage, and that the land was suitable for pasturage; and that the defendants, or either of them who have answered, or those under whom they claim, entered adversely and subsequent to the completion of said inclosure, and while the said land was being so used by said Treat prior, and, by said Dyson, after said conveyance, you will find for the plaintiff against such defendant, or defendants, provided such defendant, or defendants, was occupying the premises at the time of the commencement of this suit.

This instruction is objected to by the defendants as wholly unauthorized by the testimony, and calculated to mislead the jury.

There is no contrariety in the evidence as to the natural features of the Potrero, nor as to the acts performed by Treat or Dyson, which, it is claimed, amounted, in law, to an inclosure and to the actual possession of the land. The testimony shows the Potrero to be a peninsula, containing about one thousand acres; bounded on the north by Mission creek and bay, on the east by the bay of San Francisco, on the south by the same bay and Precita creek, and on the west by a stone wall and ditch, running from Mission creek on the north to Precita creek on the south, across the neck of the peninsula. It further appears that the wall and ditch were ancient works, probably built by the priests of the adjoining Mission of Dolores at an early day; and that in 1850, they had become considerably dilapidated, so as no longer to prevent the ingress and egress of cattle; that John Treat, or George Treat, or the two jointly, in the summer or autumn of 1850, repaired the wall and ditch, so as that, thereafter, it was sufficient to turn cattle; that they erected a gate in the wall, through which admission was had to the Potrero, and a small corral, for herding cattle, inside the wall, together with a shanty, in which the gate-keeper resided; that, immediately after the wall was repaired and the gate erected, they commenced to receive horses for pasturage and used the Potrero for that purpose — having, at times, several hundred head of horses pasturing there for hire; that, whilst the land was being thus used, John Treat relinquished to George Treat all his interest in the premises, who thereafter continued to use the land for pasturage, as it had before been used, until February, 1852, when he conveyed, by deed, to Dyson, all his interest in the property; and thereafter Dyson used the land for pasturage up to the time when the defendants entered; that the wall and ditch, together with the creeks and bay, formed an inclosure sufficient to protect and turn cattle; that, in 1850, and for several years thereafter, the Potrero afforded grass suitable for pasturage.

If the fact does not sufficiently appear in proof, the Court will take judicial notice, that the Potrero, in the year 1850, was separated from the City of San Francisco, as it then was, only by Mission creek and bay, and that it is now a portion of the city, divided into lots, blocks and streets. . . .

These being the facts of the case, do they establish, or tend to establish, in George Treat or Dyson such an actual possession of the whole Potrero, as to have justified the Court in giving the instruction above quoted?

For the plaintiff, the argument is, that the two creeks, the bay and the wall and ditch formed a perfect inclosure, capable of turning and protecting cattle, and that it would be an absurdity to hold that a fence, along the margin of the bay and creek, was necessary, in order to establish their possession, when those natural barriers formed a more perfect defense than any artificial structure could have done; that, by repairing the wall and erecting the gate, Treat and Dyson held the only means of access to the property, and that it was more suitable for pasturage than for any other purpose, in its then condition, and they used it in that way; that, by these means, they subjected the property to their exclusive dominion and control, and had the actual possession, the *possessio pedis*, until they were intruded upon by the defendants, who were trespassers without title.

On the other hand, the defendants claim that where so large a body of land is surrounded — except across a narrow neck of it — by tide waters, having a beach on which the public has a right to land and to use for any lawful purpose, a fence across the neck does not, of itself, give possession of or dominion over the whole peninsula; . . . that there having been no sufficient inclosure to constitute possession of itself, the mere temporary use of the land for pasturage, and particularly unaccompanied by a bona fide claim of title, is not, under the former decisions of this Court, such a *possessio pedis* as will maintain ejectment; that, devoting to the purpose of pasturing, merely, so large a body of land, immediately contiguous to a large city, is not such an exercise of dominion over it, nor such a subjection of it to the will and control of the party, as to constitute a *possessio pedis*. . . .

We have carefully considered the able and ingenious argument of the defendants' counsel, to the effect that the tide waters of the bay, with a beach in front of them, on which the public was free to land, and to use for any legitimate purpose, would not constitute a sufficient barrier on that side to form a portion of a complete inclosure, in a legal sense. But we think their proposition is not tenable. If it were, the result would be that a tract of land, completely inclosed with a substantial fence on three of its sides, and with the fourth side fronting on the ocean, could not be held to be inclosed; or that an island in the ocean could not be deemed to be sufficiently inclosed, unless it had precipitous cliffs, or some sufficient artificial inclosure all around it. A proposition cannot be sound, which necessarily leads to such absurd results. . . .

This brings us to the consideration of what we deem to be the most important and difficult point in the case. We assume that the Court, in the instruction on which we have been commenting, clearly intended to say to the jury — and that the jury so understood it — that if Treat repaired the wall and ditch, and if these, together with the creeks and waters of the bay, formed a sufficient inclosure to turn cattle, and if the land was suitable for pasturage, and was used by Treat and afterwards by Dyson for that purpose, up to the time of the entry by the defendants, without title, that, in that event, it resulted, as a conclusion of law, that there had been established in Dyson such a *possessio pedis* as entitled the plaintiff to recover. For the reasons already stated, we must assume that the facts referred to in the instruction were satisfactorily proved. But did the court draw a correct conclusion of law from these facts? Conceding every fact hypothetically stated in the instruction to have been proved, Did Dyson have such a *possessio pedis* as entitled him to recover? . . .

It is clearly established, both by reason and authority, that the acts of ownership and dominion over land, which may be sufficient to constitute an actual possession, vary according to the condition, size and locality of the tract. If it contains but one acre, and have upon it a valuable quarry of stone or marble, and be not adapted to any other use than as a quarry, and if it be openly claimed and actually and notoriously used for that purpose, for a reasonable time, this might be such an act of dominion over it as to establish an actual possession, even though there was no inclosure or residence upon it. So if it be a small parcel, containing a mine, the working of the mine, in the usual manner, might establish an actual possession at common law, without the aid of our mining laws and in the absence of any inclosure. But if the tract contain one thousand acres, with a mine or a quarry on one margin of it, no one would maintain that the mere working of the mine or quarry, without other acts of ownership, would establish a possession of the whole tract. . . .

If Treat had inclosed the Potrero by a fence or ditch entirely around it, and sufficient to turn cattle, it would not admit of discussion, that, by the inclosure alone, and without other acts of dominion, he would have established an actual possession of the land. An inclosure of that character, is, in itself, sufficient proof of an actual possession. But it is so, only, because the erection of the artificial barrier is an open, notorious act of dominion, proclaiming in unmistakable terms to the public that the land is appropriated and set apart from the adjoining lands for the exclusive use of the person who erected the barrier. A mere intention to occupy land, however openly proclaimed, is not possession. The intention must be carried into actual execution by such open, unequivocal and notorious acts of dominion, as plainly indicate to the public that the person who performs them has appropriated the land and claims the exclusive dominion over it. Anything short of this, is not what the law denominates actual possession. . . .

The whole theory of a *possessio pedis* rests upon the assumption that the acts of dominion which establish it, are such open, notorious acts of ownership, as usually accompany the possession of real property, and naturally spring from a claim of exclusive dominion. They must not only carry with them the usual indicia of ownership, but they must be open, notorious and unequivocal, so as to notify the public that the land is appropriated. If these be not necessary ingredients in a *possessio pedis*, and if a fence across the neck of a peninsula, however large or howsoever situate, be all that is requisite to establish such a possession, no reason is perceived why a fence across the isthmus of Darien might not be held to establish a possession in fact of the continent of North America. . . .

The general principle pervading all this class of cases, where the inclosure consists wholly or partially of natural barriers, is, that the acts of dominion and ownership which establish a *possessio pedis* must correspond, in a reasonable degree, with the size of the tract, its condition and appropriate use, and must be such as usually accompany the ownership of land similarly situated. But, in such cases, it is the peculiar province of the jury, under proper instructions from the Court, to decide whether or not the acts of dominion relied upon, considering the size of the tract, its peculiar condition and appropriate use, were of such a character as usually accompany the ownership of lands similarly situated. As already stated, the erection of a fence across the neck of a small peninsula, might, of itself, under certain circumstances, be a sufficient act of dominion to establish an actual possession. But, in such cases, there can be no rule of universal application, and each case must depend on its own circumstances; and where an inclosure, consisting partly of natural and partly of artificial obstructions, is relied upon as, in itself, establishing a *possessio pedis*, it is the province of the jury, upon all the proofs, and considering the quantity, locality and character of the land, to decide whether or not the artificial barriers were sufficient to notify the public that the land was appropriated, and to impart to the claim of appropriation the notoriety and indicia of ownership which constitute so important an element in a *possessio pedis*. But, in the case at bar, this question was not submitted to the jury. . . . The Court should have instructed the jury, that, if all the facts hypothetically stated in the second instruction were true, it was the province of the jury to decide, considering the quantity, quality and character of the land, whether or not these acts of dominion were sufficient and had the effect, upon the facts proved, to give notice to the public that Treat, first, and Dyson, as his successor in interest, had appropriated the land and claimed the exclusive dominion over it; and if this be answered in the affirmative, then, that there had been established in Treat, first, and afterwards in Dyson, an actual possession. . . .

For these reasons, the judgment should be reversed and a new trial ordered.

2. The Ideology of Ownership

J. LOCKE, THE SECOND TREATISE OF GOVERNMENT (1689):

28. He that is nourished by the Acorns he pickt up under an Oak, or the Apples he gathered from the Trees in the Wood, has certainly appropriated them to himself. No Body can deny but the nourishment is his. I ask then, When did they begin to be his? When he digested? Or when he eat? Or when he boiled? Or when he brought them home? Or when he pickt them up? And 'tis plain, if the first gathering made them not his, nothing else could. That *labour* put a distinction between them and common. That added something to them more than Nature, the common Mother of all, had done; and so they became his private right. And will any one say he had no right to those Acorns or Apples he thus appropriated, because he had not the consent of all Mankind to make them his? Was it a Robbery thus to assume to himself what belonged to all in Common? If such a consent as that was necessary, Man had starved, notwithstanding the Plenty God had given him. We see in *Commons,* which remain so by Compact, that 'tis the taking any part of what is common, and removing it out of the state Nature leaves it in, which *begins the Property;* without which the Common is of no use. And the taking of this or that part, does not depend on the express consent of all the Commoners. Thus the Grass my Horse has bit; the Turfs my Servant has cut; and the Ore I have digg'd in any place where I have a right to them in common with others, become my *Property,* without the assignation or consent of any body. The *labour* that was mine, removing them out of that common state they were in, hath *fixed* my *Property* in them. . . .

32. But the *chief matter of Property* being now not the Fruits of the Earth, and the Beasts that subsist on it, but the *Earth it self;* as that which takes in and carries with it all the rest: I think it is plain, that *Property* in that too is acquired as the former. *As much Land* as a Man Tills, Plants, Improves, Cultivates, and can use the Product of, so much is his *Property.* He by his Labour does, as it were, inclose it from the Common. Nor will it invalidate his right to say, Every body else has an equal Title to it; and therefore he cannot appropriate, he cannot inclose, without the

Consent of all his Fellow-Commoners, all Mankind. God, when he gave
the World in common to all Mankind, commanded Man also to labour,
and the penury of his Condition required it of him. God and his Reason
commanded him to subdue the Earth, *i.e.* improve it for the benefit of
Life, and therein lay out something upon it that was his own, his labour.
He that in Obedience to this Command of God, subdued, tilled and
sowed any part of it, thereby annexed to it something that was his
Property, which another had no Title to, nor could without injury take
from him. . . .

40. Nor is it so strange, as perhaps before consideration it may
appear, that the *Property of labour* should be able to over-ballance the
Community of Land. For 'tis *Labour* indeed that *puts the difference of value*
on every thing; and let any one consider, what the difference is between
an Acre of Land planted with Tobacco, or Sugar, sown with Wheat or
Barley; and an Acre of the same Land lying in common, without any
Husbandry upon it, and he will find, that the improvement of *labour*
makes the far greater part of *the value.* I think it will be but a very modest
Computation to say, that of the *Products* of the Earth useful to the Life of
Man $\frac{9}{10}$ are the *effects of labour:* nay, if we will rightly estimate things as
they come to our use, and cast up the several Expences about them,
what in them is purely owing to *Nature,* and what to *labour,* we shall
find, that in most of them $\frac{99}{100}$ are wholly to be put on the account of
labour.

41. There cannot be a clearer demonstration of any thing, than
several Nations of the *Americans* are of this, who are rich in Land, and
poor in all the Comforts of Life; whom Nature having furnished as
liberally as any other people, with the materials of Plenty, *i.e.* a fruitful
Soil, apt to produce in abundance, what might serve for food, rayment,
and delight; yet for want of improving it by labour, have not one hun-
dreth part of the Conveniencies we enjoy: And a King of a large and
fruitful Territory there feeds, lodges, and is clad worse than a day
Labourer in *England.* . . .

K. MARX, PRE-CAPITALIST ECONOMIC FORMATIONS 89, 92 (1857;
1964 ed.): [O]riginally property means no more than man's attitude to
his natural conditions of production as belonging to him, as the prerequisites of his own existence; his attitude to them as natural prerequisites
of himself, which constitute, as it were, a prolongation of his body. . . .

In so far as property is merely a conscious attitude to the conditions
of production as to one's own — an attitude established by the community for the individual, proclaimed and guaranteed as law; in so far as
the existence of the producer therefore appears as an existence within
the objective conditions belonging to him, it is realised only through
production. Actual appropriation takes place not through the relationship to these conditions as expressed in thought but through the active,

real relationship to them; in the process of positing them as the conditions of man's subjective activity. . . . Property . . . therefore originally signifies a relation of the working (producing) subject . . . to the conditions of his production or reproduction as his own. Hence, according to the conditions of production, property will take different forms.

HOHFELD, FUNDAMENTAL LEGAL CONCEPTIONS AS APPLIED IN JUDICIAL REASONING, 26 Yale L.J. 710, 746-747 (1917): *A* is fee-simple owner of Blackacre. His "legal interest" or "property" relating to the tangible object that we call *land* consists of a complex aggregate of rights (or claims), privileges, powers, and immunities. *First:* A has multital legal rights, or claims, that *others*, respectively, shall *not* enter on the land, that they shall not cause physical harm to the land, etc., such others being under respective correlative legal duties. *Second:* A has an indefinite number of legal privileges of entering on the land, using the land, harming the land, etc., that is, within limits fixed by law on grounds of social and economic policy, he has privileges of doing on or to the land what he pleases; and correlative to all such legal privileges are the respective legal no-rights of other persons. *Third:* A has the legal power to alienate his legal interest to another, i.e., to extinguish his complex aggregate of jural relations and create a new and similar aggregate in the other person; also the legal power to create a life estate in another and concurrently to create a reversion in himself; also the legal power to create a privilege of entrance in any other person by giving "leave and license"; and so on indefinitely. Correlative to all such legal powers are the legal liabilities in other persons, — this meaning that the latter are subject, *nolens volens*, to the changes of jural relations involved in the exercise of *A*'s powers. *Fourth:* A has an indefinite number of legal immunities, using the term immunity in the very specific sense of non-liability or non-subjection to a power on the part of another person. Thus he has the immunity that no ordinary person can alienate *A*'s legal interest or aggregate of jural relations to another person; the immunity that no ordinary person can extinguish *A*'s own privileges of using the land; the immunity that no ordinary person can extinguish *A*'s right that another person X shall not enter on the land or, in other words, create in X a privilege of entering on the land. Correlative to all these immunities are the respective legal disabilities of other persons in general.

S. FREUD, CIVILIZATION AND ITS DISCONTENTS 112-113 (1930; Strachey ed. 1961): The communists believe that . . . if private property were abolished, all wealth held in common, and everyone allowed to share in the enjoyment of it, ill-will and hostility would disappear among men. . . . I have no concern with any economic criticisms of the communist system. . . . But I am able to recognize that the psychological premises on which the system is based are an untenable illusion. In abolishing private property we deprive the human love of aggression of one of its instruments, certainly a strong one, though certainly not the strongest; but we have in no way altered the differences in power and influence which are misused by aggressiveness, nor have we altered anything in its nature.

RADIN, PROPERTY AND PERSONHOOD, 34 Stan. L. Rev. 957, 959-961, 986-987 (1982): Most people possess certain objects they feel are almost part of themselves. These objects are closely bound up with personhood because they are part of the way we constitute ourselves as continuing personal entities in the world. . . .

One may gauge the strength or significance of someone's relationship with an object by the kind of pain that would be occasioned by its loss. On this view, an object is closely related to one's personhood if its loss causes pain that cannot be relieved by the object's replacement. . . .

The opposite of holding an object that has become a part of oneself is holding an object that is perfectly replaceable with other goods of equal market value. One holds such an object for purely instrumental reasons. The archetype of such a good is, of course, money, which is almost always held only to buy other things. . . . I shall call these theoretical opposites — property that is bound up with a person and property that is held purely instrumentally — personal property and fungible property respectively. . . .

Once we admit that a person can be bound up with an external "thing" in some constitutive sense, we can argue that by virtue of this connection the person should be accorded broad liberty with respect to control over that "thing." But here liberty follows from property for personhood; personhood is the basic concept, not liberty. Of course, if liberty is viewed not as freedom from interference, or "negative freedom," but rather as some positive will that by acting on the external world is constitutive of the person, then liberty comes closer to capturing the idea of the self being intimately bound up with things in the external world.

It intuitively appears that there is such a thing as property for personhood because people become bound up with "things." But this intuitive view does not compel the conclusion that property for personhood deserves moral recognition or legal protection, because arguably there is bad as well as good in being bound up with external objects. If there is a traditional understanding that a well-developed person must invest herself to some extent in external objects, there is no less a traditional understanding that one should not invest oneself *in the wrong way* or *to too great an extent* in external objects. Property is damnation as well as salvation, object-fetishism as well as moral groundwork. . . .

[A] personhood dichotomy comes about in the following way: A general justification of property entitlements in terms of their relationship to personhood could hold that the rights that come within the general justification form a continuum from fungible to personal. It then might hold that those rights near one end of the continuum — fungible property rights — can be overridden in some cases in which those near the other — personal property rights — cannot be. This is to argue not that fungible property rights are unrelated to personhood, but simply that distinctions are sometimes warranted depending upon the character or strength of the connection. Thus, the personhood perspective generates a hierarchy of entitlements: The more closely connected with personhood, the stronger the entitlement. . . .

Does it make sense to speak of two levels of property, personal and fungible? I think the answer is yes in many situations, no in many others. Since the personhood perspective depends partly on the subjective nature of the relationships between person and thing, it makes more sense to think of a continuum that ranges from a thing indispensable to someone's being to a thing wholly interchangeable with money. Many relationships between persons and things will fall somewhere in the middle of this continuum. Perhaps the entrepreneur factory owner has ownership of a particular factory and its machines bound up with her being to some degree. If a dichotomy telescoping this continuum to two end points is to be useful, it must be because within a given social context certain types of person-thing relationships are understood to fall close to one end or the other of the continuum, so that decisionmakers within that social context can use the dichotomy as a guide to determine which property is worthier of protection. For example, in our social context a house that is owned by someone who resides there is generally understood to be toward the personal end of the continuum. There is both a positive sense that people are bound up with their homes and a normative sense that this is not fetishistic.

Notes

1. Treasure Salvors, Inc., and Armada Research Corp. found on the continental shelf, outside United States territorial waters, an unidentified, wrecked, and abandoned vessel, thought to be the *Nuestra Senora de Atocha*, which sank in 1622 while en route from the Spanish Indies to Spain. The general principle of international and maritime law is that abandonment repudiates ownership, and a finder can take possession and title under the doctrine of *animus revertendi*, i.e., the owner has no intention of returning.

Plaintiffs sought "possession and confirmation of title against all persons. . . ." The U.S. opposed, contending that objects of antiquity "are taken in the name of the sovereign and are the property of the people as a whole, not the finders alone." But the court found no statutory basis for such an argument, especially because the location of the ship was "neither within the jurisdiction of the United States nor owned or controlled by our government." The U.S. had asserted jurisdiction over minerals under the continental shelf, but regarded the water above the shelf as high seas. Treasure Salvors, Inc. v. Abandoned Sailing Vessel, 408 F. Supp. 907 (S.D. Fla. 1976).

Further litigation, raising complicated issues of federal jurisdiction but shedding little light on the questions of ownership, included a decision in the U.S. Supreme Court. Florida Department of State v. Treasure Salvors, Inc., 458 U.S. 670 (1982).

Would you support legislation requiring Americans to turn over "found" property to the government? Taxing the profit from such finds? At what rate?

2. New York State sued Peter Vernooy and Michael Davidson seeking the return of five rare bronze Georgian cannons about to be sold at auction by Sotheby's Parke-Bernet. Vernooy and Davidson had found the cannons while scuba diving in Lake Champlain. The weapons had been manufactured in England in 1748, were captured by the French during the French and Indian War, and were aboard the French warship Muskellunge in Lake Champlain when the ship was scuttled on the approach of British forces.

New York argued that it owned the cannons because at common law property on a wrecked vessel lying in navigable waters became the property of the Crown if not claimed by the true owner within one year. Second, New York said that a scuttled enemy vessel became the property of the Crown as spoils of war. The state also argued that it owned the bed of Lake Champlain, that N.Y. Education Law §233(4) allows the state to claim objects of archeological interest found on state land, and that defendants had failed to comply with N.Y. Personal Property Law §251 regarding lost property.

Although the trial court held it to be "appalling" behavior for state officials, including the Commissioner of Education and the Attorney General, to wait 14 years (from when the cannons were found and raised to the time they were put up for auction) to sue, it held that statutes of limitations do not run against the state when it acts in a sovereign capacity. The state owns the cannons, the court ruled, but it must compensate defendants for "reasonable salvage, and all necessary expenses accrued in the preservation and keeping of the property." State v. Vernooy, N.Y.L.J., Jan. 25, 1984, at 13 (Sup. Ct.).

3. In 1978, Alaska voters approved The Alaska Homestead Act, placed on the ballot by initiative petition. The act made available to Alaska residents 30 million acres of state land: 40 acres for persons who had resided in Alaska 3 years, 80 acres for persons with 5 years of residence, and 160 acres for persons with 10 years of residence. The

court assumed that the land would be worth an average of $300 per acre. "All vacant, unappropriated, and unreserved general grant land" was to be available for homesteading until 30 percent or 30 million acres (whichever came first) passed into private ownership.

Held: The act is invalid, because initiative cannot be used, under the Alaska Constitution, "to dedicate revenue, make or repeal appropriations," and this was an attempt to make an appropriation. Justice Rabinowitz, concurring, would also have struck down the distinction according to length of residence, as a violation of "the equal protection clause of the Alaska Constitution by infringing on the right to travel to this state and make one's home here." Thomas v. Bailey, 595 P.2d 1 (Alaska 1979).

B. TITLE VERSUS POSSESSION

1. *Relativity of Title*

Especially in a disorderly frontier society, it is easy for there to be competing claims of possession. How does the law rank those claims? What is title? Is there a thing called title that always prevails against the thing called possession, or are both title and possession "relative"?

Tapscott v. Lessee of Cobbs, *infra*, is the most challenging case in this book, and one of the most difficult you will confront during your time in law school.

◆ TAPSCOTT v. LESSEE OF COBBS
52 Va. (11 Gratt.) 172 (1854)

This was an action of ejectment in the Circuit court of Buckingham county, brought in February 1846, by the lessee of Elizabeth A. Cobbs and others against William H. Tapscott. Upon the trial the defendant demurred to the evidence. It appears that Thomas Anderson died in 1800, having made a will, by which he appointed several persons his executors, of whom John Harris, Robert Rives and Nathaniel Anderson qualified as such. By his will his executors were authorized to sell his real estate.

At the time of Thomas Anderson's death the land in controversy had been surveyed for him, and in 1802 a patent was issued therefor to Harris, Rives and N. Anderson as executors. Some time between the years 1820 and 1825, the executors sold the land at public auction, when it was knocked off to Robert Rives; though it appears from a contract between Rives and Sarah Lewis, dated in September 1825, that the land had, prior to that date, been sold by the executors to Mrs. Lewis for three hundred and sixty-seven dollars and fifty cents. This contract was for the sale by Mrs. Lewis to Rives of her dower interest in another tract of land, for which Rives was to pay to the executors of Thomas Anderson the sum of two hundred and seventeen dollars and fifty cents in part of her purchase. In a short time after her purchase she moved upon the land, built upon and improved it, and continued in possession until 1835, when she died. In 1825 the executor Harris was dead, and Nathaniel Anderson died in 1831, leaving Rives surviving him. And it appears that in an account settled by a commissioner in a suit by the devisees and legatees of Thomas Anderson against the executors of Robert Rives, there was an item under date of the 28th of August 1826, charging Rives with the whole amount of the purchase money, in which it is said, "The whole not yet collected, but Robert Rives assumes the liability."

There is no evidence that the heirs of Mrs. Lewis [one of whom is Mrs. Cobbs] were in possession of the land after her death, except as it may be inferred from the fact that she had been living upon the land from the time of her purchase until her death, and that she died upon it.

The proof was that [Tapscott] took possession of the land about the year 1842, without, so far as appears, any pretense of title. He made an entry with the surveyor of the county in December 1844, with a view to obtain a patent for it.

The court gave a judgment upon the demurrer for the plaintiffs, and Tapscott thereupon applied to this court for a supersedeas, which was allowed.

DANIEL, J. It is no doubt true, as a general rule, that the right of a plaintiff in ejectment to recover, rests on the strength of his own title, and is not established by the exhibition of defects in the title of the defendant, and that the defendant may maintain his defense by simply showing that the title is not in the plaintiff, but in some one else. And the rule is usually thus broadly stated by the authorities, without qualification. There are, however, exceptions to the rule as thus announced, as well established as the rule itself. As when the defendant has entered under the title of the plaintiff he cannot set up a title in a third person in contradiction to that under which he entered. Other instances might be cited in which it is equally as well settled that the defendant would be stopped from showing defects in the title of the plaintiff. In such cases, the plaintiff may, and often does recover, not by the exhibition of a title good in itself, but by showing that the relations between himself and the defendant are such that the latter cannot question it. The relation between the parties stands in the place of title; and though the title of the plaintiff is tainted with vices or defects that would prove fatal to his recovery in a controversy with any other defendant in peaceable possession, it is yet all sufficient in a litigation with one who entered into the possession under it, or otherwise stands so related to it that the law will not allow him to plead its defects in his defense.

Whether the case of an intrusion by a stranger without title, on a peaceable possession, is not one to meet the exigencies of which the courts will recognize a still further qualification or explanation of the rule requiring the plaintiff to recover only on the strength of his own title, is a question which, I believe, has not as yet been decided by this court. . . .

In this country . . . I have found no case in which the question seems to have been more fully examined or maturely considered than in Sowden, &c. v. McMillan's heirs, 4 Dana's R. 456 . . . [where it is asserted that earlier cases]

> establish unquestionably the right of the plaintiff to recover when it appears that he was in possession, and that the defendant entered upon and ousted his possession, without title or authority to enter; and prove that when the possession of the plaintiff and an entry upon it by the defendant are shown, the right of recovery cannot be resisted by showing that there is or may be an outstanding title in another; but only by showing that the defendant himself either has title or authority to enter under the title.
>
> It is a natural principle of justice, that he who is in possession has the right to maintain it, and if wrongfully expelled, to regain it by entry on the wrongdoer. When titles are acknowledged as separate and distinct from the possession, this right of maintaining and regaining the possession is, of course, subject to the exception that it cannot be exercised against the real owner, in competition with whose title it wholly fails. But surely it is not accordant with the principles of justice, that he who ousts a previous possession, should be permitted to defend his wrongful possession against the claim of restitution merely by showing that a stranger, and not the previous possessor whom he has ousted, was entitled to the possession. The law protects a peaceable possession against all except him who has the actual right to the possession, and no other can rightfully disturb or intrude upon it. While the peaceable possession continues, it is protected against a claimant in the action of ejectment, by permitting the defendant to show that a third person and not the claimant has the right. But if the claimant, instead of resorting to his action, attempt to gain the possession by entering upon and ousting the existing peaceable possession, he does not thereby acquire a rightful or a peaceable possession. The law does not protect him against the prior possessor. Neither does it indulge any presumption in his favor, nor permit him to gain any advantage by his own wrongful act. . . .

In this state of the law, untrammeled as we are by any decisions of our own courts, I feel free to adopt that rule which seems to me best calculated to attain the ends of justice. . . . I am disposed to follow those decisions which uphold a peaceable possession for the protection as well of a plaintiff as of a defendant in ejectment, rather than those which invite disorderly scrambles for the possession, and clothe a mere trespasser with the means of maintaining his wrong, by showing defects, however slight, in the title of him on whose peaceable possession he has intruded without shadow of authority or title.

The authorities in support of the maintenance of ejectment upon the force of a mere prior possession, however, hold it essential that the prior possession must have been removed by the entry or intrusion of the defendant; and that the entry under which the defendant holds the possession must have been a trespass upon the prior possession. And it is also said that constructive possession is not sufficient to maintain trespass to real property; that actual possession is required, and hence that where the injury is done to an heir or devisee by an abator, before he has entered, he cannot maintain trespass until his re-entry. 2 Tucker's Comm. 191. An apparent difficulty, therefore, in the way of a recovery by the plaintiffs, arises from the absence of positive proof of their possession at the time of the defendant's entry. It is to be observed, however, that there is no proof to the contrary. Mrs. Lewis died in possession of the premises, and there is no proof that they were vacant at the time of the defendant's entry. And in Gilbert's Tenures 37, (in note,) it is stated, as the law, that as the heir has the right to the hereditaments descending, the law presumes that he has the possession also. The presumption may indeed, like all other presumptions, be rebutted: but if the possession be not shown to be in another, the law concludes it to be in the heir.

The presumption is but a fair and reasonable one; and does, I think, arise here; and as the only evidence tending to show that the defendant sets up any pretense of right to the land, is the certificate of the surveyor of Buckingham, of an entry by the defendant, for the same, in his office, in December 1844; and his possession of the land must, according to the evidence, have commenced at least as early as some time in the year 1842; it seems to me that he must be regarded as standing in the attitude of a mere intruder on the possession of the plaintiffs.

Whether we might not in this case presume the whole of the purchase money to be paid, and regard the plaintiffs as having a perfect equitable title to the premises, and in that view as entitled to recover by force of such title; or whether we might not resort to the still further presumption in their favor, of a conveyance of the legal title, are questions which I have not thought it necessary to consider; the view, which I have already taken of the case, being sufficient, in my opinion, to justify us in affirming the judgment.

Allen, Moncure, and Samuels, JJ. concurred in the opinion of Daniel, J.

Lee, J. dissented.

Judgment Affirmed.

2.   The Remedy of Ejectment

Why was the action brought by "Lessee of Cobbs"? The answer is complex, and requires a discussion of the medieval roots of land law.

The adjudication of property rights originally took place in local courts maintained by feudal lords. As the King began to assert central authority over the realm, new forms of action were developed that enlarged the jurisdiction of the royal courts.

The earliest writs were essentially administrative commands to alleged wrongdoers from feudal courts to do justice in a particular matter. The King's court could punish a failure to obey the writ. A significant step occurred with the writ of right *praecipe quod reddat.* According to Plucknett:

> This writ completely ignores the feudal lord and is directed to the sheriff of the county where the land lies; he is instructed to command the defendant to render to the plaintiff the land which he claims, justly and without delay, and if he fails to do so the sheriff is to summon him before the King or his justices to show cause, and the sheriff is to return the original writ together with the names of the summoners who witnessed its service. By the time we get to this form it is clear that we have only a slight disguise for a writ virtually initiating litigation in the King's Court in complete disregard of the lawful rights — property rights as they then were — of the feudal lords. The writ of right *praecipe quod reddat,* therefore, has its beginning in somewhat discreditable circumstances; the Crown, by these writs, deprived feudal lords of their rightful jurisdiction. Thus it was that the insurgent barons extorted from King John a promise in the Great Charter that henceforward the writ called *praecipe* should not issue in such wise that a lord lost his court; though retained in all succeeding charters, this clause had little effect. [T. F. T. Plucknett, A Concise History of the Common Law 356 (5th ed. 1956).]

The writ became increasingly popular after Henry II introduced a procedure permitting an impleaded tenant to have the issue tried before a jury of 12 or 16 knights of the neighborhood. This early form of jury trial was available as an alternative to trial by battle, which remained available in the royal courts and continued as the normal practice in the feudal courts.

The next important development was the introduction of the writ of novel disseisin in 1166. It took the following form:

> The King to the Sheriff, Greetings! *D* has complained to us that *T* has disseised him of his free tenement in the Manor of Dale unjustly and without a judgment since. . . . And so we order you that, so long as *D* shall give you security for prosecuting his claim you should cause that tenement to be reseised with the chattels which were taken in it (i.e. that the chattels should be restored) and the same tenement with the chattels to be in peace until the first assize when our justices shall come into those parts. And meanwhile you should cause twelve free and lawful men of that neighbourhood to view that tenement, and cause their names to be put into the writ. And summon them by good summoners that they be before the

justices aforesaid at the assize aforesaid to make recognition [*recognitio*] thereupon. And put by gages and safe pledges the aforesaid *T*, or if he shall not be found, his bailiff, that he be there to hear that recognition. And have there the names of the summoners, the pledges, and this writ. [A. W. B. Simpson, An Introduction to the History of the Land Law 27 (1961).]

Novel disseisin offered several important advantages over earlier writs. There was no option of trial by battle and less opportunity for delay. In addition, the scope of the action was narrower.

When a writ of right was sought, each party put forward his best possible title, perhaps delving far back into history to do so; the losing party and his heirs would be barred from ever putting that title in issue again. For a writ of novel disseisin, however, the demandant (plaintiff) claimed a novel (recent) disseisin (dispossession) by the tenant (defendant), who was now seised of the disputed land. For the jury the only question was whether the tenant had disseised the demandant within the short period of limitation. If he had, the tenant had only a few defenses. Thus, the action was a speedier and simpler one than earlier writs, effective for its purposes, yet less drastic in its consequences.

Note that the writ said that *T* had disseised him of his free tenement. Part II discusses the various estates in land. For now it is only necessary to be aware that "free tenement" excluded the termor — the person who had taken a lease for a period of years. Novel disseisin was not available to the termor. Legal historians are not certain why, but it is known that the termor was looked down upon in medieval times. This was because a lessor-lessee agreement often was made to circumvent usury statutes. The moneylender advanced a sum to the landholder and in return acquired use of the land for a number of years sufficient to recapture the amount paid for the lease, plus interest.

Various remedies were available to the termor, but they were less convenient and less comprehensive than those available to one seised of a free tenement. This state of affairs gradually changed, particularly with the increasing use of husbandry leases after the Black Death in the fourteenth century. The termor obtained protection through a special form of trespass, *de ejectione firmae.*

Over time this remedy, which came to be called ejectment, began to appeal to those seised of freehold tenements. The body of law concerning novel disseisin had grown considerably, and the writ had ceased to be speedy and convenient. But ejectment could only be brought by a termor. Thus, a disseised freeholder might rent the property to a friend, solely to have the termor bring an action in ejectment. By the seventeenth century, it was sufficient to allege having created a term, without actually conducting the ritual. And so, as you may well have suspected, the action in Tapscott v. Cobbs was not brought by Cobbs' lessee, but by

Cobbs, carrying on a legal fiction shaped by the necessities of medieval procedure.

Note

For correspondence on this subject between the greatest legal historians of the old and new worlds, see the letter from F. W. Maitland to J. B. Ames, reprinted in Gossip about Legal History, 2 Camb. L.J. 1, 5 (1926):

> 15 Brookside
> Cambridge
> 6th May, 1888
>
> Dear Sir,
>
> . . . But as to "the bare possessor" — meaning thereby one who has no title — surely he had the assize. Suppose that A is the true owner and that B without a shadow of right disseises him — then A has a brief interval allowed him for re-ejectment — but from the very moment of the disseisin B is seised as regards all others, and if X turns him out, then B will have the assize against X. . . . Even against A, B will be protected so soon as a brief interval has elapsed. . . .
>
> As regards trespass, . . . my notion . . . was this, that possession, bare possession, had been quite enough for the plaintiff in trespass, but that when under a cloud of fictions trespass (in the form of ejectment) was made to do the duty of a proprietary action, the old principle was for a while confused by the maxim (appropriate only to proprietary actions) that a plaintiff must recover on the strength of his own title and not on the weakness of the defendant's; but then that further reflection set the old principle free again in the form that "title" is a relative term, and that in the case stated above [A is the owner, B without any title turns him out, and then C without any title turns B out] B has good title *as against C.* . . .
>
> Believe me,
> Yours very truly,
> F. W. Maitland

F. POLLOCK, AN ESSAY ON POSSESSION IN THE COMMON LAW 47-50 (1888): Possession of land is of two kinds. Seisin signifies in the common law possession, but one cannot be seised, in the language of modern lawyers, as of any interest less than freehold.

Where a tenant occupies a close under a lease for years, the tenant has possession of the close, so that not only a stranger but the freeholder himself may be guilty of a trespass against him, but the freeholder is still seised, or, as the judges could say as late as 1490, possessed, of the freehold. The fundamental maxim that there can not be two possessions of the same thing at the same time is evaded, successfully or not, by treating the land itself and the reversion as different things. Mr. F. W. Maitland's research has thrown much light on this curious compromise between incompatible ideas. He has shown by abundant examples that in the thirteenth century seisin and possession were absolutely synonymous terms, and that as late as the fifteenth century seisin of chattels was commonly spoken of in pleading. But as early as the thirteenth century the introduction of tenant-farming raised for thinking English lawyers the question who had possession, the landlord or the tenant. Bracton, following Roman authority and the Roman distinction between *possidere*, i.e. possession of law, and *in possessione esse*, i.e., physical possession, in one passage boldly said of the tenant-farmer "he does not possess, though he is in seisin:" he is like a bailiff or servant. But in another passage, which is followed by Fleta, we find the theory of a double seisin: "each one of them without prejudice to the other may be in seisin of the same tenement; one for a term of years, the other as a fee or a free tenement." Some words which follow this sentence in Fleta, and are absurdly thrust into it in the printed text of Bracton, try to represent the tenant's interest as of the nature of usufruct, so that "it is no part of the dominium." They may be an early gloss of some clerk still clinging to the Roman theory. But in the early part of the chapter the farmer's interest has been described as *usufruct or use and occupation;* and the theory of a concurrent seisin "one as a free tenant and the other as a usufruct" is found in the notes of a collector of cases who, if not Bracton himself, was in some way closely connected with his work and opinions. In the present state of Bracton's text it is hardly possible to decide whether the statement which occurs earlier or that which occurs later in the book represents Bracton's deliberate opinion. In any case, practical need carried the day. It would not do to say that the freeholder had parted with his seisin, for that would have cut him off from using in support of his title the convenient possessory remedies given by the assize of novel disseisin and other actions of the same class. According to the later authorities, though a man who has made a lease for years "cannot of right meddle with the demesne nor the fruits thereof," he may have an assize if the termor is ejected, and may plead that he was seised in his demesne as of fee. It would not do to say that the farmer had no possession, for he too must have an effectual remedy against intruders; if he is not exactly disseised when he is disturbed without right, it is something very like it: "if one ejects a tenant for years from his term, he shall receive seisin with damages because such an infringement does not differ much from a disseisin though there is a lord of the property" (note the Romanizing language) "the assize of novel disseisin lies against any ejector, and the tenant has a remedy by this writ," — that is, the writ of ejectment. Thus it was settled that the lessee had a kind of seisin and yet the lessor did not lose the seisin which he had before. It must be remembered that gradations of freehold tenure had already made men familiar with the conception of the lord being seised of rent and service while the tenant was seised of the land itself. Not before Littleton's time (if so early) it became the usage to confine the term seisin to estates of freehold: and accordingly we have a double terminology, corresponding to a double set of rights, and (so long as the real actions were in practical use) also of remedies.

An occupying freeholder is both seised and possessed.

A freeholder who has let his land for years is seised, or possessed, of the freehold, but not possessed of the land.

A lessee for years possesses the land even as against the freehold-er. . . .

A trespasser who has acquired *de facto* possession without title is (subject to some minute variations of terminology in particular cases) a disseisor, and has a real though wrongful seisin.

An heir, remainderman, or reversioner, who by descent, or by the determination of a precedent particular estate of freehold, has become entitled to the freehold in possession, but has not actually entered, is said to have "seisin in law," provided that no one else has taken possession.

O. KAHN-FREUND, INTRODUCTION TO K. RENNER, THE INSTITUTIONS OF PRIVATE LAW AND THEIR SOCIAL FUNCTIONS 18-20 (1949): [A]ll legal systems based on Roman law [confine] the term "ownership" to tangible things. [Continental thought] protests against the "watering down" of this concept, its extension to what English law calls "choses in action", such as debts, patents, copyright, or shares in a company. The English lawyer does not find it incongruous to say that a claim for the repayment of a loan, a mortgage upon another man's land, or a share in a limited company belongs to a person's "property". . . . [T]he comprehensive English term "property" has no equivalent in the German language. A man may be the "owner" of the piece of paper (the share warrant) which embodies his right of membership in a company. The membership right itself is not "property." "Property" which is not ownership of tangible objects plays a dominant part in modern economic life. Economic control has largely shifted from the "owner" as such to those who, in English terminology, "own" choses in action, not "choses in possession."

C. ADVERSE POSSESSION

At some point, if the "owner" of land ignores his or her rights and if another possesses and uses the land, the claim of the "bare possessor" ought to prevail over that of the indifferent "owner." What is that point?

1. Two Honest Buyers

◆ LESSEE OF EWING v. BURNET
36 U.S. (11 Pet.) 41 (1837)

BALDWIN, Justice, delivered the opinion of the court. — In the court below, this was an action of ejectment, brought in November 1834, by the lessor of the plaintiff, to recover possession of lot No. 209, in the city of Cincinnati; the legal title to which is admitted to have been in John Cleves Symmes [the original grantee of the United States, for all the land on which the city of Cincinnati is erected,] under whom both parties claimed; the plaintiff, by a deed dated 11th of June 1798, to Samuel Foreman, who, on the next day, conveyed to Samuel Williams, whose right, after his death, became vested in the plaintiff; the defendant claimed by a deed to himself, dated 21st of May 1803, and an adverse possession of twenty-one years before the bringing of the suit.

It was in evidence, that the lot in controversy is situated on the corner of Third and Vine Streets; fronting on the former 198, on the latter, 98 feet; the part on Third street is level for a short distance, but descends towards the south along a steep bank, from forty to fifty feet, to its south line; the side of it was washed in gullies, over and around which the people of the place passed and repassed at pleasure. The bed of the lot was principally sand and gravel, with but little loam or soil; the lot was not fenced, nor had any building or improvement been erected or made upon it, until within a few years before suit brought; a fence could have been kept up on the level ground on the top of the hill on Third street, but not on its declivity, on account of the deep gullies washed in the bank; and its principal use and value was in the convenience of digging sand and gravel for the inhabitants. Third street separated this lot from the one on which the defendant resided from 1804, for many years, his mansion fronting on that street; he paid the taxes upon this lot from 1810 until 1834, inclusive; and from the date of the deed from Symmes, until the trial, claimed it as his own. During this time, he also claimed the exclusive right of digging and removing sand and gravel from the lot; giving permission to some, refusing it to others; he brought actions of trespass against those who had done it, and at different times made leases to different persons, for the purpose of taking sand and gravel therefrom, besides taking it for his own use, as he pleased. This had been done by others, without his permission, but there was no evidence of his acquiescence in the claim of any person to take or remove the sand or gravel, or that he had ever intermitted his claim to the exclusive right of doing so; on the contrary, several witnesses testified to his continued assertion of right to the lot; their knowledge of his exclusive claim, and their ignorance of any adverse claim, for more than twenty-one years before the present suit was brought. They

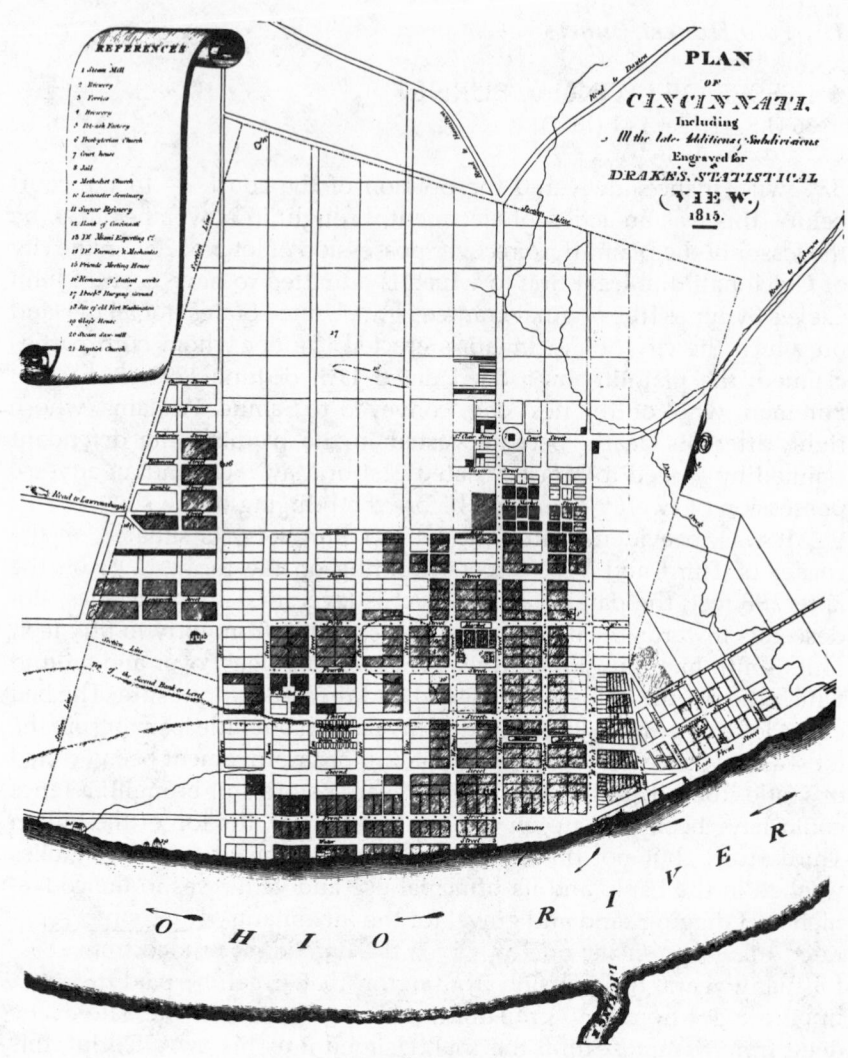

FIGURE 3-1
Plan of Cincinnati (1815)

further stated, as their conclusion from these facts, that the defendant had, from 1800, or 1807, in the words of one witness, "had possession of the lot;" of another, that since 1804, "he was as perfectly and exclusively in possession as any person could possibly be of a lot not built on or inclosed;" and of a third, "that since 1811, he had always been in the most rigid possession of the lot in dispute; a similar possession to other possessions on the hill lot." It was further in evidence, that Samuel Williams, under whom the plaintiff claimed, lived in Cincinnati, from 1803, until his death in 1824; was informed of defendant having obtained a deed from Symmes, in 1803, soon after it was obtained, and knew of his claim to the lot; but there was no evidence that he ever made an entry upon it, demanded possession or exercised or assumed any exercise of ownership over it; though he declared to one witness, produced by plaintiff, that the lot was his, and he intended to claim and improve it, when he was able. This declaration was repeated often, from 1803, till the time of his death, and on his death-bed; and it appeared, that he was, during all this time, very poor; it also appeared in evidence, by the plaintiff's witness, that the defendant was informed, that Williams owned the lot, before the deed from Symmes, in 1803, and after he had made the purchase.

This is the substance of the evidence given at the trial, and returned with the record and a bill of exceptions, stating that it contains all the evidence offered in the cause; whereupon, the plaintiff's counsel moved the court to instruct the jury, that on this evidence the plaintiff was entitled to a verdict; also, that the evidence offered by the plaintiff and defendant was not sufficient, in law, to establish an adverse possession by the defendant; which motions the court overruled. This forms the first ground of exception by the plaintiff to the overruling his motions: 1. The refusal of the court to instruct the jury that he was entitled to recover; 2. That the defendant had made out an adverse possession. . . .

Now, as the jury might have refused credence to the only witness who testified to the notice given to the defendant of Williams's ownership of the lot in 1803, and of his subsequent assertion of claim, and intention to improve it; the testimony of this witness must be thrown out of the case, in testing the correctness of the court in overruling this motion; otherwise, we should hold the court below to have erred, in instructing the jury on a matter exclusively for their consideration — the credibility of a witness, or how far his evidence tended to prove a fact, if they deemed him credible. This view of the case throws the plaintiff back to his deed, as the only evidence of title; on the legal effect of which, the court were bound to instruct the jury as a matter of law, which is the only question to be considered on this exception.

It is clear, that the plaintiff had the elder legal title to the lot in dispute, and that it gave him a right of possession, as well as the legal seisin and possession thereof, co-extensively with his right; which continued till he was ousted by an actual adverse possession (6 Pet. 743); or his right of possession had been in some other way barred. It cannot be doubted, that from the evidence adduced by the defendant, it was competent for the jury to infer these facts — that he had claimed this lot under color and claim of title, from 1804 until 1834; had exercised acts of ownership on and over it, during this whole period; that his claim was known to Williams and to the plaintiff; was visible, of public notoriety, for twenty years previous to the death of Williams. And if the jury did not credit the plaintiff's witness, they might also find that the defendant had no actual notice of Williams's claim; that it was unknown to the inhabitants of the place, while that of the defendants was known; and that Williams never did claim the lot, to assert a right to it, from 1803 until his death in 1824. The jury might also draw the same conclusion from these facts, as the witnesses did; that the defendant was, during the whole time, in possession of the lot, as strictly, perfectly and exclusively as any person could be of a lot not inclosed or built upon; or as the situation of the lot would admit of. The plaintiff must, therefore, rely on a deed of which he had given no notice, and in opposition to all the evidence of the defendant, and every fact which a jury could find, that would show a right of possession in him, either by the presumption of a release or conveyance of the elder legal title, or by an adverse possession. . . .

On the next motion, the only question presented is on the legal sufficiency of the evidence to make out an ouster of the legal seisin and possession of Williams by the defendant; and a continued adverse possession for twenty-one years before suit brought. An entry by one man on the land of another, is an ouster of the legal possession arising from the title, or not, according to the intention with which it is done; if made, under claim and color of right, it is an ouster, otherwise, it is a mere trespass; in legal language, the intention guides the entry and fixes its character. . . .

It is well settled, that to constitute an adverse possession, there need not be a fence, building or other improvement made; it suffices for this purpose, that visible and notorious acts of ownership are exercised over the premises in controversy, for twenty-one years, after an entry under claim and color of title. So much depends on the nature and situation of the property, the uses to which it can be applied, or to which the owner or claimant may choose to apply it, that it is difficult to lay down any precise rule, adapted to all cases. But it may with safety be said, that where acts of ownership have been done upon land, which, from their nature, indicate a notorious claim of property in it, and are continued for twenty-one years, with the knowledge of an adverse claimant, without interruption, or an adverse entry by him, for twenty-one years; such acts are evidence of an ouster of a former owner, and an actual adverse possession against him; if the jury shall think, that the property was not susceptible of a more strict or definite possession than had been so taken and held. Neither actual occupation, cultivation nor residence, are necessary to constitute actual possession when the property is so situated as not to admit of any permanent useful improvement, and the continued claim of the party has been evidenced by public acts of ownership, such as he would exercise over property which he claimed in his own right, and would not exercise over property which he did not claim. Whether this was the situation of the lot in question, or such was the nature of the acts done, was the peculiar province of the jury; the evidence, in our opinion, was legally sufficient to draw the inference that such were the facts of the case, and if found specially, would have entitled the defendant to the judgment of the court in his favor; they, of course, did not err in refusing to instruct the jury that the evidence was not sufficient to make out an adverse possession. . . .

It has also been urged, in argument, that as the defendant had notice of the claim of Williams, his possession was not fair and honest, and so not protected by the statute. This admits of two answers: 1. The jury were authorized to negative any notice; 2. Though there was such notice of a prior deed, as would make a subsequent one inoperative to pass any title, yet an adverse possession for twenty-one years, under claim and color of title, merely void, is a bar; the statutory protection being necessary, only where the defendant has no other title but possession, during the period prescribed. The judgment of the circuit court is, therefore, affirmed.

Notes

1. What law was the Supreme Court applying to this diversity case? In Green v. Neal's Lessee, 31 U.S. (6 Pet.) 291 (1832), the Court had held itself obliged to follow Tennessee decisions construing a state statute affecting land titles. During the reign of Swift v. Tyson, 16 Pet. (41 U.S.) 1 (1842), federal courts accepted state court interpretations "where a course of decisions, whether founded upon statutes or not, have become rules of property as laid down by the highest courts of the State, by which is meant those rules governing the descent, transfer, or sale of property, and the rules which affect the title and possession thereto. . . ." Bucher v. Cheshire R.R., 125 U.S. 555 (1888). There was much ambiguity about the dividing line between this realm of "local law," where the federal courts applied state decisions, and the Swift v. Tyson realm ("general principles of commercial law"), where federal common law was to be found and applied.

2. John Cleve Symmes, a hero of the War of 1812, had earlier obtained from the United States what was known as the Miami Purchase

— the land north of the Ohio River, between the Miami and Little Miami Rivers. Symmes sold land profligately: selling tracts not within his grant, and (as in Ewing v. Burnet) selling some land twice. Symmes, whose daughter married William Henry Harrison, rejected the laws of Newton, and proposed instead the "hollow earth" theory: that the earth has an interior, reachable through large holes at the North and South Poles, where "we will find a warm and rich land, stocked with thrifty vegetables and animals, if not men." Symmes obtained many adherents and some investors in his theory, but Congress finally decided not to commit public funds to the search for this world, although it was attracted by the possibility of "placing Old Glory on those interior planets." Hitler was said to have been an adherent of Symmes' hollow-earth theory.

2. Adverse Possession as a Legal Doctrine

a. Concept

Alpheus has good title to Blackacre, but he has not been occupying the land. Blanche enters the land and uses it for a period of years. Is there a point at which the legal system should grant Blanche a claim to Blackacre stronger than that of Alpheus? Adverse possession is the general term for the group of rules, some statutory and some judge-made, that define the circumstances in which Blanche comes to have title that prevails over the earlier title of Alpheus.

In one sense, obtaining title by adverse possession is only the application of a statute of limitations. Alpheus had a cause of action against Blanche, but he slept on his rights and did not sue. Therefore, his cause of action is extinguished. But while adverse possession reflects the policies that underlie all limitation statutes — encourage timely lawsuits, deter reliance on stale evidence, grant emotional repose — it also draws on concepts generally relevant to issues of the private possession and ownership of that special resource called land. Thus the specific rules of adverse possession doctrine turn on the behavior of the adverse possessor — what was his use? how much of the land did he occupy? did he reasonably believe he had a right to remain? — as well as on whether it is fair to deprive the title holder of "his" land — should he have known of the hostile possession? was he excusably prevented from asserting his rights?

The hornbook statement is that title through adverse possession requires (1) actual possession for the statutory period, often 20 years; (2) regular and uninterrupted possession; (3) "open and notorious" possession, giving reasonable notice to the owner and to the community; and (4) "hostile" possession, without permission from the owner. In some

states an additional requirement is imposed: that the possession be with
claim of right. If you were writing an adverse possession statute, would
you require a claim of right?

b. History

The Statute Westminster I, c. 39 (1275), fixed the beginning of the reign
of Richard I, 3d September 1189, as the earliest date a plaintiff seeking
the recovery of land could set up seisin of his ancestor as the basis of a
writ of right. The statute fixed other dates of limitation for other writs.
Fixing a stated date before which a plaintiff could not show seisin had an
obvious disadvantage: as time passed the period of limitation increased.
The Statute 32 Henry VIII, c.2 (1540), met this difficulty by providing:

> That no manner of person or persons shall from henceforth sue, have,
> or maintain any writ of right, or make any prescription, title or claim . . .
> and declare and alledge any further seisin or possession of his or their
> ancestor or predecessor, but only of the seisin or possession of his ancestor
> or predecessor, which hath been, or now is, or shall be seised . . . within
> threescore years next before the teste of the same writ, or next before the
> said prescription title or claim so thereafter to be sued, commenced,
> brought, made or had.

The Statute 32 Henry VIII did not apply to actions of ejectment but
only to the older actions, which were gradually being displaced by ejectment. The Statute of Limitations, 21 Jac. 1, c.16 (1623), enacted "for
quieting of men's estates and avoiding of suits," barred ejectment by
restricting the right of entry on which the plaintiff's right to sue in
ejectment depended. This was amended by 3 & 4 Wm. IV, c.27 (1833),
which included a provision giving title to the possessor after the running
of the period. But both this statute and the Real Property Limitation Act
of 1874, 37 & 38 Vict., c. 57, which cut the period of limitation to 12
years, came too late to serve as a model for the older states in the United
States. Hence Ohio Revised Code §2305.04 (1954) provides:

> An action to recover the title to or possession of real property shall be
> brought within twenty-one years after the cause thereof accrued, but if a
> person entitled to bring such action, at the time the cause thereof accrues,
> is within the age of minority, of unsound mind, or imprisoned, such
> person, after the expiration of twenty-one years from the time the cause of
> action accrues, may bring such action within ten years after such disability
> is removed.

Compare New York Civil Practice Law §212(a) (1978): "An action to
recover real property or its possession cannot be commenced unless the

plaintiff, or his predecessor in interest, was seized or possessed of the premises within ten years before the commencement of the action."

c. Explanation

1 J. S. Mill, Principles of Political Economy 214-215 (1848; Hadley ed., 1900):

§2. Before proceeding to consider the things which the principle of individual property does not include, we must specify one more thing which it does include: and this is, that a title, after a certain period, should be given by prescription. According to the fundamental idea of property, indeed, nothing ought to be treated as such, which has been acquired by force of fraud, or appropriated in ignorance of a prior title vested in some other person; but it is necessary to the security of rightful possessors, that they should not be molested by charges of wrongful acquisition, when by the lapse of time witnesses must have perished or been lost sight of, and the real character of the transaction can no longer be cleared up. Possession which has not been legally questioned within a moderate number of years, ought to be, as by the laws of all nations it is, a complete title. Even when the acquisition was wrongful, the dispossession, after a generation has elapsed, of the probably bona fide possessors, by the revival of a claim which had been long dormant, would generally be a greater injustice, and almost always a greater private and public mischief, than leaving the original wrong without atonement. It may seem hard, that a claim, originally just, should be defeated by mere lapse of time; but there is a time after which, (even looking at the individual case, and without regard to the general effect on the security of possessors,) the balance of hardship turns the other way. . . .

Letter from O. W. Holmes to William James, Apr. 1, 1907, from M. Lerner, The Mind and Faith of Justice Holmes 417 (1943):

I say that truth, friendship, and the statute of limitations have a common root in time. The true explanation of title by prescription seems to me to be that man, like a tree in the cleft of a rock, gradually shapes his roots to his surroundings, and when the roots have grown to a certain size, can't be displaced without cutting at his life. The law used to look with disfavor on the statute of limitations, but I have been in the habit of saying it is one of the most sacred and indubitable principles that we have, which used to lead my predecessor Field to say that Holmes didn't value any title that was not based on fraud or force.

Salmond's Jurisprudence 414-416 (2d ed. 1907):

Prescription may be defined as the effect of lapse of time in creating and destroying rights; it is the operation of time as a vestitive fact. It is of two kinds, namely (1) positive or acquisitive prescription and (2) negative or extinctive prescription. The former is the creation of a right, the latter is the destruction of one, by the lapse of time. An example of the former is the acquisition of a right of way by the *de facto* use of it for twenty years. An instance of the latter is the destruction of the right to sue for a debt after six years from the time at which it first became payable.

Lapse of time, therefore, has two opposite effects. In positive prescription it is a title of right, but in negative prescription it is a divestitive fact. Whether it shall operate in the one way or in the other depends on whether it is or is not accompanied by *possession*. Positive prescription is the investitive operation of lapse of time *with* possession, while negative prescription is the divestitive operation of lapse of time *without* possession. Long possession creates rights, and long want of possession destroys them. . . .

In many cases the two forms of prescription coincide. The property which one person loses through long dispossession is often at the same time acquired by some one else through long possession. Yet this is not always so, and it is necessary in many instances to know whether legal effect is given to long possession, in which case the prescription is positive, or to long want of possession, in which case the prescription is negative. I may, for example, be continuously out of possession of my land for twelve years, without any other single person having continuously held possession of it for that length of time. It may have been in the hands of a series of trespassers against me and against each other. In this case, if the legally recognised form of prescription is positive, it is inoperative, and I retain my ownership. But if the law recognises negative prescription instead of positive (as in this case our own system does) my title will be extinguished. Who in such circumstances will acquire the right which I thus lose, depends not on the law of prescription, but on the rules as to the acquisition of things which have no owner. The doctrine that prior possession is a good title against all but the true owner, will confer on the first of a series of adverse possessors a good title against all the world, so soon as the title of the true owner has been extinguished by negative prescription.

Problems

1. In 1883 "some young people . . . discovered what afterward proved to be the entrance to the cavern since known as Marengo Cave. . . . Within a week after discovery of the cave, it was explored, and the fact of its existence received wide publicity through newspaper articles, and otherwise." The cave was developed with walks and since 1883 has been used by the successive owners who advertised the cave and charged admission for entering the cave.

Ross, the owner of land lying some 700 feet from the mouth of the cave, first visited the cave in 1895, paying admission as he did on subsequent visits. He bought his adjoining tract in 1908. However, in 1929

Ross brought suit against the cave company; the cave was surveyed. The survey showed that a part of the cave did extend under Ross's land. For 25 years before Ross bought and 21 years thereafter the cave was in the exclusive possession of the cave company and its predecessors in title. The decision affirmed a jury verdict for Ross. The court said, "The fact that appellee had knowledge that appellant was claiming to be the owner of the 'Marengo Cave,' and advertised it to the general public, was no knowledge to him that it was in possession of appellee's land or any part of it. We are of the opinion, that appellant's possession . . . was not open, notorious, or exclusive. . . ." Marengo Cave v. Ross, 212 Ind. 624, 10 N.E.2d 917 (1937).

2. Defendants' garage, built in 1937, encroached on plaintiff's land by 1.4 feet at the rear and 2 feet at the front. The eaves encroached an additional foot.

Plaintiff, who bought his house in 1967, discovered the encroachment in 1973 and immediately sued. The Indiana Supreme Court affirmed a decision that defendants obtained, by adverse possession, the land occupied by the garage. But the court reversed the trial court's award of an additional 4 feet and 2 inches beyond the garage, on which the defendants had been mowing the grass and raking leaves. These activities, said the supreme court, were insufficient to establish adverse possession. Defendants did, however, win a prescriptive easement for their eaves.

The court below had drawn the line midway between plaintiff's and defendants' garages. "However Solomon-like the [lower court] judgment may be as a rational resolution of an irrational dispute between quarreling neighbors, the judgment cannot stand. Solomon, it must be considered, was not bound by our laws governing the ownership of real property." McCarty v. Sheets, 423 N.E.2d 297 (Ind. 1981).

3. A garage company bought land from a farmer that it thought it needed for a road. The farmer sold his remaining land to plaintiff, who planted crops on the entire tract: what he bought, plus what the farmer had earlier sold. Shortly before the 12 years' limitation period expired, the garage company abandoned plans for the road, and wrote to plaintiff offering to sell to him the piece of land that it had bought but that he was using. Plaintiff waited for the 12 years to elapse before replying, and then claimed title through adverse possession.

The court of appeal, per Lord Denning, M.R., held that even had plaintiff been in adverse possession, his failure to reply to the letter would have defeated his title. But it said that the garage company's "use" of the parcel had merely been to wait for the road project. Therefore, plaintiff never established possession adverse to *that use*, and so adverse possession never began to run in his favor. Wallis's Cayton Bay Holiday Camp Ltd. v. Shell-Mex and B.P. Ltd., [1974] 3 W.L.R. 387 (C.A.).

4. James and his wife and children owned a tract as tenants in common. In 1931 defendant Fallon recovered a judgment against James, and the land was sold by a sheriff under execution. Fallon purchased at the sheriff's sale and received a sheriff's deed purporting to convey the entire interest in the property. Thereafter he was "in the actual, visible, distant, hostile, exclusive, continuous and uninterrupted possession" of the land and paid all taxes thereon. Plaintiffs, the wife and children of James, sued, asserting their ownership of the property. Fallon claimed title by adverse possession under an 18 year statute of limitation. But the Colorado Supreme Court held that Fallon's possession had been adverse to James, but not to the wife and children. Fallon v. Davidson, 137 Colo. 48, 320 P.2d 976 (1958). But see McCree v. Jones, 103 Ill. App. 3d 66, 430 N.E.2d 676 (1981). Reconsider this issue after examining the details of tenancies in common, in Chapter 19.

5. Owner sold adjoining parcels of land to plaintiff and defendant. Plaintiff used the land up to a certain fence that he assumed was the boundary. In different years plaintiff raised crops on portions of it. But it was later determined that defendant held record title to six acres on plaintiff's side of the fence. The cross-examination of plaintiff by defendant's lawyer included the following:

Q: I want to be sure I understand. You claimed ownership up to the fence and you still claim it because that was what was described to you as being the land that was being sold to you?

A: That's correct.

Q: Now, did you have any intention to claim title to any land that was not yours, that belonged to somebody else?

A: No. I don't want to claim something that belongs to anybody else.

Q: If it is now established that the defendant owns this six acres, do you have any intention of claiming title to it?

A: That he owns it? Then that would mean that I would have to get mine all surveyed to see whether I had forty acres.

Q: Well, it might, yes.

A: That's what I can't —

Q: What I am getting at is: Have you intended all these years to get something that you did not own as your own?

A: Why, no.

Q: You intended only to claim what was your own, and you thought it was to that line?

A: That's right.

Held: Plaintiff's use of the six acres was intermittent, not continuous. Also, plaintiff showed no intention to claim title to the disputed parcels; a mistake does not lead to hostile possession. Ennis v. Stanley, 346 Mich. 296, 78 N.W.2d 114 (1956).

6. Nisbet and Potts entered a contract for the sale of a tract of land. On the date prescribed for the "closing," Nisbet presented Potts with an

abstract of title showing that the property had been owned by Kidd; that Headde had possessed it adversely to Kidd for the specified period; and that a series of valid conveyances had brought Headde's title to Nisbet.

Potts wanted to build on the land. After the contract was signed, but before title passed, neighbors informed Potts that they held covenants on the land, obtained from Kidd, that gave them the right to prevent the construction Potts had in mind. Potts therefore refused to take title, claiming Nisbet was not delivering marketable title. Nisbet sued for specific performance, asserting that Headde's adverse possession had terminated the neighbors' covenants as well as Kidd's fee. The court of appeal ruled for Potts: "[U]nless and until the right of the covenantee has been in some way infringed, . . . there is no reason either in principle or in fairness, why his right should be in any way affected." In re Nisbet and Potts' Contract, [1906] 1 Ch. 386 (C.A.).

7. In 1928, Katarzyna Lewicki sold 43 acres of farmland in Cumberland, Rhode Island, to Adam Marszalkowski. Included in the sale were "warranty covenants." Mrs. Lewicki says that for 40 years after the conveyance, she and her husband continued to use that lot: They "mowed hay, planted oats, maintained a garden, and fed the cattle." The Rhode Island Supreme Court said Mrs. Lewicki did not re-acquire title by adverse possession. "Some affirmative action [indicating] to the grantee that the grantor's occupancy is hostile to the grantee's title" was required. The court relied heavily on the Rhode Island statute, Gen. Laws 1956 §§34-11-15, providing that a warranty deed commits the grantor to a promise that "the grantee . . . shall at all times after the delivery of the deed peaceably and quietly have and enjoy the deeded premises. . . ." Lewicki v. Marszalkowski, 455 A.2d 307 (R.I. 1983).

8. In 1882, Cornelius Corwin sold land to the Grand Rapids and Indiana Rail Road Company. The deed said that "whenever the said . . . Company . . . shall fail to maintain [its] Passenger Depot . . . upon said lot . . . then this deed shall be void, and the said Real Estate shall revert to the said C. Corwin, his heirs or assigns." The passenger depot was closed in 1957. In 1980, the Penn Central Railroad, successor in interest to the Grand Rapids and Indiana Rail Road Company, sold the real estate to Poole. Poole sued to quiet his title.

Corwin argued that he had the right to assume that the railroad's continued possession was subservient to his interest until he was notified that possession was under a claim hostile to his possibility of reverter. Therefore, he said, the railroad did not acquire an unfettered fee simple by adverse possession. But an Indiana appellate court said that if hostile acts are "so manifest and notorious that a reasonable owner should have been aware of them, no further notice is required." Poole's uncontested allegation that the closing of the depot was common knowledge "required finding constructive notice as a matter of law." The court held that since this established hostile possession, and therefore title by adverse possession, summary judgment for Poole should have been awarded. Poole v. Corwin, 447 N.E.2d 1150 (Ind. App. 1983).

d. Paying Taxes

Sometimes, the paying of real estate taxes is one of the factors weighed by a court when it must decide between a prior owner and an adverse possessor.

In Slatin's Properties, Inc. v. Hassler, 53 Ill. 2d 325, 291 N.E.2d 641 (1972), the following statute was found to be relevant: "Whenever a person having color of title, made in good faith, to vacant and unoccupied land, shall pay taxes legally assessed thereon for seven successive years, he or she shall be deemed and adjudged to be the legal owner. . . ." Ill. Rev. Stat. ch. 83, §7 (1965). Plaintiff had obtained title to certain vacant city lots from Barry, as had the defendants. Plaintiff had recorded the deed first, but while the defendants had paid all taxes and assessments on the land for 9 years, plaintiff had paid nothing. The land remained vacant for 40 years following Barry's sales. While reaffirming the doctrine that actual possession of the property is necessary for taking by adverse possession, the Illinois Supreme Court nonetheless held that it would be inequitable to allow plaintiff's suit. The court reasoned that since the tax payments were matters of public record and the plaintiff was experienced in real estate and title matters, "the plaintiff should have been put on inquiry as to defendant's adverse claims."

In Rhode Island, Picerne bought the Sylvestres' home at a tax sale and paid the real estate taxes for 11 years. He did nothing to remove the Sylvestres. Under Rhode Island law the tax-sale purchaser's "title" is initially security for repayment by the tax-delinquent owner. After a year the holder can make the title absolute by seeking possession or rent, or by foreclosing the right of redemption. Even though Picerne had paid taxes on the home, the state supreme court remanded for a determination of whether the Sylvestres' occupation had been overt enough to have come to the plaintiff's attention. Picerne v. Sylvestre, 113 R.I. 598, 324 A.2d 617 (1974).

e. Tacking

To establish continuous possession for the statutory period, the adverse possessor can combine his or her period of possession with that of predecessor, as long as there is privity of estate between the possessors. For such purposes privity means only a transfer of interest — the statute of frauds is not a limitation. Of course, each party must have been in

possession adversely to the owner. Thus, if one possessor orally transfers possession to another, Brand v. Prince, 35 N.Y.2d 634, 324 N.E.2d
314, 364 N.Y.S.2d 826 (1974), or if a landowner transfers a home on lot
two with a deed to lot *one*, Howard v. Kunto, 3 Wash. App. 393, 477 P.2d
210 (1970), there is privity and the second possessor can include the
length of the predecessor's possession in meeting the statutory period.
"Tacking" is not permitted where one party has ousted another, or
where the original party had abandoned possession and was replaced
immediately by a third party.

f. Disabilities of the Owner

When at the time the adverse possession began the true owner was
unable to bring a lawsuit, most state statutes extend the period of limitation. Only the disabilities specified in the statute will operate to extend
the period. Generally, if the true owner is constrained by infancy, incar-
ceration, or insanity, he or she may challenge the possessor within the
statutory period or within ten years after the disability has been removed, whichever is longer. But a disability arising after the adverse
possession has begun does not toll or extend the statute of limitations.

D. EASEMENT BY PRESCRIPTION: "OWNERSHIP" OF SUNLIGHT

♦ PARKER & EDGARTON v. FOOTE
  19 Wend. 309 (N.Y. Sup. Ct. 1838)

This was an action on the case for stopping lights in a dwelling house,
tried at the Oneida circuit in April, 1836, before the Hon. Hiram Denio,
then one of the circuit judges.

   In 1808 the defendant being the owner of two village lots situate in
the village of Clinton, adjoining each other, sold one of them to Joseph
Stebbins, who in the same year erected a dwelling house thereon on the
line adjoining the other lot with windows in it overlooking the other lot.
The defendant also in the same year built an addition to a house which
stood on the lot which he retained, leaving a space of about sixteen feet
between the house erected by Stebbins and the addition put up by
himself. This space was subsequently occupied by the defendant as an
alley leading to buildings situate on the rear of his lot, and was so used
by him until the year 1832, when (twenty-four years after the erection of
the house by Stebbins,) he erected a store on the alley, filling up the
whole space between the two houses, and consequently stopping the

lights in the house erected by Stebbins. At the time of the erection of the store, the plaintiffs were the owners of the lot originally conveyed to Stebbins, by the title derived from him, and were in the actual possession thereof, and brought this action for the stopping of the lights. Stebbins (the original purchaser from the defendant,) was a witness for the plaintiffs, and on his cross-examination, testified that he never had any written agreement, deed or writing granting permission to have his windows overlook the defendant's lot, and that nothing was ever said upon the subject. The village of Clinton is built upon a square called Clinton Green, the sides of the square being laid out into village lots; and contained at the time of the trial about 1000 inhabitants. On motion for a nonsuit, the defendant's counsel insisted that there was no evidence of a user authorizing the presumption of a grant as to the windows; that the user in this case was merely permissive, which explained and rebutted all presumption of a grant. That if the user, in the absence of other evidence, authorized the presumption of a grant, still that here the presumption was rebutted by the proof, that in fact there never had been a grant. The circuit judge expressed a doubt whether the modern English doctrine in regard to stopping lights, was applicable to the growing villages of this country, but said he would rule in favor of the plaintiffs, and leave the question to the determination of this court. He also decided that the fact, whether there was or was not a grant in writing as to the windows, was not for the jury to determine; that the law presumed it from the user, and it could not be rebutted by proving that none had in truth been executed. After the evidence was closed, the judge declined leaving to the jury the question of presumption of right, and instructed them that the plaintiffs were entitled to their verdict. The jury accordingly found a verdict for the plaintiffs, with $225 damages. The defendant having excepted to the decisions of the judge, now moved for a new trial. . . .

By the Court, BRONSON, J. The modern doctrine of presuming a right, by grant or otherwise, to easements and incorporeal hereditaments after twenty years of uninterrupted adverse enjoyment, exerts a much wider influence in quieting possession than the old doctrine of title by prescription, which depended on immemorial usage. The period of 20 years has been adopted by the court in analogy to the statute limiting an entry into lands; but as the statute does not apply to incorporeal rights, the adverse user is not regarded as a legal bar, but only as a ground for presuming a right, either by grant or in some other form. . . .

To authorize the presumption, the enjoyment of the easement must not only be uninterrupted for the period of 20 years, but it must be adverse, not by leave or favor, but under a claim or assertion of right, and it must be with the knowledge and acquiescence of the owner. . . .

The presumption we are considering is a mixed one of law and fact.

The inference that the right is in him who has the enjoyment, so long as
nothing appears to the contrary, is a natural one — it is a presumption of
fact. But adverse enjoyment, when left to exert only its natural force as
mere presumptive evidence, can never conclude the true owner. No
length of possession could work such a consequence. Hence the necessity of fixing on some definite period of enjoyment, and making that
operate as a presumptive bar to the rightful owner. This part of the rule
is wholly artificial; it is a presumption of mere law. In general, questions
depending upon mixed presumptions of this description must be submitted to the jury, under proper instructions from the court. The difference between length of time which operates as a bar to a claim, and that
which is only used by way of evidence, was very clearly stated by Lord
Mansfield, in the Mayor &c. v. Horner, Cowp. 102. "A jury is concluded," he says,

> by length of time that operates as a bar, as where the statute of limitations
> is pleaded in bar to a debt; though the jury is satisfied that the debt is due
> and unpaid, it is still a bar. So in the case of prescription, if it be time out of
> mind, a jury is bound to conclude the right from that prescription, if there
> could be a legal commencement of the right. But length of time used
> merely by way of evidence, may be left to the consideration of a jury to be
> credited or not, and to draw their inference one way or the other, accord-
> ing to circumstances. . . .

Willes, J. mentioned a case before him, in which he held uninterrupted
possession of a pew for 20 years to be presumptive evidence merely; in
which opinion he was afterwards confirmed by the C.B. The other
judges concurred; and Gould J., before whom the action was tried, said,
he never had an idea but it was a question for a jury; and he compared it
to the case of trover, where a demand and refusal are evidence of, but
not an actual conversion. . . .

   In a plain case, where there is no evidence to repel the presumption
arising from 20 years uninterrupted adverse user of an incorporeal right,
the judge may very properly instruct the jury that it is their duty to find
in favor of the party who has had the enjoyment; but still it is a question
for the jury. The judge erred in this case in wholly withdrawing that
question from the consideration of the jury. On this ground, if no other,
the verdict must be set aside. . . .

   Most of the cases on the subject we have been considering, relate to
ways, commons, markets, water-courses, and the like, where the user
or enjoyment, if not rightful, has been an immediate and continuing
injury to the person against whom the presumption is made. His property has either been invaded, or his beneficial interest in it has been
rendered less valuable. The injury has been of such a character that he
might have immediate redress by action. But in the case of windows

overlooking the land of another, the injury, if any, is merely ideal or imaginary. The light and air which they admit are not the subjects of property beyond the moment of actual occupancy; and for overlooking one's privacy no action can be maintained. The party has no remedy but to build on the adjoining land opposite the offensive window. . . . Upon what principle the courts in England have applied the same rule of presumption to two classes of cases so essentially different in character, I have been unable to discover. If one commit a daily trespass on the land of another, under a claim of right to pass over, or feed his cattle upon it, or divert the water from his mill, or throw it back upon his land or machinery; in these and the like cases, long continued acquiescence affords strong presumptive evidence of right. But in the case of lights, there is no adverse user, nor indeed any use whatever of another's property; and no foundation is laid for indulging any presumption against the rightful owner. . . .

The learned judges who have laid down this doctrine have not told us upon what principle or analogy in the law it can be maintained. They tell us that a man may build at the extremity of his own land, and that he may lawfully have windows looking out upon the lands of his neighbor. The reason why he may lawfully have such windows, must be, because he does his neighbor no wrong; and indeed, so it is adjudged as we have already seen; and yet, somehow or other, by the exercise of a lawful right in his own land for 20 years, he acquires a beneficial interest in the land of his neighbor. The original proprietor is still seized of the fee, with the privilege of paying taxes and assessments: but the right to build on the land, without which city and village lots are of little or no value, has been destroyed by a lawful window. How much land can thus be rendered useless to the owner, remains yet to be settled. Now what is the acquiescence which concludes the owner? No one has trespassed upon his land, or done him a legal injury of any kind. He has submitted to nothing but the exercise of a lawful right on the part of his neighbor. How then has he forfeited the beneficial interest in his property? He has neglected to incur the expense of building a wall 20 or 50 feet high, as the case may be — not for his own benefit, but for the sole purpose of annoying his neighbor. That was his only remedy. A wanton act of this kind, although done in one's own land, is calculated to render a man odious. . . .

There is, I think, no principle upon which the modern English doctrine on the subject of lights can be supported. It is an anomaly in the law. It may do well enough in England; and I see that it has recently been sanctioned with some qualification, by an act of parliament. But it cannot be applied in the growing cities and villages of this country, without working the most mischievous consequences. It has never, I think, been deemed a part of our law. Nor do I find that it has been adopted in any of the states. It cannot be necessary to cite cases to prove that those portions of the common law of England which are hostile to the spirit of our institutions, or which are not adapted to the existing state of things in this country, form no part of our law. And besides, it would be difficult to prove that the rule in question was known to the common law previous to the 19th of April, 1775. Const. N.Y., art. 7, §13. There were two *nisi prius* decisions at an earlier day, but the doctrine was not sanctioned in Westminster Hall until 1786, when the case of Darwin v. Upton was decided by the K.B. 2 Saund. 175, note (2). This was clearly a departure from the old law. . . .

There is one peculiar feature in the case at bar. It appears affirmatively that there never was any grant, writing or agreement about the use of the lights. A grant may under circumstances be presumed, although, as Lord Mansfield once said, the court does not really think a grant has been made. But it remains to be decided that a right by grant or otherwise can be presumed when it plainly appears that it never existed. If this had been the case of a way, common, or the like, and there had actually been an uninterrupted adverse user for 20 years under a claim of right, to which the defendant had submitted, I do not intend to say that proof that no grant was in fact made would have overturned the action. It will be time enough to decide that question when it shall be presented. But in this case the evidence of Stebbins, who built the house, in connection with the other facts which appeared on the trial, proved most satisfactorily that the windows were never enjoyed under a claim of right, but only as a matter of favor. If there was anything to leave to the jury, they could not have hesitated a moment about their verdict. But I think the plaintiffs should have been non-suited.

Notes

1. See H.R. 11677, 94th Cong., 2d Sess. (1976), introduced by Congressman Moakley of Massachusetts:

§2. No State or local zoning law, regulation, ordinance, or other provision may permit the construction of any building or other object within the jurisdiction of such State or locality in any location or manner which would obstruct or otherwise interfere with sunlight necessary for the operation of any solar heating equipment, solar cooling equipment, or combined solar heating and cooling equipment which is in use on any building on the date on which any permit or other authorization for such construction is issued (or on the date of such construction in any case in which no such permit or other authorization for such construction is required under the applicable law, regulation, ordinance, or other provision).

Sample Document 3-1
Notice Posted Annually on Gates to Harvard Yard

NOTICE

President and Fellows of Harvard College, a Massachusetts
corporation, apprehending that a right of way or other easement
may be acquired by custom, use, or otherwise, in or over its land in
Cambridge, Massachusetts, on which are located Claverly Hall,
College or Senior House and Apley Court, bounded and described
as follows: Southwesterly by the junction of Mt. Auburn and Bow
Streets; Southeasterly by Linden Street; Northerly, Southwesterly,
Northerly and Southeasterly by land now or formerly of Trustees
of Delphic Trust; Northerly by land now or formerly of Trustees of
Hasty Pudding Club; Northwesterly by Holyoke Street; Southerly
and Northwesterly by land now or formerly of Whouley; and
Westerly by a passageway extending in a Northerly direction from
Mt. Auburn Street by some person or class of persons, hereby
gives public notice under General Laws, (Ter. Ed.) Chapter 187,
Section 3, of its intention to dispute any such right or easement and
to prevent the acquisition of the same.

President and Fellows of Harvard College.

A TRUE COPY, ATTEST: By

_____   _____
DEPUTY SHERIFF   s/Robert A. Silverman
                               AGENT

2. Under Britain's 1832 Prescription Act, the access of light to a
building or residence for 20 years without interruption, and without the
written consent of the adjacent property owner, gave the owner of the
building or residence the absolute right to that light. 2 & 3 Wm. 4, c. 71
(1832).

This provision hindered rebuilding after World War II. In 1959, it
was revised. For claims to light arising between 1958 and 1963, the
statutory period was extended to 27 years to give landowners more time
to rebuild. Further, a new procedure was initiated allowing landowners
to post a notice identifying their servient land and a dominant building.
The notice serves as the equivalent of a new structure of specified size
and location on the servient land. While the notice is in effect, the owner
of the affected building may sue to establish a claim to light, just as if the
light had been obstructed. Rights of Light Act, 7 & 8 Eliz. 2, c. 56 (1959).

3. Seeley, Comparative Aspects of Access to Sunlight: the United States, Great Britain, and Japan, 21 Harv. Intl. L.J. 687 (1980):

Japan, whose name proclaims it to be the birthplace of the sun, has evolved the appreciation of sunlight into a legal concept. . . . The landmark sunlight case Mitamura v. Suzuki preceded and set the stage for other anti-pollution successes. . . . In *Mitamura*, plaintiff's interest in access to enough sunlight for a constitutionally mandated "wholesome life" was held to override defendant's longstanding right to use his property as he chose by the Tokyo High Court, and later by the Supreme Court.

Defendant Suzuki began a second story addition to his Tokyo home. His neighbor to the north, Mitamura, petitioned the Tokyo municipal government to force a halt to Suzuki's addition, as Mitamura's light and ventilation were being adversely affected by the construction. The defendant ignored orders from the Governor of Tokyo to suspend construction. Because of the loss of ventilation and sunshine, Mitamura's family's health was detrimentally affected,[145] and he was forced to move. . . .

. . . Despite the defendant's open violations of the Building Code, the Tokyo High Court found no provisions therein for remedies for injury or damages suffered as a result of the loss of sunlight and ventilation. Instead, the court held that access to light was a fundamental right because "sunlight and ventilation are worthy of protection under the law as fundamental and necessary for life, profit, and the enjoyment of a pleasant and healthy life."

The court based its decision on the doctrine of "abuse of right" (Kenri no ranyo). This doctrine balances the rights of a landowner against the duties of neighboring landowners to bear the sundry inconveniences that may arise from the landowner's exercise of his rights. However, the adjacent property owner can no longer be expected to put up with these inconveniences when the limit of human endurance is reached. At that point, the offender has abused his rights and is liable to the injured party for compensation or damages. . . . The Building Standard Law was passed in 1950 to deal with the sudden growth of Japanese cities. As the sunlight became important to homeowners, they put pressure on the Diet, which passed a "sunshine amendment" in 1976. The amendment sets forth the maximum daily hours a newly built structure may shadow previously built ones. Local zoning authorities are permitted to reduce the hours of shade allowed by the BSL, and more than three hundred Japanese cities have adopted more restrictive standards governing hours of shade.

Apparently Japan's construction industry thought that raising the Tokyo height limit, now 33 feet in many residential neighborhoods, would give their business a boost. Also, the industry wanted local officials to speed their mediation processes for determining fair compen-

---

145. The court found the plaintiff suffered damages because his utility bills increased, his family's health was adversely affected, and the growth of trees in his garden was adversely affected.

sation for lost sunshine. A district court judge ordered Tokyo Metropolitan Government to pay a construction company $50,000 for allowing a sunshine case to drag on for months. N.Y. Times, Sunny Side of the Street is Very Dear to Japanese, July 28, 1983.

4. When the Eden Roc Hotel in Miami Beach constructed a 14-story addition, casting a shadow on the beach of the adjacent Fountainbleu, should the Fountainbleu have had a cause of action for interference with light and air? In Fountainbleu Hotel Corp. v. Forty-Five Twenty-Five, Inc., a Florida court held that there was no cause of action for interference with light and air from a structure serving a "useful and beneficial purpose." 114 So. 2d 357 (Fla. Dist. Ct. App. 1959).

5. Sears sought to build its 110-story office tower in Chicago. Plaintiff sued, saying it would block his television reception. *Held:* Absent legislation, landowner can build, even if the construction interferes with the path of television signals. People ex rel. Hoogasian v. Sears, Roebuck & Co., 52 Ill. 2d 301, 287 N.E.2d 677, *cert. denied,* 409 U.S. 1001 (1972).

◆ PRAH v. MARETTI,
108 Wis. 2d 223, 321 N.W.2d 182 (1982)

ABRAHAMSON, Justice. This appeal from a judgment of the circuit court for Waukesha county, Max Raskin, circuit judge, was certified to this court by the court of appeals, as presenting an issue of first impression, namely, whether an owner of a solar-heated residence states a claim upon which relief can be granted when he asserts that his neighbor's proposed construction of a residence (which conforms to existing deed restrictions and local ordinances) interferes with his access to an unobstructed path for sunlight across the neighbor's property. This case thus involves a conflict between one landowner (Glenn Prah, the plaintiff) interested in unobstructed access to sunlight across adjoining property as a natural source of energy and an adjoining landowner (Richard D. Maretti, the defendant) interested in the development of his land.

The circuit court concluded that the plaintiff presented no claim upon which relief could be granted and granted summary judgment for the defendant. We reverse the judgment of the circuit court and remand the cause to the circuit court for further proceedings.

According to the complaint, the plaintiff is the owner of a residence which was constructed during the years 1978-1979. The complaint alleges that the residence has a solar system which includes collectors on the roof to supply energy for heat and hot water and that after the plaintiff built his solar-heated house, the defendant purchased the lot adjacent to and immediately to the south of the plaintiff's lot and commenced planning construction of a home. The complaint further states that when the plaintiff learned of defendant's plans to build a house he advised the defendant that if the house were built at the proposed location, defendant's house would substantially and adversely affect the integrity of plaintiff's solar system and could cause plaintiff other damage. Nevertheless, the defendant began construction. The complaint further alleges that the plaintiff is entitled to "unrestricted use of the sun and its solar power" and demands judgment for injunctive relief and damages. . . .

The record made on the motion reveals the following additional facts: Plaintiff's home was the first residence built in the subdivision, and although plaintiff did not build his house in the center of the lot it was built in accordance with applicable restrictions. Plaintiff advised defendant that if the defendant's home were built at the proposed site it would cause a shadowing effect on the solar collectors which would reduce the efficiency of the system and possibly damage the system. To avoid these adverse effects, plaintiff requested defendant to locate his home an additional several feet away from the plaintiff's lot line, the exact number being disputed. Plaintiff and defendant failed to reach an agreement on the location of defendant's home before defendant started construction. The Architectural Control Committee of the subdivision and the Planning Commission of the City of Muskego approved the defendant's plans for his home, including its location on the lot. After such approval, the defendant apparently changed the grade of the property without prior notice to the Architectural Control Committee. The problem with defendant's proposed construction, as far as the plaintiff's interests are concerned, arises from a combination of the grade and the distance of defendant's home from the defendant's lot line.

The circuit court denied plaintiff's motion for injunctive relief, declared it would entertain a motion for summary judgment and thereafter entered judgment in favor of the defendant. . . .

We consider first whether the complaint states a claim for relief based on common law private nuisance. This state has long recognized that an owner of land does not have an absolute or unlimited right to use the land in a way which injures the rights of others. The rights of neighboring landowners are relative; the uses by one must not unreasonably impair the uses or enjoyment of the other. When one landowner's use of his or her property unreasonably interferes with another's enjoyment of his or her property, that use is said to be a private nuisance.

The private nuisance doctrine has traditionally been employed in this state to balance the conflicting rights of landowners, and this court has recently adopted the analysis of private nuisance set forth in the Restatement (Second) of Torts.

The Restatement defines private nuisance as "a nontrespassory invasion of another's interest in the private use and enjoyment of land." Restatement (Second) of Torts sec. 821D (1977). The phrase "interest in the private uses and enjoyment of land" as used in sec. 821D is broadly defined to include any disturbance of the enjoyment of property. . . .

Although the defendant's obstruction of the plaintiff's access to sunlight appears to fall within the Restatement's broad concept of a private nuisance as a nontrespassory invasion of another's interest in the private use and enjoyment of land, the defendant asserts that he has a right to develop his property in compliance with statutes, ordinances and private covenants without regard to the effect of such development upon the plaintiff's access to sunlight. In essence, the defendant is asking this court to hold that the private nuisance doctrine is not applicable in the instant case and that his right to develop his land is a right which is *per se* superior to his neighbor's interest in access to sunlight. This position is expressed in the maxim *"cujus est solum, ejus est usque ad coelum et ad infernos,"* that is, the owner of land owns up to the sky and down to the center of the earth. The rights of the surface owner are, however, not unlimited.

The defendant is not completely correct in asserting that the common law did not protect a landowner's access to sunlight across adjoining property. At English common law a landowner could acquire a right to receive sunlight across adjoining land by both express agreement and under the judge-made doctrine of "ancient lights." Under the doctrine of ancient lights if the landowner had received sunlight across adjoining property for a specified period of time, the landowner was entitled to continue to receive unobstructed access to sunlight across the adjoining property. Under the doctrine the landowner acquired a negative prescriptive easement and could prevent the adjoining landowner from obstructing access to light.

Although American courts have not been as receptive to protecting a landowner's access to sunlight as the English courts, American courts have afforded some protection to a landowner's interest in access to sunlight. American courts honor express easements to sunlight. American courts initially enforced the English common law doctrine of ancient lights, but later every state which considered the doctrine repudiated it as inconsistent with the needs of a developing country. Indeed, for just that reason this court concluded that an easement to light and air over adjacent property could not be created or acquired by prescription and has been unwilling to recognize such an easement by implication. . . .

Many jurisdictions in this country have protected a landowner from malicious obstruction of access to light (the spite fence cases) under the common law private nuisance doctrine. . . .

This court's reluctance in the nineteenth and early part of the twentieth century to provide broader protection for a landowner's access to sunlight was premised on three policy considerations. First, the right of landowners to use their property as they wished, as long as they did not cause physical damage to a neighbor, was jealously guarded.

Second, sunlight was valued only for aesthetic enjoyment or as illumination. Since artificial light could be used for illumination, loss of sunlight was at most a personal annoyance which was given little, if any, weight by society.

Third, society had a significant interest in not restricting or impeding land development. . . .

These three policies are no longer fully accepted or applicable. They reflect factual circumstances and social priorities that are now obsolete.

First, society has increasingly regulated the use of land by the landowner for the general welfare.

Second, access to sunlight has taken on a new significance in recent years. In this case the plaintiff seeks to protect access to sunlight, not for aesthetic reasons or as a source of illumination but as a source of energy. Access to sunlight as an energy source is of significance both to the landowner who invests in solar collectors and to a society which has an interest in developing alternative sources of energy.[11]

Third, the policy of favoring unhindered private development in an expanding economy is no longer in harmony with the realities of our society. The need for easy and rapid development is not as great today as it once was, while our perception of the value of sunlight as a source of energy has increased significantly.

Courts should not implement obsolete policies that have lost their vigor over the course of the years. The law of private nuisance is better suited to resolve landowners' disputes about property development in the 1980's than is a rigid rule which does not recognize a landowner's interest in access to sunlight. . . .

We therefore hold that private nuisance law, that is, the reasonable use doctrine as set forth in the Restatement, is applicable to the instant case. Recognition of a nuisance claim for unreasonable obstruction of access to sunlight will not prevent land development or unduly hinder the use of adjoining land. It will promote the reasonable use and enjoyment of land in a manner suitable to the 1980's. That obstruction of access to light might be found to constitute a nuisance in certain circumstances does not mean that it will be or must be found to constitute a nuisance under all circumstances. The result in each case depends on whether the conduct complained of is unreasonable.

Accordingly we hold that the plaintiff in this case has stated a claim under which relief can be granted. Nonetheless we do not determine whether the plaintiff in this case is entitled to relief. In order to be entitled to relief the plaintiff must prove the elements required to estab-

---

11. State and federal governments are encouraging the use of the sun as a significant source of energy. In this state the legislature has granted tax benefits to encourage the utilization of solar energy.

The federal government has also recognized the importance of solar energy and currently encourages its utilization by means of tax benefits, direct subsidies and government loans for solar projects.

lish actionable nuisance, and the conduct of the defendant herein must be judged by the reasonable use doctrine. . . .

Although the memorandum decision of the circuit court in the instant case is unclear, it appears that the circuit court recognized that the common law private nuisance doctrine was applicable but concluded that defendant's conduct was not unreasonable. The circuit court apparently attempted to balance the utility of the defendant's conduct with the gravity of the harm. Sec. 826, Restatement (Second) of Torts (1977). The defendant urges us to accept the circuit court's balance as adequate. We decline to do so.

The circuit court concluded that because the defendant's proposed house was in conformity with zoning regulations, building codes and deed restrictions, the defendant's use of the land was reasonable. This court has concluded that a landowner's compliance with zoning laws does not automatically bar a nuisance claim. Compliance with the law "is not the controlling factor, though it is, of course, entitled to some weight." The circuit court also concluded that the plaintiff could have avoided any harm by locating his own house in a better place. Again, plaintiff's ability to avoid the harm is a relevant but not a conclusive factor.

Furthermore, our examination of the record leads us to conclude that the record does not furnish an adequate basis for the circuit court to apply the proper legal principles on summary judgment. The application of the reasonable use standard in nuisance cases normally requires a full exposition of all underlying facts and circumstances. Too little is known in this case of such matters as the extent of the harm to the plaintiff, the suitability of solar heat in that neighborhood, the availability of remedies to the plaintiff, and the costs to the defendant of avoiding the harm. Summary judgment is not an appropriate procedural vehicle in this case when the circuit court must weigh evidence which has not been presented at trial.

CALLOW, Justice (dissenting). The majority has adopted the Restatement's reasonable use doctrine to grant an owner of a solar heated home a cause of action against his neighbor who, in acting entirely within the applicable ordinances and statutes, seeks to design and build his home in such a location that it may, at various times during the day, shade the plaintiff's solar collector, thereby impeding the efficiency of his heating system during several months of the year. Because I believe the facts of this case clearly reveal that a cause of action for private nuisance will not lie, I dissent. . . .

I firmly believe that a landowner's right to use his property within the limits of ordinances, statutes, and restrictions of record where such use is necessary to serve his legitimate needs is a fundamental precept of a free society which this court should strive to uphold.

As one commentator has suggested:

It is fashionable to dismiss such values as deriving from a bygone era in which people valued development as a "goal in itself," but current market prices for real estate, and more particularly the premiums paid for land whose zoning permits intensive use, suggest that people still place very high values on such rights.

Williams, *Solar Access and Property Rights: A Maverick Analysis*, 11 Conn. L. Rev. 430, 443 (1979) (footnote omitted). . . .

Regarding the third policy the majority apparently believes is obsolete (that society has a significant interest in not restricting land development), it cites State v. Deetz, 66 Wis. 2d 1, 224 N.W. 2d 407 (1974). I concede the law may be tending to recognize the value of aesthetics over increased volume development and that an individual may not use his land in such a way as to harm the *public*. The instant case, however, deals with a *private* benefit. . . .

It is clear that community planners are acutely aware of the present housing shortages, particularly among those two groups with limited financial resources, the young and the elderly. While the majority's policy arguments may be directed to a cause of action for public nuisance, we are presented with a private nuisance case which I believe is distinguishable in this regard.[3] . . .

I believe the facts of the instant controversy present the classic case of the owner of a solar collector who fails to take any action to protect his investment. There is nothing in the record to indicate that Mr. Prah disclosed his situation to Mr. Maretti prior to Maretti's purchase of the lot or attempted to secure protection for his solar collector prior to Maretti's submission of his building plans to the architectural committee. Such inaction should be considered a significant factor in determining whether a cause of action exists.

The majority's failure to recognize the need for notice may perpetuate a vicious cycle. Maretti may feel compelled to sell his lot because of Prah's solar collector's interference with his plans to build his family home. If so, Maretti will not be obliged to inform prospective purchasers of the problem. Certainly, such information will reduce the value of his land. If the presence of collectors is sufficient notice, it cannot be said that the seller of the lot has a duty to disclose information peculiarly

---

3. I am amused at the majority's contention that what constitutes a nuisance today would have been accepted without question in earlier times. This calls to mind the fact that, in early days of travel by horses, the first automobiles were considered nuisances. Later, when automobile travel became developed, the horse became the nuisance. This makes me wonder if we are examining the proper nuisance in the case before us. In other words, could it be said that the solar energy user is creating the nuisance when others must conform their homes to accommodate his use? I note that solar panel glare may temporarily blind automobile drivers, reflect into adjacent buildings causing excessive heat, and otherwise irritate neighbors. Certainly in these instances the solar heating system constitutes the nuisance.

within his knowledge. I do not believe that an adjacent lot owner should be obliged to experience the substantial economic loss resulting from the lot being rendered unbuildable by the contour of the land as it relates to the location and design of the adjoining home using solar collectors.[8]

E. ECONOMIC ANALYSIS OF PROPERTY RIGHTS

DEMSETZ, SOME ASPECTS OF PROPERTY RIGHTS, 9 J. Law & Econ. 61, 62 (1966): Crucially involved [in a private property system] is the notion that individuals have control over the use to which scarce resources (including ideas) can be put, and that this right of control is saleable or transferable. A private property right system requires the prior consent of "owners" before their property can be affected by others. . . . The role of the body politic in this system is twofold. Firstly, the government or courts must help decide which individuals possess what property rights and, therefore, who has the power to claim that his rights are affected by others. Secondly, property rights so assigned must be protected by the police power of the state or the owners must be allowed to protect property rights themselves. Presumably the best mix of public and private protection will depend on ethical and other considerations.

There are three important implications of a private property system that are valid in a world in which all property rights are assigned and in which the cost of exchanging and of policing property rights are zero. A private property system under such conditions, implies that (1) the value of all harmful and beneficial effects of alternative uses of property rights will be brought to bear on their owners, (2) to the extent that owners of property rights are utility maximizers, property rights will be used efficiently, and (3) the mix of output that is produced will be independent of the distribution of property rights among persons except insofar as changes in the distribution of wealth affect demand patterns.

R. POSNER, ECONOMIC ANALYSIS OF LAW 16-18 (1972): . . . Property rights are never exclusive, if only because exclusive property rights would so often be incompatible. If a railroad is to enjoy the exclu-

Locke?

---

8. Mr. Prah could have avoided this litigation by building his own home in the center of his lot instead of only ten feet from the Maretti lot line and/or by purchasing the adjoining lot for his own protection. Mr. Maretti has already moved the proposed location of his home over an additional ten feet to accommodate Mr. Prah's solar collector, and he testified that moving the home any further would interfere with his view of the lake on which the property faces.

sive use of its right of way it must be permitted to emit engine sparks without legal limitation. The value of its property will be impaired otherwise. But if it is permitted to emit engine sparks the value of adjacent farmland will be impaired because of the fire hazard created by the sparks. Is the emission of sparks an incident of the railroad's property right or an invasion of the farmer's? Does anything turn on the answer? Suppose that the right to emit sparks, by enabling the railroad to dispense with costly spark-arresting equipment, would increase the value of its property by $100 but reduce the value of the farmer's property by $50 because it would prevent him from growing crops close to the tracks. If the farmer has a legal right to be free from engine sparks, the railroad presumably will offer to pay and the farmer will accept compensation for the surrender of his right. Since the right to prevent spark emissions is worth only $50 to the farmer but imposes costs on the railroad of $100, a sale of the farmer's right at any price between $50 and $100 will make both parties better off. If instead of the farmer's having a right to be free from sparks the railroad has a legal right to emit sparks, no transaction will occur. The farmer will not pay more than $50 for the railroad's right and the railroad will not accept less than $100. Thus, whichever way the legal right is assigned, the result, in terms of resource use, is the same: the railroad emits sparks and the farmer moves his crop.

The principle is not affected by reversing the numbers. Assume that the right to emit sparks would increase the value of the railroad's property by only $50, but would reduce the value of the farmer's property by $100. If the railroad has a right to emit sparks, the farmer will offer to pay and the railroad will accept some price between $50 and $100 for the surrender of the railroad's right. If instead the farmer has a right to be free from emissions, there will be no transaction since the farmer would insist on a minimum payment of $100 and the railroad will pay no more than $50.

Whatever the relative values of the competing uses, it seems that the initial assignment of legal rights does not affect which use ultimately prevails. The efficient, or value-maximizing, accommodation of the conflict will be chosen whichever party is granted the legal right to exclude interference by the other.[1]

1. This was demonstrated in Ronald Coase's important article, The Problem of Social Cost, 3 J. Law & Econ. 1 (1960). The article makes three other important points which are sometimes overlooked, relating to the case in which the costs of transferring the property right are so high that transfer is not feasible. (a) Placing liability on the party who causes the damage (the railroad in our example) may not produce the efficient solution to the conflict. (The reader can verify this by referring to our first example and assuming that the farmer has the property right and cannot, due to heavy transaction costs, transfer it to the railroad.) (b) The common law of nuisance can be understood as an attempt to increase the value of resource use by assigning property rights to those parties to conflicting land

But it does not follow that the initial assignment of rights is immaterial from an economic standpoint. Since transactions are not costless, efficiency is promoted by assigning the legal right to the party who would buy it — the railroad in our first hypothetical and the farmer in the second — were it assigned initially to the other party. Moreover, as we shall see, transaction costs are sometimes so high as to make transactions impracticable. In such a case the initial assignment of rights is final.

These observations suggest an economic principle for deciding, in cases of conflicting land (or other property) uses, which party shall have the right to exclude the other. The right should be assigned to the party whose use is the more valuable — the party, stated otherwise, for whom discontinuance of the interference would be most costly. By assigning rights in accordance with this principle the law can anticipate and thus obviate the necessity for a market transaction. Transaction costs are minimized *when the law (1) assigns the right to the party who would buy it from the other party if it were assigned to the other party instead and if transaction costs were zero, or (2) alternatively, places liability on the party who, if he had the right and transaction costs were zero, would sell it to the other party. . . .*

Note

Calabresi and Melamed, in Property Rules, Liability Rules, and Inalienability: One View of the Cathedral, 85 Harv. L. Rev. 1089 (1972), argue that property and tort concepts can be viewed in terms of a larger structure of societal assignment of entitlements. Specifically, "an entitlement is protected by a property rule to the extent that someone who wishes to remove the entitlement from its holder must buy it from him in a voluntary transaction in which the value of the entitlement is agreed upon by the seller . . . [and] whenever someone may destroy the initial entitlement if he is willing to pay an objectively determined value for it,

---

uses in whose hands the rights are most valuable. (c) In deciding whether governmental intervention in the economic system is appropriate, it is never sufficient to demonstrate that, without intervention, the market would operate imperfectly; government also operates imperfectly so what is necessary is a comparison between the actual workings of market and government in the particular setting.

A qualification of the Coasian analysis should be mentioned here. The initial assignment of rights, even where transaction costs are zero so that efficiency is not affected, may affect the relative wealth of the parties and this may affect the use of resources in two ways. First, if the parties do not spend their money in identical ways, a shift of wealth between them will alter demand for the various goods and services that they buy, however slightly. Second, where the right ends up may depend on how the initial assignment is made, if the value of the right represents a large fraction of the wealth of either party. The extreme example is the right to a barrel of water as between two dying men in a desert. This point is developed in E. J. Mishan, Pareto Optimality and the Law, 19 Oxford Econ. Papers (n.s.) 225 (1967). Neither point undermines Coase's conclusion that efficiency is unaffected by the rule of liability if transaction costs are zero.

an entitlement is protected by a liability rule." The authors also identify a third class of entitlements: those which are inalienable, and which the legal system will not allow to be transferred.

How should a society determine which of its resources should be the subject of individual entitlements, and which of these should be protected by property rules, liability rules, or inalienability? Calabresi and Melamed say that the decision should be based upon considerations of economic efficiency, distributional preferences, and "other justice considerations." They suggest that, while there will be normative differences as to issues of distribution and of "other justice considerations," the use of the economic efficiency criterion for assigning entitlements should be analyzed as follows: "(1) economic efficiency standing alone would dictate that set of entitlements which favors knowledgeable choices between social benefits and the social costs of obtaining them, and between social costs and the social costs of avoiding them; (2) this implies, in the absence of certainty as to whether a benefit is worth its costs to society; that the cost should be put on the party or activity best located to make such a cost-benefit analysis; (3) in particular contexts like accidents or pollution, this suggests putting costs on the party or activity which can most cheaply avoid them; (4) in the absence of certainty as to who that party or activity is, the costs should be put on the party or activity which can with the lowest transaction costs act in the market to correct an error in entitlements by inducing the party who can avoid social costs most cheaply to do so; and (5) since we are in an area where by hypothesis markets do not work perfectly — there are transaction costs — a decision will often have to be made on whether market transactions or collective fiat is most likely to bring us closer to the Pareto-optimal result the 'perfect' market would reach." Id. at 1096-1097.

POLINSKY, ECONOMIC ANALYSIS AS A POTENTIALLY DEFECTIVE PRODUCT: A BUYER'S GUIDE TO POSNER'S *ECONOMIC ANALYSIS OF LAW*, 87 Harv. L. Rev. 1655, 1665-1679 (1974): Posner's methodological theme can be summarized: If transaction costs are zero the structure of the law does not matter because efficiency will result in any case. If the market does not yield efficient results because of high transaction costs, design the law to minimize these costs. If the market still does not work, design the law to "mimic" the market. Compensation is not important except insofar as it is required to achieve efficiency.

Despite the importance of the market in Posner's analysis he does not discuss systematically the conditions required for the market to work or the sense in which a market outcome is normatively appealing (whether achieved directly through the market or indirectly through the law.) . . .

A simple model of competitive behavior provides a comprehensible view of the interactions between consumers and producers within an economic system. . . .

The economy is in equilibrium when supply equals demand for each factor of production (where consumers are the suppliers and producers are the demanders) and each final commodity (where producers are the suppliers and consumers are the demanders). The prices at which supply equals demand in all markets are the competitive market prices, and given these prices, no consumer or producer will desire to alter his behavior in any way. . . .

Will a competitive equilibrium exist (i.e., is there a set of prices which will clear all markets?), and if so, will the resulting configuration be Pareto efficient and socially optimal? Three further sets of assumptions will be useful in order to answer these questions. These are not the only assumptions required, but they are the ones most likely to be invalid in the real world, so they will be considered explicitly. One of these is the *zero transaction costs assumption*. For purposes of this assumption transaction costs are all the costs which inhibit competitive markets from working. It implies, for example, that consumers and producers are able to obtain perfect information about market prices and product quality at no cost, and that the process of exchange is itself costless. The second of these assumptions is the *convexity assumption*. It limits the structure of the consumer's preferences and of the producer's technology. For example, it rules out the following possibility for a consumer's preferences. Suppose that a consumer prefers to swim in a clean river, but after pollution exceeds a certain level he prefers to take up another form of recreation. Once he quits swimming in the river he no longer cares how dirty the river becomes. The last of the assumptions is the *zero* *redistribution cost assumption*. It states that the process of redistributing initial factor endowments (income) among consumers is not costly in the sense that it does not distort behavior, or involve administrative cost. It precludes the use of any form of redistribution which affects consumer behavior in any way except by increasing or decreasing the consumer's budget.

. . . Thus the paradigm reduces questions of public policy to the determination of the most desirable distribution of income. This decision involves a value judgment about whether one person's welfare should be increased at the expense of another's, a judgment outside the scope of the economist's professional expertise. . . .

Limitations of the competitive model for the analysis of the law may be organized around failures of the three key assumptions — zero transaction costs, convexity, and zero redistribution costs. . . .

The most important implication of transaction costs, one properly emphasized by Posner, is that markets may not exist, or, if they do exist, may not work properly. Analyzing the nature of these market failures and their impact on the achievement of economic efficiency requires

identifying the particular form of transaction cost in the market under
consideration. Markets for two different types of commodities (insurance and public goods) which have two different types of transaction
costs (information and exclusion) illustrate this point.

If there were no transaction costs insurance markets would exist for
every possible risk. Because transaction costs are positive, a failure in
insurance markets, known as "moral hazard," arises. The owner of
insurance tends to behave in a way which increases the probability and
magnitude of the adverse event against which he is insuring himself. . . .
Because information costs preclude taking account of every contingency, insurers will be willing to sell policies only if the premium reflects
increased expected damage due to moral hazard. Consumers' demand
for insurance is based on their expected damage in the absence of insurance, and therefore they may be unwilling to pay as much as the company requires to provide a policy. Thus insurance markets may not exist
at all for protection against certain risks, such as smoking in bed and
leaving oil-soaked rags in one's garage. Insurance markets which do
exist will operate somewhat imperfectly because individuals will take
fewer precautions than would be efficient. . . .

When transaction costs lead to market imperfections, the most
efficient response is often not to mimic the market. Each case must be
examined in detail for the sources of the market failure, and an appropriate remedy designed in light of them. Often the best compromise in
practice is quite different from any conceivable outcome in a zero transaction costs setting. . . .

The behavior of parties who are affected by externalities illustrates
why markets fail due to nonconvexities. The party suffering the ill effects of an externality can often increase his welfare by leaving the vicinity of the externality. If thereafter the party no longer cares how
unpleasant the externality becomes, then his preferences fail to satisfy
the convexity assumption. . . .

When the convexity assumption is satisfied, the assignment of
property rights in an externality situation may create an artifical market,
provided that the transaction costs of market exchanges are zero. Such a
market would lead to a competitive equilibrium and the attainment of
efficiency. When nonconvexities are present there may be no competitive equilibrium at all, or, if there is one, it may be inefficient. . . .

The redistribution of income may have two distinct effects on
prices. First, under the new distribution of income, a new competitive
equilibrium results in which prices and quantities differ from those
under the previous equilibrium. Second, for any given change in
the income distribution the method of redistribution itself may affect
prices. . . .

Very little can be said *a priori* about the magnitudes of the costs
associated with various redistributive methods, but a few examples il-

lustrate the nature of these costs. The major distorting effect of the income tax is to increase the price of purchasable commodities relative to the price of leisure (which is the opportunity cost of not working), thereby causing persons to work less hard, everything else being equal. Excise taxes — taxes on specific factors or commodities — may also be used to achieve income redistribution, although typically they are not used for that purpose. These too cause distortions by artificially changing the price of the item taxed. Similar distortions occur when redistribution is effected through expenditures. . . .

In a world without redistribution costs the social optimum could be achieved by first using lump-sum transfers to attain the desired income distribution and then allowing competitive markets to achieve efficiency. This is no longer possible if the process of moving to the desired distribution itself causes distortions. . . .

Since redistribution is costly, the problem of designing the law, even within the economist's framework, is one of trading off efficiency and equity. . . .

To avoid consideration of distributional consequences, it is not sufficient to appeal to the fact that the gainers could compensate the losers and still be better off, even though no compensation is actually paid. . . .

An alternative argument is that each consumer can expect to come out ahead in the long run if the efficiency criterion is used to formulate legal rules. It is argued that an individual who loses from one change in legal rules is likely to gain from another. Since improving efficiency implies an excess of total gains over total losses, each consumer can expect to gain on the average. There is no assurance, however, that each person will in fact gain but only a presumption that he could expect to gain. Even after numerous changes in the law, there will in general be some individuals who are net losers. The problem is qualitatively the same as before — having to trade off efficiency and equity to improve the resulting income distribution if it is not satisfactory. The only difference is a quantitative one; more persons may be net gainers, but not everyone can be assured of being a net gainer unless compensation for losses is paid with respect to each change or after the bundle of changes.

. . . The competitive market paradigm, which is the basis of Posner's approach, requires a number of stringent assumptions, many of which are likely to fail in the context of the real world problems which Posner analyzes. These failures arise not only in the analysis of legal problems, but also in many other problems to which economic analysis is applied. However, the crucial assumptions are more likely to fail in those areas in which the law plays an important role. Because Posner does not make the limitations of the paradigm sufficiently explicit, readers not fully aware of them may accept his conclusions uncritically or may extrapolate his analysis to draw conclusions unwarranted in reality.

If the assumptions of the competitive market model were fulfilled, the law would play a relatively minor role — it would merely redistribute income and have no effect on efficiency. In the real world, however, the law is important precisely because many of these do fail. . . .

◆ KENNEDY & MICHELMAN, ARE PROPERTY AND CONTRACT EFFICIENT?
8 Hofstra L. Rev. 711, 713-714, 750, 764-770 (1980)

. . . The literature of the contemporary law and economics movement deals with both the general question and problems of specific application. It is distinguished from its forbears both by its self-conscious choice of a norm of economic virtue ("efficiency") and by its elaboration of techniques for economic analysis of legal material. . . . The arguments that concern us are those purporting to justify the legal institutions in question by reference only (a) to a very weak, highly plausible value judgment that we should do things that make or could make everyone affected more satisfied than they would otherwise be, and (b) to a very weak, highly plausible factual judgment that people tend most of the time to act as though they had goals and were trying to achieve them — i.e., that people are rational maximizers of satisfactions. . . . Any argument for the economic virtue ("efficiency") of any legal title must depend on specific assumptions about the actual wants and factual circumstances of the persons affected by the choice among possible rules — that is, that the efficiency of private property and free contract cannot be deduced from the sole factual supposition of rational maximizing behavior. . . . Much legal and related policy-analytic literature reflects and reinforces the view that certain legal institutions (e.g., private property, free contract) are in some sense *generally* or *presumptively* efficient, while others (e.g., central regulatory command, commonses) are generally or presumptively inefficient, for a population of rational maximizers. . . . Any notion of the presumptive efficiency of private property and free contract must be untenable. Any *actually* efficient regime, though it may well contain rules fairly characterizable as private property and free contract, must contain them in combination with rules drawn from realms perceived as *opposite* to private property/free contract (viz., unowned commonses and collective controls) so that there is no more reason for awarding the palm of "presumptive efficiency" to private property/free contract than to its opposites. . . .

We define two nondirective alternatives to a *private property/free contract* order (PPFC), each occupying one extreme on a spectrum of logical possibilities. At one pole there is the *state of nature* (SON), in which the only "rule" is that every person is free to do or take whatever she can with whatever strength and cunning she has. At the other pole is the whole *world* — all resources, labor, and products — *owned in common* by everyone (WOC), so that no one can do or use anything (or for that matter refrain from doing or using anything) without the consent of everyone else. . . . Both SON and WOC are instances of initial situations defined by general rules, from which the only permitted developments are those arising from self-motivated individual action taken subject to the rules, with no intervention allowed. . . .

Reflecting separately on the questions of boundaries, composition, and structure, one is led to like conclusions each time. First, the actual legal orders familiar to us do not correspond to PPFC. Our legal system, in particular, constricts PPFC within boundaries outside which there is SON or WOC. . . .

Second, it seems overwhelmingly likely that at least some of these deviations from PPFC are motivated by an accurate assessment of the disastrous efficiency consequences of taking PPFC seriously as a design for an entire legal order. A PPFC order is likely to be efficient only insofar as it has been deliberately worked over — restricted, qualified, and specified — with a view to making it efficient, only insofar as the right matters have been excluded from its range, the right limits imposed on decomposition of holdings, the right mix specified of liability and nonliability for consequences. Working in the requisite exclusions, limits, and mixes means introducing elements of SON and WOC into the order. . . . Thus in whatever sense PPFC can be said to be efficient, the same can be said of both SON and WOC.

It is obvious that real legal systems never attempt a global, domain-covering version of PPFC. Here are some salient ways in which they fall short: (a) They establish commonses, SON-like zones of universal *in rem* privilege . . . (b) They establish WOC-like areas of collective compulsion. . . .

These cases pose a problem for the thesis that PPFC is efficient for rational maximizers because they are cases in which it would be *possible* to apply a regime of property and contract but in which judges and legislators refuse to do so. That leaves us with two possible ways to defend the efficiency thesis. The first is to insist that the exclusions from PPFC are, indeed, *all* inefficient but justifiable even so by reason of their service to some nonefficiency aim or value. The second is to admit that at least some of the exclusions make sense from the standpoint of efficiency. . . .

It seems, in short, that we have here a case illustrating Wittgenstein's reputed dictum that no rule can determine its own application. The property regime is a set of rules concerning what to do about property; it is not a set of rules concerning what should and should not be property. If the efficiency of property depends on the rules being applied to the right things, then without a new set of rules about *which* things, we can't say anything significant about property's efficiency in general.

Just as all real legal systems exclude some parts of PPFC's possible range from its actual domain, so do they all impose restrictions on the decomposition of possible objects of ownership into parts that can be separately owned. . . . Our system does permit decomposition very liberally, *including decomposition of the right/privilege coupling that our Hohfeldian specification for property treated as atomic.* . . .

As with boundary exclusions, the zones of tolerance for subatomic decomposition all represent the order's acceptance of elements of SON and WOC. . . .

Suppose that both the boundary and composition problems have been solved in some unproblematic way. . . . We could then, supposedly, define a private property ideal type as follows: There is a determinate class of objects; the objects are not legally subdivisible; each object in the class belongs to a sole owner; each owner has *in rem* privileges over the object that exactly correspond with his *in rem* rights over the object — a symmetrical right/privilege. We now address the question whether it is possible to say that such a regime is efficient, even supposing that the "correct" boundaries and composition rules have been chosen.

The problem we face is that of excuses, defenses, and *damnum absque injuria*. Real legal systems all seem to contain nonliability rules of the following types:

(a) General excuses for intentional invasion of rights (e.g., duress, self-defense, necessity, competition, mistake).
(b) The defense of "no proximate cause."
(c) The absence in many or most cases of liability for failure to act — even, in some cases, when the non-act is chosen consciously in order to inflict injury on a legally protected interest.
(d) The excuses of "inevitable accident," "accident," and "no malice," each applying in some cases but not others.

The existence of these forms of *damnum absque injuria* means that as a matter of fact there are no classes of objects with respect to which there is *full* symmetry of rights and privileges. They give rise to a wide variety of situations in which I am privileged to use my X in a particular way, but have no right so to use it. I can use the X to inflict damage on another person without having to pay compensation, but the other person is privileged to resist the injury by interfering with my use, rather than being under a duty to let me be. . . .

Having found the existence of asymmetry by reason of the existence of privileges without symmetrical rights, we naturally expect also to come upon rights without symmetrical privileges, and of course we do. . . . Rather than a situation in which I can do it to myself but not to you, while you do it to yourself but not to me, we are in a situation where no one can do it at all, even when it is arguable that no one else is affected.

These cases, we may note, are WOC-like, just as the cases of universal privilege to act innocently and non-negligently (or under duress, or in self-defense, or competitively, or passively), despite adverse consequences for another's enjoyment of his things, can be described as pockets of SON. Thus the situation here seems to resemble closely that which we encountered in exploring the boundary and composition questions: As to all three questions, there appears to be a choice between explaining observed deviations from the pure form of PPFC order as all inefficient but justifiable on other grounds, and admitting that without at least some of the deviations the order could not possibly be considered efficient; and since the first line is utterly implausible we are forced to the second, which is tantamount to admitting that the circumstantially efficient order is, in principle, no less SON or WOC than it is PP. . . .

The reason for this nihilistic conclusion is not empirical or technical but mental and conceptual: In the frame of mind in which one sees an order as more or less efficiently adapted to circumstantial facts respecting wants and proclivities, one *has* to see it as *intervention* — as a *regulatory* phenomenon. An efficient order, we have shown, will always contain elements of cognizable nondirective orders — SON, WOC, PPFC. No doubt others could be invented which would do the conceptual work as well — but in an efficient order these elements will not be combined in accordance with any cognizable rule or set of rules expressible through any short list of parsimonious, axiomatic formulas or principles. The *combination* must be *ad hoc*, deliberately contrived, and from time to time recontrived, to fit the shifting mosaic of wants and proclivities (and technology, and resources, etc., etc.). But to go about the task of continually choosing and combining these pieces of PPFC, SON, and WOC, with a view to maximizing some want-regarding social objective function like total wealth (or total welfare, or per-capita welfare, or equal-per-capita wealth) is, precisely, to be engaged in intervention. The case is not, then, that WOC stands for total regulation, SON for aimless disorder, and PPFC for nondirective order or freedom-under-law. The case is that, taken separately, these are all conceivable as non-directive orders, but mixed together *ad hoc* they are all ingredients of regulation. Insofar as they have anything whatever to do with efficiency, private property and free contract are species of intervention.

F. PUBLIC ACCESS TO BEACHES

◆ OPINION OF THE JUSTICES
365 Mass. 681, 313 N.E. 2d 561 (1974)

To the Honorable the House of Representatives of the Commonwealth of Massachusetts:

The Justices of the Supreme Judicial Court respectfully submit this reply to the question set forth in an order adopted by the House on May 8, 1974, and transmitted to us on May 10, 1974. The order recites the pendency before the General Court of a bill, a copy of which has been transmitted to us with the order. The bill is entitled, "An Act authorizing public right-of-passage along certain coastline of the Commonwealth" (House No. 481). . . .

The bill declares that the reserved interests of the public in the land along the coastline between the mean high water line and the extreme low water line include a "public on-foot free right-of-passage." This "right-of-passage" is only to be exercised after sunrise and before one-half hour after sunset and is not to be exercised in those areas designated by the Commissioner of the Department of Natural Resources as of critical ecological significance and so posted. It is not to be exercised where there exists a structure or enclosure authorized by law, or an agricultural fence enclosing livestock, if such areas are clearly posted. An attempt to prevent the exercise of this right of passage is made punishable by fine, and the burden of proof in any action concerning the exclusion of the exercise of the right is to be on the party seeking to exclude or limit it. Interference with or making unsafe such passage is made unlawful, and a civil remedy is provided to any person affected by such action. Littering while exercising the right of passage is prohibited. The limited tort liability of G.L. c.21, §17C, is extended to coastal owners with respect to persons exercising the "right-of-passage" except for injuries caused by a violation of the proposed act.

The bill further provides that it is not to be construed as altering existing statutory or common law property or personal rights or remedies. It then states that any person having a recorded interest in any land affected may "within two years from the effective date of this act" petition the Superior Court under G.L. c.79 "to determine whether . . . the activities authorized herein constitute an injury for which the owner is entitled to compensation under said chapter 79." Finally, the bill requires the Commissioner of Public Works to record a notice of its adoption, prior to its effective date, in every county where coastline land is required to be recorded. He is also required to give such notice by publication within sixty days after its effective date for three consecutive weeks in newspapers in cities and towns containing affected coastal land.

The order asserts that grave doubt exists as to the constitutionality of the bill if enacted into law and propounds the following question: "Would the pending Bill if enacted into law violate Article X of the Bill of Rights of the Constitution of the Commonwealth or the Fourteenth Amendment to the Constitution of the United States?"

At common law, private ownership in coastal land extended only as far as mean high water line. Beyond that, ownership was in the Crown but subject to the rights of the public to use the coastal waters for fishing and navigation. . . . When title was transferred to private persons it remained impressed with these public rights. . . . The property inherent in the Crown in England was passed by charter to the Massachusetts Bay Colony and ultimately to the Commonwealth. . . .

In the 1640's, in order to encourage littoral owners to build wharves, the colonial authorities took the extraordinary step of extending private titles to encompass land as far as mean low water line or 100 rods from the mean high water line, whichever was the lesser measure. . . . This was accomplished by what has become known as the colonial ordinance of 1641-47, which is found in the 1649 codification, The Book of the General Lawes and Libertyes, at p. 50:

> Every Inhabitant who is an housholder shall have free fishing and fowling in any great ponds, bayes, Coves and Rivers, so farr as the Sea ebbs and flowes, within the precincts of the towne where they dwell, unles the freemen of the same Town or the General Court have otherwise appropriated them. . . . The which clearly to determine, It is Declared, That in all *Creeks*, *Coves* and other places, about and upon *Salt-water*, where the Sea ebbs and flowes, the proprietor of the land adjoyning, shall have propriety to the low-water mark, where the Sea doth not ebb above a hundred Rods, and not more wheresoever it ebbs further. Provided that such proprietor shall not by this liberty, have power to stop or hinder the passage of boates or other vessels, in or through any Sea, Creeks, or Coves, to other mens houses or lands.

Although strictly the ordinance was limited to the area of the Massachusetts Bay Colony, it has long been interpreted as effecting a grant of the tidal land to all coastal owners in the Commonwealth. . . . The language of the ordinance well illustrates the notion, previously alluded to, of reserved public right. It expressly specifies that the public is to retain the rights of fishing, fowling and navigation. Notwithstanding these limitations and the use of such ambiguous terms as "propriety" and "liberty," there is ample judicial authority to the effect that the ordinance is properly construed as granting the benefitted owners a fee in the seashore to the extent described and subject to the public rights reserved. . . . If, therefore, the right of passage authorized by the bill is, as it declares, merely an exercise of existing public rights, and not a taking of private property, it must be a natural derivative of the rights preserved by the colonial ordinance. It has been held proper to interfere with the private property rights of coastal owners in the tidal area for purposes reasonably related to the protection or promotion of fishing or navigation without paying compensation. . . . An "on-foot right-of-passage" is not so related to these public rights. The cases interpreting the right of the public in navigation all deal with the use in boats or other vessels of the area below mean high water mark "when covered with tide water." . . . Thus the right of passage over dry land at periods of low tide cannot be reasonably included as one of the traditional rights of navigation.

We have frequently had occasion to declare the limited nature of public rights in the seashore. . . . These limitations are also evident in comparing Weston v. Sampson, 8 Cush. 347 (1851), with Porter v. Shehan, 7 Gray 435 (1856), both written by Chief Justice Shaw. In the *Weston* case, the defendants entered upon the plaintiffs' tidal land by boat, and their digging for clams was held to be an exercise of the reserved public right of fishing. In the *Porter* case, however, it was deemed a trespass for the defendant to enter and take five cords of muscle [sic] mud "consisting of living and dead shell fish . . . and the soil or clay in which they were found," and used principally as a fertilizer. . . . The Chief Justice wrote that this exceeded the public rights in fishing, and that there was "no right to take the soil, or fish shells, part of the soil, except as slight portions of the soil would necessarily and ordinarily be attached to shell fish, when taken."

We are unable to find any authority that the rights of the public include a right to walk on the beach. In a case presenting a very similar question to that raised by the bill, it was held that the public rights in the seashore do not include a right to use otherwise private beaches for public bathing. . . . We have considered an able argument made in the brief of one of the *amici curiae* that we should interpret the colonial ordinance as vesting in the Commonwealth the right to allow all significant public uses in the seashore. It is contended that while fishing, fowling and navigation may have exhausted these uses in 1647, these public uses change with time and now must be deemed to include the important public interest in recreation. Whatever may be the propriety of such an interpretation with respect to public rights in littoral land held by the State, . . . we think the cases we have cited make clear that the grant to private parties effected by the colonial ordinance has never been interpreted to provide the littoral owners only such uncertain and ephemeral rights as would result from such an interpretation. . . .

It is next necessary to inquire whether the authorization of the right of passage provided by the bill, while not within the public rights reserved by the colonial ordinance, is nonetheless a proper exercise of the Commonwealth's police power and, as such, does not require that compensation be paid to the private owners. . . . The elusive border between the police power of the State and the prohibition against taking of property without compensation has been the subject of extensive litigation and commentary. . . . But these difficulties need not concern us here. The permanent physical intrusion into the property of private persons, which the bill would establish, is a taking of property within even the most narrow construction of that phrase possible under the Constitutions of the Commonwealth and of the United States.

It is true that the bill does not completely deprive private owners of all use of their seashore property in the sense that a formal taking does. But the case is readily distinguishable from such regulation as merely prohibits some particular use or uses which are harmful to the public. . . . The interference with private property here involves a wholesale denial of an owner's right to exclude the public. If a possessory interest in real property has any meaning at all it must include the general right to exclude others. . . .

Even if we were to hold that compensation to private owners for the taking of this public easement were provided in the bill it would still be constitutionally defective, for the procedure proposed is inadequate both in the scope of its potential compensation and the notice accorded to property owners of their right to recover damages.

The only property owners given an opportunity to seek damages are those having a recorded interest in affected property. It is obvious that this omits all property owners who hold their title by unrecorded deed or adverse possession. Either manner of acquiring property gives good title. . . .

Furthermore, with respect to those owners as well as to those of recorded interests, it is a matter of serious question whether the method of notice to affected property owners is sufficient. . . . The bill provides only constructive notice by recording and publication. . . .

We answer the question "Yes."

G. Joseph Tauro
Paul C. Reardon
Francis J. Quirico
Robert Braucher
Edward F. Hennessey
Herbert P. Wilkins

Notes

1. Defendant was building a high-rise condominium right up to the property line. Plaintiff was building a three-story residence in the center of his lot. Plaintiff sued, alleging trespass by construction workers' scaffolding, and fear that a negligent workman could dump objects into his yard. *Held:* No cause of action. Citing United States v. Causby, 328 U.S. 256 (1946), the Illinois appellate court said plaintiff owns "only as much air space . . . as he can practicably use." To constitute trespass "an intrusion has to . . . subtract from the owner's use. . . ." Geller v. Brownstone Condominium Assn. 82 Ill. App. 3d 334, 402 N.E.2d 807 (1980), 91 Ill. App. 3d 823, 415 N.E.2d 20 (1980).

2. See Johnson v. Seifert, 257 Minn. 159, 100 N.W.2d 689 (1960),

where the owner of land adjoining a nonnavigable lake said he owned the bed of the lake extending out from his shoreland and therefore could fence that bed and exclude other riparian owners from fishing and swimming in "his" water. The court disagreed: "an abutting owner on a nonnavigable lake has the right to use the entire surface of the lake for all suitable and reasonable purposes in common with all other riparian owners."

What if the State Recreation Department now buys a short stretch of lakefront land, and permits public access so popular that the value of Seifert's land is substantially reduced?

3. Can Opinion of the Justices be distinguished from Nantucket Conservation Foundation, Inc. v. Russell Management, Inc., 380 Mass. 212, 402 N.E.2d 501 (1980)? There, defendant owned an easement for ingress and egress along a 50-foot-wide private way across plaintiff's land. Massachusetts had enacted in 1975 Chapter 187, §5 of its General Laws, saying that any owner with a right of ingress and egress by deed should also have "the right by implication" to install gas, telephone, and electrical lines along the way. The statute was held constitutional, even though retrospective. The court said that the common law rule forbidding utility lines along easements of access "ignores the essential role certain basic utilities play today in facilitating the use and enjoyment of land."

4. How is the high-water line determined? See Dolphin Lane Assn. v. Town of Southampton, 37 N.Y.2d 292, 333 N.E.2d 358, 372 N.Y.S.2d 52 (1975):

> Attaching real significance as we do to the importance of stability and predictability in matters involving title to real property, we hold that the location of the boundary to this shore-side property depends on a combination of the verbal formulation of the boundary line — i.e., the high-water line — and the application of the traditional and customary method by which that verbal formulation has been put in practice in the past to locate the boundary line along the shore. . . . Thus, to recognize, as the town's argument must, that the type-of-grass test for location of the high-water mark may one day be replaced by an even more sophisticated and refined test for determining the high-water line, with a consequent shift again in the on-the-site location of a northern boundary line, is to introduce an element of uncertainty and unpredictability quite foreign to the law of conveyancing.
>
> The evidence in this case was really not disputed that prior to this litigation it had been normal practice to locate the high-water line by reference to the line of vegetation. If a change is to be made in the procedures for locating shore-side boundary lines to conform more precisely to hydrographic data, in our view, such innovation should be left to the Legislature.

5. Property cases have a way of asking questions such as, "Is a large body of water known as Grand Lake-Six Mile Lake a stream or a lake?" In State v. Placid Oil Co., 300 So. 2d 154 (La. 1974), *cert. denied,* 419 U.S. 1110 (1975), the Louisiana supreme court changed a long-standing doctrine on that question. The matter was important because in Louisiana private riparian owners along streams have title down to the ordinary low-water mark, while along lakes they own only to the high-water mark. What sources should a court look to in answering this kind of question? More precisely, what reasons for decision are appropriate when a court changes old doctrine on such an issue? The Louisiana decision was praised as a "positive development" because it "should have the practical effect of transferring a substantial amount of land from private to state ownership." Note, 49 Tul. L. Rev. 208, 213 (1974). Is this an acceptable reason? A sufficient reason? See also United States v. Alaska, 422 U.S. 184 (1975), holding that Cook Inlet is not a "historic bay" because Russia, America, and Alaska have rarely exercised sovereignty over the waters. Therefore, the U.S. has paramount rights to land beneath the waters of the seaward portion of the inlet, and can dispose of the oil and natural gas recently found there.

6. Rights to oil revenues from the continental shelf off the eastern end of Long Island depend on whether Long Island is legally an island or a peninsula. If it is an island, the federal government owns 172 square miles of continental shelf. But if it is a peninsula, then the waters in dispute are controlled by Rhode Island and New York.

States control offshore waters for 3 miles from the beach. From 3 miles to 200 miles, the federal government has jurisdiction.

Rhode Island's argument, which prevailed in U.S. district court but must be litigated further, is that "Long Island is a bloody island surrounded by water, but that bridges, cables, tunnels and other connections between Manhattan and Long Island make it legally part of the mainland." Wall Street J., Mar. 3, 1983. See also Warner v. Replinger, 397 F. Supp. 350 (D.R.I. 1975).

7. Generally, neither adverse possession nor prescription can be pleaded against the government. The policy underlying adverse possession — to reward those who make productive use of land — is superseded by the governmental interest in preserving public lands. But in Askew v. Sonson, 409 So. 2d 7 (Fla. 1982), the Florida Supreme Court interpreted the Marketable Record Title Act (MRTA), which includes Florida's rules for acquiring ownership by adverse possession, as applying to state lands reserved for schools. The court held that under the Florida Constitution, the legislature was not prohibited from making MRTA applicable to the state. Thus the plaintiffs, having met the requirements for adverse possession under the MRTA, acquired title to reserved school property by their 30 years adverse possession of the site.

◆ STATE EX REL. THORNTON v. HAY
254 Or. 584, 462 P.2d 671 (1969)

GOODWIN, Justice. William and Georgianna Hay, the owners of a tourist facility at Cannon Beach, appeal from a decree which enjoins them from constructing fences or other improvements in the dry-sand area between the sixteen-foot elevation contour line and the ordinary high-tide line of the Pacific Ocean.

The issue is whether the state has the power to prevent the defendant landowners from enclosing the dry-sand area contained within the legal description of their ocean-front property. . . .

The defendant landowners concede that the State Highway Commission has standing to represent the rights of the public in this litigation, ORS 390.620, and that all tideland lying seaward of the ordinary, or mean high-tide line is a state recreation area as defined in ORS 390.720.[1] . . .

The trial court found that the public had acquired, over the years, an easement for recreational purposes to go upon and enjoy the dry-sand area, and that this easement was appurtenant to the wet-sand portion of the beach which is admittedly owned by the state and designated as a "state recreation area."

Because we hold that the trial court correctly found in favor of the state on the rights of the public in the dry-sand area, it follows that the state has an equitable right to protect the public in the enjoyment of those rights by causing the removal of fences and other obstacles. . . .

The dry-sand area in Oregon has been enjoyed by the general public as a recreational adjunct of the wet-sand or foreshore area since the beginning of the state's political history. The first European settlers on these shores found the aboriginal inhabitants using the foreshore for clam-digging and the dry-sand area for their cooking fires. The newcomers continued these customs after statehood. Thus, from the time of the earliest settlement to the present day, the general public has assumed that the dry-sand area was a part of the public beach, and the public has used the dry-sand area for picnics, gathering wood, building warming fires, and generally as a headquarters from which to supervise children or to range out over the foreshore as the tides advance and recede. In the Cannon Beach vicinity, state and local officers have policed the dry

---

1. ORS 390.720 provides:

   Ownership of the shore of the Pacific Ocean between ordinary high tide and extreme low tide, and from the Oregon and Washington state line on the north to the Oregon and California state line on the south, excepting such portions as may have been disposed of by the state prior to July 5, 1947, is vested in the State of Oregon, and is declared to be a state recreation area. No portion of such ocean shore shall be alienated by any of the agencies of the state except as provided by law.

sand, and municipal sanitary crews have attempted to keep the area reasonably free from man-made litter.

Perhaps one explanation for the evolution of the custom of the public to use the dry-sand area for recreational purposes is that the area could not be used conveniently by its owners for any other purpose. The dry-sand area is unstable in its seaward boundaries, unsafe during winter storms, and for the most part unfit for the construction of permanent structures. While the vegetation line remains relatively fixed, the western edge of the dry-sand area is subject to dramatic moves eastward or westward in response to erosion and accretion. For example, evidence in the trial below indicated that between April 1966 and August 1967 the seaward edge of the dry-sand area involved in this litigation moved westward 180 feet. At other points along the shore, the evidence showed, the seaward edge of the dry-sand area could move an equal distance to the east in a similar period of time.

Until very recently, no question concerning the right of the public to enjoy the dry-sand area appears to have been brought before the courts of this state. The public's assumption that the dry sand as well as the foreshore was "public property" had been reinforced by early judicial decisions. See Shively v. Bowlby, 152 U.S. 1, 14 S. Ct. 548, 38 L. Ed. 331 (1894), which affirmed Bowlby v. Shively, 22 Or. 410, 30 P. 154 (1892). These cases held that landowners claiming under federal patents owned seaward only to the "high-water" line, a line that was then assumed to be the vegetation line.

In 1935, the United States Supreme Court held that a federal patent conveyed title to land farther seaward, to the mean high-tide line. Borax, Ltd. v. Los Angeles, 296 U.S. 10, 56 S. Ct. 23, 80 L. Ed. 9 (1935). While this decision may have expanded seaward the record ownership of upland landowners, it was apparently little noticed by Oregonians. In any event, the *Borax* decision had no discernible effect on the actual practices of Oregon beachgoers and upland property owners.

Recently, however, the scarcity of ocean-front building sites has attracted substantial private investments in resort facilities. Resort owners like these defendants now desire to reserve for their paying guests the recreational advantages that accrue to the dry-sand portions of their deeded property. Consequently, in 1967, public debate and political activity resulted in legislative attempts to resolve conflicts between public and private interests in the dry-sand area:

ORS 390.610 "(1) The Legislative Assembly hereby declares it is the public policy of the State of Oregon to forever preserve and maintain the sovereignty of the state heretofore existing over the seashore and ocean beaches of the state from the Columbia River on the North to the Oregon-California line on the South so that the public may have the free and uninterrupted use thereof.

"(2) The Legislative Assembly recognizes that over the years the public has made frequent and uninterrupted use of lands abutting, adjacent and contiguous to the public highways and state recreation areas and recognizes, further, that where such use has been sufficient to create easements in the public through dedication, prescription, grant or otherwise, that it is in the public interest to protect and preserve such public easements as a permanent part of Oregon's recreational resources.

"(3) Accordingly, the Legislative Assembly hereby declares that all public rights and easements in those lands described in subsection (2) of this section are confirmed and declared vested exclusively in the State of Oregon and shall be held and administered in the same manner as those lands described in ORS 390.720. . . ."

The state concedes that such legislation cannot divest a person of his rights in land, Hughes v. Washington, 389 U.S. 290, 88 S. Ct. 438, 19 L. Ed. 2d 530 (1967), and that the defendants' record title, which includes the dry-sand area, extends seaward to the ordinary or mean high-tide line.

The landowners likewise concede that since 1899 the public's rights in the foreshore have been confirmed by law as well as by custom and usage. Oregon Laws 1899, p. 3, provided:

"That the shore of the Pacific ocean, between ordinary high and extreme low tides, and from the Columbia river on the north to the south boundary line of Clatsop county on the south, is hereby declared a public highway, and shall forever remain open as such to the public."

The disputed area is *sui generis*. While the foreshore is "owned" by the state, and the upland is "owned" by the patentee or record-title holder, neither can be said to "own" the full bundle of rights normally connoted by the term "estate in fee simple." . . .

One group of precedents relied upon in part by the state and by the trial court can be called the "implied-dedication" cases. The doctrine of implied dedication is well known to the law in this state and elsewhere. See cases collected in Parks, The Law of Dedication in Oregon, 20 Or. L. Rev. 111 (1941). Dedication, however, whether express or implied, rests upon an intent to dedicate. In the case at bar, it is unlikely that the landowners thought they had anything to dedicate, until 1967, when the notoriety of legislative debates about the public's rights in the dry-sand area sent a number of ocean-front landowners to the offices of their legal advisers.

A second group of cases relied upon by the state, but rejected by the trial court, deals with the possibility of a landowner's losing the exclusive possession and enjoyment of his land through the development of prescriptive easements in the public.

In Oregon, as in most common-law jurisdictions, an easement can be created in favor of one person in the land of another by uninterrupted use and enjoyment of the land in a particular manner for the statutory period, so long as the user is open, adverse, under claim of right, but without authority of law or consent of the owner. . . . In Oregon, the prescriptive period is ten years. ORS 12.050. The public use of the disputed land in the case at bar is admitted to be continuous for more than sixty years. There is no suggestion in the record that anyone's permission was sought or given; rather, the public used the land under a claim of right. Therefore, if the public can acquire an easement by prescription, the requirements for such an acquisition have been met in connection with the specific tract of land involved in this case.

The owners argue, however, that the general public, not being subject to actions in trespass and ejectment, cannot acquire rights by prescription, because the statute of limitations is irrelevant when an action does not lie.

While it may not be feasible for a landowner to sue the general public, it is nonetheless possible by means of signs and fences to prevent or minimize public invasions of private land for recreational purposes. In Oregon, moreover, the courts and the Legislative Assembly have both recognized that the public can acquire prescriptive easements in private land, at least for roads and highways. . . .

Another statute codifies a policy favoring the acquisition by prescription of public recreational easements in beach lands. See ORS 390.610. While such a statute cannot create public rights at the expense of a private landowner the statute can, and does, express legislative approval of the common-law doctrine of prescription where the facts justify its application. Consequently, we conclude that the law in Oregon, regardless of the generalizations that may apply elsewhere,[5] does not preclude the creation of prescriptive easements in beach land for public recreational use.

Because many elements of prescription are present in this case, the state has relied upon the doctrine in support of the decree below. We believe, however, that there is a better legal basis for affirming the decree. The most cogent basis for the decision in this case is the English doctrine of custom. Strictly construed, prescription applies only to the specific tract of land before the court, and doubtful prescription cases

---

5. See, e.g., Sanchez v. Taylor, 377 F.2d 733, 738 (10th Cir. 1967), holding that the general public cannot acquire grazing rights in unfenced land. Among other reasons assigned by authorities cited in Sanchez v. Taylor are these: prescription would violate the rule against perpetuities because no grantee could ever convey the land free of the easement; and prescription rests on the fiction of a "lost grant," which state of affairs cannot apply to the general public. The first argument can as well be made against the public's acquiring rights by express dedication; and the second argument applies equally to the fictional aspects of the doctrine of implied dedication. Both arguments are properly ignored in cases dealing with roads and highways, because the utility of roads and the public interest in keeping them open outweigh the policy favoring formal over informal transfers of interests in land.

could fill the courts for years with tract-by-tract litigation. An established custom, on the other hand, can be proven with reference to a larger region. Ocean-front lands from the northern to the southern border of the state ought to be treated uniformly.

The other reason which commends the doctrine of custom over that of prescription as the principal basis for the decision in this case is the unique nature of the lands in question. This case deals solely with the dry-sand area along Pacific shore, and this land has been used by the public as public recreational land according to an unbroken custom running back in time as long as the land has been inhabited. . . .

Because so much of our law is the product of legislation, we sometimes lose sight of the importance of custom as a source of law in our society. It seems particularly appropriate in the case at bar to look to an ancient and accepted custom in this state as the source of a rule of law. The rule in this case, based upon custom, is salutary in confirming a public right, and at the same time it takes from no man anything which he has had a legitimate reason to regard as exclusively his.

DENECKE, Justice (specially concurring). I agree with the decision of the majority; however, I disagree with basing the decision upon the English doctrine of "customary rights." . . .

I base the public's right upon the following factors: (1) long usage by the public of the dry sands area, not necessarily on all the Oregon beaches, but wherever the public uses the beach; (2) a universal and long held belief by the public in the public's right to such use; (3) long and universal acquiescence by the upland owners in such public use; and (4) the extreme desirability to the public of the right to the use of the dry sands. When this combination exists, as it does here, I conclude that the public has the right to use the dry sands.

Admittedly, this is a new concept as applied to use of the dry sands of a beach; however, it is not new as applied to other public usages. In Luscher v. Reynolds, 153 Or. 625, 56 P.2d 1158 (1963), we held that regardless of who owns the bed of a lake, if it is capable of being boated, the public has the right to boat it.

> . . . There are hundreds of similar beautiful, small inland lakes in this state well adapted for recreational purposes, but which will never be used as highways of commerce in the ordinary acceptation of such terms. As stated in Lamprey v. State, 52 Minn. 181, 53 N.W. 1139, . . . "To hand over all these lakes to private ownership, under any old or narrow test of navigability, would be a great wrong upon the public for all time, the extent of which cannot, perhaps, be now even anticipated." Regardless of the ownership of the bed, the public has the paramount right to the use of the waters of the lake for the purpose of transportation and commerce.

In Collins v. Gerhardt, 237 Mich. 38, 211 N.W. 116 (1926), the defendant was wading Pine River and fishing. The plaintiff, who owned the land on both sides and the bed of Pine River, sued defendant for trespass. The court held for the defendant:

> From this it follows that the common-law doctrine, viz., that the right of fishing in navigable waters follows the ownership of the soil, does not prevail in this state. It is immaterial who owns the soil in our navigable rivers. The trust remains. From the beginning the title was impressed with this trust for the preservation of the public right of fishing and other public rights which all citizens enjoyed in tidal waters under the common law. . . .

These rights of the public in tidelands and in the beds of navigable streams have been called "jus publicum" and we have consistently and recently reaffirmed their existence. . . . The right of public use continues although title to the property passes into private ownership and nothing in the chain of title reserves or notifies anyone of this public right.

In a recent treatise on waters and water rights the authors state:

> The principle that the public has an interest in tidelands and banks of navigable waters and a right to use them for purposes for which there is a substantial public demand may be derived from the fact that the public won a right to passage over the shore for access to the sea for fishing when this was the area of substantial public demand. As time goes by, opportunities for much more extensive uses of these lands become available to the public. The assertion by the public of a right to enjoy additional uses is met by the assertion that the public right is defined and limited by precedent based upon past uses and past demand. But such a limitation confuses the application of the principle under given circumstances with the principle itself. . . . The words of Justice Cardozo, expressed in a different context nearly a half-century ago, are relevant today in our application of this law: "We may not suffer it to petrify at the cost of its animating principle." [1 Clark, Waters and Water Rights 202 (1967).]

Note

Orienta Beach Club, infra, shows the traditional American rule, rejected in *Hay.* Plaintiffs alleged that for more than 50 years inhabitants of Orienta Point, in Mamaroneck, New York, had used a parcel of land for access to Long Island Sound.

> A careful reading of the English authorities convinces one that the custom had its origin in the fact that from time immemorial the use had been permitted; that because of the length of time the use had existed any records of statutes creating the right had been destroyed; a presumption that the use had been duly authorized was, therefore, created.
> The necessity for such a fiction does not exist in this state. England is of the Old World; our State is of the New. Its statutes have not been lost or

destroyed. Its recording acts have been in existence since early in its history.

[C]onsidering our extensive lines of coast . . . the possibility of turning such enjoyment into prescriptive . . . right on the part of the public would open a field of litigation which no community could endure. What is still worse in a moral point of view, it would be perverting neighborhood forbearance and good nature, to the destruction of important rights. [Gillies v. Orienta Beach Club, 159 Misc. 675, 289 N.Y.S. 733 (Sup. Ct. 1935), quoting from Pearsall v. Post, 20 Wend. 111, 135 (1838).]

◆ MATTHEWS v. BAY HEAD IMPROVEMENT ASSOCIATION
95 N.J. 306, 471 A.2d 355, *cert. denied*, 105 S. Ct. 93 (1984)

The opinion of the Court was delivered by SCHREIBER, J.

The public trust doctrine acknowledges that the ownership, dominion and sovereignty over land flowed by tidal waters, which extend to the mean high water mark, is vested in the State in trust for the people. The public's right to use the tidal lands and water encompasses navigation, fishing and recreational uses, including bathing, swimming and other shore activities. Borough of Neptune City v. Borough of Avon-by-the Sea, 61 N.J. 296, 309 (1972). In *Avon* we held that the public trust applied to the municipally-owned dry sand beach immediately landward of the high water mark. The major issue in this case is whether, ancillary to the public's right to enjoy the tidal lands, the public has a right to gain access through and to use the dry sand area not owned by a municipality but by a quasi-public body.

The Borough of Point Pleasant instituted this suit against the Borough of Bay Head and the Bay Head Improvement Association . . . , generally asserting that the defendants prevented Point Pleasant inhabitants from gaining access to the Atlantic Ocean and the beachfront in Bay Head. The proceeding was dismissed as to the Borough of Bay Head because it did not own or control the beach. Subsequently, Virginia Matthews, a resident of Point Pleasant who desired to swim and bathe at the Bay Head beach, joined as a party plaintiff, and Stanley Van Ness, as Public Advocate, joined as plaintiff-intervenor. When the Borough of Point Pleasant ceased pursuing the litigation, the Public Advocate became the primary moving party. . . .

The Borough of Bay Head . . . borders the Atlantic Ocean. Adjacent to it on the north is the Borough of Point Pleasant Beach, on the south the Borough of Mantoloking, and on the west Barnegat Bay. Bay Head consists of a fairly narrow strip of land, 6,667 feet long (about 1¼ miles). A beach runs along its entire length adjacent to the Atlantic Ocean. There are 76 separate parcels of land that border the beach. All except six are owned by private individuals. Title to those six is vested in the Association.

The Association was founded in 1910 and incorporated as a nonprofit corporation in 1932. Its certificate of incorporation states that its purposes are

> the improving and beautifying of the Borough of Bay Head, New Jersey, cleaning, policing and otherwise making attractive and safe the bathing beaches in said Borough, and the doing of any act which may be found necessary or desirable for the greater convenience, comfort and enjoyment of the residents.

Its constitution delineates the Association's object to promote the best interests of the Borough and "in so doing to own property, operate bathing beaches, hire life guards, beach cleaners and policemen. . . ."

Nine streets in the Borough, which are perpendicular to the beach, end at the dry sand. The Association owns the land commencing at the end of seven of these streets for the width of each street and extending through the upper dry sand to the mean high water line, the beginning of the wet sand area or foreshore. In addition, the Association owns the fee in six shore front properties, three of which are contiguous and have a frontage aggregating 310 feet. Many owners of beachfront property executed and delivered to the Association leases of the upper dry sand area. These leases are revocable by either party to the lease on thirty days' notice. Some owners have not executed such leases and have not permitted the Association to use their beaches. Some also have acquired riparian grants from the State extending approximately 1000 feet east of the high water line.

The Association controls and supervises its beach property between the third week in June and Labor Day. It engages about 40 employees who serve as lifeguards, beach police and beach cleaners. Lifeguards, stationed at five operating beaches, indicate by use of flags whether the ocean condition is dangerous (red), requires caution (yellow), or is satisfactory (green). In addition to observing and, if need be, assisting those in the water, when called upon lifeguards render first aid. Beach cleaners are engaged to rake and keep the beach clean of debris. Beach police are stationed at the entrances to the beaches where the public streets lead into the beach to ensure that only Association members or their guests enter. Some beach police patrol the beaches to enforce its membership rules.

Membership is generally limited to residents of Bay Head. Class A members are property owners. Class B are non-owners. Large families (six or more) pay $90 per year and small families pay $60 per year. Upon application residents are routinely accepted. Membership is evidenced by badges that signify permission to use the beaches. Members, which include local hotels, motels and inns, can also acquire badges for guests. The charge for each guest badge is $12. Members of the Bay Head Fire Company, Bay Head Borough employees, and teachers in the munici-pality's school system have been issued beach badges irrespective of residency.

Except for fishermen, who are permitted to walk though the upper dry sand area to the foreshore, only the membership may use the beach between 10:00 a.m. and 5:30 p.m. during the summer season. The public is permitted to use the Association's beach from 5:30 p.m. to 10:00 a.m. during the summer and, with no hourly restrictions, between Labor Day and mid-June.

No attempt has ever been made to stop anyone from occupying the terrain east of the high water mark. During certain parts of the day, when the tide is low, the foreshore could consist of about 50 feet of sand not being flowed by the water. The public could gain access to the foreshore by coming from the Borough of Point Pleasant Beach on the north or from the Borough of Mantoloking on the south.

Association membership totals between 4,800 to 5,000. The Associa-tion President testified during depositions that its restrictive policy, in existence since 1932, was due to limited parking facilities and to the overcrowding of the beaches. The Association's avowed purpose was to provide the beach for the residents of Bay Head.

There is also a public boardwalk, about one-third of a mile long, parallel to the ocean on the westerly side of the dry sand area. The boardwalk is owned and maintained by the municipality. . . .

In Borough of Neptune City v. Borough of Avon-by-the-Sea, 61 N.J. 296, 303 (1972), Justice Hall alluded to the ancient principle "that land covered by tidal waters belonged to the sovereign, but for the common use of all the people." The genesis of this principle is found in Roman jurisprudence, which held that "[b]y the law of nature" "the air, run-ning water, the sea, and consequently the shores of the sea," were "common to mankind." Justinian, *Institutes* 2.1.1 (T. Sandars trans. 1st Am. ed. 1876). No one was forbidden access to the sea, and everyone could use the seashore "to dry his nets there, and haul them from the sea. . . ." . . . The seashore was not private property, but "subject to the same law as the sea itself, and the sand or ground beneath it." . . . This underlying concept was applied in New Jersey in Arnold v. Mundy, 6 N.J.L. 1 (Sup. Ct. 1821).

The defendant in *Arnold* tested the plaintiff's claim of an exclusive right to harvest oysters by taking some oysters that the plaintiff had planted in beds in the Raritan River adjacent to his farm in Perth Am-boy. The oyster beds extended about 150 feet below the ordinary low water mark. The tide ebbed and flowed over it. The defendant's motion for a nonsuit was granted. The Supreme Court denied the plaintiff's subsequent motion to set aside the nonsuit.

Chief Justice Kirkpatrick, in an extensive opinion, referred to the grant by Charles II of the land comprising New Jersey with "all rivers, harbors, waters, fishings, etc., and of all other royalties, so far as the king had estate, right, title or interest therein" to the Duke of York. The duke had been delegated the same power as the king with respect to the land, and by virtue of the charter could divide and grant only those properties and interests that the king could. The Chief Justice's analysis then turned to the power of the English king. According to English law, public property consisted of two classes. Some was necessary for the state's use, and the remainder was common property available to all citizens. Chief Justice Kirkpatrick wrote that "[o]f this latter kind, according to the writers upon the law of nature and of nations, and upon the civil law, are the air, the running water, the sea, the fish and the wild beasts." . . . He argued that "though this title, strictly speaking, is in the sovereign, yet the use is common to all the people." . . . He pointed out the significant difference between public property necessary for the state and common property:

> The title of both these, for the greater order, and, perhaps, of necessity, is placed in the hands of the sovereign power, but it is placed there for different purposes. The citizen cannot enter upon the domain of the crown and apply it, or any part of it, to his immediate use. He cannot go into the king's forests and fall and carry away the trees, though it is the public property; it is placed in the hands of the king for a different purpose; it is the domain of the crown, a source of revenue; so neither can the king intrude upon the common property, thus understood, and appropriate it to himself, or to the fiscal purposes of the nation, the enjoyment of it is a natural right which cannot be infringed or taken away, unless by arbitrary power; and that, in theory at least, could not exist in a free government, such as England has always claimed to be.

The Chief Justice traced the use of common property by the kings and concluded that appropriation of common property by William the Conqueror and his successors was questionable and that the Magna Charta rectified the prior improper conduct by providing "that where the banks of rivers had first been defended in his time, (that is, when they had first been fenced in, and shut against the common use, in his time) they should be from thenceforth laid open." . . . A charter of Henry III confirmed this principle at least to the extent that only grants of common property made before the reign of Henry II were valid.

Chief Justice Kirkpatrick concluded that all navigable rivers in which the tide ebbs and flows and the coasts of the sea, including the water and land under the water, are "common to all the citizens, and that each [citizen] has a right to use them according to his necessities, subject only to the laws which regulate that use. . . ."

It has been said that "[h]ealth, recreation and sports are encompassed in and intimately related to the general welfare of a well-balanced state." Extension of the public trust doctrine to include bathing, swimming and other shore activities is consonant with and furthers the general welfare. The public's right to enjoy these privileges must be respected.

In order to exercise these rights guaranteed by the public trust doctrine, the public must have access to municipally-owned dry sand areas as well as the foreshore. The extension of the public trust doctrine to include municipally-owned dry sand areas was necessitated by our conclusion that enjoyment of rights in the foreshore is inseparable from use of dry sand beaches. . . .

In *Avon* . . . our finding of public rights in dry sand areas was specifically and appropriately limited to those beaches owned by a municipality. We now address the extent of the public's interest in privately-owned dry sand beaches. This interest may take one of two forms. . . .

Exercise of the public's right to swim and bathe below the mean high water mark may depend upon a right to pass across the upland beach. Without some means of access the public right to use the foreshore would be meaningless. To say that the public trust doctrine entitles the public to swim in the ocean and to use the foreshore in connection therewith without assuring the public of a feasible access route would seriously impinge on, if not effectively eliminate, the rights of the public trust doctrine. This does not mean the public has an unrestricted right to cross at will over any and all property bordering on the common property. The public interest is satisfied so long as there is reasonable access to the sea. . . . We see no reason why rights under the public trust doctrine to use of the upland dry sand area should be limited to municipally-owned property. It is true that the private owner's interest in the upland dry sand area is not identical to that of a municipality. Nonetheless, where use of dry sand is essential or reasonably necessary for enjoyment of the ocean, the doctrine warrants the public's use of the upland dry sand area subject to an accommodation of the interests of the owner.

We perceive no need to attempt to apply notions of prescription, dedication, or custom as an alternative to application of the public trust doctrine. Archaic judicial responses are not an answer to a modern social problem. Rather, we perceive the public trust doctrine not to be "fixed or static," but one to "be molded and extended to meet changing conditions and needs of the public it was created to benefit." . . .

Precisely what privately-owned upland sand area will be available and required to satisfy the public's rights under the public trust doctrine will depend on the circumstances. Location of the dry sand area in relation to the foreshore, extent and availability of publicly-owned upland sand area, nature and extent of the public demand, and usage of the upland sand land by the owner are all factors to be weighed and considered in fixing the contours of the usage of the upper sand.

Today, recognizing the increasing demand for our State's beaches and the dynamic nature of the public trust doctrine, we find that the public must be given both access to and use of privately-owned dry sand areas as reasonably necessary. While the public's rights in private beaches are not co-extensive with the rights enjoyed in municipal beaches, private landowners may not in all instances prevent the public from exercising its rights under the public trust doctrine. The public must be afforded reasonable access to the foreshore as well as a suitable area for recreation on the dry sand. . . .

By limiting membership only to residents and foreclosing the public, the [Bay Head] Association is acting in conflict with the public good and contrary to the strong public policy "in favor of encouraging and expanding public access to and use of shoreline areas." Indeed, the Association is frustrating the public's right under the public trust doctrine. It should not be permitted to do so.

Accordingly, membership in the Association must be open to the public at large. . . . However, the Association shall also make available a reasonable quantity of daily as well as seasonal badges to the nonresident public. Its decision with respect to the number of daily and seasonal badges to be afforded to nonresidents should take into account all relevant matters, such as the public demand and the number of bathers and swimmers that may be safely and reasonably accommodated on the Association's property, whether owned or leased. The Association may continue to charge reasonable fees to cover its costs of lifeguards, beach cleaners, patrols, equipment, insurance, and administrative expenses. The fees fixed may not discriminate in any respect between residents and nonresidents. The Association may continue to enforce its regulations regarding cleanliness, safety, and other reasonable measures concerning the public use of the beach. In this connection, it would be entirely appropriate, in the formulation and adoption of such reasonable regulations concerning the public's use of the beaches, to encourage the participation and cooperation of all private beachfront property owners, regardless of their membership in or affiliation with the Association.

F. HIRSCH, SOCIAL LIMITS TO GROWTH 2-7, 10, 19-29 (1976): The structural characteristic in question is that as the level of average consumption rises, an increasing portion of consumption takes on a social as well as an individual aspect. That is to say, the satisfaction that individuals derive from goods and services depends in increasing measure not only on their own consumption but on consumption by others as well. . . .

So long as material privation is widespread, conquest of material scarcity is the dominant concern. As demands for purely private goods are increasingly satisfied, demands for goods and facilities with a public (social) character become increasingly active. These public demands make themselves felt through individual demands on the political system or through the market mechanism in the same way as do the demands for purely private goods. Individuals acquire both sets of goods without distinction, except where public goods are provided by public or collective action; even there, individuals may seek to increase their own share by private purchases. . . .

The compelling attraction of economic growth in its institutionalized modern form has been as a superior substitute for redistribution. Whereas the masses today could never get close to what the well-to-do have today, even by expropriating all of it, they can, in the conventional view, get most if not all the way there with patience in a not too distant tomorrow, through the magic of compound growth. [O]nce this growth brings mass consumption to the point where it causes problems of congestion in the widest sense — bluntly, where consumption or jobholding by others tends to crowd you out — then the key to personal welfare is again the ability to stay ahead of the crowd. . . .

[A]ddition to the material goods that can be expanded for all will, in itself, increase the scramble for those goods and facilities that cannot be so expanded. Taking part in the scramble is fully rational for any individual in his own actions, since in these actions he never confronts the distinction between what is available as a result of getting ahead of others and what is available from a general advance shared by all. . . .

Certain goods and facilities from which individuals derive satisfaction are subject to absolute limitations in supply, deriving from one of a number of sources. The first though not the most significant such source of scarcity is physical availability. . . .

Thus the frustration in affluence results from its very success in satisfying previously dominant material needs. This frustration is usually thought of as essentially a psychological phenomenon, a matter of our subjective internal assessment. What we previously had to struggle for now comes easily, so we appreciate it less.

A second classification of consumer scarcity is social: consumer demand is concentrated on particular goods and facilities that are limited in absolute supply not by physical but by social factors, including the satisfaction engendered by scarcity as such. Such social limits exist in the sense that an increase in physical availability of these goods or facilities, either in absolute terms or in relation to dimensions such as population or physical space, changes their characteristics in such a way that a given amount of use yields less satisfaction. This is equivalent to a limitation on absolute supply of a product or facility of given "quality," and it is in this sense that it is regarded here as a social limitation.

I. Physical scarcity (natural landscape; Old Masters)

II. Social scarcity

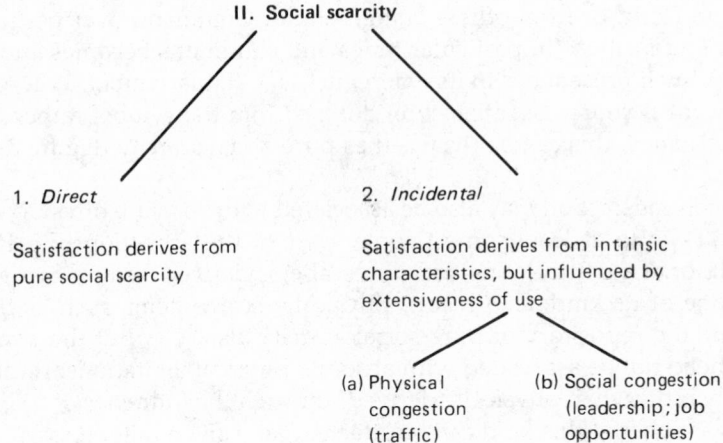

1. *Direct*

Satisfaction derives from
pure social scarcity

2. *Incidental*

Satisfaction derives from intrinsic
characteristics, but influenced by
extensiveness of use

(a) Physical
congestion
(traffic)

(b) Social congestion
(leadership; job
opportunities)

III. Allocation processes

Excess demand contained by:

A. *Auction*

B. *Crowding*

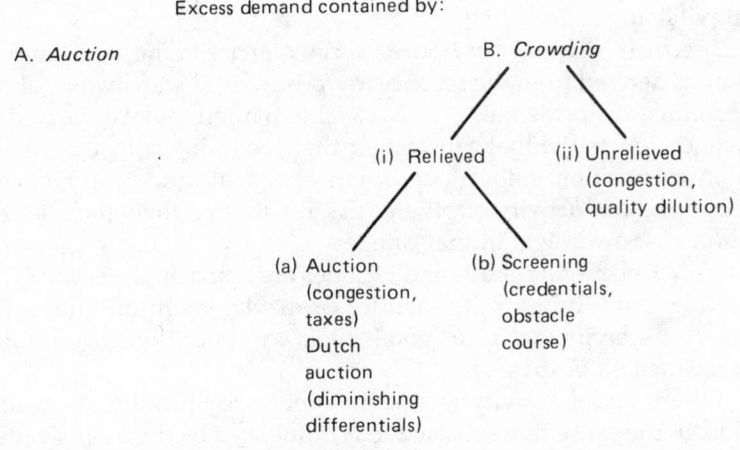

(i) Relieved

(ii) Unrelieved
(congestion,
quality dilution)

(a) Auction
(congestion,
taxes)
Dutch
auction
(diminishing
differentials)

(b) Screening
(credentials,
obstacle
course)

FIGURE 3-2
A categorization of consumption scarcity

This social limitation may be derived, most directly and most familiarly, from psychological motives of various kinds, notably envy, emulation, or pride. Satisfaction is derived from relative position alone, of being in front, or from others being behind. Command over particular goods and facilities in particular times and conditions becomes an indicator of such precedence in its emergence as a status symbol. Where the sole or main source of satisfaction derives from the symbol rather than the substance, this can be regarded as pure social scarcity [Figure 3-2, II (1)].

Such satisfaction may also be associated with absolute physical scarcities. Thus to at least some people, part of the attraction of a Rembrandt, or of a particular natural landscape, is derived from its being the only one of its kind; as a result, physically scarce items such as these become the repository of pure social scarcity also. . . . But the scarcity itself need not be associated with absolute physical limitations. It can be socially rather than physically derived, through the influence of fashion. Thus, a cachet of this kind can be attached, at a given time, to particular antiques which cannot be replicated, but derive their scarcity *value* only from the (changeable) fashion that designates them as a sought after emblem. . . . Scarcity is, so to say, deliberately created and in a sense manipulated.

These are examples of "pure" social scarcity in the sense that satisfaction is derived from the scarcity itself. But social scarcity may also be a by-product, or incidental. . . . A social limitation may be derived from influences on individual satisfaction that are independent of the satisfaction or position enjoyed by others and that are yet influenced by consumption or activity of others. Essentially the phenomenon of congestion or crowding is in that category. . . .

. . . All economic goods and facilities are scarce in the sense of being attainable only through the sacrifice or displacement of other satisfactions. It is scarcity that gives goods their economic dimension. More of this means less of that.

Where social scarcity is not pure but a by-product of positional goods, in the sense that satisfaction is influenced by the extensiveness of use by others, the resultant congestion or crowding reduces the "quality" as perceived by the consumers. This process of crowding can then have a number of different results. It may induce a deliberate attempt to preserve the initial quality by restrictions of various kinds to access to the goods or activity. . . .

Crowding may be avoided in a second and quite different way in cases where the scarce facility is itself of fixed quality for some reason. . . . There is, in principle, no reason why these scarcities too should not be allocated by auction.

4 ◆ PROPERTY IN WATER

Contemporary property issues often concern claims to intangible, even evanescent, resources in contexts making shared possession or use inevitable. Think of rights to ideas, to computer programs, to genetic codes, to light and air, and to permission to build 500 feet above the ground. In contrast, we sometimes think that "old" property involved unique and tangible "things" that could be adapted in individual needs. But English and American law has many centuries of experience allocating claims to the water in flowing rivers. The history of water law shows society struggling to adapt doctrines to circumstances and to mediate among conflicting values and goals. It therefore provides important analogies for contemporary choices.

A. ENGLISH UNDERGROUND WATER

◆ Acton v. Blundell
  12 Mees. and W. 324, 152 Eng. Rep. 1223 (Exch. 1843)

TINDAL, C.J. The question raised before us on this bill of exceptions is one of equal novelty and importance. The plaintiff below, who is also the plaintiff in error, in his action on the case, declared in the first count for the disturbance of his right to the water of certain underground springs, streams, and watercourses, which, as he alleged, ought of right to run, flow, and percolate into the closes of the plaintiff, for supplying certain mills with water; and in the second count for draining off the water of a certain spring or well of water in a certain close of the plaintiff, by reason of the possession of which close, as he alleged, he ought of right to have the use, benefit, and enjoyment of the water of the said spring or well for the convenient use of his close. The defendants by their pleas traversed the rights in the manner alleged in those counts respectively. At the trial the plaintiff proved, that, within twenty years before the commencement of the suit, viz. in the latter end of 1821, a former owner and occupier of certain land and a cotton-mill, now belonging to the plaintiff, had sunk and made in such land a well for raising water for the working of the mill; and that the defendants, in the year 1837, had sunk a coal-pit in the land of one of the defendants at about three-quarters of a mile from the plaintiff's well, and about three years after sunk a second at a somewhat less distance; the consequence of which sinkings was, that, by the first, the supply of water was considerably diminished, and by the second was rendered altogether insufficient for the purposes of the mill. The learned Judge before whom the cause was tried directed the jury, that, if the defendants had proceeded and acted in the usual and proper manner on the land, for the purpose of working and winning a coal-mine therein, they might lawfully do so, and that the plaintiff's evidence was not sufficient to support the allegations in his declaration as traversed by the second and third pleas. Against this direction of the Judge the counsel for the plaintiff tendered the bill of exceptions which has been argued before us. And after hearing such argument and consideration of the case, we are of opinion that the direction of the learned Judge was correct in point of law.

The question argued before us has been in substance this: whether the right to the enjoyment of an underground spring, or of a well supplied by such underground spring, is governed by the same rule of law as that which applies to, and regulates, a water-course flowing on the surface.

The rule of law which governs the enjoyment of a stream flowing in its natural course over the surface of land belonging to different proprietors is well established; each proprietor of the land has a right to the advantage of the stream flowing in its natural course over his land, to use the same as he pleases, for any purposes of his own not inconsistent with a similar right in the proprietors of the land above or below; so that, neither can any proprietor above diminish the quantity or injure the quality of the water which would otherwise naturally descend, nor can any proprietor below throw back the water without the license or the grant of the proprietor above. . . . And if the right to the enjoyment of underground springs, or to a well supplied thereby, is to be governed by the same law, then undoubtedly the defendants could not justify the sinking of the coal-pits, and the direction given by the learned Judge would be wrong.

But we think, on considering the grounds and origin of the law which is held to govern running streams, the consequences which would result if the same law is made applicable to springs beneath the surface, and, lastly, the authorities to be found in the books, so far as any inference can be drawn from them bearing on the point now under discussion, that there is a marked and substantial difference between the two cases, and that they are not to be governed by the same rule of law.

The ground and origin of the law which governs streams running in their natural course would seem to be this, that the right enjoyed by the several proprietors of the lands over which they flow is, and always has been, public and notorious: that the enjoyment has been long continued — in ordinary cases, indeed, time out of mind — and uninterrupted; each man knowing what he receives and what has always been received from the higher lands, and what he transmits and what has always been transmitted to the lower. The rule, therefore, either assumes for its foundation the implied assent and agreement of the proprietors of the different lands from all ages, or perhaps it may be considered as a rule of positive law, (which would seem to be the opinion of Fleta and of Blackstone), the origin of which is lost by the progress of time; or it may not be unfitly treated, as laid down by Mr. Justice Story, in his judgment in the case of Tyler v. Wilkinson, in the courts of the United States (4 Mason's (American) Reports, 401), as "an incident to the land; and that whoever seeks to found an exclusive use must establish a rightful appropriation in some manner known and admitted by the law." But in the case of a well sunk by a proprietor in his own land, the water which feeds it from a neighbouring soil does not flow openly in the sight of the neighbouring proprietor, but through the hidden veins of the earth beneath its surface; no man can tell what changes these underground sources have undergone in the progress of time; it may well be, that it is only yesterday's date, that they first took the course and direction which enabled them to supply the well: again, no proprietor knows what portion of water is taken beneath his own soil: how much he gives originally, or how much he transmits only, or how much he receives: on the contrary, until the well is sunk, and the water collected by draining into it, there cannot properly be said, with reference to the well, to be any flow of water at all. In the case, therefore, of the well, there can be no ground for implying any mutual consent or agreement, for ages past, between the owners of the several lands beneath which the underground springs may exist, which is one of the foundations on which the law as to running streams is supposed to be built; nor, for the same reason, can any trace of a positive law be inferred from long-continued acquiescence and submission, whilst the very existence of the underground springs or of the well may be unknown to the proprietors of the soil.

But the difference between the two cases with respect to the consequences, if the same law is to be applied to both, is still more apparent. In the case of the running stream, the owner of the soil merely transmits the water over its surface: he receives as much from his higher neighbour as he sends down to his neighbour below: he is neither better nor worse: the level of the water remains the same. But if the man who sinks the well in his own land can acquire by that act an absolute and indefeasible right to the water that collects in it, he has the power of preventing his neighbour from making any use of the spring in his own soil which shall interfere with the enjoyment of the well. He has the power, still further, of debarring the owner of the land in which the spring is first found, or through which it is transmitted, from draining his land for the proper cultivation of the soil: and thus by an act which is voluntary on his part, and which may be entirely unsuspected by his neighbour, he may impose on such neighbour the necessity of bearing a heavy expense, if the latter has erected machinery for the purposes of mining, and discovers, when too late, that the appropriation of the water has already been made. Further, the advantage on one side, and the detriment to the other, may bear no proportion. The well may be sunk to supply a cottage, or a drinking-place for cattle; whilst the owner of the adjoining land may be prevented from winning metals and minerals of inestimable value. And, lastly, there is no limit of space within which the claim of right to an underground spring can be confined: in the present case, the nearest coal-pit is at the distance of half a mile from the well: it is obvious the law must equally apply if there is an interval of many miles.

Considering, therefore, the state of circumstances upon which the law is grounded in the one case to be entirely dissimilar from those which exist in the other; and that the application of the same rule to both would lead, in many cases, to consequences at once unreasonable and unjust; we feel ourselves warranted in holding, upon principle, that the case now under discussion does not fall within the rule which obtains as to surface streams nor is it to be governed by analogy therewith. . . .

No case has been cited on either side bearing directly on the subject in dispute. . . .

The Roman law forms no rule, binding in itself, upon the subjects of these realms; but, in deciding a case upon principle, where no direct authority can be cited from our books, it affords no small evidence of the soundness of the conclusion at which we have arrived, if it proves to be supported by that law, the fruit of the researches of the most learned men, the collective wisdom of ages and the groundwork of the municipal law of most of the countries in Europe.

The authority of one at least of the learned Roman lawyers appears decisive upon the point in favour of the defendants; of some others the opinion is expressed with more obscurity. In the Digest, lib. 39, tit. 3, *De aequa et aquae pluviae arcandae*, s.12, "*Denique Marcellus scribit, Cum eo, qui in suo fodiens, vicini fontem avertit, nihil posse agi: nec de dolo actionem, et sane non debet habere; si non animo vicini nocendi, sed suum agrum meliorem faciendi, id fecit."* . . .

It is scarcely necessary to say, that we intimate no opinion whatever as to what might be the rule of law, if there had been an uninterrupted user of the right for more than the last twenty years; but, confining ourselves strictly to the facts stated in the bill of exceptions, we think the present case, for the reasons above given, is not to be governed by the law which applies to rivers and flowing streams, but that it rather falls within that principle, which gives to the owner of the soil all that lies beneath his surface; that the land immediately below is his property, whether it is solid rock, or porous ground, or venous earth, or part soil, part water; that the person who owns the surface may dig therein, and apply all that is there found to his own purposes at his free will and pleasure; and that if, in the exercise of such right, he intercepts or drains off the water collected from underground springs in his neighbour's well, this inconvenience to his neighbour falls within the description of *damnum absque injuria*, which cannot become the ground of an action.

We think, therefore, the direction given by the learned judge at the trial was correct, and that the judgment already given for the defendants in the Court below must be affirmed.

Notes

1. In Dickinson v. Grand Junction Canal Co., 7 Exch. 282, 155 Eng. Rep. 953 (1852), the defendant company had dug a large well on its own property, to increase the water level of a canal running between the Gade and Bulbourne rivers. With the aid of pumps and a steam engine, the company had then diverted into the canal the groundwaters that otherwise would have flowed into the Bulbourne River. Plaintiff mill owners, downstream of this diversion, were thus deprived of the quantity of water that ordinarily powered their mills. Because the groundwaters were known to form part of the river, the court characterized the well as a diversion and recognized a cause of action against the canal company. Whether the water had been prevented from joining the river or had already formed a part of it, "[t]he mill-owners were entitled to the benefit of the stream in its natural course; and they are deprived of part

*The quotation from the Digest appearing here is translated (rather freely) in 9 Scott, The Civil Law (1932) as follows:

> In conclusion, Marcellus says that when anyone, while excavating upon his own land, diverts a vein of water belonging to his neighbour, no action can be brought against him, not even one on the ground of malice. And it is evident that he should not have such a right of action, where his neighbour did not intend to injure him, but did the work for the purpose of improving his own property.

of that benefit if the natural supply of the stream is taken away." Attempting to distinguish Acton v. Blundell, Chief Baron Pollock said that in the instant case the water was taken "after it formed part of the stream"; also, "if, indeed, it had appeared that the Company was ignorant, and could not by a degree of care have ascertained" the effect of its well, *Dickinson* might have come out differently.

2. In Chasemore v. Richards, 7 H.L.C. 349, 11 Eng. Rep. 140 (1859), the town of Croyden had dug a well upstream from Chasemore's mill. The town's use of the groundwater for fresh water supplies depleted the Wandle River, injuring the plaintiff's mill operations. The court found that the plaintiff had no rights against the town of Croyden, distinguishing groundwater, which does not flow in definite channels, from surface water. Owners may freely use groundwater under their property. Acton v. Blundell was relied upon, and *Dickinson* was mentioned but not effectively distinguished. Lord Wensleydale emphasized that "as the great interests in society require that the cultivation of every man's land should be encouraged, . . . the owner must be permitted to dig in his own soil."

B. UNITED STATES SURFACE WATER

◆ EVANS v. MERRIWEATHER
4 Ill. 492 (1842)

Lockwood, Justice, delivered the opinion of the Court: This was an action on the *case*, brought in the Greene Circuit Court, by Merriweather against Evans, for obstructing and diverting a water course. The plaintiff obtained a verdict, and judgment was rendered thereon. On the trial the defendant excepted to the instructions asked for and given, at the instance of the plaintiff. The defendant also excepted, because instructions, that were asked by him, were refused. After the cause was brought into this Court, the parties agreed upon the following statement of facts, as having been proved on the trial, to wit:

> It is agreed between the parties to this suit, that the following is the statement of facts proved at the trial in this case, and that the same shall be considered as part of the record by the Court, in the adjudication of this cause. . . . Smith & Baker, in 1834, bought of T. Carlin six acres of land, through which a branch ran, and erected a stream mill thereon. They depended upon a well and the branch for water in running their engine. . . . About one or two years afterwards, John Evans bought of T. Carlin six acres of land, on the same branch, above and immediately adjoining the lot owned by Smith & Baker, and erected thereon a steam mill, depending upon a well and the branch for water in running his engine.

Smith & Baker, after the erection of Evans' mill, in 1836 or 1837, sold the mill and appurtenances to Merriweather, for about $8,000. Evans' mill was supposed to be worth $12,000. Ordinarily there was an abundance of water for both mills; but in the fall of 1837, there being a drought, the branch failed, so far that it did not afford water sufficient to run the upper mill continually. Evans directed his hands not to stop, or divert the water, in the branch; but one of them employed about the mill did make a dam across the branch, just below Evans' mill, and thereby diverted all the water in the branch into Evans' well. Evans was at home, half a mile from the mill, and was frequently about his mill, and evidence was introduced conducing to prove that he might have known that the water of the branch was diverted into his well. After the diversion of the water into Evans' well, as aforesaid, the branch went dry below, and Merriweather's mill could not and did not run, in consequence of it, more than one day in a week, and was then supplied with water from his well. Merriweather then brought this suit, in three or four weeks after the putting of the dam across the branch for the diversion of the water, and obtained a verdict for $150. This suit, it is admitted, is the first between the parties litigating the right as to the use of the water. It is further agreed, that the branch afforded usually sufficient water for the supply of both mills, without materially affecting the size of the current, though the branch was not depended upon exclusively for that purpose. Furthermore, that at the time of the grievances complained of by the plaintiff below, the defendant had water hauled in part for the supply of his boilers. That the dam was made below the defendant's well, across the branch, which diverted as well the water hauled and poured out into the branch above the well, as the water of the branch, into the defendant's well.

Upon this state of facts, the question is presented, as to what extent riparian proprietors, upon a stream not navigable, can use the water of such stream? The branch mentioned in the agreed statement of facts, is a small natural stream of water, not furnishing, at all seasons of the year, a supply of water sufficient for both mills. There are no facts in the case showing that the water is wanted for any other than milling purposes, and for those purposes to be converted into steam, and thus entirely consumed. In an early case decided in England, it is laid down that "A water course begins 'ex jure naturae,' and having taken a certain course naturally, cannot be diverted." The language of all the authorities is, that water flows in its natural course, and should be permitted thus to flow, so that all through whose land it naturally flows, may enjoy the privilege of using it. The property in the water, therefore, by virtue of the riparian ownership, is in its nature usufructuary, and consists, in general, not so much of the fluid itself, as of the advantage of its impetus. A riparian proprietor, therefore, though he has an undoubted right to use the water for hydraulic or manufacturing purposes, must so use it as to do no injury to any other riparian proprietor. Some decisions, in laying down the rights of riparian proprietors of water courses, have gone so far as to restrict their right in the use of water flowing over their land, so that there shall be no diminution in the quantity of the water, and no obstruction to its course. The decisions last referred to cannot, however, be considered as furnishing the true doctrine on this subject. Mr. Justice Story, in delivering the opinion of the Court, in the case of Tyler v. Wilkinson, says,

I do not mean to be understood as holding the doctrine that there can be no diminution whatever, and no obstruction of impediment whatever, by a riparian proprietor in the use of water as it flows; for that would be to deny any valuable use of it. There may be, and there must be, of that which is common to all, a reasonable use. The true test of the principle and extent of the use is, whether it is to the injury of the other proprietors or not. There may be diminution in quantity, or a retardation or acceleration of the natural current, indispensable for the general and valuable use of the water, perfectly consistent with the use of the common right. The diminution, retardation, or acceleration, not positively and sensibly injurious, by diminishing the value of the common right, is an implied element in the right of using the stream at all. The law here, as in many other cases, acts with a reasonable reference to public convenience and general good, and is not betrayed into a narrow strictness, subversive of common use, nor into an extravagant looseness, which would destroy private rights.

The same learned judge further says, "That of a thing common by nature, there may be an appropriation by general consent or grant. Mere priority of appropriation of running water, without such consent or grant, confers no exclusive right" . . .

Each riparian proprietor is bound to make such a use of running water, as to do as little injury to those below him, as is consistent with a valuable benefit to himself. The use must be a reasonable one. Now the question fairly arises, is that a reasonable use of running water by the upper proprietor, by which the fluid itself is entirely consumed? To answer this question satisfactorily, it is proper to consider the wants of man in regard to the element of water. These wants are either natural or artificial. Natural are such as are absolutely necessary . . . to his existence. Artificial, such only, as by supplying them, his comfort and prosperity are increased. To quench thirst, and for household purposes, water is absolutely indispensable. In civilized life, water for cattle is also necessary. These wants must be supplied, or both man and beast will perish.

The supply of man's artificial wants is not essential to his existence; it is not indispensable; he could live if water was not employed in irrigating lands, or in propelling his machinery. In countries differently situated from ours, with a hot and arid climate, water doubtless is absolutely indispensable to the cultivation of the soil, and in them, water for irrigation would be a natural want. Here it might increase the products of the soil, but it is by no means essential, and cannot therefore be considered a natural want of man. So of manufactures, they promote the prosperity and comfort of mankind, but cannot be considered absolutely necessary to his existence; nor need the machinery which he employs be set in motion by steam.

From these premises would result this conclusion; that an individual owning a spring on his land, from which water flows in a current through his neighbor's land, would have the right to use the whole of it, if necessary to satisfy his natural wants. He may consume all the water for his domestic purposes, including water for his stock. If he desires to use it for irrigation or manufactures, and there be a lower proprietor to whom its use is essential to supply his natural wants, or for his stock, he must use the water so as to leave enough for such lower proprietor. Where the stream is small, and does not supply water more than sufficient to answer the natural wants of the different proprietors living on it, none of the proprietors can use the water for either irrigation or manufactures. So far then as natural wants are concerned, there is no difficulty in furnishing a rule by which riparian proprietors may use flowing water to supply such natural wants. Each proprietor in his turn may, if necessary, consume all the water for these purposes. But where the water is not wanted to supply natural wants, and there is not sufficient for each proprietor living on the stream, to carry on his manufacturing purposes, how shall the water be divided? We have seen that without a contract or grant, neither has a right to use all the water; all have a right to participate in its benefits. Where all have a right to participate in a common benefit, and none can have an exclusive enjoyment, no rule, from the very nature of the case, can be laid down, as to how much each may use without infringing upon the rights of others. In such cases, the question must be left to the judgment of the jury, whether the party complained of has used, under all the circumstances, more than his just proportion.

It appears from the facts agreed on, that Evans obstructed the water by a dam, and diverted the whole into his well. This diversion, according to all the cases, both English and American, was clearly illegal. For this diversion, an action will lie. It, however, was contended that Evans forbid the construction of the dam, by which the water was diverted into his well. If a servant do an act against the consent of the master, the latter is not liable. In this case, however, a jury might fairly infer from the fact, that as Evans lived near the mill, and was frequently at it, he must have been conversant of the manner in which his mill was supplied with water, and that he either countermanded the instructions, or acquiesced in the construction of the dam, after it was erected. Having availed himself of the illegal act of his servant, the law presumes he authorized it. Having arrived at the conclusion that an action will lie in behalf of Merriweather against Evans, for obstructing and diverting the water course mentioned in the plaintiff's declaration, I have not deemed it necessary to examine the instructions given by the Court, to see if they accord with the principles above laid down. Having decided that the plaintiff below has a right to recover on the facts, whether the instructions were right or wrong, would not vary that result. It is possible that if the true principles which govern this action had been correctly given to the jury, the damages might have been either less or more than the jury have given; but in this case, as the damages are small, the Court ought not, where justice has upon the whole been done, to send the case back, to see if a jury, upon another trial, would not give less.

For these reasons, I am of opinion that the judgment ought to be affirmed with costs.

The eastern half of the United States adopted from England the system of property rights in flowing water known as "riparianism." Rights to use flowing water arise from ownership of adjoining (that is, "riparian") land. The system has been subjected to numerous modifications and alterations, especially in response to particular locally felt needs and practices. But a hornbook summary of riparianism would divide the doctrine into two standard subsystems, "natural flow" and "reasonable use." According to the natural flow rule (said to be the English rule, but by no means uniformly enforced there), each riparian owner has a right to have the stream flow past his land in the same quantity and quality that it flowed without human alteration. Thus no owner can use the water in a way that interferes with the natural flow to the detriment of another owner. Because "natural flow" appeared to restrict economically valuable uses, American courts enunciated the doctrine of "reasonable use," which asserted that each owner could use the water in a manner that was reasonable, considering the needs and uses of other owners. "Reasonable use" requires that courts — as in Evans v. Merriweather — announce that certain uses are socially more valuable than others. In both kinds of riparian schemes, earlier users have no preference over later ones, and nonuse forfeits no rights.

The riparian system was rejected in the dry western states, where the profound need to transport water for mining and irrigation barred a system that saved all the water for land bordering streams, and where the general scarcity of water seemed to require assuring a secure supply to anyone contemplating investment. Thus, the western states developed a system of water rights called "appropriation," under which rights are created by taking water for any beneficial use, and are lost by ceasing use. Water can be transported. And as among competing users, priority in time is determinative. When the water supply is reduced, and there is only enough for the user who began exploitation first, all users who began later must cease their use.

Consider the relative merits of the reasonable use and prior appropriation doctrines. Which is more likely to lead to certainty in property rights? Which will produce more litigation? Achieve economic efficiency? Be more responsive to the needs of the general public? Preserve the environment?

Another doctrine emerged in the western United States: "correlative rights." In a correlative rights jurisdiction all surface owners over a common underground water basin have rights to the underground water; the amount that a single owner may use depends on the proportion of the basin's surface area that his land surface covers.

Under what circumstances will a correlative rights doctrine yield different results from a reasonable use doctrine?

B. CARDOZO, THE GROWTH OF THE LAW 117-120 (1924): Sooner or later, if the demands of social utility are sufficiently urgent, if the operation of an existing rule is sufficiently productive of hardship or inconvenience, utility will tend to triumph. . . . We have a conspicuous illustration in the law of waters in our western states. "Two systems of water law are in force within the United States — the riparian and the appropriation systems." The system first named prevails in thirty-one of the forty-eight states. Its fundamental principal is "that each riparian proprietor has an equal right to make a reasonable use of the waters of the stream, subject to the equal right of the other riparian proprietors likewise to make a reasonable use." Some of the arid states of the west found this system unsuited to their needs. Division of the water "into small quantities among the various water users and on the general principle of equality of right" would be a division "so minute as not to be of advantage to anybody." "It is better in such a region that some have enough and others go without, than that the division should be so minute as to be of no real economic value." The appropriation system is built upon the recognition of this truth. Its fundamental principle is "that the water user who first puts to beneficial use — irrigation, mining, manufacturing, power, household, or other economic use — the water of a stream, acquires thereby the first right to the water, to the extent reasonably necessary to his use, and that he who is the second to put the water of the stream to beneficial use, acquires the second right, a right similar to the first right, but subordinate thereto, and he who is the third to put it to use acquires the third right, a right subordinate to the other two, and so on throughout the entire series of uses." Here we have the conscious departure from a known rule, and the deliberate adoption of a new one, in obedience to the promptings of a social need so obvious and so insistent as to overrun the ancient channel and cut a new one for itself. [Quoting from various treatises and cases.]

Notes

1. Plaintiff, owner of a mill on a small stream, sued defendant, an upper riparian proprietor on the same stream, for wrongful diversion of water therefrom. Defendant diverted 60,000 gallons of water daily by pumping it from a spring confluent to the stream. The water was pumped to land owned by defendant one mile away, for domestic uses of a boys' school. Diminution or change in the natural flow by an upstream owner "cannot exceed that which arises from reasonable conduct in the light of all circumstances." Therefore, exceptions were overruled to a trial court instruction that "the defendant's right was confined to a reasonable use of the water for the benefit of its land adjoining the water course . . . and did not extend to taking it for use upon other premises." Stratton v. Mt. Hermon Boys' School, 216 Mass. 83, 103 N.E. 87 (1913).

2. Defendants manufactured cardboard, discharging their waste into the Raisin River. Plaintiff operated a pond near the river below defendants' mills for the storage and feeding of carp. Many of plaintiff's fish were killed by the wastes. "[T]he use made of the stream by the defendants as above stated is not a reasonable one, when complained of by a lower proprietor having riparian rights thereto." But:

Monroe is a city of about 13,000 population. Its principal industries are the mills of the defendants. There are eight of these, in which about 3,000 persons are employed. Defendants' investment in these plants is about $15,000,000. The proof satisfies us that there is no way in which their waste can be treated and purified on their own premises so as to permit the plants to be operated with reasonable profit. Seven of defendants' mills were erected before plaintiff established its carp pond in 1916. The eighth was built in 1918.

The plaintiff company has a capital stock of $10,000. It employs from one to five men. While the record does not contain a list of its stockbrokers, it appears that Mr. Sterling has had control of it. He had long been a resident of Monroe, and had full knowledge of defendants' industries and the extent to which the city was dependent upon them for its prosperity.

While plaintiff's business, if operated without the loss incident to the pollution of the stream by the defendants and the city, would doubtless prove a profitable one, we cannot but agree with the trial court "that the equities in this case would be against granting a permanent injunction." It is apparent that the plaintiff may be recompensed for such loss as it will sustain by a denial of such relief. It is also apparent that the granting of it will work a great injury, entirely disproportionate to that sustained by plaintiff, upon the defendants, and that it will also seriously affect the prosperity of the city. [Monroe Carp Pond Co. v. River Raisin Paper Co., 240 Mich. 279, 215 N.W. 325, (1927).]

3. A subsidiary of American Metal Climax owned the surface estate of a piece of property known as Peabody 43. From 1943 to 1957, Peabody 43 had been used to obtain access to #5 Coal Seam. During that period, refuse material was hand picked from the raw coal and spread over an 18-acre area, from 1 to 8 feet thick. The refuse material absorbed rainfall and gradually released water as seepage, along with a mineral commonly known as pyrite. The seepage entered Brushy Creek, where, because of the pyrite, it killed fish.

The 1970 Illinois Constitution grants every person an inherent right to a clean and healthful environment. By statute, the legislature stated its purpose to purify, cleanse, and enhance the waters of Illinois, and granted the Pollution Control Board the power to make and enforce rules. The agency found the company guilty of violating the act and ordered it to cease and desist, to pay a penalty of $141.66, and to submit an abatement plan. The appellate court affirmed. Meadowlark Farms, Inc. v. Illinois Pollution Control Board, 17 Ill. App. 3d 851, 308 N.E.2d 829 (1974).

4. If a downstream landowner has a right to the natural flow of water, can a landowner rely on the weather that nature will send, and can that owner win a lawsuit against efforts at "weather modification"? In Slutsky v. City of New York, 197 Misc. 730, 97 N.Y.S.2d 238 (Sup. Ct. 1950), a mountain resort owner sought to stop the city from seeding near his resort in its effort to collect more rainfall in its water supply catchment. The judge said Slutsky had no right to "his" clouds, and that he had not proven harm. But see Southwest Weather Research, Inc. v. Duncan, 319 S.W.2d 940 (Tex. Civ. App. 1958), aff'd sub nom. Southwest Weather Research, Inc. v. Jones, 160 Tex. 104, 327 S.W.2d 417 (1959), finding that the landowner did have rights to nature's rainfall likely to be infringed by defendant's hail-suppression seeding. On the potential for interstate legal disputes growing out of weather modification projects see Davis, Weather Modification: Interstate Legal Issues, 15 Idaho L. Rev. 419 (1979).

C. ARIZONA UNDERGROUND WATER

Few people initially expected groundwater to play an important role in the Arizona economy; the territorial constitution of 1864 makes no reference to it in enumerating the waters that were public property and subject to prior appropriation. In 1919, the legislature formulated a distinction between definite underground channels and percolating water; the former were public, and subject to prior appropriation; the latter came with land ownership, and were owned absolutely. Later court cases attempted to sharpen the distinction, but the resulting system was inherently unpredictable and economically irrational.

As the importance of ground water became clearer, various groups began calling for a legislative ground water code that would prevent speculative overdevelopment. Those who opposed codes were generally the more recent developers of land, who would have had inferior rights under any scheme based on the doctrine of prior appropriation. Many were seeking short-term profits, with knowledge that the resources eventually would be exhausted.

The Ground Water Code of 1948 was recognized as a stopgap measure. It allowed designation of crucial ground water areas (which would not have a reasonably safe supply at the present rate of withdrawal) where development of new wells would be limited, but did not restrict the quantity that could be pumped from existing wells. Many lawyers doubted the constitutionality of the code.

This was the context for the Bristor v. Cheatham litigation. Bristor was the earlier domestic user; Cheatham was pumping water from his land to other areas. Bristor's well went dry. Cheatham relied on Acton v. Blundell. Bristor urged the concept of correlative rights, and a rule that Cheatham could only use underground water on his own land, and not so as to injure Bristor. A number of *amici curiae* claimed that the time was right for the court to declare public ownership of ground water and hold that rights to use it could be obtained by prior appropriation. Two years after the case was brought, the supreme court agreed with the *amici curiae* by a 3-2 vote.

Reaction was immediate, particularly from business interests facing ruin from the new rules. Public debate was intense, some justices received physical threats, and the uncertainty deferred investment in Arizona land. Then it was announced that the court would grant a rehearing. The story is told in Mann, Law and Politics of Ground Water in Arizona, 2 Ariz. L. Rev. 241 (1960).

♦ BRISTOR v. CHEATHAM
75 Ariz. 227, 255 P.2d 173 (1953)

Windes, Justice. The appeal is from an order of the lower court in sustaining a motion to dismiss plaintiffs' complaint. For the original majority and minority opinions, see 73 Ariz. 238, 240 P.2d 185. The substance of the allegations of the complaint are set forth therein. Rehearing was granted. Whenever the term ground water is used herein it shall be construed to mean what is commonly called natural percolating water, and when the term majority is used reference is made to the majority original opinion.

The only questions presented by the pleadings, by the assignments of error and by the contentions of plaintiffs in their briefs are whether *Issue* the plaintiffs have the right to invoke the doctrine of reasonable use or correlative rights and whether, having alleged in the second cause of action an underground stream and prior use of the water thereof, they have alleged an appropriation thereof. It was never alleged in the complaint nor contended by the plaintiffs in assignment of error or briefs that they had appropriated percolating water. This issue was apparently introduced into the case by *amici curiae* who have no right to create, extend or enlarge the issues. . . .

Without sanctioning the right of the court, under the issues as thus presented, to re-examine the field of ground water law, since such has been done we will treat it as a legitimate issue.

The majority hold that ground waters are public notwithstanding this court has ruled to the contrary for the past forty-nine years. . . .

Whether we should . . . after approximately fifty years' operation under an announced rule, depart therefrom depends upon many questions, the most important of which is the protection of property rights acquired upon the faith of this court's announcement of the law. . . .

It is generally so well known that we take judicial notice that, with faith in . . . this court, many and large investments have been made in the development of ground waters. Under these circumstances the court's announcement of the rule becomes a rule of property, and rights acquired thereunder should not be disturbed "unless the law is such as to leave the court no alternative," and when a decision does become a rule of property, the rights acquired thereunder are entitled to protection under the law as declared. The majority opinion seems to recognize that the users of ground water developed under these conditions are entitled to protection but takes the position that they will receive better protection under the law of prior appropriation.

This brings us to the question whether, even if it were assumed ground waters are public, it is legally possible to acquire any rights thereto under the law of prior appropriation. After deciding that such waters are now and always have been public, the majority proceeds to hold that because they have always been public and have been put to use, they have been appropriated as of the respective dates that beneficial use began. This conclusion is based upon the proposition that because the legislature has not seen fit to declare ground water, as a class of water, subject to appropriation nor provide the steps for the acquisition of appropriate rights, plaintiffs have appropriated under some law of custom and usage, because congress had declared them public and subject to appropriation according to custom and usage prevailing in the arid West. We believe this to be unsound for several reasons. First, we can find no authority for the assumption that there exists any custom and usage to divert ground waters for irrigation purposes and thereby secure a prior right thereto. Under both the civil and common law, ground water belonged to the owner of the soil. Second, even if there had existed such a custom, it cannot prevail nor operate contrary to legislative rule.

In 1864, the territorial legislature provided a rule as to what waters were subject to appropriation, for what purposes they could be appropriated and that they could only be appropriated exclusively under such regulations and restrictions as the legislature provided. Article 22, Territorial Bill of Rights, Section 1, Chapter 55, Howell's Code. The classes of water by this law authorized to be appropriated were streams, lakes and ponds capable of beneficial use for irrigation. During succeeding years, other classes were added and made available for appropriation such as underground streams, flood waters, and spring waters. Session Laws 1919, Chapter 164, Section 1; Session Laws 1921, Chapter 64, Section 1.

The legislature has thus provided laws for the acquisition of public waters, and if there ever existed a custom and usage which authorized the appropriation of these waters (which we do not admit), such cannot be given the force of law contrary to the statute. When the legislature classifies waters that are subject to and available for appropriation, it is a limitation on the right to so acquire waters not classified for such purpose. . . .

We therefore cannot agree with the majority in holding that ground water is subject to appropriation. By every rule of statutory construction of which we have knowledge, the legislature has in effect said that it is not. When waters are classified for appropriation, it operates as a statutory limitation and excludes all waters not included therein. To say otherwise would permit the court to amend the statute by adding thereto other classes, which of course is strictly a legislative function. . . .

The majority seems to think that the congressional Act of 1877, having severed ground waters from the soil, likewise carried with it a right to appropriate the same. Even if the premise were true that such waters are thus severed, the conclusion that the Act also gives some rights to appropriate is unsound.

The case of California Oregon Power Co. v. Beaver Portland Cement Co., 295 U.S. 142, upon which the majority relies so strongly, recognizes that the source of the right to appropriate must come from the state. Therein the court said:

> . . . "Congress cannot enforce either rule upon any state," the full power of choice must remain with the state. The Desert Land Act does not bind or purport to bind the states to any policy. It simply recognizes and gives sanction, in so far as the United States and its future grantees are concerned, to the state and local doctrine of appropriation, and seeks to remove what otherwise might be an impediment to its full and successful operation. . . .

The state of Arizona through its legislature has adopted its policy and local doctrine to the effect that ground waters are not subject to appropriation. It seems the only answer, therefore, is that a prior right to the use of ground waters cannot now be acquired and never could have been acquired under the law of prior appropriation. We hold, therefore, that such waters are not subject to any law of appropriation. Consequently the protection offered by the majority does not exist, and they have no protection except that offered by the common law as heretofore enunciated in Howard v. Perrin, 8 Ariz. 347, 76 P. 469.

It is claimed that if we do not change the law, ground waters will be exhausted and the legislature is shackled and powerless to enact a ground water code. If the legislature is shackled, it is the constitution that imposes the impediment. The court has no right to pull the rug from under the owner and release the constitutional obstructions, if any. It is the court's duty to protect constitutional rights. Possibly the only source of power the legislature possesses is the police power for the general welfare. Such power has been repeatedly used in numerous instances to limit the exercise of property rights. It has been exercised in the regulation of water. We do not mean to say whether or to what extent such police power may be used to affect the rights involved herein. That is not before us. Should it ever be presented we will decide the matter.

With reference to the dismissal of the complaint, we consider the first cause of action thereof. This cause alleges that the plaintiffs since the year 1916 sank certain wells which supplied them with water for domestic purposes; that during the years 1948 and 1949 the defendants sank on their lands a number of large wells for irrigation purposes; that by the operation thereof the water has been drawn from under plaintiffs' lands causing the level to drop to the extent that plaintiffs were deprived of such waters for domestic purposes; that defendants are transporting the water thus pumped from under plaintiffs' land to a distance of approximately three miles for the development and irrigation of lands not theretofore irrigated; that the waters pumped by the defendants are not used for any beneficial purpose upon the lands from which the same is taken and that the plaintiffs have been suffering and will continue to suffer damages.

Whether the foregoing states a cause of action depends upon whether this court is going to follow the English common-law rule that the owner of lands overlying subterranean waters may extract the same for any purpose he chooses with a resulting damage to an adjoining owner without liability therefor, or whether we adopt what is called the American rule that one may extract such water for a reasonable, beneficial use of the land from which the same is taken. This court has never passed upon the question. . . .

A great majority of the states which in recent years have been presented with this problem adhere to the principle that the owner of lands overlying ground waters may freely, without liability to an adjoining user, use the same without limitation and without liability to another owner, providing his use thereof is for the purpose of reasonably putting the land from which the water is taken to a beneficial use. . . .

Some courts have extended the doctrine by limiting the taking of water, when there is a scarcity thereof, to only the landowner's proportionate share thereof. The former is the doctrine of reasonable use and the latter is the doctrine of correlative rights. The terms are often used interchangeably, but they are distinct doctrines. We think the better rule is that of reasonable use as distinguished from the doctrine of correlative rights. . . .

We have held many times that when not bound by previous decision or legislative enactment we would follow the Restatement of the Law, Ingalls v. Neidlinger, 70 Ariz. 40, 216 P. 2d 387, and this subject is quite thoroughly considered in Restatement of Law of Torts, Volume IV, Chapter 41, Topic 4, Page 387. Section 860 thereof says: "A possessor of land who, in using the subterranean water therein, intentionally causes substantial harm to a possessor of other land through invasion of the other's interest in the use of subterranean water in his land, is liable to the other if, but only if, the harmful use of water is unreasonable in respect to the other possessor."

The principal difficulty in the application of the reasonable use doctrine is in determining what is reasonable use. There are various uses that have been held reasonable or unreasonable depending upon the nature of the use. What is a reasonable use must depend to a great extent upon many factors, such as the persons involved, the nature of their use and all the facts and circumstances pertinent to the issue. . . .

[The rule of reasonable use] does not prevent the extraction of ground water subjacent to the soil so long as it is taken in connection with a beneficial enjoyment of the land from which it is taken. If it is diverted for the purpose of making reasonable use of the land from which it is taken, there is no liability incurred to an adjoining owner for a resulting damage. As stated in Canada v. City of Shawnee, 179 Okl. 53, 64 P.2d 694 (1936):

> [T]he rule of reasonable use as applied to percolating waters "does not prevent the proper use by any landowner of the percolating waters subjacent to his soil in agriculture, manufacturing, irrigation, or otherwise; nor does it prevent any reasonable development of his land by mining or the like, although the underground water of neighboring proprietors may thus be interfered with or diverted; but it does prevent the withdrawal of underground waters for distribution or sale for uses not connected with any beneficial ownership or enjoyment of the land whence they are taken, if it thereby result that the owner of adjacent or neighboring land is inter-

fered with in his right to the reasonable user of subsurface water upon his land, or if his wells, springs, or streams are thereby materially diminished in flow or his land is rendered so arid as to be less valuable for agriculture, pasturage, or other legitimate uses."

We hold, therefore, that the first cause of action states sufficient facts to warrant relief if supported by the proper evidence.

Concerning the second cause of action, plaintiffs allege that at various times since 1916, they sank their wells for the purpose of supplying themselves with domestic water from an underground stream and that defendants are pumping from the same source. It is apparent plaintiffs are attempting to allege prior appropriation of underground stream water. It is not clearly so stated but applying the doctrine of reasonable intendment and considering our new liberal rules of pleading, we so construe these allegations. Certainly it will be necessary for the plaintiffs to prove prior appropriation in accordance with the law in existence at the respective times they claim such appropriations were made before they can prevail on this basis.

Judgment is reversed with directions that the complaint be reinstated and that further proceedings be had in accordance with the principles announced.

Stanford, C.J., and La Prade, J., concur.

Phelps and Udall, Justices, dissenting. For the sake of clarity we shall term the court's opinion of January 12, 1952 as the majority opinion and shall designate the present court's opinion on rehearing as the prevailing opinion.

We held in the majority opinion that the lower court erred in dismissing the plaintiffs' complaint as to the first cause of action and to that extent we now agree with the prevailing opinion which arrives at the same conclusion. However, the basis for our holding is so diametrically opposed to the rationale of the prevailing opinion authored by Justice Windes that we are impelled to register our disagreement with the principles enunciated therein.

There has never been disagreement between any of the members of the court that the second cause of action stated a proper "claim for relief," and that the lower court erred in dismissing that cause of action instead of putting plaintiffs to their proof.

At the outset let it be known that in the intervening months, since handing down the majority opinion we have completely re-examined the law relative to percolating waters in Arizona and are even more firmly of the opinion (1) that the Congressional Desert Land Act of 1877 effected a severance from the land of all waters upon *and under* the public domain; (2) that percolating waters being migratory were not thereafter entitled to be considered as inherent in the soil or a component part of the earth and thereby the property of the owner of the overlying soil, as was held by this court in the case of Howard v. Perrin, 1904, *supra;* (3) that the Perrin decision and the later cases following it should be expressly overruled; (4) that inasmuch as this never was the law the rule of *stare decisis* should not be applied; and (5), that no rights have been acquired thereunder which have ripened into "a rule of property." Nor is there anything in the prevailing opinion that would cause us to change the pronouncement contained in the original majority opinion to the effect, (a) that at least since 1877 percolating waters have been and are public in character; (b) are subject to appropriation and application to beneficial use under the acknowledged and accepted customs and usages of this state until the legislature prescribes other methods; and (c) that no act of the legislature of the territory or of the state of Arizona was necessary to invest percolating waters with the character of public ownership.

Without reiterating what has been previously said we shall attempt to confine this dissent to pointing out the weaknesses, as we see them, in the prevailing opinion.

First, it cannot be said that lakes or pools underlying the lands located in the valleys of Arizona fed by percolating waters for centuries upon centuries and eons upon eons were not a source of water supply in existence when the Desert Land Act was passed in 1877 as much so as now, nor that they were not plainly embraced within the language of the act. . . .

With respect to the application of the law of prior appropriation to underground waters the prevailing opinion makes the startling declaration that ". . . we can find no authority for the assumption that there exists any custom and usage to divert ground waters for irrigation purposes and thereby secure a prior right thereto. . . . [E]ven if there had existed such a custom, it cannot prevail nor operate contrary to legislative rule." It also declares that "Under both the civil and common law, ground water belonged to the owner of the soil," citing Kinney on Irrigation and Water Rights, 2d Ed., Vol. 1, section 563. An examination of this section in our opinion fails to confirm the statement above quoted.

This court in the case of Clough v. Wing, 2 Ariz. 371, 17 P. 453, 455, decided in 1888, after an exhaustive recitation of the history of irrigation stated that:

> . . . From "time whereof the memory of man runneth not to the contrary," the rights of riparian owners were settled in the common law; and the right to appropriate and use water for irrigation has been recognized longer than history, and since earlier than tradition. . . . The same was found to prevail in Mexico among the Aztecs, the Toltecs, the Vaquis, and other tribes at the time of the conquest, and remained undisturbed in the jurisprudence of that country until now. . . .

. . . Up to about a third of a century ago, and but recently before this enactment [the act of the Arizona legislature of 1864], the territory of Arizona had been subject to the laws and customs of Mexico, and the common law had been unknown; and that law has never been, and is not now, suited to conditions that exist here, so far as the same applies to the uses of water. (Citing cases.)

The "local customs" of the act of 1866 [act of Congress], so far at least as it refers to rights to the use of water, is not a mere usage or custom, requiring proofs of undisturbed continuance beyond the memory of man. 1 Greenl. Ev. §128. The courts take knowledge of them as of the public laws. . . . 1 Greenl. Ev. §5. . . .

The above quotation makes it doubly clear that the citations of authorities in the prevailing opinion from riparian right jurisdictions can have no application to water problems in Arizona where the doctrine of prior appropriation has prevailed since before the Spanish conquest of Mexico.

It is our position that the act of the legislature in declaring certain of the waters of Arizona to be public is a voluntary recognition of a pre-existing right rather than the establishment of a new one and was therefore unnecessary except for regulatory purpose. . . .

The prevailing opinion, after holding that the rule first announced in Howard v. Perrin has now ripened into a "rule of property" very cautiously opines, before embracing the reasonable use doctrine, that for the future "Possibly the only source of power the legislature possesses (to regulate the use of water) is the police power for the general welfare." If this be true there are rough times ahead for the reason that Arizona will be on an uncharted sea. While there are isolated instances where police power has been invoked to regulate water to solve a particular local problem, our research attests that no jurisdiction in the United States has attempted to regulate on a statewide basis the use of waters, either surface or percolating, under its inherent police power.

The magnitude of the regulatory task ahead becomes more apparent when it is realized that three-fourths of the irrigated crops grown in Arizona last year were produced from pumped waters. And it becomes even more appalling when we consider that the volume of underground waters being annually withdrawn is many times greater than the recharge. We predict that the mad race to "mine" percolating waters which are our greatest natural resource will continue unabated until such time as these waters are declared to be public in character and suitable regulatory measures are adopted. We are confident that the inexorable judgment of time will confirm the views expressed in the original majority opinion and in this dissent.

It is asserted in the prevailing opinion that a great majority of the states confronted with this problem in recent years have adopted the reasonable use doctrine. As applied to riparian right jurisdictions this is probably a correct statement. We note however that the˙jurisdictions cited in support of the assertion are from the Atlantic and Pacific seaboards where too much rather than too little water is the problem. It is noticeable that the arid states of the West are not included. The great majority of the latter do not stop short of prior appropriation and beneficial use in regulating the use of both their surface and percolating waters.

The outcome of *Bristor* made it difficult for growing cities to purchase outlying land and transport groundwater for the use of their thirsty residents. Regarding Tucson's problems, see Farmers Investment Co. v. Bettwy, 113 Ariz. 520, 558 P.2d 14 (1976).

The problems of the cities and fears that too much water was being extracted from available sources finally resulted in enactment of a new Arizona groundwater code in 1980.

Arizona Governor Bruce Babbit said, "In the Old West, we're going overnight from a laissez-faire system, a system where everybody used whatever they wanted wherever they wanted, to the most comprehensive ground-water management system of any state in the American West."

The new law resulted from a compromise among farm, mine, and urban interests, stimulated by a threat from Interior Secretary Cecil Andrus that without a new law he would delay the Central Arizona project, a vast federal undertaking to divert Colorado River water to Arizona's central and southern basins. With underground water making up more than 60 percent of Arizona's water supply, the state is currently consuming 2.5 million acre-feet more per year than is replenished by nature.

Among the provisions of the new law are the following:

(a) A statewide management and conservation program, with civil and criminal penalties for violation, intended to lead by the year 2025 to consumption of only as much groundwater as is replenished;

(b) In water-short areas, a pump tax and mandatory conservation for farms, industry, and mines, and per capita consumption limits for cities;

(c) No new growth where there is no assured supply;

(d) No new irrigated agriculture in certain areas, although existing farms are "grandfathered" and can sell their rights with their land.

Ariz. Groundwater Code §§45-401 to 45-637 (1980).

One consequence of the 1980 statute was that the City of Prescott was permitted to obtain water from land it owned 17 miles away in the Chino Valley. Nearby landowners formed a town and sued, saying "that the [1980] Act takes property without due process of law and without just compensation." The act was upheld against the constitutional challenges in Town of Chino Valley v. City of Prescott, 131 Ariz. 78, 638 P.2d 1324 (1982), *appeal dismissed,* 457 U.S. 1101 (1982). The court drew an analogy between percolating underground water and wild animals: "free to roam as they please, they are the property of no one." But its principal argument was that regulation of scarce water is like regulation of land use, and it relied heavily on the constitutionality of zoning in upholding the new water law.

Arizona's latest plan includes an effort to reduce consumption. Residents of Phoenix consume 267 gallons per capita per day, while Tucsonians use only 160 gallons. The goal is 140 gallons per day by the year 2025. To do this, there must be controversial changes in "life styles." Rules promulgated in 1983 say that golf courses can no longer be all grass, that private pools cannot exceed a certain size, that highway medians may no longer be covered with grass, and that no more private ponds and lakes — a major prestige item in real estate developments — can be dug. But the main effort is to reduce consumption by the agricultural sector which currently uses 89 percent of the state's water. The goal is to cut irrigated farmland from 1.3 million acres to 800,000 acres by the year 2025. N. Y. Times, Jan. 30, 1984.

Meanwhile, as part of the effort to encourage population growth and industry at the expense of agriculture, the state is building Palo Verde Nuclear Generating Station, the only nuclear power complex without a natural source of cooling-water. It will require 90 million gallons of water a day, much of which will be sewage pumped 37 miles from Phoenix. Letter to editor of the N.Y. Times from Raymond B. Wrabley, Feb. 17, 1984.

SHUPE, WASTE IN WESTERN WATER LAW: A BLUEPRINT FOR CHANGE, 61 Or. L. Rev. 483, 485-486, 492, 510-511 (1982): Because of the abundant rainfall in the East, the common law concept of riparian rights was well-suited to the American colonies. Under this doctrine, riparian landowners were entitled to reasonable use of the natural flow of watercourses, subject to the restriction that downstream riparians not be impaired by such use. Although the riparian system allowed only limited removal and consumption of streamflow, it did not inhibit agricultural development in the East, where rainfall provided sufficient moisture for farming. But as settlers moved across the Great Plains, they encountered a different set of conditions that required a new approach to water allocation. Most areas west of the 100th meridian were too arid to support natural crop growth. Consequently, western farming generally required the removal of large quantities of water from rivers and streams for irrigation. Diversions of such magnitude, however, contravened the riparian doctrine's provision that downstream users not be impaired by upstream withdrawals. Furthermore, vast tracks of potentially valuable western agricultural and mining lands were nonriparian, thus not entitled to any water under the doctrine. With these limitations, it became obvious that existing water law lacked the flexibility needed for developing the resources of the West.

An alternative to the restrictive nature of riparian rights arrived in the form of the prior appropriation doctrine. This doctrine, developed during the California goldrush of the 1850s, held that the first person to divert and use streamflow gained a legally protected right to continued use in subsequent years. The senior water right was strictly enforceable against future diverters, so long as a valid appropriation had been made initially. The legal requirements of an appropriation simply were a physical diversion of the water, an intent to use the flow, and an application of the water to some beneficial purpose.

This doctrine of "prior in time, prior in right" proved an effective technique for encouraging exploitation of the West's natural resources. Not only did it reward the quickest to act, but it added a measure of certainty regarding relative rights. Also, the prior appropriation doctrine allowed for more intensive use of water than did the riparian system. No longer were diversions restricted to use on lands contiguous to watercourses, nor were limits placed on the appropriable amount. Each of these features of the doctrine was consistent with the "open-the-West" ethic of the latter half of the nineteenth century. What the new system did not encourage, however, was efficient use of water. . . .

In order to eliminate wasteful irrigation in the arid West, courts must stop treating the volume of water lost in inefficient customary systems as part of the vested water right. Farmers should be allowed to appropriate only as much water as is reasonably needed under modern irrigation practices. Fortunately, a common law framework already exists that will permit the reduction of excessive water appropriations while avoiding constitutional prohibitions. This framework and its interface with statutory law are discussed in the following sections. The analysis involves a five-step progression as summarized below:

1) Early irrigators' inviolate property interest was their right to accrue the benefits from watering their crops. The quantity required to derive such benefit constituted the protectable water right.

2) After technologies developed that allowed for more efficient conveyance and application of the water, the use of the old, water-intensive irrigation practices became a privilege rather than a part of the irrigators' vested right.

3) With the full appropriation of local water supplies by later development, the privilege afforded the inefficient system was lost and any further use of the excess water by that system would constitute waste.

4) Following passage of a forfeiture statute and the running of the stipulated period, the wasteful amount was no longer part of the water right and reverted to the control of the state appropriation system.
5) Courts and administrative agencies must now determine how much of prior water rights was forfeited as waste, and allow diversion of only as much water as is reasonably needed under modern irrigation practices. . . .

The preceding blueprint indicates that the legal framework exists either for courts to take action against wasteful water use or for administrative bodies to implement the program through forfeiture proceedings. State legislatures, as well, should take steps to become involved in the process. Limiting existing water rights can have significant economic consequences, and concurrent legislation would help to ease the potential burden. The state may wish to set up a revolving loan fund or provide direct subsidies for modernizing irrigation systems. Funds could be earmarked for research into efficient agronomy techniques, and programs established to advise irrigators on implementing conservation measures.

Several western states have already recognized the importance of providing aid to irrigators. For instance, since 1955 Wyoming has made more than $60 million available for private construction of irrigation improvements. Idaho, New Mexico, Utah, Washington, and Colorado have also appropriated substantial funds for grants and loans to irrigators. Although much of the funding has been spent in the past on developing new sources of water (e.g., reservoir projects), the emphasis in recent authorizations has shifted to encouraging efficient utilization of existing supplies.

In order to further help irrigators absorb the economic impact of a water conservation program, the legislature may choose to grant a grace period before allowing a state administrative agency to undertake forfeiture proceedings. This would give irrigators time to modernize and either apply the saved water to additional acreage or sell the excess right. Such additional usage or sale, however, would be restricted by laws limiting water use changes to those that do not adversely affect other appropriators. For example, an irrigator could not recover and reuse surface runoff if downstream users have historically relied upon this return flow for their supply. In addition, application of the saved water to other acreage would be prohibited in jurisdictions recognizing the appurtenancy rule. Nonetheless, this rule could be overridden by the legislature, if so desired, and additional measures enacted to allow the irrigators who modernize to receive some economic benefits accruing from the conserved waters.

Notes

1. An Idaho statute had "appropriated" in trust for the people certain unappropriated waters of the Malad Canyon, having declared their preservation for scenic beauty and recreation to be a beneficial use. When the Department of Parks sought to carry out the statutory mandate, and the Idaho Water Users Association protested, the Department of Water Administration determined that in Idaho there cannot be a valid appropriation of water without at least a proposed physical diversion. The supreme court disagreed, one concurring opinion quoting: "If nature accomplishes a result which is recognized and utilized, a change of process by man would seem unnecessary." State Dept. of Parks v. Idaho Dept. of Water Administration, 96 Idaho 440, 530 P.2d 924 (1974) (Bakes, J., concurring, and quoting Empire Water & Power Co. v. Cascade Town Co., 205 F. 123 (8th Cir. 1913)).

2. The Texas Supreme Court applied to the case before it the common law rule (for which it cited Acton v. Blundell) that "in the absence of willful waste or malicious injury, a land-owner has the right to withdraw ground water from wells on his own land without liability for resulting subsidence to his neighbor's land." But for future cases, the court enunciated a new rule: liability according to a standard of negligence (as well as for willful waste or malicious injury). The court was strongly influenced by the development of legislative regulation of water extraction — for example, rules regarding spacing of wells and quantity withdrawn. But it did not speak to whether negligence will now be provable by conduct that does not offend some legislative or regulatory rule. A dissenting justice would have found for plaintiffs on the theory that their right to lateral support was violated when the defendants caused subsidence of their surface. Friendswood Development Co. v. Smith-Southwest Indus., 576 S.W.2d 21 (Tex. 1978).

3. The inadequacies of the basic doctrines of water law have led to a number of eclectic proposals. One example is the Model Water Code. The MWC suggests a standard of "reasonable-beneficial use," which is defined as "use of water in such a quantity as is necessary for economic and efficient utilization, for a purpose and in a manner which is both reasonable and consistent with the public interest." F. Maloney, R. Ausness & J. Morris, Model Water Code §1.03(4) (1972).

Perceiving a need for unified long-range planning, the code envisions a State Water Resources Board, which would formulate state water use and water quality plans. Water would be a "public trust," with the board empowered to issue short- and long-term permits for consumption and discharge, in accordance with the established plan. Sinking and operation of wells would be regulated. The board would have discretionary emergency powers for extraordinary weather conditions.

MISS. REV. STAT. (1972): [The following sections of the Mississippi code present an example of a statutory scheme much like that proposed in the Model Water Code.]

§51-3-1

It is hereby declared that the general welfare of the people of the state of Mississippi requires that the water resources of the state be put to beneficial use to the fullest extent of which they are capable, that the waste or unreasonable use, or unreasonable method of use, of water be prevented, that the conservation of such water be exercised with the view to the reasonable and beneficial use thereof in the interest of the people, and that the public and private funds for the promotion and expansion of the beneficial use of water resources shall be invested to the end that the best interests and welfare of the people are served.

Water occurring in any watercourse, lake, or other natural water body of the state is hereby declared to be among the basic resources of this state and subject to appropriation in accordance with the provisions of this chapter; and the control and development and use of water for all beneficial purposes shall be in the state, which, in the exercise of its police powers, shall take such measures as shall effectuate full utilization and protection of the water resources of Mississippi.

§51-3-3

(e) "Beneficial use" — The application of water to a useful purpose that inures to the benefit of the water user and subject to his dominion and control, but does not include the waste of water.

(f) "Appropriator" — The person who obtains a permit from the board authorizing him to take possession by diversion or otherwise and to use and apply an allotted quantity of water for a designated beneficial use, and who makes actual use of the water for such purpose.

(g) "Appropriation" —

(1) The use of a specific amount of water at a specific time and at a specific place, authorized and allotted by the board for a designated beneficial purpose within the specific limits as to quantity, time, place, and rate of diversion and withdrawal.

(2) The right to continue the use of water having actually been applied to any beneficial use as of April 6, 1956, or within three years prior thereto to the extent of the beneficial use made thereof. It is not the intent of this chapter that any person making use of any watercourse for waste disposal or in pollution abatement, on said date, shall be construed as having any vested right to pollute the waters of the watercourse.

(3) The right to take and use water for beneficial purposes where a person is bona fide engaged in the construction of works for the actual application of water to a beneficial use as of April 6, 1956, provided such

works shall be completed and water is actually applied for such use within three years after said date, with extension of not more than seven years in the discretion of the board. It is not the intent, however, to validate any claim to the use of water, or for rights of construction looking to the use of water, not lawful on said date.

§51-3-7

(1) No right to appropriate or use water subject to appropriation shall be initiated or acquired except upon compliance with the provisions of this chapter, and no person shall take water from a stream, lake, or other watercourse without having a valid right to do so. However, any person or persons claiming their rights under subsection (g)(2) of section 51-3-3 where that person had begun to make beneficial use of water as of April 6, 1956, or within three years prior thereto, or after April 6, 1956, until December 31, 1958, shall file their claim with the board of water commissioners on or before December 31, 1958; and after said date of December 31, 1958, claims may be filed with the board, but the priority of all claims will be determined by the date the claim is received by the board. Any person convicted of violating the provisions hereof shall be fined not to exceed one hundred dollars ($100.00), or be imprisoned not to exceed thirty days, or both, in the discretion of the court. Nothing herein shall interfere with the customary use of water for domestic purposes, and the user of water for domestic purposes may elect to establish a right to the use of such water under the procedures provided in this chapter. Nothing herein shall operate to deprive any landowner of the right to the use of the water from a spring arising on his land so long as such use does not interfere with the right of any water user below. Nothing herein shall interfere with a landowner's right to place a dam across a gully on his property or across a stream that originates on his property so long as provision is made for continued established average minimum stream flow, if and when such flow is required to protect the rights of water users below.

(2) Subject to the common law or other lawful water rights of others, any person may build and maintain a dam on any stream having a minimum flow of not more than one half million gallons of water per day and utilize up to three hundred acre feet of the impounded water without a permit from the board so long as such action does not affect the established average minimum flow in the stream below the dam. However, any such person who seeks to build and maintain a dam on such stream within the territorial limits of any watercourse lying in whole or in part within a levee district duly constituted under the laws of this state shall first obtain permission from the levee board of such levee district.

(3) The board shall have the authority to permit the appropriation of water of any stream only in excess of the established average minimum

flow as based upon records or computations by the board. However, exceptions may be made for domestic and municipal users. The board may authorize any appropriator to use the established minimum flow upon written assurance that such water will be immediately returned to the stream in substantially the same amount to insure the maintenance at all times of the average minimum flow. The board may authorize an appropriator to use the established minimum flow for industrial purposes when such water shall be returned within such reasonable time, as specified by the board in its authorization, to the stream at a point downstream from the place of withdrawal, where the board shall find that such appropriation will not result in any substantial detriment to property owners affected thereby or to the public interest.

(4) The board shall have the authority to permit the appropriation of water of any lake only in excess of the established average minimum lake level as based upon records or computations by the board. However, exceptions may be made for domestic and municipal users. The board, upon affording a hearing to interested parties, may authorize any appropriator to use below the established average minimum level when such use will not affect plans for the proper utilization of the water resources of the state, or the board may establish a level above the established average minimum lake level, after affording an opportunity for a hearing, where plans for the proper utilization of the water resources of the state require it.

§51-3-11

The right of the appropriator and his successors to the use of water shall terminate when he ceases for three consecutive years to use it for the specific beneficial purpose authorized in his permit or license. However, upon his application prior to the expiration of said three year period for extension of said permit or license, the board may grant such extension without the loss of priority.

§51-3-13

Appropriation of surface waters of the state shall not constitute absolute ownership or absolute rights of use of such waters, but such waters shall remain subject to the principle of beneficial use. It shall be the duty of the board to approve all applications made in such form as shall meet the requirements of this chapter and such rules and regulations as shall be promulgated by the board and which contemplate the utilization of water for beneficial purposes, within reasonable limitations, provided the proposed use does not prejudicially and unreasonably affect the public interest. If it is determined that the proposed use of the water sought to be appropriated is not for beneficial purposes, is not within reasonable limitations, or is detrimental to the public interest, it shall be the duty of the board to enter an order rejecting such application or requiring its modification.

§51-3-15

For the administration of this chapter there is hereby created a board of water commissioners of the State of Mississippi, consisting of seven members appointed by the governor, by and with the advice and consent of the senate, whose terms of office shall be for a period of four years. . . .

Notes

Compare the Mississippi Statute to the Systematic Arrangement of the Socialist National Environment in the German Democratic Republic (National Environmental Act, May 14, 1970), from Sand, The Socialist Response: Environmental Protection Law in the German Democratic Republic, 3 Ecol. L.Q. 451, 500-501 (1973):

Article V: Water Use and Protection

Section 24 (Objectives)

Water, including groundwater, shall be efficiently used and protected as an irreplaceable basis of the social reproduction process, particularly for the supply of drinking water, industrial water, and irrigation of socialist agricultural enterprises, as well as for inland shipping and fishing. Conservation of its quality shall be ensured for the continuous development of the national economy, for the promotion of health and recreation of citizens, of physical culture, and of sports. Utilisation of water resources, protection and cultivation of waters and their embankments, improvement of water quality, and efficient use of water constitute permanent duties of government and economic authorities and enterprises in concert with the National Front, social organizations, and citizens.

Section 25 (Utilisation of water resources and water allocation)

(1) Responsible government authorities and enterprises shall ensure that water resources are conserved — particularly by means of a system of biological and technological measures including economic regulations — that their usable proportion is increased, improved in quality, and used efficiently.

(2) In case of interference with the water economy of the landscape as a result of production measures by industry, agriculture, or other sectors, enterprises shall strive to exclude, to the extent possible, detrimental effects on the social use in terms of quantity and quality of water resources, or undertake other measures to safeguard the water supply.

(3) To meet the water demands of the national economy, economical use of water, particularly by industry, shall be ensured by means of appropriate methods based on the highest scientific-technological standards.

Section 26 (Water use and water quality conservation)

(1) Utilisation of waters by water extraction, inflow of water and effluents, and other measures influencing water quality, or by the raising

or lowering of water levels shall proceed in accordance with social requirements. The competent government authorities shall regulate water use based on government permits, ensure the supervision of water uses, and cooperate with citizens and social organizations in implementing the functions of water protection.

D.   RIGHTS TO DISCHARGE SURFACE WATER

◆ YONADI v. HOMESTEAD COUNTRY HOMES
35 N.J. Super. 514, 114 A.2d 564 (App. Div. 1955)

CLAPP, S.J.A.D. This appeal has to do with the law of casual surface waters. The principal question presented (to state the case very generally) is whether a person improving a tract of land and constructing and maintaining drains therein is to be charged with liability for a resultant increase in the flow of surface water which runs off the tract upon plaintiffs' lands.

Plaintiffs own a golf course and restaurant located on the south side of Allaire Road, Spring Lake Heights. The tract mentioned, consisting of 40 acres, lying across the road on the north side, had been farming land until 1950, but since then the private corporate defendants, or one of them, have erected on it 169 houses. Generally speaking, the natural drainage of this land is southerly, passing from this tract through ditches and a swale once existing on the property now constituting the golf course, and so eventually to the Atlantic Ocean. There was testimony that the run-off from improved residential areas, such as the development here with its catch basins and sub-surface drains, is about 3½ times that coming from the more absorbent soil of the farm land formerly here. In times of heavy rain, excess water has produced flood conditions on plaintiffs' property.

The court sitting without a jury gave judgment for the plaintiff against the borough and the two private corporations, awarding damages of $2,500 against all three defendants, and

(a) restraining them from "using or permitting the artificial collection of waters, and from collecting and diverting it thereby on the lands of the plaintiffs, to the harm of the plaintiffs," and

(b) ordering defendants "to accomplish this work" (sic) within 90 days. . . .

The general rule is that neither the diversion nor the altered transmission, repulsion or retention of surface water gives rise to an actionable injury. Generally therefore he who improves or alters land is not subjected to liability because of the consequences of his acts upon the flow of surface water.

Under this rule it matters not that the flow of water upon plaintiffs' property is much increased or accelerated or its force aggravated.

In pursuance of this rule, it has been held that the mere filling in of a tract of land "to such an extent as to work a change in the topography of the land, and to cause the surface water to run in a southerly, instead of, as formerly, in an easterly course," is not actionable.

There are or may be a number of exceptions to this rule. But we need consider only one of them.

This exception arises where a defendant improving or altering land interferes with the flow of surface water, not by making a change in the grade or surface of the land, but by means of drains, ditches or other artificial contrivances for the very purpose of transmitting the water. Under this exception, a defendant renders himself absolutely liable if by means of such an artificial device he causes surface water to be carried in a body large enough to do substantial injury (usually drainage from a large tract) and thereby casts it on plaintiff's lands away from where it otherwise would have flowed. . . .

But this exception does not apply where the surface water is brought to the locality substantially where it otherwise would have flowed. In such a case we are thrown back upon the general rule. Thus, if through a drain or other artificial means, a defendant effects a concentration in the flow of surface water but brings it to the locality substantially where it otherwise would have flowed, the damage is not actionable.

While the New Jersey cases do not deal with the matter explicitly, we conclude that where surface water is concentrated through a drain or other artificial means and is conducted to some place substantially where it otherwise would have flowed, the defendant will not be liable even though by reason of improvements he has made in the land, the water is brought there in larger quantities and with greater force than would have occurred prior to the improvements. The policies underlying the general rule come to bear here. What reasonably could the upland proprietor or occupant do in the present case with this excess water? Rather than require him to dispose of it — and so perhaps require him to secure the cooperation of a number of lowland properties through which the water must eventually be brought — the burden is cast on each lowland proprietor to protect his own land. . . .

There are three rules in this country as to surface water. First, there is the Massachusetts and New Jersey rule — the general rule above stated — adopted in some 22 jurisdictions. It is known as the common enemy rule, after a phrase employed by Beasley, C.J., in Town of Union v. Durkes, 38 N.J.L. 21, 22 (Sup. Ct. 1875), which, though apparently inaccurate in its allusion, nevertheless is a not inappropriate appellation of the fundamental concept of the rule. This rule obviously favors the improver of property, at the expense of neighbors who are affected by his disposition of the surface water.

Second, there is the civil law rule prevailing in some measure in 18 states, including Illinois and Pennsylvania. Under it the proprietor of the higher land has a natural servitude in the lower land to accommodate the natural flow (and no more than the natural flow) of surface water from his land. This servitude, the proprietor of the lowland cannot obstruct.

There is a third rule in force only in two jurisdictions, nevertheless representative also of a recent tendency in the law of other jurisdictions. Under it a person altering his land is placed under a duty in connection with surface water not to act unreasonably under the circumstances. . . . The strong public policies favoring the development of land, which underlie the common enemy doctrine, not to speak of the practicalities of the doctrine, have made themselves felt under the rule of reasonable user also. So under the latter rule the erection of buildings in an urban locality is regarded as of such high utility that in the absence of exceptional circumstances, the resultant invasion of another's enjoyment of land, through surface waters, is not actionable. Restatement of Torts, §833b. Thus, under the doctrine of reasonable user there are rules, limited it is true, but nevertheless representative of a crystallization of judicial opinion, as to what under certain circumstances is reasonable or unreasonable as a matter of law. In our view the common enemy doctrine and the exception to it above stated are crystallizations of this very sort.

The problem before us then is simply to apply the above stated rule and exception to the circumstances here. Of the 40 acres, 28 and another two acres still drain to the locality substantially where they would otherwise drain, had there been no development. In these 30 acres, as above indicated, not only has there been an increase in the flow of the surface water as a result of the development, but catchbasins and drains have been constructed and the land seems in places to have been elevated; however, in our view, the plaintiffs cannot complain of any of these acts. Furthermore the mere fact that at one point a level 15-inch pipe was tied into a 12-inch pipe running under Allaire Road (it has been said that these two pipes have recently been disconnected) creates at most a concentration of the water which, as above indicated, is not actionable. . . .

The next question in the case is whether there is any liability with respect to the ten acres remaining from the 40, after deducting the 30 acres mentioned. . . .

If the drainage water from these ten acres has been carried away from the place where it otherwise would flow, defendants may relieve themselves of liability as to the same in the future, provided they rechannel this water back substantially to that place — that is, to the place where under the engineer's original design of the development, it was intended to go. This follows from what has already been said.

Reversed and remanded.

TUCKER v. BADOIAN, 376 Mass. 907, 384 N.E.2d 1195 (1978) (Kaplan, J., concurring): The common enemy rule had only questionable support in the common law when it was first sponsored by this court in the mid-nineteenth century. Being assimilated to conceptions of property rather than tort, it exhibited from the beginning a deplorable rigidity. In its substance, however, it was anarchic. Perhaps a common enemy doctrine served originally a public purpose by stimulating or assisting entrepreneurship in the exploitation of land. But, as Brennan, J. (now Mr. Justice Brennan), intimated in Armstrong v. Francis Corp., 20 N.J. 320, 120 A.2d 4 (1956), at a matured stage of the economy there is little reason why costs of land development "should be borne in every case by adjoining landowners rather than by those who engage in such projects for profit."

As might be expected, jurisdictions espousing the rule have civilized it in one way or another, not always with explicit recognition of what they were doing. This court allowed some "exceptions," and no doubt we often reached sensible results. A like process of adjustment or amelioration could be discerned with respect to an unsatisfactory "natural flow" rule in vogue in another group of jurisdictions. This started at the opposite end and imposed liability on a possessor for interfering to the detriment of his neighbor with the drainage of surface waters in their natural course.

In practice and application, then, if not in terms, both rules tended in some degree to reach a plane of reason. Still the formulary statements on either side confused the issues and impaired the results. Therefore, with encouragement from competent scholars, a respectable number of courts over the past thirty years and more have abandoned the polar positions and adopted, instead, a "reasonable use" standard which introduces, in the resolution of quarrels between landowners about surface waters, the considerations typical of the law of private nuisance. On such lines the question was treated in the Restatement of Torts as promulgated in 1939. . . .

Ordinarily a change of decisional law falls into place and is applied to past as well as to subsequent transactions or occurrences. In the present situation, however, we propose to alter a rule of long standing on which parties may have relied. Accordingly we think the new standard should be reserved for prospective application, that is, for conduct occurring hereafter, excepting future conduct so related in a continuum with past conduct that it would be unjust to apply the new standard to it. We do not apply the new standard to the instant case (which would ntail reversing the judgment appealed from and remanding the matter for further proceedings) because the parties did not raise the question of a departure from the existing rule and were content to litigate within its bounds.

Notes

1. In Armstrong v. Francis Corp., 20 N.J. 320, 120 A.2d 4, (1956), Justice William J. Brennan, Jr., wrote for the court:

> It is, of course, true that society has a great interest that land shall be developed for the greater good. It is therefore properly a consideration in these cases whether the utility of the possessor's use of his land outweighs the gravity of the harm which results from his alteration of the flow of surface waters. . . . But while today's mass home building projects, of which the Francis development is typical, are assuredly in the social good, no reason suggests itself why, in justice, the economic costs incident to the expulsion of surface waters in the transformation of the rural or semi-rural areas of our state into urban or suburban communities should be borne in every case by adjoining landowners rather than by those who engage in such projects for profit. Social progress and the common well being are in actuality better served by a just and right balancing of the competing interests according to the general principles of fairness and common sense which attend the application of the rule of reason.

2. See Keys v. Romley, 64 Cal. 2d 396, 412 P.2d 529, 50 Cal. Rptr. 273 (1966): "In the total spectrum of American case law, California may be considered a devotee of a modified civil law rule. Our rule has the advantage of predictability, in that responsibility for diversion of surface waters is fixed, all things being relatively equal."

3. A statute reads: "The owner of the land owns water standing thereon, or flowing over or under its surface, but not forming a definite stream. Water running in a definite stream, formed by nature over or under the surface, may be used by him as long as it remains there; but he may not prevent the natural flow of the stream, or of the natural spring from which it commences its definite course, nor pursue nor pollute the same." What theory of property interests has the legislature adopted with respect to percolating waters?

4. The Alabama Supreme Court applied the tort doctrine of nuisance where the pumping of groundwater in a quarry caused the sinking of homes a half-mile away. The trial court had found for the defendant quarry under a rule that a landowner can drain percolating waters so long as his actions are reasonable. The Alabama Supreme Court reversed, saying that the traditional rule, "carried to its logical extension, . . . would allow a quarry owner willfully to sink the City of

Birmingham with impunity. . . ." The court said that the old rule should be replaced by "the rule of liability developed by the law of nuisance." It pointed to Alabama Code §6-5-120 (1975) for a definition of nuisance as being "anything that works hurt, inconvenience or damage to another. The fact that the act done may otherwise be lawful does not keep it from being a nuisance. The inconvenience complained of . . . should be such as would affect an ordinary reasonable man." Henderson v. Wade Sand & Gravel Co., 388 So. 2d 900 (Ala. 1980).

E. RIGHTS TO WATER GOOD AGAINST THE GOVERNMENT

What claims to property are protected, constitutionally or otherwise, against the government "taking" or diminishing them? Cases considering this question arise throughout the book; the subject is then addressed in depth in Chapter 22.

◆ UNITED STATES v. WILLOW RIVER POWER CO.
324 U.S. 499 (1945)

MR. JUSTICE JACKSON delivered the opinion of the Court. The Willow River Power Company has been awarded $25,000 by the Court of Claims as just compensation for impaired efficiency of its hydroelectric plant caused by the action of the United States in raising the water level of the St. Croix River. Reality of damage and reasonableness of the award are not in issue. Our question is whether the damage is the result of a "taking" of private property, for which just compensation is required by the Fifth Amendment.

Willow River in its natural state was a non-navigable stream, which flowed to within a few rods of the St. Croix River, turned and roughly paralleled it for something less than a mile, and then emptied into the St. Croix. Many years ago an earth dam was thrown across the Willow about a half-mile above its natural mouth. A new mouth was cut across the narrow neck which separated the two rivers and a dam was built across the artificial channel close to or upon the banks of the St. Croix. Here also was built a mill, which operated under the head produced in the pool by the two dams, which obstructed both the natural and the artificial channel of the Willow River.

These lands and appurtenant rights were acquired by the Willow River Power Company, a public utility corporation of the State of Wisconsin, and were devoted to hydroelectric generation for supply of the neighborhood. The plant was the lowest of four on Willow River operated by the Company as an integrated system. The powerhouse was located on land owned by the Company above ordinary high water of the St. Croix. Mechanical energy for generation of electrical energy was developed by water in falling from the artificial level of non-navigable Willow River to the natural level of navigable St. Croix River. The elevation of the head water when at the crest of the gates was 689 feet above mean sea level. The operating head varied because elevation of the tail water was governed by the fluctuating level of the St. Croix. When that river was low, the maximum head was developed, and was 22.5 feet; when the river was at flood stage, the operating head diminished to as little as eight feet. The ordinary high-water mark is found to have been 672 feet, and the head available above that was seventeen feet.

The Government, in pursuance of a Congressional plan to improve navigation, in August of 1938 had completed what is known as the Red Wing Dam in the upper Mississippi, into which the St. Croix flows. This dam was some thirty miles downstream, but it created a pool which extended upstream on the St. Croix beyond respondent's plant at an ordinary elevation of 675 feet. Thus the water level maintained by the Government in the St. Croix was approximately three feet above its ordinary high-water level at claimant's property. By thus raising the level at which tail waters must flow off from claimant's plant, the Government reduced the operating head by three feet, using ordinary high water as the standard, and diminished the plant's capacity to produce electric energy. The Company was obliged to supplement its production by purchase from other sources.

Loss of power was made the only basis of the award. The Court of Claims found as a fact that "The value of the loss in power as a result of the raising of the level of the St. Croix River by three feet above ordinary high water was $25,000 at the time and place of taking," and it rendered judgment for that amount. There is no finding that any fast lands were flooded or that other injury was done to property or that claimant otherwise was deprived of any use of its property. It is true that the water level was above high-water mark on the St. Croix River banks and on claimant's structures, but damage to land as land or to structures as such is not shown to be more than nominal and accounts for no part of the award. The Court held that the Government "had a right to raise the level of the river to ordinary high-water mark with impunity, but it is liable for the taking or deprivation of such property rights as may have resulted from raising the level beyond that point." Turning, then, to ascertain what property right had been "taken," the Court referred to United States v. Cress, 243 U.S. 316, which it said was identical in facts, and held it had no option but to follow it and that "It results that plaintiff is entitled to recover the value of the decrease in the head of its dam."

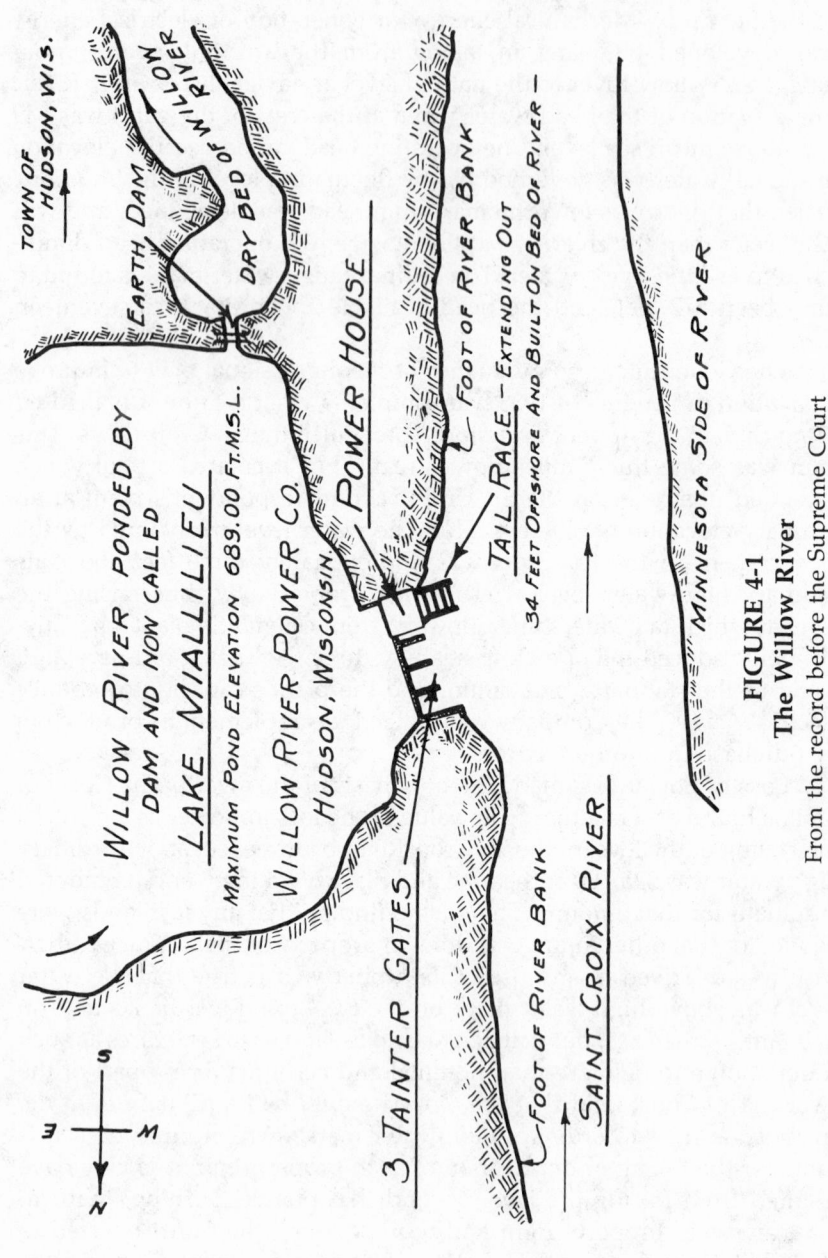

FIGURE 4-1
The Willow River
From the record before the Supreme Court

The Fifth Amendment, which requires just compensation where private property is taken for public use, undertakes to redistribute certain economic losses inflicted by public improvements so that they will fall upon the public rather than wholly upon those who happen to lie in the path of the project. It does not undertake, however, to socialize all losses, but those only which result from a taking of property. If damages from any other cause are to be absorbed by the public, they must be assumed by act of Congress and may not be awarded by the courts merely by implication from the constitutional provision. The court below thought that decrease of head under the circumstances was a "taking" of such a "property right," and that is the contention of the claimant here.

It is clear, of course, that a head of water has value and that the Company has an economic interest in keeping the St. Croix at the lower level. But not all economic interests are "property rights"; only those economic advantages are "rights" which have the law back of them, and only when they are so recognized may courts compel others to forbear from interfering with them or to compensate for their invasion. The law long has recognized that the right of ownership in land may carry with it a legal right to enjoy some benefits from adjacent waters. But that a closed catalogue of abstract and absolute "property rights" in water hovers over a given piece of shore land, good against all the world, is not in this day a permissible assumption. We cannot start the process of decision by calling such a claim as we have here a "property right"; whether it is a property right is really the question to be answered. Such economic uses are rights only when they are legally protected interests. Whether they are such interests may depend on the claimant's rights in the land to which he claims the water rights to be appurtenant or incidental; on the navigable or nonnavigable nature of the waters from which he advantages; on the substance of the enjoyment thereof for which he claims legal protection; on the legal relations of the adversary claimed to be under a duty to observe or compensate his interests; and on whether the conflict is with another private riparian interest or with a public interest in navigation. The claimant's assertion that its interest in a power head amounts to a "property right" is made under circumstances not present in any case before considered by this Court.

Claimant is the owner of lands riparian to the St. Croix River, and under the law of Wisconsin, in which the lands lie, the shore owner also has title to the bed of the stream.

The case seems to have been tried on the theory that the Company may also claim because of interference with its rights as a riparian owner on the Willow. But the Government has not interfered with any natural flow of the Willow past claimant's lands. Where it was riparian owner along Willow's natural channel claimant already had created an artificial level much above the Government level. If claimant's land along the

Willow was at all affected it was at the point where the land was riparian to the artificial channel, just back of the shore line of the St. Croix, where the land had been cut away to install the dam and power plant and to utilize the advantages of being riparian to the St. Croix. We think the claimant's maximum and only interest in the level of the St. Croix arises from its riparian position thereon and is not helped by the fact that its utilization of riparian lands on the St. Croix involves conducting over them at artificial levels waters from the Willow.

The property right asserted to be appurtenant to claimant's land is that described in United States v. Cress, 243 U.S. 316, 330, as "the right to have the water flow away from the mill dam unobstructed, except as in the course of nature" and held in that case to be an "inseparable part" of the land. The argument here is put that the waters of the St. Croix were backed up into claimant's tailrace, causing damage. But if a dyke kept the waters of the St. Croix out of the tailrace entirely it would not help. The water falling from the Willow must go somewhere, and the head may be preserved only by having the St. Croix channel serve as a run-off for the tail waters. The run-off of claimant's water may be said to be obstructed by the presence of an increased level of Government-impounded water at the end of claimant's discharge pipes. The resulting damage may be passed on to the Government only if the riparian owner's interest in "having the water flow away" unobstructed above the high-water line is a legally protected one.

The basic doctrine of riparian rights in flowing streams prevails with minor variations in thirty-one states of the Union. It chiefly was evolved to settle conflicts between parties, both of whom were riparian owners. Equality of right between such claimants was the essence of the resulting water law. "The fundamental principle of this system is that each riparian proprietor has an equal right to make a reasonable use of the waters of the stream, subject to the equal right of the other riparian proprietors likewise to make a reasonable use." With this basic principle as a bench mark, particular rights to use flowing water on riparian lands for domestic purposes and for power were defined, each right in every riparian owner subject to the same right in others above and to a corresponding duty to those below.

The doctrine of riparian rights attained its maximum authority on non-navigable streams. . . . Such streams, like the lands, were fenced in, and while the waters might show resentment by carrying away a few spans of fence in the spring, the riparian owner's rights in such streams were acknowledged by the custom of the countryside as well as recognized by the law. In such surroundings and as between such owners equality of benefits from flowing waters was sought in the rule that each was entitled to their natural flow, subject only to a reasonable riparian use which must not substantially diminish their quantity or impair their quality. It was in such a stream that this Court found Cress as a landowner under the law of Kentucky possessed "the right to have the water flow away from the mill dam unobstructed, except as in the course of nature." 243 U.S. 316, 330.

Cress owned riparian lands and the bed as well of a non-navigable creek in Kentucky. He built a dam which pooled the water and diverted it to his headrace; after it turned the wheel of his mill, it was returned to the stream by his tailrace. The Government built a dam in the navigable Kentucky River which backed up the water in this non-navigable tributary to a point one foot below the crest of the mill dam, leaving an unworkable head. The Court concluded that Cress was entitled to compensation as for a taking. It found that Cress had the right as a riparian owner to the natural flow-off of the water in this non-navigable stream. The *Cress* case is significant in that it measured the rights of a riparian owner against the Government in improving navigation by the standard which had been evolved to measure the rights of riparian owners against each other. The rights of the Government at that location were held to be no greater than those of a riparian owner, and therefore, of course, not paramount to the rights of Cress.

We are of opinion that the *Cress* case does not govern this one and that there is no warrant for applying it, as the claimant asks, or for overruling it, as the Government intimates would be desirable. The Government there was charged with the consequences of changing the level of a non-navigable stream; here it is sought to be charged with the same consequences from changing the level in a navigable one. In the former case the navigation interest was held not to be a dominant one at the property damaged; here dominance of the navigation interest at the St. Croix is clear. And the claimant in this case cannot stand in the *Cress* shoes unless it can establish the same right to have the navigable St. Croix flow tail waters away at natural levels that Cress had to have the non-navigable stream run off his tail waters at natural levels. This could only be done by an extension of the doctrine of the *Cress* case. . . .

On navigable streams a different right intervenes. While riparian owners on navigable streams usually were held to have the same rights to be free from interferences of other riparian owners as on non-navigable streams, it was recognized from the beginning that all riparian interests were subject to a dominant public interest in navigation. The consequences of the latter upon the former have been the subject of frequent litigation. . . .

However, in 1913 this Court decided United States v. Chandler-Dunbar Co., 229 U.S. 53. It involved the claim that water power inherent in a navigable stream due to its fall in passing riparian lands belongs to the shore owner as an appurtenant to his lands. The Court set aside questions as to the right of riparian owners on non-navigable streams and all questions as to the rights of riparian owners on either navigable or non-navigable streams as between each other. And it laid aside as irrelevant whether the shore owner did or did not have a technical title to the bed of the river which would pass with it "as a shadow follows a substance." It declared that "In neither event can there be said to arise any ownership of the river. Ownership of a private stream wholly upon the lands of an individual is conceivable; but that the running water in a great navigable stream is capable of private ownership is inconceivable." 229 U.S. at 62, 69. This Court then took a view quite in line with the trend of former decisions there reviewed, that a strategic position for the development of power does not give rise to right to maintain it as against interference by the United States in aid of navigation. . . . The *Chandler-Dunbar* case held that the shore owner had no appurtenant property right in two natural levels of water in front of its lands or to the use of the natural difference between as a head for power production. In this case the claimant asserts a similar right to one natural level in front of his lands and a right of ownership in the difference between that and the artificial level of the impounded water of the Willow River. It constituted a privilege or a convenience, enjoyed for many years, permissible so long as compatible with navigation interests, but it is not an interest protected by law when it becomes inconsistent with plans authorized by Congress for improvement of navigation.

It is conceded that the riparian owner has no right as against improvements of navigation to maintenance of a level below high-water mark, but it is claimed that there is a riparian right to use the stream for run-off of water at this level. High-water mark bounds the bed of the river. Lands above it are fast lands and to flood them is a taking for which compensation must be paid. But the award here does not purport to compensate a flooding of fast lands or impairment of their value. Lands below that level are subject always to a dominant servitude in the interests of navigation and its exercise calls for no compensation. . . .

Rights, property or otherwise, which are absolute against all the world are certainly rare, and water rights are not among them. Whatever rights may be as between equals such as riparian owners, they are not the measure of riparian rights on a navigable stream relative to the function of the Government in improving navigation. Where these interests conflict they are not to be reconciled as between equals, but the private interest must give way to a superior right, or perhaps it would be more accurate to say that as against the Government such private interest is not a right at all.

Operations of the Government in aid of navigation ofttimes inflict serious damage or inconvenience or interfere with advantages formerly enjoyed by riparian owners, but damage alone gives courts no power to require compensation where there is not an actual taking of property. . . . Such losses may be compensated by legislative authority, not by force of the Constitution alone.

The uncompensated damages sustained by this riparian owner on a public waterway are not different from those often suffered without indemnification by owners abutting on public highways by land. It has been held in nearly every state in the Union that "there can be no recovery for damages to abutting property resulting from a mere change of grade in the street in front of it, there being no physical injury to the property itself, and the change being authorized by law." This appears to be the law of Wisconsin. It would be strange if the State of Wisconsin is free to raise an adjacent land highway without compensation but the United States may not exercise an analogous power to raise a highway by water without making compensation where neither takes claimant's lands, but each cuts off access to and use of a natural level.

We hold that claimant's interest or advantage in the high-water level of the St. Croix River as a run-off for tail waters to maintain its power head is not a right protected by law and that the award below based exclusively on the loss in value thereof must be reversed.

Mr. Justice Reed concurs in the result on the ground that the United States has not taken property of the respondent.

MR. JUSTICE ROBERTS. . . . The respondent owned the land on either side of the Willow River at and above the point where its dam was constructed. Under the law of Wisconsin the respondent owned the bed of Willow River, and both by common and statute law of Wisconsin it had the right to erect and use the dam. That right was property; and such a right recognized as private property by the law of a state is one which under the Constitution the federal government is bound to recognize.

Unless United States v. Cress, 243 U.S. 316, is to be disregarded or overruled, the respondent is entitled to recover for the property taken by the reduction of the efficiency of its dam due to the raising of the high-water mark. If the respondent's power dam had been in Willow River at a distance of one hundred yards or more above the confluence of the two streams, there can be no question that the decision in the *Cress* case would require payment for the injury done to its water power. Since under local law the owner of the land and the dam was entitled to have the water of the nonnavigable stream flow below his dam at the natural level of the Willow River, which is affected by the natural level of the St. Croix, the raising of that level by navigation works in the St. Croix invaded the respondent's rights. This is the basis of decision in the *Cress* case. The fact that the respondent's dam is close to the high-water mark of the St. Croix River can not call for a different result.

The court concludes that the *Cress* case is inapplicable by ignoring the finding of the trial court that the increase in level of the St. Croix above high-water mark has diminished the head of respondent's dam by three feet. But to reach its conclusion the court must also disregard the natural law of hydraulics that water seeks its own level. At the confluence of the two rivers at normal high water of the St. Croix, both the

St. Croix and the Willow are at the same level. Any increase in the level of the St. Croix above high-water mark must result in raising the natural level of the Willow to some extent. The court below has found that the increase in the level of the St. Croix operates to diminish the head at respondent's dam by the specified amount. The facts thus established are in all relevant respects precisely those on the basis of which this court sustained the recovery of damages in the *Cress* case.

If the fact is that respondent discharges the water from its power plant through a tailrace extending below high-water mark of the St. Croix, that fact is irrelevant to the problem presented. Respondent claims, and the court below has sustained, only the right to have the flow of the Willow maintained at its natural level. That level has been increased by raising the level of the St. Croix above its high-water mark. The increase in the level of the St. Croix above high-water mark has operated to raise the level below the respondent's dam to an extent which has damaged respondent by diminishing the power head. To that extent respondent has suffered damage and is entitled to recover on principles announced in the *Cress* case.

United States v. Cress has stood for twenty-eight years as a declaration of the law applicable in circumstances precisely similar to those here disclosed. I think it is a right decision if the United States, under the Constitution, must pay for the destruction of a property right arising out of the lawful use of waters not regulable by the federal government because they are not navigable.

The Chief Justice concurs in this opinion.

Notes

1. *Willow River* was argued for the government by Paul Freund, then an assistant to the solicitor general. At the foot of the typed notes which Freund used at the argument is this handwritten addendum: "The flow of a nav. stream is in no sense private property. Excl[uding] riparian owners from its benefits without compens. is entirely within the govt's discr."

2. "A division of watercourses into navigable and nonnavigable is merely a method of dividing them into public and private, which is the more natural classification. . . . Rivers . . . are navigable when they are used . . . , in their ordinary condition, as highways for commerce." Nevertheless, when forced to decide whether the Little Miami is navigable (if it is, defendant's concrete causeway unlawfully interfered with passage of canoes rented from plaintiff's canoe livery), the Ohio court of appeals held that "modern utilization of our waters . . . requires that our courts . . . consider their recreational use as well as the more traditional criteria of commercial use. . . . [Therefore,] Ohio holds these waters in

trust for those Ohioans who wish to use the stream for all legitimate uses, be they commercial, transportational, or recreational." State ex rel. Brown v. Newport Concrete Co., 44 Ohio App. 2d 121, 336 N.E.2d 453 (1975).

Can *Newport Concrete* be squared with *Dolphin Lane,* p.116 *supra?*

3. The Second Treaty of Fort Laramie, signed in 1868, established a reservation of roughly 8 million acres in southern Montana "for the absolute and undisturbed use and occupation" by the Crow Tribe, and said that no non-Indians "shall ever be permitted to pass over, settle upon, or reside in" the reservation. But 1887 and 1920 U.S. statutes allowed reservation land to be patented in fee to individual Indian allottees, who could alienate to non-Indians after they held the land for 25 years. Today 28 percent of the land is held by non-Indians.

When the tribe and the State of Montana came in conflict over control of hunting and fishing within the reservation, the Supreme Court held:

(a) Conveyance by the U.S. to the tribe of land riparian to a navigable river carried no interest in the riverbed, since the conveyance did not explicitly refer to the riverbed. Ownership of the bed of a navigable river is "an incident of sovereignty." After a state enters the Union, title to the land under the river is governed by state law. Thus, title to the bed of the Big Horn River passed from the U.S. to Montana upon its admission to the Union.

(b) Because the U.S. retained "a navigational easement in the navigable waters," the words of the 1868 treaty, "whatever they seem to mean literally, do not give the Indians the exclusive right to occupy all the territory within the described boundaries . . . even if exclusivity were the same as ownership. . . ."

(c) No concept of "inherent sovereignty" supports tribal control over land now owned by non-Indians. "Exercise of tribal power beyond what is necessary to protect tribal self-government or to control internal relations is inconsistent with the dependent status of the tribes. . . ."

Justices Blackmun, Brennan, and Marshall dissented, relying heavily on the proposition that the terms of a treaty between the U.S. and an Indian tribe must be construed "in the sense in which they would naturally be understood by the Indians," words they traced to Jones v. Meehan, 175 U.S. 1 (1899), and which they said would certainly require a holding that the bed of the Big Horn passed to the Crow Tribe in 1868, especially since the U.S. repeatedly spoke to the Indians of "your country," "your land," and "your territory." Montana v. United States, 450 U.S. 544 (1981).

Part 6 considers in depth the ambiguous line between takings of property, for which the Constitution insists on compensation, and uncompensated police-power regulation. To put *Willow River* in context, however, it may be useful to recognize that when the state builds a highway, it raises and lowers the value of nearby land. Normally owners receive windfall gains and losses without being taxed or compensated. But if the state physically takes a parcel of land, it must pay for that parcel. Sometimes, the price is higher if the owner's retained land loses value because of traffic, and sometimes the price is lower if the retained land gains value because of the new transportation amenity. For an analysis of possible theoretical bases for the apparent arbitrarinesses of compensation law see Michelman, Property, Utility, and Fairness: Comments on the Ethical Foundations of "Just Compensation Law," 80 Harv. L. Rev. 1165 (1967). As an example from the horde of compensation cases, see La Briola v. State, 36 N.Y.2d 328, 328 N.E.2d 781, 368 N.Y.S.2d 147 (1975):

La Briola owned land zoned for retail business along Route 22 in Westchester County. The highway was relocated, requiring the state to "take" by eminent domain less than one-third of an acre of La Briola's 24-acre tract. But after the relocation, La Briola owned a reduced corner frontage on the old road and a short spur connection to the new route. The property's value was reduced, and it was rezoned for light industrial use. The court of appeals said that the issue was "whether that diminution was caused by compensable loss of suitable access or by noncompensable highway relocation and diversion of traffic." An appellate division decision for plaintiff was reversed, 4 to 2. The court held: "That La Briola's property would no longer be profitably used for retail business was a noncompensable misfortune. For the light industrial use still feasible, the access provided was found suitable. . . ."

Consider also the claim of plaintiffs who owned a gift shop in Massachusetts that abutted Route 10. When the road was straightened, the gift shop — which had been 9 feet from the highway — found itself on a connector-road 215 feet from Route 10 and 10 feet higher in grade. The visibility of the gift shop from the road was greatly reduced. In addition, the state refused permission to cut down trees (on state land) blocking the visibility.

An appraiser testified that after the relocation, the highest and best use for the property was for storage. He also testified that the road relocation reduced the value of the property as a whole, even though the value of the plaintiffs' adjoining residence increased.

Since 1786, Massachusetts statutes had provided for compensation for damages caused "by the laying out, altering, or discontinuing of any highway, . . . by taking . . . or by injuring it in any manner" and also for "set-off [of] the benefit, if any, to the property . . . by reason of such laying out. . . ." But since 1918 the law has provided compensation only for injury "special and peculiar to such parcel." Justice Holmes had held in Stanwood v. Malden, 157 Mass. 17, 31 N.E. 702 (1892), that "only the loss of access — the comparatively palpable injury — should be paid for, and not the advantage which the land owner had had the luck to enjoy of being where the crowd was. . . ."

The court in the instant case held: "We do not deal here in absolutes. . . . [W]e have everywhere about us instances of particular injuries following upon governmental acts which by common understanding are not expected to be paid for out of the public treasury. . . . [By] an intuitive or lay perception about the attributes of private property, . . . traffic flow would not be thought of as property. . . ." Malone v. Commonwealth, 378 Mass. 74, 389 N.E.2d 975 (1979)(Kaplan, J.).

F. PUBLIC TRUST

Is there "property" that is not available for private appropriation because it must remain "public"? Such a proposition was asserted in 1892 in the *Illinois Central* case and has achieved new life recently in a series of cases discussing public trusts over coastal and inland wetlands. Compare the following cases to the discussion of this issue in Matthews v. Bay Head Improvement Association p.124 *supra*.

◆ ILLINOIS CENTRAL RAILROAD v. ILLINOIS
146 U.S. 387 (1892)

At one time the existence of tide waters was deemed essential in determining the admiralty jurisdiction of courts in England. That doctrine is now repudiated in this country as wholly inapplicable to our condition. In England the ebb and flow of the tide constitute the legal test of the navigability of waters. There no waters are navigable in fact, at least to any great extent, which are not subject to the tide. . . .

But in this country the case is different. Some of our rivers are navigable for great distances above the flow of the tide; indeed, for hundreds of miles, by the largest vessels used in commerce. . . .

The Great Lakes are not in any appreciable respect affected by the tide, and yet on their waters, as said above, a large commerce is carried on, exceeding in many instances the entire commerce of States on the borders of the sea. When the reason of the limitation of admiralty jurisdiction in England was found inapplicable to the condition of navigable waters in this country, the limitation and all its incidents were discarded. So also, by the common law, the doctrine of the dominion over and ownership by the crown of lands within the realm under tide waters is not founded upon the existence of the tide over the lands, but upon the fact that the waters are navigable, tide waters and navigable waters, as already said, being used as synonymous terms in England. The public being interested in the use of such waters, the possession by private individuals of lands under them could not be permitted except by license of the crown, which could alone exercise such dominion over the waters as would insure freedom in their use so far as consistent with the public interest. The doctrine is founded upon the necessity of preserving to the public the use of navigable waters from private interruption and encroachment, a reason as applicable to navigable fresh waters as to waters moved by the tide. We hold, therefore, that the same doctrine as to the dominion and sovereignty over and ownership of lands under the navigable waters of the Great Lakes applies, which obtains at the common law as to the dominion and sovereignty over and ownership of lands under tide waters on the borders of the sea, and that the lands are held by the same right in the one case as in the other, and subject to the same trusts and limitations. . . .

That the State holds the title to the lands under the navigable waters of Lake Michigan, within its limits, in the same manner that the State holds title to soils under tide water, by the common law, we have already shown, and that title necessarily carries with it control over the waters above them whenever the lands are subjected to use. But it is a title different in character from that which the State holds in lands intended for sale. It is different from the title which the United States hold in the public lands which are open to preemption and sale. It is a title held in trust for the people of the State that they may enjoy the navigation of the waters, carry on commerce over them, and have liberty of fishing therein freed from the obstruction or interference of private parties. The interest of the people in the navigation of the waters and in commerce over them may be improved in many instances by the erection of wharves, docks and piers therein, for which purpose the State may grant parcels of the submerged lands; and, so long as their disposition is made for such purpose, no valid objections can be made to the grants. It is grants of parcels of lands under navigable waters, that may afford foundation for wharves, piers, docks and other structures in aid of commerce, and grants of parcels which, being occupied, do not substantially impair the public interest in the lands and waters remaining, that are chiefly considered and sustained in the adjudged cases as a valid exercise of legislative power consistently with the trust to the public upon which such lands are held by the State. But that is a very different doctrine from the one which would sanction the abdication of the general control of the State over lands under the navigable waters of an entire harbor or bay, or of a sea or lake. Such abdication is not consistent with the exercise of that trust which requires the government of the State to preserve such waters for the use of the public. The trust devolving upon the State for the public, and which can only be discharged by the management and control of property in which the public has an interest, cannot be relinquished by a transfer of the property. The control of the State for the purposes of the trust can never be lost, except as to such parcels as are used in promoting the interests of the public therein, or can be disposed of without any substantial impairment of the public interest in the lands and waters remaining. It is only by observing the distinction between a grant of such parcels for the improvement of the public interest, or which when occupied do not substantially impair the public interest in the lands and waters remaining, and a grant of the whole property in which the public is interested, that the language of the adjudged cases can be reconciled. General language sometimes found in opinions of the courts, expressive of absolute ownership and control by the State of lands under navigable waters, irrespective of any trust as to their use and disposition, must be read and construed with reference to the special facts of the particular cases. A grant of all the lands under the navigable waters of a State has never been adjudged to be within the legislative power; and any attempted grant of the kind would be held, if not absolutely void on its face, as subject to revocation. The State can no more abdicate its trust over property in which the whole people are interested, like navigable waters and soils under them, so as to leave them entirely under the use and control of private parties, except in the instance of parcels mentioned for the improvement of the navigation and use of the waters, or when parcels can be disposed of without impairment of the public interest in what remains, than it can abdicate its police powers in the administration of government and the preservation of the peace. In the administration of government the use of such powers may for a limited period be delegated to a municipality or other body, but there always remains with the State the right to revoke those powers and exercise them in a more direct manner, and one more conformable to its wishes. So with trusts connected with public property, or property of a special character, like lands under navigable waters, they cannot be placed entirely beyond the direction and control of the State.

The harbor of Chicago is of immense value to the people of the State of Illinois in the facilities it affords to its vast and constantly increasing commerce; and the idea that its legislature can deprive the State of control over its bed and waters and place the same in the hands of a private corporation created for a different purpose, one limited to trans-portation of passengers and freight between distant points and the city, is a proposition that cannot be defended.

The area of the submerged lands proposed to be ceded by the act in question to the railroad company embraces something more than a thousand acres, being, as stated by counsel, more than three times the area of the outer harbor, and not only including all of that harbor but embracing adjoining submerged lands which will, in all probability, be hereafter included in the harbor. It is as large as that embraced by all the merchandise docks along the Thames at London; is much larger than that included in the famous docks and basins at Liverpool; is twice that of the port of Marseilles, and nearly if not quite equal to the pier area along the water front of the city of New York. And the arrivals and clearings of vessels at the port exceed in number those of New York, and are equal to those of New York and Boston combined. Chicago has nearly twenty-five per cent of the lake carrying trade as compared with the arrivals and clearings of all the leading ports of our great inland seas. In the year ending June 30, 1886, the joint arrivals and clearances of vessels at that port amounted to twenty-two thousand and ninety-six, with a tonnage of over seven millions; and in 1890 the tonnage of the vessels reached nearly nine millions. As stated by counsel, since the passage of the Lake Front Act, in 1869, the population of the city has increased nearly a million souls, and the increase of commerce has kept pace with it. It is hardly conceivable that the legislature can divest the State of the control and management of this harbor and vest it absolutely in a private corporation. Surely an act of the legislature transferring the title to its submerged lands and the power claimed by the railroad company, to a foreign State or nation would be repudiated, without hesitation, as a gross perversion of the trust over the property under which it is held. So would a similar transfer to a corporation of another State. It would not be listened to that the control and management of the harbor of that great city — a subject of concern to the whole people of the State — should thus be placed elsewhere than in the State itself. All the objections which can be urged to such attempted transfer may be urged to a transfer to a private corporation like the railroad company in this case.

Any grant of the kind is necessarily revocable, and the exercise of the trust by which the property was held by the State can be resumed at any time. Undoubtedly there may be expenses incurred in improvements made under such a grant which the State ought to pay; but, be that as it may, the power to resume the trust whenever the State judges best is, we think, incontrovertible. The position advanced by the railroad company in support of its claim to the ownership of the submerged lands and the right to the erection of wharves, piers, and docks at its pleasure, or for its business in the harbor of Chicago, would place every harbor in the country at the mercy of a majority of the legislature of the State in which the harbor is situated.

We cannot, it is true, cite any authority where a grant of this kind has been held invalid, for we believe that no instance exists where the harbor of a great city and its commerce have been allowed to pass into the control of any private corporation. But the decisions are numerous which declare that such property is held by the State, by virtue of its sovereignty, in trust for the public. The ownership of the navigable waters of the harbor and of the lands under them is a subject of public concern to the whole people of the State. The trust with which they are held, therefore, is governmental and cannot be alienated, except in those instances mentioned of parcels used in the improvement of the interest thus held, or when parcels can be disposed of without detriment to the public interest in the lands and waters remaining. . . .

◆ NATIONAL AUDUBON SOCIETY v. SUPERIOR COURT
33 Cal. 3d 419, 658 P.2d 709, 189 Cal. Rptr. 346 (1983)

BROUSSARD, Justice. Mono Lake, the second largest lake in California, sits at the base of the Sierra Nevada escarpment near the eastern entrance to Yosemite National Park. The lake is saline; it contains no fish but supports a large population of brine shrimp which feed vast numbers of nesting and migratory birds. Islands in the lake protect a large breeding colony of California gulls, and the lake itself serves as a haven on the migration route for thousands of Northern Phalarope, Wilson's Phalarope, and Eared Greve. Towers and spires of tufa on the north and south shores are matters of geological interest and a tourist attraction.

Although Mono Lake receives some water from rain and snow on the lake surface, historically most of its supply came from snowmelt in the Sierra Nevada. Five freshwater streams — Mill, Lee Vining, Walker, Parker and Rush Creeks — arise near the crest of the range and carry the annual runoff to the west shore of the lake. In 1940, however, the Division of Water Resources, the predecessor to the present California Water Resources Board, granted the Department of Water and Power of the City of Los Angeles (hereafter DWP) a permit to appropriate virtually the entire flow of four of the five streams flowing into the lake. DWP promptly constructed facilities to divert about half the flow of these streams into DWP's Owens Valley aqueduct. In 1970 DWP completed a second diversion tunnel, and since that time has taken virtually the entire flow of these streams.

As a result of these diversions, the level of the lake has dropped; the surface area has diminished by one-third; one of the two principal islands in the lake has become a peninsula, exposing the gull rookery there to coyotes and other predators and causing the gulls to abandon the former island. The ultimate effect of continued diversions is a matter of intense dispute, but there seems little doubt that both the scenic beauty and the ecological values of Mono Lake are imperiled.

Plaintiffs filed suit in superior court to enjoin the DWP diversions on the theory that the shores, bed and waters of Mono Lake are protected by a public trust. Plaintiffs' suit was transferred to the federal district court, which requested that the state courts determine the relationship between the public trust doctrine and the water rights system, and decide whether plaintiffs must exhaust administrative remedies before the Water Board prior to filing suit. The superior court then entered summary judgments against plaintiffs on both matters, ruling that the public trust doctrine offered no independent basis for challenging the DWP diversions, and that plaintiffs had failed to exhaust administrative remedies. Plaintiffs petitioned us directly for writ of mandate to review that decision; in view of the importance of the issues presented, we issued an alternative writ.

This case brings together for the first time two systems of legal thought: the appropriative water rights system which since the days of the gold rush has dominated California water law, and the public trust doctrine which, after evolving as a shield for the protection of tidelands, now extends its protective scope to navigable lakes. Ever since we first recognized that the public trust protects environmental and recreational values, the two systems of legal thought have been on a collision course. They meet in a unique and dramatic setting which highlights the clash of values. Mono Lake is a scenic and ecological treasure of national significance, imperiled by continued diversions of water; yet, the need of Los Angeles for water is apparent, its reliance on rights granted by the board evident, the cost of curtailing diversions substantial.

Attempting to integrate the teachings and values of both the public trust and the appropriative water rights system, we have arrived at certain conclusions which we briefly summarize here. In our opinion, the core of the public trust doctrine is the state's authority as sovereign to exercise a continuous supervision and control over the navigable waters of the state and the lands underlying those waters. This authority applies to the waters tributary to Mono Lake and bars DWP or any other party from claiming a vested right to divert waters once it becomes clear that such diversions harm the interests protected by the public trust. The corollary rule which evolved in tideland and lakeshore cases barring conveyance of rights free of the trust except to serve trust purposes cannot, however, apply without modification to flowing waters. The prosperity and habitability of much of this state requires the diversion of great quantities of water from its streams for purposes unconnected to any navigation, commerce, fishing, recreation, or ecological use relating to the source stream. The state must have the power to grant nonvested usufructuary rights to appropriate water even if diversions harm public trust uses. Approval of such diversion without considering public trust values, however, may result in needless destruction of those values. Accordingly, we believe that before state courts and agencies approve water diversions they should consider the effect of such diversions upon interests protected by the public trust, and attempt, so far so feasible, to avoid or minimize any harm to those interests.

The water rights enjoyed by DWP were granted, the diversion was

commenced, and has continued to the present without any consideration of the impact upon the public trust. An objective study and reconsideration of the water rights in the Mono Basin is long overdue. The
water law of California — which we conceive to be an integration including both the public trust doctrine and the board-administered appropriative rights system — permits such a reconsideration; the values
underlying that integration require it. . . .

"By the law of nature these things are common to mankind — the
air, running water, the sea and consequently the shores of the sea."
(Institutes of Justinian 2.1.1.) From this origin in Roman law, the English
common law evolved the concept of the public trust, under which the
sovereign owns "all of its navigable waterways and the lands lying
beneath them 'as trustee of a public trust for the benefit of the people.' "
The State of California acquired title as trustee to such lands and waterways upon its admission to the union; from the earliest days its judicial
decisions have recognized and enforced the trust obligation. . . .

The objective of the public trust has evolved in tandem with the
changing public perception of the values and uses of waterways.

> [P]ublic trust easements [were] traditionally defined in terms of navi-
> gation, commerce and fisheries. They have been held to include the right
> to fish, hunt, bathe, swim, to use for boating and general recreation pur-
> poses the navigable waters of the state, and to use the bottom of the
> navigable waters for anchoring, standing, or other purposes.

We went on, however, to hold that the traditional triad of uses —
navigation, commerce and fishing — did not limit the public interest in
the trust res. In language of special importance to the present setting,
we stated that

> [t]he public uses to which tidelands are subject are sufficiently flexible
> to encompass changing public needs. In administering the trust the state is
> not burdened with an outmoded classification favoring one mode of utili-
> zation over another. There is a growing public recognition that one of the
> most important public uses of the tidelands — a use encompassed within
> the tidelands trust — is the preservation of those lands in their natural
> state, so that they may serve as ecological units for scientific study, as
> open space, and as environments which provide food and habitat for birds
> and marine life, and which favorably affect the scenery and climate of the
> area. . . . [Marks v. Whitney, 6 Cal. 3d 251, 491 P.2d 374, 98 Cal. Rptr. 790
> (1971).]

As we noted recently in City of Berkeley v. Superior Court, *supra*, 26 Cal.
3d 515, 162 Cal. Rptr. 327, 606 P.2d 362, the decision of the United States
Supreme Court in Illinois Central Railroad Company v. Illinois, *supra*,
146 U.S. 387, 13 S. Ct. 110, 36 L. Ed. 1018, "remains the primary authority even today, almost nine decades after it was decided.". . .

Finally, in our recent decision in City of Berkeley v. Superior Court, *supra,* we considered whether deeds executed by the Board of Tidelands Commissioners pursuant to an 1870 act conferred title free of the trust. Applying the principles of earlier decisions, we held that the grantees' title was subject to the trust, both because the Legislature had not made clear its intention to authorize a conveyance free of the trust and because the 1870 act and the conveyances under it were not intended to further trust purposes.

Once again we rejected the claim that establishment of the public trust constituted a taking of property for which compensation was required: "We do not divest anyone of title to property; the consequence of our decision will be only that some landowners whose predecessors in interest acquired property under the 1870 act will hold it subject to the public trust."[22]

In summary, the foregoing cases amply demonstrate the continuing power of the state as administrator of the public trust, a power which extends to the revocation of previously granted rights or to the enforcement of the trust against lands long thought free of the trust. Except for those rare instances in which a grantee may acquire a right to use former trust property free of trust restrictions, the grantee holds subject to the trust, and while he may assert a vested right to the servient estate (the right of use subject to the trust) and to any improvements he erects, he can claim no vested right to bar recognition of the trust or state action to carry out its purposes.

Since the public trust doctrine does not prevent the state from choosing between trust uses the Attorney General of California, seeking to maximize state power under the trust, argues for a broad concept of trust uses. In his view, "trust uses" encompass all public uses, so that in practical effect the doctrine would impose no restrictions on the state's ability to allocate trust property. Most decisions and commentators assume that "trust uses" relate to uses and activities in the vicinity of the lake, stream, or tidal reach at issue.

The tideland cases make this point clear; after City of Berkeley v. Superior Court, *supra,* no one could contend that the state could grant tidelands free of the trust merely because the grant served some public purpose, such as increasing tax revenues, or because the grantee might put the property to a commercial use.

Thus, the public trust is more than an affirmation of state power to use public property for public purposes. It is an affirmation of the duty of the state to protect the people's common heritage of streams, lakes, marshlands and tidelands, surrendering that right of protection only in

---

22. We noted, however, that "any improvements made on such lands could not be appropriated by the state without compensation."

rare cases when the abandonment of that right is consistent with the purposes of the trust. . . .

The state as sovereign retains continuing supervisory control over its navigable waters and the lands beneath those waters. This principle, fundamental to the concept of the public trust, applies to rights in flowing waters as well as to rights in tidelands and lakeshores; it prevents any party from acquiring a vested right to appropriate water in a manner harmful to the interests protected by the public trust.

As a matter of current and historical necessity, the Legislature, acting directly or through an authorized agency such as the Water Board, has the power to grant usufructuary licenses that will permit an appropriator to take water from flowing streams and use that water in a distant part of the state, even though this taking does not promote, and may unavoidably harm, the trust uses at the source stream. The population and economy of this state depend upon the appropriation of vast quantities of water for uses unrelated to in-stream trust values. California's Constitution, its statutes, decisions, and commentators all emphasize the need to make efficient use of California's limited water resources: all recognize, at least implicitly, that efficient use requires diverting water from in-stream uses. Now that the economy and population centers of this state have developed in reliance upon appropriated water, it would be disingenuous to hold that such appropriations are and have always been improper to the extent that they harm public trust uses, and can be justified only upon theories of reliance or estoppel.

The state has an affirmative duty to take the public trust into account in the planning and allocation of water resources, and to protect public trust uses whenever feasible. Just as the history of this state shows that appropriation may be necessary for efficient use of water despite unavoidable harm to public trust values, it demonstrates that an appropriative water rights system administered without consideration of the public trust may cause unnecessary and unjustified harm to trust interests.

As a matter of practical necessity the state may have to approve appropriations despite foreseeable harm to public trust uses. In so doing, however, the state must bear in mind its duty as trustee to consider the effect of the taking on the public trust and to preserve, so far as consistent with the public interest, the uses protected by the trust.

Once the state has approved an appropriation, the public trust imposes a duty of continuing supervision over the taking and use of the appropriated water. In exercising its sovereign power to allocate water resources in the public interest, the state is not confined by past allocation decisions which may be incorrect in light of current knowledge or inconsistent with current needs. . . .

It is clear that some responsible body ought to reconsider the allocation of the waters of the Mono Basin. No vested rights bar such reconsideration. We recognize the substantial concerns voiced by Los Angeles — the city's need for water, its reliance upon the 1940 board decision, the cost both in terms of money and environmental impact of obtaining water elsewhere. Such concerns must enter into any allocation decision. We hold only that they do not preclude a reconsideration and reallocation which also takes into account the impact of water diversion on the Mono Lake environment.

Notes

1. When the City of Los Angeles wanted to dredge a lagoon and build a seawall without having to exercise its right to eminent domain, it filed an action for declaratory relief and to quiet title. Claiming a public easement over the lagoon for recreation, commerce, navigation, fishing, and the passage of water, the city argued that the lagoon was an "arm of the sea" and therefore subject to the tides. The California Supreme Court accepted the trial court's finding of fact that the lagoon was indeed "tidelands." In deciding whether the lagoon was a subject of the public trust, the court first noted that Mexico, at the time of cession of California to the United States, had a law declaring the public's right to use of the tidelands. Thus the title that had been ceded was subject to the public trust. The United States had acquired the public trust as part of the "bundle of sticks" in the title. When the United States government later granted the land to individuals, it could only give what it had, which was land restricted by the public trust. Even if the language of the grants had seemed to be an unrestricted fee, and even if the individual holders had relied and invested, the public interest remained. City of Los Angeles v. Venice Peninsula Properties, 31 Cal. 3d 288, 644 P.2d 792, 182 Cal. Rptr. 599 (1982).

See, however, note 22 in National Audubon v. Superior Court, p. 186 *supra*, stating that the state must pay when its public trust use of land appropriates "improvements" that the private owner has made.

2. New Jersey permits tidal land to be sold to private owners, but since 1844 it has earmarked receipts from such sales for its public schools. When certain coastal land became extremely valuable because of the Atlantic City gambling boom, attention was focused on land of uncertain ownership. For example, what should be considered the status of land that was "flowed by the tide" many years ago, but on which substantial private investment has occurred? By referendum, New Jersey voters adopted in 1981 a constitutional amendment, N.J. Const., art. VIII, §V, par. 1, providing as follows: "No lands that were formerly tidal flowed, but which have not been tidal flowed at any time for a period of 40 years, shall be deemed riparian lands, . . . and the passage of that period shall be a good and sufficient bar to any such claim. . . ."

Validity of the constitutional amendment was upheld in Dickinson v. Fund for the Support of Free Public Schools, 95 N.J. 65, 469 A.2d 1 (1983).

As to land flowed within 40 years, to which the state retained claims, homeowners sought a constitutional amendment permitting them to purchase the rights to the lands at prices that would be determined by the legislature and could be set at less than fair market value. That attempt was defeated by the voters in 1982. As part of a large-scale effort to straighten out coastal land titles, the Tidewaters Resource Council has settled with individual homeowners for an average of $1,722, while casinos have paid a total $5 million. N.Y. Times, Nov. 7, 1982.

◆ SUMMA CORP. v. CALIFORNIA EX REL. STATE
LANDS COMMISSION
104 S. Ct. 1751 (1984)

JUSTICE REHNQUIST delivered the opinion of the Court. Petitioner owns the fee title to property known as the Ballona Lagoon, a narrow body of water connected to Marina del Rey, a man-made harbor located in a part of the City of Los Angeles called Venice. Venice is located on the Pacific Ocean between the Los Angeles International Airport and the City of Santa Monica. The present case arises from a lawsuit brought by respondent City of Los Angeles against petitioner Summa Corp. in a state court, in which the City alleged that it held an easement in the Ballona Lagoon for commerce, navigation, and fishing, for the passage of fresh waters to the Venice Canals, and for water recreation. The State of California, joined as a defendant as required by state law, filed a cross-complaint alleging that it had acquired an interest in the lagoon for commerce, navigation, and fishing upon its admission to the Union, that it held this interest in trust for the public, and that it had granted this interest to the City of Los Angeles. The City's complaint indicated that it wanted to dredge the lagoon and make other improvements without having to exercise its power of eminent domain over petitioner's property. The trial court ruled in favor of respondents, finding that the lagoon was subject to the public trust easement claimed by the City and the State, who had the right to construct improvements in the lagoon without exercising the power of eminent domain or compensating the landowners. The Supreme Court of California affirmed the ruling of the trial court.

In the Supreme Court of California, petitioner asserted that the Ballona Lagoon had never been tideland, that even if it had been tideland, Mexican law imposed no servitude on the fee interest by reason of that fact, and that even if it were tideland and subject to a servitude under Mexican law, such a servitude was forfeited by the failure of the

State to assert it in the federal patent proceedings. The Supreme Court of California ruled against petitioner on all three of these grounds. We now reverse that judgment, holding that even if it is assumed that the Ballona Lagoon was part of tidelands subject by Mexican law to the servitude described by the Supreme Court of California, the State's claim to such a servitude must have been presented in the federal patent proceeding in order to survive the issue of a fee patent.[1]

Petitioner's title to the lagoon, like all the land in Marina del Rey, dates back to 1839, when the Mexican Governor of California granted to Augustin and Ignacio Machado and Felipe and Tomas Talamantes a property known as the Rancho Ballona.[2] The land comprising the Rancho Ballona became part of the United States following the war between the United States and Mexico, which was formally ended by the Treaty of Guadalupe Hidalgo in 1848. Under the terms of the Treaty of Guadalupe Hidalgo the United States undertook to protect the property rights of Mexican landowners, Treaty of Guadalupe Hidalgo, Art. VIII, 9 Stat. 929, at the same time settlers were moving into California in large numbers to exploit the mineral wealth and other resources of the new territory. Mexican grants encompassed well over 10,000,000 acres in California and included some of the best land suitable for development. H. R. Rep. No. 1, 33d Cong., 2d Sess., 4-5 (1854). As we wrote long ago:

> The country was new, and rich in mineral wealth, and attracted settlers, whose industry and enterprise produced an unparalleled state of pros-

1. Respondents argue that the decision below presents simply a question concerning an incident of title, which even though relating to a patent issued under a federal statute raises only a question of state law. . . . These cases all held, quite properly in our view, that questions of riparian water rights under patents issued under the 1851 Act did not raise a substantial federal question merely because the conflicting claims were based upon such patents. But the controversy in the present case, unlike those cases, turns on the proper construction of the Act of March 3, 1851. . . . The opinion below clearly recognized as much, for the California Supreme Court wrote, "under the Act of 1851, the federal government succeeded to Mexico's right in the tidelands granted to the defendants' predecessors upon annexation of California," an interest that "was acquired by California upon its admission to statehood."

Thus, our jurisdiction is based on the need to determine whether the provisions of the 1851 Act operate to preclude California from now asserting its public trust easement. . . .

2. The Rancho Ballona occupied an area of approximately 14,000 acres and included a tidelands area of about 2,000 acres within its boundaries. The present-day Ballona Lagoon is virtually all that remains of the former tidelands, with filling and development or natural conditions transforming most of much larger lagoon area into dry land. Although respondent Los Angeles claims that the present controversy involves only what remains of the old lagoon, a fair reading of California law suggests that the State's claimed public trust servitude can be extended over land no longer subject to the tides if the land was tidelands when California became a state.

The Mexican grantees acquired title through a formal process that began with a petition to the Mexican Governor of California. Their petition was forwarded to the City Council of Los Angeles, whose committee on vacant lands approved the request. Formal vesting of title took place after the Rancho had been inspected, a Mexican judge had completed "walking the boundaries," and the conveyance duly registered.

perity. The enhanced value given to the whole surface of the country by the discovery of gold, made it necessary to ascertain and settle all private land claims, so that the real estate belonging to individuals could be separated from the public domain. Peralta v. United States, 3 Wall. 434, 439 (1865).

To fulfill its obligations under the Treaty of Guadalupe Hidalgo and to provide for an orderly settlement of Mexican land claims, Congress passed the Act of March 3, 1851, setting up a comprehensive claims settlement procedure. Under the terms of the Act, a Board of Land Commissioners was established with the power to decide the rights of "each and every person claiming lands in California by virtue of any right or title derived from the Spanish or Mexican government. . . ." The Board was to decide the validity of any claim according to "the laws, usages, and customs" of Mexico, while parties before the Board had the right to appeal to the District Court for a *de novo* determination of their rights, and to appeal to this Court. Claimants were required to present their claims within two years, however, or have their claims barred. The final decree of the Board, or any patent issued under the Act, was also a conclusive adjudication of the rights of the claimant as against the United States, but not against the interests of third parties with superior titles.

In 1852 the Machados and the Talamantes petitioned the Board for confirmation of their title under the Act. Following a hearing, the petition was granted by the Board and affirmed by the United States District Court on appeal. . . . The Secretary of the Interior subsequently approved the survey and in 1873 a patent was issued confirming title in the Rancho Ballona to the original Mexican grantees. Significantly, the federal patent issued to the Machados and Talamantes made no mention of any public trust interest such as the one asserted by California in the present proceedings.

The public trust easement claimed by California in this lawsuit has been interpreted to apply to all lands which were tidelands at the time California became a state, irrespective of the present character of the land. Through this easement, the State has an overriding power to enter upon the property and possess it, to make physical changes in the property, and to control how the property is used. Although the landowner retains legal title to the property, he controls little more than the naked fee, for any proposed private use remains subject to the right of the State or any member of the public to assert the State's public trust easement.

The question we face is whether a property interest so substantially in derogation of the fee interest patented to petitioner's predecessors can survive the patent proceedings conducted pursuant to the statute implementing the Treaty of Guadalupe Hidalgo. We think it cannot. The federal government, of course, cannot dispose of a right possessed by the State under the equal footing doctrine of the United States Constitution. Thus, an ordinary federal patent purporting to convey tidelands located within a state to a private individual is invalid, since the United States holds such tidelands only in trust for the state. But . . . [p]atents confirmed under the authority of the 1851 Act were issued "pursuant to the authority reserved to the United States to enable it to discharge its international duty with respect to land which, although tidelands, had not passed to the State."

This fundamental distinction reflects an important aspect of the 1851 Act enacted by Congress. While the 1851 Act was intended to implement this country's obligations under the Treaty of Guadalupe Hidalgo, the 1851 Act also served an overriding purpose of providing repose to land titles that originated with Mexican grants. As the Court noted in Peralta v. United States, 3 Wall. 434 (1865), the territory in California was undergoing a period of rapid development and exploitation, primarily as a result of the finding of gold at Sutter's Mill in 1848. It was essential to determine which lands were private property and which lands were in the public domain in order that interested parties could determine what land was available from the government. The 1851 Act was intended "to place the titles to land in California upon a stable foundation, and to give the parties who possess them an opportunity of placing them on the records of this country, in a manner and form that will prevent future controversy."

California argues that since its public trust servitude is a sovereign right, the interest did not have to be reserved expressly on the federal patent to survive the confirmation proceedings.[4] [But we] hold that California cannot at this late date assert its public trust easement over petitioner's property, when petitioner's predecessors-in-interest had their interest confirmed without any mention of such an easement in proceedings taken pursuant to the Act of 1851. The interest claimed by California is one of such substantial magnitude that regardless of the fact that the claim is asserted by the State in its sovereign capacity, this interest . . . must have been presented in the patent proceeding or be

---

4. In support of this argument the State cites to Montana v. United States, 450 U.S. 544 (1981), and Illinois Central R. v. Illinois, 146 U.S. 387 (1892), in support of its proposition that its public trust servitude survived the 1851 Act confirmation proceedings. While Montana v. United States and Illinois Central R. v. Illinois support the proposition that alienation of the beds of navigable waters will not be lightly inferred, property underlying navigable waters can be conveyed in recognition of an "international duty." Whether the Ballona Lagoon was navigable under federal law in 1850 is open to speculation. The trial court found only that the present-day lagoon was navigable, while respondent Los Angeles concedes that the lagoon was not navigable in 1850. The obligation of the United States to respect the property rights of Mexican citizens was, of course, just such an international obligation, made express by the Treaty of Guadalupe Hidalgo and inherent in the law of nations. . . .

barred. Accordingly, the judgment of the Supreme Court of California is reversed, and the case is remanded to that court for further proceedings not inconsistent with this opinion.

G. PUBLIC TRUST VERSUS PRIVATE INVESTMENT

◆ KAISER AETNA v. UNITED STATES
444 U.S. 164 (1979)

Mr. Justice REHNQUIST delivered the opinion of the Court. The Hawaii Kai Marina was developed by the dredging and filling of Kuapa Pond, which was a shallow lagoon separated from Maunalua Bay and the Pacific Ocean by a barrier beach. Although under Hawaii law Kuapa Pond was private property, the Court of Appeals for the Ninth Circuit held that when petitioners converted the pond into a marina and thereby connected it to the bay, it became subject to the "navigational servitude" of the Federal Government. Thus, the public acquired a right of access to what was once petitioners' private pond. We granted *certiorari* because of the importance of the issue and a conflict concerning the scope and nature of the servitude.

Kuapa Pond was apparently created in the late Pleistocene Period, near the end of the ice age, when the rising sea level caused the shoreline to retreat, and partial erosion of the headlands adjacent to the bay formed sediment that accreted to form a barrier beach at the mouth of the pond, creating a lagoon. It covered 523 acres on the island of Oahu, Hawaii, and extended approximately two miles inland from Maunalua Bay and the Pacific Ocean. The pond was contiguous to the bay, which is a navigable waterway of the United States, but was separated from it by the barrier beach.

Early Hawaiians used the lagoon as a fishpond and reinforced the natural sandbar with stone walls. Prior to the annexation of Hawaii, there were two openings from the pond to Maunalua Bay. The fishpond's managers placed removable sluice gates in the stone walls across these openings. Water from the bay and ocean entered the pond through the gates during high tide, and during low tide the current flow reversed toward the ocean. The Hawaiians used the tidal action to raise and catch fish such as mullet.

Kuapa Pond, and other Hawaiian fishponds, have always been considered to be private property by landowners and by the Hawaiian government. Such ponds were once an integral part of the Hawaiian feudal system. And in 1848 they were allotted as parts of large land units, known as "ahupuaas," by King Kamehameha III during the Great

Mahele or royal land division. Titles to the fishponds were recognized to the same extent and in the same manner as rights in more orthodox fast land. Kuapa Pond was part of an ahupuaa that eventually vested in Bernice Pauahi Bishop and on her death formed a part of the trust corpus of petitioner Bishop Estate, the present owner.

In 1961, Bishop Estate leased a 6,000-acre area, which included Kuapa Pond, to petitioner Kaiser Aetna for subdivision development. The development is now known as "Hawaii Kai." Kaiser Aetna dredged and filled parts of Kuapa Pond, erected retaining walls, and built bridges within the development to create the Hawaii Kai Marina. Kaiser Aetna increased the average depth of the channel from two to six feet. It also created accommodations for pleasure boats and eliminated the sluice gates.

When petitioners notified the Corps of Engineers of their plans in 1961, the Corps advised them they were not required to obtain permits for the development of and operations in Kuapa Pond. Kaiser Aetna subsequently informed the Corps that it planned to dredge an 8-foot-deep channel connecting Kuapa Pond to Maunalua Bay and the Pacific Ocean, and to increase the clearance of a bridge of the Kalanianaole Highway — which had been constructed during the early 1900's along the barrier beach separating Kuapa Pond from the bay and ocean — to a maximum of 13.5 feet over the mean sea level. These improvements were made in order to allow boats from the marina to enter into and return from the bay, as well as to provide better waters. The Corps acquiesced in the proposals, its chief of construction commenting only that the "deepening of the channel may cause erosion of the beach."

At the time of trial, a marina-style community of approximately 22,000 persons surrounded Kuapa Pond. It included approximately 1,500 marina waterfront lot lessees. The waterfront lot lessees, along with at least 86 nonmarina lot lessees from Hawaii Kai and 56 boat-owners who are not residents of Hawaii Kai, pay fees for maintenance of the pond and for patrol boats that remove floating debris, enforce boating regulations, and maintain the privacy and security of the pond. Kaiser Aetna controls access to and use of the marina. It has generally not permitted commercial use, except for a small vessel, the *Marina Queen*, which could carry 25 passengers and was used for about five years to promote sales of marina lots and for a brief period by marina shopping center merchants to attract people to their shopping facilities.

In 1972, a dispute arose between petitioners and the Corps concerning whether (1) petitioners were required to obtain authorization from the Corps, in accordance with §10 of the Rivers and Harbors Appropriation Act of 1899, 33 U.S.C. §403, for future construction, excavation, or filling in the marina, and (2) petitioners were precluded from denying the public access to the pond because, as a result of the improvements, it had become a navigable water of the United States. The dispute foreseeably ripened into a lawsuit by the United States Government against petitioners in the United States District Court for the District of Hawaii.

In light of its expansive authority under the Commerce Clause, there is no question but that Congress could assure the public a free right of access to the Hawaii Kai Marina if it so chose. Whether a statute or regulation that went so far amounted to a "taking," however, is an entirely separate question. Pennsylvania Coal Co. v. Mahon, 260 U.S. 393, 415 (1922). As was recently pointed out in Penn Central Transportation Co. v. New York City, 438 U.S. 104 (1978), this Court has generally "been unable to develop any 'set formula' for determining when 'justice and fairness' require that economic injuries caused by public action be compensated by the government, rather than remain disproportionately concentrated on a few persons." Rather, it has examined the "taking" question by engaging in essentially ad hoc, factual inquiries that have identified several factors — such as the economic impact of the regulation, its interference with reasonable investment backed expectations, and the character of the governmental action — that have particular significance. When the "taking" question has involved the exercise of the public right of navigation over interstate waters that constitute highways for commerce, however, this Court has held in many cases that compensation may not be required as a result of the federal navigational servitude.

The navigational servitude is an expression of the notion that the determination whether a taking has occurred must take into consideration the important public interest in the flow of interstate waters that in their natural condition are in fact capable of supporting public navigation. See United States v. Cress, 243 U.S. 316 (1917). Thus, in United States v. Chandler-Dunbar Co. [229 U.S. at 69 (1913)], this Court stated that "the running water in a great navigable stream is [incapable] of private ownership. . . ."

There is no denying that the strict logic of the more recent cases limiting the Government's liability to pay damages for riparian access, if carried to its ultimate conclusion, might completely swallow up any private claim for "just compensation" under the Fifth Amendment even in a situation as different from the riparian condemnation cases as this one. But, as Mr. Justice Holmes observed in a very different context, the life of the law has not been logic, it has been experience. The navigational servitude, which exists by virtue of the Commerce Clause in navigable streams, gives rise to an authority in the Government to assure that such streams retain their capacity to serve as continuous highways for the purpose of navigation in interstate commerce. Thus, when the government acquires fast lands to improve navigation, it is not required under the Eminent Domain Clause to compensate landowners for certain elements of damage attributable to riparian location, such as the land's value as a hydroelectric site or a port site. But none of these cases ever doubted that when the Government wished to acquire fast lands, it was required by the Eminent Domain Clause of the Fifth Amendment to condemn and pay fair value for that interest. The nature of the navigational servitude when invoked by the Government in condemnation cases is summarized as well as anywhere in United States v. Willow River Co., 324 U.S. 499, 502 (1945):

> It is clear, of course, that a head of water has value and that the Company has an economic interest in keeping the St. Croix at the lower level. But not all economic interests are "property rights"; only those economic advantages are "rights" which have the law back of them, and only when they are so recognized may courts compel others to forbear from interfering with them or to compensate for their invasion.

We think, however, that when the Government makes the naked assertion it does here, that assertion collides with not merely an "economic advantage" but an "economic advantage" that has the law back of it to such an extent that courts may "compel others to forbear from interfering with [it] or to compensate for [its] invasion." United States v. Willow River Co., supra, at 502.

Here, the Government's attempt to create a public right of access to the improved pond goes so far beyond ordinary regulation or improvement for navigation as to amount to a taking under the logic of Pennsylvania Coal Co. v. Mahon, 260 U.S. 393 (1922). More than one factor contributes to this result. It is clear that prior to its improvement, Kuapa Pond was incapable of being used as a continuous highway for the purpose of navigation in interstate commerce. Its maximum depth at high tide was a mere two feet, it was separated from the adjacent bay and ocean by a natural barrier beach, and its principal commercial value was limited to fishing. It consequently is not the sort of "great navigable stream" that this Court has previously recognized as being "[incapable] of private ownership." And, as previously noted, Kuapa Pond has always been considered to be private property under Hawaiian law. Thus, the interest of petitioners in the now dredged marina is strikingly similar to that of owners of fast land adjacent to navigable water.

We have not the slightest doubt that the Government could have refused to allow such dredging on the ground that it would have impaired navigation in the bay, or could have conditioned its approval of the dredging on petitioners' agreement to comply with various measures that it deemed appropriate for the promotion of navigation. But what petitioners now have is a body of water that was private property under Hawaiian law, linked to navigable water by a channel dredged by them with the consent of the Government. While the consent of individual officials representing the United States cannot "estop" the United States, it can lead to the fruition of a number of expectancies embodied in the concept of "property" — expectancies that, if sufficiently important, the Government must condemn and pay for before it takes over the management of the landowner's property. In this case, we hold that the "right to exclude," so universally held to be a fundamental element of the property right, falls within this category of interests that the Government cannot take without compensation. This is not a case in which the Government is exercising its regulatory power in a manner that will cause an insubstantial devaluation of petitioners' private property; rather, the imposition of the navigational servitude in this context will result in an actual invasion of the privately owned marina. And even if the Government physically invades only an easement in property, it must nonetheless pay just compensation. Thus, if the Government wishes to make what was formerly Kuapa Pond into a public aquatic park after petitioners have proceeded as far as they have here, it may not, without invoking its eminent domain power and paying just compensation, require them to allow free access to the dredged pond while petitioners' agreement with their customers calls for an annual $72 regular fee.

Mr. Justice Blackmun, with whom Mr. Justice Brennan and Mr. Justice Marshall join, dissenting. . . .

I take it the Court must concede that, at least for regulatory purposes, the pond in its current condition is "navigable water" because it is now "navigable in fact."

I would add that the pond was "navigable water" prior to development of the present marina because it was subject to the ebb and flow of the tide. . . .

The Court holds, in essence, that the extent of the servitude does not depend on whether a waterway is navigable under any of the tests, but on whether the navigable waterway is "natural" or privately developed. In view of the fact that Kuapa Pond originally was created by natural forces, and that its separation from the Bay has been maintained by the interaction of natural forces and human effort, neither characterization seems particularly apt in this case. One could accept the Court's approach, however, and still find that the servitude extends to Kuapa Pond, by virtue of its status prior to development under the ebb-and-flow test. Nevertheless, I think the Court's reasoning on this point is flawed. In my view, the power we describe by the term "navigational servitude" extends to the limits of interstate commerce by water; accordingly, I would hold that it is coextensive with the "navigable waters of the United States."

The Court in *Twin City Power Co.* recognized that what is at issue is a matter of power, not of property. The servitude, in order to safeguard the Federal Government's paramount control over waters used in interstate commerce, limits the power of the States to create conflicting interests based on local law. That control does not depend on the form of the water body or the manner in which it was created, but on the fact of navigability and the corresponding commercial significance the waterway attains. Wherever that commerce can occur, be it Kuapa Pond or Honolulu Harbor, the navigational servitude must extend. . . .

Petitioners do not question the Federal Government's plenary control over the waters of the Bay, and they have no vested right in access to its open water. Since the value of the pond and the motive for improving it lie in access to a highway of commerce, I am drawn to the conclusion that the petitioners' interest in the improved waters of the pond is not subject to compensation. Whatever expectancy petitioners may have had in control over the pond for use as a fishery was surrendered in exchange for . . . access when they cut a channel into the Bay.

In contrast, the Government's interest in vindicating a public right of access to the pond is substantial. It is the very interest in maintaining "common highways, . . . forever free." After today's decision, it is open to any developer to claim that private improvements to a waterway navigable in interstate commerce have transformed "navigable water of the United States" into private property, at least to the extent that he may charge for access to the portion improved. Such appropriation of navigable waters for private use directly injures the freedom of commerce that the navigational servitude is intended to safeguard. . . .

Notes

1. In 1854, the U.S. government transferred to the Omaha Indians 3 million acres in Blackbird Hills, Territory of Nebraska, on the west bank of the Missouri River. The eastern boundary of the reservation was fixed as the "thalweg" of the river, the principal channel of navigation. The river moved east and west, but mostly west. As land that formerly had been in the reservation and then was under the river dried out on the Iowa side, non-Indians occupied, improved, and farmed it. In 1975, these non-Indians were dispossessed by the tribe with help from the Bureau of Indian Affairs. Lawsuits followed, requiring construction of a rarely used 145-year-old statute, 25 U.S.C. §194: "In all trials about the right of property in which an Indian may be a party on one side, and a white person on the other, the burden of proof shall rest upon the white person, whenever the Indian shall make out a presumption of title in himself or the fact of previous possession or ownership."

Held: (a) "White person" in the statute includes individuals and corporations — but not the State of Iowa.

(b) The private non-Indian litigants must therefore shoulder the burden of persuasion as well as the burden of coming forward once the tribe has made a prima facie case of prior title or possession.

(c) Federal law governs, but should borrow state law as the federal rule of decision.

(d) The river change was by accretion, as determined by Nebraska law, so the Iowa takers get the land.

[handwritten marginalia: accretion/gradual, avulsion/sudden]

Justice Blackmun, concurring, wanted to make clear an issue apparently left open by the Court, that "white persons" includes black and oriental persons. Wilson v. Omaha Indian Tribe, 442 U.S. 653 (1979).

"Accretion," a doctrine relevant in *Omaha Tribe*, is the addition of soil by the gradual action of natural forces. When soil is added by accretion to a coastal parcel, the parcel's owner gains new territory. Similarly, when a river gradually moves away from a riparian owner, the owner's territory increases, preserving the riparian status. The opposing doctrine is "avulsion": the sudden gain or loss of land by dramatic change in a river's course or by some major coastal change. When avulsion occurs, boundaries and titles to land remain where they were. Thus when a river suddenly carves a new channel, an owner of riverside land can become, overnight, the owner of land along a dry bed. For discussion of accretion and avulsion in the context of the question of whether federal or state law determines the rules of property law as to land formerly granted by the United States, see Bonelli Cattle Co. v. Arizona, 414 U.S. 313 (1973); Oregon ex rel. State Land Board v. Corvallis Sand & Gravel Co., 429 U.S. 363 (1977).

2. Puma Volcano erupted in 1955, its lava overflowing the shoreline and adding 7.9 acres of new land to the island of Hawaii. In 1960 the Zimrings bought land that had been on the coast before the lava flow, entered upon the disputed lava extension, and made improvements including bulldozing and planting of trees and shrubs. The state sued to quiet title in 1968.

Held: (a) Before 1840, to King Kamehameha III "belonged all the land from one end of the Islands to the other, though it was not his own private property. It belonged to the chiefs and the people in common, of whom [the King] was the head, and had the management. . . ."

(b) With the Constitution of 1840, a regime of private title was instituted, under pressure from "foreign residents." The rearrangement of the land system included "a land mahele, or division, [which] was necessary for the prosperity of the Kingdom."

(c) Any land not granted pursuant to the Great Mahele or thereafter remains in the public domain. The exception is acquisition through operation of common law, for Hawaii Revised Statutes §1-1 reads: "The common law of England, as ascertained by English and American decisions is declared to be the common law of the State of Hawaii in all cases, except as otherwise expressly provided by the Constitution or laws of the United States, or by the laws of the State, or fixed by Hawaiian judicial precedent, or established by Hawaiian usage."

(d) Too few lava flows occurred in the nineteenth century to permit a conclusion about traditional Hawaiian practice on this question.

(e) "No court sitting at common law has had occasion to deal with the question of lava extensions."

(f) Giving lava extensions to shoreline owners would be inequitable: Many who are damaged by lava have nothing added to their land.

Giving the boon to the state will give the legislature funds with which to fashion a fair compensation system.

(g) Lava extensions go to the state "in public trust . . . for the benefit, use, and enjoyment of all the people." The land would be devoted "to actual public uses, e.g., recreation. Sale . . . would be permissible only . . . [for] a valid public purpose."

One dissenting judge concluded that the state's delay in pressing its claim created an equitable estoppel. He also found a problem in the chain of title. The State of Hawaii took by the statehood act of 1959. This gave Hawaii "all the public lands and other property," defined in the act as "limited to the lands and properties that were ceded to the United States by the Republic of Hawaii . . . July 7, 1898 . . . or that have been acquired in exchange for lands or properties so ceded. . . ." Since this land came into existence only in 1955, how can it be included? State by Kobayashi v. Zimring, 58 Haw. 106, 566 P.2d 725 (1977).

3. Plaintiff's property originally was bordered on the south by a creek. Beyond the creek was a spit, and beyond the spit was Long Island Sound. In a series of storms between 1938 and 1955 the spit was destroyed, after which the plaintiffs' property bordered the sound. Plaintiffs then claimed ownership of the 250 feet of beach that had been built up by the storms. Since 1959, however, the Town of Fairfield had been treating the beach as public property, maintaining a lifeguard station and keeping the area clean.

The Connecticut Supreme Court affirmed a judgment for the town holding that the beach was created by accretion; therefore, plaintiffs had title up to the high-water mark. Also, the town's seasonal use for 18 years was a well-organized activity, sufficient to create title by adverse possession. Roche v. Town of Fairfield, 186 Conn. 490, 442 A.2d 911 (1982).

4. The size of the Great Salt Lake in Utah has ranged from 1,100 square miles to 2,300 square miles. As of 1983, the lake was rising, gobbling up hundreds of thousands of acres of shore and threatening industries, parks, resorts, and highways, as well as vital waterfowl nesting areas. Utah estimated that another one-foot rise would impose costs of $30 million. In 1979, the legislature enacted a statute that the Wall Street Journal (March 29, 1983) interpreted as "forbidding the lake to rise higher than 4,202 feet above mean sea level." In fact, the statute, Utah Code Ann. §65-8a (Supp. 1983), first defined "lake" to mean "the Great Salt Lake and its environs . . . within that outer perimeter established by the 4212 feet elevation meander line," and then ordered the Department of Natural Resources to maintain the lake below that level. In February 1983, the Lake became an outlaw. "The laughter," said an unnamed state official quoted in the Journal, "could be heard all the way to Montana."

II ◆ ESTATES AND THE LANDLORD-TENANT ESTATE

What is property?

Holmes tells us that a page of history is worth a volume of logic. For understanding the current system of land law, and for working to alter it, an understanding of real property's feudal origins is essential.

Relationships among individuals concerning land constituted the basic fabric of medieval society, assigning wealth and power and shaping the system of government. In England, a system of feudal landholding was imposed by William the Conqueror and his Norman army. Aspects of that system survived the economic and social transformations of nine centuries as well as transportation across the Atlantic. This Part describes and analyzes the unique Anglo-American system of land ownership, focusing both on specific rules that affect (or infest) modern land transactions and on fundamental ideas that have remained relatively constant over the centuries and that underlie our system of rights and responsibilities toward land. We present some of this material in the words of its classic exponents: Blackstone in England, Kent and Walker in America. These scholars wrote about a system that was alive for them; they thus communicate its central aspects with an assurance and a conviction that no twentieth century author can match.

The key to medieval society was the *estate*, a term derived from the word "status." An individual's status was defined by *tenurial* relations between grantors and grantees. "He who has land, is said to hold it rather than to own it." For example, a lord was granted tenure over vast acreage by the King. He thus had the right, enforcible by the King's peace, to receive income and homage from persons who farmed that land. But as he was obligated to supply knights at the King's summons, so he had obligations to his farmers — to protect their safety and to administer justice in a manorial court, for example. The lord's "estate"

He was obligate to supply knights.
+ he had obligatins to protect safety to farmers

imposed a large number of relationships, all understood in terms of land.

Modern property law, too, is concerned with the societal assignment of regularized legal consequences to private transactions and relationships. In 1150, a "fee simple" estate in land meant certain well-understood relationships. In 1250, and 1350, and 1450, it meant that also, though in each century the detailed rules were different. So now the fee simple owner, or the life tenant, or the holder of a one-year lease has a standardized circumstance, only parts of which can be varied by individual contractual provision.

For most persons today, "property" means shelter, whether a single-family house, a rented apartment, a condominium, or a dormitory room. Decisions about the location, construction, and maintenance of housing, about who is to live in what housing, and at what price paid to whom, are matters of intense social controversy. Much of the remainder of this course is devoted to these issues. In this Part, you are introduced first to the catalogue of freehold estates: the fee simple, the fee tail, and the life estate. The Part then explores in detail a standardized "estate" relationship that had little dignity until the past fifty years but is today vital and fundamental, the "term of years" or landlord-tenant relationship. Especially in the context of urban housing inhabited by the poor, the fairness and efficiency of that relationship has been challenged, and in the past decade significant changes have occurred. Thus Part 2 seeks to teach about the idea of tenures and estates, and the way they develop and change in response to social pressures and social needs, by emphasizing recent developments affecting the landlord-tenant estate.

5 ◆ THE ESTATE CONCEPT

A. KINDS OF INHERITANCE

◆ JOHNSON v. WHITON
159 Mass. 424, 34 N.E. 542 (1893)

HOLMES, J. This is an action to recover a deposit paid under an agreement to purchase land. The land in question passed under the seventh clause of the will of Royal Whiton to his five grandchildren, and a deed executed by them was tendered to the plaintiff, but was refused on the ground that one of the grandchildren, Sarah A. Whiton, could not convey a fee simple absolute, and this action is brought to try the question. The clause of the will referred to is as follows: "After the decease of all my children, I give, devise, and bequeath to my granddaughter, Sarah A. Whiton, and her heirs on her father's side, one-third part of all my estate, both real and personal, and to my other grandchildren and their heirs respectively the remainder, to be divided in equal parts between them."

We see no room for doubt that the legal title passed by the foregoing clause. We think it equally plain that the words "and her heirs on her father's side" are words of limitation, and not words of purchase. The only serious question is whether the effect of them was to give Sarah A. Whiton merely a qualified fee, and whether by reason of the qualification she is unable to convey a fee simple. We do not think that it would be profitable to follow the discussions to be found in 1 Prest. Est. 449 et seq., and Challis, Real Prop. 215 et seq. By the old English law, to take land by descent a man must be of the blood of the first purchaser; Co. Lit. 12a; 2 Bl. Com. 220; and by the St. 3 & 4 Will. IV. c. 106, §2, descent is traced from the purchaser. For instance, if the land had been acquired in fee simple by Sarah A. Whiton's father, it could have descended from her only to her heirs on her father's side. The English rule means that

203

inherited property does not pass from one line to the other, and is like the rule of the French customary law, *Propres ne remontent pas.* P. Viollet, Hist. du Droit Civil Franç. (2d ed.) 845. In this state of the law of descent it was no great stretch to allow a limitation in the first instance to Sarah of a fee with the same descendible quality that it would have had in the case supposed. . . . Especially is this true if, as Mr. Challis argues, the grantee under such a limitation could convey a fee simple, just as he or she could have done if the estate actually had descended from the father. But our statute of descent looks no further than the person himself who died seised of or entitled to the estate. In other words, inherited property may pass from one line to the other in Massachusetts. Pub. Sts. c. 125. The analogy on which is founded the argument for the possibility of limitations like that under discussion is wanting. A man cannot create a new kind of inheritance. Co. Lit. 27. Com. Dig. Estates by Grant (A 6). These and other authorities show, too, that except in the case of a grant by the King, if the words "on her father's side" do not effect the purpose intended, they are to be rejected, leaving the estate a fee simple, which was Mr. Washburn's opinion. 1 Washb. Real Prop. (5th ed.) 61. Certainly it would seem that in this Commonwealth an estate descending only to heirs on the father's side was a new kind of inheritance.

What we have to consider, however, is not the question of descent, but that of alienability; and that question brings a further consideration into view. It would be most unfortunate and unexpected if it should be discovered at this late day that it was possible to impose such a qualification upon a fee, and to put it out of the power of the owners to give a clear title for generations. In the more familiar case of an estate tail, the Legislature has acted and the statute has been carried to the farthest verge by construction. Pub. Sts. c. 120, §15. Coombs v. Anderson, 138 Mass. 376. It is not too much to say that it would be plainly contrary to the policy of the law of Massachusetts to deny the power of Sarah A. Whiton to convey an unqualified fee.

Judgment for defendant.

A layperson's tendency is to define real property by its physical dimensions — its place in space. But the lawyer's "estates" identify duration. Originally, all estates were held by the tenant for his life only. However, as the Normans settled in England, barons and lesser lords sought to assure the status of their children and grandchildren. They also sought the power to alienate their estates to others. Over several centuries, interests clashed and combined to create a list of permitted "estates" each designating a unique potential duration.

The quantum of an estate, its durational definition, is signified by the words of limitation, the part of a conveyance that defines what estate the grantor intends to create in the grantee. Because the law recognized only a finite number of estates, the words of limitation of each convey-ance had to be fit into a regular pattern. An imaginative or arbitrary grantor could not create a new estate. The interpretation of words of limitation followed specific rules — for example, *inter vivos* conveyance was permitted unless the holder's estate had been established with cer-tain words. A conveyance transferred a fee simple only if the grantor used the words "and his heirs," which were interpreted at an early date to signify an estate of potentially infinite duration, the "largest" estate possible. Furthermore, Johnson v. Whiton illustrates the common law maxim that new kinds of legal estates could not be created; grantors had to work within the traditional forms. Consider, however, as you read about the various estates, whether Royal Whiton could have achieved his objectives by using the available common law estates.

Words of purchase are the part of a conveyance that identifies the person who receives the estate conveyed. Typically, words of purchase might be the name of the grantee, or other words that indicate who will take the interest, such as "my spouse," or "the surviving children of." "Purchase" does not refer to the type of conveyance; the grantee signi-fied may be a donee or a buyer. Sometimes, words of limitation and words of purchase merged: "to *A*" was sufficient to create a life estate in *A*.

B. THE FEUDAL BACKGROUND

◆ SIR WILLIAM BLACKSTONE, COMMENTARIES ON THE LAWS OF ENGLAND
Book the Second: Of the Rights of Things, Chapter the Fourth:
Of the Feudal System 44, 53-58 (1766)*

It is impossible to understand, with any degree of accuracy, either the civil constitution of this kingdom, or the laws which regulate its landed property, without some general acquaintance with the nature and doc-trine of feuds, or the feudal law: a system so universally received

---

* "In the fourteen centuries since Justinian's *Institutes*," writes Librarian of Congress Daniel Boorstin,

> Blackstone's Commentaries are the most important attempt in western civilization to reduce to short and rational form the complex legal institutions of an entire society. And Justinian's role in the reception of the civil law in western Europe was Blackstone's in the reception of the common law in America. . . . [M]any an early American lawyer might have said, with Chancellor Kent, that 'he owed his reputa-tion to the fact that, when studying law . . . he had but one book, Blackstone's Commentaries, but that one book he mastered.' . . . When Judge Tapping Reeve lectured to the first law school in America at Litchfield, Connecticut, he gave his

206 ◆ 5. The Estate Concept

throughout Europe, upwards of twelve centuries ago, that Sir Henry Spelman does not scruple to call it the law of nations in our western world. This chapter will be therefore dedicated to this inquiry. And though, in the course of our observations in this and many other parts of the present book, we may have occasion to search pretty highly into the antiquities of our English jurisprudence, yet surely no industrious student will imagine his time mis-employed, when he is led to consider that the obsolete doctrines of our laws are frequently the foundation, upon which what remains is erected; and that it is impracticable to comprehend many rules of the modern law, in a scholarlike scientifical manner, without having recourse to the ancient. Nor will these researches be

---

students the substance of Blackstone. . . . [Reeve's] notes were carried west to Ohio to comprise the law library of the frontier practitioner. . . .

The great reputation of Blackstone (1723–1780) rests on his four volumes. Ironically, this most famous of lawyers had little initial success at the bar, quitting London altogether in 1753 to provide at Oxford the first lectures on English law ever given in a university. With notes of the lectures circulating and a pirated printing threatened — "Copies have been multiplied," the author complained, "in their nature imperfect, if not erroneous; some of which have fallen into mercenary hands, and become the object of clandestine sale" — Blackstone published the first volume of the Commentaries in 1765. It achieved immediate success on both sides of the Atlantic; in his Conciliation speech in 1776, Edmund Burke stated that nearly as many copies had been sold in America as in England.

Blackstone's later career included nine years in the House of Commons, where he described himself as "amid the Rage of Contesting Parties, a man of Moderation." He opposed repeal of the Stamp Act and supported the expulsion of John Wilkes. Knighted in 1770, Blackstone spent his last years as a judge of Common Pleas.

To some, Blackstone seemed a mixed blessing. Jefferson was concerned that Blackstone's eloquence and clarity might strengthen the position of English Common Law — with its monarchial and aristocratic traditions — in the new nation. John Quincy Adams, wondering if the lucidity of the Commentaries might prove a trap, noted in his diary that it was a "very improper" book to put into the hands of a student just beginning the study of law but of "an inestimable advantage" to the profession.

See also Kennedy, "The Structure of Blackstone's Commentaries," 28 Buffalo L. Rev. 205, 210-211 (1979):

Blackstone is important on three distinct grounds. First, he was a pivotal figure in the development of what I will call the liberal mode of American legal thought. His work set out together, for the first time in English, all the themes that right to the present day characterize attempts to legitimate the status quo through doctrinal exegesis. Second, he presented these familiar arguments and categories as parts of a larger structure that is quite unfamiliar to the modern reader. By analyzing that structure, we can get a sense of the contingency of our accustomed modes of thought in approaching what seem the most elementary legal issues.

Third, Blackstone is supremely unconvincing. Although he made many contributions to the utopian enterprise of legality, his Commentaries as a whole quite patently attempt to "naturalize" purely social phenomena. They restate as "freedom" what we see as servitude. And they cast as rational order what we see as something like chaos. At least since Bentham's Fragment on Government, critics have linked these traits of the Commentaries to Blackstone's desire to legitimate the legal status quo of the England of his day. Thus Blackstone serves both as a convenient starting point for the substantive history of American legal thought and as a relatively easy object for the method of discovering hidden political intentions beneath the surface of legal exposition.

altogether void of rational entertainment as well as use: as in viewing the majestic ruins of Rome or Athens, or Balbec or Palmyra, it administers both pleasure and instruction to compare them with the draughts of the same edifices, in their pristine proportion and splendor. . . .

The grand and fundamental maxim of all feodal tenure is this; that all lands were originally granted out by the sovereign, and are therefore holden, either mediately or immediately, of the crown. The grantor was called the proprietor, or lord; being he who retained the dominion or ultimate property of the feud or fee: and the grantee, who had only the use and possession, according to the terms of the grant, was stiled the feudatory or vasal, which was only another name for the tenant or holder of the lands; though, on account of the prejudices we have justly conceived against the doctrines that were afterwards gifted on this system, we now use the word vasal opprobriously, as synonymous to slave or bondman. The manner of the grant was by words of gratuitous and pure donation, *dedi et concessi;* which are still the operative words in our

The Honourable
SIR Wᴹ BLACKSTONE Knight
One of the JUSTICES
of the Court of Common Pleas.

PHOTOGRAPH 5-1
Sir William Blackstone

modern infeodations or deeds of feoffment. This was perfected by the ceremony of corporal investure, or open and notorious delivery of possession in the presence of the other vasals, which perpetuated among them the area of the new acquisition, at a time when the art of writing was very little known: and therefore the evidence of property was reposed in the memory of the neighbourhood; who, in case of a disputed title, were afterwards called upon to decide the difference, not only according to external proofs, adduced by the parties litigant, but also by the internal testimony of their own private knowledge.

Besides an oath of fealty, or profession of faith to the lord, which was the parent of our oath of allegiance, the vasal or tenant upon investiture did usually homage to his lord; openly and humbly kneeling, being ungirt, uncovered, and holding up his hands both together between those of the lord, who sate before him; and there professing that "he did become his man, from that day forth, of life and limb and earthly honour:" and then he received a kiss from his lord. Which ceremony was denominated *homagium*, or manhood, by the feudists, from the stated form of words, *devenio vester homo*.

When the tenant had thus professed himself to be the man of his superior or lord, the next consideration was concerning the service, which, as such, he was bound to render, in recompense for the land he held. This, in pure, proper, and original feuds, was only twofold: to follow, or do suit to, the lord in his courts in time of peace; and in his armies or warlike retinue, when necessity called him to the field. The lord was, in early times, the legislator and judge over all his feudatories: and therefore the vasals of the interior lords were bound by their fealty to attend their domestic courts baron, (which were instituted in every manor or barony, for doing speedy and effectual justice to all the tenants) in order as well to answer such complaints as might be alleged against themselves, as to form a jury or homage for the trial of their fellow-tenants; . . . The military branch of service consisted in attending the lord to the wars, if called upon, with such a retinue, and for such a number of days, as were stipulated at the first donation, in proportion to the quantity of the land.

At the first introduction of feuds, as they were gratuitous, so also they were precarious and held at the will of the lord, who was the sole judge whether his vasal performed his services faithfully. Then they became certain, for one or more years. . . . But, when the general migration was pretty well over, and a peaceable possession of their new-acquired settlements had introduced new customs and manners; when the fertility of the soil had encouraged the study of husbandry, and an affection for the spots they had cultivated began naturally to arise in the tillers: a more permanent degree of property was introduced, and feuds began now to be granted for the life of the feudatory. But still feuds were not yet hereditary; though frequently granted, by the favour of the lord, to the children of the former possessor; till in process of time it became unusual, and was therefore thought hard, to reject the heir, if he were capable to perform the services: and therefore infants, women, and professed monks, who were incapable of bearing arms, were also incapable of succeeding to a genuine feud. But the heir, when admitted to the feud which his ancestors possessed, used generally to pay a fine or acknowledgement to the lord, in horses, arms, money, and the like, for such renewal of the feud: which was called a relief, because it reestablished the inheritance, or, in the words of the feodal writers, *"incertam et caducam hereditatem relevabat."* This relief was afterwards, when feuds became absolutely hereditary, continued on the death of the tenant, though the original foundation of it had ceased.

For in process of time feuds came by degrees to be universally extended, beyond the life of the first vasal, to his sons, or perhaps to such one of them, as the lord should name; and in this case the form of the donation was strictly observed; for if a feud was given to a man and his sons, all his sons succeeded him in equal portions; and as they died off, their shares reverted to the lord, and did not descend to their children, or even to their surviving brothers, as not being specified in the donation. But when such a feud was given to a man, and his heirs, in general terms, then a more extended rule of succession took place; and when a feudatory died, his male descendants in infinitum were admitted to the succession. When any such descendant, who thus had succeeded, died, his male descendants were also admitted in the first place; and, in defect of them, such of his male collateral kindred as were of the blood or lineage of the first feudatory, but no others. For this was an unalterable maxim in feodal succession, that "none was capable of inheriting a feud, but such as was the blood of, that is, lineally descended from the first feudatory." . . .

Other qualities of feuds were, that the feudatory could not aliene or dispose of his feud; neither could be exchange, nor yet mortgage, nor even devise it by will, without the consent of the lord. For, the reason of conferring the feud being the personal abilities of the feudatory to serve in war, it was not fit he should be at liberty to transfer this gift, either from himself, or his posterity who were presumed to inherit his valour, to others who might prove less able. And, as the feodal obligation was looked upon as reciprocal, the feudatory being entitled to the lord's protection, in return for his own fealty and service; therefore the lord could no more transfer his seignory or protection without consent of his vasal, than the vasal could his feud without consent of his lord: it being equally unreasonable, that the lord should extend his protection to a person to whom he had exceptions, and that the vasal should owe subjection to a superior not of his own choosing.

These were the principal, and very simple, qualities of the genuine or original feuds; being then all of a military nature, and in the hands of military persons: though the feudatories, being under frequent incapacities of cultivating and manuring their own lands, soon found it necessary to commit part of them to inferior tenants; obliging them to such returns in service, corn, cattle, or money, as might enable the chief feudatories to attend their military duties without distraction: which returns, or *reditus*, were the original of rents. And by this means the feodal polity was greatly extended; these inferior feudatories being under similar obligations of fealty, to do suit of court, to answer the stipulated renders or rent-service, and to promote the welfare of their immediate superiors or lords. But this at the same time demolished the ancient simplicity of feuds; and an inroad being once made upon their constitution, it subjected them, in a course of time, to great varieties and innovations. . . .

But as soon as the feudal system came to be considered in the light of a civil establishment, rather than as a military plan, the ingenuity of the same ages, which perplexed all theology with the subtilty of scholastic disquisitions, and bewildered philosophy in the mazes of metaphysical jargon, began also to exert its influence on this copious and fruitful subject: in pursuance of which, the most refined and oppressive consequences were drawn from what originally was a plan of simplicity and liberty, equally beneficial to both lord and tenant, and prudently calculated for their mutual protection and defence.

◆ JAMES KENT, COMMENTARIES ON AMERICAN LAW
Vol. 3, Part VI: Of the Law Concerning Real Property,
Lecture LIII: Of the History of the Law of Tenure 501-510 (5th ed. 1844)*

2. OF THE HISTORY OF FEUDAL TENURES IN ENGLAND

England was distinguished above every part of Europe for the universal establishment of the feudal tenures. There is no presumption or admission in the English law, of the existence of allodial lands. They are all held by some feudal tenure. There were traces of feudal grants, and

---

* "James Kent (1763-1847) felt called upon to engage in the strategic work of placing a seething urban democracy under the constraint of the common law. An ardent Federalist (and, later, Whig), he was profoundly distrustful of democracy with its 'inflammatory appeals to the worst passions of the worst men.' His opposition to the extension of the franchise at the N.Y. constitutional convention of 1821 is taken as the model of American conservatism at bay. In 1814 he was appointed to the newly established Court of Chancery. Here he remained until 1823, when the constitutional convention, by imposing a mandatory retirement age of 60, forced him to retire. From 1826 to 1830 he wrote his monumental Commentaries on American Law, published in four volumes. This work established him as the American Blackstone. It went through six editions before his death, eight more until the last one in 1873, edited by Holmes." Golden Age of American Law 101 (C. Haar, ed., 1965).

of the relation of lord and vassal, in the time of the Anglo-Saxons, but the formal and regular establishment of feudal tenures in their genuine character, and with all their fruits and services, was in the reign of William the Conqueror.

The tenures which were authoritatively established in England, in the time of the Conqueror, were principally of two kinds, according to the services annexed. They were either tenures by knight service, in which the services, though occasionally uncertain, were altogether of a military nature, and esteemed highly honourable, according to the martial spirit of the times; or they were tenures by socage, in which the services were defined and certain, and generally of a praedial or pacific nature. Tenure by knight service, in addition to the obligation of fealty and the military service of forty days in a year, was subject to certain hard conditions. The tenant was bound to afford aid to his lord by the payment of money, when his lord stood in need of it, on certain emergent calls, as when he married his daughter, when he made his son a

PHOTOGRAPH 5-2
James Kent

knight, or when he was taken prisoner. So, when a tenant died, his heir at law was obliged to pay a relief to the lord, being in the nature of a compensation for being permitted to succeed to the inheritance. If the heir was under age, the lord was entitled to the wardship of the heir, and he took to himself the profits of the land during the minority. Various modes were devised to elude the hardships of this guardianship in chivalry, incident to the tenure by knight service. The lord had also a right to dispose of his infant ward in marriage, and if the latter refused, he or she forfeited as much as was arbitrarily assessed for the value of the match. If the tenant aliened his land, he was liable to pay a fine to the lord, for the privilege of selling. Lastly, if the tenant died, without leaving an heir competent to perform the feudal services, or was convicted of treason or felony, the land escheated, or reverted to the feudal lord. The greatest part of the lands in England were held by this tenure by knight service; and several of these fruits and consequences of the feudal tenure, belonged also to tenure in socage. . . . The abuses of the feudal connexion took place equally in other parts of Europe; but the spirit of rapacity met with a more steady and determined resistance, by the English of the Saxon blood, than by any other people. This resistance produced the memorable national compact of Magna Carta, which corrected the feudal policy, and checked many grievances of the feudal tenures; and the intelligence and intrepidity of the House of Commons, subsequent to the era of the great charter, enabled the nation to struggle with better success than any other people against the enormous oppression of the system.

A feoffment in fee did not originally pass an estate in the sense we now use it. It was only an estate to be enjoyed as a benefice, without the power of alienation, in prejudice of the heir or the lord; and the heir took it as an usufructuary interest, and in default of heirs the tenure became extinct, and the land reverted to the lord. The heir took by purchase, and independent of the ancestor, who could not alien, nor could the lord alien the seignory without the consent of the tenant. This restraint on alienation was a violent and unnatural state of things, and contrary to the nature and value of property, and the inherent and universal love of independence. It arose partly from favour to the heir, and partly from favour to the lord, and the genius of the feudal system was originally so strong in favour of restraint upon alienation, that by a general ordinance mentioned in the Book of Fiefs, the hand of him who knowingly wrote a deed of alienation, was directed to be struck off.

The first step taken to mitigate the severe restriction upon alienation of the feudal estate, was the power of alienation by the tenant with leave of the lord, and this tended to leave the heir dependent upon the ancestor. The right of alienation was first applied to the lands acquired by the tenant by purchase; and Glanville says, that in his time, it was, generally speaking, lawful for a person to alien a reasonable part of his land by inheritance, or purchase, and if he had no heirs of his body, he might alien the whole of his purchased lands. If, however, he had a son and heir, he could not disinherit him, and alien the whole even of his purchased lands. . . .

Successive improvements in the character of the estate, and the condition of the tenant, greatly relieved the nation from some of the prominent evils of the feudal investiture. . . . At length, upon the restoration of Charles II, tenure by knight service, with all its grievous incidents, was by statute abolished, and the tenure of land was, for the most part, turned into free and common socage, and every thing oppressive in that tenure was also abolished. The statute of 12 Charles II essentially put an end to the feudal system in England, although some fictions, (and they are scarcely any thing more) founded on the ancient feudal relation and dependence, are still retained in the socage tenures.

3. OF THE DOCTRINE OF TENURE IN THESE UNITED STATES

. . . [M]ost of the feudal incidents and consequences of socage tenure, are expressly abolished in New York, by the act of 1787, already mentioned; and they are all annihilated by statute in Connecticut; and they have never existed, or they have ceased to exist, in all essential respects, in every other state. The only feudal fictions and services which appear to be retained in this state, consist of the feudal principle, that the lands in socage are held of some superior or lord, to whom the obligation of fealty, and to pay a determinate rent, are due. The act of 1787 provided, that the socage lands were not to be deemed discharged of "any rents certain, or other services incident, or belonging to tenure in common socage, due to the people of this state, or any mean lord, or other person, or the fealty or distresses incident thereunto." The lord paramount of all socage land is none other than the people of this state, and to them, and only, the duty of fealty ought to be rendered; and the quit-rents which were due to the king on all colonial grants, and to which the people succeeded at the revolution, have been gradually diminished by commutation, under various acts of the legislature, and are now nearly, if not entirely extinguished.

A. W. B. SIMPSON, AN INTRODUCTION TO THE HISTORY OF THE LAND LAW 21, 51 (1961): The history of tenure passes through a number of stages. In the early formative period before and after the Conquest the relationship of lord and man forms the basis of the whole organization of the country, and the tenures created form the bond of economic, military, and spiritual co-operation between high and low. Oppression and exaction are not absent, but they are abuses of a fundamentally rational system. With the decline in the value of the services and the rise of an economy based upon the payment of wages, the feudal structure tends to atrophy, and the incidents of tenure assume an increasing importance; in the field of private law a ceaseless battle is waged between those who seek to evade them, and those who seek to profit from them. . . .

In Glanvil's time [c. 1187] it is doubtful whether a tenant was entitled to alienate his holding without the consent of his lord; to be on the safe side it was wise to secure the lord's consent to a gift, but it was not perhaps essential if the gift was a reasonable one which did not seriously affect the lord's interests. . . .

In Bracton's time [c. 1250] it appears that in practice a lord could not do anything about an alienation which displeased him, and thus from the mid-thirteenth century onwards the fee has become an alienable fee; this situation was finally recognized by the Statute of Quia Emptores in 1290, which lays down that, ". . . from henceforth it shall be lawful for every freeman to sell at his own pleasure his lands and tenements, or part of them." But the Statute was devised so that lords should in future suffer no loss by alienation, for it provides that in all unconditional grants of a fee (later this means grants in fee simple) the grantee shall, by operation of law, take by substitution, and hold of the grantor's lord, and not of the grantor. This solution to the problem is a striking illustration of the lack of importance which by this time was attached to the personal relationship of lord and tenant; lords were more interested in protecting their incidents than in selecting their tenants.

C. GENERAL PRINCIPLES

◆ TIMOTHY WALKER, INTRODUCTION TO
AMERICAN LAW, DESIGNED AS A FIRST BOOK
FOR STUDENTS
Part Fourth: The Law of Property, Lecture Twenty-First:
Estates with Respect to Duration 266-269 (2d ed. 1846)*

§129. NATURE OF ESTATES

The inquiry next in order, relates to the various kinds of estates. The term, estate, when applied to realty, signifies the interest which the owner has therein: so that if I grant all my estate in a certain parcel of

---

* "The life story of Timothy Walker (1806-1856) could be narrated as a homily on the virtues of industry. At the age of sixteen he could look back on years of work on the family farm in Wilmington, Massachusetts, but no time spent on formal education. Yet when he graduated from Harvard College in 1826 he was first in his class. Three years later he entered Harvard Law School as a member of the first class since its reorganization. There he studied under Joseph Story, to whom he later dedicated his famous treatise on American law. One of his classmates was the elder Holmes, whose sharply critical son was to

land, all my interest thereby passes, without any other words. In common language, the term is used in a broader sense. Thus, when we speak of the estate of a certain person, we mean by it, all he is worth, whether of personalty or realty. But at present we are concerned with estates in their technical acceptation: and here they divide themselves into various classes, depending first, upon their duration; secondly, upon their commencement; thirdly, upon the number of owners; and fourthly, upon the conditions which may be annexed to them. . . . It has been customary to make a more general division of estates into two classes; namely, freehold estates, and estates less than freehold; . . . This doctrine originated in feudal reasons, which have long since ceased to exist. As a feud, when once created, could not be terminated by the mere will of the lord, whatever could be held as a feud, was called a frank tenement or freehold. Now feuds could not be conferred for a term of years, but were either for life or hereditary; and hence freeholds included only estates in fee, and for life. Again feuds were always conferred by corporeal investiture; and hence by the common law, freeholds could not be created without livery of seisin. This term, *seisin, seisina,* originally signified actual possession of land under a feudal grant. But when feuds became hereditary, and the heir succeeded by law to the rights of the ancestor, a distinction was made between seisin *in fact,* which was the actual possession before mentioned, and seisin *in law,* which was the right of possession acquired by the heir before entry, but not perfected into actual possession until entry. A similar distinction is said to prevail now, where the ceremony of livery of seisin is still in use, which signifies that formal delivery of possession required to perfect the conveyance of a freehold. The parties, grantor and grantee, with their witnesses, go to or upon the land, and the grantor actually delivers to the grantee a key, twig, or some other thing, as a symbol of the delivery of the land. But the case was entirely different with estates for years; not being created with feudal solemnities, they were held by the most precarious tenure; it depended upon the will of the feudal owner to terminate the tenancy when he pleased; and though he should violate

---

comment that Walker's book was the best general practical approach to the law that he could find in his student days.

"Walker was of Pilgrim stock, and it may not be a distortion to view him as a latter-day pilgrim transplanting the legal culture of the East to the then Western section of the country. (In evaluating the hypothesis of the Western frontier's influence on democratic culture, this type of Eastern export — people and patterns of life — must be heavily weighted.) He emigrated to Cincinnati, Ohio, in 1830, where he later established the first law school in the West and the fourth oldest presently existing law school in the country. In 1843 he launched a scholarly legal publication, the Western Law Journal. This was a major vehicle through which the newer society confronted Eastern legal ideas, and was the forum for many articles agitating for reform in legal procedures and institutions." Golden Age of American Law 51-52 (C. Haar ed., 1965).

WESTERN LAW JOURNAL.

No. 1.   OCTOBER, 1843.   Vol. I.

INTRODUCTORY.

At the July Term of the U. S. Circuit Court in Cincinnati, a proposition was made by the Hon. Thomas L. Hamer, that a Law Periodical should be started here, to serve as an organ of communication among Western Lawyers. The result of this movement was the issuing of the following Prospectus, which is here inserted for future reference.

PROSPECTUS OF THE WESTERN LAW JOURNAL.
TO BE PUBLISHED AT CINCINNATI, OHIO.

The undersigned propose to publish a Monthly Periodical, under the above title, which shall be wholly devoted to Jurisprudence.— They have engaged, as Editor, TIMOTHY WALKER, Esq., LATE PRESIDENT JUDGE OF THE NINTH JUDICIAL CIRCUIT, AND NOW PROFESSOR OF LAW IN THE CINCINNATI COLLEGE.

The object of the work will be to gather from, and diffuse among the Lawyers of the West, whatever is most worthy of note in their profession. To this end, they are, one and all, invited and urged to furnish Reports of interesting Cases, Notices of new Law Books, and Biographical Sketches of deceased members of the profession.

Should subscriptions justify it, the first number will appear on the first of October 1843, and thenceforward the work will be published regularly on the first of each month. Each number will contain forty-eight octavo pages, printed in the best manner, upon a superior paper, and will be sent promptly by mail or otherwise, according to order. Twelve numbers will make a volume of ordinary size, for which an index and title page will be provided.

The price will be THREE DOLLARS per annum, payable in advance. This rule must be strictly complied with. Remittances can always be made through Post Masters, who are authorized to frank letters containing money for subscriptions to periodicals. The first year's subscription must be paid immediately on receipt of the first number, or a second number will not be forwarded.

The names of subscribers should be handed in before the first of September next.

All communications relating to the WESTERN LAW JOURNAL must be addressed to   DESILVER & BURR,
Booksellers and Publishers.

In accordance with these promises, the first number is now submitted to the public. In some respects it is hardly a fair specimen of what the Journal proposes to be. I would gladly make it more *Western*, and less *Ohioan*. This I cannot do without assistance from the profession in other States, which could not be expected for the first number; but which, I trust, may be counted upon hereafter. I rely for success upon a general co-operation of the BENCH and BAR, not merely in the way of *subscriptions*, but in *the furnishing of matter*. And on this last point, I wish it to be distinctly understood, *that no article will be published anonymously.* Every contributor must take the responsibility of what he furnishes, be it for praise or censure. This is but bare justice to all concerned. With regard to subscriptions, the publishers desire me to state explicitly, *that they must be paid in advance.* The subscriptions can be transmitted through the Post Office free of charge; and unless this be done on receipt of the first number, the second will not be sent. The publishers further desire me to state, that future subscribers, on remitting the price, can be supplied with the back numbers.   T. WALKER, EDITOR.

SAMPLE DOCUMENT 5-1
Opening pages of the Western Law Journal (1843)

an express agreement, the tenant had no remedy for the recovery of possession. An estate for years, therefore, when held by so frail and slavish a tenure, could with no propriety be called a freehold. And such continued to be the law until the year 1530, when it was altered by act of Parliament; and the tenant for years was made as secure in his possession as a tenant for life. From that time, the real difference between freehold and other estates ceased; but the technical difference in the mode of creating them continues to this day in England, and perhaps in many of the states; and from this difference resulted another, namely, that freeholds could not be made to commence at a future time, while other estates could. The reason was that livery of seisin, being in its nature a present act, could not have a future operation; whereas, estates for years, requiring no livery of seisin, might commence at any time the parties should agree.

6 ◆ FREEHOLD ESTATES

A. THE FEE SIMPLE ABSOLUTE

Though the classification of estates by "freehold dignity" is clear, only a wavering line separates freehold from nonfreehold estates. The holder of a freehold is said to have *seisin* in the property, yet seisin is a term that was never satisfactorily defined. See pages 72-74 *supra*. However, *livery of seisin*, the delivery to the grantee of a twig or some other tangible symbol, in front of witnesses gathered at the property, served a practical function in the time before recorded deeds — livery of seisin announced to the world the creation of a freehold estate. The freehold estates were simply those feudal estates whose tenants could bring *real actions* in the King's courts.

◆ T. WALKER, INTRODUCTION TO AMERICAN LAW
269-270

§130. ESTATES IN FEE

An estate in fee, is one, which, at the death of its owner, if not otherwise disposed of by him, descends to his heirs . . . so that an estate in fee, is the same thing as an <u>estate of inheritance</u>. . . . [W]here it is created *by deed*, the word *heirs* is indispensable, unless otherwise provided by statute; which is not the case [in Ohio]. This is an inflexible rule of the common law, and no words of perpetuity, will supply the place of the word *heirs*, except in the grant to corporations, where the word *successors*, though not essential, is usually substituted. Accordingly, if in creating this estate by deed the word *heirs* happens to be omitted, however clear may be the intention to create a fee, the grantee will take only a life estate. But in regard to wills, this severity is relaxed, on account of

219

the hurry and want of advice with which they are often made; and there, any words of perpetuity, signifying an intention to create a fee, will have that effect. Several of the states, have, by express provision, put deeds upon the same footing as wills, in this respect; and I cannot help looking upon the common law rule as arbitrary and unjust. It is certainly in direct opposition to one of the prevailing rules of interpreting contracts, which is, to construe them most strongly against the maker or grantor, and most beneficially for the other party. But its origin is to be traced to the feudal system. . . .

What has now been said, applies to all estates in fee. But it is usual to divide these estates into two classes, *fees simple* and *fees conditional*. Since, however, conditions may be annexed to every other species of estate, as well as an estate in fee, I have thought it better to consider conditional fees, in connection with other conditional estates, in a separate division. At present, therefore, I am only concerned with estates in fee simple. This is the highest possible interest, which a man can have in real property, whether corporeal or incorporeal. It includes all interests present and future. It forms a unit or whole, of which all other estates are but fractions or parts. It comes to the owner with the unlimited power of alienation during life; and unless he does something to incumber it, passes in the same absolute character to his heirs. Such estates are obviously more in harmony with the free spirit of our institutions, than those which are clogged with conditions and limitations. It does not suit the genius of our citizens, to be put under restrictions with regard to the disposition of property. They prefer to be the absolute masters of what they call their own. Hence those "fettered inheritances," which are so common in England, are rare in this country. The prevailing estate is a fee simple. And this is one leading cause of the exceeding simplicity of our land system.

Example

O to A and his heirs (the fee simple absolute)

Grants in fee simple absolute are of potentially infinite duration, are freely alienable, can be inherited by any heir of the tenant, and are given without any conditions that might divest the tenant later. As previously noted, in an *inter vivos* conveyance the words of limitation "and his heirs" were a prerequisite to creating an estate in fee simple. However, one might well ask why both the "*A*" part and the "heirs" part are not words of purchase. Is *O* giving something to the heirs as well as to *A*? If that were the case, *A* could alienate only a life estate. You will not find a logical answer to this question. In part to favor free alienation, the courts by 1225 interpreted "and his heirs" as words of limitation. Then, in 1290, the State of Quia Emptores made a fee simple freely alienable, so long as done through substitution, rather than subinfeudation. This was done through eliminating a feudal incident, the fine a vassal paid his lord for alienating. By substitution, the grantee stepped into the grantor's shoes, assuming the grantor's relationship with his lord; thus no new tenurial relationship was created between the grantor and the grantee. Note, however, that Quia Emptores did not apply to the King's relationship with his tenants-in-chief, who thus could still create sub-tenures, but could not alienate without paying a fine to the King. The rights incident to a fee simple absolute developed gradually over the centuries; the effect of Quia Emptores over time was to eliminate inter-mediate tenures, those lodged between the fee simple tenant and the sovereign.

Today, fees simple are held directly from the state, except for anach-ronisms in a few states, especially the former proprietary colonies of Maryland and Pennsylvania. Since Lord Baltimore and William Penn took directly from the King, and were therefore exempt from Quia Emp-tores, they were permitted to establish certain subinfeudations that sur-vive to this day.

◆ VAN RENSSELAER v. HAYS
19 N.Y. 68 (1859)

Appeal from a judgment of the Supreme Court in the third district. The action was commenced in May, 1855, and was brought to recover rent arising upon a conveyance in fee, alleged to be in arrear for sixteen years to the 1st day of January, 1855. The case was tried before Mr. Justice William F. Allen, without a jury, in January, 1857.

The plaintiff gave in evidence an indenture, dated February 15, 1796, by which Stephen Van Rensselaer, the elder, the father of the complainant, in consideration of five shillings, lawful money, and of the yearly rents, covenants, reservations and conditions contained in the indenture, granted, bargained, sold, released and confirmed unto Jacob Dietz, a certain farm or lot of ground, in Berne, in the county of Albany, containing two hundred and seventy-four acres, habendum to said Dietz, his heirs and assigns forever; "yielding and paying therefor yearly and every year during the continuance of this grant, unto the said Stephen Van Rensselaer, his heirs or assigns," the yearly rent of thirty bushels, &c., of good winter wheat, to be delivered, &c., four fat fowls, and one day's service with carriage and horses. There is a covenant to pay the rent, in these words:

> And the said party of the second part [Dietz], for himself, his heirs, ex-ecutors, administrators and assigns, doth covenant, grant and agree to and with the said Stephen Van Rensselaer, his heirs and assigns, . . . that

> he, the said party of the second part, his heirs, executors, administrators and assigns, will, from time to time, and at all times hereafter, well and truly pay, or cause to be paid, unto the said Stephen Van Rensselaer, his heirs and assigns, the yearly rent above reserved, at the days and times, and in the manner aforesaid.

There is a covenant on the part of the grantee to pay all losses upon the premises, and to indemnify the grantor in respect thereto. There was also a covenant of warranty for quiet enjoyment on the part of the grantees, running to the heirs and assigns of both parties; and there is a clause authorizing the grantor, his heirs or assigns, to distrain if the rent shall be behind for twenty-eight days next after the days of payment; or, at his option, to prosecute for a recovery of it in a court of record; and also that if no sufficient distress can be found on the premises, or if there should be a breach of any of the covenants of the grantee, it should be lawful for the grantor, his heirs and assigns, to reenter, and to have and enjoy the premises as of his former estate, and to put out and remove the grantee, his heirs and assigns; and in that case the indenture is to be void. There were other provisions in the instrument, not necessary to be stated. Other evidence was given, and at the close of the trial, the judge found, besides the execution and delivery of the indenture, that the said grantor, Stephen Van Rensselaer, the elder, died on the 26th day of January, 1839; and that by virtue of his last will and testament, duly executed the 18th day of April, 1837, the plaintiff became seised in fee and owner of the rent reserved upon the indenture from the time of his death; that the defendant, before January 1, 1840, by assignment, became owner of one hundred and twenty-eight acres, parcel of the granted premises, and continued such assignee until the time of the commencement of the action; and that the proper proportion of the rent for that part of the premises owned by the defendant, for the period mentioned, with the interest, was $483.07, for which he directed judgment for the plaintiff to be entered. The judgment being affirmed at a general term of the third district, the defendant appealed here.

By the Court. Denio, J. The defendant's . . . argument is, in effect, that the law does not permit arrangements by which a rent shall be reserved upon a conveyance in fee, and that where it is attempted the reservation does not affect the title to the land, but the conveyance is absolute and unconditional. . . . We have a legislative declaration, in an act of 1805, passed about ten years after this conveyance, that grants in fee reserving rents had then long been in use in this State; and the design of the Legislature by that enactment was, not only to render such grants thereafter available according to their intention, but to resolve, in favor of such transactions, the doubts which it is recited had been entertained respecting their validity. Still, if, by a stubborn principle of law, a burden in the form of an annual payment cannot be attached to the ownership of land held in fee simple, or if the right to enforce such payment cannot be made transferable by the party in whom it is vested, effect must be given to the rule, though it may have been unknown to the parties and to the Legislature; unless indeed the interposition of the latter, by the statute which has been mentioned, can lawfully operate retrospectively upon the conveyance under consideration. It is not denied but that, by the early common law of England, conveyances in all respects like the present would have created the precise rights and obligations claimed by the plaintiff; but it is insisted that the act respecting tenures, called the statute of *quia emptores,* enacted in the eighteenth year of King Edward I, and which has been adopted in this country, rendered such transactions no longer possible. The principles of that statute have, in my opinion, always been the law of this country, as well during its colonial condition as after it became an independent State. A little attention to the preexisting state of the law will show that this must necessarily have been so. In the early vigor of the feudal system, a tenant in fee could not alienate the feud without the consent of his immediate superior; but this extreme rigor was soon afterwards relaxed, and it was also avoided by the practice of subinfeudation, which consisted in the tenant enfeoffing another to hold of himself by fealty and such services as might be reserved by the act of feoffment. Thus a new tenure was created upon every alienation; and thence there arose a series of lords of the same lands, the first, called the chief lords, holding immediately of the sovereign: the next grade holding of them; and so on, each alienation creating another lord and another tenant. This practice was considered detrimental to the great lords, as it deprived them, to a certain extent, of the fruits of the tenure, such as escheats, marriages, wardships, and the like, which, when due from the terretenants, accrued to the next immediate superior. This was attempted to be remedied by the 32d chapter of the Great Charter of Henry III (A.D. 1225), which declared that no freeman should thenceforth give or sell any more of his land, but so that of the residue of the lands the lord of the fee might have the service due to him which belonged to the fee. The next important change was the statute of *quia emptores,* enacted in 1290, which, after reciting that "forasmuch as purchasers of lands and tenements (*quia emptores terrarum et tenementorum*), of the fees of great men and other lords had many times entered into their fees to the prejudice of the lords," to be holden of the feoffors and not of the chief lords, by means of which these chief lords many times lost their escheats, &c., "which thing seemed very hard and extreme unto these lords and other great men," &c., enacted that from henceforth it should be lawful for every freeman to sell at his own pleasure his lands and tenements, or part of them, so that the feoffee should hold the same lands and tenements of the chief lord of the same fee by such services and customs as his feoffor held before. The effect of this important enactment was, that thenceforth no new tenure of lands which had already been granted by the sovereign could be created. Every subsequent alienation placed the feoffee in the same feudal relation which his feoffor before occupied; that is, he held of the same superior lord by the same services, and not of his feoffor. The system of tenures then existing was left untouched, but the progress of expansion under the practice of subinfeudation was arrested. Our ancestors, in emigrating to this country, brought with them such parts of the common law and such of the English statutes as were of a general nature and applicable to their situation, and when the first Constitution of this State came to be framed, all such parts of the common law of England and of Great Britain and of the acts of the Colonial Legislature as together formed the law of the Colony at the breaking out of the Revolution, were declared to be the law of this State, subject, of course, to alteration by the Legislature. . . . [W]ith the exception of the tenure arising upon royal grants, and such as might be created by the King's immediate grantees under express license from the Crown, I am of opinion that the law forbidding the creating of new tenants by means of subinfeudation was always the law of the Colony, and that it was the law of this State, as well before as after the passage of our act concerning tenures, in 1787. A contrary theory would lead to the most absurd conclusions. We should have to hold that the feudal system, during the whole colonial period, and for the first ten years of the State government, existed here in a condition of vigor which had been unknown in England for more than three centuries before the first settlement of this country. . . .

We are then to ascertain the effect of a conveyance in fee reserving rent, upon the assumption that the statue of *quia emptores* applies to such transactions. In the first place, no reversion, in the sense of the law of tenures, is created in favor of the grantor; and as the right to distrain is incident to the reversion, and without one it cannot exist of common right, the relation created by this conveyance did not itself authorize a distress. The fiction of fealty did not exist. The rent in terms reserved was not a rent-service. It was, however, a valid rent-charge. According to the language of Littleton,

> if a man, by deed indented at this day, maketh a feoffment in fee, and by the same indenture reserveth to him and to his heirs a certain rent, and that if the rent be behind it shall be lawful for him and his heirs to distrain, &c., such a rent is a rent-charge, because such lands or tenements are charged with such distress by force of the writing only, and not of common right. . . .

And the law is the same where the conveyance is by deed of bargain and sale under the statute of uses. Mr. Hargrave, in his note to this part of the Commentaries, expresses the opinion that a proper fee farm rent cannot be reserved upon a conveyance in fee, since the statute of *quia emptores;* but he concedes that where a conveyance in fee contains a power to distrain and to reenter, the rent would be good as a rent-charge. Blackstone says that upon such a conveyance the land is liable to distress, not of common right, but by virtue of the clause in the deed. . . .

These authorities establish the position that upon the conveyance under consideration a valid rent was reserved, available to the grantor by means of the clause of distress. This rent, though not strictly an estate in the land is nevertheless a hereditament, and in the absence of a valid alienation by the person in whose favor it is reserved, it descends to his heirs. . . .

It was stated upon the argument that the questions which have been discussed were suggested by the decision of this court in the case of De Peyster v. Michael (2 Seld. 467); and the defendant's counsel insisted that his views were sustained by the judgment in that case. The point determined was, that a condition in a conveyance in fee reserving rent, providing that the grantee and his assigns should not sell or dispose of the land without first offering it to the grantor, his representatives or assigns, and that upon every sale to another either the seller or purchaser should pay to the grantor, or those representing him, one-fourth part of the purchase price, was void as repugnant to the estate granted and an illegal restraint upon alienation. The action was ejectment to recover the premises, and the plaintiff was defeated. I have attentively examined the reasoning of the learned Chief Judge who delivered the opinion, in nearly all of which I concur, as I do entirely in the result. I consider the judgment as standing firmly upon the position that a condition to pay a quarter of the value of the land, including all the improvements which might be put upon it upon every alienation, however frequent, which the circumstances of the owner might oblige or incline him to make, is substantially equivalent to a total restraint upon alienation, and that it is quite repugnant to the nature of a fee simple estate. The Chief Judge was careful to distinguish such a restraint upon alienation from the reservation of an annual rent. "Rent," he said, "is separable from the ownership in fee of the land. The reservation of rent does not affect the alienation of the tenant's interest in the land. The reservation of the sale-money restrains, and may destroy it." Again, he said: "The covenant of the lessee to pay, *which runs with the land*, and the lessor's right to reenter for the non-payment, are practically a sufficient security for the rent." If the reasoning of the opinion gives a somewhat greater effect to the statute of *quia emptores*, and some other acts referred to, than I have attributed to them, it does not affect the conclusion which was arrived at. . . .

The result of the examination which we have given to this case is, that these covenants are available in favor of the plaintiff, and that the defendant, as the owner under Dietz of a portion of the land granted, is liable in this action for a breach of them: and we, therefore, affirm the judgment of the Supreme Court. . . .

A. W. B. SIMPSON, AN INTRODUCTION TO THE HISTORY OF THE LAND LAW, 73-74 (1961): There was another form of landholding at a rent known to early English law, and it has an odd history; the institution is known as fee farm. A tenant was said to hold at fee farm when he held heritably (in fee) in return for a perpetual rent due to his lord. The rent was rent service, and not a rent charge, for it was a tenurial service due to the lord, and carried with it a right to distrain at common law, or as the old books put it, "of common right." . . .

Fee farm was killed by the Statute of Quia Emptores (1290). The nature of the fee which the tenant had was uncomplicated; we would say the tenant's interest was a fee simple. After Quia Emptores it was no longer possible for a subject to subinfeudate for a fee simple, so that grants in fee farm, reserving rent service to the grantor as lord, could no longer be made. What had previously been a common practice passed almost wholly out of use, and previously created tenures in fee farm became treated as a type of socage tenure. In Scotland, where Quia Emptores did not apply, *feu-farm* has become the predominant tenure today. Yet even in England the practical effects of Quia Emptores could be bypassed to some extent; land could be granted in fee simple but be charged with a perpetual rent-charge in favour of the grantor, and this practice has survived until modern times in the north of England.

The excerpts from Van Rensselaer v. Hays do not include the substantial portion of the opinion which discussed the issue of whether the devisee of the grantor who reserved a claim to rent could bring an action for that rent against an assignee of the original grantee. The question turned upon interpretation of an act of 1805, which Stephen Van Rensselaer III "helped to enact." See H. Christman, Tin Horns and Calico 9 (1945).

You may wish to examine the entire opinion after our consideration of covenants running with land and covenants in gross in Part 6.

H. CHRISTMAN, TIN HORNS AND CALICO 2-14 (1945): The Patroon System which Stephen [Van Rensselaer III] and his contemporaries inherited had been engrafted on America by Kiliaen Van Rensselaer in 1629, long after it had been discarded in Holland. . . . Of six patroonships granted, his was the only one to survive the first six years, for although he never crossed the ocean to his dominions, he was as fortunate in choosing his deputies as he had been in selecting his location.

Tenants imported to secure his title were under absolute control of his agents. They were compelled to buy all supplies from the patroon's commissary at usurious prices, grind their grain at the patroon's mill, and pay over to him part of all crops and increase in livestock. . . .

As the land was cleared and farms became productive, the tribute paid by Kiliaen's slowly growing nucleus of settlers added measurably to his fortune. "I would not like to have my people get too wise and figure out their master's profit, especially in matters in which they themselves are somewhat interested," he wrote in 1629 to William Kieft, director of New Netherland.

After the British seized New Netherland in 1664, the changes were largely superficial. . . .

[I]n 1685 the governor granted a patent transforming the patroonship into an English manor and the patroon into the lord of the manor. His civil rights were restricted a bit, but there was no change in the relations between landlord and tenant.

The English almost outdid their predecessors in saddling the valley with big estates, for in addition to nine actual manors, they handed out millions of acres in patents to lesser members of the Hudson River aristocracy. It was regarded as good policy to place large tracts in the hands of gentlemen of weight and consideration, who would naturally farm out their lands to tenants, a method which would create subordination and, as the last of the colonial governors expressed it, "counterpoise in some measure the general levelling spirit that so prevails in some of His Majesty's governments."

Even the Revolution did not weaken the feudal hold of the big landowners. It merely stripped them of baronial honors and privileges. The rent-distressed tenants of New York State gave themselves and their supplies to the struggle; . . . [but] found themselves betrayed in victory, when the new government became a bulwark for the rich and the middle class against the "despised proletariat" and the rising tide of democracy.

Alexander Hamilton, John Jay, and the Livingstons worked unceasingly to keep New York the most conservative commonwealth in the new Union. In 1777 the people of the state guaranteed that nothing in the state constitution should be construed to affect any of the grants made by the authority of the king or his predecessors.

Two years later, however, under Governor George Clinton, the estates of Tories who had been loyal to the Crown during the Revolution were confiscated. In 1780, these and the lands acquired from foreclosures, tax sales, and Indian purchases were promised as bounty for Revolutionary services, but the land office was not created until four years later. By that time, the choicest tracts had been taken by prominent Federalists to satisfy their war claims, and great blocks had been sold to speculators and corporations for a pittance. Wherever impoverished veterans turned, they found the speculators had been there first. The tenant system spread, in flagrant disregard of the broader economic interests of the state. Highly skilled settlers fleeing Old World oppression and class distinctions avoided New York, rejecting its terms of perpetual tribute for the use of soil and water power. Still the great landowners would offer only leases.

Thus it was that when Stephen Van Rensselaer III came of age on November 1, 1785, Rensselaerwyck was as extensive as it had been at the death of Kiliaen in 1646, and had grown vastly in wealth and influence. . . .

The great manor had always returned income enough to support its lords in luxury, but the farms were few. Only scattered settlers had gone beyond the fertile valley lands to clear the heights of the Helderbergs, where thousands of untouched acres still awaited the ax and the plow. East of the Hudson, thousands more stretched across the rolling hills. Stephen now announced a "liberal" program to people the rest of his seven hundred thousand acres. He would give the patriots of the Revolution homesteads without cost; only after the farms became productive would he ask any compensation.

Surveyors were sent over the hills; farms of one hundred and twenty acres each were blocked out; exaggerated reports were issued about the fertility of the soil, the salubrity of the climate. Men began to come, and to each the patroon said: "Go and find you a situation. You may occupy it for seven years free. Then come in at the office, and I will give you a durable lease with a moderate wheat rent." Before long, nearly three thousand farms were taken, and villages sprang up around church spires.

Seven years went by, and the tenants came in for their "durable leases." By this time, protected by the new Federal Constitution which he had helped to frame, Alexander Hamilton had perfected for his brother-in-law a "lease" that would bind the new tenants permanently to the estate. In effect, its terms did not differ radically from those offered by the first patroon to his original settlers. By calling the contract an "incomplete sale," Stephen Van Rensselaer adroitly sidestepped the issue of feudalism, which had been outlawed in New York State in 1782 by the abolition of entail and primogeniture. He "sold" the property to the farmer and his heirs and assigns forever, on the following conditions:

As "purchase" price for the title to and the use of the soil, the tenant was to pay ten to fourteen bushels of winter wheat annually, and four fat fowls; and he was to give one day's service each year with team and wagon. He was to pay all taxes, and was to use the land for agricultural purposes only. The patroon specifically reserved to himself all wood, mineral, and water rights, and the right of re-entry to exploit these resources. The tenant could not sell the property, but only his contract of incomplete sale, with its terms unaltered. A "quarter-sale" clause restricted him still further: if he wished to sell, the landlord had the option of collecting one-fourth of the sale price or recovering full title to the property at three-quarters of the market price. Thus the landlord kept for himself all the advantages of landownership while saddling the "tenant" with all the obligations, such as taxes and road-building. . . .

Any offer to buy the land outright was scorned, for no investment could be so secure for the landlord as this perpetual interest in the produce of his land. Only a few tenants had the courage and the hardihood to refuse the leases and turn to the wilderness to begin their toil anew. The rest remained in a serfdom which was, for all practical purposes, complete. . . .

Stephen Van Rensselaer was too realistic not to know that the semifeudal power of the Hudson Valley aristocracy was an anachronism, and that a single act of provocation might crystallize democratic opposition. Knowing the history of his title, he was constantly harried by doubts of its legality. . . . [Therefore, he avoided] forcing issues whenever he could, earning thereby the name of "Good Patroon." In hard times he let the rents accumulate. Even when the depression of 1837 pinched him so critically that he complained to Van Buren, then President of the United States, the Good Patroon could not be persuaded to press the tenants for back rents. . . . The Good Patroon could well afford philanthropy. His rule over Rensselaerwyck had paid him an estimated forty-one million dollars. With Hamilton's aid he had extended his holdings to include extensive tracts in northern New York and considerable real estate in New York City. He was counted by many the richest man in America.

The will of Stephen Van Rensselaer III directed that back rents be collected in order to pay the debts of his estate. As his sons attempted to exact the rents, an Anti-Rent resistance movement began which gradually encompassed thousands of tenant farmers. The tenants tried to accomplish their goals through electoral politics and appeals to the legislature, but met with little success. During this time, the electoral approach was supplemented by the use of groups of tenants in Indian costumes, who blocked rent collectors and sheriffs from serving eviction notices and distraining tenant goods. Tar and featherings were common, and several deaths occurred before the issues were resolved.

The Anti-Rent movement reached its greatest level of militancy in the mid-1840s, and some of its leaders dreamed of merging it with groups advocating public ownership of land and abolition of slavery, in order to form a new political party. However, the strength of the most radical element of the movement was substantially diminished after 1845; in that year, after an incident in which a deputy sheriff was killed, 200 Anti-Renters were indicted, half of them for felony-murder. At the end of their trials, two were sentenced to death (though later pardoned), and more than 60 received prison sentences or fines. After this crippling of the independent Anti-Rent leadership, Democratic and Whig politicians found it easier to channel the movement into more conventional forms of political activity.

De Peyster v. Michael, see page 225 supra, was a rare judicial victory for the Anti-Renters; Van Rensselaer v. Hays is far more typical of the tenant treatment in court, even after the tenant-advocated reform of popular election of the judiciary was achieved.

SUTHERLAND, TENANTRY OF THE NEW YORK MANORS: A CHAPTER OF LEGAL HISTORY, 41 Cornell L.Q. 620, 636 (1956): The Good Patroon owed almost as much when he died as the arrears in rent, approaching $400,000, which were then owing to him. [Colonel Walter] Church [who bought out Stephen Van Rensselaer IV's rights for $210,000] found the pickings in the west manor so slight that he was unable to carry out his original commitment for the purchase price.

The Van Rensselaer heir on the east side of the Hudson made an assignment for his creditors in 1848, and Colonel Church finally agreed to buy his rights, nominally amounting to more than $200,000, for less than fifty cents on the dollar. The next year this was scaled down to $57,303.07. Church still found payment of the price difficult: by 1863 the East Manor claims had been divided among twenty-one different owners; they sold for five to twenty-five cents on the dollar. Church continued to struggle to collect rents with diminishing success until his death in comparative financial straits in 1890. The expense of collecting small claims for rent by levy and sale must have been considerable even when it was ultimately successful. Most landlords decided to sell out. Of the 3,325 farms in Albany County shown in the census of 1880, 2,635 were then occupied and worked by their owners and only 690 were held upon lease. Stephen Van Rensselaer alone had had twice that many farms under lease in Albany County in 1846. By 1880 in Delaware County where the rent troubles of the '40's had reached their greatest intensity, there were only 688 leased farms out of a total of 5,264. The proportion of leased farms was no greater than that in any other portion of the state or in other eastern states.

B. THE FEE TAIL

◆ LONG v. LONG
45 Ohio St. 2d 165, 343 N.E.2d 100 (1976)

Plaintiff-appellees herein, Howard W. Long and Paul H. Olinger, the grandsons of Henry Long, commenced a declaratory judgment action in the Court of Common Pleas of Darke County, Probate Division, against the defendant-appellant herein, Bessie Long, the widow and beneficiary of Eugene Long, the deceased brother of appellee, Howard W. Long, to determine the ownership of certain real property.

The undisputed facts are as follows:

On April 2, 1919, Henry Long conveyed three separate tracts of land in fee tail to each of his three children, Jesse Long, Edward W. Long and Emma Long Olinger. The latter two were survived by living children who took their respective tracts in fee simple, pursuant to R.C. 2131.08. Their parcels are not involved in the present controversy.

The granting clause in the deed from Henry Long to Jesse Long, which is similar to those conveying the other parcels to the other children, reads, in part: ". . . to . . . Jesse S. Long, and the children of his body begotten, and their heirs and assigns forever. . . ." Henry Long died testate in August 1932. His will contained no general residuary clause, but provided in Item IV, as follows:

> At the decease of my wife I will and direct that my executor sell all my real estate, at public or private sale as deemed best at the time, and reduce all my personal estate into money, and from said funds then pay, — 1st to my then living grandchildren the sum of Three Thousand Dollars ($3,000.00) to be divided equally among such grand-children and the residue to my three children, or their issue, if any be deceased with issue — if any of my children at the time of such division, be deceased, leaving no issue, no part of said funds shall pass to the estate of such deceased.

Edward Long died intestate in March 1946, survived by his wife, Emma, and sons, Howard and Eugene. Emma Long died testate on July 3, 1964, survived by Howard and Eugene. Her will contained a clause dividing her residuary estate equally between her sons. Eugene died testate in October 1966 without issue, and was survived by his wife, Bessie Long. His will made Bessie Long his sole beneficiary and specifically mentioned the real estate in controversy.

Emma Long Olinger was predeceased by her husband and died intestate on October 19, 1954, survived by a son, Paul H. Olinger.

In 1945, Jesse Long executed a quitclaim deed conveying whatever interest he had in the property in question to Rosella Long, who died testate and made Marie Ethel Brown and her husband, John Brown, her sole beneficiaries. The Browns subsequently executed a quitclaim deed conveying whatever interest they had in the property to Howard W. Long and his wife, Esther Naomi Long.

Jesse Long died intestate on March 4, 1974, without issue.

The appellant, Bessie Long, maintains that, "where a grantor deeds real estate to his son and to the children of his body begotten, their heirs and assigns forever, and such son dies without having sired a child, a possibility of reverter remains in the original grantor of such fee tail estate which is a descendible, devisable estate at the death of the original grantor of the estate tail." Appellant contends that, from the time Henry Long conveyed the fee tail estate to Jesse Long, there remained in him, as the grantor, a "possibility of reverter." Appellant argues that this "possibility of reverter" was a descendible, devisable interest and, therefore, passed at the grantor's death to his heirs existing at that time. Appellant contends that Item IV of Henry Long's will expressed an intention to convey the residue of his estate only to those surviving children who had issue and, therefore, Jesse Long's conveyance was ineffective. Appellant maintains that the possibility of reverter following Jesse Long's fee tail descended or was devised, one-half to Edward Long and one-half to Emma Long Olinger.

Appellant claims, through her deceased husband, Eugene Long, a one-fourth interest in the property from Edward's portion. Appellant also maintains that Howard W. Long received the other one-fourth interest from Edward's portion and that Paul Olinger, Emma Long Olinger's son, received, by descent, Emma's one-half interest in the possibility of reverter.

The Probate Court determined that a possibility of reverter is not an estate of inheritance and that, upon the happening of the contingency, the grantee's death without issue, the property passes to the next of kin and heirs at law of the grantor then living — in the present case the appellees, Howard Long and Paul Olinger.

J.J.P. CORRIGAN, Justice. The unique issue in this case concerns the nature of the interest remaining in the grantor, Henry Long, after the creation by deed of a fee tail estate which was conveyed by the grantor to his son "Jesse S. Long, and the children of his body begotten, and their heirs and assigns forever."

The parties agree that the estate created . . . was a fee tail.

Appellant maintains that the interest remaining in the grantor is a "possibility of reverter" which is a descendible, devisable estate at the death of the original grantor of the estate tail. Appellant contends that, upon the death of the first donee in tail without issue, the interest then passes to the heirs of the grantor living at his death, and to their descendants.

The appellees, too, maintain that the interest remaining in the grantor of a fee tail estate is a possibility of reverter. Appellees contend, however, that this possibility of reverter was not of sufficient quality to descend to an heir until the donee in tail dies without issue. At this point, appellees argue, the possibility ripens into a fee simple estate in the grantor and, where he has predeceased the donee in tail, the estate then passes by the law of intestate succession to his heirs living at the time of the ripening of the possibility. . . .

Considerable confusion exists in the present case because of the term used to designate the nature of the grantor's future interest in the property conveyed.

At early common law, prior to the enactment of the Statute of Westminster, 13 Edward I. Chapter 1, *De Donis Conditionalibus*, in 1285, the transfer of a fee restrained to some particular heirs exclusive of others, e.g., to the heirs of a man's body, created an estate designated a fee simple conditional.

The future interest in the grantor of a conditional fee at common law was generally called a possibility of reversion or right of reverter. The usual practice at common law, however, was for the tenant in tail to alien the land conveyed and afterward repurchase, taking an absolute estate in the land which would descend to his heirs generally and prevent any reversion to the donor. To prevent this practice, the statute *de donis* was enacted, imposing a restraint upon the power of alienation by the tenant in tail. Prior to the enactment of the statute, a fee simple conditional became absolute upon the birth of issue. By operation of the statute the tenant now held an estate tail and the donor had a reversion of fee simple expectant on the failure of the issue in tail. The tenant could no longer alien, upon his having issue, but the feud (estate) was to remain to the issue according to the form of the gift, i.e., the issue of the donee in tail took *per formam doni* (by the form of the gift) or from the grantor rather than through any particular tenant in tail. The statute preserved the estate for the benefit of the issue of the grantee and the reversion for the benefit of the donor and his heirs by declaring that the intention of the donor manifestly expressed according to the form of the deed should be observed.

The real source of the title was the donor, himself, who always retained a reversion expectant upon the failure of issue.

It should be noted that the statute *de donis* did not create the estate tail but rather gave it perpetuity.

More importantly, for purposes of the present case, the statute *de donis* converted the donor's bare possibility of reversion or right of reverter into a reversion or fee simple expectant upon failure of issue. This distinction is important because a reversion in fee is a vested interest or estate and is descendible, alienable or assignable by deed or conveyance, and is also devisable.

A reversion is the residue of an estate left in the grantor or other transferor, to commence in possession after the determination of some particular estate transferred by him. A reversion arises only by operation of law and is a vested right.

A reversion arises whenever a person having a vested estate transfers to another a lesser vested estate. Since the reversion is the undisposed of portion of a vested estate, it follows that all reversions are vested interests. A reversion is said to be vested because there is no condition precedent to the taking effect in possession other than the termination of the preceding estates. This does not mean, however, that every reversion is certain to take effect in possession and enjoyment. The distinguishing feature of the reversion is that it is not subject to a condition precedent to its taking effect in possession, and all other conditions defeating a reversion are regarded as conditions subsequent.

A reversion is historically distinguishable from a possibility of reverter in that a reversion arises when the estate transferred is of a lesser quantum than the transferor owns. A possibility of reverter arises when the estate conveyed is of the (same) quantum as the transferor owns.

In Ohio, the term "possibility of reverter" is used to denominate the future interest remaining in the transferor of a "qualified fee."

Ohio cases have held that this interest is not an estate but only the possibility of having an estate at a future time, and that the estate is vested in the grantee, subject to divestment at a future time.

The possibility of reverter is regarded as a lesser interest than the reversion because of the nature of the fee transferred. The term "qualified fee" is used to designate those fees which descend as fees simple but which will, or may, terminate or be subject to termination upon the occurrence of a stated event. Such fees include fees simple determinable, fees simple subject to condition subsequent, fees simple subject to executory limitation and conditional fees, in those jurisdictions in which the fee tail has been completely abolished and the predecessor conditional fee is still recognized. Qualified fees do not include the fee simple absolute or the fee tail.

Possibilities of reverter and the right of entry for condition broken following a fee simple condition subsequent were not alienable *inter vivos* or devisable prior to the enactment of R.C. 2131.04 (G.C. 10512-4) in 1932. Both, however, appear always to have been capable of descent, and either interest might be released to the holder of the possessory interest in the land. These interests are clearly distinguishable in their incidents from the reversion which is [a] vested estate, descendible, alienable, assignable and devisable. . . .

The only remaining issue to consider is whether the Ohio enactment of 1811 (10 Ohio Laws 7),* modifying fee tail estates, has had any effect on the reversionary interest in the grantor.

In Pollock v. Speidel, 17 Ohio St. 439, this court recognized the continued existence of estates tail in Ohio, subject to the statutory modification enacted in 1811, and now embodied in R.C. 2131.08, which

---

*"AN ACT to restrict the entailment of real estate.

Sect. 1 Be it enacted by the General Assembly of the state of Ohio. That from and after the taking effect of this act, no estate in fee simple, fee tail, or any lesser estate in lands or tenements, lying within this state, shall be given or granted by deed or will to any person or persons, but such as are in being, or to the immediate issue or descendants of such as are in being at the time of making such deed or will, and that all estates given in tail shall be and remain an absolute estate in fee simple to the issue of the first donee in tail. ·

This act to take effect and be in force from and after the first day of June next. . . . December 17, 1811."

converted estates tail into fees simple in the hands of the issue of the first donee in tail. Subsequent decisions . . . made it clear that the statutory enactment did not change the nature of the estate tail in the donee in tail from an inheritable estate to an estate for life merely but restricted the entailment to the immediate issue of such donee.

Ohio courts have also recognized the existence of a reversion in the grantor of an estate tail. . . .

In accordance with the undisputed authority that the interest created in the grantor of a common-law fee tail estate is a vested reversion, and in view of the decisions to the effect that the Ohio enactment restricting fee tail estates does not alter the fundamental nature of the estate tail in the first donee in tail, we hold that such reversions are vested estates fully descendible, devisable and alienable *inter vivos*.

As a result, in the present case, the series of conveyances begun by Henry Long's deceased son, Jesse Long, were effective to convey his one-third reversionary interest in the property to appellee Howard W. Long, and Esther Naomi Long, one-sixth to each.

As to Henry Long's son, Edward Long, who died intestate, his one-third reversionary interest in the property descended, one-half or a one-sixth share to his son, appellee Howard W. Long, and the other one-half interest or one-sixth share to his other son, Eugene Long. Eugene Long died testate in 1966, specifically devising his estate including the one-sixth share of the reversion to his wife, appellant Bessie Long.

As to Henry Long's daughter, Emma Long Olinger, who died intestate, her one-third share of the reversion descended to her son, appellee Paul H. Olinger.

The present ownership of the realty in question rests, therefore, in the following undivided interests:

1. Esther Naomi Long, wife of Howard W. Long . . . . . one-sixth (from Jesse's portion)
2. Howard W. Long (Appellee) . . . . . one-sixth (from Jesse's portion) and . . . . . one-sixth (from Edward's portion) Howard W. Long's Total Interest is . . . . . one-third
3. Bessie Long (Appellant) . . . . . one-sixth (from Edward's portion)
4. Paul H. Olinger . . . . . one-third (Emma Long Olinger's portion)

Examples

(a) *O to A and the heirs of his body* (fee tail)
(b) *O to A and the male heirs of his body* (fee tail male)
(c) *O to A and the heirs of his body by his wife Mary* (fee tail special)

*oldest
heir*

The fee tail — along with primogeniture — was the legal basis of the English manorial system that succeeded feudalism as the basic political and economic order. It was the legal instrumentality for preserving a landed aristocracy by keeping property in a continual family line, and preventing its dissipation at the whim of a particular generation.

The fee tail experienced a checkered history. Favoring free alienation, the early common law courts defeated the intent of the grantor by holding that a fee simple conditional, as the conveyance "O to A and the heirs of his body" was called, became a fee simple absolute in A as soon as A had issue, fulfilling the "condition." In 1285 landowners desiring to fetter their offspring achieved the Statute De Donis which abolished the fee simple conditional and created the fee tail. The statute was effective until the fifteenth century, when through a fraudulent legal proceeding tenants were able to "dock the entail" and break the familial hold. (However, other means, notably the strict settlement, were used in England until 1925 to perpetuate family holdings.) As Long v. Long illustrates, American states have eliminated the fee tail by converting it into other estates, though South Carolina, for example, does not recognize De Donis and retains the fee simple conditional.

LETTER TO JAMES BOSWELL FROM DR. JOHNSON: [James Boswell's father, a Scottish judge, in 1776 wished to entail the Boswell family lands, as was then permitted by Scottish law. Because of marriage articles, he required Boswell's consent to do so. Boswell and his father disagreed about how narrow to make the restriction. The senior Boswell desired a general entail, while James Boswell "had a zealous partiality for heirs male." James, a lawyer, feared "disagreeable consequences" from continued opposition to his father. He wrote to his friend Dr. Johnson, who was not a lawyer, for advice. Part of Johnson's reply follows.]

Dear Sir,

Land is, like any other possession, by natural right wholly in the power of its present owner; and may be sold, given, or bequeathed, absolutely or conditionally, as judgement shall direct, or passion incite.

But natural right would avail little without the protection of law; and the primary notion of law is restraint in the exercise of natural right. A man is therefore, in society, not fully master of what he calls his own, but he still retains all the power which law does not take from him.

In the exercise of the right which law either leaves or gives, regard is to be paid to moral obligations.

Of the estate which we are now considering, your father still retains such possession, with such power over it, that he can sell it, and do with the money what he will, without any legal impediment. But when he extends his power beyond his own life, by settling the order of succession, the law makes your consent necessary.

Let us suppose that he sells the land to risk the money in some specious adventure, and in that adventure loses the whole; his posterity would be disappointed; but they could not think themselves injured or robbed. If he spent it upon vice or pleasure, his successors could only call him vicious and voluptuous; they could not say that he was injurious or unjust.

He that may do more, may do less. He that, by selling or squandering, may disinherit a whole family, may certainly disinherit part, by a partial settlement.

Laws are formed by the manners and exigencies of particular times, and it is but accidental that they last longer than their causes: the limitation of feudal succession to the male arose from the obligation of the tenant to attend his chief in war.

As times and opinions are always changing, I know not whether it be not usurpation to prescribe rules to posterity, by presuming to judge of what we cannot know: and I know not whether I fully approve either your design or your father's, to limit that succession which descended to you unlimited. If we are to leave *sartum tectum* to posterity, what we have without any merit of our own received from our ancestors, should not choice and free-will be kept unviolated? Is land to be treated with more reverence than liberty? — If this consideration should restrain your father from disinheriting some of the males, does it leave you the power of disinheriting all the females? . . .

If, therefore, you ask by what right your father admits daughters to inheritance, ask yourself, first, by what right you require them to be excluded? . . .

These, dear Sir, are my thoughts, immethodical and deliberative; but, perhaps, you may find in them some glimmering of evidence.

I cannot, however, but again recommend to you a conference with Lord Hailes, whom you know to be both a Lawyer and a Christian.

Make my compliments to Mrs. Boswell, though she does not love me. I am, Sir, your affectionate servant,

Sam. Johnson

C. THE LIFE ESTATE

◆ WALKER, INTRODUCTION TO AMERICAN LAW
270-273

§131. ESTATES FOR LIFE

Estates for life rank next in importance to estates in fee. We have seen, that for feudal reasons, they are esteemed of higher dignity than the longest estate for years. An estate for life is so much taken off from a complete estate in fee. The future estate in fee expectant on the termination of the life estate, is called either a reversion or remainder, as will be explained hereafter; and the two together constitute one complete estate in fee. An estate for life may either be for the life of him who has it, or for the life of a third person. In the first case, the owner is called tenant for life, simply; in the second, tenant for another's life, or in law French, *tenant pur autre vie;* while he for whose life the estate is held, is called *cestui que vie.* Both these estates are of freehold dignity, though the former is justly regarded as the preferable estate, because it certainly must last as long as the owner lives, while the latter may not. But connected with an estate for another's life, is one curious question. Suppose the owner dies before the man for whose life it is held; to whom does the residue of this estate belong? It does not revert to the grantor, for the time has not expired; and it does not descend to the heirs of the grantee, unless they are expressly mentioned. This was the reasoning of the ancient common law; and to solve the difficulty, any person was permitted to take possession by way of special occupancy, as of a vacant estate, and hold it till the death of him by whose life the estate was measured. In England, and in many of the states, this doctrine has been altered by statute. In this state we have no provision on the subject; but yet I would venture to say that our courts would never recognize so absurd a doctrine, as to allow a stranger to take possession. . . . Estates for life may be created either by the act of the parties, or by the operation of law. Thus if I grant land to you for the term of your life, I create in you an estate for life by express words. If I grant land to you without any specification of time, I create in you an estate for life, by legal construction. For it cannot be a fee, because it has not the word *heirs;* and it cannot be an estate for years, because the years are not specified. It is therefore construed as a life estate. There are but two estates for life by the operation of law, namely, dower and curtesy; both resulting from marriage, and both having the same general incidents as other life estates. . . .

Termination. An estate for life, in this country, terminates only with the natural death of the person. We know no such thing as civil death under the English law. . . .

Estovers. A tenant for life has a right to take reasonable estovers; that is, wood and timber necessary for the purpose of building, burning, ploughing, and fencing; but [not] to sell it. The general principle is, that he is entitled to nothing more than what is necessary for the temporary enjoyment of the estate. . . .

Emblements. On the death of a tenant for life his representatives are entitled to the emblements not yet severed from the land; that is, to those annual crops which were the immediate fruits of his labor; such as grain, garden-roots, and the like. Grass and fruits are not emblements, because they do not owe their existence to the annual cultivation of man. . . .

Alienation. A tenant for life, unless the contrary be stipulated, has the power of disposing of his entire estate, or any less portion. And if he undertakes to create an estate in fee, this does not work a forfeiture. The common law doctrine of forfeiture, by attempting to grant a greater estate than one has, never existed in this state, and probably not in this country. . . . If therefore a tenant for life undertakes to convey a greater estate than he has, the conveyance will be good for so much as he has.

Incumbrances. If a tenant for life, takes an estate charged with an incumbrance, he is not required to pay off the incumbrance; but only to keep down the interest, leaving the principal to be paid by the owner of the fee. . . .

Waste. A tenant for life is liable for waste. In general terms, waste may be defined to be, a spoiling or destroying of the estate with respect to houses, wood, or soil, to the lasting injury of the inheritance. But no damage resulting from the act of God, as lightning or tempest; or from public enemies, as an invading army; or from the reversioner himself, is waste. There are two kinds of waste, voluntary and permissive. Voluntary waste is that which results from actual commission, as felling timber, defacing buildings, opening mines, and changing the course of husbandry. Permissive waste is that which results from omission, as suffering buildings or other improvements to go to decay. But in every provision against waste, estovers are of course excepted. And it has been held that where timber has been cut down and sold, to purchase boards for making repairs, this is not waste. The circumstances of this country have also made one change in the law, respecting waste; which is, that in case of wild lands, the tenant may clear a reasonable portion, for the purpose of cultivation, without being guilty of waste. With respect to repairs, in the absence of any special agreement between the tenant and the next in estate, the rule is, that the tenant shall keep the premises in as good condition as he found them, inevitable accidents only excepted. And where there is a special agreement to repair, the tenant is not excused even by inevitable accident, unless he so stipulates. The obligation of the tenant to preserve the premises from waste extends also to the acts of strangers, for which he is liable, having his remedy against them. In some of the states, waste is guarded against by the statutory penalty of forfeiture of the place wasted and treble damages.

Examples

(a) *O to A* (life estate)

(b) *O to A for life* (life estate)

(c) *O to A for the life of B* (life estate *pur autre vie*)

The life estate, unlike the fee tail, is still a viable estate and plays a prominent role in family settlements. Although the concept of a life

estate is not difficult to understand, the life estate has a complex dimension — the ambiguous relationship between the life tenant and the
reversioner or the remainderman. The person who will take on termination of the life estate has interests to be protected during the life tenancy,
and much of the law of life estates defines the relationship between the
tenant and the holder of the future interest. The doctrines of estovers,
emblements, waste, and so forth apportion economic benefits and
liabilities between the present and the future. Also, at times courts must
apportion between the tenancy and the future interest both costs, such
as an assessment for a permanent improvement, and benefits, such as a
damage award from a trespasser. Typically, courts in such cases refer to
actuarial tables.

Perhaps the most interesting question today about legal life estates
is whether we should have them at all. Consider the problems that life
estates present to those who would like to develop the property. In
contrast to modern estates for years, no one knows just how long life
estates will last, which makes alienation of the interest difficult. But does
this argument wrongly presume that property rules should be judged
solely by their impact on land development?

◆ MELMS v. PABST BREWING CO.
104 Wis. 7, 79 N.W. 738 (1899)

This is an action for waste, brought by reversioners against the defendant, which is the owner of an estate for the life of another in a quarter
of an acre of land in the city of Milwaukee. The waste claimed is the
destruction of a dwelling-house upon the land, and the grading of the
same down to the level of the street. The complaint demands double
damages, under sec. 3176, Stats. 1898.

The quarter of an acre of land in question is situated upon Virginia
street, in the city of Milwaukee, and was the homestead of one Charles
T. Melms, deceased. The house thereon was a large brick building built
by Melms in the year 1864, and cost more than $20,000. At the time of
the building of the house, Melms owned the adjoining real estate, and
also owned a brewery upon a part of the premises. Charles T. Melms
died in the year 1869, leaving his estate involved in financial difficulties.
After his decease, both the brewery and the homestead were sold and
conveyed to the Pabst Brewing Company, but it was held in the action of
Melms v. Pabst B. Co., 93 Wis. 140, that the brewing company only
acquired Mrs. Melms's life estate in the homestead, and that the plaintiffs in this action were the owners of the fee, subject to such life estate.
As to the brewery property, it was held in an action under the same title,
decided at the same time, and reported in 93 Wis. 153, that the brewing
company acquired the full title in fee. The homestead consists of a piece

of land ninety feet square, in the center of which the aforesaid dwelling house stood; and this parcel is connected with Virginia street on the south by a strip forty-five feet wide and sixty feet long, making an exact quarter of an acre.

It clearly appears by the evidence that after the purchase of this land by the brewing company the general character of real estate upon Virginia street about the homestead rapidly changed, so that soon after the year 1890 it became wholly undesirable and unprofitable as residence property. Factories and railway tracks increased in the vicinity, and the balance of the property was built up with brewing buildings, until the quarter of an acre homestead in question became an isolated lot and building, standing from twenty to thirty feet above the level of the street, the balance of the property having been graded down in order to fit it for business purposes. The evidence shows without material dispute that, owing to these circumstances, the residence, which was at one time a handsome and desirable one, became of no practical value, and would not rent for enough to pay the taxes and insurance thereon; whereas, if the property were cut down to the level of the street, so as to be capable of being used as business property, it would again be useful, and its value would be largely enhanced. Under these circumstances, and prior to the judgment in the former action, the defendant removed the building and graded down the property to about the level of the street, and these are the acts which it is claimed constitute waste. . . .

WINSLOW, J. Our statutes recognize waste, and provide a remedy by action and the recovery of double damages therefor; but they do not define it. It may be either voluntary or permissive, and may be of houses, gardens, orchards, lands, or woods; but, in order to ascertain whether a given act constitutes waste or not, recourse must be had to the common law as expounded by the text-books and decisions. In the present case a large dwelling house, expensive when constructed, has been destroyed, and the ground has been graded down, by the owner of the life estate, in order to make the property serve business purposes. That these acts would constitute waste under ordinary circumstances cannot be doubted. It is not necessary to delve deeply into the Year Books, or philosophize extensively as to the meaning of early judicial utterances, in order to arrive at this conclusion. The following definition of waste was approved by this court in Bandlow v. Thieme, 53 Wis. 57: "It may be defined to be any act or omission of duty by a tenant of land which does a lasting injury to the freehold, tends to the permanent loss of the owner of the fee, or to destroy or lessen the value of the inheritance, or to destroy the identity of the property, or impair the evidence of title." . . . And in Brock v. Dole, 66 Wis. 142, it was also said that "any material change in the nature and character of the buildngs made by the tenant is waste, although the value of the property should be enhanced by the alteration."

242 • 6. Freehold Estates

These recent judicial utterances in this court settle the general rules which govern waste, without difficulty, and it may be said, also, that these rules are in accord with the general current of the authorities elsewhere. But, while they are correct as general expressions of the law upon the subject, and were properly applicable to the cases under consideration, it must be remembered that they are general rules only, and, like most general propositions, are not to be accepted without limitation or reserve under any and all circumstances. Thus the ancient English rule which prevented the tenant from converting a meadow into arable land was early softened down, and the doctrine of meliorating waste was adopted, which, without changing the legal definition of waste, still allowed the tenant to change the course of husbandry upon the estate if such change be for the betterment of the estate. Again, and in accordance with this same principle, the rule that any change in a building upon the premises constitutes waste has been greatly modified, even in England; and it is now well settled that, while such change may constitute technical waste, still it will not be enjoined in equity when it clearly appears that the change will be, in effect, a meliorating change which rather improves the inheritance than injures it. Following the same general line of reasoning, it was early held in the United States that, while the English doctrine as to waste was a part of our common law, still the cutting of timber in order to clear up wild land and fit it for cultivation, if consonant with the rules of good husbandry, was not waste, although such acts would clearly have been waste in England.

These familiar examples of departure from ancient rules will serve to show that, while definitions have remained much the same, the law upon the subject of waste is not an unchanging and unchangeable code, which was crystallized for all time in the days of feudal tenures, but that it is subject to such reasonable modifications as may be demanded by the growth of civilization and varying conditions. And so it is now laid down that the same act may be waste in one part of the country while in another it is a legitimate use of the land, and that the usages and customs of each community enter largely into the settlement of the question. This is entirely consistent with, and in fact springs from, the central idea upon which the disability of waste is now, and always has been, founded, namely, the preservation of the property for the benefit of the owner of the future estate without permanent injury to it. This element will be found in all the definitions of waste, namely, that it must be an act resulting in permanent injury to the inheritance or future estate. . . . But the principle that the reversioner or remainderman is ordinarily to receive the identical estate, or, in other words, that the identity of the property is not to be destroyed, still remains, and it has been said that changes in the nature of buildings, though enhancing the value of the property, will constitute waste if they change the identity of the estate. This principle was enforced in the last-named case, where it was held that a tenant from year to year of a room in a frame building would be enjoined from constructing a chimney in the building against the objection of his landlord. The importance of this rule to the landlord or owner of the future estate cannot be denied. Especially is it valuable and essential to the protection of a landlord who rents his premises for a short time. He has fitted his premises for certain uses. He leases them for such uses, and he is entitled to receive them back at the end of the term still fitted for those uses; and he may well say that he does not choose to have a different property returned to him from that which he leased, even if, upon the taking of testimony, it might be found of greater value by reason of the change. Many cases will be found sustaining this rule; and that it is a wholesome rule of law, operating to prevent lawless acts on the part of tenants, cannot be doubted, nor is it intended to depart therefrom in this decision. The case now before us, however, bears little likeness to such a case. : . . .

There are no contract relations in the present case. The defendants are the grantees of a life estate, and their rights may continue for a number of years. The evidence shows that the property became valueless for the purpose of residence property as the result of the growth and development of a great city. Business and manufacturing interests advanced and surrounded the once elegant mansion, until it stood isolated and alone, standing upon just enough ground to support it, and surrounded by factories and railway tracks, absolutely undesirable as a residence and incapable of any use as business property. Here was a complete change of conditions, not produced by the tenant, but resulting from causes which none could control. Can it be reasonably or logically said that this entire change of condition is to be completely ignored, and the ironclad rule applied that the tenant can make no change in the uses of the property because he will destroy its identity? Must the tenant stand by and preserve the useless dwelling-house, so that he may at some future time turn it over to the reversioner, equally useless? Certainly, all the analogies are to the contrary. As we have before seen, the cutting of timber, which in England was considered waste, has become in this country an act which may be waste or not, according to the surrounding conditions and the rules of good husbandry; and the same rule applies to the change of a meadow to arable land. The changes of conditions which justify these departures from early inflexible rules are no more marked nor complete than is the change of conditions which destroys the value of residence property as such and renders it only useful for business purposes. Suppose the house in question had been so situated that it could have been remodeled into business property; would any court of equity have enjoined such remodeling under the circumstances here shown, or ought any court to render a judgment for damages for such an act? Clearly, we think not. Again, suppose an orchard to have become permanently unproductive through disease or death of the trees, and the land to have become far more valuable, by reason of new conditions as a vegetable garden or wheat field, is the life tenant to be compelled to preserve or renew the useless orchard, and forego the advantages to be derived from a different use? Or suppose a farm to have become absolutely unprofitable by reason of change of market conditions as a grain farm, but very valuable as a tobacco plantation, would it be waste for the life tenant to change the use accordingly, and remodel a now useless barn or granary into a tobacco shed? All these questions naturally suggest their own answer, and it is certainly difficult to see why, if change of conditions is so potent in the case of timber, orchards, or kinds of crops, it should be of no effect in the case of buildings similarly affected. . . .

In the present case this consideration was regarded by the trial court· as controlling, and we are satisfied that this is the right view. This case is not to be construed as justifying a tenant in making substantial changes in the leasehold property, or the buildings thereon, to suit his own whim or convenience, because, perchance, he may be able to show that the change is in some degree beneficial. Under all ordinary circumstances the landlord or reversioner, even in the absence of any contract, is entitled to receive the property at the close of the tenancy substantially in the condition in which it was when the tenant received it; but when, as here, there has occurred a complete and permanent change of surrounding conditions, which has deprived the property of its value and usefulness as previously used, the question whether a life tenant, not bound by contract to restore the property in the same condition in which he received it, has been guilty of waste in making changes necessary to make the property useful, is a question of fact for the jury under proper instructions, or for the court where, as in the present case, the question is tried by the court.

Is there an independent body of "property law" doctrine that is more than the application of tort, contract, and some criminal doctrine in circumstances concerning land? The question is worth occasional attention as this course proceeds. *Melms* suggests one part of the answer: property law involves the public assignment of regularized legal consequences to private transactions that may be quite diverse. Thus it often poses a conflict between the claims of regularity — predictability, administrative simplicity, "neutrality" — and irregular facts. Why was *Melms* a difficult case? Can the arguments for the reversioner be put more strongly than those the court described and answered? Who should decide the division of rights and obligations between life tenant and remainderman? If circumstances suggest the utility of an altered division, is judicial reconsideration the appropriate mechanism?

Notes

1. A residential property had been conveyed by Becker to herself as life tenant, remainder in fee simple to Alfred and Diana Scheinberg. Becker insured with Home Insurance Co. against "all Direct Loss by Fire" but "not in any event for more than the interest of the insured." The remaindermen did not insure.

The house caught fire and received extensive damage. Becker was killed in the fire, 19 minutes after it began. The court held: "Becker insured the property in the full amount of its value against loss by fire during her lifetime and when that contingent event occurred prior to her death . . . the loss necessarily accrued in Becker's favor prior to her demise without regard to the length of time she lived after the fire began." To whom should Becker's executor distribute the money? Home Insurance Co. v. Adler, 269 Md. 715, 309 A.2d 751 (1973).

2. Farmland was owned by Jacob Richardson for his life, then by his son Charles Richardson in fee simple. Jacob entered into a written contract with his second wife's son, Christopher Scroggham, renting the farm on a cash annual basis of $4,375. On October 24, 1970, Jacob Richardson died. Charles Richardson went immediately to the farm where he found Scroggham starting to plow the middle field. "At that time words were exchanged about title and ownership and the right of [Scroggham] to continue on the farm. . . . [Scroggham] immediately ceased plowing. . . . In June, 1971, [Scroggham] returned to the farm to harvest his hay crop and was mowing in the north field when the sheriff of Shelby County came out and ordered him to stop mowing."

An Indiana court of appeals, per Judge Lowdermilk, held that growing annual crops belonging to a life tenant are his personal property, and his interest in them survives the termination of his estate. Pursuant to this interest, Scroggham had an absolute right to return to the land to harvest the crops. Richardson v. Scroggham, 307 N.E.2d 80 (Ind. App. 1974).

But, in an Illinois case, after life tenant Pearl Johnson died on August 12, 1969, with corn and soybeans growing on her 65-acre tract, a court directed 164/365 of the purchase price to Pearl Johnson's estate and the rest to the remaindermen, with adjustments to take into account fertilizer purchased by the life tenant and taxes paid by the remaindermen. The fraction, 164/365, represented the days Pearl Johnson had lived of a year long crop-sharing farm lease. Ralston Purina Co. v. Killam, 10 Ill. App. 3d 397, 293 N.E.2d 750 (1973).

3. Testator devised house and land to his wife for life, but provided that his son by a prior marriage should have one room in the house during the wife's lifetime, and that on her death the property should go to the son in fee simple if he had issue, otherwise to him for life, and

then one-half each to the testator's and his wife's nearest blood relatives. Two years after probate, the son murdered the wife.

The court's guide to apportioning the property was the maxim, "no man should profit by his own wrong." Therefore, the son could not take as a devisee of the wife; and the son should receive only the value of his right to occupy one room, plus the actuarial value of his remainder interest if the wife had lived to her normal life expectancy. The wife's estate received the value of her interest for the period of her expected life, and whether the son received the property in fee was postponed to see whether he would have issue before her hypothetical date of death. (His long prison sentence may have made this unlikely.) In re Estate of Moses, 13 Ill. App. 3d 137, 300 N.E.2d 473 (1973).

D.   CONDITIONAL ESTATES

◆ BLACKSTONE, COMMENTARIES
152-155

Besides the several divisions of estates, in point of interest, there is also another species still remaining, which is called an estate upon condition; being such whose existence depends upon the happening or not happening of some uncertain event, whereby the estate may be either originally created, or enlarged, or finally defeated. And these conditional estates I have chosen to reserve till last, because they are indeed more properly qualifications of other estates, than a distinct species of themselves; seeing that any quantity of interest, a fee, a freehold, or a term of years, may depend upon these provisional restrictions. . . .

I. Estates upon condition implied in law, are where a grant of an estate has a condition annexed to it inseparably, from its essence and constitution, although no condition be expressed in words. As if a grant be made to a man of an office, generally, without adding other words; the law tacitly annexes hereto a secret condition, that the grantee shall duly execute his office, on breach of which condition it is lawful for the grantor, or his heirs, to oust him, and grant it to another person. . . .

II. An estate on condition expressed in the grant itself, is where an estate is granted, either in fee-simple or otherwise, with an express qualification annexed, whereby the estate granted shall either commence, be enlarged, or be defeated, upon performance or breach of such qualification or condition. These conditions are therefore either precedent, or subsequent. Precedent are such as must happen or be performed before the estate can vest or be enlarged; subsequent are such, by the failure or non-performance of which an estate already vested may be defeated. Thus, if an estate for life be limited to A upon his marriage with *B*, the marriage is a precedent condition, and till that happens no estate is vested in *A*. Or, if a man grant to his lessee for years, that upon payment of a hundred marks within the term he shall have the fee, this also is a condition precedent, and the fee-simple passeth not till the hundred marks be paid. But if a man grant an estate in fee-simple, reserving to himself and his heirs a certain rent; and that, if such rent be not paid at the times limited, it shall be lawful for him and his heirs to re-enter, and avoid the estate; in this case the grantee and his heirs have an estate upon condition subsequent, which is defeasible if the condition be not strictly performed. To this class may also be referred all base fees, and fees simple conditional at the common law. Thus an estate to a man and his heirs, tenants of the manor of Dale, is an estate on condition that he and his heirs continue tenants of that manor. . . . [O]n the breach of any of these subsequent conditions by the failure of these contingencies; by the grantee's not continuing tenant of the manor of Dale, . . . the estates which were respectively vested in each grantee are wholly determined and void.

A distinction is however made between a condition in deed and a limitation, which Littleton denominates also a condition in law. For when an estate is so expressly confined and limited by the words of its creation, that it cannot endure for any longer time than till the contingency happens upon which the estate is to fail, this is denominated a limitation: as when land is granted to a man, so long as he is parson of Dale, or while he continues unmarried, or until out of the rents and profits he shall have made 500£ and the like. In such cases the estate determines as soon as the contingency happens, (when he ceases to be parson, marries a wife, or has received the 500£) and the next subsequent estate, which depends upon such determination, becomes immediately vested, without any act to be done by him who is next in expectancy. But when an estate is, strictly speaking, upon condition in deed (as if granted expressly upon condition to be void upon the payment of 40£ by the grantor, or so that the grantee continues unmarried, or provided he goes to York, etc.) the law permits it to endure beyond the time when such contingency happens, unless the grantor or his heirs or assigns take advantage of the breach of the condition, and make either an entry or a claim in order to avoid the estate.

◆ WALKER, INTRODUCTION TO AMERICAN LAW
288-291

§142. CONDITIONS IN GENERAL

The most important rules relating to conditions are the following.

1. Conditions must be annexed at the time of creating the estate, and not afterwards; because when an estate is once created, the grant-

or's power is at an end. Accordingly, if the conditions are contained in a separate deed, both must be executed at the same time.

2. Conditions must operate upon the whole estate. If I should grant you an estate in fee, with a provision that upon the happening of a certain event, your estate should cease for a certain number of years, this would not be good, it is said, because it would destroy the unity of the estate. But a condition may operate upon part of the land, and not upon the rest. Thus one half might be made to revert, upon a certain event. There may be good reason for this distinction under the technical rules of the common law, but I can perceive none in the nature of the subject.

3. Conditions can only be reserved to the grantor and his heirs. Except by statutory provision, which we have not, they cannot be reserved to strangers. The reason assigned is, that estates upon condition, do not, *ipso facto*, cease upon the happening of the condition, but only when there has been an entry for condition broken, or some act equivalent thereto, as the commencement of an action. In order to discourage champerty and maintenance, or the fomenting of litigation, it was a maxim of the English law, as we have seen, that no right of action could be assigned by one person to another. Consequently the right of entry for condition broken, could not be reserved to a stranger. But here the reason of this rule does not exist, because we have no law against champerty or maintenance. . . .

4. Conditions which are impossible at the time of making them, or which afterwards become impossible by the act of God, or by the act of the grantor himself, are void; and an estate already vested thus becomes absolute. . . . Thus if I should grant you an estate, upon condition that within five years you should marry a certain woman, and she should be dead at the time, or should die within the five years; or I should marry her; in either case you would hold the estate discharged of the condition.

5. Conditions, the performance of which is unlawful, are void. . . .

6. Conditions which are repugnant to the nature of the estate, are void. Thus if I grant you an estate in fee, upon condition that you shall not part with it, or shall not receive the profits of it, these conditions would be void for repugnancy, since the rights of alienation, and of taking the profits, are the essential incidents of an estate in fee. But the grantor may prohibit alienation, to a particular person; for this is not within the reason of the rule. . . .

7. Conditions in absolute prevention of marriage, are void on grounds of public policy, except in the case of widows taking lands from their deceased husbands. But the grantor may provide that the grantee shall not marry without his consent; because this does not absolutely prevent marriage.

8. Conditions may be performed by any person having an interest

in the subject matter. And if a particular time be appointed, the performance must be at or before the time. The law is strict on this subject, though equity will relieve against mere failure in point of time.

9. Equity will relieve against all forfeitures for breach of conditions, where a compensation can be made in damages; and this renders the legal doctrines respecting conditions of little practical consequence.

10. When the condition has been broken, the grantor may, by his own act, debar himself from taking advantage of it. Thus, where a lease contains a clause of re-entry, for non-payment of rent at a certain time, and the lessor accepts rent afterwards, he cannot enter for condition broken.

◆ HAGAMAN v. BOARD OF EDUCATION
117 N.J. Super. 446, 285 A.2d 63 (1971)

LANE, J.A.D. The complaint seeks possession of real property conveyed by plaintiff's parents to defendant on October 20, 1925. Both parties moved for summary judgment. The trial court . . . granted defendant's motion. The judgment that was entered "ORDERED that Summary Judgment be and is hereby granted to the defendant, Board of Education of the Township of Woodbridge dismissing plaintiff's complaint." Plaintiff appeals.

The deed to defendant contained a provision:

> It is the understanding of the parties to this conveyance that the hereinabove described land is conveyed solely for the purpose of being used for the erection and maintenance of a public school or schools and that the Board of Education of Woodbridge Township, N.J., will erect a school thereon on or before the school year of 1926 and use such building for school purposes.

From the affidavits and admissions in the pleadings it was uncontroverted that defendant erected a school building on the property and used the property for school purposes until approximately 1968. In that year the school building was closed. The students who formerly would have attended the school began to attend two new schools within the area. At the time of the trial the property in question was used as a recreational park or playground. It was equipped with swings, a sliding board, monkey bars and basketball courts. During the summer it was supervised by a full-time playground supervisor. Organized and supervised play activities were carried on. On March 2, 1971 after the judgment was rendered the school building was destroyed by fire.

Plaintiff argues that the deed expresses a clear and unequivocal intention to convey a fee simple determinable or a fee simple subject to a condition subsequent and that he is entitled to possession because the property is no longer being used for the maintenance of a public school. . . .

In determining the meaning of a deed, prime consideration is the intent of the parties. . . .

An estate in fee simple determinable is an estate in fee simple which automatically determines upon the occurrence of a given event. The grantor retains a possibility of reverter upon the occurrence of the stated event. . . . Generally, the intent to create such an estate is indicated by the use of words denoting duration of time such as "while," "during," "so long as." . . . "The absence of some one of these phraseologies makes it likely that a court will find a covenant, a trust, or some other type of interest less drastic in its sanctions." 2 Powell, Real Property, §187 at 45-47. However, ". . . particular forms of expression standing alone and without resort to the purpose of the instrument in question are not determinative. . . ."

Words of limitation merely stating the purpose for which the land is conveyed usually do not indicate an intent to create an estate in fee simple determinable although other language in the instrument, the amount of the consideration and the circumstances surrounding the conveyance may indicate such an intent. . . .

When a conveyance contains only a clause of condition or of covenant, such clause does not usually indicate an intent to create a fee simple determinable. Restatement, Property, §44, comment n, at 130.

 An estate in fee simple subject to a condition subsequent is an estate in fee simple which upon the occurrence of a given event gives to the grantor or his successor in interest the right to reenter and terminate the estate. Upon the occurrence of the given event, the forfeiture of the estate is not automatic. . . . The intent to create such an estate may be indicated by the use of such words as "on condition that," "provided that." . . . However, such language is not necessarily determinative. . . . Generally, an intent to create a fee simple subject to a condition subsequent is established when the conveyance contains one of the above phrases and a provision that if the given event occurs the grantor may enter and terminate or has a right to re-enter. . . . A mere statement of the use to which the conveyed land is to be devoted is not sufficient to create an estate in fee simple subject to a condition subsequent. . . . Absent clear intention to create a fee simple subject to a condition subsequent, a conveyance with words of condition may be found to create a covenant, a trust, or a mere precatory expression. . . .

Language in an instrument which is alleged to create a fee simple determinable or a fee simple subject to a condition subsequent is strictly construed. "A recognized rule of construction indicates that an instrument, when a choice exists, is to be construed against rather than in favor of a forfeiture." . . .

If a choice is between an estate in fee simple determinable and an estate on condition subsequent, the latter is preferred. . . . Where it is doubtful whether a clause in a deed is a covenant or a condition, the former is preferred. . . .

When a condition in a deed is relied upon to defeat an estate, it should be strictly construed and its violation must be clearly established. . . .

In the present case there are no words indicating an intent to create a fee simple determinable or a fee simple subject to a condition subsequent. There are no words creating either a right of re-entry or a possibility of a reversion.

Plaintiff does not have a right to possession to the property under the deed. This holding by the trial court was correct.

In its decision upon which the judgment was based, the trial court raised an issue that was not in the pleadings. The trial court suggested that the defendant held "a fee simple absolute subject to a trust for the charitable purpose of maintaining an educational facility." The opinion granted leave to plaintiff to amend his complaint to seek the enforcement of a charitable trust; and to the defendant, to answer and counterclaim for a declaratory judgment or for instructions whether under the circumstances a public playground may be substituted for a school use under the doctrine of *cy pres*. Plaintiff filed a written "Declination of Permission to Amend." No counterclaim was filed by defendant. In stating that plaintiff could amend his complaint to seek the enforcement of a charitable trust, the trial court was in error. Generally, heirs of a settlor cannot enforce a charitable trust. . . . A suit to enforce a charitable trust may be brought by the Attorney General, by the trustee or by one having a special interest in its enforcement. . . . Defendant cross-appeals from so much of the judgment that "adjudges that, the deed from the plaintiff's parents to the defendant, Board of Education does not establish a fee simple estate in the defendant-respondent, Board of Education." No counterclaim was filed by defendant and such relief was not sought. It is inappropriate to seek for the first time on appeal a declaration of defendant's interest in the property. A determination on that question may be made in a proceeding properly brought at a later time seeking such relief. The failure to file a counterclaim in this action will not be a bar to such action.

The judgment is affirmed.

The various conditions that can be attached to an estate at the time of its creation are qualifications, not estates themselves. All estates, freehold and nonfreehold, can be conditioned. However, for the sake of simplicity, the dicussion of conditions can focus on the various types of the fee simple.

Examples

(a) O to A and his heirs so long as the property is used for residential purposes

This conveyance creates a fee simple determinable, known also as a fee simple on a special limitation. The outstanding characteristic of a determinable estate is that the estate terminates automatically, and reverts back to the grantor, upon violation of the limitation. These special limitations are signified by words such as "so long as," "until," or "while," indicating a limitation inseparable from the whole of the conveyance. The future interest retained by the grantor is called a possibility of reverter (discussed in Chapter 13 with the other future interests). The fee simple determinable is a viable estate today, but scholars have argued that the Statute of Quia Emptores should have had the same effect on determinable fees as it had on feudal tenures, since the aim of the special limitation is to confer on the grantor a continuing interest in the use of the property.

(b) O to A and his heirs, but if the property is used for nonresidential purposes, O and his heirs shall have a right of entry and repossession

This conveyance is said to create a fee simple subject to a condition subsequent. At first glance, it appears to create the identical interests in grantor and grantee as the fee simple determinable, but the grantor's interest is described as a power of termination, or right of entry, since it is a future interest that does not operate automatically, as does the possibility of reverter. If the condition is violated, the grantor or his heirs must act to terminate the estate; otherwise, the estate remains with the grantee or his heirs. What effect would the distinction between these two estates have on the operation of statutes of limitation and adverse possession?

(c) O to A and his heirs so long as the property is used for residential purposes, then to B and his heirs

This conveyance creates a fee simple with an executory limitation, quite similar to the following example.

(d) O to A and his heirs, but if the property is used for nonresidential purposes, B and his heirs shall have a right of entry and repossession

This creates a fee simple subject to an executory limitation. The executory limitation is a future interest created for a third person. Before the Statute of Uses of 1536 (see Part 4), the distinction between example (c) and (d) was especially important because executory limitations in conveyances were not recognized by common law courts. In a conveyance such as example (c), this left a fee simple determinable, since the special limitation was deemed not separable; but a condition subsequent was regarded as a separate part of the conveyance, thus leaving A in (d) with a fee simple absolute.

Summary of Freehold Interests

	Limitation	Present Interests	Future Interests In Grantor	Future Interests In Third Person
(A) 1.	B and his heirs	fee simple absolute	none	none
2.	B and his heirs so long as the property is used for residential purposes	fee simple determinable (also called, fee simple on a special limitation)	possibility of reverter	none
3.	B and his heirs, but if the property is not used for residential purposes, A and his heirs shall have a right of entry and repossession	fee simple subject to a condition subsequent	power of termination (right of entry)	none
4.	B and his heirs so long as the property is used for residential purposes, then to C and his heirs	fee simple with an executory limitation	none	executory interest
5.	B and his heirs, but if the property is not used for residential purposes, C and his heirs shall have a right of entry and repossession	fee simple subject to an executory limitation	none	executory interest

Summary of Freehold Interests (continued)

Limitation	Present Interests	Future Interests	
		In Grantor	*In Third Person*
(B) 1. *B* and the heirs of his body			
(a) 1225-1285	fee simple conditional	?	none
(b) 1285-1472	fee tail	reversion	remainder
(c) strict settlement, 1650-1925			
2. *B* and the heirs (male) (female) of his body	fee tail (male) (female)	reversion	remainder
3. *B* and the heirs of his body by his wife *W*	fee tail special	reversion	remainder
(C) 1. *B*	life estate	reversion	remainder or executory interest
2. *B* for the life of *X*	life estate pur autre vie	reversion	remainder or executory interest

7 ◆ LANDLORD AND TENANT AT COMMON LAW

A. NONFREEHOLD ESTATES

◆ WALKER, INTRODUCTION TO AMERICAN LAW
273-275

§132. ESTATES FOR YEARS

An estate for years has been defined to be, a contract for the possession and profits of land, for a certain period. Its distinguishing characteristic is, that it must expire at a fixed period or terminus, which is always ascertained at the creation of the estate; hence the estate itself is called a term, and the tenant a termor. This estate is never created by the operation of law, but always by the act of the parties. The instrument creating it is called a lease, and the parties lessor and lessee, or landlord and tenant. These latter terms are derived from the feudal system, though the relation itself did not exist under that system, all feuds being freehold. An estate for years originally differed from a freehold in the five following particulars. 1. Livery of seisin, as we have seen, was not necessary in creating it. Hence the tenant could not be said to be seised, but merely possessed of the land. He had no interest in the soil itself, but merely in the profits of the soil. His estate was therefore treated as a chattel; and this technical distinction still continues, though the reason has ceased, livery of seisin not being now necessary in the creation of any estate. 2. An estate for years might be made to commence at a future time, while a freehold could not. But this distinction, as we have seen, no longer exists. 3. An estate for years was originally held, as we have seen, by a precarious tenure: but now the law makes this tenant as secure in his possession as the tenant of a freehold. 4. An actual entry by the tenant was necessary to perfect this estate. But now an actual entry is not required in any case. The execution and delivery of the lease, perfects the title of the lessee to all intents and purposes. 5. It made no difference, as to the nature of this estate, whether it were for only a part of a year, or for any number of years. It might be for a month, or for a thousand years; but it was still no more or less than an estate for years, with precisely the same legal incidents. In fact, by a very common practice, this estate could be so created as to last for ever, without altering its character. This is the case with what are called perpetual leases, in which a certain term is created, renewable forever. Yet at common law these estates, although they may continue for ever, are nothing more than estates for years. The fee still remains in the lessor, and the lessee has only a chattel interest. But by our statute, these permanent leasehold estates are made subject to the same law of descent and distribution, and of sale on execution or by decree, as estates in fee. Though as to dower and curtesy, and in all other respects but those above mentioned, they still continue to be chattel interests. The incidents of estates for years are nearly the same as those of estates for life, except in regard to emblements. Thus tenants for years, in the absence of a special agreement to the contrary, have the same right to estovers, the same power of underletting, are in the same manner exempt from forfeiture, for creating a greater estate, and are equally liable for waste. . . .

Rent. But there is one additional incident, belonging sometimes to estates for life, and generally to estates for years, which remains to be described. I mean rent. According to Blackstone, rent is "a certain profit issuing yearly out of lands and tenements corporeal;" and there are three kinds of rent, namely, rent-service, where the fee remains in the landlord, and the tenant is bound to render some corporeal service in partial or full return for the use of land, which service may be enforced by distress; rent-charge, where the fee is granted with a reservation of rent, and with a special clause of distress charging the rent upon the land; and rent-seck, where the fee is granted with a reservation of rent, and without a clause of distress. The term distress, here signifies a summary mode allowed to the landlord, of seizing and selling the tenant's property to satisfy the rent which he owes. But in this State [Ohio], and several other states, the power of enforcing payment by distress is confined to the collection of public dues; and the landlord stands on the same footing as any other creditor. Accordingly, the foregoing distinctions are of little importance; and we may consider rent simply as a periodical compensation, in money or otherwise, agreed to be given by the tenant to the landlord for the use of realty, the payment of which may be enforced like any other demand. I say agreed to be given, because where one occupies another's land without a lease containing a special agreement to pay a fixed rent, the compensation which may be recovered, is not in the shape of rent, but of damages in an action for use and occupation, or for mesne profits. . . . When the relation of landlord and tenant has been created, the estate of the landlord is denominated a reversion, to which rent is said to be incident. If therefore he conveys the reversion, the future rent passes with it, and when he dies it goes to his heirs; but it is otherwise if the rent be already due. If the tenant be evicted by a paramount title in a stranger, or actually expelled by the landlord, his obligation to pay rent ceases; but no destruction of the premises by fire, flood, or other inevitable accident will discharge the obligation, unless the lease contains a provision to that effect. Where the lease provides for a forfeiture in case of non-payment of the rent when due, a tender or readiness to pay on the premises at any time, before sunset on the day stipulated, will be sufficient. The tenant is not obliged to seek the landlord away from the premises unless he agrees so to do, but he may make such tender, and it will be good. When leased property becomes divided, either by the act of the landlord or by operation of law, if the parties cannot agree upon an apportionment of rent, it must be made by a jury.

§133. ESTATES AT WILL

An estate at will was originally where the tenant occupied at the mere pleasure of him who had the next estate; and who could terminate the tenancy at any moment without previous notice. Such a connection between landlord and tenant harmonized perfectly with the arbitrary notions of a landed aristocracy. It had but one redeeming quality, and that was with regard to emblements. The tenant at will, having no knowledge when he might be obliged to quit the premises, was entitled to emblements, on the same ground as the representatives of a tenant for life. But as notions of liberty began to gain ground, the slavish character of this tenancy became gradually changed. It was first settled that an estate at will was equally at the will of both parties; and that neither could terminate the tenancy without fair notice to the other. The next improvement was to determine, that, unless there was an express agreement to hold at will, all tenancies for no stipulated term, should be construed as periodical tenancies from year to year, or some shorter period, according to the facts of the case. The establishment of this wholesome doctrine is a virtual abolition of estates at will; and it has been fully recognized in this state. . . . We have two ways of dispossessing a refractory tenant; namely, by the action of ejectment, and of forcible detainer. In ejectment, our state requires ten days' notice before the commencement of the term to which the appearance is to be made; and in forcible detainer, three days' notice before the commencement of the suit; but this is a different thing from notice to quit. Whatever this be, it must be so given as to expire before or at the time the period expires; for if the tenant has been allowed to enter upon a new period without notice, he cannot be dispossessed until the end of the period. And the chief criterion to determine whether a tenancy is from year to year, from quarter to quarter, or from month to month, is the pay-day or rent. . . .

§134.   ESTATES AT SUFFERANCE

An estate at sufferance is where one comes rightfully into possession of land, but holds over after his interest is determined. A tenant at sufferance differs from a mere intruder, in this, that he is not a trespasser. But he has no interest capable of being transferred or defended; and it is said that independently of statutory provision, he is not liable to pay rent. We have no statute on the subject; but the doctrine is so absurd on the face of it, that I presume our courts would not recognize it. The tenant could not indeed be sued for rent technically speaking, under the lease, because it has expired; but I have no doubt he might be liable in an action for use and occupation. At common law, this tenant is not entitled to notice to quit. But here, this point is of very little importance; because . . . there must be ten or three days' notice, as the case may be, before he can be dispossessed by action. The landlord may indeed enter at any time, without notice, and will not thereby become a trespasser; and if he can turn the tenant out peaceably, he will thus acquire possession immediately. But if the tenant refuses to go out, he cannot use force upon his person; for though we have no statute making forcible entry an indictable offence, yet in the case supposed, the landlord could not justify an assault and battery. Unless, therefore, he can expel the tenant at sufferance peaceably, he must give the required notice, and then bring his action. This tenant therefore has an undue advantage over his landlord. In England and in many of the states, a penalty of double rent is imposed by statute, for holding over; while here, there is not only no penalty, but in our course of proceeding, an obstinate tenant cannot be expelled under perhaps several months. This is an evil which calls loudly for remedy.

Examples

(a) *O to A for 10 years* (estate for years)

The original concept underlying the estate for years was that the lessee purchased from the lessor a *term*. This was, of course, a durational concept, but the term of years established not only a specified and definite period of tenancy, but also a bundle of rights and duties unique to the leasehold. These rights and duties are discussed in detail in the cases that follow.

(b) *O to A at the will of O* (estate at will)

(c) *O to A from month to month* (estate from period to period, or the "periodic estate")

The estate at will was a variation of the estate for years, advantageous to the grantor, satisfying a desire for more flexibility than a fixed term. The estate from period to period, a cross between the estates for years and at will, allowed either landlord or tenant a "grace period" when the other wanted to terminate the tenancy.

(d) *Holdover* (tenancy at sufferance)

Walker disliked legal recognition of the holdover tenant, especially since it could make eviction by the landlord difficult. Yet one effect of recognizing the estate was that the holdover tenant could not establish rights against the landlord by adverse possession.

Summary of Nonfreehold Interests

Limitation	Present Interests	Future Interests	
		In Grantor	In Third Person
B for 10 years	estate for years	reversion	remainder
B at the will of A	tenancy at will	reversion	
B from month to month	periodic tenancy	reversion	
Holdover	tenant at sufferance		

B. ASSIGNMENT AND SUBLEASE

◆ SAMUELS v. OTTINGER
169 Cal. 209, 146 P. 638 (1915)

SLOSS, J. The plaintiff appeals from a judgment in favor of the defendant. The judgment disposed of three separate actions, which, with the consent of the parties, had been consolidated for trial. The appeal is on the judgment roll.

The actions were brought to recover installments on monthly rent accruing under a written lease of real property. The three proceedings differed only in the months for which rental was claimed.

A jury trial having been waived, the court made findings as follows: On December 20, 1906, D. Samuels Realty Company, a corporation, as lessor, leased to the defendants, as lessees, a certain lot in the city of San Francisco. A copy of the lease is set out in the answers and referred to by the findings. The term of the lease was ten years, commencing on the 20th day of December, 1906. The rent of the premises was $150 per month, payable in advance, for the first five years of the term, and $175 per month, payable in advance, for the next five years. . . .

The defendants went into possession of the premises under the lease, and paid the monthly installments of rent to and including the

19th day of May, 1908. On that day they sold and assigned the lease to one Altschular. The lessor was, at the same time, notified of the assignment. Altschular paid the rent for the month commencing May 20, 1908, and said payment was received and accepted by the lessor. The monthly installments of rent payable on the 20th days of the successive months from June, 1908, to March, 1910, have not been paid. . . .

The single question presented for decision is whether the defendants, the original lessees, are absolved from liability to pay rent by their assignment to Altschular, and the payment by Altschular to the lessor of one month's rent. The general rule of law governing the controversy is settled beyond the possibility of dispute. A lease has a dual character — it presents the aspect of a contract and also that of a conveyance.

> Consequently the lease has two sets of rights and obligations — one comprising those growing out of the relation of landlord and tenant, and said to be based on the "privity of estate," and the other comprising those growing out of the express stipulations of the lease, and so said to be based on "privity of contract."

Tiffany on Real Property, §46.

An obligation to pay rent, without an express agreement to that end, arises from the mere occupancy, as tenant, of the premises. A lessee who has not agreed to pay rent is, by his transfer to an assignee, with the consent of landlord, relieved of any further obligation to pay rent. Such obligation is thereafter upon the assignee who has come into "privity of estate" with the landlord. But where the lessee has expressly agreed to pay rent, his liability under his contract remains, notwithstanding an assignment with the consent of the lessor. . . .

The test of the assigning lessee's liability is, then, whether he has, in the lease, agreed to pay rent during the term. The rule of law is sometimes phrased thus: The obligation to pay rent remains on the lessee, after his assignment, when the obligation was created by his express agreement. It does not survive an assignment with the lessor's consent when the obligation is implied. . . .

The lease in question was executed by the lessees, as well as by the lessor. It begins by stating that the lessor leases the premises to the lessees, for the term of 10 years, at the monthly rental above stated, "payable in advance on the twentieth day of each and every month." By subsequent clauses the lessees agree to pay all bills for water, gas, and electricity furnished to the premises, and all taxes on improvements to be erected by said lessees. The privilege of subleasing is expressly given, as is permission to erect buildings, which, if they comply with certain conditions, are to be purchased by the lessor at the expiration of the term. The lessees agree to insure the improvements, "and said insurance shall be made payable to the lessor and the lessees jointly, for the purpose of securing the said lessor in the payment of the rents herein stipulated. . . ." By another clause it is agreed that the improvements to be erected "shall be security for the rent herein stipulated to be paid. . . ." Finally, it is agreed that, if the lessees hold over beyond the term provided in the lease, such holding over shall be deemed merely a tenancy from month to month, "and at the same monthly rental that shall have been payable hereunder by said lessees immediately prior to such holding over."

If it is possible to express a contractual obligation to pay rent by any form of words other than a direct promise, in exact terms, to pay such rent, the language we have quoted from the lease before us imposes that obligation on the lessees. The lessor agrees to lease the premises to the lessees at a given rental, "payable" at stated times. The writing is signed by the lessees as well as by the lessor. . . .

But beyond this, there are various other provisions in the lease plainly indicating the intention and understanding of the parties that the lessees were bound to pay the rent. Insurance is to be taken out for the purpose of securing the lessor in the "payment of the rents herein stipulated." Improvements are to be security for the rent "herein stipulated to be paid." A holding over shall be deemed a tenancy from month to month at the same monthly rental as shall have been "payable hereunder by said lessees" prior to such holding over. We find, first, a reference to the payment of "rents herein stipulated," then a provision for security for "rent herein stipulated to be paid," and finally a clause which speaks of "rents payable hereunder by said lessees." These expressions afford a convincing showing that the parties to the lease believed and understood that the writing embodied a "stipulation" for the payment of rents, and that it made such rents payable by the lessees. The obligation to pay rent is not implied from the relation of landlord and tenant, but is expressed by the words used by the parties in their writing. . . .

The judgment is reversed, with directions to the court below to enter judgment in favor of the plaintiff as prayed in the three several complaints.

Note

Mrs. Davis leased land and buildings in El Paso to Dallas Brewery for three years, at a rent of $100 per month. "For $300.00 to it in hand paid" the brewery did "hereby sublet, assign and transfer the said above premises and assign and transfer the above said lease" to Lou Vidal, who agreed "to pay the rents in said lease agreed to be paid." Vidal later vacated, and Mrs. Davis sued him for rent for the remainder of the term. The court said that because the brewery retained a right to reenter if

Vidal violated, the transfer from Dallas Brewery to Vidal was not an assignment but a sublease. Therefore Mrs. Davis and Vidal were not in privity of estate, and she could not recover from him. Davis v. Vidal, 105 Tex. 444, 151 S.W. 290 (1912). Can you think of another theory under which Mrs. Davis might sue Vidal today?

PHILBRICK, CHANGING CONCEPTIONS OF PROPERTY IN LAW, 86 U. Pa. L. Rev. 691, 699-703 (1938): The *dominium* of Roman Law — that is the *dominium* of the quiritary law (*dominium ex jure Quiritium*) to which that word was almost wholly confined — was an absolute right in private property. No holder of temporary rights in land, therefore, whatever their nature, could have *dominium*. Likewise, the Romans never classified under *dominium* mere limited and definite rights of use in the land of another. . . .

Utterly different was the situation in Germanic law. In the earlier centuries of the medieval period the transfer of land titles was either impossible or so impeded by restrictions as to minimize its value in exchange. Its value lay almost exclusively in its produce. We know that in England the distribution among tenants of lands either privately owned in a strict sense or at least controlled by local potentates goes back to the earliest English occupation of England. We know that the giving out of land to persons for life, holding immediate enjoyment, with rights of future enjoyment held by other persons, was well established before 1200 A.D. Leaseholds for years were also then becoming important. This separation of title from unified and complete enjoyment, and consequent distribution of the produce of the land among different persons under tenancies of some form, apparently characterized Germanic land law on the continent from the time individual ownership had permitted the accumulation of landed estates of any considerable extent. Inevitably, partial ownership was claimed by those who shared in the use of land; and partial title was conceded to them. Control, actual and protected by law, directed to the use of a thing was "the final and the central idea" in the medieval land law. It existed in degrees infinitely varied, but in essence there was no difference between complete title and a right, definite or indefinite, to use land — even the land of another. Ownership was a rubric covering all instances.

Under that law, therefore, all persons sharing in enjoyment held, together, the complete title; and each was owner of his particular interest, be it what it might and according to its nature. Likewise, as respect rights *in re aliena*, which Roman law did not treat as owned by the person enjoying them (nor, therefore, by anyone), but only as incumbrances upon the ownership of the thing in which such rights existed: in Germanic law they were, in Gierke's phrase, "splinters of ownership".

And the preceding statements are equally true of our law, which takes its fundamental concepts of possession and ownership directly from the medieval German law; to which it is much nearer, in fact, than is the present law of Germany. Enjoyment content, use, is the essence and the basis of all title, of all proprietary rights in our law. This brings it very near to the understanding and expectation of the common man, as it ought to be. Question any man, and he will yield the opinion that the sole reason for owning property is to use or (which is enjoyment in another form) to sell it. He will agree that title is only a shell that covers and protects a kernel of enjoyments. These enjoyments are today mainly economic; although of course they may be æsthetic, and under older conditions they were in part both political and honorific in England, and in this country political. In their economic form, enjoyments of land appear, of course, in a variety of guises. The tenant for years, or even at will, has the liberties of an actual occupant and may consume the produce of the land; but the reversioner, his landlord, collects the rent, and it is waste if the tenant wrongfully so uses the land that the consequences of his acts will outlast the tenancy and, therefore, do damage to the reversioner. Holders of present estates of future possessory enjoyment have no liberties dependent upon occupation; but their present estates may be vested rights, indestructible and alienable, and in that form they may share by a sale in the economic values of the title; and if their rights be contingent instead of vested, still they share, albeit in lesser measure. A tenant for years owns his leasehold interest in the land; his reversioner owns, and can convey, no more than a title subject thereto. If the existing estates in the land are those of A for twenty years, of B for life, and then of C in fee simple, only the three together can convey a *complete* title. In the absence of such a conveyance A's right is good against everybody during his term, as thereafter B's and C's rights will successively be good. Thus, as in medieval law, ownership is a rubric covering all instances of apportioned use: one may own any interest, and either literally against the whole world, or only against the world generally with exceptions of one or more persons holding better rights. . . . All this is the root of our fundamental doctrine that title is no more than relatively better right to immediate possession (and so of user) — or, in case of rights *in re aliena,* simply a better right of enjoyment — as between two contestants actually litigating that issue; with possible similar subsequent litigations involving another party (or other parties) simply ignored and postponed. To possess, even without any original title whatever, is to be owner against the world generally; against all save those who have a title higher than such possessory title — perhaps merely an older possession. Our law, save in a few rare situations, has never known more than the relative rights to possession (hence, to use) of A and B, and then of B and C, and so on — successive parties to successive litigations.

The doctrine of divided ownership, based upon apportioned use, sprang from the actual economic conditions of medieval times. In it the medieval Germanic law gave us the most fundamental single character-istic of the present Anglo-American law of property. It became such merely because of a particularly logical development in our law of the distinction between general title and immediate enjoyment. It has re-mained such because it conforms to economic justice and human expec-tations. Four great doctrines have shaped our law: seisin (possession), tenure, uses, and estates. Of these only the first can even be conceived of apart from the concept of divided ownership. In fact, all four have operated solely through that concept; their creative power has been wholly due to it; practically speaking, all sprang from it. Our unique law of trusts, with title in trustee and use in beneficiary, is only the apotheosis of the medieval distinction. And what is true of land is true, in only lesser degree, of personal property.

♦ PALMER v. 309 EAST 87TH STREET CO.
112 Misc. 2d 667, 447 N.Y.S.2d 1000 (Sup. Ct. 1982)

RYP, Justice:
. . . The facts are substantially undisputed, as follows. On Decem-ber 5, 1977, tenant and landlord entered into a Real Estate Board of New York, Inc. standard form of apartment lease (1973) for a one bedroom, rent-stabilized apartment 4J, premises No. 307 East 87th Street, New York, New York which contains over four residential units. Said lease was for a two year term, effective January 1, 1978 and ending December 31, 1980, at a monthly rental of $365.00, with one month security deposit and guaranteed by tenant's mother, Margaret E. Palmer.

Pertinent paragraph "16" of said lease relevantly provides:

Assignment, Mortgage, etc.:

16. Except as permitted by Real Property Law Section 226-b, Tenant, for itself . . . , successors and assigns, expressly covenants that it shall not assign, . . . nor underlet . . . or permit the demised premises . . . to be used by others without the prior written consent of Landlord; such consent shall not be unreasonably withheld in each instance. If this lease be as-signed, or if the demised premises . . . be underlet or occupied by anybody other than Tenant, Landlord may, after default by Tenant, collect rent from the assignee, under-tenant or occupant, and apply the net amount collected to the rent herein reserved, but no such assignment, underlet-ting, occupancy or collection shall be deemed a waiver of this covenant, or the acceptance of the assignee, under-tenant or occupant as tenant, or a release of Tenant from the further performance by Tenant of covenants on the part of Tenant herein contained. The consent of Landlord to an assign-ment or underletting shall not in any wise be construed to relieve Tenant from obtaining the express consent in writing of Landlord to any further assignment or underletting.

Said lease was subsequently renewed for a one year term ending December 31, 1981.

Thereafter, on December 16 to 17, 1981, tenant and landlord, again, duly executed a two year renewal, effective January 1, 1982 through December 31, 1983, of said lease at a monthly rental of $457.82, pursuant to the Rent Guidelines Board under the Rent Stabilization Law of 1969, as amended and a ninety day cooperative plan cancellation clause under RSC §61, subd. 7.

Prior thereto, by letter dated October 8 and mailed October 15, 1981, by certified mail, return receipt requested, enclosing tenant's guarantor's consent to such subletting, dated October 9, 1981, tenant formally sent landlord a notice to renew and sublet said lease under paragraph 16 thereunder and RPL §226-b. Such proposed sublease was to be effective February 1, 1982 for a period of nine months while tenant marries, lives and works with her prospective banker husband originally in Nairobi, Kenya (later transferred to London, England) with expressed intent to return to subject apartment. The proposed sublessee is one Anthony E. Davis, Esq., an English solicitor, member of the New York Bar and partner.

Thereafter, landlord's managing agent, A. Eisenger, by certified mail, return receipt requested, refused to consent to tenant's proposed sublessee, claiming landlord has "a number of people who have expressed their need for a one-room apartment and there is no reason why the landlord should show preference for Mr. Davis, a sub-tenant or new tenant over our candidates for the apartment".

"Pursuant to the requirements of law, having given these reasons for denying you the right to sublet the landlord here, offers to release you from the lease."

Thereafter, on November 24, 1981, tenant in response to landlord's November 12, 1981 denial letter rejected landlord's offer of release from her subject lease.

Thereafter, as noted above, on December 16 to 17, 1981, landlord and tenant duly executed a RSL two year lease, renewal, effective January 1, 1982 through December 31, 1983 including an RSC §61, subd. 7 ninety (90) day cooperative cancellation clause.

Section 226-b of the Real Property Law (Right to sublease or assign):

1. A tenant renting a residence in a dwelling having four or more residential units shall have the right to sublease or assign his premises, subject to the written consent of the landlord given in advance of the sublease or assignment. Such consent shall not be unreasonably withheld. If the landlord unreasonably withholds consent for such sublease or assignment, the landlord must release the tenant from the lease upon request of the tenant.
2. The tenant shall inform the landlord of his intent to sublease or assign by mailing a notice of such intent by registered or certified mail. Such

request shall be accompanied by the written consent thereto of any co-tenant or guarantor of such lease and a statement of the name, business and home address of the proposed sublessee or assignee. Within ten days after the mailing of such request, the landlord may ask the sender thereof for additional information as will enable the landlord to determine if rejection of such request shall be unreasonable. Within thirty days after the mailing of the request for consent, or of the additional information reasonably asked for by the landlord, whichever is later, the landlord shall send a notice to the sender thereof of his consent or, if he does not consent, his reasons therefor. Landlord's failure to send such a notice shall be deemed to be a consent to the proposed subletting or assignment. If the landlord consents, the premises may be sublet or assigned in accordance with the request, but the tenant thereunder, shall nevertheless remain liable for the performance of tenant's obligation under said lease.

This Court, in the first RPL §226-b legislative interpretation, Kruger v. Page Management Co., 105 Misc. 2d 14, 433 N.Y.S.2d 295, analyzed in depth case law history transposed into RPL §226-b and set forth the standard of reason governing a landlord's unreasonable withholding of consent to assign or sublet requiring such to be "factual and objective based upon the proposed sublessee(s)' financial responsibility, identity or suitability for the particular apartment or building, legality of the proposed use or nature of the occupancy or any other sound real estate business. . . ." While confined to subleases such, although reserved therein, is applicable to assignments. . . .

The fulcrum issue presented to this Court is whether, under the parties' lease, applicable statute and the facts and circumstances set forth in the motion papers, landlord's withholding of consent based upon an alleged prior "waiting list" is unreasonable. As noted above, under the 1981-2 tight residential housing market, the right to [approve] or bar a sublease is a valuable one. . . .

This Court finds this case factually and legally distinguishable from Meredith v. 985 Fifth Avenue, Inc. In *Meredith*, the landlord claimed an established prior "lengthy waiting list" and an over two year commitment for the first three bedroom apartment available to a named, identified and investigated candidate. In this case, landlord generally refers to "a number of people who have expressed their need for a one bedroom apartment." In addition, *Meredith* involved a permanent assignment, rather than a temporary sublet herein with a transfer of a leasehold and rent stabilized tenancy in a rental, rather than a prospective cooperative building herein. While RPL §226-b makes no distinction between an assignment and sublet, the permanent consequences of an assignment, as distinct from the temporary consequences of a sublet, is a factor for the Court to consider whether to determine this motion summarily or by reference. The Court notes that the prospective nominee, an English solicitor and partner in a New York law firm has equal or greater financial responsibility than tenant.

This Court further considers the fact, although minimized by the parties, that the real object of contention may not be a valuable rental leasehold but the possession, purchase and prospective sale of an even more valuable one bedroom co-operative apartment in the upper East Side of Manhattan, which this tenant of four years in good standing, would be entitled to purchase at an "insider's price". It further appears to this Court that the trigger for tenant's RPL §226-b relief request herein is her pending marriage which, as a matter of public policy, should commence, at least, with a fiscal blessing and not, contrary to past federal income tax, cause an economic penalty. Finally, tenant alleges, although landlord disputes, she intends to return with her marital partner, to the leasehold.

After careful consideration and review of all papers, pleadings, RPL §226-b, its parallel clause in above-cited paragraph 16 of subject lease, all relevant and material facts and circumstances submitted herein this Court finds and declares:

1. Tenant herein has duly complied with the requirements of RPL §226-b, by mailing on October 15, 1981 by certified mail, a notice of intent of sublease, dated October 8, 1981, including a guarantor's consent, dated October 9, 1981.
2. Landlord's response, dated November 12, 1981, that "a number of people who have expressed their need for a one bedroom apartment and there is no reason why the landlord should show preference for Mr. Davis a subtenant or new tenant over our candidates for the apartment" was an unreasonable withholding of consent, under RPL §226-b.
3. Landlord's said response, dated November 12, 1981, shall be deemed, as a matter of law under RPL §226-b a consent to tenant's request for a nine months' sublease, effective February 1, 1982 to the proposed sublessee only, . . .

Accordingly, for the foregoing reasons, tenant is granted declaratory judgment to the extent and upon the conditions set forth herein above, and landlord's cross-motion to dismiss tenant's action is denied.

Notes

1. Look again at Real Property Law §226-b *supra*. Subsection 2 says that the landlord's failure to send notice "shall be deemed to be a consent. . . ." But subsection 1 says only that if the landlord unreasonably withholds consent, "the landlord must release the tenant from the lease. . . ." How does the court in *Palmer* explain ordering the landlord to permit the sublease?
2. After an Appellate Division decision consistent with *Palmer*,

Kreitman v. Einy, 92 A.D.2d 801, 460 N.Y.S.2d 46 (1983), the landlord's lawyer said, "We have a tenant who is now is Florida, with no intention of ever returning, deciding who will have that apartment. What's left? Considering the housing shortage in New York, we don't think the major qualification for getting an apartment is that you are a friend of the tenant or are willing to pay key money." N.Y. Times, March 18, 1983.

3. A tenant of a rent-stabilized apartment sued for possession at the expiration of a subtenancy. The subtenant took what the court called the "startling position that he may not be evicted except upon one of the special grounds set forth in . . . the Rent Stabilization Code."

This would mean, said the court, "that one sublets at one's own peril. Although the Landlord dragon has finally been vanquished [citing Real Property Law §226-b], another dragon lies in wait."

The court held that "startling or not, . . . [subtenant's] position is correct. A prime tenant has all of the obligations of an owner. A subtenant has all of the rights of a tenant." But a prime tenant also has the statutory protection of the Rent Stabilization Code, which allows an "owner" to refuse to renew a lease in order to occupy the unit himself. That does not help this prime tenant, the court said: "Petitioner has not established that she wishes to move back from Northport. Rather she has merely shown that she wants the added convenience of a *pied-a-terre* in town." Lindstrom v. Conte, 113 Misc. 2d 139, 448 N.Y.S.2d 636 (Civ. Ct. 1982).

4. Rosefan Construction Corp. v. Salazar, 114 Misc. 2d 959, 452 N.Y.S.2d 1016 (Civ. Ct. 1982), held that according to N.Y. Real Property Law §236, executors of the estate of a deceased tenant may be refused permission to assign or sublet the apartment, but if the landlord unreasonably refuses consent, the lease "shall be deemed terminated" and the estate discharged from further liability for rent.

5. The New York legislature apparently took the view posed as a question in Note 1 *supra*. In 1983 it replaced Real Property Law §226-b with these provisions:

> 1. Unless a greater right to assign is conferred by the lease, a tenant renting a residence may not assign his lease without the written consent of the owner, which consent may be unconditionally withheld without cause provided that the owner shall release the tenant from the lease . . . which release shall be the sole remedy of the tenant. If the owner reasonably withholds consent, there shall be no assignment and the tenant shall not be released from the lease.
>
> 2. (a) A tenant . . . shall have the right to sublease . . . subject to . . . consent of the landlord. . . . Such consent shall not be unreasonably withheld. . . .
>
> (c) . . . If the landlord consents, . . . the tenant . . . shall nevertheless remain liable for the performance of tenant's obligations under said lease.

. . . If the landlord unreasonably withholds consent, the tenant may sublet in accordance with the request. . . .

6. Any provision of a lease or rental agreement purporting to waive a provision of this section is null and void. . . ."

1983 N.Y. Laws 403, §37.

At the same time, the legislature amended the Rent Stabilization Law to provide that a rent stabilization tenant can only charge a subtenant "the legal regulated rent plus a ten percent surcharge . . . if the unit sublet was furnished with the tenant's furniture," and that subleasing is allowed only where the prime tenant "intends to occupy it as [his primary residence] at the expiration of the sublease." 1983 N.Y. Laws 402, §57.

6. A ten-year lease for restaurant premises beginning January 1, 1964, had given the tenant an option to renew for twenty-four more years by providing notice "in writing by registered or certified mail six months prior" to the end of the first term. Through negligence, the tenant failed to submit the prescribed notice that he was exercising the option. The landlord wrote to the tenant on November 12, 1973, saying it assumed tenant would vacate the premises on January 1, 1974. On November 16, 1973, tenant sent written notice of his intention to renew. Landlord refused to honor the late notice.

Held: Granting possession to the landlord would work a forfeiture, and a court of equity is empowered to grant tenant relief even if he has been negligent. However, in this instance, there should be a new trial on the issue of possible prejudice to the landlord.

J.N.A. Realty Corp. v. Cross Bay Chelsea, Inc., 42 N.Y.2d 392, 366 N.E.2d 1313, 397 N.Y.S.2d 958 (1977) (4-3). The court was influenced by the landlord's apparent knowledge that the date for renewal was approaching and the landlord's decision not to call this to the tenant's attention. Judge Breitel wrote a stinging dissent.

C.   RIGHTS AND DUTIES

♦ PARADINE v. JANE
Aleyn 27, 82 Eng. Rep. 897 (K.B. 1647)

In debt the plaintiff declares upon a lease for years rendring rent at the four usual feasts; and for rent behind for three years, ending at the Feast of the Annunciation, 21 Car. brings his action; the defendant pleads, that a certain German prince, by name Prince Rupert, an alien born, enemy to the King and kingdom, had invaded the realm with an hostile army of men; and with the same force did enter upon the defendant's possession, and him expelled, and held out of possession from the 19 of July 18 Car. till the Feast of the Annunciation, 21 Car. whereby he could not take the profits; whereupon the plaintiff demurred, and the plea was resolved insufficient. . . .

It was resolved, that the matter of the plea was insufficient; for though the whole army had been alien enemies, yet he ought to pay his rent. And this difference was taken, that where the law creates a duty or charge, and the party is disabled to perform it without any default in him, and hath no remedy over, there the law will excuse him. . . . Now the rent is a duty created by the parties upon the reservation, and had there been a covenant to pay it, there had been no question but the lessee must have made it good, notwithstanding the interruption by enemies, for the law would not protect him beyond his own agreement, no more than in the case of reparations; this reservation then being a covenant in law, and whereupon an action of covenant hath been maintained (as Roll said) it is all one as if there had been an actual covenant. Another reason was added, that as the lessee is to have the advantage of casual profits, so he must run the hazard of casual losses, and not lay the whole burthen of them upon his lessor; and *Dyer* 56.6. was cited for this purpose, that though the land be surrounded, or gained by the sea, or made barren by wildfire, yet the lessor shall have his whole rent: and judgment was given for the plaintiff.

Paradine v. Jane was a minor legal skirmish of the English Civil War. The case was decided during a lull in the fighting, after Parliament had defeated Charles I but before his last military adventure and execution.

In 1647 fighting had gone on for almost five years and many tenants were unable or unwilling to pay their rent. At the same time Parliament and its army were at odds over a demand by some soldiers for "indemnity." Since an army not commanded by the King rested on dubious legal foundations, officers were afraid that they would be sued by civilians for the damage caused by military operations. In 1647 one such case came before the King's Bench, and the Commons had to intervene and order it dismissed.

Although the *Paradine* court still called itself "King's Bench," it was not the King's court. Prince Rupert, described in the case report as "enemy to the King," was in fact Charles' nephew and best general. The "alien armies" were the armies of the King, composed almost exclusively of native Englishmen. Despite its hostility to the King's cause, Parliament had not yet imagined a basis for traditional common law rights outside the old framework of royal authority. Thus Parliament went on granting land to its adherents in the name of the King even when the grantees were being rewarded precisely for fighting against the King. (After the King was executed, in early 1649, Parliament began to grant land in its own name, as "custodians of the liberties of England," and the name of the court was changed from "King's Bench" to "Upper Bench.")

The judges who decided *Paradine*, though not extremists, were sympathetic to Parliament. King Charles had difficulty persuading judges to leave London and work for him in Oxford, but Parliament had equal trouble getting respected common lawyers to enforce its laws. Many judges simply retired to their country homes. On at least one occasion, not a single judge of the King's Bench could be found to hold court; the judicial backlog got worse and worse — by 1648 it was estimated Chancery was 8,000 cases behind.

Most of the old judges had been impeached by Parliament in 1643, and the two judges who sat for Paradine v. Jane (half the King's Bench's usual strength) had been appointed after the war began. The first was Francis Bacon, a distant relative of the illustrious Lord Chancellor, who was to be so shocked by the execution of King Charles that he would resign from the bench. The other was Justice Rolle, the leading parliamentary judge of the period. Cromwell eventually forced Rolle to retire after the judge refused to preside at the trial of a group of Royalists who had captured Rolle but spared his life.

◆ DYETT v. PENDLETON
8 Cow. 727 (N.Y. 1826)

CRARY, Senator. The question in this cause appears to me to depend upon the conduct of the parties. The enjoyment of the tenant is the consideration for which he agreed to pay rent. If he is deprived of that enjoyment by the wrongful act of the landlord, the consideration has failed; and whether it was an unnecessary and voluntary abandonment of the premises on the part of the tenant, or compelled by the moral turpitude of the landlord, is the only question material to be considered.

The facts offered to be proved on the trial are, substantially, that in February, 1820, from time to time, and at sundry times, the plaintiff introduced into the house, (two rooms upon the second floor and two rooms upon the third floor whereof had been leased to the defendant,) divers lewd women or prostitutes, and kept and detained them in the said house all night, for the purpose of prostitution; that the said lewd women or prostitutes would frequently enter the said house in the day time, and after staying all night, would leave the same by day-light in the morning; that the plaintiff sometimes introduced other men into the said premises, who, together with him, kept company with the said lewd women or prostitutes during the night; that on such occasions, the plaintiff and the said lewd women or prostitutes, being in company in certain parts of the said house, not included in the lease to the defendant, but adjacent thereto, and in the occupation or use of the plaintiff, were accustomed to make a great deal of indecent noise and disturbance, the said women or prostitutes often screaming extravagantly, and so as to be heard throughout the house, and by the near neighbors, and frequently using obscene or vulgar language so loud as to be understood at a considerable distance; that such noise and riotous proceedings, being from time to time continued all night, greatly disturbed the rest of persons sleeping in other parts of the said house, and particularly in those parts thereof demised to the defendant; that the practices aforesaid were matters of conversation and reproach in the neighborhood, and were of nature to draw, and did draw, odium and infamy upon the said house, as being a place of ill fame, so that it was no longer respectable for moral and decent persons to dwell or enter therein; that all the said immoral, indecent and unlawful practices and proceedings were by the procurement or with the permission and concurrence of the plaintiff; that the defendant, being a person of good and respectable character, was compelled, by the repetition of the said indecent practices and proceedings, to leave the said premises, and did, for that cause, leave the same on or about the beginning of March, 1820, after which he did not return thereto, &c.

This evidence, being objected to by the plaintiff's counsel, was rejected by the court, and is now to be considered as true.

The plea was an eviction; and the supreme court have decided this evidence did not support it, and was, therefore, properly rejected. The view that I have taken of it has led me to a different conclusion. The supreme court consider the plaintiff guilty of an offence, and that "the police of the city, upon the complaint of the defendant, would have instantly taken the plaintiff and his associates into custody, and punished them by fine and imprisonment, as often as the offence was repeated;" and for that reason supposed there was no moral necessity for abandoning the premises. This remedy is believed to be not only very imperfect, but particularly objectionable on principle, as affording to vice every indulgence, at the expense of virtue. It will be recollected that the place of prostitution was the dwelling house of the plaintiff, who occupied the first floor. Fine, and even imprisonment, then, unless perpetual, would not prevent him from returning to it; and if he should return, perfectly reclaimed, which is scarcely possible, yet the imputation would rest upon the defendant, of remaining under the same roof with him. But if the plaintiff should return unreclaimed, which is most probable, he would be very likely to re-commence his old business of prostitution, in which the defendant must come in for his full share, at least in public estimation.

Something is due to the dignity of judicial tribunals, not so much for the sake of those whose duty it is to preside, as for the sake of that justice which it is their duty to administer. Judicial robes can never inspire confidence, if the proper sense of right and wrong is not manifested. . . .

The whole science of law consists in the application of a few simple principles to the "affairs and bosoms of men." In Collins v. Blantern, (2 Wils. R. 350,) it is said by lord chief justice Wilmot, that "all writers upon our law agree in this: no polluted hand shall touch the pure fountains of justice." I should lay hold upon this principle, if there was no other, for the purpose of chastising vice and impudence, on the one hand, and protecting virtue and innocence, on the other. When the defendant is told that every right, when withheld, shall have its remedy, and every injury its proper redress, and that personal security, which includes reputation, is one of his absolute rights, and then told he must live in a brothel, against his will, or, at least, pay rent for it, he cannot but see the disparity between the text and the comment, and if the one is right, the other must be wrong.

If the evidence offered does not technically prove an eviction, yet, as there is no other plea under which the defence can be made, for the sake of giving effect to it, I should resort not to the statute law, nor to the common law, but to the great principles of morality, on which both are founded; and if, in the long tract of ages which are past, I could find no case parallel with the present, I should decide against the plaintiff, satisfied that if the same case had ever existed, the principal actor in it had not aspired to immortality by publishing his own infamy.

SPENCER, Senator. It seems to be conceded that the only plea which could be interposed by the defendant below, to let in the defence which he offered, if any would answer that purpose, was that the plaintiff had entered in and upon the demised premises, and ejected and put out the defendant. Such a plea was filed; and it is contended on the one side, that it must be literally proved, and an actual entry and expulsion established: while on the other side it is insisted, that a constructive entry and expulsion is sufficient, and that the facts which tended to prove it, should have been left to the jury. . . .

I cannot omit the opportunity presented by this case, of observing, that it appears to me to be one of those within the view of the framers of our constitution, in the organization of this court. When this court, of last resort, was declared to consist of the senators, with the chancellor and judges, it must have occurred, that the largest proportion of its members would be citizens not belonging to the legal profession. And it must, therefore, have been intended to collect here, a body of sound practical common sense, which would not overthrow law but which would apply the principles and reasons of the law according to the justice of each case, without regard to the technical refinements and arbitrary and fictitious rules, which will always grow upon professional men. And herein I conceive, is the great excellence of this court; that whenever it perceives a rule established by the inferior courts, pushed to such an extent as to produce positive injustice, it is within its power, as it most certainly will always be its disposition, to rescind or modify such rule. Several signal examples of the exercise of this power might be cited in the decisions of this court. Were this, then, a case in which the law was considered settled by the supreme court that nothing but a physical turning a tenant out of possession would exonerate him from the payment of his rent, it would be precisely such as would require and justify the interposition of this court to correct it; not by making law, but by applying its familiar and elementary principles to a new case. Suppose the landlord had established a hospital for the small pox, the plague, or the yellow fever, in the remaining part of this house; suppose he had made a deposit of gunpowder, under the tenant, or had introduced some offensive and pestilential materials of the most dangerous nature; can there by any hesitation in saying that if, by such means, he had driven the tenant from his habitation, he should not recover for the use of that house, of which, by his own wrong, he had deprived his tenant? It would need nothing but common sense and common justice to decide it. No man shall derive benefit from his own wrong. . . .

COLDEN, Senator. It is to be remarked, that the letting was from the 1st of November, 1818, to the 1st of November, 1820; at least the terms of the lease did not compel the lessee to keep the premises longer than to the last mentioned date. The rents had been paid to the 1st of February, 1820, so that the controversy is as to the three ensuing quarters of that year.

The proof offered, related only to the month of February, or from time to time and at sundry times, in and about that month. There was no further offer to prove how long the evil practices had continued. Indeed, as it was stated that it would be shewn that the lessee left the premises on the 1st of March, the offer must be considered as referring to sundry times in the month of February. There was no offer to prove that the lessee would have been interrupted in the enjoyment of the premises during the residue of the term.

It is conceded, on all hands, that to excuse the non-performance of a covenant to pay rent, an entry of the lessor, and an eviction of the lessee must be pleaded. But the plaintiff in error contends that the evidence he offered, should have been received as proof of an entry and eviction. This doctrine appears to be entirely new, and no case was cited to show that it was not so. Indeed, the counsel of the plaintiff in error seemed to appeal to the moral, rather than to the municipal law. And if we were to decide this case according to the dictates of morality, we might be disposed to pronounce a judgment in his favor. It is true that the moral law and the law of the land should not be at variance; but if they be so, it is not for us, in our judicial capacity, to reconcile them. We are, in rendering our judgments, not to determine as we may think the law of our country should be, but as we find it established; and the question now presented for our decision is, whether a lessee finding himself temporarily disturbed in the enjoyment of the demised premises by the misconduct or immoral practices of the lessor, may abandon the tenement for the whole term, and be exonerated from the payment of rent. If this question were to be answered in the affirmative, it would, in my opinion, introduce a new and very extensive chapter in the law of landlord and tenant; for if the encouragement or practice of lewdness, on premises under the same roof with the tenements leased, would warrant an abdication by the tenant, and release him from his covenant to pay rent, there is no reason why, if the landlord should by any other means render the occupation of the premises inconvenient or uncomfortable, the same consequences should not ensue. It would be so if the landlord were to maintain a house of ill fame adjoining or opposite to, or in the same street with the demised premises; if he were to set up a noisy or noxious manufactory near the tenements he had let; or if the landlord should happen to have the plague of a scolding wife under the same roof with his tenant, the tenant might feel himself authorized to leave the premises, and claim an exoneration from the payment of rent. . . .

Were the evidence to be admitted under this plea, it would be carrying legal fiction farther, I believe, than it ever had been carried, and farther than is consistent with any notions of justice.

The plaintiff finding that the allegation of the defendant, in answer to the demand for rent, was, that he had been turned out of possession, and kept out by the plaintiff himself, might have gone to trial without testimony, resting on his knowledge that no such facts existed, or with witnesses to prove that the allegations were entirely untrue. But when the cause is opened, he learns, for the first time, that the allegation that he turned the defendant out of possession was a mere fiction, and that he has to defend himself against the charge of having kept a bawdy-house? If the plaintiff had been apprised that this was the fact on which the defendant relied, are we to intend that he could have brought no testimony to contradict the allegations of the defendant?

If the facts alleged by the defendant would form a defence to the action, it is not possible that the rules of pleading are so absurd as to exclude the defendant from putting them on the record in the form of a plea. It cannot be that the science of special pleading holds a party to allege that his adversary entered on premises, drove him off, and kept him out, when he means to prove no such fact; but, on the contrary, that he left the premises voluntarily, and abandoned them of his own free will, because the plaintiff had offended him by permitting and participating in immoral practices in apartments under the same roof with the demised premises. There are fictions of law sanctioned by great antiquity, which we are obliged to maintain, though they are such a violation of truth and common sense as to subject legal science to contempt and

odium. I think we should add to the number of these, if we were to
countenance so violent a fiction as that on which the defendant relies.

But a majority were for reversal.

Whereupon

It was ordered, that the judgment of the supreme court be reversed;
and that a *venire de novo* should issue in the court below.

[Judgment reversed by vote of 16 to 6.]

◆ JACOBS v. MORAND
59 Misc. 200, 110 N.Y.S. 208 (Sup. Ct. 1908)

GIEGERICH, J. The action was brought to recover the sum of $50, alleged
to be due as rent for the month of November, 1907, for an apartment
occupied by the defendant under a lease from the plaintiff. On behalf of
the defendant evidence was given that the apartment, including the
beds and closets, and all the rooms, was overrun with water bugs and
bedbugs. The complaint was dismissed, with costs, and the judgment is
sought to be supported on the ground that the presence of the vermin
constituted a constructive eviction.

The apartment in suit was not under the control of the plaintiff, and
no evidence was given of any express covenant in the lease to keep the
apartment free from vermin; and in the absence of such a covenant the
lessee, under the circumstances detailed above and in the absence of
fraud, deceit, or wrongdoing on the part of the plaintiff, ran the risk of
the condition of the property in that regard. . . . In Vanderbilt v. Persse,
3 E.D. Smith, 428, the court said that, although a bad smell in the
pantry, and the kitchen being too hot with the stove in it, and bad smells
from the front window, a stagnant pond of water near the place, bad
smell from fish, and vermin in the bedrooms, were all matters that
might have given some trouble to eradicate, yet none of them could be
held sufficient to relieve the tenant from his liability, or to come within
the rule that defines an eviction. Pomeroy v. Tyler, 9 N.Y. St. Rep. 514,
was also a case very similar in its facts to the present one, and it was
held, McAdam, C.J., writing the opinion, that the fact that the rooms
occupied by the tenant were overrun with vermin, namely, bedbugs,
cockroaches, croton bugs, and red ants, making it inconvenient to in-
habit the premises and rendering them untenantable, did not constitute
a constructive eviction of the tenant. The following remarks of Chief
Justice McAdam, in the course of such opinion, are especially applicable
to the present case (page 515):

> The Legislature has passed a statute relieving tenants from their com-
> mon law obligations, where the demised premises have been destroyed by
> fire, tempest, or other sudden and unexpected event (Laws 1860, p.592,

c.345; Suydam v. Jackson, 54 N.Y. 453); but the legislative sense of relief to tenants has not as yet reached the case of rats, mice, bugs, roaches, or other vermin, and all questions as to them must be decided according to the wisdom of the common law. The inconvenience is one to which all more or less are subject at times, but which, with ordinary skill and attention, may be abated by the tenant.

The judgment should therefore be reversed, and a new trial ordered, with costs to the appellant to abide the event. All concur.

◆ REMEDCO CORP. v. BRYN MAWR HOTEL CORP.
45 Misc. 2d 586, 257 N.Y.S.2d 525 (Civ. Ct. 1965)

SHAPIRO, Judge. By this holdover summary proceeding, the landlord seeks to bring to an end the lease of the entire building located at 420 West 121st Street, New York City, which lease has thirteen years to run, because of the long course of conduct of roomers involving narcotics addiction, prostitution, attempted rape, homicide and other disreputable occurrences.

Although adjacent to one of our leading institutions of learning and culture, the premises, operated as the Bryn Mawr Hotel, are located in a section of this city where many happenings have taken place, dangerous to the life, security and comfort of people living there and those who travel through it. The subject premises have been marked by the Police Department as a focal point for the gathering of persons bent upon committing immoral, illegal and dangerous acts. The record is replete with repeated arrests of roomer-occupants for narcotics addiction, for prostitution and other heinous crimes.

No one hearing the testimony elicited at this trial can help but shudder at the degradation which has befallen the inhabitants of this section of our city. Conditions in this area had come to that unhappy pass where the local people, including the university and other institutions, banded together to establish a private 24-hour security patrol. When citizens band together to protect themselves because the conditions are so severe as to vitiate even the most diligent and comprehensive efforts of the municipal departments charged with the protection and security of the local citizenry, then, indeed, this court is most sensitive to their plight.

In the face of these reprehensible and highly dangerous circumstances, the tenant challenges the jurisdiction of this court to hear this proceeding. The tenant further claims that this is a valuable lease of an entire building possessing a monetary level of upwards of $100,000 and hence the landlord seeks a forfeiture of tenant's substantial property. The tenant also asserts technical objections, claiming that the lease merely calls for tenant's diligent efforts after notice to cure the complained of conditions, and not their actual alleviation.

Responding to the evidence plainly showing repeated occurrences of inimical and dangerous behavior, tenant says that after such occasions came to its attention it took steps to remove the offending occupant. But tenant admits nothing was done and no procedure adopted to screen out potentially undesirable occupants. All that was required of any roomer was the payment of one week's rent in advance. Hardly indeed can this be a method by which undesirable roomers would be excluded from the building. Tenant in effect says that inherent in the operation of a rooming house is the inevitable attraction, as occupants, of narcotic addicts, prostitutes and other malodorous and evil characters. With rather callous attitude, the tenant affirms that this is the "nature of the beast," that thereby the tenant automatically acquires an exculpatory shield against landlord's and the community's efforts to rid the area of this blight.

Manifestly, this argument would sustain and protect evil and wrongdoing by giving it a base for operation — which in effect has happened here. The vital question really is: Can the landlord terminate a tenancy where the permitted use, though on its face a legal one, actually turns out to be a haven for degradation dangerous to the entire community?

Tenant's answer to this question is that the landlord is helpless so long as the tenant, after the offending acts are committed regardless of their continuity and repetition, calls in the police or takes other steps to terminate the occupancy. Thus the attitude of the tenant is that it need do nothing to prevent the blight but merely take action after the corrupt acts have exploded into grievous antisocial behavior.

Unless there is the most persuasive basis therefor, tenant should not have available such a defense to excuse it from adopting a more effective and rigorous tenant selection procedure. It could never have been intended that technical lease provisions can and are to be the device by which the tenant can ignore its obligations to the public and the community, not only to cure evil conditions after their eruption, but also to take reasonably effective measures to prevent their occurrence.

Tenant asserts the theory that the provisions of this lease with regard to its termination set up conditions subsequent as distinct from conditional limitations, and that the former call for a forfeiture and not an expiration of the term of the tenancy. Tenant goes on to argue that summary proceedings will not lie to give force to conditions subsequent and that hence this court has no jurisdiction.

Veiled in language offtimes confusing and contradictory, the doctrines distinguishing condition from conditional limitations have become perplexing in their application. But basic in all of the determinations is the search for the intentions of the parties as to whether the specified term shall be accelerated to its close if the prohibited or pro-scribed circumstances are found to exist, or the tenancy is to continue dependent upon an option or choice solely resting with the landlord, accompanied by a consequent enforced right of re-entry and for-feiture. . . .

Unlike many cases where the breach of the lease gave landlord only the right of re-entry, here upon the breach "the term . . . shall im-mediately cease and determine. . . ." Manifestly this lease requires no re-entry to bring it to an end — its end is specifically brought about *in haec verba.* By verbalizing the distinction between "termination" and "expiration," massive difficulties have crept into the law. Rather, em-phasis should rest not on whether the landlord has an option to call for an earlier "expiration" or for a sudden "termination," but whether the landlord-tenant relationship is cut off by re-entry alone, or, it sooner ends under the specific lease terms because of the breach of its restrictive provisions. . . .

Preserved even from the very beginning of the New York Summary Proceedings Statute was the availability of summary proceedings to oust a tenant of premises used for prostitution, or "house or place of assigna-tion for lewd persons." That the Bryn Mawr Hotel was used as the rendezvous for roomers bent on dissolute and profligate behavior is clear; that this summary proceeding could be maintained under Subd. 5 of Sec. 711 of the Real Property Actions and Proceedings Law, and under the Multiple Dwelling Law, §352, is equally clear.

From the early beginnings, the summary proceedings statute was deemed to be remedial and its purposes not to be easily defeated. As its title plainly indicates, the state intended the proceeding to be summary, short, sharp and decisive; this legislative intent was and is to be given full effect.

Consonant with its purposes and in accord with legislative intent, this court holds that it has jurisdiction over this proceeding because under the lease terms the tenancy had expired and, even if this not be so, the petition and proof are sufficient under Subd. 5 of Sec. 711 of the Real Property Actions and Proceedings Law, to warrant a final judgment for landlord.

Judgment for landlord against the tenant and subtenants. Issuance of warrant stayed to March 31, 1965. Use and occupancy to be paid at present rental.

◆ PEOPLE EX REL. TUTTLE v. WALTON
2 Thompson & Cook 533 (N.Y. Sup. Ct. 1874)

DANIELS, J. The affidavit presented to the justice, on behalf of the land-lord, in the proceedings taken before him for the removal of his tenant, for the nonpayment of rent, contained a statement of all the facts required to bring the case within the statute, and the person who made it swore positively to the fact that he was the agent of the landlord. It was, within the construction of the statute adopted by the courts, sufficient to give the justice jurisdiction of the proceedings. Upon the affidavit the justice issued his summons, in the form prescribed, which was served upon the tenant and under tenants named in the proceedings, and upon its return day the tenant appeared and filed his own affidavit, simply controverting the fact that the rent claimed was due; and that was denied because the tenant had tendered one-half the rent before the proceedings were taken, and had an off-set to the other half for improvements upon the premises, which the landlord had agreed to pay, a claim of $150 for the use of the premises, which the landlord had also agreed to pay, and for certain services of the tenant and his clerks. The justice held that this did not contain a legal answer to the application made by the landlord, and in that he was clearly right, for the affidavit, so far as it depended upon the off-set, in substance admitted that the rent was due and unpaid. As long as the demands mentioned in the tenant's affidavit were unapplied to the rent due, both they and the rent were entirely separate and independent demands. The statutes relating to the allowance of off-sets and counter-claims have no application to the proceedings provided for the removal of tenants for the nonpayment of rent. They are solely applicable to actions, and to such actions only as are mentioned in the statutes.

The determination of the justice was correct, and the proceedings should be affirmed, with costs.

◆ SUMMARY PROCEEDINGS TO RECOVER THE POSSESSION OF LAND IN CERTAIN CASES: OF POSSIBLE ENTRIES AND DETAINERS
3 N.Y. Rev. Stats. tit. X, art. 1st (6th ed. 1875)

§28   Any tenant or lessee at will, or at sufferance, or for any part of a year, or for one or more years, of any houses, land or tenements . . . may be removed from such premises by any judge of the county courts of the county, or by any justice of the peace of the city or town where the premises are situated, or by any mayor . . . in the manner hereinafter prescribed in the following cases:

1. Where such person shall hold over and continue in possession of the demised premises, or any part thereof, after the expiration of this term, without the permission of the landlord;
2. Where such person shall hold over . . . after any default in the payment of rent . . . and a demand of such rent shall have been

made, or three days' notice in writing . . . shall have been served . . . on the person owing the same . . . ;

3. Where the tenant or lessee of a term of three years, or less, shall have taken the benefit of any insolvent act. . . .

§29 Any landlord or lessor . . . may make oath in writing, of the facts, which . . . authorize the removal of a tenant. . . .

§30 On receiving such affidavit such officer shall issue his summons . . . requiring any person in possession . . . to remove from the same, or to show cause . . . within such time as shall appear reasonable, not less than three nor more than five days . . . ; provided, however, that in the cases where a person continues in possession . . . after the expiration of his term . . . the magistrate, if the summons be issued on the day the term expires or on the next day thereafter, may direct such summons to be made returnable on the same day (at any time after twelve o'clock noon and before six o'clock in the afternoon).

§33 If at the time appointed . . . no sufficient cause be shown to the contrary, and due proof of the service of such summons be made . . . he shall thereupon issue his warrant to the sheriff of the county. . . .

§34 Any person in possession . . . may, at the time appointed in such summons for showing cause, file an affidavit with the magistrate who issued the same, denying the facts . . . and the matters thus controverted may be tried by the magistrate, or by a jury; provided either party . . . shall . . . demand a jury, and at the time of such demand, pay to such magistrate the necessary costs and expenses of obtaining such jury.

§44 The issuing of such warrant of removal shall be stayed in the case of a proceeding for the non-payment of rent, if the person owing such rent shall . . . pay the rent due and all the costs and charges of the proceedings. . . .

§47 The supreme court may award a certiorari for the purpose of examining any adjudication made . . . but the proceedings on any such application shall not be stayed or suspended by such writ. . . .

§49 In all cases of an application pursuant to . . . this article, the prevailing party shall recover costs. . . .

§52 The proceedings before such justice may be removed by appeal to the county court. . . . But . . . in order to stay the issuing of such warrant or execution, there shall, in case of appeal by the tenant, be security also given for the payment of all rent accruing or to accrue upon said premises subsequent to the said application to such justice.

MAXWELL v. SIMONS, 77 Misc. 2d 184, 353 N.Y.S.2d 589 (Civ. Ct. 1973): Prior to 1820, the only remedy which a landlord had was by action in ejectment. That was, of course, an expensive and dilatory proceeding which, in many instances amounted to a denial of justice. By degrees, the remedy has been extended until the statute now covers a variety of cases such as holding over after title has been perfected under a sale on execution, or under foreclosure, or under agreement to work land on shares, or where property has been squatted upon, or where an owner or tenant of premises in the neighborhood of premises used or occupied as a bawdy house is authorized to institute proceedings. . . . The effect of the various revisions was to bring summary proceedings within the range of our remedial procedure. They are still statutory proceedings in the prosecution of which the requirements of the state must be met and they are usually instituted in Courts of circumscribed jurisdiction where the right of act depends upon the sufficiency of the record. . . .

The fact that the landlord has commenced actions at law for all rents in arrears at the time a summary proceeding for the non-payment of rent was commenced was held not to constitute a bar to the summary proceeding on the ground of election of remedies. . . . Conversely, the landlord's right to sue the tenant for arrears under a contract cause of action remains inviolate, where, as in this case, the landlord sought summary proceedings first. The causes of action for arrears in rent for more than three months should be commenced by an action at law in the other Part of this Court where a money judgment only can be rendered and not in the Landlord and Tenant Portion of this Court where an eviction can take place. It is unconscionable for a landlord to permit his tenant to amass large sums of arrears, which total the tenant cannot be expected to pay in one lump sum within five days. This is true especially in cases where an eviction order would mandate a decontrolled apartment status through the operation of the Court's eviction order.

Accordingly, I have rendered judgment in favor of the landlord in each of the above cases for a three month period immediately prior to the commencement of the action as demanded in the within petition and precept and have dismissed the suit for all prior months with leave to sue in the proper forum.

Notes

1. Minnie McCall had given a lease "for as many years as desired by the party of the second part from Nov. 1926" at the yearly rent of $300. Tenant Gamester had signed nothing. McCall sold to Foley, who had notice of the lease to Gamester. Foley refused rent from Gamester and served notice to vacate. "[W]here the lessee is not bound for any definite period, . . . the landlord is not prevented from ending the relation." Foley v. Gamester, 271 Mass. 55, 170 N.E. 799 (1930).

2. Plaintiff alleged that he was in lawful occupation of a store in Boston, and that defendant employed persons to throw "him and the contents of his store" into the street. Defendant said plaintiff had been a

tenant at will, and had remained on the premises after receiving notice that the tenancy was at an end. The court said that since plaintiff had no right to remain, he cannot sue "even if the defendant was actuated by malice," because the plaintiff sustained "no legal injury." Groustra v. Bourges, 141 Mass. 7, 4 N.E. 623 (1886).

3. When tenant's term expired, on February 1, 1906, he had removed six wagonloads of household goods, and was making every effort to leave, but was detained by the sickness of his wife and child, who could not be removed without endangering their lives. Landlord sued to eject. The jury found for the tenant, but then an Indiana appellate court reversed, finding the defense (act of God) impermissible. "[I]f a tenant for a definite period of time remains in possession after the expiration of the term, without the landlord's consent, the landlord may elect either to consider the tenant a trespasser and bring the proper action to remove him from the leased premises, or to consider the tenancy renewed and recover the rent." Gifford v. Bingham, 42 Ind. App. 37, 84 N.E. 1099 (1908).

4. "Squatting" is the term for taking up residence "without any colour of right . . . [except] that he was homeless and that this house of land was standing empty." McPhail v. Persons, Names Unknown, 3 [1973] W.L.R. 71 (Ct. App.). The law, of course, is clear:

> If homelessness were once admitted as a defence to trespass, no one's house could be safe. . . . So the courts must, for the sake of law and order, take a firm stand. They must refuse to admit the plea of necessity to the hungry and the homeless: and trust that their distress will be relieved by the charitable and the good. [Southwark Borough Council v. Williams, [1971] Ch. 734 (Ct. App.).]

The owner invaded by squatters has two choices. He can repel them by force, so long as he uses no more than is reasonably necessary; or he can sue in the action once called ejectment, now in England known as an action for the recovery of land. "[S]eeing that the owner could take possession at once without the help of the courts, it is plain that, when he does come to the courts, he should not be in any worse position. The courts should give him possession at once, else he would be tempted to do it himself." McPhail v. Persons, Names Unknown, *supra,* affirming a refusal to give the squatters four weeks to find another home. 3 [1973] W.L.R. at 75.

Writing in *McPhail,* Lawton, L.J. said:

> Were I a cadi dispensing justice under a palm tree I might have been able to solve the problems which arise in this case. I might have ordered the plaintiff, Mr. McPhail, to forgo the profits which he seeks to make by converting 4 Thornhill Square, Islington, into flats and the Bristol Corpora-

tion to postpone the demolition of 23 Normandy Road for the purpose of extending the playing fields of a school. Cadis do not sit in this court. The problem has had to be solved by the application of principle; and in my judgment the solution is to be found in first principles, even though those principles have been encrusted, and partly hidden, by the legal dust of centuries. . . . [H]e who sought equity had to show that the common law proceedings were impinging upon some right or interest which he had. . . . What equitable right or interest has a trespasser? . . . Forcible entry has been a crime since the Forcible Entry Act of 1381. . . .

Lord Justice Lawton's views produced this reply, Case Note, 89 Law Q. Rev. 460 (1973):

[T]his is not the first occasion on which the Court of Appeal has spoken of cadis in somewhat disparaging — or is it envious? — terms: . . . Cadis would surely protest that they, too, had to have regard for principle and precedent. For civil cases this was the Mohammedan canon law which was superior even to the dictates of the rulers, let alone the whims of the judges. One cadi was dramatically reminded of this. It is recorded of the Caliph Omar that "to vindicate the majesty of the law he dismissed the Cadi who rose from his seat out of respect for him when he was appearing before him in the capacity of a suitor." The cadis and the Court of Appeal may have more in common than is sometimes supposed.

5. On the medieval law of self-help, see F. W. Maitland, The Beatitude of Seisin, 4 L.Q. Rev. 24, 28-30 (1888), also in 1 Collected Papers of F. W. Maitland 407, 415-417 (1911):

Now in order that we may understand the spirit of this assize as administered in Bracton's day, we had better at once put the extreme case, which is also the simplest case: — A is the true owner, or very tenant in fee simple, of land and is seised of it; he lives on it and cultivates it himself; there comes one B who has no right whatever; he casts A out and keeps him out, by force and arms. When, we must ask, does A cease to be seised and when does B begin to be seised? Doubtless in one sense or for one purpose, A is disseised so soon as he is put off the land; he can at once complain to a court of law that B has disseised him. Indeed to found such a complaint no actual ouster was necessary; had he repulsed B he might still have complained of a disseisin. The assize serves the purpose of an interdict for retaining, as well as that of an interdict for recovering possession; had B but entered with an intent to assume possession this would have been disseisin enough. In many cases the mere troubling of possession is a sufficient disseisin, if the person seised choose to complain of it as such. But even when A has been extruded from the land, B is not at once seised (at least as regards A), that is to say, he is not protected by the assize (at least as against A); if within a certain limited time A returns and ejects B, B will have no ground of complaint. . . . Really there seems to be a set of hard and fast rules about the matter. A must turn B out within four days; otherwise B will have a seisin protected by the assize. Such is the case if A was actually on the land and was himself cast out. If however he was away from the land when the disseisin took place, then a longer time will be allowed him. In the first place, he will not be disseised until the act of disseisin is brought to his knowledge. In the second place, he will then have a reasonable time within which to come to the land, and after that he will have his four days. The "reasonable" time is in several cases determined by the parallel rules about essoins. Thus the man who is in Gascony or on a pilgrimage to Compostella has forty days, two floods and an ebb, fifteen days and then the four days. Bracton, if I understand him rightly, seems to think that for a man in England fifteen days would always be reasonable, but says that at the present time this rule is not observed. The four days he tells us are allowed a man for the purpose of collecting friends and arms. Fleta and Britton repeat, though not very clearly, this curious doctrine; four days seems still the fixed time within which a person who has himself been cast out of land may lawfully enter upon and eject his ejector.

Mr. Nichols in his fine edition of Britton has supplied a gloss from a Cambridge MS., which there is some reason for attributing to John of Longueville, a justice of Edward the Second's time. The first words of it are very interesting — "Where the disseisin is done in the presence of the disseisee, the disseisor must be ejected within five days; because the law of ancient time granted that the disseisee should go one day to the east, the second day to the west, the third day to the south, and the fourth day to the north, to seek succour of his friends all the country round."

6. Issues of self-help often turn on the extent of an individual's right to use property.

During the 1968 New York City teachers' strike, the Board of Education declared that the schools were open. Horelick, a teacher who opposed the strike, sought entry to Washington Irving High School, but was denied admission by the custodian. Horelick entered through a basement window that had been broken by a student that morning. The New York Court of Appeals said "the issue turns on whether the affected teachers had a 'license' or 'privilege' to open the school by surreptitious entry and force, and not whether they had a right or duty to be in the school." By 4-3 vote, it upheld a conviction for criminal trespass. People v. Horelick, 30 N.Y.2d 453, 285 N.E.2d 864, 334 N.Y.S.2d 623 (1972), *cert. denied*, 410 U.S. 943 (1973). A writ of habeas corpus granted in U.S. district court was reversed by the court of appeals. United States ex rel. Horelick v. Criminal Court of the City of New York, 507 F.2d 37 (2d Cir. 1974).

Consider the propositions of "bad old landlord-tenant law":

a) No implied landlord promise as to the condition of the premises at the outset of the tenancy;

b) No implied landlord obligation to maintain the condition of the premises during the tenancy;
c) Independence of covenants: even where the landlord has obligations, they cannot be pleaded as a defense to a major tenant violation such as non-payment of rent;
d) Summary process: eviction for non-payment of rent or for holding over gets court priority, sometimes in a specialized court.

What social and economic assumptions and situations explain these doctrines? To what extent are those reasons relevant in urban housing situations today? How would you argue for changes in the doctrines? Twenty years of landlord-tenant law "reform" is the subject of the next chapter.

8 ◆ CURRENT CONTROVERSY OVER LANDLORD-TENANT LAW: TOWARD A WARRANTY OF HABITABILITY

A. LEGAL REGULATION OF URBAN HOUSING

◆ NEW YORK CITY PLANNING COMMISSION,
NEIGHBORHOOD PRESERVATION IN
NEW YORK CITY
25-31, 35-44 (A. Garvin ed., 1973)

HOUSING REHABILITATION

Physical deterioration always occurs as housing ages, but some building types are more easily maintained and rehabilitated than others. A brownstone may currently be a run-down rooming house, but if the owner wants to convert it to floor-through apartments or a single-family home, it can be a very desirable building. On the other hand, a well-maintained tenement can be a pleasant home, but it is likely to have poorer light, ventilation, and room layout than buildings originally designed with higher standards. Construction materials also have significance for maintenance and rehabilitation. Wooden buildings, for example, generally have a shorter life than masonry structures. Thus in order to analyze the potential success and long-term impact of housing preservation efforts, the quality of the building stock as originally designed and built must be understood.

EARLY CONCEPTS

The significance of this caveat is not inherent in housing rehabilitation, and it is more important in New York than many other cities. For if the City had been developed as envisioned by the State Commission* that designed the street grid for Manhattan in 1811, the quality of the building stock would not be a major factor in creating a neighborhood preservation strategy for the City. The Commission established rectangular residential blocks and sold land in lots of 25 by 100 feet. They envisioned these blocks built up with rowhouses 25 feet wide and no more than 50 feet deep. All rooms in these buildings would receive light and air from 60-foot wide streets or 100-foot wide avenues on the front, and spacious rear yards on the back [see Figure 8-1]. But the Commission's regulations covered only the street system, not building type and size nor lot subdivisions. They assumed that legal controls beyond street and block lines were unnecessary.

TENEMENTS

But, when massive immigration in the 19th century bloated the demand for low-rent housing, developers responded by cramming the

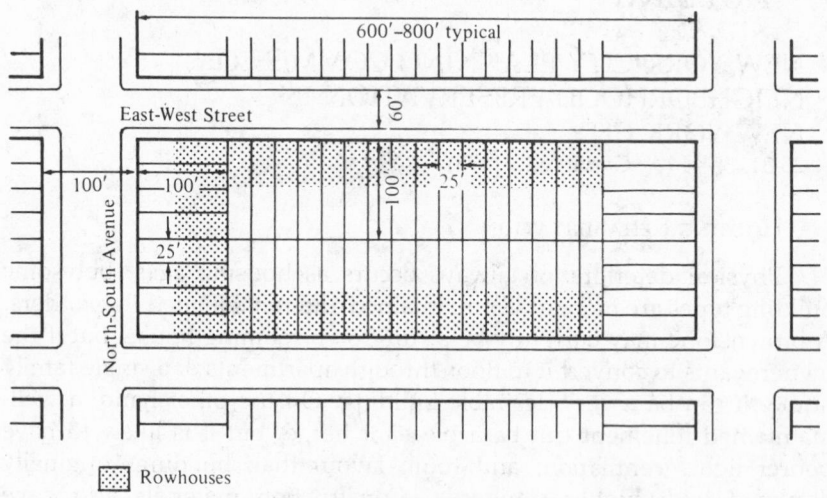

☷ Rowhouses

FIGURE 8-1
Typical New York City block

---

* In 1807 the N.Y. State Legislature appointed Simon De Witt, Gouverneur Morris, and John Rutherford as a committee to prepare a "final and conclusive" map for the extension of N.Y.C. They hired John Randall, Jr. to prepare what has since become the common grid for the City.

maximum number of rooms onto their land. Lots were subdivided. Where once three buildings were planned for a 75 by 100-foot parcel, now there were four buildings 18 feet, 9 inches wide, or five buildings 15 feet wide. Instead of rowhouses two rooms and 50 feet deep, tenements extended 90 feet and eight or more rooms deep, almost the full extent of the lot. This created a cramped series of walk-through rooms without natural ventilation [see Figure 8-2].

Children suffocated in fires that sucked the oxygen from their rooms. Thousands died from tuberculosis, cholera, small pox, and a variety of infectious diseases that spread in these overcrowded tenement slums. Conditions were almost as bad in "model tenements" built by benevolent reformers. Gotham Court, built in 1851 for the express purpose of rescuing the poor from such noxious conditions, is described by Jacob Riis:

> A double row of five-story tenements, back to back under a common roof, extending back from the street two hundred and thirty-four feet, with barred openings in the dividing wall, so that the tenants may see but cannot get at each other from the stairs, makes the "court." Alleys — one wider by a couple of feet than the other, whence the distinction Single and Double Alley — skirt the barracks on either side.
>
> In 1862, ten years after it was finished, a sanitary official counted 146 cases of sickness in the court, including "all kinds of infectious disease," from small pox down, and reported that of 138 children born in it, in less than three years 61 had died, mostly before they were one year old. Seven years later the inspector of the district reported to the Board of Health that "nearly ten per cent of the population is sent to the public hospitals each year."

HOUSING LAWS

Conditions grew so bad that in 1867 New York State passed the first Tenement House Act which provided at least three square feet of transom window for each room (provided the window opened onto another room which had a window providing access to an air shaft), one water source in the house or yard, and an approved fire exit. This law, also known as the Old Tenement Law, was amended in 1879 to ensure a window opening directly onto a 28-inch air shaft and minimum room sizes of 60 square feet. In 1901, the State decided that all such buildings were unfit for human habitation and passed a New Tenement Law that required one water closet per apartment, replaced the air shaft with court yards providing natural light as well as ventilation, and limited lot coverage to 70%. Finally, in 1929, a new State Multiple Dwelling Law prohibited the construction of tenements in New York City.

The 1929 law required that every building with three or more apartments have a water closet and bath and that every room for cooking

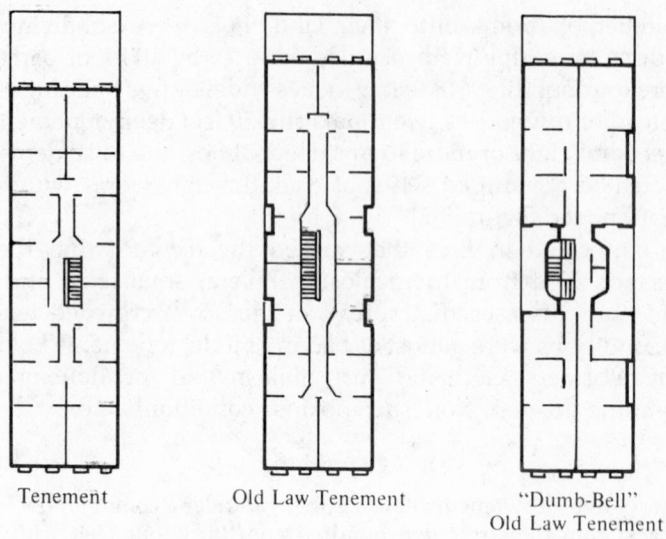

Tenement   Old Law Tenement   "Dumb-Bell"
                                            Old Law Tenement

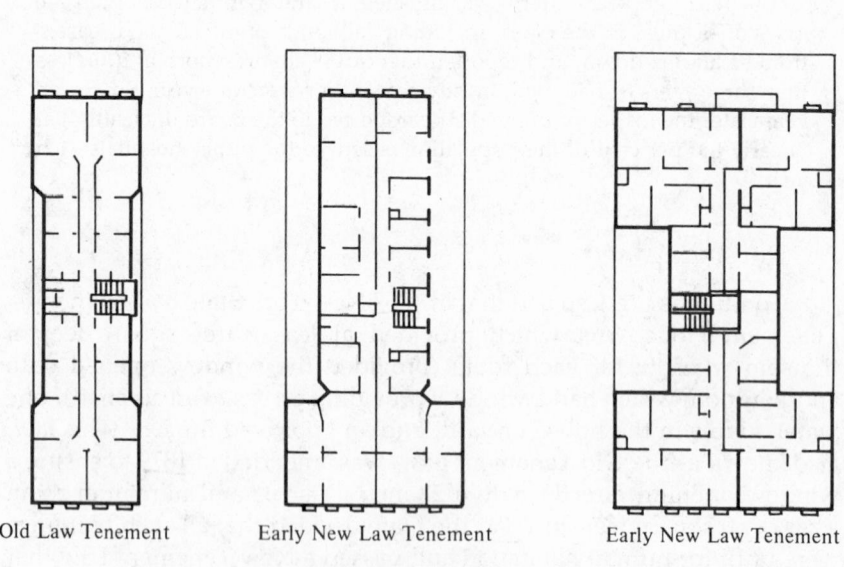

Old Law Tenement   Early New Law Tenement   Early New Law Tenement

FIGURE 8-2
Typical apartment layouts

have a sink with running water. It also mandated light and ventilation for every room by means of at least one window opening directly on a street, court or yard. Regulations specified an adequate size for these courts and yards. Instead of the 28-inch air shafts of the Old Laws (1867-1901) and the 4-foot wide courts of the New Laws (1901-1929), buildings constructed after 1929 opened on inner courts measuring at least 30 by 36 feet if completely enclosed, or 20 by 30 feet if on the lot line.

The City's Housing Stock

As of 1973, these laws left the City with a legacy of 315,358 apartments in 36,771 Old Law Tenement buildings, 806,223 apartments in 46,979 New Law Tenement buildings, and 734,402 apartments in 8,773 multiple dwellings built after 1929. In addition, there are 387,961 one-family and 221,501 two-family homes in New York City, built without having to conform to the regulations for multiple dwellings.

Post-1929 multiple dwellings were built to standards that ensure their continued usability for generations to come, given normal maintenance. Most of the later New Law buildings, with ample court yards, elevators, and through-ventilated apartments, except for age and deterioration, also remain desirable homes.

Old Law Tenements present greater problems. Ideally, converting Old Laws to desirable apartments requires gutting the building, removing substantial parts of the structure, and completely reconstructing the interior. But this is usually a highly impractical and expensive solution. At current rates of production, the City cannot expect to replace some 300,000 low-rent Old Law units for some time. Moreover, when these apartments are air-conditioned, they become more habitable. Thus, while Old law buildings may not be built to current housing standards, the City has little realistic choice but to maintain them in the best condition possible. . . .

◆ G. STERNLIEB, THE TENEMENT LANDLORD
79, 80-82, 88, 93-96 (1966)

The profitability of investment in slum properties is as much a function of financial leverage as the percentage of return on gross income. In the next chapter tenement trading and financing are discussed in more detail, but it is worthwhile noticing here, for example, that if a tenement was purchased for four times its gross rent roll, a fairly generous multiplier, the yield before depreciation and financing charges based on the data presented would be 10 percent, i.e., 40 percent of 25 percent. If, instead of paying cash, the investor were able to secure a mortgage for 50 percent of the purchase price at a 6 percent interest figure, the yield would go up to 14 percent on his cash investment. Rapkin estimates that old-law tenements return 9.3 percent on the total consideration in the West Side Urban Renewal Project. Brownstones return an estimated 10.7 percent and all types of elevator apartments combined return 9.3 percent. . . .

To determine the return on the total value of tenement parcels required some method of assessing the value. . . . [B]ased on the thirty-two parcels examined . . . two approaches to this problem are presented. The first uses the assessment value which is nominally 100 percent; the second uses a multiplier of four times gross income, which in terms of the current market is undoubtedly high. On the former base the thirty-two parcels, which were examined earlier, yield an average return of 12.04 percent and a median of 8.65 percent; on the latter basis the equivalent figures are 8.53 percent and 7.25 percent. Again it should be noted that there is a wide range within the interquartile figure.

In sum then, tenement parcels are returning, before debt service and depreciation, approximately 40 percent of the gross rentals received by the landlord. The actual return on investment in terms of the overall parcel value is clearly in the neighborhood of 10 to 12 percent. The range of variation both in expenses and in net return is considerable. A major factor affecting this is the variation of gross income as a function of the vacancy rates. It is the vacancy rate which determines a substantial part of the upward flexibility of the rent structure as well as the extent of gross rental. Let us examine this very significant function in detail. . . .

The effect of high vacancy rates is much more complex than might be thought at first glance. As yet, for example, they have rarely resulted in rent reductions. As Grebler pointed out, a substantial exposure to high vacancy rates over time is required before the market adjusts price to meet the decreased demand. On the other hand, the high vacancy rate certainly inhibits rent increases. The fear of raising rents in a weak market is compounded of two elements, the possibility of ending up with substantial vacancies, and, perhaps even more significantly, the fear that in order to secure tenants at the increased rates the landlord must take in lower categories of tenantry.

One owner stated: "The only man who can afford the increased rates around here would be the man without roots, a drifter, and they're no good." *The availability of housing for Negroes in better areas of Newark, as well as in the surrounding suburbs, limits the number of people with capacity and willingness to pay high rents in the slum areas. The willingness of tenement owners to make improvements, therefore, is substantially inhibited by the feeling that there would be limited demand for better, i.e., higher rent, apartments.* The controller of a small hospital who owns two parcels in our sample area typified the attitude when he claimed: "Any increase in rents immediately results in vacancies even with the improvements; that's why the tenants are willing to stay in cold-water flats. This type of tenant cannot afford the increase in rents to offset taxes for improvements. The financial economy of the people don't permit it. They're big families with little or no employment."

The fear of losing the tenants one knows for the tenants one doesn't know, upon raising rents, also serves as an inhibitor. The attitude of a fifty-nine-year-old Portuguese resident-owner and construction worker was representative of a substantial number of landlords. He said: "I couldn't raise the rents because I would get bad tenants, and that's the worst thing you can have." Faced with reassessment on this particular parcel and a lid on rents, this owner maintains the place but is very loath to put money into it. . . .

It is the risk factor, typified by the vacant parcel, which raises the required threshold of return on investment in slum properties. In a sense, the very weakness of the market has increased the rewards which potential buyers of slum tenements require in return for their investment. The risks also, as shall be seen again and again in the following chapters, limit the kind of investor who is attracted to slum tenements. Both of these limitations are increased by the fear of housing inspection. One observer put it very aptly:

> Landlords may suddenly be confronted with enthusiastic, if often short-lived, campaigns to enforce long dormant occupancy [and] building codes. Such campaigns are not inherently undesirable, nor is the rental market unable to adjust to consistent standards of code enforcement. But sporadic drives, together with the wide gulf that exists between the standard re-cited in statutory codes and actual enforcement, create many uncertainties; uncertainty is a notoriously uncongenial climate for investors.

The high rate of current return demanded by investors in slum tenements can be summarized as a compound of the fear of costly code crackdowns; the basic weakness of the market, both in terms of rental increases and securing full tenancy; the risk of outright loss through the complete abandonment of a parcel, and in substantial part, the pejoratives which society heaps upon the "slum lord." All of these combine to shape the nature of the trading market in slum tenements — the buying and selling, the maintenance and will to rehabilitate, the very characteristics of the landlords who become involved in tenements — all are closely shaped and defined by the realities of the market.

In sum, high vacancy rates have been looked foward to by urban planners who have felt strongly that the major inhibitor to appropriate code enforcement and rehabilitation efforts was the lack of housing for those displaced. While this potential is now being made available through the actions of the market, the landlord's will and desire to upgrade his parcels, with some exceptions discussed, are being eroded by the relative lack of profitability of those parcels. Faced with a weak market, the entrepreneur can do one of three things:

1. Sell out, or
2. Do as little as possible in terms of new investment and wait for "better times," or
3. Upgrade his holdings so as to attract either higher paying or a more stable tenantry.

Which shall the landlord choose?

B. LANDLORD'S LIABILITY IN TORT: FROM THE COMMON LAW TO THE HOUSING CODE

The cases that follow tell the story of change in the law of landlord and tenant relations in the District of Columbia. It is pedagogically useful to see the development of the law in one jurisdiction. Students can consider at each stage what approaches they would try next if they were representing poor tenants who were clients at a legal services office, or if they were representing landlords. Also, because of the District of Columbia's special status as a federal enclave, these landlord-tenant cases were considered by a federal court of appeals. As you will see, some of these judicial opinions were written for the law reviews and the property casebooks. But keep in mind as you read the cases that similar developments in the law were also occurring by judicial decision and by statute in some other jurisdictions. Material in the later part of this chapter shows approaches to landlord-tenant issues in several states.

◆ BOWLES v. MAHONEY
  202 F.2d 320 (D.C. Cir. 1952), *cert. denied*, 344 U.S. 935 (1953)

MILLER, Circuit Judge. The appellant, Sarah Edna Bowles, is the owner of a parcel of ground at 2320 H Street, N.W., in the District of Columbia. The lot is some 6 feet higher than the level of the traveled portion of H Street, and the residence thereon extends to the front property line. In front of the house the publicly owned "parking"[1] rises somewhat abruptly from the front sidewalk so that a flight of nine steps is required to reach the front door from the sidewalk — a distance at street level of about 20 feet. Thus the parking in front of the residence is a rather high sloping bank of earth between the sidewalk and the property line, which

---

1. This word is used to describe the portion of the street which lies between the sidewalk and the property line.

seems to the passersby to be the front yard of the resident. Technically, however, the parking is a part of the street owned by the United States and controlled by the District of Columbia.

On one side, the dwelling at 2320 H Street is attached to the house on the adjoining lot. Along that side line of the property is a passageway two and one-half feet wide which extends from the front sidewalk through the parking and under the house through a tunnel-like opening. This passageway, which gives access from the sidewalk to the rear of the premises is on the level of H Street. From the sidewalk to the house, the passageway is protected from the rises with the slope of the bank until it reaches, at the house, a height of about 6 feet. A permit for the erection of the retaining wall in the parking was issued by the District of Columbia on February 18, 1896. It may be presumed that the then owner of the property at 2320 H Street constructed the wall soon after that date.

On December 15, 1936, B. F. Saul Company, apparently the renting agent for the owner, Mrs. Bowles, leased the entire premises at 2320 H Street to one Luke Gaither. The lease, a copy of which is in the record, does not obligate the landlord to make repairs. There is no statute im-

PHOTOGRAPH 8-1
The *Bowles* site (1977)

posing that duty on a landlord. Gaither's sister, Mrs. Helen Armstrong, who had lived in the house some years before the date of the lease, continued thereafter to occupy it with her brother. On March 30, 1948, Mrs. Armstrong's son, Ralph Mahoney, who was then seven years old and who lived at 2320 H Street with his mother and uncle, was at play in the passageway above described at a point perhaps half way between the property line and the front sidewalk, which was therefore in the area known as the parking. A portion of the retaining wall collapsed and struck him, inflicting serious injuries.

Through his mother as next friend, the child brought this tort action against Mrs. Bowles, the owner of the property, and against the District of Columbia. It was alleged in the complaint that Mrs. Bowles erected the brick retaining wall in the publicly owned parking with the knowledge and consent of the District of Columbia ". . . for the enhancement of value and benefit of premises 2320 H Street, N.W. owned by defendant, Sarah Edna Bowles.

"That as the result of the defendants' negligence and failure to keep said wall in good repair, on March 30, 1948, the said wall fell, collapsed and crumbled upon the plaintiff, Ralph Mahoney, while the plaintiff was using the aforesaid abutting and adjoining sidewalk for a lawful and proper purpose."

Thus the plaintiff's theory is seen to be this: Mrs. Bowles, having constructed the wall in the parking for the benefit of her property, was under a duty to maintain it in a safe condition; she violated her duty by negligently failing to keep the wall in repair; as a result of her negligence the wall collapsed and injured tenant's invitee; she is therefore liable in damages to the invitee. The District of Columbia, says the complaint, permitted the structure to be erected, and negligently failed to keep it in repair.

Mrs. Armstrong testified at the trial that two years before the accident she had noticed a crack in the retaining wall which she attributed to an explosion which had occurred in a nearby electric "sewer." Although she did not regard the condition as dangerous, she informed B. F. Saul Company that the wall had cracked and was told it would not be repaired. No notice of the crack in the wall was given to the District of Columbia. Mrs. Armstrong said that on previous occasions B. F. Saul Company had caused minor repairs to be made to the premises. There was no other evidence tending to show what caused a portion of the wall to fall. Mrs. Armstrong, who at the time was seated at the front window of the house, said she saw the wall suddenly collapse. Ralph's aunt testified to the same effect.

The defendants' motions for a directed verdict, made at the conclusion of the plaintiff's evidence, were denied. Mrs. Bowles stood on her motion and introduced no evidence. The District of Columbia proceeded with proof, and at the end of all the evidence both motions were renewed and again denied. Over the objection of the defendant, the trial judge instructed the jury on the doctrine of *res ipsa loquitur*. Having been so instructed, the jury found for the plaintiff child in the sum of $2,500.00 against both defendants. These appeals are from the judgment entered pursuant to the verdict. Both defendants complain of the District Court's failure to direct a verdict in their favor and of the instruction on *res ipsa*. The District of Columbia assigns other related errors.

As to Mrs. Bowles, Judge Groner, speaking for this court, said, "before the owner of the premises can be held liable [for injuries due to a defect therein], there must be a failure on his part to perform a duty which the law imposes." We must therefore ascertain whether Mrs. Bowles owed the child the duty of maintaining the wall in good repair. The plaintiff, Ralph Mahoney, was living in the house at the invitation of his uncle, who was Mrs. Bowles' tenant, so he was using the appurtenant passageway as the tenant's invitee. The rule is that the duties and liabilities of a landlord to persons on the leased premises by the invitation of the tenant are those owed to the tenant himself. It follows that Mrs. Bowles is not liable for the child's injuries unless she would have been liable to her tenant, Luke Gaither, had he been injured under similar circumstances.

We have seen that Mrs. Bowles had not agreed to repair or maintain the demised premises. It is not suggested that she fraudulently concealed from Gaither, at the time the lease was executed, a defect in the retaining wall which was known to her and not to him; in fact it is not suggested that the wall was defective when the lease was made in 1936. The first indication of a defective condition was the crack in the wall which Mrs. Armstrong noticed in 1946. So, if the crack indicated a defective condition, it was one which arose during the term of the lease. Absent any statutory or contract duty, the lessor is not responsible for an injury resulting from a defect which developed during the term. . . .

In the foregoing, we have treated the case as though the accident had occurred on the premises owned by Mrs. Bowles and leased to Gaither. That the child was injured in the parking area and not on the premises proper, we regard as immaterial for the reason that Mrs. Bowles owed Gaither no greater duty with regard to maintaining the wall in the parking than with respect to keeping the actual premises in repair. As to the latter, we have seen she owed him no duty at all. . . . It follows from what has been said that the trial judge erred in denying Mrs. Bowles' motion for a directed verdict at the conclusion of the plaintiff's evidence.

As to the District of Columbia. The District had control of the publicly owned parking which was servient to the private easement therein enjoyed by the owner of 2320 H Street. The local authorities permitted the owner to erect the wall at his own expense. As between the owner of the premises and the District, there can be no doubt that the former had the duty of maintaining the retaining wall in good repair. When Mrs. Bowles conveyed the property and its appurtenances to Gaither, she transferred to him, and he assumed, the primary duty of keeping the wall safe. So, if Gaither had been injured by the collapse of the wall due to his own negligent failure to repair it, it would hardly be said he could recover from the District. The child had no greater right against the District than Gaither would have had in similar circumstances. The trial judge should have peremptorily instructed the jury to return a verdict in favor of the District of Columbia.

This conclusion makes it unnecessary for us to consider whether it was the District's duty to make regular inspections of the wall, and whether it had constructive notice of the defect in time to have caused repairs which would have prevented the accident. Nor is it material that the court erroneously included in its charge to the jury an instruction on *res ipsa loquitur*.

Reversed and remanded.

BAZELON, Circuit Judge (dissenting). The key to the decision of the court, relieving both the landlord and the District of Columbia from liability, lies in its adherence to the rule at common law that "[a]bsent any statutory or contract duty, the lessor is not responsible for an injury resulting from a defect which developed during the term." I think that rule is an anachronism which has lived on through *stare decisis* alone rather than through pragmatic adjustment to "the felt necessities of [our] time." I would therefore discard it and cast the presumptive burden of liability upon the landlord. This, I think, is the command of the realities and mores of our day.

Courts have gradually recognized, at least in part, that the exalted position which the landlord held at early common law is discordant with the needs of a later day. At early common law a lessee was regarded as having merely a personal right against the lessor. But as a result of several remedies that were created in the lessee's favor, he came to be regarded as having rights *in rem*, and the lease "was regarded as a sale of the demised premises for the term." Upon this thesis, the courts held that a lease was "like the sale of specified personal property to be delivered", and applied the same concept of *caveat emptor* that prevailed generally in that day with respect to the sale of all chattels. As a corollary of this concept, courts generally held that the "destruction or any depreciation of [the] value [of the leased premises], other than such depreciation occasioned by a fault of the lessor, was entirely the loss of the lessee."

"[B]oth the English and the American law have broken almost entirely away from the ancient rule of *caveat emptor*" with respect to the sale of chattels generally. To some extent this development has been reflected in the law governing landlord and tenant relations. For example, now "the lessor, like a vendor, is under the obligation to disclose to the lessee [not only] concealed dangerous conditions existing when possession is transferred, of which he has knowledge . . . ." but also any "information [in his possession] which would lead a reasonable man to suspect that the danger exists . . . ." But with respect to the landlord's responsibility for the condition of the premises during the term of the lease, courts have failed to reflect this development. As a result, the common law in this respect still lags behind the modern notion that in general one who sells an article is presumed to warrant that it is good for the purpose for which it is sold. In order to keep pace, the law should recognize that when one pays for the temporary use of a dwelling, the parties contemplate that insofar as reasonable care on the part of the owner can assure it, the dwelling will be safe and habitable, not only at the time . . . possession is delivered but throughout the period for which payment is made. It is fair to presume that no individual would voluntarily choose to live in a dwelling that had become unsafe for human habitation. The community's enlightened self-interest requires the same presumption. It follows that, at least in the absence of express provision to the contrary, a landlord who leases property should be held to a continuing obligation to exercise reasonable care to provide that which the parties intended he should provide, namely, a safe and habitable dwelling. Applying this view to the circumstances of the present case, the landlord would be liable for the injuries to little Ralph Mahoney as the tenant's invitee. For the lease did not expressly make the tenant responsible for repairs and there is no doubt that the owner of this dilapidated dwelling failed to exercise reasonable care to prevent the collapse of the cracked retaining wall. And since the court's reason for excusing the District of Columbia from liability is that the tenant, and not the landlord, had the duty to repair, that reason would no longer be valid. . . .

Two reasons have been advanced to justify perpetuation of the rule at common law under modern day conditions. First, it is said that the tenant should bear the responsibility for repair during the term of the lease because his control and possession of the premises give him the opportunity to know their condition, whereas the landlord has no such opportunity. This reason might have some validity if the landlord had no right to go upon the premises. But if the landlord is presumed to have the duty to repair, then the concomitant right to enter upon the premises for inspection and repair would be necessarily implied. And, in any case, the landlord can always reserve the right to enter the premises in order to inspect and repair them. Indeed, the case at bar shows that the landlord did enter to make repairs from time to time, not that he was ever refused such entry. And insofar as "notice" is the reason for the rule, it bears emphasis that the landlord had specific notice of the defect which caused the injuries in this case.

The second and a more sophisticated reason for relieving the land-

investment
discouragement

lord from liability is the hypothesis that "it is still socially desirable not to discourage investment in and ownership of real estate, particularly private dwellings." This objective may well be desirable. But it is a fallacious oversimplification to suppose that the common law rule has much to do with the rate of investment in real property. On the other hand, it seems clear to me that the rule operates to defeat the interests of utility and justice. "Upon whom is the loss to be placed, more justly than upon the landlord? Upon the tenant who, because of his poverty . . . risks his own neck to live in the house? Upon the tenant's equally poor guest, the mailman, the visiting nurse, etc.?" Courts are not impervious to the unequal bargaining position of the parties in interpreting their agreements. For, as Mr. Justice Cardozo said, "Rules derived by a process of logical deduction from pre-established conceptions of contract and obligation have broken down before the slow and steady and erosive action of utility and justice." This court illustrated that in Kay v. Cain, where we said that ". . . it is doubtful whether a clause which did undertake to exempt a landlord from responsibility for such negligence would now be valid. The acute housing shortage in and near the District of Columbia gives the landlord so great a bargaining advantage over the tenant that such an exemption might be held invalid on grounds of public policy." There is no reason to adopt an inconsistent view where, as here, the dwelling constitutes the entire premises and there is no clause expressly exempting the landlord from liability. . . .

It may be fairly asked, should not the courts of the District of Columbia await a congressional change of this rule? Mr. Justice Sutherland provided the answer to this query in Funk v. United States, when he said,

> It may be said that the court should continue to enforce the old rule, however contrary to modern experience and thought, and however opposed, in principle, to the general current of legislation and of judicial opinion it may have become, *leaving to Congress the responsibility of changing it*. Of course, Congress has that power; but, if Congress fails to act, as it has failed in respect of the matter now under review, and the court be called upon to decide the question, is it not the duty of the court, if it possess the power, to decide it in accordance with present-day standards of wisdom and justice rather than in accordance with some outworn and antiquated rule of the past? . . .

There is no fixed line dividing the sphere of action as between the legislature and the courts for effecting needed change of a common law rule. The line should not be marked in accordance with "metaphysical conceptions of the nature of judge-made law, nor by the fetish of some implacable tenet, such as that of the division of governmental powers, but by considerations of convenience, of utility, and of the deepest sentiments of justice." "Change of this character should not be left to the Legislature." "If judges have woefully misinterpreted the mores of their day, or if the mores of their day are no longer those of ours, they ought not to tie, in helpless submission, the hands of their successors."

It is undoubtedly true that many landlords have shaped their conduct in reliance upon the rule which I would discard. This consideration is entitled to some weight. But, in my view, it cannot outweigh the social and economic need for shifting the distribution of the risk. To those landlords who have acted in good faith there may undoubtedly be some hardship. But in our realistic experience, they are possessed of the better means to discharge this burden. We need give slight consideration to other landlords who would employ the rule to press their advantage to the extent of permitting a known hazard to exist in callous disregard of the safety of fellow human beings who are obviously without the means to protect themselves.

Note

In the fall of 1981, a New York Times column asked, "What do you call the grassy strip between the curb and the sidewalk?" It proposed some answers: "tree-lawn," according to a Mt. Holyoke professor; "berm," from a southerner; "median," from a New Englander; also, "treebox," "C box," and "dog run." And, from a man from the Pacific Northwest, "the parking strip, or just the parking."

◆ HOUSING REGULATIONS OF THE DISTRICT OF COLUMBIA
(1970)

SEC. 1202 — WATERPROOF FLOORS IN TOILETS

The owner of a building used for residential purposes shall provide each water closet compartment, privy, toilet room or bathroom in such building with a waterproof floor surface and wall base, such base to be at least three inches in height and such floor surface to consist of one of the following: (1) smooth-finished tile or masonry effectively sealed so as to have a nonporous surface, laid in a manner to be free from cracks or open joints, and tightly joined to the base; (2) tongue-and-groove hardwood flooring that is tightly laid without open cracks or joints, tightly joined to the base, and both the base and surface covered with a seal coat of waterproof finish; or (3) linoleum, plastic or rubber floor covering, or linoleum, asphalt, rubber or plastic floor tiles, firmly cemented to a smooth substantial subfloor, laid without overlapping or open joints, and tightly joined to the base. "Linoleum" as used herein means a floor covering made of special preparations of linseed oil, gum, coloring matter, and wood flour, firmly affixed to a cloth or feltpaper base, and does not include enameled and cottonlinter composition coverings.

Sec. 2202 — Light

Each habitable room shall have a glass area transmitting natural light equivalent to that which would be transmitted by a clear glass area at least equal to 1/10 of the floor area served, consisting of one or more windows, glazed doors, glazed doors with either or both side lights or transoms, or other glass construction facing directly to the outside: *Provided*, That (1) rooms opening on enclosed porches and meeting the lighting requirements of Article 501-01-e of the 1941 Building Code, as amended . . . , and (2) rooms lighted through sunporches and meeting the lighting requirements of Section 3-515 of the 1961 Building Code, as amended . . . , shall be deemed to have adequate natural light. The sash area of openable windows, side lights, or transoms, the horizontal protection of the glass area of skylights, and in all other instances the gross glass area, shall be used in computing the required glass area. Any portion of any glass area facing directly on any wall, portion of a structure, or other light obstruction less than three feet from such glass area, shall not be included as contributing to the required natural light. At least 50 percent of the required glass area shall be a window, glazed door, side light or transom, each glazed with clear glass. Obscure glass, glass blocks, or other approved translucent material may be used to transmit up to 50 percent of the required natural light.

Sec. 2301 — Use and Occupancy

No owner, licensee, or tenant shall occupy or permit the occupancy of any habitation in violation of these regulations.

Sec. 2504 — Interior Walls and Ceilings

Each interior wall or ceiling shall be structurally sound and free of loose plaster or other loose structural or surfacing material. Each interior wall or ceiling shall be free of holes and wide cracks.

Sec. 2510 — Gutters and Downspouts

All gutters and downspouts shall be properly connected and be maintained in good condition, free of holes and obstructions. Water shall be conveyed off premises in accordance with plumbing regulations.

SEC. 2512 — PAINTING OF WOOD SURFACES

All exterior wood surfaces shall be kept painted, varnished, shellacked, or covered with other preservative, unless any such wood is customarily used in its natural state.

SEC. 2602A — TENANT RESPONSIBILITY

In addition to the tenant's responsibility under Section 2601 and 2602 the tenant shall specifically be responsible for the following:

2602A.1 Keeping that part of the premises which he occupies and uses as clean and sanitary as the conditions of the premises permit;

2602A.2 disposing from his dwelling unit all rubbish, garbage, and other organic or flammable waste, in a clean, safe and sanitary manner;

2602A.3 keeping all plumbing fixtures as clean and sanitary as their condition permits; . . .

SEC. 2605.4 — LEAD PAINT

The owner of a residential building shall maintain the interior surfaces of the building free of lead or lead in its compounds in any quality of more than one milligram per square centimeter (1 mg/cm^2) or in any quantity sufficient to constitute a hazard to the health of any inhabitant of, or visitor to, the building.

◆ WHETZEL v. JESS FISHER MANAGEMENT CO.
282 F.2d 943 (D.C. Cir. 1960)

BAZELON, Circuit Judge. In Bowles v. Mahoney, this court adhered to the common-law rule that "absent any statutory or contract duty, the lessor is not responsible for an injury resulting from a defect which developed during the term." Since that case was decided, the Commissioners of the District of Columbia have promulgated regulations concerning maintenance and repair of residential property. The primary question here presented is whether these regulations impose a "statu- ʰ tory . . . duty" on the lessor not presented in Bowles v. Mahoney. We conclude that they do.

The issue arises upon an appeal from a summary judgment entered against the plaintiffs below. Their amended complaint alleged that on March 1, 1956, Audrey Whetzel rented an apartment from the appellee for $75.00 per month upon a one-year lease which did not affirmatively place the burden of repairs, other than those caused by the tenant's

304 ♦ 8. Landlord-Tenant Law

negligence, on either party.[2] On June 30, 1956, four months after she entered into possession, the entire bedroom ceiling fell, causing the injuries of which she complains. The principal theory of her action is that the appellee, with knowledge of the defect, negligently permitted the ceiling to remain in an unsafe condition.

Appellant contends that the Housing Regulations establish a standard of conduct for the landlord, which, if negligently breached allows an injured tenant to recover. They rely heavily on the landmark case of Altz v. Lieberson, 1922, 233 N.Y. 16, 134 N.E. 703, 704.

That case also involved a tenant injured by a falling ceiling. Judge Cardozo, writing for the New York Court of Appeals, held that the New York Tenement House Law, which provided that "every tenement house and all the parts thereof shall be kept in good repair," thus "changed the ancient rule" and imposed upon landlords a duty that "extends to all whom there was a purpose to protect." That statute did not specify who had the duty of repair; nor did it speak of tort liability. It only authorized penalties in criminal enforcement proceedings. Nevertheless, the court held that:

"The Legislative must have known that unless repairs in the rooms of the poor were made by the landlord, they would not be made by anyone. The duty imposed became commensurate with the need. The right to seek redress is not limited to the city or its officers." . . .

The courts have not agreed, however, on the precise effect to be given a breach of a statute. A majority of American courts hold that the unexcused violation of a statute which is intended to protect a class of persons, of which the plaintiff is a member, against the type of harm which has in fact occurred is neligence per se. That is to say, such violation is negligence as a matter of law and the jury must be so instructed. But a substantial and growing number of jurisdictions hold that violation of a penal statute is "only evidence of negligence which the jury may accept or reject as it sees fit."

Commentators have pointed out that the per se rule may create serious rigidities and inequities. Strictly applied, the per se rule can, for instance, render negligent as a matter of law a defendant who has taken all due precautions, and bar recovery of a plaintiff who is likewise free from fault in all but a technical sense. Courts adhering to the per se rule

---

2. The lease provided that the lessee would "keep the premises in good order and condition and surrender the same at the expiration of the term herein in the same order in which they are received, *usual wear and tear and damage resulting from acts not caused by the Tenant's negligence excepted.*" (Emphasis supplied.) The landlord reserved the right of access to the premises "at any time for the purpose of inspection . . . or for the purpose of making any repairs the landlord considers necessary or desirable." The tenant agreed to give the landlord "prompt notice of any defects or breakage in the structure, equipment or fixtures of said premises," and promised not to make structural alterations or additions without permission.

have generally recognized its inadequacies and developed such doctrines as "statutory purpose" and "justifiable violation" in an effort to return to the jury responsibility for determining whether reasonable care was exercised in the circumstances. . . .

A review of these cases makes it clear that in this jurisdiction the rather rigid doctrine of negligence *per se* has been tempered by important limitations. Our law is clearly moving in the direction of leaving more and more of the question of negligence as derived from statutory standards for the jury to consider.

Turning to the instant case, we must determine the authority of the District of Columbia Housing Regulations and their effect upon the landlord's duty of care toward his tenants. The Housing Regulations were established and authorized by an order of the Commissioners of the District, dated August 11, 1955. They are arranged in eight chapters. Chapter 1 contains uniform definitions. Chapter 2 is the "Housing Code of the District of Columbia." It applies "to every premises or part thereof, occupied, used or held out for use as a place of abode for human beings," and lays down minimum standards of repair, sanitation and occupancy. The following chapters of the Housing Regulations concern the licensing of premises in which a "housing business" is conducted. . . .

The D.C. Code authorizes the Commissioners to promulgate licensing regulations for dwellings containing more than two families, or rooming houses accommodating four or more persons. Since the instant case involves an apartment building housing more than two families, these licensing regulations and the Housing Code (chapter 2) incorporated therein apply.

Turning now to the Housing Regulations themselves, §2101 declares:

> The Commissioners of the District of Columbia hereby find and declare that there exist residential buildings and areas within said District which are slums or are otherwise blighted, and . . . which are deteriorating and are in danger of becoming slums or otherwise blighted. . . .
>
> The Commissioners further find and declare that such unfortunate conditions are due, among other circumstances, to . . . : dilapidation, inadequate maintenance, overcrowding, inadequate toilet facilities, inadequate bathing or washing facilities, inadequate heating, insufficient protection against fire hazards, inadequate lighting and ventilation, and other insanitary or unsafe conditions. . . .
>
> The Commissioners, accordingly, promulgate these regulations for the purpose of preserving and promoting the public health, safety, welfare, and morals.[14]

14. For a similar expression of community policy on the national level, see 50 Stat. 888 (1937), as amended, 42 U.S.C.A. §1401, concerning the Federal low rent housing program:

For each violation of these standards the regulations provide a maximum penalty of a $300 fine or ten days imprisonment. Housing Regulations §2104. See D.C. Code §§1-224a, 47-2347 (1951).

Upon whom are the duties specified by the regulations imposed? Some are upon the landlord alone. Under §2304, "No persons shall rent or offer to rent any habitation, or the furnishings thereof, unless such habitation and its furnishings are in a clean, safe and sanitary condition, in repair, and free from rodents or vermin." At the very least, this imposes an obligation upon the landlord to put the premises in safe condition prior to their rental. A second duty imposed upon the landlord alone is found in Article 240 dealing with facilities, utilities and services. "The owner or licensee of each residential building shall provide and maintain the facilities, utilities and services required by this part. Each such facility or utility shall be properly and safely installed, and be maintained in a safe and good working condition." Housing Regulations §2401. Such facilities include hot water, plumbing, and heating (where not under the control of the occupant). For reasons which will appear from our discussion of the facts, *infra*, we think there was enough evidence that appellant's injuries proximately resulted from the landlord's failure to put the premises in safe condition prior to their rental, or from its failure to maintain the heating system in good repair, to permit the appellant to go to trial. Whether breach of these regulations is negligence *per se* or evidence of negligence will depend upon the facts developed at trial, applied in accordance with the standards which we have discussed.

The regulations also impose other obligations which are extended to both the landlord and tenant in order to achieve their broad purposes. Section 2301 provides that "No owner, licensee, or tenant shall occupy or permit the occupancy of any habitation in violation of these regulations." Section 2501 directs, *inter alia*, that:

> Every premises accommodating one or more inhabitations shall be maintained and kept in repair so as to provide decent living accommodations for the occupants. This part of the Code contemplates more than mere basic repairs and maintenance to keep out the elements; its purpose is to include repairs and maintenance designed to make a premises or neighborhood healthy and safe.

And more specifically §2504 requires: "Each interior wall or ceiling shall be structurally sound and free of loose plaster or other loose structural or

---

"It is declared to be the policy of the United States . . . to remedy the unsafe and insanitary housing conditions and the acute shortage of decent, safe, and sanitary dwellings for families of low income, in urban and rural nonfarm areas, that are injurious to the health, safety, and morals of the citizens of the Nation." See also 63 Stat. 413, 42 U.S.C.A. §1441 (slum clearance and urban renewal).

surfacing material. Each interior wall or ceiling shall be free of holes and wide cracks."

This it appears that §2301 imposes upon the appellee a duty of care toward its tenants. This duty can be satisfied either by making the necessary repairs or by terminating use of the premises as a place of human habitation. Breach of that duty is, according to the principles which we have discussed, at least evidence of negligence.

But §2301 also creates a duty of care which the appellant owes to herself. Breach of this duty is likewise at least evidence of contributory negligence. The question then is, does her contributory negligence so clearly appear from the face of the complaint that she is not entitled to go to trial? We think not.

In the first place, even if she were contributorily negligent per se, there would remain for the jury the question of proximate cause. Second, the pleadings and affidavits which constitute the present record do not provide an adequate basis for determining whether the plaintiff-appellant was contributorily negligent as a matter of law by occupying non-conforming premises. It is possible that facts may be developed at trial which would warrant a charge of negligence or contributory negligence as a matter of law. But we think that these are questions generally for the jury to resolve upon consideration of all the circumstances bearing on negligence and contributory negligence — including but by no means limited to the regulatory violation, reasonable efforts if any to comply with the regulations, and circumstances excusing their violation.

For example, recovery would be barred if the jury finds that in the total circumstance of the case the tenant unreasonably exposed herself to danger by failing to vacate the premises or to keep them in repair. Some of the more obviously relevant circumstances would include the lease provisions, if any, concerning the duty to repair and the landlord's right of entry for that purpose; the latent or patent character of the defect and tenant's knowledge, or opportunity for knowledge thereof; who repaired previous defects, if any; the amount of rental and term of lease, on the one hand, against the extent and nature of the defect and cost of repair on the other; and the bargaining position of the parties in entering into the lease. In the present case, the jury would also consider, for example, the fact that the defective ceiling is a common wall with the floor . . . above, over which a tenant has virtually no control.

Appellee contends, however, that even if the jury must weigh the duty imposed by the Housing Regulations upon the lessee, summary judgment was nonetheless appropriate because there are uncontradicted affidavits in the record showing that appellee had no notice of the defect in the ceiling. We think actual knowledge is not required for liability; it is enough if, in the exercise of reasonable care, appellee should have known that the condition of the ceiling violated the standards of the Housing Code.

We cannot say that upon a trial a jury could not reasonably find that appellee should have known of the condition of the ceiling. The bathroom ceiling, located just off the bedroom in appellant's apartment, had fallen and been repaired not long before appellant took possession. On New Year's Eve of 1956, just two months before appellant moved in, the livingroom ceiling of the adjoining apartment also fell. On April 1, 1956, appellant noticed a leak in her bedroom ceiling, and reported it to the janitor who was able to stop the leak by adjusting the radiator in the apartment above. But there is no evidence that he then inspected appellant's ceiling to determine if it had been weakened. Just before appellant moved in, appellee hired a contractor to inspect and repair the plaster in appellant's apartment. The contractor's affidavit, executed three years after the event, stated that he "carefully inspected and examined the entire apartment" and found "the plaster in the ceiling of the bedroom . . . in good sound condition." . . . In view of the fact that the ceiling fell only four months after the alleged inspection, the jury might reasonably find that the inspection was negligently performed.

It follows from all that we have said that the District Court erred in granting summary judgment on the first count of appellant's amended complaint. We therefore reverse the judgment as to that count and remand with directions to proceed to trial.

Wilbur K. Miller, Circuit Judge, dissents.

Notes

1. Ceiling plaster is an interior nonstructural item, so the landlord of an art gallery was not liable for damages to tenant's paintings that occurred when a six-by-six-foot section of ceiling fell. Baxter v. Illinois Police Federation, 63 Ill. App. 3d 819, 380 N.E.2d 832 (1978).

2. Tort exculpatory clauses in residential leases violate public policy in California because the landlord should be primarily responsible for maintaining safe and habitable housing and because the tenant has unequal bargaining strength. Henrioulle v. Marin Ventures, Inc., 20 Cal. 3d 512, 573 P.2d 465, 143 Cal. Rptr. 247 (1978).

3. A student at Pine Manor College was awarded a tort judgment of $29,000 against the college for injuries suffered when she was raped. The award was based on a theory of negligent failure by the college to provide appropriate security. (The trial judge had reduced the jury's damage award, which had been $175,000.) The student had chosen to live in a dormitory in which male visitors were allowed to stay overnight on weekends. It was uncertain whether the offender was someone who had been admitted as a visitor by another student. Mullins v. Pine Manor College, 389 Mass. 47, 449 N.E.2d 331 (1983).

See also Miller v. State, 62 N.Y.2d 506, 467 N.E.2d 493, 478

N.Y.S.2d 829 (1984), upholding an award of $25,000 to a student who had been raped in a dormitory room at the State University of New York at Stony Brook. The university was held to have negligently failed to keep the dormitory's outer doors locked, thus permitting the assailant to gain access to a laundry room where he confronted the student with a knife and forced her to accompany him to an upstairs room.

The Court of Appeals based the state's duty on its proprietary role as landlord, thus distinguishing Bass v. City of New York, 38 A.D.2d 407, 330 N.Y.S.2d 569 (1972), aff'd, 32 N.Y.2d 894, 300 N.E.2d 154, 346 N.Y.S.2d 814 (1973), which held New York City immune from the tort claim of a rape victim who had alleged that a Housing Authority police- man was at lunch instead of patrolling. Providing police protection is a traditional governmental function, said the court, for which the government is immune from suit for negligence, while serving as landlord is a proprietary function for which the state is as liable for suit as a private landlord.

4. A landlord is not responsible in tort when one tenant's dog bites the child of another tenant. Royer v. Pryor, 427 N.E.2d 1112 (Ind. App. 1981).

5. For a review of case law concerning the tort liability of a municipality for its failure to enforce housing or building codes, see Dinsky v. Framingham, 386 Mass. 801, 438 N.E.2d 51 (1982). The majority view is that there is no such cause of action. But see Garrett v. Holiday Inns, Inc., 58 N.Y.2d 253, 447 N.E.2d 717, 460 N.Y.S.2d 774 (1983).

◆ KANELOS v. KETTLER
406 F.2d 951 (D.C. Cir. 1968)

ROBINSON, Circuit Judge. Appellant sued appellee for damages on account of personal injuries sustained in a fall allegedly caused by negligent failure to maintain the safety of an apartment which appellee had leased to appellant. The offending condition was the bathroom door sill which, though perhaps in good order when appellant took possession, soon thereafter was in a state of deterioration. On three separate occasions prior to her fall, appellant reported the defect to appellee and asked that it be corrected, but nothing was done about it. Then came the fateful day on which appellant, in her words, was "going back into the bathroom . . . when I got my bedroom slipper caught in the sill and went down."

Appellant's litigative theory was that appellee's disregard of appellant's requests for the repair was violative of the District of Columbia Housing Regulations. Witnesses at the trial testified to the condition of the door sill in descriptive terms plainly connoting the peril that ultimately overtook appellant. When appellant rested her case, however, appellee moved for a directed verdict on the hypothesis that no negligence on his part had been shown. The trial judge granted the motion on the ground that appellant had assumed the risk of injury from the faulty door sill. This ruling we must test upon the view of the evidence that best supports appellant's claim upon this appeal. . . .

Risks, in legal contemplation, are assumed, not simply because they inhere in the situation out of which the claimant's injury arises, but because the claimant, with knowledge of the risk and full appreciation of its dangers, is willing to accept and gamble on it. Thus, in common with the general American law on the subject, we have rejected applications of the assumed risk doctrine where the exposure, even to a recognized hazard, was not voluntary. And

> the plaintiff's acceptance of the risk is not to be regarded as voluntary where the defendant's tortious conduct had forced upon him a choice of two courses of conduct, which leaves him no reasonable alternative to taking his chances. A defendant who, by his own wrong, has compelled the plaintiff to choose between two evils cannot be permitted to say that the plaintiff is barred from recovery because he has made the choice.

So, "[t]o call this defense into play requires a showing that the person charged has no duty to protect the other from the risk," and our decisions have given this requirement full sway. The citizen who travels over public streets and sidewalks does not assume the risk of injury as against the municipality legally charged with keeping them in safe condition. . . . These decisions are but applications of the rule barring assumption of risk as a viable doctrine "where the plaintiff," whether tenant or not, "is compelled to accept the risk in order to exercise or protect a right or privilege, of which the defendant has no privilege to deprive him." For "[o]ne's acceptance of a risk of harm created by another's nonperformance of duty does not represent a free choice where there is no feasible alternative save to sacrifice an interest which the duty exists ultimately to subserve." Quite obviously, unless these considerations are to govern cases like that at bar, the responsibilities placed upon landlords by the Housing Regulations are effectively nullified by the mere circumstance that the tenant remains in possession.

Thus we are guided unfailingly to the conclusion that direction of the verdict against appellant was error. Appellee owed appellant the obligation, mandated by the Housing Regulations, to maintain the leased apartment, including the bathroom door sill, in a reasonably safe condition. Appellant's evidence was of a caliber sufficient to require submission for the jury's determination of the issue whether that duty had been dishonored. If it was, appellee cannot now avoid liability by the suggestion that appellant was at liberty to avert the danger by moving out. She could not, in the face of appellee's affirmative duty to exert care, be held to have voluntarily assumed the risk of injury posed by his negligence.

We reverse the judgment appealed from and remand the case to the District Court for a new trial.

Wilbur K. Miller, Senior Circuit Judge, concurs in the result.

C.   THE LEASE AS A CONTRACT IN VIOLATION OF THE HOUSING CODE

◆ BROWN v. SOUTHALL REALTY CO.
   237 A.2d 834 (D.C. 1968)

Florence Wagman Roisman, Washington, D.C., for appellant. Thomas E. Willging and Michael Frank were on the brief, for appellant.

No appearance for appellee.

QUINN, Judge. This appeal arises out of an action for possession brought by appellee-landlord, against appellant-tenant, Mrs. Brown, for nonpayment of rent. The parties stipulated, at the time of trial, that the rent was in the arrears in the amount of $230.00. Mrs. Brown contended, however, that no rent was due under the lease because it was an illegal contract. The court held to the contrary and awarded appellee possession for nonpayment of rent. . . .

. . . Mrs. Brown [has] moved from the premises and [does] not wish to be returned to possession. . . . [But] because the validity of the lease and the determination that rent is owing will be irrevocably established in this case if the judgment of the trial court is allowed to stand, we feel that this appeal is timely made.

Although appellant notes a number of errors, we consider the allegation that the trial court erred in failing to declare the lease agreement void as an illegal contract both meritorious and completely dispositive, and for this reason we reverse.

The evidence developed, at the trial, revealed that prior to the signing of the lease agreement, appellee was on notice that certain Housing Code violations existed on the premises in question. An inspector for the District of Columbia Housing Division of the Department of Licenses and Inspections testified that the violations, an obstructed commode, a broken railing and insufficient ceiling height in the basement, existed at lease some months prior to the lease agreement and had not been abated at the time of trial. He also stated that the basement violations prohibited the use of the entire basement as a dwelling place. Counsel for appellant at the trial below elicited an admission from the appellee that "he told the defendant after the lease had been signed that the back room of the basement was habitable despite the Housing Code Violations." In addition, a Mr. Sinkler Penn, the owner of the premises in question, was called as an adverse witness by the defense. He testified that "he had submitted a sworn statement to the Housing Division on December 8, 1964 to the effect that the basement was unoccupied at the time and would continue to be kept vacant until the violations were corrected."

This evidence having been established and uncontroverted, appellant contends that the lease should have been declared unenforceable because it was entered into in contravention to the District of Columbia Housing Regulations, and knowingly so.

Section 2304 of the District of Columbia Housing Regulations reads as follows: "No persons shall rent or offer to rent any habitation, or the furnishings thereof, unless such habitation and its furnishings are in a clean, safe and sanitary condition, in repair, and free from rodents or vermin."

Section 2501 of these same Regulations, states:

> Every premises accommodating one or more habitations shall be maintained and kept in repair so as to provide decent living accommodations for the occupants. This part of the Code contemplates more than mere basic repairs and maintenance to keep out the elements; its purpose is to include repairs and maintenance designed to make a premises or neighborhood healthy and safe.

It appears that the violations known by appellee to be existing on the leasehold at the time of the signing of the lease agreement were of a nature to make the "habitation" unsafe and unsanitary. Neither had the premises been maintained or repaired to the degree contemplated by the regulations, i.e., "designed to make a premises . . . healthy and safe." The lease contract was, therefore, entered into in violation of the Housing Regulations requiring that they be safe and sanitary and that they be properly maintained. . . .

. . . To uphold the validity of this lease agreement, in light of the defects known to be existing on the leasehold prior to the agreement (i.e., obstructed commode, broken railing, and insufficient ceiling height in the basement) would be to flout the evident purposes for which Sections 2304 and 2501 were enacted. The more reasonable view is, therefore, that where such conditions exist on a leasehold prior to an agreement to lease, the letting of such premises constitutes a violation of Sections 2304 and 2501 of the Housing Regulations, and that these Sections do indeed "imply a prohibition" so as "to render the prohibited act void." Neither does there exist any reason to treat a lease agreement differently from any other contract in this regard.

Thus, for this reason and those stated above, we reverse.

◆ DIAMOND HOUSING CORP. v. ROBINSON
257 A.2d 492 (D.C. 1969)

Hood, Chief Judge. Appellant-landlord initiated two successive suits for possession of an unfurnished house leased to appellee-tenant which resulted in judgment in both cases for appellee. In the first suit appellant sought possession under a written lease for nonpayment of rent. Appellee raised two defenses to the claim for possession: (1) She had not waived her statutory right of thirty days' notice to quit; and (2) that the written lease was void and unenforceable because it was an illegal agreement. The jury in the trial below rendered special verdicts in favor of appellee on each defense.

Appellee's first defense is that the lease provision for waiver of the statutory right of thirty days' notice to quit in the event the tenant fails to pay the agreed upon rent was unconscionable under the circumstances of this case. Appellee testified at trial that she had a limited education and that she did not understand the term "notice to quit" and several other terms contained in the lease. She admitted that she did not attempt to ascertain the meaning of the lease before signing it.

The general rule is that, in the absence of fraud, duress or mistake, "[o]ne who signs a contract which he had an opportunity to read and understand is bound by its provisions" unless enforcement of the agreement should be withheld because the terms of the contract are unconscionable. Since there is no evidence in the record of fraud, duress or mistake, and appellee testified that she had an opportunity to read the lease before signing it, the issue before us is whether the notice to quit waiver provision is an unconscionable term. . . . In the present case the waiver of notice to quit provision is not hidden or obscured by the other provisions of the printed lease agreement, and attention is drawn to the waiver provision by the fact that the words "notice to quit" are printed in a larger and bolder typeface. There appears to be no reason why appellee should not be bound by her signed agreement. We therefore hold that it was error for the trial court to submit the question of appellee's waiver of notice to quit to the jury.

Appellee relies on our decision in Brown v. Southall Realty Co. as the basis of her second defense that the lease is void and unenforceable. In *Brown* we held that where a landlord leases a premises knowing that Housing Code violations exist on the premises which render it unsafe and unsanitary, such lease is illegal and void and cannot be the basis of the landlord's cause of action.

In the present case, the jury made a special finding that there were substantial violations of the Housing Regulations existing on the premises at the time that the lease was signed, "that those violations were of a quality and kind sufficient to render the premises unsafe and unsanitary, and that [appellant] actually knew or should have known of the existence of those violations." It is appellant's contention that even if there were defective conditions on the leased premises which significantly impaired its habitability, the fact that he had not received official notice of the existence of Housing Code violations from the city's housing inspectors would distinguish the present case from the facts in *Brown*, and would preclude the jury's finding that the lease was void and unenforceable. Appellant is correct that in *Brown* there had been official citations of Housing Code violations. However, our opinion was based on the fact that the lease agreement had knowingly been made in violation of a housing regulation. The illegality found in *Brown* was not based on the existence of conditions which violated the Housing Regulations per se — a technical or minor violation would not render the lease void — but rather on violations coupled with the purpose of the Regulations which prohibited the leasing of uninhabitable dwellings. Violations of the Housing Regulations may exist even though city officials have not inspected the premises and cited the defective conditions. Consequently, the rationale of *Brown* must logically be applied to the present case. Therefore, the jury's special verdict that the lease is void and unenforceable must be upheld.

Subsequent to the jury's verdict in favor of appellee, appellant filed two post trial motions: The first was for judgment n. o. v. on the grounds that appellee's successful defense of illegal contract was a rescission of the contract, and therefore appellee was required to relinquish possession of the leased premises; and the second motion was for judgment of possession and assessment of damages for trespass. The trial court denied both motions, and appellant claims error.

Appellant contends that the determination that a lease is void and unenforceable results in a rescission of the lease agreement, and requires the tenant to return possession of the premises. We do not agree. It is well established that an agreement entered into in violation of the law creates no rights upon the wrongdoer. The defense of illegality does not rescind the illegal agreement, but merely prevents a party from using the courts to enforce such an agreement.

Appellant's final argument is that the determination that the lease is void terminates the landlord-tenant relationship between the parties and causes appellee to become a trespasser on appellant's property. Such an argument, however, is contrary to the great weight of authority. The generally accepted view is that entry upon a premises under a void and unenforceable lease creates a tenancy at will. However, in this jurisdiction an estate at will must be created by express contract, and can arise by implication of law in only one specified situation not here applicable; but we do have a statutory estate by sufferance which is in the nature of an estate from month to month or an estate of will. We hold that appellee, having entered possession under a void and unenforceable lease, was not a trespasser but became a tenant at sufferance. Consequently, appellant was not entitled to relief under its theory that appellee be treated as a trespasser.

In view of the fact that our opinion in Brown v. Southall Realty Co., *supra*, has caused some confusion regarding the proper procedure for a landlord to regain possession when the lease has been held illegal and unenforceable, we add the following. When it is established that a lease is void and unenforceable under the Brown v. Southall ruling, the tenant becomes a tenant at sufferance and the tenancy, like any other tenancy at sufferance, may be terminated on thirty days' notice. The Housing Regulations do not compel an owner of housing property to rent his property. Where, as here, it has been determined that the property when rented was not habitable, that is, not safe and sanitary, and should not have been rented, and if the landlord is unwilling or unable to put the property in a habitable condition, he may and should promptly terminate the tenancy and withdraw the property from the rental market, because the Regulations forbid both the rental and the occupancy of such premises.

Affirmed.

Have the legal services lawyers helped their clients? Obviously, not very much. What should they do next?

♦ JAVINS v. FIRST NATIONAL REALTY CORP.
428 F.2d 1071 (D.C. Cir. 1970)

WRIGHT, Circuit Judge: These cases present the question whether housing code violations which arise during the term of a lease have any effect upon the tenant's obligation to pay rent. The Landlord and Tenant Branch of the District of Columbia Court of General Sessions ruled proof of such violations inadmissible when proffered as a defense to an eviction action for nonpayment of rent. The District of Columbia Court of Appeals upheld this ruling. Saunders v. First National Realty Corp., 245 A.2d 836 (1968).

Because of the importance of the question presented, we granted appellants' petitions for leave to appeal. We now reverse and hold that a warranty of habitability, measured by the standards set out in the Housing Regulations for the District of Columbia, is implied by operation of law into leases of urban dwelling units covered by those Regulations and that breach of this warranty gives rise to the usual remedies for breach of contract.

The facts revealed by the record are simple. By separate written

PHOTOGRAPH 8-2
Clifton Terrace Apartments

leases,[2] each of the appellants rented an apartment in a three-building apartment complex in Northwest Washington known as Clifton Terrace. The landlord, First National Realty Corporation, filed separate actions in the Landlord and Tenant Branch of the Court of General Sessions on April 8, 1966, seeking possession on the ground that each of the appellants had defaulted in the payment of rent due for the month of April. The tenants, appellants here, admitted that they had not paid the landlord any rent for April. However, they alleged numerous violations of the Housing Regulations as "an equitable defense or [a] claim by way of recoupment or set-off in an amount equal to the rent claim," as provided in the rules of the Court of General Session. They offered to prove

> [t]hat there are approximately 1500 violations of the Housing Regulations of the District of Columbia in the building at Clifton Terrace, where Defendant resides some affecting the premises of this Defendant directly, others

---

2. A clause in the lease provided that the tenant waived the statutory 30-day notice to quit. 45 D.C. Code §908 (1967) expressly permits waiver of this notice. Appellants' answer put in issue the validity of the waivers. In view of our disposition, we have no occasion to pass upon this aspect of the case.

PHOTOGRAPH 8-3
The *Javins* property (1976)

indirectly, and all tending to establish a course of conduct of violation of
the Housing Regulations to the damage of Defendants. . . .

Appellants conceded at trial, however, that this offer of proof reached
only violations which had arisen since the term of the lease had commenced. The Court of General Sessions refused appellants' offer of
proof and entered judgment for the landlord. The District of Columbia
Court of Appeals affirmed, rejecting the argument made by appellants
that the landlord was under a contractual duty to maintain the premises
in compliance with the Housing Regulations.

Since, in traditional analysis, a lease was the conveyance of an
interest in land, courts have usually utilized the special rules governing
real property transactions to resolve controversies involving leases.
However, as the Supreme Court has noted in another context, "the
body of private property law . . . , more than almost any other branch of
law, has been shaped by distinctions whose validity is largely historical." Courts have a duty to reappraise old doctrines in the light of the
facts and values of contemporary life — particularly old common law
doctrines which the courts themselves created and developed. As we
have said before, "[T]he continued vitality of the common law . . .

depends upon its ability to reflect contemporary community values and ethics."

The assumption of landlord-tenant law, derived from feudal property law, that a lease primarily conveyed to the tenant an interest in land may have been reasonable in a rural, agrarian society; it may continue to be reasonable in some leases involving farming or commercial land. In these cases, the value of the lease to the tenant is the land itself. But in the case of the modern apartment dweller, the value of the lease is that it gives him a place to live. The city dweller who seeks to lease an apartment on the third floor of a tenement has little interest in the land 30 or 40 feet below, or even in the bare right to possession within the four walls of his apartment. When American city dwellers, both rich and poor, seek "shelter" today, they seek a well known package of goods and services — a package which includes not merely walls and ceilings, but also adequate heat, light and ventilation, serviceable plumbing facilities, secure windows and doors, proper sanitation, and proper maintenance. . . .

Some courts have realized that certain of the old rules of property law governing leases are inappropriate for today's transactions. In order to reach results more in accord with the legitimate expectations of the parties and the standards of the community, courts have been gradually introducing more modern precepts of contract law in interpreting leases. Proceeding piecemeal has, however, led to confusion where "decisions are frequently conflicting, not because of a healthy disagreement on social policy, but because of the lingering impact of rules whose policies are long since dead."

In our judgment the trend toward treating leases as contracts is wise and well considered. Our holding in this case reflects a belief that leases of urban dwelling units should be interpreted and construed like any other contract.[13]

Modern contract law has recognized that the buyer of goods and services in an industrial society must rely upon the skill and honesty of the supplier to assure that goods and services purchased are of adequate quality. In interpreting most contracts, courts have sought to protect the legitimate expectations of the buyer and have steadily widened the

13. This approach does not deny the possible importance of the fact that land is involved in a transaction. The interpretation and construction of contracts between private parties has always required courts to be sensitive and responsive to myriad different factors. We believe contract doctrines allow courts to be properly sensitive to all relevant factors in interpreting lease obligations.

We also intend no alteration of statutory or case law definitions of the term "real property" for purposes of statutes or decisions on recordation, descent, conveyancing, creditors' rights, etc. We contemplate only that contract law is to determine the rights and obligations of the parties to the lease agreement, as between themselves. The civil law has always viewed the lease as a contract, and in our judgment that perspective has proved superior to that of the common law.

seller's responsibility for the quality of goods and services through implied warranties of fitness and merchantability. . . .

The rigid doctrines of real property law have tended to inhibit the
application of implied warranties to transactions involving real estate.
Now, however, courts have begun to hold sellers and developers of real
property responsible for the quality of their product. For example, builders of new homes have recently been held liable to purchasers for improper construction on the ground that the builders had breached an
implied warranty of fitness. In other cases courts have held builders of
new homes liable for breach of an implied warranty that all local building regulations had been complied with. And following the developments in other areas, very recent decisions and commentary suggest the
possible extension of liability to parties other than the immediate seller
for improper construction of residential real estate.

Despite this trend in the sale of real estate, many courts have been
unwilling to imply warranties of quality, specifically a warranty of
habitability, into leases of apartments. Recent decisions have offered no
convincing explanation for their refusal, rather they have relied without
discussion upon the old common law rule that the lessor is not obligated
to repair unless he covenants to do so in the written lease contract.
However, the Supreme Courts of at least two states, in recent and well
reasoned opinions, have held landlords to implied warranties of quality
in housing leases. Lemle v. Breeden, S. Ct. Hawaii, 462 P.2d 470 (1969);
Reste Realty Corp. v. Cooper, 53 N.J. 444, 251 A.2d 268 (1969).

In our judgment, the old no-repair rule cannot coexist with the
obligations imposed on the landlord by a typical modern housing code, *H*
and must be abandoned in favor of an implied warranty of habitability.
In the District of Columbia, the standards of this warranty are set out in
the Housing Regulations.

In our judgment the common law itself must recognize the landlord's obligation to keep his premises in a habitable condition. This
conclusion is compelled by three separate considerations. First, we believe that the old rule was based on certain factual assumptions which
are no longer true; on its own terms, it can no longer be justified.
Second, we believe that the consumer protection cases discussed above
require that the old rule be abandoned in order to bring residential
landlord-tenant law into harmony with the principles on which those
cases rest. Third, we think that the nature of today's urban housing
market also dictates abandonment of the old rule.

The common law rule absolving the lessor of all obligation to repair
originated in the early Middle Ages.[30] Such a rule was perhaps well

30. The rule was "settled" by 1485. 3 W. Holdsworth, A History of English Law 122-
123 (6th ed. 1934). The common law rule discussed in text originated in the even older rule
prohibiting the tenant from committing waste. The writ of waste expanded as the tenant's

suited to an agrarian economy; the land was more important[31] than whatever small living structure was included in the leasehold, and the tenant farmer was fully capable of making repairs himself. These historical facts were the basis on which the common law constructed its rule; they also provided the necessary prerequisites for its application.[33]

Court decisions in the late 1800's began to recognize that the factual assumptions of the common law were no longer accurate in some cases. For example, the common law, since it assumed that the land was the most important part of the leasehold, required a tenant to pay rent even if any building on the land was destroyed. Faced with such a rule and the ludicrous results it produced, in 1863 the New York Court of Appeals declined to hold that an upper story tenant was obliged to continue paying rent after his apartment building burned down. The court simply pointed out that the urban tenant had no interest in the land, only in the attached building. . . .

These as well as other similar cases demonstrate that some courts began some time ago to question the common law's assumptions that the land was the most important feature of a leasehold and that the tenant could feasibly make any necessary repairs himself. Where those assumptions no longer reflect contemporary housing patterns, the courts have created exceptions to the general rule that landlords have no duty to keep their premises in repair.

It is overdue for courts to admit that these assumptions are no longer true with regard to all urban housing. Today's urban tenants, the vast majority of whom live in multiple dwelling houses, are interested, not in the land, but solely in "a house suitable for occupation." Furthermore, today's city dweller usually has a single, specialized skill unrelated to maintenance work; he is unable to make repairs like the "jack-of-all-trades" farmer who was the common law's model of the lessee. Further, unlike his agrarian predecessor who often remained on one piece of land for his entire life, urban tenants today are more mobile than ever before. A tenant's tenure in a specific apartment will often not be sufficient to justify efforts at repairs. In addition, the increasing com-

---

right in possession grew stronger. Eventually, in order to protect the landowner's reversionary interest, the tenant became obligated to make repairs and liable to eviction and damages if he failed to do so.

31. The land was so central to the original common law conception of a leasehold that rent was viewed as "issuing" from the land: "[T]he governing idea is that the land is bound to pay the rent. . . . We may almost go to the length of saying that the land pays it through [the tenant's] hand." 2 F. Pollock & F. Maitland, The History of English Law 131 (2d ed. 1923).

33. Even the old common law courts responded with a different rule for a landlord-tenant relationship which did not conform to the model of the usual agrarian lease. Much more substantial obligations were placed upon the keepers of inns (the only multiple dwelling houses known to the common law). Their guests were interested solely in shelter and could not be expected to make their own repairs.

plexity of today's dwellings renders them much more difficult to repair than the structures of earlier times. In a multiple dwelling repair may require access to equipment and areas in the control of the landlord. Low and middle income tenants, even if they were interested in making repairs, would be unable to obtain any financing for major repairs since they have no long-term interest in the property.

Our approach to the common law of landlord and tenant ought to be aided by principles derived from the consumer protection cases referred to above. In a lease contract, a tenant seeks to purchase from his landlord shelter for a specified period of time. The landlord sells housing as a commercial businessman and has much greater opportunity, incentive and capacity to inspect and maintain the condition of his building. Moreover, the tenant must rely upon the skill and *bona fides* of his landlord at least as much as a car buyer must rely upon the car manufacturer. In dealing with major problems, such as heating, plumbing, electrical or structural defects, the tenant's position corresponds precisely with "the ordinary consumer who cannot be expected to have the knowledge or capacity or even the opportunity to make adequate inspection of mechanical instrumentalities, like automobiles, and to decide for himself whether they are reasonably fit for the designed purpose." Henningsen v. Bloomfield Motors, Inc., 32 N.J. 358, 375, 161 A.2d 69, 78 (1960).[42]

Since a lease contract specifies a particular period of time during which the tenant has a right to use his apartment for shelter, he may legitimately expect that the apartment will be fit for habitation for the time period for which it is rented. We point out that in the present cases there is no allegation that appellants' apartments were in poor condition or in violation of the housing code at the commencement of the leases. Since the lessees continue to pay the same rent, they were entitled to expect that the landlord would continue to keep the premises in their beginning condition during the lease term. It is precisely such expectations that the law now recognizes as deserving of formal, legal protection.

Even beyond the rationale of traditional products liability law, the relationship of landlord and tenant suggests further compelling reasons for the law's protection of the tenants' legitimate expectations of quality. The inequality in bargaining power between landlord and tenant has been well documented. Tenants have very little leverage to enforce demands for better housing. Various impediments to competition in the rental housing market, such as racial and class discrimination and stan-

---

42. Nor should the average tenant be thought capable of "inspecting" plaster, floorboards, roofing, kitchen appliances, etc. To the extent, however, that some defects *are* obvious, the law must take note of the present housing shortage. Tenants may have no real alternative but to accept such housing with the expectation that the landlord will make necessary repairs. Where this is so, *caveat emptor* must of necessity be rejected.

dardized form leases, mean that landlords place tenants in a take it or leave it situation. The increasingly severe shortage of adequate housing further increases the landlord's bargaining power and escalates the need for maintaining and improving the existing stock. Finally, the findings by various studies of the social impact of bad housing has led to the realization that poor housing is detrimental to the whole society, not merely to the unlucky one who must suffer the daily indignity of living in a slum.

Thus we are led by our inspection of the relevant legal principles and precedents to the conclusion that the old common law rule imposing an obligation upon the lessee to repair during the lease term was really never intended to apply to residential urban leaseholds. Contract principles established in other areas of the law provide a more rational framework for the apportionment of landlord-tenant responsibilities; they strongly suggest that a warranty of habitability be implied into all contracts[49] for urban dwellings.

We believe, in any event, that the District's housing code requires that a warranty of habitability be implied in the leases of all housing that it covers. The housing code — formally designated the Housing Regulations of the District of Columbia — was established and authorized by the Commissioners of the District of Columbia on August 11, 1955. Since that time, the code has been updated by numerous orders of the Commissioners. The 75 pages of the Regulations provide a comprehensive regulatory scheme setting forth in some detail: (a) the standards which housing in the District of Columbia must meet; (b) which party, the lessor or the lessee, must meet each standard; and (c) a system of inspections, notifications and criminal penalties. The Regulations themselves are silent on the question of private remedies.

Two previous decisions of this court, however, have held that the Housing Regulations create legal rights and duties enforceable in tort by private parties. . . .

The District of Columbia Court of Appeals gave further effect to the Housing Regulations in Brown v. Southall Realty Co., 237 A.2d 834 (1968). . . . Viewing the lease as a contract, the District of Columbia Court of Appeals held that the premises were let in violation of Sections 2304[53] and 2501 of the Regulations and that the lease, therefore, was void as an illegal contract. In the light of *Brown*, it is clear not only that the housing code creates privately enforceable duties as held in *Whetzel*, but that the basic validity of every housing contract depends upon substantial compliance with the housing code at the beginning of the lease

49. We need not consider the provisions of the written lease governing repairs since this implied warranty of the landlord could not be excluded.
53. "No person shall rent or offer to rent any habitation, or the furnishings thereof, unless such habitation and its furnishings are in a clean, safe and sanitary condition, in repair, and free from rodents or vermin."

term. The *Brown* court relied particularly upon Section 2501 of the Regulations which provides:

> Every premises accommodating one or more habitations shall be maintained and kept in repair so as to provide decent living accommodations for the occupants. This part of this Code contemplates more than mere basic repairs and maintenance to keep out the elements; its purpose is to include repairs and maintenance designed to make a premise or neighborhood healthy and safe.

By its terms, this section applies to maintenance and repair during the lease term. Under the *Brown* holding, serious failure to comply with this section before the lease term begins renders the contract void. We think it untenable to find that this section has no effect on the contract after it has been signed. To the contrary, by signing the lease the landlord has undertaken a continuing obligation to the tenant to maintain the premises in accordance with all applicable law.

This principle of implied warranty is well established. Courts often imply relevant law into contracts to provide a remedy for any damage caused by one party's illegal conduct.[56] . . .

[T]he housing code must be read into housing contracts — a holding also required by the purposes and the structure of the code itself. The duties imposed by the Housing Regulations may not be waived or shifted by agreement if the Regulations specifically place the duty upon the lessor. Criminal penalties are provided if these duties are ignored. This regulatory structure was established by the Commissioners because, in their judgment, the grave conditions in the housing market required serious action. Yet official enforcement of the housing code has been far from uniformly effective. Innumerable studies have documented the desperate condition of rental housing in the District of Columbia and in the nation. . . .

We therefore hold that the Housing Regulations imply a warranty of habitability, measured by the standards which they set out, into leases of all housing that they cover.

In the present cases, the landlord sued for possession for nonpayment of rent. Under contract principles,[61] however, the tenant's obligation to pay rent is dependent upon the landlord's performance of his obligations, including his warranty to maintain the premises in habitable

---

56. As a general proposition, it is undoubtedly true that parties to a contract intend that applicable law will be complied with by both sides. We recognize, however, that reading statutory provisions into private contracts may have little factual support in the intentions of the particular parties now before us. But, for reasons of public policy, warranties are often implied into contracts by operation of law in order to meet generally prevailing standards of honesty and fair dealing. When the public policy has been enacted into law like the housing code, that policy will usually have deep roots in the expectations and intentions of most people.

61. In extending all contract remedies for breach to the parties to a lease, we include an action for specific performance of the landlord's implied warranty of habitability.

condition. In order to determine whether any rent is owed to the land-lord, the tenants must be given an opportunity to prove the housing code violations alleged as breach of the landlord's warranty.[62]

At trial, the finder of fact must make two findings: (1) whether the alleged violations[63] existed during the period for which past due rent is claimed, and (2) what portion, if any or all, of the tenant's obligation to pay rent was suspended by the landlord's breach. If no part of the tenant's rental obligation is found to have been suspended, then a judg-ment for possession may issue forthwith. On the other hand, if the jury determines that the entire rental obligation has been extinguished by the landlord's total breach, then the action for possession on the ground of nonpayment must fail.[64]

The jury may find that part of the tenant's rental obligation has been suspended but that part of the unpaid back rent is indeed owned to the landlord. In these circumstances, no judgment for possession should issue if the tenant agrees to pay the partial rent found to be due. If the tenant refuses to pay the partial amount, a judgment for possession may then be entered.

The judgment of the District of Columbia Court of Appeals is re-versed and the cases are remanded for further proceedings consistent with this opinion.[67]

62. To be relevant, of course, the violations must affect the tenant's apartment or common areas which the tenant uses. Moreover, the contract principle that no one may benefit from his own wrong will allow the landlord to defend by proving the damage was caused by the tenant's wrongful action. However, violations resulting from inadequate repairs or materials which disintegrate under normal use would not be assignable to the tenant. Also we agree with the District of Columbia Court of Appeals that the tenant's private rights do not depend on official inspection or official finding of violation by the city government.

63. The jury should be instructed that one or two minor violations standing alone which do not affect habitability are *de minimis* and would not entitle the tenant to a reduction in rent.

64. As soon as the landlord made the necessary repairs rent would again become due. Our holding, of course, affects only eviction for nonpayment of rent. The landlord is free to seek eviction at the termination of the lease or on any other legal ground.

67. Appellants in the present cases offered to pay rent into the registry of the court during the present action. We think this is an excellent protective procedure. If the tenant defends against an action for possession on the basis of breach of the landlord's warranty of habitability, the trial court may require the tenant to make future rent payments into the registry of the court as they become due; such a procedure would be appropriate only while the tenant remains in possession. The escrowed money will, however, represent rent for the period between the time the landlord files suit and the time the case comes to trial. In the normal course of litigation, the only factual question at trial would be the condition of the apartment during the time the landlord alleged rent was due and not paid.

As a general rule, the escrowed money should be apportioned between the landlord and the tenant after trial on the basis of the finding of rent actually due for the period at issue in the suit. To insure fair apportionment, however, we think either party should be permitted to amend its complaint or answer at any time before trial, to allege a change in the condition of the apartment. In this event, the finder of fact should make a separate finding as to the condition of the apartment at the time at which the amendment was filed. This new finding will have no effect upon the original action; it will only affect the distribution of the escrowed rent paid after the filing of the amendment.

SIEGEL, IS THE MODERN LEASE A CONTRACT OR A CONVEY-ANCE? — A HISTORICAL INQUIRY, 52 J. Urb. Law 649, 650, 668–670 (1975): [C]ontrary to the conventional wisdom, current landlord-tenant law is modern, commercial, and already grounded in contract doctrine. Real property analysis of leasing disputes does occur, but it is insignificant compared to leasing's dominant contract basis. Moreover, it originated in the nineteenth century to resolve a selected group of leasing problems (primarily associated with the then recent emergence of multiple-occupancy leasing) for which contract law provided inapt analogies. Therefore, the landlord-tenant reformers' battle cry, "from conveyance to contract," is illusory, and the basis of the movement that is occurring and should occur must be reconceptualized.

That modern leasing law is neither feudal, agrarian, nor grounded in real property doctrines is to be expected. The ancient "special rules" governing real property transactions applied to freehold estates. Modern leasing estates (the term of years, periodic tenancy and tenancy at will) are all nonfreehold, and thus exempt from the "special rules." For example, leases for a term, unlike freehold leases, could commence in futuro and descend as personalty. . . . [The general independence of lease covenants] resulted from superimposing the nineteenth century summary proceeding for possession of real property over the part performance doctrine. Typically, these proceedings do not permit presentation of any counterclaims. The simple question before the court is whether rent is owed. The issue is whether something excuses performance of the rent covenant, not whether something reduces the amount due. Only a defense, e.g., breach of a dependent covenant, is relevant; not a counterclaim, e.g., breach of an independent covenant. This exclusion of counterclaims, not the independence of lease covenants, is the modern anomaly.

It is said that the summary proceeding's exclusion of counterclaims is "a concomitant of the inflexible and highly technical common law pleading system." But the rise of modern summary proceedings, particularly the exclusion of counterclaims, post-dates the expansion of recoupment and the collapse of common law civil practice. Moreover, nineteenth century summary proceedings are part of a more general movement in the law of forfeiture.

In the eighteenth century, the legal system "abhorred a forfeiture." Law courts limited forfeitures in a variety of ways. With limited exception, rights of re-entry had to be expressly reserved. To perfect a forfeiture for nonpayment of rent, the lessor had to meet several strict, technical requirements, such as making demand for rent "before sunset of the day on which the rent is due." Even when a forfeiture occurred at law, Equity freely granted relief to the tenant. Legislation designed to strengthen the lessor's position was limited in scope. The common law "niceties" precedent to bringing an ejectment for the nonpayment of rent were done away with only when half-year's rent was in arrearage and there was insufficient distress on the premises. Statutes granted rights of entry only for waste and in summary proceedings. And, summary proceedings were limited to situations where the rent reserved was equal to three-fourths the yearly value of the premises, was half-year in arrearage and the tenant had abandoned the premises leaving insufficient distress behind.

In the nineteenth century, however, only law courts continued to disfavor forfeitures. In fact, by integrating recoupment and counterclaims with ejectment actions, law courts poured new wine into old bottles. But Equity, concluding that "anciently, [Equity] corrected men's contracts without any foundation," virtually abandoned its jurisdiction to intervene. . . .

Legislative changes were equally dramatic. The common law requirements of demand for rent were dropped entirely. Express reservation of the right of entry became unnecessary in cases involving the breach of rent covenant. Some states even abrogated the express reservation requirement for all breaches so that, effectively, the scope of summary proceedings was greatly enlarged.

Some of these dramatic changes in the law of forfeiture may be explained by reference to movements in contract law and civil practice. But others, including the exclusion of counterclaims from summary proceedings are not. Indeed, they are counter to these movements. The exclusion of counterclaims is a product of unique legislation, and it seems a product of nineteenth century economic and social policy because the lessor's position receives a unique degree of protection. Whether this protection represents a hidden economic subsidy for real estate capital, or social protection from its consumers, it is a product of nineteenth century contract law and legislation.

Notes

1. Compare Judge Wright's efforts *supra* to the conclusion drawn by Lord Coke:

> But now copiholders stand upon a sure ground, now they weigh not their Lord's displeasure, they shake not at every suddaine blast of wind, they eate, drinke, and sleepe securely; onely drawing a speciall care of the maine chance (viz.) to performe carefully what duties and services soever their Tenure doth exact, and Custome doth require; then let Lord Frowne, the Copy holder cares not, knowing himselfe safe and not within any danger, for if the Lord's anger frow to expulsion, the Law hath provided severall weapons of remedy; for it is at his election either to sue a Subpena or an Action of Trespasse against the Lord. Time hath dealt very favorably with Copy holders in diver respects. [Coke, Compleate Copyholder,

Sec. 9 (1641), quoted in J. Commons, Legal Foundations of Capitalism 222 (1924).]

2. For a doctrinal approach more conventional than that taken in *Javins* see National Carriers Ltd. v. Panalpina (Northern) Ltd., [1981] 1 All E.R. 161 (House of Lords). There the tenants had leased a warehouse for ten years from 1 January 1974 at an annual rent of £6,500 for the first five years and £13,300 for the second five years. The landlord had given a covenant of quiet enjoyment in the lease. The tenant's promise to pay rent was unconditional except for the event of destruction of the premises by fire.

In May 1979 the City of Hull closed the street that gave the only access to the warehouse. The city did this because another building, a Victorian warehouse, was in dangerous condition. Demolition of the dangerous building took almost two years, because the building was a listed historic structure, and permission was required from the Secretary of State for the Environment, who first had to hold a hearing.

The tenants stopped paying rent until they could again use the warehouse. The landlord subsequently sued for unpaid rent.

The House of Lords refused to say that a lease could *never* be frustrated. Viscount Hailsham, the Lord Chancellor, said, "I come down on the side of the 'hardly ever' school of thought." Citing cases back to Paradine v. Jane, page 269 *supra*, he said he had been unable to find a reported English case where a lease had ever been held to have been frustrated.

> I hope this fact will act as a suitable deterrent to the litigious, eager to make legal history by being first in this field. But I am comforted by the reflexion of the authority referred to in the Compleat Angler on the subject of strawberries: "Doubtless God could have made a better berry, but doubtless God never did."

Lord Simon of Glaisdale suggested a fact situation in which tenant would be freed from his promise to pay rent:

> There are several places on the coast of England where sea erosion has undermined a cliff causing property of the top of the cliff to be totally lost for occupation; obviously occupation of a dwelling house is something significantly different in nature from its acqualung contemplation after it has suffered a sea change.

But Lord Hailsham, Lord Simon, and their colleagues were clear that the facts before them did not show frustration. The tenants lost use of the warehouse for two years, but would then have three more years remaining on their lease. Thus the landlord recovered a judgment for the rent that tenants had withheld.

(No United States case was cited by any of the five Law Lords who gave opinions. The judges seemed unacquainted with the *Javins* doctrine, although they did make references to Corbin and Williston.)

3. Introducing the Housing of the Working Classes Bill 1885 in the House of Lords, the Marquess of Salisbury described it as "a provision of considerable value" that would remove "the anomaly" caused by "a curious peculiarity of the law" that implied a warranty of fitness in the letting of furnished but not unfurnished premises. Hansard 3rd Ser. 1885, vol. 299, col. 892. The 1885 provision is now section 6 of The Housing Act 1957. In the 1885 debate, opposition was led by Lord Bramwell, who described the provision as "contrary to the ordinary principle of caveat emptor — altogether an unwarranted interference with freedom of contract . . . this mischievous, grandmotherly legislation . . . the best thing for . . . working men was to teach them to look after themselves." Id., vol. 301, cols. 5-6. Since 1885, "the effect of judicial interpretation has been to confine the warranty of fitness to the narrowest possible limits." Reynolds, Statutory Covenants of Fitness and Repair: Social Legislation and the Judges, 37 Mod. L. Rev. 377 (1974).

4. In Lindsey v. Normet, 405 U.S. 56 (1972), tenants attempted to achieve a *Javins*-like result as a matter of federal constitutional law. The Supreme Court rejected both equal protection and due process challenges to Oregon's Forcible Entry and Wrongful Detainer (FED) procedure for summary eviction of tenants. The Court thus refused to give the tenants a right to argue, before eviction, that their nonpayment of rent was justified by a Portland Bureau of Buildings declaration that the dwelling unit was unfit for habitation.

Writing for five justices, Justice White said that Oregon did not deny due process by restricting the issue in FED actions to whether the tenant has paid rent:

> The tenant is barred from raising claims . . . that the landlord has failed to maintain the premises, but the landlord is also barred from claiming back rent. . . . The tenant is not foreclosed from instituting his own action against the landlord and litigating his right to damages or other relief in that action.

The court also rejected the equal protection claim:

> The statute potentially applies to all tenants, rich and poor, commercial and noncommercial . . . . The landlord-tenant relationship was one of the few areas where the right to self-help was recognized by the common law . . . An alternative legal remedy to prevent such breaches of the peace has appeared to be an overriding necessity to many legislators and judges.

Finally, the Court refused to test the state's classification by a more stringent standard than rationality:

We do not denigrate the importance of decent, safe, and sanitary housing. But . . . we are unable to perceive . . . any constitutional guarantee of access to dwellings of a particular quality, or any recognition of the right of a tenant to occupy the real property of his landlord beyond the term of his lease without the payment of rent. . . .

The Court did invalidate one detail of the Oregon process. Civil appellants in Oregon were required to promise to pay damages and costs, but a FED defendant wishing to appeal was required to give security for *double* the rental value of the premises until final judgment. If the landlord won on appeal, he or she got to keep the double rent. The Supreme Court said that this double-bond provision was an arbitrary, irrational, and thus unconstitutional discrimination against the class of FED appellants.

(In 1973, Oregon passed comprehensive landlord-tenant reform legislation. Ore. Rev. Stat. §§91.700-91.895, 105.105-105.160. The legislation details landlord and tenant obligations and gives tenants the right in an action for possession or for rent to counterclaim based on the rental agreement or the landlord's violation of statutory duties.

The speed of eviction actions was slowed somewhat by the legislature. Personal service of process must take place three to seven days before trial. Or, process can be posted at the tenant's dwelling not less than seven or more then ten days before trial. In addition, a continuance may now be granted if the tenant pays rent into the court registry until the matter is resolved.)

5. When Milwaukee enforced its housing code, plaintiff tenants were forced to vacate. The Court of Appeals for the Seventh Circuit held that the city's actions constituted a taking of the tenants' property and that therefore it was required to pay them compensation. The court said:

[T]he City placed a disproportionately heavy burden on those individual members of the community who have little or no choice but to live in low cost, often substandard, housing. The fairness dictated by the Fifth Amendment requires that the economic burden borne by the plaintiffs for the benefit of the community be distributed among those benefited. [Devines v. Maier, 665 F.2d 138 (7th Cir. 1981)]

After a district court decision on remand, the case returned to a different Seventh Circuit panel where the earlier decision was reversed. The court held the city's regulation valid and that enforcement of it did not amount to a taking of property requiring compensation. In its opinion the court was able to rely on dicta in Loretto v. TelePrompter Manhattan CATV Corp., 458 U.S. 419 (1982), Chapter 22 *infra*, but justices left little doubt about their feelings that the earlier decision had involved a misreading of the Constitution. Devines v. Maier, 728 F.2d 876 (7th Cir. 1984).

6. In 1983 New York City marshals — private individuals licensed by the city — carried out 33,000 court-ordered evictions. The marshal receives $56.55 from the landlord for each eviction. The New York Times described the work of Woodrow Gist, a retired police detective, who performed evictions two days a week and repossessed utility meters on other days. His income was $249,795 gross and $107,861 net. N.Y. Times, Feb. 12, 1984.

7. In Japan, laws and procedures make tenant eviction difficult. A real estate broker borrowed heavily to buy a house at a foreclosure auction for $440,000. When the family occupying the house demanded $125,000 to leave, the broker allegedly killed the two adults and three of their children. Wall Street J., July 12, 1983.

D. LANDLORD-TENANT DOCTRINE AFTER *JAVINS*

1. The Implied Warranty of Habitability

MINN. STAT. ANN. §504.18(1) (Supp. 1975-1976): In every lease or license of residential premises, whether in writing or parol, the lessor or licensor covenants:

(a) That the premises and all common areas are fit for the use intended by the parties.

(b) To keep the premises in reasonable repair during the term of the lease or license, except when the disrepair has been caused by the willful, malicious, or irresponsible conduct of the lessee or licensee or a person under his direction or control.

(c) To maintain the premises in compliance with the applicable health and safety laws of the state and of the local units of government where the premises are located during the term of the lease or license, except when violation of the health and safety laws has been caused by the willful, malicious, or irresponsible conduct of the lessee or licensee or a person under his direction or control.

The parties to a lease or license of residential premises may not waive or modify the covenants imposed by this section.

MEASE v. FOX, 200 N.W.2d 791 (Iowa 1972): Under these circumstances we hold the landlord impliedly warrants at the outset of the lease that there are no latent defects in facilities and utilities vital to the use of the premises for residential purposes and that these essential features shall remain during the entire term in such condition to maintain the habitability of the dwelling. Further, the implied warranty we perceive in the lease situation is a representation there neither is nor shall be during the term a violation of applicable housing law, ordinance or regulation which shall render the premises unsafe, or unsanitary and unfit for living therein. . . .

As we have indicated, the breach of warranty must be of such substantial nature as to render the premises unsafe or unsanitary, and thus unfit for habitation. This will usually be a fact question to be determined by the circumstances of each case.

One such circumstance would be whether the alleged defect violated housing laws, regulations or ordinances. Other factors pertinent in testing the effect and materiality of the alleged breach include:

a. the nature of the deficiency or defect,
b. its effect on safety and sanitation,
c. the length of time for which it persisted,
d. the age of the structure,
e. the amount of the rent,
f. whether tenant voluntarily, knowingly and intelligently waived the defects, or is estopped to raise the question of the breach, and
g. whether the defects or deficiencies resulted from unusual, abnormal or malicious use by the tenant.

BERZITO v. GAMBINO, 63 N.J. 460, 308 A.2d 17 (1973): Not every defect or inconvenience will be deemed to constitute a breach of the covenant of habitability. The condition complained of must be such as truly to render the premises uninhabitable in the eyes of a reasonable person.

The *Berzito* court went on to paraphrase the same standards laid down in Mease v. Fox. Consider why such factors as age of structure and amount of rent should affect the question of whether a reasonable person would consider a structure uninhabitable.

BOSTON HOUSING AUTHORITY v. HEMINGWAY, 363 Mass. 184, 293 N.E.2d 831 (1973): Proof of any violation of [the State Statutory Code and any local health regulations] would usually constitute compelling evidence that the apartment was not in habitable condition. . . .

Notes

1. The *Javins* defense is not waivable. See, e.g., Houston Realty Corp. v. Castor, 94 Misc. 2d 115, 404 N.Y.S.2d 796 (Civ. Ct. 1978) (warranty of habitability is a non-waivable owner obligation); Teller v.

McCoy, 253 S.E.2d 114 (W. Va. 1978) ("Certainly no one can waive the obligations imposed by law upon landlords, and no one, by contract or otherwise, can agree to permit a landlord to break the law.").

2. The implied warranty of habitability established by *Javins* is limited to only those conditions that actually affect the ability of the tenant to live in a residential unit, essentially those conditions regulated by the housing code. It does not apply to services, such as air conditioning, that are not essential to habitability. See Winchester Management Corp. v. Staten, 361 A.2d 187 (D.C. 1976) ("Our decision today does no[t] repudiate the tenant's right to seek redress for the landlord's failure to provide the promised air conditioning service. . . . We hold merely that such redress may not be sought by means of an equitable defense to an action for possession for nonpayment of rent, for such a grievance is insufficient to justify the withholding of rent and defeat a landlord's possessory action.").

3. A St. Louis ordinance required that every dwelling unit "shall have a tub or shower bath in good working condition properly connected to approved hot and cold water and sewer systems in the toilet room or in a separate room adjacent to such dwelling unit." Ord. 51637, §391.040. Defendant's properties were not in compliance; appealing a criminal conviction, he claimed the ordinance was unreasonably arbitrary and took his property for public use without just compensation. The Supreme Court of Missouri concluded that:

> These buildings have no sale value, and no loan value. The buildings are 70 years old. No one will purchase them and people simply do not want to live in that neighborhood. This evidence, though coming from the defendant himself, is uncontroverted and we accept it. The locality has been largely vandalized and many of the buildings are vacant. When a building becomes vacant it is almost immediately vandalized and, as defendant said, it "disappears." Most of defendant's tenants are living on welfare or social security. This record does not show that any tenants have complained of existing conditions; they apparently do have flush toilets and lavatories with hot and cold water. The cost to defendant of the improvements demanded would total approximately $7,800 for each building, according to defendant's testimony. This figure was objected to as hearsay, but estimates had been received and defendant was an experienced real estate operator and owner. The evidence was admissible. Also, according to two witnesses who actually made estimates, the total cost of the improvements so estimated would total $7,260 per building. In the alteration the kitchens would be reduced to "closet" size. There was testimony from the defendant that in order to recoup such expense, he would have to charge monthly rentals of $60 over a five-year period and that this was simply not obtainable. The net result would seem to be vacancies, vandalism, and probably a total loss of the buildings.
>
> The problem here is not actually one of public health; it is wholly different from those cases involving outside privies, sewage, etc. While

the situation is by no means ideal, it really involves a matter of inconvenience to those tenants who choose to pay a minimum rent in return for incomplete facilities. The tenants may still bathe if they want to, and we are not convinced of any great danger that diseases will be spread. In conclusion, we hold that the part of §391.040 of Ordinance 51637 first quoted herein (tub or shower connected to approved hot and cold water and sewer systems) is unconstitutional as applied to these two properties; this, for the reason that it is unreasonable, arbitrary and confiscatory as so applied, and consequently a deprivation of due process; and that, as so applied, it would have no substantial or reasonable relationship to the public health, welfare or safety. [City of St. Louis v. Brune, 515 S.W.2d 471 (Mo. 1974).]

4. Holding that a tenant's right to abate rent does not depend on a showing that the landlord was at fault or acted in bad faith, the Massachusetts Supreme Judicial Court commented:

> The landlord suggests, and the amicus Greater Boston Real Estate Board argues at length, that to make the landlord the insurer of apartment maintenance will have deleterious economic effects on landlords and on the housing market generally. Increased costs derived from the warranty will result in increased rents. Older buildings, whose maintenance is hardest to ensure, tend to house low income tenants who cannot pay increased rents. Thus, imposing full warranty protection will ultimately reduce the stock of low income housing.
>
> This argument assumes that tenants will frequently enforce the rent abatement remedy or that landlords will spend a great deal of money on preventive maintenance. Yet empirical evidence tends to show a very low rate of tenant enforcement. Abbott, Housing Policy, Housing Codes and Tenant Remedies: An Integration, 56 B.U.L. Rev. 1, 63 (1976). Hirsch, Hirsch & Margolis, Regression Analysis of the Effects of Habitability Laws Upon Rent: An Empirical Observation on the Ackerman-Komesar Debate, 63 Cal. L. Rev. 1098, 1130 (1975). A study has failed to find a statistically significant relationship between the presence of most habitability laws, including rent abatement, and increased rents. Hirsch, Hirsch, & Margolis, supra at 1130-1132. In addition, we question the virtue of relying on a theory of economic efficiency at the expense of legal analysis. Precedent, legislative policy, and common law principles support the result we reach today. See Michelman, Norms and Normativity in the Economic Theory of Law, 62 Minn. L. Rev. 1015, 1015 (1978) ("[W]ell-conducted, systematic, convincing, behaviorally focused research can entrap as well as liberate, can help engender as well as dispel false belief about social reality, insofar as it invites the reduction of reality to observed regularities of behavior"). [Berman & Sons, Inc. v. Jefferson, 379 Mass. 196, 396 N.E.2d 981 (1979).]

5. Building maintenance and janitorial employees were on strike for 17 days. There were numerous violations of housing and sanitation codes, and the city declared a health emergency.

Held: Failure of landlord to provide adequate service, especially garbage removal, authorized an abatement of 10 percent of tenants' rent for the relevant period. Park West Management Corp. v. Mitchell, 47 N.Y.2d 316, 391 N.E.2d 1288, 418 N.Y.S.2d 310, *cert. denied,* 444 U.S. 992 (1979).

The New York statute, Real Property Law §235-b, provides:

1. In every written or oral lease or rental agreement for residential premises the landlord or lessor shall be deemed to covenant and warrant that the premises so leased or rented and all areas used in connection therewith in common with other tenants or residents are fit for human habitation and for the uses reasonably intended by the parties and that the occupants of such premises shall not be subjected to any conditions which would be dangerous, hazardous or detrimental to their life, health or safety. When any such condition has been caused by the misconduct of the tenant or lessee or persons under his direction or control, it shall not constitute a breach of such covenants and warranties.
2. Any agreement by a lessee or tenant of a dwelling waiving or modifying his rights as set forth in this section shall be void as contrary to public policy.
3. In determining the amount of damages sustained by a tenant as a result of a breach of the warranty set forth in this section, the court need not require any expert testimony.

6. Plaintiff landlords bought a 30-unit apartment building on Ocean Front Walk in Venice, California. They tried to raise rents, and tenants pleaded "wall cracks, peeling paint, water leaks, heating and electrical fixture problems, rodents and cockroaches, and the lack of sufficient heat." The trial court instructed the jury that the tenant may not defend against an eviction action on the basis of landlord breach of the implied warranty of habitability unless "[t]he defective condition was unknown to the tenant at the time of the occupancy of his or her apartment." The trial court also said that the tenant's defense is available only after the landlord has had a "reasonable time" to correct the defects. The California Supreme Court reversed on both issues, allowing these tenants the defense.

Justice William Clark, dissenting on the issue of tenant knowledge of defects, wrote:

> In a free market community, the primary determinant of agreed rent is the physical condition of the premises. The lessor is ordinarily aware of rent charged for comparable properties in nearby locations. The tenant chooses his apartment in light of rent demanded for comparable premises, aware of other apartments offering more or fewer advantages. The relationship between physical condition of the premises and rentals is illus-

trated by the facts of this case. So long as the rents remained low, the tenants paid the rent notwithstanding the physical conditions assertedly rendering the premises uninhabitable.

Should the tenant be permitted to conclude his bargain aware of the shortcomings of the premises, then later require the lessor to provide improved property at the earlier agreed rental?

Only the most compelling circumstances should prevent the tenant and landlord from freely agreeing the premises shall be leased in whatever condition for commensurate rent, both aware that better premises would call for higher rent. For example, in some of the mild weather areas, tenants may be willing to forego heating facilities in view of the low rent charged. Similarly, willing parties should not be prevented from agreeing the tenant will undertake improving the premises for commensurate rent.

Civil Code section 1941 setting forth landlord duty to place premises in habitable condition provides the duty is imposed "in the absence of an agreement to the contrary." [Knight v. Hallsthammar, 29 Cal. 3d 46, 623 P.2d 268, 171 Cal. Rptr. 707 (1981).]

7. The homeless Welborn family, including three children, approached Father Goosens at St. Mary's Church, Indianapolis. He found them temporary quarters in a house owned by the Society for the Propagation of the Faith. An oral lease was agreed to, at $55 per month. The church was slow with promised repairs. For some time, no rent was paid. After the Welborns moved out, the society sued and won a judgment for $365 in agreed but unpaid rent. An appellate court affirmed, rejecting the Welborns' defense of housing code non-compliance on the grounds that there was no showing that a better place was even impliedly warranted or promised, that the fair rental value of the premises was less than the agreed rent, or that the landlord's "part performance" was worth less than the rent tenants had promised to pay. Welborn v. Society for the Propagation of the Faith, 411 N.E.2d 1267 (Ind. App. 1980).

8. Referring to a landlord as a "slumlord" or "slum landlord" is not defamatory because it is capable of an innocent construction. Even if the statements charged the landlord with the crime of criminal housing management, they would not be libel per se since housing mismanagement is not a crime of moral turpitude. Rasky v. CBS, Inc., 103 Ill. App. 3d 577, 431 N.E.2d 1055 (1981), *cert. denied*, 459 U.S. 864 (1982).

2. Reach of the Standard

The most interesting "advance" from *Javins* is the cases imposing responsibility on the landlord for physical security of the premises. See, e.g., Kline v. 1500 Massachusetts Avenue Apartment Corp., 439 F.2d 477 (D.C. Cir. 1970) ("In the case at bar we place the duty of taking protective measures guarding the entire premises and the areas peculiarly under the landlord's control against the perpetration of criminal acts upon the landlord, the party to the lease contract who has the effective capacity to perform these necessary acts."); and Trentacost v. Brussel, 82 N.J. 214, 412 A.2d 436 (1980) ("Under modern living conditions, an apartment is clearly not habitable unless it provides a reasonable measure of security from the risk of criminal intrusion.").

But see: Williams v. William J. Davis, Inc., 275 A.2d 231 (D.C. 1971) (reliance on *Javins* and *Kline* for protection against crime is misplaced where the tenants seek to force the landlord to take safety measures not present at the beginning of the lease); Hall v. Frankoi, 69 Misc. 2d 470, 330 N.Y.S.2d 637 (Civ. Ct. 1972) (an implied warranty of habitability is not the same as an implied warranty against crimes committed by third persons; lack of front door lock is "not so closely connected with the result"—mugging of tenant-plaintiffs in public area—to support liability).

Notes

1. *Javins* and *Kline* apply to a student dormitory. Duarte v. State, 88 Cal. App. 3d 473, 151 Cal. Rptr. 727 (1979).

2. Does *Javins* apply to leases from the government? Massachusetts, earlier, had said yes. Boston Housing Authority v. Hemingway, 363 Mass. 184, 293 N.E.2d 831 (1973). But see Alexander v. U.S. Department of Housing and Urban Development, 555 F.2d 166 (7th Cir. 1977), *aff'd on other grounds*, 441 U.S. 39 (1979).

3. To what landlord-tenant relations does an implied warranty apply? Interstate Restaurants obtained in 1961 a 21-year leasehold in Halsa Corporation's Skyline Inn, on I Street in southwest Washington, to operate a restaurant, coffee shop, and cocktail lounge.

In 1970 Halsa sought possession, alleging breaches of the lease. Included were Interstate's failure to operate on weekends, as the lease required; part of the rent computation was a percentage of gross receipts. Interstate defended that even if it breached, it should be able to show Halsa's failures to supply adequate heat and air conditioning, and to prevent drafts and leaks in bad weather.

The court of appeals affirmed the trial court's refusal to permit evidence of violations by Halsa. "It is settled law that unless a contrary intention is expressed, the covenants in a lease are independent. . . . The rationale of [Javins] does not, in our view, extend to a commercial lease. . . ." Interstate Restaurants, Inc. v. Halsa Corp., 309 A.2d 108 (D.C. 1973).

Similarly, in Pleasure Driveway & Park Dist. of Peoria v. Kurek, 27 Ill. App. 3d 60, 325 N.E.2d 650 (1975), an appellate court refused to extend Illinois' version of *Javins* to the attempt by golf course professionals to retain possession of the concession shop at a public course beyond their contractual term while litigating their claim to a continuing employment relationship as greenskeepers. And in Clark Oil & Refining Corp. v. Thomas, 25 Ill. App. 3d 428, 323 N.E.2d 479 (1975), a gasoline station tenant being evicted for nonpayment of rent was denied the opportunity to assert, in the forcible entry and detainer proceeding, antitrust violations by the landlord oil company.

Further, some states have expressly excluded long-term leases, agricultural leases, and single-family houses from statutorily created warranties of habitability.

4. Lindsay v. Normet, p. 328 *supra*, seems to hold that there is no federal constitutional right to decent housing. Article XVIII of the New York Constitution says ". . . the legislature may provide in such a manner, by such means and upon such terms and conditions as it may prescribe for low rent housing . . . for persons of low income. . . ."

No case has held that this section *requires* the state to provide housing, but Article VII, §1 reads, "The aid, care and support of the needy are public concerns and shall be provided by the state and by such of its subdivisions, and in such manner and by such means, as the legislature may from time to time determine."

Applying this provision, Kahn v. Smith, 60 App. Div. 2d 869, 401 N.Y.S.2d 264 (1978), held that "Unless the Department of Social Services can show that petitioner is not in need of the emergency public assistance and care which he is unable to provide for himself, it must furnish him assistance. . . . [T]he department, in its discretion, may deny emergency assistance for rental arrears and instead rehouse the applicant in other housing accommodations appropriate for his best interests. . . ."

3. Remedies

Javins represents judicial adoption of a particular remedy for housing code violations: the tenant remains in possession and pays reduced rent or no rent at all.

Courts have taken a variety of approaches to the problem of fixing the amount of the rent abatement in the warranty of habitability. This may be due in part to the differing policies that come into play; they include compensating the tenant, encouraging the landlord to rehabilitate the property, and preserving some scope for freedom of contract.

One method used for measuring damages is for the tenant to recover any rent charges in excess of the "fair market value" of the premises in their unsafe or unsanitary condition. See Berzito v. Gambino, 63 N.J. 460, 308 A.2d 17 (1973). In addition to the problem of securing expert testimony so that a fair market value can be determined, this method may result in lower damages for a tenant who is a good bargainer and manages to sign a lease calling for relatively low rent. Consider also whether this conflicts with the general rule that a warranty of habitability cannot be waived.

The approach some other courts have taken is to abate an amount that is the difference between the fair market rental value of the premises *as warranted* and the fair market value of the premises *as is*. See, e,g., Mease v. Fox, 200 N.W.2d 791 (Iowa 1972). Note that this makes the agreed-upon rent irrelevant, except insofar as it aids in establishing fair market value. This method is potentially very harsh on landlords since a tenant who is a good bargainer might conceivably end up paying no rent at all.

The percentage diminution rule assumes that the agreed-upon rent is the fair market value of the premises *as warranted*. The rent is then reduced by a certain percentage, corresponding to the amount of use lost. Instead of relying on expert testimony, judges will generally use rough approximations in making this determination.

There is a wide disparity between tenant and landlord's testimony as to the extent of diminution of service, but landlord admits that heat, hot water, elevator service and incinerator use failed at various times during the period December 1969 to March 1970, and that repairs were made from time to time. Had landlord produced records of repair bills, more precise determination of the periods during which service failed might have been possible. Tenant testified that in the child's bedroom there was no heat during the entire period; that complaint was made to the superintendent without avail, and that the child slept in the living room by reason thereof. He testified that there was no hot water for substantial periods in November, December and March, as the result of which water was heated on the stove for bathing; that the living room lacked heat in November and December; that two out of three elevators failed to function in November, December and two weeks in March, and that the incinerator was defective throughout the period.

The superintendent denied that the breakdowns were for such extended periods. He said that the heating system never broke down for more than six-hour periods; that a service repaired the elevators promptly; that the incinerator broke down for a day to a day and one-half in November, and two weeks in December, during which garbage cans were used. He attributed much of the difficulty with the incinerator to vandalism.

I am convinced that tenant exaggerated, and that the superintendent testified from ignorance. I find as a fact that there was a breach of the covenant of habitability, and that the diminution in rent of 25% is a fair amount. There will therefore be a judgment that tenant is indebted to landlord for rent in the amount of $433. If that amount is not paid within three days, a warrant for possession will issue. No costs. [Academy Spires, Inc. v. Brown, 111 N.J. Super. 477, 268 A.2d 556 (Dist. Ct. 1970).]

The Second Restatement's approach combines the two approaches discussed above: The amount of use lost is determined by a comparison of the fair market value of the premises as warranted and as is; the rent is then reduced by the same percentage.

Consider the following hypothetical. A tenant rents an apartment at $140 per month. After a few years, the landlord allows the apartment to become dilapidated, while the value of the land has increased. The warranted fair market value of the premises is now $200 per month, but the value in its present condition is only $100. Under the "pay-for-as-is" approach the tenant would be entitled to an abatement of $40. The benefit of the bargain approach would give the tenant a $100 rent reduction. The Restatement (Second) method would allow the tenant a $70 rent reduction.

Finally, some commentators have suggested an entirely different approach, and argued for tort damages for discomfort and annoyance.

MOSKOVITZ, THE IMPLIED WARRANTY OF HABITABILITY: A NEW DOCTRINE RAISING NEW ISSUES, 62 Calif. L. Rev. 1444, 1470-1473 (1974):

A New Proposal: Discomfort and Annoyance

Generally, the residential tenant who has suffered a breach of the warranty does not lose money. He instead cannot bathe as frequently as he would like or at all if there is inadequate hot water; he must worry about rodents harassing his children or spreading disease if the premises are infested; or he must avoid certain rooms or worry about catching a cold if there is inadequate weather protection or heat. Thus discomfort and annoyance are the common injuries caused by each breach and hence the true nature of the general damages the tenant is claiming.

While it is somewhat unusual to allow compensation for such injuries in an action for breach of contract, it should be allowed here. First, damages for discomfort and annoyance have been allowed where the breach of contract is also a nuisance, as it often appears to be here. Second, the implied warranty theory is essentially a tort-contract hybrid concept, a concept which has been used to justify, in the sales of goods, damages for mental suffering caused by the breach of an implied warranty of fitness for the purpose intended. Finally, damages for a very *Tort* similar injury — mental suffering — have been allowed in a breach of contract action where the subject of the contract directly concerned the comfort of the aggrieved party.

Another advantage of the discomfort and annoyance approach is that the tenant could in many cases prove his general damages by the same evidence used to prove the seriousness of the defects — their effect on safety and sanitation and the length of time they persisted.

Nor need precedent be wholly abandoned in order to adopt this suggested new approach. Although reduction in use does seem logically more suited to the commercial rather than the residential tenant, certainly the tenant's ability to use the facilities of the premises has a direct bearing on how much discomfort and inconvenience has been suffered. Therefore, any evidence of percentage reduction in use is relevant to the ultimate determination. Evidence of difference in value, however, seems out of place. Market value has no bearing on the actual physical discomfort and annoyance caused by the breach. Moreover, it is highly unlikely that the tenant is emotionally or even financially concerned about any drop in the market value of the premises. The typical residential tenant rents his dwelling not for the monetary gain, but to live in. Evidence of difference in value, therefore, has little or no probative value in determining actual damage, and should accordingly be discounted or discarded altogether as a determinant of tenant injury.

Placing a dollar value on the injury caused in a given case by a tenant's discomfort and annoyance is admittedly quite difficult. This difficulty is not, however, sufficient reason to disallow such damages. Fact-finders face a similar problem every day where damages for pain and suffering are claimed in personal injury trials. The law recognizes the difficulty involved here, but trusts the good judgment of the fact-finder to set damages for pain and suffering in a reasonable amount.

Using the discomfort and annoyance approach, a court could assess damages at an amount equaling — or even exceeding — the contract rent, and thus reduce the reasonable rent to zero. This should *not* be viewed as "giving the tenant something for nothing." The tenant has given his discomfort and annoyance in amounts which the fact-finder could quantify as exceeding the contract rent. One would not think of limiting an award for the pain and suffering of a plaintiff injured by a defective ten-dollar electric iron to $9.99 to prevent him from getting the iron "for nothing."

Generally, courts have not adopted this method. But see Simon v. Solomon, 385 Mass 91, 431 N.E.2d 556 (1982).

MCKENNA v. BEGIN, 5 Mass. App. 304, 362 N.E.2d 548 (1977): Basically, [the trial judge] computed the damages by finding the fair rental value of the defective premises to be the rent agreed upon less the amortized cost of repairing the major code violations. Thus McKenna's damages became the cost of repairing the major defects amortized over the remaining useful life of the building. Rather than measuring the damages by amortizing the cost to Begin of remedying the defects, we believe that the damages should have been calculated in a manner which more closely reflects the diminution in the value of McKenna's use and enjoyment of the premises. One of the established aims of determining damages for breach of contract is to put the injured party in the position he would have been in if performance had been rendered as promised. . . .

To fashion a measure of damages which more closely reflects the actual injury suffered by McKenna we adopt a percentage reduction of use approach, under which McKenna's rent is to be reduced by a percentage reflecting the diminution in the value of the use and enjoyment of the leased premises by reason of the existence of defects which gave rise to the breach of warranty of habitability. . . .

BROWN, J. (concurring): I concur with the majority that in general it is appropriate to remand cases involving breaches of the warranty of habitability to the Superior Court to allow it to determine the portion of rent to be rebated to the tenant. However, it seems to me that under the reasoning of Boston Housing Auth. v. Hemingway, 363 Mass. 184, 293 N.E.2d 831 (1973), the rental value of the unit must be zero when the board of health condemns the apartment. . . .

Finally, where a contract is in violation of a statute and public policy, it is illegal and unenforceable. A lease agreement which is knowingly made despite the existence of violations of the sanitary code which make the dwelling uninhabitable is an illegal agreement which is unenforceable.

———————

The *Javins* court combined the remedies of rent withholding and rent abatement, but they are different.

Rent withholding by one or more tenants is a means of providing indirect pressure to compel a landlord to make repairs. A number of states have developed statutory guidelines for rent withholding, making use of escrow accounts to provide security for the landlord with indigent tenants.

Rent withholding is a remedy well suited for coordinated activity by tenants and for forcing the major repairs that tenants cannot finance. However, it faces two important drawbacks. Rent withholding is rarely effective immediately, and is thus ill suited for emergencies. Worse, in a low-profit building where cost of repairs is substantial, a resort to rent withholding may induce the landlord to abandon the building.

Rent abatement plays two remedial roles. A court awarding rent abatement is providing compensatory damages for breach of warranty. In addition, the presence of the remedy may serve to deter landlords from allowing buildings to deteriorate. Abatement was raised as a counterclaim in *Javins*, but an affirmative action for breach of warranty and retroactive abatement may also be brought. (It is unclear whether such a remedy would remain in existence if tenants actually began to bring suits with any frequency.)

a. Repair and Deduct

Under certain circumstances the most rapid and convenient means to assure the correction of housing code violations may be for the tenant to make the repairs himself and then deduct the cost of repairs from rent payments. A number of states now have some form of repair-and-deduct remedy available. Compare the following approaches.

Mass. Gen. Laws Ann. Ch. 111, §127L (Supp. 1975):

> When violations of the standards of fitness for human habitation as established in the state sanitary code, or of other applicable laws, ordinances, by-laws, rules or regulations, may endanger or materially impair the health, safety or well-being of a tenant of residential premises and are so certified by the board of health or local code enforcement agency, or in the city of Boston by the commissioner of housing inspection, or by a court of law, and if the owner or his agent has been notified in writing of the existence of the violations and has failed to begin all necessary repairs or to contract in writing with a third party for such repairs within five days after such notice, and to substantially complete all necessary repairs within fourteen days after such notice, unless a board of health, local code enforcement agency or court has ordered that said violations be corrected within a shorter period, in which case said period shall govern, the tenant or tenants may repair or have repaired the defects or conditions constituting the violations. The tenant or tenants may subsequently deduct from any rent which may subsequently become due, subject to the provisions of the following paragraph, an amount necessary to pay for such repairs. The tenant or tenants may, alternatively in such cases, treat the lease or rental agreement as abrogated, pay only the fair value of their use and occupation and vacate the premises within a reasonable time.
>
> A tenant may not deduct pursuant to this section an amount greater than four months' rent in any twelve-month period, or period of occupancy, whichever is shorter, from rent due to the owner. . . .
>
> Any provision of a residential lease or rental agreement whereby a tenant, lessee, or occupant enters into a covenant, agreement or contract, the effect of which is to waive the benefits of any provision of this section, shall be against public policy and void; except that a covenant in any lease of two years' duration not counting any renewal periods, in which the tenant undertakes to make certain defined repairs or renovations in consideration for a substantially lower rent, shall not be against public policy nor void.

Okla. Stat. Ann. tit. 41, §121(B) (1978):

> If there is a material noncompliance by the landlord . . . which . . .
> materially affects health and the breach is remediable by repairs, the rea-
> sonable cost of which is less than $100, the tenant may notify the landlord
> of his intention to correct the condition at the landlord's expense after the
> expiration of 14 days.

Does either statute deal adequately with the problem of large and
expensive repairs or with the need for tenant cooperative activity in
repairs of common areas? What happens under each statute if the tenant
incurs expenses that the court later finds excessive, or if inadequate
repairs give rise to tort liability?

b. The Administrative Sanction

ABBOTT, HOUSING POLICY, HOUSING CODES AND TENANT
REMEDIES: AN INTEGRATION, 56 B.U.L. Rev. 1, 49-50 (1976): Initially, code enforcement remedies were administratively enforced. Early
tenement house laws empowered the board of health to order premises
vacated that were not in code compliance once the owner had been
notified of the violation and had failed to repair within a reasonable
time. Vacated structures were then ordered demolished if they had not
been repaired within six months. If the owner failed to comply, the
municipality was usually authorized to board up the building and eventually demolish it. The cost in doing so became a lien against the property.

The order to vacate, followed by demolition, is a drastic remedy; it
removes dwelling units from the housing stock, temporarily or permanently, and leaves the tenants homeless. Unless the community has
standard relocation housing into which the displaced families can move,
their eviction may be politically unpopular and futile in improving their
housing conditions. They will be forced to absorb the costs, psychological and monetary, of moving and may end up in equally substandard
housing. Thus, to be effective, the remedy needs a very high vacancy
rate — estimated at over twenty-five percent — in standard housing to
avoid these harsh consequences. For example, vacate orders were used
effectively in New York City in the early 1900s and again in the 1930s
when such high vacancy rates existed in the housing market. But such
high vacancy rates are unlikely to obtain today.

As a code enforcement remedy, a vacate order can play into the
hands of a recalcitrant landlord who wishes to rid himself of troublesome tenants without resort to the eviction process. By allowing his
building to become seriously substandard, the landlord can trigger an
order to vacate that would then allow him to remodel or tear down the

vacant structure. Yet the vacate order can be a powerful sanction because it cuts off entirely the landlord's rent revenues. However, it must be a credible threat to effect code compliance; at present, because of housing market conditions, it seldom is.

c. The Criminal Sanction

F. GRAD, LEGAL REMEDIES FOR HOUSING CODE VIOLATIONS 24, 26, 29-30 (Natl. Commn. on Urban Problems, 1968): Practices with respect to criminal prosecution differ widely from jurisdiction to jurisdiction. Although it is true in every state and every city that not every uncorrected housing violation is prosecuted, the practice of selecting cases for prosecution differs considerably, with some large cities bringing thousands of cases each year, and others a mere handful. . . .

Most housing laws and housing codes authorize both fines and jail terms. A number limit jail terms to cases in which the fine is not paid, and a smaller number provide for fines only.

Although in some jurisdictions jail terms up to six months may be authorized, most commonly 30 days is the maximum jail sentence that may be imposed for a housing violation. But, whatever the length of time authorized, the actual imposition of jail sentences is so unusual and infrequent as to play a relatively insignificant part in code enforcement. A jail sentence for housing code violations is almost invariably noted in the newspapers because of its unusual nature, and in the recent past, at least, an instance or two of jail sentences have been so noted in New York City and in Washington, D.C. It is fair to say that jail sentences pose no real threat to the overwhelming mass of housing violators.

In the main, the situation is not too different with respect to the imposition of fines. Although fines ranging up to $500 or even $1,000 per violation may be authorized, only very minor fines are imposed in most jurisdictions. . . .

The effectiveness of the criminal sanction — just like the effectiveness of all other sanctions — can be gauged only by reference to the major goals of code enforcement; namely, the restoration and maintenance of healthful and decent housing conditions in existing dwellings. Are criminal penalties effective in bringing about the repair of violation-ridden buildings, or the maintenance of dwellings in accordance with code standards? They generally [are] not, for reasons that inhere both in the practical and theoretical aspects of the sanction. . . .

The failure of the criminal sanction in code enforcement is largely due to its conceptual and logical inappropriateness. Sentencing practices in housing cases no doubt reflect this problem. Criminal courts are unwilling to recognize housing violations as true "crimes," and, in the traditional sense, this is not an indefensible attitude. However inexact the age-old distinction may be in the criminal law between *malum in se* —

the true crime, the "wrong in and of itself" like murder, assault, robbery, or larceny — and *malum prohibitum* — a wrong which is wrongful merely because it has been prohibited by law, but which does not necessarily bespeak inherent moral delinquency — it is clear that the unintentional failure to observe a traffic sign, to curb one's dog, and to replace a broken windowpane in the hallway of a multiple dwelling falls into the latter category. Whether we adhere to the *malum in se–malum prohibitum* distinction or not, the "true" crimes are generally characterized by criminal intent, by a guilty mind or *mens rea;* the other category, in the main, consists of crimes of omission — a failure or neglect to comply with some positive requirements of law. . . .

Thus, the nature of the criminal remedy and its lack of effectiveness in code enforcement are interrelated. It is obvious that the volume and nature of housing violations make it practically impossible to look for intent and wrongful knowledge on the part of the owner in every case. It follows that if we continue to rely on criminal prosecutions, the doctrine of strict liability will be essential. But strict liability — the definition of "absolute" crimes regardless of intent — invariably leads to a trivializing of the offense, to judicial nullification by a refusal to impose penalties that are capable of deterrence. The criminal sanction in housing code enforcement thus becomes incapable of drawing clear distinctions between the hard-core recalcitrant and the less serious occasional offender who needs to be prodded into compliance.

d. Receivership

Receivership can provide a direct and immediate remedy for serious housing code violations. A receivership statute establishes a formal procedure by which a court can appoint an individual or body to act as receiver of a building's rent roll and make the necessary repairs, after which the building ownership is returned to the landlord. (Why is it returned?)

The most serious difficulties with receivership programs occur when the rent flow from an apartment building is insufficient to finance emergency repairs. Thus New York City has developed a revolving fund for receivership repairs. The cost of repair is advanced from the fund, and gradually repaid from future rental income. However, the New York experience has been that buildings in need of emergency repairs are often encumbered with mortgages, liens, and taxes, and little money is ever recovered. For details see Grad, New Sanctions and Remedies in Housing Code Enforcement, 3 Urb. Law. 577 (1971).

An interesting variant of receivership is the Landlord Security Deposit Act, which has operated in parts of New Jersey in recent years. Under this legislation, landlords are required to give the municipality a security deposit for each apartment operated. This deposit is then available for emergency repairs without the expenditure of city funds. While the city holds the deposit, interest is paid to the landlord (a benefit tenants usually do not receive on their security deposits). The existence of the fund seems to encourage landlords to maintain their buildings in order to avoid city-made repairs with their money. However, the existence of the fund cannot compel landlords to invest in repairs when return on investment is inadequate; thus this type of statute seems not to answer the problems of marginal and dilapidated housing. A discussion of the LSDA is found in Apartment House Council v. Mayor and Council of Ridgefield, 123 N.J. Super. 87, 301 A.2d 484 (Law Div. 1973), aff'd per curiam, 128 N.J. Super. 192, 319 A.2d 507 (App. Div. 1974), and in Blumberg and Robbins, Beyond URLTA: A Program for Achieving Real Tenant Goals, 11 Harv. Civ. Rights-Civ. Lib. L. Rev. 1, 30-35 (1976).

e. Specific Performance

Specific performance is suggested in *Javins* as a remedy that should be available for breach of warranty. Plainly there are circumstances in which all remedies at law are inadequate for the tenant. Where violations of the housing code are serious, immediate action is necessary, and rent withholding neither spurs landlord action nor provides sufficient funds for repair, a decree of specific performance would seem appropriate. These factors must be balanced against the landlord's capacity to carry out the performance and the court's ability to supervise. Nevertheless, it seems clear that specific performance is a potentially effective and presently underutilized remedy.

f. Involving the Mortgagee

BLUMBERG & ROBBINS, BEYOND URLTA: A PROGRAM FOR ACHIEVING REAL TENANT GOALS, 11 Harv. Civ. Rights-Civ. Lib. L. Rev. 1, 35-39 (1976): Tenant-mortgagee negotiating is a method by which tenants can involve mortgagees in the rehabilitation of deteriorated residential buildings. The strategy is based upon the legal right of tenants pursuant to the warranty of habitability to withhold rent or to seek rent abatement against the landlord-mortgagor when serious housing defects exist. Continued rent withholding or abatement decreases the rent flow available to the landlord, thus placing a financially marginal landlord in serious danger of defaulting on the mortgage payments. Tenants who exercise their right to decent housing may thus be forcing foreclosure by the mortgagee. When foreclosure becomes a real possibility the mortgagee is compelled to become involved with the problems of the building, the tenants, and the landlord-mortgagor, often for the first time.

g.   Tenant Unions

NOTE, TENANT UNIONS: COLLECTIVE BARGAINING AND THE LOW-INCOME TENANT, 77 Yale L.J. 1368, 1383-1385, 1395-1396 (1968): Can the tenant union obtain housing improvements where more traditional legal remedies have failed? Even if the landlord has profits the loss of which will not drive him from the market, he will fight any effort to extract them. And even where the union seeks only to improve housing by lowering operating costs and contributing its own effort, it will have to convince the landlord that good faith bargaining is not against his interest. Whether the union will be able to lead the landlord to the negotiating table, and what it will obtain once there, will hinge on the strength of the union, the type of landlord, conditions in the housing market, and the building's state of deterioration. The union derives its strength from the only source available to it: collective action. To maximize its power, it must organize a significant proportion of the buildings owned or managed by the landlord it confronts. Unless it can do so, the union probably cannot obtain the leverage to bring the landlord to the negotiating table.

Widespread picketing and rent withholding are the most potent forces to convince the landlord to bargain. Even if both tactics encounter no resistance in the courts, how likely are they to be effective? The landlord has three major weapons at his disposal to break a recognition drive by the union. Chief among them is eviction. . . .

Second, the landlord may simply cease to service his building. . . .

Third, and most drastically, the landlord may threaten to abandon the building or to take it off the market — a threat made more credible if he has already stopped servicing the structure. . . .

Against the tactics available to the landlord, the union can pitch its weapons of rent withholding and picketing. The former is likely to be the more potent; the landlord's need for a steady flow of rent money to meet mortgage payments will make him feel the pinch rapidly and painfully when his revenue is cut off. But picketing, although not so powerful a tool as in the labor context, will also have its impact. Besides the social and political pressures on the landlord that inevitably accompany a strike, the publicity and discord it generates, especially when accompanied by a rent-withholding campaign, may stimulate the threat of a code enforcement crackdown which might be more drastic in its impact than the tenants' demands. . . .

The final negotiation of a collective agreement with the landlord represents the fruition of the tenant union's efforts. The contracts vary widely in sophistication, specific terms, and the number of buildings covered. The typical agreement contains the following provisions:

Substantive promises
— a union commitment to encourage and oversee tenant efforts in responsible apartment maintenance;

— a landlord commitment to make certain initial repairs and to meet basic maintenance standards thereafter;
— a maximum rent scale for the life of the contract;
— a union commitment not to strike;

Enforcement provisions
— machinery for the regular transmission of tenant complaints and demands to the landlord;
— an arbitration board to resolve disputes over grievances with power to compel repairs;
— a procedure for rent withholding if the landlord fails to comply with the agreement;

Landlord-union relations
— landlord recognition of the union as exclusive bargaining agent;
— a landlord commitment not to discriminate against union members;
— a requirement that the landlord inform the tenant union of the addresses of all buildings owned and managed by him, and of the names of all new tenants as they move in.

Increasingly, collective bargaining agreements provide for a dues check-off by the landlord.

Most important to the union is the landlord's acceptance of binding arbitration and the private enforcement mechanism of the rent withholding provision; their combined effect produces considerable economic pressure on the landlord to make necessary repairs rather than delay or take the matter into court.

4. Procedure

The District of Columbia Court Reform and Criminal Procedure Act of 1970, 84 Stat. 552, was interpreted by the D.C. Court of Appeals as removing the right of jury trial in actions for the recovery of the possession of real estate. But the Supreme Court found this in violation of the Seventh Amendment, and so jury trials à la *Javins* have been restored. Pernell v. Southall Realty, 416 U.S. 363 (1974).

When a D.C. landlord sues for possession after *Javins*, should the tenant be required to prepay rent into the registry of the court before being allowed to defend? The issue was considered in Bell v. Tsintolas Realty Co., 430 F.2d 474 (D.C. Cir. 1970).

As arguments in favor of requiring a protective order for prepayment, the court listed "the emerging non-summary nature of the suit for possession, the concomitant severe disadvantage in which the landlord has been placed during such litigation, and the potential for dilatory tactics which judicial innovation in this area has bred. . . ." It also cited factors that should discourage use of the protective order:

that such a prepayment requirement is extraordinary in the course of civil litigation, that it has a tendency indirectly to constrict the tenant's right to proceed *in forma pauperis*, a right which equal protection considerations have recently led us to defend, that it carries with it, especially in the context of landlord-tenant litigation, a substantial risk of precluding litigation of meritorious defenses, that it also carries a substantial risk of upsetting the precarious balance of tactics in landlord-tenant litigation.

The court of appeals concluded that it was appropriate to grant a protective order

only when the tenant has either asked for a jury trial or asserted a defense based on violations of the housing code, and only upon motion of the landlord and after notice and opportunity for oral argument by both parties. . . . In making a determination of need, the trial court may properly consider the amount of rent alleged to be due, the number of months the landlord has not received even a partial rental payment, the reasonableness of the rent for the premises, the amount of the landlord's monthly obligations for the premises, whether the tenant has been allowed to proceed *in forma pauperis*, and whether the landlord faces a substantial threat of foreclosure.

Even if the landlord has adequately demonstrated his need for a protective order, the trial judge must compare that need with the apparent merits of the defense based on housing code violations. Relevant considerations would be whether the housing code violations alleged are *de minimis* or substantial, whether the landlord has been notified of the existence of the defects, and, if so, his response to that notice, and the date, if known, of the last repair or renovation relating to the alleged defect.

When a protective order is granted, how much should the tenant be required to pay?

[I]n the ordinary course of events . . . the tenant will be called upon to pay into the court registry each month the amount which he originally contracted to pay as rent. However . . . a lesser amount would be desirable when the tenant makes a very strong showing that the condition of the dwelling is in violation of Housing Regulation norms.

What will be the appropriate prepayment procedure at the appellate stages of the litigation?

Certainly if the landlord has been accorded summary judgment . . . or other judgment on the merits, the case for requiring prepayment of rent is strengthened. Of course, if the appeals court is of the opinion that the grant of summary or other judgment is erroneous on its face, it may dissolve the prepayment order or its equivalent on a motion for summary reversal or stay or other seasonable motion. And, similarly, if the tenant prevails at the trial level, any prepayment order will be discontinued.

It is hard to enforce *Javins* rights without legal representation. Yet representation for the poor is at best incomplete. The following opinion resulted from an effort by the Legal Services Institute to give poor tenants enough guidance to represent themselves. (The institute, located in the Jamaica Plain neighborhood of Boston, was a combined effort of the U.S. Legal Services Corporation and the Harvard and Northeastern University Law Schools.)

BABE JULIAN v. CHARLES DONOVAN, Summary Process No. 16955, Massachusetts Housing Court Dept., Boston Division, June 23, 1980: [*Order on motion to introduce further evidence.*]

Lawrence D. Shubow, Justice of Boston Housing Court: After completion of the trial of this summary process action on May 30, 1980, the Defendant (tenant) has filed (June 6, 1980) a Motion to Introduce Further Evidence. At the trial there was evidence of unpaid rent in the two-family dwelling for many months. The Motion recites that the movant is "being assisted by paralegal and other staff at the Legal Services Institute," and the Motion is accompanied by affidavits and other documents obviously prepared by a lawyer. The affidavit of an attorney asserts that legal advice and consultative services have been provided the tenant but that "No attorney in this office is able to properly prepare this case and provide representation to Ms. Chubbuck . . . who cannot afford an attorney." The supporting materials strongly suggest the Defendant may well have had substantial defenses and counterclaims which she did not assert. The case has been pending (by reason of a delay in transfer from the West Roxbury Division) since February 14, 1980.

The Court is mindful of the important and promising mission being undertaken by the Legal Services Institute. See "Progress, Amidst Chaos, at Legal Services Institute," 70 Harv. L.S. Rec. 10 (May 2, 1980 at page 1). The Court is aware of the problem of the need for representation threatening to engulf available legal service resources. See McNally, "Why We Need Mandatory Pro Bono," 8 M.L.W. 907 (June 9, 1980).

But individual lawyers cannot be permitted to determine for themselves the proper parameters of legal representation.

The reasons become manifest in a case like this where counsel in effect does enough "lawyering" to determine that a possible miscarriage of justice impends, and then indicates to the Court, "It's your problem, I am too busy to deal with it." Trial Courts do not have the luxury of restricting their existing caseload, the better to discharge their obligations to pending matters, but must deal with all who properly invoke their powers. The proper quantum of legal representation, similarly, cannot be left to the conscience of the individual practitioner. The decisions of ethical committees, the rules and decisions of disciplinary agencies, the common law of professional liability all make up a body of controlling principles on the degree to which a lawyer, once the relationship is established, may be permitted to define the limits of the professional service he or she is to provide. It seems to me no difference should be recognized for publicly chartered offices.

A further consideration made clear by the history of this case is that the mode of legal representation adopted, even if permissible, undermines a necessary element of the adversary process without which it would be gravely crippled: i.e., continuing communication and negotiation between counsel. Attorneys often educate one another about the true state of the facts and applicable law. Each is then better able to counsel his or her own client and bring the controversy to resolution without the burden of trial, saving litigation for the statistically rare case in which one party, or both, insist on remaining rooted on untenable ground. Not even a phone call appears to have been made by tenant's counsel in this case. Opposing counsel cannot be faulted on this score because his opponent was, until he receives this Order, operating with a hidden hand.

The papers filed and other forms of participation in the pending case going back to February, 1980, by the law office of which the tenant's attorney is director are deemed to constitute an appearance in the case. Counsel is, therefore, pursuant to Mass. R. Civ. P. No. 5d, directed to furnish copies of the papers prepared by her (or under her supervision) to counsel for the Plaintiff, and the Clerk is requested to assign the pending motion for early hearing.

Counsel for both sides are requested to confer prior to hearing on the motion and to be prepared to report on any agreement reached.

After vehement protests from Legal Services Institute lawyers, Judge Shubow withdrew his opinion shortly after it was issued.

E. *DIAMOND HOUSING* AFTER *JAVINS:* IS THE LEASE "VOID AND UNENFORCEABLE" AFTER ALL?

◆ ROBINSON v. DIAMOND HOUSING CORP.
463 F.2d 853 (D.C. Cir. 1972)

WRIGHT, Circuit Judge. In Edwards v. Habib, 397 F.2d 687 (1968), cert. denied, 393 U.S. 1016 (1969), this court held that a tenant may assert the retaliatory motivation of his landlord as a defense to an otherwise proper eviction. In Brown v. Southall Realty Co., D.C. App., 237 A.2d

834 (1968), the District of Columbia Court of Appeals held that a lease purporting to convey property burdened with substantial housing code violations was illegal and void and that hence the landlord was not entitled to gain possession for rent due under the invalid lease. The case before us involves the intersection of these two principles. Specifically, it raises the question whether a landlord who has been frustrated in his effort to evict a tenant for nonpayment of rent by successful assertion of a *Southall Realty* defense may automatically accomplish the same goal by serving a 30-day notice to quit. . . .

If lawsuits were won by perseverance alone, Diamond Housing could hardly lose this suit. Appellee has been attempting to evict Mrs. Robinson for over three and a half years. It has proceeded under no fewer than three legal theories and has remained undaunted through an adverse jury verdict, a dismissal of its action by the Court of General Sessions, an adverse decision by the District of Columbia Court of Appeals, and action by the District of Columbia City Council which seemingly cut the heart out of its case.

The saga begins on May 2, 1968, when Mrs. Robinson and her four children moved into a row house owned by Diamond Housing in Northwest Washington. Mrs. Robinson signed a lease making her a month-to-month tenant with the apparent understanding that the landlord would repair the deteriorating condition of the premises.

When the landlord failed to keep this promise, Mrs. Robinson began withholding rent, and Diamond Housing sued for possession. Mrs. Robinson defended on the ground that substantial housing violations existed at the time the lease was signed and that the lease was therefore unenforceable under the principles announced in Brown v. Southall Realty Co., *supra*. Specifically, Mrs. Robinson introduced evidence showing that large pieces of plaster were missing throughout the house, that there was no step from the front walk to the front porch, that the front porch was shaky and unsafe, that there was a wall in the back bedroom which was not attached to the ceiling and which moved back and forth when pressed, that nails protruded along the side of the stairway, that there was a pane of glass missing from the living room window, and that the window frame in the kitchen was so far out of position that one could see into the back yard through the space between it and the wall. At the completion of the trial, the jury returned a special verdict finding that housing code violations existed at the inception of the lease rendering the premises unsafe and unsanitary. The trial court then granted judgment to Mrs. Robinson, as required by *Southall Realty*.

Unwilling to admit defeat, Diamond Housing instituted a second suit for possession on the theory that, since the lease was void, Mrs. Robinson was a trespasser and hence no longer entitled to possession. When the trial court granted Mrs. Robinson's motion to dismiss, Diamond Housing appealed to the District of Columbia Court of Appeals.

That court affirmed, holding that "an agreement entered into in violation of the law creates no rights upon the wrongdoer. The defense of illegality does not rescind the illegal agreement, but merely prevents a party from using the courts to enforce such an agreement." It followed that Mrs. Robinson, "having entered possession under a void and unenforceable lease, was not a trespasser but became a tenant at sufferance." The court added, however, that Mrs. Robinson's tenancy,

> like any other tenancy at sufferance, may be terminated on thirty days' notice. The Housing Regulations do not compel an owner of housing property to rent his property. Where, as here, it has been determined that the property when rented was not habitable, that is, not safe and sanitary, and should not have been rented, and if the landlord is unwilling or unable to put the property in a habitable condition, he may and should promptly terminate the tenancy and withdraw the property from the rental market, because the Regulations forbid both the rental and the occupancy of such premises.

Seizing upon this dicta, Diamond Housing instituted a third action for possession, this time on the basis of a 30-day notice. In support of its action, Diamond filed an affidavit stating that it was unwilling to make the repairs necessary to put the housing in compliance with the housing code and that it presently intended to take the unit off the rental market. In defense, Mrs. Robinson asserted that she was being evicted in retaliation for successfully asserting her *Southall Realty* rights in the previous actions, and that the eviction was therefore illegal under the principles announced in Edwards v. Habib, *supra*. Mrs. Robinson also argued that the eviction was barred under general equitable principles since Diamond Housing, having allowed its housing to fall into disrepair, lacked the requisite "clean hands."

On this record, Diamond Housing moved for summary judgment. In an oral opinion, Judge Hyde recognized that "there wouldn't be but one way this issue [Diamond's retaliatory motive] could be decided by the jury, because as a matter of fact, I should think that if the landlord is honest at all, he would admit that he's upset, angry, wanted the tenant out of there." Nonetheless, the court found that "[i]t would seem to be the height of absurdity to permit retaliation, at this juncture, even to be entertained," and granted Diamond's motion.

While this decision was on appeal to the District of Columbia Court of Appeals, Mrs. Robinson apparently vacated the premises. However, the precise circumstances surrounding her move are not clear on this record. Mrs. Robinson alleges that she was forced to leave involuntarily by the continued existence of the unremedied housing code violations. Diamond Housing asserts that Mrs. Robinson voluntarily made the premises uninhabitable by failing to pay her heating bills which led to a discontinuance of heat and the freezing of all pipes in the building.

Whatever the truth of these competing contentions, the District of Columbia Court of Appeals apparently found that they had no effect on the justiciability of the controversy, since that court proceeded to affirm the judgment of the Court of General Sessions on the merits. The court found that the procedures followed by Diamond were in accord with the statutory requirements for recovery of property from a tenant at sufferance and that the retaliatory defense of Edwards v. Habib was unavailable as a matter of law in this situation.

A panel of this court recently had occasion to observe that there is an "apparently rising incidence of possessory actions based on notices to quit following closely on the heels of possessory actions based on nonpayment of rent." This trend is disturbing because, if judicially encouraged, it would vitiate tenants' rights recognized in *Southall Realty* and *Javins* and now protected by statute in the District of Columbia. . . . The *Javins* and *Southall Realty* decisions — as well as the District of Columbia regulations patterned after them — were based on the express premise that private remedies for housing code violations would increase the stock of livable low-cost housing in the District. If exercise of those remedies leads instead to eviction in the District, the great goal of "a decent home and a suitable living environment for every American family" will be frustrated.

Of course, if the housing market is structured in such a way that it is impossible for landlords to absorb the cost of bringing their units into compliance with the housing code, there may be nothing a court can do to prevent vigorous code enforcement from driving low-cost housing off the market. But the most recent scholarship on the subject indicates this danger is largely imagined. In fact, it appears that vigorous code enforcement plays little or no role in the decrease in low-cost housing stock. When code enforcement is seriously pursued, market forces generally prevent landlords from passing on their increased costs through rent increases. See generally Ackerman, Regulating Slum Housing Markets on Behalf of the Poor: Of Housing Codes, Housing Subsidies and Income Redistribution Policy, 80 Yale L.J. 1093 (1971). The danger stems not from the possibility that landlords might take low-cost units off the market altogether, but rather from the possibility that they will do so selectively in order to "make an example" of a troublesome tenant who has the temerity to assert his legal rights in court. We can be fairly confident that most landlords will find ownership of property sufficiently profitable — even with vigorous code enforcement — to remain in business. But it is undoubtedly true that the same landlords would be able to make a greater profit if the housing code were enforced laxly or not at all. There is thus a real danger that landlords may find it in their interest to sacrifice the profits derived from operation of a few units in order to intimidate the rest of their tenants.

Fortunately, this is a danger with which the law is better equipped to deal. While the judiciary may be powerless to control landlords who no longer wish to remain landlords, it can prevent landlords from conducting their business in a way that chills the legally protected rights of tenants. Indeed, this court's decision in Edwards v. Habib, *supra*, was premised on the belief that retaliatory evictions had a "chilling effect" on assertion of rights protected by the housing code, and that the courts could and should eliminate this inhibition. The *Edwards* court expressly recognized the vital role which private tenants play in the District's system of housing code enforcement, and held that it would violate congressional intent to permit eviction of tenants for the purpose of preventing exercise of private remedies.

It would thus appear, at first blush at least, that the *Edwards* principle should control disposition of this case. Applying this principle Diamond Housing would prevail if it were able to prove to the satisfaction of a jury that it evicted Mrs. Robinson because it could not afford to repair the premises, or for some other valid reason, or for no reason at all. But questions of motivation are particularly inappropriate for resolution on a motion for summary judgment. There is also the possibility — indeed, the trial judge viewed it as a near certainty — that the jury would find Mrs. Robinson's eviction to be based on an illicit motive. Given the legal sufficiency of the *Edwards* defense, Mrs. Robinson should have been permitted to make her case if she could, and the factual issue should have been left in the hands of a jury.

This argument assumes, however, that an *Edwards* defense is in fact, legally sufficient in this situation. Although the broad principles which underlie *Edwards* would seem squarely applicable, it is possible that something special about this fact pattern would make it unwise or impermissible to utilize *Edwards* here. Diamond Housing takes the position that this case is, in fact, special and that the special circumstances surrounding it make an application of *Edwards* unjust. Diamond's argument begins with the premise — apparently shared by the Distict of Columbia Court of Appeals — that *Edwards* should be narrowly "limited to its facts." Since *Edwards* involved reporting of code violations to city officials while this case involves setting up those violations as a defense to an action for eviction, it is contended that *Edwards* does not compel reversal here. Moreover, Diamond argues that, even if *Edwards* is more broadly read, it still should not be applied to a case such as this where the landlord is prevented from collecting rent by *Southall Realty*, refuses to repair the premises, and wishes to take the housing off the market altogether. Closely allied to this contention is the further argument that Mrs. Robinson is precluded from remaining in possession by Section 2301 of the Housing Regulations which makes it illegal to occupy premises which are in violation of the Regulations. Finally, Diamond argues that in any event this case is now moot since Mrs. Robinson has voluntarily surrendered possession and Diamond has chosen to forego any claim it might have to back rent.

We have carefully examined each of these arguments and have

concluded that none of them sufficiently distinguishes this case from *Edwards* or precludes application of the District of Columbia law against retaliatory evictions. If we resolve all reasonable doubts in favor of appellant — as we must when reviewing a summary judgment — it becomes plain that a jury might find Diamond Housing to be using the eviction machinery to punish Mrs. Robinson for exercising her legal rights. *Edwards* squarely holds that the state's judicial processes may not be so used, and nothing which has transpired since *Edwards* was decided has caused us to change our view. Indeed, if anything, the creation by the District of Columbia City Council of new private remedies for code violations since *Edwards* reinforces our belief in the necessity for a broad retaliatory eviction defense. If the housing code were effectuated solely by a system of comprehensive public enforcement, the situation might perhaps be different. But by legislating a system of private remedies conforming to the *Javins* and *Southall Realty* decisions, the City Council has made plain that the code is to be enforced in large part through the actions of private tenants. Having put at least some of its eggs in the private enforcement basket, the legislature should not at the same time be taken as having authorized use of legal processes by those who seek to frustrate private enforcement. The right to a decent home is far too vital for us to assume that government has taken away with one hand what it purports to grant with the other. . . .

It must nonetheless be conceded that implementing the legislative will in this fact situation leads to some difficulties and ambiguities. For example, Diamond Housing argues that permitting a retaliatory eviction defense here may mean that it will never be able to recover possession of its property. Nonreceipt of rent is a continuing injury, Diamond argues, and it will always want to remove the tenant so as to remove the source of injury. Yet ironically, so long as it is motivated by this goal, the *Edwards* defense will prevent achievement of it. Thus Diamond fears that its shotgun marriage to Mrs. Robinson may last till death do them part.

Moreover, Diamond points out, it is not trying to evict Mrs. Robinson so that it may rent the premises to someone else. It does not want a quickie divorce in order to permit a hasty remarriage. Rather, if freed from Mrs. Robinson, Diamond promises to beat a strategic retreat to a monastery where it will go and sin no more. Thus Diamond says that it intends to take the unit off the market altogether when Mrs. Robinson leaves — the very thing which this court has suggested a landlord do when he is unwilling or unable to repair the premises. There is nothing in the Housing Regulations which prevents it from going out of business, Diamond argues. Whatever limitations the law imposes on how it chooses its tenants, Diamond claims an absolute right to choose not to have any tenants.

In order to clarify these and other ambiguities inherent in the *Ed-*

wards defense, attorneys for Mrs. Robinson have suggested that we formulate comprehensive guidelines for the circumstances under which a landlord may evict his tenants when the premises contain unremedied housing code violations. We respectfully decline this invitation. We do so primarily because we think the *Edwards* rule, as supplemented by District law, is largely self-explanatory and its ramifications are best elucidated on a case-by-case basis. We are also motivated, however, by the fear, generated in part by this case, that any such guidelines would become the basis for mechanical legal decisions by judges, where we believe the matter is best left to the sound discretion of juries under proper instructions. Whether the landlord's action is retaliatory is, after all, a question of fact, and we would not be justified in taking it away from the jury merely because it is "hard." . . . This is especially true where, as here, the matter for decision involves a complex of moral and empirical judgments best left in the hands of representatives of the community as a whole. . . . But while we are unwilling to write comprehensive guidelines for application of the *Edwards* defense, we do feel it may be useful to clarify some of the confusion which has evidently surrounded it. These clarifications should, in turn, be incorporated into appropriate instructions which the trial judge should give to the jury when it considers the underlying factual question. First, then, it should be noted that the *Edwards* defense deals with the landlord's subjective state of mind — that is, with his motive. If the landlord's actions are motivated by a desire to punish the tenant for exercising his rights or to chill the exercise of similar rights by other tenants, then they are impermissible. It is commonplace, however, that a jury can judge a landlord's state of mind only by examining its objective manifestations. Thus when the landlord's conduct is "inherently destructive" of tenants' rights, or unavoidably chills their exercise, the jury may, under well recognized principles, presume that the landlord intended this result. . . .

An unexplained eviction following successful assertion of a *Javins* or *Southall Realty* defense falls within this inherently destructive category and hence gives rise to the presumption. Once the presumption is established, it is then up to the landlord to rebut it by demonstrating that he is motivated by some legitimate business purpose rather than by the illicit motive which would otherwise be presumed. . . . We wish to emphasize, however, that the landlord's desire to remove a tenant who is not paying rent is not such a legitimate purpose. *Southall Realty* and the housing code guarantee the right of a tenant to remain in possession without paying rent when the premises are burdened with substantial housing code violations making them unsafe and unsanitary. The landlord of such premises who evicts his tenant because he will not pay rent is in effect evicting him for asserting his legal right to refuse to pay rent. This, of course, is the very sort of reason which, according to *Edwards* and the housing code, will not support an eviction. Thus Diamond

Housing is correct when it asserts it will never be able to evict Mrs. Robinson so long as it is motivated by a desire to rid itself of a tenant who is not paying rent. But it does not follow that Diamond will be burdened by its unwanted tenant forever. If Diamond comes forward with a legitimate business justification — other than the mere desire to get rid of a tenant exercising *Southall Realty* rights — it may be able to convince a jury that it is motivated by this proper concern. For example, if Diamond brought the premises up to housing code standards so that rent was again due and then evicted the tenant for some unrelated, lawful reason, the eviction would be permissible. Similarly, if Diamond were to make a convincing showing that it was for some reason impossible or unfeasible to make repairs, it would have a legitimate reason for evicting the tenant and taking the unit off the market.

It does not follow, however, that mere desire to take the unit off the market is by itself a legitimate business reason which will justify an eviction. Expression of such a desire begs the further question of why the landlord wishes to remove the unit. If he wishes to remove the unit for some sound business reason, then of course he is free to do so. But such a removal, following a tenant's *Southall Realty* defense, is as inherently destructive of tenants' rights as an ordinary eviction. Therefore, a landlord who fails to come forward with a substantial business reason for removing a unit from the market — such as, for example, his financial inability to make the necessary repairs — may be presumed to have done so for an illicit reason. . . . Thus the landlord's mere allegation that he is removing the unit from the market because he cannot afford to make repairs does not mean that the jury will find that he is in fact unable to make the necessary repairs. Moreover, even if the jury makes such a finding, it still does not follow that judgment for the landlord is compelled. We must remember that we are dealing with a question of subjective motive, and that objective factors are relevant only as indicia of motive. Thus the mere existence of a legitimate reason for the landlord's actions will not help him if the jury finds that he was in fact motivated by some illegitimate reason. In cases of mixed motives, the jury will have the difficult task of weighing one against the other and determining which was the causative factor. . . .

None of this is to say that the landlord may not go out of business entirely if he wishes to do so or that the jury is authorized to inspect his motives if he chooses to commit economic harakiri. There would be severe constitutional problems with a rule of law which required an entrepreneur to remain in business against his will. But in a closely analogous area, the Supreme Court has distinguished sharply between a businessman's absolute right to go out of business altogether and his more limited right to discontinue part of his enterprise so as to benefit the rest of it.

The closing of an entire business, even though discriminatory, ends the employer-employee relationship; the force of such a closing is entirely spent as to that business when termination of the enterprise takes place. On the other hand, a discriminatory partial closing may have repercussions on what remains of the business, affording employer leverage for discouraging the free exercise of §7 rights among the remaining employees. . . . [Textile Workers Union v. Darlington Manufacturing Co., 380 U.S. 263, 274-275 (1965).]

Thus we hold that the landlord's right to discontinue rental of all his units in no way justifies a partial closing designed to intimidate the remaining tenants. . . .

It must be recognized that in some situations exercise of the sort of *Edwards* defense outlined above may lead to an impasse. If the landlord is unwilling, but not unable, to repair code violations, he will probably be prevented from either evicting the tenant or collecting rent. The result arguably might be a tenant who lives indefinitely in substandard premises without paying the landlord for the leasehold interest.[24]

Diamond argues that such a solution represents poor public policy and a poor reading of the applicable statutes. So long as the landlord is not receiving rent, the argument goes, he will certainly not be able to finance repairs. Yet so long as he cannot make repairs, he will not be able to collect rent. Unable to break out of this vicious circle, the landlord is likely to abandon the building altogether without even bothering with an attempted eviction. Diamond contends that this unfortunate result was widely precluded by the legislature when it approved Section 2301 of the housing code: "No owner, licensee, or tenant shall occupy or permit the occupancy of any habitation in violation of these regulations." Diamond argues that since this section prohibits Mrs. Robinson from remaining in her house and Diamond from allowing her to remain there, an eviction must be proper even though — indeed, for the very reason that — there are unremedied housing code violations on the premises. Although superficially persuasive, on closer analysis this argument turns out to be built on a series of non sequiturs. Section 2301 cannot be read in isolation. It is part of a larger scheme which is clearly designed to protect tenants and encourage them to demand their rights, not to punish them. True, Section 2301 makes it illegal for a tenant to remain in a unit burdened with code violations, and there are procedures available through which the city government can force such a tenant to vacate the premises. But it does not follow that Section 2301

24. This puts to one side the possibility, which need not be discussed here, that the landlord may be able to secure payment for the actual value of the leased premises on a *quantum meruit* theory.

should therefore be interpreted as authorizing retaliatory evictions by landlords, particularly where another section of the same code makes retaliatory evictions unlawful. The housing code plainly places the primary responsibility for repair of housing violations on the landlord.

Under ordinary estoppel principles, the landlord can hardly rely on his own wrongful neglect of this duty as a ground for evicting his tenant. Indeed, such principles of estoppel underlie the opinions of this court in *Edwards* and *Javins* and of the District of Columbia Court of Appeals in *Southall Realty* since in all of those cases the landlord was prevented from evicting his tenant despite housing code violations which put the premises within the scope of Section 2301. Nor is Diamond helped by the language in Section 2301 prohibiting landlords from "permit[ting] the occupancy" of premises with code violations. Diamond argues that it can hardly be required to do something which the law itself prohibits. But the suppressed premise in this reasoning is that Diamond can avoid violating Section 2301 only by evicting the tenant. If this were in fact true — that is, if Diamond were unable to repair the premises — then, under the principles outlined above, an eviction would be permissible. But Diamond has failed to show that the situation is posed by this case. If the landlord is able to repair the premises, another method is available to him for complying with the requirements of Section 2301. Since a retaliatory eviction would be unlawful under *Edwards* and under the housing code, the landlord must choose the only lawful method of compliance — i.e., he must repair the premises.

Thus it is clear that Diamond cannot utilize Section 2301 to overcome an *Edwards* defense and justify an eviction. Nonetheless, if we accepted Diamond's assertion that our ruling today would lead to many families living indefinitely in substandard housing without paying rent, we would be deeply troubled. Even if the landlord is estopped from asserting Section 2301, it is still clear that that section expresses a public policy against long term occupancy of substandard housing. We would be evading our duty if our decisions were to undermine this legislatively declared goal. Fortunately, however, we do not share Diamond's gloomy assessment of the effects of our decision. All substandard housing in the District can be divided into two categories: those units which the landlord is unable to repair, and those units which the landlord could, but will not, repair. We submit that nothing in our decision today necessitates long term occupancy of housing in either of these categories. In situations where the landlord is unable to repair the premises, he has a legitimate business justification for taking the unit off the market, and he can therefore meet his responsibility under Section 2301 by evicting his tenants. In situations where the landlord is able but unwilling to repair the premises, he has, by hypothesis, made them uninhabitable and hence constructively deprived the tenant of possession. It should be obvious that a landlord may no more constructively evict a tenant for retaliatory purposes than he may actually so evict him. It follows that if the tenant is entitled to possession, he is also entitled to have the premises made habitable through a code enforcement action by housing authorities or a proper suit by the tenant. It is clear, then, that whether the landlord is unable to repair the premises or simply unwilling, the policy of Section 2301 can be respected without authorizing evictions which violate *Southall Realty, Edwards,* and the housing code itself. We must keep constantly in mind that the purpose of the housing code is to increase rather than decrease the stock of habitable housing in the District of Columbia. Given this purpose, it would be surprising indeed if the code blocked development of fair and effective weapons to fight the mounting housing crisis. . . .

We do not pretend that allowing Mrs. Robinson to assert an *Edwards* defense will solve the housing crisis in the District of Columbia. That crisis is the product of a constellation of social and economic forces over which no court — and indeed perhaps no legislature — can exercise full control. But while the judicial process is not a *deus ex machina* which can magically solve problems where the legislature and the executive have failed, neither is it a mere game of wits to be played without regard for the well-being of the helpless spectators. We cannot expect judges to solve the housing dilemma, but at least they should avoid affirmative action which makes it worse. The District's legislative body has formulated a comprehensive plan, including criminal sanctions, public inspections, subsidies and rent withholding, to tackle our housing difficulties. In the end, that plan may not work. But if it fails, at least the failure should be caused by inherent weaknesses rather than by judicial subversion.

Thus all we hold today is that when the legislature creates a broad based scheme for dealing with a problem in the public interest, courts should not permit private, selfishly motivated litigants to undermine it. This result is required by the clear wording of the applicable statute, by the dictates of legislatively declared social policy, and, in the final analysis, by respect for the separation of powers and the rule of law.

Reversed and remanded with instructions.

ROBB, Circuit Judge (dissenting). . . . The landlord, Diamond Housing, served a proper notice to quit on a tenant by sufferance, who refused to pay rent. In the ensuing action for possession the tenant answered, claiming that the action was retaliatory and demanding a jury trial. The landlord moved for summary judgment, supporting the motion with an affidavit referring to the notice to quit and stating that the landlord was unwilling to make any repairs to the property and did not presently wish to rent it. No affidavit in opposition was filed by the tenant, and the court accordingly granted the motion for summary judgment. I think this ruling was correct, because there was no material issue of fact as to the landlord's motive.

I cannot accept the proposition espoused by the majority that when a landlord states under oath and without contradiction that he wishes to remove a housing unit from the market it will be presumed that his reasons are "illicit," unless he is able to prove to the satisfaction of a jury that he is financially unable to make necessary repairs or has some other "substantial business reason" for removing the unit from the market. I find no warrant in law for any such presumption or requirement of proof.

The theory of the majority seems to be that if not an outlaw a landlord is at least a public utility, subject to regulation by the court in conformity with its concept of public convenience and necessity. I reject that notion, which in practical application will commit to the discretion of a jury the management of a landlord's business and property.

The majority suggests that its decision will promote the development of more and better low-cost housing. This reasoning passes my understanding. In my judgment the majority's Draconian treatment of landlords will inevitably discourage investment in housing for rental purposes.

Note

For insight into the concerns that motivated Judge Wright in his *Javins* and *Robinson* decisions, see the letter he wrote to Professor Edward Rabin, of the University of California at Davis, printed in Rabin, The Revolution in Residential Landlord-Tenant Law: Causes and Consequences, 69 Cornell L. Rev. 517, 549 (1984):

J. Skelly Wright
United States Circuit Judge
October 14, 1982

Professor Edward H. Rabin
School of Law
University of California, Davis
Davis, California 95616

Dear Professor Rabin:

Why the revolution in landlord-tenant law is largely traceable to the 1960's rather than decades before I really cannot say with any degree of certainty. Unquestionably the Vietnam War and the civil rights movement of the 1960's did cause people to question existing institutions and authorities. And perhaps this inquisition reached the judiciary itself. Obviously, judges cannot be unaware of what all people know and feel.

With reference to your specific question, I was indeed influenced by the fact that, during the nationwide racial turmoil of the sixties and the unrest caused by the injustice of racially selective service in Vietnam, most of the tenants in Washington, D.C. slums were poor and black and most of the landlords were rich and white. There is no doubt in my mind that these conditions played a subconscious role in influencing my landlord and tenant decisions.

I came to Washington in April 1962 after being born and raised in New Orleans, Louisiana for 51 years. I had never been exposed, either as a judge or as a lawyer, to the local practice of law which, of course, included landlord and tenant cases. I was Assistant U.S. Attorney, U.S. Attorney, and then U.S. District Court judge in New Orleans before I joined the U.S. Court of Appeals in Washington. It was my first exposure to landlord and tenant cases, the U.S. Court of Appeals here being a writ court to the local court system at the time. I didn't like what I saw, and I did what I could to ameliorate, if not eliminate, the injustice involved in the way many of the poor were required to live in the nation's capital.

I offer no apology for not following more closely the legal precedents which had cooperated in creating the conditions that I found unjust.

Sincerely,
s/J. Skelly Wright

F.   JUST CAUSE AND THE EVICTION PROCESS

On the issue of statutory interpretation referred to in Robinson v. Diamond Housing Corp. — whether Congress should be held to have created a right to be free of retaliatory evictions — see Edwards v. Habib, 397 F.2d 687 (D.C. Cir. 1968) (Wright, J.), cert. denied, 393 U.S. 1016 (1969). Edwards contains an interesting essay by Judge Wright on the question — which he scrupulously refrains from deciding — whether there is a constitutional right not to be evicted for complaining to the government. We will discuss the issue of "state action" later, in conjunction with Shelley v. Kraemer, at p. 1071 infra.

A number of states have developed protection against retaliatory measures for tenants who have asserted legal rights. Substantial variations exist in the types of behavior that are protected, and the remedies available to the tenant facing retaliatory conduct.

ILL. REV. STAT. Ch. 80 §71 (1973):

TERMINATION OF, OR REFUSAL TO RENEW, LEASE —
PROHIBITION — VALIDITY OF PROVISIONS IN LEASE

It is declared to be against the public policy of the State for a landlord to terminate or refuse to renew a lease or tenancy of property used as a residence on the ground that the tenant has complained to any governmental authority of a bona fide violation of any applicable building code, health ordinance, or similar regulation. Any provision in any lease, or any agreement or understanding, purporting to permit the landlord to terminate or refuse to renew a lease or tenancy for such reason is void.

OHIO REV. CODE ANN. §5321.02 (Page Supp. 1974):

(A) A landlord may not retaliate against a tenant by increasing the tenant's rent, decreasing services that are due to the tenant, or bringing or threatening to bring an action for possession of the tenant's premises because:

(1) The tenant has complained to an appropriate governmental agency of a violation of a building, housing, health, or safety code that is applicable to the premises, and the violation materially affects health and safety;

(2) The tenant has complained to the landlord of any violation of section 5321.04 of the Revised Code;

(3) The tenant joined with other tenants for the purpose of negotiating or dealing collectively with the landlord on any of the terms and conditions of a rental agreement.

(B) If a landlord acts in violation of division (A) of this section the tenant may:

(1) Use the retaliatory action of the landlord as a defense to an action by the landlord to recover possession of the premises;

(2) Recover possession of the premises; or

(3) Terminate the rental agreement.

In addition, the tenant may recover from the landlord any actual damages together with reasonable attorneys' fees.

(C) Nothing in division (A) of this section shall prohibit a landlord from increasing the rent to reflect the cost of improvements installed by the landlord in or about the premises or to reflect an increase in other costs of operation of the premises.

At common law a tenancy at will could be terminated at any time and a landlord could refuse to renew a lease for any reason. A statute protecting tenants from retaliatory conduct does not provide security from arbitrary or capricious refusals to renew by a landlord. New Jersey has developed specific and limited criteria that justify the removal of tenants.

N.J. STAT. ANN. §2A:18-61.1 (Supp. 1976): No lessee or tenant or the assigns, undertenants or legal representative of such lessee or tenant may be removed by the court or the Superior Court from any house, building, mobile home or land in a mobile home park or tenement leased for residential purposes, other than owner-occupied premises with not more than two rental units or a hotel, motel or other guest house or part thereof rented to a transient guest or seasonal tenant, except upon establishment of one of the following grounds as good cause:

a. The person fails to pay rent due and owing under the lease whether the same be oral or written;

b. The person has continued to be, after written notice to cease, so disorderly as to destroy the peace and quiet of the occupants or other tenants living in said house or neighborhood;

c. The person has willfully or by reason of gross negligence caused or allowed destruction, damage or injury to the premises;

d. The person has continued, after written notice to cease, to substantially violate or breach any of the landlord's rules and regulations governing said premises, provided such rules and regulations are reasonable and have been accepted in writing by the tenant or made a part of the lease at the beginning of the lease term;

e. The person has continued, after written notice to cease, to substantially violate or breach any of the covenants or agreements contained in the lease for the premises where a right of re-entry is reserved to the landlord in the lease for a violation of such covenant or agreement, provided that such covenant or agreement is reasonable and was contained in the lease at the beginning of the lease term;

f. The person has failed to pay rent after a valid notice to quit and notice of increase of said rent, provided the increase in rent is not unconscionable and complies with any and all other laws or municipal ordinances governing rent increases;

g. The landlord or owner (1) seeks to permanently board up or demolish the premises because he has been cited by local or State housing inspectors for substantial violations affecting the health and safety of tenants and it is economically unfeasible for the owner to eliminate the violations; (2) seeks to comply with local or State housing inspectors who have cited him for substantial violations affecting the health and safety of tenants and it is unfeasible to so comply without removing the tenant . . . ; (4) is a governmental agency which seeks to permanently retire the premises from the rental market pursuant to a redevelopment- or land clearance plan in a blighted area . . . ;

i. The landlord or owner proposes, at the termination of a lease, reasonable changes of substance in the terms and conditions of the lease, including specifically any change in the term thereof, which the tenant, after written notice, refuses to accept . . . ;

k. The landlord or owner of the building is converting from the rental market to a condominium or a cooperative . . . ;

m. The landlord or owner conditioned the tenancy upon and in consideration for the tenant's employment by the landlord or owner as superintendent, janitor or in some other capacity and such employment is being terminated.

Notes

1. On retaliation, see Holmes v. District of Columbia, 354 A.2d 858 (D.C. 1976) (improper for landlord to remove an apartment from the market five months after being cited for housing code violations involving impermissibly high levels of lead in paint in the unit); Alteri v. Layton, 35 Conn. Supp. 261, 408 A.2d 18 (1979) ("This court holds that repairs required to conform a dwelling unit to basic structural, mechanical and housing code regulations are the type of repairs contemplated by the legislature and which raise the presumption of retaliatory [eviction]"; the presumption would not be raised by a tenant's request that a bath tub drain be unclogged, followed by eviction for nonpayment of rent); Parkin v. Fitzgerald, 307 Minn. 423, 240 N.W.2d 828 (1976) ("A landlord must establish by a fair preponderance of the evidence a substantial non-retaliatory reason for the eviction, arising at or within a reasonably short time before service of the notice to quit. A non-retaliatory reason is a reason wholly unrelated to and unmotivated by any good-faith activity on the part of the tenant protected by the statute. . . .").

2. It was adequate ground for eviction from a rent-controlled apartment that tenant struck landlord's adult son with a four-foot long closet pole. "Although Harrison has been beyond reproach as a tenant for many years with this one grave exception, rent control legislation does not vest him with a right to engage in more than one serious incident of misconduct before he can be evicted." Driscoll v. Harrison, 417 N.E.2d 26 (Mass. App. 1981).

3. Douglas, tenant in a National Capital Housing Authority project in Washington, fell more than a year behind in rent payments. When the agency sought possession, tenant contended that the agency had violated its implied warranty of habitability due to deficiencies in wiring, plumbing, and plastering. The trial court found total unpaid rent of $868.67, allowed a 15 percent *Javins* setoff, and concluded that tenant owed $756.54. The court issued a judgment for possession but stayed execution for two years, during which tenant was to pay current rents plus $25 per month toward the past-due obligation. The D.C. Court of Appeals reversed: "All accrued past rent must be unconditionally tendered before any stay of execution can issue." National Capital Housing Auth. v. Douglas, 333 A.2d 55 (D.C. 1975).

4. Landlord offered rent-controlled tenant money to move. The tenant refused, calling the landlord's attention to a falling ceiling. When

the landlord did not repair, the tenant replaced the ceiling with a new one, thinner than called for in the housing code. He also installed a new light fixture, a new closet, and a small frame around the window. The landlord said these changes violated a substantial obligation of the tenancy and sought eviction. Three courts ruled for the landlord, but the New York Court of Appeals reversed, 4-3. Judge Fuchsberg wrote that no lease provision banned alterations. Rather, the only relevant provision was a city administrative rule permitting eviction for violations "willful and injurious to the landlord," and the tenant's actions here were not injurious. He reviewed cases on voluntary waste but found waste had not been committed because there was no "change as to affect a vital and substantial part of the premises, . . . as would affect the very realty itself. . . ."

Judge Cooke, dissenting, said that "it is obvious that the removal of the ceiling and its reconstruction with sheetrock of insufficient thickness to satisfy the fire code constituted waste," and that the lack of code compliance could prevent landlord from re-leasing if tenant vacated, and so it was a substantial injury. Rumiche Corp. v. Eisenreich, 40 N.Y.2d 174, 352 N.E.2d 125, 386 N.Y.S.2d 208 (1976).

G.   ECONOMIC CONSEQUENCES OF LANDLORD-TENANT LAW REFORM

ACKERMAN, REGULATING SLUM HOUSING MARKETS ON BEHALF OF THE POOR: OF HOUSING CODES, HOUSING SUBSIDIES AND INCOME REDISTRIBUTION POLICY, 80 Yale L.J. 1093, 1102-1106, 1113-1116 (1971): Imagine a city called Athens whose slums are concentrated in one geographic area that we shall call Slumville. While the residents of Slumville are extremely mobile within the confines of the slum district, Athenians living outside Slumville are extremely reluctant to move into the area even if there is a significant improvement in housing quality. Of course, if there is an enormous change in the character of the neighborhood, the city's residents may change their view of Slumville. But a moderate change will not lead them to discard their fears about the quality of life, as well as the quality of housing, enjoyed by the area's inhabitants.

While the middle-class Athenian's substantial reluctance to live in Slumville is fundamental to much of the argument that follows, several additional assumptions will be altered at subsequent stages of this essay. For purposes of the present discussion, then, assume (1) both landlords and tenants act rationally in their self-interest; (2) no landlord or group of landlords has successfully established a monopoly or oligopoly position in the rental market; (3) tenants are aware of the range of prices and quality levels of accommodations offered for rent in Slumville and experience no significant cost in moving from one part of Slumville to another; (4) all of Slumville's accommodations are not only slums, but are *equally* slummy; (5) similarly, all of Slumville's tenants inflict *equal* damage upon the physical structures of the houses in which they reside; (6) a significant number of poor provincials are not entering Athens from the outlands nor are Slumvillites emigrating to the hinterlands; (7) *each* and *every* landlord in Slumville earns a rate of return on his investment which substantially exceeds the return available when the property is used for other purposes; indeed (8) even if the landlords are forced to bring their residential properties up to code, their rate of return would still exceed that available for any other use of the property; and (9) no landlord will find it more profitable to abandon his building entirely when faced with the necessity of investing substantial sums to bring his tenement up to code. . . .

We are now in a position to trace the economic consequences of a code enforcement program in Slumville. Given the model which has been developed, it follows that when the costs of code improvements are imposed upon Slumville's landlords *none* of them will have an incentive to remove their properties from the rental housing market. For we have stipulated that even after code costs are taken into account, the return on slum investment still exceeds the rate of return available when the land is used for other purposes or not used at all. Since the imposition of code costs upon the landlords does not induce a fall in the supply of housing, rent levels will be determined by the effect of code enforcement upon the demand for housing.

Two different demand responses can be anticipated, depending upon the extent to which the housing code is enforced. First, assume that the code is enforced strictly only in one part (Area X) of Slumville and that the rest of Slumville (Area Y) is entirely ignored by the housing code inspectorate. In this case, one would expect that some of the residents of Y will find X a more attractive place than formerly and will bid the rents up in Area X. Those residents of X who find the new rent levels too steep for their taste will of course move to Y, where apartments have been vacated by those moving into the newly improved housing in X. Consequently, a program of selective housing code enforcement in Slumville will, in fact, partially fulfill the expectations of those administrators who doubt the desirability of code enforcement: rents will increase in the target area and tenants who cannot "afford" the higher rents will leave the area to find new abodes in the now slummier sections of Slumville.

If, however, one assumes that the housing code is enforced strictly in all of Slumville, the same result will not follow. Since we have assumed that before the code was enforced, houses in Areas X and Y were equally dilapidated, the comprehensive enforcement of the code throughout Areas X and Y will raise the quality of housing in all parts of Slumville to an equal degree, thereby providing no special incentive for a resident of Area Y to want to move to Area X. Thus, rents will not rise because of competition *among* Slumville residents as occurred in the case of partial code enforcement just discussed.

Indeed rents will not rise *at all* in Slumville if only a single further condition is met. Paradoxically, code enforcement will have "zero rent impact" if and only if there exists a class of Slumville tenants who do *not* believe that code enforcement will significantly improve their lives. A simple mathematical example will make this clear. Assume that, before the code is enforced, two types of families live in Slumville's 100,000 rental units: 90,000 families (the "homelovers") would be willing to pay a significant amount of money for code housing; in contrast, 10,000 families (the "lukewarm" families) would not be willing to pay extra rent for improved housing. This is not to say that even the lukewarm do not recognize that they will benefit from code enforcement — the improvement is simply not significant enough in their minds to warrant allocation of any more of their scarce funds to purchase it.

Now imagine that all of Slumville's landlords seek to pass their code costs on to tenants by raising rents by $25. While the 90,000 homelovers initially respond by paying the premium, the 10,000 lukewarm families act differently. Rather than paying the higher rent, they choose to pair up and share apartments instead, thus leaving 5000 units vacant. The lukewarm families will take this course since they believe that half an apartment at a lower rent is a better deal than a whole apartment at the inflated rental.

When the 10,000 lukewarm families decide to double-up, however, the owners of the 5000 vacant apartments are faced with a serious problem. Since no new residents have (under our assumptions) been attracted to Slumville as a result of code enforcement, there is no reason to expect that they will successfully fill their apartments if they persist in demanding the $25 premium. Rather, a landlord can rent his units in only one of two ways: (a) by inducing one of the homelovers to move by cutting the premium below the $25 level or (b) by cutting the rent sufficiently to induce one of the lukewarm families to prefer an entire apartment to its more crowded quarters. It should be apparent that if a given landlord fills a vacant apartment by offering one of the homelovers a better deal than his present landlord, the competitive dynamic will continue, for the owner of the newly vacated apartment will find himself in the same bleak position as his now successful competitor once occupied. It is only when prices are set low enough to induce the lukewarm families to resume their former habits and live in individual apartments that the economic situation will regain equilibrium. But if a significant number of lukewarm families are willing to spend no additional money for the code improvements, equilibrium will not be attained until the competing landlords absorb all of the code costs and rent all of their units at the pre-code price. Q.E.D. . . .

Until now, we have ignored the housing market in surrounding Athens. As our model becomes more complex, however, we can no longer afford this luxury. Activities in the larger housing market may well determine the extent to which the government must subsidize low income housing in support of vigorous code enforcement within Slumville. For in order to attain "zero rent impact," code enforcement need not rely solely upon government subsidy to make up the 5000 unit deficit; it is possible that the private sector will make available units which were previously inhabited by the upper classes of Athens, thereby making up part or all of the deficit without public subsidy.

To make this point clear, imagine that Slumville is surrounded by a lower-middle-class community (Middleburg) composed of decent buildings which do not at present violate the housing code, which in turn is surrounded by an upper-class zone (Snobtown). As a result of new construction for the rich and upper-middle class, a number of Snobtown houses, formerly occupied by these groups, may open up for the lower-middle-class Athenians who previously resided around the borders of Slumville. As the lower-middle class moves to the dwellings once occupied by their betters, Middleburg landlords will find it profitable to rent to the "Slumville-types" they shunned before. In short, some of the impact of new construction for the rich will "trickle down" to the poor as the lower-middle class move to the homes formerly occupied by the well-to-do.

The rate at which housing can be expected to "trickle down" from Middleburgers to Slumvillites will depend — among other things — upon the degree to which the more privileged Athenians believe that new housing offers a higher level of amenity than that provided by their present dwellings, the birth rate experienced by Athenians of both high and moderate income, the willingness of the lower-middle-class families bordering Slumville to move, and the intensity with which Middleburg landlords discriminate against ghetto émigrés. Whether the number of dwelling units trickling down is greater than, less than, or equal to, the number of units removed from the market as a result of strict code enforcement is an empirical question which cannot be answered *a priori*. Assuming, for the moment, that the houses trickling down are equal in number to the houses removed from the market, the rent level in the now-expanding Slumville will be a function of the quality of the houses which have recently been made available to Slumville residents. If the "ex-Middleburg" houses are equal in quality to the Slumville units which have been improved to code requirements, rent levels will remain unchanged as a result of code enforcement for the reasons previously considered. If the quality of the "new" housing is higher than that prevailing in a code enforced Slumville, rents will increase to the extent that Slumville residents are willing to allocate a larger share of their budget in order to purchase higher quality housing. Thus, the owners of the "ex-Middleburg" units will be constrained to rent them at the prevailing rent level or remove the units from the rental market altogether if there is no demand for "supercode" housing within Slumville. It should be emphasized, therefore, that rents will not rise unless a segment of the Slumville community really values the better housing that has trickled down.

Of course, if the number of housing units "trickling down" to Slumville is less than the number of dwellings removed from the market by code enforcement, the area will still confront a "housing shortage" as a result of code enforcement, and the authorities will be faced with the dilemma which has already been described — they will enforce the code only at the cost of requiring the poor to pay higher rents or live in the streets or double-up or skip rent more frequently than in the past. In order to avoid this dilemma, the government must make up the difference between the number of houses withdrawn from the market and the number of houses trickling down into Slumville through a subsidy program. If the public sector fulfills this task, the paradoxical conclusion reached in our earlier discussion remains intact: while a selective program of code enforcement will raise rents in the target area, a comprehensive enforcement plan will not.

Up to the present point, we have only considered "trickle down" from a perspective which gives substantial comfort to the code enforcement proponent. But, alas, there is a more troublesome aspect to this phenomenon which is revealed when the code enforcement administrator stops asking "what can 'trickle down' do for me?" and considers what his program is doing to the trickle: will code enforcement increase the trickle to a flood of "new" housing for Slumvillites or will the code regime reduce the trickle to a droplet?

The general answer to this question seems clear: code enforcement will significantly diminish the trickle to the extent that the Middleburg landlord believes that Slumville-type tenants will wreak greater havoc upon his buildings than will the more sober Middleburgers. Insomuch as this is true, code costs will be heavier if the building becomes part of an expanding Slumville than if it remains in the lower-middle-class sector. And the greater the anticipated code cost differential, the more willing a landlord will be to continue renting his unit to the Middleburger at a lower price than he can extract from a Slumvillite, thereby attenuating the trickle down rate.

This unfortunate tendency of code enforcement may, however, itself be checked by two important factors. First, effective enforcement of civil rights laws assuring Slumvillites "equal access" to Athens' housing may make efforts at price discrimination between "Slumville-types" and "Middleburger" tenants illegal, and therefore costly, to the Middleburg lessor. Second, successful code enforcement in Slumville may itself have an impact upon the psychology of the Middleburg landlord. Whereas, in the pre-code past, each time a Middleburg lessor found his way into Slumville he was greeted by signs of obvious disrepair which he was apt to assign to tenant vandalism, the number of cases of scandalous living conditions will have been markedly reduced by a successful code enforcement-subsidy scheme, thereby (perhaps) inducing the Middleburger to revise his estimate of the degree of lower-class vandalism. Since the trickle down effect will only be influenced by the *anticipated* code cost differential, the creation of a more favorable image of the lower-class tenant in the landlord's eye (by whatever means) will diminish the differential, thereby reducing code enforcement's unfavorable impact upon the trickle down.

MEYERS, THE COVENANT OF HABITABILITY AND THE AMERICAN LAW INSTITUTE, 27 Stan. L. Rev. 879, 889-893 (1975): Let us consider the probable economic consequences of the Restatement rules.

Four categories of rental housing may be identified, one of which is unaffected by the covenant of habitability and therefore need not be considered further. That category consists of dwellings that substantially comply with the housing code and are considered "suitable" for residential purposes.

The other three categories of housing will be affected by the covenant and consist of:

1) dwellings that do not comply with the housing code and are considered unsuitable for residential use, but that can be brought up to code standards by additional investment that can be recovered through higher rents.

2) dwellings that do not comply with the housing code and are considered unsuitable for residential use but that can be brought up to code standards by an expenditure that will reduce the landlord's rate of return (because rents cannot be raised sufficiently to cover repair costs) but will not eliminate a positive return on sunk capital.

3) dwellings that do not comply with the housing code and are considered unsuitable for residential use, for which the costs of repair to meet code standards (together with other expenses) will result in a negative return on sunk capital.

No one knows how the nation's substandard housing stock is divided among these three categories, and the proportions are likely to vary from city to city. Whatever those proportions may be, some portion of the housing stock will fall into category (3) and will be withdrawn from the market because of the imposition of the duty of habitability. To the extent such withdrawal occurs, low-income tenants as a class are hurt, not helped, by the Restatement rules. It is the further contention here that application of the Restatement rules to the other two categories of slum housing will also adversely affect the interests of low-income tenants, certainly in the long run.

As to rental housing in category (1), housing that can be profitably improved, the Restatement says, in effect, that such housing cannot be rented in substandard condition. Therefore, the landlord will improve the property and charge higher rents. The class of tenants theretofore occupying the premises will either lose occupancy because they cannot afford the new rents or will remain in possession and have less disposable income for other goods and services. In the latter case, the Restatement makes a judgment for the tenant, that he should (must) spend more money on housing and less on clothes, food, recreation, and other items, even though left to his own devices he would and previously did make the opposite choice. Where courts derive the authority to make this choice for tenants and why it is a better choice than the tenants' own is not apparent.

Rental housing in category (2) — housing that can be improved by expenditures reducing, although not eliminating, the landlord's return — presents different considerations. Here low-income tenants as a class are initially benefited by the Restatement rules. As long as the landlord recovers from rents all of his out-of-pocket expenses, including the cost of repairs plus interest on the investment in repairs, he is likely to make the repairs in order to protect his equity in the property. Even if his equity is zero (because no one will buy the property), he may still invest in repairs if the rents cover all costs, including as costs the return the landlord would have received by investing the repair money in some other venture. . . . In the long run, however, unless rents fully reflect the costs of the additional repairs required by the Restatement, the quantity of category (2) property will decline. First, because of the lower profit position, the operating costs associated with increasing building age will take their toll faster than normal and the building will be prematurely forced into a deficit position and removed from the market. Second, no new category (2) property will be built; while present owners need only cover their operating costs, potential owners must be able to cover their initial capital expenses.

Category (3) consists of housing unsuitable for residential use (under the Restatement rules) for which the cost of repairs (when added to other operating expenses) exceeds the rental income that may be obtained from the property. This housing will be abandoned sooner or later, the timing depending on the landlord's perceptions and the financing arrangements for the property.

If the property is not mortgaged, the property will be abandoned as soon as the landlord concludes that his deficit position is irreversible.

Once the property starts to lose money, the only reason for holding onto it is the expectation that sometime in the near future, the situation will turn around, and by an amount in excess of the losses previously suffered. For this reversal to occur it is probably necessary for rents to rise, which by hypothesis cannot happen for property in category (3).

If the property is mortgaged, the mortgagor will default, leaving the lending institution to take over. The lending institution will operate the property as long as rental income exceeds costs (including the cost of Restatement mandated repairs plus interest), thereby reducing the bad-debt loss the lender would otherwise suffer. The lender can afford to operate the property when the mortgagor-landlord could not, because the lender obviously does not have to pay himself interest. All the lender requires is a positive return on irretrievably sunk capital so as to reduce the unpaid balance on principal.

When neither the landlord without a mortgage nor the foreclosing mortgagee can break even on the property, the residuary legatee is the state. The state can take over the property for taxes, remove it from the tax rolls, and in theory pay for the Restatement repairs out of rental income not reduced by taxes. The state's ability to continue operation of the property depends, of course, on its ability either to divert public funds from former objects of support or to increase taxes to subsidize low-rent housing. Empirical evidence of what actually happens to slum housing after the state takes it over for taxes is lacking, but the prospects are probaby poor that the properties will remain in the housing stock, for central city expenses are rising faster than tax revenues. Moreover, as cities increase the tax rate more rental properties slip into a deficit position, with landlords refusing to invest in repairs and ultimately abandoning the property to the city for taxes. Thus tax foreclosures tend to result in a vicious circle unless substandard structures are demolished after the city acquires them; city expenses rise, real estate taxes rise, and more structures are abandoned for taxes, to start the process all over again.

R. POSNER, ECONOMIC ANALYSIS OF LAW 356-359 (2d ed. 1977):

§16.8 Wealth Redistribution by Liability Rules: The Case of Housing Code Enforcement

Housing codes specify minimum standards of housing — though whether in order to ensure a decent minimum level of safety and sanitation or to subsidize the building trades is a matter of debate. Legal scholarship has been imaginative in suggesting devices by which the violators of housing codes could be subjected to sanctions that would greatly reduce the incidence of violation. To deal with the problem of substandard housing by legal sanction has the additional attraction of enabling, or seeming to enable, a principal manifestation of poverty to be eliminated without any public expenditure.

The effects of housing code enforcement are shown graphically in Figure [8-3]. D_1 is the market demand curve for low income housing before enforcement. It is negatively sloped because not all the slum's residents would leave if price rose as a result of an increase in the landlord's marginal costs. MC_1 is the landlords' pre-enforcement marginal cost curve and is positively sloped to reflect the fact that the production of slum rental housing units involves the use of some specialized resources, in particular land, that would be worth less in any other use.

Enforcement of the housing code has two main effects on the market depicted in Figure [8-3].[2] First, by improving the quality of the housing units, it increases the demand for them, i.e., the quantity purchased at any given price. Second, by increasing the landlord's maintenance costs, which are marginal costs (they vary with the number of housing units provided), enforcement shifts the marginal cost curve in the market upward. This shift is shown in Figure [8-3] as being large in relation to the shift in the demand curve, on the plausible assumption that if quantity demanded were highly responsive to an increase in the quality of the housing provided, the landlords would upgrade quality voluntarily and there would be no need to enforce a housing code. Both demand and supply in Figure [8-3] are depicted as being rather elastic, on the

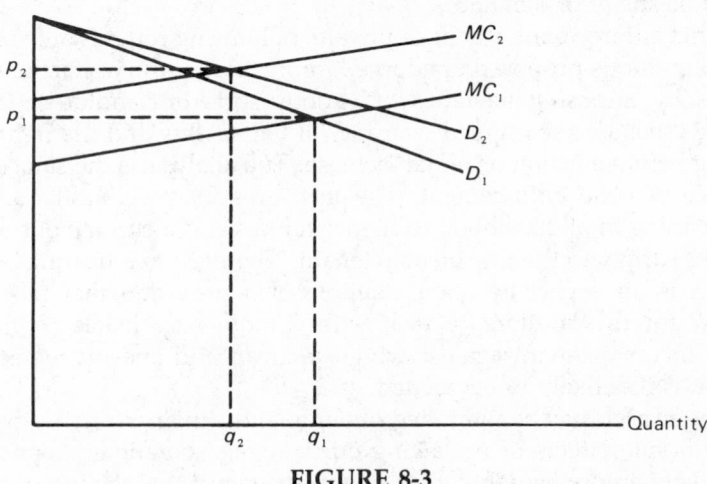

FIGURE 8-3

2. A third effect is a reduction in the rent of land received by the landlords (assuming they are the owners of the land). The irony here is that these "rentiers" include a number of almost-poor people for whom ownership of slum property represents the first stage in the escape from poverty.

(again plausible) assumptions that slum dwellers lack the resources to pay substantially higher rentals and that slum rentals are already so depressed in relation to costs that a further reduction in those rentals would cause many landlords to withdraw from the low income housing market (for example, by abandonment of their property to the city).

Given these assumptions, housing code enforcement leads to a substantial reduction in the supply of low income housing (from q_1 to q_2) coupled with a substantial rise in the price of the remaining supply (from p_1 to p_2). The quantity effect is actually understated (though by the same token the price effect is overstated) in Figure [8-3]: some of the higher quality supply brought about by housing code enforcement may be rented to the nonpoor.[4] These effects could be offset by rent supplements, but such a measure would deprive the program of its politically attractive quality of entailing no public expenditures. Admittedly, the *magnitude* of the effects shown in Figure [8-3] depends on the (arbitrary) location of the curves. It has even been suggested that demand might be perfectly elastic in the relevant region (implying no price effect of housing code enforcement) because the slightest increase would induce many tenants to double up. But since doubling up is costly (it involves forgoing the value of the greater space and privacy of single-family occupancy), tenants would surely be willing to pay something to avoid being forced to double up — i.e., a somewhat higher rental. This implies a less than perfectly elastic demand. What little empirical evidence there is suggests that Figure [8-3] provides a closer approximation to the actual conditions of the slum housing market than a model which assumes perfect elasticity of demand.

Strict enforcement, public or private, of housing codes is only one of several methods proposed or adopted for increasing the welfare of slum tenants by imposing liabilities of various sorts on landlords. Other methods include the implied warranty of habitability and the right to a hearing before eviction or rental increase. The analysis is the same as in the case of code enforcement. The measures increase the landlord's costs leading in all likelihood to higher rentals and a curtailment of the housing supply to the low income tenant. The right to a hearing before eviction is an especially good example of a provision that makes it cheaper for the landlord to deal with a more responsible (normally higher income) tenant against whom a cheap and speedy remedy of eviction is less likely to be needed.

The reader may be reminded of our analysis in an earlier chapter of the economic effects of outlawing efficient but sometimes oppressive methods of enforcing debts. Both analyses suggest that the use of liabil-

---

4. Might a covert purpose of housing codes be to increase the supply of middle income housing at the expense of people of low income? Cf. George J. Stigler, Director's Law of Public Income Redistribution, 13 J. Law & Econ. 1 (1970).

ity rules or other legal sanctions to redistribute income from wealthy to poor is likely to miscarry. A rule of liability is like an excise tax: it induces a contraction in output and increase in price. The party made liable, even if not poor himself (but that, as we have seen, is possible, too) may be able to shift much of the cost of the liability to the poor in the form of higher prices or reduced opportunities. The result may be a capricious redistribution of income and wealth within the class of poor people themselves and an overall reduction in their welfare.

G. STERNLIEB & R. BURCHELL, RESIDENTIAL ABANDONMENT: THE TENEMENT LANDLORD REVISITED xvi-xvii, xviii, xxii-xxiv (1973) (from the introduction and summary): In Newark, New Jersey, a key to the abandonment process appears to be prior property tax arrearage. Also contributing to the abandonment process is the heavy presence of nonwhite tenants resident in white-owned structures whose cost schedule includes funds allocated for "arm's length" operation, that is, either professionally managed or employing a professional rent collector.

Following this selection criteria in order of importance is a locational variable which expresses abandonment as a function of areas of increasing adjacent housing deterioration, i.e., once the tax arrearage, the fact of arm's length operation, and the tenant/owner racial profile of rental urban housing have been established as corollaries of abandonment, then location of the parcel seems to play an important part. Another important index which arises in areas of increasing abandonment is the lack of a mortgage or significant monetary interest in the property.

It appears, after examining this and previous indices, that abandonment may well be the nail in the coffin of the "classic" view of the tenement landlord. . . .

It also does *not* appear to hold that succeeding waves of tenement landlords were milking parcels and from this deriving substantial income. It may well be that if there were once a tenement landlord, in the classic sense, he is fast disappearing. There appears to be a greater tendency for abandoned parcels to have been owned by people who had at least ten years' experience in the real estate market and who had incomes in 1964 in excess of $8,000, largely contributed to by their real estate holdings. These current owners wanted to sell their buildings eight to ten years prior to abandonment and could not. Today they bitterly complain that the tenantry, and not taxes or other city ills, is preventing them from improving upon or recouping all or a portion of the parcel's value. . . .

One of the more satisfying folk figures of our time is that of the slumlord. This is an individual who popularly is supposed to dominate the low income private housing stock, and who has not only grown wealthy historically because of his tenure, but is currently securing a more than adequate return on his properties. The myth is satisfying because it leads to the belief that the major input necessary to provide more adequate standards of maintenance and operating behavior is to get this overfed individual to disgorge some of his excess earnings; the basic pie of rents is adequate both to support owner interests in holding on to his parcels and continuing their operation while still providing the tenants with adequate service inputs. The bulk of governmental measures in the older housing sphere has revolved around this concept, whether it is tax abatement in order to assure the owner that improvements will not be overassessed, long-term inexpensive loans for essential repairs in line with code enforcement efforts, or any of the more localized activities along these same lines. All of them essentially are based on the belief in the desirability, not only from a social point of view but also from the owner's economic point of view, of holding onto his properties. They presume a basic economic viability in operating low income housing. Thus governmental intervention has essentially been enabling legislation not to change present yields, but rather to permit better services and improved structures without altering the basic rent/expense ratios. . . .

In reality the changes in form and function of the older city and the folkways of its inhabitants, the great migration patterns which have dominated the demographic considerations in and about the United States metropolitan areas for decades, and, more recently, urban racial unrest, have occasioned a housing market situation of virtual stagnation. The combination of risk, decreasing profitability, and loss of potential for capital gains has substantially restricted the kinds of professional owners who are willing to invest in slum properties. It takes a highly insensitive individual to become a professional nonresident owner of slum property, in the light of present societal attitudes. This is not an individual who is easily influenced to invest his money unless an appropriate return can be secured.

There is as yet, however, no adequate replacement for these hard core tenement owners. The minority owner . . . , frequently buying for residence rather than income purposes, is avoiding the worst areas of the city. This leaves a definite gap as to who will manage hard core, urban realty. City-employed bureaucrats have characteristically done a poor job at housing management. The condition and solvency of housing run by local authorities attest to this.

The Tort Sanction

Sax and Hiestand, in Slumlordism as a Tort, 65 Mich. L. Rev. 869 (1967), argue that it is not possible for the private sector to provide adequate housing for the poor and maintain the profit level necessary for sustained investment in slum housing. Therefore they posit a different goal: "We are not out to reform the landlord (who, we agree, cannot afford to provide standard housing for the poor); we seek to create a pressure situation leading to additional legislative subsidization of low cost housing." Sax, Slumlordism as a Tort — A Brief Response, 66 Mich. L. Rev. 465, 467 (1968).

The "pressure situation" suggested by the authors is judicial creation of a tort of slumlordism. Such a tort could provide direct compensation for the indigent tenant in unlivable conditions, avoid the paternalism that characterizes housing code enforcement, and force landlords to choose between making reasonable efforts to conform to housing codes and leaving the slumlord business. Further, requiring nonnegligent behavior of tenant-plaintiffs may lead to improved tenant conduct.

The authors justify their proposed application of pressure on slum landlords as follows:

> Those who propose action against slum landlords are often met with the argument that the owners of these properties are not evildoers, but simply businessmen in a high-risk market who must, as a matter of economic survival, take rather rigorous measures. From this, it is often urged that those who attack "slumlords" are simply tugging an emotional string and are oblivious to objective economic facts. We hope to avoid these charges by making our position perfectly explicit: We do not characterize the slum landlord as a conscious or willing evildoer; we agree that he is probably doing precisely what a rational profit-seeking businessman in his circumstances would feel required to do. We simply say that if it is true that slum ownership is a business which requires the maintenance of such indecent conditions, then this is a business which needs to be eliminated. Moreover, let us not be deluded by the landlord's continued emphasis on the economic pressures which the slum housing business imposes on one who is in it; let us recognize that what we are condemning him for is going into (or staying in) such a business. Nothing forced him into buying a slum, except his own profit expectations. If he inherited such properties or found himself a landlord in a deteriorating neighborhood, nothing forced him to stay except his willingness to subordinate the life of his tenants to the prospect of some economic loss. As long as a landlord is willing to see his tenants' children bitten by rats in the night rather than take his losses and get out of the business — and that is the choice which our potential defendants have made — we see no need to wonder whether an injustice would be done in characterizing them as tortfeasors. [Sax and Hiestand, supra, 65 Mich. L. Rev. at 892-893.]

A study evaluating the impact of Green v. Superior Court, 10 Cal. 3d 616, 517 P.2d 1168, 111 Cal. Rptr. 704 (1974), which established the implied warranty of habitability in California, reached the following conclusions:

The single most important characteristic of the present eviction-unlawful detainer process is that in most cases the tenant does nothing. Either the action goes to default, or it simply is dropped. . . .

The high incidence of dropped and defaulted cases points to the extremely important fact that in most unlawful detainer suits, the substantive law is of little importance. This finding can be attributed most directly to the scarcity of legal services for the poor. People who are threatened with eviction typically do not receive legal advice, and consequently neither know nor assert their rights. Underrepresentation of the poor limits the effects that any legal doctrine might have on their problems. Thus, any evaluation of *Green*'s impact on contested cases must be tempered by the recognition that the great majority of unlawful detainer actions go uncontested.

Green may have an impact on the housing market even if habitability issues seldom are raised in unlawful detainer actions — the defense allowed in *Green* may encourage some landlords to maintain their premises in a habitable condition, while other landlords who allow their dwellings to deteriorate may be reluctant to initiate suit knowing that the tenant may raise a valid defense. However, it is only the fear of a successful defense in a contested case that provides the impetus for such landlord behavior. If the high incidence of tenant nonresponse to unlawful detainer complaints continues, landlords will discount greatly the possibility of a successful habitability defense, and *Green* will not affect their conduct significantly. . . . *Green* appears to be a classic example of a "progressive" judicial move unknown and relatively unimportant to the very people it was intended to assist. Even when raised, the uninhabitability defense has had only a moderate impact on case outcomes. As a result, it is doubtful that *Green* has affected the housing market greatly. It is neither accomplishing its presumed goal of "decent housing" nor resulting in the massive dislocation of the housing market predicted by its critics. [Note, The Great *Green* Hope: The Implied Warranty of Habitability in Practice, 28 Stan, L. Rev. 729, 739-741, 776-777 (1976).]

MOSIER & SOBLE, MODERN LEGISLATION, METROPOLITAN COURT, MINISCULE RESULTS: A STUDY OF DETROIT'S LANDLORD-TENANT COURT, 7 U. Mich. J.L. Ref. 8, 61, 63 (1973): One inescapable conclusion from the study results is that in 1970 and 1971 the reform legislation passed in Michigan was not meeting the goals that had been set for it in 1968. The new statutory defenses and warranties affected Detroit tenants, and thus landlords, very little. As before the legislation, landlords continued filing a large number of cases in Detroit Landlord-Tenant Court, and writs of eviction actually increased slightly. The court continued to serve the landlords as before, and the new defenses were only slightly utilized. In over 90 percent of the cases filed, the landlords did not have to contend with any tenant defenses, old or new; and in only approximately 3 percent of the cases filed did landlords have one of the new defenses, either landlord breach or retaliation, raised against them. Even considering only the cases where the tenant appeared and contested the action (20 percent of cases filed), the landlords need not have expected many fierce legal battles: less than 35 percent of the tenants who appeared raised any defense, and less than 13 percent raised one of the new defenses.

The outcomes of the cases studied show even more clearly how miniscule was the effect of the new legislation. Of the cases started, 97 percent resulted in the landlord's obtaining all he sought, by voluntary dismissal, default, or taking judgment in a contested case. In contested cases, 85 percent resulted in complete victory for the landlord. So the study showed that neither the new defenses nor the old defenses significantly affected the outcome of court cases.

The study proves false the prediction of one commentator that if defenses such as Michigan enacted in 1968 were allowed, "a substantial proportion of eviction suits would become complicated by fact-dominated squabbles," and "the present court system would be swamped." It can also be safely concluded from this study that this type of legislation, implemented under conditions such as those prevailing in Detroit Landlord-Tenant Court in 1970-71 and probably in most other summary proceedings courts, cannot meet the goal of improving the condition of housing. . . .

The disparities in help given to landlords and tenants and the treatment of late landlords and tenants are an indication of the perhaps inevitable bias of the court toward the landlord. Most of the judges and court personnel have a middle-class background, and they have become familiar with many landlords and attorneys appearing regularly in the court. The court had years of experience as a vehicle for rent collection and eviction where no defenses could be raised. The judges and clerks repeatedly hear about tenants who fail to pay rent or do damage to the premises, while they probably never have the opportunity to observe the actual conditions of the housing that the landlords are renting. Thus, another conclusion from the study is that if reform legislation is to have meaning, it must not rely on the actions of a court that has neither the experience nor the inclination to give the legislation full effect.

For major efforts to assess the consequences of landlord-tenant law reform, see Hirsch, Hirsch, and Margolis, Regression Analysis of the Effect of Habitability Laws Upon Rent: An Empirical Observation on the Ackerman-Komesar Debate, 63 Calif. L. Rev. 1098 (1975); Brakel and McIntyre, URLTA (Uniform Residential Landlord Tenant Act) in Operation: Oregon and Ohio, 1980 Am. B. Foundation Res. J. 559. The latter study was preceded by a comment from John M. McCale of the National Conference of Commissioners on State Laws:

[M]any of the expectations that underlay URLTA were unrealistic. It was too much to expect major economic impact particularly. . . . The new law is generally perceived as fairer than the common law, even by many land-lords and their representatives. At least some elements of the tenant population seem willing to organize, without fear of retaliation. Problems with security deposits have been minimized. Some of the worst slumlords seem to have been put out of business.

But there is not much evidence that the law has positively influenced the general quality of housing. . . .

See also one item from Mr. Brakel's research conducted in Portland, Oregon (Table 8-1).

HIRSCH, HIRSCH AND MARGOLIS, REGRESSION ANALYSIS OF THE EFFECTS OF HABITABILITY LAWS UPON RENT, 63 Calif. L. Rev. 1098, 1125, 1130-1131 (1975): In order to determine whether increased costs associated with minimum housing quality laws were in fact passed on to low-income tenants, housing expenditures of low-income households were analyzed with the aid of multiple regression techniques. The analysis was conducted on data from a survey of 5,000 households undertaken in the years 1968-72 by the University of Michigan Survey Research Center. From the 5,000 households we selected all low-income households that live in rented dwellings in metropolitan areas with populations greater than 50,000 and that live within 30 miles of the central business district. From this sample, households were removed if data were missing or if income/rent ratios indicated probable error in the measurement of either one or both variables. . . .

Two conclusions stand out from the empirical results. First, the regression equation we constructed is a relatively good one — it can explain a large percentage of the variation in rents paid by low-income tenants in the United States in 1972, and it does so with a relatively high degree of confidence. Second, given the strength of the explanatory power of the equation, we can say with a relatively high degree of confidence that in the early 1970's the presence or absence of receivership laws had a statistically significant effect on the rents paid by low-income tenants. Thus, *ceteris paribus*, rents in states with receivership laws were, on the average, about 12 percent higher than in those without such laws. Clearly, these empirical results support neither Judge Wright's statement about the effects of housing codes, nor Professor Ackerman's formulation of the problem.

The same confidence cannot be expressed in relation to repair and deduct and rent withholding remedies. A number of explanations may be offered to account for the lack of a strong relationship between the availability of the repair and deduct and rent withholding remedies and levels of rent. The most logical explanation, and the one most consistent with the sketchy empirical information which exists on the subject, is

TABLE 8-1
Sample of 100 FED Cases from the Multnomah County Court,
Portland, 1978-79

	No.
Reasons for landlord's action:	
24-hour notice for nonpayment of rent (only ground)	69
24-hour notice for nonpayment of rent plus other grounds	10
30-day notice "for cause"	11
30-day notice, month-to-month tenancy	8
24-hour notice for irreparable damage by tenant	5
No information of grounds in record	8
Total	100
Outcome of landlords' action:	
Landlord wins "restitution" (includes 29 default judgments against tenants; 14 "stipulated judgments" for restitution; 4 stipulated judgments for restitution, not to be executed if tenant fulfills other conditions of judgment (all Housing Authority cases))	79
Landlord wins other favorable result	2
Tenant wins (includes 2 landlord "no shows"; 1 stipulated judgment on balance favoring tenant)	3
Neither party wins (includes mixture of no disposition yet, no discernible outcome in record, a few "no shows" either party or other dismissals, and no-win settlements)	16
Total	100
Special parties or representatives:	
Housing Authority cases (all but 2 stipulated judgments with restitution to landlord, not to be executed if tenant meets other conditions)	6
Legal Aid clients (all but 1 case stipulated judgments of restitution to landlord, but not back rent or attorney's fees to be paid by tenant)	9
Other noteworthy aspects:	
Record shows tenant's property forcibly moved	5

Source: Brakel & McIntyre, URLTA in Operation: Oregon and Ohio, 1980 Am. B. Foundation Res. J. 559, 581. Used with permission.

that repair and deduct and rent withholding remedies are not being used by tenants to any great extent. If these remedies are not widely used, no real costs would be imposed on landlords, and thus there would be no increased costs to be passed on to tenants.

If tenant-initiated code enforcement remedies are not widely used by tenants (or at least were not frequently used by tenants from 1968 to 1972, the years included in this study), the question then arises as to the reasons for their lack of use. Housing and legal service agencies often point to the lack of information and resources on the part of poor tenants. If costs are indeed passed on to low-income tenants, as suggested by the experience with receivership laws, a greater availability of information and resources for indigent tenants may result in higher rents being charged. Thus, if legal service organizations increase the probability that tenants will invoke habitability laws, such organizations may hurt, rather than help, their clients, at least to the extent of indirectly giving impetus to an increase in rent.

There is another possible explanation for the infrequent use of such remedies, however. Tenants may indeed know of the availability of such remedies and in addition perceive the potentially counterproductive consequences of invoking such remedies. Thus, the infrequent use of tenant-initiated code enforcement mechanisms may be a reflection of a foresighted perception of self-interest.

Note

Cf. N. Mandelstam, Hope Against Hope 128 (1970):

> I came back not to the hotel, but to a "room" which M. had managed to find to serve us as a temporary accommodation. It consisted of a glassed-over veranda in a large tumbledown house that belonged to the best cook in town. . . . He was a tired, sick old man who no longer had any appetite for food, and lived in one room of his house — all the others were occupied by tenants who for a long time had been paying him the nominal rent fixed by law. As the owner, he had to do all repairs at his own expense, and in summer he let the veranda just to make ends meet. His one hope was that the place might be pulled down or taken over by the housing department of the local Soviet, but no local Soviet in its right mind would want to saddle itself with a ruin like this. So the last private owner of a large house in Voronezh was miserably going to the dogs, and his only dream was to become an ordinary tenant in his own house, which would in any case soon be pulled down.

H. THE MASSZONIA v. WASHINGTON LITIGATION

The judicial attempt to reform landlord-tenant relations in the District of Columbia reached its apogee in a series of cases each titled Masszonia v. Washington. In that dispute, the landlord had ceased attempting to collect rent, but also ceased paying for water, gas, and

PHOTOGRAPH 8-4
The *Masszonia* site (1976)

electricity. Tenants sued Mayor Walter Washington of Washington. The city had found more than 1,000 housing code violations on the premises.

Judge Gerhard Gesell in U.S. District Court concluded that the court was "without power to direct the gas and electrical utility companies to continue service without payment." When the city corporation counsel suggested that the tenants organize themselves and pay for the utility services, Judge Gesell responded saying that since "many of the tenants lead a marginal existence and changes of occupancy may well occur, there is no probability that a stable solution can be achieved by following this suggested course." The judge concluded that the mayor had discretionary authority to pay the utilities, fix the building, and "assess the costs as a tax lien on the property." He held that in the circumstances, failure to exercise discretionary authority "would be an abuse of discretion."

The judge had been unmoved by the corporation counsel's statement that 100,000 persons lived in the district "under conditions quite comparable to those which this complaint portrays," and that the city had an inadequate budget for the tasks the judge was assigning. Masszonia v. Washington, 315 F. Supp. 529 (D.D.C. 1970).

After discovering that fixing the boiler would cost $100,000, the city ordered the tenants to vacate within six days pursuant to the Housing Regulations. Forty-five of the tenants were referred to the Family Relocation Office. The second action in the case resulted in the court's refusal to block the evictions pending a showing that the city had found adequate replacement housing. The court limited the earlier decision to a rule that the city must supply utilities for an emergency period, but not on a "permanent, continuing basis." Masszonia v. Washington, 321 F. Supp. 965 (D.D.C. 1971).

The final *Masszonia* opinion was from the U.S. Court of Appeals. A senior judge for the District of Montana, sitting by designation, found the issues being appealed from the second district court decision to be moot. The premises had been condemned and razed, and Mrs. Masszonia had "moved to an address unknown on May 17, 1971." Masszonia v. Washington, 476 F.2d 915 (D.C. Cir. 1973).

III ◆ HOUSING AS A PUBLIC UTILITY

What is property?

As Part 2 shows, the recent restructuring of landlord-tenant doctrine illustrates the traditional role estate law has played in the formation of standardized relationships appropriate to contemporary conditions and values. But the landlord-tenant story also evinces a modern concern with the social importance of the tenant's possession of a premises, even at the expense of the social importance of the landlord's title. The wider society regulates property holdings because of its perception of fairness, entitlement, efficiency, equality, and externality. Suddenly, as so often is the case with current property law, we move from private law to public law, from the law of estates to administrative law. This part of the book considers four recent public controversies concerning housing law. In each example, an argument is made that public intervention should replace the landlord's traditional role. Throughout, an important question to keep in mind is whether government has the will, the capacity, and the resources to achieve the ends it proclaims.

9 ◆ RENT CONTROL

A. CONSTITUTIONAL LEGITIMACY

◆ BLOCK v. HIRSH
  256 U.S. 135 (1921)

Mr. Justice HOLMES delivered the opinion of the court. This is a proceeding brought by the defendant in error, Hirsh, to recover possession of the cellar and first floor of a building on F Street in Washington which the plaintiff in error, Block, holds over after the expiration of a lease to him. Hirsh bought the building while the lease was running, and on December 15, 1919, notified Block that he should require possession on December 31, when the lease expired. Block declined to surrender the premises, relying upon the Act of October 22, 1919, c.80, Title II — "District of Columbia Rents." That is also the ground of his defence in this Court, and the question is whether the statute is constitutional, or, as held by the Court of Appeals, an attempt to authorize the taking of property not for public use and without due process of law, and for this and other reasons void.

By §109 of the act the right of a tenant to occupy any hotel, apartment, or "rental property," i.e., any building or part thereof, other than hotel or apartment, is to continue notwithstanding the expiration of his term, at the option of the tenant, subject to regulation by the Commission appointed by the act, so long as he pays the rent and performs the conditions as fixed by the lease or as modified by the Commission. It is provided in the same section that the owner shall have the right to possession "for actual and *bona fide* occupancy by himself, or his wife, children, or dependents . . . upon giving thirty days' notice in writing." According to his affidavit Hirsh wanted the premises for his own use, but he did not see fit to give the thirty days' notice because he denied the validity of the act. The statute embodies a scheme or code which it is needless to set forth, but it should be stated that it ends with the declaration in §122 that the provisions of Title II are made necessary by emergencies growing out of the war, resulting in rental conditions in the District dangerous to the public health and burdensome to public officers, employees and accessories, and thereby embarrassing the Federal Government in the transaction of the public business. As emergency legislation the Title is to end in two years unless sooner repealed. . . .

The general proposition to be maintained is that circumstances have clothed the letting of buildings in the District of Columbia with a public interest so great as to justify regulation by law. Plainly circumstances may so change in time or so differ in space as to clothe with such an interest what at other times or in other places would be a matter of purely private concern. . . .

The fact that tangible property is also visible tends to give a rigidity to our conception of our rights in it that we do not attach to others less concretely clothed. But the notion that the former are exempt from the legislative modification required from time to time in civilized life is contradicted not only by the doctrine of eminent domain, under which what is taken is paid for, but by that of the police power in its proper sense, under which property rights may be cut down, and to that extent taken, without pay. Under the police power the right to erect buildings in a certain quarter of a city may be limited to from eighty to one hundred feet. Safe pillars may be required in coal mines. Billboards in cities may be regulated. Water-sheds in the country may be kept clear. These cases are enough to establish that a public exigency will justify the legislature in restricting property rights in land to a certain extent without compensation. But if to answer one need the legislature may limit height to answer another it may limit rent. We do not perceive any reason for denying the justification held good in the foregoing cases to a law limiting the property rights now in question if the public exigency requires that. The reasons are of a different nature but they certainly are not less pressing. Congress has stated the unquestionable embarrassment of Government and danger to the public health in the existing condition of things. The space in Washington is necessarily monopolized in comparatively few hands, and letting portions of it is as much a business as any other. Housing is a necessary of life. All the elements of a public interest justifying some degree of public control are present. The only matter that seems to us open to debate is whether the statute goes too far. For just as there comes a point at which the police power ceases and leaves only that of eminent domain, it may be conceded that regulations of the present sort pressed to a certain height might amount to a taking without due process of law.

Perhaps it would be too strict to deal with this case as concerning only the requirement of thirty days' notice. For although the plaintiff

alleged that he wanted the premises for his own use the defendant
denied it and might have prevailed upon that issue under the act. The
general question to which we have adverted must be decided, if not in
this then in the next case, and it should be disposed of now. — The main
point against the law is that tenants are allowed to remain in possession
at the same rent that they have been paying, unless modified by the
Commission established by the act, and that thus the use of the land and
the right of the owner to do what he will with his own and to make what
contracts he pleases are cut down. But if the public interest be established the regulation of rates is one of the first forms in which it is
asserted, and the validity of such regulation has been settled since
Munn v. Illinois, 94 U.S. 113. It is said that a grain elevator may go out of
business whereas here the use is fastened upon the land. The power to
go out of business, when it exists, is an illusory answer to gas companies
and waterworks, but we need not stop at that. The regulation is put and
justified only as a temporary measure. A limit in time, to tide over a
passing trouble, well may justify a law that could not be upheld as a
permanent change.

Machinery is provided to secure to the landlord a reasonable rent. It
may be assumed that the interpretation of "reasonable" will deprive him
in part at least of the power of profiting by the sudden influx of people to
Washington caused by the needs of Government and the war, and thus
of a right usually incident to fortunately situated property — of a part of
the value of his property as defined in International Harvester Co. v.
Kentucky, 234 U.S. 222. But while it is unjust to pursue such profits
from a national misfortune with sweeping denunciations, the policy of
restricting them has been embodied in taxation and is accepted. It goes
little if at all farther than the restriction put upon the rights of the owner
of money by the more debatable usury laws. The preference given to the
tenant in possession is an almost necessary incident of the policy and is
traditional in English law. If the tenant remained subject to the landlord's power to evict, the attempt to limit the landlord's demands would
fail.

Assuming that the end in view otherwise justified the means
adopted by Congress, we have no concern of course with the question
whether those means were the wisest, whether they may not cost more
than they come to, or will effect the result desired. It is enough that we
are not warranted in saying that legislation that has been resorted to for
the same purpose all over the world, is futile or has no reasonable
relation to the relief sought. . . .

Mr. Justice McKENNA: The Chief Justice, Mr. Justice Van Devanter,
Mr. Justice McReynolds and I dissent from the opinion and judgment of
the court. The grounds of dissent are the explicit provisions of the Constitution of the United States; the specifications of the grounds are the
irresistible deductions from those provisions and, we think, would re-

quire no expression but for the opposition of those whose judgments challenge attention. . . .

The statute in the present case is denominated "The Rent Law" and its purpose is to permit a lessee to continue in possession of leased premises after the expiration of his term, against the demand of his landlord and in direct opposition to the covenants of the lease, so long as he pays the rent and performs the conditions as fixed by the lease or as modified by a commission created by the statute. This is contrary to every conception of leases that the world has ever entertained, and of the reciprocal rights and obligations of lessor and·lessee.

As already declared, the provisions of the Constitution seem so direct and definite as to need no reinforcing words and to leave no other inquiry than, Does the statute under review come within their prohibition? It is asserted, that the statute has been made necessary by the conditions resulting from the "Imperial German war." The thought instantly comes that the country has had other wars with resulting embarrassments, yet they did not induce the relaxation of constitutional requirements nor the exercise of arbitrary power. Constitutional restraints were increased, not diminished. However, it may be admitted that the conditions presented a problem and induced an appeal for government remedy. But we must bear in mind that the Constitution is, as we have shown, a restraint upon government, purposely provided and declared upon consideration of all the consequences of what it prohibits and permits, making the restraints upon government the rights of the governed. And this careful adjustment of power and rights makes the Constitution what it was intended to be and is, a real charter of liberty, receiving and deserving the praise that has been given it as "the most wonderful work ever struck off at any given time by the brain and purpose of man." And we add that more than a century of trial "has certainly proven the sagacity of the constructors, and the stubborn strength of the fabric."

The "strength of the fabric" can not be assigned to any one provision, it is the contribution of all, and, therefore, it is not the expression of too much anxiety to declare that a violation of any of its prohibitions is an evil — an evil in the circumstance of violation, of greater evil because of its example and malign instruction. And against the first step to it this court has warned, expressing a maxim of experience, — *"Withstand beginnings."* Boyd v. United States, 116 U.S. 616, 635. Who can know to what end they will conduct?

The facts of this litigation point the warning. Recurring to them, we may ask, Of what concern is it to the public health or the operations of the Federal Government who shall occupy a cellar, and a room above it, for business purposes in the City of Washington? — (the question in this case); and, Why is it the solicitude of the police power of the State of New York to keep from competition an apartment in the City of New

York? — (the question in the other case). The answer is, to supply homes to the homeless. It does not satisfy. If the statute keeps a tenant in, it keeps a tenant out, indeed, this is its assumption. Its only basis is, that tenants are more numerous than landlords and that in some way this proportion, it is assumed, makes a tyranny in the landlord, and an oppression to the tenant, notwithstanding the tenant is only required to perform a contract entered into, not under the statute, but before the statute; and that the condition is remedied by rent fixing — value adjustment — by the power of the Government. And this, it is the view of the opinion, has justification because "space in Washington is limited" and "housing is a necessary of life." A causative and remedial relation in the circumstances we are unable to see. We do see that the effect and evil of the statute is that it withdraws the dominion of property from its owner, superseding the contracts that he confidently made under the law then existing and subjecting them to the fiat of a subsequent law.

If such exercise of government be legal, what exercise of government is illegal? Houses are a necessary of life, but other things are as necessary. May they too be taken from the direction of their owners and disposed of by the Government? Who supplies them, and upon what inducement? And, when supplied, may those who get them under promise of return, and who had no hand or expense in their supply, dictate the terms of retention or use, and be bound by no agreement concerning them?

An affirmative answer seems to be the requirement of the decision. If the public interest may be concerned, as in the statute under review, with the control of any form of property, it can be concerned with the control of all forms of property. And, certainly, in the first instance, the necessity or expediency of control must be a matter of legislative judgment. But, however, not to go beyond the case — if the public interest can extend a lease it can compel a lease; the difference is only in degree and boldness. In one as much as in the other, there is a violation of the positive and absolute right of the owner of the property. And it would seem, necessarily, if either can be done, unoccupied houses or unoccupied space in occupied houses can be appropriated. The efficacy of either to afford homes for the homeless cannot be disputed. In response to an inquiry from the bench, counsel replied that the experiment had been tried or was being tried in a European country. It is to be remembered, that the legality of power must be estimated not by what it will do but by what it can do.

The prospect expands and dismays when we pass outside of considerations applicable to the local and narrow conditions in the District of Columbia. It is the assertion of the statute that the Federal Government is embarrassed in the transaction of its business, but, as we have said, a New York statute is submitted to us and counsel have referred to the legislation of six other States. And, there is intimation in the opinion that Congress in its enactment has imitated the laws of other countries. The facts are significant and suggest the inquiry, Have conditions come, not only to the District of Columbia, embarrassing the Federal Government, but to the world as well, that are not amenable to passing palliatives, so that socialism, or some form of socialism, is the only permanent corrective or accommodation? It is indeed strange that this court, in effect, is called upon to make way for it and, through the instrument of a constitution based on personal rights and the purposeful encouragement of individual incentive and energy, to declare legal a power exerted for their destruction. The inquiry occurs, Have we come to the realization of the observation that "War unless it be fought for liberty is the most deadly enemy of liberty"?

1 HOLMES-LASKI LETTERS 331-332 (M. deW. Howe ed., 1953):

Washington, D.C., May 8, 1921

My beloved Laski:

For once, four or five days, including a week-end when I suppose a vessel sails for England, have gone by after a letter from you before I answered. The reason is that I have been in such a spasm over three interesting cases that I could do nothing else till I finished them. The first was on the constitutionality of an Estate Tax levied by Congress. The next on the validity of conduct charged against a Reserve Bank as intended to compel the plaintiffs — State banks — to come into the system — and collect and remit the proceeds of checks from a distance without a charge. The cases took concentration to get them stated to my liking. After these came an easier one that I took to relieve the C.J. on business of retreating to the wall when defending one's life. I finished that this morning. I am pretty well satisfied with all of them and with a recent one that I wrote upholding the constitutionality of the Emergency Housing legislation enabling tenants to hold over. McKenna shrieked over the downfall of the Constitution[4] — yet a few days later he said something to me about everything being a question of circumstances that showed that he understood the business as well as anyone. But he not infrequently recurs to the tyro's question: Where are you going to draw the line? — as if all life were not the marking of grades between black and white. My satisfaction does not mean any great conceit, but simply that I watch myself to see if I am keeping up to the mark. No reading of course. I got a copy of the original edition of Moby Dick in fair condition at Lowdermilk's $3.50 — as a tribute to Melville — and my

4. . . . Writing to Felix Frankfurter on April 20, 1921, Holmes made this further comment on the decision in Block v. Hirsh: "I was content with my statement and made no changes after receiving the dissent, although it criticized my opinion, which I think bad form."

wife has sent for the French Gauguin's Noa Noa which is interesting in the illustrations and even in the translation. Gauguin thought — I don't doubt sincerely — that in Tahiti he got back to the classics and away from the degeneracy of civilization — I ain't quite sure about it — and of course myself prefer civilization with all its defects to Tahiti in all its glory — and that they did have damned handsome women in those parts I devoutly believe especially remembering photographs that Stevenson many years ago sent to a friend of his and mine. Well, my lad, I am tired — more than I ought to be — and so instead of duties or reading I mean to stretch myself out and try to sleep. I think it tends to take me in my innards when I get over-wrought. Your feeling of the imminence of civil war I trust was unwarranted. Who was the "She" who also was at the luncheon [with] Morley, Asquith, and McDonald? Was it Mrs. Asquith? I don't quite understand what follows "And as always with the eager word of Leslie Stephen who of all their friends, seems to be closest to their hearts." I didn't know that Mrs. Asquith ever knew L. S. which seems queer if your sentence means what it seems to. Who is Beale? The Beale of the Harvard Law School? I have just run my eye over a learned study of his on the law of retreating to the wall. It has a little more veneration for the texts and for human life than I have but seems a good analysis of the old law. Why should any remark about Adams prick me? My wife gave me those two volumes but I have passed by on the other side hitherto and intend to stay there. Now for a little rest.

Yours as ever,
O.W.H.

Notes

1. In Block v. Hirsh, Holmes cited Munn v. Illinois, which upheld regulation of grain warehouse prices with the argument, "When . . . one devotes his property to a use in which the public has an interest, he, in effect, grants to the public an interest in that use, and must submit to be controlled by the public for the common good." 94 U.S. 113, 126 (1877). Justice Field dissented:

> If this be sound law, if there be no protection, either in the principles upon which our republican government is founded, or in the prohibitions of the Constitution against such invasion of private rights, all property and all business in the State are held at the mercy of a majority of its legislature. The public has no greater interest in the use of buildings for the storage of grain than it has in the use of buildings for the residences of families, nor, indeed, any thing like so great an interest; and, according to the doctrine announced, the legislature may fix the rent of all tenements used for residences, without reference to the cost of their erection. If the

owner does not like the rates prescribed, he may cease renting his houses. He has granted to the public, says the court, an interest in the use of the buildings. . . . [Id. at 140-141.]

2. Price controls usually pass constitutional muster. For example, the 1971 Nixon "freeze" was upheld in Amalgamated Meat Cutters v. Connally, 337 F. Supp. 737 (D.D.C. 1971). But some state courts have struck down rent control ordinances because of the absence of a sufficient showing of housing emergency. See, e.g., City of Miami Beach v. Fleetwood Hotel, Inc., 261 So. 2d 801 (Fla. 1972); City of Miami Beach v. Forte Towers, 305 So. 2d 764 (Fla. 1974).

A rent stabilization ordinance adopted in Berkeley, California, was struck down by a court of appeals on the ground that the "inexcusably cumbersome" administrative procedures that landlords had to follow to obtain rent increases were constitutionally unsatisfactory. The court held that "delays in considering and acting upon individual petitions would inevitably cause delays in providing a fair return to the landlord and would therefore be confiscatory." Fisher v. City of Berkeley, 148 Cal. App. 3d 267, 195 Cal. Rptr. 836 (1983).

◆ FRESH POND SHOPPING CENTER, INC., v. CALLAHAN
104 S. Ct. 218 (1983)

The appeal is dismissed for want of a substantial federal question.

Justice REHNQUIST, dissenting.

Appellant, Fresh Pond Shopping Center, Inc. signed a purchase agreement in June, 1979 whereby it would acquire a six-unit apartment building located adjacent to some property it already owned. Appellant planned to demolish the building and pave over the lot to provide parking to a commercial tenant of the shopping center. Because the apartment units were rent-controlled rental housing, under the terms of Cambridge City Ordinance 926 appellant first had to obtain permission from the Cambridge Rent Control Board to remove the property from the rental housing market. Although at the time the removal permit was sought only one of the six units was occupied, the Board denied the permit. . . . I would note probable jurisdiction in this case because I believe the case presents important and difficult questions concerning the application of the Takings Clause of the Fifth and Fourteenth Amendments of the Constitution, which have not been decided before by this Court. They might be postponed or avoided if the case were here on certiorari, but the case is an appeal; we act on the merits whatever we do.

The primary feature of the Cambridge rent control statute, 1976 Mass. Acts, ch. 36, is to place virtually all residential rental property in Cambridge under control of the Cambridge Rent Control Board, whose members are appellees here. Owners of rent-controlled property are also prohibited from evicting tenants without first obtaining a certificate of eviction from the Rent Control Board. The statute limits issuance of eviction certificates to circumstances where tenants have committed certain improper acts. It preserves the landlord's right to obtain a certificate of eviction to recover possession of the property only for occupancy by the owner or certain of his family members, or if the property is to be removed from the housing market through demolition or otherwise.

Although the state enabling statute preserves in limited fashion a landlord's traditional right to evict a tenant in order to occupy a rental unit personally, Cambridge City Ordinance 926 eliminated the landlord's right to evict a tenant save when the Rent Control Board first issues a "removal" permit. Ordinance 926 delegates virtually unfettered discretion to the Board to determine whether to grant a removal permit. The Board may consider the benefits of denying removal to the tenants protected by rent control, the hardship upon existing tenants of the units sought to be removed, and the effect of removal on the proclaimed housing shortage in Cambridge. Nowhere does the ordinance suggest that these considerations be balanced against the landlord's right to put his property to other uses. In short, Ordinance 926 permits denying a "removal" permit in any situation.

The combined effect of the limitations imposed by the state enabling statute and Ordinance 926 is to deny appellant use of his property. Appellant, as a corporate entity, simply cannot occupy the remaining apartment for personal use. In effect, then, the Rent Control Board has determined that until the remaining tenant decides to leave, appellant will be unable to vacate and demolish the building. In my view this deprives appellant of the use of its property in a manner closely analogous to a permanent physical invasion, like that involved in *Loretto v. Teleprompter Manhattan CATV Corp.*, 458 U.S. 419 (1982). In *Teleprompter* we were presented with the question whether a New York law that authorized a cable television company to install cable facilities on other persons' property without permission or effective compensation constituted a taking in violation of the Fifth and Fourteenth Amendments. Though the physical invasion was minor, we "conclude[d] that a permanent physical occupation authorized by government is a taking without regard to the public interests that it may serve." . . . We called a permanent physical occupation of another's property "the most serious form of invasion of an owner's property interest."

As the Cambridge ordinance operates in this case, I fail to see how it works anything but a physical occupation of appellant's property. First, appellant's right to evict the tenant was limited by state law to two circumstances: occupation of the rental unit by the owner or certain members of his family, or demolition. The first of these rights is not available to appellant. The second, demolition, is controlled by Cambridge Ordinance 926, and under the administration of that ordinance by the Cambridge Rent Control Board, appellant has been denied the right to remove the unit from the housing market by demolition. It is not certain whether the Rent Control Board would, if the tenant decided to leave, determine that a demolition permit should issue, but it is clear that until the tenant decides to leave of his own volition, appellant is unable to possess the property.

There is little to distinguish this case from the situation confronting the Court in *Teleprompter*. As in *Teleprompter*, the power to end or terminate the physical invasion is under the control of a private party. As in New York, the Massachusetts legislature can alter the rent control statute to provide appellant with some other means of restoring control of his property. But neither of these factors moved the Court away from its holding in *Teleprompter* that the physical invasion amounted to a taking. I must conclude, as the Court did in *Teleprompter*, that Ordinance 926 has effected a permanent physical invasion of appellant's property.

It might also be argued that the rent control provisions are justified by the emergency housing shortage in Cambridge, but the very fact that there is no foreseeable end to the emergency takes this case outside the Court's holding in Block v. Hirsh, 256 U.S. 135 (1921). At issue in *Block* was the constitutionality of a rent control statute enacted by Congress to regulate rents and rental practices in the District of Columbia. Like the rent control practices employed in Cambridge, the regulations disputed in *Block* fixed rents and denied the landlord the right to evict a tenant except to allow the owner or a member of his family to occupy the unit. We held the rent control statute constitutional because it was enacted to deal with a wartime emergency housing shortage. We noted that "[a] limit in time, to tide over a passing trouble, may well justify a law that could not be upheld as a permanent change." . . . Thus, although we upheld a regulatory scheme in *Block* that is remarkably similar to that presently in force in the City of Cambridge, we reserved judgment as to whether such a regulatory scheme would be constitutional if it were made part of a permanent scheme. The Cambridge rent control ordinance presents the question thus reserved.

The provision in the Massachusetts statute ensuring a fair net operating income to the landlord does not change the result that should attend this case. In previous decisions we have recognized that property ownership carries with it a bundle of rights, including the right "to possess, use and dispose of it." . . . Though no issue is raised here that the rent paid by the tenant is insufficient, that fact does not end the inquiry. What has taken place is a transfer of control over the reversionary interest retained by appellant. This power to exclude is "one of the most treasured strands in an owner's bundle of property rights, . . . [because] even though the owner may retain the bare legal right to dispose of the occupied space by transfer or sale, the permanent occupation of that space by a stranger would ordinarily empty the right of any value, since the purchaser will also be unable to make any use of the property." Nothing in the rent control provisions requires the Board to compensate appellant for the loss of control over the use of its property.

Notes

1. What is the constitutionally protected minimum rent level? See Troy Hills Village v. Township Council, 68 N.J. 604, 350 A.2d 34 (1975):

> Rent control begins with the premise that rents are being unfairly inflated as a result of failure in the free operation of the rental housing market. . . . A standard of valuation which itself incorporates this failure will quickly defeat the purpose of rent control. Thus, valuation based on inflated rents [and itself justifying rent increases] would inevitably and erroneously lead the courts to a conclusion that a regulation which fails to permit such inflated rents is confiscatory. . . . [The relevant value for determining minimum rents is] the worth of the property in the context of a hypothetical market in which the supply of available rental housing is just adequate to meet the needs of the various categories of persons actively desiring to rent apartments in the municipality.

See also Niles v. Boston Rent Control Administrator, 374 N.E.2d 296 (Mass. App. 1978): "A rate which makes it impossible for an efficient operator to stay in business or derive any profit whatever for shareholders is confiscatory. . . . [T]he administrator is not required . . . to assure a fair return on fair market value. . . ."

2. Tenants are not the only ones who seek ways to benefit from the details of English rent law. The Rent Acts apply only if exclusive possession is granted to a tenant. In one case, the landlords offered a "license . . . notwithstanding that such use be in common with the Licensor." The licensees, two young men, were assured that the language was "just a legal formality," and no other person would in fact enter the flat.

The landlords later sought a possession order for the flat, arguing that the men had no tenancy. The court held that although the documents were ambiguous, the facts indicated that the landlords had never intended to exercise their theoretical right of entry and that therefore a joint tenancy protected by the Rent Acts existed. Walsh v. Griffiths-Jones, [1972] 2 All E.R. 1002 (Lambeth County Court).

For discussion of a series of such cases, not consistently decided, and showing judges "torn between a desire to uphold contractual arrangements and an awareness, however dimly perceived, that the Rent

Acts have a social purpose that should not be too easily thwarted," see Partington, Non-Exclusive Occupation Agreements, 42 Modern L. Rev. 331 (1979).

3. *Held:* The state may constitutionally bar "scalping" of tickets to sports events. State v. Major, 243 Ga. 255, 253 S.E.2d 724 (1979), rejecting Tyson & Brother v. Banton, 273 U.S. 418 (1927) (freedom to contract except as to matters affected with "a public interest").

4. Who "owns" a tenant's rights under rent control? In England there has been controversy over situations in which, for example, a 76-year-old and a 26-year-old share quarters, and then the 26-year-old takes over the 76-year-old's rights. The statute says that upon a tenant's death, his or her rights devolve upon "a member of the original tenant's family." The House of Lords said the test was whether there was a "familial nexus." A commentator said this creates "a strange exception, in many ways, to the rule against perpetuities."

The actual case was extraordinary. In 1925, Salter, J., had written that it "may have to be determined some day what limit is to be put on these words 'tenant's family,' whether they are equivalent to 'household' or whether they are limited as meaning blood relations. . . ." Salter v. Lask, [1925] 1 K.B. 584, 587. He could not have realized that 50 years later his own widow would create the case. Lady Salter, then 76, took in a 26-year-old man in 1958. Their "platonic cohabitation" lasted 18 years. The young man called her "Aunt Nora." She died at 94, but the court refused to let him have the apartment. "The line must be drawn somewhere," said Lord Justice Browne, when the court of appeal acted on the case, [1979] 1 W.L.R. 3. Carega Properties S.A. v. Sharratt, [1979] 1 W.L.R. 928 (House of Lords); Tennant, Cohabitation and the Rent Act, 1980 Camb. L.J. 31.

Compare Zimmerman v. Burton, 107 Misc. 2d 401, 434 N.Y.S.2d 127 (Civ. Ct. 1980), where a woman holding rights under rent control died, and the court refused to permit eviction of the man with whom she had maintained "partnership . . . akin to that of husband and wife, absent the legal formality of marriage." Said the court, "The law must keep abreast of changing moral standards."

5. When New York City takes rental housing because the landlord is in arrears on property tax, "the city shall be seized of an estate in fee simple. . . ." Housing taken by the city is called *in rem* housing.

The city sought to "restructure" *in rem* rents "in order to reduce the shortfall between the current rent revenues . . . and the costs of operation and maintenance. . . ." A goal was "to make such buildings self-sufficient and to return them to the private sector." The increases were in excess of those allowed under rent control, but the rent control law permitted the city as landlord to impose the increases.

Tenants sued, saying they had a constitutionally protected property interest in the controlled rent level. The federal district court said that even if they had such an interest, they had received adequate due process before the increases occurred. The court also held that the Equal Protection Clause was not violated when the city in effect exempted itself from rent control. Sidberry v. Koch, 539 F. Supp. 413 (S.D.N.Y. 1982).

As a result of such takings, New York City in 1983 held title to some 4,000 occupied buildings and about 6,000 unoccupied ones. It had 40,000 apartments containing 120,000 residents, and spent $150 million per year to run them. N.Y. Times, Nov. 27, 1983.

B.   ECONOMIC LEGITIMACY

1.   Setting the Price

How should a "controlled" rent be set? Experience suggests that the range of alternatives is limited:

a. Freezing rents at their level on the date controls are adopted.

"Generally, the base rent for any residence is the rent charged . . . in the most recent rent payment interval before August 15, 1971." CCH Economic Controls Reporter ¶6515 (1972).

b. Freezing them at their level on some other date.

"It is strongly argued to us that the six month rollback feature of [Mass. Gen. Laws 1970, ch. 842 §6(1)] violates equal protection and due process of the law. . . . Institution of a rollback provides a safeguard against freezing last minute rent increases into controlled rent levels and carries the advantage of setting rents 'at levels which landlords and tenants had worked out for themselves by free bargaining in a competitive market' . . . at a time either before undue rent increases commenced or at least before they became so evident." Marshal House, Inc. v. Rent Control Bd., 358 Mass. 686, 266 N.E.2d 876 (1971).

c. At levels that provide owners a specified rate of return on their investment.

"The . . . objection is that [the controlled rent] deprives the plaintiff of a reasonable return. . . . Deprivation is spelled out in two ways: first, because under prior statutes the larger base figure representing the purchase price was usable; and, second, because prior adjudications under those statutes fixed a value on which a just return was to be calculated. No question of fact is here presented. The essential allegations — that the earlier statutes in this instance allowed the purchase price to be used; that it was so used; that the present statute prevents such use; and that a return based on the assessed value under the existing assessment will be less than one based on the purchase price — are all facts which are not in dispute. And there are no other facts necessary for decision.

"Obviating the paradox of a perpetual emergency, not here questioned, the right of the legislature to control rents is no longer open to challenge. Nor is the method of accomplishing this result by freezing rents as of a given date. Relief against hardship arising from this method is only mandated where the hardship amounts to deprivation — not a reduction in income per se but only such a reduction which in practical effect can be equated with a taking of the property. There is no constitutional guarantee of the preservation of the return on any property short of the limitation indicated.

"In fixing the conditions under which hardship can be relieved the legislature has always put limitations on the instances in which the purchase price may be used as a base. Among these has always been a requirement that the sale be one within a period reasonably close in time to the application. Such a restriction is hardly questionable. Nor can it be questionable that the legislative body can itself fix the period that is reasonable instead of leaving it to the authority, the courts or anyone else. Barring a determination which is patently unreasonable, such a legislative finding is final. As the passage of time changes a date from current to stale, the cut-off date may so reflect. The fact that there have been applications at times where the sale was reasonably close to the cut-off date does not operate to give a vested interest in that cut-off date. . . ." Plaza Management Co. v. City Rent Agency, 31 A. D. 2d 347, 298 N.Y.S.2d 162, *aff'd*, 25 N.Y.2d 630, 254 N.E.2d 227, 306 N.Y.S.2d 11 (1969).

"In July, 1970, the City of New York adopted Local Law 30, effecting major changes in its rent control laws. The changes were precipitated by several studies indicating massive housing disinvestment or abandonment attributable in large part to uneconomic rents. . . . [A] major feature . . . concerned the adoption of a computerized system of rent control — the MBR system — providing for establishment of maximum base rents (MBR) for each rent-controlled building in the city, and, on the basis of a complex formula, equitable allocation of this building-wide MBR to individual controlled units within the building yielding an individual unit or apartment MBR. The landlord's assured return on capital value was also increased from 6.0 percent to 8.5 percent. Individual apartment rents were permitted to rise automatically to their computer determined MBR at the rate of 7½ percent per year. Maximum rents which are already at or above the computed MBR remain unchanged until the MBR, as adjusted from time to time pursuant to Rent Regulations, exceeds the current maximum rent." 241 East 22nd St. Corp. v. City Rent Agency, 33 N.Y.2d 134, 305 N.E.2d 760, 350 N.Y.S.2d 631 (1973).

d. At levels which authorize specified cost-based increases above rents in existence on a given date.

"Boston Rent Control Administrator John S. Grace announced today he will allow landlords to increase rents . . . this year to cover rising fuel costs.

"Grace, however, stressed that the fuel costs will be shared equally by owners and tenants during 1974.

". . . He said it might be a good idea for banks to come to [land-lords'] aid by deferring payments on mortgage principals during the heating season." Boston Globe, Jan. 10, 1974, at 12, col. 1.

  e. By specifying some political process to which the determination of rent level is to be delegated.

"The main difference between the Rent Stabilization Law of 1969 and its predecessor is that while the 1962 statute is administered entirely by a city agency, the 1969 law is administered in part by an association made up of apartment owners, but under close and detailed supervision and control of official city agencies.

"A somewhat larger permissible return on investment is possible under the 1969 act. Consistently with guidelines required to be pre-scribed, increases over the May 31, 1968 rent may be allowed on re-newed leases or new leases not exceeding 10 percent for a two-year lease or 15 percent for a three-year lease. Certain other kinds of vacancies result in smaller percentage increases. These limitations continue until July 1, 1970. In vacancies occurring after that date, increases may be fixed by administrative action at levels other than those prescribed in the statute.

"The association which is authorized by the act to play a part in rent control is precisely prescribed as a 'Real Estate Industry Stabilization Association.' This group may be either a corporation or an association and shall have as members the owners of not less than 40 percent of the dwelling units affected by the 1969 statute. It shall be registered with the Housing and Development Administration, a city agency which was in existence before the enactment of the 1969 act. . . .

"The statute also establishes a Rent Guidelines Board of nine mem-bers, all appointed by the Mayor and paid by the city, no member of which may be a person who owns real estate covered by the statute or is an officer of a tenants' organization. Its function is to prescribe guide-lines for rent increases within the prescribed limits before July 1, 1970, and to review the problem of rent increases once annually and to estab-lish different levels thereafter.

"Membership by owners of multiple dwellings in the Real Estate Industry Association is voluntary, but if an owner does not join an association the dwelling becomes subject to normal rent control under title Y of chapter 51, in which case the City Rent Agency shall establish the maximum rent on the basis of the rent charged May 31, 1968. . . .

"The ultimate success, or even the utility of the statutory mecha-nism which brings an industry association into an active role or regula-tive responsibility, may be arguable one way or another. But fair latitude should be allowed by the court to the legislative body to generate new and imaginative mechanisms addressed to municipal problems. 'Novelty is no argument against constitutionality.'" 8200 Realty Corp. v. Lindsay, 27 N.Y.2d 124, 261 N.E.2d 647, 313 N.Y.S.2d 733, *app. dism.*, 400 U.S. 962 (1970).

f. By the consequence of the bureaucratic arrangements that are created.

"A major landlord group announced yesterday that it had begun court action to force immediate city approval of a large backlog of rent-rise applications submitted by owners who had made significant improvements in their rent-controlled buildings.

"The group . . . noted that the owners were entitled by law to get rent increases for such improvements. But, the group said, the Department of Rent and Housing Maintenance was far behind in processing the applications, in some cases having failed to dispose of applications for work completed two years ago.

"A spokesman for the city department . . . contended that landlord actions, such as the new court suits, had themselves contributed to the backlog because they had 'tied up' city personnel." New York Times, Dec. 10, 1973.

g. According to how much each tenant ought to pay.

"New York City's Local Law No. 30 and Local Law No. 31 of 1970 were enacted together and became effective on August 1, 1970. The former provided, insofar as here relevant, for general increases in maximum rents up to a limit of 15 percent of the July 31, 1970 maximum rent. The other enactment, Local Law No. 31, exempts a certain class of older persons from Local Law No. 30's increases. More specifically, it exempts from such rent increases any tenant 62 years of age or older, not the recipient of public assistance, whose total annual income — when added to that of other members of the household — does not exceed $4,500, after taxes, and who pays more than one-third of such income for rent. . . .

"We find without substance the plaintiff's principal contention that the exemption accorded to persons 62 years of age or older amounts to a taking of property without compensation on the asserted ground — to quote from the plaintiffs' brief — that it 'effects a reduction in the rent of certain tenants at the expense of their landlords.' Actually, Local Law No. 31 calls for no 'reduction'; it merely provides that for the period of its limited duration — as already noted, until January 1, 1972 — elderly tenants (who meet the other conditions specified) are to be exempt from rent increases which might otherwise be imposed in accordance with Local Law No. 30. . . . Indeed, such older tenants will be required to pay the same rent that they were obligated to pay prior to the enactment of the 1970 legislation, under the then local law which this court, also in the face of a due process attack, sustained as constitutional. . . .

"Nor is there any justification for the charge that Local Law No. 31 deprives the plaintiffs of equal protection of the laws. . . . Certainly, the classification effected by the local law under consideration has such reasonable basis; it has a substantial relation to a legitimate public purpose, namely, the prevention of severe hardship to aging needy citizens resulting from the shortage of low and moderately priced housing accommodations. As bearing on the reasonableness of a classification based on age or income, we but note the many laws which provide for public assistance, social security payments, reduction in real estate taxes for elderly home owners and double exemption on the computation of Federal, State and city income taxes and other protective legislation based wholly on the age or economic need of the recipient." Parrino v. Lindsay, 29 N.Y.2d 30, 272 N.E.2d 67, 323 N.Y.S.2d 689 (1971).

See also Winningham v. U.S. Dept. of HUD, 512 F.2d 617 (5th Cir. 1975):

"The rent supplement program provides financial assistance to six categories of persons meeting specified income requirements and moving into housing financed under certain federal programs. . . .

"In December 1972, Mrs. Winningham, her second husband, and Mrs. Winningham's five children by her first husband moved into Presidential Plaza, a 'section 236' housing development. Although the 'fair market' rent for their apartment was $161.69 per month, the Winninghams were charged only $116.46, the 'basic' monthly rent. After taking up residence at Presidential Plaza, a series of misfortunes beset Mrs. Winningham, including a divorce from her second husband and the termination of child support payments from her first husband. These reverses rendered Mrs. Winningham unable to pay even the basic rent, which was raised to $129.00 on January 1, 1974. The district court found that 'Mrs. Winningham cannot afford to pay anything but a very nominal rent.'

"Confronted with the prospect of having to move her family out of Presidential Plaza, Mrs. Winningham applied for rent supplement assistance. Such assistance would have reduced her rent to $37.00 per month. Because Mrs. Winningham previously had not occupied substandard housing and because she did not fall within any of the other five categories of eligible recipients, her application for a rent supplement was denied by the project owner. . . . Mrs. Winningham contends that, if she is denied rent supplement assistance, she will have to move into substandard housing. She therefore claims that the rent supplement program is unconstitutional as applied to her because the statutory distinction between 'section 236' tenants formerly residing in substandard housing and those such as herself who subsequently will have to locate in substandard housing is not fairly related to the object of the rent supplement program. . . .

"Occupants of substandard housing have a present need of assistance substantiated by their immediate condition. Persons such as Mrs.

Winningham, on the other hand, face only the possibility of being forced into substandard housing.

"They may well find suitable accommodations either under other governmental programs or through assistance of friends or relatives. Painful as the situation may be, Congress is not constitutionally obligated to solve all social problems, especially at one time. It may, as it did here, 'select one phase of one field and apply a remedy there, neglecting the others.'"

2. Consequences

a. What are the arguments for and against each of these methods of fixing rents? Is there some master formula that can take account of the values reflected in all of them? For the argument that the effort itself is unwise, see the testimony of John F. Kain, Professor of Economics at Harvard University, before the Joint Committee on Local Affairs of the Great and General Court of the Commonwealth of Massachusetts, January 26, 1970:

"I find my position today deeply troubling. I have been asked to testify on the economic ramifications of rent control without having at my disposal a clear statement and diagnosis of the problem and without being able to insure that alternative, and I believe better, methods of dealing with the low-income housing problem will be given serious consideration.

"Recent declines in the purchasing power of the dollar have put a financial squeeze on low-income households, particularly those, such as the elderly, living on fixed incomes. These rapid price increases have combined with a tight housing market to produce even larger increases in rents. The tight housing market is primarily the result of federal anti-inflationary policies. A heavy reliance on high interest rates to combat inflation has discouraged housing construction and thereby caused a rise in the price of low-income housing.

"The general increase in housing costs has been aggravated in a few locales by special demand pressures. The most widely recognized of these is that associated with the growth of the student population. Thus, the greatest pressure for rent control comes from the Back Bay, Allston-Brighton, Brookline, Cambridge, and more recently Somerville, where the student populations are large and visible. Whether rent increases in these areas are all that disproportionate, or whether it is just that the presence of students gives the residents of these neighborhoods an obvious group to blame for rent hikes, is less certain than might be imagined. The fondness of students for political organization may also partially explain the considerable interest in rent control in communities and neighborhoods where they reside.

"Still, it is probably true that rents in these neighborhoods have increased more rapidly than in the region as a whole. Differences in rent increases by community are not unusual and in normal times would attract little attention. The present tight housing market, however, causes serious adjustment problems. Households who live in communities experiencing unusual rent increases, such as Cambridge, have little to choose from in adjoining communities. Ironically, the problem may have been aggravated by the intense interest in rent control. Since landlords are reluctant to raise the rents of good long-term tenants, their rents usually lag behind those charged new occupants. But the widespread discussion of rent control may have induced many landlords to raise rents more rapidly out of a fear of having rents frozen below market levels.

"The most pervasive rationale for unusual action at this time is that the impact of national anti-inflationary policy may be very uneven. Dependence on high interest rates to combat inflation may have caused the price of housing to rise more than the price of less capital-intensive goods. As a result, low-income renters, lacking the protection of homeownership, may be bearing a disproportionate share of the burden of these anti-inflationary measures. The case for public action becomes even more compelling if, as rent control proponents assert, many low-income families are being *seriously* injured by abnormal rent increases.

"Presumably the intent of rent-control legislation is to protect certain low-income households from rent increases they cannot afford. Since these persons are clearly a minority of all renters, it is not hard to demonstrate that rent control is a clumsy, inefficient, and probably inequitable means of providing them assistance. Moreover, it is not difficult, in principle, to develop efficient and equitable programs for providing these impacted households with as much assistance as is deemed necessary or desirable.

"The difficulty is whether these more efficient and equitable ways of providing assistance to 'deserving' low-income households are politically feasible. Rent control, as a way of dealing with the low-income housing problem, has one overwhelming political advantage. Its costs and consequences are poorly understood, particularly by the electorate. It gives the impression of being costless, or nearly so. This is, of course, not true. The costs are simply more difficult to calculate and perceive, and they may take longer to appear. Many individuals will imagine they will benefit from rent control when actually the opposite will be true.

"There is still another aspect of this debate over rent control that I find disconcerting. There is probably a strong temptation for the state government to 'solve' the low-income housing crisis by passing rent control. In this way, the state government simply passes the buck to the cities and towns. Thus, we have a problem which is caused by the federal government and which the state ducks by telling the local governments they must solve it. This is indefensible. Local governments are the least prepared to solve the problem of all levels of government. The low-income housing problem is unevenly distributed among local governments. The communities with the most serious problems have the least fiscal capacity. The most severe charge against rent control is that it will weaken the capacity of these low-income communities to deal with their problems in the future. Rent control will have little effect on high-income communities, such as Newton, Belmont, and Weston; but its effects on the fiscal capacity of low-income communities, such as Boston and Somerville, could be ruinous.

"If you feel the problem is serious enough to pass legislation permitting local governments to pass rent-control laws, you should be willing to pass legislation that effectively deals with the low-income housing problem thereby making rent-control legislation in individual cities and towns unnecessary. If you are unwilling to do so, I can only conclude either that you do not believe the problem is really a serious one or that you are not accepting your responsibilities.

"As I indicated previously, it is fairly easy to develop programs for dealing with the plight of low-income renters faced with abnormal rent increases that are both less expensive and more equitable than rent control. However, if I conclude the state government will not act in a meaningful way, then it is far more difficult for me to evaluate rent control. It is easy to show that rent control is a poor method of dealing with the current situation. It is far more difficult to demonstrate conclusively that it is worse than doing nothing. I suspect it is, but I could argue the case with much more conviction if I felt sure the state government would develop meaningful alternative programs of assistance for low-income households hurt by rapid rent increases."

b. As to the entire New York story, see 89 Christopher Inc. v. Joy, 35 N.Y.2d 213, 318 N.E.2d 776, 360 N.Y.S.2d 612 (1974):

"The patchwork of rent-control legislation in recent years has created an impenetrable thicket, confusing not only to laymen but to lawyers. Most important, under legitimate political pressures and the stress of economic and social tensions, the rational resolution of policy considerations vital to the well-being of the people in the City of New York [has] been handled on a day-to-day basis, and often by temporary makeshifts. As a consequence, the legislation contains serious gaps, not readily filled by interpretation based on intention, because there was none, or even by judicial construction to make reasonable and workable schemes that are self-abortive as designed."

c. The existence of rent control inevitably requires additional regulation of the landlord-tenant relationship, to substitute for disciplining functions performed by price adjustment. For example, if rents are below-market, landlords are too free to evict tenants, and this circumstance is greatly magnified if a change from one tenant to another is the occasion for a rent increase.

See, e.g., Gentile v. Rent Control Board, 365 Mass. 343, 312 N.E.2d 210 (1974):

"The tenant argues that no certificate of eviction should have been issued [by the Rent Control Board] because late payment of rent, even chronic late payment of rent, is not a statutory ground for the issuance of such a certificate. . . . The tenant argues that his rent was paid up when the certificate of eviction was issued and that late payment of rent cannot have been intended by the legislature as a ground for eviction from a controlled rental unit.

"We believe that the tenant's failure to pay rent on time 'nearly every month' for a year . . . justifies issuance of a certificate of eviction. . . .

". . . We believe that the Legislature did not intend that there be an adversary hearing before a rent control board considering an application for a certificate of eviction . . ."

See also Mayo v. Boston Rent Control Administrator, 314 N.E.2d 118 (Mass. 1974):

"The twenty units are located in the Custom House Block [in Long Wharf in the city of Boston]. . . .

". . . [O]ne of the principal purposes of the act is to preserve and expand the supply of housing for families of low and moderate income. The . . . twenty units presently carry rents from $145 to $315 a month. If the proposed renovation takes place, rents on the units will increase by at least $120 to $125 a month. . . . The total number of available units, at any and all rental levels, would not be increased by the rehabilitation: the net effect would be to convert twenty low and moderate rental units into twenty high-rent units. Clearly the administrator could not validly permit evictions in these circumstances.

"The landlord emphasizes evidence . . . showing that the apartments . . . have plumbing which needs modern replacements and have unsafe firewalls. However, there is no evidence whatsoever that public authorities have directed that any changes must be made in the interests of health or safety."

Chief Judge Tauro dissented:

"The practical effect of denying the certificates of eviction in this case is to compel the landlord to dedicate his property indefinitely to tenants of low and moderate income. For the time being, the landlord's twenty rental units have, in effect, been converted from private to public housing. This amounts to a *pro tanto* taking for which the landlord is entitled to compensation."

On the other hand, the same court permitted evictions for the purpose of permitting a conversion from rent-controlled tenancy to owner-occupied condominium, so as to "accommodate the Act to a policy of encouraging home ownership." Zussman v. Rent Control Board, 326 N.E.2d 876 (Mass. 1975). (See p.419 *infra*.)

d. See also Lynn, Mass., Daily Evening Item, March 1, 1973, at 3 (concerning a rent-control petition):

> Citizens of Lynn
> Beware of What You Sign Your Name To
> It has come to our attention that there may be a
> Communist
> Action Group
> Infiltrating in the City of Lynn
> Before You Sign Anything
> We Strongly Urge You
> To Consult With Your Attorney
> A Public Service Donation By The Concerned Citizen Committee of Lynn

10 ◆ CHOICE OF TENANT

◆ HUDSON VIEW PROPERTIES v. WEISS
109 Misc. 2d 589, 442 N.Y.S.2d 367 (Sup. Ct. 1981)

PER CURIAM: The record before us is sparse and its principal elements are easily recounted. Landlord served a notice to cure, dated January 24, 1980, upon Julia Weiss "and all other occupants" of the apartment here at issue. That notice to cure stated, ". . . you are violating a substantial obligation of your tenancy . . . , viz., you are allowing a person who is not a tenant to reside in and occupy the premises." The January 24, 1980 notice afforded tenant 10 days to cure the alleged violation. On February 5, 1980, landlord served upon the tenant a thirty day notice of termination, which purported to terminate the subject tenancy on March 17, 1980, on the ground that the violation set forth in the January 24, 1980 notice had not been cured. The instant holdover proceeding was commenced after the tenant failed to surrender the premises as demanded in the February 5, 1980 notice of termination. The petition indicates that the premises are subject to rent control.

Tenant Weiss moved to dismiss the petition for failure to state a cause of action. In support of that motion Ms. Weiss submitted an affidavit, dated April 21, 1980, in which she states, upon information and belief, that the unauthorized occupant referred to by the landlord is one Jack A. Wertheimer ". . . who lives in my apartment, who did not sign the lease, and to whom I am not related by blood or marriage." Ms. Weiss goes on to allege in her affidavit in support of the motion to dismiss, again upon information and belief, that

    . . . the landlord through his attorney has stated that if I marry Mr. Wertheimer, he will withdraw his claim that I have violated the lease and will not seek to evict me. If I remain single, this action will continue. I am moving to dismiss on the grounds that these actions violate the State

411

Human Rights Law [Executive Law] §296(5)(a) and the City Human Rights Law §B1-7.0(5a) which prohibit discrimination in housing on the basis of marital status.

Finally Ms. Weiss notes in her affidavit of April 21, 1980 that she does not believe that the nature of her relationship with Mr. Wertheimer is relevant to her motion. She states, however, that the Court has inquired into that issue, and she goes on to note that Mr. Wertheimer and I have a "close and loving relationship."

In an affidavit submitted on behalf of the landlord by the managing agent for the subject premises, in opposition to tenant's motion to dismiss the petition, it is stated that Ms. Weiss moved into the apartment at issue on or about February 1, 1967 pursuant to a written lease between the then landlord and her husband, Lawrence Weiss. Ms. Weiss was never a signatory to that lease. Mr. Weiss subsequently vacated the premises, but it is unknown whether Mr. Weiss and Ms. Weiss are legally separated or divorced (whether Ms. Weiss or Mr. Wertheimer are single or married is not revealed in the record; what is clear is that they are not married to one another). Thereafter and shortly before the commencement of this proceeding an "unauthorized occupant", identified in the caption as "John Doe" (i.e., Mr. Wertheimer) moved into the apartment.

Landlord, through its managing agent's affidavit in opposition to tenant's motion to dismiss the petition, professes no concern as to the nature of the relationship between the unauthorized occupant of the apartment and Ms. Weiss, other than that he is not a member of the immediate family of the tenant. Landlord notes however, that were he (the unauthorized occupant) a member of the tenant's immediate family, there would be no basis for the proceeding.

Although the lease underlying Ms. Weiss' tenancy has not been included in the record on appeal, the lease, as quoted in the opinion of the Court below, contains a restrictive covenant that ". . . the demised premises and any part thereof shall be occupied only by tenant and members of the immediate family of tenant. . . ." The occupancy of Ms. Weiss — she not having been a party to the original lease — was sanctioned by virtue of her status as a member of the original tenant's immediate family. The New York State Attorney General intervened in this proceeding and, in both the Court below and on this appeal, has joined with the tenant in arguing that the petition fails to state a cause of action (citing State Human Rights Law [Executive Law] §296[5][a]).

Section 296(5)(a) of the State Human Rights Law [Executive Law] provides that:

It shall be an unlawful discriminatory practice for the owner . . . or managing agent of, or other person having the right to sell, rent, or lease a housing accommodation . . . or any agent or employee thereof:

(1) To refuse to sell, rent, lease or otherwise deny to or withhold from any person or group of persons such a housing accommodation because of the . . . marital status of such person or persons [L.1975 ch. 803, eff. on the 60th day after August 9, 1975]. . . .

The pleading at issue is not defective upon its face. Landlord seeks to enforce a restrictive covenant contained in the lease executed at the inception of the subject tenancy. In the case of a statutory tenancy — such as that of the tenant Weiss —

> . . . with the exceptions of the duration of the term, and the amount of rent payable, the rule established by the weight of authority is that insofar as the provisions of a lease which has expired are not in conflict with the then prevailing emergency rent statutes, and are not confined to the period of the expired lease, they are projected into the statutory tenancy, and will continue in effect during the term of the statutory tenancy. [Rausch, New York Landlord and Tenant 2d ed. §286]

The law favors free and unrestricted use of property, and all doubts and ambiguities in a lease will be resolved in favor of the natural right to free use and enjoyment of premises against restrictions. A landlord, however, does have the right to limit a tenant's use of the premises and where covenants restricting the use of property are reasonable and not contrary to public policy, they will be enforced by the courts. Indeed it has long been held that parties to a lease may, by express provision therein, restrict the uses to which the lessee may put the demised premises, and lease provisions restricting the use of premises to "tenant and members of tenant's immediate family" — the very provision here sought to be enforced by the landlord — have consistently been sustained. . . . Tenant alludes to no judicial or statutory authority which expressly proscribes or declares it to be against public policy for landlord to limit the use of demised premises to the tenant or tenants and members of his or their immediate family. . . .

We are cognizant that §300 of the State Human Rights Law [Executive Law] provides that "the provisions of this article [including of course §296(5)(a)] shall be construed liberally for the accomplishment of the purposes thereof" and that §B1-11.0 of the City Law on Human Rights similarly so provides. . . . There is nonetheless little in this sparse record to suggest that the landlord, in seeking to enforce the restrictive covenant in the lease limiting occupancy to the tenant and members of tenant's immediate family, had any interest in the marital status of the tenant Weiss or the occupant Wertheimer, other than that Wertheimer was not a member of Weiss' immediate family. An interest in ascertaining whether an occupant qualifies for occupancy of a demised premises, under a lease provision authorizing occupancy by tenant and members of tenant's immediate family (i.e., whether the occupant is a spouse, son, parent or other relation within the scope of "immediate family") does not *ipso facto* connote discrimination on the basis of "marital status"; thus we are not persuaded by this sparse record that there has been a showing of discrimination by the landlord against the tenant upon the basis of her "marital status". While clearly no cause of action lies under a restrictive covenant in a lease limiting occupancy to the tenant and members of tenant's immediate family, where the tenant has married a newly arrived occupant, it does not follow that a landlord is automatically precluded by §296(5)(a) from enforcing such a restrictive covenant where the tenant and the new occupant are, for whatever reason, unmarried. In summary, landlord's cause of action predicated upon the covenant in the specified lease restricting occupancy of the subject premises to the tenant and members of tenant's immediate family does not appear to us to constitute discrimination per se on the basis of tenant's "marital status." . . .

ASCH, Justice, dissenting. . . . I find unpersuasive the remonstrances by landlord that the lower court's decision has the effect of nullifying a landlord's right to pass upon and approve those who are to occupy his premises. Certainly, the existing lease clause restricting occupancy to close family members, impinges to a large degree on a landlord's veto over those who are to share in the premises. A close family member may be just as objectionable as an unrelated party deciding to share house with an unmarried mate. But, as the Court noted below, all things being equal, discrimination on the basis of marital status is precisely what HRL §296 proscribes. In short, that the objectionable occupant is unrelated by marriage to tenant may not, consistent with the Human Rights Law be used as a predicate for ouster.

Landlord's final challenge to the dismissal of its petition focuses on the rent controlled status of the premises in dispute. It was never the intent of the legislature, argues landlord to extend the benefits of those laws to lovers. To the contrary, contends landlord, the statutory structure reveals a clear bias in favor of bestowing rent advantages on the families and spouses of rent control tenants. Prime reliance is placed by landlord on §56 of New York City Rent and Eviction Regulations which states that where a tenant no longer occupies his apartment, a certificate of eviction may issue, except when the remaining occupant is either the surviving spouse or some other member of the deceased tenant's family. . . .

While these regulations do show a pro-family bias, they have no role to play under the facts of this case. Tenant Weiss has neither died nor vacated unit 15H. The Human Rights Law permits Wertheimer to occupy the apartment. Hence, he falls within the broad definition of tenant spelled out in §Y51-3.0m of New York City's Rent and Rehabilitation Law and is entitled to continue residing in the apartment. Whether, if Ms. Weiss left the apartment, Wertheimer could maintain his possession is a knotty question which need not be addressed here. For purposes of this case, it is sufficient to note that under §296 of the HRL, Ms. Weiss and Wertheimer are completely within their rights in staying in apartment 15H.

As a postscript, it should be noted that the grounds for the dissent are fairly narrow. Concededly, the occupants of the apartment "maintain a close and loving relationship." Yet, it is indisputable that the landlord required a formal marriage as the essential condition for continuing the tenancy. The marriage certificate does not always supply a litmus test for love. Further, under the Human Rights Law, it cannot serve as the key which opens the door to the tenancy of an apartment.

The landlord still has ample discretion to select and reject tenants provided that he does not use categories interdicted under the law, such as, marital status, in screening their suitability.

I would affirm the lower court's dismissal of the petition.

Subsequently the appellate division of the supreme court reversed in a unanimous decision, relying on the dissent of Justice Asch, 86 A.D.2d 803, 448 N.Y.S.2d 649 (1982). On appeal, the New York Court of Appeals reversed again, reinstating the landlord's petition to evict. 59 N.Y.2d 733, 450 N.E.2d 234, 463 N.Y.S.2d 428 (1983). The court stated that the landlord had not discriminated in violation of the Human Rights law:

> The landlord received the right by virtue of the covenant in the lease to restrict the occupants and the tenant agreed to this restriction. Were the additional tenant a female unrelated to the tenant, the lease would be violated without reference to marriage. The fact that the additional tenant here involved is a man with whom the tenant has a loving relationship is simply irrelevant.

Other New York cases include Avest Seventh Corp. v. Ringelheim, 109 Misc. 2d 284, 440 N.Y.S.2d 159 (Civ. Ct. 1981) (lesbian lover is not eligible to remain as "member of [tenant's] immediate family"; "to hold otherwise, this or any other court would lend itself to the ultimate destruction of the family unit, the foundation of society"), *reversed mem.*, relying on *Chin, infra*, 116 Misc. 2d 402, 458 N.Y.S.2d 903 (App. Term 1982); 420 East 80th Co. v. Chin, 115 Misc. 2d 195, 455 N.Y.S.2d 42, *aff'd*, 97 A.D.2d 390, 468 N.Y.S.2d 9 (1983) ("Realities of urban life [that] allow many different types of nontraditional families" mean that male tenant who shares an apartment with a homosexual lover has not committed substantial violation of lease and therefore cannot be evicted); Evangelista Associates v. Bland, 117 Misc. 2d 558, 458 N.Y.S.2d 996 (Civ. Ct. 1983) (Male tenant who began living with male friend committed substantial violation of lease requirement limiting occupancy to immediate family; New York law does not bar discrimination based on sexual preference.); Yorkshire House Assoc. v. Lulkin, 114 Misc. 2d 40, 450 N.Y.S.2d 962 (Civ. Ct. 1982) (lover of tenant allowed to stay after tenant leaves, because *if* they had been married spouse would have been allowed to stay); Young v. Carruth, 113 Misc. 2d 586, 452 N.Y.S.2d 978 (App. Term 1982), *aff'd*, 89 A.D.2d 466, 455 N.Y.S.2d 776 (1982) (executor allowed to evict woman with whom decedent had lived extra-maritally); L.V. Realty v. Desommosy, 119 Misc. 2d 213, 462 N.Y.S.2d 584 (Civ. Ct. 1983) (landlord could not evict lover while tenant was alive, but need not grant surviving lover renewal lease); Leonedas Realty Corp. v. Brodowsky, 115 Misc. 2d 88, 454 N.Y.S.2d 183 (Civ. Ct. 1982) (singles-only provision is invalid discrimination according to marital status).

Note

Held: No illegal discrimination in refusing to *sell* a house to an unmarried couple. McFadden v. Elma Country Club, 26 Wash. App. 195, 613 P.2d 146 (1980); Prince George's County v. Greenbelt Homes, Inc., 49 Md. App. 314, 431 A.2d 745 (1981).

◆ 1983 NEW YORK LAWS CH. 403

§235-f. Unlawful restrictions on occupancy. 1. As used in this section, the terms:

(a) "Tenant" means a person occupying or entitled to occupy a residential rental premises who is either a party to the lease or rental agreement for such premises or is a statutory tenant pursuant to the emergency housing rent control law or the city rent and rehabilitation law or article seven-c of the multiple dwelling law.

(b) "Occupant" means a person, other than a tenant or a member of a tenant's immediate family, occupying a premises with the consent of the tenant or tenants.

2. It shall be unlawful for a landlord to restrict occupancy of residential premises, by express lease terms of otherwise, to a tenant or tenants or to such tenants and immediate family. Any such restriction in a lease or rental agreement entered into or renewed before or after the effective date of this section shall be unenforceable as against public policy.

3. Any lease or rental agreement for residential premises entered into by one tenant shall be construed to permit occupancy by the tenant, immediate family of the tenant, one additional occupant, and dependent children of the occupant.

4. Any lease or rental agreement for residential premises entered into by two or more tenants shall be construed to permit occupancy by tenants, immediate family of tenants, occupants and dependent children of occupants; provided that the total number of tenants and occupants, excluding occupants' dependent children, does not exceed the number of tenants specified in the current lease or rental agreement, and that at least one tenant or a tenants' spouse occupies the premises as his primary residence.

5. The tenant shall inform the landlord of the name of any occupant within thirty days following the commencement of occupancy by such person or within thirty days following a request by the landlord.

6. No occupant nor occupant's dependent child shall, without express written permission of the landlord, acquire any right to continued occupancy in the event that the tenant vacates the premises or acquire any other rights of tenancy; provided that nothing in this section shall be construed to reduce or impair any right or remedy otherwise available to any person residing in any housing accommodation on the effective date of this section which accrued prior to such date.

7. Any provision of a lease or rental agreement purporting to waive a provision of this section is null and void.

8. Nothing in this section shall be construed as invalidating or impairing the operation of, or the right of a landlord to restrict occupancy in order to comply with federal, state or local laws, regulations, ordinances or codes.

9. Any person aggrieved by a violation of this section may maintain an action in any court of competent jurisdiction for:

(a)   an injunction to enjoin and restrain such unlawful practice;
(b)   actual damages sustained as a result of such unlawful practice; and
(c)   court costs.

Notes

1. Does this statute overrule the New York Court of Appeals' *Weiss* decision? Does it resolve all of the issues raised in the above cases? What if a New York landlord refuses to rent a vacant apartment to an unmarried heterosexual or homosexual couple?

2. Why didn't the New York legislature explicitly outlaw housing discrimination based on sexual preference? See Wis. Stat. Ann. §101.22 (West 1983); D.C. Code §1-2515 (1981).

3. Could the New York courts have interpreted "marital status" differently? See Hess v. Fair Employment & Housing Commission, 138 Cal. App. 3d 232, 187 Cal. Rptr. 712 (1982) (marital status includes unmarried couples); Loveland v. Leslie, 21 Wash. App. 84, 583 P.2d 664 (1978) (marital status includes two men); Hubert v. Williams, 133 Cal.

App. 3d 1, 184 Cal. Rptr. 161 (1982) (civil rights statute interpreted to prohibit all arbitrary discrimination including that based on a person's homosexuality). In Marina Point, Ltd. v. Wolfson, 30 Cal. 3d 721, 640 P.2d 115, 180 Cal. Rptr. 496 (1982), the California Supreme Court held that California's anti-discrimination law applies to "all persons" and bars a landlord from enforcing a "no children" policy. Justice Richardson, dissenting, asked: "Do our middle aged or older citizens, having worked long and hard, having raised their own children, having paid both their taxes and their dues to society retain a right to spend their remaining years in a relatively quiet, peaceful and tranquil environment of their own choice?"

4. Would protection of unmarried homosexual and heterosexual couples "lend itself to the ultimate destruction of the family unit"? In Atkisson v. Kern County Housing Authority, 59 Cal. App. 3d 89, 130 Cal. Rptr. 375 (1976), the court noted that a ban against unmarried, cohabitating adults would include a couple with children of their own. The court said, "As such, it would effectively prevent one of the parents from living with and raising in a close intimate relationship his or her own children."

5. What should be the scope of protections afforded to "quasi-marital" relationships? Should the tenants have to prove they have a "close and loving" relationship? See Yorkshire House Assoc. v. Lulkin, 114 Misc. 2d 40, 450 N.Y.S.2d 933 (Civ. Ct. 1982) (court suggests that a sworn statement by tenants should give rise to an irrebuttable presumption that such a relationship does exist). Should the protection be limited to those with a "close and loving" relationship? See King v. Menachem, 113 Misc. 2d 63, 450 N.Y.S.2d 933 (App. Term 1981) (landlord claimed that having a live-in nurse violated terms of tenancy).

6. Should Congress pass a federal statute to protect homosexual and heterosexual couples? What about families with children, welfare recipients, or handicapped persons? Should the protection extend to pets? What about a deaf or blind person who needs a dog?

7. Can the evictions by New York landlords be explained on a basis other than discrimination? In Leonedas Realty Corp. v. Brodowsky, 115 Misc. 2d 88, 454 N.Y.S.2d 103 (Civ. Ct. 1982), the court said, "[The landlord] maintains that he is not seeking to evict the tenants because of their marital status but is willing to permit them to remain provided they sign a lease and pay the appropriate vacancy rent increase which the tenant has refused to do."

11 ◆ CONDOMINIUM CONVERSION

The contemporary estate relationship called condominium is discussed in Chapter 20. This chapter, however, deals with the widespread conversion of rental housing to condominiums that has led to efforts to protect tenants from being forced into move-or-buy situations.

◆ ZUSSMAN v. RENT CONTROL BOARD
367 Mass. 561, 326 N.E.2d 876 (1975)

BRAUCHER, Justice. A Brookline landlord, subject to rent control under St. 1970, c.842 (the Act), sought certificates of eviction for the purpose of converting "controlled rental units" into condominiums. The Rent Control Board of Brookline (the board) denied the applications, and the landlord sought judicial review. Like the Municipal Court of Brookline and the Superior Court, we hold that in the circumstances "the landlord seeks to recover possession for . . . just cause," that "his purpose is not in conflict with the provisions and purposes" of the Act, and that the certificates of eviction should therefore issue under §9(a)(10) of the Act. . . .

Zussman borrowed $950,000 · in construction and permanent financing, refurbished hallways, improved electrical systems, and modernized units as they became vacant. He demonstrated his willingness to do all work in a manner least likely to inconvenience the tenants, and offered each tenant a preferential opportunity to buy at a lower price than that offered to the public, including favorable financing and an offer to repurchase after two years at the same price if the purchaser was dissatisfied. He has offered any tenant not desiring to purchase a full year to vacate. Because of his inability to recover possession, he has lost sales and has returned deposits. . . . The board and the tenants contend that this case is governed by Mayo v. Boston Rent Control Admr., 365

Mass. 575, 314 N.E.2d 118 (1974). There we declared that a landlord's purpose of "optional upgrading" of controlled rental units was "in conflict with the provisions and purposes" of the Act, and therefore did not constitute "just cause" for eviction under §9(a)(10). The *Mayo* case would be more directly in point if the landlord here sought to evict his tenants in order to remove all the controlled rental units temporarily from the housing market, to upgrade them and then to reintroduce them into the housing market as condominiums for families with higher incomes. We do not rule on such a case. But the conversion proposed here is piecemeal, unit by unit, and we think it need not be in conflict with the provisions and purposes of the act, even if there is some rehabilitation or "optional upgrading" in the process.

Several provisions of the Act indicate a purpose to accommodate the Act to a policy of encouraging home ownership. . . . Condominiums offer the city dweller significant advantages over rental housing. Condominium ownership may be well suited to the housing problems of low income families. The Legislature has provided for condominiums in G.L. c.183A. We conclude that accommodation of the Act to a policy of encouraging home ownership in condominium form is not in conflict with its provisions and purposes. . . .

◆ GRACE v. TOWN OF BROOKLINE
379 Mass. 43, 399 N.E.2d 1038 (1979)

LIACOS, Justice. A condominium developer, a condominium owner and a potential condominium purchaser challenge, as unauthorized by statute and prohibited by the Massachusetts and the United States Constitutions, two amendments to art. XXXVIII of the by-laws of the town of Brookline. The disputed amendments protect tenants by regulating the procedure for their eviction from apartments converted into condominium units. We uphold their validity. . . .

The pertinent facts stipulated are as follows. From 1970 until December 31, 1975, the town of Brookline generally regulated and controlled rents and evictions under the general rent control enabling provisions of St. 1970, c.842. On December 16, 1975, a Brookline special town meeting rescinded its approval of c.842. In its place, under the authority specifically granted to Brookline by St. 1970, c.843, the town meeting adopted art. XXXVIII of the Brookline by-laws (referred to hereafter as the "by-law"). Brookline has regulated rents and evictions pursuant to c.843 and the by-law since January 1, 1976.

Section 9(a) of the by-law enumerates the bases on which the rent control board may issue certificates of eviction with regard to rent-controlled housing units. Prior to July 25, 1978, §9(a) provided two grounds for eviction of tenants residing in rent controlled apartments which were slated for, or had already undergone, conversion to condominiums. Section 9(a)(8) allowed a landlord to obtain a certificate of eviction if he sought to occupy a unit for himself or a member of his immediate family; section 9(a)(10) authorized a landlord to bring an action to recover possession of a unit "for any other just cause." The first of these provisions permitted a purchaser of a newly converted condominium unit who sought occupancy to apply for a certificate of eviction. The second allowed a developer to seek certificates of eviction for an entire building intended for conversion to condominium units. The rent control board of Brookline routinely granted developers such certificates upon compliance with particular guidelines it had promulgated.

On July 25, 1978, a special town meeting of Brookline voted to amend §9(a)(8) and (10) of the by-law. The effect of the amendment to §9(a)(10) was to render certificates of eviction unavailable to condominium developers. At the same time, the amendment to §9(a)(8) preserves, for the condominium purchaser who seeks to occupy the unit, the opportunity to evict a tenant who refuses to vacate voluntarily. However, if the tenant was in possession of the unit when the new landlord acquired ownership, that tenant is protected by a mandatory six-month stay of issuance of a certificate of eviction. The amendment to §9(a)(8) also provides for an additional six-month delay if the board determines that a hardship exists. After approval by the Attorney General, pursuant to G.L. c.40, §32, both amendments took effect on September 27, 1978.

The plaintiff Grace is a developer of a condominium project in Brookline. On January 13, 1978, he purchased several buildings in order to convert the thirty-five apartments therein for sale as condominiums. After entering into purchase and sale agreements with prospective purchasers who were not tenants and who intended to occupy the units, Grace applied to the board for certificates of eviction. In each case decided before July 25, 1978, on finding compliance with the guidelines, the board granted Grace a certificate of eviction.

Prior to enactment of the by-law amendments, the plaintiff Lonabocker contracted to buy one of the units owned by Grace. She obtained a commitment for mortgage financing and sold her residence, expecting to occupy the condominium. After July 25, 1978, Lonabocker and Grace were disqualified from applying for a certificate of eviction. Because she was unable to obtain occupancy of the unit, Lonabocker's mortgage financing was cancelled. She has not purchased the unit.

The plaintiff Ehrenworth purchased a unit from Grace on October 20, 1978, in order to occupy it as his residence. At the time of the purchase, the unit was occupied by a tenant. Ehrenworth filed an application for a certificate of eviction which was approved by the board on December 19, 1978. As of March 2, 1979, the date of the parties' stipulation, the board had not issued a certificate of eviction, by virtue of the operation of §9(a)(8), as amended. Since purchasing the unit from Grace, and until at least March 2, 1979, Ehrenworth received rent from the tenant occupying the unit. The rental receipts, however, were insufficient to offset the monthly carrying charges incurred by Ehrenworth on the unit. Grace agreed to bear the difference between the rents collected and the costs incurred for a period of one year from the passage of title.

On November 14, 1978, a Brookline special town meeting voted to amend the by-law further by imposing a general six-month moratorium on the issuance of any certificate of eviction against a tenant who was in possession of an apartment when it was purchased as a condominium unit. The moratorium, which was approved by the Attorney General on December 28, 1978, bore an expiration date of June 15, 1979.

The plaintiffs bear an onerous burden in seeking to invalidate the by-law amendments. We have consistently stated that in the judicial review of municipal by-laws and ordinances "every presumption is to be made in favor of their validity, and that their enforcement will not be refused unless it is shown beyond reasonable doubt that they conflict with the applicable enabling act or the Constitution." Crall v. Leominster, 362 Mass. 95, 102, 284 N.E.2d 610, 615 (1972), and cases cited. In seeking to meet their burden, the plaintiffs rely heavily on our decision in Zussman v. Rent Control Bd. of Brookline, 367 Mass. 561, 326 N.E.2d 876 (1975), where we struck down eviction restrictions similar to those presented here. *Zussman*, however, is distinguishable in at least one critical respect. The court in *Zussman* ruled invalid emergency regulations promulgated by the Brookline rent control board under authority that the board presumed had been granted by St. 1970, c.842, a statute of Statewide application. According to the court, by enacting regulations which tend to discourage condominium coversion, the Board had accorded insufficient recognition to the policy, implicit in c.842, of encouraging home ownership. The regulations foundered on that single premise.

The by-law amendments under consideration here face no such obstacle. Unlike the regulations in *Zussman*, the by-law amendments were enacted under authority granted in c.843 especially to Brookline for the purpose of enabling that town to confront, singularly, its housing difficulties. The two chapters differ in crucial respects. As we noted in Marshal House, Inc. v. Rent Control Bd. of Brookline, 358 Mass. at 697, 266 N.E.2d at 884 [1971]:

Chapter 843 states that "a serious public emergency exists in the town of Brookline with respect to the housing of a substantial number of the citizens of said town." It goes on to describe the emergency as created in part by an "expanding student population . . . [and] a substantial elderly population," causes not assigned in the comparable statement of emergency in c.842. Chapter 843 under §2 grants the town broad general regulatory powers, unencumbered by the various restrictions and exemptions contained in §3 of c.842, to deal with its particular housing crisis. It is apparent from a comparison of §§1 and 2 of c.843 and comparable sections of c.842 that the problem in Brookline was unique. . . .

Furthermore, none of the provisions cited in *Zussman* as indicating the c.842 policy of encouragment of home ownership is present in c.843. See *Zussman, supra* 367 Mass. at 566-567, 326 N.E.2d 876. Absent provisions to the same effect, we decline to read such a policy into c.843.

The plaintiffs also claim that the by-law amendments are unauthorized by c.843 because they obstruct the intent made explicit in §2, that "evictions may be regulated by the rent board so as to remove hardships or correct inequities for both *the owner* and tenants of such housing accommodations" (emphasis supplied). We agree that the interests of condominium developers and purchasers are to be given due consideration under c.843. It is clear, however, that the major thrust of the act was directed at the need to control "abnormally high rents" and the "substantial and increasing shortage of rental housing accommodations" which most severely afflict "families of low and moderate income and elderly on fixed income." See c.843, §1. By retarding the pace of condominium conversion, the by-law amendments further this purpose. In doing so, moreover, they fairly accommodate the interests of building owners and condominium developers and purchasers. They do not deprive landlords of their reasonable profits. Nor do they preclude condominium conversion altogether. Conversion is permissible and may proceed unimpeded when the tenant chooses to buy the unit or vacates voluntarily. This accommodation to the interests of condominium developers and purchasers of condominium units is particularly significant since such conversions, while avoiding the hardships incidental to eviction of tenants, have a nonetheless deleterious effect on the rental housing market.

We hold, therefore, that the by-law amendments are both consistent with and authorized by St. 1970, c.843.

G.L. c.183A. The plaintiffs also assert that the tendency of the by-law amendments to decelerate condominium conversion conflicts with the purpose of G.L. c.183A, entitled "Condominiums." We disagree. Chapter 183A is a neutral provision, neither favoring nor disfavoring condominium conversion. The apparent purpose of the statute was to clarify the legal status of the condominium in light of its peculiar characteristics, and not to grant this hybrid form of property ownership exceptional protection from social legislation. The language in §4 of c.183A, cited by the plaintiffs, that each unit owner of a condominium "shall be entitled to the exclusive ownership and possession of his unit" does not contradict this view. In the context of the entire section and the act as a whole, the evident intent of these words is to define the rights and responsibilities of condominium owners in a particular building vis-à-vis one another, and not to insulate them, uniquely, from the reach of rent and eviction control. . . .

The plaintiffs' "taking" argument rests on an apparent distinction between the regulation of use and the transfer of rights. They suggest that the amendments are illegal because, rather than regulate what uses are or are not permitted, the amendments determine who, as between a tenant in possession and an owner, shall enjoy a permitted use. In effect, the plaintiffs contend, the amendments transfer the right to possess from the owner to the tenant and compel the condominium owner to become a landlord.

The United States Supreme Court consistently has upheld rent control statutes as proper exercises of the police power in times of public emergency. This court also has upheld such acts, including the enabling legislation for the local provisions challenged today. The import of these cases is that a shortage of housing threatens the public interest and that legislation which preserves the rental market for low, moderate, and fixed income persons promotes health, safety, and welfare generally. In short, a housing crisis justifies the exercise of the police power.

A particular provision, nevertheless, may go too far. . . . In a strict sense, the amendments do effect a transfer of rights incident to ownership: the tenant in possession at the time of conversion is permitted to remain in possession even though the owner seeks recovery for his own personal use. In our view, however, this redistribution of rights is not unlike the redistribution of rights effected by rent and eviction control generally.

◆ LOETERMAN v. TOWN OF BROOKLINE
524 F. Supp. 1325 (D. Mass. 1981), *cert. denied*, 456 U.S. 906 (1982)

McNaught, District Judge. This matter is before the court on the parties' cross motions for summary judgment. The plaintiffs are Ben and Mardi Loeterman, purchasers of a condominium unit in Brookline, Massachusetts, and the defendants are the Town of Brookline (the Town) and the Rent Control Board of Brookline (Rent Control Board). The Attorney General of Massachusetts has also intervened in this action as a defendant. The plaintiffs seek a declaration that the Town's bylaw amendment prohibiting owners of individual condominium units from recovering possession of their units from tenants under certain conditions is unconstitutional as being a violation of their Fifth and Fourteenth Amendment rights, and an injunction against the enforcement of the bylaw amendment by the Town or its agents or employees.

The bylaw amendment (the so-called Ban Amendment) and its predecessors were discussed by the court in the case of Chan v. Town of Brookline, 484 F. Supp. 1283 (D. Mass. 1980), wherein the court denied preliminary injunctive relief against the Town with respect to plaintiffs who had purchased their condominium prior to the Ban Amendment's enactment by the Town. The present action was consolidated with the *Chan* case in November, 1980. Before reaching the issue of the constitutionality of the Ban Amendment with respect to the Chans, the *Chan* action was dismissed for mootness in December, 1980, as the tenant occupying the Chans' unit voluntarily vacated the premises. Consequently, the court is not called upon in the instant case to decide the constitutionality of the ordinance as applied to persons who purchased their units with the intent to occupy them in accordance with then applicable eviction procedures (the Six Plus Six Amendment), but who may be subject to a permanent prohibition against evicting tenants in possession by the subsequent enactment of the Ban Amendment.

The gist of the Ban Amendment, amending section 9(a)(8) of Article XXXVIII of the Town bylaws (Rent and Eviction Control Bylaw), is that the owner of an individual condominium unit is precluded from recovering possession of his unit from a tenant who has occupied it continuously since the time before the recording of the master condominium deed. The tenant has the equivalent of a life tenancy in the property so long as the amendment is in effect, and the owner may only recover possession for the use and occupancy of himself or other family members designated in the bylaw provision upon a tenant's voluntary departure or death. The Ban Amendment was approved at a town meeting on May 7, 1979. It was enacted as part of the Town's Rent and Eviction Control Bylaw and applied only to controlled rental units as defined in section 3(b) of Article XXXVIII.

There is no dispute among the parties as to the facts relating to the Loetermans' purchase of the condominium and its occupancy by a tenant at the time of sale. The plaintiffs entered into a purchase and sale agreement on March 29, 1979 to purchase the unit for $35,000 in a rent controlled building for the purpose of occupying it as their personal residence. They took title to the unit on May 17, 1979, ten days after the Ban Amendment was passed at the Brookline town meeting. Plaintiffs do not dispute that they knew of the enactment of the amendment at the time they took title to their unit. At the time of sale the unit was, and continues to be occupied by a tenant who has lived there continuously since a time prior to the recording of the master condominium deed. Plaintiffs still desire to occupy the unit for dwelling purposes. The tenant, however, has refused to vacate the premises voluntarily.

Section 6 of the bylaw provides that the rents established for controlled rental units shall be adjusted "to assure that rents . . . are established at levels which yield to landlords a fair net operating income for such units." Prior to November 27, 1979, the tenant occupying the Loetermans' unit paid a monthly rent of $315.00. On November 27, 1979, plaintiffs were granted a rent increase by the Brookline Rent Control Board of $96.00 per month, raising the monthly maximum rent to $411.00. Thereafter, on June 30, 1981, plaintiffs received a rent increase of $110.00 per month, increasing the monthly maximum rent to $521.00.

The plaintiffs argue that the amendment unlawfully effects a redistribution of property by transferring from the owner to the tenant the right to use the property in a particular way for a public purpose. They do not dispute the existence of an increasing shortage of rental housing accommodations in the Town, exacerbated by a rapid and an increasing rate of conversion of rental units to condominiums, or that such a rental housing shortage poses a threat to the public health, safety, and welfare, particularly that of the elderly and low income households. The thrust of their opposition to the Ban Amendment is that the amendment, unlike its predecessor, the "Six Plus Six" Amendment, effectively prohibits an owner from ever occupying his unit and that such a prohibition constitutes a "taking" of property violative of the Fifth and Fourteenth Amendments. According to plaintiffs, the fact that the Ban Amendment may operate to extinguish an owner's right of possession altogether distinguishes the present case from other cases where courts have upheld the government's right to prohibit particular uses of property, but where the owner nevertheless remains in possession or retains the right to use and occupy the premises he owns. Plaintiffs further urge that the Town's grant to the tenant of a right to occupy the premises indefinitely compels a property owner to dedicate his property indefinitely to the rental market, a practice held unlawful in another context in Rivera v. R. Cobian Chinea and Co., 181 F.2d 974 (1st Cir. 1950).

The defendants and defendant-intervenor respond that the Ban Amendment does not operate as a taking of property in that the bylaw serves a legitimate public purpose of assuring an adequate supply of rental housing and allows purchasers of individual condominium units the right to receive rent and enjoy all other traditional incidents of ownership except occupancy. It is argued that a prohibition of only one use does not render plaintiffs' property worthless so as to amount to a taking requiring compensation. Defendants also contend that the plaintiffs here, as distinguished from the property owner in Kaiser Aetna v. United States, 444 U.S. 164 (1979), had no legitimate investment-backed expectation that has been thwarted by the Town. In this regard defendants focus upon the chronology of events surrounding the Loetermans' purchase of their unit.

The private interest asserted by the Loetermans is the right to use and occupy premises to which they lawfully took title and the correlative right to exclude others. The right to exclude has been recognized as an important element of private property ownership. Kaiser Aetna v. United States, *supra*. An examination of the facts in this case, however, leads me to conclude that this right is not compensable under the Fifth and Fourteenth Amendments. First of all, the Loetermans had no legitimate *expectation* of occupying their condominium at the time they purchased it. While the Loetermans entered into the purchase and sale agreement for the condominium unit before the Town enacted the Ban Amendment, the actual purchase of the property occurred ten days after the amendment was passed at the Brookline town meeting. Plaintiffs, therefore, were on notice that they would not be able to evict the tenant occupying the unit and reasonably knew or should have known that the continued use of their unit for rental housing was mandated by the Ban Amendment. Under these circumstances they had no legitimate expectation of occupying the unit themselves. . . .

In connection with the Loetermans' argument that the Ban Amendment goes "too far" in restricting a well recognized element of private property ownership by preventing occupancy of the premises by the owners themselves, the court finds it significant that the Ban Amendment does not operate to deny the Loetermans an economically viable and reasonable use of their property. Under the applicable rent control bylaws, plaintiffs here are entitled to a fair net operating income from their unit and retain other economic benefits ordinarily associated with the ownership of rental property. I am thus not persuaded that the Ban Amendment goes too far in restricting the owners' use of their property, particularly where there is no question that the amendment serves a legitimate public purpose of slowing the rate of reduction of rental housing accommodations in Brookline pending the Town's further study of the problem in consideration of long-range solutions to the increasing shortage of rental housing. While the Ban Amendment undeniably affects the present and future value of plaintiffs' property, I am not persuaded that the amendment unduly interferes with plaintiffs' rights so as to amount to a taking of property without just compensation. . . .

The Court of Appeals for the First Circuit remanded for reconsideration in light of Loretto v. Teleprompter Manhattan CATV Corp., 458 U.S. 419 (1982), see Chapter 22, p.1279. The district court again granted the town's motion for summary judgment. By the time the case returned to the court of appeals, the tenant had vacated and the apartment was available for occupancy by the Loetermans. The court held that the case had become moot. Loeterman v. Town of Brookline, 709 F.2d 116 (1st Cir. 1983).

Notes

1. San Francisco's condominium ordinance provides for lower income households by requiring developers converting buildings with more than fifty units to reserve ten percent of the units for low- and moderate-income housing. The ordinance further provides that any unit occupied by low- or moderate-income persons prior to conversion must be priced so that the unit is not removed from the city's low- and moderate-income housing stock. San Francisco Mun. Code §§1341, 1385(b). See also Bryant, California and Federal Lower Income Housing Laws: A Compilation and Analysis (Los Angeles County Bar Assoc. 1978).

2. New York's takes a different approach to protecting tenants when buildings are changed over to cooperative or condominium ownership. State law provides for "eviction plans," under which tenants can be evicted at the end of their current leases, and for "non-eviction plans," under which occupants desiring to remain renters do so as tenants under a building ownership arrangement that gradually becomes dominated by occupants. After recent amendments to the law, an eviction plan can be implemented after 51 percent of the tenants approve, and a non-eviction plan after 15 percent agree. The effect is that the economic gains from conversion to a cooperative or a condominium are to be shared between owners and tenants, because the owner must make an attractive offer to tenants to obtain their participation. See N.Y. Gen. Bus. Law §352-4eeee (1982).

12 ◆ PUBLIC HOUSING

A. BACKGROUND

◆ FRIEDMAN, PUBLIC HOUSING AND THE POOR: AN OVERVIEW
54 Calif. L. Rev. 642, 645-652 (1966)

The public housing law is one of a vaguely defined group of statutes called "social" or "welfare" legislation.

It would be a mistake to suppose (if anyone did) that the Wagner-Steagall Act arose solely out of a gradual persuasion of decent-minded people that the slums were odious, crowded, and evil, and that the federal government had a duty to relieve the sufferings of the poor. The social and economic conditions in the slums provided the opportunity, the background, and much of the emotive power of the law. Yet reformers had long dreamed in vain of public housing. And the slums were surely no worse than they had been in the nineteenth century, though possibly they were larger.

In 1937 the country was suffering from a deep and dangerous depression. Fully one-quarter of the work force was unemployed during the worst days of the depression. In the spring of 1933, thirteen to fifteen million were unemployed. Millions of families were barely making a living. The number of "poor people" in the country had been vastly increased; indeed, many of the "poor people" were formerly members of the middle class, who had enjoyed prosperity in the twenties. They retained their middle-class culture and their outlook, their articulateness, their habit of expressing their desires at the polls. There were, therefore, millions of candidates for public housing who did not belong (as later was true) to the class of the "problem poor"; rather they were members of what we might call the submerged middle class. The attractiveness of public housing was enormously enhanced because the potential clientele was itself enormous, composed of millions of relatively articulate citizens, angry and dispirited at their unjust descent into poverty. Public housing was not supported by the dregs of society; a discontented army of men and women of high demands and high expectations stood ready to insist on decent housing from government or at least stood ready to approve and defend it. The political climate was receptive to federal planning and federal housing — not so much as a matter of radical ideology, but out of a demand for positive programs to eliminate the "undeserved" privations of the unaccustomed poor.

Moreover, business was stagnant in the thirties. Programs of social welfare and relief were tested by their ability to create new jobs and prime the business pump as much as by their inherent welfare virtues. Public works programs were exceedingly popular for this reason. A vast federal program of house building naturally received the enthusiastic support of manufacturers of building supplies and workers in the building trades. The normal opposition to "socialized" housing made its appearance in debate, but it was weak and somewhat muted. Nonetheless, business support for the act was conditioned upon the act being so structured as to avoid any actual government competition with business. Homes would be built only for those who could not possibly afford to buy them on their own. A clear wall must separate the public and the private sector. This too was only partly ideological. Government, it was felt, should not cut into the markets of private industry; it must stimulate fresh demand and make fresh jobs — otherwise the effect of the program on the economy would be wasted.

During the depression, the volume of private housing construction was very low. In 1925, 900,000 housing units were constructed; in 1934, only 60,000. Yet in one sense no housing shortage developed. During much of the depression, plenty of apartments stood vacant. People who were poor doubled up with relatives, lived in "Hoovervilles" and shanties, returned to rural areas, and in general failed to consume the housing supply. Rents were extremely low. The high vacancy rate posed a potential danger for the program. If public construction increased the housing supply during a period in which many dwellings stood vacant, rents would decrease still more and vacancies would increase. In a decade willing to kill baby pigs and impose acreage controls on farmers, one could hardly expect to see government flooding the housing market with new units. And in fact, the Wagner-Steagall Act was careful to avoid the problem of over-supply. No units were to be built without destroying "dwellings . . . substantially equal in number to the number of newly contructed dwellings provided by the project." This provision — the so-called "equivalent elimination" provision — killed two birds with one stone. It neutralized potential opposition from landlords and the housing industry by removing the danger of oversupply; at the same time, by making slum clearance a part of the law, it appealed to those whose desire for public housing stemmed from their loathing of the slums and slum conditions. The Wagner-Steagall Act was thus shaped by the force of concrete social conditions; what emerged was a program geared to the needs of the submerged middle class, tied to slum clearance, and purged of any element of possible competition with business.

Constitutional difficulties played a part in determining one of the most notable features of the program — its decentralization. From 1933 on, the Public Works Administration had run its own public housing program. In 1935 a federal district court case held that the federal government had no power under the constitution to clear land and build public housing. It was not proper, said the court, for the federal government "to construct buildings in a state for the purpose of selling or leasing them to private citizens for occupancy as homes." The federal government never appealed this decision. In 1935 the government's prospect of sympathetic treatment by the United States Supreme Court seemed bleak; attempting to overturn the adverse housing decision might risk the whole program of public works. On the other hand, no important legal barriers stood in the way of a decentralized program. Washington could supply money and a certain amount of benign control; title to property and the motive force in condemnation could remain vested in local public agencies. A key New York state decision strengthened this view, distinguished the federal cases as inapplicable to state power. Moreover, decentralization was politically attractive to those who dreaded further expansion of the "federal octopus."

Financial considerations had an important impact on the design of the housing law. If the federal government had made outright grants to local authorities to build houses, immense amounts of money would have been immediately required. Under the act, however, local authorities were invited to borrow money through bond issues; with the proceeds, they were to acquire sites, clear them, and put up houses. The federal government would enter into "contracts" with local housing authorities, under which the federal government would agree to make annual contributions for a long period of time. The federal government would pay (in essence) enough money for the interest on the bonds and the amortization of the principal. Operating expenses for the housing projects would come out of current rents. In this way, federal contributions would be kept relatively small; housing could be built on the installment plan, and paid for over a period of fifty or sixty years.

Note, too, that the tenants were only partially subsidized. They were not given "free" housing. Each tenant had to pay his rent. Project rents had to be sufficient to pay operating costs — maintenance, administration, and payments in lieu of taxes to local government for fire and police protection and other municipal services. Though the federal act was discreetly silent on the subject, the rent requirement meant that the unemployed and the paupers were not welcome in public housing.

They could not pay the rent, any more than in private housing. There are "some people," said Senator Wagner, "who we cannot possibly reach; I mean those who have no means to pay the rent. . . . [O]bviously this bill cannot provide housing for those who cannot pay the rent minus the subsidy allowed." The projects were for poor but honest workers — the members of the submerged middle class, biding their time until the day when they regained their rightful income level. The tenants were not to receive any "charity." The difference between a dole and a subsidy is psychologically powerful, whether or not the distinction is good economics. The working class residents of public housing were not to receive a gift from the government, but their rightful due as citizens.

Public housing, arguably, was no more "charitable" than the free land of the homestead act of 1862 — an earlier form of middle-class subsidy. Decent, sanitary apartments were a stepping-stone to a fee simple cottage — the American dream. Perhaps a radical fringe of housing reformers looked on public housing as something more fundamentally "public"; but the core of support lay in an old and conservative tradition.

If this general analysis is correct, what would happen to public housing if a rising standard of living released the submerged middle class from dependence on government shelter? Public housing would be inherited by the permanent poor. The empty rooms would pass to those who had at first been disdained — the unemployed, "problem" families, those from broken homes. The program could adapt only with difficulty to its new conditions, because it had been originally designed for a different clientele. To suit the programs to the needs of the new tenant would require fresh legislation; and yet change would be difficult to enact and to implement precisely because the new clientele would be so poor, so powerless, so inarticulate. The political attractiveness of public housing would diminish. Maladaptations to reality in the program would disenchant housing reformers; they would declare the program a failure and abandon it to search out fresh cures for bad housing and slums.

All this is precisely what has happened. . . . The new tenants were precisely those who had the least power in our society, the least potent voice in the councils of city hall. The middle-class masses, moreover, were spending their sweat and treasure in a wild flight from the slums and their residents. Now that they had attained the status of suburban property owners, they had no intention of giving up their property values and their hard-won status by allowing their former neighbors (and even less desirable people) to move in. The slums were not to follow them into the suburbs. Race and income prejudice was by no means confined to the suburbs. It flourished in the city, too, particularly in the little enclaves of frame houses that formed ethnically homogeneous, proud, and self-contained neighborhoods. These sub-cities would also resist public housing in their midst. Public housing no longer meant homes for less fortunate friends and neighbors, but rather, intrusions of "foreigners," the problem poor and those least welcome "forbidden neighbors," the lower class Negro. Public housing not only lost its political appeal but what was left of the program was confined to the core of the city. Public housing remained tied to slum clearance and rebuilding out of necessity. The suburbs and the middle-class areas of the city had shut their doors. Vacant land could not be used for sites unless the land happened to lie in skid row or a Negro neighborhood.

H. AARON, SHELTER AND SUBSIDIES: WHO BENEFITS FROM FEDERAL HOUSING POLICIES? 112-113 (1972): Before 1969, local housing authorities were required to meet current operating expenses out of rents and utility charges collected from tenants and to remit any excess over current operating expenses to the federal government. More than 84 percent of annual contributions were offset by such remissions in 1948 and 1949, but only about 2 percent in the aggregate in fiscal year 1971. Many housing authorities, particularly in large cities, could not cover operating expenses out of rents. As a result, Congress in 1969 and 1970 specifically authorized payments to defray them. In addition, Congress stipulated that public housing rents should not exceed 25 percent of tenant income and agreed to appropriate additional funds to reimburse housing authorities for the resulting loss of revenues. Such supplementary payments are anticipated to add $170 million during fiscal year 1973 to the approximately $950 million in fixed annual contributions. Due to various offsetting amounts, total annual contributions are estimated at 1.1 billion.

The form of the federal subsidy offers local housing authorities little incentive for efficient planning and operation. Before 1969 the federal willingness to bear all capital costs but no operating costs encouraged local authorities to minimize maintenance through construction design, even if additional capital costs outweighed future savings in maintenance. Construction guidelines issued by HUD probably narrowed opportunities for abuse. The 1969 and 1970 provisions reduced this problem but created a new one. They commit the federal government to pay the excess (up to a certain maximum) of operating expenses over rents, offering little incentive to efficient management. A subsidy equal to some proportion of total (capital plus operating) expenses or a subsidy directed to tenants in housing projects would correct this deficiency; in either case, the requirement that all residual receipts be returned to HUD would have to be relaxed if profit incentives were to have any effect.

◆ MANIGO v. NEW YORK CITY HOUSING
AUTHORITY
51 Misc. 2d 829, 273 N.Y.S.2d 1003 (Sup. Ct. 1966), *aff'd*, 27 A.D.2d
803, 279 N.Y.S.2d 1014, *cert. denied*, 389 U.S. 1008 (1967)

MURPHY, Justice. Petitioner seeks a review and annulment of the determination of the New York City Housing Authority denying her and her
family admission to tenancy in a public housing [project] operated by
respondent.

Petitioner contends that she is qualified for tenancy and has complied with all of the required application procedures and that the standards used by respondent to determine qualifications of tenancy deny
her and her family the equal protection guaranteed by the 14th Amendment of the Constitution of the United States in that the said standards
are arbitrary, capricious, unreasonable and unrelated to the declared
purpose and public policy of the respondent.

Respondent is a public corporation organized and existing by virtue
of the Public Housing Law of the State of New York. Pursuant to its legal
authority respondent owns and operates low rent public housing within
the City of New York to provide housing accommodations in such properties for families of low income who qualify pursuant to law and to
regulations made by the said respondent. Respondent, in the operation
of its properties, has established eligibility requirements for applicants.
These regulations and requirements are contained in Authority Res No.
12-9-683 entitled "Resolution Relating to Desirability as a Ground for
Eligibility" and have been made a part of the record herein. Section 1 of
the said resolution sets forth that non-desirability standards and procedures have been established to insure the health, safety, morals and
comfort of public housing tenants, to protect the property of the Authority and to facilitate the proper administration by the Authority of its
projects. The standards for judging non-desirability are set forth in Section 2 of the said resolution as follows:

> Section 2. *Ground for Eligibility*. It shall be a ground for eligibility for
> admission or continued occupancy in any Authority project, that the ten-
> ant or applicant is or will be a desirable tenant. The standard to be used in
> approving eligibility for admission or continued occupancy of a family
> shall be that the family will not or does not constitute (1) a detriment to the
> health, safety or morals of its neighbors or the community, (2) an adverse
> influence upon sound family and community life, (3) a source of danger to
> the peaceful occupation of the other tenants, (4) a source of danger or
> cause of damage to the premises or property of the Authority, or (5) a
> nuisance. In making such determination consideration shall be given to
> the family composition, parental control over children, family stability,
> medical and other past history, reputation, conduct and behavior, criminal
> record, if any, occupation of wage earners, and any other data or informa-
> tion with respect to the family that has a bearing upon its desirability,

including its conduct or behavior while residing in a project. Any applicant or tenant determined to be ineligible by virtue of the standard herein set forth shall be declared to be ineligible on the ground of Non-Desirability.

There can be no doubt that the respondent, to protect the large concentration of children and elderly persons who reside within its properties, must take steps to prevent the development of unsafe conditions therein. Without a proper screening of prospective tenants the dangers to those persons residing therein would be multiplied many times over. . . .

In the course of its routine investigation relating to the desirability of the petitioner as a tenant the respondent discovered, among other things, that petitioner's husband, during the past eight years, has been arrested seven times. On four of these occasions he has been adjudicated a youthful offender or a juvenile delinquent. On at least two occasions he has been incarcerated. In addition to the four juvenile and youthful offender offenses, he was, in 1964, arrested for disorderly conduct, found guilty and sentenced to ten days in the Workhouse. In July of 1965 he was arrested for possession of drugs, which charge was ultimately dismissed. The record further reveals that the first juvenile delinquency adjudication was as a result of an altercation with one of the respondent's Public Housing Guards.

Respondent, in applying the facts in the instant case to the eligibility resolution above set forth, has concluded that the background of petitioner's husband makes a clear case of non-desirability within the standards and regulations provided by the respondent. This court agrees with the fundamental proposition advanced by petitioner that adjudication of a person as a youthful offender or juvenile delinquent, standing by itself, cannot be utilized to operate as a forfeiture of any right or privilege nor to disqualify that person from certain rights specified in the applicable statutes. However, this does not mean that an applicant's entire behavior pattern over a period of years may not be the proper subject of scrutiny by an administrative agency before granting a right or privilege such as eligibility to public housing. . . .

Accordingly, the court finds that in the circumstances presented the actions of the respondent were reasonable and the standards applied by said respondent with respect to petitioner's application were applied reasonably and justified the action taken by the said respondent. The petition is dismissed.

Notes

1. Thomas v. Housing Authority, 282 F. Supp. 575 (E.D. Ark. 1967), struck down the Housing Authority's policy of denying admission to unwed mothers.

The prohibition . . . is absolute. . . . It completely overlooks the possibility that the mother has reformed, or that if placed in better surroundings she may lead a more conventional life.

. . . The absence of illegitimate children from a family group does not establish the morality of the members of that group. . . .

More basically, an indiscriminate denial of access to public housing to families unfortunate enough to have or acquire one or more illegitimate children would be to deprive of the real or supposed benefits of the program many of the very people who need it most — the poorest and most ignorant of the poor.

Is the policy bad (1) because the rule is too broad, (2) because it is not broad enough, (3) because the matter is outside the authority's proper concern, (4) because these are precisely the families the authority should seek to house, or (5) for some other reason or reasons?

2. "Whereas the financial solvency of the Louisville Authority, because of housing a majority of its residents in income ranges extremely below the operating costs of the authority, has reached a point where the solvency of the authority is in jeopardy . . .", the authority sought qualifying applicants who would fit within a scheduled capacity to pay rent that would provide enough income to pay operating bills. This ranged from 30 percent of units paying $0 to $30 per month, to 30 percent paying above $61 per month. The authority's actions were held in violation of the policies implicit in national housing legislation. Fletcher v. Housing Authority, 491 F.2d 793 (6th Cir.), *vacated and remanded*, 419 U.S. 865 (1974), *reinstated*, 525 F.2d 532 (6th Cir. 1975).

But see Boyd v. Lefrak Organization, 509 F.2d 1110 (2d Cir.), *cert. denied*, 423 U.S. 896 (1975), holding that a private landlord can use financial criteria to pick tenants, even where they exclude almost all recipients of AFDC benefits and many black and Puerto Rican families.

B.   PEREZ v. BOSTON HOUSING AUTHORITY: A CASE STUDY IN INSTITUTIONAL REFORM LITIGATION*

1.   *Background to the* Perez *Suit*

On February 7, 1975, Armando Perez and eight other named tenants of developments operated by the Boston Housing Authority (BHA) filed a

*This case study, which constitutes the remainder of this chapter, was written by Eric T. Schneiderman of the Harvard Law School class of 1982. It was prepared under the auspices of the Harvard Law School Program on the Legal Profession. The cooperation of Richard Bluestein, Howard Cohen, Arthur Johnson, Bruce Mohl, Leslie Newman, and Judge Paul Garrity is appreciated.

complaint, on behalf of all BHA tenants, seeking relief from widespread violations of the Massachusetts Sanitary Code. The tenants, represented by Greater Boston Legal Services (GBLS) lawyers, brought their suit as a class action in the Housing Court of the City of Boston before Chief Judge Paul Garrity. Their complaint alleged that the Sanitary Code violations "caused irreparable physical and/or emotional injury" to persons residing in the developments and requested broad injunctive relief against the Housing Authority and the State Department of Community Affairs (DCA).

The *Perez* case represented a new legal approach by GBLS housing lawyers to addressing the deplorable conditions in Boston's public housing. In the late 1960s and early 1970s the BHA became known as one of the worst housing authorities in the country. By the mid-1970s it was often cited as the worst. In 1967, a coalition of public interest organizations funded a study of the BHA that stated:

> Many of Boston's housing projects (particularly those for the non-elderly) are in need of major and minor repairs, and in some instances wholesale remodeling. The quality of maintenance in most projects is far below acceptable standards . . . hiring policies at the BHA remain essentially "closed". . . most Housing Authority positions are regarded as being in the patronage category, to be filled by directive from City Hall. . . . The life tenure system for housing authority employees, enacted in 1962, has led to severe personnel problems at the BHA. The system leads to poor work performance and inadequate supervisory mechanisms. [Citizens' Housing and Planning Association, Public Housing at the Crossroads: The Boston Housing Authority (1967).]

Other reports arrived at similar conclusions and a 1972 Comprehensive Consolidated Management Review Report by the U.S. Department of Housing and Urban Development was extremely critical of the authority in most areas of its operations. The BHA's housing units were not just poorly managed — many were dangerous and unsanitary, clearly in violation of the Massachusetts Sanitary Code, Mass. Gen. Laws Ann. ch. 111 §127. The authority's vacancy rate increased year by year, with the boarded up apartments and vandalism that accompanied vacancies encouraging further abandonment. Some apartments lacked windows that could be opened in the summer, others were missing windows completely. Piles of debris and rubbish, often set on fire by vandals, filled many halls, basements, and courtyards. Heat and hot water were inadequate and in some buildings non-existent. Rats, roaches, and packs of wild dogs inhabited the premises. GBLS lawyers represented individual tenants in numerous suits to force compliance with the state sanitary code, but the housing stock continued to deteriorate.

In 1973 and 1974 GBLS lawyers, along with attorneys representing BHA tenant organizations, filed several suits to force general improvements in the operation of the BHA. In West Broadway Task Force

PHOTOGRAPH 12-1
A Boston Housing Authority project in 1984

Inc. v. Commissioner, 363 Mass. 745, 297 N.E.2d 505 (1973), a local tenants group* brought a class action to "have the Superior Court declare and enforce by continuing injunction an obligation on the part of the defendants [the BHA and the Massachusetts Department of Community Affairs, the state agency responsible for most BHA funds] to maintain the development in sound condition." The plaintiffs argued that the Massachusetts statutes setting out the purposes, powers, and responsibilities of the BHA and DCA (Mass. Gen. Laws Ann. ch. 121B) imposed obligations on the state to fund and supervise the BHA's

*BHA developments have both local and city-wide tenant organizations. The West Broadway Task Force and Mission Hill Tenants' Organization are examples of local groups that represent tenants in particular developments. The Tenants Policy Council (TPC), which intervened in the *Perez* case, is a city wide organization of BHA tenants.

provision of housing that complied with the state sanitary code. The Superior Court rejected these claims and the plaintiffs appealed.

The Massachusetts Supreme Judicial Court affirmed the Superior Court's dismissal of the suit. The court acknowledged that "health or life" was at stake. But it said that "more effective, albeit less heroic, procedures are available" than major judicial intervention. The court looked with hope at the recent state regulations, at tenant remedies under the Massachusetts version of *Javins* (see Chapter 8, p.315), and at a Massachusetts statute permitting payment of rent "to the clerk of court, to be disbursed to effectuate removal of the [housing code] violation."

West Broadway, along with other cases brought by tenants against the BHA at about the same time, represented a strategy of seeking to establish "entitlements" to a particular standard of housing and to force the provision of funds from the state and federal governments to meet that standard. According to a GBLS lawyer who had been involved in this litigation, by late 1974 it was clear the courts were no longer receptive to this line of attack. In the early 1970s, cases held that landlords have a continuing duty to tenants to maintain housing in a decent, habitable condition. However, other cases held that the state could not be forced to allocate funds to ensure that this duty was met in public housing. The state and federal courts in which relief was sought were simply unwilling to interfere with what they viewed as essentially political decisions of resource allocation. For example, in Boston Housing Tenants Policy Council v. Lynn, 388 F. Supp. 493 (D. Mass. 1974), a suit in which tenants sought to hold the U.S. Department of Housing and Urban Development to standards similar to those urged for the state defendants in *West Broadway,* the Federal District Court for Massachusetts wrote:

> One can only sympathize with the plight of the tenants residing in Boston's low-income housing projects. The projects are mismanaged and in a poor state of repair. Yet the federal courts cannot pretend to be the cure-all for America's housing ills. Federal courts lack the expertise, the staff, and the Congressional mandate to do the job. On the other hand, the Housing Court for the City of Boston has been established by state legislation, which is better suited to solve the enormous housing problems encountered by the tenants of Boston. Yet in the last analysis, long range answers can best be provided by the "political branches" of government. It is they who have the resources, the duty, and the power to make significant changes in the field of housing.

2. Perez I

After several months of digesting the decisions rejecting their entitlement theories, GBLS lawyers, working closely with a group of tenants at the Mission Hill development, brought the *Perez* suit. *Perez* advanced yet another theory aimed at forcing the State Department of Community Affairs to allocate sufficient funds to bring the BHA developments into compliance with the Sanitary Code. This time the tenants' attorneys asserted that the Mass. Gen. Laws ch. 111 §127N, inserted in the Sanitary Code in 1974, required DCA to fund court-ordered BHA rehabilitation. The new provision stated that "any individual, trust or corporation, partnership or other person who, acting alone or with another, has the authority to decide whether to rehabilitate, or sell or otherwise dispose of the premises" would, if the owner of property was unable for financial reasons to provide the relief ordered by a court, "be jointly and severally liable for taking any action or paying any damages ordered by the Court."

Perez differed from earlier litigation against the BHA because, in addition to this new "entitlement" argument, the GBLS lawyers bringing the suit focused on the possibility of securing injunctive relief for the authority's failure to use the funds it already had to remedy widespread Sanitary Code violations — one of the routes suggested by the Supreme Judicial Court opinion in *West Broadway*. The BHA had a large budget throughout the early 1970s but it was so poorly managed that funds often seemed not to reach their intended targets. The U.S. Department of Housing and Urban Development had begun a major program to rebuild public housing in 1969. According to one report, by 1979 the BHA had only spent $28 million of the $42 million allocated to it under the program. The authority defended itself in court and in the press by saying that its problems resulted from lack of funds, but by the time of the *Perez* case tenants' attorneys had recognized that the BHA's problems resulted from incompetence and corruption at least as much as from a lack of money. The GBLS lawyers who represented individual tenants in their suits against the BHA for collapsed ceilings, lack of heat and hot water, inadequate lighting, and other code violations were already litigating to re-direct and improve the management of existing BHA funds. In a sense, *Perez* represented a recognition that suits by individual tenants were an inadequate means to attack the authority's deep management problems and that, even if no more funds were available, a class action for broad injunctive relief was needed.

Judge Paul Garrity, before whom the case was brought, had a long background in Massachusetts housing law. He had worked as a legal services attorney, contributed to legislation providing legal protection to tenants, and was appointed the first judge of the Housing Court of the City of Boston when that court was established in 1972. After a lengthy hearing, which included visits by the judge to several BHA developments, the BHA was ordered to take immediate action to remedy the numerous violations of the state Sanitary Code in its housing developments. With limited exceptions, the Department of Community Affairs was enjoined from committing $105 million of its borrowing authority that was intended, but had not yet been committed, for the development of low-income housing throughout the state.

The DCA appealed the order against it to the Massachusetts Supreme Judicial Court which held that the Mass. Gen. Laws Ann. ch. 111 §127N could not be construed to require the state to fund BHA rehabilitation. The court then remanded to Judge Garrity, writing that:

> The result we have reached is clearly required by the law. Nevertheless, the ramifications of our decision are disturbing. The Commonwealth cannot be required to expend funds for rehabilitation of BHA property; yet hundreds, and probably thousands, of tenants are living in substandard units which the judge has characterized as "not decent." Without adequate funding, the alternatives appear equally unacceptable: either the tenants continue to live in conditions which are unlawful under the sanitary code, or the substandard units are to be withdrawn from use, with the accompanying probability of many persons left homeless.
>
> Conditions in certain BHA projects are such as to justify the use of the adjectives "massive" and "critical." The judge has found that the great majority of the residential units owned and operated by the BHA, as well as the buildings themselves, "are not decent, nor are they safe and nor are they in compliance with the provisions of the State Sanitary Code." A substantial percentage of the rental units are unoccupied, with vacancies in one project as high as sixty per cent. The background is one of numerous crimes of violence and widespread vandalism. Vandalism has virtually destroyed hundreds of apartments, and large segments of the buildings themselves. The judge found that the residents did not perpetrate the vandalism.
>
> These conditions directly affect a substantial percentage of the residents of Boston. The BHA owns and operates nineteen Federally aided developments for families of low income with a total of 10,348 dwelling units (seventy-three per cent of such units in the Commonwealth), ten State aided developments for families of low income with a total of 3,681 units (twenty-seven per cent of such units in the Commonwealth), twenty-five Federally aided developments for elderly persons of low income with a total of 2,613 units (ninety-four per cent of such units in the Commonwealth), and two State aided developments for elderly persons of low income with a total of 160 units (sixty per cent of such units in the Commonwealth). The BHA also leases from private landlords 2,655 dwelling units pursuant to various Federal programs (ninety-seven per cent of such units in the Commonwealth), and fifty-nine units pursuant to various State programs (three per cent of such units in the Commonwealth). Residents living in BHA owned and leased housing projects comprise in excess of ten per cent of the total population of Boston.
>
> With these conditions in mind the question remains as to the proper disposition of this case, aside from the fact that the complaints must be dismissed as to the State defendants. Jurisdiction of the subject matter (violations of the sanitary code) resides in the Housing Court, of course, and that court's powers embrace such matters, relating to both the problem and the cure of sanitary code violations, as vandalism, crime, alleged

mismanagement, and the marshalling of tenant cooperation. Furthermore, the Housing Court judge has demonstrated, in his considerable efforts up to this point, both sympathetic understanding and competence directed toward the special problems of the BHA. Therefore, it is appropriate for us to remand the case to the judge below for such further proceedings, as to the BHA only, as he deems appropriate in the circumstances.

The judge entered a final decree, but it is clear from representations of counsel before us that the judge may well intend to retain jurisdiction of the matter. Apparently the preparation of plans for solution of some of the BHA problems has been ordered by the judge and we understand that a master has been or will be appointed to that end.

Of course, the future proceedings under this complaint can be binding only on the BHA. It is an understatement to say that our decision to order the dismissal of the complaint as to the State defendants limits the utility of further proceedings, since adequate funds to implement certain court orders are not available. As the judge found, "BHA is unable for financial reasons to comply with orders made by this Court in this case pursuant to G.L. c. 111, §127H to maintain its developments in compliance with the State Sanitary Code and to provide security to its tenants." Nevertheless, further proceedings, despite the lack of availability of State funds as decided in this case, may result in appropriate orders against BHA related to the sanitary code. Moreover, additional proceedings may well offer guidance and precedent for future cases involving not only mandatory action by BHA, but also discretionary action by the legislative and executive branches.

The final decree of the Housing Court of the City of Boston is reversed as to the State defendants and the complaint is dismissed as to those defendants. The injunction against the State defendants is vacated. The case is remanded to the Housing Court for further proceedings as to the BHA in the discretion of the judge and consistent with this opinion. [Perez v. Boston Housing Authority, 368 Mass. 333, 331 N.E.2d 801, *app. dismissed sub nom.* Perez v. Bateman, 423 U.S. 1009 (1975).]

3. Interim Remedial Action

Judge Garrity and the GBLS lawyers representing the *Perez* tenant class had recognized before the Supreme Judicial Court rendered its decision, which became known as *Perez I*, that a reversal on the funding issue was possible, even likely. The judge therefore began to issue interim orders, which did not depend on the high court's funding decision, while the appeal was pending.

Among other things, Judge Garrity directed the BHA to do the following:

to develop criteria for identification of occupied apartments where conditions are such that the health, welfare and/or safety of the tenants is/are in serious jeopardy . . . [and] to prepare a program for speedy inspection of

every tenanted apartment in all of BHA's developments in order to identify apartments where such conditions exist and to prepare a plan for
immediate rectification of such conditions.

The BHA, as ordered, filed its written responses to the interim
orders on and after April 11, 1975, but these were incomplete, inaccurate, and late. The judge considered the BHA's responses to his initial
orders so inadequate that after consultations with the tenants, lawyers,
and BHA representatives involved in the suit, he requested the parties
to meet to discuss the possible appointment of a master to "assist" the
BHA in its efforts to comply with court orders. The tenant plaintiffs filed
an application for the appointment of a master and in an order of reference dated May 22, 1975, the judge appointed Robert B. Whittlesey, a
well-respected city planner and engineer, to the position.

On a long-range level, the master began to prepare a comprehensive, detailed report and plan for the reformation of the BHA. On a more
immediate level, the GBLS lawyers, who were in touch with various
tenant groups, and the Tenants Policy Council (TPC), a city-wide BHA
tenants' organization that was allowed to enter the case as a plaintiff-
intervenor, began to request discrete injunctive orders for a variety of
specific problems. Some of these problems, such as tenant selection
procedures and security, involved BHA operations city-wide. Some
problems were specific to one or two buildings: Roofs were falling in,
windows missing, and in the Orchard Park development there was little
or no hot water. The problem of the Orchard Park boiler is often cited as
an example of the BHA's inability to resolve problems. Five years after
the *Perez* suit began, and ten years after work was begun on the boiler,
there was still inadequate hot water in Orchard Park.

The GBLS and TPC lawyers, along with their tenant clients, worked
with the master's staff and the judge to prepare interim plans and orders
to address these and other problems. Between May 22, 1975, and September 1, 1976, the court issued 25 interim orders to the BHA. Judge
Garrity, who by this time was quite familiar with the BHA's capabilities
and conditions, dispensed with many procedural formalities during this
period. He conducted numerous ongoing hearings on a variety of
identified problem areas and initiated some orders to the BHA himself,
without waiting for formal requests by the parties.

The BHA failed to comply with nearly every order issued during
this period. Its failure to follow court orders led to hearings, contempt
citations, and findings by the court, including the following:

It is abundantly clear from the evidence in the many hearings in this case
that the BHA has insufficient funds and management expertise to maintain adequately and to provide security to its existing developments many
of which are in a shocking state of disrepair. . . . [Order dated February 20,
1976.]

BHA has sufficient resources to comply with those portions of the December 2nd Orders requiring relocation from or repair of occupied uninhabitable units and resolution of the "squatter issue." BHA's failure to comply resulted, in my opinion, from less than adequate planning, coordination, direction, supervision and accountability at BHA's upper staff echelons. . . . Accordingly on the above facts, I find and rule BHA was and is in contempt of the Orders dated and made December 2, 1975 in this case. . . . [Findings, Rulings and Orders dated April 16, 1976.]

[A] number of "crises" have developed which have required the direct intervention and assistance of the Master. . . . The February 11, 1976 Report [by the master] summarized many of the BHA's weaknesses which were dramatized by these "crises." These weaknesses include lack of planning and coordination in the operation of the BHA and a failure to effectively direct, supervise and make accountable the employees of the BHA. I find these weaknesses seriously exacerbate BHA's extreme financial problems and impede its ability to carry out the orders of this Court required to rectify the conditions described in the original and subsequent findings made in this case. . . . [Order dated March 23, 1976.]

On July 1, 1976, while the lawyers for the *Perez* plaintiff class were concluding from these contempt hearings that attempts to get the BHA to comply with injunctions were a waste of time, the master issued his five-volume report. This report found that the BHA board had failed to provide policy direction and leadership in most areas of operation — including maintenance, budgeting, tenant selection, and modernization. The report analyzed BHA operations in some detail, including some issues such as the racial composition of the BHA's waiting list, which the BHA had never examined, and proposed extensive reorganization and new procedures in many areas.

The report stated that "there are major problems in the capability of the BHA to communicate, implement and administer major policy decisions and programs within the Authority," and that the master's staff had "discovered little evidence that the board is fully aware of the scope and seriousness of these problems or has provided the leadership necessary to resolve these major problems." A major overhaul of the entire Authority was clearly required if the BHA was to comply with the minimum legal standards for decent housing.

According to Bruce Mohl, a lead GBLS attorney at this stage of the *Perez* case, it was at this point that the strategy developed by the plaintiff's attorneys a year earlier was abandoned and a receivership was identified as the plaintiffs' goal. The reorganization of the BHA, which the master's report identified as essential, was clearly beyond the capacity of an agency that could not even follow court orders to inventory supplies and repair windows.

The BHA, which had relied on its own attorneys thus far in the suit, retained the well-known Boston firm of Choate, Hall & Stewart shortly after the Master's report came out. The new BHA counsel moved to dismiss for lack of jurisdiction and raised other procedural objections to the conduct of the suit. The plaintiffs' attorneys moved at about the same time for the appointment of a receiver to take over the responsibilities of the BHA Board and Administrator, the top official of the authority, appointed by and responsible to the five member board. The judge set a hearing on the receivership issue for mid-September, 1976.

GBLS, the master's staff, and the BHA constituted three separate forces, each pulling in a different direction. Prior to the date set for the receivership hearing, however, a coalition of sorts was formed between the master and the BHA's lawyers to work out a settlement that would implement the master's report through a consent decree. The judge was receptive to this approach, which was generally seen as a last effort to address the BHA's problems without attempting a judicial take-over of the agency through a receivership. Informal negotiations among the parties, the master, and the judge, right up until the day that had been set for the hearing on receivership, finally ended in an agreement by all parties to negotiate such a settlement.

4. The Consent Decree

The parties, the master, and Judge Garrity entered negotiations for a consent decree in September 1976. Nine months later, after hundreds of hours of negotiation, they agreed on a 291-page document that provided detailed plans for the revitalization of most areas of BHA operations.

The master and his staff were given major responsibility for monitoring the BHA's performance under the consent decree. The BHA was required to keep the master "fully informed" of all information pertaining to or affecting the implementation of any part of the decree, and to inform him "immediately . . . where requested . . . of any decision, action or proposed decision or action which [was] reasonably expected to substantially affect either the financial condition of the BHA or the operations of its developments, insofar as related to areas covered" by the decree. The master was also given a role in the development of job descriptions and in the hiring and promotion of upper and mid-level BHA management personnel.

The decree provided that, in the event of a dispute between one of the parties and the master over the interpretation of the decree or concerning non-compliance with any part of it, a special dispute resolution process could be invoked. If the master of a party filed a written statement with the judge describing the nature of the dispute and the requested resolution, Judge Garrity was to evaluate the dispute and then hold a formal or informal hearing on the matter. The judge was given broad discretion to set the terms of the hearing, to restrict the presentation of evidence, and to frame "remedial" and "punitive" orders.

The consent decree was viewed from the start with mixed feelings on the part of the tenant-plaintiffs' attorneys. Bruce Mohl, who participated in the negotiation of the decree, recalled that, early in the negotiations, the BHA's lawyers began to try to use the dispute resolution processes in the decree to insulate the authority from further remedial action by the court. Everyone involved in the negotiations became so committed to the process of developing and implementing the consent decree that it became difficult to argue for the preservation of sanctions for non-compliance, such as receivership, that would undercut the operation of the decree itself. In fact, the final document did not provide for the appointment of a receiver as a sanction if the BHA failed to comply. At one point in the negotiations the GBLS attorneys walked out to protest the BHA's attempts to foreclose the possibility of a receivership. They succeeded in keeping only one door open for such a step — the decree could be vacated for non-compliance and the court could then proceed to institute any of its ordinary legal or equitable remedies. This was the route finally taken when the decree broke down 18 months after it went into effect on June 1, 1977.

The consent decree had actually begun to break down early in its 18 month existence. After the administrator of the BHA resigned in September 1977, the board refused to follow the hiring procedures set out in the decree. After months of vacillation and obstruction, which the Supreme Judicial Court later described as "farcical," the board was finally ordered by Judge Garrity, on March 6, 1978, to act on the vacancy within a week's time. Bradley Biggs was then appointed to the position, but the board refused to cooperate with him in various matters, including the appointment of a deputy administrator and efforts to reduce the board's requests to BHA staff on behalf of individual tenants. Biggs resigned in October 1978, and the BHA was without a permanent administrator for the rest of the life of the decree.

There were 29 formal modifications of the decree between June 1977 and July 1978, most of them extending the deadlines for various submissions by the BHA. The master's biannual reports on progress under the decree became more and more critical of the BHA's efforts. By November 1978 the master had filed 26 notices of substantial non-compliance with various provisions of the agreement. Finally, on December 28 the plaintiffs' attorneys filed a motion to vacate the consent decree and, as further relief, to have a receiver appointed. The formal basis of the motion to vacate was §10A of the decree. It provided that the decree, which had a stated life of three years,

> shall be vacated at any time upon the application of any party, if such party demonstrates that, because of a change of law or any other reason, its further functioning will in all likelihood be so substantially unworkable that it will not substantially achieve the significant particular purposes of the plans.

5.   Perez II — *The Superior Court**

After several months of discovery, the trial on the motion to vacate the consent decree and appoint a receiver began on March 26, 1979. At the 34 day trial, the GBLS lawyers presented their evidence of the BHA's non-compliance with the decree and showed, through depositions and the testimony of 2 members of the BHA board, a shocking level of BHA ignorance about the consent decree's provisions. Members of the BHA board testified that they did not know which of the consent decree's plans had been complied with, and that they had not even read the master's semiannual report or the sub-plans they were responsible for submitting. One board member did not know what a fiscal year is or what parentheses around numbers on a balance sheet signify, and therefore did not know the BHA was operating at a deficit in various areas.

The plaintiffs also called BHA tenants to testify about the continued deterioration of housing conditions since the *Perez* suit began. In his discussion of this testimony Judge Garrity found that:

> Each tenant who testified at the hearings on the Application to Vacate recounted a housing horror story. The conditions in their apartments and in their developments were and are indecent, unsafe and unsanitary and are in violation of almost every provision of the State Sanitary Code. If the BHA were a private landlord it surely would have been driven out of business long ago or its Board jailed or most likely both. The tenants also testified about the crime and vandalism which plague the developments where they live and make a mockery of the quality of life in those developments. Some tenants testified that it was unsafe to leave their apartments either by day or at night. One elderly resident of the Franklin Field development testified that she and her neighbors had to be bused and escorted to a local supermarket otherwise she and they would be mugged and robbed. Vandalism has also taken its toll. Another tenant, a young person who resides at the Maverick development, testified how a sewer cover had been vandalized, how it was allowed to remain in that condition for several months, how he observed a small child fall into the open sewer and how he rescued the child. By way of further example, a tenant of the Franklin Hill development testified of a fire being set in a large accumulation of trash in the basement area of her building and of the 14 year old girl residing in the first floor apartment being overcome by the smoke from the fire and rushed to a hospital. The tenant residing at the Maverick development testified about the susceptibility of his ten-month old son to colds since his birth as a result of inadequate heat in his apartment.

---

*Judge Garrity was appointed to the Massachusetts Superior Court in October 1976. In view of his experience with the BHA suit, and with the consent of the parties, the Supreme Judicial court allowed him to retain jurisdiction of *Perez* and transfer it from the Boston Housing Court to the Superior Court.

The conditions at the BHA's development in all likelihood cause social disintegration as well as the physical and psychological suffering exemplified above. The resident of the Franklin Field development who testified of the trash fire in the basement of her building also recounted her observations of a four-year old child about to set fire to a dumpster filled with trash. Almost every tenant who testified indicated that the physical deterioration of his or her development had accelerated at an increasing rate in the past two or three years. Those tenants also testified that the BHA was not responsive to specific and generalized requests for maintenance assistance and that security by way of a police presence was nonexistent.

The BHA's attorneys argued that the authority was in substantial compliance with many parts of the consent decree and that, in any event, appointment of a receiver was beyond the court's power. The BHA also accused the master and his staff of hindering BHA efforts to comply, and of attempting to "take over" the authority.

In a lengthy statement of findings, rulings, opinion, and orders issued on July 25, Judge Garrity held for the tenant-plaintiffs on all issues. The judge discussed the roles of individual board members in some detail and found that they had failed to perform adequately under the decree. He also found that the BHA's politically-connected acting administrator, Kevin Feeley — whom the board had actually sought to appoint as administrator and whose term was extended over the objection of the master — did not meet the administrative requirements of the decree. Finally, after examining in great detail the BHA's failure to achieve specific consent decree requirements, the judge stated that in light of all the circumstances of the case the appointment of a receiver was now necessary.

At this stage of the proceedings in this litigation appointment of a Receiver is the only possible remedy offering relief to the Tenants. The background and history of this case indicates beyond any doubt the futility of relying upon other remedies. The hope expressed by the District Court Judge in Boston Public Housing Tenants' Policy Council v. Lynn, that "long range answers can best be provided by the political branches of government" has not been fulfilled. The voting public does not appear to hold elected officials accountable for the failures of public housing, and the bureaucrats from HUD and the DCA, who are appointed by elected officials and who have the power to force the BHA and the Board to change their ways, have been notably unable and/or unwilling to do so. In fact, those bureaucrats have funded at enormous financial cost the outside legal representation of the BHA in opposing the management and other reforms sought by this litigation, which reforms those same bureaucrats have been urging upon the BHA for years, and they will probably fund, probably at enormous financial cost, any appeal of this Decision.

The history of this case and the repeated efforts by the Tenants over the years in seeking and in following up every remedy short of receivership in order to obtain safe, sanitary and decent housing as mandated by law requires that they be permitted the only remedy which has not yet been attempted. As found above, the indescribable conditions existing in the BHA's developments which cause incalculable human suffering have worsened. In *Perez*, the Supreme Judicial Court noted two unacceptable alternatives: "either the tenants continue to live in conditions which are unlawful under the Sanitary Code, or the substandard units are to be withdrawn from use." Receivership offers the only hope for remedying those unlawful conditions; otherwise, withdrawal of the substandard units from use will be required.

Finally, the Board's alleged gross mismanagement, nonfeasance, incompetence and irresponsibility have been shown to exist beyond any question. While this case was under advisement, on July 2, 1979, the Board, in utter disregard of the Consent Decree and apparently without any consideration of the consequences, authorized its Chairperson to extend all existing employment agreements with senior management employees for a period of two years for "morale" reasons. That action, of which the Court was informed by correspondence from the Master and the BHA, confirms as well as several pages of findings would confirm the allegations of the Tenants, and necessitates certain portions of the Orders set out below. It amounts as well to a blatant attempt to frustrate the authority of the Court.

In sum, on the facts, the Tenants have shown both extraordinary circumstances and the employment of every other conceivable remedy without avail, which compels the remedy of receivership if permitted as a matter of law. . . .

Whether or not a receiver may be appointed for the BHA is apparently a matter of first impression in this Commonwealth. In *West Broadway Task Force, Inc.*, the Court noted "We express no opinion as to whether a receiver may be appointed for a public housing development or any part of it." In my opinion, on the facts of this case, Massachusetts law permits the appointment of a receiver pursuant to G.L. c.111, §127H and by virtue of the inherent power of the Superior Court. This action is brought in part pursuant to §127H to enforce the State Sanitary Code, a law of the Commonwealth, in the BHA's developments. G.L. c.111, §§127A-127N "reflect a comprehensive legislative attempt to effectuate compliance with minimum health and safety standards for residential premises". . . . Section 127H specifically authorizes this Court in proceedings under c.111 to appoint a receiver in a petition to enforce the State Sanitary Code "with such powers and duties as the Court shall determine" as permitted by §127I. While §127H does not specifically include government landlords as being subject to its terms neither does it exclude such landlords from its coverage. . . .

The Court understands and realizes that receivership is an extraordinary remedy and amounts to a significant intervention into the affairs of what is traditionally considered the province of another body of government. For these reasons, the Court intends that the receivership granted as a remedy in this case shall continue for no longer than is absolutely necessary to achieve the relief to which the Tenants are entitled under law.

Judge Garrity followed this opinion with several orders. He vacated the Consent decree and recertified the plaintiff class, stating that:

1. The Plaintiff Class is hereby recertified.
2. It is further determined that the Plainiff Class is comprised of all residential tenants, whether or not under lease, who now reside or who in the future may reside in dwelling units and buildings owned, operated and/or leased by the BHA in which conditions exist or may in the future exist not substantially caused by those tenants, which conditions endanger and/or materially impair their health, safety or well-being, in violation of the State Sanitary Code and other relevant laws. That Class is certified for purposes of granting relief to such a class but not for the purposes of granting individualized relief to individual tenants.
3. The Court finds that the Class is so numerous that joinder of all members is impracticable; that there are questions of law and fact common to the Class; that the claims of the representative Plaintiffs are typical of the claims of the Class; that although the representative Plaintiffs are unaware of every detail concerning this case, the representative Plaintiffs will fairly and adequately protect the interests of the Class; that question of law or fact common to the members of the Class predominate over any questions affecting only individual members; and a class action is superior to other available methods for the fair and efficient adjudication of the controversy between the Parties and in fact it is the only method which will achieve such adjudication.
4. The Court further determines that, under this class recertification, any member of the Class who, solely on his or her own behalf, seeks judicial relief, including but not limited to damages, based in whole or in substantial part on alleged violations of the State Sanitary Code, shall seek such relief in an action independent of this case in any appropriate court.

The judge redesignated the master and gave him substantial responsibility for aiding in the hiring of a receiver. A Housing Advisory Committee was ordered to be established, with its members to be appointed at the same time as the receiver. Several "interim orders" were also issued to prevent the BHA Board and Administrator from taking actions that would impede later efforts to bring BHA housing into compliance with the Sanitary Code before the receiver was installed.

The BHA immediately appealed the vacation of the consent decree and the order to appoint a receiver.

6. Perez II — *The Supreme Judicial Court*

On appeal, the Massachusetts Supreme Judicial Court upheld Judge
Garrity's order to appoint a receiver. Writing for the court, Justice Benjamin Kaplan reviewed the history of the case and then addressed the
legal basis for a receivership.

◆ PEREZ v. BOSTON HOUSING AUTHORITY
379 Mass. 703, 400 N.E.2d 1231 (1980)

II. DISCUSSION OF THE APPLICABLE LAW

A. *BHA's Liability Established.* Although in certain respects a public
body, BHA in carrying on its housing functions is submissible to and
must abide by the ordinary substantive law of the Commonwealth —
the rules of contract, tort, and so forth. In its relations with its tenants,
BHA has rights and duties like those of other landlords: this appears
from many decided cases. And, like other landlords, BHA is under
duties as prescribed by G.L. c.111, §§127A-127N, including the duty to
maintain residential properties in accordance with the minimal standards established by the State sanitary code. Early in the present litigation — when the judge entered the judgment in the Boston Housing
Court from which the "State defendants" took the first *Perez* appeal —
there was a judicial determination that BHA was seriously in breach of the
basic obligation of G.L. c.111, §127H, and that situation continues to this day.

B. *Equitable Remedies.* BHA's liability being established, the problem
posed by this important litigation has been to find remedies appropriate
and efficient to restore the properties as far as possible to the levels
prescribed for human habitation. It must be confessed with remorse, not
unmixed with shame, that this problem has proved intractable to this
date. . . .

2. *Amenability to equitable remedy of receivership.* . . .

(a) *Sections 127H(d) and 127I.* The plaintiffs, addressing themselves
to this question of power or jurisdiction, suggest that it is promptly
answered by §127H(d): "The court may . . . (d) appoint a receiver." Then
they cite §127I: "Upon appointment such receiver shall post such bond
as may be deemed sufficient by the court, shall forthwith collect all rents
and profits of the property as the court shall direct and use all or any of
such funds, or funds received from the commonwealth as hereinafter
provided,[26] to enable such property to meet the standards of fitness for

26. The reference is to G.L. c.111, §127J (receiver may petition court for leave to apply
for financial assistance from the Commonwealth, through the Department of Public
Health, to supplement the rent funds for the purpose of effectuating repair and rehabilitation).

human habitation. A receiver may be a person, partnership or corporation." The riposte is that §127I seems to look to a mere rent receiver of a particular property and — as the parties were agreed in argument before us — no property-by-property receiverships, whether of the simple "rent" variety or of a type endowed with more ample powers, could possibly meet effectively the problems confronting BHA: receivership, if that remedy is to be used at all, must be single and entire. On a superficial view, therefore, §§127H(d) and 127I may appear inappropriate as a basis for a general receivership.

Nevertheless, there is strength in the position that while §127I is naturally geared to the prospect of many homely occasions for rent receiverships of single private properties which become offensive to the sanitary code, the section, especially in the light of its second sentence ("such powers and duties as the court shall determine"), can be read together with §127H(d) to empower the court on compelling facts to install a receivership of broader coverage, not limited to a single property or to the rents. Suppose a case where a private landlord has a number of properties in what amounts to single ownership, some or all of the properties are in violation, and unitary administration beyond mere collection and use of rents is needed under court supervision. We do not exclude the possibility that §§127H(d) and 127I may suffice for the appointment of a single receiver to do a complete job; and on that reading of the statutes the same may hold with respect to BHA as an entity.

(b) *Section 127H(a) and general equity powers.* However, the question under those cited statutes need not be labored, because another and very satisfactory source of power exists for the appointment of a unitary receiver for BHA. That is §127H(a) itself — the injunctive provision which invokes general equity powers. The power to compel affirmative action by injunction draws with it a power in the court to call to its assistance any agents or officers — we may call them parajudicial officers — whose services appear to be reasonably necessary to attain a legitimate objective. (Indeed the power may be said to inhere in a court whether sitting on the "law" or "equity" side according to the historical division.) . . .

Still further, it is characteristic of decrees in the fields of institutional reform that they appoint sundry parajudicial officers to assist the court not only in delineating remedies, but often in conducting or overseeing the actual implementation of the remedies. These agents or officers of the court are given functions accommodated to the particular needs. They are called by different names: masters, special masters, examiners, experts, monitors, referees, commissioners, administrators, observers, visitors, ombudsmen, committees, panels, etc. Significantly, the court adjuncts referred to have, as a group, been called "neoreceivers." The point to be made, again, is that the enjoined officials for practical purposes are replaced as to function — here, quite visibly — in the degree needed to attain or restore legality.[29] . . .

. . . A combination of conditions existed here . . . that looked finally to a receivership remedy. There had been massive trouble with eliciting performance of injunctive orders and finally of a comprehensive decree. There could be little doubt that to persist in that course — retention of the consent decree or reversion to a regime of injunction without consent — could end only in frustration. True leadership of BHA had in fact lapsed. Be it noted that the question was not whether members of the Board were not trying hard. The statutory rights of tenants were not to be equated merely with the Board's best efforts. The tenants were entitled to a leadership that had the potential for reaching out to achieve the objectives set by the law. Receivership had not been decided upon precipitately; although earlier sought by the plaintiffs, it had been refused until experience with the consent decree under the existing BHA management established to the satisfaction of the judge that a change of command was indispensable. The Board cannot justly complain of being superseded when it failed, over a long period and after fair opportunity, to secure performance to the level of the injunctive orders and then the consent decree, a decree not thrust upon it but voluntarily adopted. . . .

Tied to the "separation" [of powers] argument, and not too slyly, is an intimation that the courts would do well to stay out of this housing problem, for if the receivership meets with little more success than the current administration of BHA, then the courts will be substituted for BHA as the target of criticism; and the question is left not squarely stated but immanent whether that would be good for the courts. Amid these tears shed by anticipation for the courts, we acknowledge the possibility that a receivership will not succeed, but the facts of record suggest to us the certainty that the present administration has failed and would very probably continue to do so. It becomes a conscientious duty, within the law, even at the risk implied, to allow the receivership experiment to go forward as a last resort.

C. *Collateral Matters. 1. Claim of bias.* In the course of the proceedings, BHA made unsuccessful applications to the judge to disqualify himself, and to this court (under our superintendence power) to disqualify him, on the ground of his alleged bias. The grievance is renewed on this appeal as a reason for reversing the judgment. No doubt the judge

29. The mechanisms at work in the creation of a neoreceivership or, in the more extreme case, a receivership of a public institution, are fairly clear. The political process has failed to produce an institution conforming to law, and those subjected to the illegality, who are usually politically powerless (cf. United States v. Carolene Prods. Co., 304 U.S. 144, 152 n.4 [1938]), turn to the courts for the vindication of their rights. Injunctive remedies are called for, but the judge lacks expertness in the particular field, and lacks time even when he chances to have the knowledge. Hence the appointment of adjunct officers who supply expert knowledge and sometimes implicitly encourage acceptance by the parties and the general public of the results of the judicial intervention.

in the course of the proceedings below formed a negative impression of BHA, that is, of members of its Board and of certain of its employees, based on his appraisal of their performance. But that is not a ground for the assertion of a disqualifying bias. Nor is it a ground for demanding recusal that a judge in an equity cause expresses his views with a certain amount of vehemence. Here that vehemence undoubtedly was fueled, first, by the judge's frustration at what he took to be the poor reaction of the BHA people to his orders and directions and latterly to the requirements of the consent decree, and, second, by his plain concern for the human beings affected by the litigation. We think the judge's indulgence in very emphatic criticism was not helpful and we suggest that that style of utterance should be abandoned for the future. But, upon consideration, the judge felt that he could maintain his impartiality and had done so, and we do not reach any contrary conclusion.

2. "*Ex parte*" *communications.* BHA also attacks the judgment on the ground that the judge on several occasions had conversations about the case outside the usual judicial setting where representatives of both sides are present. The judge was in constant touch with the master but we think it was understood, and was in fact provided in the consent decree itself (although not with entire clarity), that there could be private consultations between the judge and master. Indeed such an understood arrangement would seem natural against the background of the case. However the judge on several occasions also had conversations with BHA people (in the majority of instances the master was also present). In the absence of an understanding with the parties about such encounters, we think they should not have taken place. But the transgressions appear to us to have been unthinking rather than venal, and we do not believe they affected the substance of the proceedings one way or the other. To reverse the judgment on this account and reopen proceedings before a judge lacking the five years' experience would be a profligate waste of time and resources.

We do not condone such communications, but the nature of the case suggests some palliation of the misbehavior. This was not a standard lawsuit. It was a massive, long-continuing litigation which has approximated the type involving institutional reform. . . .

D. *Conclusion.* It is right and proper that BHA should be operated as the Legislature declared it should be. But there has been a breakdown, resulting in widespread violations of law by BHA, which necessitates and therefore must evoke extraordinary action. To say that this court has been most reluctant to approve the temporary receivership is to understate the matter. No judge or court could enjoy the prospect of interfering with local authority and assuming a measure of supervision over a large outside enterprise, least of all one sliding downhill. Nevertheless the violations of law are there, and on the facts remedial efforts cannot stop short of receivership.

A receivership ought to be able to do a better job with the funds becoming available than has been done by BHA in the past, but we repeat what we said on the first appeal: inadequate funding will pose ultimately the cruelest of dilemmas affecting large numbers of Boston citizens. . . . We can do no more than express the hope that the governmental sources which furnish funding, as well as those which provide services, will be sensitive to these consequences and give all feasible help to the receivership.[39]

The judgment . . . is affirmed.

7.   Establishment of the Receivership

The master began placing advertisements for a receiver while the appeal to the Supreme Judicial Court in *Perez II* was pending. Interviews were conducted, references checked, and on February 5, 1980, shortly after the Supreme Judicial Court issued its *Perez II* opinion, Judge Garrity appointed Lewis Harwood (Harry) Spence to the position. In his order of February 5, the judge stated that:

> The Receiver shall take any and all actions necessary, desirable and appropriate to bring conditions in housing units owned or operated by the BHA into substantial compliance with the State Sanitary Code and with all other provisions of applicable federal, state, and local laws regulating the condition and habitability of residential premises.

The court's order granted the receiver "all powers and authority necessary and available to provide relief to the plaintiff class of tenants" and instructed him to meet regularly with the leadership of the TPC and with counsel for the plaintiff class. A Housing Advisory Committee was also established to monitor the BHA's needs and progress and to advise the judge and receiver. The master and his staff were commended for their work on the case and discharged.

Judge Garrity retained jurisdiction of the *Perez* case and, as is traditional in receiverships, acquired the power to review any legal claims or charges "arising out of any action taken by the Receiver in the performance of his duties." All actions against the receiver by creditors, BHA

---

39. There is perhaps an augury of solid cooperation with the receivership in the fact that the Executive Office of Communities and Development (speaking for DCA) in a letter of July 27, 1979, to the chairperson of BHA, ordered BHA not to expend funds from the State subsidy (or from the rents) for external legal services in pursuing an appeal from the judgment. Similarly HUD in a letter dated July 26, 1979, to the chairperson said that it would not concur in any request to pursue an appeal and that BHA was not allowed to use Federal funds for that purpose. It added: "I [regional administrator] urge the Authority to give its fullest support to the Court's Order and to the Receiver when he or she is appointed and I assure you that you can count on HUD's cooperation and support during this difficult period."

employees, or anyone else were henceforth to be submitted to the judge and to proceed only if he consented.

Harry Spence, the new receiver, was only 33 years old when he took over the ailing authority. A graduate of Harvard Law School, Spence had served as executive director of the housing authorities in both Cambridge and Somerville, Massachusetts, before coming to the BHA. His appointment was welcomed by the TPC and by the director of the HUD area office. Boston Mayor Kevin White, who had appointed a majority of the BHA board that Spence displaced, said of Judge Garrity's takeover of the authority: "That's all right. If they want it, they can have it."

Howard Cohen, a housing lawyer who had worked with Spence as general counsel to the Cambridge Housing Authority was hired to help set up the receivership. In an interview he described the BHA at the time Spence was appointed:

> It really was a shambles. It was Europe after World War I. People were sort of wandering around . . . anything that had gone on while the master was there had essentially stopped while the receivership issue was pending. Everybody had essentially given up and the Master's people were looking for jobs. . . . Basically what they needed was somebody to make decisions. I remember Harry and I used to get together . . . and we'd meet with staff people from 5 to 7. I would [meet with them on] legal and planning issues. He would do it every night. And we would make decisions. People would come in with a list of things and it was like we were Padrones or something. They would come in and say "We need authority to do such and such. Yes or No?" . . . As long as decisions get made sometimes it's good for the organization. There had been an absolute absence of leadership in the Authority. There just wasn't any administration. . . .

The receiver moved quickly to restore lines of authority in the BHA and to establish channels between the new administration and the BHA tenants. Spence began to hold "receivership meetings," the equivalent of board meetings, at which tenants could see their questions and grievances directly addressed by the receiver and his top staff. New planners and administrators were hired, and a detailed analysis of the BHA's needs and resources was begun.

Harry Spence brought a broad social vision of the future of public housing to the BHA. The administrative and management reforms he and his staff developed were important but, in many people's eyes, the most important change was the infusion of a sense of mission into the agency.

SPEECH AT THE ANNUAL MEETING OF THE UNITED COMMUNITY PLANNING CORPORATION (1980): What, then, is the task of this Receivership? Traditionally, in the law of bankruptcy, from which the model of receivership is derived, receivership can serve either of two functions: the restoration, or the liquidation, of the troubled enterprise. In the weeks since I have undertaken my responsibilities, I have encountered an alarming number of persons, persons in positions of substantial power, who assume the task of this receivership is the liquidation of public housing as a publicly-held inventory of housing for the poor. That assumption is sufficiently widespread that I believe it needs to be confronted and examined directly.

The argument for liquidation is a simple one: the present state of Boston's public housing is adequate evidence of the incapacity of public enterprise to efficiently manage the stock. Furthermore, that incapacity derives both from public incompetence, and from a structural flaw inherent in the concept of public housing. That structural flaw is the belief that large, poor communities can ever be orderly and attractive. The liquidators would argue that it is only common sense and realism to dispose of the public housing stock, by sale to the private sector, which will both achieve economic integration of the developments (the so-called mixed-income solution) and manage them with the efficiency of the private sector. . . .

The so-called mixed-income approach is not, in truth, a *solution* to the problem of public housing; it is largely an *elimination* of the problem of public housing. It begins by withdrawing from 75% of the task — for the redevelopment plan usually reduces to ¼ of their original number the units available for low income occupancy. The mixed-income alternative is roughly 25% more sophisticated than the argument of those who say to me: "Tear it all down and get rid of those people."

And as to the vaunted efficiency of private endeavor, I do not deny it in many fields of activity. But in the area of assisted housing, private enterprise has no more enviable a record than the public sector. My most immediate previous professional engagement was as a private developer and manager of subsidized housing. While I worked with an excellent firm, what I saw of the industry in general dispelled any romantic fantasies I might have had about private capacities. This City has ample proof, in its distressed 221(d)(3) and 236 housing stock, and in waterfront luxury apartments as well, that private management is no more assured of competence and efficiency in housing than public enterprise.

The private, mixed-income model may be appropriate in certain unusual and specific circumstances. But let us not seek false comfort in illusions that we are solving the problems of the poor by displacing them; or in the ascription of magical powers to private endeavor. The problem is harder than that, it requires more of us as a community than that, it goes to the heart of our relationship to the poor communities we are considering.

I would propose that the task of this receivership is not the liquidation of the public housing stock and the communities it is intended to serve, but rather the restoration of the public housing stock and the poor communities which occupy public housing. That restoration, as in a bankruptcy, can only occur if we understand what went wrong, to bring us to this brink of disaster.

[Spence then discussed the youth gangs, drug pushers, and perpetrators of racially-motivated violence that dominated many BHA developments.]

These groups in shifting and varying alliances maintain control of much of the public housing property in Boston. They have never been challenged in a coherent and a consistent way by the government to whom the poor have surrendered their proxy for the use of force. In light of their willingness to resort to high levels of violence to maintain their control, it is no wonder that the poor themselves have been unable to recover the territory, in the absence of governmental support. If we liquidate the public housing stock we will have accomplished the cruelest injustice of all. We will have withdrawn the power to contain the violence in their midst, and then punished them with exile for the violence that has ensued.

What is the origin of the withdrawal of ordering authority in governmental support in public housing? Let me briefly and much too simply recount the history. Public housing developments were for a period of years maintained by a system of benevolent or malevolent despotisms. The authority of the housing manager was absolute. If it was wisely and beneficially used in support of the needs of the community, it was a blessing. If it was malevolently abused, it was cruel tyranny. In either event it bore all the hallmarks of unlimited authority and it was subject to constant individual, class and, most of all, racial abuse.

In the course of the last two decades that unrestrained authority was appropriately challenged. But rather than that challenge resulting in the development of ordering mechanisms which are grounded in and reflect the needs of public housing communities, governmental authority was instead withdrawn. In the face of appropriate challenge to its previously tyrannical and often racist nature, the government withdrew in a destructive abdication of responsibility for the safety and well-being of poor communities. By so withdrawing [from] public housing, the government has allowed public housing developments to become a no man's land, ruled by those extra-legal groups I earlier described. Communities suffered; our minority communities were subjected to a particularly comprehensive, unrestrained, and therefore savage withdrawal of government support.

Our task is not to complete the already advanced destruction of these poor communities. It is instead to resume the government's previously abdicated responsibility for the protection and safety of the residents of public housing in the City of Boston. We must find ways to establish ordering authorities that reflect the needs of these communities, and are integrated into their daily lives. Those ordering authorities cannot be instruments of enforced acquiescense to intolerable and inhumane conditions. Quite the opposite, they must establish a protective cordon, within which the community of poor persons can exercise their creative energies. The establishment of such a liberating order can only be accomplished by the use of governmental authority in support of and in conjuction with the communities that authority is intended to serve. If we can accomplish that, we will restore our public housing developments not only physically but humanly and we may, if it is not too late, reconcile in some small measure, our previous savage breach of faith with the poor in our community.

The receivership placed the GBLS lawyers, who had now been representing the tenant class for five years, in a peculiar and unprecedented position. Bruce Mohl recalled that while there had been a defendant, the old BHA, the GBLS role had been fairly straightforward. It was litigating to force the BHA to comply with very basic court orders and there was a "knee-jerk presumption" that legal maneuvers by the BHA and their lawyers were probably contrary to the interests of the tenants. There had not been much need for formal notice to the members of the tenant class of the suit's progress during the period prior to receivership. Notice was sent to all class members when the consent decree was proposed, but, on the whole, the BHA's response to the litigation was so poor that there was little real progress to give notice of.

All this changed when the receiver was appointed. The administration of the housing authority against whom the tenants' lawyers had been struggling was now their remedy. It was *their* administration. Recognizing this, the GBLS attorneys working on the case decided to give the new receiver some room in which to operate. In Bruce Mohl's words, they determined that it would be foolish to begin immediately to "nickel and dime the receiver to death."

GBLS lawyer Leslie Newman described the process of class representation that evolved at this stage of the litigation as consisting of a variety of informal and formal mechanisms by which the plaintiffs' lawyers communicated what the receiver was doing to the tenants and received tenant input in return. Formal letters were sent to the named plaintiffs explaining the receiverships policies and GBLS lawyers who had links to various tenant groups conferred informally with them. In addition, individual tenants' legal complaints continued to be brought to various GBLS offices.

The problem of individual tenants' claims was especially troublesome at this stage. GBLS was, in a sense, responsible for seeing that the new BHA administration acted in the best interest of the tenant class as a whole. Yet they had traditionally provided the major vehicle by which individual tenants could take legal action to contest decisions by the housing authority. Shortly after the receiver was appointed the GBLS lead counsel wrote a "conflicts memo" to the entire staff of the legal services agency which stated:

> The class recertification in Perez v. BHA in the July 26, 1979 Order . . . tracks in relevant part the class certification of the Consent Decree. The class, as now certified, includes all present and future BHA tenants and is defined, in part, in terms of the relief to be granted, namely, class-wide relief. The present class certification specifically excludes individualized relief to individual tenants within the context of Perez. Individual actions related to the state sanitary code would simply not be part of the Perez case but may be litigated outside of and independent of, Perez. This is consistent with the way GBLS has handled individual sanitary code claims under the Consent Decree and such individual claims should not present serious conflict problems.
>
> Two other limitations in the Perez Consent Decree on the bringing of other class actions against BHA and on the seeking of relief inconsistent with the Consent Decree, while no longer part of an order, are, we believe, embodied in traditional ethical restraints on conflicts of interest (DR 5-105) and generalized notions of collateral estoppel/res judicata. While the ethical restrictions do not run to class members, the restrictions certainly would prohibit GBLS as a "firm" from representing individual BHA tenants either in a competing class action or in a challenge to existing or future orders in Perez. It is clear that GBLS, in representing the class plaintiffs, cannot also represent individual interests which might challenge the relief sought by, or granted to, Perez class plaintiffs, inside or outside of Perez. Representation of such individual interests would put GBLS in the untenable position of representing the class client's interests in Perez and interests antagonistic or potentially antagonistic to those interests, either in separate forums, or potentially in the same forum, in Perez. . . .
>
> Even in the context of individual sanitary code cases, however, there may well arise certain limitations in the representation. It is clear, for example, that we could not seek to join similar claims in bringing another class action against BHA or take similar actions against BHA on behalf of groups of tenants. Nor could we seek another appointment of a receiver or similar relief under G.L. c.111 §127H. Likewise, counseling a project-wide or city-wide rent strike, as opposed to individual counseling on rent withholding, or the representation of so-called "squatters," would also put GBLS in a conflict of interest. Similarly difficult, but less direct, would be a challenge by an individual BHA tenant to a policy or procedure developed by the receiver in Perez in which the tenant claims he or she was adversely affected by the procedure. In the context of Perez, we could and should handle any of these matters, if after consultation with the class, the judgment is that a particular course of action is in the best interests of that

class. The problem, of course, is that the class interest and the individual tenant interest may vary. This problem is particularly severe when the procedure is one which may have been developed or adopted by the receiver in conjunction with the plaintiffs in *Perez*, although it is not confined to such situations since plaintiffs may well be called on to take a position on any such matter in *Perez*. In short, while we can, consistent with the Code of Professional Responsibility, handle individual sanitary code cases, both defensively in evictions and offensively in independent actions, we can do so only within the parameters of the conflict problems presented by our ongoing representation in *Perez*. In the ordinary eviction case or affirmative sanitary code case this should not be a problem and the representation should be able to be undertaken consistent with DR 5-105. . . .

Our preliminary assessment of our obligations under, and the limitations imposed by, the order of appointment follows.

With respect to individual code enforcement actions, we may represent individual clients, members of the class, in such individual code matters as defenses to evictions and as affirmative sanitary code complaints with the understanding that such representation must not be inconsistent with the representation of the class in *Perez*. Potential clients must be fully advised of this limitation and assent to the representation.

With respect to non sanitary code matters, there are serious conflicts presented, both actual and potential. With respect to non BHA tenants, GBLS should avoid taking all such cases. With respect to BHA tenants, the only way any such matter may be taken is as part of the class presentation in *Perez*, and any such matter should be reviewed with *Perez* attorneys for such a determination. In that instance the individual is not the client except as a member of the class and the interest we represent is that of the class, not his/her individual interest, although the interests may well coincide. In the event we do not take the matter as part of *Perez*, we should make referral to Volunteer Lawyers or other appropriate referral.

Before bringing any affirmative action against BHA, GBLS attorneys should discuss the particular case with one or more of *Perez* counsel to ensure that we are not in a present or potential future conflict with *Perez*. Where there is any doubt about the conflict, we should seek other representation for the individual tenant. . . .

The GBLS lawyers and Judge Garrity were both extremely supportive of the new receiver in public and the press, as were the BHA's tenant organizations. Most BHA tenants interviewed at the time expressed hope that the new receiver would improve the BHA, and often asserted that he could do no worse than the old, politically controlled board. Underneath these positive public expressions, however, there was a certain amount of uncertainty on everyone's part about what would happen next. The issue of what the receiver was going to do if one was appointed had never been briefed and argued during the trial. As it turned out, Harry Spence proved quite capable of figuring out what needed to be done to get the BHA moving again, but Howard

Cohen, among others, reported that, in the early days of the receivership there was a sense of urgency and a need for immediate improvements on the part of Judge Garrity and GBLS lawyers who had been wrestling with the case for years. The judge and legal services lawyers had been attacking the BHA's problem from the outside, but they were now responsible for its operations and for all future failures. Cohen later remembered that

> a lot of the pressure on Harry [Spence] was from those two sources [GBLS and the judge] sort of saying "don't let us down, guy." . . . You could see that they were really very nervous about Harry . . . the people around now were sort of viewing him as the archangel. They had to, because if [the BHA] went down now, what would GBLS do? What would the judge do? What if all of a sudden riots break out, like in the schools, or the tenants start picketing the judge's house? . . . One of the problems with the attack on the [old BHA] board members was that if you say [the BHA's problems] were because they were stupid, now I'm there, and I'm smart its got to stop . . . everybody said it was a ten-year problem but I don't think anybody meant that meant ten years of people getting shot in public housing, drug pushing going on, or housing being abandoned. It was a ten-year problem but the cure would start day one. That was everybody's thought. And the acute problems we could resolve on day five and then we'd have ten years of nursing the patient back to health.

8. The Emergency Eviction and Injunction Procedure

In this atmosphere of urgent "retooling" in all areas of BHA activity, the issue of crime in the housing projects was identified by Spence and others as the most urgent of all the issues facing the receivership. As indicated by his speech to the United Community Planning Corporation, Harry Spence envisioned the issue of security and tenant safety in broad ideological terms. Judge Garrity, who had described control of the crime problem as the "sine qua non" for improvements in BHA housing, held similar views. On May 29, 1980, the receiver, along with counsel for the plaintiff class and the Tenant Policy Council, requested that Judge Garrity adopt an emergency eviction and injunction procedure to expedite evictions of tenants charged with committing violent crimes. In his affidavit in support of the new procedure Spence stated:

> The restoration of a reasonable level of order and safety to the public housing communities for which the Boston Housing Authority is responsible is the first priority of this receivership. It is a necessary pre-requisite to further improvement of the physical conditions of the properties. The Authority is seeking to establish, with some reasonable success, improved working relationships between its staff and the staff of the Boston Police Department. Nonetheless, it is my own judgment and the judgment of

other participants both with public housing and police experience, that firm, fair, but swift enforcement of the lease may be the single most important vehicle for the accomplishment of the restoration of order in our projects. The application of police powers through criminal actions cannot serve as the sole security vehicle to end the present intolerable human conditions in the BHA's properties.

A hearing, attended by the parties who had requested the emergency procedure, was held before Judge Garrity, who approved their request on June 3, 1980. The judge found that a state of emergency with regard to safety and security existed in many BHA developments and that a speedy eviction process for tenants accused of committing serious crimes was critical to the success of the receivership.

The new eviction procedure was invoked when the BHA filed an *ex parte* application with Judge Garrity alleging that a tenant had committed or threatened to commit certain serious crimes of violence in or near a BHA development. If the judge approved the application and the procedure operated without delays, the BHA could get an order to evict within six days of the filing of the application, cutting the time for the fastest possible eviction by three to four weeks. The pre-eviction grievance hearing usually held before BHA evictions was to be omitted under the new procedure, as was discovery other than that allowed by a specific order of the court. Unlike regular evictions, these actions would not be transferable to the Housing Court of the City of Boston. They were all to be filed as limited interventions in *Perez* and tried before Judge Garrity.

The first tenants against whom the emergency eviction procedures were invoked were George and Irene Reeder, 30-year residents of the BHA's Bunker Hill housing project in Charlestown. The Reeder's son, John, was charged with breaking into the apartment of another tenant on the evening of May 2, 1980, and with slashing the resident when she refused to allow him to hide there from the police, who were seeking him for a murder he was accused of having committed earlier that evening. The BHA's affidavit to invoke the emergency eviction procedure described in detail John Reeder's illegal acts as well as the threats against the victim made by a companion of his to discourage her from pressing charges. John Reeder was arrested the day after his alleged crimes and was incarcerated throughout the BHA's eviction proceedings. The eviction sought was directed against his parents and the two youngest Reeder children, who lived at home.

Greater Boston Legal Services took the position that representing tenants accused of anti-social conduct under the emergency eviction procedure would be against the interest of the plaintiff class as a whole that they represented. GBLS therefore refused to represent the Reeders. Another legal services agency, the Association of Neighborhood Law

Clinics (ANLC), which was in the process of closing down its operations, agreed to find a lawyer to represent the Reeders. Just before it went out of business ANLC persuaded Arthur Johnson, a private attorney with experience in landlord-tenant law, to take the case.

Meanwhile, Howard Cohen, who had drafted the emergency eviction procedure, began to have doubts about the wisdom of pursuing the Reeder eviction as the procedure's first test case. He approached Art Johnson, the Reeder's lawyer, about a settlement, and after some discussion they agreed that if the Reeders would leave Charlestown and find an apartment that qualified for a BHA "leased housing" subsidy, the BHA would pay for it under that program. On July 18, when the settlement was presented to Judge Garrity, he refused to approve it, stating that tenants who adversely affect security "should be dealt with speedily and harshly."

After several delays, one caused by the failure of the BHA tenant who had been the victim of the May 2 slashing to attend the trial and one because George Reeder had suffered a heart attack, the Reeders were tried before Judge Garrity and a jury.

PEREZ v. BHA; BHA v. REEDER, Suffolk Superior Court (August 7, 1980): [Judge Garrity gave the following charge to the Jury.] . . . Before I begin my instructions, I have two preliminary remarks. Both of these very, very able lawyers indicated that this was a tough case. It is a tough case, and I am certain that is why emotions ran somewhat high during the conduct of this not so long trial. There were many objections made, and if I was going to be one of the very able advocates on either side of this issue, I am sure I would have made just as many objections. Where I allowed an objection doesn't mean that I was correct. It means that I agreed with the attorney in the particular context.

I really respect these two lawyers. I think they are very able advocates, and I think they did a good job for and on behalf of their clients and I compliment them for what they did.

Now, when I was a little kid there was a president in this country whom people say had a sign on his desk and that sign said, "The buck stops here." There should be a sign on the jury box in this case, especially in this case, because the buck stops where you are. You have to decide this case. You have to set the standards. You establish the values. It is that simple. It is your job.

. Now, when I was a lawyer not so very long ago in the late 1960's I traveled up to the State Legislature and I testified before several committees. At that time I represented tenants of public housing and I told those legislators because of the abuses by the Boston Housing Authority and other housing authorities across the state, because of the arbitrary way in which those housing authorities were evicting tenants, it was important to set standards. It was important that if you were a tenant of public housing that you should not be evicted unless there was good cause to be evicted and I quote to you a provision from Chapter 121(B) of the General Laws in this black book, and I represent to you that I wrote this in the late 60's, and this was lobbied for and it was enacted. It was approved by the governor at that time and it states, "The tenancy of a tenant of a public housing authority shall not be terminated without cause and without reasons therefor given to said tenant in writing." Do you understand what I am saying? And when I became a judge a few years after that, in 1975 there was a case filed when I was the Chief Judge of the Housing Court for the City of Boston, which is on the tenth floor of this building, there was a case filed by an attorney seeking to have the housing authority rectify conditions in the various housing developments around this city. You are all residents of Boston. I am a resident of Boston. I am probably the only judge in the Superior Court that I know at the present time who remains a resident of this city. You have seen those projects. I drive by them. You may have friends living in them. I do. They are terrible.

In 1979 after several years of involvement as a judge with that case, I ordered that the Housing Authority be put into receivership, and in 1980, I was confirmed by the Supreme Court of this state, and early in 1980, I appointed a Receiver to run the Authority, who yesterday filed his six-month report, which I have glanced at periodically during the course of this trial.

There is one thing I have learned as the judge involved in that case over the past several years is that as bad as the physical conditions that exist in public housing in the City of Boston in 1975 and 1977 or in 1980 the [violence] is worse, which troubles people more, which makes it bad for tenants. It is an absolute travesty as to the total absence of safety and security, and I think you know that because of that, a request was filed before me a few months ago, and I was asked to establish an emergency eviction procedure, and this is the first case to be heard under that emergency eviction procedure.

Let me tell you what is not part of this case. What is not part of this case is where the Reeders are going to live if they in fact are evicted. That has nothing to do with this case at all. The fact that they have lived in the BHA development in Charlestown for several years has nothing to do with this case. They may have lived there for six months. They may have lived there for 60 years. That has absolutely nothing to do with your decision.

Finally, the fact that John Reeder, I gather is in the Billerica House of Correction and is no longer living with them has nothing to do with this case at all.

Let me tell you what has to do with this case. What has to do with this case is the first question that I am going to be putting to you. You will have this paper with you.

The first question is 1. "Did the defendant's son, John Reeder, who was then living with them on May 2d, 1980, unlawfully break and enter the apartment of Shirley Landenburg, then also a tenant at the Charlestown development and did he physically slash her throat and harm her without any justification or excuse?" Yes or no.

The second question: "Did John Reeder have a reputation for violence to persons and/or to property his parents knew of or should have known?"

The third question: "Did the occupancy of John Reeder in the plaintiff's development, that BHA development, as a member of the defendant's household, did it constitute or amount to a reasonable likelihood of serious or repeated interference with the rights of other tenants or amount to the creation or maintenance of a serious threat to other tenants?"

There is a lease there. Could I have the exhibits, please?

This lease between the Housing Authority and the Reeder family permits the Housing Authority to evict a tenant for one of several reasons. One of those reasons is if there is a reasonable likelihood of serious repeated interference with the rights of other tenants by John Reeder living with his family, and the other relevant provision, by John Reeder living with his family, is there the creation or the maintenance of a serious threat to the health or safety of other tenants?

The Housing Authority does not have to prove that it was likely that John Reeder was going to slash Shirley Landenburg's throat by his continuing to live there. Do you understand that? Okay.

Finally, "Has what has occurred here, is it a violation of that lease between the Housing Authority and the Reeder family? Should the Housing Authority be permitted to evict the Reeder family for cause shown or for that cause?"

Please circle the answers, "Yes" or "No," "Yes" or "No," "Yes" or "No," "Yes" or "No," to the four questions. Then your foreman, she signs it, and she puts today's date on it. Those are the questions. Do you understand them? Do you understand what you have to decide? Is there any question at all? No, I don't think there is, but if there is, raise your hands. Okay.

The jury found for the BHA on all four questions and evicted the Reeders, whose attorney immediately sought a stay of execution and an appeal. Judge Garrity initially denied the stay but, when the Supreme Judicial Court of Massachusetts agreed to take the case as an expedited appeal, the BHA agreed to stay the execution pending the high court's decision.

9. Spence v. Reeder

During the summer of 1980, as the BHA introduced and began to utilize the emergency eviction procedure, Boston's "progressive" legal community became divided over the wisdom of such an approach to the problem of crime in public housing. Many members of GBLS and other legal services organizations that traditionally had represented tenants against landlords, public or private, objected to the introduction of a process that they saw as undercutting years of work to provide extensive procedural safeguards to tenants threatened with evictions. Elimination of the grievance hearing before a panel composed of fellow tenants and BHA employees, and the vast reduction in the time required for eviction proceedings, even if justified by "emergency" conditions, were viewed as mistakes by many lawyers and tenant advocates who had spent years arguing that these safeguards were needed to protect the basic due process rights of public housing tenants.

Some efforts were made to smooth out the differences over these issues but there was little success. A meeting was held at the Massachusetts Law Reform Institute among several lawyers from that organization who opposed the new eviction procedure and the receiver. One participant described the session as "two non-intersecting lines of argument."

A group of lawyers from the Massachusetts Law Reform Institute and various other legal services agencies in eastern Massachusetts who were opposed to the positions GBLS and the receiver were taking on the *Reeder* case began to meet in September. Ultimately, they filed a lengthy *amicus* brief with the Supreme Judicial Court when it heard the *Reeder* appeal. Briefs supporting the receiver's position were filed by the BHA, GBLS, the Tenant Policy Council, a local tenant organization from the Bromley-Heath development, and the Massachusetts Secretary of Communities and Development. After hearing oral arguments on the expedited appeal of Judge Garrity's decision, the Supreme Judicial Court reversed the lower court, holding that the emergency eviction procedure had been improperly adopted.

◆ SPENCE v. REEDER
382 Mass. 398, 416 N.E.2d 914 (1981)

WILKINS, J. By this action, the Boston Housing Authority (BHA), acting through its court-appointed receiver, sought to recover possession of residential premises in the Charlestown Bunker Hill development leased under a written lease to the defendants (Reeders). This eviction proceeding was commenced as an adjunct to the long-continuing *Perez* litigation concerning housing conditions in BHA developments. . . .

In adopting the emergency eviction procedure, the judge made certain findings based on three sources: an affidavit filed by the receiver in support of the parties' joint motion, evidence concerning safety and security received in the course of many hearings in the *Perez* proceeding, and information provided by the receiver in many meetings with the judge. A hearing was held on the day the joint motion was filed. It does not appear that anyone attended or was represented at the hearing other than the parties who favored the allowance of the joint motion. Nor does it appear that attention was paid to whether the interests of class members who might have opposed the motion should have been represented in the course of considering whether to enter the order establishing the emergency eviction procedure. . . .

Under the terms of the order, the emergency eviction procedure was to apply to cases in which the BHA alleged that a tenant or a member of a tenant's household, or both, committed or threatened to commit certain serious crimes of violence in or nearby a BHA development or committed certain drug offenses in a BHA development. [The judge] directed that the BHA submit an *ex parte* application to invoke the emergency eviction procedure as to a particular tenant, with notice to the plaintiff class and to the Tenants Policy Council that they could appear and be heard. Use of the emergency eviction procedure would be authorized if the court "finds that there is sufficient cause to believe that use of the Procedure is warranted." A tenant's lease could be terminated on forty-eight hours' written notice. That notice would state the specific reasons for the termination, although the BHA could assert other reasons at any subsequent hearing. The BHA was relieved from offering to hold and from holding a private conference or grievance hearing concerning the termination and eviction.

At the end of the forty-eight hours' notice period, the BHA was authorized to file a summons and complaint for summary process "as a limited intervention in Perez v. BHA." The tenant was required to file an answer within forty-eight hours after service of the summons. Discovery was available only by order of the court, but the judge indicated that he would allow reasonable and necessary discovery. The trial of the eviction action was to be set no later than forty-eight hours after the time to answer. . . .

1. *The effect of the order on the Reeders.* The BHA has not argued generally that the Reeders were bound by the order adopting the emergency eviction procedure and thus foreclosed from challenging the procedure. Rather the BHA contends that the Reeders had an unrestricted right to challenge the emergency eviction procedure within the eviction action itself. One might well question the efficacy of a system designed for the expeditious disposition of certain eviction actions which permitted every such case to turn into a challenge to the propriety of a comprehensive order establishing procedures for an entire class of

cases. Further, one might question the reasonableness of a system that allowed a given tenant to challenge the application of the emergency eviction procedures only before a judge who already had approved those procedures generally and who, in an *ex parte* proceeding, had authorized the application of those procedures to the individual tenant specifically. In any event, the judge appears to have treated as being before him, the Reeders' challenges to (a) the failure of the BHA to offer a pre-termination hearing as provided in G.L. c 121B, §32, (b) the reasonableness of the shortened time periods for taking various procedural steps, (c) the reasonableness of limitations on pretrial discovery, and (d) the appropriateness of evicting them because of the conduct of their adult son. On the other hand, the judge dealt with the Reeders' challenge to the validity of the order itself, ruling, for example, that the order was valid even if the Reeders had not received notice of the proposed order. Such a ruling would seem to have made it unnecessary for the judge to pass on the Reeders' general or facial challenges to the emergency eviction procedure.

Because the judge made no rulings of law or written statement of what he thought was properly before him, we are not able to determine with certainty what effect he gave to the order establishing the emergency eviction procedure when he passed on the Reeders' various challenges. We know that, in the course of argument on one of the Reeders' motions to dismiss, the judge said that the order was drafted to provide procedural due process; that the eviction procedure was ordered after a joint application of the BHA, the plaintiff class, and the plaintiff Tenants Policy Council; and that there was "a vast amount of literature with respect to representation by counsel in a class action which justifies what occurred here." He then rejected the Reeders' due process challenge to the order establishing the emergency eviction procedure.

We conclude then that because the judge determined that the manner in which the emergency eviction procedure had been adopted met the requisites of due process, he did not give full consideration to the Reeders' subsequent challenges to the substance of the emergency eviction procedure. We turn then to consider whether, as to the Reeders, due process requirements were met in the adoption of the emergency eviction procedure.

The Reeders argue that, if they are to be bound by the order establishing the emergency eviction procedure, due process of law requires their interests to have been fairly and adequately represented during consideration of the request for entry of the order. They do not insist, in this court, that due process of law required them to have received notice of the proposed order. In this they are correct, because the principal concern is the fairness and adequacy of the representation of their interests rather than whether they received proper notice. Hansberry v. Lee, 311 U.S. 32, 41-42 (1940). . . . Rule 23(d) of the Massachusetts Rules of

Civil Procedure, 365 Mass. 767 (1974), reflects similar considerations. In his discretion, a judge may require the giving of notice of particular proceedings in an action, but notice is not required in all instances. If the Reeders' interests were fairly and adequately represented, and in this and other ways procedural due process demands were met, the judge reasonably could have concluded in his discretion that notice to the Reeders, and other similarly situated class members, was not required.[13] If, however, the representation of the Reeders' position was not fair and adequate, they, and others similarly situated, cannot be bound by the emergency eviction order.

We conclude that the interests of the Reeders, and persons similarly situated, were not adequately represented when on July 7, 1980, the judge acted on the joint motion requesting the establishment of the emergency eviction procedure. The Reeders were, of course, members of the class of tenants represented in the case. The request of the parties was no doubt representative of the views of a vast majority of the class. That fact, however, is not conclusive. A class representative has the responsibility to protect the interests of all class members. In turn, counsel for a class has a continuing obligation to each class member. . . .

At the time the emergency eviction procedure was under consideration by the court, events had occurred involving the Reeders that made their position on adoption of the emergency eviction procedure contrary to the position advanced by the class representatives. Their son allegedly had committed a serious crime in May, 1980, which, if proved, would have justified application to them of the proposed emergency eviction procedure. The Reeders thus had a significant interest in opposing adoption of any order authorizing the emergency eviction procedure.

Nowhere in the record, however, is there any indication that the position of persons such as the Reeders was adequately presented to the court. Various contentions might have been advanced on behalf of their position, but were not. Argument might have been made that forceful use of normal eviction procedures would substantially achieve the desired goal; that the scope of the order was too broad because it authorized eviction even where the threat to public safety had been eliminated; that improved public safety might be achieved by other, less drastic, means; that any deterrent effect of such an order would have no

13. The class representatives argue that, earlier in the *Perez* litigation, the Reeders and other class members received adequate notice that the emergency eviction procedure, or something like it, might be adopted. A notice sent to class members earlier in the *Perez* litigation that the "BHA will evict nuisance tenants who destroy property and threaten other tenants" did not give adequate notice of the possibility of an order suspending regular eviction procedures. Similarly, the justified, long-standing concern, shown in the record, over the serious problem of security in BHA housing does not constitute notice. A class member is not obliged to monitor the litigation to be certain that his interests are being protected.

impact when applied to events occurring before its entry; and that the order's asserted conflict with the requirements of leases, statutes, and rules should be addressed and perhaps resolved by changes in those conflicting leases, statutes, and rules. Whether these challenges would have been successful, we cannot say. We can say that the interests of the persons in the position of the Reeders should have been represented in the proceedings, and because those interests were not represented, the Reeders are not bound by the order and could not fairly be subjected to its terms. Consequently, the Reeders' case should not have been tried pursuant to the emergency eviction procedure and the judgment against them must be reversed.

2. *The authority of the class to waive rights.* Although what we have said disposes of the Reeders' appeal, we think it appropriate to consider certain matters argued by the parties that may bear on the future operation of the receivership and of any emergency eviction procedure. One of these subjects concerns how far the plaintiff class may effectively agree to surrender certain rights.

A person may waive his statutory and even his constitutional rights. See Johnson v. Zerbst, 304 U.S. 458, 464 (1938). . . . In the course of civil litigation, a party may waive rights merely by failing to assert them. . . .

[W]ith proper compliance with requirements of due process and court rules, the plaintiff class could waive a tenant's rights concerning lease termination set forth in the BHA's leases with its tenants. Such a waiver could not have been binding on persons in the status of the Reeders because, as we have said, a waiver would be against the interest of persons who might be subjected to the emergency eviction procedure for acts committed prior to its implementation. Consideration would have to be given as well to the interests of class members, not immediately subject to eviction by application of the emergency eviction procedure, who might oppose the procedure as a matter of principle, even though its possible effect on them would be only prospective and conditional. Careful consideration would also have to be given to whether the class was fairly and adequately represented in the proceeding and whether notice to the class should be given under Mass. R. Civ. P. 23(c), 365 Mass. 767 (1974). The fairness of the class's waiver of procedural rights contained in court rules concerning pretrial discovery (assuming the rules are not amended) and the class's agreement to expedite hearings of emergency eviction cases might have to be tested, on a case by case basis, in order to assure that procedural due process was met. But we see no objection, within the limits of due process, to the class agreeing to accept lease modifications that permit different procedural rules to govern emergency eviction proceedings based on future misconduct specifically described in those rules.

Such a waiver is, in many respects, similar to a settlement — a surrender of certain rights by the class in exchange for certain benefits. Before approving such a waiver, then, the judge would have to demonstrate on the record why he concluded, in his discretion, that the solution was fair and reasonable. We add that an amendment of the form of lease used by the BHA might be an effective supplement to any waiver approved by the class and authorized by the court. A lease amendment would provide notice to all tenants and would be permissible under the form of lease appearing in the record as a change required to comply with government "regulations," in this case a court order.

Notwithstanding the possibility that certain statutory rights might be subject to the doctrine of waiver, the attempted waiver in advance of a tenant's right under G.L. c.121B, §32, to request a hearing by the BHA prior to termination of his tenancy must be rejected. The class has no greater authority to waive a tenant's right to such a pre-termination hearing than does the tenant himself. Section 32 was enacted to provide certain procedural safeguards for tenants in public housing. In various circumstances, courts have long refused to give effect to purported waivers of statutory rights where enforcement of the particular waiver would do violence to the public policy underlying the legislative enactment. In our opinion, public policy considerations demand that an agreement in advance to waive the statutory right to a pretermination hearing before the BHA must be regarded as unenforceable. To accept such a waiver as valid would destroy the very purpose of the statute.

3. *The authority of the court to enter orders.* We think it is also appropriate for us to discuss, in general terms, the authority of a judge to enter orders in an institutional receivership proceeding and particularly an order of the character involved in this case. The institutional receivership in this case differs from a traditional receivership, and the limits of judicial authority in a receivership such as is involved in the *Perez* case are not well defined in decided cases. Indeed, the receivership of the BHA itself differs from those institutional receiverships established to assure that constitutional rights are protected. In constitutionally based receiverships, administrative rules and statutory provisions inconsistent with the fulfilment of constitutional mandates appropriately may be modified or set aside by court order. In the *Perez* receivership, however, no constitutional ruling underlies the order establishing the receivership. The receivership was ordered solely to achieve statutory goals. . . .

. . . The bold step of creating the receivership in the compelling circumstances fully set forth in our opinion in *Perez II* cannot appropriately be followed by a timid view of what the court may do in an attempt to make the receivership successful. Judicial authority to enter implementing orders is inherent in the equity power of the courts. That authority, as to the *Perez* litigation, is further found in G.L. c.111, §127H(*a*), which authorizes injunctions where rental housing exists in violation of certain standards and the condition of the housing may endanger or materially impair a tenant's or the public's health or well-being.

We reject the Reeders' contention that an emergency eviction procedure would be beyond the scope of the receivership and thus beyond
the authority of the court. . . .

We consider then, in this context, the attempted abrogation by the
emergency eviction procedure of a tenant's statutory right to request a
hearing by the BHA at least fifteen days prior to any termination of his
tenancy (except for nonpayment of rent). G.L. c.121B, §32. We do not
accept the BHA's argument that the receivership itself immunizes the
court and the receiver from compliance with statutes and regulations
that bear on the operations of the BHA. . . .

We see no justification for a court to disregard or overrule the requirements of §32. As we have said, the Legislature has prescribed
procedural requirements concerning the termination of leases of tenants
in public housing. The fact that the Commonwealth might have adopted
other means of meeting Federal requirements concerning lease termination procedures does not justify nullifying the provisions of §32. On the
record, the judge does not appear to have given any consideration to the
conflict between his order and §32. We are unable to perceive any basis
on which §32 properly can be swept aside by judicial order. If, as we
have said, as a matter of public policy, the tenant himself may not
effectively waive his statutory right to a hearing before his lease is terminated, surely as a matter of public policy a court should not be able to
impose a "waiver" on him. The solution lies in an amendment of §32, or
in the development of an emergency eviction procedure that does not
contravene §32.

4. *Bias of the judge.* We see no indication that the judge should not
have presided at the trial of the Reeder case. The fact that he appointed
the receiver and approved the emergency eviction procedure did not
require him to disqualify himself. We do not know what the judge
learned in the course of considering the receiver's *ex parte* application
that the Reeders be subject to the terms of the emergency eviction procedure. However, even if the trial had been jury waived, we would regard
the matter of disqualification as largely within the discretion of the
judge. Of course, the greater a judge's involvement with extraneous
pretrial matters the closer will be the scrutiny given to the fairness of the
proceeding.

Any showing that the judge was motivated by a desire to set an
example by evicting the Reeders would present a serious problem. We
note the judge's introductory remarks to the jury concerning public
housing problems in Boston, the need to appoint a receiver for the BHA,
the travesty of the lack of safety and security for BHA tenants, the
necessity of establishing an emergency eviction procedure, and the fact
that the Reeder case was the first one brought under the emergency
procedure. None of these remarks had any bearing on the questions
before the jury.

5. *Eviction for the acts of another household member.* The Reeders chal-

lenged the propriety of evicting them because of the criminal conduct of their adult son who resided with them. They claim that they may be evicted only for good cause and that the acts of their son do not constitute good cause to evict them. We assume any eviction of persons in the position of the Reeders must be based on good cause reasonably related to the protection of some legitimate interest of the public landlord. If the criminal acts were performed by a tenant's relative who was not resident in the household at the time he committed those acts, there might well be no "cause" to evict the tenant. There is on the other hand, authority suggesting that the situation is different when the miscreant is a member of the tenant's household. When the judge presented the Reeder case to the jury, he added a condition to the right to evict them that was not within the terms of the lease. He required that, to evict the Reeders, the jury must find that the Reeders knew or should have known of their son's propensity for violence to persons or property. This additional condition tended to establish a degree of culpability in the Reeders for the continued antisocial behavior of their son.

We do not know which conditions, if any, might hereafter be adopted for triggering the application of an emergency eviction procedure or terminating a BHA lease. We limit our comments to a few general observations. Although a tenant might not be liable for the misconduct of a person not a resident of the household, a tenant could properly be evicted for the acts of a household member in breach of the terms of the lease. In the interests of achieving safety in BHA projects, grounds for eviction may rationally be found in the wrongful conduct of household members other than the tenant, at least where the tenant knew or should have known of the violent tendencies of the other household member. The public interest may be served by a general rule allowing an eviction when, in the terms of the BHA lease, there is a "[r]easonable likelihood of serious repeated interference with the rights of other tenants" or the "[c]reation or maintenance of a serious threat to the health or safety of other tenants." These will be questions to be answered by the trier of fact and tested on appeal as to whether the evidence warranted such a finding. The notion that interference with or threats to the rights of other tenants justifying eviction can only come from a signatory of the lease (or his or her minor children) is itself illogical. Surely, a public housing authority cannot be left helpless to rectify a serious threat to the safety of other tenants simply because the signatory of the lease happens not to be the source of the threat. . . .

The judgment against the Reeders is reversed, and judgment shall be entered for the defendants.

So ordered.

10.   Post-Reeder *Adjustments*

a.   The Boston Housing Authority

The BHA receivership continued and, by most accounts, grew more effective and successful during the period in which the Reeder case was being litigated. Harry Spence fought against an attempt by Mayor Kevin White to cut the BHA out of Boston's Community Development Block Grant funds, securing $2 million for security in the developments. During these months much of the BHA's top management was replaced and the process of decentralizing the agency's decision-making authority was begun, an effort intended to give project managers and tenants more of a voice.

A great deal had changed in the BHA by the time the Supreme Judicial Court issued its opinion in Spence v. Reeder in February 1981. Richard Bluestein, who took over the BHA's legal affairs as general counsel in September 1980, described in an interview the legal posture the BHA took after *Reeder* as less aggressive on the issue of receivership power than was suggested by some of the arguments made on its behalf in that case:

> What I have held to is the notion that we'd better start as soon as possible, and . . . for me that was the day I got there, figuring out ways to function within the existing structure, and that to the extent we found that we couldn't function within the existing structure we should do our damndest to change the structure, not just for the receivership, but for the BHA. I wasn't sure we had a whole lot of extraordinary powers to begin with and I wanted to learn how to use the powers we'd have after receivership. It didn't do me any good to hide behind the receivership shield to do that. . . .

The BHA also backed off a bit from the legal positions argued on its behalf during *Reeder* concerning evictions. Bluestein expressed his view of the *Reeder* appeal as follows:

> Philosophically, that emergency eviction procedure [at issue in Spence v. Reeder] does not fit into the framework that I set out for myself when I got here, and it's not been the one that I've used. . . . [W]e tried to shape the appeal in a way that would answer some questions that existed in the case [such as] what kinds of statutes receivers have to abide by and what kinds they don't have to abide by . . . and to shape it so it would give us answers to some procedural questions along the way. It [the Reeder opinion] really wasn't that helpful on those kinds of things, but the larger goal was to get the SJC to write an opinion that said "you lost because the law required that we make you lose. Your remedy is up the street with the legislature. Take this opinion and go to the legislature." That [strategy] worked out rather nicely. . . .

The BHA did go to the legislature after Spence v. Reeder to modify the statutory requirement for a pre-eviction grievance hearing. On November 5, 1981, the Massachusetts legislature approved the following act, introduced at the request of the receiver.

Mass. Acts of 1981, Ch. 510

Whereas, The deferred operation of this act would tend to defeat its purpose, which is to immediately allow the waiver of hearings relative to terminating tenancies of housing authority tenants in certain situations, therefore it is hereby declared to be an emergency law, necessary for the immediate preservation of the public convenience.

Be it enacted, etc. as follows:

The sixth paragraph of section 32 of chapter 121B of the General Laws, as appearing in section 1 of chapter 751 of the acts of 1969, is hereby amended by adding the following four sentences: Notwithstanding other provisions of this paragraph, the executive director of the housing authority may petition the housing authority's hearing tribunal authorized to hold hearings under this paragraph to waive said hearing. Said petition shall be considered *ex-parte*. If the hearing tribunal determines, based on affidavits or other information provided by the housing authority that there is reasonable cause to believe that the tenant or a member of the tenants household has (1) caused physical harm to another tenant or employee of the housing authority, (2) threatened to seriously physically harm another tenant or housing authority employee, or the property of either, (3) destroyed, vandalized or stolen property of a tenant or the housing authority which thereby creates or maintains a serious threat to the health or safety of a tenant or employee of the housing authority, (4) on or near housing authority property, possessed or carried a weapon . . . or possessed or used an explosive or incendiary device . . . or (5) on or near housing authority property, unlawfully possessed, sold, or possessed with intent to distribute a controlled substance . . . then the hearing tribunal may waive said hearing, and permit the housing authority to commence an action for possession of the premises in the district, superior or housing court. In any such action, the court may, if it determines, after a trial on the merits, that the tenant or a member of the tenant's household did not commit any of the acts set forth above, remand the case to the hearing tribunal for a hearing. Any regulation of any agency of the commonwealth or subdivision thereof, or any provision in any lease between the tenant and a housing authority contrary to the provisions of this paragraph, shall be void and against public policy.

The BHA then instituted a special fast-track eviction procedure to apply the standard rules for summary process in the least possible time.

Notes

1. Consider the strategy Bluestein described for the *Reeder* appeal and the long term legal goals he suggested for the receivership. What did the BHA really lose in Spence v. Reeder?

2. Consider the above legislation in the light of the fact that it applies to all public housing authorities in Massachusetts. What did the pro-tenant lawyers who opposed the BHA in Spence v. Reeder really gain?

3. For later litigation concerning evictions from Boston public housing, see Spence v. Gormley, 387 Mass. 258, 439 N.E.2d 741 (1982) (eviction because of violent acts by members of tenants' households upheld); Spence v. O'Brien, 446 N.E.2d 1070 (Mass. App. 1983) (eviction for allowing person living in apartment to use apartment for sale of marijuana upheld).

b. Greater Boston Legal Services

The GBLS lawyers serving as counsel for the *Perez* plaintiff class also had some adjustments to make in light of the *Reeder* case. The issues of adequacy of representation and conflicting interests within the class were central to the Supreme Judicial Court's opinion, but that opinion contained little in the way of practical guidelines for the class representatives. GBLS certainly became more sensitive to these issues and, after *Reeder*, raised the possibility several times to Judge Garrity of conflicting interests within the class.

The controversy that began in Spence v. Reeder over the propriety of a legal services organization assuming the role GBLS assumed in the receivership phase of *Perez* continued. Leslie Newman described in an interview the GBLS decision to continue to serve as legal representative of the class as the most realistic way to help provide decent housing for all BHA tenants:

> We already don't represent everybody who walks in our door. We have undertaken to represent a class of people here, and we're representing 50,000 people in some form. It's not the way we usually represent people, which is with their individual problems . . . but we are representing 50,000 people and have succeeded in getting class-wide relief. . . . The institution which was our adversary is now our remedy, and that necessitates the establishment of a different kind of relationship. There are many legal services attorneys who feel that to work at all with an institution is to be co-opted. And there are many who understand being a legal aid lawyer to mean being an independent attorney with full control over your own cases as they come in the door. Having to coordinate individual

cases with [class representation], in which the first client is the class, creates hierarchical problems in this legal services program because it defies traditional expectations that attorneys have full independence in their representation of individual clients that they undertake to represent. Those two tensions always exist.

I believe very strongly that *Perez* provides a unique opportunity now and that being able to work with the institution is one of the things that makes *Perez* the special opportunity that it is for the public housing tenants in Boston. It's always necessary to be mindful of the threat of co-optation, of being too easily absorbed into the institution's conceptual framework. But the fact is that the time for adversarial action has passed in many ways. We pushed it as far as we could. If the Boston Housing Authority is to make it now, it has to be through a co-operative effort between the tenants and the Authority. It's not just a matter of buildings in which the landlord has a requirement to provide specific services, and as long as they are provided everything will be fine. The problem is more complex.

I believe very strongly, and this is why I represent individual tenant groups as a part of my representation of the class, that ultimately it has to be the tenants who monitor the Boston Housing Authority, because some-day the lawyers will be gone. The case will be over and our formal role as pro-tectors of the tenants' legal rights will end. If, in that time, we can create a situation in which, through resident organization and participation, not only do residents have a greater investment in their developments but also a greater sense of empowerment relative to the institution itself because they have negotiated and won battles on the expenditure of moderniza-tion funds, on the priorities for redevelopment and rehabilitation and various other issues — then *Perez* will have accomplished something.

Note

Is Leslie Newman's vision of the proper role for GBLS in *Perez* an appropriate one for a legal services organization? Who else could per-form it?

c. George and Irene Reeder

The Supreme Judicial Court's decision did not end the Reeders' prob-lems with the BHA. The authority attempted to evict them again in 1981, this time by the regular eviction process. At the first stage of these proceedings, which were based on the same charges as the previous year's eviction action, a BHA grievance panel composed of three tenants and two BHA employees voted four to one against the eviction. The Reeders were allowed to stay in their apartment.

Shortly after this final attempt to evict the Reeders, Art Johnson applied to Judge Garrity for an award of attorneys' fees for his work in Spence v. Reeder. The initial fee Johnson received when he took the case had not even covered his work on the trial, and by the time he had filed his application for fees, he, his partners, and student law clerks had put in hundreds of hours of unpaid work on the appeal. Several different theories were presented that could have justified the award of fees, including the suggestion that the Reeders' case had conferred the benefit of adequate representation on all members of the plaintiff class.

Judge Garrity rejected the request for any attorney's fees. After discussing the law in the area and dismissing the suggested rationales for a fee award to the Reeders' lawyers, he wrote:

> With respect to the Reeders' second, third, and fourth claims which all seem to assert that the Reeders, in representing a so-called minority portion of the tenants' class, both functioned as "private attorneys general" or as "public interest litigants" and also conferred a substantial benefit upon the tenants' class as a whole by their [the Reeders'] successful appeal which invalidated the emergency eviction procedures jointly requested by the plaintiffs' tenants' class and the plaintiff Tenants Policy Council, I note that under the terms of the order establishing the emergency eviction procedures, those procedures were to apply to situations where, as indicated in footnote 5 in *Reeder,* a tenant "(1) physically harmed another tenant(s) or employee(s) of the BHA in or nearby a development operated by the BHA; (2) committed acts of serious violence against the property of another tenant(s) or employee(s) of the BHA in or nearby a development operated by the BHA; (3) threatened to seriously physically harm another tenant(s) or employee(s) of the BHA in or nearby a development operated by the BHA; or (4) carried or kept upon the premises or any common area or development of the BHA a Class A, Class B, or Class C controlled substance as defined in G.L. c.94c §31 or a dangerous weapon as defined in G.L. c.269 §10(a), (b) or (k)."
>
> On the basis of reports to me by the Receiver and by his staff, after views of several of the BHA's developments, and after conversations with scores of residents of those developments, I specifically find, as I have so often found in the past, that both the actuality and the fear of serious crime are pervasive in most of the BHA's developments. Murders, rapes, robberies, and home invasions are commonplace and because the criminal justice system has failed and continues to fail utterly in dealing with such crimes and in providing any semblance of protection to the BHA's tenants the Receiver is compelled to employ the eviction process to provide some semblance of social control and order in the BHA's developments. The findings of fact in support of the establishment of the BHA's emergency eviction procedures underscore those observations. The Reeders' reliance upon a "private attorneys general" theory is misplaced. To suggest that the Reeders sought either to benefit the plaintiff tenants' class or in fact did so by their undermining of the BHA's efforts to respond to the situations which cause the life of the typical BHA tenant to be a hell on earth is inherently contradictory. To claim that the Reeders acted in the public interest is inconsistent with what members of the public perceive to be in their interest. . . .
>
> On the basis of the above findings and rulings, the Reeders' motion is ORDERED denied.

Problem

Judge Garrity's strong personal feelings about the proper course for the BHA receivership were evident throughout the *Reeder* case. Consider the jury charge and the opinion on attorney's fees. Is Judge Garrity fulfilling his proper role as a judge? Why do we care about "propriety" in a situation like this anyway?

11. Changes at BHA under a Court-Appointed Receiver

Twice yearly, the receiver issued a report to the Suffolk Superior Court, outlining progress at the BHA. In the Sixth Semi-Annual Report, issued in February 1983, Harry Spence discussed progress in the three-phased program to improve housing resources. The first phase, or diagnostic stage, defined the proposed course of action for the latter stages of the program. The second, or restoration phase, begun in the second year of the receivership, was ongoing. Work at three housing developments, demolishing some high-story structures, cleaning out and rehabilitating others was progressing (see photograph 12-2). In 1982, more than 500 previously vacant units were reoccupied, and the BHA was planning on a similar increase in 1983. Another related project was the redevelopment of the Columbia Point project. The BHA was reviewing three proposals to convert the project to mixed-income housing, and it was expected to begin redevelopment shortly.

The third phase, or preservation stage, was to be the restructuring of operating systems to prevent the further decline of housing units. The field management operations and tenant selection operations were the primary focus of these anticipated changes.

Also, the BHA won a suit against the City of Boston, for the city's failure to collect trash. Under the court order, the BHA was hoping to reduce its trash collection costs. Harry Spence commented that,

> We expect to be able to reduce our trash collection costs by as much as half a million dollars as a result of this order, thereby allowing us to greatly improve the quality of our trash collection and our severely underfunded extermination program. It is my hope that we might be able to demonstrate to our residents this summer that we are able to make substantial inroads in our battle against man's oldest enemy, the cockroach.

On February 24, 1984, Judge Garrity extended the receivership for a fifth year saying that the additional year was intended to permit an orderly return of authority to the city government.

At the hearing that preceded the extension, GBLS lawyer Leslie Newman said, "in some cases, conditions are still grievously poor." She

PHOTOGRAPH 12-2
A Boston Housing Authority project in 1984

asked the judge to require the BHA to meet specific standards in ten areas. Rodney J. Solomon, BHA acting general counsel, said that court-ordered performance standards would "bring about a flurry of activity [but] we don't believe they would bring about lasting change." Judge Garrity said the two sides should meet and try to agree on "bench-marks" for BHA performance, but he added that he was reluctant to issue an order to the BHA on the matter. Boston Globe, Feb. 25, 1984.

Meanwhile, BHA was considering major changes in the way it selects tenants, "a change designed to give a preference to public-housing-eligible families at the higher end of the income scale." Boston Globe, Aug. 6, 1983. The goal was to give "a preference to the working poor" that would "help to end the isolation of many public housing projects." Ibid. In 1983, 25 percent of public housing families had an employed member. The BHA was considering a policy of admitting two "working poor" families for every one that depended entirely on welfare. Ibid.

12.   *Conclusion*

On October 18, 1984, Judge Garrity ended his five-year receivership and control of the Housing Authority was returned to city government. Boston had elected to office a new mayor, Raymond Flynn — with whom Judge Garrity had a good relationship — who appointed a state representative, Doris Bunte, to the position of BHA Administrator. Bunte was thought to be the first former public housing tenant as well as the first black woman to head a major housing authority in the United States.

IV ◆ CONTROLLING THE FUTURE: OF DEAD HANDS AND QUICK TRUSTEES

What is property?

People seek immortality. Property — land, buildings, corporate shares, money — sometimes lasts longer than a lifetime, and so can be a vehicle for extending a person's significance beyond mortal life. Directing construction of a pyramid (or a memorial law school building) may reflect different motivations from seeking to control disposition of a family farm, but each is an attempt to tell the world how property should be used when its owner is no longer alive.

Each generation is in the ambiguous position of pressing to loosen the fetters imposed on property by its ancestors while trying to establish restrictions that will bind its children. Property law is the battleground for this war between the generations.

This Part considers the war between the generations in a variety of doctrinal and institutional contexts. Repeatedly, English and American judges have had to answer the question: to what extent should the dead hand of the past be permitted to control property today? Answering it, they have had to respond to royal revenue needs, the preferences of landowners, and the need for freely alienable property to finance development in a capitalist economy.

The principal subject of Part Three is the *trust*, the modern name for an arrangement of great significance in England for nearly a millenium and in America since the early seventeenth century. A trust is a device for separating the management of property from its enjoyment. As the idea of the *estate* emphasizes the place of a property holder in a chain of privileges and obligations, so the trust is a peculiarly Anglo-American expression of property as responsibility, a conceptual and practical vehicle for controlling property for a purpose other than one's own consumption. The trustee of a hospital, college, foundation, or church — like the trustee charged with an infant's or an incompetent's assets — demonstrates the idea of property holding as a limited, responsible, purposive activity. As society, in response to its density and its perils, comes more and more to understand the interrelatedness of modern life, and so to charge the possessors of property with new obligations and responsibilities, the doctrines and institutions that develop are likely to draw heavily on traditional ideas of trusteeship.

13 ◆ FUTURE INTERESTS

Individuals who convey or devise property often desire to retain controls over the use or further alienation of the property. The law's attitude to this desire has been ambivalent, allowing "dead hand" control through some legal devices, while confining its effect with yet other doctrines. A grantor who ties up property creates an interest in the property, one that represents the imprint of the present on the future; such a *future interest* is a potential right to enter into possession of the land. In this sense it is a present interest, here and now, with a present value susceptible to actuarial calculation. But the interest is "in expectance" rather than "in possession." Future interests may now be retained by the grantor and his or her heirs or created for third parties. Again, there is a common law hierarchy. A grantor may reserve three types: *possibility of reverter, power of termination,* and *reversion.* A third person may have one of two types, a *remainder,* either vested or contingent, or an *executory interest.*

A. POSSIBILITIES OF REVERTER AND POWERS OF TERMINATION

◆ CHARLOTTE PARK AND RECREATION COMMISSION v. BARRINGER
242 N.C. 311, 88 S.E.2d 114 (1955), *cert. den. sub nom.*
Leeper v. Charlotte Park and Recreation Commission, 350 U.S. 983
(1956)

On 22 May 1929 the defendant Barringer, and wife, by deed properly recorded, conveyed as a gift certain lands therein described to plaintiff for use as a park, playground and recreational system of the city of

Charlotte to be known as Revolution Park. This deed in the granting clause conveys the land to the plaintiff here "upon the terms and conditions, and for the uses and purposes, as hereinafter fully set forth." The *habendum* clause is to have and to hold the land "upon the following terms and conditions, and for the following uses and purposes, and none other," which are set forth as follows: 1. The land conveyed by this deed, together with other lands conveyed to plaintiff by W. T. Shore, and wife, T. C. Wilson, and wife, Abbott Realty Co. and the city of Charlotte shall be maintained and operated by plaintiff as an integral part of a park, playground and recreational area, to be known as Revolution Park, "for the use of, and to be used and enjoyed by persons of the white race only." 2. Here follows the other conditions of the offer. Then the deed contains this language:

> In the event that the said lands comprising the said Revolution Park area as aforesaid, being all of the lands hereinbefore referred to, shall not be kept and maintained as a park, playground and/or recreational area, at an average expenditure of five thousand dollars ($5,000) per year, for the eight-year period as aforesaid, and/or in the event that the said lands and all of them shall not be kept, used and maintained for park, playground and/or recreational purposes, for use by the white race only, and if such disuse or non-maintenance continue for any period as long as one year, and/or should the party of the second part, or its successors, fail to construct or have constructed the roadway above referred to, within the time specified above, then and in either one or more of said events, the lands hereby conveyed shall revert in fee simple to the said Osmond L. Barringer, his heirs or assigns; provided, however, that before said lands, in any such event, shall revert to the said Osmond L. Barringer and as a condition precedent to the reversion of the said lands in any such event, the said Osmond L. Barringer, his heirs or assigns, shall pay unto the party of the second part or its successors the sum of thirty-five hundred dollars ($3500).

On 22 May 1929 W. T. Shore, and wife, and T. C. Wilson, and wife, by deed properly recorded, conveyed as a gift certain lands therein described to plaintiff upon the terms and conditions and for the same uses and purposes as set forth in the defendant Barringer's deed. The provisions in this deed as to the use of the land, and the language as to reversion to the donors, are similar to the Barringer deed, except there is no provision that as a condition precedent to a reversion the grantors shall pay any money to the grantee. A number of years later a controversy arose between W. T. Shore and T. C. Wilson on the one side and the plaintiff here on the other over this land they conveyed as a gift. Action was instituted by W. T. Shore and T. C. Wilson against the plaintiff here, which action was compromised and settled by the plaintiff here, the defendant in that case, paying to W. T. Shore $3,600 for all rights of reversion, forfeiture, re-entry and interest which Shore had, has, or might have in the lands he conveyed by gift, and paying to the heirs of Wilson $2,400 for the same rights. As a part of the compromise and settlement, W. T. Shore and the heirs of Wilson, by separate deeds, remised, released and forever quit-claimed unto the plaintiff here all rights of reversion, forfeiture, entry, re-entry, title, interest, equity and estate and all other rights of every nature, kind and character, which they had, now have, or might have hereafter in the said lands.

On 22 May 1929 Abbott Realty Company, by deed properly recorded, conveyed as a gift certain lands therein described to plaintiff upon the terms and conditions and for the same uses and purposes, and for use of the white race only, as set forth in the defendant Barringer's deed. This deed contains a reverter provision, but it does not provide that if the lands conveyed are used by members of a nonwhite race that the lands conveyed as a gift shall revert back to the grantor. Nor does it contain a provision that as a condition precedent to reversion Abbott Realty Company shall pay to the grantee any money.

②abbott

On 22 May 1929 the city of Charlotte conveyed to plaintiff certain adjacent lands owned by it to form a part of Revolution Park. This park is composed of this land and the lands conveyed by Barringer, Shore, Wilson and Abbott Realty Company. The city's deed provides that should the lands conveyed by it and the lands conveyed by the other parties named above . . . not at any time for 12 consecutive months be used for park, playground or recreational purposes for use by persons of the white race only, then the land conveyed by the city shall cease to be a park, playground, etc., and shall revert to the city of Charlotte. . . .

③ Charlotte

In December 1951 all the defendants, except Barringer, Abbott Realty Company and the city of Charlotte presented to plaintiff a petition stating that they are negroes, and because they are negroes, they have been denied the right to use this golf course, in violation of their constitutional rights, and demanding that they be permitted to use this golf course.

Plaintiff by operation of law is charged with the duty of operating and maintaining recreational facilities for the citizens of Charlotte, and does not desire to deprive any of its citizens of their legal rights, nor does plaintiff desire to lose by reverter any of the properties entrusted to it for recreational purposes, nor does it desire to fail to comply with the terms of any gifts made to it by any of its citizens. Therefore, by reason of the aforesaid petition the plaintiff immediately instituted suit against the grantors of the lands composing Revolution Park to obtain a judicial determination of the effect of allowing negroes to use the golf course in said park, because of the reverter provisions and the restrictions as to use in their deeds. The appellants were made parties to the suit. Pending a final decision in such suit plaintiff refused petitioner's request.

PARKER, Justice. . . . We shall discuss first the Barringer Deed, which by reference, as well as all the other deeds mentioned in the statement of facts, is incorporated in the findings of fact, and made a part thereof. The first question presented is: Does the Barringer Deed create a fee determinable on special limitations, as decided by the Trial Judge?

This Court said . . . : "Whenever a fee is so qualified as to be made to determine, or liable to be defeated, upon the happening of some contingent event or act, the fee is said to be base, qualified or determinable. Hall v. Turner, 110 N.C. 292, 14 S.E. 791."

> An estate in fee simple determinable, sometimes referred to as a base or a qualified fee, is created by any limitation which, in an otherwise effective conveyance of land, creates an estate in fee simple and provides that the estate shall automatically expire upon the occurrence of a stated event. . . . No set formula is necessary for the creation of the limitation, any words expressive of the grantor's intent that the estate shall terminate on the occurrence of the event being sufficient. . . . So, when land is granted for certain purposes, as for a schoolhouse, a church, a public building, or the like, and it is evidently the grantor's intention that it shall be used for such purposes only, and that, on the cessation of such use, the estate shall end, without any re-entry by the grantor, an estate of the kind now under consideration is created. It is necessary, it has been said, that the event named as terminating the estate be such that it may by possibility never happen at all, since it is an essential characteristic of a fee that it may possibly endure forever. . . . Tiffany, Law of Real Property 3d ed. §220.

Barringer by clear and express words in his deed limited in the granting clause and in the *habendum* clause the estate granted, and in express language provided for a reverter of the estate granted by him, to him or his heirs, in the event of a breach of the expressed limitations. It seems plain that his intention, as expressed in his deed, was that plaintiff should have the land as long as it was not used in breach of the limitations of the grant, and, if such limitations, or any of them, were broken, the estate should automatically revert to the grantor by virtue of the limitations of the deed. In our opinion, Barringer conveyed to plaintiff a fee determinable upon special limitations.

It is a distinct characteristic of a fee determinable upon limitation that the estate automatically reverts at once on the occurrence of the event by which it is limited, by virtue of the limitation in the written instrument creating such fee, and the entire fee automatically ceases and determines by its own limitations. No action on the part of the creator of the estate is required, in such event, to terminate the estate.

According to the deed of gift "Osmond L. Barringer, his heirs and assigns" have a possibility of reverter in the determinable fee he conveyed to plaintiff. It has been held that such possibility of reverter is not void for remoteness, and does not violate the rule against perpetuities. The land was Barringer's, and no rights of creditors being involved, and the gift not being induced by fraud or undue influence, he had the right to give it away if he chose, and to convey to plaintiff by deed a fee determinable upon valid limitations, and by such limitations provide that his bounty shall be enjoyed only by those whom he intended to enjoy it. . . .

If negroes use the Bonnie Brae Golf Course, the determinable fee conveyed to plaintiff by Barringer, and his wife, automatically will cease and terminate by its own limitation expressed in the deed, and the estate granted automatically will revert to Barringer, by virtue of the limitation in the deed, provided he complies with the condition precedent by paying to plaintiff $3,500, as provided in the deed. The operation of this reversion provision is not by any judicial enforcement by the State Courts of North Carolina, and Shelley v. Kraemer, 334 U.S. 1, has no application. We do not see how any rights of appellants under the 14th Amendment to the U.S. Constitution, Section 1, or any rights secured to them by Title 42 U.S.C.A. §§1981, 1983, are violated.

If negroes use Bonnie Brae Golf Course, to hold that the fee does not revert back to Barringer by virtue of the limitation in the deed would be to deprive him of his property without adequate compensation and due process in violation of the rights guaranteed to him by the 5th Amendment to the U.S. Constitution and by Art. 1, Sec. 17 of the N.C. Constitution, and to rewrite his deed by judicial fiat. . . .

Now as to the Abbott Realty Company deed. This deed conveyed as a gift certain lands to plaintiff upon the same terms and conditions, and for the same uses and purposes, and for the white race only, as set forth in the Barringer deed. This deed contains a reverter provision, if there is a violation of certain limitations of the estate conveyed, but the reverter provision does not provide that, if the lands of Revolution Park are used by members of a nonwhite race, the lands conveyed by Abbott Realty Company to plaintiff shall revert to the grantor. In our opinion, the estate conveyed by Abbott Realty Company to plaintiff is a fee determinable upon certain expressed limitations set forth in the deed, with a possibility of reverter to Abbott Realty Company if the limitations expressed in the deed are violated and the reverter provision states that such violations will cause a reverter. That was the conclusion of law of the Trial Judge, and the appellants' assignment of error No. 2 thereto is overruled. However, the reverter provision does not require a reverter to Abbott Realty Company, if the lands of Revolution Park are used by negroes. Therefore, if negroes use Bonnie Brae Golf Course, title to the lands conveyed by Abbott Realty Company to plaintiff will not revert to the grantor. . . .

The appellants' assignment of error No. 7 is to this conclusion of law of the Trial Judge, that the deed from the city of Charlotte to plaintiff created a valid determinable fee with the possibility of a reverter, and that as the city of Charlotte has only one municipal golf course, the use of Bonnie Brae Golf Course by negroes will not cause a reversion of title to the property conveyed by the city of Charlotte to plaintiff, for that said reversionary clause in said deed is, under such circumstances void as being in violation of the 14th Amendment to the U.S. Constitution.

From this conclusion of law the city of Charlotte and the plaintiff did not appeal. We do not see in what way appellants have been aggrieved by this conclusion of law, and their assignment of error thereto is overruled.

The *possibility of reverter* is the interest retained after a determinable estate, while the *power of termination* is the future interest reserved after an estate subject to a condition subsequent. They differ, by traditional emphasis, in that the possibility of reverter is said to operate automatically, while the power of termination is deemed effective only when exercised voluntarily by its holder.

At common law, these reserved interests were recognized — albeit grudgingly. They were "mere expectancies," not sufficiently substantial to be alienable *inter vivos* or devised; they could only descend to heirs at law. Today, however, statutes and decisions in most states permit alienation by any means of all future interests. For further discussion of these issues, see Long v. Long, p. 230 *supra*.

B. REVERSIONS

◆ WALKER, INTRODUCTION TO AMERICAN LAW
277-278

§135. ESTATES IN REVERSION

Estates are divided, with respect to their commencement, into estates in possession, in reversion, and in remainder. Of estates in possession there is nothing to be said. All the remarks hitherto made, apply to estates in the actual possession of the owner. This is their most natural and obvious situation. But the first three of the foregoing estates, namely, estates in fee, for life, and for years, while they are in the present occupation of one person, may belong in expectancy, either in reversion or remainder, to another. To these accordingly we turn our attention. An estate in reversion may be defined to be, the residue of an estate remaining in the grantor or his heirs, to come to his or their possession, after the determination of some particular estate granted away. It grows out of this legal maxim with regard to property, that whatever interest a man has, and does not dispose of, remains in him and his representatives. A reversion may be in fee, for life, or for years. Thus if I have an estate in fee, and grant you any smaller estate, the reversion in fee still remains in me. If I have an estate for life, and grant you any smaller estate, the reversion for life still continues in me; and if I have an estate for years, and grant you an estate for a less number of years, the reversion for years still continues in me. In this way there may be any number of reversions existing in the same state, in the same manner as a unit may be divided into any number of parts; and all these estates in reversion, added to the estate in possession, make together only one fee simple estate in possession. An estate in reversion is considered as a present interest, though it can only take effect in future; and as such, is transferable and descendible in the same manner as an estate in possession.

Examples

In each example, *O* starts with a fee simple absolute:

(a) O to A for life (O has a reversion)

A reversion is, as Walker stated, the "residue" of the grantor's estate after he has conveyed part of his total estate. "Residue" once again refers to duration.

(b) O to A and the heirs of his body

Though a fee tail is a potentially infinite estate, nevertheless *O* retains a reversion that awaits the possibility that *A*'s line will expire.

(c) O to A for ten years

When seisin was all important, a freeholder who granted a non-freehold estate was said to retain his freehold, subject to the non-freehold term. In this example *O* would have had a fee simple subject to a term of ten years. Seisin is not so important now, and we simply say that the grantor of a term for years retains a reversion.

(d) O to A for life; A to B for 99 years

O clearly has a reversion in fee, but what does *A* have, and how secure is *B*'s lease? On the hierarchy, a life estate is "larger" than any term for years, so even if *A* is eighty years old, *A* has a reversion. *B's term for years will expire if A dies before the lease is up.*

The distinction between a reversion and a possibility of reverter is subtle and not necessarily logical. Though it is clear that the grantor of a fee simple determinable reserved a future interest, the fee simple determinable was held to be as "large" an estate as the fee simple absolute. The grantor gave away everything, so he had no reversion, but nevertheless retained something. This "mere possibility," as already noted, was so insubstantial that the possibility of reverter was neither alienable nor devisable. A reversion, however, was a substantial portion of infinite duration, and thus a true estate in expectancy.

C. REMAINDERS

1. Creation

♦ WALKER, INTRODUCTION TO AMERICAN LAW
278-282

§136. ESTATES IN REMAINDER

An estate in remainder may be defined to be an estate limited by the grantor to take effect and be enjoyed by the grantee, after another previous estate shall be terminated. For example, if I grant land to you for life, and then to your brother and his heirs, the latter estate is a remainder. The estate which precedes the remainder is called a particular estate. Remainders differ from reversions in this, that they are always created by the express act of the parties, while reversions result from the operation of law; and also in this, that remainders are never limited to the grantor, while reversions are always reserved to him or his heirs. In other words, a remainder is something granted; a reversion is something reserved. Estates in remainder form by far the most abstruse and intricate subject, connected with the law of realty. They had their origin in the English fondness for family settlements. It is not uncommon to find in such settlements eight or ten remainders limited one after the other, in order to prevent the possibility of the estate passing out of the family of the grantor. Fortunately, the spirit of our institutions is utterly opposed to these entangled and cumbrous arrangements; and accordingly our books contain few discussions on the subject. In this state, so far as I know, there has not been a single case; not from any legal prohibition, but from the general disposition of our citizens to keep property as little trammelled as possible. On this account, I shall attempt no more than to give a very general statement of the leading properties belonging to remainders.

To whom remainders may be limited. 1. In this state we have a statutory restriction, "that no estate shall be given or granted by deed or will to any persons but such as are in being, or the immediate issue or descendants of such as are in being, at the time of making such deed or will." There is some ambiguity in these words. . . . We have had no construction of this statute; but from the strong aversion the law manifests to perpetuities, . . . I should presume that our legislature intended to restrict the limitation of estates to persons in being and their children. 2. Another restriction grows out of the rule in Shelley's case, which may be thus stated. Whenever a person, either by deed or will, takes an estate for life, and in the same instrument there is a remainder limited, either immediately or otherwise, to his heirs in fee, that person takes the whole estate in fee. This rule is said to have been established as early as 1325. But the case from which the rule took its name is one reported by Coke. . . . [T]hough professedly a rule of construction, adopted to effectuate the intention of the parties, its obvious tendency is to frustrate such intention, by converting what was meant for a life estate into fee simple. . . . [T[here is scarcely a principle of our law which has been the subject of so much controversy. But I am at present concerned with this rule only so far as it is connected with remainders. The result of its existence is, that remainders in fee cannot be limited by deed to the heirs of the same person to whom the life estate is granted; for this would be construed to be an estate in fee simple. . . .

How remainders are created. It is a fundamental property of remainders, that they must always be created by the same instrument or act, which creates the particular estate; for if by one instrument I should grant a present estate to you, and by another the future estate to someone else, this last would not be the creation of a remainder, but the grant of a reversion growing out of the first grant. . . .

The leading properties of remainders created by deed, are as follows. 1. There must be a present particular estate to precede the remainder. This is implied in the very term; something must be taken out, to leave a remainder. Such is the reason usually given; and in mathematics it would be perfectly satisfactory. But the student of law, who perceives no inherent difficulty in creating a future estate, after a present estate reserved to the grantor, will require some further explanation. The necessity then, for a particular estate, only exists where the freehold is to pass in remainder; and then it results from the doctrine before referred to, that a freehold cannot be made to commence in future. Accordingly, when a man wishes to convey a freehold, to commence at a future time, he must first create a particular estate, to continue until he wishes the next estate to commence, and then limit the freehold thereon. In so doing, livery of seisin is made to the particular tenant, and enures to the benefit of the remainder-man. Such is the artificial reasoning upon which the whole system of remainders is founded. But under our law, this reason for creating a particular estate, for the mere purpose of limiting remainders thereon, does not exist, because we do not make livery of seisin. I may grant an estate of freehold, to commence at any time I please; and although this would not be a remainder, it would answer precisely the same purpose. This fact certainly renders the law of remainders unnecessary here, but whether it alters that law in any respect, remains to be decided. 2. This particular estate must be at least an estate for years; for an estate at will or sufferance, having no certain measure of duration, is of too slender a nature to support a remainder; since it would depend upon the pleasure of the grantor, whether the remainder should ever take effect at all. 3. This particular estate must be less than a fee simple; for after a fee simple nothing can remain; hence it follows that the greatest estate upon which a remainder can be limited is a conditional fee. 4. This particular estate must not fail or be defeated before its natural termination; for when the particular estate fails, the remainder also fails. The one is said to support the other, and the maturity of the particular estate, may be likened to a condition precedent, which must be fulfilled, before the remainder can take effect. This rule seems to be entirely arbitrary, and founded in no substantial reason. The idea that one estate supports the other, is purely metaphorical; it does not have this effect from any inherent necessity, but merely because the law so ordains. The consequence is to place all the remainder-men more or less at the mercy of him who has the first estate; and to destroy the whole chain because one link happens to fail. This can only be obviated by the cumbrous arrangement of appointing trustees to preserve the remainders; an expedient now universally adopted in creating these estates, but which I have not room particularly to describe. 5. The remainder must vest in the grantee, either during the continuance of the particular estate, or at the instant of its termination. The reason is, that the particular estate and the remainder, being created by the same act, are considered but one entire estate, divided into parts; and if there could be an interval or hiatus between the expiration of the particular estate and the commencement of the remainder, there would be an intermediate reversion in the grantor, which would destroy the unity of his grant. This rule, like the foregoing, seems to be purely arbitrary. The reason here given would be good in mathematics, but need not be adopted in law. What harm could possibly arise from allowing the grantor to enjoy the intervening estate, until by the terms of the grant the remainder-man could take it, and then giving it to him? There is surely no necessity for breaking up the whole grant, when the deficiency could be so easily supplied; yet such is the law; and its effect can only be obviated, as before, by the appointment of trustees to preserve the remainders. These several rules, and particularly the last, give rise to the distinction between vested and contingent remainders, which I shall now proceed to explain.

Example

O to A and the heirs of his body, then to B and his heirs (B has a remainder in fee simple)

Prior to the development of executory interests after the Statute of

Uses (1536), the remainder was the only future interest a grantor could grant to a person other than himself. In fact, the remainder itself was not possible until sometime after the Statute De Donis (1285), when courts began to allow the grant, along with a fee tail, of a remainder (with most of the rights of a reversion) to a third person. A grantor with a reversion could always convey it separately to a third person, but along with it went a tenurial relationship with the holder of the possessory estate. A remainder was construed differently; there was no tenure between the present possessor and the remainderman. Remainders today have the "content" of a reversion, but they must be grants to third persons made simultaneously with the grant of the "particular" estate.

2. Varieties

♦ WALKER, INTRODUCTION TO AMERICAN LAW
282-284

§137. VESTED AND CONTINGENT REMAINDERS

A vested remainder is where a present interest passes to a determinate person to be enjoyed in future. Thus, if I grant an estate to you for life, with remainder to your brother and his heirs in fee, your brother acquires a present interest which he may dispose of at pleasure, though it can only be enjoyed by him and his heirs or assigns after your death. In this case, you perceive there is no doubt that the remainder will take effect at the moment your particular estate expires. In other words, the moment you die, your brother or his representatives will be ready to take, since the law will not presume an entire failure of heirs. On account of this certainty, the remainder is considered as vesting at once; and becomes as much a present interest, as a reversion is. A contingent remainder is where no present interest passes, on account of the uncertainty whether there will be any one to take it, when the particular estate expires. Thus if I grant an estate to you for life, with remainder to the heirs of your brother in fee; here, as it is doubtful whether your brother will die before you, and as he can have no heirs while he lives, the remainder to his heirs is contingent. If he dies before you, the remainder at once vests in his heirs, and becomes in them a disposable interest; but if he survives you, the remainder never vests at all; because the particular estate has previously terminated. In this case, the remainder is contingent, because limited to an uncertain person. It may likewise be contingent, by being limited upon an uncertain event. Thus if I give you an estate for life, with a remainder to your brother if he survives you, here the uncertainty whether your brother will survive you, makes his remainder contingent. Whenever the contingency upon which the remainder depends is changed into certainty, the remainder vests of itself in the person to whom it is limited, without any act by him; but until then, his interest being a mere possibility, is not the subject of bargain and sale.

. . . The view I have taken of estates in remainder, is too brief and general to do any thing more than excite your curiosity to examine further; unless perhaps it should lead you to discuss the policy of adhering to rules, when the reasons of them no longer exist. There is clearly no absolute necessity for perpetuating a branch of law so purely arbitrary and technical. A few brief statutory provisions would enable persons to make future dispositions of realty, as easily as of personalty, and to any extent which might be deemed expedient. Let it be expressly provided, that any estate might be made, by deed or will, to commence at a future period; and that where several successive estates should thus be created, the failure of any one should not affect the rest; but the lapsed estate should revert to the grantor or his heirs, until the next estate could take effect; and the whole fabric of remainders would fall to the ground. I hope the day is not far distant, when such a reform will be undertaken.

The law of vested remainders is truly "abstruse and intricate," what Cromwell is said to have called "a tortuous and ungodly jumble." We can ascribe this unfortunate condition to the conflict between dead-hand control and free alienation, coupled with the most mystical manifestations of an evanescent concept, seisin. Yet as one studies the various types of remainders, and the root distinction between vested and contingent, one should neither condescend to the intricacies of common lawyering nor throw up one's hands in frustration or horror. The distinction between vested and contingent remainders, and the restrictions on the latter, were a primitive system for preventing *perpetuities*, dead-hand control for generation after generation. It took several centuries, and the demise of feudal tenures, to effect a simpler system to accomplish this necessary and often politically unpopular task.

The common law of remainders has been modified by statutes, and there are today other devices for future management of wealth. Real property no longer dominates our economic system. Yet it is worth considering the following examples and reflecting on the reasons for the bygone importance of the rules they represent.

Examples

(a) *O to A for life, then to B and his heirs* (B has a vested remainder in fee simple)

(b) O to A for life, then to the heirs of B (The heirs have a contingent remainder in fee simple)

(c) O to A for life, then to B and his heirs if he marries C (B has a contingent remainder in fee simple)

Example *(a)* is Walker's prototype of a vested remainder. It satisfies two criteria: The person who will take on termination of the particular estate, B, is ascertained, and he is ready to take immediately upon natural termination of that estate. Example *(b)* is Walker's example of a contingent remainder: the heirs of B are not ascertained until B dies. Similarly, in *(c)* B's remainder will not vest until he marries C. The problem with a contingent remainder was that if it did not vest immediately upon termination of the prior estate, it was destroyed; in our example, the full fee simple would revert back to O or his heirs, and would not spring back when the heirs were ascertained or B married C.

A remainder might also suffer artificial destruction. A premature determination of the particular estate could be brought about by *forfeiture, surrender,* or *merger,* thereby destroying any contingent remainders supported by it. Forfeiture was a tortious conveyance, by which a tenant for life or in tail purported to convey a fee simple. Surrender occurred when a tenant for life surrendered his life estate to a vested remainder, the estate thereby ceasing to exist as a particular estate. Merger, which has significant modern applications, occurs if a freehold estate comes into the hands of the same person holding a fee simple remainder or reversion. The freehold coalesces with the greater estate, thus ceases to exist, and thereby destroys intermediate contingent remainders.

The destructibility rule may be harsh, but it is rooted in conveyancing by common law feoffment, with livery of seisin. A grantee could not be enfeoffed *in futuro,* because livery of seisin had to occur on the property between grantor and grantee. The courts allowed remainders as exceptions to this rule because the path of seisin was at least "continuous." Seisin passed as usual to the particular estate; then, on the natural termination of that estate, it "enured" to the vested remainderman. However, there could be no gap in seisin, no "abeyance"; if the remainderman was not ready to take on termination, seisin could not be suspended until he was ready. Continuity of seisin was important to the feudal lord, because only a tenant who was seised would perform services. The courts used seisin to defeat the intentions of the grantor, in the interest of unifying the ownership of estates and thus facilitating alienation. Statutes and court decisions since the middle of the nineteenth century have rejected destructibility in most American jurisdictions, although the rule is still recognized in a handful of states.

Even so restricted, contingent remainders were voided by the courts until the fifteenth century. The difficulty was that if the ultimate heirs of the complete fee simple were not ascertained, one could not "locate" the fee simple of the original grantor, since the essential quality of holding a fee simple was inheritance. Even after the courts had acquiesced to contingent remainders, they groped for solutions to this logical problem. Some courts, perhaps in their own frustration, announced that the fee simple was *in nubibus* (in the clouds), or *in gremio legis* (in the bosom of the law). Though there is no solution to the problem, by modern analysis the fee simple remains with the grantor until the remainder vests.

(d) O to A for ten years, then to B and his heirs

A nonfreehold estate could not technically be the basis for a freehold remainder because seisin could not pass *in futuro*; the ten-year period would constitute a gap in seisin. At common law *B* took a fee simple, subject to *A*'s term of years.

(e) O to A and his heirs so long as used for residential purposes, then to B and his heirs

At common law, the interest remaining after conveyance of a fee simple determinable was too slight to be a reversion; see p. 490 *supra*. By feudal reasoning, the interest could also not be granted as a remainder to a third person, *B* in this example. Not until the sixteenth century did the law courts recognize an interest for *B*, see p. 503 *infra*.

(f) O to A for life, then one day later to B and his heirs

B has no remainder because of the one-day gap in seisin; *O* has a reversion.

(g) O to A for life, then to the children of B and their heirs

So long as *B* has no children, the nonexistent children have a contingent remainder. As soon as a child is born, the remainder vests in that child, but it is a "vested remainder subject to open" because when *B* has more children, each takes a vested interest in the property. The heirs of a vested remainderman inherit the remainder even if the remainderman dies before the remainder becomes possessory. However, children of *B* who are born after the remainder vests in possession in the older children do not share in the property.

(h) O to A for life, then to such children of A as A will appoint, and without any appointment by A, to A's children in equal shares

A's children have a "vested remainder subject to divestment." Their interest in equal shares is vested because the law favors vesting; if *A* exercises his power of appointment, some children may be divested. The difference between this vested remainder and a contingent remainder is hardly obvious, but it has at times been quite important.

3. The Rule in Shelley's Case and the Doctrine of Worthier Title

Disputes over "freedom of alienation" often arose in tax cases, when large landowners sought to protect their income from feudal incidents.

These incidents, such as relief and wardship, were due from those who took by inheritance, but not from takers by purchase. Thus alienations that bypassed inheritance could defeat collection of the incidents. The clearest evasions were by grantors who still sought to transfer the property to their heirs. Two famous judge-made doctrines, the Rule in Shelley's Case and the Doctrine of Worthier Title, blocked specific arrangements for evading incidents with the use of remainders.

Shelley's Case, 1 Co. Rep. 93b, 76 Eng. Rep. 206 (K.B. 1581), is authority for a rule much older than the case; the rule dates to at least 1366. If O conveyed or devised a life estate in land to A, and with the same conveyance or devise limited a remainder in the property to the heirs of A, the rule held that A, not his heirs, had a remainder in fee simple. As A also took a life estate under the first part of the gift, that life estate merged with his remainder so as to give him an immediate fee simple in possession. Thus "O to A for life and then to the heirs of A" became "O to A and his heirs." When A died, his heirs inherited the fee simple from him, rather than taking from O "by purchase." The rule has been abolished in England and in at least 44 American states.

Like the Rule in Shelley's Case, the Doctrine of Worthier Title proscribed devises of land by T to those who would be his heirs at law. If he did so (presumably to protect the incidents) the heirs took as heirs rather than as devisees. The doctrine also had an *inter vivos* branch; when a grantor limited a remainder to those who would be his heirs at law, the courts converted the remainder into a reversion. For example "O to A for life, then to the heirs of O"; by the doctrine, O had a reversion that the heirs would inherit when O died. This *inter vivos* branch is now a rule of construction rather than a rule of law, a rebuttable presumption that the grantor intended to retain a reversion. See Cardozo's opinion in Doctor v. Hughes, 225 N.Y. 305, 122 N.E. 221 (1919). As for the name of the doctrine, apparently one's title to land was "worthier" if more obligations were appended to it.

◆ EVANS v. GILES
   83 Ill. 2d 448, 415 N.E.2d 354 (1980)

KLUCZYNSKI, Justice. . . . This case concerns title to 320 acres of Macon County farmland. At issue is the construction on the will of Sard Giles who died November 22, 1925. Article Third of his will devised the land to his daughter Leta Timmons for life, ". . . with remainder over to the heirs of the body of her, the said Leta Timmons, and in the event of the death of the said Leta Timmons without issue, then in that event, the real estate herein . . . I give, devise and bequeath to Elmo S. Giles for and during his natural life with remainder over to the heirs of the body of him, the said Elmo S. Giles." The parties agree that this devise created a life estate in Leta Timmons followed by alternate contingent remainders.

On April 8, 1972, Leta G. Timmons died never having had children. The parties agree that this caused the failure of the first contingent remainder to the heirs of her body. Previously on February 9, 1951, Elmo S. Giles, son of Sard Giles, died leaving Elmo S. Giles, Jr., the only child ever born to him. On February 26, 1968 also prior to Leta's death, Elmo S. Giles, Jr., died never having had children. The precise question to be decided is whether all estates after the life estate of Leta Timmons failed causing the title to the tract, in the absence of a residuary clause, to revert to the heirs of Sard Giles, thus enabling plaintiffs as devisees of Leta Timmons to take her one-half interest in that reversion, or whether defendants, the devisees of the contingent remainder interest of Elmo S. Giles, Jr., take through him and are entitled to the remainder in fee.

The circuit court ruled that Sard Giles' will created alternative contingent remainders and that both remainders had failed. The court reasoned that the first contingent remainder, to the heirs of the body of Leta Timmons, failed at the date of her death without issue. The court further reasoned that the alternate contingent remainder, to Elmo S. Giles, Sr., for life with remainder to the heirs of his body, failed because both he and Elmo S. Giles, Jr., predeceased Leta Timmons. The court accordingly ruled that the failure of both remainders caused the property to revert to Sard Giles, to pass by intestacy to Leta Timmons and Elmo S. Giles, Jr., and thereafter to be distributed under the wills of Leta Timmons and Elmo S. Giles, Jr. The court then entered its decree partitioning the property, as requested by plaintiffs. The appellate court, one justice dissenting, reversed the judgment of the circuit court. Relying primarily upon the decision of the court in Hofing v. Willis (1964), 31 Ill. 2d 365, 201 N.E.2d 852, and the public policy against partial intestacy, the appellate court reasoned that a contingent remainderman, such as Elmo S. Giles, Jr., in the absence of an express provision by the testator, need not survive the life tenant in possession, Leta Timmons. The appellate court therefore ruled that the property in its entirety should pass under the will of Sard Giles to Elmo S. Giles, Jr., and thereafter according to the will of Elmo S. Giles, Jr., to defendants. We affirm.

The parties agree that the devise in question created alternative contingent remainders, and they agree that the first contingent remainder failed on the death of Leta Timmons without issue. Plaintiffs contend, however, that a condition precedent to vesting of the alternative remainder of Elmo S. Giles, Jr., is that he and Elmo S. Giles, Sr., survive Leta Timmons.

As noted by the appellate court, a threshold issue in characterizing the respective interests of the parties is the application of the Rule in Shelley's Case. That rule, in effect at the date of testator's death, has been defined as follows: "In any instrument, if a freehold be limited to the ancestor for life, and the inheritance to his heirs, either mediately or immediately, the first taker takes the whole estate; if it be limited to the heirs of his body, he takes a fee tail; if to his heirs, a fee simple." 1 Preston on Estates, 263. The rule expressed, as noted by one commentator, is a condensed statement of the common law, for it is not the Rule in Shelley's Case which creates in the first taker a fee or a fee tail, but the operation of the doctrine of merger. The Rule in Shelley's Case operates only on the contingent remainder given to the heirs of the ancestor, converting the contingent remainder into a vested remainder in the ancestor himself. The doctrine of merger then operates to vest in the first taker a fee or fee tail. The Rule in Shelley's Case is applicable to remainders limited to the heirs of one's body and therefore operates to transfer the remainders in fee tail to the life tenants, Leta Timmons and Elmo S. Giles, Sr. The doctrine of merger operates to give these takers alternative estates in fee tail.

Also in effect at the death of Sard Giles, and applicable to the devise created, was the Illinois entailment statute (Ill. Rev. Stat. 1925, ch. 30, par. 5). The statute provided:

> In cases where, by the common law, any person or persons might hereafter become seized, in fee tail, of any lands, tenements or hereditaments, by virtue of any devise, gift, grant or other conveyance, hereafter to be made, or by any other means whatsoever, such person or persons, instead of being or becoming seized thereof in fee tail, shall be deemed and adjudged to be, and become seized thereof, for his or her natural life only, and the remainder shall pass in fee simple absolute, to the person or persons to whom the estate tail would, on the death of the first grantee, devisee, or donee in tail, first pass, according to the course of the common law, by virtue of such devise, gift, grant or conveyance.

As was stated in Moore v. Reddell (1913), 259 Ill. 36, 44, 102 N.E. 257, "[T]he purpose of the act was to provide that issue which was in existence at the time of the grant or should be born afterward should be invested with the fee simple and the reversion in the grantor be destroyed." As the entailment statute applies to the present devise, the fee tail to Leta Timmons is converted to a life estate in Leta with a contingent remainder in fee in her children. The parties agree, and the appellate court determined, that the death of Leta Timmons without issue destroyed the contingent remainder in the heirs of her body. This conclusion is clearly proper.

We also agree with the appellate court that the entailment statute operated on the limitation to Elmo S. Giles, Sr. Although this point is not disputed in this court, both the trial court and the dissenting justice in the appellate court, relying upon the literal language of the entailment statute, believed that the operation of the provision was triggered only when the taker became "seized in possession." The legislature's inclusion of persons who "might hereafter become seized" belies any argument that actual possession is necessary, and we do not believe that the legislature intended that the entailment statute would be rendered inoperable simply because Elmo S. Giles, Sr., never actually took possession of the property. We believe that the purpose of the statute, to vest the issue with the fee simple at the time of the devise or as soon as they should be born in order to destroy the reversion in the grantor, can best be accomplished by applying the statute to the limitation in favor of Elmo S. Giles, Sr.

To summarize, the interests involved here are a life estate in Leta Timmons, contingent remainder in fee in her children, a contingent gift over to Elmo S. Giles, Sr., for life upon a definite failure of issue of Leta Timmons, and a contingent remainder in fee in Elmo S. Giles, Jr. . . .

In *Hofing*, this court . . . ascertained the grantor's intent and determined that the language of the deed there in question indicated an intent to grant a fee simple estate, that the interests intended should be considered of an inheritable quality, and that the interests created were therefore not contingent upon survivorship of the remaindermen. In sum, the effect of *Hofing* is to eliminate the implied condition of survivorship as enunciated in our prior cases where the intent of the transferor is to transfer an interest in fee simple.

In the present case, the operation of the entailment statute, independent of the intent of the testator, transfers an interest in fee and, as previously noted, the purpose of this statute is to destroy the reversion in the grantor. In light of the purpose of this provision, and the transfer of a fee by its operation, we believe that the devise falls within the rule of *Hofing*, and we are unwilling to imply a condition of survivorship in Elmo S. Giles, Jr. Plaintiffs' contention that Elmo S. Giles, Sr., must survive Leta Timmons is likewise without merit. To hold otherwise would defeat the policy against destruction of remainders. The failure of this estate will not destroy the contingent interest in Elmo S. Giles, Jr. Plaintiffs do not argue, nor do we find, any expressed intent of the testator which would require survival of Elmo S. Giles, Jr.

For the foregoing reasons, the judgment of the appellate court is affirmed.

Note

Illinois abolished the Rule in Shelley's Case in 1953, Ill. Rev. Stat. 1981, ch. 30, ¶186, but the abolition had no retroactive application, and the Rule remains applicable to instruments executed and delivered prior to 1953.

D. EXECUTORY INTERESTS

◆ R. E. MEGARRY AND H. W. R. WADE, THE LAW
OF REAL PROPERTY
162-163 (4th ed., 1975)

. . . At common law future interests by way of remainder were hedged about by many technical restrictions, derived mainly from feudal law. It was impossible to create an estate which might cut short another estate, or spring up in the future without any estate being granted to anyone in the meantime. A conveyance "to A when he marries," for example, was entirely ineffective if A was unmarried. But these rules were not followed by equity, and before 1535 such interests could be created in equity by means of uses, known as shifting and springing uses. By a shifting use a preceding interest could be cut short, as in a grant "to A and his heirs to the use of B for life (or in fee) but if B inherits Blackacre then to the use of C for life (or in fee)." By a springing use a grant could be made, for example, "to A and his heirs to the use of B when he marries," or "to the use of B at 21." After 1535 the courts of law were in a difficulty. The Statute of Uses, 1535, provided that the *cestui que use* should have legal estates similar to those which they had in the use, yet the estates which existed in the use in many cases infringed the common law rules. Ultimately, with one important qualification, the same liberty was allowed at law to executed uses as equity allowed to unexecuted uses.

In this way the scope of legal conveyances was greatly extended by the addition of this new group of legal future interests. By the employment of uses more elaborate settlements became possible. These future interests created by way of uses were called "executory interests" because they remained executory (i.e., not executed) until the prescribed time arrived; thereupon the feoffee became seised to the use of the beneficiary, the State executed the use, and the beneficiary took a legal estate. "Instead of the land stifling the activity of uses, the latter have imparted their mercurial properties to the land." The common law judges were thus forced to inquire what the rules of equity were, for so far as concerned executed uses, the rules of equity became the rules of the law also.

Remainders are "successive." They always follow the normal termination of a preceding estate, while executory interests may appear suddenly to divest an estate in possession. Medieval legal theory had permitted neither a gap nor a lapse in the seisin. The Statute of Uses thus removed many technical restrictions clogging common law future interests by way of remainder. Compare the following examples of legal executory interests with the remainders on pp. 496-498 *supra.*

Examples

(a) O to A for life, then one day after A's death, to B and his heirs

B in this example has a *springing* executory interest which, of course, was not possible with remainders, because of the gap in seisin of one day.

(b) O to A and his heirs, the estate to commence when A climbs Mt. Everest

With executory interests, freeholds can commence *in futuro*. This is another example of a springing interest.

(c) O to A for life, but if B climbs Mt. Everest, to B and his heirs

A has a life estate subject to B's *shifting* executory interest.

(d) O to A so long as used for residential purposes, then to B and his heirs

The executory interest following a fee simple determinable is the one executory interest that is successive, since B will take after the normal termination of A's estate.

In 1620 the courts held that, unlike contingent remainders, executory interests were *not destructible*. The indestructibility of executory interests was a great advantage for grantors, but other judicial doctrines tended to limit the effectiveness of indestructibility. By one doctrine, called the Rule in Purefoy v. Rogers, the courts refused to "save" destructible contingent remainders by construing them as executory interests, if at the time of its creation it was possible that the interest would vest in the future under the rules of common law remainders. For example:

(e) O to A for life, then to B and his heirs if B marries C

Because of the bias in favor of contingent remainders, B does not have an executory interest, because, looking from the time of conveyance, he could marry C before A dies and then take through a remainder. However, if he does not marry in time, his contingent remainder is destroyed when A dies. If he had had an executory interest, however, it would spring back whenever he married C, regardless of the time since O had had his reversion.

14 ◆ EQUITABLE ESTATES

A. LAW AND EQUITY

◆ WALKER, INTRODUCTION TO AMERICAN LAW
298-299

§150 . . . The estates before described . . . are strictly legal estates; that is, such as courts of law can recognize and enforce. And in the earliest period of the English law, no other estates were known. But the institution of a court of chancery has given rise to another kind of estates, which may be denominated equitable, and which now occupy a very important place in the law of realty. It is not common in the books, to find such a title as equitable estates; but I have selected it for the purpose of discussing a variety of rules relating to property, which could not well be embraced under any other head; and which are essential to a proper understanding of this branch of law. By an equitable estate is meant any right or interest in land, which, not having the properties of a legal estate, requires the aid of a <u>court</u> of <u>chancery</u> to make it available. What the requisites of a legal estate are will be explained hereafter. It may be laid down in the meantime as a general proposition, that whenever one man has a legal title to land, to which another, on the established principles of equity, has a right, the latter may, by recourse to a court of chancery, render his equitable title available against the legal title. In all such cases, the owner of the legal estate is held to be a trustee, for the owner of the equitable estate: and chancery will compel him to execute the trust, for the use of the latter. Hence equitable estates have acquired the name of uses or trusts; under which name their properties will be now considered.

The Historical Distinction Between Law and Equity

The law that we now call *equitable* had its earliest origins in the centuries after the Norman Conquest when there were several competing sources of law and authority. At that time the developing common law was the king's nationwide law that gradually supplanted localized custom. The common law courts were the king's courts, used with permission of the king by those who wanted to have the national authority judge their cases. Equity derived from the administrative structure of the king's courts.

The chancellor was the king's highest officer, and it was to the chancellor and his *clerks* that petitioners went to obtain the *writ* that opened the doors to the law courts. The law courts and chancery thus were not differentiated; they both served the king's prerogative to secure justice for his subjects. This relationship existed until the thirteenth century, by which time the law courts had established themselves as the ordinary forums for justice.

The common lawyers resented the power of the chancellor to make new writs and recognize new rights, so they moved to restrict this power. But as the common law became rigid and its jurisdiction enclosed, chancery began to serve, in the fourteenth century, the same function vis-à-vis the law courts that the common law had served vis-à-vis local justice in the twelfth century: securing justice on appeal to the good graces of the king. Chancery had other functions as well; as the role of the church in secular affairs declined, and the jurisdiction of the ecclesiastical courts contracted, chancery took over adjudication of many matters of "conscience," including enforcement of promises and administration of the estates of decedents. In addition, though the king could not be sued in his own courts, a subject wronged by the king could plead humbly for justice through the chancellor.

By 1400 the court of chancery was well established, and all through the fifteenth century, a time of political chaos and Civil War, it developed further. It seems that only the professional common lawyers were upset about chancery; its more flexible doctrines, and the relief it could give from the law courts, were quite helpful to many who sought ways to protect their interests in uncertain times. The chancellor recognized the *use*, with which landowners devised real property while avoiding the feudal incidents due on the descent of land to heirs. However, in 1485 Henry Tudor ascended to the throne, and began to assemble in England the modern, centralized state; consequently, in the following century there were radical changes in the respective roles of the law courts and chancery.

C. DICKENS, BLEAK HOUSE 109-110 (1853; Signet ed. 1964):

"Of course, Esther," he said, "you don't understand this Chancery business?"

And of course I shook my head.

"I don't know who does," he returned. "The lawyers have twisted it into such a state of bedevilment that the original merits of the case have long disappeared from the face of the earth. It's about a will and the trusts under a will — or it was once. It's about nothing but costs now. We are always appearing, and disappearing, and swearing, and interrogating, and filing, and cross-filing, and arguing, and sealing, and motioning, and referring, and reporting, and revolving about the Lord Chancellor and all his satellites, and equitably waltzing ourselves off to dusty death, about costs. That's the great question. All the rest, by some extraordinary means, has melted away."

"But it was, sir," said I, to bring him back, for he began to rub his head, "about a will?"

"Why, yes, it was about a will when it was about anything," he returned. "A certain Jarndyce, in an evil hour, made a great fortune, and made a great will. In the question how the trusts under that will are to be administered, the fortune left by the will is squandered away; the legatees under the will are reduced to such a miserable condition that they would be sufficiently punished if they had committed an enormous crime in having money left them, and the will itself is made a dead letter. All through the deplorable cause, everything that everybody in it, except one man, knows already is referred to that only one man who don't know it to find out — all through the deplorable cause, everybody must have copies, over and over again, of everything that has accumulated about it in the way of cartloads of papers (or must pay for them without having them, which is the usual course, for nobody wants them) and must go down the middle and up again through such an infernal country-dance of costs and fees and nonsense and corruption as was never dreamed of in the wildest visions of a witch's Sabbath. Equity sends questions to law, law sends questions back to equity; law finds it can't do this, equity finds it can't do that; neither can so much as say it can't do anything, without this solicitor instructing and this counsel appearing for A, and that solicitor instructing and counsel appearing for B; and so on through the whole alphabet, like the history of the apple pie. And thus, through years and years, and lives and lives, everything goes on, constantly beginning over and over again, and nothing ever ends. And we can't get out of the suit on any terms, for we are made parties to it, and *must be* parties to it, whether we like it or not. But it won't do to think of it! When my great uncle, poor Tom Jarndyce, began to think of it, it was the beginning of the end!"

B. USES AND THE STATUTE OF USES

◆ F. BACON,* READING ON THE STATUTE OF USES
(1600) in Law Tracts, 299, 302, 307 (1737)

The nature of a use is best discerned by considering what it is not, and then what it is; for it is the nature of all human science and knowledge to proceed most safely by negative and exclusive, to what is affirmative and inclusive. . . .

It followeth to consider the parts and properties of an use: wherein by the consent of all books, as it was distinctly delivered by Justice Walmsley in 36 of Elizabeth: That a trust consisteth upon three parts.

—The first, that the feoffee will suffer the feoffor to take the profits.

—The second, that the feoffee upon request of the feoffor, or notice of his will, will execute the estates to the feoffor, or his heirs, or any other by his direction.

—The third, that if the feoffee be disseised, and so the feoffor disturbed, the feoffee will re-enter, or bring an action to recontinue the possession. So that those three, pernancy of profits, execution of estates, and defence of the land, are the three points of trust.

*Applied to Francis Bacon, 1567-1626, Lord Chancellor from 1617 to 1621, the term "renaissance man" is a triviality. Though he was neither a scientist nor a significant patron of science, Bacon is perhaps best remembered for his role in the scientific revolution. As author of Novum Organum (1620), an early expression of modern experimental philosophy, he was hailed by later seventeenth century English natural philosophers as the prophet of the new science, and the spirit of his inductive method was enthusiastically adopted by the infant Royal Society. But Bacon was also a lawyer, admitted to Gray's Inn at age fifteen, and a political theorist actively involved with the political conflicts of his day. As much as any individual, Bacon closed the door on medieval thought and institutions in England. Politically, Bacon was a statist, a believer in the prerogatives of royal authority. His lifelong adversary was Edward Coke, Chief Justice of Common Pleas and of King's Bench during the reign of James I. Coke oppposed the Tudor-Stuart state with the essentially medieval common law. The conflict led to political crisis in 1616; the immediate issue was the jurisdiction of Chancery, and the independence of the common law judges. Bacon — then attorney-general — and the King and the Chancellor successfully asserted the powers of the state. Yet Bacon, like Machiavelli, ultimately failed at practical politics. His genius was flawed by fascination with authority and the perquisites of power, and his tenure as Lord Chancellor ended with impeachment and conviction for accepting bribes. In 1626, while collecting snow to experiment with its effects on preserving the flesh of a fowl, he caught cold and died of bronchitis.

FIGURE 14-1
Francis Bacon

1. History of the Use

◆ A. W. B. SIMPSON, AN INTRODUCTION TO THE
HISTORY OF THE LAND LAW
164, 166, 171-172 (1961)

A variety of explanations have been given for the prevalence of feoffments to uses in the Middle Ages. The Crusades, it has been suggested,
encouraged the practice by taking landowners out of the country and
making it imperative that they left somebody at home in control of their
lands. The Franciscan Friars have also been pointed to, for they were not
allowed to own property other than their convents, but could have lands
held to their use without infringing the rules of their order. Dishonesty
also played some part. One who was proposing to indulge in treason-
able enterprises could seek to avoid the chance of his lands being forfeit
to the Crown for treason by conveying them away to a blameless confed-
erate, to be held to his use. By the fifteenth century it becomes clear that
most uses were created for one of four main reasons: they could be
employed to assist in simple fraud; they could be used to avoid feudal
dues; they could be used to gain a power of devise over land; and they
could be used to facilitate the creation of settlements of land. But before
these reasons can be explained we must first see how the Chancellor
came to protect the use and develop a body of equitable principles
around the institution. . . .

The use simply could not be fitted into the common law scheme of
things, for the doctrine of estates and the doctrine of seisin left no place
for the separation of beneficial enjoyment from legal title. The simplest
form of use would arise when A enfeoffed B of Blackacre to the use of C.
By the feoffment the legal estate vested in B, upon whom the seisin had
been conferred by the livery of seisin. Until seisin had passed to C he
could not possibly obtain any estate in the land, and if of course B did
make a conveyance and pass the seisin to C, then B would step out of
the picture completely, which was hardly A's intention. If B let C into
possession without any formal conveyance then the only legal category
into which C could be fitted was that of tenant at will of B, and this
meant that C could be thrown out by B whenever B wished. The root of
the common law's difficulty lay in the fact that the landowner's
beneficial interest was protected by protecting seisin; the person who
had seisin could recover that seisin specifically in the real actions if he
were disseised, or disturbed in some other way. The *cestui que use* did
not have seisin, and thus he could not use the actions which gave
specific recovery, nor were there forms of action capable of protecting a
beneficial interest divorced from seisin.

The intervention of the legislature was confined to the introduction
of measures directed towards the prevention of fraudulent feoffments to

uses, so that it was to the Chancellor that petitions for the protection of uses were directed. Since it was settled in the fifteenth century (and recognized earlier) that the common law courts would not uphold uses as such, the person who made a feoffment to uses was clearly reposing a trust or confidence in the feoffee, which it was unconscionable, though not illegal, for him to break. Thus it was the very impotence of the common law which provided the basis upon which the Chancellor could intervene in the name of good conscience and equity, and require the feoffee to hold the land for the benefit of the *cestui que use* and allow him to take the profits. He could enforce his decrees by threat of imprisonment, and his mode of procedure by interrogation under oath was a potent method for discovering the nature and scope of the trust reposed in the feoffee, and whether or not his behavior was conscionable. . . . In the later half of the fifteenth century the Chancellors began to develop some consistent principles which governed their readiness to intervene, and once this begins to be the case it is clear that the *cestui que use* has come to obtain a species of protected interest which will be defended consistently and predictably — that is, a species of property. . . .

The use had originated as a personal confidence or trust placed by one person in the other, and even when a use became a species of property it continued to bear marks of this origin. Thus it never came to bind the land itself; rather, it was conceived to bind the conscience of persons into whose hands the land came. This conception is illustrated by the rule that quite irrespective of notice a use was only binding upon persons who came to the land *through* those in whom the confidence had been originally reposed. Thus if a feoffee to uses sold the land to another who took with notice that person would be bound, but if the feoffee was disseised by some rogue, who might well know of the use, such a disseisor was not bound by the use. . . . [N]o use could arise unless at the time of its creation there was some person in whom the creator of the use had reposed his confidence; there could be no use which attached simply to the land, and not to some person. Thus there was nothing to resemble the modern system under which a trust can arise without a trustee. . . .

In one particular, however, there was a definite and extremely important settled rule, and that was that uses could be disposed of by will; common law estates, of course, could not. Thus by conveying his lands to feoffees to his own use a landowner at once acquired a power of devise over his beneficial interest, and it is generally admitted that this power of devise was the most potent attraction of putting lands in use.

The employment of the use to avoid the feudal dues was widespread. Normally there would be a number of feoffees to uses, and they would hold as joint tenants. As an insurance against fraud eminent lawyers were often used as feoffees and, no doubt, were paid for their services. By choosing such respectable persons and not putting his trust in a single feoffee the feoffor could have considerable confidence that his wishes would be observed without the need for litigation. Now at law the feoffees were the persons who had the legal estate, and it was from them that the lord must look for his feudal services and incidents. By the fifteenth century the services were usually not worth exacting, but the incidents were. The plurality of feoffees had the effect, however, of denying to the lord wardship, marriage, relief, primer seisin, and escheat. This was because of the *ius adcrescendi* — the rule that when one joint tenant died his interest accrued to the surviving joint tenants, and did not pass to his heir, so that the legal estate never passed by descent at all; thus no minor ever inherited the legal estate so as to be in ward, and no heir ever had to pay relief and so on.

[I]n 1535 an attempt was made to argue before the Exchequer Chamber and the Chancellor the general proposition that manipulation of uses calculated to defraud the Crown of feudal revenue was covinous and void, or as we should say, contrary to public policy. But the judges adopted the attitude which has become traditional and would not accept this argument. It came to be realized that radical legislation was the only possible answer to the problem.

Such legislation was forced through Parliament in 1535 in the form of two Statutes, the Statute of Uses and the Statute of Enrolments. The second of these two Statutes is best considered as a sub-provision of the first. The basic principle embodied in this legislation was brilliantly simple in conception — it was to vest the legal estate in the *cestui que use* and take it away from the feoffees. This approach was not entirely without precedent. Earlier Statutes had adopted the expedient of treating the *cestui que use* (for some purposes) *as if he had* the legal estate.

2.   *The Statute and Executed Uses*

◆ AN ACT CONCERNING USES AND WILLS
27 Hen. 8, c.10 (1535)

Where by the common laws of this realm, lands, tenements, and hereditaments be not devisable by testament, nor ought to be transferred from one to another, but by solemn livery and seisin, matter of record, writing sufficient made bona fide, without covin or fraud; yet nevertheless divers and sundry imaginations, subtle inventions, and practices have been used, whereby the hereditaments of this realm have been conveyed from one to another by fraudulent feoffments, fines, recoveries, and other assurances craftily made to secret uses, intents, and trusts; and also by wills and testaments, sometime made by *nude parolx* and words, sometime by signs and tokens, and sometime by writing, and for the most part made by such persons as be visited with sickness,

in their extreme agonies and pains, or at such time as they have had
scantly any good memory or remembrance; at which times they being
provoked by greedy and covetous persons lying in wait about them, do
many times dispose indiscreetly and unadvisedly their lands and inheritances; by reason whereof, and by occasion of which fraudulent feoffments, fines, recoveries, and other like assurances to uses, confidences,
and trusts, divers and many heirs have been unjustly at sundry times
disherited, the lords have lost their wards, marriages, reliefs, harriots,
escheats, aids *pur fair fitz chivalier* and *pur file marier*, and scantly any
person can be certainly assured of any lands by them purchased, nor
know surely against whom they shall use their actions or executions for
their rights, titles, and duties; also men married have lost their tenancies
by the curtesy, women their dowers, manifest perjuries by trial of such
secret wills and uses have been committed; the King's Highness hath
lost the profits and advantages of the lands of persons attainted, and of
the lands craftily put in feoffments to the uses of aliens born, and
also the profits of waste for a year and a day of lands of felons attainted,
and the lords their escheats thereof; and many other inconveniences
have happened, and daily do increase among the King's subjects, to their
great trouble and inquietness, and to the utter subversion of the ancient
common laws of this realm; for the extirping [eradicate] and extinguishment of all
such subtle practised feoffments, fines, recoveries, abuses, and errors
heretofore used and accustomed in this realm, to the subversion of the
good and ancient laws of the same, and to the intent that the King's
Highness or any other his subjects of this realm, shall not in any wise
hereafter, by any means or inventions be deceived, damaged, or hurt,
by reason of such trusts, uses, or confidences: It may please the King's
most royal Majesty, that it may be enacted by his Highness, by the
assent of the Lords Spiritual and Temporal, and the Commons, in this
present parliament assembled, and by the authority of the same, in
manner and form following: that is to say, that where any person or
persons stand or be seised, or at any time hereafter shall happen to be
seised, of and in any honours, castles, manors, lands, tenements, rents,
services, reversions, remainders, or other hereditaments, to the use,
confidence, or trust of any other person or persons, or of any body
politick, by reason of any bargain, sale, feoffment, fine, recovery, covenant, contract, agreement, will, or otherwise, by any manner means
whatsoever it be; that in every such case, all and every such person and
persons, and bodies politick, that have or hereafter shall have any such
use, confidence, or trust, in fee simple, fee tail, for term of life, or for
years, or otherwise; or any use, confidence, or trust, in remainder or
reverter, shall from henceforth stand and be seised, deemed, and adjudged in lawful seisin, estate, and possession of and in the same honours, castles, manors, lands, tenements, rents, services, reversions,
remainders, and hereditaments, with their appurtenances, to all intents,

constructions, and purposes in the law, of and in such like estates, as they had or shall have in use, trust, or confidence of or in the same: and that the estate, title, right, and possession that was in such person or persons that were or hereafter shall be seised of any lands, tenements, or hereditaments, to the use, confidence, or trust of any such person or persons, or of any body politick, be from henceforth clearly deemed and adjudged to be in him or them that have, or hereafter shall have such use, confidence, or trust, after such quality, manner, form, and condition as they had before, in or to the use, confidence, or trust that was in them.

The Statute of Uses transferred legal title to vast acreage. Did it therefore "take" property in violation of common law restrictions on Parliament's authority? The issue was difficult for Tudor judges. The most interesting case was Wimbish v. Tailbois, 1 Plowden 39, 75 Eng. Rep. 63 (K.B. 1551). The pleadings began:

> Elizabeth Tailbois, late of Golthough, in the County aforesaid, Widow, was attached to answer Thomas Wimbish, Esquire, and Elizabeth his Wife, of a Plea, wherefore with Force and Arms the Close of them the said Thomas and Elizabeth she broke, and their Grass to the Value of £40 there lately growing with certain Cattle eat up, tread down, and destroyed, and other Wrongs to them did, to the great Damage of the said Thomas and Elizabeth, and against the Peace of the Lord Henry the Eighth, late King of England, Father of the Lord the King now. . . .

The judges upheld the Statute of Uses against constitutional attack as follows:

> And when the Statute was made, it gave the Land to them that had the Use. It is to be seen then, who shall be adjudged in Law the Donor after the Execution of the Possession to the Use. And, Sir, the Parliament, (which is nothing but a Court) may not be adjudged the Donor. For what the Parliament did was only a Conveyance of the Land from one to another, and a Conveyance by Parliament does not make the Parliament Donor; but it seems to me that the Feoffees to Use shall be the Donors, for when a Gift is made by Parliament, every Person in the Realm is privy to it, and assents to it, but yet the Thing shall pass from him that has the most Right and Authority to give it.

F. BACON, READING ON THE STATUTE OF USES (1600) in Law Tracts 299, 324-325 (1737): This statute, as it is the statute which of all others hath the greatest power and operation over the heritages of the realm, so howsoever it hath been by the humour of the time perverted in exposition, yet in itself is most perfectly and exactly conceived and penned of any law in the books. 'Tis induced with the most declaring and persuading preamble, 'tis consisting and standing upon the wisest and fittest ordinances, and qualified with the most foreseeing and circumspect savings and provisoes: and lastly 'tis the best ponder'd in all the words and clauses of it of any statute that I find.

BORDWELL, THE REPEAL OF THE STATUTE OF USES, 39 Harv. L. Rev. 466, 466 (1926): For three centuries and a half the Statute of Uses had plagued students when the worm turned. A young student, barely sixteen, resolved that he would put a end to the Statute of Uses should he ever be in a position to do so. As Lord Chancellor that student was able to carry out his resolution. With a precocity that is amazing, the future Lord Birkenhead, for that student was he, came to that resolution on the first day of his study of real property, the latter part of the day being devoted to the Statute of Uses. He says that on his way home, as he carried with him the text that he had been reading, Williams on Real Property, he surveyed the Statute of Uses from every conceivable point of view and came to the conclusion "that it was the barbarous, if necessary, invention of a number of scholastic legal pedants, but that it had no contact of any kind with our modern life."

W. HOLDSWORTH, AN HISTORICAL INTRODUCTION TO THE LAND LAW 151-155 (1927): Thus, at the close of the medieval period, the development of uses and trusts had given rise to the equitable ownership of English law. Through the medium of trustees landowners had gained a large new series of powers over their property; and they could use these powers by the simple machinery of a direction to the feoffees to uses or trustees, which might be quite informal. Some of the problems, to which the rise of this new form of ownership had given rise, had been dealt with by the Legislature. We shall now see that it was its fiscal consequences which, in 1535, were the chief cause for the passing of the statute of Uses — the statute which has shaped the whole future history of uses and trusts of land. . . .

Because at later periods in the history of the law some of the objects of the statute were frustrated, either by the new development of equitable doctrines which were called for by altered legal and social conditions, or by the ingenuity of conveyancers, its effects have been sometimes unduly minimized. The student is told almost in one breath that the only effect of the statute was to add three words to a conveyance, and that it is the foundation of the modern system of conveyancing. . . .

The immediate cause for the passing of the statute of Uses must be looked for in Henry VIII's fiscal necessities — just as the immediate cause for his Reformation legislation must be looked for in his matrimonial necessities. He wanted money badly, and the restoration of his feudal revenue (which was after all his own property) seemed to promise a permanent increase in the royal revenue. His earlier measures, proposed to attain this object, failed to pass the House of Commons, since they aroused the hostility of two very powerful interests in that House — the interest of the landowners and the interest of the lawyers. The statute of Uses of 1535 was a new and different attempt to tackle the problem. Henry won over the common lawyers to his side by playing upon the jealousy which they felt for the Chancery, and by producing a scheme for annexing the legal estate to certain uses of land, which gave their courts jurisdiction over the uses to which the legal estate had been thus annexed. By these means Henry got the statute through Parliament. At the same time he tried to induce Parliament to pass an elaborate bill for the registration of conveyances. If it had been passed, and had been efficiently carried out, we should have had to-day a series of county registers which would have considerably simplified the land law.

R. E. MEGARRY & H. W. R. WADE, THE LAW OF REAL PROPERTY 163-165 (4th ed., 1975): [T]he Statute of Uses brought many unforeseen advantages in its train, and "conveyancers soon began to make a servant of the Statute." Such were its powers, when fully understood, that conveyances themselves were refashioned in more convenient if not in simpler form. The principal forms of conveyance at common law were the feoffment with livery of seisin and the grant by deed. . . .

A feoffment had the disadvantages that it was public, "which must have been distressing in transactions of delicacy," and that it demanded actual entry on the land by both parties, or their attorneys. This was often inconvenient. For example, where both parties were at York and the land lay in Cornwall, long journeys would be necessary or else the appointment of attorneys; in the latter case the parties would not know at what precise time the transfer took effect. And feoffments were often impeached for some failure in the formalities of livery. Professional ingenuity was therefore applied in searching for some means of conveying land which should be private and which should operate merely by the execution of a deed. . . .

The Statute of Uses . . . provided that the *cestui que use* should be "deemed and adjudged in lawful seisin, estate *and possession*" for the equivalent legal estate. Therefore if matters were so arranged that V became seised to the use of P, the legal estate would be vested in P forthwith by virtue of the Statute. The Statute was clearly a powerful engine for transferring legal estates, and the following new forms of conveyance came into use.

(1) BARGAIN AND SALE

If V contracted to sell land to P, and P paid the price (which at first had to be the full value, but later might be nominal, e.g., twelve pence or a peppercorn), *V* was said to have "bargained and sold" the land to *P*. Equity deemed *V* to be seised to the use of *P*, much as today *V* is said to be trustee for *P* until the land is duly conveyed in accordance with the contract. The use was then executed and *P* took the legal estate both secretly and without entry on the land. This possibility was foreseen by the authors of the Statute of Uses and in the same session the Statute of Enrolments, 1535, was passed. This provided that from July 31, 1536, no bargain and sale of freeholds was to be effective unless in writing indented (i.e., made by indenture), sealed and within six months enrolled in one of the King's Courts of Record at Westminster or in the county where the land was situated. Thereafter entry on the land but not publicity could be avoided by a bargain and sale enrolled. . . .

(2) COVENANT TO STAND SEISED

After some hesitation it was settled in 1565 that if a tenant in fee simple covenanted to stand seised of his land in favour of some near relative, the "good consideration" of natural love and affection sufficed to raise a use in favour of the relative; the use was then executed and the legal estate vested in the relative. This type of conveyance was of limited application as it could not be employed to convey land to strangers; and, like the bargain and sale enrolled, it could not carry any further uses under the Statute. But where it could be used it had the advantage of not requiring enrolment.

Though the bargain and sale was not secret after 1535, and the covenant to stand seised was good only between relatives, more complicated conveyances — notably the *lease and release* — eventually allowed grantors to avoid even these defects.

Examples of Executed Uses

(a) *A conveys by common law feoffment to B, C, and D for the use of E*
(b) *A bargains and sells to B and his heirs*
(c) *A covenants to stand seised for the use of B, his brother, and his heirs in consideration of natural love and affection*

C. THE MODERN TRUST

The statute did not purport to do away with all uses, and the concept continued to evolve during succeeding centuries. The result is the modern trust. It is a fair question whether the survival of the trust, and its wide use today, result solely from past and present tax advantages, or whether separation of the management and enjoyment of property, represented by a split between legal and equitable title, serves broader social purposes. Consider F. H. Lawson, Introduction to the Law of Property 10 (1958):

> If property is given to trustees to hold in trust for beneficiaries the trustees are said, now mainly for historical reasons, to have the legal estate, and the beneficiaries the equitable interest. The former is merely a way of explaining that the trustees are the managers of the property and can act commercially as owners of it, enjoying wide powers of alienating it in the market; while the latter means that the beneficiaries have the beneficial ownership, which implies that they can enjoy the use and possession of it and draw an income from it. Thus by means of the trust the legal estate can be separated from the equitable interest in property and the former vested in trustees as managers of the property, while the latter is vested in beneficiaries who enjoy it. Having gone so far, Parliament could insist on a high degree of concentration as far as the legal estate is concerned, so as to confer on the managers an almost complete control over the trust property, while allowing dispersal of the equitable interest within very wide limits among several beneficiaries who take either concurrently or in succession to each other.

Does the fragmentation inherent in the trust mediate between the developmental concern with free alienation and the desire for dead-hand control? Does it do so adequately, or does the trust create new problems that diminish its effectiveness? What happens when the trust concept, venerable as it is, provides the machinery for the modern social welfare system?

1. Evolution of the Trust: Unexecuted Uses

The Statute of Uses returned to the common lawyers their real property practice. Then, in 1540, the Statute of Wills extended legal jurisdiction to devises of land. Yet the statute had not abolished uses and the court of chancery was not closed. Equity was not completely out of the picture; almost immediately after passage of the statute, enterprising property owners discovered, developed, and exploited exceptions to the execution of uses. By 1700 this process had produced the modern trust.

◆ SYMSON v. TURNER
1 Eq. Cas. Ab. 383, note, 21 Eng. Rep. 1119 (1700)

But notwithstanding this Statute, there are three Ways of creating an Use or a Trust, which still remains as at Common Law, and is a Creature of the Court of Equity, and subject only to their Controul and Direction: 1st, Where a Man seised in Fee raises a Term for Years, and limits it in Trust for A. &c., for this the Statute cannot execute, the Termor not being seised. 2dly, Where Lands are limited to the Use of A. in Trust, to permit B. to receive the Rents and Profits; for the Statute can only execute the first Use. 3dly, Where Lands are limited to Trustees to receive and pay over the Rents and Profits to such and such Persons; for here the Lands must remain in them to answer these Purposes; and these points were agreed to.

SILVESTER v. WILSON, 2 T.R. 444, 450-451, 100 Eng. Rep. 239, 242-243 (K.B. 1788): Then taking the former authorities to be unshaken, the case of Symson v. Turner, Eq. Cas. Abr. 383., and which is recognized in 2 Bl. Com. 336., is in point to the present. But there seems to be a circumstance in the present case which makes it still stronger; for it is not barely to receive and pay, but the testator directs that such rents, issues, and profits, shall be applied for the subsistence and maintenance of the said John Wilson. The testator therefore seems to mean that the trustees should be invested with some sort of discretion with respect to the application. And if the tenant for life had proved dissolute and extravagant, and had squandered his money in gaming, to the defrauding of his honest creditors, it is by no means clear that the trustees would not have been justified, either in a Court of Law or Equity, in paying such creditors, before they had paid over the surplus to the tenant for life; as the testator seems to have had some jealousy of his son's conduct, and to have wished that the trustees should have an eye to the application of the money. Therefore we are all of opinion that the judgment must be for the defendant.

A. W. B. SIMPSON, AN INTRODUCTION TO THE HISTORY OF THE LAND LAW 182-183 (1961): In 1580 the judges and chief baron were asked by the Chancellor whether uses declared on a term of years were executed by the Statute, as where lands were conveyed to A for a term of a thousand years to the use of B and his heirs. Their opinion was that [*nonfreehold*] such uses were not covered by the Statute. The doctrinal explanation of this, as it came to be settled, was that a termor was not seised, and the Statute clearly only spoke of situations where one person was *seised* to the use of another, and omitted to mention situations where one person was *possessed* to the use of another. In the early seventeenth century the Court of Chancery came to protect such uses, under the name of trusts; the position is stated in this way: "Although *cestui que use* of a term of years be not within the State of Uses, rather therefore he shall have remedy in Chancery." . . . .

Quite soon after 1535 another form of use which was not executed [*active*] was discovered. If a feoffee to uses had active duties to perform as would be the case if lands were conveyed to B with a direction that he collect the rents and profits and pay them to C, then it was held that the use was not executed. The explanation which has been given for this was that the feoffee could not in such a case before the Statute have conveyed the lands to C without a breach of trust, and that the Statute only did universally what the feoffee could himself have done privately without breaking trust. [These active uses did not form a large or important class, however, and represent only a minor fault in the Statute.]

Examples of Unexecuted Uses

(a) *A conveys by common law feoffment to B for 100 years for the use of C for 100 years, then to D and his heirs for the use of E and his heirs*

At common law before the statute, since B had only a nonfreehold term, C's trust term is not executed, since B was not *seised* to his use. D had a legal fee simple subject to B's term of years. After the statute, since D was seised, E's interest was executed and he now held the legal fee simple to become possessory after 100 years.

(b) *A conveys by common law feoffment to B and his heirs to pay the income to C for life, then to convey the land to D and his heirs*

Since B had responsibilities, this is an example of an *active trust*, and both C and D have unexecuted equitable estates.

(c) *A to B for the use of C in trust for D*

This is an example of the famous "use on a use," the third type of use on real property not executed by the statute. By the eighteenth century, after the demise of feudal incidents, the courts would execute only the first use, thus legal title lodged in C as trustee for D. In Doe v. Passingham, 6 B. & C. 305, 108 Eng. Rep. 465 (K.B. 1827), the court held that the even simpler conveyance, "A unto and to the use of B and his heirs in trust for C and his heirs," was sufficient to create a trust for the benefit of C.

(d) *A transfers to B and his heirs 100 shares of General Motors common stock in trust for C*

Uses in personal property where, as with nonfreehold estates, there was no seisin, were never executed by the statute.

Problem

Which uses are executed in the following conveyances, and which remain unexecuted?

(a) *O conveys "to B and his heirs to the use of C for life then to the use of D and his heirs"*

(b) *O conveys "to B for ten years to the use of C for ten years then to D and his heirs for the use of E and his heirs"*

(c) O conveys "to B for life to the use of C for B's life then to D and his heirs for the use of E and his heirs"

2. Modern Trust Doctrine

a. Creation

◆ WALKER, INTRODUCTION TO AMERICAN LAW
   301-306

. . . I shall consider equitable estates under two heads, express trusts and implied trusts; confining myself to a very general outline of their nature and properties.

§152. EXPRESS TRUSTS

Our *statute of frauds* . . . requires all transactions relating to land, to be expressed in writing. The English statute of frauds contained a special exception in regard to trusts. Our statute does not make this exception, but it is held to be implied. The doctrine is so universal, that implied trusts will be enforced in equity, that without citing authorities to prove it, I shall take it for granted; and shall therefore speak of express trusts as a distinct class. In the creation of every express trust, three parties are concerned; first, the person who creates the trust, and who is called the *grantor;* secondly, the person who is to execute the trust, and who is called the *trustee;* thirdly, the person for whose benefit the trust is made, and who has been designated by the awkward phrase of *cestui que trust;* in the place of which, I shall substitute the term *beneficiary.* The parties will then be grantor, trustee, and beneficiary. . . .

The republican habits of our citizens being opposed to complicated family settlements, we have very few express trusts created by deed, though they occasionally occur. But trusts created by will are more frequent. The leading motive for creating a trust is to prevent property from being improvidently squandered. If a father wishes to provide with certainty for a child about to marry, and for the issue of such marriage, instead of conveying property to the child directly, he conveys it to trustees, with a declaration of his wishes; and thus while he gives the annual income to the married couple, he secures the principal to their children. . . . [A] little reflection will convince any one of the very great utility of this description of estates.

§153. IMPLIED TRUSTS

Implied trusts, as their name imports, are those which result from the established doctrines of equity, without any declaration by the parties, . . . They are sometimes called *resulting trusts*, and are chiefly upheld to prevent fraud. In most cases, the question whether there be an implied trust or not, depends upon circumstances connected with the consideration of real contracts. The following are the cases in which implied trusts have been most generally sustained.

If I purchase land, and take the title in my own name, but you pay the consideration, I become thereby a trustee for you.

If being already your general trustee, I purchase land in my own name with money belonging to you, I hold this land as trustee for you.

If I convey land to you without any consideration, you become a trustee for me.

If I contract with you for the purchase of real estate, by title bond, or otherwise, you thereby become a trustee for me, until the legal conveyance is made. And the same is true, if through a mistake you make me a defective conveyance. You hold the legal title in trust for me, until a good conveyance is made.

If I convey land to you when I have not the legal title; and afterwards acquire the legal title, I hold it in trust for you, and the same doctrine extends to my heirs taking by descent from me.

If I convey land to you, and take no collateral security for the payment of the purchase money, you become a trustee for me, until the purchase money is paid. But it is otherwise, if I do any thing to manifest an intention not to rely upon the land for security. This is called an *equitable lien*.

If I, being your debtor, deposit my title deeds with you, I thereby become a trustee for you until the debt is paid. This is called an *equitable mortgage*, but it is of little consequence in this country, owing to the difficulty of affecting another claimant with notice of such deposit.

If I convey land to a trustee, and declare the trust as to a part, there is a resulting trust to me for the residue. If the conveyance be upon such trusts as I shall afterwards declare, and I fail to declare them, there is a resulting trust to me for the whole. And generally, if I create a trust for any particular purpose, there is a resulting trust to me as soon as that purpose is accomplished. . . .

For the sake of simplicity, the foregoing remarks have related exclusively to realty. But trusts may be created of personalty, to the same extent, and nearly on the same principles, as of realty. In fact, courts of chancery, for the purpose of giving complete effect to settlements in trust for any of the purposes aforementioned, will sometimes virtually reverse the distinctions between the two kinds of property, by treating realty as personalty, and personalty as realty. From the nature of personalty, moreover, it must be obvious, that where infants or married women are concerned, the best way to secure personalty for them, so that they may be certain of enjoying the proceeds, is to place it in the hands of trustees. We have seen that the guardian or husband has only a limited power over realty; but with regard to personalty it is nearly absolute; and therefore the motives for creating trusts of the latter, are often stronger than with respect to the former.

◆ FARKAS v. WILLIAMS
5 Ill. 2d 417, 125 N.E.2d 600 (1955)

HERSHEY, Justice. This is an appeal from a decision of the Appellate Court, First District, which affirmed a decree of the circuit court of Cook County finding that certain declarations of. trust executed by Albert B. Farkas and naming Richard J. Williams as beneficiary were invalid and that Regina Farkas and Victor Farkas, as coadministrators of the estate of said Albert B. Farkas, were the owners of the property referred to in said trust instruments, being certain shares of capital stock of Investors Mutual, Inc.

Said coadministrators, herein referred to as plaintiffs, filed a complaint in the circuit court of Cook County for a declaratory decree and other relief against said Richard J. Williams and Investors Mutual, Inc., herein referred to as defendants. The plaintiffs asked the court to declare their legal rights, as coadministrators, in four stock certificates issued by Investors Mutual, Inc. in the name of "Albert B. Farkas, as trustee for Richard J. Williams" and which were issued pursuant to written declarations of trust. The decree of the circuit court found that said declarations were testamentary in character, and not having been executed with the formalities of a will, were invalid, and directed that the stock be awarded to the plaintiffs as an asset of the estate of said Albert B. Farkas. . . .

Albert B. Farkas died intestate at the age of sixty-seven years, a resident of Chicago, leaving as his only heirs-at-law brothers, sisters, a nephew and a niece. Although retired at the time of his death, he had for many years practiced veterinary medicine and operated a veterinarian establishment in Chicago. During a considerable portion of that time, he employed the defendant Williams, who was not related to him.

On four occasions (December 8, 1948; February 7, 1949; February 14, 1950; and March 1, 1950) Farkas purchased stock of Investors Mutual, Inc. At the time of each purchase he executed a written application to Investors Mutual, Inc., instructing them to issue the stock in his name "as trustee for Richard J. Williams." Investors Mutual, Inc., by its agent, accepted each of these applications in writing by signature on the face of the application. Coincident with the execution of these applications, Farkas signed separate declarations of trust, all of which were identical except as to dates. The terms of said trust instruments are as follows:

Declaration of Trust — Revocable. I, the undersigned, having purchased or declared my intention to purchase certain shares of capital stock of Investors Mutual, Inc. (the Company), and having directed that the certificate for said stock be issued in my name as trustee for Richard J. Williams as beneficiary, whose address is 1704 W. North Ave., Chicago, Ill., under this Declaration of Trust Do Hereby Declare that the terms and conditions upon which I shall hold said stock in trust and any additional stock resulting from reinvestments of cash dividends upon such original or additional shares are as follows:

(1) During my lifetime all cash dividends are to be paid to me individually for my own personal account and use; provided, however, that any such additional stock purchased under an authorized reinvestment of cash dividends shall become a part of and subject to this trust.

(2) Upon my death the title to any stock subject hereto and the right to any subsequent payments or distributions shall be vested absolutely in the beneficiary. The record date for the payment of dividends, rather than the date of declaration of the dividend, shall, with reference to my death, determine whether any particular dividend shall be payable to my estate or to the beneficiary.

(3) During my lifetime I reserve the right, as trustee, to vote, sell, redeem, exchange or otherwise deal in or with the stock subject hereto, but upon any sale or redemption of said stock or any part thereof, the trust hereby declared shall terminate as to the stock sold or redeemed, and I shall be entitled to retain the proceeds of sale or redemption for my own personal account and use.

(4) I reserve the right at any time to change the beneficiary or revoke this trust, but it is understood that no change of beneficiary and no revocation of this trust except by death of the beneficiary, shall be effective as to the Company for any purpose unless and until written notice thereof in such form as the Company shall prescribe is delivered to the Company at Minneapolis, Minnesota. The decease of the beneficiary before my death shall operate as a revocation of this trust.

(5) In the event this trust shall be revoked or otherwise terminated, said stock and all rights and privileges thereunder shall belong to and be exercised by me in my individual capacity.

(6) The Company shall not be liable for the validity or existence of any trust created by me, and any payment or other consideration made or given by the Company to me as trustee or otherwise, in connection with said stock or any cash dividends thereon, or in the event of my death prior to revocation, to the beneficiary, shall to the extent of such payment fully release and discharge the Company from liability with respect to said stock or any cash dividends thereon.

The applications and declarations of trust were delivered to Investors Mutual, Inc., and held by the company until Farkas's death. The stock certificates were issued in the name of Farkas as "trustee for Richard J. Williams" and were discovered in a safety-deposit box of Farkas after his death, along with other securities, some of which were in the name of Williams alone. . . .

First, upon execution of these trust instruments did defendant Williams presently acquire an interest in the subject matter of the intended trusts? If no interest passed to Williams before the death of Farkas, the intended trusts are testamentary and hence invalid for failure to comply with the statute on wills. But considering the terms of these instruments we believe Farkas did intend to presently give Williams an interest in the property referred to. For it may be said, at the very least, that upon his executing one of these instruments, he showed an intention to presently part with some of the incidents of ownership in the stock. Immediately after the execution of each of these instruments, he could not deal with the stock therein referred to the same as if he owned the property absolutely, but only in accordance with the terms of the instrument. He purported to set himself up as trustee of the stock for the benefit of Williams, and the stock was registered in his name as trustee for Williams. Thus assuming to act as trustee, he is held to have intended to take on those obligations which are expressly set out in the instrument, as well as those fiduciary obligations implied by law. In addition, he manifested an intention to bind himself to having this property pass upon his death to Williams, unless he changed the beneficiary or revoked the trust, and then such change of beneficiary or revocation was not to be effective as to Investors Mutual, Inc., unless and until written notice thereof in such form as the company prescribed was delivered to them at Minneapolis, Minnesota. An absolute owner can dispose of his property, either in his lifetime or by will, in any way he sees fit without notifying or securing approval from anyone and without being held to the duties of a fiduciary in so doing.

It seems to follow that what incidents of ownership Farkas intended to relinquish, in a sense he intended Williams to acquire. That is, Williams was to be the beneficiary to whom Farkas was to be obligated, and unless Farkas revoked the instrument in the manner therein set out or the instrument was otherwise terminated in a manner therein provided for, upon Farkas's death Williams was to become absolute owner of the trust property. It is difficult to name this interest of Williams, nor is there any reason for so doing so long as it passed to him immediately upon the creation of the trust. As stated in 4 Powell, The Law of Real Property, at page 87: "Interests of beneficiaries of private express trusts run the gamut from valuable substantialities to evanescent hopes. Such a beneficiary may have any one of an almost infinite variety of the possible aggregates of rights, privileges, powers and immunities."

An additional problem is presented here, however, for it is to be noted that the trust instruments provide: "The decease of the beneficiary before my death shall operate as a revocation of this trust." The plaintiffs argue that the presence of this provision removes the only possible distinction which might have been drawn between these instruments and a will. Being thus conditioned on his surviving, it is argued that the "interest" of Williams until the death of Farkas was a mere expectancy. Conversely, they assert, the interest of Farkas in the securities until his death was precisely the same as that of a testator who bequeaths securities by his will, since he had all the rights accruing to an absolute owner.

Admittedly, had this provision been absent the interest of Williams would have been greater, since he would then have had an inheritable interest in the lifetime of Farkas. But to say his interest would have been greater is not to say that he here did not have a beneficial interest, properly so-called, during the lifetime of Farkas. [The provision purports to set up but another "contingency" which would serve to terminate the trust.] The disposition is not testamentary and the intended trust is valid, even though the interest of the beneficiary is contingent upon the existence of a certain state of facts at the time of the settlor's death. Restatement of the Law of Trusts, section 56, comment f. In an example contained in the previous reference, the authors of the Restatement have referred to the interest of a beneficiary under a trust who must survive the settlor (and where the settlor receives the income for life) as a contingent equitable interest in remainder. . . .

Second, did Farkas retain such control over the subject matter of the trust as to render said trust instruments attempted testamentary dispositions?

In each of these trust instruments, Farkas reserved to himself as settlor the following powers: (1) the right to receive during his lifetime all cash dividends; (2) the right at any time to change the beneficiary or revoke the trust; and (3) upon sale or redemption of any portion of the trust property, the right to retain the proceeds therefrom for his own use.

Additionally, Farkas reserved the right to act as sole trustee, and in such capacity, he was accorded the right to vote, sell, redeem, exchange or otherwise deal in the stock which formed the subject matter of the trust.

We shall consider first those enumerated powers which Farkas reserved to himself as settlor.

It is well established that the retention by the settlor of the power to revoke, even when coupled with the reservation of a life interest in the trust property, does not render the trust inoperative for want of execution as a will.

Only when it is thought that there are additional reservations present of such a substantial nature as to amount to the retention of full ownership is a court likely to invalidate an _inter vivos_ trust by reason of its not being executed as a will. . . .

It is obvious that a settlor with the power to revoke and to amend the trust at any time is, for all practical purpose, in a position to exert considerable control over the trustee regarding the administration of the trust. For anything believed to be inimicable to his best interests can be thwarted or prevented by simply revoking the trust or amending it in such a way as to conform to his wishes. Indeed, it seems that many of those powers which from time to time have been viewed as "additional powers" are already, in a sense, virtually contained within the overriding power of revocation or the power to amend the trust. Consider, for example, the following: (1) the power to consume the principal; (2) the power to sell or mortgage the trust property and appropriate the proceeds; (3) the power to appoint or remove trustees; (4) the power to supervise and direct investments; and (5) the power to otherwise direct and supervise the trustee in the administration of the trust. Actually, any of the above powers could readily be assumed by a settlor with the reserved power of revocation through the simple expedient of revoking the trust, and then, as absolute owner of the subject matter, doing with the property as he chooses. Even though no actual termination of the trust is effectuated, however, it could hardly be questioned but that the mere existence of this power in the settlor is sufficient to enable his influence to be felt in a practical way in the administration of the trust. . . .

In the case at bar, the power of Farkas to vote, sell, redeem, exchange or otherwise deal in the stock was reserved to him as trustee, and it was only upon sale or redemption that he was entitled to keep the proceeds for his own use. Thus, the control reserved is not as great as in those cases where said power is reserved to the owner as settlor. For as trustee he must so conduct himself in accordance with standards applicable to trustees generally. It is not a valid objection to this to say that Williams would never question Farkas' conduct, inasmuch as Farkas could then revoke the trust and destroy what interest Williams has. Such a possibility exists in any case where the settlor has the power of revocation. Still, Williams has rights the same as any beneficiary, although it may not be feasible for him to exercise them. Moreover, it is entirely possible that he might in certain situations have a right to hold Farkas' estate liable for breaches of trust committed by Farkas during his lifetime. In this regard, consider what would happen if, without having revoked the trust, Farkas as trustee had given the stock away without receiving any consideration therefor, had pledged the stock improperly for his own personal debt and allowed it to be lost by foreclosure or had exchanged the stock for another security or other worthless property in such manner as to constitute gross impropriety and gross negligence. In such instances, it would seem in accordance with the terms of those instruments that Williams would have had an enforceable claim against Farkas' estate for whatever damage had been suffered. Contrast this with the rights of a legatee or devisee under a will. The testator could waste the property or do anything with it he wished during his lifetime without incurring any liability to those designated by the will to inherit the property. In any event, if Farkas as settlor could reserve the power to sell or otherwise deal with the property and retain the proceeds, which the cases indicate he could, then it necessarily follows that he should have the right to sell or otherwise deal with the property as trustee and retain the proceeds from a sale or redemption without having the instruments rendered invalid as testamentary dispositions.

Another factor often considered in determining whether an *inter vivos* trust is an attempted testamentary disposition is the formality of the transaction. . . . Historically, the purpose behind the enactment of the statute on wills was the prevention of fraud. The requirement as to witnesses was deemed necessary because a will is ordinarily an expression of the secret wish of the testator, signed out of the presence of all concerned. The possibility of forgery and fraud are ever present in such situations. Here, Farkas executed four separate applications for stock of Investors Mutual, Inc., in which he directed that the stock be issued in his name as trustee for Williams, and he executed four separate declarations of trust in which he declared he was holding said stock in trust for Williams. The stock certificates in question were issued in his name as trustee for Williams. He thus manifested his intention in a solemn and formal manner.

For the reasons stated, we conclude that these trust declarations executed by Farkas constituted valid *inter vivos* trusts and were not attempted testamentary dispositions. It must be conceded that they have, in the words of Mr. Justice Holmes in Bromley v. Mitchell, 155 Mass. 509, 30 N.E. 83, a "testamentary look." Moreover, it must be admitted that the line should be drawn somewhere, but after a study of this case we do not believe that point has here been reached.

Reversed and remanded, with directions.

Note

Ernest G. Sullivan and Mary A. Sullivan had been separated for many years when Mr. Sullivan died. During his life he had put ownership of his house in an *inter vivos* trust much like that in Farkas v. Williams. He was sole trustee, net income was paid to him during his life, and trustee was to pay him principal at his request. He could revoke the trust. At Mr. Sullivan's death, the successor trustee was to pay anything left to George F. Cronin Sr. and Harold J. Cronin.

When Mr. Sullivan died, leaving a will saying that he "intentionally neglected to make provision for my wife . . . ," Mrs. Sullivan sought to exercise her statutory right to a share of his estate, but virtually all his assets were in the trust.

The Massachusetts Supreme Judicial Court held that the trust "was not testamentary in character" and was "a valid *inter vivos* trust." As to this case, the court followed precedents and denied the surviving spouse "any claim against the assets of a valid *inter vivos* trust created by the surviving spouse, even where the deceased spouse alone retained substantial rights and powers. . . ." But for the future, the court said that in these circumstances, the surviving spouse's statutory share would be based on assets contained in trusts like this one. Sullivan v. Burkin, 460 N.E.2d 572 (Mass. 1984).

In drafting the Restatement (Second) of Property, the American Law Institute in 1982 divided 63 to 60 against the position taken in *Sullivan*. See Sullivan v. Burkin, 460 N.E.2d at 576 n.4.

b. Fiduciary Responsibility

◆ BLANKENSHIP v. BOYLE
329 F. Supp. 1089 (D.D.C. 1971)

GESELL, District Judge. This is a derivative class action brought on behalf of coal miners who have a present or future right to benefits as provided by the United Mine Workers of America Welfare and Retirement Fund of 1950. Plaintiffs have qualified under Rule 23.2 of the Federal Rules of Civil Procedure. Jurisdiction is founded on diversity and on the general jurisdiction of this Court, 11 D.C. Code §521, in effect at the time suit was filed.

Defendants are the Fund and its present and certain past trustees; the United Mine Workers of America; and the National Bank of Washington and a former president of that Bank. . . .

I. BACKGROUND

The Fund was created by the terms of the National Bituminous Coal Wage Agreement of 1950, executed at Washington, D.C., March 5, 1950, beween the Union and numerous coal operators. It is an irrevocable trust established pursuant to Section 302(c) of the Labor-Management Relations Act of 1947, 29 U.S.C. §186(c), and has been continuously in operation with only slight modifications since its creation.

The Fund is administered by three trustees: one designated by the Union, one designated by the coal operators, and the third a "neutral party designated by the other two." The Union representative is named Chairman of the Board of Trustees by the terms of the trust. Each trustee, once selected, serves for the term of the Agreement subject only to resignation, death, or an inability or unwillingness to serve. The original trustees named in the Agreement were Charles A. Owen for the Operators, now deceased; John L. Lewis for the Union, now deceased; and Miss Josephine Roche. The present trustees are W. A. (Tony) Boyle, representing the Union; C. W. Davis, representing the Operators; and Roche, who still serves.

Each coal operator signatory to the Agreement (there are approximately fifty-five operator signatories) is required to pay a royalty (originally thirty cents, and now forty cents per ton of coal mined) into the Fund. These royalty payments represent in excess of ninety-seven percent of the total receipts of the Fund, the remainder being income from investments. In the year ending June 30, 1968, royalty receipts totalled $163.1 million and investment income totalled $4.7 million. Total benefit expenditures amounted to $152 million.

In general, the purpose of the Fund is to pay various benefits, "from principal or income or both," to employees of coal operators, their families and dependents. These benefits cover medical and hospital care, pensions, compensation for work-related injuries or illness, death or disability, wage losses, etc. The trustees have considerable discretion to determine the types and levels of benefits that will be recognized. While prior or present membership in the Union is not a prerequisite to receiving welfare payments, more than ninety-five percent of the beneficiaries were or are Union members.

The Fund has maintained a large staff based mainly in Washington, D.C., which carries out the day-to-day work under policies set by the trustees. Roche, the neutral trustee, is also Administrator of the Fund serving at an additional salary in this full-time position. Thomas Ryan, the Fund's Comptroller, is the senior staff member next in line.

The trustees hold irregular meetings, usually at the Fund's offices. Formal minutes are prepared and circulated for approval. In the past, a more detailed and revealing record of discussions among the trustees has been prepared and maintained in the files of the Fund by the Fund's counsel, who attended all meetings. The Fund is regularly audited, and a printed annual report summarizing the audit and other developments was published and widely disseminated to beneficiaries, Union representatives, and coal operators, as well as to interested persons in public life.

From the outset the trustees contemplated that the Fund would operate on a "pay-as-you-go" basis — that is, that the various benefits would be paid out largely from royalty receipts rather than solely from income earned on accumulated capital. Always extremely liquid, the Fund invested some of its growing funds in United States Government securities and purchased certificates of deposit. It also purchased a few public utility common stocks, and in very recent years invested some amounts in tax-free municipal securities. . . .

From its creation in 1950, the Fund has done all of its banking business with the National Bank of Washington. In fact, for more than twenty years it has been the Bank's largest customer. When this lawsuit was brought, the Fund had about $28 million in checking accounts and $50 million in time deposits in the Bank. The Bank was at all times owned and controlled by the Union which presently holds 74 percent of

Union controlled bank -

the voting stock. Several Union officials serve on the Board of Directors of the Bank, and the Union and many of its locals also carry substantial accounts there. Boyle, President of the Union, is also Chairman of the Board of Trustees of the Fund and until recently was a Director of the Bank. Representatives of the Fund have also served as Directors of the Bank, including the Fund's house counsel and its Comptroller. The Fund occupies office space rented from the Union for a nominal amount, located in close proximity to the Union's offices.

The precise duties and obligations of the trustees are not specified in any of the operative documents creating the Fund and are only suggested by the designation of the Fund as an "irrevocable trust." There appears to have been an initial recognition by the trustees of the implications of this term. Lewis, who was by far the dominant factor in the development and administration of the Fund, stated at Board meetings that neither the Union's nor the Operators' representative was responsible to any special interest except that of the beneficiaries. He declared that each trustee should act solely in the best interests of the Fund, that the day-to-day affairs of the Fund were to be kept confidential by the trustees, that minutes were not to be circulated outside the Fund, and that the Fund should be soundly and conservatively managed with the long-term best interests of the beneficiaries as the exclusive objective. While he ignored these strictures on a number of occasions, as will appear, his view is still accepted by counsel for the Fund in this action, who took the position at oral argument that the duties of the trustees are equivalent to the duties of a trustee under a testamentary trust. Counsel stated, "You can't be just a little bit loyal. Once you are a trustee, you are a trustee, and you cannot consider what is good for the Union, what is good for the operators, what is good for the Bank, anybody but the trust."

This view, which corresponds with plaintiffs' position, is not accepted by all parties. While acknowledging that a trustee must be "punctilious," counsel for some of the parties urge that trustees as representatives of labor or management may properly operate the Fund so as to give their special interests collateral advantages (e.g., managing trust funds so as to increase tonnage of Union-mined coal), and that this is not inconsistent with fiduciary responsibilities since such actions ultimately assist beneficiaries by raising royalty income. But there is nothing in the Labor-Management Relations Act or other federal statutes or in their legislative history which can be said to alleviate the otherwise strict common-law fiduciary responsibilities of trustees appointed for employee welfare or pension funds developed by collective bargaining. . . .

It is true that trustees are allowed considerable discretion in administering a trust as large and complex as the Fund. In determining the nature and levels of benefits that will be paid by a welfare fund and the rules governing eligibility for benefits, the trustees must make decisions of major importance to the coal industry as well as to the beneficiaries, and their actions are valid unless arbitrary or capricious. On these matters, trustee representatives of the Union and the Operators may have honest differences in judgment as to what is best for the beneficiaries. Congress anticipated such differences in enacting §302(c) of the Labor-Management Relations Act, and sought to temper them by the anticipated neutrality of the third trustee. The congressional scheme was thus designed not to alter, but to reinforce "the most fundamental duty owed by the trustee": the duty of undivided loyalty to the beneficiaries. This is the duty to which defendant trustees in this case must be held.

Before dealing in detail with the specific breaches of trust alleged, a general comment concerning the conduct of the trustees is appropriate to place the instances of alleged misfeasance into proper context. It has already been noted that the trustees did not hold regular meetings but only met subject to the call of the Chairman. There was, accordingly, no set pattern for deciding policy questions, and often matters of considerable import were resolved between meetings by Roche and Lewis without even consulting the Operator trustee.

The Fund's affairs were dominated by Lewis until his death in 1969. Roche never once disagreed with him. Over a period of years, primarily at Lewis' urging, the Fund became entangled with Union policies and practices in ways that undermined the independence of the trustees. This resulted in working arrangements between the Fund and the Union that served the Union to the disadvantage of the beneficiaries. Conflicts of interest were openly tolerated and their implications generally ignored.[4] Not only was all the money of the Fund placed in the Union's Bank without any consideration of alternative banking services and facilities that might be available, but Lewis felt no scruple in recommending that the Fund invest in securities in which the Union and Lewis, as trustee for the Union's investments, had an interest. Personnel of the Fund went on the Bank's board without hindrance, thus affiliating themselves with a Union business venture. In short, the Fund proceeded without any clear understanding of the trustee's exclusive duty to the beneficiaries, and its affairs were so loosely controlled that abuses, mistakes and inattention to detail occurred.

II.   ACCUMULATION OF EXCESSIVE CASH

The major breach of trust of which plaintiffs complain is the Fund's accumulation of excessive amounts of cash. A basic duty of trustees is to invest trust funds so that they will be productive of income. . . .

---

4. In one instance, Roche was momentarily troubled by Ryan's going on the Bank board but when she took this up hesitantly with Lewis he "just smiled," and Roche let the matter drop.

It is contended that the trustees failed to invest cash that was available to generate income for the beneficiaries, and in total disregard of their duty allowed large sums to remain in checking accounts at the Bank without interest. It is further claimed that this breach of trust was carried out pursuant to a conspiracy among certain trustees, the Union, and the Bank through its President, and that all these parties are jointly liable for the Fund's loss of income resulting from the failure to invest.

That enormous cash balances were accumulated and held at the Bank over the twenty-year period is not disputed. The following figures are representative.

Fiscal Year	Amount of Cash in Demand Deposits at End of Year	Percentage of Cash to the Fund's Total Resources
1951	$29,000,000	29%
1956	30,000,000	23
1961	14,000,000	14
1966	50,000,000	34
1967	75,000,000	44
1968	70,000,000	39
1969	32,000,000	18

The beneficiaries were in no way assisted by these cash accumulations, while the Union and the Bank profited; and in view of the fiduciary obligation to maximize the trust income by prudent investment, the burden of justifying the conduct is clearly on the trustees.

Three explanations were seriously presented in justification of the cash accumulations: the trustees' general concern as to the future course of labor relations and other developments in the coal industry which might make it necessary to have money readily at hand on short notice; tax factors; and what was characterized as inadvertence or accident. None of these explanations will withstand analysis.

(a) *Uncertainty about the future.* Prior to 1950, strikes and labor disputes had caused mine shutdowns, placing heavy demands on the then-existing welfare programs. Any repetition of these or similar conditions would have shut off royalty payments, perhaps for a considerable period. While this factor could therefore justify the trustees in maintaining a substantial, highly liquid reserve, if affords no justification for the failure of the trustees to put the large accumulations of excess cash to work for the beneficiaries. Roche testified that she favored maintaining an amount equal to several months' expenditures in cash, because "that is the only way you can be sure." Such naiveté by a trustee is unacceptable, particularly in light of the trustees' knowledge that short-term Government securities, which the evidence showed were redeemable on one-half hour notice, for example, were readily available and would have generated substantial income for the Fund while still assuring maximum liquidity.] . .

(b) *Tax considerations.* The Fund has from the beginning been competently advised by experienced outside tax counsel. Naturally its return was examined by field audit from time to time. The Fund first sought an exemption from income tax as a charitable trust. This was denied in 1954, after a long delay while the requested ruling was being processed at the Treasury Department. This negative ruling was prospective, and thereafter the Fund understood that it would have to pay taxes on any amount of investment income that exceeded its administrative expenses. In fact, investment income never exceeded administrative expense and indeed was usually well below. In one year the spread was $2.4 million. It was obvious that even if income exceeded expenses and taxes became due on the excess, the Fund would have profited to the extent of its after-tax income.] . .

(c) *Accident or inadvertence.* There was no proof to support this desperate theory which the Fund itself does not advance and which in any event is in effect an admission of failure to adhere to minimum fiduciary standards of care and skill in administering the trust. 2 Scott on Trusts §174 (3d ed. 1967). The Fund's Comptroller stoutly denies accident or inadvertence, and the proof shows that the trustee well knew at all times that cash was steadily accumulating.

Under the most charitable view, this accident theory can help to account only for the staggering accumulations of cash in the period 1966 to 1968, when Lewis was in failing health and the trustees met infrequently. However, as is clear from the discussion of the conspiracy aspects of this case, *infra,* these accumulations were only an extension of a conscious, longstanding policy of the trustees. . . . The inference is also unavoidable that Lewis made more than a mistake of judgment as a trustee. He acted to benefit the Bank and to enhance its prestige and indirectly the prestige of the Union, not simply to keep money needed by the Fund in a safe place. The minutes show that he knew the large demand deposits were unnecessary for any legitimate purpose of the Fund. Moreover, he was not lacking in financial sophistication. He had been president of a bank himself and the record shows his many financial dealings and the manner in which, as President of the Union, he utilized the considerable financial resources of the Union for the Union's benefit. The conclusion is clear that Lewis, in concert with Roche, used the Fund's resources to benefit the Union's Bank and to enhance the Union's economic power in disregard of the paramount and exclusive needs of the beneficiaries which he was charged as Chairman of the Board of Trustees to protect.

Lewis acted for the Union when he entered into the conspiracy. A conspiracy once formed is presumed to continue; to escape continuing liability, a party must affirmatively withdraw from the conspiracy and seek to avoid its effects. The Union did not withdraw from the conspiracy; it had full power to end this breach of trust, yet it knowingly perpetuated the breach and continued to reap the benefits thereof.

Any doubt as to Lewis' motivation is fully dissipated by other evidence showing respects in which the Fund was used to benefit the Union during Lewis' chairmanship, to be discussed later. There is no suggestion that Lewis personally benefited, but he allowed his dedication to the Union's future and penchant for financial manipulation to lead him and through him the Union into conduct that denied the beneficiaries the maximum benefits of the Fund. A finding of conspiracy to maintain excessive cash at the Bank, justifying an award of damages against the Union in favor of the beneficiaries, is required. . . .

To summarize this aspect of the case, the Court finds: an agreement among Lewis . . . and Roche to maintain on deposit at the Bank substantial sums in interest-free accounts, without relation to the real needs of the Fund for liquidity or otherwise, for the benefit of the Union and the Bank and in disregard of the best interests of the beneficiaries; knowing participation in the breach of trust by the Union and the Bank, beginning in 1950 and continuing at least until this lawsuit was filed; and resulting injury to the beneficiaries measured by the loss of income on funds wrongfully maintained in interest-free accounts. . . .

III.   OTHER BREACHES OF TRUST

This issue relates to the Fund's purchases of stock of certain electric utility companies, principally Cleveland Electric Illuminating Company and Kansas City Power & Light Company. While these stocks are on the list approved for trustees, the propriety of these investments is challenged on the ground that they were made primarily for the purpose of benefiting the Union and the operators, and assisting them in their efforts to force public utilities to burn Union-mined coal. The investments have declined in value and are said to have been in violation of the trustees' duty of undivided loyalty to the beneficiaries.

In the late 1950's and early 1960's, the Union was engaged in a vigorous campaign to force public utility companies to purchase Union-mined coal. Public relations and organizational campaigns to this end were pressed vigorously in several cities. Lewis, then a trustee, worked closely with Cyrus S. Eaton, a Cleveland businessman. It is undisputed that between February and April 1955 the Fund purchased 30,000 shares of Cleveland Electric, and in March of that year the Union loaned Eaton money to enable him to buy an additional 20,000 shares. Eaton then went on the Board of Directors of Cleveland Electric. Similarly, between January and March 1955 the Fund purchased 55,000 shares of Kansas City Power & Light, and in June of the same year the Union loaned

Eaton money to buy an additional 27,000 shares. In each of the years from 1956 to 1965 the Fund gave a general proxy for all of its shares in Cleveland Electric and Kansas City Power & Light to Eaton. The Union and Eaton were pressing the managements of each company to force them to buy Union-mined coal. The Fund purchased both Cleveland Electric and Kansas City Power & Light stock on the recommendation of Lewis, who was then fully familiar with the Union's activities affecting these companies and proxies were given to the Union by the Fund at Lewis' request.

Schmidt, who became a trustee of the Fund in 1958, was president of the principal coal operator standing to benefit from Cleveland Electric's additional purchases of Union-mined coal. He was acquainted with the activities of the Fund and of the Union with respect to Cleveland Electric, and actively encouraged them. When the Union's campaign to push Union-mined coal focused on Cleveland Electric in 1962 and 1963, the Fund purchased an additional 90,000 shares, with the hearty approval of Schmidt.

Further indication that these particular challenged stock purchases were made primarily for the collateral benefits they gave the Union is found in a general course of conduct. Lewis and Widman, the Union man spearheading the efforts to force utilities to buy Union-mined coal, discussed some seventeen utility companies on the Fund's investment list, looking toward the possibility of obtaining proxies from fifteen. Proxies were in fact given the Union by the Fund not only on Cleveland Electric and Kansas City Power & Light, but on the shares the Fund held in Union Electric, Ohio Edison, West Penn Electric, Southern Company and Consolidated Edison. The intimate relationship between the Union's financial and organizing activities and the utility investment activities of the trustees demonstrates that the Fund was acting primarily for the collateral benefit of the Union and the signatory operators in making most of its utility stock acquisitions. These activities present a clear case of self-dealing on the part of trustees Lewis and Schmidt, and constituted a breach of trust. Roche knowingly consented to the investments, and must also be held liable. The Union is likewise liable for conspiring to effectuate and benefit by this breach of trust. . . .

One of the principal subjects of inquiry at the trial involved the circumstances under which monthly pensions were raised from $115 to $150 on June 24, 1969. This $35 increase was not without consequences, since it involved an additional annual disbursement from the Fund of approximately $30 million. Plaintiffs do not seek a rollback of the pension increase, but assert that the motives for which it was made, and the manner in which it was made, are grounds for removal of Boyle as a trustee, and for monetary relief from Boyle, Judy, and the Union for any injuries the Fund may suffer as a result of the action. A full discussion of the incident is required.

Roche broke her hip early in June, 1969, and for most of that month was recuperating at the Washington Hospital Center. She was nonetheless in frequent contact with her office by telephone and although immobile was otherwise fully functional. Lewis, still a trustee, was at home in Alexandria where he had remained more or less continuously for many months. He was alert but his health was failing. No trustee meeting had been held since February, 1969. Schmidt, the Operator trustee, had resigned on that date and a vacancy existed. On June 4, 1969, defendant Judy was installed as Schmidt's successor at a brief semi-social meeting held at Lewis' home. Roche, already hospitalized, knew of the meeting and approved of Judy's designation, but could not attend.   Boyle, Judy, Roche

Lewis died on June 11, 1969, and Boyle, who had been president of the Union since 1963, was designated as the Union's trustee representative, and hence Chairman of the Board of Trustees of the Fund, at a meeting of Union officials on June 23. Boyle had received some general information concerning the Fund's operations which led him to feel that a sizable pension increase could be financed. As an energetic Union leader, he was confident that if additional money were needed, the operators could be forced to increase their royalty payments when the next collective bargaining agreement was negotiated. He felt the unexpended balance of the Fund was far too large, and that a pension increase was long overdue. Indeed, at Union meetings and elsewhere he had promised that if he ever had anything to do with the matter he would increase pensions at the earliest possible opportunity. Boyle had urged Lewis to raise the amount of the pension but Lewis had refused to act.

When Lewis died and Boyle was named trustee, an election contest for presidency of the Union was looming. Boyle undoubtedly recognized that if he delivered on his pension promises to the rank and file, his position would be strengthened in the campaign. These election considerations account for the timing of his actions, but they were not the primary factor motivating Boyle. He genuinely believed that a pension increase should be made in the interests of the miner beneficiaries. Boyle knew that Roche was opposed to a pension increase, but with her hospitalized he was in a position to force the issue with Operator trustee Judy, and undoubtedly felt that the end — that is, the increase in pensions — justified the means. Even if Judy refused to go along, the Union's position in subsequent bargaining would be strengthened. Thus, Boyle decided to see if he could bully it through. As soon as he was designated trustee, Boyle called a meeting of the trustees for the next day at his offices at the Union.

Judy approved the increase in a private session with Boyle immediately before the formal meeting, under circumstances which will be mentioned later. The increase was formally approved a few minutes later and an announcement was thereafter sent out over Boyle's name to all pensioners and potential beneficiaries.

This action was taken in unnecessary haste. The trustees did not adequately consider the implications of their action, and while the increase was not wholly irresponsible it was not approached with adequate regard for the trustees' fiduciary obligations. Roche was not consulted or even advised of the action in advance, and in fact continued vigorously to oppose the pension increase. No detailed projections of the Fund's long-term ability to pay were made, nor were possible alternative changes in benefit payments considered. The trustees took no contemporaneous steps partially to offset the added payout by eliminating unnecessary administrative expenses or by investing cash in income-producing securities. In short, the increase was handled as an arrangement between labor and management with little recognition of its fiscal and fiduciary aspects. . . .

The most revealing document in this entire episode is the full text of the press release which the Fund's public relations man issued on the day of the pension increase. It reads as follows:

> Washington, D.C. — W. A. "Tony" Boyle, President of the United Mine Workers of America, succeeded John L. Lewis today as the Chief Executive Officer and Trustee of the Union's Welfare and Retirement Fund, and immediately boosted the pension of retired soft coal miners from $115 to $150 monthly.
>
> The new pension rate will be effective August 1. It was voted at the first session of the Trustees attended by the Union chief. He was chosen trustee at a meeting of the International Executive Board yesterday, and as chief executive officer of the Fund, as set forth under the UMWA contract with the bituminous coal industry, called a meeting of the Trustees, and the pension boost was adopted. Other trustees are George Judy, for the coal operators, and Josephine Roche, also director of the Fund, as the neutral.
>
> Pensions now are going to approximately 70,000 retired soft coal miners. Last year, the Fund paid out $96 million in this benefit alone. Other benefits are complete hospital care for miners and their families, and death benefits to widows and survivors.
>
> Chairman Boyle also called for an immediate in-depth study of all benefits of the 23-year-old Fund, with complete analysis of the entire program for miners, their widows and families. He has received scores of suggestions for possibly improving the benefits at a series of rallies in the coal fields of West Virginia, Pennsylvania and Illinois in recent months.
>
> The new chief executive of the Fund, like his predecessor, will accept no pay for serving as Trustee.

Nothing could more blatantly expose the realities of what had occurred in this instance and had been occurring for some time. However correct or incorrect the pension increase decision may have been, it reflected the Union's influence over Fund policy and the loss of independence that the Fund's continuous deferences to the Union's self-interest had by this time achieved. . . .

V.   RELIEF

. . . No considerations of equity intervene to bar prospective remedies for mismanagement of the Fund by its trustees. The Fund has been seriously compromised. It has failed to develop a coherent investment policy geared to immediate or long-term goals. It has collaborated with the Union contrary to the trustees' fiduciary duties, and has left excessive sums of money on deposit with the Union's Bank in order to assist the Union. In their day-to-day decisions, the trustees have overlooked their exclusive obligation to the beneficiaries by improperly aiding the Union to collect back dues and by cutting off certain beneficiaries unfairly.

Alongside these serious deficiencies must be placed the pioneer role of the Fund, which by constant effort has led in the development of a broad program of welfare benefits for a distressed segment of the working population. The many beneficial and well-motivated actions cannot, however, excuse the serious lapses which have resulted in obvious detriments to many beneficiaries. There is an urgent need for reformation of policies and practices which only changes in the composition of the Board of Trustees, an adjustment of its banking relationship, and other equitable relief can accomplish.

Further proceedings must be conducted on the measure of damages, but as the Court indicated before trial it is desirable at this stage to establish the nature of equitable relief which must be taken for the protection of the beneficiaries. Equitable relief shall take the following form.

Neither Boyle nor Roche shall continue to serve as a trustee. Each shall be replaced by June 30, 1971, under the following procedures. A new trustee must first be named by the Union. Consonant with the provisions of the Agreement, the new Union trustee and the existing trustee representing the Operators shall then select a new neutral trustee. The neutral trustee shall be designated on or before June 15, 1971, and the designation will then be submitted for approval by this Court before the new trustee takes office on June 30.

The newly constituted Board of Trustees selected as required by the decree shall then immediately determine whether or not Roche shall continue as Administrator of the Fund. No trustee shall serve as Administrator after June 30, 1971.

Upon the selection of a replacement for Boyle and the neutral trustee, the newly constituted Board of Trustees shall be required to obtain independent professional advice to assist them in developing an

540 ♦ 14. Equitable Estates

investment policy for creating maximum income consistent with the prudent investment of the Fund's assets, and such a program shall be promptly put into effect.

The Fund shall by June 30, 1971, cease maintaining banking accounts with or doing any further business of any kind with the National Bank of Washington. Following termination of this relationship, the Fund shall not have any account in a bank in which either the Union, any coal operator or any trustee has controlling or substantial stock interest. No employee, representative or trustee of the Fund shall have any official connection with the bank or banks used by the Fund after June 30, 1971. The Fund shall not maintain non-interest-bearing accounts in any bank or other depository which are in excess of the amount reasonably necessary to cover immediate administrative expenses and to pay required taxes and benefits on a current basis.

A general injunction shall be framed enjoining the trustees from the practices here found to be breaches of trust and generally prohibiting the trustees from operating the Fund in a manner designed in whole or in part to afford collateral advantages to the Union or the operators.

Counsel are directed to confer and prepare a proposed form of decree carrying out the equitable relief here specified. This proposed decree shall be presented to the Court and any disagreements as to form settled on May 13, 1971, at 4:00 p.m. On May 21, 1971, plaintiffs shall furnish the Court and defendants with a precise statement of the amounts of compensatory damages and attorneys' fees and expenses claimed in light of this Opinion, a statement of the method used to compute the claims, and a list of witnesses to be called at the damages phase of this proceeding. No punitive damages will be awarded. A hearing as to compensatory damages is set for June 21, 1971, at 9:30 a.m.

Why was it a breach of trust for John L. Lewis to use pension fund money to benefit the union? Indeed, if he used the money to buy utility stocks and kept the utilities burning coal, weren't his investments justifiable even in respect to the short-term interests of pensioners? If Judge Gesell is imposing a conception of political legitimacy — that decisions about the trust should be made by persons visibly responsible to current beneficiaries and not to the future beneficiaries who still work in the mines — is his source for such a rule the trust instrument itself, a statute, or some common law doctrine?

Regarding Josephine Roche, see S. Alinsky, John L. Lewis 60-61 (1950):

> In 1924 Lewis got the operators of Illinois, Indiana, Ohio, and western Pennsylvania to agree to a three-year wage contract. This contract, known as the Jacksonville agreement, was hailed as a great victory as it would

protect the wages of the miners for the next three-year period. Shortly afterward, the agreement became another scrap of paper as the operators violated it again and again, all except one coal operator who sided with and tried to help the union. This operator, a woman named Josephine Roche, was president of the Rocky Mountain Fuel Company. Acting on the basis of ideals, she signed and honored a two-year contract with the union. In later years, when the company ran into financial difficulties the union reciprocated by setting up a private corporation . . . and siphoned large sums of money into Miss Roche's mines to try to keep her properties afloat. There was more than sheer altruism involved, as Lewis well knew that the union miners' jobs were dependent upon the continuance of operations by the company.

Ralph Nader was a leader of the movement for private pension reform. See, for example, his remarks before the Sixth Annual Conference on Employee Benefits, New York City, May 24, 1972, from R. Nader & K. Blackwell, You and Your Pension 158 (1973):

In terms of dollar impact, the private pension system represents one of the most comprehensive consumer frauds that many Americans will encounter in their lifetime. And I use the term "fraud" advisedly.

Those of you who sell, service, and administer private pension plans, as well as those who negotiate and establish plans, have seriously and deliberately misrepresented the nature of this pension system. The industry has induced some 30 million Americans to rely on the system's promise of retirement security knowing full well that the system can afford to provide that security to very few. At least one-half of all persons participating in private pension plans will not receive pension benefits when they retire. More than one-half of all persons who receive private pension benefits receive less than $1000 a year. The majority of pension plans do not provide for benefits for dependent widows or widowers, or provide very limited benefits. This vast . . . system — heavily subsidized by an annual Federal tax subsidy of well over 3 billion dollars a year — is hurting too many people unnecessarily and unfairly.

Finally, national legislation was enacted as part of the Internal Revenue Code. See Note, Fiduciary Standards and the Prudent Man Rule Under the Employment Retirement Income Security Act of 1974, 88 Harv. L. Rev. 960, 960-961, 964 (1975):

At the end of 1973, . . . more than 35 million employees were covered by the private pension system. Federal regulation of this system was limited primarily to the indirect control exerted by awarding tax benefits to pension plans that complied with specified conditions. Since the only sanction for violation of the Internal Revenue Code's standards was withdrawal of a plan's tax-exempt status — a drastic action whose primary impact would have been on the intended beneficiaries — the sanction was rarely invoked, raising questions about the effectiveness of federal regulation. Responding to concern that this indirect regulation insufficiently protected employees' interests, Congress passed the Employment Retirement Income Security Act of 1974 (ERISA). ERISA imposes far-reaching uniform standards governing the operation of pension plans in order to assure that employees will receive anticipated benefits when they retire or when a plan is terminated. . . .

In addition to prohibiting certain transactions, the new law contains less well-defined standards governing the investment decisions of plan fiduciaries. Fiduciaries are required to discharge their duties for the exclusive purpose of providing benefits to plan participants and beneficiaries and "with the care, skill, prudence, and diligence under the circumstances then prevailing that a prudent man acting in a like capacity and familiar with such matters would use in the conduct of an enterprise of a like character and with like aims." The Act further obliges fiduciaries to diversify plan assets when it is prudent to do so and to abide by the provisions of the documents that establish the plan, but only insofar as those provisions are consistent with ERISA.

Neither the Act nor its legislative history, however, clearly indicates how any of these more general fiduciary standards is to be interpreted. . . .

For prescience about the consequences of "reform" in the ERISA mold, see S. Harriss, Economic Effects of Estate and Gift Taxation, in Joint Committee on the Economic Report, Federal Tax Policy for Economic Growth and Stability 855 (1955):

One major economic effect of estate taxes results from the opportunity under the law to reduce the total tax over the years, reduce it substantially, by placing property in trust. Consequently, the use of trusts is stimulated by the taxes in their present form. Although there is no doubt about the tendency, no data for measuring it are available. Thus, knowing that over 25 percent of gifts reported on 1950 gift tax returns were of property in trust, we still cannot say how much of this use of trusts was due to the tax system. Certainly some, probably much! And the extent will grow as the tax-saving advantages of trusts are recognized more widely and as wills now being made come into effect.

What, then, is the economic significance of trusteeship of wealth? More cautious and conservative investment is one result. Although trusts made today generally permit investment beyond the restrictive limits of the past, the tendency is to stick to relatively "high quality" assets. Another, and related, is greater emphasis on rationality in making investment decisions; specialized, technically competent personnel generally guide the decision making. While the wisdom of trustees will vary widely, their influence will make the preservation of wealth more likely than if heirs were given greater responsibility and freedom for investment. The dissipation of inheritances that can come from foolish investment or reckless spending by heirs who are free to use their property is largely prevented by trusteeing wealth. The economy as a whole, as well as the particular families involved, will benefit from any such reduction of folly and waste.

On the other hand, the conservative and restricted nature of trusts removes wealth from markets where it might be available for more venturesome and risky investment. Fortunes in trust cannot, as a rule, be used for financing some of the most dynamic parts of the economy. Even the beneficiary of a trust seeking capital for his own business often cannot use assets which under a freer system would have been available to him. Yet it is the large concentration of wealth that can finance the scrutiny of new ventures and afford to take the extreme risks that are involved in true economic pioneering.[58] Of course, there is no way to determine how much, if any, of the wealth now in trust for rich families would in fact be used to finance dynamic venture intelligently were it not for trustification. It is easy, perhaps, to romanticize a bit about the part existing fortunes would play in financing the expansion of economic frontiers, especially by new businesses. There can be no doubt, however, that much wealth now in trust cannot conceivably be used for such purposes; in addition there are assets which in fact will not be used for dynamic economic growth even through the trustees are not absolutely prohibited from doing so.

However, there develops a group — not large in relation to the whole population — receiving income (about $2 billion a year before income tax) from trusts whose capital assets they do not fully own or control and may not consume. Although the social and economic effects of such a development are not obvious, they will hardly assume the relative importance of those associated with rentier groups in some civilizations in the past.

As to the future, consider the comments of James E. Joseph, president of the Council on Foundations, as reported in the Wall Street Journal, April 5, 1984:

In the late 1980s, the battle for control of pension fund investments may become America's central economic and social justice issue. The most recent assessment put its present worth at $700 billion, growing at $300 million a day. Total assets are expected to reach $3 trillion by 1995. This means that it is now larger than the combined gross national product of the U.K. and France.

Notes

1. Plaintiffs, civil service employees' organizations, sued on behalf of their members' interests in retirement funds. By statute, the state

58. Giant corporations now perform some of the venturesome undertakings once left more to individuals; the giants seeking funds for expansion may at times get them by sale of new common stock to trusts. There is little basis for judging how adequately established firms do the job or what gaps they leave that might be filled by use of private fortunes. My own feeling, which may be largely prejudice, is that innumerable opportunities will not be developed by firms large enough to draw, directly or indirectly, on wealth in trust.

comptroller was "trustee" of the funds, with authority to invest in securities. A 1975 law directed the comptroller to purchase $125 million in bonds of the new Municipal Assistance Corporation, created to ease New York City's financial plight. The court of appeals held that "to strip . . . the comptroller . . . of his personal responsibility" to choose investments "is to remove a safeguard integral to the scheme of maintaining the security of the sources of benefits," and therefore an unconstitutional infringement of the contract rights of participants in the retirement system. Sgaglione v. Levitt, 37 N.Y.2d 507, 337 N.E.2d 592 (1975).

But when the comptroller then exercised his restored discretion to purchase the bonds, the same court approved. Westchester Chapter, Civil Service Employees Assn. v. Levitt, 37 N.Y.2d 519, 337 N.E.2d 748, 375 N.Y.S.2d 294 (1975).

Is it unconstitutional for the legislature to relieve the comptroller of liability as a fiduciary in choosing investments? Is it appropriate for union leader-trustees to consider, in selecting investments, the likelihood that keeping New York City from insolvency will maximize the number of future jobs? Can such decisions be distinguished from the actions of John L. Lewis castigated by Judge Gesell?

Estimates of the total assets held by private pension plans and profit-sharing plans range upwards from $250 billion. S. Murray, Analysis of the Pension Reform Act of 1974 1-4 (1974). For the argument that pension fund ownership of a substantial share of the nation's industrial and financial assets has made America's economy socialist, see P. Drucker, The Unseen Revolution: How Pension Fund Socialism Came to America (1975). One should consider, however, that most private pension funds are managed by bank trust departments. See, generally, L. D. Jones, Bank Trust Activity and the Public Interest (1971) and U.S. Congress, H.R. Committee on Banking and Currency, Subcommittee on Domestic Finance, Commercial Banks and Their Trust Activities: Emerging Influence on the American Economy (1968).

Upholding investment by trustees of municipal pension funds in New York City securities: Withers v. Teachers' Retirement System, 447 F. Supp. 1248 (S.D.N.Y. 1978), aff'd, 595 F.2d 1210 (2d Cir. 1979).

2. Teamsters at End of Line as Vegas Angels, Variety, March 31, 1976:

> Reno, March 30. The Teamsters Union, with more than $210,000,000 in loans and loan commitments to Nevada casinos, is the gaming industry's No. 1 financial backer, but its days may be numbered. Federal pension law reforms, current investigations into the union's biggest pension fund, and even hassles between the casinos and their employees are prompting second thoughts by the Teamsters and club operators.
>
> There have been no known commitments of new Teamster money in more than a year in the state. That shows "a more cautious approach" by the Teamsters Central States, Southeast and Southwest Areas Pension Fund, says state Gaming Commission Chairman Pete Echeverria.

"I don't want to call it a negative approach, but it's certainly a more cautious approach, in view of the pension reform act and some of the Federal investigations into the fund," Echeverria says. . . .

The possible loss of that loan resource — a key factor in the Nevada gaming industry's rapid growth over the past decade — is prompting club operators to look elsewhere for longterm loans at reasonable rates. . . .

The search for new financing has also been spurred as a result of the recent labor strike which affected many major Las Vegas casinos. Teamster Union members honored picket lines — in some cases at clubs where the Teamsters pension fund loaned money.

"That's a case of the dog biting its own tail," said one industry spokesman. . . .

Echeverria says pension fund money has not usually presented a problem for the state because it can be easily traced. The money comes from the $22 weekly contributions made for each of the 400,000 Teamster Union members.

3. The secretary of labor sued a Teamsters pension trust fund pursuant to ERISA to prevent a loan of $20 million to finance a 1,000 room hotel and casino on the "strip" in Las Vegas. The court enjoined the loan, citing the act's requirement that assets be diversified and the fact that this loan would be for 34 percent of the total principal of the fund. Marshall v. Teamsters Local 282 Pension Trust Fund, 458 F. Supp. 986 (E.D.N.Y. 1978).

c. Limitations on Grantor Sovereignty

The settlor uses the terms of the trust to control the future actions of trustees and beneficiaries. Circumstances change, however, and the directions of the settlor may come to seem detrimental to the public, or merely inconvenient for the beneficiaries or trustees. The next three cases illustrate typical problems of this sort, and some of the doctrines courts have employed to adjust the settlor's intentions to circumstances that he may never have envisioned. Courts interpret, sometimes altering, the intentions of property owners when dealing with wills, contracts, and covenants. Is there, or should there be, a greater or lesser leeway when interpreting trust instruments?

◆ WESLEY UNITED METHODIST CHURCH v. HARVARD COLLEGE
366 Mass. 247, 316 N.E.2d 620 (1974)

TAURO, Chief Justice. This is a bill in equity brought by the board of trustees of the Wesley United Methodist Church, as trustees under a charitable trust created by the will of one Harold E. Colson, seeking modification of the terms of the trust under the doctrine of (cy pres) The defendant Harvard College did not file an answer, and the Attorney General waived his right to be heard. The sole heirs at law of Harold E. Colson, Harold C. Guppy, Sr., and Mary F. Smith, contend that the doctrine of *cy pres* is inapplicable and that a resulting trust should be declared in their favor. The Probate Court granted the plaintiff the requested relief, and the heirs at law have appealed. We affirm.

The case is before us on a statement of agreed material facts which may be summarized as follows. Harold E. Colson died on December 28, 1968. His will, executed in September, 1957, contained the following provision:

> Fourth: All the rest, residue and remainder of my estate, of whatsoever kind and wheresoever situate, I give, devise and bequeath unto Wesley Methodist Church of Salem, Massachusetts, to be used by the Board of Trustees of said church to establish a fund to be designated as the "Frances L. Colson Memorial Scholarship Fund" and both the principal and income of such fund shall be used by said Board of Trustees to provide one five-hundred dollar scholarship each year to assist one worthy male member of the congregation or communicant of said church, to be selected each year at the discretion of said Board of Trustees, to attend Harvard College, Cambridge, Massachusetts for undergraduate education. In the event that the annual income from said fund shall exceed five hundred dollars, then the income in excess of that required for the scholarship above referred to shall be accumulated until such excess income exceeds the sum of five hundred dollars, at which time said Board of Trustees may, at its discretion, provide a second five-hundred dollar scholarship, subject to the qualifications and limitations as above provided.

Frances L. Colson was the testator's mother. Both she and the testator had been members of the Wesley United Methodist Church, he having joined on December 29, 1907. When his will was executed in September, 1957, the decedent had a small estate, with modest investment in United States Savings Bonds. In time, his net worth increased significantly, and as of July 11, 1972, the funds given to the Wesley United Methodist Church for trust purposes exceeded $55,000, producing an annual income approximating $3,200.

To date, the church has given out no scholarships. In fact, it has not even received any applications from students or prospective students. It has only 236 members, most of whom are adults. The tuition charge at Harvard College has risen substantially since 1957, and as of 1973 was $2,600 a year. In 1957 the college did not admit women, but it does today.

The Probate Court found that "the express terms of the trust . . . are literally impracticable of operation in limiting the beneficiaries to male members or communicants of Wesley Methodist Church," and that "the testator's intention to provide scholarships for students attending Harvard College as a memorial for his mother may be fulfilled to promote and accomplish the general charitable intent of the testator under the application of *cy pres*." It was ordered that "the Board of Trustees of the Petitioner apply income and accumulations of the trust fund in the awarding of annual scholarships, in their discretion, unlimited in amount, to worthy male or female applicants, not restricted to members or communicants of the petitioner if there are no such applicants, for undergraduate or graduate education in Harvard University."

The defendant heirs at law argue that both the findings as to impracticability and general charitable intent are erroneous. Each is a necessary element for the application of the *cy pres* doctrine . . . *Cy pres* will not apply, however, if the trust remains capable of meaningful application, or if, despite impracticability, there is a lack of general charitable intent on the testator's part. In the latter situation, ". . . in the absence of any limitation over or other provision, the legacy lapses."

We hold that the Probate Court's findings were warranted and the decree was not erroneous. . . . This and other courts have found impracticability where a present and probably continuing lack of specified beneficiaries serve effectively to freeze disbursement of charitable funds. . . . This rule is a sound one, as no purpose, least of all the settlor's, is served by tying up funds intended for charitable use with the thin thread of a theoretically possible (but unlikely) change in circumstances. We believe that in the instant case, in view of the size and character of the Wesley United Methodist Church membership, the Probate Court was correct in its finding that the Frances L. Colson trust is impracticable.

Moreover, we believe that the settlor displayed a general charitable intent, as distinguished from an intent "limited to . . . a specific charitable purpose." Ultimately, the question is whether the settlor would have preferred that his bequest be applied to a like charitable purpose in the event that his original scheme did not work out, or would have instead desired that the unused funds be diverted to private use. This analysis is often difficult since more often than not the settlor, fully expecting his scheme to be effective, never contemplates alternative dispositions, or at least fails to include them in his testamentary design. This appears to be the case here, as the settlor's will contains neither an express statement of general charitable intent, nor specific instructions for the disposition of the trust funds in the event of failure or impracticability. Thus, the general charitable intent, or lack of it, must be inferred from the language of the trust provisions contained in the will, and from the language of the will as a whole.

We are satisfied that the settlor would have wished that the funds be applied to a like charitable purpose rather than be removed from charitable use entirely. . . . The decedent bequeathed his eyes to the

Wills Eye Hospital of Philadelphia to be used for scientific research, and the rest of his mortal remains to the Cox Institute of the University of Pennsylvania for the same purpose. We conclude on the basis of all of these considerations, including his desire to establish a memorial to his deceased mother, that the decedent possessed a general intent to have his estate applied to charitable ends, and that he " '. . . would attach so much more importance to the object of the gift than to the mechanism by which he intended to accomplish it that he would prefer to alter the mechanism to the extent necessary to save the object.' "

————————

Was the primary purpose of the memorial to the testator's mother to benefit the church membership or Harvard students? Considering that in 1957 women were attending classes at Harvard, but that at the time of the order in 1974 the school did not formally admit women undergraduates, did the court fairly interpret the testator's intent when it ordered distribution of scholarships regardless of sex?

With regard to the *cy pres* doctrine, consider the history of the will of U.S. Senator A. O. Bacon, of Georgia. The will, dated 1911, devised property in trust to the city of Macon for the creation of a public park for exclusive use of the white people of that city. In 1966, the Supreme Court held that Macon's operation of the park on a racially discriminatory basis violated the Fourteenth Amendment. Evans v. Newton, 382 U.S. 296 (1966). The Supreme Court of Georgia subsequently ruled that the senator's intention to provide a park for whites only had become impossible to fulfill, that accordingly the trust had failed, and that the parkland and other trust property reverted by operation of law to the heirs of the senator. Evans v. Abney, 224 Ga. 826, 165 S.E.2d 160 (1968). The Supreme Court affirmed, stating "the loss of charitable trusts . . . is part of the price we pay for permitting deceased persons to exercise a continuing control over assets owned by them at death. This aspect of freedom of testation, like most things, has its advantages and disadvantages." Evans v. Abney, 396 U.S. 435, 447 (1970). Justice Brennan, in dissent, said the prior *Evans* case had found that the senator, in expressing his testamentary intent, had taken advantage of a specific Georgia statute enacted expressly to permit the creation of trusts for park purposes for the enjoyment of one race; as such, the state of Georgia was "significantly involved" in both the discriminatory bequest and its "reverter." 396 U.S. at 458-459.

An interesting context in which past donative intention clashes with present perceived reality concerns property held by or in trust for religious institutions. Schisms — doctrinal and otherwise — occur regularly. Often two or more groups contend that they are the "true" successor to the earlier institution, and therefore entitled to use the building or benefit from the financial assets. Courts are hindered from resolving these disputes by First Amendment hostility to official judicial determination of religious truth or purity. These controversies took on the added color of a Johnson v. M'Intosh appeal to relevant sovereignties when some American communicants in hierarchical Eastern European churches sought to deny the authority of new church leaders appointed under influence of communist governments. See, e.g., Kedroff v. Saint Nicholas Cathedral, 344 U.S. 94 (1952), where the dispute was between an archbishop of the Russian Orthodox Church in North America elected by the American churches, and one appointed by the patriarch of Moscow and all Russia. A New York statute, characterized by the Supreme Court as "legislative application of a *cy pres* doctrine to this trust," attempted to transfer control of the New York Russian Orthodox churches from Moscow to New York. The Supreme Court invalidated the statute as an unconstitutional legislative interference in religious matters. See also Serbian Eastern Orthodox Diocese v. Milivojevich, 426 U.S. 696 (1976), finding impermissible as an interference with religious liberty the efforts of Illinois courts to resolve a dispute over possession of the Monastery of St. Sava, in Libertyville, Illinois, between the church judicatory and a defrocked bishop.

Note

Clark Wilson's 1969 will created a trust, the income of which was to pay college expenses for "five young men who shall have graduated from Canastota High School. . . ." The New York Court of Appeals held that the school district, unwilling to serve as trustee for male-only awards, should be replaced with a private trustee, and that the actions of the judicial system in facilitating implementation of the grantor's wishes were not unconstitutional official participation in a discriminatory scheme. In re Estate of Wilson, 59 N.Y.2d 461, 452 N.E.2d 1228, 465 N.Y.S.2d 900 (1983).

♦ IN RE PULITZER'S ESTATE
139 Misc. 575, 249 N.Y.S. 87 (Sur. Ct. 1931), *aff'd*, 237 App. Div. 808, 260 N.Y.S. 975 (1932)

FOLEY, Surrogate. . . . Joseph Pulitzer died in the year 1911. He left a will and four codicils which were admitted to probate by this court on November 29, 1911. The provisions directly pertinent to the issues here are contained in the first codicil, which is dated March 23, 1909. By its terms he gave the shares of the capital stock of the Press Publishing Company, which were owned by him, and his shares of the Pulitzer Publishing Company, of St. Louis, in trust for the life of each of the two youngest of his sons, Joseph Pulitzer, Jr., and Herbert Pulitzer. The period of the two lives mentioned was defined by him as the "trust term." There were directions to pay the income in certain fractional shares to his three sons and to certain other persons. Further provisions were made for payment to the male descendants of the sons in case of the death of any of the sons during the "trust term." Upon the expiration of the "trust term" there was a direction to divide the said stock under varying conditions. If one of the sons survives, he is to take "the shares of stock of said Companies" held for his benefit, and the remainder is to be divided among the male descendants of his sons and daughters. Certain other provisions for the vesting of the remainders and for gifts over are contained, which are not important here.

To distinguish it from the residuary trust, the particular trust here has been called the "Newspaper Trust." Its trustees are the testator's three sons, Ralph Pulitzer, Herbert Pulitzer, and Joseph Pulitzer, Jr. The Pulitzer Publishing Company publishes the St. Louis Post Dispatch. The Press Publishing Company publishes the New York World, the Sunday World, and the Evening World. The trustees of the so-called "Newspaper Trust" hold within the trust a very large majority of shares of the Press Publishing Company. The remaining shares are owned by the trustees individually. The paragraph particularly sought to be construed here, which deals with the powers of the trustees and the limitations thereon, is contained in article seventh of the codicil of March 23, 1909, and reads as follows:

> I further authorize and empower my Executors and Trustees to whom I have hereinbefore bequeathed my stock in the Pulitzer Publishing Company of St. Louis, at any time, and from time to time, to sell and dispose of said stock, or any part thereof, at public or private sale, at such prices and on such terms as they may think best, and to hold the proceeds of any stock sold in trust for the beneficiaries for whom such shares were held in lieu thereof, and upon the same trusts. This power of sale is not to be construed as in any respect mandatory, but purely discretionary. This power of sale, however, is limited to the said stock of the Pulitzer Publishing Company of St. Louis, and shall not be taken to authorize or empower the sale or disposition under any circumstances whatever, by the Trustees of any stock of the Press Publishing Company, publisher of "The World" newspaper. I particularly enjoin upon my sons and my descendants the duty of preserving, perfecting and perpetuating "The World" newspaper (to the maintenance and upbuilding of which I have sacrificed my health and strength) in the same spirit in which I have striven to create and conduct it as a public institution, from motives higher than mere gain, it having been my desire that it should be at all times conducted in a spirit of independence and with a view to inculcating high standards and public spirit among the people and their official representatives, and it is my earnest wish that said newspaper shall hereafter be conducted upon the same principles.

There are fifteen remaindermen in existence. One of them is an adult; the other fourteen are infants. Because of a possible adversity of interest, they are represented here by two separate special guardians. The adult life tenants and remainderman join in requesting the relief sought by the trustees.

Counsel for the trustees contend that the express denial of a power of sale contained in the paragraph was modified and cut down, as a matter of testamentary intent, by Mr. Pulitzer in its subsequent language, wherein he expressed his desire and his earnest wish as to the perpetuation of the paper and the standards and ideals for its management by his sons and their descendants. . . .

But I prefer to place my determination here upon broader grounds and upon the power of a court of equity, in emergencies, to protect the beneficiaries of a trust from serious loss, or a total destruction of a substantial asset of the corpus. The law, in the case of necessity, reads into the will an implied power of sale. The law also assumes that a testator had sufficient foresight to realize that securities bequeathed to a trustee may become so unproductive or so diminished in value as to authorize their sale where extraordinary circumstances develop, or crisis occurs. Such was the law in this state prior to the making of Mr. Pulitzer's will. He is charged with knowledge of it. . . .

The same rule applies to emergencies in trusts not only where there is an absence of a power of sale in a will, but also where there is a prohibition against sale. It has been satisfactorily established by the evidence before me that the continuance of the publication of the newspapers, which are the principal assets of the Press Publishing Company, will in all probability lead to a serious impairment or the destruction of a large part of the trust estate. The dominant purpose of Mr. Pulitzer must have been the maintenance of a fair income for his children and the ultimate reception of the unimpaired corpus by the remaindermen. Permanence of the trust and ultimate enjoyment by his grandchildren were intended. A man of his sagacity and business ability could not have intended that from mere vanity, the publication of the newspapers, with which his name and efforts had been associated, should be persisted in until the entire trust asset was destroyed or wrecked by bankruptcy or dissolution. His expectation was that his New York newspapers would flourish. Despite his optimism, he must have contemplated that they might become entirely unprofitable and their disposal would be required to avert a complete loss of the trust asset. The power of a court of equity, with its jurisdiction over trusts, to save the beneficiaries in such a situation has been repeatedly sustained in New York and other jurisdictions. . . .

The extreme circumstances in the pending case surely justify the alternative of disregarding the directions of the testator, if mandatory, and reading into the will a power of sale. Briefly summarized, the proofs submitted to me show that the losses in the business operations of the three newspapers owned by the Press Publishing Company for the five years from 1926 to 1930 averaged $811,822.10 per year. In 1929 the loss was $1,062,749.80. In 1930 the loss was $1,975,604.77. In 1930 the loss grew, despite economies effected that year, aggregating $1,250,000. The advertising lineage of the three newspapers has greatly declined in recent years. . . . The reserves of the corporation have diminished to the extent of $3,025,000 in the past five years. The present reserves, it is stated, would not permit continued publication of the newspapers for more than three months. . . .

I accordingly hold, in this phase of the decision, that the terms of the will and codicils do not prohibit the trustees from disposing of any assets of the Press Publishing Company, that the trustees have general power and authority to act in the conveyance of the assets proposed to be sold, and that this court, in the exercise of its equitable jurisdiction, should authorize them by an appropriate direction in the decree to exercise such general authority.

H. J. MANKIEWICZ & O. WELLES, CITIZEN KANE, THE SHOOTING SCRIPT 182 (1974):

Kane: . . . I am the publisher of the "Inquirer." As such, it is my duty — I'll let you in on a little secret, it is also my pleasure — to see to it that the decent, hardworking people of this city are not robbed blind by a group of money-mad pirates because, God help them, they have no one to look after their interests! . . . I think I'm the man to do it. You see I have money and property. If I don't defend the interests of the underprivileged, somebody else will — maybe somebody *without* any money or property — and that would be too bad.

Thatcher: . . . I happened to see your consolidated statement this morning, Charles. Don't you think it's rather unwise to continue this philanthropic enterprise — this "Inquirer" — that's costing you one million dollars a year?

Kane: You're right. We did los[e] a million dollars last year. We expect to lose a million next year, too. You know, Mr. Thatcher — at the rate of a million a year — we'll have to close this place — in sixty years.

W. A. SWANBERG, PULITZER 411-418 (1967):
Which was the real man — the front-page sensationalist or the schoolmaster-idealist of the editorial page? Could one really reconcile the millionaire capitalist, the palace-dweller, the man of yachts and private cars, with the Pulitzer who attacked capitalists and trusts? . . .

. . . Henry Watterson noted the difficulties experts were having in determining the value of Pulitzer's newspapers to make an appraisal of the estate because (as one of the appraisers, Melville Stone, admitted) Pulitzer's own contribution to their value was priceless, impossible to estimate. . . .

. . . There was much speculation about the size of his estate, estimates running from thirty to eighty millions. Surprise was general when it was appraised at a comparatively modest $18,525,116. Those who felt that the morning, Evening and Sunday Worlds must have returned a million-dollar annual profit were also surprised to learn that the average net profit . . . for the years 1908 to 1911 was $536,580, the flourishing Post-Dispatch in St. Louis being not far behind in showing an annual average of $408,456 for the same period. The estate would of course have been larger but for the family's luxurious mode of life. The cost of maintaining the *Liberty* was estimated at nearly $200,000 a year, while the bill for the homes in New York, Bar Harbor, Jekyll Island and the best villa at Cap Martin came to around $350,000 annually. No one estimated the amount Pulitzer had paid to physicians for himself and his often ailing family, and for scores of stays at European spas, but that total alone would obviously have represented a sizable fortune.

He left $100,000 to Jabez Dunningham, $20,000 to Dr. Hosmer and $100,000 to be divided among his secretary-companions and his leading recruiter, James M. Tuohy. His earlier bequest of $50,000 to Alfred Butes had been canceled when Butes left him. He left $50,000 for the fountain which now ornaments the Plaza at 59th Street, and $25,000 for a statue of Jefferson, a Democratic father whom he felt was neglected in the nation's largest Democratic city. Another $1,000,000 went to Columbia University for its school of journalism, not yet begun; and a fund of $250,000 to provide scholarships and annual prizes for outstanding journalistic, historical, musical and dramatic work. A half-million was given the Metropolitan Museum of Art, and a like sum to the Philharmonic Society, the donor urging that its programs be not too severely classical and that they be "open to the public at reduced rates, and will also receive my favorite composers, Beethoven, Wagner and Liszt."

Kate Pulitzer was given the income of a fund of $2,500,000, the two daughters that of $1,500,000 and the residuary estate was left in trust for the grandchildren. The wife of Joseph Pulitzer Jr., the former Elinor Wickham, received $250,000, perhaps being favored because she would come into no such family inheritance as would Ralph's wife. The stipulations that startled observers were those relating to the sons and to the newspapers. The will read:

> I particularly enjoin upon my sons and my descendants the duty of preserving, perfecting and perpetuating The World newspaper, to the maintenance and publishing of which I have sacrificed my health and strength, in the same spirit in which I have striven to create and conduct it as a public institution, from motives higher than mere gain. . . .

His partiality for Herbert made a flurry of news headlines. The capital stock of the New York and St. Louis newspapers was left in trust for the sons, Herbert being given six-tenths, Ralph two-tenths and

Joseph one-tenth, the remaining tenth to be sold later at "liberal terms" to "the principal editors or managers" felt by the trustees to be most deserving. However, none of the sons was given actual control of the newspapers, this being left in the hands of four trustees — J. Angus Shaw, the St. Louis attorney Frederick N. Judson, Judge Harrington Putnam of Brooklyn, and the New York attorney George L. Rives, president of the Board of Trustees of Columbia University. Charles Evans Hughes had declined his $100,000 trusteeship because in 1910 he had become a justice of the Supreme Court. Judson would serve as trustee for three years, when Joseph Jr. would become 30 and would replace him. Shaw would serve for six years, when Herbert Pulitzer would become 21 and take his place. Ralph, now 32, was the only one of the brothers not given a trusteeship then or at any time in the future. . . .

The annual profits of the World trio sank from $500,000 in 1922 to half that in 1925. It could hardly have been gratifying to the two hard-working brothers that Herbert, who contributed little effort, drew by far the largest share of profit. In 1924, Herbert paid an income tax of $198,000, while Ralph paid $83,000. In 1925, the morning World raised its price to three cents although its competitors held at two cents. It was a disastrous move. Until then, Senior had still held top morning circulation with 404,000. By 1926 it was down to 285,000. In 1927 the price was dropped to two cents again, but the recovery of circulation was small. . . .

Ultimately the three Worlds were sold to the Scripps-Howard bidders for $5,000,000. This meant only the diluted perpetuation of the Evening World in the new World-Telegram. The Sunday World was dead. *The* World, the mighty Senior, the heart and soul of Joseph Pulitzer, was dead. Its last front page, dated Friday, February 27, 1931, still displayed the Goddess of Liberty between the two faces of the globe on its nameplate, but below it was a statement signed by Ralph, Joseph and Herbert as trustees pointing to "inexorable" economic conditions and ending:

> The trustees cannot pretend that it is anything but a painful duty to pass the World newspapers into other hands. But there is a fortunate mitigation in the spirit of the new ownership which is thoroughly hospitable to the World tradition. May it carry on that tradition with the fullest measure of public service and success.

The World had outlived Joseph Pulitzer by 19 years and four months. The Post-Dispatch, which he had several times tried to sell and to which he devoted much less attention, survived — and still does — as a vigorous leader among afternoon papers, perpetuating also the famous name of its founder in its present owner, the third Joseph Pulitzer.

The Pulitzer Building, no longer housing a newspaper, continued rather forlornly as an office building. As one former Evening World man, Emmet Crozier, described it, "It resembled a once beautiful and vivacious woman who had lost her interest in life." It was razed in 1955 to gain space for a new approach to the Brooklyn Bridge.

Note

Mrs. Vair's will left $100,000 to the Massachusetts Society for the Prevention of Cruelty to Animals, $75,000 to the Cleveland Health Museum, $25,000 to Harvard Law School, and the residue, about $5 million, to Case Western Reserve University Medical School. It also provided: "If, at . . . my death, I shall own . . . 307 West Avenue, Elyria, Ohio, I direct my Executors . . . to cause the house to be razed, and to sell the land. . . ." Her lawyer testified that Mrs. Vair saw the neighborhood changing, with large older homes being converted to offices, nursing homes, and rooming homes, and did not want this to happen to her house — built originally in 1837 and extended in 1868 in the "Italianate Renaissance Revival" or "Romano-Tuscan" style. After her death, the house was entered by the Ohio Historical Society in the National Register of Historic Places kept by the National Park Service. This listing restricts demolition of such properties as part of a federal project but does not limit the rights of private owners.

Held: Mrs. Vair's purpose was not capricious or irrational, and was not "repugnant, contrary to public policy." The executors would be permitted to raze the house. The executors would also be acting lawfully, however, if they transferred the property to the Lorain County Historical Society with restrictions assuring its maintenance as Mrs. Vair knew it. National City Bank v. Case Western Reserve University, 2 Ohio Op. 3d 100, 369 N.E.2d 814 (Ohio C.P. 1976).

◆ HOWARD v. SPRAGINS
350 So. 2d 318 (Ala. 1977)

BLOODWORTH, Justice. Appellants, Amy Camelia Howard, et al., appeal from a judgment authorizing and ordering appellee, First Alabama Bank of Huntsville, N. A. (Bank), as trustee, to pay a judgment for child support out of the corpus of two trusts.

The issue presented is whether the trustee, Bank, may legally pay child support payments from the corpus of the two trusts, notwithstanding the spendthrift provision[1] in each trust. We hold that the

---

1. Tit. 58, §1, Code of Alabama 1940, limits the amount protected by a spendthrift trust to $1,800.00 annually.

trustee may do so with respect to the 1970 testamentary trust. We, therefore, affirm in part and reverse in part.

On March 20, 1976, appellee, Anna Ruth W. Spragins, filed a petition for Rule Nisi against her former husband, M. B. Spragins, Jr., praying that he be found in contempt for failure to make child support payments, and seeking a judgment for unpaid child support, plus interest, attorneys' fees, and costs.

Spragins, Jr., filed an answer, in which he admitted being in arrears on child support, and a claim denominated a "third party claim" against the Bank as trustee of two *inter vivos* trusts and one testamentary trust under the will of his deceased father, Spragins, Sr., seeking construction of the trusts in regard to payment of the claim for unpaid child support. In his answer and "third party claim," as amended, Spragins, Jr., also sought to have his legal granddaughter, his legal children, and all unborn beneficiaries under the testamentary trust, made party respondents.

The Bank answered the "third party claim" of Spragins, Jr., stating that its authority, under the trusts, to pay the claim for past-due child support was unclear. The Bank then cross-claimed against all other parties. It later amended to include any possible widow of Spragins, Jr., and sought to have its authority under the trusts declared.

Three guardians *ad litem* were appointed to represent the interests of the children, grandchildren, and possible widow of Spragins, Jr., and they filed answers, denying that the corpus of the trust could be invaded to pay child support. . . .

The 1968 inter vivos trust indenture provides, *inter alia*:

Article I

The Trustee, (or such successor corporation having trust powers as shall succeed to the business of The First National Bank of Huntsville, by purchase, merger, consolidation, or change of charter or name), shall hold the above described property and such other property as may be acquired by the Trustee, *for the use and benefit of the Beneficiaries* hereinafter set forth, and said Trustee shall administer this Trust for the following purposes:

1. To pay the net income quarterly, or at such other intervals as may be determined by the Trustee, (except that said income must be paid at least once a year), to Marion B. Spragins, Jr., the said income payments to be made to Marion B. Spragins, Jr. for as long as he shall live. The Trustee shall also be fully authorized to pay to Marion B. Spragins, Jr., such sums from the principal of the trust estate as in its sole discretion shall be necessary from time to time for his medical care and reasonable support.
2. If at any time the Trustee deems it inadvisable to make the income payments direct to the said Marion B. Spragins, Jr., the Trustee is hereby authorized, in its sole discretion, to apply the net income from this Trust for the support and maintenance of said Beneficiary.

Article IV

The Trustee is relieved of making any accounting to the Courts in the administration of this Trust, and it is expressly relieved of applying to any Court for authority to carry out the provisions of this Trust, as it is intended hereby that the Trustee shall have full and complete authority to administer the Trust in the manner it deems best, without the aid or assistance of any Court.

Article VI

To the extent permitted by law, no Beneficiary under this Trust shall have the power to dispose of, or to change by way of anticipation, any interest given to him, or her, and all sums payable to any Beneficiary shall be free and clear of his, or her debts, contracts, distributions, and anticipations, and shall not be taken or reached by any legal or equitable process in satisfaction thereof. (Italics supplied.)

The 1970 testamentary trust provides, *inter alia:*

(1) The Trustee shall divide the Trust Estate into equal separate shares so as to provide one share for each then living lawful child of mine and one share for the then living lawful descendants, collectively, or each deceased child of mine, per stirpes. Each of said shares of my Trust Estate shall be administered as follows:

(a) The share of my Trust Estate held for the benefit of my son M. Beirne Spragins, Jr. shall be held in trust *for the benefit of M. Beirne Spragins, Jr. and his lawful children,* and during the lifetime of M. Beirne Spragins, Jr. my Trustee *shall pay to my said son or to his lawful children* such amounts from the *trust income or principal* as my Trustee shall determine to be necessary and advisable for the reasonable support of the said M. Beirne Spragins, Jr. and his lawful children. . . .

(2) PROVISIONS RELATING TO TRUSTS. With respect to all the trusts herein created:

(a) In making payments committed to its discretion, to or for the benefit of any beneficiary, my Trustee shall take into consideration any other income or support received, or property possessed by such beneficiary, and known to my Trustee, but the extent to which such other income, support, or property must be first used or liquidated by such beneficiary, shall be in the absolute discretion of my said Trustee.

(b) The interest of beneficiaries in principal or income shall not be subject to claims of their creditors or others, nor to legal process, and may not be voluntarily or involuntarily anticipated, alienated, or encumbered.

In a true "discretionary trust," the general rule is that the beneficiary's interest is not subject to a claim for child support. The trusts in question, here, however, are not true "discretionary trusts." A true discretionary trust

> must be distinguished from trusts where the discretion of the trustee pertains to the item or manner of the payments, or to the size of the payments needed to support the beneficiary. The trustee must be free to pay or apply or to totally exclude the beneficiary, if the trust is to be called "discretionary" in a technical sense. The language of both trusts clearly negates any impression that these trusts are true discretionary trusts. In the 1968 *inter vivos* trust indenture it is expressly provided that the income must be paid quarterly, or at such other intervals as may be determined by the Trustee, (except that said income must be paid once a year). . . .

Therefore, although the trustee is granted discretion by the terms of this trust, the mandatory provision that the income be paid at least annually clearly demonstrates that this is not a true discretionary trust. The same holds true for the 1970 testamentary trust. Although that trust vests "absolute discretion" in the trustee, Bank, nevertheless, by its express terms it is clear that the trustee, Bank, may not totally exclude the beneficiaries. Therefore, this trust, too, may not be termed a true discretionary trust, and the general rule mentioned above is applicable.

The rule is different for support or spendthrift trusts. Here, the rule is that, absent a statute, the income of a spendthrift or a support trust of which the husband is the current income beneficiary may be reached to satisfy his wife's claim for child support. It is also generally held that the corpus of the trust may be reached to satisfy the claim for child support.

The raison d'etre for these rules is articulated in several different ways. Some courts base their holdings on the settlor's intent. . . . Other courts hold that child support is not a "debt" contemplated by the spendthrift provision of the trust.

Some courts have said that it would be contrary to public policy to hold that a wife may not enforce child support claims against a recalcitrant husband. These decisions reflect the wide variety of reasons which courts have given to justify these rules.

As would be expected, some courts have refused to adopt these positions. They appear to be in the minority, however.

In the instant case, both trusts contained spendthrift provisions. It seems reasonable to assume, however, particularly with reference to the 1970 testamentary trust, that Spragins, Sr., intended to refer only to contracts or debts ordinarily made or incurred in the usual contractual or financial transaction. To assume that it was the Spragins Sr.'s intent, with respect to the 1970 trust, to deliberately allow his own son to deprive his own grandchildren of the necessary protection and support, which by law the son owed them (and who are themselves beneficiaries under the trust) is supportable neither by common sense nor by the terms of that trust.

Thus, it is that in this case, we base our decision on the 1970 testamentary trust, and need not consider the 1968 *inter vivos* trust. We have reached this conclusion for two reasons. First, the language of the 1970 testamentary trust clearly evidences the testator's intent that both corpus and income be used and that Spragins, Jr.'s children are beneficiaries. The language of the 1968 *inter vivos* trust is less conclusive. Second, the corpus of the 1970 testamentary trust is significantly larger than that of the 1968 *inter vivos* trust and can easily accommodate the lump-sum child support payment. . . .

Holding

Moreover, The claim of a wife and dependent children to support is based upon the clearest grounds of public policy. They are in quite a different position from ordinary creditors who have voluntarily extended credit. It would be shocking indeed to permit a husband to receive and enjoy the whole of the income from a large trust fund and to make no provision for his needy dependents. II Scott on Trusts, 3rd ed. §157.1, p.1210.

AFFIRMED IN PART, REVERSED AND REMANDED IN PART.

Notes

1. "If there is one sentiment, therefore, which it would seem to be the part of all in authority, and particularly of all judges, to fortify, it is the duty of keeping one's promises and paying one's debts. [Judges approving spendthrift trusts were moved] by that spirit, in short, of paternalism, which is the fundamental essence alike of spendthrift trusts and of socialism." John Chipman Gray, Restraints on the Alienation of Property iii, ix (2d ed. 1895).

"The statute of Uses was designed to suppress a mode of defrauding creditors and purchasers by putting an end, in the cases to which the statute applied, to the separation of the legal from the equitable estate." W. Holdsworth, An Historical Introduction to the Land Law 167 (1927).

"The most notable cause of Boston's commercial decline . . . is the 'spendthrift trust' decisions of Massachusetts courts . . . that a man could tie his children's inheritance up, either by deed or will, so that they could not spend or risk the principal, . . . perforce they became coupon-cutters — parasites, not promoters." F. J. Stimson, My United States 76-77 (1931).

"[T]he land being so sure tied upon the heir as that his father could not put it from him, it made the son to be disobedient, negligent, and wastful; often marrying without the father's consent, and to grow insolent in vice knowing that there could be no check of disinheriting him." Francis Bacon, Use of the Law, in Law Tracts 109, 144 (1737).

2. Asie Mahone, Jr., had vested rights in the Kansas Public Employees Retirement System. His wife and minor children had uncollected judgments against him for support payments, and sought to reach his Retirement System assets. Mahone himself had a right to withdraw the funds, and had applied to do so. But Kansas law declared Retirement System rights exempt from "execution, garnishment, or attachment, or any other process or claim whatever." The court found the exemption of these funds from attachment "not applicable when in conflict with the enforcement of a decree or claim for child support," quoting from the first Justice Harlan (in the Civil Rights Cases, 109 U.S. 3 (1883)): "The letter of the law is the body; the sense and reason of the law is the soul." The dissenting justice alleged that "public policy is the time worn friend of appellate judges in a quandary." Mahone v. Mahone, 213 Kan. 346, 517 P.2d 131 (1973).

3. Worker's compensation benefits are normally protected from garnishment by debtors. However, in Calvin v. Calvin, 6 Or. App. 572, 487 P.2d 1164 (1971), *modified on rehearing,* 6 Or. App. 572, 489 P.2d 403 (1971), a divorced woman was allowed to reach the benefits of her former husband, who had ceased support and alimony payments. Citing the preamble to the Workman's Compensation Act, the Oregon Court of Appeals found a legislative intent to provide care and support for injured workers *and* their dependents. Thus, to allow the husband to find immunity from payment in the anti-garnishment provision would have been illogical as well as contrary to public policy.

However, failing to find a similar legislative intent in the language of the Public Employees Retirement Act, the same court eight years later held that the exclusion of retirement benefits from garnishment for child support was proper. Bresnan v. Bresnan, 42 Or. App. 739, 601 P.2d 851 (1979).

15 ◆ GIFTS AND WILLS

As the preceding chapter showed, our legal system is committed to a general privilege of property owners to choose the next owner of their wealth; yet it is also committed to certain goals that are at odds with the owner's unfettered choice of succeeding holders. The law of gifts and the law of wills show this clash. One concern is formal: tradition and policy restrict the forms an owner can employ for designating successors. More interesting, perhaps, is official restriction on donation and testation because the society believes that others — spouses or children, for example — have a right to a portion of the property. This chapter considers these policies — particularly the protection of spouses — as a limitation on "owner" freedom to donate and devise. Related issues are considered, and in somewhat greater detail, in Part 5 as an aspect of the "shared ownership" that the society assigns under the labels Tenancy by the Entireties and Community Property — the estates within which married couples commonly assume the ownership and possession of real estate.

From the sixteenth century, English landowners have possessed and prized the freedom to choose their heirs. Continental law was different: Certain nearest relatives were usually "compulsory" heirs, and only a "disposable fraction" was left to the testator's decision. Max Weber noticed the distinction, and wrote in his Social Economy (1929):

> Complete, or nearly complete, liberty of testation is only recorded twice: as to Republican Rome and as to English Law; in both cases for expanding nations ruled by a landed gentry. Today the most important territory recognizing liberty of testation, is the territory of greatest economic opportunities: the United States. In Rome, liberty of testation grew up under a bellicose expansion policy which promised a living on conquered land for the disinherited; it vanished through the *legitime* rule borrowed from Greek law when Rome's colonial period was coming to an end. In English law, liberty of testation aimed at maintenance of fortunes within the great families, a goal which can be reached also by measures of a legally opposite, e.g., feudal, nature. [Quoted in Nussbaum, Liberty of Testation, 23 A.B.A.J. 183 (1937).]

American history also reflects a tradition of hostility to inheritance. See, e.g., its expression by President Franklin D. Roosevelt:

> The transmission from generation to generation of vast fortunes by will, inheritance, or gift is not consistent with the ideals and sentiments of the American people. The desire to provide security for one's self and one's family is natural and wholesome, but it is adequately served by a reasonable inheritance. Great accumulations of wealth cannot be justified on the basis of personal and family security. . . . Such inherited economic power is as inconsistent with the ideals of this generation as inherited political power was inconsistent with the ideals of the generation which established our Government. [Statement on Revenue Bill of 1935, Sen. Rep. No. 1240, 74th Cong. 1st Sess., p.2.]

Harvard economist F. W. Taussig had a different view from Roosevelt's. See 2 Principles of Economics 249 (1912):

> The ground on which inheritance is now to be defended is frankly utilitarian. In a society organized on the basis of private property, inheritance is essential to the maintenance of capital.
> It may be open to question how far inheritance is necessary for the first steps in accumulation. The motives that lead to money-making and to the initial stages of saving and investment are various: not only the safeguarding of the future for one's self and one's dependents, but social ambition, the love of distinction, the impulses to activity and to domination. But, for sustained accumulation and permanent investment, the main motives are domestic affection and family ambition. The bequest of a competence or a fortune, though often a dubious boon for the descendants, is a mainspring for its upbuilding by the ancestor. If we were to put an end to inheritance, decreeing that all estates should escheat to the public at death, the owner would commonly dissipate his property. One of the motives for its first acquisition would be gone, and certainly the chief motive for its maintenance. Why accumulate and invest for the benefit of the community at large?
> It is on this ground that the taxation of inheritance should be kept within limits.

A. GIFTS AND WILLS: REQUIREMENTS

1. Gifts: Inter Vivos *and* Causa Mortis

◆ IRONS v. SMALLPIECE
2 B. & ALD. 551, 106 Eng. Rep. 467 (K.B. 1819)

Trover for two colts. Plea, not guilty. The defendant was the executrix and residuary legatee of the plaintiff's father, and the plaintiff claimed the colts, under a verbal gift made to him by the testator twelve months before his death. The colts, however, continued to remain in possession of the father until his death. It appeared, further, that about six months before the father's death, the son having been to a neighbouring market for the purpose of purchasing hay for the colts, and finding the price of that article very high, mentioned the circumstance to his father; and that the latter agreed to furnish for the colts any hay they might want at a stipulated price, to be paid by the son. None, however, was furnished to them till within three or four days before the testator's death. Upon these facts, Abbott C.J. was of opinion, that the possession of the colts never having been delivered to the plaintiff, the property therein had not vested in him by the gift; but that it continued in the testator at the time of his death, and consequently that it passed to his executrix under the will; and the plaintiff was therefore nonsuited. . . .

ABBOTT C.J. I am of opinion, that by the law of England, in order to transfer property by gift there must either be a deed or instrument of gift, or there must be an actual delivery of the thing to the donee. Here the gift is merely verbal, and differs from a *donatio mortis causa* only in this respect, that the latter is subject to a condition, that if the donor live the thing shall be restored to him. Now, it is a well established rule of law, that a *donatio mortis causa* does not transfer the property without an actual delivery. The possession must be transferred, in point of fact; and the late case of Bunn v. Markham (2 Marsh. 532), where all the former authorities were considered, is a very strong authority upon that subject. There Sir G. Clifton had written upon the parcels containing the property the names of the parties for whom they were intended, and had requested his natural son to see the property delivered to the donees. It was therefore manifestly his intention that the property should pass to the donees; yet, as there was no actual delivery, the Court of Common Pleas held that it was not a valid gift. I cannot distinguish that case from the present, and therefore think that this property in the colts did not pass to the son by the verbal gift; and I cannot agree that the son can be charged with the hay which was provided for these colts three or four days before the father's death; for I cannot think that the tardy supply can be referred to the contract which was made so many months before.

HOLROYD J. I am also of the same opinion. In order to change the property by a gift of this description, there must be a change of possession; here there has been no change of possession. If, indeed, it could be made out that the son was chargeable for the hay provided for the colts, then the possession of the father might be considered as the possession of the son. Here, however, no hay is delivered during a long interval from the time of the contract, until within a few days of the father's death; and I cannot think that the hay so delivered is to be considered as delivered in execution of that contract made so long before, and consequently the son is not chargeable for the price of it.

BEST, J. concurred. . . .

Rule refused.

◆ IN RE DREWETT
34 Bankr. 316 (E.D. Penna. 1983)

TWARDOWSKI, Bankruptcy Judge. In this adversary proceeding, the plaintiff/trustee has filed a Complaint To Recover Property against Charles M. Drewett, who is the debtor in a Chapter 7 bankruptcy case. The trustee's Complaint essentially alleges that the debtor was the owner of a diamond as of September 16, 1980, the date that the debtor filed his voluntary Chapter 7 bankruptcy petition, but that the debtor has wrongfully refused to admit his ownership of the diamond at that time. The Complaint requests that the debtor be ordered to surrender possession of the diamond to the trustee on the basis that the diamond is property of the debtor's bankruptcy estate under section 541(a) of the Bankruptcy Code, 11 U.S.C. §541(a). However, for the reasons hereinafter given, we shall dismiss the Complaint because the debtor had made a valid gift of the diamond to his fiancee more than nineteen months before he filed his bankruptcy petition.

Prior to 1979, the debtor purchased for his own use a diamond ring for $1,500.00. The ring consisted of a diamond of slightly more than one carat and a man's band and setting. On February 6, 1979, the debtor married Marsha Toole Drewett. On February 3, 1979, the debtor told his future wife that the diamond was hers and she accepted it. However, they agreed that he would continue to wear the ring until, sometime after their marriage, they could afford to have it converted to a woman's band and setting, whereupon Mrs. Drewett would wear it as an engagement ring.

The debtor filed his voluntary Chapter 7 bankruptcy petition on September 16, 1980. As of that date, he was still wearing the diamond ring, but did not list it as his property in his bankruptcy schedules. In approximately late October, 1980, due to marital problems, Mrs. Drewett left the debtor and took the diamond ring with her. In approximately mid-January, 1981, she had the ring converted to a woman's band and setting, and began wearing it. In late January, 1981, Mr. and Mrs. Drewett resumed living together and have lived together ever since. Also, Mrs. Drewett has worn the converted diamond ring as an engagement ring from mid-January, 1981 to the present. The trustee's aforementioned Complaint To Recover Property was filed on November 20, 1981.

The issue in this case is whether or not the debtor, according to

Pennsylvania law, owned the diamond in question as of September 16, 1980, the date that he filed his bankruptcy petition. This issue turns on the question of whether or not the debtor, according to Pennsylvania law, made a valid gift of the diamond to his fiancee on February 3, 1979.

In Pennsylvania, the two elements of a valid *inter vivos* gift are (1) a present intention to make a gift, and (2) an actual or constructive delivery to the donee by which the donor releases all dominion over the property in question and invests the donee with full title to and control over it.

The trustee contends that the purported gift of the diamond in question was invalid as of the debtor's September 16, 1980 bankruptcy filing because there had been no delivery of the diamond by the debtor to Mrs. Drewett as of that time. His contention is based upon the fact that the debtor continued to wear the diamond until sometime after September 16, 1980. The trustee argues that this fact shows that the debtor had not made an effective delivery of the diamond by transferring his dominion over it to Mrs. Drewett by the time of his bankruptcy filing.

According to Pennsylvania case law, however, the donor's retention of actual physical possession of personal property is not necessarily sufficient to negate delivery of the personal property as a gift. . . .

In the present case, we find that the debtor had the requisite present intention to make a gift of the diamond to his fiancee on February 3, 1979. We also find, based upon the above-cited authorities, that he made an effective delivery of the diamond to his fiancee on that date, despite the fact that he retained physical possession of the diamond for some time thereafter. His retention of such physical possession for a time was agreed upon by both the debtor and his fiancee and, under the circumstances of this case, was not inconsistent with her continued ownership of the diamond from February 3, 1979 onward.

Therefore, the ownership of the diamond having vested in his fiancee on February 3, 1979, the debtor was not the owner of the diamond as of September 16, 1980, the date of his bankruptcy filing, and the trustee's Complaint to Recover Property shall be dismissed.

◆ FOSTER v. REISS
18 N.J. 41, 112 A.2d 553 (1955)

VANDERBILT, C.J. On April 30, 1951 the decedent, Ethel Reiss, entered a hospital in New Brunswick where she was to undergo major surgery. Just prior to going to the operating room on May 4, 1951, she wrote the following note in her native Hungarian language to her husband, the defendant herein:

My Dearest Papa:

In the kitchen, in the bottom of the cabinet, where the blue frying pan is, under the wine bottle, there is one hundred dollars. Along side the bed in my bedroom, in the rear drawer of the small table in the corner of the drawer, where my stockings are, you will find about seventy-five dollars. In my purse there is six dollars, where the coats are. Where the coats are, in a round tin box, on the floor, where the shoes are, there is two hundred dollars. This is Dianna's. Please put it in the bank for her. This is for her schooling.

The Building Loan book is yours, and the Bank book, and also the money that is here. In the red book is my son's and sister's and my brothers address. In the letter box is also my bank book.

Give Margaret my sewing machine and anything else she may want; she deserves it as she was good to me.

God be with you. God shall watch your steps. Please look out for yourself that you do not go on a bad road. I cannot stay with you. My will is in the office of the former Lawyer Anekstein, and his successor has it. There you will find out everything.

> Your Kissing, loving wife,
> Ethel Reiss   1951-5-4.

She placed the note in the drawer of a table beside her bed, at the same time asking Mrs. Agnes Tekowitz, an old friend who was also confined in the hospital, to tell her husband or daughter about it — "In case my daughter come in or my husband come in, tell them they got a note over there and take the note." That afternoon, while the wife was in the operating room unconscious under the effects of ether, the defendant came to the hospital and was told about the note by the friend. He took the note from the drawer, went home, found the cash, the savings account passbook, and the building and loan book mentioned in the note, and has retained possession of them since that time.

The wife was admittedly in a coma for three days after the operation and the testimony is in dispute as to whether or not she recovered consciousness at all before her death on the ninth day. Her daughter, her son-in-law, Mrs. Waldner, an old friend and one of her executrices who visited her every day, and Mrs. Tekowitz, who was in the ward with her, said that they could not understand her and she could not understand them. The defendant, on the other hand, testified that while she was "awful poor from ether" after the operation, "the fourth, fifth and sixth days I thought she was going to get healthy again and come home. She talked just as good as I with you." The trial judge who saw the witnesses and heard the testimony found that "After the operation and until the date of her death on May 13, 1951 she was in a coma most of the time; was unable to recognize members of her family; and unable to carry on intelligent conversations. . . . Mrs. Reiss was never able to talk or converse after coming out of the operation until her death."

The decedent's will gave $1 to the defendant and the residue of her estate to her children and grandchildren. The decedent's personal representatives and her trustees under a separation agreement with the defendant, brought this action to recover the cash, the passbook, and the building and loan book from the defendant, who in turn claimed ownership of them based on an alleged gift *causa mortis* from his wife. The trial court granted judgment for the plaintiffs, concluding that there had been no such gift. The Appellate Division of the Superior Court reversed, and we granted the plaintiff's petition for certification to the Appellate Division.

The doctrine of *donatio causa mortis* was borrowed by the Roman law from the Greeks, 2 Bl. Com. 514, and ultimately became a part of English and then American common law. . . . Blackstone has said that there is a gift *causa mortis* "when a person in his last sickness, apprehending his dissolution near, delivers or causes to be delivered to another the possession of any personal goods, to keep in case of his decease." 2 Bl. Com. 514. Justinian offered this definition:

> A gift *causa mortis* is one made in expectation of death; when a person gives upon condition that, if any fatality happen to him, the receiver shall keep the article, but that if the donor should survive, or if he should change his mind, or if the donee should die first, then the donor shall have it back again. These gifts *causa mortis* are in all respects put upon the same footing as legacies. . . . To put it briefly, a gift *causa mortis* is when a person wishes that he himself should have the gift in preference to the donee, but that the donee should have it in preference to the heir. [Walker's Just., at 119.]

. . . There is some doubt in the New Jersey cases as to whether as a result of a gift *causa mortis* the property remains in the donor until his death, . . . In any event, a gift *causa mortis* is essentially of a testamentary nature and as a practical matter the doctrine, though well established, is an invasion into the province of the statute of wills: . . .

In Ward v. Turner, 2 Ves. Sr. 431, 28 E.R. 275, 279, Lord Chancellor Hardwicke said that "it was a pity that the Statute of Frauds did not set aside all these kinds of gifts." Lord Eldon expressed the opinion that it would be an improvement of the law to strike out altogether this peculiar form of gift, but since that had not been done, he felt obliged to "examine into the subject of it." Our own Vice-Chancellor Stevenson referred to it as "that ancient legal curiosity," Dunn v. Houghton, 51 A. 71, 78 (Ch. 1902), and then later said that such gifts are "dangerous things":

> These gifts *causa mortis* are dangerous things. The law requires, before Mr. Hitt can come into this court and claim $10,000 as an ordinary testamentary gift from Mrs. Thompson, that he should produce an instru-

ment in writing signed by Mrs. Thompson, and also acknowledged with peculiar solemnity by her in the presence of two witnesses, who thereupon subscribed their names as witnesses. That is what Mr. Hitt would have to prove if he claimed a testamentary gift in the ordinary form of one-third of Mrs. Thompson's estate. And yet, in cases of these gifts *causa mortis,* it is possible that a fortune of a million dollars can be taken away from the heirs, the next of kin of a deceased person, by a stranger, who simply has possession of the fortune, claims that he received it by way of gift, and brings parol testimony to sustain that claim. . . .

The first question confronting us is whether there has been "actual, unequivocal, and complete delivery during the lifetime of the donor, wholly divesting him [her] of the possession, dominion, and control" of the property. . . .

Here there was no delivery of any kind whatsoever. We have already noted the requirement so amply established in our cases, *supra,* of "actual, unequivocal and complete delivery during the lifetime of the donor, wholly divesting her of the possession, dominion, and control" of the property. This requirement is satisfied only by delivery by the *donor,* which calls for an affirmative act on her part, not by the mere taking of possession of the property by the donee. . . .

Here we are concerned with three separate items of property — cash, a savings account represented by a bank passbook, and shares in a building and loan association represented by a book. There was no actual delivery of the cash and no delivery of the indicia of title to the savings account or the building and loan association shares. Rather, the donor set forth in an informal writing her desire to give these items to the defendant. Although the writing establishes her donative intent at the time it was written, it does not fulfill the requirement of delivery of the property, which is a separate and distinct requirement for a gift *causa mortis.* The cash, passbook, and stock book remained at the decedent's home and she made no effort to obtain them so as to effectuate a delivery to the defendant.

We disagree with the conclusion of the Appellate Division that the donee already had possession of the property, and therefore delivery was unnecessary. Assuming, but not deciding, the validity of this doctrine, we note that the house was the property of the deceased and, although defendant resided there with her, he had no knowledge of the presence of this property in the house, let alone its precise location therein; therefore it cannot be said that he had possession of the property. . . .

But it is argued that the decedent's note to her husband in the circumstances of the case was an authorization to him to take possession of the chattels mentioned therein which when coupled with his taking of possession thereof during her lifetime was in law the equivalent of the delivery required in the Roman and common law alike and by all the decisions in this State for a valid gift *causa mortis*. Without accepting this contention, it is to be noted that it has no application to the present case, because here at the time the defendant obtained her note the decedent was in the operating room under ether and, according to the finding of the trial court, *supra:* "after the operation and until the date of her death on May 13, 1951 she was in a coma most of the time; was unable to recognize members of her family; and unable to carry on intelligent conversation . . . Mrs. Reiss was never able to talk or converse after coming out of the operation until her death."

In these circumstances the note clearly failed as an authorization to the defendant to take possession of the chattels mentioned therein, since at the time he took the note from the drawer the decedent was under ether and according to the findings of the trial court unable to transact business until the time of her death. . . .

The judgment of the Appellate Division of the Superior Court is reversed and the judgment of the Chancery Division of the Superior Court will be reinstated.

JACOBS, J. (with whom Wachenfeld and William J. Brennan, Jr., JJ., agree) dissenting. The decedent Ethel Reiss was fully competent when she freely wrote the longhand note which was intended to make a gift *causa mortis* to her husband Adam Reiss. On the day the note was written her husband duly received it, located the money and books in accordance with its directions, and took personal possession of them. Nine days later Mrs. Reiss died; in the meantime her husband retained his possession and there was never any suggestion of revocation of the gift. Althought the honesty of the husband's claim is conceded and justice fairly cries out for the fulfillment of his wife's wishes, the majority opinion (while acknowledging that gifts *causa mortis* are valid in our State as elsewhere) holds that the absence of direct physical delivery of the donated articles requires that the gift be stricken down. I find neither reason nor persuasive authority anywhere which compels this untoward result. See Gulliver and Tilson, Classification of Gratuitous Transfers, 51 Yale L.J. 1, 2 (1941):

> One fundamental proposition is that, under a legal system recognizing the individualistic institution of private property and granting to the owner the power to determine his successors in ownership, the general philosophy of the courts should favor giving effect to an intentional exercise of that power. This is commonplace enough but it needs constant emphasis, for it may be obscured or neglected in inordinate preoccupation with detail or dialectic. A court absorbed in purely doctrinal arguments may lose sight of the important and desirable objective of sanctioning what the transferror wanted to do, even though it is convinced that he wanted to do it.

Harlan F. Stone, in his discussion of Delivery in Gifts of Personal Property, 20 Col. L. Rev. 196 (1920), points out that the rule requiring delivery is traceable to early notions of seisin as an element in the ownership of chattels as well as land; and he expresses the view that as the technical significance of seisin fades into the background, courts should evidence a tendency to accept other evidence in lieu of delivery as corroborative of the donative intent. Nevertheless, the artificial requirement of delivery is still widely entrenched and is defended for modern times by Mechem as a protective device to insure deliberate and unequivocal conduct by the donor and the elimination of questionable or fraudulent claims against him. But even that defense has no applicability where, as here, the donor's wishes were freely and clearly expressed in a written instrument and the donee's ensuring possession was admittedly bona fide; under these particular circumstances every consideration of public policy would seem to point towards upholding the gift. . . .

When Ethel Reiss signed the note and arranged to have her husband receive it, she did everything that could reasonably have been expected of her to effectuate the gift *causa mortis;* and while her husband might conceivably have attempted to return the donated articles to her at the hospital for immediate re-delivery to him, it would have been unnatural for him to do so. It is difficult to believe that our law would require such wholly ritualistic ceremony and I find nothing in our decisions to suggest it. The majority opinion advances the suggestion that the husband's authority to take possession of the donated articles was terminated by the wife's incapacity in the operating room and thereafter. The very reason she wrote the longhand note when she did was because she knew she would be incapacitated and wished her husband to take immediate possession, as he did. Men who enter hospitals for major surgery often execute powers of attorney to enable others to continue their business affairs during their incapacity. Any judicial doctrine which would legally terminate such power as of the inception of the incapacity would be startling indeed — it would disrupt commercial affairs and entirely without reason or purpose.

Notes

1. The hornbook statement is that a valid *inter vivos* gift requires donative intent, delivery, and acceptance. Consider each requirement in the factual context of former President Nixon's controversial transfer of his vice-presidential papers to the National Archives.

Gifts of papers acquired in the course of official business could occasion a tax deduction only if the gift was made no later than July 25, 1969. At Nixon's request, a large collection of his papers was delivered from the White House to the archives on March 27, 1969, but specific papers were not selected for donation until March 27, 1970. No deed of gift was executed and delivered until April 1970, though the deed was backdated (fraudulently, as later determined in a criminal proceeding) to April 21, 1969. The deed included restrictions limiting access to the papers and was signed by a Nixon aide. Nixon deducted $575,000 from his taxable income. See House Judiciary Committee, Rep. No. 93-1305, Impeachment of Richard M. Nixon 220-223 (1974).

Was there a gift? Of what? By whom? When? Could Nixon's lawyers have made use of Miller v. Herzfeld, 4 F.2d 355 (3d Cir. 1925)? Joseph Herzfeld, a German citizen and member of the Reichstag, owned stocks and bonds in the United States, which were held by the New York brokerage firm of Herzfeld & Stern. This Herzfeld was Joseph's brother, Felix. On February 6, 1917, three days after the United States and Germany severed diplomatic relations, Joseph Herzfeld sent a radiogram to Herzfeld & Stern: "Transfer account Felix." Felix consulted counsel, who advised him to report the property to the Alien Property Custodian as held in trust for his brother. Possession was transferred to the custodian.

After the war, Felix Herzfeld sued the custodian, asserting that the property should be transferred to him because Joseph had given it to him. Joseph testified that such had been his intention in sending the radiogram. The custodian defended, saying that even if there had been intent and delivery, Felix had not accepted the gift. The Third Circuit affirmed a decree for Felix Herzfeld:

> [I]t is not necessary . . . that the acceptance be contemporaneous with the gift in order that title may pass. When there is doubt as to whether or not the transfer was intended as a gift, the subsequent declarations of the alleged donor may be sufficient proof to show the nature of the transaction. . . . Felix Herzfeld did the perfectly natural thing in consulting counsel as to what to do with the securities transferred to him, and his counsel, in view of all the circumstances, advised him wisely. He did not assume absolute ownership of the property, but he was always willing to accept it as a gift, and has done so.

2. "At about 4:00 a.m. on the morning of March 21, 1970, Catherine Morys called Bernice Dopak and asked her to come and care for her because she was sick. . . . [O]n the day Catherine Morys went to the hospital, she gave Bernice Dopak all the keys to her [apartment] building, instructed her tenants to pay rent to Miss Dopak, showed her how to operate the boiler and told her that 'the building will be all [yours].' " On April 9, Catherine Morys executed the documents assigning to Miss Dopak her interest in the building. On May 15, Catherine died.

What general propositions should the legal system employ for this case? Are there additional facts on which the result should turn? Are you satisfied with the following declaration by an Illinois court of appeals? "[I]f a person is a fiduciary, and during that relation, as a result of it, he becomes a donee or the beneficiary of an instrument, the burden rests on him to show that the transaction which produced the gift or instrument was fair. . . ." In re Estate of Morys, 17 Ill. App. 3d 6, 307 N.E.2d 669 (1973).

Compare Dewar v. Dewar, [1975] 2 All E.R. 728 (Ch.), where Archibald and his wife, seeking a house to buy, decided to buy one in which they would live with Archibald's parents. In assembling the funds, Archibald took £500 from his mother, which she regarded as a gift and he as a loan. When she died, 13 years later, her other son, Alexander sought £250 as beneficiary of one-half her residuary estate. The court ruled for Archibald, deciding that the £500 should be treated as having been a gift.

3.   On June 22, 1964, Kenneth Berry made a warranty deed to Lee Berry of an interest in real estate. The deed said:

> In consideration . . . Lee Berry . . . [is] to pay to the grantor $500 each year for 18 years, provided, however, if the said Kenneth Berry should die . . . then said yearly payments thereafter are to be made to the said Delma Berry; and . . . upon the death of . . . Delma Berry . . . then . . . Lee Arthur Berry . . . shall . . . pay each year . . . $250 to William Harris Berry and $250 to John Kenneth Berry.

As heir of Kenneth Berry, William Berry sued, alleging that the deed was an improper testamentary disposition, not in compliance with the Probate Act. The court disagreed, saying the deed was valid because Kenneth Berry parted fully with control of the property. Had he retained, for example, the power to revoke, the arrangement would have been testamentary. Berry v. Berry, 32 Ill. App. 3d 711, 366 N.E.2d 239 (1975).

4. Did Catherine Wagner make a valid gift *causa mortis* to Robert Scherer? They had lived together for 15 years before Catherine's death in 1974. Prior to her death, which followed an automobile accident and a broken hip, Catherine had been acutely depressed and attempted suicide. She died by jumping from the roof of their apartment building.

On the morning of her suicide, Catherine had received a check for $17,400 from a lawyer who represented her in a claim arising from the accident. After her death, the check was found on the kitchen table, endorsed in blank next to two notes. One asked Scherer's pardon "for taking the easy way out." The other "bequeathed" to Scherer all her possessions incuding "the check for $17,400."

The New Jersey Supreme Court unanimously upheld the validity of the gift, citing with approval the dissent in Foster v. Reiss. Scherer v. Hyland, 75 N.J. 127, 380 A.2d 698 (1977).

2.   The Statute of Wills and "Wills Acts"

EXTRACT FROM THE WILL OF JOSEPH STORY, EXECUTED JAN. 2, 1843: I ask the President and Fellows of Harvard College to accept [this painting of Chief Justice John Marshall] as [a] memorial [of] my Reverence & Respect for that venerable Institution, at which I received my Education. — I hope it may not be improper for me here to add, that I have devoted myself, as Dane Law Professor, for the last thirteen years to the labours & duties of instruction in the Law School, & have always performed equal duties & to an equal amount with my excellent Colleagues, Mr. Professor Ashmun & Mr. Professor Greenleaf — in the Law School. When I came to Cambridge & undertook the duties of my professorship, there had not been a single Law Student there for the preceding year — There was no Law Library; but few old & imperfect works being there — The Students have since increased to a large number, & for six years last past have exceeded one Hundred a year — The Law Library now contains about Six thousand Volumes whose value cannot be deemed less than twenty five thousand Dollars — My own Salary has constantly remained limited to one thousand Dollars, (a little more than the Interest of Mr. Dane's Donation) — I have never asked or desired an increase thereof, as I was receiving a suitable Salary as a Judge of the Supreme Court of the U. States, while my Colleagues have, very properly, received a much larger sum, & of later years more than Double my own — Under these circumstances I cannot but feel, that I have contributed toward the advancement of the Law School a sum out of my earnings — which with my moderate means will be thought to absolve me from making, what otherwise I certainly should do, a pecuniary Legacy to Harvard College for the general advancement of Literature & Learning therein.

T. F. T. PLUCKNETT, A CONCISE HISTORY OF THE COMMON LAW 587 (5th ed. 1956): To the landed gentry the Statute of Uses seemed a calamity, and in the rebellion of 1536, which described itself as the "Pilgrimage of Grace", we find among numerous other grievances — the dissolution of the monasteries, the religious changes, the divorce question — a demand for the repeal of the Statute of Uses, particularly because it abolished the powers of devise hitherto enjoyed by landowners. Henry VIII was well aware of this seriousness of opposition when it came from so important a class as the country gentry. By this time the enforcement of any government policy (and Henry VIII's revolutionary policies needed a good deal of enforcement) depended very largely upon the co-operation of the local gentry, who as justices of the peace were responsible for local government. He felt that the time had come for a concession to the landed gentry, and this took the form of the Statute of Wills (1540), which conferred complete powers of devise over socage lands, and over two-thirds of land held by knight-service, accompanied by the usual provisions (based on the principle that a devisee was to be deemed as in by inheritance) to safeguard feudal dues. Three years later the statute was amended in numerous points of detail. In 1540, following the usual Tudor policy of erecting administrative courts for special business, Henry VIII established the Court of Wards, whose duties were to be the supervision of the King's feudal revenue especially as it was affected by the Statutes of Uses and Wills.

LANGBEIN, SUBSTANTIAL COMPLIANCE WITH THE WILLS ACT, 88 Harv. L. Rev. 489-492 (1975): The law of wills is notorious for its harsh and relentless formalism. The Wills Act prescribes a particular set of formalities for executing one's testament. The most minute defect in formal compliance is held to void the will, no matter how abundant the evidence that the defect was inconsequential. Probate courts do not speak of harmless error in the execution of wills. To be sure, there is considerable diversity and contradiction in the cases interpreting what acts constitute compliance with what formalities. But once a formal defect is found, Anglo-American courts have been unanimous in concluding that the attempted will fails. . . .

The formalities for witnessed wills originated in the Statute of Frauds of 1677,[1] the first Wills Act. The Wills Acts vary among common law jurisdictions in wording and detail, but in the broad outline they are similar. The statute authorizes as the primary or exclusive mode of testation the so-called "formal" or "witnessed" will. Its essentials are writing, signature, and attestation. The provisions of the will must be in writing, be it print, typescript or handwriting. The testator must sign the will in the presence of two (in a few states three) witnesses, who must then attest to the signing by their own signatures. Many statutes require the testator to "publish" the will to the witnesses, that is, to declare to them that the instrument is his will. Some statutes permit someone else to sign for the testator in his presence; most permit the testator to acknowledge to the witnesses a signature he has already made. Some statutes require that the testator subscribe or sign "at the end" of the will, raising difficulties when text follows the signature or when blank space intervenes between text and signature. A few statutes require the testator to call upon the witnesses at the execution ceremony to attest. The witnesses are often required to be "competent," meaning that they

---

1. 29 Car. II, c.3 (1677).

The Statute of Wills of 1540, 32 Hen. VIII, c.I (1540), made most real property devisable at common law for the first time. Although the statute required a writing, it was not primarily concerned with the formal requirements for such transfers. There were no formal requirements for wills of personalty, including leaseholds, until 1677. The Wills Act of 1837, 7 Will. 4 & 1 Vict., c.26 (1837), sometimes called the Statute of Victoria, separated the law of wills from the Statute of Frauds and unified the formal requirements for wills of realty and of personalty. . . .

may not themselves benefit under the will. The witnesses must sign the will; they are commonly but not invariably required to sign in the testator's presence, after the testator, and in the presence of each other. . . .

The first principle of the law of wills is freedom of testation. Although the state limits the power of testation in various ways, within the province that remains to the testamentary power, virtually the entire law of wills derives from the premise that an owner is entitled to dispose of his property as he pleases in death as in life. The many rules governing testamentary capacity and the construction of wills are directed to two broad issues of testamentary intent: did the decedent intend to make a will, and if so, what are its terms?

A tension is apparent between this principle of "free testation and the stiff, formal" requirements of the Wills Act. The classic article by Gulliver and Tilson [Classification of Gratuitous Transfers, 51 Yale L.J. 1 (1941)], pointed out that the Wills Act formalities were made necessary by the peculiar posture in which the decedent's transfer reached the court:

> If all transfers were required to be made before the court determining their validity, it is probable that no formalities except oral declarations in the presence of the court would be necessary. The court could observe the transferor, hear his statements, and clear up ambiguities by appropriate questions. . . . The fact that our judicial agencies are remote from the actual or fictitious occurrences relied on by the various claimants to the property, and so must accept second hand information, perhaps ambiguous, perhaps innocently misleading, perhaps deliberately falsified, seems to furnish the chief justification for requirements of transfer beyond evidence of oral statements of intent.

When the court is asked to implement the testator's intention, he "will inevitably be dead" and unable to authenticate or clarify his declarations, which may have been made years, even decades past. The formalities are designed to perform functions which will assure that his estate really is distributed according to his intention.

KENNEDY, LEGAL FORMALITY, 2 J. Leg. Studies 351, 355-360 (1973):
7. As I will use the term here, a formal system is one that takes it as a premise that there are only two processes of decision a theorist need take into account when he sets out to build a theory of social order. These are rule application and decision according to purposes, or substantive rationality. Decision according to rule means, in the ideal typical case, the application of per se rules, that is, decision by the selection of one (or very few) easily identifiable aspect of the situation, and the justification of the decision uniquely by appeal to the presence or absence of that element. An example of rule application is the dismissal of

a suit on an uncontested oral promise on the ground that the Statute of Frauds required a writing. At the other pole, ad hoc or substantively rational decision making involves an identification of purposes and then an assessment or weighing by the decision maker of all those aspects of the situation which he feels have some bearing on the achievement of those purposes. Some cases are those of a regional planner deciding where to locate a dam, a Congressman deciding how to vote on a tariff proposal, or a court deciding a nuisance case. . . .

12. The essence of rule application, as I defined it above, is that it is *mechanical*. The decision process is called rule application only if the actor resolutely limits himself to identifying those aspects of the situation which, per se, trigger his response. He must *never* ask whether giving this particular response, in light of the total situation including *but not limited* to the per se elements, is best. The minute he begins to look over his shoulder at the *consequences* of responding to the presence or absence of the per se elements he has moved some distance toward substantively rational decision. So long as he refuses to look over his shoulder, then from the point of view of anyone concerned with the particular consequences, anyone for whom this particular act of adjudication has a purpose, his action will — barring a providential arrangement of the universe not to be considered here — occasionally have effects on the litigants just the opposite of those desired. For example, the Statute of Frauds was intended to prevent the manufacture of evidence, but occasionally works as an escape hatch for a shady operator dealing with a legal neophyte.

13. Yet around this "absolutism" of the rule applier, his perverse self-denial, his refusal to have any purpose outside the application itself or to regard the consequences of his action, cluster many of the deepest and most intense emotions associated with legal as opposed to other kinds of process. Witness the passion aroused by legalism, bias, impartiality, fairness.

Note

The New York Court of Appeals held that a will should be admitted to probate even though decedent and his wife, intending to execute mutual wills, each executed by mistake the will intended for the other. Judge Jones, dissenting, said he was "of the conviction that the willingness of the majority in an appealing case to depart from what has been consistent precedent in the courts of the United States and England will prove troublesome in the future." Snide v. Johnson, 52 N.Y.2d 193, 418 N.E.2d 656, 437 N.Y.S.2d 63 (1981) (4-3).

◆ CALIFORNIA "STATUTORY WILL FORM"
1982 Cal. Stat. Ch. 1401 §1

CALIFORNIA STATUTORY WILL OF

_____

(Insert Your Name)

Article 1. Declaration

This is my will and I revoke any prior wills and codicils.

Article 2. Disposition of My Property

2.1. PERSONAL AND HOUSEHOLD ITEMS. I give all my furniture, furnishings, household items, personal automobiles and personal items to my spouse, if living; otherwise they shall be divided equally among my children who survive me.

2.2. CASH GIFT TO A PERSON OR CHARITY. I make the following cash gift to the person or charity in the amount stated in words and figures in the box which I have completed and signed. If I fail to sign in the box, no gift is made. If the person mentioned does not survive me, or the charity designated does not accept the gift, then no gift is made. No death tax shall be paid from this gift.

Full name of person or charity to receive cash gift (Name only one. Please print.).	*Amount of gift* $ _____ *Amount written out* _____ Dollars
	  _____ *Signature of Testator*

2.3. ALL OTHER ASSETS (MY "RESIDUARY ESTATE"). I adopt only one Property Disposition Clause in this paragraph 2.3 by writing my signature in the box next to the title of the Property Disposition Clause I wish to adopt. I sign in only one box. I write the words "not used" in the remaining boxes. If I sign in more than one box or if I fail to sign in any box, the property will go under

Property Disposition Clause (c) and I realize that means the property will be distributed as if I did not make a will.
PROPERTY DISPOSITION CLAUSES (Select one.)

(a) To my spouse if living; if not living, then to my children and the descendants of any deceased child

(b) To my children and the descendants of any deceased child. I leave nothing to my spouse, if living

(c) To be distributed as if I did not have a will

Article 3.   Nominations of Executor and Guardian

3.1. EXECUTOR (Name at least one.) I nominate the person or institution named in the first box of this paragraph 3.1 to serve as executor of this will. If that person or institution does not serve, then I nominate the others to serve in the order I list them in the other boxes.

First Executor

Second Executor

Third Executor

3.2.   GUARDIAN (If you have a child under 18 years of age, you should name at least one guardian of the child's person and at least one guardian of the child's property. The guardian of the child's person and the guardian of the child's property may, but need not, be the same. An individual can serve as guardian of either the person or the property, or as guardian of both. An institution can serve only as guardian of the property.)

If a guardian is needed for any child of mine, then I nominate the individual named in the first box of this paragraph 3.2 to serve as guardian of the person of that child, and I nominate the individual or institution named in the second box of this paragraph 3.2 to serve as guardian of the property of that child. If that person or institution does not serve, then the others shall serve in the order I list them in the other boxes.

First Guardian of the Person

First Guardian of the Property

Second Guardian of the Person

Second Guardian of the Property

Third Guardian of the Person

Third Guardian of the Property

My signature in this box means that a bond is not required for any individual executor or guardian named in this will. If I do not sign in this box, then a bond is required for each of those persons as set forth in the Probate Code.

I sign my name to this California Statutory Will on _____ at
_____
Date

_____, _____.
City   State

_____
Signature of Testator

STATEMENT OF WITNESSES (You must use two adult witnesses and three would be preferable.) Each of us declares under penalty of perjury under the laws of California that the testator signed this California statutory will in our presence, all of us being present at the same time, and we now, at the testator's request, in the testator's presence, and in the presence of each other, sign below as witnesses, declaring that the testator appears to be of sound mind and under no duress, fraud, or undue influence.

Signature _____   Residence Address: _____
Print Name   _____
   Here: _____

Signature: _____   Residence Address: _____
Print Name   _____
   Here: _____

Signature _____   Residence Address: _____
Print Name   _____
   Here: _____

PERKINS ET AL., PROPOSED UNIFORM ACTS FOR A STATUTORY WILL, STATUTORY TRUST, AND STATUTORY SHORT FORM CLAUSES, 15 Real Prop., Prob. and Tr. J. 837, 837-838 (1980): In many parts of the country increasing consideration is being given to the concept that legislation can aid the legal profession and the public by providing the means to meet the estate planning needs of many persons with small to medium sized estates by simple, short, economical and competent instruments. There is widespread recognition that the estate planning process has become too complicated and too costly for many persons. There is also too much risk of error for many lawyers who, although called upon to provide the services, are often not experts in the drafting of wills and trusts. And the lawyer's task is becoming more and more risky under the increasing hazards imposed by tax legislation and malpractice litigation. . . .

This is a proposal for what many have come to refer to as a "statutory will." However, the proposed act would not adopt a will form. There is widespread apprehension that the adoption of a statutory will form, which would lend itself to use without legal advice by purchase from a stationer, is likely to encourage dangerous misuse. This risk cannot be completely excluded under the proposed statute, nor even under present law without any new statute. However, the proposed act is drawn in a way to make it usable only by someone who knows how to make a will and to appoint executors, etc.

The proposed statute provides a widely usable scheme of disposition, which can be adopted by a simple will. It does not provide a battery of schemes or options, but it allows modifications and additions to be made by the will which adopts the statutory scheme.

The proposed act provides in effect a statutory will which leaves the entire estate to the surviving spouse, if the testator's federal adjusted gross estate (plus community property if applicable) does not exceed $250,000 or the testator leaves no issue. If the testator's federal adjusted gross estate (plus community property if applicable) exceeds $250,000 and he leaves issue, the statutory will leaves the testator's residence and tangible personal property and one-half of the residue (or all up to $25,000) to the surviving spouse and the other half of the residue in trust to pay the income to the surviving spouse for life, and principal in the discretion of the trustee, with the remainder on the death of the surviving spouse passing to the testator's issue *per stirpes*. If, however, the testator leaves any issue by a prior marriage, the surviving spouse receives one-half of the testamentary estate outright as under the Uniform Probate Code intestacy provisions. If the testator leaves no surviving spouse, the entire estate goes to the issue *per stirpes*. Distributions to the issue may be retained in trust until the distributee attains age twenty-five. In two situations the shares of children of the testator under age twenty-five may be used for them as a family unit. This is permitted on termination of the trust for a surviving spouse. It is also permitted if the testator's federal gross estate does not exceed $100,000. Otherwise, the shares of issue retained in trust are to be held as separate shares qualifying for the orphan deduction under the Internal Revenue Code, if applicable.

The special provision for decedents whose federal adjusted gross estate (plus community property if applicable) exceeds $250,000 is included not primarily out of a desire to provide a statutory scheme for such estates but to guard against the trap that a person whose estate has grown to such size may die without making a new will. A statutory will that leaves the entire estate outright to the surviving spouse without limitation could become a tax planning disaster. There is no attempt to provide a fine tuned marital deduction formula, but such a fine tuned result can often be accomplished under the statutory will through its provision for partial disclaimer by the surviving spouse or by the guardian, conservator, executor or administrator of the surviving spouse.

◆ IN RE ESTATE OF STRITTMATER
140 N.J. Eq. 94, 53 A.2d 205 (N.J. Ct. Err. & App. 1947)

Appeal from Prerogative Court.

Proceeding in the matter of the estate of Louisa F. Strittmater, deceased. From a decree of the Essex County Orphans' Court admitting to probate the will of the deceased, the contestants appealed to the Prerogative court, claiming that deceased was insane. From a decree of the Prerogative Court setting aside the probate, the proponents appeal.

Decree affirmed.

Vice Ordinary BIGELOW affirmed. His opinion follows:

This is an appeal from a decree of the Essex County Orphans' Court admitting to probate the will of Louisa F. Strittmater. Appellants challenge the decree on the ground that testatrix was insane.

The only medical witness was Dr. Sarah D. Smalley, a general practitioner who was Miss Strittmater's physican all her adult life. In her opinion, decedent suffered from paranoia of the Bleuler type of split personality. The factual evidence justifies the conclusion. But I regret not having had the benefit of an analysis of the data by a specialist in diseases of the brain.

The deceased never married. Born in 1896, she lived with her parents until their death about 1928, and seems to have had a normal childhood. She was devoted to both her parents and they to her. Her admiration and love of her parents persisted after their death to 1934, at least. Yet four years later she wrote: "My father was a corrupt, vicious, and unintelligent savage, a typical specimen of the majority of his sex. Blast his wormstinking carcass and his whole damn breed." And in 1943, she inscribed on a photograph of her mother "That Moronic she-devil that was my mother."

Numerous memoranda and comments written by decedent on the margins of books constitute the chief evidence of her mental condition. Most of them are dated in 1935, when she was 40 years old. But there are enough in later years to indicate no change in her condition. The Master who heard the case in the court below, found that the proofs demonstrated "incontrovertably her morbid aversion to men" and "feminism to a neurotic extreme." This characterization seems to me not strong enough. She regarded men as a class with an insane hatred. She looked forward to the day when women would bear children without the aid of men, and all males would be put to death at birth. Decedent's inward life, disclosed by what she wrote, found an occasional outlet such as the incident of the smashing of the clock, the killing of the pet kitten, vile language, etc. On the other hand, — and I suppose this is the split personality, — Miss Strittmater, in her dealings with her lawyer, Mr. Semel, over a period of several years, and with her bank, to cite only two examples, was entirely reasonable and normal.

Decedent, in 1925, became a member of the New Jersey branch of the National Women's Party. From 1939 to 1941, and perhaps later, she worked as a volunteer one day a week in the New York office, filing papers, etc. During this period, she spoke of leaving her estate to the Party. On October 31, 1944, she executed her last will, carrying this intention into effect. A month later, December 6, she died. Her only relatives were some cousins of whom she saw very little during the last few years of her life.

The question is whether Miss Strittmater's will is the product of her insanity. Her disease seems to have become well developed by 1936. In August of that year she wrote, "It remains for feministic organizations like the National Women's Party, to make exposure of women's 'protectors' and 'lovers' for what their vicious and contemptible selves are." She had been a member of the Women's Party for eleven years at that time, but the evidence does not show that she had taken great interest in it. I think it was her paranoic condition, especially her insane delusions about the male, that led her to leave her estate to the National Women's Party. The result is that the probate should be set aside.

Notes

1. Hattie Gerbing's will provided:

> In the event my said son's wife, Arlie Gerbing predeceases my son, Frank Gerbing, Jr., or in the event Arlie Gerbing and Frank Gerbing, Jr. are divorced and remain divorced for a period of two years, then in either event this trust shall terminate and my trustee is directed to pay, turn over and deliver the remaining principal of the trust property and all accrued dividends or interest accumulated thereon to my said son.

The Illinois Supreme Court said that a condition tending to encourage divorce is against public policy, and so void, although had "the dominant motive . . . [been] to provide support in the event of such separation or divorce the condition [would be] valid." Therefore,

> we are concerned in this case with a void condition precedent to the vesting of title to the property in Frank. . . . [W]e must attempt . . . to ascertain from the four corners of the will whether the testator intended that the gift to her son fail completely or vest absolutely upon the declaration that the divorce condition is void. . . . Although the will makes no specific reference to such an event the entire will speaks clearly of the testator's confidence in her son and her intent to provide adequately for him. . . . [Estate of Gerbing, 61 Ill. 2d 503, 337 N.E.2d 29 (1975).]

But see Shapira v. Union National Bank, 39 Ohio Misc. 28, 315 N.E.2d 825 (C.P. 1974), upholding bequests to the testator's sons on condition they marry "Jewish girls whose both parents were Jewish."

Is *Gerbing* authority for Lord Mansfield's assertion that judges in will cases "must sometimes feel that they are the only authorized interpreters of nonsense"? See Cookson v. Bingham, 3 DE G. M. & G. 668, 43 Eng. Rep. 263 (Ch. 1853).

2. Bernyce Green met Richard Richmond in 1962. She was a 36-year-old secretary, he a 49-year-old bachelor whose holdings included three radio stations. She accepted his proposal of marriage. A year later,

however, Richmond said he had a "mental hangup" about marriage, but that if she would "stay" with him, he would bequeath his entire estate to her at his death. Ms. Green agreed. Until 1971, when Richmond died, Ms. Green "kept her part of the agreement in reliance on the decedent's promise." The value of the estate was approximately $7,232,000.

The Massachusetts Supreme Judicial Court held that an oral agreement to make a will is not binding, but Green would nonetheless have a right to the fair value of her service if the agreement was legal and not contrary to public policy; that on these facts (including, e.g., the fact that the decedent took another woman with him when plaintiff could not accompany him on his annual vacation) it was appropriate to leave to the jury the issue of whether unlawful sexual relations were no part of the agreement, and only an incidental part of plaintiff's performance; and that it was not error to admit evidence of the value of the estate, to assist the jury in determining the value of plaintiff's services. Green v. Richmond, 369 Mass. 47, 337 N.E.2d 691 (1975).

3. Are estate taxes an unconstitutional taking of property?

"1. An inheritance tax is not one on property, but one on the succession. 2. The right to take property by devise or descent is the creature of the law, and not a natural right — a privilege, and therefore the authority which confers it may impose conditions upon it." Magoun v. Illinois Trust & Savings Bank, 170 U.S. 283 (1897). Justice Brewer, dissenting, objected that while imposing different tax rates on near relatives, remote relatives, and strangers was not objectionable, the statute was unconstitutional in varying the rate as to bequests to strangers according to the size of the estate.

Could the legislature of Illinois . . . enact that the property of A, on his death, should pass to the State; the property of B to some religious or charitable institution; and the property of C be divided among his children? . . . And now by this statute . . . a tax is imposed . . . unequal because not proportioned to the amount of the estate; unequal because based upon a classification purely arbitrary, to wit, that of wealth. . . .

See also Irving Trust Co. v. Day, 314 U.S. 556 (1942):

Rights of succession to the property of a deceased, whether by will or by intestacy, are of statutory creation, and the dead hand rules succession only by sufferance. Nothing in the Federal Constitution forbids the legislature of a state to limit, condition, or even abolish the power of testamentary disposition over property within its jurisdiction.

4. In In re Estate of Riley, 459 Pa. 428, 329 A.2d 511 (1974), cert. denied, 421 U.S. 971 (1975), the Pennsylvania Supreme Court struck down a so-called "mortmain" statute, which generally invalidated be-

quests to religious and charitable organizations in wills executed within 30 days of testator's death. Because the statute prohibited many testamentary gifts presenting no threat of the evils that the statute purported to minimize, and left unaffected many gifts presenting such a threat, it lacked "a fair and substantial relation" to the legislative object, and so violated the Fourteenth Amendment.

5. The District of Columbia Court of Appeals had invalidated the District of Columbia mortmain statute in French v. Doyle, 365 A.2d 621 (D.C. 1976). The Supreme Court decided, 5-4, that there was no basis for its appellate jurisdiction because a law applicable only in the District of Columbia is not a "statute of the United States." Key v. Doyle, 434 U.S. 59 (1977). Thus we still do not have Supreme Court law on this issue.

GRIFFIN, THE ABOUT TURN: SOVIET LAW OF INHERITANCE, 10 Am. J. Comp. Law 431, 431-437, 442 (1961): Marx and Engels were quite clear that there was no place for inheritance in a communist system of government. Its retention would be inconsistent with the ordained abolition of unearned income. It would be unnecessary since workers would receive compensation according to their labor, and those unable to work would be provided for by social insurance. In a system in which private property was extinct it would be redundant. Its historical function — assisting capitalists to retain power in capitalist society — would be, to say the least, outmoded.

In accordance with the Marxian view, the Soviet Regime, within four months of its coming into existence, published a decree purporting to perform the abrogation. "Inheritance, testate and intestate, is abolished. Upon the death of the owner his property (movable and immovable) becomes the property of the R.S.F.S.R." (Article I). Despite the categorical language of the first article of the decree, however, all forms of inheritance were not completely repudiated. The decree itself provided for the administration and use of an estate not exceeding 10,000 rubles to pass to the close relatives of the decedent who had lived with him, and, "until a decree of social insurance is issued" they were permitted to receive from the estate such amount as they required for their support. By way of "interpretation" of the limitation, the Commissariat for Justice directed the following year that the 10,000 ruble maximum be removed in the case of estates left by peasants.

Quite apart from the limitations contained on the face of the decree, it would appear that the stated abolition of inheritance was never given any practical application at all. Mr. A. Goykhbarg, who was practising law in Russia in the early days of the Regime, was not able to recall one instance of an estate being transferred to the R.S.F.S.R. under it. He also drew attention to the fact that the Soviet Budget for this period contained no reference to income derived from this source. Furthermore, it is clear that the newborn government simply did not have the machinery with which to regulate all Russian estates. This lack of adequate machinery probably at least partly explains the favor of lenient treatment accorded the peasants under the decree of the Commissariat of Justice, since their estates would have been the hardest of all to administer and they were well served by the peasant customary law of succession.

The form of abolition was maintained, however, and soviet jurists insisted that the abrogation was complete. The exceptions were no more than matters of social welfare. Thus an official "Explanation" of the original decree, issued on December 31st, 1918, stated the limitations to be of a "temporary character" only, and foreshadowed their abolition upon the construction of a social security system. The exceptions were said to be merely one of the forms of social aid. Similarly, Professor Serebrovsky maintained that the exceptions drawn in favor of the smaller estates and close relatives of the decedent had "nothing in common with succession; they are based on motives of a special kind, viz., the desire to give security to disabled persons who are the decedent's next of kin, provided they have had some connection, economic or as workers, with his property." It is interesting to note that, prior to the succession reform of 1945, Professor Serebrovsky was among the Russian lawyers holding that inheritance had never been abolished, at least in the case of estates of less than 10,000 rubles.

The first official recognition of inheritance rights came in 1922 with the "New Economic Policy" and one of its principal manifestations, the 1922 Civil Code. Within a narrowly defined area, inheritance was made possible whether the beneficiaries were in a state of necessity or not. . . . Notwithstanding these exceptions, the restriction placed upon the value of the estate met with "practical difficulties," and a change in policy was soon made. In 1926 the Soviet Government resolved "to aid the possibility of the continued existence of commercial and industrial enterprises after the decease of their owners and to establish more attractive conditions for the creation and influx into the country of material and resources." Accordingly the 10,000 rubles limitation was abolished by the decree of February 15th, 1926. It was replaced, however, by a gigantic increase in the inheritance tax which, though introduced in 1922, had until this time been insignificant. For estates of more than 1000 rubles the tax was placed on a progressive scale and could rise as high as 90 percent. For estates valued at less than 1000 rubles there was no tax. The inheritance tax itself was abolished in 1943, and it has never been reinstituted. The only direct fee levied upon inheritance now is the fee on the issuance of the inheritance certificate. This charge, which again is determined progressively, rises to 10 percent of the value of the bequest.

The second limitation in the 1922 Code was in respect of the class of persons entitled to inherit. Having introduced both testate and intestate succession, the Code limited the devolution of the estate in both instances to specified persons, the category of eligible heirs being the same for both means of devolution. The first capable group was the direct descendants of the decedent. This group was stated as extensively as possible. Grandchildren and great-grandchildren were in the same position as children; adopted children shared equally with natural children; and legitimate and illegitimate children shared equally. The second group comprised destitute relatives or strangers who were in fact dependent upon the decedent for a year before his death. Finally, the surviving spouse was also eligible.

An Edict of the Federal Presidium of March 14th, 1945, reformed and codified the law relating to succession. Most of the provisions of this Edict are still in force. Although, with the abolition of the inheritance tax in 1943, a major change had already taken place, the Edict represents further relaxations in many significant respects, particularly in the rules establishing the group of capable heirs. . . .

The general widening for intestate succession of the class of competent heirs resulted in a corresponding extension of the freedom of the testator who desired to plan his distribution. For the testator was at liberty to leave his property to any of the persons falling within any of the three classes, and in such shares as he desired. Consequently his range of choice was extended for the first time to his parents, brothers and sisters. At the same time, the removal of grandchildren and great-grandchildren from the eligible classes would appear to mean that the testator lost his freedom to choose any of his descendants other than his children. The Edict also provided (mirroring the provision of 1928) that the testator might not "deprive his minor children or other heirs who are unable to earn of the portion which would belong to them under intestate succession." The class whom the testator was unable to exclude was thereby extended from children to heirs unable to earn. The Communist Party was no longer specifically mentioned as a competent beneficiary of the testator's generosity, but the Edict provided that bequests could be left to "governmental agencies and public organizations," and there appears to be no doubt that the Party would come within the latter category.

By a new and important provision, the testator, if there were no persons within any of the three classes, could leave his property to any person he wished. This bud of complete freedom of choice of heirs has blossomed in the recent Draft Code of Civil Law Principles. . . .

The 1945 Edict of the R.S.F.S.R. remains the ruling enactment with respect to inheritance and the rules outlined represent the current position. A major change in one aspect is imminent, however. It represents freedom of choice of heirs. It will be recalled that, under the 1945 Edict the testator may bequeath his property to anyone he wishes only if there are no persons within the circle of heirs defined by law. By the recent Draft of Civil Law Principles of U.S.S.R. Supreme Soviet this limitation is abolished and complete freedom of choice given. The new provision is Article 95 of the Draft Principles. It is in these terms: "Every person may will all or part of his property to one or several persons, either included or not included in the circle of heirs by law, as well as to the State or to individual State organizations, collective farms or other cooperative and public organizations." At the same time, the Draft foreshadows a new limitation. This will draw the Russian position in line with traditional European legislation. The foreshadowed change is the introduction of the *legitima portio* concept into Soviet law; that is to say, it is indicated that some very close relatives of the testator will be entitled to share a portion of the estate irrespective of his wishes.

A. TROLLOPE, "MR. DOVE'S OPINION," from THE EUSTACE DIA-MONDS 226-229 (1873; 1973 ed.): "There is much error about heirlooms. Many think that any chattel may be made an heirloom by any owner of it. This is not the case. The law, however, does recognise heirlooms; — as to which the Exors. or Admors. are excluded in favour of the Successor; and when there are such heirlooms they go to the heir by special custom. Any devise of an heirloom is necessarily void, for the will takes place after death; and the heirloom is already vested in the heir by custom. We have it from Littleton, that law prefers custom to devise.

"Brooke says, that the best thing of every sort may be an heirloom, — such as the best bed, the best table, the best pot or pan.

"Coke says, that heirlooms are so by custom, and not by law.

"Spelman says, in defining an heirloom, that it may be 'Omne utensil robustius;' which would exclude a necklace.

"In the 'Termes de Ley,' it is defined as 'Ascun parcel des utensiles.'

"We are told in 'Coke upon Littleton,' that Crown jewels are heirlooms, which decision, — as far as it goes, — denies the right to other jewels.

"Certain chattels may undoubtedly be held and claimed as being in the nature of heirlooms, — as swords, pennons of honour, garter and collar of S.S. See case of the Earl of Northumberland; and that of the Pusey horn, — Pusey v. Pusey. The journals of the House of Lords, delivered officially to peers, may be so claimed. See Upton v. Lord Ferrers.

"A devisor may clearly devise or limit the possession of chattels, making them inalienable by devisees in succession. But in such cases they will become the absolute possession of the first person seized in tail, — even though an infant, and in case of death without will, would go to the Exors. Such arrangement, therefore, can only hold good for lives in existence and for 21 years afterwards. Chattels so secured would not be heirlooms. See Carr v. Lord Error, 14 Vesey, and Rowland v. Morgan.

"Lord Elson remarks, that such chattels held in families are 'rather favourites of the court.' This was in the Ormande case. Executors, therefore, even when setting aside any claim as for heirlooms, ought not to apply such property in payment of debts unless obliged.

"The law allows of claims for paraphernalia for widows, and, having adjusted such claims, seems to show that the claim may be limited.

"If a man deliver cloth to his wife, and die, she shall have it, though she had not fashioned it into the garment intended.

"Pearls and jewels, even though only worn on state occasions, may go to the widow as paraphernalia, — but with a limit. In the case of Lady Douglas, she being the daughter of an Irish Earl and widow of the King's Sergeant (temp. Car. I.), it was held that £370 was not too much, and she was allowed a diamond and a pearl chain to that value.

"In 1674, Lord Keeper Finch declared that he would never allow paraphernalia, except to the widow of a nobleman.

"But in 1721 Lord Macclesfield gave Mistress Tipping paraphernalia to the value of £200, — whether so persuaded by law and precedent, or otherwise, may be uncertain.

"Lord Talbot allowed a gold watch as paraphernalia.

"Lord Hardwicke went much further, and decided that Mrs. Northey was entitled to wear jewels to the value of £3000, — saying that value made no difference; but seems to have limited the nature of her possession in the jewels by declaring her to be entitled to wear them only when full-dressed.

"It is, I think, clear that the Eustace estate cannot claim the jewels as an heirloom. They are last mentioned, and, as far as I know, only mentioned as an heirloom, in the will of the great-grandfather of the present baronet, — if these be the diamonds then named by him. As such, he could not have devised them to the present claimant, as he died in 1820, and the present claimant is not yet two years old.

"Whether the widow could claim them as paraphernalia is more doubtful. I do not know that Lord Hardwicke's ruling would decide the case; but, if so, she would, I think, be debarred from selling, as he limits the use of jewels of lesser value than these, to the wearing of them when full-dressed. The use being limited, possession with power of alienation cannot be intended.

"The lady's claim to them as a gift from her husband amounts to nothing. If they are not hers by will, — and it seems that they are not so, — she can only hold them as paraphernalia belonging to her station.

"I presume it to be capable of proof that the diamonds were not in Scotland when Sir Florian made his will or when he died. The former fact might be used as tending to show his intention when the will was made. I understand that he did leave to his widow by will all the chattels in Portray Castle.

"15 August, 18 — "   "J.D."

When Mr. Camperdown had thrice read this opinion, he sat in his chair an unhappy old man.

B. INTESTACY

◆ IN RE WOOD'S ESTATE
164 Misc. 425, 299 N.Y.S. 195 (Sur. Ct. 1937)

FOLEY, Surrogate. In this accounting proceeding, with the objective of ultimate determination of the persons legally entitled to share in the estate of Ida E. Wood, the surrogate in his prior decision laid out the course of procedure for the orderly trial of the issues. The large number of persons claiming to be distributees of the decedent made necessary the formulation of a plan for the elimination of those not entitled to participate in the distribution of the estate. Since the decedent died intestate, the determination of the next of kin is required to be tested by the provisions of our Statute of Distribution. Citation originally issued to 1103 claimants. Of these 537 persons have filed objections to the account asserting varying degrees of kinship to the decedent and 79 claimed a right of participation as next of kin of her deceased husband, Benjamin Wood.

In my prior decision I outlined three issues for determination: first, the status of the persons claiming to be the next of kin of Benjamin Wood, the husband; second, the trial and determination of the identity of this decedent, the establishment of her maiden name, and the names and identification of her parents; third, the ascertainment of the persons, if any, establishing their relationship by blood to the decedent and their identification within the legal class of her next of kin.

The first issue was tried and determined and 5 persons were proven to be the next of kin of the predeceased husband as his direct descendants. By my decision on that phase of the proceeding 74 claimants of more distant relationship were eliminated. These proven next of kin of the husband thus become potential distributees in the event that it be finally determined that Ida E. Wood left no relation of her blood.

The second issue was then taken up for trial. . . .

Upon this issue, the contentions of the various claimants may be divided into two general questions: (1) Was Ida E. Wood born in England as Ellen Walsh, the daughter of Thomas Walsh and Ann Crawford Walsh, who were natives of Ireland? or (2) Was she born in the state of Louisiana or of Mississippi as Ida Mayfield, the daughter of Thomas H. Mayfield and Mary Ann Crawford Mayfield? . . .

Ida E. Wood died in the Herald Square Hotel in 1932. She had been a recluse for the last 30 years of her life. She left an estate of approximately $900,000. Most of it was in cash. Two alleged wills of hers were presented for probate. One was refused admission because of the forgery of her signature to it. The other failed because of inability to prove execution although the body of the will was clearly in her own handwriting and the signature authentic. She therefore died intestate. She had lived with her sister, who was known as Mary E. Mayfield. The latter died in 1931. With them also resided a woman known as Emma Wood over whose identity doubt has arisen as to whether she was the daugher or the sister of the decedent. That question is academic since she predeceased the decedent, leaving no descendants.

Ida E. Wood, at the time of her death, was 93 years of age. She was the widow of Benjamin Wood who had attained distinction in New York City as a successful stockbroker and as publisher of the former newspaper known as The New York Daily News. Ida E. Wood appears to have been associated actively with him for many years in its management and ownership. Benjamin Wood died in 1900. Fernando Wood, his brother, was mayor of the city of New York during the years 1855 to 1858. He served later in that office in the years 1860 to 1862. With this background of the history of her husband and of his family, Ida E. Wood appears from the evidence to have taken part in her earlier and middle life in public and social activities of this city. She possessed or acquired a high degree of culture. Her letters indicate refinement. She and her husband traveled extensively both in this country and abroad. She was shrewd in her business operations and prudent in the management of her large fortune. Much of the financial success of her husband was apparently due to her qualities of thrift and frugality.

There are other elements of her character which are revealed by the evidence. She was secretive of her personal affairs which was demonstrated by her living as a recluse for the last 30 years of her life. During most of that period she kept secret her whereabouts from her stepchildren and stepgrandchildren. A few years before her death she was adjudicated an incompetent. After her demise, in due course the public administrator of New York county took over her estate and he is the accounting party here. She appears to have kept her letters, checks, and bills with meticulous care. She made and retained copies of letters sent by her. Most important in the determination of this case she kept in her own handwriting, within the group of her personal papers, records of her family history and the dates and places of the births and deaths and the places of burial of her parents, her brothers, and sisters.

The only doubt created as to her identity, which has afforded a basis for the assertion of a claim by certain parties to this proceeding, is the fact that in her early years she was known as Ida E. Mayfield. Her mother, her brother, and her sister also adopted Mayfield as the family name. The evidence, however, and particularly the documentary evidence, indubitably leads to the conclusion that Ida E. Wood was born Ellen Walsh, the daughter of Thomas Walsh and Ann Crawford Walsh, and that the change of name from Walsh to Mayfield was made by herself and her family, undoubtedly influenced by her pretenses to a social standing in this community. . . . The motives of the decedent in her own actions and in her influence upon the members of her family are palpable. She was plainly actuated by her desire to suppress her humble origin and to asume an alleged social standing in the period before and after her marriage to Benjamin Wood. She spoke with pride of having danced with the Prince of Wales (later King Edward VII) during his visit to New York and of having entertained President Lincoln in her home.

It is the jest of fortune that, having attained wealth and prominence, she abandoned her pretenses at the age of 60 and retired to strict seclusion. By way of direct contrast, during her last years in her talks and writings she cherishes only the memory of her real parents and her Walsh and Crawford lineage. . . .

To summarize the entire evidence in the case it appears that three lines of proof are presented. The first is that revealed in the handwriting of Ida E. Wood with her own notations of her family history. The second line consists of the independent and uncontrovertible documentary proofs submitted by the Walsh claimants which verify, corroborate, and confirm the accuracy of the memoranda made by Mrs. Wood personally. The third line of proof as presented by the Mayfield claimants in so far as it attempts to establish relationship to the decedent lacks any contact or identification whatsoever with the blood of the decedent. No common ancestor has been shown. The first two lines of evidence coincide and the coincidence compels the conclusion found by the surrogate that Ida E. Wood was born Ellen Walsh.

The motion of the attorney for the public administrator and other counsel to strike out the notices of appearances and the objections of all the Mayfield claimants has been granted upon the merits. The surrogate specifically finds that they are not related in any manner whatsoever to the decedent here and are not persons interested in her estate. The names and numbers of such claimants may be included in the intermediate decree. Apparently they aggregate 430 persons.

Submit such intermediate decree on notice accordingly.

Notes

1. In twelfth-century England, though land could not be devised by will, to die intestate with regard to one's chattels was a great sin, because it implied that the intestate had neglected to make a final confession. Therefore, the personal property of an intestate was fair game for the king, the lords, and the ecclesiastical authorities. This policy of forfeitures was not only unseemly, but also resented by the relatives and friends of the deceased. Chapter 27 of Magna Carta (1215) mandated

distribution of the goods of intestates to relatives and friends. Today all jurisdictions have laws specifying patterns of distribution. See, e.g., Mass. Gen. Laws Ann. ch. 190 (supp. 1976):

§1. Spouse's Share of Property not Disposed of by Will

A surviving husband or wife shall, after the payment of the debts of the deceased and the charges of his last sickness and funeral and of the settlement of his estate, . . . be entitled to the following share in his real and personal property not disposed of by will:

(1) If the deceased leaves kindred and no issue, and it appears on determination by the probate court, as hereinafter provided, that the whole estate does not exceed fifty thousand dollars in value, the surviving husband or wife shall take the whole thereof; otherwise such survivor shall take fifty thousand dollars and one-half of the remaining personal and one-half of the remaining real property. If the personal property is insufficient to pay said fifty thousand dollars, the deficiency shall, upon the petition of any party in interest, be paid from the sale or mortgage, in the manner provided for the payment of debts or legacies, of any interest of the deceased in real property which he could have conveyed at the time of his death; and the surviving husband or wife shall be permitted, subject to the approval of the court, to purchase at any such sale, notwithstanding the fact that he or she is the administrator of the estate of the deceased person. . . .

(2) If the deceased leaves issue, the survivor shall take one-third of the personal and one-third of the real property.

(3) If the deceased leaves no issue and no kindred, the survivor shall take the whole.

§2. [Stipulates that Personal Property will be Distributed in the Same Proportions as Real Property.]

§3. Descent of Land, Tenements or Hereditaments

When a person dies seized of land, tenements or hereditaments, or of any right thereto, or entitled to any interest therein, in fee simple or for the life of another, not having lawfully devised the same, they shall descend as follows: . . .

(1) In equal shares to his children and to the issue of any deceased child by right of representation; and if there is no surviving child of the intestate then to all his other lineal descendants. If all such descendants are in the same degree of kindred to the intestate, they shall share the estate equally; otherwise, they shall take according to the right of representation.

(2) If he leaves no issue, in equal shares to his father and mother.

(3) If he leaves no issue and no mother, to his father.

(4) If he leaves no issue and no father, to his mother.

(5) If he leaves no issue and no father or mother, to his brothers and sisters and to the issue of any deceased brother or sister by right of repre-

sentation; and, if there is no surviving brother or sister of the intestate, to all the issue of his deceased brothers and sisters. If all such issue are in the same degree of kindred to the intestate, they shall share the estate equally, otherwise, according to the right of representation.

(6) If he leaves no issue, and no father, mother, brother or sister, and no issue of any deceased brother or sister, then to his next of kin in equal degree; but if there are two or more collateral kindred in equal degree claiming through different ancestors, those claiming through the nearest ancestor shall be preferred to those claiming through an ancestor more remote.

(7) If an intestate leaves no kindred and no widow or husband, his estate shall escheat to the commonwealth.

2. Winthrop v. Lechmere challenged the validity of a 1699 Connecticut statute providing that an intestate's real and personal property should be divided in equal shares among the intestate's children, the eldest son receiving a double share. After protracted litigation, the statute was declared null and void by the Privy Council, in London. The statute was held to be against the common and statute law of England (under which all realty descended to the eldest son of the intestate), destructive of the liberty and property of the subject, against reason, and contrary to the royal charter of the province. The case was an important stage in the development of American resistance to subordination to the mother country. See Joseph Henry Smith, Appeals to the Privy Council from the American Plantations 537-551 (1950).

3. In Labine v. Vincent, 401 U.S. 532 (1971), the Supreme Court upheld the constitutionality of Louisiana's laws that bar an illegitimate child from sharing equally with legitimates in the estate of their father who had publicly acknowledged the child. Justices Douglas, Brennan, White, and Marshall dissented, arguing that the laws violated the Equal Protection Clause, under Levy v. Louisiana, 391 U.S. 68 (1968), which invalidated a similarly discriminatory wrongful death benefits statute. In Weber v. Aetna Casualty & Surety Co., 406 U.S. 164 (1972), the Court followed *Levy* and distinguished *Labine* when it invalidated a worker's compensation law that put claims of legitimate children ahead of illegitimate. Since then, the Court has followed the *Levy-Weber* line, in the social welfare context, but *Labine* has not been overruled. See New Jersey Welfare Rights Organization v. Cahill, 411 U.S. 619 (1973), and Jimenez v. Weinberger, 417 U.S. 628 (1974).

4. In Byerly v. Tolbert, 250 N.C. 27, 108 S.E.2d 29 (1959), the question was whether a child born to a widow 322 days after her husband's death was entitled to share in the father's estate. The court concluded that the presumption "that the child was not *en ventre sa mere* when the intestate died" may be rebutted, and that the question should have been put to the jury.

C. DOWER AND CURTESY

◆ W. S. HOLDSWORTH, AN HISTORICAL INTRODUCTION TO THE LAND LAW
87-89 (1927)

At common law the wife had, after the death of her husband, the right to dower. This dower consisted of a life interest in a third of the land of which her husband had ever been solely seised during the marriage for an estate of inheritance, which issue of the marriage by the husband might inherit. There were several species of dower under the old law; but it was this form of dower, thus fixed by law, which superseded the others.

The widow's right to dower attached to all the lands of which the husband had ever been solely seised. It therefore restricted his right to alienate his property freely. The purchaser could only take the land subject to the chance that the wife might survive and assert her claim to a third of the land for her life. This was in fact the one restriction on the power of free alienation, in the interests of the family, which the common law retained. It was largely for this reason that equity (contrary to its rule of following the law) refused to admit a right to dower out of equitable estates. . . .

The husband, after the death of his wife, was entitled to an estate by the curtesy out of all his wife's estates of inheritance, provided that, (1) the wife was seised in deed of such an estate of inheritance as the issue, which the husband had by her, might have inherited; and (2) that a child was born alive during a valid marriage. The right to curtesy was extended to equitable estates. . . .

◆ CHAPLIN v. CHAPLIN
2 Eq. Cas. Ab. 384, pl. 10, 11, 24 Eng. Rep. 1040 (Ch. 1733)

But it was afterwards disclosed to the court, that the legal estate of the rent in fee was in trustees, in trust for Porter Chaplin in tail male; and that on his dying, the trust of this estate-tail descended to his only son Sir John Chaplin in tail, the husband of the plaintiff the Lady Chaplin, who (*inter al'*) brought her bill for her dower of this rent; and then the case was no more, than whether the wife of a *cestuy que trust* in tail should be endowed? . . .

It was said to have been agreed and settled, that a man should be tenant by curtesy of a trust; and it would not be pretended that there were less stronger reasons to be urged in favour of a dowress. . . .

His Lordship took notice, that by the preamble of the statute of uses (27 Hen. 8, c.10), it is recited, that by means of these uses the wife was defeated of her dower; by which it appears, that the wife of *cestuy que trust* was not dowable at common law; and if so, then as at common law an use was the same as a trust is now, it follows, that the wife can no more be endowed of a trust now, than at common law, and before the statute, she could be endowed of an use; so that here was the opinion of the whole parliament in the point; that it had been the common practice of conveyancers, agreeable hereto, to place the legal estate in trustees on purpose to prevent dower; wherefore it would be of the most dangerous consequence to titles, and throw things into confusion, contrary to former opinions, and the advice of so many eminent and learned men, to let in the claim of dower upon trust estates; that he took it to be settled, that the husband should be tenant by the curtesy of a trust, though the wife could not have dower thereof . . .; for which diversity, as he could see no reason, so neither should he have made it; but since it had prevailed, he would not alter it; that there did not appear to be so much as one single case, where abstracting from all other circumstances, it had been determined there should be dower of a trust. . . . For which reason, his Lordship dimissed the bill as to such part of it as claimed dower of the trust of this rent.

Note

The Dower Act of 1833 (3, 4 Will. 4, c.105) extended the right to dower to equitable estates, but subordinated the widow's dower interest to the husband's right to alienate the property absolutely either *inter vivos* or by will.

C. Kenny, History of the Law of Married Women's Property 80-82 (1879):

> . . . Having thus traced Curtesy into the form which it retains to our own day — an estate for life accruing to a husband in his wife's lands of inheritance, as soon as he has by her heritable issue born alive — we may turn aside to notice . . . a puzzling technicality in lawyers' definitions of curtesy. . . .
>
> The test of life, from Glanvil downwards, is made to consist, as the Prussian Code to this day makes it, in its having uttered a cry; which, says Bracton, even though born deaf and dumb it is sure to do. . . .
>
> Our English lawyers seem to have been compelled to select from the various possible proofs of life the audible one, on account of the peculiarities of their own system of evidence and procedure. Women, by a disqualification borrowed from the Canon law, were not allowed to take part in an "Inquisition." And even if they had been, midwives, according to Bracton, were so frequently suborned by widowers who wished to claim curtesy, that their testimony would have carried little weight. "The godly midwives of Egypt lied," as Bunyan puts it; and their less devout

successors retained the habits of the profession. Consequently someone else must be produced who from his own perceptions, and not from hearsay (which might merely have originated with the suborned mid-wives), could establish that the child had actually lived. But this perception could only be one of hearing, not of sight. For, as the record I have mentioned tells us — here completing what was omitted in the reasoning of Bracton — the prudery of medieval obstetrics "did not permit the presence of a male at such mysteries;" and the husband's witnesses must therefore content themselves with listening outside the "four walls" for an infantine wail.

HORWITZ, THE TRANSFORMATION IN THE CONCEPTION OF PROPERTY IN AMERICAN LAW, 1780-1860, 40 U. Chi. L. Rev. 248, 282-284 (1973): Because the value of land was increasingly determined by its productive capacity, American courts had to decide whether to follow the common law in measuring dower by the value of land divorced from its productive capacity. This issue arose in several different forms. Did unimproved lands have any greater value for purposes of measuring dower if they could be sold to speculators for a substantial price? Would the dower right be computed on the basis of existing rents and profits if speculation had raised the land's market price above any sum that could reflect its present productivity? That is, was a widow entitled, as at common law, to a life interest in one-third of the land or only to a one-third interest in the profits? Finally, how would dower be computed on land that a husband had sold in his lifetime and that, by the time of his death, had increased in value, either because of a general rise in land values or because the purchaser had improved it?

The courts wrestled with each of these questions from the beginning of the nineteenth century. In 1783, an unreported Massachusetts decision had turned back a challenge to the common law rule that a widow was entitled to dower in unimproved lands. The first clear change in the theory of land valuation appears in Leonard v. Leonard [4 Mass. 533 (1808)]. Commissioners appointed by the probate judge had appraised the relevant real estate, "a considerable part of which was woodland and unproductive.". The widow was awarded land valued at one-third of the total, though it was agreed that her actual share "comprised the most productive parts of the . . . estate." Reversing and holding that dower should be determined not by the market value but by the rents and profits of the estate, the court declared: "This rule is adapted equally to protect widows from having an unproductive part of estates assigned to them, and to guard heirs from being left, during the life of the widow without the means of support."

This rule may have appeared to be even-handed when it was announced, but in a speculative and developing economy, with the market value of land consistently above the capitalized value of its present product, dowagers would soon become victims of the theory underlying it. In Conner v. Shepard, the Supreme Judicial Court carried the new rule of *Leonard* to its logical conclusion. Overruling its decision of thirty-five years earlier, the court denied a widow's claim to a dower in unimproved lands. Since dower is to be measured by the productive value of the land, Chief Justice Parker reasoned, there could be no dower in unimproved lands. Could not the widow, if only given her traditional share, herself make the lands productive? No, said the court, for that would constitute waste. Returning for this particular situation to the discredited common law doctrine of waste, the court declared:

> [A]ccording to the principles of the common law, her estate would be forfeited if she were to cut down any of the trees valuable as timber. It would seem too that the mere change of the property from wilderness to arable or pasture land . . . might be considered waste: for the alteration of the property, *even if it became thereby more valuable,* would subject the estate in dower to forfeiture: the heir having a right to the inheritance, in the same character as it was left by the ancestor.

Thus, the widow lost either way. A utilitarian standard of value made worthless her dower rights in unimproved lands, while a nonutilitarian rule of waste made improvement impossible.

The contradictions go deeper still. In order not to rest the argument from waste entirely on outmoded rules of common law, Parker went on to argue that improvements by a tenant in dower "would be actually, as well as technically, waste of the inheritance." "[L]ands actually in a state of nature may," he said, "in a country fast increasing in its population, be more valuable than the same land would be with . . . cultivation. . . ." Parker here seemed to be suggesting that legal rules should be used to discourage and delay economic improvement as long as buyers were willing to pay more for undeveloped than for developed land. If so, his theory appears to be without support in other cases, and inconsistent with the conception of property then emerging in the case law. Indeed, the premise that underlay the changing law of waste was that it was preferable to encourage immediate improvement by tenants, even at the risk that development might prevent other future uses and thereby impair the transferability of land.

The conclusion seems inescapable that Parker's central purpose in Conner v. Shepard was to undermine the right of dower itself. "Believing that [the dower right] would operate as a clog, upon estates designed to be the subject of transfer," the court was prepared to use any method to cut off the widow's share, including reliance on dubious assumptions about the relation between market price and productive value. Perhaps the most important effect of the holding that a widow was not entitled to dower in unimproved lands, however, was to promote further the view that the value of land was exclusively a function of its productivity.

The doctrine of Conner v. Shepard was clearly an exception to a general policy of encouraging improvements by those in possession of land. That policy was most uniformly pursued in the related context of dower rights asserted against purchasers rather than heirs. For example, from the first decade of the nineteenth century, the Massachusetts courts had held that a widow could not receive any of the increase in the value of land owing to improvements made by her husband's vendee. Identical results were reached in all the other states. New York, moreover, held that a widow could not gain the advantage either of improvements or of a general increase in land values. On the other hand, the Supreme Court of Pennsylvania, which as early as 1792 had denied that dower extended to improvements, refused to deprive the widow of the benefit of general increases in land values. While courts thus divided over who should have the benefit of increasing land prices, they all agreed that — regardless of common law property doctrines — the value of improvements should be left with the developer.

◆ OPINION OF THE JUSTICES
337 Mass. 786, 151 N.E.2d 475 (1958)

To the Honorable the Senate of the Commonwealth of Massachusetts:
     The undersigned Justices of the Supreme Judicial Court respectfully submit these answers to the questions set forth in an order of the Senate dated June 18, 1958, and transmitted to us on June 20. The order refers to a pending bill, Senate No. 388, entitled "An Act to restrict dower and curtesy claims to land owned at the death of the claimant's spouse." . . .
     The order recites that a substantially identical bill, Senate No. 274 of 1956, was referred to the Judicial Council by c.10 of the Resolves of 1956; and that a majority of the Judicial Council in its thirty-second report in 1956, at pages 24-28, recommended passage but suggested the possibility of an advisory opinion of the Justices. In that report we read that the purpose of the bill "is to reduce the title problems affecting the marketability of land whether by sale or mortgage" (page 25). We there are told that these problems have two chief causes: (1) The omission of a husband or wife to declare an existing marriage and to obtain the signature of the spouse to a deed. (2) The ever growing number of migratory divorces with the attendant doubt as to their validity and the consequent uncertainty as to the legality of remarriage. The result might be described as a conveyancers' nightmare.
     Under §1 as now in effect, curtesy is a life estate of a surviving husband in one-third of all land owned by his wife during marriage unless he has joined in a deed of conveyance or "otherwise" released his right to claim curtesy; and dower is a similar life estate of a surviving wife in one-third of land owned by the husband. . . . Either curtesy or

dower may be "otherwise" released by a deed subsequent to the deed of conveyance executed either separately or jointly with the spouse. Of course, neither can exist without a valid marriage. By statute neither survives divorce. This, of course, means a valid divorce. During marriage the right to claim curtesy or dower is said to be inchoate. (At common law the phrase was curtesy initiate.) Upon the death of the spouse, or at any rate, after the later assignment of a specified one-third of the land, it is said to be consummate. Curtesy and dower, under §1 in its present form, are superior to the rights of creditors. It should be noted that nothing like curtesy or dower exists as to personal property, which a husband or wife may dispose of freely without the consent of the spouse. . . .

That the bill would violate no provision of the Federal Constitution is settled by decisions of the Supreme Court of the United States. In Randall v. Kreiger, 23 Wall, 137, at page 148, decided in 1874, it was said:

> During the life of the husband the right [of dower] is a mere expectancy or possibility. In that condition of things, the lawmaking power may deal with it as may be deemed proper. It is not a natural right. It is wholly given by law, and the power that gave it may increase, diminish, or otherwise alter it, or wholly take it away. It is upon the same footing with the expectancy of heirs, apparent or presumptive, before the death of the ancestor. Until that event occurs the law of descent and distribution may be moulded according to the will of the legislature.

In Ferry v. Spokane, Portland & Seattle Ry., 258 U.S. 314, decided in 1922, the court upheld a decision of the Circuit Court of Appeals for the Ninth Circuit, to the effect that an Oregon statute limiting the right of dower of a nonresident to land of which the husband died seised was not unconstitutional. In the *Ferry* case the Supreme Court of the United States said,

> Dower is not a privilege or immunity of citizenship, either state or federal, within the meaning of the provisions relied on [§2 of art. 4 and the Fourteenth Amendment]. At most it is a right which, while it exists, is attached to the marital contract or relation, and it always has been deemed subject to regulation by each state as respects property within its limits. Conner v. Elliott, 18 How. 591. . . . The cases recognize that the limitation of the dower right is to remove an impediment to the transfer of real estate and to assure titles against absent and probably unknown wives. . . .

According to the thirty-second report of the Judicial Council claims of dower or curtesy in this Commonwealth have almost ceased to be made; and, in fact, a claim of neither is advisable except under two special circumstances: "(1) if the deceased owned real estate, but died insolvent or so nearly so that the bulk of the real estate must be sold to pay the debts and expenses; and (2) if the deceased during his or her lifetime conveyed a considerable amount of real estate without procuring a release of curtesy or dower in the deed." Newhall, Settlement of Estates (4th ed.) §213. . . .

In the light of the shrinking significance of curtesy or dower as alternatives which must be elected by a surviving husband or wife in the estate of a deceased spouse, we cannot regard the statements quoted from our cases as precluding inchoate curtesy and inchoate dower from being viewed in this Commonwealth in the same way as in a majority of the States. We are of opinion that as a matter of public policy the Legislature can restrict them in the manner proposed. Let it be conceded that each is a valuable interest and more than a possibility. Yet each is only a contingency — a contingency of waning value — which in the usual estate today is of slight importance. We think that inchoate curtesy and inchoate dower, as contingencies before the death of the predeceasing spouse, are subject to action by the Legislature, which may make an evaluation in the public interest, and determine that any slight advantage in their retention in a relatively few cases is outweighed by the far greater benefit to the general good accruing from their restriction.

D.   STATUTORY SHARES

◆ NEWMAN v. DORE
275 N.Y. 371, 9 N.E.2d 966 (1937)

LEHMAN, Judge. The Decedent Estate Law regulates the testamentary disposition and the descent and distribution of the real and personal property of decedents. It does not limit or affect disposition of property *inter vivos*. In terms and in intent it applies only to decedents' estates. Property which did not belong to a decedent at his death and which does not become part of his estate does not come within its scope.

The share in the real and personal property of a decedent, not devised or bequeathed, which a husband or wife takes, is now fixed by section 83 of the Decedent Estate Law. Prior to the revision of the Decedent Estate Law which took effect on September 1, 1930, a decedent could by testamentary disposition effectively exclude a wife or husband from the share of the estate which would pass to her or him in case of intestacy. That was changed by section 18 of the revised Decedent Estate Law. By that section (subdivision 1) "a personal right of election is given to the surviving spouse to take his or her share of the estate as in intestacy, subject to the limitations, conditions and exceptions contained in this section." These limitations and exceptions include a case where "the testator has devised or bequeathed in trust an amount equal to or greater than the intestate share, with income thereof payable to the surviving spouse for life." Subdivision 1(b). The Legislature has declared that its intention in enacting these sections of the revised Decedent Estate Law was "to increase the share of a surviving spouse in the estate of a deceased spouse, either in a case of intestacy or by an election against the terms of the will of the deceased spouse thus enlarging property rights of such surviving spouse."

Ferdinand Straus died on July 1, 1934, leaving a last will and testament dated May 5, 1934, which contained a provision for a trust for his wife for her life of one-third of the decedent's property both real and personal. In such case the statute did not give the wife a right of election to take her share of the estate as an intestacy. She receives the income for life from a trust fund of the amount of the intestate share, but does not take the share. That share is one-third of the decedent's estate. It includes no property which does not form part of the estate at the decedent's death. The testator on June 28, 1934, three days before his death, executed trust agreements by which, in form at least, he transferred to trustees all his real and personal property. If the agreements effectively divested the settlor of title to his property, then the decedent left no estate and the widow takes nothing. The widow has challenged the validity of the transfer to the trustee. The beneficiary named in the trust agreement has brought this action to compel the trustees to carry out its terms. The trial court has found that the "trust agreements were made, executed and delivered by said Ferdinand Straus for the purpose of evading and circumventing the laws of the State of New York, and particularly sections 18 and 83 of the Decedent Estate Law." Undoubtedly the settlor's purpose was to provide that at his death his property should pass to beneficiaries named in the trust agreement to the exclusion of his wife. Under the provisions of the Decedent Estate Law the decedent could not effect the desired purpose by testamentary disposition of his property. The problem in this case is whether he has accomplished that result by creating a trust during his lifetime.

The validity of the attempted transfer depends upon whether "the laws of the State of New York and particularly sections 18 and 83 of the Decedent Estate Law" prohibit or permit such transfer. If the statute, in express language or by clear implication, prohibits the transfer, it is illegal; if the laws of the state do not prohibit it, the transfer is legal. In strict accuracy, it cannot be said that a "purpose of evading and circumventing" the law can carry any legal consequences.

> We do not speak of evasion, because, when the law draws a line, a case is on one side of it or the other, and if on the safe side is none the worse legally that a party has availed himself to the full of what the law permits. When an act is condemned as an evasion what is meant is that it is on the wrong side of the line indicated by the policy if not by the mere letter of the law. [Bullen v. Wisconsin, 240 U.S. 625, 630.]

In a subsequent case it was said of a defendant: "The fact that it desired to evade the law, as it is called, is immaterial, because the very meaning of a line in the law is that you intentionally may go as close to it as you can if you do not pass it." Superior Oil Co. v. State of Mississippi, 280 U.S. 390, 395, both opinions by Mr. Justice Holmes. Under the laws of the State of New York, and particularly sections 18 and 83 of the Decedent Estate Law, neither spouse has any immediate interest in the property of the other. The "enlarged property right" which the Legislature intended to confer is only an expectant interest dependent upon the contingency that the property to which the interest attaches becomes part of a decedent's estate. The contingency does not occur, and the expectant property right does not ripen into a property right in possession, if the owner sells or gives away the property. Defeat of a contingent expectant interest by means available under the law cannot be regarded as an unlawful "evasion" of the law. A duty imperfectly defined by law may at times be evaded or a right imperfectly protected by law may be violated with impunity, but to say that an act, lawful under common-law rules and not prohibited by any express or implied statutory provision, is in itself a "fraud" on the law or an "evasion" of the law, involves a contradiction in terms.

That does not mean, of course, that the law may not place its ban upon an intended result even though the means to effect that result may be lawful. The statute gives to a spouse a property right. The question is, how far the statute protects that right even while it remains only expectant and contingent. A right created by law may be protected by law against invasion through acts otherwise lawful. A wrong does not cease to be a wrong because it is cloaked in form of law. The test of legality, then, is whether the result is lawful and the means used to achieve that result are lawful. Here, we should point out that the courts below have not based their decision primarily upon the finding that the trust agreements were executed for the purpose of evading and circumventing the law of the state of New York. The courts have also found, and the evidence conclusively establishes, that the trust agreements were made for the purpose of depriving the decedent's widow of any rights in and to his property upon his death. Under the trust agreements executed a few days before the death of the settlor, he reserved the enjoyment of the entire income as long as he should live, and a right to revoke the trust at his will, and in general the powers granted to the trustees were in terms made "subject to the settlor's control during his life," and could be exercised "in such manner only as the settlor shall from time to time direct in writing." Thus by the trust agreement which transferred to the trustees the settlor's entire property, the settlor reserved substantially the same rights to enjoy and control the disposition of the property as he previously had possessed, and the inference is inescapable that the trust agreements were executed by the settlor, as the court has found, "with the intention and for the purpose of diminishing his estate and thereby to reduce in amount the share" of his wife in his estate upon his death and as a "contrivance to deprive . . . his widow of any rights in and to his property upon his death." They had no other purpose and substantially they had no other effect. Does the statute intend that such a transfer shall be available as a means of defeating the contingent expectant estate of a spouse? . . .

Motive or intent is an unsatisfactory test of the validity of a transfer of property. In most jurisdictions it has been rejected, sometimes for the reason that it would cast doubt upon the validity of all transfers made by a married man, outside of the regular course of business; sometimes because it is difficult to find a satisfactory logical foundation for it. Intent may, at times, be relevant in determining whether an act is fraudulent, but there can be no fraud where no right of any person is invaded. "The great weight of authority is that the intent to defeat a claim which otherwise a wife might have is not enough to defeat the deed." Since the law gives the wife only an expectant interest in the property of her husband which becomes part of his estate, and since the law does not restrict transfers of property by the husband during his life, it would seem that the only sound test of the validity of a challenged transfer is whether it is real or illusory.

The test has been formulated in different ways, but in most jurisdictions the test applied is essentially the test of whether the husband has in good faith divested himself of ownership of his property or has made an illusory transfer. . . .

Judged by the substance, not by the form, the testator's conveyance is illusory, intended only as a mask for the effective retention by the settlor of the property which in form he had conveyed. We do not attempt now to formulate any general test of how far a settlor must divest himself of his interest in the trust property to render the conveyance more than illusory. Question of whether reservation of the income or of a power of revocation, or both, might even without reservation of the power of control be sufficient to show that the transfer was not intended in good faith to divest the settlor of his property must await decision until such question arises. In this case it is clear that the settlor never intended to divest himself of his property. He was unwilling to do so even when death was near.

The judgment should be affirmed, with costs.

MASS. GEN. LAWS ANN. ch. 191 (Supp. 1976):

§15.   FILING OF WAIVER; RIGHTS UPON WAIVER

The surviving husband or wife of a deceased person, except as provided in section thirty-five or thirty-six of chapter two hundred and nine, within six months after the probate of the will of such deceased, may file in the registry of probate a writing signed by him or by her, waiving any provisions that may have been made in it for him or for her, or claiming such portion of the estate of the deceased as he or she is given the right to claim under this section, and if the deceased left issue, he or she shall thereupon take one-third of the personal and one-third of the real property; and if the deceased left kindred but no issue, he or she shall take twenty-five thousand dollars and one-half of the remaining personal and one-half of the remaining real property; except that in either case if he or she would thus take real and personal property to an amount exceeding twenty-five thousand dollars in value, he or she shall receive, in addition to that amount, only the income during his or her life of the excess of his or her share of such estate above that amount, the personal property to be held in trust and the real property vested in him or her for life, from the death of the deceased. If the deceased left no issue or kindred, the surviving husband or wife shall take twenty-five thousand dollars and one-half of the remaining personal and one half of the remaining real property absolutely. . . .

§20.   OMITTED CHILDREN

If a testator omits to provide in his will for any of his children, whether born before or after the testator's death, or for the issue of a deceased child, whether born before or after the testator's death, they shall take the same share of his estate which they would have taken if he had died intestate, unless they have been provided for by the testator in his lifetime or unless it appears that the omission was intentional and not occasioned by accident or mistake. . . .

GLENDON, MATRIMONIAL PROPERTY: A COMPARATIVE STUDY OF LAW AND SOCIAL CHANGE, 49 Tul. L. Rev. 21, 58-62 (1974): The major techniques of American law in separate property states for securing what amounts to a "reserved share" to the wife are three: dower, indefeasible share, and homestead. . . .

Because of the practical difficulties with dower, the states are coming to see other protective devices as more effective ways of securing a share in a deceased spouse's estate to the survivor. The most popular of these is the simple device, used in many European systems, of limiting the testamentary power of one spouse over a certain proportion of his property. This limitation in American law is in favor of the spouse, rather than in favor of certain groups of ascendants and descendants, as it is in the French system. The share may be fixed as a fraction of the estate, which will vary according to the circumstances. For instance, in Illinois, where children survive, the forced share of the spouse is one-third. If there are no descendants surviving, the spouse's share will be one-half. Thus, in Illinois, the forced share corresponds exactly to the share the spouse would take in the case of intestate succession. In some states the forced share is a fraction of the intestate share; in others it is a fixed sum of money, with or without a fractional share in the surplus. The exact regulation of the forced share in any state will, of course, reflect the way the legislature of the state balances the policy favoring freedom of testation against the policy favoring protection of surviving spouses. Since indigent spouses are apt to become charges of the state, it is not surprising that freedom of testation tends increasingly to be subordinated to concern for the surviving spouse.

The American system of reserved share has some disadvantages in comparison with the reserved share as it is known in some civil law systems. Its principal disadvantage is that its size depends on the size of the estate. Thus, if the husband, three days before his death, gives his entire estate to the Society for the Prevention of Cruelty to Animals, or to his mistress, the forced share of his wife is defeated. Only New York and the few states which have so far adopted the Uniform Probate Code have taken steps to protect the wife by statute against such *inter vivos* transactions. The courts in a minority of states have developed rules to protect a widow against "fraudulent" *inter vivos* transfers by the husband. From the point of view of the testator and his other dependents, the wife's forced share has a related disadvantage: sometimes a testator may provide generously for his wife by nontestamentary means, such as joint tenancies with right of survivorship or life insurance, and will leave the rest of his estate by will to other dependents. A spiteful or greedy spouse under a forced share system always has the opportunity to upset such carefully arranged estate plans by claiming against the will. Just as the courts generally will not take into consideration *inter vivos* transfers to others in order to increase the forced share, so they will not consider such transfers to the spouse in order to reduce her share. . . .

The third technique which American separate property states use to secure some financial protection to a surviving spouse is homestead. Homestead laws are an American invention. In force in nearly all states, they have as their primary purpose the protection of certain family property from the claims of creditors. But they afford some protection against transferees as well. In addition, most of them have a third function in the area of succession. They operate at the death of a householder to secure the property to a surviving spouse and children not only against creditors of the estate, but even against takers under a will made by the deceased. They function in both testate and intestate succession. The homestead right typically lasts until the remarriage or death of the surviving spouse.

The extent of the protection given by these statutes varies from state to state. Typically, they declare that the family home and household goods will be exempt from the claims of creditors and takers under a will up to a certain amount, which may be as little as $1,000 in some states or as great as $40,000 in North Dakota where there are no other restrictions on testamentary freedom. In many states the homestead allowance is so generous that it secures the whole of the average small estate to the widow and minor children, leaving no property for the will to operate on or for creditors to attach.

One other aspect of the American succession law relating to spouses ought to be noted here. During the period of administration of an estate, there is often a need to provide temporarily for the support of a widow and minor children. In view of this need, nearly all states empower the court that supervises the administration of the estate to grant support from the estate to dependents of the deceased. This device is called the widow's or family allowance. Like homestead, this device functions in both testate and intestate succession and is free of the claims of creditors and takers under the will. The amount of a widow's award can be quite large. Indeed, it can consume the whole of a small estate. In Illinois, for example, a surviving spouse is entitled for a period of nine months after the death of the decedent to "such a sum of money as the court deems reasonable for the proper support of the surviving spouse . . . in a manner suited to the condition in life of the surviving spouse and to the condition of the estate and such additional sum of money as the court deems reasonable for the proper support . . . of minor and adult children of the decedent who reside with the surviving spouse at the time of decedent's death." The statute provides that the award shall in no case be less than $2,500 for the spouse and $500 for each child, and that the spouse may, if he or she wishes, elect to take personal property of the decedent in payment of the award. Where it appears to the court that the value of all the property left by the decedent does not exceed the amount of the surviving spouse's award, the court is empowered to terminate the administration of the personal property and to order that complete title to the personal estate be vested immediately in the spouse.

Notes

1. "William J. Sellick, late of Paw Paw, Van Buren County," included the following clause in his will: "I give, devise and bequeath to my wife, Caroline Sellick, $25,000, to be used and enjoyed by her during her life and at her death to be equally divided between my nephew, Arthur F. Sellick, and my niece, Gertrude Sellick." The widow elected to take under the statute. The issue then was whether Arthur and Gertrude should immediately take their remainders, because the termina-

tion of the life estate had been accelerated by the widow's election, or whether the fund should go to the residuary legatee. The widow's statutory share had greatly diminished the residual legacy.

The court appointed a trustee to pay the income of the fund for the life of the widow to the residuary legatee, then convey the corpus to Arthur and Gertrude. Sellick v. Sellick, 207 Mich. 194, 173 N.W. 609 (1919).

2. The most interesting empirical study of wealth transmission in America is M. Sussman, J. Cates & D. Smith, The Family and Inheritance (1970). It was based on a random sampling of 5 percent of the more than 13,000 estates closed in Cuyahoga County, Ohio, Probate Court during ten months of 1964-65. Some of its conclusions have been summarized as follows:

PASLEY, BOOK REVIEW, 58 Minn. L. Rev. 1191, 1192-1194 (1974): (1) The overall ratio of testacy to intestacy was 69/31 (incidentally, the highest rate of testacy found in any such study in the United States). As was to be expected, the percentage of testacy went up with the age of the decedent. For example, no decedents in the 20-29 age group left wills, whereas 83.3 percent of decedents in the 90-99 age group died testate. However, factors other than age affected the percentage of testate estates, and most testators had had wills (often more than one) for long periods of time. The authors report that "[t]he great age for will making [among the survivors] was 31-45, the time of planning to meet future commitments, especially family obligations."

(2) In testacy cases, the most common departure from the pattern of intestate distribution was the overwhelming tendency of married testators to leave their entire estate to their spouses, relying on the spouses to care for any children.

(3) Most of the estates were relatively small. Eight-five of the 659 estates studied were $2,000 or less, 526 were between $2,000 and $60,000, and 48 were $60,000 or more. Only a few were over $100,000. The common assertion that the principal result of inheritance is to make the rich richer and the poor poorer finds no support in this study.

(4) Most beneficiaries made prudent use of their legacies, regardless of whether they were large or small. In order of frequency of occurrence, savings, living expenses, acquisition of real estate and durable goods, and education were the favored uses for legacies. In a mere one and six-tenths percent of cases were they spent on vacations.

(5) Trusts were used in only 16 of the cases. Legal life estates were created only rarely and were generally regarded as causing more trouble than they were worth.

(6) While insurance was the single most important nonprobate asset, being present in nearly three-fourths of the cases, the average amount, $5,250, was surprisingly small. The amount of insurance car-

ried tended to increase with the size of the probate estate ($19,117 average for gross estates over $60,000) but, even so, the highest figure reported was $100,000.

(7) Although this finding is apt to be disputed by those pressing for simplification of the probate process, court costs, lawyers' fees, and elapsed time for the settlement of estates seemed reasonable. However, there was almost universal condemnation of the institution of the appraiser, and taken as a group the lawyers who were interviewed seemed remarkably amenable toward further simplification of the process, and reduction of the cost, of settling estates.

(8) Although complete testamentary freedom was widely regarded as the ideal norm, most "survivors" conceded that a testator should not be allowed to disinherit his spouse or family. In practice, the general pattern was one of "both serial service and reciprocity," that is, the passing of wealth to the spouse or descendants, and the favoring of those who most needed help or who had helped the testator during his life, or at least remained close to him. In those rare cases where the testator did depart from a "normal" pattern of distribution, there seemed to be a good reason in the family circumstances. Very few survivors felt disgruntled or seriously disappointed at being given a smaller share, or no share at all.

One disturbing finding, from a sociological standpoint, is that the process of will-making and testate and intestate distribution is still largely concentrated in the white upper and middle classes. The poor, and a large proportion of blacks, simply bypass the whole process. For example, although nearly 20 percent of the population of Cuyahoga County is black, blacks accounted for less than seven percent of the sample used in the survey. While the survivors presumably made their own arrangements for dividing the decedent's property, this is apt to result in complications, especially where title to real property is involved.

16 ◆ PERPETUITIES

A. HISTORY

◆ A. W. B. SIMPSON, AN INTRODUCTION TO THE HISTORY OF THE LAND LAW
186 (1961)

The new-found flexibility in the manipulation of legal estates was not lost on the conveyancers and the landowners who employed them, and the late sixteenth and early seventeenth centuries may justly be called the age of the fantastic conveyance, for if the old common law rules could be bypassed by using the formula "to X to the use of . . .", what rules *were* to limit a man's powers of disposition over his land? Could he make it inalienable for ever, or could he make the fee simple in it jump from person to person a hundred years after his death? The chaotic state of the land law on points such as these was all the more lamentable during a period of social upheaval marked by an increase in the prosperity and social status of the lesser landowners, which, in its turn, brought an accompanying desire to "found families" and ensure that the family estate should not be alienated out of the family in the future. The courts were brought face to face with the fact that the wide powers of disposition which their interpretation of the Statutes of Uses and Wills had conferred upon landowners were being employed for their own destruction. This is the basic problem of Perpetuities, and it was not for well over a century after 1535 that a satisfactory solution of this problem began to emerge.

♦ T. F. T. PLUCKNETT, A CONCISE HISTORY OF THE COMMON LAW
596-598 (5th ed., 1956)

THE RULE AGAINST PERPETUITIES

. . . [C]hancery and the common law courts were . . . both faced by the problem of perpetuities, and so combined their forces in devising a solution, for it must be remembered that chancellors frequently consulted the common law judges in difficult cases.

The word perpetuity was for a long time vaguely used: it first becomes precise when it is used to designate attempts to produce an unbarrable entail. . . . A bill against "perpetuities" which passed its first reading in the Lords on 19 January, 1598, was directed against uses arising in one person when another person attempts to alienate. The term was then extended to analogous situations where the employment of contingent remainders, springing and shifting uses, and executory devises resulted in making the fee inalienable for a considerable length of time. An early instance of the word is in Chudleigh's Case, [1595], but the problem itself may be regarded in one sense as very much older, and indeed as being a continuation of the history of freedom of alienation. . . . Old rules thus came to be justified on newer grounds. Thus the rule in Shelley's Case was devised in mediaeval times for a feudal purpose, but its continuance was assured because it rendered the creation of perpetuities more difficult. The rule in Purefoy v. Rogers, [expressing a preference for contingent remainders, rather than executory interests, see Chapter 13, p. 504], whatever its technical justification, likewise owed its survival to similar considerations.

The first attempts to prevent perpetuities took the form of complicated rules. . . . It was hoped that rules limiting the creation and derivation of interests, coupled with rules permitting their destruction, would make undesirable settlement impossible. They probably did; but at the cost of upsetting many others which were perfectly harmless and even convenient. . . . An acute dilemma presented itself between the two dangers of permitting perpetuities and upsetting reasonable arrangements, and slowly it was being realised that the sort of rules then being developed would inevitably cut both ways. The first gleam of light appears in an argument by Davenport (later C.B.) when Child v. Baylie[1]

---

1. (1618-1623), Cro. Jac. 459; 2 Roll. R. 129; Palmer, 334; it was a devise of a term to A. and his assigns, but if A. die without issue living at his death, then to B. Both courts held that the devise over to B. was bad. Note, however, that while this was pending it was held in Pells v. Brown that corresponding limitations in a devise of a freehold were good. As Gray, Perpetuities, 119, remarks, the courts were especially suspicious of settlements of terms, and it was in connection with terms that the rule against perpetuities was first developed.

[Pells v. Brown, Cro. Jac. 590, 2 Rolle Rep. 216, 79 Eng. Rep. 504 (K.B. 1620), reversed common law precedents and recognized executory limitations on fee simples — the fee came into the Exchequer chamber. He argued that since in this case the contingency must be determined in the lifetime of a living person, then there could be no fear of a perpetuity. The argument was unsuccessful, but slowly attention began to fasten on the life in being, helped at first by the settlement of the rule that an executory devise of a term after an entailed interest was bad, although it would be good after a life interest.

A line of hesitating decisions culminated in the Duke of Norfolk's Case [3 Chan. Cas. 1, 22 Eng. Rep. 931 (Ch. 1681)] in which Lord Nottingham laid the foundations of the rule against perpetuities, not so much by defining its content, as by settling the lines upon which it was subsequently to develop. . . . In the course of his decision, Nottingham went fully into the history of the subject, and poured scorn on the mass of artificialities with which the common lawyers had encumbered it. . . . Such language must have been profoundly shocking to the common lawyers. . . . For two centuries the rule has continued to develop on that broad and reasonable basis, although Nottingham himself refused to be enticed into the discussion of hypothetical difficulties; to the question where would he stop in such cases he retorted: "I will tell you where I will stop: I will stop where-ever any visible inconvenience doth appear; for the just bounds of a fee simple upon a fee simple are not yet determined, but the first inconvenience that ariseth upon it will regulate it." Inconveniences have arisen, and the growing rule received its due measure of complexities and difficulties, but it is thanks to Lord Nottingham's courage and perception that the rule has as its basis a reasonable and simple proposition, instead of the artificial complications which the common law courts had been devising in order to meet the problem.

Such is the history, in brief outline, of the three systems of real property law controlled by the common law courts in the sixteenth and seventeenth centuries — the common law itself, uses executed under the Statute of Uses, and devises of freeholds and of terms under the Statute of Wills. Obviously they were faced with a bewildering situation, but it is difficult to show that they did anything to clarify it. All three systems raised the problem of perpetuities, but the common lawyers seemed to lack the courage, if not the penetration, to state a general solution.

————————————

In the Duke of Norfolk's Case, 1682, in which a realistic rule against perpetuities began to take shape, the chancellor, Lord Nottingham, observed:

————————————

simple subject to an executory interest — holding that the executory interest could not be destroyed by actions of the holder of the present possessory interest. Thus, a parent could give family lands in fee simple to an eldest son, with a condition that if the son had no children, the lands would go to the next son in fee simple. The childless first son could not destroy the second son's interest by alienating the land.]

> The law hath so long laboured to defeat perpetuities, that now it is become a sufficient reason of itself against any settlement to say it tends to a perpetuity . . . such perpetuities fight against God, by affecting a stability which human providence can never attain to, and are utterly against the reason and policy of the common law.

Ironically, the Duke of Norfolk's case upheld a limitation. The Earl of Arundel assumed that his eldest son, Thomas, who was *non compos mentis*, would not long outlive his father. Then the earldom and its estates would descend to Henry, the second son. If Henry became earl, the father wanted the Barony of Grostock, and its estates, to go to the fourth son, Charles, since presumably the principal estates would provide an adequate living for Henry. (The third son, Phillip, entered the church and became a cardinal.) The father therefore provided in his trust indenture for Grostock to go to Henry, on condition that if Thomas die without issue during Henry's life, Grostock should shift to Charles and the heirs male of his body.

When the earl died in 1652, Henry took control of the family estates, locked up Thomas in Padua, and obtained restoration of the title "Duke of Norfolk" from the king. By the time Thomas finally died in 1677, Henry was a duke quite uninterested in turning Grostock over to Charles. When Charles sued, Henry alleged that the limitation on Grostock was void for perpetuity under the existing common law rules; see Child v. Baylie, Cro. Jac. 459, 79 Eng. Rep. 393 (K.B. 1623). Lord Nottingham ruled for Charles, saying that there was no tendency to a perpetuity in the limitation, thus pointing the way toward a rule based on lives in being. Though the Duke of Norfolk's case upheld a limitation, the case is significant because Nottingham's lives-in-being test was gradually accepted, replacing a variety of unpredictable rules that the common law had concocted in the 1600s.

Concerning Nottingham, see 3 J. Campbell, Lives of the Lord Chancellors 339 (2d Am. ed. 1851):

> It is related of him, that he comforted himself by taking the Great Seal to bed with him, and that thus on the 7th of February, 1677, he saved it from the fate which then befell the mace, and afterwards the Great Seal itself, in the time of Lord Chancellor Thurlow, who had not treated it so tenderly. "About one in the morning," says Wood, "the Lord Chancellor Finch [Nottingham] his mace was stole out of his house in Queen Street. The Seal laid under his pillow, so the thief missed it. The famous thief that did it was Thomas Sadler, soon after taken and hanged for it at Tyburn."

Over 200 years, the Rule against Perpetuities evolved into the formula that John Chipman Gray finally carved in stone: "No interest is good unless it must vest, if at all, not later than twenty-one years after some life in being at the creation of the interest."

PHOTOGRAPH 16-1
John Chipman Gray

Learning the Rule against Perpetuities is difficult for law students. It is one of those educational challenges that is mastered when the student reaches a stage of "got it!" After that, one has difficulty remembering why the struggle was so hard. The *First Universalist* case seems to work best as a pedagogical tool: After three close readings, most students "know" the rule — not in all its tortured application, of course (only John Chipman Gray and A. James Casner have ever reached that stage), but sufficiently for applying it in ordinary life and for taking the multistate bar exam. Another useful approach to learning the rule through the materials in this chapter can be to read *First Universalist* twice, then read the text and examples that follow, and finally return to *First Universalist* for the third reading. Be comforted by the fact that generations have preceded you and survived, and by the additional fact that this is a unique moment in your legal education.

B. MECHANICS OF THE RULE

◆ FIRST UNIVERSALIST SOCIETY OF NORTH ADAMS v. BOLAND
155 Mass. 171, 29 N.E. 524 (1892)

. . . On April 9, 1842, Joseph D. Clark and twenty-five or thirty other persons formed the plaintiff society, with a constitution which adopted as the basis of its religious faith the profession of belief accepted by the General Convention of the Universalists at its session at Winchester, New Hampshire, in 1803, and provided for three trustees to be the executive power of the society and to see that all votes of the society were carried out. On April 3, 1854, Clark for the expressed consideration of nine hundred dollars conveyed the land in question by a deed containing the usual covenants to the plaintiff society

> to have and to hold to the said First Universalist Society and their assigns, so long as said real estate shall by said society or its assigns be devoted to the uses, interests, and support of those doctrines of the Christian religion embraced in the Confession of Faith adopted by the General Convention of the Universalists held at Winchester, New Hampshire, in the year eighteen hundred and three. And when said real estate shall by said society or its assigns be diverted from the uses, interests, and support aforesaid to any other interests, uses, or purposes than as aforesaid, then the title of said society or its assigns in the same shall forever cease, and be forever vested in the following named persons, and such persons shall be the legal representatives of any of such persons at the time the same so vests as aforesaid in the following undivided parts and proportions, to wit: to

Stephen M. Whipple 140/1000, Alanson Cady 140/1000, John F. Arnold 114/1000, Joseph D. Clark 70/1000 [Here followed the names of thirty-seven others after each of which was placed a fraction in thousandths]. To have and to hold the above granted premises, with the privileges and appurtenances thereto belonging, to the said grantees, their heirs and assigns, to them and their use and behoof forever, as aforesaid. . . .

Upon the land so conveyed to the plaintiff a church was erected, which from the time of its erection to the present time has been occupied and used for religious worship by the plaintiff society, without any change in the profession of faith mentioned in the deed of April 3, 1854, or in its constitution. The agreement in question was made by the parties on April 20, 1891, but the defendant, upon the tender of a deed to him from the plaintiff, refused to carry it out, on the ground, among others, that the plaintiff society never was seised in fee simple, but at most obtained only a qualified or conditional fee, and could not convey a good and clear title. . . .

ALLEN, J. The limitation over, which is contained in the deed of Clark to the plaintiff in 1854, is void for remoteness. The fact that the grantor designated himself as one of the persons amongst many others to take under this limitation, does not have the effect to make the limitation valid. He was to take with the rest, and stand upon the same footing with them.

Where there is an invalid limitation over, the general rule is that the preceding estate is to stand, unaffected by the void limitation. The estate becomes vested in the first taker, according to the terms in which it was granted or devised. There may be instances in which a void limitation might be referred to for the purpose of giving a construction to the language used in making the prior gift, provided any aid could be gained thereby. In the present case, we do not see that any such aid can be gained. The estate given to the first taker does not depend at all upon the validity or invalidity of the limitation over, and the construction of the language used is not aided by a reference thereto.

The grant to the plaintiff was to have and to hold, etc., "so long as said real estate shall by said society or its assigns be devoted to the uses, interests, and support of those doctrines of the Christian religion," as specified. "And when said real estate shall by said society or its assigns be diverted from the uses, interests, and support aforesaid to any other interests, uses, or purposes than as aforesaid, then the title of said society or its assigns in the same shall forever cease, and be forever vested in the following named persons," etc. These words do not grant an absolute fee, nor an estate on condition, but an estate which is to continue till the happening of a certain event, and then to cease. That event may happen at any time, or it may never happen. Because the estate may last forever, it is a fee. Because it may end on the happening of the event, it is what is usually called a determinable or qualified fee. The grant was not upon a condition subsequent, and no re-entry would be necessary; but by the terms of the grant the estate was to continue so long as the real estate should be devoted to the specified uses, and when it should no longer be so devoted, then the estate would cease and determine by its own limitation. Numerous illustrations of words proper to create such qualified or determinable fees are to be found in the books, one of which, as old as *Walsingham's* case, 2 Plowd. 557, is "as long as the Church of St. Paul shall stand." . . .

Since the estate of the plaintiff may determine, and since there is no valid limitation over, it follows that there is a possibility of reverter in the original grantor, Clark. This is similar to, though not quite identical with, the possibility of reverter which remains in the grantor of land upon a condition subsequent. The exact nature and incidents of this right need not now be discussed, but it represents whatever is not conveyed by the deed, and it is the possibility that the land may revert to the grantor or his heirs when the granted estate determines. . . .

Clark's possibility of reverter is not invalid for remoteness. It has been expressly held by this court, that such possibility of reverter upon breach of a condition subsequent is not within the rule against perpetuities. If there is any distinction in this respect between such possibility of reverter and that which arises upon the determination of a qualified fee, it would seem to be in favor of the latter. But they should be governed by the same rule. If one is not held void for remoteness, the other should not be. The very many cases cited in Gray, Rule against Perpetuities, §§305-312, show conclusively that the general understanding of courts and of the profession in America has been that the rule as to remoteness does not apply; though the learned author thinks this view erroneous in principle.

The modern rule applies to personal property as well as realty, and to both legal and equitable interests. It is the chief judicial weapon in imposing a limit on the dead hand in the transmission of tangible and intangible wealth. Since the rule now operates with almost mathematical precision, it can be mastered by learning a series of rules:

1. *Interests Affected by the Rule*

The rule does not restrict all interests that wait for the future to become possessory. Vested future interests are safe and, contrary to expectation, in the United States the rule does not apply to possibilities of reverter and powers of termination, regardless of how remote possession may be. The interests most vulnerable to the rule are contingent remainders and executory interests.

All vested future interests satisfy the rule, even if not vested in possession. That is, the person entitled to it need not have a right to the immediate possession of land, or to immediate income from a fund. Thus, in this context the distinction between a vested remainder subject to divestment and a contingent remainder is quite important; fortunes can turn on mere differences in phrasing. The rule is satisfied if it "vests in interest": In a gift to "B for life, remainder to the children of C for their lives, remainder to D and his heirs," all the interests satisfy the rule. D's interest may not ripen into possession until after the life of a child of C not born at the time the instrument speaks, but D's interest is a remainder to an ascertained person, and is vested at all times.

However, it should be noted that not only must the two usual conditions for a vested remainder be satisfied — the remainderman must be ascertained and the interest ready to take effect — but also the size of the benefit must be known. In other words, the possibility that the amount of the property given may vary according to future events is for the purposes of the rule treated as a contingency, and the gift fails for remoteness if the contingency might happen outside the perpetuity period. Thus, in the case of a gift to a class, if the interest of a single member of the class might possibly vest beyond the period, the whole gift fails, even for those members of the class who have satisfied any required contingency. If personalty is given "to A for life and after her death to be equally divided between all her children who shall attain the age of 25," the remainder is void even for children who are lives-in-being at the time of the gift.

Executory interests are not "vested" until they become possessory. In a conveyance "to B for life and then, forty years after B's life estate, to C and his heirs," the gift to C fails.

There is an exception to the rule in favor of charities. Where a gift is made to A charity with a gift over to B charity on remote contingency, both gifts are valid. But were either gift not to charity, the second gift would fail.

2. The Perpetuity Period

The permissible period may be extended to include all of the following: (a) lives-in-being, (b) periods of gestation, and (c) 21 years.

For a person to be a life-in-being for the purposes of the rule, it is unnecessary that he should receive any benefit from the gift, or that he be in any way associated with the beneficiary. Nor is there any restriction on the number of lives selected, provided it is reasonably possible to ascertain who they are, "for let the lives be never so many, there must be a survivor, and so it is but the length of that life." For example, a gift by a testator to such of his descendants as are living 20 years after the death of the last survivor of all the lineal descendants of Queen Victoria living at the testator's death has been held valid.

The measuring lives need not be designated as such in the instrument. Thus, a gift by will "to those of my grandchildren who attain the age of 21" is valid, since the children of the testator can be taken as lives-in-being; they are all bound to have been born by the time of the testator's death, and the gift to grandchildren presupposes the existence of children.

3. The Certainty of Vesting

There is no "wait and see" with regard to the rule. A future interest is void unless it is absolutely certain at the outset that it must vest within the permitted period. Thus, a deed must be considered at the time when it is delivered, while a will must be considered at the moment of the testator's death. If at the relevant moment there is the slightest possibility that the perpetuity period may be exceeded, the limitation is void *ab initio*, even if it is most improbable that this fact will happen and even if, as events turn out, it in fact does not. Thus, a gift "to the first son of A to become a lawyer" is void if A is alive, no matter how old A may be and even if he has a son who is due to be called to the Bar the next day.

Examples

Almost any contingency is permitted if it must become certain (or not) during lives-in-being when the interest is created plus 21 years.

Thus:

1. A *devises Blackacre to B and his heirs but if B, during his lifetime, shall convey or attempt to convey Blackacre, then to C and his heirs.*

Good.

But:

2. A *devises Blackacre to B Church so long as the church uses Blackacre as a parsonage, but if B Church ceases to do so, to C and his heirs.*

The contingency is invalid because it might vest later than lives-in-being plus 21 years.

Exceptions:

3. Reversion: A *devises Blackacre to B Church so long as the church uses Blackacre as a parsonage.*

The limitation is valid, and if the church violates the condition, the property reverts to the estate of A.

4. Remainder in another charity: Same as (3), and if a violation, to the ASPCA.

Good.

Lives-in-being *when the interest is created:*

5. A *devises a fund to such of my grandchildren who shall live to be 21.*

At A's death, his children are known (the rule has a 9-month exception for A's unborn children), so we will know who A's grandchildren are during the lives of A's children; and within those lives plus 21 years we will know which grandchildren survive to 21. Thus this is the longest contingency that can be created.

But:

6. *During his lifetime, A establishes a trust to go to such of his grandchildren who may reach the age of 21.*

The trust fails, because *A* might have more children.

Or:

7. Same as (5) except the age is 25 instead of 21.

Too long by four years.

An interest vests where it stands in succession to prior interests which are less than a fee simple:

8. *A devises Blackacre to B in fee tail male, and then to C in fee simple.*

Good, even though *C* may not take for hundreds of years, because *C's* fee simple remainder is *vested* from the outset.

Problems

not valid

1. To First Universalist Church so long as used to pursue the principles of 1803, and when diverted to Whipple, Cady, Arnold, Clark, et al. [*First Universalist, supra.*]

valid

2. To my grandchildren who reach the age of 21. (Will or *inter vivos* conveyance?)   *children - exec int.   contingrem. - eldest daughter of C is live.*

3. By will to my grandchildren for their lives, then in fee simple to the eldest daughter of *C* who survives *C*. — *Invalid*

4. To *A* and his heirs, but if the big house is torn down, to the Red Cross. Compare: To *A* and his heirs, but if the big house is torn down during the life of the last surviving descendent of Queen Victoria alive now or for 21 years thereafter, to the Red Cross.   *— invalid*

5. In 1962 to Gary Eisenmann, for and during the natural lifetime of the grantor herein or until December 1, 1990, whichever later occurs, then to. . . . [Eisenmann v. Eisenmann, 52 Ohio Misc. 119, 370 N.E.2d 788 (1977).]   *?*

6. To my friend *A* to whom I am gratified for the care she has given my horses, but only for so long as my horses who survive shall continue to receive proper care, and then. . . . *fi. invalidated under rule*   *invalid – can't use rule*

7. To my wife for life, then to my niece Mary Hall and the issue of her body lawfully begotten and to be begotten, and in default of such issue to the daughters then living of my kinsman John Jee and his wife Elizabeth Jee. [Jee v. Audley, *infra.*]   *invalid*

8. Life estate to son Edward and daughter Delana, remainder in fee simple to granddaughter Margaret May; if my children have other heirs of their bodies surviving them, these heirs shall share equally with Margaret May; if Margaret May or other grandchildren survive both my children and leave no heirs of her or their body, then to my brothers and sisters then living and to the representatives of those not living, and to Almeda Goyscan, in equal shares. [Merchants Bank v. Curtis, *infra;* "wait and see."]   *invalid?*

C. "REMORSELESS APPLICATION"

◆ JEE v. AUDLEY
1 Cox 324, 29 Eng. Rep. 1186 (Ch. 1787)

Edward Audley, by his will, bequeathed as follows,

> Also my will is that £1,000 shall be placed out at interest during the life of my wife, which interest I give her during her life, and at her death I give the said £1,000 unto my niece Mary Hall and the issue of her body lawfully begotten, and to be begotten, and in default of such issue I give the said £1,000 to be equally divided between the daughters then living of my kinsman John Jee and his wife Elizabeth Jee. . . .

It appeared that John Jee and Elizabeth Jee were living at the time of the death of the testator, had four daughters and no son, and were of a very advanced age. Mary Hall was unmarried and of the age of about 40; the wife was dead. The present bill was filed by the four daughters of John and Elizabeth Jee to have the £1000 secured for their benefit upon the event of the said Mary Hall dying without leaving children. And the question was, [whether the limitation to the daughters of John and Elizabeth Jee was not void as being too remote; and to prove it so, it was said that this was to take effect on a general failure of issue of Mary Hall; and though it was to the daughters of John and Elizabeth Jee, yet it was not confined to the daughters living at the death of the testator, and consequently it might extend to after-born daughters, in which case it would not be within the limit of a life or lives in being and 21 years afterwards, beyond which time an executory devise is void.

On the other side it was said, that though the late cases had decided that on a gift to children generally, such children as should be living at the time of the distribution of the fund should be let in, yet it would be very hard to adhere to such a rule of construction so rigidly, as to defeat the evident intention of the testator in this case, especially as there was no real possibility of John and Elizabeth Jee having children after the testator's death, they being then 70 years old; that if there were two ways of construing words, that should be adopted which would give effect to the disposition made by the testator; that the cases, which had decided that after-born children should take, proceeded on the implied intention of the testator, and never meant to give an effect to words which would totally defeat such intention.

Master of the Rolls [Sir Lloyd Kenyon]. Several cases determined by Lord Northington, Lord Camden, and the present Chancellor, have settled that children born after the death of the testator shall take a share in these cases; the difference is, where there is an immediate devise, and where there is an interest in remainder; in the former case the children living at the testator's death only shall take; in the latter those who are

living at the time the interest vests in possession; and this being now a
settled principle, I shall not strain to serve an intention at the expense of
removing the landmarks of the law; it is of infinite importance to abide
by decided cases, and perhaps more so on this subject than any other.
The general principles which apply to this case are not disputed: the
limitations of personal estate are void, unless they necessarily vest, if at
all, within a life or lives in being and 21 years or 9 or 10 months afterwards. This has been sanctioned by the opinion of judges of all times,
from the time of the Duke of Norfolk's case to the present: it is grown
reverend by age, and is not now to be broken in upon; I am desired to do
in this case something which I do not feel myself at liberty to do, namely
to suppose it impossible for persons in so advanced an age as John and
Elizabeth Jee to have children; but if this can be done in one case it may
in another, and it is a very dangerous experiment, and introductive of
the greatest inconvenience to give a latitude to such sort of conjecture.
Another thing pressed upon me, is to decide on the events which have
happened; but I cannot do this without overturning very many cases.
The single question before me is, not whether the limitation is good in
the events which have happened, but whether it was good in its creation; and if it were not, I cannot make it so. Then must this limitation, if
at all, necessarily take place within the limits prescribed by law? The
words are "in default of such issue I give the said £1,000 to be equally
divided between the daughters then living of John Jee and Elizabeth his
wife." If it had been to "daughters now living," or "who should be
living at the time of my death," it would have been very good; but as it
stands, this limitation may take in after-born daughters; this point is
clearly settled by Ellison v. Airey, and the effect of law on such limitation cannot make any difference in construing such intention. If then
this will extended to after-born daughters, is it within the rules of law?
Most certainly not, because John and Elizabeth Jee might have children
born 10 years after the testator's death, and then Mary Hall might die
without issue 50 years afterwards; in which case it would evidently
transgress the rules prescribed. I am of opinion therefore, though the
testator might possibly mean to restrain the limitation to the children
who should be living at the time of the death, I cannot, consistently with
decided cases, construe it in such restrained sense, but must intend it to
take in after-born children. This therefore not being within the rules of
law, and as I cannot judge upon subsequent events, I think the limitation void. Therefore dismiss the bill, but without costs.

Notes

1. Testatrix bequeathed money to A for life, and then to such of A's
grandchildren "living at my death or born within five years therefrom
who shall attain the age of 21." The arrangement would violate the Rule

against Perpetuities only if *A* could have a child after *T*'s death, who would become a parent within 5 years. An English court found that the bequest did not violate the rule because the Age of Marriage Act said that marriages before the age of 16 "shall be void," and so the child in question "could not lawfully be married and have lawful children." Banks v. Gaite, [1949] 1 All E.R. 459 (Ch. D.).

2. "In the United States, statistics covering 20 million births during the 10 years from 1923 to 1932 showed that no children were born to women over 55, and only 0.0001 percent of children to women over 50. In England, statistics covering 83,000 births during 1946 showed that no children were born to women over 55 and only two children to women over 50." Morris & Leach, The Rule against Perpetuities 82 n.20 (2d ed. 1962).

3. Lucas v. Hamm, 56 Cal. 2d 583, 364 P.2d 685, 15 Cal. Rptr. 821 (1961), held that it is not negligence for a lawyer to err in applying the Rule against Perpetuities, because even lawyers of ordinary skill and diligence find the rule a "technicality-ridden legal nightmare."

Justice R.E. Megarry wrote:

> An Englishman's comment on [Lucas v. Hamm] must perforce observe a proper restraint. Doubtless the Supreme Court of California is the best judge of the standard of competence which is to be expected of California lawyers of ordinary skill and capacity. . . . The standard of competence in California . . . seems to be that it is not negligent for lawyers to draft wills knowing little or nothing of the rule against perpetuities, and without consulting anyone skilled in the rule. . . . [I]t is to be hoped that on the standard of professional competence [Lucas v. Hamm] will prove to be a slur on the profession which, like the mule, will display neither pride of ancestry nor hope of posterity. [81 L.Q. Rev. 481 (1965).]

If the lawyer does commit malpractice in failing to achieve the testamentary intentions of his client, Heyer v. Flaig, 70 Cal. 2d 223, 449 P.2d 161, 74 Cal. Rptr. 225 (1969), holds that the statute of limitations starts to run from the date of the testator's death, which of course can be long after the lawyer's negligent acts occurred.

4. A variant on the Rule against Perpetuities is the Rule against Accumulations, designed to prevent a settlor from establishing a fund that will accumulate for an exceedingly long period. In Thellusson v. Woodford, 4 Ves. 227, 31 Eng. Rep. 117 (1798), 11 Ves. 112, 32 Eng. Rep. 1030 (1805), the chancellor promulgated a rule permitting a budding patriarch to accumulate a corpus only for lives-in-being plus 21 years. American courts have generally been more lenient, especially when the beneficiary is a charity. See Holdeen v. Ratterree, 270 F.2d 701 (2d Cir. 1959):

> Plaintiff, a lawyer by profession, . . . has been intensely interested in the effect of accumulation of income and the compound interest table. His

writings reflect this interest in his books, "Cult of the Clan" and "Futurite Cult." He is somewhat more practical than the economist who would speculate on the present value of one cent invested at the time of Moses. A sentence from one of his books advises that one cent today invested at four percent interest for one thousand years will become one thousand trillion dollars. Considering the fact that the money invested in only one of the trusts involved if kept invested at compound interest for one thousand years "would amount to all of the total value of the world," the trial court's wonderment as to how "two of them [the trusts] could be carried out when there is only one world" can easily be understood and shared even in this day of space exploration. Possibly other worlds will have to be discovered for plaintiff's future investments. Although plaintiff modeled his plan somewhat after that of the thrifty Benjamin Franklin who limited himself to two hundred years (1790-1990), he was not too sanguine that his trusts would not be interfered with by the courts before the day of final accounting arrived. Indeed, such an accounting would be a monumental task because an actuary testified that the corpus of the five trusts for one thousand years alone would be "nine million, nine hundred eighty-eight thousand, three hundred and eighty million billions."

5. Regarding the surviving grandchildren of Queen Victoria, the last surviving such — Princess Alice, Countess of Athlone — died in London in 1981, age 97.

6. See In re Kelly, 1932 Irish R. 255:

The remaining question concerns the validity of the following bequest: "I leave one hundred pounds sterling to my executors and trustees for the purpose of expending four pounds sterling on the support of each of my dogs per year, and I direct that my dogs be kept in the old house at Upper Tullaroan aforesaid. Should any balance remain in the hands of my trustees on the death of the last of my dogs I leave same to the Parish Priest for the time being of the Parish of Tullaroan for masses for the repose of my soul and the souls of my parents, brothers and stepfather."

Mr. Michael Comyn, for the plaintiff, contended that both the gift for the support of the dogs and the gift over, which is to take effect on the death of the last of the dogs, are void.

It will be more convenient to deal first with the gift of any possible surplus remaining over on the death of the last of the dogs. Here the question, so far as there can be any question, is strictly one of remoteness. If the lives of the dogs or other animals could be taken into account in reckoning the maximum period of "lives in being and twenty-one years afterwards" any contingent or executory interest might be properly limited, so as only to vest within the lives of specified carp, or tortoises, or other animals that might live for over a hundred years, and for twenty-one years afterwards, which, of course, is absurd. "Lives" means human lives. It was suggested that the last of the dogs could in fact not outlive the testator by more than twenty-one years. I know nothing of that. The Court does not enter into the question of a dog's expectation of life. In point of fact neighbour's dogs and cats are unpleasantly long-lived; but I have no knowledge of their precise expectation of life. Anyway the maximum period is exceeded by the lives even of specified butterflies and twenty-one years afterwards. And even, according to my decision — and, I confess, it displays this weakness on being pressed to a logical conclusion — the expiration of the life of a single butterfly, even without the twenty-one years, would be too remote, despite all the world of poetry that may be thereby destroyed. In Robinson v. Hardcastle, Lord Thurlow defined a perpetuity in these words: "What is a perpetuity, but the extending the estate beyond a life in being, and twenty-one years after?" Of course, by "a life" he means lives; and there can be no doubt that "lives" means lives of human beings, not of animals or trees in California.

D.   MODERN INTERPRETATION AND REFORM

◆ ATCHISON v. CITY OF ENGLEWOOD
170 Colo. 295, 463 P.2d 297 (1969)

Mr. Justice Groves delivered the opinion of the Court.

The plaintiffs in error brought an action against the City of Englewood and Martin-Marietta Corporation as defendants for a determination with respect to plaintiffs' preemptive right to repurchase certain lands. The district court granted defendants' motions for summary judgment on the grounds that the documentary provisions granting the rights to the plaintiffs were void as violative of the rule against perpetuities. We affirm.

In 1948 Mr. and Mrs. Atchison were, and for a number of years had been, the owners of approximately 2500 acres of land in Jefferson County, together with water rights belonging thereto. Englewood desired to acquire the water rights, but had no use for the land. However, the City concluded that it should purchase the land with the water in order to be in a possibly more favorable position when it prosecuted proceedings to change the points of diversion of the water and to change its use from irrigation to municipal purposes. A sale and purchase of the land and water from the plaintiffs to Englewood was arranged. The written documents involved gave the right to Mr. and Mrs. Atchison to repurchase the land (but without any water transferred therefrom in the meantime) upon the same terms and conditions as Englewood might be willing to sell it to a third person. Later Englewood entered into a lease of most of the land (presumably with few or no water rights) and as a part of the lease granted to Martin-Marietta an option to purchase the demised property. Still later Martin-Marietta exercised the option and purchased the land. Under the record existing as a basis for the summary judgment we treat Mr. and Mrs. Atchison as having no knowledge and not being charged with notice of the option rights granted to Martin-Marietta; and that upon obtaining knowledge or being charged with notice they made timely filing of this action. They evinced a desire to purchase the land upon the same terms as the corporation had purchased it.

. . . [U]nder our view the two principal questions presented are: (1) was the preemptive right granted Mr. and Mrs. Atchison personal, i.e., would it die with them and therefore not be violative of the rule against perpetuities; and (2), even if the preemptive right was not personal and would extend more than 21 years beyond the life of a person in being, should it be proscribed by the rule against perpetuities? We have not experienced too much difficulty in concluding that the right was not personal; but, as to the second question, the scales of decision are so evenly balanced that a little weight on either side would weigh it down. . . .

Counsel for plaintiffs argue strenuously that the preemption granted to the "Atchisons" in paragraph 11 of the December agreement and in paragraph 1 of the January agreement was a right which was granted to them personally and would die with them. They also contend that paragraph 13 of the December agreement and paragraph 3 of the January agreement relate to other portions of the agreements, but not to paragraphs 11 and 1, respectively. In other words, they submit, paragraphs 11 and 1 are severable and are things apart. Counsel further urge that stock phrases such as "heirs and assigns" should not be applied to a particular provision of a contract except upon examination of the context and surrounding facts; that these words and those similar thereto should not be applied to the provisions relating to the preemptive right as it is apparent that the parties intended that right to be personal; and that the plaintiffs are entitled to a presumption that the parties intended to have a legal and enforceable preemptive right. . . .

In the December agreement the provision "The terms and provisions hereof shall inure to the benefit of the heirs, legal representatives and assigns of the Atchisons" is definite and unambiguous. . . .

Accordingly, we hold that the preemptive right was not personal.

We now approach the question of whether the rule against perpetuities should be applied to preemptive rights. At the outset the difference between an ordinary option and a preemptive right should be noted. In a typical option the optionee has the absolute right to purchase something for a definite consideration. A preemptive right involves the creation of the privilege to purchase only on the formulation of a desire on the part of the owner to sell; and, in the case here, the holder of the right must purchase for the price at which the owner is willing to sell to a third person.

It will be recalled that there is a difference between the rule against perpetuities and the rule against restraints upon alienation. Both rules have the same fundamental purpose, namely, to keep property freely alienable; or, stated differently, each stems from a general policy which frowns upon the withdrawal of property from commerce. The rule against perpetuities invalidates interests which *vest* too remotely. The rule against restraints upon alienation relates to other unreasonable restraints. For example, *A* conveys land to *B* in fee simple with the provision that if *B* during his lifetime shall convey or attempt to convey it the land shall become the property of *C* in fee simple. This does not violate the rule against perpetuities but is violative of the rule against restraints with the result that *B* obtains a fee simple absolute. An option given to a person, his heirs and assigns, to purchase land for $5,000 with no limiting term is void under the rule against perpetuities. The reason is that, with such an option outstanding the owner dare not place substantial improvements on the land, and the likelihood of anyone purchasing it is remote. The reason for application of the rule against perpetuities to a preemptive right to purchase at an offeror's price acceptable to the owner is not supported by the same reasoning as found in the option example, thus making the case for non-application much more arguable.

The application of the rule to ordinary options is firmly established. However, so far as we are advised this is the first time that there has been before this court the question of application of the rule against perpetuities to a preemptive right to purchase at an offeror's acceptable price. The Restatement of the Law of Property makes no exception of preemptive right under the rule against perpetuities and in the comment following §413 it states, "Preemptive provisions, being analogous to options upon a condition precedent, must comply with the rule against perpetuities in so far as their maximum duration is concerned." . . .

The plaintiffs rely upon Weber v. Texas Co., 83 F.2d 807, *cert. denied,* 299 U.S. 561, and except as later mentioned it supports their position. There the owners of land leased it to Texas Company's assignor for prospecting and drilling for oil and gas. The lease was for a primary term of five years and as long thereafter as either oil or gas is or could be produced from any well on the land. The owners reserved a one-eighth royalty. The lease provided:

"The lessee is hereby given the option of purchasing all or any part of said royalty rights from the lessor at the best bona fide price offered by responsible third parties when and if offered for sale or transfer by lessor."

Texas Company acquired the lessee's interest and brought in a producing well. Prior to completion of the drilling the owners sold a one-fourth interest of their royalty to Weber for $7,000. As soon as Texas Company learned of this they tendered $7,000 for the interest sold. The tender was refused. Texas Company then sued for specific performance. It was held that the preemptive right was valid and enforceable. The

court concluded that when an option simply gives an oil and gas lessee
the prior right to take the lessor's royalty interest at the same price the
lessor could and would secure from another purchaser, there is no restraint of free alienation by the lessor. The option, therefore, according
to the court, should not be objectionable as a perpetuity. . . .

We have held that before us is an inheritable preemptive right without limit as to time. It is in no manner connected with any land owned
by Mr. and Mrs. Atchison. While they reserved one-half of the mineral
rights, this interest can be sold at any time; and following a sale there
will be no land title interest of record to give any clue as to the identity of
future successors in interest to the preemptive right. We feel that at
some point in the infinite time at which Englewood might in the future
conclude to sell the land, ascertaining and locating the owners of the
preemptive right would be an unreasonable task. As a result, there
would be a sufficiently unreasonable restraint upon the transferability of
the property as to justify imposition of the rule against perpetuities. It
may be said that we are stating a rule against alienation and giving it a
label of the rule against perpetuities. Be that as it may, the result is the
same.

It is to be noted that in Weber v. Texas Company, *supra*, the identity
of the owners of interests involved could be ascertained — or at least
with some reasonable investigation discovered — from the record title to
the mineral rights and royalties. Our conclusion might be different here
if the ownership of the preemptive right followed the title to designated
real property; or, if it were restricted to a limited term found to be
reasonable, albeit longer than a life in being plus 21 years. Be that as it
may, we rule merely that a contractual right, granted to A and his heirs
and assigns, unlimited as to time, to purchase land upon the same terms
as the owner could and would sell to a third person, is void.

Notes

1. Plaintiffs and defendants had entered into a written agreement
in which defendants agreed to lease to plaintiffs for a period of ten years
a building to be constructed by defendant. The agreement provided,
"Upon completion of said building, lessor shall forthwith cause a notice
of completion to be recorded, and the term of this lease shall commence
upon the recording of said notice of completion." The court said, without substantial discussion, that it would not apply the Rule against
Perpetuities to the agreement. Wong v. DiGrazia, 60 Cal. 2d 525, 386
P.2d 817, 35 Cal. Rptr. 241 (1963).

2. An indefinite option to buy land, not appurtenant to a lease, has
been characterized as an interest that would become possessory only
upon its exercise and therefore void under the rule. London & South

Western Ry. v. Gomm, [1882] 20 Ch. D. 562. For other points of view see Leach, Perpetuities in a Nutshell, 51 Harv. L. Rev. 638, 660 (1938), and Berg, Long-Term Options and the Rule Against Perpetuities, 37 Calif. L. Rev. 1 (1949).

3. Quarto Mining held the rights to minerals under Litman's land in Monroe County, Ohio, pursuant to a 1906 purchase, along with options to purchase surface land when needed to extract coal. Then Quarto sought to exercise the options and to build an overhead conveyor belt. The court rejected a challenge premised on the rule:

> A bare option to purchase land which is unlimited as to time is void as an impermissible restraint upon alienation, but an option which is appurtenant to a mineral estate and is limited to the necessary and reasonable use of the overlying surface estate for the exercise of mining rights is a presently vested part of the . . . estate, and is not void as a restraint on alienation. [Quarto Mining Co. v. Litman, 42 Ohio St. 2d 73, 326 N.E.2d 676 (1975).]

4. A lease had given the tenant an option to add additional retail space within 90 days of the 5th, 10th, 15th, 20th, or 25th anniversary of the commencement of the lease. When the tenant tried to exercise the option after 15 years, the landlord claimed a violation of the Rule against Perpetuities.

The Colorado Supreme Court said the tenant had been given 5 separate options, and the first 3 were valid. The court also said that the rule does not apply in Colorado to lessee options to buy or extend a lease, but does apply where as here the tenant has an option to take new space. Crossroads Shopping Center v. Montgomery Ward, 646 P.2d 330 (Colo. 1981).

5. Plaintiff and defendant owned contiguous parcels of land in Buffalo. The defendant had given plaintiff, its successors and assigns, an irrevocable option to purchase "all or any part" of a 20-foot srip along the defendant's southerly boundary at a market price to be determined at the time of purchase. Also, the defendant had promised not to build structures or other improvements on the strip during the life of the option. Plaintiff sought specific performance.

The Appellate Division said the option did not illegally suspend the power of alienation, since at any time plaintiff and defendant could have conveyed an absolute fee simple. But the court also said that the option, unlimited in time, violated the rule against remoteness in vesting. It interpreted the New York perpetuities law as including an exemption for long-lasting options. The court declined to modify the option so that it would be valid for a period of 21 years. Buffalo Seminary v. McCarthy, 86 A.D.2d 435, 451 N.Y.S.2d 457 (1982), aff'd mem., 58 N.Y.2d 867, 447 N.E.2d 76, 460 N.Y.S.2d 528 (1983).

6. In *Buffalo Seminary*, the irrevocable option to purchase land that was found to violate New York's Rule against Perpetuities was con-

tained in a deed of sale. Would it make any difference if the option, rather than being included in a deed, had been written into a 60-year timber lease and was exercisable within the period of the lease? The Georgia Supreme Court distinguished between an "option in gross" and an "option appendant" to hold that the rule did not apply to a long-term option contained in a lease. Underlying the court's opinion was the following view.

> The wisdom and legal logic . . . for extending the rule's applicability to a commercial setting is at best questionable. In today's world of complex and sophisticated real estate dealings, it is important that we do not broaden the rule against perpetuities to the point that its effect will be the opposite of its intended purpose. The rule came into being in order to control family property transfers which limited the rights of certain generations to alienate the property. Therefore, the thrust of the rule is to encourage the right of free dealings in real estate interest. To apply the rule to options contained in leases could very well have a reverse effect. Neither lives in being nor twenty-one years has any relevance to the commercial situation. This is particularly true when the holder of the beneficial interest in the property is able to utilize and develop his interest to its fullest, as is the case of a lessee who holds an option to purchase a leasehold. [St. Regis Paper Co. v. Brown, 247 Ga. 361, 276 S.E.2d 24 (1981).]

7. In return for $10, Isaac and Bonnie Prather had granted to Robert and Isabel Robbins "the first right of refusal of purchasing" certain real estate.

The Supreme Court of Washington refused to apply the Rule against Perpetuities to rights of first refusal, saying that unlike an option, such an interest does not allow the buyer to require an unwilling seller to part with the land. Thus, the interference with alienation is "so light that the major policies furthered by freedom of alienation are not infringed. . . ." But the court said that such contracts should be "presumed as intended to last only for a reasonable time." As to what constitutes "a reasonable time," the court said, "each case should be judged on its facts" and ruled that in the instant case, where the sale took place only five years after the first-refusal agreement, the agreement was valid and binding. Robroy Land Co. v. Prather, 95 Wash. 2d 66, 622 P.2d 367 (1980).

◆ MERCHANTS NATIONAL BANK v. CURTIS
98 N.H. 225, 97 A.2d 207 (1953)

. . . Petition, for partition of certain real estate situated at the corner of Elm and Manchester Streets in Manchester. The real estate was sold and a portion of the proceeds of the sale amounting to $32,975.11, together with accumulating interest, is in the hands of the clerk of the Superior Court for distribution in accordance with the ruling of the Supreme Court on certain stipulated facts agreed to by all the parties. On the basis of the stipulated facts, and the exhibits, the Court (Wheeler, C.J.) transferred without ruling the following question of law: "What individuals are entitled to participate in the distribution of the trust moneys deposited with the Clerk of Court, and in what proportions are they entitled to share"?

The petition was originally brought by the plaintiff in March 1914, claiming an undivided two-thirds interest in said real estate, the defendant Delana B. Curtis owning an undivided eleven fifty-fourths interest and the devisees under the will of Margaret A. Harrington a seven fifty-fourths interest. Margaret A. Harrington had previously died in 1902, leaving a will which was duly probated. At her death she owned the undivided seven fifty-fourths interest in this real estate. Under the provisions of her will her only children, a son, Edward Harrington, and a daughter, the abovementioned Delana B. Curtis, received a life estate in this real estate. By clause fourth the remainder was devised "to my Grand Daughter Margaret May Curtis and her heirs forever." The will further provided:

> Fifth: In the event of either of my children having other heirs of their body, surviving them such heir or heirs shall share equally with Margaret May Curtis, and in that event I give, bequeath and devise my estate to them, and their heirs, on the death of my children.
>
> Sixth: If my Grand Daughter Margaret May Curtis or other grand children shall survive both of my children and shall have and leave no heirs of her or their body, then and in that event, I give, bequeath and devise all my estate unto my brothers and sisters then living and to the representatives of those not living, and to my late husband's niece, Almeda S. Goyscan formerly Almeda S. Harrington, in equal shares. . . .

The said Almeda S. Goyscan predeceased the testatrix leaving no issue. The testatrix' son, the said Edward W. Harrington, survived the testatrix and died leaving no issue. The testatrix' daughter, the said Delana B. Curtis, also survived the testatrix and died leaving no children other than her said daughter, Margaret. Margaret was twice married and, at the time of her death without issue, on January 16, 1951, her name was Margaret May Curtis Reynolds Vreeland.

The testatrix, Margaret A. Harrington, had three sisters and three brothers, who were living or who had issue living at the time of her death, namely: Abigail Bond Chandler, Nancy Bond Corliss, Maria Bond Hill, James B. Bond, Jonathan Bond and John R. Bond. All of these brothers and sisters left representatives in interest in this case, with the exception of Nancy Bond Corliss, who died on July 1, 1910, leaving an only child, George W. Corliss, who died unmarried and without issue on September 6, 1922. Accordingly, the parties to this proceeding are the representatives in interest of five brothers and sisters of Margaret A. Harrington, who were living at the death of Margaret May Curtis Reynolds Vreeland on January 16, 1951. The representatives of these brothers and sisters have been stipulated by the parties.

Subsequent to the filing of the petition for partition and before the sale of the real estate, the defendant Delana B. Curtis secured certain deeds from the then living representatives of Abigail Bond Chandler, Maria Bond Hill, James E. Bond and Nancy Bond Corliss, four of the six brothers and sisters of Margaret A. Harrington. These conveyances refer to the sixth clause of the will of Margaret A. Harrington for their title. The later deed from Delana B. Curtis to William E. Quirin, purporting to convey an undivided one-third interest in the premises, excepted and reserved whatever title the heirs of Jonathan Bond and John Bond had in the premises by virtue of the will of Margaret A. Harrington.

Pursuant to the petition for partition the premises were sold at public auction for $297,500. The plaintiff bank was the purchaser and as owner of an undivided two-thirds interest in the premises sold, it was required to pay only one-third of the purchase price, $99,166.67, which was deposited with the clerk of court. In accordance with the prayer in the petition of the said William E. Quirin and on the strength of the conveyances offered in support of his petition, the Court decreed in October, 1914, that of the fund eleven-eighteenths thereof ($60,601.85) represented the individual interest of Delana B. Curtis and that it should be paid to Quirin without prejudice to further rights claimed by the said William E. Quirin in seven-eighteenths of this fund ($38,564.82) said latter sum representing the interest of the . . . Harrington estate.

This fund of approximately $38,000 was thereafter administered by a trustee appointed by the court to pay the income to William E. Quirin as he claimed to be entitled to such income until the death of Margaret May Curtis Reynolds (Vreeland). The trustee continued to pay the income thereof to William E. Quirin and his assignees until the death of Margaret Vreeland on January 16, 1951. On September 2, 1924, William E. Quirin assigned all his interest in the trust fund to his wife Grace. . .

KENISON, Chief Justice. The Rule against Perpetuities, hereinafter called the rule, prevails in this state, but it has never been "remorselessly applied" as advocated by Gray in "The Rule against Perpetuities" (4th ed.) §629. The genesis of the modified rule in New Hampshire began in 1891 when a gift of a remainder interest to grandchildren reaching forty years of age, which offended the rule, was cut down to a gift to grandchildren reaching twenty-one years of age so as to not offend the rule. This decision was bitterly assailed by Gray in his treatise (appendix G) since he thought it was a dangerous thing to tamper with this ancient English rule "which is concatenated with almost mathematical precision." . . .

The rationale of the case was that, wherever possible, a will should be construed to carry out the primary intent to accomplish a legal testamentary disposition even though the will may have inadvertently exposed a secondary intent to accomplish the testamentary disposition in an ineffective manner. That rationale has been applied in many recent will cases that have not involved the rule itself. . . . The rule is a technical one, difficult of application and is often enforced to frustrate testamentary intent although the policy of the rule may not require such enforcement in a particular case. It is not surprising, therefore, that there has been an increasing tendency to avoid the application of the rule by various judicial techniques. There is a constructional preference for considering interests vested rather than contingent. "The public interest in keeping *the destructive force of the rule against perpetuities within reasonable limits* is a considerable present factor supporting the public interest in that construction which accomplishes the earlier vesting." 3 Restatement, Property, §243 comment i. If a gift is made upon alternative contingencies, one of which might be remote, while the other is not, the gift is valid where the second contingency actually happens. This doctrine is used to prevent the application of the rule in many cases. Annotation 64 A.L.R. 1077. "Essentially this represents a revulsion against the rule requiring absolute certainty of vesting as viewed from the creation of the interest. . . . Courts have a strong tendency to 'wait and see' wherever possible." 6 American Law of Property (1952) §24.54. These techniques have the salutary effect of avoiding the punitive and technical aspects of the rule but at the same time confirming the policy and purpose of the rule within reasonable limits.

Clause sixth of the will is capable of at least two possible constructions. The first construction is that clause sixth created two contingencies upon which it would take effect: one to occur, if at all, on the death of Margaret May Curtis; the other to occur, if at all, on the death of unborn grandchildren. Since the first contingency actually occurred and is within the period of perpetuities, the gift may be considered valid. Under this construction the event occurs at the death of Margaret May Curtis, a life in being, and clause sixth would not be considered violative of the rule.

The second possible construction of this sixth clause is the one urged by the Bean-Quirin interests. They argue that the will gives the brothers and sisters an executory interest upon a single contingency which may occur at the death of as yet unborn grandchildren. While this is not the only construction that the clause is susceptible of, it is not a labored one. There is no doubt that, if there had been another grandchild who died after Margaret May Curtis without leaving heirs of his body, this event would have occurred beyond the period allowed by the rule against perpetuities.

Assuming this second construction to be permissible, we come to the crucial question whether we are justified in deciding the perpetuities issue on the facts which actually occurred rather than on facts that might have happened viewed as of the death of the testator. There is little case authority for deciding upon facts occurring after the testator's death in a case such as the one before us. However, recognized modern commentators present convincing arguments for doing so. . . . There is no precedent in this state that compels us to close our eyes to facts occurring after the death of the testator.

In the present case we are called on to determine the validity of a clause of a will that did not in fact tie up property beyond the permissible limit of lives in being plus twenty-one years. There is no logical justification for deciding the problem as of the date of the death of the testator on facts that might have happened rather than the facts which actually happened. It is difficult to see how the public welfare is threatened by a vesting that might have been postponed beyond the period of perpetuities but actually was not. . . .

At the death of the survivor of the life tenants, Edward Harrington and Delana B. Curtis, both of whom were lives in being at testatrix' death, it became certain that no grandchildren of the testatrix would be born after her death. This in turn made it certain that the gift in clause sixth of the will would in fact vest at the death of Margaret May Curtis Reynolds Vreeland, also a life in being at testatrix' death. Consistent with the principles above stated, the facts existing at the death of the two life tenants are taken into consideration in applying the rule.

We therefore conclude that clause sixth does not violate the rule against perpetuities. The individuals who are entitled to participate in the distribution of the trust moneys and the extent of their interests are to be determined under this clause.

Since Almeda S. Goyscan predeceased the testatrix leaving no issue and since the testatrix' sister, Nancy Bond Corliss and her only child George died without issue before the death of Margaret, the division is to be made among the representatives in interest of five brothers and sisters of the testatrix as stated in In re Harrington's Estate, 97 N.H. 184, 187.

The brother Jonathan is represented by two grandchildren whose interests are equal. Similarly the brother John is represented by two grandchildren whose interests are likewise equal. The interests of these representatives of the two brothers are unaffected by any conveyances. Consequently, the representatives of each brother share equally in one-fifth of the fund.

The sister Maria is survived by three grandchildren, all children of George E. Hill, who conveyed his interest in 1914, but predeceased Margaret. Similarly the brother James B. is survived by two grandchildren, both children of Arthur J., who conveyed his interest in 1914, but predeceased Margaret.

The sister Abigail is survived by three children and a granddaughter representing a deceased child all of whom conveyed their interests in 1914, the granddaughter's interest being conveyed by a guardian's deed.

While it was the common law rule that future contingent interests were not alienable, this is not the majority rule today. More recent cases in this state indicate the growing tendency to uphold conveyances of unvested rights. Accordingly it is held that the deeds given in 1914 were effective to convey whatever interests the grantors then had, which interests were contingent upon the grantors surviving Margaret. Since those who were the representatives of the sister Abigail in 1914, all survived Margaret, the interests conveyed by their deeds belonged at the time of vesting to the successors of the grantee, now the Quirin and Bean interests. These interests are entitled to one-fifth of the fund. On the other hand since the children of the sister Maria and the brother James B. who conveyed in 1914, predeceased Margaret, no interests vested in them and Quirin and Bean, the successors of the grantee, took nothing from them. The representatives of this brother and sister living at the death of Margaret take under clause sixth of the will. The three representatives of Maria are each entitled to one-fifteenth of the fund and the two representatives of James B. are each entitled to one-tenth.

The Quirin and Bean one-fifth part of the fund is to be divided between them in accordance with the ancillary stipulation which they filed.

Case discharged.

All concurred.

The American Law Institute has, after heated debate, adopted the wait-and-see approach to the Rule against Perpetuities in statutory form by slightly amending Gray's statement of the rule: "[A] donative transfer of an interest in property fails, if the interest does not vest within the period of the rule against perpetuities." Restatement (Second) of Property — Donative Transfers §1.4 (1983).

Some states have adopted the Restatement (Second)'s statutory approach. See Va. Code §55-13.3A (1983 Cum. Supp.); Act of Apr. 22, 1983, S.F. 433, 1983 Iowa Leg. Serv. 90 (West) (to be codified at Iowa Code §558.68). Pennsylvania was the first state to pass a wait-and-see statute. See 20 Pa. Cons. Stat. Ann. §6104(b) (Purdon 1975). For more discussion of the Pennsylvania approach, see In re Estate of Pearson, *infra*.

What effect should a legislative adoption of the wait-and-see approach have on judicial interpretation of a state's common law Rule against Perpetuities? Compare Connecticut Bank & Trust Co. v. Brody, 174 Conn. 616, 392 A.2d 445 (1978) ("[t]he so-called 'wait and see' or 'second look' doctrine . . . is not the common-law rule in Connecticut," despite the legislative adoption of such a statute after the document in question was executed), with Warner v. Whitman, 353 Mass. 468, 233 N.E.2d 14 (1968) ("Although the [Massachusetts wait-and-see] statute operates prospectively, the Legislature has clearly expressed the policy of the Commonwealth and we feel that this court is justified in applying that policy to the provision under consideration.").

For an excellent discussion of all the issues raised by wait-and-see legislation, see Maudsley, Perpetuities: Reforming the Common Law Rule — How to Wait and See, 60 Cornell L. Rev. 355 (1975), and Fetters, Perpetuities: The Wait-and-See Disaster, 60 Cornell L. Rev. 380 (1975). See also American Law Institute Proceedings 1978, at 222-278, 280-307 (1979); id. 1979, at 424-81 (1980).

◆ IN RE ESTATE OF PEARSON
442 Pa. 172, 275 A.2d 336 (1971)

JONES, Justice. Robert Pearson [testator] died on July 27, 1967, leaving a holographic instrument dated January 7, 1958, and entitled "Will and Testimony" [will], which was admitted to probate and letters of administration c. t. a. were granted to Dauphin Deposit Trust Company [administrator]. Testator, a childless widower, was survived by six brothers and sisters, thirteen nephews and nieces and twenty-nine grandnephews and grandnieces.

The controversial portions of the will prompting these appeals are:

[2] It is the hope and prayer, that my estate, be placed in trust for the benefit of the legal heirs, entitled to succeed to my estate.

[3] It is the further instruction that the proceeds of my estate be placed in a Trust Fund, under the management of a reliable Agency or Banking Firm, and administered throughout the life and period of the Estate, as long as there are living legal heirs. The heirs or beneficiary to share the income from the Trust Fund.

[4] The rate or partition shall be apportioned according to the number of living nephews and neices [sic], and thereafter equally proportioned to the surviving heirs. There shall be an exception provided in the aforestated declaration, in the event of special hardships. The first apportionment of the income from the Trust Fund shall accrue to the benefit of the brothers and sisters, during their life.

[7] When the Trust Fund has fulfilled its obligation to the heirs, and thereby spent its usefulness of the legal requirements, the estate shall be awarded to benevolent organizations, educational Institutions, and Charities [hereinafter collectively termed "Charities"].

The administrator filed its first and partial account and a petition for proposed distribution wherein it posed questions to be determined by the auditing judge and its suggested interpretation of testator's intent. Thereafter, exceptions to the proposed distribution were advanced by the parties to these appeals. In its order, accompanied by an opinion, the court below rendered the following interpretation of testator's will: (1) testator created a valid trust; (2) the income from the trust fund is to be distributed among those of the testator's brothers and sisters who had children surviving at the time of testator's death with each share to be determined according to their respective number of said children; (3) upon the respective deaths of testator's brothers and sisters, their shares of income are to be paid in equal proportion to their children for their lives or to the heirs of any deceased child and so forth to testator's heirs ad infinitum; and (4) testator intended that, upon the death of his last collateral descendant, the corpus of the trust should be paid to charities. However, applying the Rule Against Perpetuities *at the time of testator's death*, the lower court voided the gifts to descendants after nephews and nieces as well as the gifts to charities and ordered a distribution of the corpus of the trust under the laws of intestate succession upon the death of testator's last surviving nephew or niece.

Initially we must determine whether the testator intended to create a trust, and, specifically, whether the possibly precatory quality of the words "hope and prayer" in paragraph two renders the trust invalid because of the lack of enforceable duties. . . .

An examination of paragraphs three, four and seven reveals an elaborate, albeit confusing, scheme of distribution imposing very definite duties on the trustee and convinces us of the propriety of the conclusion of the court below that a valid trust was *created*. . . .

In the case at bar, only the brothers and sisters could be "heirs" under the Intestate Act of 1947 since *all* testator's brothers and sisters have survived him and they could take to the exclusion of all later descendants.

However, to apply this statutory rule of interpretation would, in our view, ignore the plain language of paragraph four which demonstrates an intent to provide for the nephews and nieces as well as their issue. In the light of the language employed . . . we do not believe testator intended to limit participation in the estate to the brothers and sisters alone.

Further construing testator's intent, we must next determine whether testator intended *all* or *some* or *none* of his brothers and sisters to have a life estate in the income produced by the corpus. This jumble of theories is made possible by the nettlesome fourth paragraph wherein testator provided for the apportionment of income "according to the number of living nephews and neices [*sic*]." From this language the appellees are able to argue that the primary object of testator's bounty was his nieces and nephews with only a secondary interest in their parent's well-being, especially as all testator's brothers and sisters were advanced in years. Thus, appellees' argument, accepted by the lower court, is that only those brothers and sisters *with children* are entitled to share and that appellant Clara Leonard is excluded as she is childless. The guardian and trustee *ad litem*, one of the appellants, makes a more radical interpretation of this language and proposes that *no* brother or sister is entitled to share in the estate while other appellants suggest that *all* brothers and sisters are to share equally.

Because the testator directed in paragraph four that "the *first* apportionment of the income from the Trust Fund shall accrue to the benefit of the brothers and sisters," (emphasis added) we deem the position of the guardian to be untenable. However, owing to the troublesome and ambiguous first sentence of paragraph four, any further interpretation of testator's intent can only be accomplished by resort to the canons of construction.

Throughout the will testator referred to his "heirs" or "the brothers and sisters" without ever intimating the exclusion of appellant Clara Leonard. Had this result been intended, a more direct method than this intricate, euphemistic scheme could have been employed. Moreover, this Court has created both a presumption and a canon of construction that an heir is not to be disinherited except by plain words or necessary implication. In this vein we are not persuaded by the initial placative conclusion of the lower court that by the testator's appointment of appellant Clara Leonard as "first administratrix" he essentially "include[d] her in his will . . . by entitling her to fees and commissions directly from the estate." To accept this reasoning would ignore the basic concept that the commission payable to a personal representative is purely a *fee for services performed* and does not constitute a legacy in any sense of the word — the amount of the commission must be commensurate with the services actually performed by the personal representative. . . . We are convinced that testator did not intend to disinherit his sister, Clara Leonard, and did not intend that she be the recipient of his bounty only by receiving a commission as a personal representative. . . . In our view, a more accurate exposition of testator's scheme is achieved if the last sentence of paragraph four is placed first, which would make the fourth paragraph read as follows:

> The first apportionment of the income from the Trust Fund shall accrue to the benefit of the brothers and sisters, during their life. The rate or partition shall [then] be apportioned according to the number of living nephews and nieces, and thereafter equally proportioned to the surviving heirs. There shall be an exception provided in the aforesaid declaration, in the event of special hardships.

This rearrangement accords with our previous interpretation of testator's intent to be that *all* the brothers and sisters should share equally, or per capita, in the first life estates of income and that testator's "partition" language indicates an intent that the nieces and nephews, the recipients of the second life estates, should also share per capita as representatives of their parents. However, as testator has directed that income "shall accrue to the benefit of the brothers and sisters, during their life," we believe that *no* nephew or niece will take until the death of *the last surviving brother or sister* and not immediately upon the death of his or her parent. Lastly, we conclude from testator's language in paragraphs three ("Trust Fund . . . [to be] administered throughout the life and period of the Estate") and four ("thereafter *equally* apportioned to the surviving heirs") that testator intended class gifts of successive life estates, per capita, to his collateral descendants *ad infinitum*. Thereafter, and only then, a gift over of the remainder was intended for the charities.

At this stage we are squarely confronted, for the first time, with the controversial "wait and see" version of the Rule Against Perpetuities. So much has been already written on the history and development of this subject that any further discussion would be unduly repetitious. Nonetheless, the statute cannot be understood and applied without reference to the classic statement of the common law Rule Against Perpetuities as set forth in Gray, The Rule Against Perpetuities, §201 (4th ed. 1942) (hereinafter "Gray"): "No interest is good unless it must vest, if at all, not later than twenty-one years after some life in being at the creation of the interest." The relevant portions of the statute provide:

Rule against perpetuities

(a) General. No interest shall be void as a perpetuity except as herein provided.
(b) Void interest — exceptions. Upon the expiration of the period allowed by the common law rule against perpetuities as measured by actual rather than possible events any interest not then vested and any interest to members of a class the membership of which is then subject to increase shall be void. This subsection shall not apply to:
(1) Interest exempt at common law. Interests which would not have been subject to the common law rule against perpetuities.

Estates Act of 1947, Act of April 24, 1947, P.L. 100, §4, 20 P.S. §301.4. . . .

The court below, in derogation of the "wait and see" statute, proceeded to a determination of the legality of all the future interests *upon testator's death*. The lower court's rationale was the necessity to pass on the eligibility of the charities to take under the will since the extent of their taking will affect the tax liability of the estate. . . .

Although its underlying premise is incorrect, the opinion of the court below effectively mirroring the common law's emphasis on possibilities at the beginning of the period rather than actualities at the end of the period, provides us with an opportunity to contrast the common law and statutory Rule Against Perpetuities. As correctly noted by the lower court, the respective interests devised and bequeathed to testator's brothers and sisters and nephews and nieces must necessarily vest within the period provided by the Rule Against Perpetuities and are valid: (1) the brothers and sisters because the previous death of testator's parents ensures that testator can have no other brothers and sisters; and (2) the nephews and nieces because no other nephews and nieces can be born after the death of the last surviving brother or sister, and the interest of the nephews and nieces must vest, if not immediately, within the period enunciated by the Rule Against Perpetuities. The thought implicit in this rationale is that only the brothers and sisters could qualify as measuring lives since the prior demise of their parents precludes the possibility of a "fertile octogenarian" adding yet another member to the class of brothers and sisters. Leach, Perpetuities in a Nutshell, 51 Harv. L. Rev. 638, 643-44 (1938); see, Jee v. Audley, 1 Cox 324, 29 Eng. Rep. 690 (1787). However, under the common law rule, the nephews and nieces could not be measuring lives since there was a *possibility* of "fertile octogenarian" parents (brothers and sisters) giving birth to an additional nephew and/or niece after testator's death. Thus, any interest to follow the interest of the nephews and nieces, including the remainder over to the charities, if contingent, would fall victim to the Rule Against Perpetuities. It is toward the prevention of such results that the General Assembly enacted the "wait and see" version of the Rule Against Perpetuities. In our view, three possible situations could occur by waiting and seeing.

First, if no additional nephews and nieces are born, not only do the brothers and sisters qualify as measuring lives *but also* the six nephews and nieces. Thus, the interest given to the grandnephews and grandnieces must necessarily vest within twenty-one years following the death of the last surviving nephew or niece since membership in the class of grandnephews and grandnieces could not, thereafter, increase. The gift to the charities, if contingent, however, would be valid only if all the grandnephews and grandnieces should produce no offspring.

Secondly, if no additional nephews and nieces *and* grandnephews and grandnieces are born, not only do the brothers and sisters *and* nieces and nephews qualify as measuring lives *but also* the twenty-nine grandnephews and grandnieces. In this situation, the interest to great-grandnephews and great-grandnieces would be valid since that interest must necessarily vest within twenty-one years after the death of the last surviving grandnephew or grandniece. As before, the gift to charities, if contingent, would be invalidated if any of the great-grandnephews or great-grandnieces should produce offspring.

③ Thirdly, if any of the brothers and sisters should prove to be "fertile octogenarians," then the common law's stress on *possibilities* coincides with the statute's emphasis on *actualities* and our earlier discussion of the opinion of the court below controls.

Since which of the three situations will eventuate is unpredictable, it is necessary that the "wait and see" rule be applied. In failing to do so, the court below fell in error.

④ Finally we reach the fourth level of discussion: if any interest be found violative of the Rule Against Perpetuities, what disposition will be made of the corpus? It was the theory of the lower court that the intended distribution of trust income after the extinction of testator's nephews and nieces, along with the gift over in remainder to the charities, violated the Rule Against Perpetuities and that, upon the death of the last surviving nephew or niece, the corpus would pass by intestacy. Again the court below ignored the Estates Act of 1947. Section 5(c) of that Act provides: "Other void interests. Any other void interest shall vest in the person or persons entitled to the income at the expiration of the period described in section 4(b) ('Wait and see')."

Moreover, if the charitable remainder is vested, that interest is valid and Section 5(a) would then control: "Valid interests following void interests. A valid interest following a void interest in income shall be accelerated to the termination date of the last preceding valid interest."

Since we cannot now determine with certainty what interests do not violate the Rule Against Perpetuities, we cannot determine this issue except to note that the court below's conclusion was erroneous in this respect.

Notes

1. Professor Louis Lusky of Columbia Law School told the American Law Institute that his classroom approach to the wait-and-see problem is as follows:

> [W]hen my class and I come to this case in the book, I tell them what a pediatrician is supposed to tell a mother who has a two and a half year old child. That, you know, is the impossible age, and there is really nothing you can do except to hope that the child gets through it and the mother does too. The advice is that there is really nothing for the doctor to do except support the mother. So when the class comes to this, I tell them the day before I assign it to read that they are not to try to unravel the complexities of the opinion, they are not to try to rationalize the apparent mistakes that have resulted from those complexities; that they are simply to take it as an example of the burden that unlimited wait and see imposes on a court. The Pennsylvania Supreme Court is one of the most highly respected appellate courts in the country, and if you would examine their

performance in that case, I think you will sympathize with them rather than condemn them. [American Law Institute Proceedings 1978, at 261 (1979).]

2. The problem created by the Pennsylvania legislature's failure to include any reference to who could be considered a measuring life for the perpetuities period has been addressed by the Restatement (Second) of Property, which includes a statutory list of permissible measuring lives. Restatement (Second) of Property — Donative Transfers §1.3 (1983). For a discussion of the proper measuring lives under wait-and-see legislation, see Note, Measuring Lives Under Wait-and-See Versions of the Rule Against Perpetuities, 60 Wash. U.L.Q. 577 (1982).

3. Other courts have taken a less drastic approach to reforming the Rule against Perpetuities than the one chosen by the New Hampshire court in *Merchants Bank*, p. 631 *supra*. For example, examine the case of a testator who died in 1954, survived by his wife and sixteen children. When suit was brought in 1967, his issue, including children, grandchildren, and great grandchildren, numbered one hundred and thirty-five. The will provided: "This trust shall cease upon the death of my wife or thirty years from the date of my death, whichever shall last occur. . . ." On termination, three-fourths was to go to the survivors of his four sons, and one-fourth to the survivors of his twelve daughters.

The court asked "whether the orthodox common law Rule against Perpetuities will be strictly applied" in Hawaii? Its answer:

> This "common law" . . . does not remain in a somnolent and sedentary state . . . the genius of the common law . . . is its capacity for orderly growth. . . . As a judge made rule of law, [the Rule against Perpetuities] is not so firmly ensconced in Hawaii that this court cannot deal with it like any other rule of judicial origin which must change with the times.

The court therefore performed "equitable approximation" on the trust, and altered the testator's thirty-year term to twenty-one years. Justice Kobayashi, dissenting, called this "tenuous reasoning . . . to attempt to justify a gross violation of the Rule." In re Quan Yee Hop, 52 Haw. 40, 469 P.2d 183 (1970).

4. The West Virginia Supreme Court of Appeals has established four conditions that must be met before it will perform "equitable modification" to revise a devise or bequest so that it does not violate the rule. They include the following:

(1) The testator's intent is expressed in the instrument or can be readily determined by a court;
(2) The testator's general intent does not violate the rule against perpetuities;

(3) The testator's particular intent, which does violate the rule, is not a critical aspect of the testamentary scheme; and

(4) The proposed modification will effectuate the testator's general intent, will avoid the consequences of intestacy, and will conform to the policy considerations underlying the rule.

Berry v. Union National Bank, 262 S.E.2d 766 (W. Va. 1980).

5. Legislatures have followed a *Berry*-like approach in amending the common law. For example, the New York statute provides:

> Where an estate would, except for this section, be invalid because made to depend, for its vesting or its duration, upon any person attaining or failing to attain an age in excess of twenty-one years, the age contingency shall be reduced to twenty-one years as to any or all persons subject to such contingency. [N.Y. Est., Powers & Trust Law §9-1.2 (McKinney 1967).]

6. Some statutes combine a wait-and-see approach with the approach taken by the Hawaii court in In re Quan Yee Hop. For example, the Kentucky Rule against Perpetuities states:

> In determining whether an interest would violate the rule against perpetuities the period of perpetuities shall be measured by actual rather than possible events; Provided, however, the period shall not be measured by any lives whose continuance does not have a causal relationship to the vesting or failure of the interest. Any interest which would violate said rule as thus modified shall be reformed, within the limits of that rule, to approximate most closely the intention of the creator of the interest. [Ky. Rev. Stat. Ann. §381.216 (1972).]

7. Other specific "hazards" within the operation of the rule have been identified and dealt with by statute. For example, a statute can limit the age at which a person can be deemed capable of reproduction. See, e.g., N.Y. Est., Powers & Trusts Law §9-1.3(e)(1) (McKinney 1967) (lower limit of 14 for males and limits of 12 to 55 for females); Idaho Code §55-111 (1979) (". . . there shall be no presumption that a person is capable of having children at any state of adult life."). In addition, the "all-or-nothing" rule of gifts to classes can be amended by statute, so that members of a class whose interests have vested by the end of the period may take, while all others are excluded. See, e.g., [English] Perpetuities and Accumulations Act of 1964, c.55, §§4(3) to 4(4).

8. Some jurisdictions have set an absolute limit within which an interest must vest. "No interest in real or personal property which must vest, if at all, not later than 60 years after the creation of the interest violates Section 715.2 [which codifies the common law rule] of this code." Cal. Civ. Code §715.6 (West 1982). For the English approach, see

Perpetuities and Accumulations Act of 1964, c.55, §1 (a maximum period of 80 years).

9. One state legislature has declared that "the common law rule against perpetuities is not in force in this state." Wis. Stat. §700.16(5) (1981).

10. With the general reduction of the age of majority from twenty-one to eighteen, it can now be argued that the hallowed formula "lives-in-being plus twenty-one years," a definition that has survived its sesquicentennial (see Cadell v. Palmer, 1 Cl. & F. 372, 6 Eng. Rep. 956 (H.L. 1833), should now be reduced by three years. For an argument against such a drastic event, see Soled, Effect of Reduction of the Age of Majority on the Permissible Period of the Rule Against Perpetuities, 34 Md. L. Rev. 245 (1974).

11. For an extensive discussion of perpetuities reform, one that examines all of the approaches noted in this chapter and that treats favorably the Restatement (Second)'s wait-and-see approach, see Waggoner, Perpetuities Reform, 81 Mich. L. Rev. 1718 (1983).

E.   RULE AND REASON

◆ L. M. SIMES, PUBLIC POLICY AND THE DEAD HAND
32-33, 40-41, 55-56, 58-59 (1955)

In the halls of University College, University of London, prominently displayed within a glass case, are the bones of the great legal philosopher, Jeremy Bentham. The skeleton is clad in the garments which the great man wore in life. A wax replica of his head is substituted for his skull. His bony fingers grasp the walking stick, which he called "Dapple." On the glass case is a typewritten extract from his will, stating that the testator desired to have his preserved figure, on certain occasions, placed in a chair at gatherings of his friends and disciples, for the purpose of commemorating his philosophy. It is said that this direction is still observed at banquets in his honor. I know of no more vivid illustration of the influence of the dead hand. One can picture that extraordinary scene in which the skeleton of a man, dead for over a century, sits at the head of the board. Literally the hand of the dead presides.

When the subject matter of dead hand control is not philosophic ideas, but property, much less bizarre devices are employed. The testator, by the terms of his will, uses the trust, the condition, the special limitation, and the future interest. By these means, he seeks to impose his wishes upon the property of future generations.

But our legal system, having recognized all these devices of remote control, also provides a whole arsenal of rules, designed to strike down unwanted creations of the dead hand. There are rules against direct restraints on alienation, against conditions in restraint of marriage, against conditions and limitations generally contrary to public policy. There are other rules restricting the duration of honorary trusts and trusts for accumulation.

By far the most important of these rules, however, is that which restricts the creation of contingent future interests. It is the Rule against Perpetuities. . . .

What public policy actuates this rule? If we are to content ourselves with the terse and sometimes superficial pronouncements on the subject scattered through the books, the policy of the Rule has never been in doubt. Ever since it first emerged in the Duke of Norfolk's Case, it has been declared to be a rule in furtherance of the alienability of property. . . .

Now, if the policy of the Rule against perpetuities is to make property productive, just how far is this policy advanced in the application of the Rule today? Is property still taken out of commerce by remote contingent future interests? *I believe it is no exaggeration to say that, at the present time, due to changes both in the nature of capital investments and in the law, the proposition that contingent future interests make property unproductive is rarely true in the United States and almost never true in England.* . . .

In the first place, the future interest with which the Rule against Perpetuities is concerned is nearly always an equitable interest in a trust. The modern trust instrument, if well drawn, will contain broad powers of sale and reinvestment. While the beneficiary who has an equitable estate subject to a future interest may have difficulty in selling his property, that does not make it unproductive. As a practical matter, the trustee will have an absolute legal estate which he can sell, and will be empowered to reinvest the proceeds. While at one time in the history of the law, in the absence of express authorization in the trust instrument, the trustee's powers of reinvestment were extremely limited, today the rapidly extending "prudent man rule" gives the trustee a wide field of selection in making trust investments productive.

Moreover, not only is the trustee empowered by the terms of any well drawn trust instrument to sell and reinvest in productive property; the law requires him to do so. One of the duties imposed by law upon trustees is to use reasonable care in making the trust property productive.

Suppose, however, that the trust instrument is not well drawn, and no express powers of alienation are given to the trustee. Still the trust property is not necessarily taken out of commerce. The law recognizes that, when circumstances change in a manner unforeseen by the settlor, the trustee may secure permission of the court to sell. . . .

Now, so far as the common law is concerned, it is perfectly clear that the existence of a power in a trustee to sell and reinvest does not take the case out of the Rule against Perpetuities. Courts have rarely discussed the proposition except in connection with statutory rules against perpetuities. When they have done so, they have ordinarily dismissed it with the terse observation that, of course, the contingent character of the equitable interest renders it inalienable, without telling us why that sort of inalienability is objectionable. . . .

If alienability for purposes of productivity is not the justification of the modern Rule against Perpetuities, then what is the public policy which justifies it? . . .

There are, in my opinion, . . . two other bases for the social policy of the Rule, the force of which can scarcely be denied.

First, the Rule against Perpetuities strikes a fair balance between the desires of members of the present generation, and similar desires of succeeding generations, to do what they wish with the property which they enjoy. In our first lecture, we saw that one of the most common human wants is the desire to distribute one's property at death without restriction in whatever manner he desires. Indeed, we can go farther, and say that there is a policy in favor of permitting people to create future interests by will, as well as present interests, because that also accords with human desires. The difficulty here is that, if we give free rein to the desires of one generation to create future interests, the members of succeeding generations will receive the property in a restricted state. They will thus be unable to create all the future interests they wish. Perhaps, they may not even be able to devise it at all. Hence, to come most nearly to satisfying the desires of people of all generations, we must strike a fair balance between unrestricted testamentary disposition of property by the present generation and unrestricted disposition by future generations. In a sense this is a policy of alienability, but it is not alienability for productivity. It is alienability to enable people to do what they please at death with the property which they enjoy in life. As Kohler says in his treatise on the Philosophy of Law: "The far-reaching hand of a testator who would enforce his will in distant future generations destroys the liberty of other individuals, and presumes to make rules for distant times."

But, in my opinion, a second and even more important reason for the Rule is this. It is socially desirable that the wealth of the world be controlled by its living members and not by the dead. I know of no better statement of that doctrine than the language of Thomas Jefferson, contained in a letter to James Madison, when he said: "The earth belongs always to the living generation. They may manage it then, and what proceeds from it, as they please during their usufruct."

◆ W. B. LEACH, THE RULE AGAINST PERPETUITIES AND GIFTS TO CLASSES
51 Harv. L. Rev. 1329, 1353 n.67 (1938)

I have recently had a somewhat extended correspondence with a friend who sits on the highest bench of his state and for whose ability and candor I have equally high regard. . . . His view was that he was justified in striking down an essentially harmless gift in adherence to a rigid application of the Rule. Mine was that a relatively small dose of judicial ingenuity could have saved the gift and that the case was one in which the court might well be astute to carry out the intent of the testator. What troubled me, however, was the following, offered in support of his position: "In reference to property law I am a conservative. In reference to public law my inclinations would be quite the contrary." I don't know just what that word "conservative" means; but I vaguely dislike it, particularly in the context of correspondence in which it was used. I get two impressions from it, both possibly unjustified: (1) a testator of wealth and the objects of his bounty have no rights that a man is bound to respect, (2) in reference to the Rule against Perpetuities it is preferable to follow blindly a line of authority established outside the jurisdiction than to re-examine the problem from the point of view of reason and analogy. . . . There is no question that the Rule against Perpetuities is rich men's law. But until the "public law" to which my judicial friend refers liquidates rich men or abolishes the transmission of their property upon death, property law should be administered by the courts in accordance with its announced fundamental principle: to transmit property to those persons to whom the testator intended it to go except so far as some consideration of public policy necessarily forbids. To my mind, it should be recognized that the Rule against Perpetuities is an expression in mathematical terms of a consideration of public policy; where the substance is not offended a court should, whenever possible, avoid a holding that the form of the Rule invalidates the gift. There is no reason why the attitude of a court with reference to a will under the Rule against Perpetuities should differ from its attitude with reference to legislation under a constitution. Presumptions of validity are in order in both cases. Public and private law are aspects of a single judicial process.

V ◆ LAND IN COMMERCE

What is property?

For many persons, it is their capital stake: their economic achievement and security; their gamble on inflation and growth. Property is capital in stocks and bonds and savings accounts and pension plans. Legal regulation of these sorts of wealth is considered briefly in Parts 4, 5, and 7. But for most American families, the principal "property" is land and a residence. Routine house sales provide a significant part of the income for many lawyers. Lately, with economic considerations putting new single-family housing beyond the reach of most of the population, and with new lifestyles supplementing the nuclear family, emphasis has shifted to multi-family developments of various sorts. More and more, lawyers spend their time and earn their income representing "developers": dealmakers whose social function is acquiring land, obtaining public and private permissions to build, collecting financial commitments, choosing and supervising contractors, gauging the market, navigating the maze of government subsidy programs, and establishing a framework for ownership and maintenance. Each of these tasks is bounded by law, and each imposes a need for legal services. Altogether, this realm of property law lets the attorney be business advisor, dealmaker, negotiator, cautious reality-constrainer, lobbyist, fileclerk, and litigator, as his or her inclinations, skills, and clients dictate.

In this chapter you see aspects of commercial real estate practice, ranging from a single-family house transaction through a subsidized apartment complex to an entire new community. This is not an advanced course in real estate transactions, and certainly not in the federal income tax provisions that are so important to real estate finance. But you can get basic background here, adequate depth on a few of the most important aspects of land transfer and development, and commercial perspectives on land law and land lawyering that should complement the insights you are gaining elsewhere in the course.

17 ◆ BUYING A HOUSE

Problem: Mr. & Ms. Ambitious

In 1985 Mr. Ambitious, a graduate student, and Ms. Ambitious, a stockbroker, decided to move from their apartment in Baltimore into a house in Columbia, Maryland. On Monday Ms. *A* noticed a "principals only" ad in the Daily News listing a split-level house for $100,000. She *invitation* telephoned and made an appointment to see the owner, Mr. Bailout, the next morning. *covenants* ①

The *A*'s liked the house. The neighborhood was a pleasant subdivision, well kept by its residents. The *A*'s were both pleased with *B*'s taste in decorating, which would enable them to save on redecorating costs. The livingroom-diningroom floor was covered with an oriental rug that was an excellent match with the room's wallpaper and drapery. *B* made a special point of commenting on the rug's good condition and how it would complement any furniture that the *A*'s might bring into the house. *B* also explained that the house had had some trouble with its wiring, but had been rewired two years ago when he and his late wife had put new light fixtures in the livingroom and study. He even offered to show the *A*'s the old fixtures in the closet upstairs. The *A*'s were pleased to find that the bedrooms and the livingroom-diningroom all had window air conditioners. Other appliances in the house, the dishwasher, washer and dryer, stove, refrigerator and the gas water heater, were all fairly new and in good shape, which would help the *A*'s' budget.

Although the interior plan of the house and the neighborhood seemed perfect, the *A*'s were a bit uncomfortable with the appearance of the front of the house. The *A*'s mentioned this to *B*, who suggested adding on a front porch. Ms. *A* had seen this done at the house of one of her friends, and thought that this would be a good solution to the house's lack of character. The only real doubts that the *A*'s had were about evidence of water damage in the second floor bedroom. Mr. *B* said that there had been a leak, but that he had fixed it. He seemed reluctant to allow the *A*'s to have someone come in to examine the roof.

The lot itself was at the edge of the subdivision and bordered a wooded area. In the backyard was a fence which ran along the edge of the woods. Mr. *B* said that the property extended about 10 feet beyond the fence into the woods, to certain trees. The *A*'s saw that all of those owning property along the woods seemed to keep their fences uniform with the line where Mr. *B*'s was. After looking through and around the house and speaking at length with Mr. *B*, the *A*'s left and said that they would get back to him within 48 hours.

Tuesday morning the *A*'s decided to follow up on another ad. This one listed a two-story frame and brick house in a "quiet area" of Columbia. The *A*'s went to see the broker, Mr. Oiler. Oiler suggested they drive to the house with him. Within a few minutes, they found themselves on *B*'s street with the broker's hand pointing out the same house which they had visited earlier. The broker gave the listing price as $105,000. When the *A*'s balked at this figure, he seemed to take them into his confidence and said that he knew that they really wanted that sort of house. He explained that he had known the owner for quite a while, and was sure that an offer of $95,000 would be accepted.

Oiler emphasized the pleasant atmosphere of the neighborhood, the quality of the schools, and the convenience of the commuter bus. He explained that the developer-builder was an outstandingly honest man who had "old fashioned pride" in his workmanship. The *A*'s, when asked if they wanted to look inside the house, pleaded another appointment.

The ride back consisted of some more vague remarks from the broker and an invitation to the *A*'s to come back at their earliest convenience to look more closely at the house. Just before they parted company, the broker pulled Mr. *A* aside and said that, although he was not supposed to mention it, *B* was going to move into an apartment in Washington after he sold the house. Therefore, *B* was planning to leave behind his power mower and the furniture in the study and extra bedroom without additional cost. The broker said that *B* was not mentioning this because he wanted to use the articles for last-ditch bargaining, if the sale should come to that. The broker also warned that two other couples had already looked at the house, and that he would be obliged to convey all offers to the owner.

Tuesday afternoon, the *A*'s walk into your office, and explain the facts given above. They tell you that they are unsure about the whole house-purchasing process, explaining that they have lived in apartments since their marriage. Should they use the broker for the transaction or do it themselves with Mr. *B*? They ask whether $95,000 is a fair price for such a house, whether they should try to negotiate the price down, and who should do any such negotiating. They are worried that while they make some sort of offer, the house will go to another bidder whom they might have been willing to outbid if given the chance.

Before the *A*'s become owners of Mr. Bailout's house, they will encounter a great many legal doctrines and relations: they will negotiate with the seller, perhaps using a *broker* as intermediary; they will make an *offer* for the house; the offer will be accepted; they and the seller will sign a contract, often called a *purchase and sale agreement*; they will arrange to obtain the funds, which usually means borrowing money from a financial institution in return for a *mortgage* or *deed of trust* on the property; they will investigate the *title*, to find out from the *recording office* (and perhaps elsewhere) whether Mr. Bailout really owns what he says he owns; then they will *close*, at a relatively formal ceremony at which a *deed* is issued from Mr. Bailout to the *A*'s; that deed will describe the extent of the commitments, called *warranties*, that Mr. *B* is making to the *A*'s.

This chapter presents basic information on all of these subjects. Surrounding the material are the questions raised by Chief Justice Burger several years ago in a famous speech: Have we made the process of transferring real estate far too complicated and expensive? Why does it cost so much more — in money and time and worry — to transfer a $100,000 house than to transfer a much less tangible and mobile commodity, $100,000 of General Motors stock?

A. BROKERS AND LAWYERS

Individuals selling houses sometimes try to sell through their own devices, including friends and newspapers. As soon as they advertise, they are approached by brokers, who promise to sell speedily and ask for an "exclusive"—meaning that they will get a fee if the house is sold. The American Bar Foundation, not exactly a disinterested source, finds so much confusion in relations between sellers and brokers that it believes the house seller should have legal representation before signing the contract with a broker. American Bar Foundation, The Proper Role of the Lawyer — Real Estate Transactions 3-4 (1974). This rarely occurs. Instead, the seller will sign a standard form proffered by the broker, or will engage him or her orally. But what do brokers do? What are they legally authorized to do? For whom is Mr. Oiler working when he talks so silkily to Mr. and Ms. *A*? At what stage, if any, is it essential that the *A*'s retain a lawyer?

◆ TRISTRAM'S LANDING, INC. v. WAIT
367 Mass. 622, 327 N.E.2d 727 (1975)

Tauro, Chief Justice. This is an action in contract seeking to recover a brokerage commission alleged to be due to the plaintiffs from the defendant. . . . The judge found for the plaintiffs in the full amount of the commission. The defendant . . . appealed.

The facts briefly are these: The plaintiffs are real estate brokers doing business in Nantucket. The defendant owned real estate on the island which she desired to sell. In the past, the plaintiffs acted as brokers for the defendant when she rented the same premises.

The plaintiffs heard that the defendant's property was for sale, and in the spring of 1972 the plaintiff Van der Wolk telephoned the defendant and asked for authority to show it. The defendant agreed that the plaintiffs could act as brokers, although not as exclusive brokers, and told them that the price for the property was $110,000. During this conversation there was no mention of a commission. The defendant knew that the normal brokerage commission in Nantucket was five percent of the sale price.

In the early months of 1973, Van der Wolk located a prospective buyer, Louise L. Cashman (Cashman), who indicated that she was interested in purchasing the defendant's property. Her written offer of $100,000, dated April 29, was conveyed to the defendant. Shortly thereafter, the defendant's husband and attorney wrote to the plaintiffs that "a counter-offer of $105,000 with an October 1st closing" should be made to Cashman. Within a few weeks the counter-offer was orally accepted, and a purchase and sale agreement was drawn up by Van der Wolk.

The agreement was executed by Cashman and was returned to the plaintiffs with a check for $10,500, representing a ten percent down payment. The agreement was then presented by the plaintiffs to the defendant, who signed it after reviewing it with her attorney. The down payment check was thereafter turned over to the defendant.

The purchase and sale agreement signed by the parties called for an October 1, 1973, closing date. On September 22, the defendant signed a fifteen day extension of the closing date, which was communicated to Cashman by the plaintiffs. Cashman did not sign the extension. On October 1, 1973, the defendant appeared at the registry of deeds with a deed to the property. Cashman did not appear for the closing and thereafter refused to go through with the purchase. No formal action has been taken by the defendant to enforce the agreement or to recover damages for its breach, although the defendant has retained the down payment.

Van der Wolk presented the defendant with a bill for commission in the amount of $5,250, five percent of the agreed sales price. The defendant, through her attorney, refused to pay, stating that "[t]here has been no sale and consequently the 5 percent commission has not been earned." The plaintiffs then brought this action to recover the commission.

In the course of dealings between the plaintiffs and the defendant there was no mention of commission. The only reference to commission is found in the purchase and sale agreement signed by Cashman and the defendant, which reads as follows: "It is understood that a broker's commission of five (5) percent on the said sale is to be paid to . . . [the broker] by the said seller." The plaintiffs contend that, having produced a buyer who was ready, willing and able to purchase the property, and who was in fact accepted by the seller, they are entitled to their full commission. The defendant argues that no commission was earned because the sale was not consummated. We agree with the defendant, and reverse the finding by the judge below.

1. The general rule regarding whether a broker is entitled to a commission from one attempting to sell real estate is that, absent special circumstances, the broker "is entitled to a commission if he produces a customer ready, able, and willing to buy upon the terms and for the price given the broker by the owner." . . . In the past, this rule has been construed to mean that once a customer is produced by the broker and accepted by the seller, the commission is earned, whether or not the sale is actually consummated. . . . Furthermore, execution of a purchase and sale agreement is usually seen as conclusive evidence of the seller's acceptance of the buyer. . . .

Despite these well established and often cited rules, we have held that "[t]he owner is not helpless" to protect himself from these consequences. "He may, by appropriate language in his dealings with the broker, limit his liability for payment of a commission to the situation where not only is the broker obligated to find a customer ready, willing and able to purchase on the owner's terms and for his prices, but also it is provided that no commission is to become due until the customer actually takes a conveyance and pays therefor."

In the application of these rules to the instant case, we believe that the broker here is not entitled to a commission. We cannot construe the purchase and sale agreement as an unconditional acceptance by the seller of the buyer, as the agreement itself contained conditional language. The purchase and sale agreement provided that the commission was to be paid "on the said sale," and we construe this language as requiring that the said sale be consummated before the commission is earned. . . .

To the extent that there are cases, unique on their facts, which may appear inconsistent with this holding and seem to indicate a contrary result, we choose not to follow them.

In light of what we have said, we construe the language "on the said sale" as providing for a "special agreement," or as creating "special circumstances," wherein consummation of the sale became a condition precedent for the broker to earn his commission. Accordingly, since the sale was not consummated, the plaintiffs were not entitled to recover the amount specified in the purchase and sale agreement.[5]

2. Although what we have said to this point is determinative of the rights of the parties, we note that the relationship and obligations of real estate owners and brokers *inter se* has been the "subject of frequent litigation." . . . We believe, however, that it is both appropriate and necessary at this time to clarify the law, and we now join the growing minority of States who have adopted the rule of Ellsworth Dobbs, Inc. v. Johnson, 50 N.J. 528, 236 A.2d 843 (1967).

In the *Ellsworth* case, the New Jersey court faced the task of clarifying the law regarding the legal relationships between sellers and brokers in real estate transactions. In order to formulate a just and proper rule, the court examined the realities of such transactions. The court noted that "ordinarily when an owner of property lists it with a broker for sale, his expectation is that the money for the payment of commission will come out of the proceeds of the sale." It quoted with approval from the opinion of Lord Justice Denning, in Dennis Reed, Ltd. v. Goody, [1950] 2 K.B. 277, 284-285, where he stated:

> When a house owner puts his house into the hands of an estate agent, the ordinary understanding is that the agent is only to receive a commission if he succeeds in effecting a sale. . . . The common understanding of men is . . . that the agent's commission is payable out of the purchase price. . . . The house-owner wants to find a man who will actually buy his house and pay for it. He does not want a man who will only make an offer or sign a contract. He wants a purchaser "able to purchase and able to complete as well."

The court went on to say that the principle binding

> the seller to pay commission if he signs a contract of sale with the broker's customer, regardless of the customer's financial ability, puts the burden on the wrong shoulders. Since the broker's duty to the owner is to produce a prospective buyer who is financially able to pay the purchase price and take title, a right in the owner to assume such capacity when the broker presents his purchase ought to be recognized.

Reason and Justice dictate that it should be the broker who bears the burden of producing a purchaser who is not only ready, willing and able

---

5. We note here that the count of *quantum meruit* was waived at trial, and the action proceeded on the written contract only.

at the time of the negotiations, but who also consummates the sale at the time of closing.

. . .Thus, we adopt the following rules:

> When a broker is engaged by an owner of property to find a purchaser for it, the broker earns his commission when (a) he produces a purchaser ready, willing and able to buy on the terms fixed by the owner, (b) the purchaser enters into a binding contract with the owner to do so, and (c) the purchaser completes the transaction by closing the title in accordance with the provisions of the contract. If the contract is not consummated because of lack of financial ability of the buyer to perform or because of any other default of his . . . there is no right to commission against the seller. On the other hand, if the failure of completion of the contract results from the wrongful act or interference of the seller, the broker's claim is valid and must be paid. . . .

We recognize that this rule could be easily circumvented by language to the contrary in purchase and sale agreements or in agreements between sellers and brokers. In many States a signed writing is required for an agreement to pay a commission to a real estate broker. Such a requirement may be worthy of legislative consideration, but we do not think we should establish such a requirement by judicial decision. Informal agreements fairly made between people of equal skill and understanding serve a useful purpose. But many sellers, unlike brokers, are involved in real estate transactions infrequently, perhaps only once in a lifetime, and are thus unfamiliar with their legal rights. In such cases agreements by the seller to pay a commission even though the purchaser defaults are to be scrutinized carefully. If not fairly made, such agreements may be unconscionable or against public policy.

L. FRIEDMAN, CONTRACT LAW IN AMERICA 46-50 (1964): The most striking aspect of the labor and service [appellate cases in Wisconsin between 1905 and 1915] was the ubiquitousness of the real estate brokers. In eighteen cases brokers brought suit to collect their commissions. The use of real estate brokers was common during the period. Of the thousands of sales through brokers every year, only a handful are litigated, even fewer were appealed. Nonetheless, compared with other occupations, the brokers took up far more than their fair share of the court's time.

The basic reason can be found partly in the nature of the business, partly in consideration of the type of brokers who litigated. The brokerage business was relatively disorganized. Entry into this business specialty was free to all. Professional organizations had not assumed control and the state did not yet license brokers. The nature of the business, indeed, was not conducive to internal control. The potential customers were a fluid, constantly shifting group. Buying and selling were usually non-recurring acts; the stabilizing effect of a "course of dealing" was lacking. The business required little specialized knowledge, despite what the "professionals" said. Any layman could fill in printed forms of ordinary deeds and learn how to handle a land transfer with a little experience. Then, too, Wisconsin (and America in general) had a long tradition of part-timers dabbling in real estate.

The land marketing and brokerage business was rich and colorful. At one end of the scale the large land companies of the north were highly organized and rationalized. The Tomahawk Land Company, which flourished after 1910, selected settlers, financed them, even rented them stump clearing machines. J. L. Gates sold land through agents who received $1 an acre for their pains. In the cities and small towns, there were dealers who operated regular brokerage businesses over the years, as well as part-time dealers, some of whom sold a lot or two and then quit. In the palmy days of land speculation, the farmer was lightly attached to the soil; land to him was (relatively speaking) emotionally colorless; every man was a potential land dealer. Perhaps the great number of fly-by-night brokers was an inheritance from this by-gone age. At any rate, real estate was an attractive side-line, not only for complete amateurs, but also for insurance men, lawyers, and stockbrokers. Thus we meet in one case with William J. Willis of Fond du Lac, who began by plastering and calcimining houses and ended by selling them. It is easy to see why brokers were harder to "organize" than doctors and lawyers.

Of these various types of brokers, our eighteen cases concern, primarily, only one: the part-time or marginal operator. These were litigants like one Zitske, who devoted "full time" to real estate. But his contract was oral; he had no office and no records. He lived "just outside . . . New London in Outagamie County. . . . I travel on foot, sometimes with a team, and sometimes on the cars." The cases show great variations in the commissions charged, a situation which hints at that most dreaded of occupational diseases, price-cutting. Commissions seemed to range from 2 per cent to 5 per cent; the magnitude of the sale made a difference. In some cases the seller fixed a minimum sale price and the broker took everything he could get over that price, or split the excess fifty-fifty with the owner. Undoubtedly, the part-time and marginal brokers had the most price flexibility; a man like Zitske had no overhead to worry about. Many of the part-timers were probably out only to earn fast, occasional dollars. But in a disorganized market the "regulars" had not much chance to maintain their own rates. A broker of Green Bay testified frankly, if ungrammatically: "We have not at all times regular ironclad rules which governs us all in our actions. It depends on the people I am dealing with, and the amount of property, etc." Undoubtedly, another problem faced by the brokers was widespread public misunderstanding of the schedules of rates (indeed, of the nature of the brokerage commission altogether). The occasional buyer and seller of a house might view the broker's commission as an unjust exaction, a large price paid for a trifling amount of work. Nor did the public readily accept the broker's claim — more or less agreed to by the courts — that the commission was earned if he brought a buyer to the seller, even if the broker did not actively negotiate, or if the seller backed out of the deal. These problems were most critical for the marginal operators, whose business methods were the loosest. Such a broker was not a member of a real estate "board," thus not sympathetic to the "gentlemen's agreements" of the trade; he haggled about rates and service, undercut the regulars, competed with them for available business, and brought the whole corps of brokers into disrepute through "unprofessional" conduct. . . .

Interestingly enough, in the years 1955-1958 the brokers' cases continued to come before the court. Unlike the brokers of 1905-1915, the new crop of broker-plaintiffs were regularly licensed brokers, members of an active professional group, with established businesses and fairly standardized business practices. Regulation, licensing, and tighter internal control had driven away the marginal brokers, but the inherent problems of customer relations were not so easy to cure. In one 1958 case the broker claimed commissions on repeated renewals of a lease first executed in 1937. Probably the client was thoroughly disgusted with these "unearned" commissions. In other cases, it is clear that to a certain extent the brokers had brought their troubles onto their own heads. In five of these cases the customer's defense was based on a special section of the Statute of Frauds, passed in 1917, and applying only to real estate brokers. The "reputable" brokers themselves had hatched the statute, as a weapon against the marginal and part-time brokers who so plagued them. Forty years later, through a cruel irony, the licensed brokers themselves felt the major bite of the statute. . . .

◆ CHICAGO BAR ASSOCIATION v. QUINLAN AND TYSON, INC.
34 Ill. 2d 116, 214 N.E.2d 771 (1966)

PER CURIAM: The Chicago Bar Association filed a complaint in the circuit court of Cook County to enjoin a real-estate brokerage firm, Quinlan and Tyson, Inc., from engaging in the unauthorized practice of law. After a lengthy hearing before a master in chancery it was found that the activities in question, performed in connection with negotiating purchases and sales of real estate for consumers, constitute the practice of law. A decree was entered as prayed, except that the defendant was permitted to fill in the blanks of customary offer forms and contract forms as a necessary incident to its business. Upon review in the appellate court that part of the decree was reversed which allowed the filling in of forms, the court holding that none of the challenged services could be performed by persons not licensed to practice law. We have granted leave to appeal. The Illinois State Bar Association, the Chicago Real Estate Board and others have appeared and filed briefs as *amici curiae*.

The defendant is a corporation employing some fifty or sixty persons of which three are licensed real-estate brokers and twenty-three are licensed real-estate salesmen. In conducting its business defendant prepares offers to purchase real estate, draws contracts of purchase and sale, prepares deeds and other instruments necessary to clear or transfer title, and supervises the closing of the transaction. No separate fee is charged for these services, the defendant's compensation consisting solely of brokerage commissions. . . .

The question is not one of first impression in this State. It was settled by our decision in People ex rel. Illinois State Bar Association v. Schafer, 404 Ill. 45, 87 N.E.2d 773, where a licensed real-estate broker was held in contempt of court for preparing contracts, deeds, notes and mortgages in transactions for which he received a broker's commission. This court found unacceptable the contention that the drawing of such instruments was proper because done in connection with his real-estate business. Rejected also was the argument which considers those acts to be more or less mechanical and routine, requiring no legal knowledge or skill. We pointed out that

> Those who prepare instruments which affect titles to real estate have many points to consider. A transaction which at first seems simple may upon investigation be found to be quite involved. One who merely fills in certain blanks when other pertinent information should be elicited and considered is rendering little service but is acting in a manner calculated to produce trouble.

Except for the matter of filling in blanks on the customary preliminary contract-of-sale form, which we shall hereinafter discuss, we agree with the appellate court that the *Schafer* case is not distinguishable from the case at bar. . . .

We think, however, that in one respect, the prohibition in the appellate court's opinion is too broad. In the *Schafer* case this court did not in so many words discuss the preliminary or earnest money contract form, nor did we specifically condemn the mere filling in of the blanks on such forms. The decree of the trial court in the case at bar, permitting real-estate brokers to fill in the blanks of whatever form of such contract is customarily used in the community and to make appropriate deletions from such contract to conform to the facts, is approved. In the usual situation where the broker is employed to find a purchaser he performs this service when he produces a prospect ready, willing and able to buy upon the terms proposed by the seller. The execution of an offer or preliminary contract is an evidencing or recording of this service in bringing together the buyer and seller. It coincides with the job the broker was employed to perform and which he is licensed to perform, and in practice it marks the point at which he becomes entitled to his commission. It seems reasonable therefore that he be authorized to draft this offer or preliminary contract, where this involves merely the filling in of blank forms. . . .

But when the broker has secured the signatures on the usual form of preliminary contract or offer to purchase, completed by the insertion of necessary factual data, he has fully performed his obligation as broker. The drawing or filling in of blanks on deeds, mortgages, and other legal instruments subsequently executed requires the peculiar skill of a lawyer and constitutes the practice of law. Such instruments are often muniments of title and become matters of permanent record. They are not ordinarily executed and delivered until after title has been examined and approved by the attorney for the purchaser. Their preparation is not incidental to the performance of brokerage services but falls outside the scope of the broker's function. . . .

Drafting and attending to the execution of instruments relating to real-estate titles are within the practice of law, and neither corporations nor any other persons unlicensed to practice the profession may engage therein. Nor does the fact that standardized forms are usually employed make these services an incident of the real-estate broker business. Many aspects of law practice are conducted through the use of forms, and not all of the matters handled require extensive investigation of the law. But by his training the lawyer is equipped to recognize when this is and when it is not the case. Neither counsel nor *amici* have suggested any practicable way in which an exception to the general rule can be made where only the use of forms is involved, or where the transaction is a "simple" one. Mere simplicity cannot be the basis for drawing boundaries to the practice of a profession. A pharmacist, for example, might be competent to prescribe for many of the simpler ailments, but it takes a medical background to recognize when the ailment is simple. Protection of the public requires that only licensed physicians may prescribe or treat for any ailment, regardless of complexity or simplicity. And protection of the public requires a similar approach when the practice of law is involved.

UNDERWOOD, Justice (dissenting): The opinion of this court permits real estate brokers to prepare contracts for the purchase and sale of real estate by "filling the blanks" in, and making "appropriate deletions" from form contracts customarily used in the community and to secure the signatures of the parties thereon. It prohibits explanation by the brokers of the provisions of the contract and bars them from preparing any other documents subsequent to the contract. Actually, the contract

between the parties is the fundamental instrument in a real-estate transaction and determines their future rights and obligations. It seems to me
somewhat anomalous to permit the broker to prepare the controlling
agreement but not those which it controls. Be that as it may, the practical
result of this decision will be a binding contract executed by the parties
without informed consideration of the serious questions involved except
in those instances where the buyer or seller is aware of the inherent
hazards and consults his attorney before signing the contract.

Note

In State Bar v. Arizona Land Title & Trust Co., 90 Ariz. 76, 366 P.2d
1 (1961), the Arizona Supreme Court denied brokers the authority to
draft instruments creating legal rights and responsibilities, and also the
authority to fill in blanks on standard forms. The realtors obtained
109,000 signatures for the constitutional proposition giving them "the
right to draft or fill out and complete, without charge, any and all instruments . . . including . . . preliminary purchase agreements . . . , deeds,
mortgages, leases. . . ." Ariz. Const. art. 26, §1. The bar opposed with
vigor, arguing:

> The real estate agents in their petition are asking for a constitutional
> guarantee of the right to engage in the practice of real estate law without
> the responsibility imposed upon lawyers by their education, canons of
> ethics, and court supervision. It is the public interest, and not that of
> lawyers, which is involved in this Proposition.

The proposition passed, 224,177 to 61,316.
See Marks, The Lawyers and the Realtors: Arizona's Experience, 49
A.B.A.J. 139 (1963).

◆ GOLDFARB v. VIRGINIA STATE BAR
421 U.S. 733 (1975)

Mr. Chief Justice BURGER delivered the opinion of the Court. We granted
certiorari to decide whether a minimum fee schedule for lawyers published by the Fairfax County Bar Association and enforced by the Virginia State Bar violates §1 of the Sherman Act, 15 U.S.C. §1. The Court of
Appeals held that, although the fee schedule and enforcement mechanism substantially restrained competition among lawyers, publication of
the schedule by the County Bar was outside the scope of the Act because
the practice of law is not "trade or commerce," and enforcement of the
schedule by the State Bar was exempt from the Sherman Act as state
action. . . .

In 1971 petitioners, husband and wife, contracted to buy a home in Fairfax County, Virginia.* The financing agency required them to secure title insurance; this required a title examination, and only a member of the Virginia State Bar could legally perform that service. Petitioners therefore contacted a lawyer who quoted them the precise fee suggested in a minimum fee schedule published by respondent Fairfax County Bar Association; the lawyer told them that it was his policy to keep his charges in line with the minimum fee schedule which provided for a fee of 1 percent of the value of the property involved. Petitioners then tried to find a lawyer who would examine the title for less than the fee fixed by the schedule. They sent letters to 36 other Fairfax County lawyers requesting their fees. Nineteen replied, and none indicated that he would charge less than the rate fixed by the schedule; several stated that they knew of no attorney who would do so.

The fee schedule the lawyers referred to is a list of recommended minimum prices for common legal services. Respondent Fairfax County Bar Association published the fee schedule although, as a purely voluntary association of attorneys, the County Bar has no formal power to enforce it. Enforcement has been provided by respondent Virginia State Bar which is the administrative agency through which the Virginia Supreme Court regulates the practice of law in that State; membership in the State Bar is required in order to practice in Virginia. Although the State Bar has never taken formal disciplinary action to compel adherence to any fee schedule, it has published reports[4] condoning fee schedules, and has issued two ethical opinions indicating fee schedules cannot be ignored. The most recent opinion states that "evidence that an attorney *habitually* charges less than the suggested minimum fee schedule

---

*The house was in Reston, the "new community" near Dulles Airport that is, with Columbia, Md., one of the two "new towns" in the Washington area.

4. In 1962 the State Bar published a minimum fee schedule report that listed a series of fees and stated that they "represent the considered judgment of the Commitee [on Economics of Law Practice] as to a fair minimum fee in each instance." The report stated, however, that the fees were not mandatory, and it recommended only that the State Bar *consider* adopting such a schedule. Nevertheless, shortly thereafter the County Bar adopted its own minimum fee schedule that purported to be "a conscientious effort to show lawyers in their true perspective of dignity, training and integrity." The suggested fees for title examination were virtually identical to those in the State Bar report. . . .

In 1969 the State Bar published a second fee schedule report that, as it candidly stated, "reflect[ed] a general scaling up of fees for legal services." The report again stated that no local bar association was bound by its recommendations; however, respondent County Bar again quickly moved to publish an updated minimum fee schedule, and generally to raise fees. The new schedule stated that the fees were not mandatory, but tempered that by referring again to Opinion 98. This time the schedule also stated that lawyers should feel free to charge *more* than the recommended fees; and to avoid condemnation of higher fees charged by some lawyers, it cautioned County Bar members that "to . . . publicly criticize lawyers who charge more than the suggested fees herein might in itself be evidence of solicitation. . . ."

adopted by his local bar association raises a presumption that such lawyer is guilty of misconduct. . . ."

Because petitioners could not find a lawyer willing to charge a fee lower than the schedule dictated they had their title examined by the lawyer they had first contacted. They then brought this class action against the State Bar and the County Bar alleging that the operation of the minimum fee schedule, as applied to fees for legal services relating to residential real estate transactions, constitutes price fixing in violation of §1 of the Sherman Act. Petitioners sought both injunctive relief and damages. . . .

The County Bar argues that Congress never intended to include the learned professions within the terms "trade or commerce" in §1 of the Sherman Act, and therefore the sale of professional services is exempt from the Act. . . . Also, the County Bar maintains that competition is inconsistent with the practice of a profession because enhancing profit is not the goal of professional activities; the goal is to provide services necessary to the community. That, indeed, is the classic basis traditionally advanced to distinguish professions from trades, businesses, and other occupations, but it loses some of its force when used to support the fee control activities involved here.

In arguing that learned professions are not "trade or commerce" the County Bar seeks a total exclusion from antitrust regulation. Whether state regulation is active or dormant, real or theoretical, lawyers would be able to adopt anticompetitive practices with impunity. We cannot find support for the proposition that Congress intended any such sweeping exclusion. The nature of an occupation, standing alone, does not provide sanctuary from the Sherman Act, . . . nor is the public service aspect of professional practice controlling in determining whether §1 includes professions. . . . Congress intended to strike as broadly as it could in §1 of the Sherman Act, and to read into it so wide an exemption as that urged on us would be at odds with that purpose . . . . Whatever else it may be, the examination of a land title is a service; the exchange of such service for money is "commerce" in the most common usage of that word. It is no disparagement of the practice of law as a profession to acknowledge that it has this business aspect. . . . In the modern world it cannot be denied that the activities of lawyers play an important part in commercial intercourse, and that anticompetitive activities by lawyers may exert a restraint on commerce. . . .

The threshold inquiry in determining if an anticompetitive activity is state action of the type the Sherman Act was not meant to proscribe is whether the activity is required by the State acting as sovereign.

Here we need not inquire further into the state action question because it cannot fairly be said that the State of Virginia through its Supreme Court Rules required the anticompetitive activities of either respondent. Respondents have pointed to no Virginia statute requiring their activities; state law simply does not refer to fees, leaving regulation of the profession to the Virginia Supreme Court; although the Supreme Court's ethical codes mention advisory fee schedules they do not direct either respondent to supply them, or require the type of price floor which arose from respondents' activities. Although the State Bar apparently has been granted the power to issue ethical opinions there is no indication in this record that the Virginia Supreme Court approves the opinions. Respondents' arguments, at most, constitute the contention that their activities complemented the objective of the ethical codes. In our view that is not state action for Sherman Act purposes. It is not enough that, as the County Bar puts it, anticompetitive conduct is "prompted" by state action; rather, anticompetitive activities must be compelled by direction of the State acting as a sovereign. . . .

The judgment of the Court of Appeals is reversed.

◆ IN RE LANZA
65 N.J. 347, 322 A.2d 445 (1974)

PER CURIAM. The Bergen County Ethics Committee filed a presentment with this Court against respondent, Guy J. Lanza, who has been a practicing member of the bar of this State since 1954.

The Committee specifically found that respondent's conduct violated DR 5-105. This Disciplinary Rule forbids an attorney to represent adverse interests, except under certain very carefully circumscribed conditions.[1]

In April or May of 1971, Elizabeth F. Greene consulted respondent with respect to the sale of her residence property in Palisades Park, New Jersey. Mr. Lanza agreed to act for her. In due course a contract, apparently prepared by a broker, was signed by Mrs. Greene as seller as well as by the prospective purchasers, James and Joan Connolly. The execu-

---

1. The Disciplinary Rules of the Code of Professional Responsibility became effective in New Jersey on September 13, 1971. Respondent's criticized conduct took place earlier in the year 1971 and hence was governed by the Canons of Professional Ethics then in force. Canon 6, the predecessor of DR 5-105, read as follows:

6. *Adverse Influences and Conflicting Interests*
It is the duty of a lawyer at the time of retainer to disclose to the client all the circumstances of his relations to the parties, and any interest in or connection with the controversy, which might influence the client in the selection of counsel.

It is unprofessional to represent conflicting interests, except by express consent of all concerned given after a full disclosure of the facts. Within the meaning of this canon, a lawyer represents conflicting interests when, in behalf of one client, it is his duty to contend for that which duty to another client requires him to oppose.

The obligation to represent the client with undivided fidelity and not to divulge his secrets or confidences forbids also the subsequent acceptance of retainers or employment from others in matters adversely affecting any interest of the client with respect to which confidence has been reposed.

tion and delivery of the contract took place in Mr. Lanza's office, although he seems to have played little or no part in the negotiation of its terms. By this time he had agreed with the Connollys that he would represent them, as well as Mrs. Greene, in completing the transaction. The testimony is conflicting as to whether or not Mrs. Greene had been told of this dual representation at the time she signed the contract. Mr. Lanza says that she had been told, but according to her recollection she only learned of this at a later date from Mrs. Connolly. In any event it is quite clear that respondent agreed to act for the purchasers before discussing the question of such additional representation with Mrs. Greene.

The contract as originally drawn provided for a closing date in late July, 1971. At Mrs. Greene's request this date was postponed to September 1. A short time later, circumstances having again changed, Mrs. Greene found that she would now prefer the original date. This proved satisfactory to the purchasers but Mr. Connolly told Mrs. Greene that at this earlier date he would not have in hand funds sufficient to make up the full purchase price of $36,000. Of this sum he would lack $1,000. He suggested, however, that the parties might close title upon the earlier date if Mrs. Greene would accept, as part of the purchase price, a check for $1,000 postdated approximately 30 days. Mrs. Greene was personally agreeable to this. She consulted respondent who advised her that he saw no reason why she should not follow this course.

The closing accordingly took place late in July and in accordance with the foregoing arrangement, Mrs. Greene received, as part of the purchase price, Mr. Connolly's check in the sum of $1,000 dated August 31, 1971. Shortly after this latter date she deposited the check for collection and it was returned because of insufficient funds. When questioned, Mr. Connolly said that after he and his wife had taken possession of the property they discovered a serious water condition in the cellar. He added that Mrs. Greene had made an explicit representation that the cellar was at all times dry. For this reason he refused to make good the check, saying that it would cost $1,000 to rectify the condition in the cellar. Mrs. Greene denied that she had ever made any representation whatsoever. She immediately got in touch with respondent who did nothing effective on her behalf. She then retained other counsel and has subsequently initiated legal proceedings against the Connollys.

We find respondent's conduct to have been unprofessional in two respects. In the first place, the way in which he undertook the dual representation failed to meet the standards imposed upon an attorney who elects to follow such a course. In the second place, after the latent conflict of interests of the two clients had become acute, he nevertheless continued to represent both parties. At that point, rather than going forward with the matter as he did, he should have withdrawn altogether.

Mr. Lanza first undertook to act for the seller, Mrs. Greene. This immediately placed upon him an obligation to represent her with undivided fidelity. Despite this obligation, he later agreed, without prior consultation with Mrs. Greene, to represent Mr. and Mrs. Connolly, whose interest in the matter was of course potentially adverse to that of his client. He should not have undertaken to represent the purchasers until he had initially conferred with Mrs. Greene. He should have first explained to her all the facts and indicated in specific detail all the areas of potential conflict that foreseeably might arise. He should also have made her aware that if indeed any of these contingencies should thereafter eventuate and not prove susceptible of ready solution in a manner fair and agreeable to all concerned, it would then become his professional duty immediately to cease acting for all parties. Only after such a conference with his client, and following her informed consent, would he have been at liberty to consider representing the purchasers. They, too, were entitled to the same explanation as is set forth above, as well as being told of respondent's existing attorney-client relationship with the seller.

The second instance of misconduct arose after respondent learned that the purchasers would not be able to pay the full purchase price in cash at the time of closing title. At that point adequate representation of the seller required that her attorney first strongly insist on her behalf that cash be forthcoming. Failing this, and if the seller persisted in her wish to close upon the earlier date, her attorney should have vigorously urged the execution and delivery to her of a mortgage from the purchasers in the amount of $1,000, or of other adequate security, in order to protect her interest pending receipt of the full cash payment. We think it fair to assume that had respondent not found himself in a position of conflicting loyalties, his representation of the seller would have taken some such course. Had the purchasers persisted in their unwillingness to pay the full amount in cash at the time of closing and had they also refused to execute and deliver a mortgage or other security, respondent should have immediately withdrawn from the matter, advising both parties to secure independent counsel of their respective choosing. At that point in time it would have clearly been impossible for any single attorney adequately and fairly to represent both sides. . . .

For the reasons set forth above, we deem respondent's conduct to merit censure. He is hereby reprimanded.

PASHMAN, J. (concurring). . . . I believe that if a conflict is perpetually lurking somewhere in the background, an attorney is likely to be swayed or adversely affected thereby, whether consciously or unconsciously. I, therefore, choose not to exempt so-called potential conflicts under DR 5-105(C). Because of the admittedly inherent nature of a buyer-seller situation and the dangers involved, true impartiality is only an ideal and not an actuality. No matter how honest and well intentioned an attorney is, the possibility for conflict always exists. Commencing with the negotiation of contract terms to the preparation and execution of that contract to sell, and then to the closing itself which may involve breached warranties as to incompleted work or delays or failure of payment, or warranties to be effective after the closing, or innumerable other complications, the attorney is dealing with two or more conflicting interests. To believe otherwise is illusory.

It is virtually impossible for one attorney in any manner and under any circumstances to faithfully and with undivided allegiance represent both a buyer and seller. This concurrence, therefore, stands for the position of the majority and further holds that dual representation in a buyer-seller situation should be totally forbidden. The reasons for this seem to me fairly obvious. In this type of transaction, it is most certainly in the public interest to safeguard and protect both parties from any abuses, whether they be ill-advised or inadvertent. The potential conflict in home buying or selling may never come to fruition. However, when it does surface, both sides explode in anger and accusations. The attorney will then withdraw, leaving the situation no better than when it occurred and . . . probably a bit worse. This is not fair to either party.

It is my contention that neither buyer nor seller can ever possibly fully appreciate all the complexities involved. That is precisely the reason why full disclosure and informed consent are illusory. What most people typically do is rely upon the representation of their attorney when he reassures them that everything will be properly handled. However, the attorney is, unfortunately, not a clairvoyant who can foresee problem areas, although he realizes that there is certainly the potential for genuine conflict. Even where his motives are of the highest, as they usually are, and in good faith believes that he can effect a meeting of the minds, he really is not sure. Because of that dangerous uncertainty, I believe attorneys would, generally, welcome this prohibition against potential conflict. . . .

Note

For discussion of the application of *Goldfarb* to real estate brokers in New Orleans, see McLain v. Real Estate Board of New Orleans, Inc., 444 U.S. 232 (1979).

B. THE ORIGINS OF COLUMBIA NEW TOWN

On a different scale are the problems with brokers when dealing with a large assemblage of land, such as is required for a regional shopping center, a planned unit development, or a new community.

The secrecy — in this case necessary to protect the buyer — is manifest in the origins of Columbia, Maryland, perhaps the most prominent example of new city development in the United States. Columbia began as over 150 separate parcels of land, mostly farms, located midway between Washington, D.C., and Baltimore. It embodies a dream that is in large part social: a city which combines the richness and excitement found only in urban areas with the sense of community of a small town. There is a financial aspect of the dream as well: build a carefully planned city, with superior living environment, and people will respond, giving the developer not just a profit but a very large profit.

G. BRECKENFELD, COLUMBIA AND THE NEW CITIES 236-242 (1971): [James Rouse, developer of Columbia,] figured at the time that he would need at least $18 million to buy 12,000 acres of Howard County, the minimum that he felt would accommodate a city of 100,000. He calculated that it would take him twelve years and at least $42 million to see the project through. Despite the growth of his mortgage and shopping center business, such a sum was far beyond his means. But Rouse also projected an ultimate pretax profit of $67 million — $54 million cash and $13 million in commercial property on which mortgage debt would have been retired. Rouse elaborated these dreams and hopes in twenty loose-leaf pages of a green leather-bound notebook. Then he went shopping for money.

His first approach was to David Rockefeller, then president of Chase Manhattan Bank. Rouse was not seeking financial help from Chase. Banks are prohibited by law from making loans secured by undeveloped acreage. He did hope that the Rockefeller brothers, with their millions of personal investment capital, might be interested. Although Rouse hoped to obtain his major financing elsewhere, he told Rockefeller that additional funds might still be needed. The Rockefellers expressed interest, but events took another course. Armed with his green book and his unfailing eloquence, Columbia's builder turned to Frazar Wilde, chairman of Connecticut General Life Insurance Company (1968 assets five billion dollars). In two decades of doing business with Jim Rouse, the insurance company had already helped to finance seven Rouse-built projects, including the first enclosed shopping center mall at Harundale and the dramatically successful Cherry Hill. Rouse had solid arguments. There was an enormous potential profit if the new town proved successful. "There is no developer in America that can do this," Rouse argued. "The real resources available to the city-building business are the great life insurance companies; therefore if this is to be done you must provide the money, not 80 percent or 90 percent of the money, but all of the money. Whatever we can put up in this is a pittance. We will do the planning and administer the program, but we need your financing."

What if Rouse could not assemble a suitable site or win permission

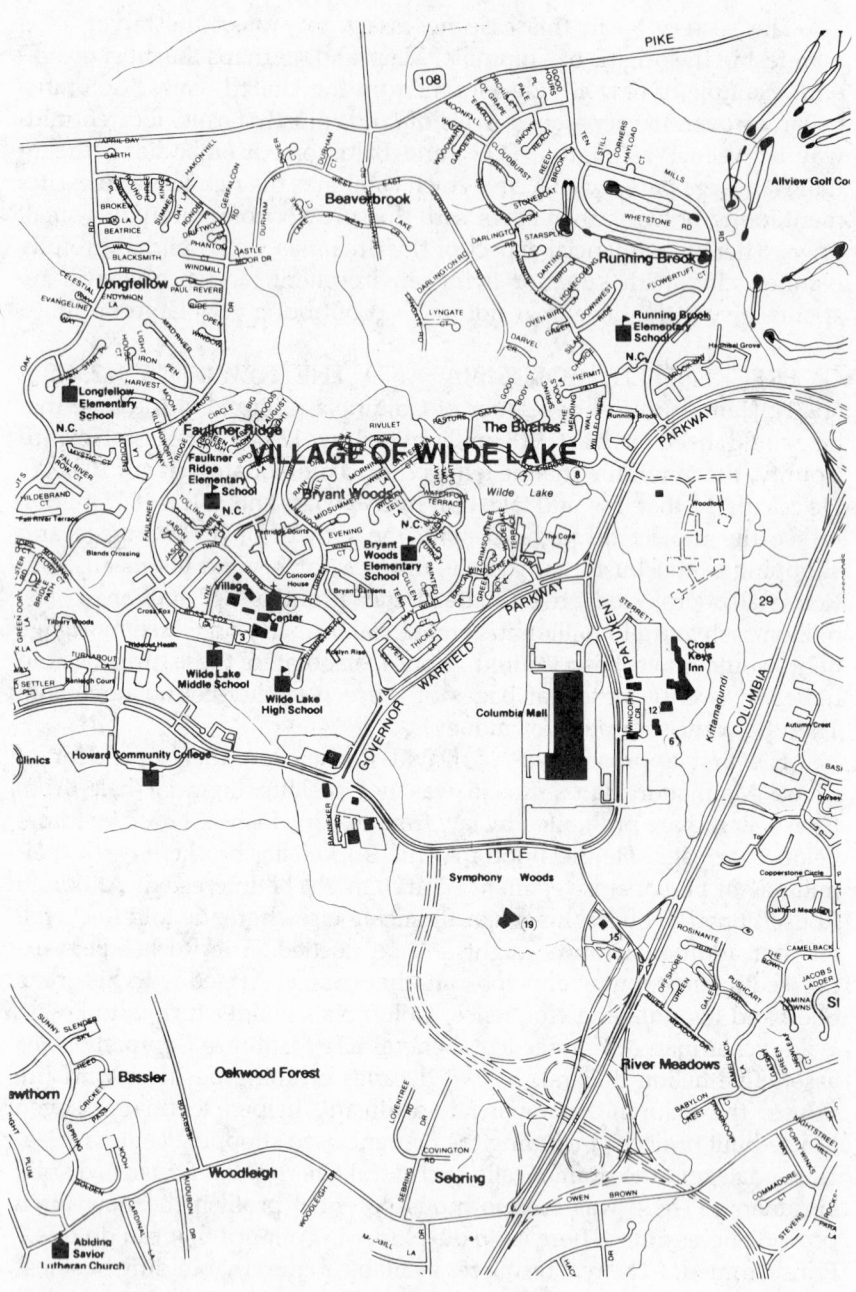

FIGURE 17-1
Columbia, Maryland

from Howard County to build the town? Columbia's founder had a persuasive answer for that contingency, too. He proposed to pay no more than $1500 an acre for the land. "How can you lose money on land bought at that price?" he asked Wilde. "If you sit on it you will make money. The worst that can happen is that you will get rich slowly."

In return for his huge loan, Rouse proposed to give Connecticut General an option to buy 50,000 shares of Community Research and Development common stock at a favorable $9 per share. Wilde was interested, but he insisted on a bigger share of the ownership and profit. Rouse countered with a second proposal: why not create a land-development company jointly owned by CRD and Connecticut General? That arrangement was adopted, and in January 1963 the insurance company agreed in writing to advance $18 million to buy the land. Profits would be split 50-50, but Connecticut General would name three directors of the jointly owned Howard Research and Development Corporation (HRD), Rouse only two. Though Rouse had the responsibility of managing the company that created Columbia, control of the venture remained in Hartford. . . .

Whether Connecticut General really exposed itself to much risk is debatable, but Rouse took a large gamble for a company the size of his. Rouse had to manage the project and pay for the $750,000 administrative overhead of planning and development. His target was land costing no more than $1500 an acre. He was allowed to buy land at an average price of not more than $2000 an acre; he could not pay more than $3000 an acre for any single parcel without specific approval from Hartford. Moreover, it was up to him to produce a financial and physical plan for the new city that Connecticut General would approve, or at worst forfeit his time and money. "We were shooting craps with them," Rouse told me. . . .

"I laid it out as a military maneuver," recalls [John Jones, a partner in the Baltimore firm of Piper and Marbury, which had represented Rouse for 20 years]." I divided the 'target land' into segments. I didn't want any one real estate dealer to get a clear idea of what we were up to." It was a tactic, he explained, that he had learned from his colonel in counterintelligence. Then Jones enlisted half a dozen realty men. Without giving them a hint as to what client he was representing, he told them, "In this area (a different area for each agent), we will accept offers to sell property. If the price is right we will buy." He deliberately avoided saying how much he would pay, but he had a plan: no more than $1000 per acre until Rouse had acquired a considerable holding, after which the price could gradually move up to higher and higher levels. "For a while the $1000 plateau held," says Jones, "so we began buying." Some property was acquired in the name of Jones' law firm, but Jones bought most of the Columbia site in the names of six dummy corporations formed for that purpose. Maryland allows any three individuals to incorporate, so Jones picked Piper Marbury secretaries or other lawyers "whom I knew very well." As a further touch of camouflage, he gave the dummy corporations misleading names: Alimco, Potomac Estate, Howard Estate, The Cedar Farms Company, Farmingdale, and Serenity Acres. Explains Jones, "We picked corny names, suggesting small real estate developers."

That was only the beginning of the security rigmarole. To prevent an observant bank clerk or officer from detecting the millions that Connecticut General was advancing to Rouse, Jack Jones arranged to have the money paid to one of the dummy corporations. Then he funneled the money this way and that, through a labyrinth of corporations and accounts in various Baltimore banks. Jones explains,

> First some money might go to Maryland National Bank. Then I would get a Maryland National cashier's check drawn to the account of another one of the dummy corporations in Union Trust. Then from Union Trust a cashier's check made out to the order of Jack Jones. Then the money might go back to Maryland National for another dummy account.

To accentuate the security, Jones even established an extra personal checking account at First National, for which he alone could sign checks. "Then I'd draw personal checks to pay for the properties," he says. "Hardly anybody can decipher my signature." . . .

To keep the secret from leaking out at Rouse's office, all maps, plans, and contracts involving Columbia were kept in a locked, unmarked office in the First National Bank Building. Only three persons had a key to what became known in the Rouse organization as Shangri-La. For months no waste paper was allowed to leave the room, lest a charwoman stumble on Rouse's buying blitz. Though the secret command post had a telephone, elaborate precautions surrounded its use; a wrong number, answered, could have prompted unfortunate curiosity by people who should not know about the secret land buying. A secretary phoning her boss at Shangri-La had to start the conversation herself, after somebody lifted the receiver from its cradle.

C. CONTRACTING TO PURCHASE

1. Binding Agreements

As Mr. & Ms. Ambitious consider Mr. Bailout's house, they are under pressure from the broker to "make an offer." When they are ready to do so, he is ready with a standard printed form on which they enter their bid. Forms of the sort reproduced below are used in most simple real

Greater Boston Real Estate Board

OFFER TO PURCHASE REAL ESTATE

TO_____
(Seller and Spouse)

_____

_____ DATE_____

The property herein referred to is identified as follows: ....

....

....

....

I hereby offer to buy said property, which has been offered to me by _____

_____ as your Broker, under the following terms and conditions:

1. I will pay therefore $_____, of which
   (a) $............is paid herewith as a deposit to bind this Offer.
   (b) $............is to be paid as an additional deposit upon the execution of the Purchase and Sale Agreement provided for below.
   (c) $............is to be paid at the time of delivery of the Deed in cash.
   (d) $............

   (e) $............Total Purchase Price

2. This Offer is good until _____ A.M./P.M. on _____ 19____, at or before which time a copy hereof shall be signed by you, the seller and your (husband) (wife), signifying acceptance of this Offer, and returned to me forthwith; otherwise this Offer shall be considered as rejected and the money deposited herewith shall be returned to me forthwith.

3. The parties hereto shall, on or before _____ A.M./P.M. _____ 19____, execute the Standard Form of Purchase and Sale Agreement recommended by the Greater Boston Real Estate Board which, when executed, shall be the agreement between the parties hereto.

4. A good and sufficient Deed, conveying a good and clear record and marketable title shall be delivered at 12:00 Noon on _____ 19____, at the appropriate Registry of Deeds, unless some other time and place are mutually agreed upon in writing.

5. If I do not fulfill my obligations under this Offer, the above mentioned deposit shall forthwith become your property without recourse to either party.

6. Time is of the essence hereof.

7. ....
(Additional terms and conditions, if any)

....

....

WITNESS my hand and seal.

SIGNED_____
(Buyer)

(ADDRESS)   (PHONE NO.)

This Offer is hereby accepted upon the foregoing terms and conditions and the receipt of the deposit of $_____ is hereby acknowledged at _____ A.M./P.M. on _____ 19____.

WITNESS my (our) hand(s) and seal(s)

_____   _____
(Seller's Spouse)   (Seller)

RECEIPT FOR DEPOSIT

_____19____

Received from _____ the sum of $_____ as deposit
(Buyer)
under the terms and conditions of the above Offer.
SELLER'S COPY

_____
(Broker)

SAMPLE DOCUMENT 17-1
Offer to Purchase

estate transactions. Indeed, the lawyer who seeks to "start from scratch" and create a new document would be regarded skeptically by other lawyers and would add large sums to the client's bill.

After there has been offer and acceptance, the parties are then likely to sign a "purchase and sale agreement." After there is a contract, common law tradition performs a sleight of hand that has no analogue in the law of personal property. Suddenly, ownership of the land and house separates into one set of rights called "legal title," remaining with Bailout until the deed is transferred at the "closing," and another set of rights called "equitable title," which moves immediately to the purchasers. The idea of legal and equitable title is only a shorthand way of saying that the A's probably do not have possession yet, but they certainly have enforceable interests in the property, and that among these interests is the historic willingness of the equity courts to give specific performance, and so to compel transfer to the A's if Mr. Bailout later attempts to renege on the sale.

[handwritten margin note: specific performance enforced]

Problem: Offer to Purchase

If the A's submit an offer to purchase on the form shown on page 673, and Mr. Bailout accepts, is there a contract? Where will all the supplementary terms come from: whether the A's get the air conditioners, and what happens if the seller turns out not to have good title, and whether the A's can get out of the transaction if they can't get a mortgage? Would you let a client become this committed on so important a transaction with so casual a document? If not, do you have to advise them to stop seeking this house?

Greater Boston Real Estate Board

PURCHASE and SALE
AGREEMENT

. . . .
SELLER

. . . .
BUYER

. . . .
Property Address

. . . .
Date of Agreement

. . . .
Date for Delivery of Deed

INSTRUCTIONS TO BUYER

If you are giving a mortgage, your spouse must join in signing it and so should be present at time of passing title.

Bring at the appointed time to the place designated for completing the transaction
1. A certified or Bank's Check (if acceptable to the SELLER) drawn payable to your order and one hundred dollars in cash, the total amount to equal the amount of payment to be made at time of passing title.
2. Sufficient additional cash to pay for apportionment of rents, taxes, water rates, insurance premiums, and other adjustments, attorney's bill, plot plans, and recording fees.

It is customary for the BUYER to pay for drawing any mortgage given by him and fees for recording his deed and purchase money mortgage. He also pays for examination of title and for Tax Collector's report showing whether there are any municipal liens or unpaid taxes.

SAMPLE DOCUMENT 17-2
Purchase and Sale Agreement

This _____ day of _____ 19___

1. PARTIES
(fill in)

hereinafter called the SELLER, agrees to SELL and

hereinafter called the BUYER or PURCHASER, agrees to BUY, upon the terms hereinafter set forth, the following described premises:

2. DESCRIPTION
(fill in and include title reference)

3. BUILDINGS, STRUCTURES, IMPROVEMENTS, FIXTURES

(fill in or delete)

Included in the sale as a part of said premises are the buildings, structures, and improvements now thereon, and the fixtures belonging to the SELLER and used in connection therewith including, if any, all venetian blinds, window shades, screens, screen doors, storm windows and doors, awnings, shutters, furnaces, heaters, heating equipment, stoves, ranges, oil and gas burners and fixtures appurtenant thereto, hot water heaters, plumbing and bathroom fixtures, electric and other lighting fixtures, mantels, outside television antennas, fences, gates, trees, shrubs, plants, and, if built in, air conditioning equipment, ventilators, garbage disposers, dishwashers, washing machines and driers, and
but excluding

4. TITLE DEED
(fill in)

* Include here by specific reference any restrictions, easements, rights and obligations in party walls not included in (b), leases, municipal and other liens,

Said premises are to be conveyed by a good and sufficient _____ deed running to the BUYER, or to the nominee designated by the BUYER by written notice to the SELLER at least seven _____ days before the deed is to be delivered as herein provided, and said deed shall convey a good and clear record and marketable title thereto, free from encumbrances, except

(a) Provisions of existing building and zoning laws; —
(b) Existing rights and obligations in party walls which are not the subject of written agreement;

676

other encumbrances, and make provision to protect SELLER against BUYER'S breach of SELLER'S covenants in leases, where necessary.

(c) Such taxes for the then current year as are not due and payable on the date of the delivery of such deed;

(d) Any liens for municipal betterments assessed after the date of this agreement;

*(e)

5. PLANS

If said deed refers to a plan necessary to be recorded therewith the SELLER shall deliver such plan with the deed in form adequate for recording or registration.

6. REGISTERED TITLE

In addition to the foregoing, if the title to said premises is registered, said deed shall be in form sufficient to entitle the BUYER to a Certificate of Title of said premises, and the SELLER shall deliver with said deed all instruments, if any, necessary to enable the BUYER to obtain such Certificate of Title.

7. PURCHASE PRICE
(fill in): space is allowed to write out the amounts if desired

(provide for payment by certified or Bank's Check acceptable to the SELLER, if required)

The agreed purchase price for said premises is

dollars, of which

$ have been paid as a deposit this day and

$ are to be paid at the time of delivery of the deed in cash.

$

$ TOTAL

677

8. TIME FOR PERFORMANCE; DELIVERY OF DEED *(fill in)*

Such deed is to be delivered at   o'clock   M. on the   day of   19   , at the   Registry of Deeds, unless otherwise agreed upon in writing. It is agreed that time is of the essence of this agreement.

9. POSSESSION and CONDITION of PREMISES *(attach list of exceptions, if any)*

Full possession of said premises free of all tenants and occupants, except as herein provided, is to be delivered at the time of the delivery of the deed, said premises to be then (a) in the same condition as they now are, reasonable use and wear thereof excepted, and (b) not in violation of said building and zoning laws, and (c) in compliance with the provisions of any instrument referred to in clause 4 hereof.

10. EXTENSION TO PERFECT TITLE OR MAKE PREMISES CONFORM *(Change period of time if desired.)*

If the SELLER shall be unable to give title or to make conveyance, or to deliver possession of the premises, all as herein stipulated, or if at the time of the delivery of the deed the premises do not conform with the provisions hereof, then any payments made under this agreement shall be refunded and all other obligations of the parties hereto shall cease and this agreement shall be void and without recourse to the parties hereto, unless the SELLER elects to use reasonable efforts to remove any defects in title, or to deliver possession as provided herein, or to make the said premises conform to the provisions hereof, as the case may be, in which event the SELLER shall give written notice thereof to the BUYER at or before the time for performance hereunder, and thereupon the time for performance hereof shall be extended for a period of thirty   days.

11. FAILURE TO PERFECT TITLE OR MAKE PREMISES CONFORM, etc.

If at the expiration of the extended time the SELLER shall have failed so to remove any defects in title, deliver possession, or make the premises conform, as the case may be, all as herein agreed, or if at any time during the period of this agreement or any extension thereof, the holder of a mortgage on said premises shall refuse to permit the insurance proceeds, if any, to be used for such purposes, then, at the BUYER'S option, any payments made under this agreement shall be forthwith refunded and all other obligations of all parties hereto shall cease and this agreement shall be void without recourse to the parties hereto.

678

12. BUYER'S ELECTION TO ACCEPT TITLE

The BUYER shall have the election, at either the original or any extended time for performance, to accept such title as the SELLER can deliver to the said premises in their then condition and to pay therefor the purchase price without deduction, in which case the SELLER shall convey such title, except that in the event of such conveyance in accord with the provisions of this clause, if the said premises shall have been damaged by fire or casualty insured against, then the SELLER shall, unless the SELLER has previously restored the premises to their former condition, either

(a) pay over or assign to the BUYER, on delivery of the deed, all amounts recovered or recoverable on account of such insurance, less any amounts reasonably expended by the SELLER for any partial restoration, or

(b) if a holder of a mortgage on said premises shall not permit the insurance proceeds or a part thereof to be used to restore the said premises to their former condition or to be so paid over or assigned, give to the BUYER a credit against the purchase price, on delivery of the deed, equal to said amounts so recovered or recoverable and retained by the holder of the said mortgage less any amounts reasonably expended by the SELLER for any partial restoration.

13. ACCEPTANCE OF DEED

The acceptance of a deed by the BUYER or his nominee as the case may be, shall be deemed to be a full performance and discharge of every agreement and obligation herein contained or expressed, except such as are, by the terms hereof, to be performed after the delivery of said deed.

14. USE OF PURCHASE MONEY TO CLEAR TITLE

To enable the SELLER to make conveyance as herein provided, the SELLER may, at the time of delivery of the deed, use the purchase money or any portion thereof to clear the title of any or all encumbrances or interests, provided that all instruments so procured are recorded simultaneously with the delivery of said deed.

679

15. INSURANCE
* Insert amount
(list additional types of insurance and amounts as agreed)

Until the delivery of the deed, the SELLER shall maintain insurance on said premises as follows:

Type of Insurance	Amount of Coverage
(a) Fire	* $
(b) Extended coverage	*
(c)	

16. ASSIGNMENT OF INSURANCE
(delete entire clause if insurance is not to be assigned)

Unless otherwise notified in writing by the BUYER at least seven   days before the time for delivery of the deed, and unless prevented from doing so by the refusal of the insurance company(s) involved to issue the same, the SELLER shall assign such insurance and deliver binders therefor in proper form to the BUYER at the time for performance of this agreement. In the event of refusal by the insurance company(s) to issue the same, the SELLER shall give notice thereof to the BUYER at least two   business days before the time for performance of this agreement.

17. ADJUSTMENTS
(list operating expenses, if any, or attach schedule)

Collected rents, mortgage interest, prepaid premiums on insurance if assigned as herein provided, water and sewer use charges, operating expenses (if any) according to the schedule attached hereto or set forth below, and taxes for the then current year, shall be apportioned and fuel value shall be adjusted, as of the day of performance of this agreement   and the net amount thereof shall be added to or deducted from, as the case may be, the purchase price payable by the BUYER at the time of delivery of the deed. Uncollected rents for the current rental period shall be apportioned if and when collected by either party.

18. ADJUSTMENT OF UNASSESSED AND ABATED TAXES

If the amount of said taxes is not known at the time of the delivery of the deed, they shall be apportioned on the basis of the taxes assessed for the preceding year, with a reapportionment as soon as the new tax rate and valuation can be ascertained; and, if the taxes which are to be apportioned shall thereafter be reduced by abatement, the amount of such abatement, less the reasonable cost of obtaining the same, shall be apportioned between the parties, provided that neither party shall be obligated to institute or prosecute proceedings for an abatement unless herein otherwise agreed.

680

19. **BROKER'S FEE**
(fill in fee with dollar amount or percentage; also name of Broker(s))

A broker's fee for professional services of
is due from the SELLER to

the Broker(s) herein, but if the SELLER pursuant to the terms of clause 22 hereof retains the deposits made hereunder by the BUYER, said Broker(s) shall be entitled to receive from the SELLER an amount equal to one half the amount so retained or an amount equal to the broker's fee for professional services according to this contract, whichever is the lesser.

20. **BROKER(S) WARRANTY**
(fill in name)

The Broker(s) named herein
warrant(s) that he (they) is (are) duly licensed as such by the Commonwealth of Massachusetts.

21. **DEPOSIT**
(fill in, or delete reference to broker(s) if SELLER holds deposit)

All deposits made hereunder shall be held by the Broker(s)
as agent for the SELLER, subject to the terms of this agreement and shall be duly accounted for at the time for performance of this agreement.

22. **BUYER'S DEFAULT; DAMAGES**

If the BUYER shall fail to fulfill the BUYER'S agreements herein, all deposits made hereunder by the BUYER shall be retained by the SELLER as liquidated damages unless within thirty days after the time for performance of this agreement or any extension hereof, the SELLER otherwise notifies the BUYER in writing.

23. **VETERANS FINANCING**
(fill in blank spaces or delete entire clause)

The BUYER, being a Veteran, intends to use his so-called Veterans Administration loan benefits to finance the purchase of said premises; it is understood and agreed that if on or before _____ a Certificate of Reasonable Value for not less than the purchase price shall not be issued by the Veterans Administration Loan Guaranty Division and if an accredited lending institution shall not approve and accept a mortgage loan of $_____ , payable in _____ years at a rate of interest not to exceed _____ % per year, based upon the aforesaid Certificate of Reasonable Value, then all payments hereunder by the BUYER shall be forthwith refunded and all other obligations of all parties hereto shall cease and this agreement shall be void and without recourse to the parties hereto. Provided, however, that in the event the purchase price exceeds the Reasonable Value determination, the BUYER shall have the option of proceeding with the purchase of the property subject to procuring a mortgage loan as above-stated, but in a sum not exceeding the Reasonable Value determination.

24. **F.H.A. FINANCING**
(fill in blank spaces or delete Clauses 24 & 25)

The BUYER agrees to apply promptly for a U.S. Government Federal Housing Administration insured loan for not less than $_____ , payable in _____ years at a rate of interest not to exceed _____ % per year, and if he shall not be able to obtain a firm commitment for such loan on or before _____ , then at the BUYER'S option, all payments hereunder by the BUYER shall be forthwith refunded and all other obligations of all parties hereto shall cease and this agreement shall be void and without recourse to the parties hereto.

25. **F.H.A. APPRAISAL STATEMENT**
(fill in amount or delete Clauses 24 & 25)

(the wording of this clause is required verbatim by F.H.A. Rules & Regulations)

It is expressly agreed that, notwithstanding any other provisions of this contract, the PURCHASER shall not be obligated to complete the purchase of the property described herein or to incur any penalty by forfeiture of earnest money deposits or otherwise, unless the SELLER has delivered to the PURCHASER a written statement issued by the Federal Housing Commissioner setting forth the appraised value of the property for mortgage insurance purposes of not less than $_____ , which statement the SELLER hereby agrees to deliver to the PURCHASER promptly after such appraised value statement is made available to the SELLER. The PURCHASER shall, however, have the privilege and option of proceeding with the consummation of this contract without regard to the amount of the appraised valuation made by the Federal Housing Commissioner.

26. SALE OF PERSONAL PROPERTY
(fill in and attach list or delete entire clause)

The BUYER agrees to buy from the SELLER the articles of personal property enumerated on the attached list for the price of $ and the SELLER agrees to deliver to the BUYER upon delivery of the deed hereunder, a warranty bill of sale therefor on payment of said price. The provisions of this clause shall constitute an agreement separate and apart from the provisions herein contained with respect to the real estate, and any breach of the terms and conditions of this clause shall have no effect on the provisions of this agreement with respect to the real estate.

27. RELEASE BY HUSBAND OR WIFE

The SELLER'S spouse hereby agrees to join in said deed and to release and convey all statutory and other rights and interests in said premises.

28. BROKER AS PARTY

The broker(s) named herein, join(s) in this agreement and become(s) a party hereto, in so far as any provisions of this agreement expressly apply to him (them), and to any amendments or modifications of such provisions to which he (they) agree(s) in writing.

29. LIABILITY OF TRUSTEE, SHAREHOLDER, BENEFICIARY, etc.

If the SELLER or BUYER executes this agreement in a representative or fiduciary capacity, only the principal or the estate represented shall be bound, and neither the SELLER or BUYER so executing, nor any shareholder or beneficiary of any trust, shall be personally liable for any obligation, express or implied, hereunder.

30. CONSTRUCTION OF AGREEMENT
* delete "triplicate" and substitute "quadruplicate" if required. (See "Instructions in General", 1.)

This instrument, executed in triplicate*   is to be construed as a Massachusetts contract, is to take effect as a sealed instrument, sets forth the entire contract between the parties, is binding upon and enures to the benefit of the parties hereto and their respective heirs, devisees, executors, administrators, successors and assigns, and may be cancelled, modified or amended only by a written instrument executed by both the SELLER and the BUYER. If two or more persons are named herein as BUYER their obligations hereunder shall be joint and several. The captions and marginal notes are used only as a matter of convenience and are not to be considered a part of this agreement or to be used in determining the intent of the parties to it.

683

31. ADDITIONAL PROVISIONS

.... SELLER

.... BUYER

Husband or Wife of Seller

Husband or Wife of Buyer

....

Broker

Problems: Purchase and Sale Agreement

1. Suppose the buyer pays a deposit of $2,000. What happens if he later reneges and refuses to go through with the purchase? Will the seller be permitted to keep the $2,000 as liquidated damages, or would that be barred as a penalty? Would your answer be different if, as a result of the buyer's default, seller later sells the property for a considerably larger price? Compare Kraft v. Michael, 166 Pa. Super. 57, 70 A.2d 425 (1950) (defaulting buyer forfeits deposit even where seller resells at a higher price; court suggests that 10 percent can be forfeited, but that 15 percent might be a penalty), with Freedman v. Rector, Wardens and Vestrymen, 37 Cal. 2d 16, 230 P.2d 629 (1951) (willingly defaulting buyer recovers deposit in excess of seller's actual damages and broker's commission).

2. Buyer pays a deposit of $2,000 and agrees to purchase a $40,000 house by March 25. On March 25, buyer fails to close. Due to tight money conditions, seller does not find another buyer until six months later and must sell for $35,000. Can seller sue first buyer for $3,000? Can first buyer defend with the argument that seller waived these damages by turning to other potential buyers rather than suing him for specific performance?

Sample Document 17-3 is a reproduction of the entire contract for sale of one of the largest (and last) tracts of land in Columbia. Jones signed as attorney for Alimco, Inc. (Alaska Iron Mines Co.), one of the dummy corporations used by the developer, the Rouse Company, to acquire secretly the land that ultimately became the new city.

See G. Breckenfeld, Columbia and the New Cities 244 (1971):

"At last," says Jack Jones, "we came to the Big Bear, Isidore Gudelsky. He wanted $5 million for his 1000 acres. By this time it was obvious that a big land assembly was going on, and he was a shrewd bargainer." Moxley saw Gudelsky several times, usually in his auto, in a restaurant, or a drugstore. On Jones's instructions, Moxley offered $1,750,000 in a property swap. Gudelsky allowed that maybe he'd take $4 million. "Finally," says Jones, "I told Moxley that this deal had to be done." It was an understatement. Unbeknown to him, Gudelsky held the key Columbia land: the town center, symphony hall, glade lake site, and shopping district. Moxley arranged for Gudelsky to meet Jones at Baltimore's Friendship Airport forty-five minutes before Jones was to fly to West Germany on other legal business.

The negotiations began late and moved slowly. Gudelsky complained: "I don't have my lawyer with me." At length, he asked, "Will you pay $3 million?" Jones would, even though the $3000 an acre price was painful. "My wife was frantic," he recalls. "She was aboard and they were

8/14/63

For five dollars and other good and valuable consideration

I, Isadore Gudelsky, on behalf of Rhodes-Fletcher Corp, D. & S. Enterprises, Inc. and Charles Waugh, agree to sell the property designated on this plat of Rhodes-Fletcher Corp of approximately 93.73 acres, D. & S. Enterprises, Inc. of approximately 801.51 acres, and Charles Waugh of approximately 106.11 acres on the following terms: The sales price of $3000 per acre or $3,000,000 payable 29% down at settlement, the balance to be paid over a four year period in equal annual installments with interest at 6% payable semi-annually. All other details to be formalized in a formal contract of sale within a 15 day period, at which time a deposit of 5% will be made to secure the contract. I reserve the right to have the aforesaid terms changed to $3,000,000 cash at settlement. I further reserve the right to accept as part of the cash price of $3,000,000 any one or all of these properties which I may select, not limiting this selection to any specific number of properties or dollar value of the properties selected as shown on exhibit "B" attached hereto. If this selection is made, the $3,000,000 will be reduced by the price shown on said exhibit "B" on those properties selected. All of the above terms and conditions are acceptable to all mine. Inc. settlement is to be made in 60 days from said date.

witness
By: Robert H. Morley
By: Robert H. Morley

By John Winston
Isadore Gudelsky

SAMPLE DOCUMENT 17-3
The Gudelsky contract as written on a restaurant placemat

announcing the flight departure." With Moxley looking on, Jones wrote out a "contract of sale" on the back of a handy scrap of paper, leaving numerous blank spaces for facts Moxley had to fill in later. The deal was with one of the dummy corporations, Alimco. Jones caught his overseas flight, but, he says, "I had to pound on the door of the plane to get in."

Moxley filled in the blanks and, adds Jones, "That's all the contract we ever had with Gudelsky" — a hand-scrawled document from an airport lunch counter ending with the final admonition, "reduce to final form in 15 days." Gudelsky later tried to renege on the deal, partly on the ground that some of the terms were not expressed. An argument ensued over whether the contract was enforceable. As a result, says Jones, "We let him dictate the rest of the terms." Though the contract required the Rouse organization to pay the full price within 30 days, Jones did manage to persuade Gudelsky not to record the transaction immediately — a step that would have exposed the land assembly.

After 15 months, Columbia owned 14,000 acres, 10 percent of Howard County; the average price per acre of land had been $1,450. The site resembled a piece of Swiss cheese, with the 13 existing settlements and various unacquired portions constituting the holes. Nevertheless, instead of random, disorderly growth, a comprehensive plan was adopted, with neighborhoods as the building blocks.

Problem

A 350-acre tract located within the area that Rouse plans to develop as Columbia is presently being used as a cattle-breeding farm. It is owned by Mr. and Mrs. X and Mr. and Mrs. Y (Mr. X and Mrs. Y are brother and sister; they inherited the land when their mother died). In negotiating with the X's and Y's, Rouse has learned the following:

a) The X's and Y's believe that land is the only reasonably safe way to hold wealth; therefore, they are hesitant about exchanging their land for cash, which they would then have to invest in something riskier.

b) They might be willing to exchange their land for another piece of property, but only if they are reasonably sure that it will be a sound, income-producing property. Thus, they would prefer a developed property that will produce rental income.

c) Because of inflation, any extended payment agreement should provide for a cost-of-living adjustment.

Some of Rouse's requirements may conflict with those of the X's and Y's:

d) Flexibility is important to Rouse. While he realizes that the sellers may desire a lease arrangement rather than a straight sale, he feels he cannot be tied to such an arrangement if, for example, he wishes to develop the tract for single family homes.

e) The area is presently zoned for agricultural and large-lot single family residential uses. Since there is no guarantee that his "New Town" zoning plan will be adopted by Howard County, Rouse is in no position to promise that he can develop any or all of the property as income producing rental property.

f) Rouse does not want to be tied down to any particular development plan, nor does he want to be forced by rent-payment provisions to have to develop the entire tract at once.

g) Even if he agrees to take the property as a leasehold, Rouse would at some time like to be able to obtain the fee to all or the greater part of the tract.

Draft a suitable agreement.

Note

Option agreement said: "In consideration of the sum of $10,000.00 paid by the Optionee to the Optionor, . . . the Optionor hereby grants to the Optionee the exclusive option to purchase the real property described in Exhibit 1 hereto on the terms and conditions contained in said Real Estate Sale Contract." A standard form contract was attached. The agreement also provided for a purchase price of $700,000.

Optionor, Roosevelt Hospital in Chicago, tried to bargain about contract terms, especially since it had been offered $125,000 more for the land by a third party, but the court held that it would be appropriate to award specific performance to an optionee in these circumstances. Farley v. Roosevelt Memorial Hospital, 67 Ill. App. 3d 700, 384 N.E.2d 1352 (1978).

2. The Statute of Frauds

MARYLAND LAWS (1974):

§5-103. ASSIGNMENT, GRANT, OR SURRENDER OF INTEREST IN PROPERTY

No corporeal estate, leasehold or freehold, or incorporeal interest in land may be assigned, granted, or surrendered, unless it is in writing signed by the party assigning, granting, or surrendering it, or his agent lawfully authorized by writing, or by act and operation of law.

§5-104. EXECUTORY CONTRACTS

No action may be brought on any contract for the sale or disposition of land or of any interest in or concerning land unless the contract or agreement on which the action is brought, or some memorandum or note of it, is in writing and signed by the party to be charged or some other person lawfully authorized by him.

§5-105.   DECLARATIONS OF TRUST

Except as provided in §5-107 [resulting or constructive trusts], every declaration of trust, or amendment to it, respecting land shall be manifested . . . by a writing signed by the party who by law is enabled to declare the trust, or by his last will in writing, or else it is void.

NATIONAL CONFERENCE OF COMMISSIONERS ON UNIFORM STATE LAWS, UNIFORM LAND TRANSACTIONS ACT §2-201 (1975): (a) Notwithstanding agreement to the contrary and except as provided in subsection (b), a contract to convey real estate is not enforceable by judicial proceeding unless there is a writing signed by the party against whom enforcement is sought or by the party's representative which:

(1)   contains a description of the real estate that is sufficiently definite to make possible an identification of the real estate with reasonable certainty;

(2)   except as to an option to renew a lease, states the price or a method of fixing the price; and

(3)   is sufficiently definite to indicate with reasonable certainty that a contract to convey has been made by the parties.

(b)   A contract not evidenced by a writing satisfying the requirements of subsection (a), but which is valid in other respects, is enforceable if:

(1)   it is for the conveyance of real estate for one year or less;

(2)   the buyer has taken possession of the real estate, and has paid all or a part of the contract price;

(3)   the buyer has accepted a deed from the seller;

(4)   the party seeking to enforce a contract, in reasonable reliance upon the contract and upon the continuing assent of the party against whom enforcement is sought has changed his position to his detriment to the extent that an unjust result can be avoided only by enforcing the contract; or

(5)   the party against whom enforcement is sought admits in his pleading, testimony, or otherwise in court that the contract for conveyance was made.

Problem

Suppose the A's and Mr. Bailout enter into an oral agreement for the purchase of the house, and the A's pay $5,000 down, receiving the following receipt:

"Feb. 1, 1977. For the sum of $95,000. I agree to sell my house located at 100 Kennedy Road, Columbia, Md. Received as earnest money $5,000. Signed, Barnaby Bailout."

The A's tender $90,000 and Mr. Bailout refuses to go forward with the transaction. Can the A's win a suit for specific performance?

3. Equitable Conversion

◆ GRIGGS LAND CO. v. SMITH
46 Wash. 185, 89 P. 477 (1907)

Root, J. In his lifetime one John Bruster entered into a contract to convey an undivided half interest in certain land to one Bruce A. Griggs. . . . Thereafter Bruster died, and respondent Smith was appointed his administrator by the superior court of Okanogan county, and duly qualified. Under Ballinger's Ann. Codes & St. §§6381-6391, said Griggs filed his petition for the specific performance of decedent's contract with him; and such proceedings were had, in accordance with said statutes, that specific performance was decreed. No appeal having been taken, the administrator executed a deed of said undivided one-half interest to Griggs. . . .

The only question presented upon appeal is this: Did the enactment of section 4640 et seq., Ballinger's Ann. Codes & St., repeal section 6381 et seq.? Section 6381 reads as follows: "if any person who is bound by contract, in writing, to convey any real property, shall die before making the conveyance, the superior court of the county in which such real estate or any portion thereof is situate may make a decree authorizing and directing his executor or administrator to convey such real property to the person entitled thereto." The sections following this set forth the procedure necessary to secure a decree for, and a deed of, conveyance. Section 4640, enacted in 1895, reads as follows:

> When a person dies seized of land, tenements or hereditaments, or any right thereto or entitled to any interest therein in fee or for the life of another, his title shall vest immediately in his heirs or devisees, subject to his debts, family allowance, expenses of administration and any other charges for which such real estate is liable under existing laws. No administration of the estate of such decedent, and no decree of distribution or other findings or order of any court shall be necessary in any case to vest such title in the heirs or devisees instantly upon the death of such decedent: Provided, that no person shall be deemed a devisee until the will has been probated. The title and right to possession of such lands, tenements, or hereditaments so vested in such heirs or devisees, together with the rents, issues and profits thereof, shall be good and valid against all persons claiming adversely to the claims of any such heirs, or devisees, ex- •

cepting only the executor or administrator when appointed, and persons lawfully claiming under such executor or administrator; and any one or more of such heirs or devisees, or their grantees, jointly or severally, may sue for and recover their respective shares or interests in any such lands, tenements, or hereditaments and the rents, issues and profits thereof, whether letters testamentary or of administration be granted or not, from any person except the executor or administrator and those lawfully claiming under such executor or administrator.

Respondents urge, and the trial court held, that the last-quoted section had the effect of repealing section 6381 et seq., and that the decree of the court and the deed made in pursuance thereof were invalid and of no effect inasmuch as the heirs of the decedent Bruster were not made parties to the proceeding. Appellant contends that section 4640 et seq. are not inconsistent with section 6381 et seq., and that the latter were not repealed. It invokes the doctrine of equitable conversion, and cites, among other authorities, Story's Equity Jurisprudence (13th ed.), 790 and 1212, where Mr. Justice Story, among other things, says,

> There is another consideration which is incident to this subject and to which courts of equity have given an attention and effect proportioned to its importance. In the view of courts of law, contracts respecting lands or other things of which a specific execution will be decreed in equity are considered as simply executory agreements, and as not attaching to the property in any manner as an incident, or as a present or future charge, but courts of equity regard them in a very different light. They treat them for most purposes precisely as if they had been specifically executed. Thus, if a man has entered into a valid contract for the purchase of land, he is treated in equity as the equitable owner of the land, and the vendor is treated as the owner of the money. The purchaser may devise it as land even before the conveyance is made, and it passes by descent to his heir as land. The vendor is deemed in equity to stand seised of it for the benefit of the purchaser, and the trust (as has already been stated) attaches to the land so as to bind the heir of the vendor and everyone claiming under him as a purchaser with notice of the trust. The heir of the purchaser may come into equity and insist upon a specific performance of the contract; and unless some other circumstances affect the case he may require the purchase money to be paid out of the personal estate of the purchaser in the hands of his personal representative. On the other hand, the vendor may come into equity for a specific performance of the contract on the other side and to have the money paid; for the remedy in cases of specific performance is mutual, and the purchase money is treated as the personal estate of the vendor and goes as such to his personal representative. Another class of cases illustrating the doctrine of implied trusts is that which embraces what is commonly called the equitable conversion of property. By this is meant an implied or equitable change of property from real to personal, or from personal to real, so that each is considered as transferable, transmissible, and descendible, according to its new charac-

ter as it arises out of the contracts or other intentions of the parties. This change is a mere consequence of the common doctrine of courts of equity that where things are agreed to be done they are to be treated for many purposes as if they were actually done. Thus . . . where a contract is made for the sale of land, the vendor is in equity immediately deemed a trustee for the vendee of the real estate, and the vendee is deemed a trustee for the vendor of the purchase money. Under such circumstance the vendee is treated as the owner of the land, and it is devisable and descendible as his real estate. On the other hand, the money is treated as the personal estate of the vendor, and as subject to the like modes of disposition by him as other personalty, and is distributable in the same manner on his death.

We think appellant's contention must be upheld. Repeals by implication are not favored. There is nothing in the law of 1895 which indicates any intention to repeal the provisions of section 6381 et seq. The latter were statutes dealing with contracts for conveyance of real estate after the grantor's decease. The statute of 1895, general in its character, provided for the descent of the title to real estate immediately to the heirs. It was admitted that an administrator would have power to sell the property to pay debts of the estate incurred by the decedent in his lifetime. The contract that he made to convey this property was an obligation which he left unfilled at the time of his death. There would seem to be no good reason why the administrator, whose province it is to settle up the affairs of the state, should not adjust this matter. Section 6381 provides that he should so do. The purpose of section 4640, to vest title to real estate in the heirs immediately upon the death of the ancestor, should not be held to contravene the objects of section 6381 et seq. In this state a mortgage upon real estate is but a lien, the title to the mortgaged property remaining in the mortgagor, and, of course, descending to the heirs immediately upon his death. But in the case at bar, the owner of the land has made a contract to convey and he could leave to his heirs only the interest then owned which was virtually but the right to the proceeds — the holder of the contract being entitled to have the land conveyed to him upon paying the purchase price. In such cases the courts have treated the property, for purposes of administration, as personal rather than real. . . .

The judgment of the honorable superior court is reversed, and the cause remanded with instructions to overrule the demurrer, and to proceed in accordance with this opinion.

Notes

1. Buyer paid $100 for a 60-day option to purchase. Seller died. Seller's will provided for her real property to go to X and her personal

property to Y. Did equitable conversion turn seller's interest in the land into personalty? In Eddington v. Turner, 27 Del. Ch. 411, 38 A.2d 738 (1944), the court held that equitable conversion would occur only at the exercise of the option, and that the property therefore passes as real property, subject to an obligation on X to convey the property (and receive the purchase price) if buyer exercises the option.

2. Seller sold 160 acres to buyer, with the price to be paid in 5 annual installments. Seller kept title, but buyer took possession immediately. Seller sued to stop buyer from cutting timber. The court said buyer could not cut the timber if its removal threatened the security for seller's interest, and that in America, with widely fluctuating land values, to assure "sufficient security . . . there should be a much broader margin between the amount of the debt and the value of the property mortgaged for its security than is considered sufficient in [England]." Moses v. Johnson, 88 Ala. 517, 7 So. 146 (1890).

3. S contracted to sell P the Arizona Orchard, including all water and ditch rights, and all improvements. Before the closing, the packing plant and warehouse burned down. The court accepted

the so-called majority rule . . . that the risk of loss falls on the vendee . . . upon the theory of an equitable conversion, whereby the vendor's interest in the property has been converted by the contract from realty into personalty and the vendor holds merely the bare legal title in trust for the vendee, who holds the equitable title; or upon the theory that the beneficial incidents of ownership are in the vendee. [Ross v. Bumstead, 65 Ariz. 61, 173 P.2d 765 (1946).]

4. See N.Y. Gen. Oblig. Law (1964):

§5-1311. *Uniform Vendor and Purchaser Risk Act*

1. Any contract for the purchase and sale or exchange of realty shall be interpreted, unless the contract expressly provides otherwise, as including an agreement that the parties shall have the following rights and duties:

a. When neither the legal title nor the possession of the subject matter of the contract has been transferred to the purchaser: (1) if all or a material part thereof is destroyed without fault of the purchaser or is taken by eminent domain, the vendor cannot enforce the contract, and the purchaser is entitled to recover any portion of the price that he has paid; but nothing herein contained shall be deemed to deprive the vendor of any right to recover damages against the purchaser for any breach of contract by the purchaser prior to the destruction or taking; (2) if an immaterial part thereof is destroyed without fault of the purchaser or is taken by eminent domain, neither the vendor nor the purchaser is thereby deprived of the right to enforce the contract; but there shall be, to the extent of the destruction or taking, an abatement of the purchase price.

b. When either the legal title or the possession of the subject matter of the contract has been transferred to the purchaser, if all or any part thereof is destroyed without fault of the vendor or is taken by eminent domain, the purchaser is not thereby relieved from a duty to pay the price, nor is he thereby entitled to recover any portion thereof that he has paid; but nothing herein contained shall be deemed to deprive the purchaser of any right to recover damages against the vendor for any breach of contract by the vendor prior to the destruction or taking.

D.   ESTABLISHING TITLE

1.   Recording Systems

Once they are parties to a contract, Mr. & Ms. Ambitious need a "title search" to determine whether Mr. Bailout owns what he has committed himself to sell them. At the same time, whatever savings bank the A's approach for a mortgage will commission a title search. In some states, the buyer and the lender jointly commission a search. For this search it is necessary to go to the office of the Registry of Deeds, usually located in the county seat, which provides a public record of transactions affecting title to land.

The job of the deed registry is to copy verbatim whatever title documents are submitted for "recording," and then place them in order in a bound volume without regard to the names of the parties or the location of the parcels. When the system began, records were few and simple — a Vermont case of 1836 discusses the 5 volumes of documents then in existence. By contrast, in 1949 in Los Angeles County, 794,306 documents were recorded.

The only available access to these voluminous records is through official indices. By far the most common index is the Grantor-Grantee Index, which is compiled according to the names of the persons referred to in the documents. As the name implies, there are actually two separate indices, one alphabetical by grantor, the other by grantee. When a grantee records a property transaction in order to protect his interests, the clerk will list the document in each index. Opposite the name indexed appears the date of recording, the name of the other party to the transaction, the volume and page on which the material is copied, a brief description of the property, and other identifying notations required by the practice of the local registry sample. (See Sample Document 17-4.)

In establishing the chain of title, the searcher begins by working back from the present owner in the grantee index to an owner some years back so far as seems necessary in order that earlier claims are cut

SAMPLE DOCUMENT 17-4
Grantor Index

GRANTOR INDEX TO LAND RECORDS — Howard County, Maryland

COTTCO UNIVERSAL INDEX No. 3-25 © 1956
Colt Data Processed Indexes
Sold by The Paul Company, Baltimore, Md.

[09 025 001 R]   Entry Sheet Identification No.

GRANTOR SURNAME	GIVEN NAMES ABCDEFGH	GIVEN NAMES IJKLMNO	GIVEN NAMES PQRSTUVWXYZ	AP	GRANTEE	AP	KIND OF INSTRUMENT	MO	DAY	YEAR	VOL	PAGE	BRIEF DESCRIPTION (Vol.-Page refers to Original Mortgage or Trust)
Guarnieri	Carolyn D Francis				Edmondson Fed Sav & Ln Assn		Mtg	Aug	9	68	493	197	27000.00 Lot 10 Chatham
	******				***********								
Gubrud	Faye E				John W Steele III Tr	O	Deed of Trust	Oct	5	70	541	646	Lt 306 Thunder Hill 27600.00
Gubrud	Arnold E Faye E				Merritt Savings & Ln Assoc		Mtg	May	31	73	637	743	Lt 10 Bk B Allview Ests 62000
Gubrud	Arnold E Faye E				Birnie E Williams	W	Deed	May	31	73	638	82	Lt 306 V of OM Sec 1
	******				***********								
Gude	France K	Lawson H		O	Monumental Life Ins Co		Mtg	Mar	28	66	451	202	20500.00
Gude		Mary L			Hazel M McClintic		Deed	Sep	27	67	476	112	Lot 4 Savage
Gude	France K	Lawson H			Balto Gas & Elec Co		Fin Statmt	Aug	14	70	538	454	
	******				***********								
Gudelsky	Homer				Thomas W Ligon	O	Mtg	May	27	65	436	26	493186.80
Gudelsky	Homer				How Res & Dev Corp	O	Conf Deed	Nov	29	67	479	495	
	******				***********								
Gudmore		Nancy L	Patrick H		John N Bowers Inc		Deed	Aug	7	72	603	196	Lt 40 Blk P Allview
	******				************								

off by the statute of limitations and, in some circumstances, back to the original grant from the United States or some other sovereign; and then forward in the grantor index to ascertain whether any owner has made a conveyance affecting the title that the buyer will claim if she buys.

As an example, assume that the *A*'s purchase the house from Mr. Bailout, and now wish to mortgage it to the First National Bank. The bank employs you to check for clouds on the title. You begin by looking for Mr. Bailout in the grantee index. The entry looks something like this;

Date of Recording	Grantee	Grantor	Instrument	Brief Land Description	Liber	Folio
3/24/64	Horace Bailout	Smith, John and Nan	deed	¼ acre, 2nd election district	WWH 172	546

This leads the title searcher to the deed from the Smiths to Bailout. This deed may contain restrictions of interest to the bank. The deed may or may not indicate from whom the Smiths took title; if it does not, by checking the grantee index back from 1964, the searcher should find a record of the deed by which the Smiths acquired title. This process of checking each grantor in the grantee index (or in the probate index) continues until the searcher feels confident that the chain is clear. A search of the grantee index for John Smith might be fruitless, if for example Smith took by inheritance. Only a check of the probate records would locate this transaction; unless the deed from the Smiths to Bailout refers to the will, it might be difficult to locate.

The searcher then turns to the grantor index, beginning with the last grantor found in the grantee index. This search has two purposes: to locate prior transfers of title that may invalidate the chain, and to locate encumbrances on the property. For example, assume that Carol Bensinger was the predecessor in title to the Smiths and that she took her deed from William Jones. Before giving his deed to Bensinger, though, Jones had given a deed to Darrell Johnson, who had recorded it. The chain of title in the grantee index would look like this: Ambitious from Bailout from Smith from Bensinger from Jones. Jones to Johnson to. . . . This can be located only through the grantor index.

Similarly, Jones may have given a mortgage to Bank. Unless the grantor index later shows a release of mortgage from Bank to Jones, that mortgage has priority over one that First National would give. Similarly, long-term leases, easements, and other encumbrances conveyed by a prior owner in the chain of title would show up in the grantor index.

If the title is deemed clear, and the bank gives the mortgage, the entry in the grantor index would look like this:

Date of Recording	Grantor	Grantee	Instrument	Brief Land Description	Liber	Folio
10/1/76	John & Mary Ambitious	First Natl. Bank	deed of trust	¼ acre, 2nd election district	WWH 173	14

A word of caution: this weaving between the indices is not as easy as it seems. Among the complications:

(1) Change of name of a person in the chain, whether by marriage, divorce, legal change of name, use of nickname, etc.;

(2) Besides conveyance by will, problems of intestacy, divorce, partition, adverse possession, and the like, which normally will not be reflected in the grantor-grantee index;

(3) Many liens against the property recorded in a completely different system: tax liens, mechanics liens, judgments, and highway right-of-way condemnations, for example.

Instead of or in addition to a grantor-grantee index system, some jurisdictions utilize a Tract or Block Index, which keys the instruments to the parcels of land rather than to the names of the parties. In such states, the searcher begins with a map of the county or city in the recorder's office, from which is located the number of the block and the boundaries and number of each lot within the block. A page in the index volume covers each numbered tract, and lists the volume and page numbers of each recorded instrument relating to that tract. (See Figure 17-2 and Sample Document 17-5).

The title searcher's aim is to use the indices to find the documents in the chain of title. Then he or she makes extracts of the pertinent parts, for ultimate evaluation.

2. Recording Statutes

What happens when an owner sells a tract of land twice? At common law, first in time was the rule for determining priorities. If *O*, the true owner, conveyed to *A* for valuable consideration, and then tried to sell to *B*, *A* would prevail over *B* even if *B* had no notice of the earlier sale to *A*. With the delivery of the first deed, ran the metaphysics, the grantor conveyed all he owned. Water could not rise higher than its source!

This rule was incompatible with a market economy in which commercial transfer of land occurred frequently, and so recording acts modified the doctrines. Now the first purchaser was required to "record" his deed. Once he did so, he was protected against later purchasers. And they were protected because they could check at the record office and discover that the alleged owner had already sold. The statutes fall into three main classifications,* set forth below.

---

*Sometimes a fourth category is listed, the so-called period of grace statute, which declares a deed invalid against a good faith purchaser unless recorded within 15 days of the closing. Since the only example, Del. Code Ann. titl. 25, §153, has been repealed, 56 Del. Laws 318 (1968), we treat "period of grace" as a footnote and not as a category.

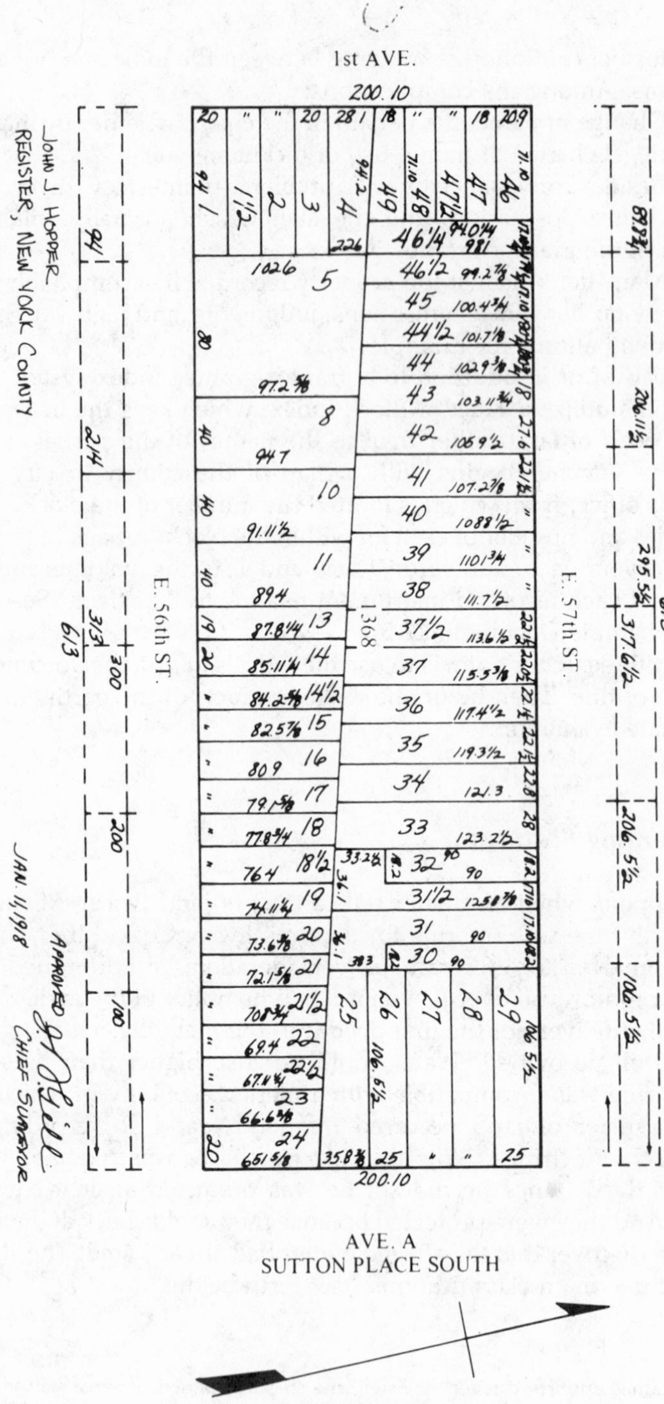

FIGURE 17-2
The Sutton Townhouse site on New York's tract index map

SAMPLE DOCUMENT 17-5
Mortgage Register

REGISTER NEW YORK COUNTY   MORTGAGES   BLOCK 1368   LOT NO. 5   PAGE 1

MORTGAGOR	MORTGAGEE	AMOUNT	DATE OF RECORD	LIBER	PAGE	NOTES
CHATHAM ASSOCIATES, INC.	HANOVER EQUITIES CORPORATION	$680,000.	July 1 1965	6395	232	
CHATHAM ASSOCIATES, INC.	OXFORD ASSOCIATES INC.	$235,000	Oct. 4 1965	6421	54	
OXFORD ASSOCIATES INC.	JACKSON Willard T.		Oct. 4 1965	6421	52	Assigns 6421mp54 Now Due $235,000.00
HANOVER EQUITIES CORPORATION	FRANKLIN NATIONAL BANK		Nov. 5, 1965	6430	19	Asgn 6395mp232 due $680,000.
FRANKLIN NATIONAL BANK	GIBRALTAR CREDIT CORP.		July 12, 1966	80	448	Asgn Mtge 6395mp232
CHATHAM ASSOCIATES	GIBRALTAR CREDIT CORP.		July 12, 1966	80	450	Extns. Mtge 6395 232

continued on page 2

1. *Notice Statutes.* A subsequent purchaser, who has no notice of the prior instrument, prevails over a prior grantee who has not recorded. Thus if O sells to A, who does not record, and then O sells to B, B wins against A unless B had notice of the earlier transaction. See, e.g., Mass. Gen. Laws Ann. Ch. 183, §4 (West 1977):

> A conveyance of an estate in fee simple, fee tail or for life, or a lease for a term of seven years, . . . shall not be valid as against any person, except the grantor or lessor, his heirs and devisees and persons having actual notice of it, unless it . . . is recorded in the registry of deeds for the county or district in which the land to which it relates lies.

2. *Race Statutes.* The first person to record wins. Thus if O sells to A who does not record, and then to B who records, B wins. But if B also delays in recording, and A records first, A wins. See, e.g., N.C. Stat. §47-18 (Michie 1984):

> (a) No (i) conveyance of land, or (ii) contract to convey, or (iii) option to convey, or (iv) lease of land for more than three years shall be valid to pass any property interest as against lien creditors or purchasers for a valuable consideration from the donor, bargainor or lessor but from the time of registration thereof in the county where the land lies. . . .

3. *Race-Notice Statute.* The second purchaser wins if he (1) takes without notice, and also (2) records first. See, e.g., Cal. Civ. Code §1214 (West 1982):

> Every conveyance of real property, other than a lease for a term not exceeding one year, is void as against any subsequent purchaser or mortgagee of the same property, or any part thereof, in good faith and for a valuable consideration, whose conveyance is first duly recorded. . . .

Problems

1. Bailout conveys to the A's, who do not record; he then conveys to X, who records immediately. Who prevails under each of the foregoing statutes?

2. Bailout conveys to the A's, who do not record; he then conveys to X, who also does not record. Subsequently, Bailout conveys to Z. Who prevails under each statute?

3. Bailout conveys to the A's, who do not record; he then conveys to X, who after learning of the deed to the A's, records. Who prevails under each statute?

4. Bailout conveys to the A's who do not record; Bailout conveys to

X, who has no knowledge of *A*'s deed but who also does not record immediately. *A* records; *X* records and sells to *Z*.

5. Bailout conveys to the *A*'s, who do not record; he then conveys to *X*. *X* had actual notice of the Bailout-*A*'s transaction when he purchased, but he records first. The *A*'s then record. *X* sells to *Z*. Who prevails under each statute?

6. Bailout conveys to the *A*'s, who do not record. Bailout gives a mortgage to First National Bank, and receives $25,000 in cash. Who prevails under each statute in suit between the *A*'s and the bank?

Note

The most interesting of these problems is number 4. Why does *Z* win in a notice jurisdiction? When *Z* bought, *Z* could have discovered the existence of the deed from Bailout to *A*. But a person who purchases from a seller protected under the recording act should have the same rights as his or her grantor. This rule is necessary if the recording act is to give *X* the benefit of his or her bargain by giving protection when he or she seeks to sell Blackacre. Of course if Bailout repurchases Blackacre from *X*, Bailout will not prevail over *A*. There is too much risk of collusion; and *B*, having sold to *A*, simply cannot be permitted to win a lawsuit against *A* even if *A* has behaved badly by not recording.

3.   *Recording Disputes*

◆ MORSE v. CURTIS
140 Mass. 112, 2 N.E. 929 (1885)

MORTON, C.J. This is a writ of entry. Both parties derive their title from one Hall. On August 8, 1872, Hall mortgaged the land to the demandant. On September 7, 1875, Hall mortgaged the land to one Clark, who had notice of the earlier mortgage. The mortgage to Clark was recorded on January 31, 1876. The mortgage to the demandant was recorded on September 8, 1876.* On October 4, 1881, Clark assigned his mortgage to the tenant, who had no actual notice of the mortgage to the demandant. . . . [W]hich of these titles has priority? . . .

---

*The preceding is an accurate report of the case, from the official reporter. In one of the rare errors in the West reporter system, the unofficial report, 2 N.E. 929, says in the sixth line "September 8, 1875," instead of September 8, 1876. With the year wrongly stated, the discussion in the opinion makes no sense.

Upon careful consideration, the reasons upon which the earlier cases were decided seem to us the more satisfactory, because they best follow the spirit of our registry laws and the practice of the profession under them. The earliest registry laws provided that no conveyance of land shall be good and effectual in law "against any other person or persons but the grantor or grantors, and their heirs only, unless the deed or deeds thereof be acknowledged and recorded in manner aforesaid." St. 1783, c.37, §4.

Under this statute, the court, at an early period, held that the recording was designed to take the place of the notorious act of livery of seisin; and that, though by the first deed the title passed out of the grantor, as against itself, yet he could, if such deed was not recorded, convey a good title to an innocent purchaser who received and recorded his deed. But the court also held that a prior unrecorded deed would be valid against a second purchaser who took his deed with a knowledge of the prior deed, thus engrafting an exception upon the statute.

This exception was adopted on the ground that it was a fraud in the second grantee to take a deed, if he had knowledge of the prior deed. As Chief Justice Shaw forcibly says, in Lawrence v. Stratton, 6 Cush. 163, the rule is "put upon the ground, that a party with such notice could not take a deed without fraud, the objection was not to the nature of the conveyance, but to the honesty of the taker; and, therefore, if the estate had passed through such taker to a bona fide purchaser, without fraud, the conveyance was held valid."

This exception by judicial exposition was afterwards engrafted upon the statutes, and somewhat extended, by the Legislature. It is to be observed that, in each of these revisions, it is provided that an unrecorded prior deed is not valid against any persons except the grantor, his heirs and devisees, "and persons having actual notice" of it. The reason why the statute requires actual notice to a second purchaser, in order to defeat his title, is apparent: its purpose is that his title shall not prevail against the prior deed, if he has been guilty of a fraud upon the first grantee; and he could not be guilty of such fraud, unless he had actual notice of the first deed.

Now, in the case before us, it is found as a fact that the tenant had no actual knowledge of the prior mortgage to the demandant at the time he took his assignment from Clark; but it is contended that he had constructive notice, because the demandant's mortgage was recorded before such assignment.

It was held in Connecticut v. Bradish that such record was evidence of actual notice, but was not of itself enough to show actual notice, and to charge the assignee of the second deed with a fraud upon the holder of the first unrecorded deed. This seems to us to accord with the spirit of our registry laws, and with the uniform understanding of and practice under them by the profession.

These laws not only provide that deeds must be recorded, but they also prescribe the method in which the records shall be kept and indexes prepared for public inspection and examination. There are indexes of grantors and grantees, so that, in searching a title, the examiner is obliged to run down the list of grantors, or run backward through the list of grantees. If he can start with an owner who is known to have a good title, as, in the case at bar, he could start with Hall, he is obliged to run through the index of grantors until he finds a conveyance by the owner of the land in question. After such conveyance, the former owner becomes a stranger to the title, and the examiner must follow down the name of the new owner to see if he has conveyed the land, and so on. It would be a hardship to require an examiner to follow in the indexes of grantors the names of every person who, at any time, through perhaps a long chain of title, was the owner of the land.

We do not think this is the practical construction which lawyers and conveyancers have given to our registry laws. The inconveniences of such a construction would be much greater than would be the inconvenience of requiring a person, who has neglected to record his prior deed for a time, to record it, and to bring a bill in equity to set aside the subsequent deed, if it was taken in fraud of his rights.

The better rule, and the one the least likely to create confusion of titles, seems to us to be, that, if a purchaser, upon examining the registry, find a conveyance from the owner of the land to his grantor, which gives him a perfect record title completed by what the law, at the time it is recorded, regards as equivalent to a livery of seisin, he is entitled to rely upon such record title, and is not obliged to search the records afterwards, in order to see if there has been any prior unrecorded deed of the original owner. . . .

We are therefore of opinion, that, in the case at bar, the tenant has the better title; and, according to the terms of the report, the verdict ordered for the demandant must be set aside, and a new trial granted.

CROSS, THE RECORD "CHAIN OF TITLE" HYPOCRISY, 57 Colum. L. Rev. 787, 787-789, 799-800 (1957): Anyone reading part of the mass of recording act cases in almost any American jurisdiction will be confronted with the "chain of title" rationale often invoked to resolve priority between competing claimants to interests in land. The assertion is that a subsequent purchaser will have priority over an earlier claimant to the same title unless the antecedent claim is revealed within the "chain" of the title which the subsequent purchaser believes he is getting. The concept has been evolved apparently to effect some practical protection by the recording acts. These acts commonly provide that an instrument shall be ineffective against certain competing claimants unless the direction of the statute is followed. The statute may make the instrument "void" as to the competitor or may state that if the statutory direction is followed the record of an instrument shall be notice to all the world. The chain of title concept is commonly used without regard to the possible importance of the particular form of statute.

From the rule that all conveyances are "innocent" it must follow that a current claimant can prevail only if he can establish that ownership has in fact passed from the sovereign (theoretically) through his predecessors to himself, and hence that there is a chain or sequence of transactions ending in him. The record chain of title concept has an additional connotation, that of defining the length of each link in the sense of fixing the period of time for search in the records against a particular owner. Rather than strictly a chain of transfers it connotes a chain of owners or persons interested in the title. The typical statute says nothing of chain of title — it appears by a judicial gloss which has done much to conceal the inadequacy of the protection afforded by the facts. Consequently the needed corrections are not pressed. . . .

From the practical necessities of search in the public records has evolved the meaning definitive of the length of each link. This is the method: to determine whether a prospective vendor has the interest he purports to have, the records are examined to discover the sequence of transfers which support his assertion of title. Unless the origin of his title is known the search must extend backwards in time looking for the record of a conveyance to the vendor; then continuing backwards, search is made for the record of the instrument to which the vendor's grantor was the grantee, and continuing similarly as to each predecessor until the transfer from the sovereign is discovered, or in older states, far enough back until an apparently firm "root" is located. In an earlier time this must have involved thumbing through the actual volumes of the record, but since indexing has been directed by the legislatures, the initial search for the persons has been in the indexes. The history of transfer now discovered, the process is reversed and search is made to determine what each of the various owners did with or to the title during the period of his apparent ownership. As to each owner there should be a small overlap in time, i.e., the search is made from the day before execution of the deed to him (not the day of recording) until the day after recording of the deed from him (not the day of execution).

Thus the length of the respective links is identified. A transaction by the then owner fairly discoverable of record within the duration of his link is in the chain of title, but all other transactions, though reflected in the records in fact, are not in the chain of title. Under this approach the prospective purchaser has no concern with instruments thus determined to be out of the chain of title. . . . And where search or examination is made directly from the public records this meaning is apparently adopted to control the extent of search.

Since it is not now practicable to search in the actual record or transcription books, if it ever was for long, this then is the resulting proposition: A prospective purchaser can be confident he will get good title from his vendor if an examination of the indexes in the indicated manner, and a study of the transactions thereby discovered, reveals a chain of title without infirmity. But is this so? I suggest that to assert that such a "chain of title" assures ownership in the vendor is sheer hypocrisy. . . .

Where statutes prescribe tract or numerical indexes rather than, or in addition to, alphabetical or name indexes, the chain of title reasoning is totally impertinent because all transactions relating to the particular tract are readily discoverable. And of course when the record information is in fact secured through the use of tract indexes even though privately prepared, the careful subsequent purchaser will probably have actual notice of the competing claim, thus making constructive notice from the record more theoretically, than actually, important. Where search is made from public records with name indexes, the lack of more reported difficulties must result from absence of real difficulties, disqualification of the subsequent purchaser because of notice external to the record, or resolution of the controversy without litigation or without appeal.

A title claimant's protection by the record ought to be as complete as practicable, against both the hazards of the past and of the future. As a minimum the statutes should provide for three things: first, the keeping of tract indexes, thus eliminating the need for chain of title rationalizing; second, proper indexing as an essential part of recording; and third, specific placement of the burden of full recording on the claimant under the instrument, he being the only person who can as a practical matter determine that it is done. There are more things that profitably can and may be done in the future. Thus, it is perhaps not wholly unrealistic to hope that a revised interest in the problems may result in widespread legislative elimination of the record chain of title hypocrisy.

◆ AYER v. PHILADELPHIA & BOSTON
FACE BRICK CO.
159 Mass. 84, 34 N.E. 177 (1893)

HOLMES, J. When this case was before us the first time, 157 Mass. 57, it was assumed by the tenant that the only question was whether the covenant of warranty in the second mortgage should be construed as warranting against the first mortgage. No attempt was made to deny that, if it was so construed, the title afterwards acquired by the mortgagor would enure to the benefit of the second mortgagee under the established American doctrine. The tenant now desires to reopen the agreed facts for the purpose of showing that after a breach of the covenant in the second mortgage, and before he repurchased the land, the mortgagor went into bankruptcy and got his discharge. The judge below ruled that the discharge was immaterial, and for that reason alone declined to reopen the agreed statement, and the case comes before us upon an exception to that ruling.

The tenant's counsel frankly avow their own opinion that the discharge in bankruptcy makes no difference. But they say that the enuring of an after acquired title by virtue of a covenant of warranty must be due either to a representation or to a promise contained in the covenant, and that if it is due to the former, which they deem the correct doctrine, then they are entitled to judgment on the agreed statement of facts as it stands, on the ground that there can be no estoppel by an instrument when the truth appears on the face of it, and that in this case the deed showed that the grantor was conveying land subject to a mortgage. If, however, contrary to their opinion, the title enures by reason of the promise in the covenant, or to prevent circuity of action, then they say the provision is discharged by the discharge in bankruptcy.

However anomalous what we have called the American doctrine may be, it is settled in this State as well as elsewhere. It is settled also that a discharge in bankruptcy has no effect on this operation of the covenant of warranty in an ordinary deed where the warranty is coextensive with the grant. It would be to introduce further technicality into an artificial doctrine if a different rule should be applied where the conveyance is of land subject to a mortgage against which the grantor covenants to warrant and defend. No reason has been offered for such a distinction, nor do we perceive any.

But it is said that the operation of the covenant must be rested on some general principle, and cannot be left to stand simply as an unjustified peculiarity of a particular transaction without analogies elsewhere in the law, and that this general principle can be found only in the doctrine of estoppel by representation, if it is held, as the cases cited and many others show, that the estoppel does not depend on personal liability for damages.

If the American rule is an anomaly, it gains no strength by being referred to a principle which does not justify it in fact and by sound reasoning. The title may be said to enure by way of estoppel when explaining the reason why a discharge in bankruptcy does not affect this operation of the warranty; but if so, the existence of the estoppel does not rest on the prevention of fraud or on the fact of a representation actually believed to be true. It is a technical effect of a technical representation, the extent of which is determined by the scope of the words devoted to making it. A subsequent title would enure to the grantee when the grant was of an unencumbered fee although the parties agreed by parol that there was a mortgage outstanding; and this shows that the estoppel is determined by the scope of the conventional assertion, not by any question of fraud or of actual belief. But the scope of the conventional assertion is determined by the scope of the warranty which contains it. Usually the warranty is of what is granted, and therefore the scope of it is determined by the scope of the description. But this is not necessarily so; and when the warranty says that the grantor is to be taken as assuring you that he owns and will defend you in the unencumbered fee, it does not matter that by the same deed he avows the assertion not to be the fact. The warranty is intended to fix the extent of responsibility assumed, and by that the grantor makes himself answerable for the fact being true. In short, if a man by a deed says, I hereby estop myself to deny a fact, it does not matter that he recites as a preliminary that the fact is not true. The difference between a warranty and an ordinary statement in a deed is, that the operation and effect of the latter depends on the whole context of the deed, whereas the warranty is put in for the express purpose of estopping the grantor to the extent of its words. The reason "why the estoppel should operate, is, that such was the obvious intention of the parties."

If a general covenant of warranty following a conveyance of only the grantor's right, title, and interest were made in such a form that it was construed as more extensive than the conveyance, there would be an estoppel coextensive with the covenant. So in the case of a deed by an heir presumptive of his expectancy with a covenant of warranty. In this case, of course, there is no pretence that the grantor has a title coextensive with his warranty. In Lincoln v. Emerson, 108 Mass. 87, a first mortgage was mentioned in the covenant against encumbrances in a second mortgage, but was not excepted from the covenant of warranty. The title of the mortgagor under a foreclosure of the first mortgage was held to enure to an assignee of the second mortgage. Here the deed disclosed the truth, and for the purposes of the tenant's argument it cannot matter what part of the deed discloses the truth, unless it should be suggested that a covenant of warranty cannot be made more extensive than the grant, which was held not to be the law in our former decision.

The question remains whether the tenant stands better as a purchaser without actual notice, assuming that he had not actual notice of the second mortgage.

> It has been the settled law of this Commonwealth for nearly forty years, that, under a deed with covenants of warranty from one capable of executing it, a title afterwards acquired by the grantor inures by way of estoppel to the grantee, not only as against the grantor, but also as against one holding by descent or grant from him after acquiring the new title. Somes v. Skinner, 3 Pick. 52. We are aware that this rule, especially as applied to subsequent grantees, while followed in some States, has been criticised in others. But it has been too long established and acted on in Massachusetts to be changed, except by legislation. [Knight v. Thayer, 125 Mass. 25, 27.]

It is urged for the tenant that this rule should not be extended. But if it is a bad rule, that is no reason for making a bad exception to it. As the title would have enured as against a subsequent purchaser from the mortgagor had his deed made no mention of the mortgage, and as by our decision his covenant of warranty operates by way of estoppel notwithstanding the mention of the mortgage, no intelligible reason can be stated why the estoppel should bind a purchaser without actual notice in the former case, and not bind him in the latter.

Upon the whole case, we are of opinion that the demandant is entitled to judgment.

Note

See R. Swain, 1949 Supplement to Crocker's Notes on Common Forms, Sixth (Conveyancers') Edition 95-96 (1949):

> Thus we have an example of a variance between law and practice in which the conveyancers are clearly right and the law is clearly wrong. The logical result of the law is that title examiners, to be entirely safe, must search the records before the date when any individual in the chain acquired title, to see if he, or an ancestor of his ever gave a warranty deed. It is not even safe, in theory, to stop when the individual grantor must have been unborn. Thanks to the doctrine of lineal warranty, the heir may be estopped by his ancestor's warranty, or that of his wife's ancestor! The wretched examiner would have to search the index under each name in the chain of title clear back to the opening of the Registry in 1639, and he will probably never then find a deed by an ancestor with a different name.
>
> Do conveyancers do this? They do not. The cost of such examination would exceed the value of the land. Perhaps they hope that by ignoring the specter of estoppel by deed, they can prevent it from materializing. Perhaps they have been taking comfort in the thought that warranty deeds are becoming unfashionable in urban Massachusetts. Nevertheless, mortgages are as common as ever, and the statutory mortgage covenants are capable of feeding an estoppel. . . .

◆ TRAMONTOZZI v. D'AMICIS
344 Mass. 514, 183 N.E.2d 295 (1962)

SPIEGEL, Justice. This is an action of contract to recover a deposit made by the plaintiff under a contract to purchase land and buildings owned by the defendant and located at 107 Adams Street, Lexington. . . .

The evidence is herewith summarized. The contract of purchase and sale was entered into on September 13, 1958, at which time a deposit of $500 was made. The premises were to be conveyed on November 12, 1958, "by a good and sufficient deed conveying a good and clear record and marketable title thereto free from encumbrances" with certain exceptions not here pertinent. There were also provisions that, "[i]f the seller shall be unable to give title or to make conveyance as . . . stipulated, any payments made under this agreement shall be refunded, and all other obligations of either party hereunto shall cease"; and, "[i]f buyer is unable to pass papers on or before November 12, 1958, their [*sic*] deposit is to be forfeited."

In 1913 a previous owner of the premises died and in the probate of his estate on March 25, 1913, an inventory was filed in the Middlesex probate registry which listed the premises in question with the following notation: "estate on Adams Street subject to the following mortgages, Mrs. C. G. Wiswell, $3,000.00; Mrs. E. S. Smith, $1600.00; Cambridge Savings Bank, $400.00." There is no record in the appropriate registry of deeds of the Smith mortgage. There is no evidence that such a mortgage is still outstanding nor, indeed, is there any evidence that such a mortgage was ever executed.

The heirs of the owner who died in 1913 "conveyed the fee to one Burnham, and following mesne conveyances, the defendant acquired the title."

The trial judge found that, "[o]n the facts, . . . there is actual notice of a previous mortgage"; and that "even if it should be decided that the notice of the mortgage in the inventory was not sufficient to give the parties actual notice, it raises a sufficient doubt so that the defendant can not give a clear record, as called for in the agreement." . . .

The issue before us is whether the reference to an unrecorded mortgage appearing in the 1913 probate inventory prevents the defendant from giving a good and clear record title.

"A good and clear record title free from all encumbrances means a title which on the record itself can be again sold as free from obvious defects, and substantial doubts." . . .

Under our recording statute an unrecorded mortgage is invalid as against third parties who do not have "actual notice" of it. The unrecorded Smith mortgage cannot be asserted as adversely affecting the defendant's title unless it is shown that he had actual notice of it. The plaintiff, being the party relying upon an alleged unrecorded mortgage, has the burden of proving that the defendant had actual notice of such a mortgage. . . ."The 'actual notice' of the statute has been construed with considerable strictness. . . . Knowledge of facts which would ordinarily put a party upon inquiry is not enough."

The sole basis for the judge's finding of actual notice is the existence of the reference to the Smith mortgage appearing in the probate inventory. The mere existence of such reference cannot constitute "actual notice" within the meaning of the recording statute.

It was error to rule that the defendant was unable to give good and clear record title because of the reference to an unrecorded mortgage in the 1913 probate inventory. . . .

Notes

1. In June 1972, the Smiths signed a five-year lease on a one-bedroom apartment in Columbia at $200 per month. By oral agreement with the landlady, they prepaid $12,000 for the five-year tenancy. In September 1972, the building was conveyed to Cambrian Realty Corp. The Smiths refused to pay rent for October to their new landlords. Cambrian sued on the written lease. The Smiths replied that Cambrian had a duty to inquire into any special arrangements existing at the time of purchase. Who should prevail? See Martinique Realty Corp. v. Hull, 64 N.J. Super. 599, 166 A.2d 803 (1960) (purchaser of leasehold is under duty of inquiry that is not discharged by mere examination of the written lease).

2. When Harry Jones divorced his wife, Margaret, the decree stated that he was to maintain the house and property for Margaret and their son, Harry, Jr. The decree further stated, "In the event said Harry Jones dies or remarries, then, in that event, his interest in the house and property shall be conveyed to his son Harry Jones, Jr."

Harry, Sr., remarried 90 days after his divorce, and he and his second wife Doris mortgaged the house to the Girard Trust Bank. The bank recorded. Harry, Jr., who had at all times lived with his mother on the property, later brought suit against the bank to quiet title to the land that he claimed to hold in fee simple absolute. See First Federal Savings & Loan Association of Miami v. Fisher, 60 So. 2d 496 (Fla. 1952) (bank under a duty of inquiry and may be held to have had constructive notice of the son's interest).

Problem

O gives A a mortgage on Blackacre as security for an obligation to repay $7,000. A does not record. O gives B a mortgage for $5,000. B has actual notice of A's mortgage. B records. O gives C a mortgage for $3,000. C does not have actual notice of A. C records. In a jurisdiction with a notice-type recording statute, Blackacre is foreclosed, and brings $10,000 at auction. Who gets the money? For one solution see Day v. Munson, 14 Ohio St. 488 (1863), where the court gave C the amount available above B's claim, and then gave A first claim on what remained. Can you propose a different resolution?

◆ HAUCK v. CRAWFORD
75 S.D. 202, 62 N.W.2d 92 (1973)

RUDOLPH, Judge. Although in form an action to quiet title, the real purpose of this action is to cancel and set aside a certain mineral deed admittedly signed by plaintiff and certain other deeds transferring the mineral rights by the grantee named in the original deed. No one has questioned the form of the action. The trial court entered judgment cancelling the deeds and defendants have appealed.

Cancellation was asked because of alleged fraud, and it was upon this basis that the trial court entered its judgment. The defendants contend, first, that there was no fraud and second, that the mineral rights were transferred to a bona fide purchaser for value and are not, therefore, subject to cancellation even though obtained by fraud in the first instance.

The facts most favorable in support of the judgment of the trial court are as follows: Plaintiff is a farmer owning and operating a farm located partly in South Dakota and partly in North Dakota. He lives on that part of the farm located in South Dakota in McPherson County. Plaintiff is 44 years old, has an 8th grade education, married and has a family. His farm consists of two sections of land which he purchased at three different times.

On May 23, 1951, while plaintiff was at a neighbor's place, three men approached him and discussed leasing plaintiff's land for oil and gas. A Mr. Crawford was the principal spokesman. Plaintiff testified that after some discussion Crawford offered 25¢ an acre for a lease. Plaintiff agreed, and one of the men apparently prepared the necessary papers on a typewriter while sitting in the back seat of the car. When the papers were prepared they were clamped to a board or pad and presented to plaintiff while in the car for signing. Printed forms were used which contained much fine print. The man who prepared the papers indicated where plaintiff should sign, and after signing in one place, partially turned the signed sheet and asked plaintiff to sign again, stating this second sheet was a part of the lease, which plaintiff believed. Plaintiff testified that no mention was ever made of a mineral deed and to this extent is corroborated by Crawford who in response to the question, "Did you ever describe to Mr. Hauck one of the instruments as a mineral deed?", answered, "No, sir." Separate instruments were required for the land in each state. Plaintiff never received a copy of any of the instruments he signed.

It now appears that somehow plaintiff had signed a mineral deed conveying one-half the minerals in his land to D. W. Crawford. This deed was filed for record June 1, 1951, but on May 29, 1951, Crawford, the grantee, conveyed such mineral rights to the defendants White and Duncan at Gainsville, Texas. The trial court made no finding related to the knowledge of White and Duncan concerning the conditions under which Duncan obtained the deed, but decided the case on the basis that they were in fact bona fide purchasers for value. This statement of the facts is sufficient for our present purpose.

We are concerned with a type of fraud which the trial court, texts and decided cases refer to as "fraud in the factum" or "fraud in the execution" as distinguished from "fraud in the inducement." This type of fraud relates to misrepresentation of the contents of a document by which one is induced to sign a paper thinking that it is other than it really is. It was this type of fraud with which this court was dealing in the case of Federal Land Bank v. Houck, 68 S.D. 449, 4 N.W.2d 213, 218. In this cited case we held that, as between the original parties, when a person is fraudulently induced to sign a paper believing that it is something other than it really is "the contractual knot was never tied" and such paper or instrument is not only voidable but actually void. In that case it was further held in conformity with prior holdings that "neither reason nor policy justifies the reception of a showing of negligence on the part of him who is overreached, as a countervailent or neutralizer of fraud." In other words, the perpetrator of the fraud cannot avoid his acts by a showing that the person upon whom the fraud was committed was negligent.

The Houck case, we are convinced, settles the issue of fraud. Accepting as a verity testimony of the plaintiff the misrepresentation and trickery of Crawford was complete. Crawford not only misrepresented the effect of the papers plaintiff signed, but by "manipulation of the papers" as found by the trial court tricked plaintiff into signing the deed thinking it was the lease. Under the rule of the Houck case plaintiff's negligence, if any, does not neutralize this fraud. As stated in the Houck case there was "no intention to do the act or say the words which manifest a volition to assent." It must therefore be held that as between Houck, the grantor, and Crawford, the grantee, the deed was void.

The deed being void as distinguished from voidable it had no effect whatsoever, conveyed nothing to Crawford, and he in turn had nothing to convey to White and Duncan. As stated by Judge McCoy in the case of Highrock v. Gavin, 43 S.D. 315, 346, 179 N.W. 12, 23,

> The grantee under this void deed was as powerless to transmit title as would be the thief of stolen property. Said deed had no more force or effect than a forged deed, and, in principle, was legally analogous to a forged deed. The recording statutes furnish no protection to those who claim as innocent purchasers under a forged or otherwise void deed, where the true owner has been guilty of no negligence or acts sufficient to create an estoppel.

Throughout these proceedings appellant has contended that plaintiff is an intelligent farmer, operating a large farm, and that if he failed to detect the fact that he signed a deed such failure was due to his negligence and therefore he should not be permitted to prevail in these proceedings. We have pointed out above that plaintiff's negligence will not neutralize the fraud, or give validity to the deed, but we are convinced that this holding is not decisive as against a purchaser for value without notice. . . .

[E]ven though the deed is void if plaintiff were negligent or committed acts sufficient to create an estoppel he should bear the brunt of such negligence, rather than a bona fide purchaser. . . .

As we view this case, therefore, we must revert to the issue of whether plaintiff was negligent when he affixed his signature to this deed not knowing that it was a deed he signed. On this issue the trial court made no specific determination. Whether plaintiff was negligent under all the facts and circumstances presented by this record we believe to be a question of fact which should be determined by the trial court. The question is, did plaintiff act as a person of reasonable and ordinary care, endowed with plaintiff's capacity and intelligence, would usually act under like circumstances?

We are not inclined to accept the trial court's holding that the manner in which plaintiff's signature was obtained constituted a forgery. Such holding is a minority view, and seems to us unsound. We believe the rule we have announced in Federal Land Bank v. Houck, supra, and in this opinion will better sustain the ends of justice. Our holding, we believe, recognizes actualities. The signature was the real signature of the plaintiff. True, plaintiff was induced to sign by a false representation, but to hold a signature thus obtained a forgery seems artificial and out of harmony with the actual facts.

The judgment appealed from is reversed.

All the Judges concur.

The preceding case is but one of dozens in which men and women have been capable of the most careless, if not stupid, behavior with regard to the asset prized above all others — land. In Houston v. Mentelos, 318 So. 2d 427 (Fla. App. 1975), for example, plaintiff, under the impression that she was leasing her property for use in filming a motion picture with Paramount Studios, signed documents that purported to embody terms of an oral lease agreement but were actually a "Sale of Property Agreement" and a "Warranty Deed." In this context an ounce of prevention is not merely a cliché: flagrant frauds may be impossible to undo once the rights of a bona fide purchaser have intervened, and those perpetrating the fraud may be unavailable or unable to give satisfaction.

Arbitrary technicalities may determine whether a supposed bona fide purchaser or the defrauded prior grantor will prevail.

Obviously the best advice to a client is that he or she sign nothing that purports to deal with the land without being perfectly certain what is being signed.

For example, where possession is consistent with the recording, the bona fide purchaser may not have to go further in his inquiry. Dixon v. Kaufman, 58 N.W.2d 797 (N.D. 1953). Many cases in which the bona fide purchaser's interest is defeated are decided on the ground that the grant by the allegedly defrauded grantor was void *ab initio*. See, e.g., Erickson v. Bohne, 130 Cal. App. 2d 553, 279 P.2d 619 (1955) (incapacity of grantor), and Trout v. Taylor, 220 Cal. 652, 32 P.2d 968 (1934) (grantee undesignated at time of execution and acknowledgment).

Sometimes, the problem is caused by human error. Rice lent $6000 to Taylor, who pledged as security his equity in Blackacre. Rice had the instrument recorded, but under the title of "Note and pledge as security" in the Registry index, rather than under "Mortgage of real property." One year later Taylor applied for a loan to Mortgage Company, which agreed to make the loan. The company wrote a deed of trust for the property, and it was properly recorded as a mortgage. Rice then sued to have his loan deemed the prior encumbrance. The issue was whether Mortgage Company had constructive notice of the pledge to Rice because it was recorded.

The court held that there was no constructive notice because the pledge, if it was to be a real property mortgage, was improperly indexed. Rice v. Taylor, 220 Cal. 629, 32 P.2d 381 (1934).

Suppose the A's fail to record. Bailout then conveys to X, a bona fide purchaser, who records immediately. X then conveys to C, who has actual knowledge of the deed from Bailout to the A's. Who prevails? Suppose it was Bailout himself who repurchased from X; what result?

Should recording be a final act or does a property owner have an obligation to insure that the recording will actually impart notice to those searching the title? Suppose all records have been destroyed by fire; must an owner re-record or face the loss of his property? For a holding suggesting that he must, see Kentucky Coal & Timber Development Co. v. Conley, 184 Ky. 274, 211 S.W. 734 (1919).

If an instrument is indexed under the wrong name, is the grantee protected against a subsequent bona fide purchaser? Compare Jones v. Folks, 149 Va. 140, 140 S.E. 126 (1927) (yes: "the admission to record is in law notice . . . to the world . . . , though the clerical act [of indexing] . . . be never performed"), with Mortensen v. Lingo, 99 F. Supp. 585 (D. Alaska 1951) (no: "all the prescribed steps, including indexing, had to be performed before the record could constitute constructive notice . . . ; a deed might as well be buried in the earth as in a mass of records without a clue to its whereabouts").

Recording acts vary in identifying those to whom their protection runs. Bona fide purchasers are always protected; usually mortgagees are also. Jurisdictions split as to "creditors" and "lessees." The "any person" category of the Massachusetts statute produced controversy.

States also disagree about the nature of the document, for only unrecorded recordable instruments are cut off by a failure to record. For example, if the *A*'s should record their contract of sale, what protection is offered them by the statute? And what of a deed legally recorded but not properly acknowledged? See Messersmith v. Smith, 60 N.W.2d 276 (N.D. 1953) ("In the absence of the fact of acknowledgment the deed was not entitled to be recorded, regardless of the recital in the certificate. The deed not being entitled to be recorded, the record thereof did not constitute notice of its execution.").

R. CHANDLER, FAREWELL MY LOVELY 89-90 (Ballantine ed. 1975): I looked at my watch once more. It was more than time for lunch. My stomach burned from the last drink. I wasn't hungry. I lit a cigarette. It tasted like a plumber's handkerchief. I nodded across the office at Mr. Rembrandt, then I reached for my hat and went out. I was halfway to the elevator before the thought hit me. It hit me without any reason or sense, like a dropped brick. I stopped and leaned against the marbled wall and pushed by hat around on my head and suddenly I laughed.

A girl passing me on the way from the elevators back to her work turned and gave me one of those looks which are supposed to make your spine feel like a run in a stocking. I waved my hand at her and went back to my office and grabbed the phone. I called up a man I knew who worked on the Lot Books of a title company.

"Can you find a property by the address alone?" I asked him.

"Sure. We have a cross index. What is it?"

"1644 West 54th Place. I'd like to know a little something about the condition of the title."

"I'd better call you back. What's that number?"

He called back in about three minutes.

"Get your pencil out," he said. "It's Lot 8 of Block 11 of Caraday's Addition to the Maplewood Tract Number 4. The owner of record, subject to certain things, is Jessie Pierce Florian, widow."

"Yeah. What things?"

"Second half taxes, two ten-year street improvement bonds, one storm drain assessment bond also ten year, none of these delinquents, also a first trust deed of $2600."

"You mean one of those things where they can sell you out in ten minutes' notice?"

"Not quite that quick, but a lot quicker than a mortgage. There's nothing unusual about it except the amount. It's high for that neighborhood, unless it's a new house."

"It's a very old house and in bad repair," I said. "I'd say fifteen hundred would buy the place."

"Then it's distinctly unusual, because the refinancing was done only four years ago."

"Okey, who holds it? Some investment company?"

"No. An individual. Man named Lindsay Marriott, a single man. Okey?"

I forget what I said to him or what thanks I made. They probably sounded like words. I sat there, just staring at the wall.

My stomach suddenly felt fine. I was hungry. I went down to the Mansion House Coffee Shop and ate lunch and got my car out of the parking lot next to my building.

I drove south and east, towards West 54th Place. I didn't carry any liquor with me this time.

Note

In a public-trust litigation in Hempstead, N.Y., developers attempting to prove 300 years of ownership were foiled when the town's 18th century land records were found to be unreadable. The county museum director said "mice or other deterioration" was the cause. Newsday, Nov. 9, 1978.

E. MARKETABLE TITLE

Suppose that when the title is searched on behalf of Mr. & Ms. Ambitious, a cloud is discovered. Under paragraph 4 of the Purchase and Sale Agreement, Mr. Bailout is obliged to convey "good and clear record and marketable title . . . free from encumbrances. . . ." But how dark must the cloud be to permit the A's to decline to take title and ask for the return of their deposit?

♦ TRI-STATE HOTEL CO. v. SPHINX INVESTMENT CO.
212 Kan. 234, 510 P.2d 1223 (1973)

KAUL, Justice. This is an action to recover a deposit made under the terms of option purchase contracts entered into between the plaintiffs-appellants, . . . and the defendant-appellee. The Fourth National Bank and Trust Company received the funds in question from the escrow agent, who was permitted to withdraw from the litigation with the consent of all parties. The Tri-State Hotel Company, Inc. . . . own interests in property known as the Broadview Hotel in Wichita and certain adjacent tracts and are the vendors in the option purchase contracts in question. . . .

The tracts of real estate involved in the option contracts, for purposes of identification, will be referred to as Tracts *A, B, C* and *D*. In negotiations leading up to the consummation of the option purchase contracts, plaintiffs-appellants were represented by Mr. R. C. McCormick, chairman of the board of directors of the Tri-State Hotel Company, Inc., which owned the Broadview Hotel. Negotiations for defendant-Sphinx were conducted primarily by Donald L. Herrick, treasurer and a member of the board of directors of Sphinx.

In December 1969 McCormick and Herrick reached an agreement in general terms for option purchase contracts of the properties involved. McCormick contacted John F. Eberhardt, a member of a Wichita law firm, and requested him to draw contracts on the basis of the general terms which had been agreed upon and which were summarized in a memo submitted to Eberhardt. . . .

It was soon discovered that a part of Tract *A*, upon which the Broadview is located, was not covered by any of the abstracts — as Eberhardt described the situation "we had abstracts that kept going to this place on all sides and we couldn't find anything that covered that particular tract." Efforts were made through the abstract company to locate the missing portion. Eberhardt had several more conversations with McCormick who was positive that he had complete abstracts of title. He told Eberhardt that he (McCormick) thought at one time they had already had a quiet title suit involving the same thing. Eberhardt testified that it took a month or two to locate all the abstracts on the property and finally it was necessary to have an abstract made. Ultimately, on April 16, 1970, a title opinion was rendered. The opinion was drafted in letter form by Mr. Eberhardt, addressed to Herrick and a copy sent to McCormick. The opinion revealed four merchantable title defects, three of which were said to be of no significance and could easily be cured before May 1, 1970, the cutoff date under the terms of the contract.

The fourth merchantable title defect which gives rise to this controversy was described by Eberhardt in this fashion:

> Although it is of no practical significance, the fourth merchantable title defect raises problems which cannot be remedied by May 1. As is explained in comment "(2)" of our title opinion covering Tract *A*, on June 30, 1925, The Arkansas Valley Improvement Company conveyed to the Siedhoff Hotel Company part of Holmes Addition (which is bounded by the Arkansas River on the west, by the south line of the NE/4 of Section 20-27S-1E on the north, by Waco Avenue on the east, and by Douglas Avenue on the south). However, in this deed the grantor excepted and retained a small wedge of land described by metes and bounds as set out in comment "(2)". When the Siedhoff Hotel Company reconveyed this part of Holmes Addition to The Tri-State Hotel Company, Inc. on July 31, 1964, the deed

again excepted this same wedge of ground that is 10'5" wide (north and south) at its east end, 2'1" wide at its west end, 30' long on its southern side, and 25' long on its northern side. From that time to this there has been no deed of any sort covering this diagonal strip of land, title to which is still vested in The Arkansas Valley Improvement Company, a Kansas corporation which is no longer in existence. So you can visualize this strip more readily I enclose a Zerox copy of a plat of Holmes Addition on which our troublesome wedge of land appears as a diagonal red mark immediately north of Lots 5 and 6. This strip is underneath the hotel improvements on Tract A. Beyond all shadow of doubt Tri-State has long since acquired indefeasible title to this strip by adverse possession, continued occupancy, and payment of real property taxes thereon. Nevertheless, since we can no longer obtain a quit-claim deed from the record title owner, our only remedy is to file quiet title proceedings. This, too, presents no problem whatever, except that it will require a minimum of 60 days to file suit, obtain service by publication, and secure judgment quieting Tri-State's title against The Arkansas Valley Improvement Company and its unknown successors, trustees, and assigns. By the same token, it is impossible to rectify this title defect by May 1, or even by May 15.

Inasmuch as this defect cannot be removed by May 1, under paragraph "3" of the Sphinx-Tri-State base contract Sphinx has until May 15 to decide whether to cancel or retain its option. I would hope, though, that you can give me Sphinx' decision much sooner than May 15. Certainly I must know very quickly whether or not it will be necessary for Tri-State to prepay the last half of 1969 real property taxes and to prepay the two escrow contracts prior to May 1. Nor do I want to file quiet title proceedings until I know whether or not Sphinx will waive this one title defect, conditioned upon our promptly instituting and prosecuting quiet title action to final judgment at the sole cost of Tri-State. In this connection, having to represent both the seller and buyer puts me in an unhappy predicament. I must say, however, that I would strongly recommend that you waive this defect and accept Tri-State's title, conditioned upon Tri-State's authorizing us to conduct quiet title proceedings, even if I were representing Sphinx alone because the defect, although technically a "merchantable" one, is of no real consequence whatever and can easily be removed by a routine title suit.

The board of directors of Sphinx met on May 7, 1970, and considered the action which should be taken on Eberhardt's letter relating to the title defects. The action of Sphinx is reflected in the minutes of the board meeting and the deposition testimony of Herrick and Albert A. Kaine, Jr., vice-president and director. The discussion at the meeting centered around the problems Sphinx might encounter if it waived the defects in terms of being able to retain the financing commitment which Sphinx had previously arranged on the property. One of the directors, Glenn Jones, an attorney, warned of difficulties that might be encountered in various situations that were under negotiations by reason of not having merchantable title to the property.

Mr. Herrick testified that he had communicated with the correspondent for a mortgage lender on the property and was told that there would be a risk of having the mortgage lender back out completely or raise the interest rate, or require more personal signatures on the loan, or otherwise change existing commitments. The discussion culminated in a resolution adopted by the board of directors as follows:

> BE IT RESOLVED, that WHEREAS the Tri-State Hotel Company, Inc. through its attorney, John F. Eberhardt, had indicated it cannot deliver merchantable title by May 1, 1970, and WHEREAS under the Sphinx-Tri-State base contract, Sphinx Investment Co., Inc. has the option of waiving the defect or cancelling the contract, Sphinx hereby elects not to waive the defect and authorizes its President to send notices of this fact by certified mail to all interested parties and to demand the return of its $100,000 option money plus interest from the escrow agent, John F. Eberhardt.

Thereafter, Sphinx sent notice of their election to terminate the contracts to the respective parties and made formal demand for the return of the option money paid in escrow to Eberhardt.

In the meantime, Eberhardt informed McCormick that he was going to hold the option deposit a few days and unless McCormick commenced litigation he was going to return the money to Sphinx. Thereafter this litigation was promptly instigated. . . .

The basic question on appeal is whether the outstanding fee title to an irregularly shaped strip of land approximately 6'6" × 30' × 2' × 25', which now lies beneath an addition to the Broadview Hotel constructed in 1952, amounts to a merchantable defect which could not be cured within the time limit specified in the contract. . . .

The contracts in this case are clear, specific and unambiguous. The language is neither doubtful nor obscure. They obligated the vendors to furnish abstracts disclosing good and merchantable title in fee simple. The terms "merchantable title" and "marketable title" are interchangeable when used in the context of a land contract, and they denote the same quality of title to be furnished.

Where a contract for the sale and purchase of land provides that the vendor shall furnish vendee or his representative an abstract disclosing a good and marketable title in fee simple, such as the contract here, the abstract must show on its face a marketable title in the vendor. . . . A good or merchantable title within the meaning of a contract of sale, in the absence of provisions to the contrary, generally means a record title.

There can be no doubt regarding what constitutes a marketable or merchantable title in this jurisdiction. This court has been confronted with the question on many occasions, most recently in the case of Darby v. Keeran, 211 Kan. 133, where we held:

"A marketable title is one which is free from reasonable doubt and will not expose the party who holds it to the hazards of litigation." . . .

In the instant case, it is undisputed that Tri-State does not have title to the small irregular tract in question, the title to which remains in

Arkansas Valley Improvement Company. In other words, title to the problem tract is outstanding. Tri-State says the defect could be cured or is extinguished by adverse possession; that it is not a defect of substantial character which might cause injury to the buyer: and thus can not serve as a ground for cancellation by Sphinx. We cannot agree. In all probability, as Tri-State says, adverse possession could be established showing that the outstanding title in this case is barred. But the question is not whether adverse possession is or could be established by affidavits or a quiet title suit, it is whether, when delivered to Eberhardt, the abstracts disclosed a merchantable title which Sphinx must accept. . . .

We rest our decision on the hypotheses that Tri-State failed to furnish abstracts disclosing a marketable title; that the defect was not remedied by May 1; and that Sphinx exercised its discretionary right to cancel prior to May 15, all as provided for in the explicit terms of the contract.

The judgment is affirmed.

Note

If the seller does not deliver marketable title, and the buyer must pay more to obtain a comparable house, can the buyer recover damages? See Wroth v. Tyler, p.880 *infra*.

F. CURING RECORDING PROBLEMS

Although old unresolved claims rarely produce disaster, the possibility that this may occur forces title examiners to conduct a search extending far beyond the limits of probable live interests. This fly specking by the legal system results in terminating transactions that would otherwise take place and always results in higher prices for the homeowner.

Consumer ignorance of the pitfalls has been matched by apathy on the part of the legal profession. But there are a number of ways by which land titles can be cleared of imperfections and consumers afforded protection. The existing system of land transfers is not satisfactory, and should be an urgent subject of law reform.

1. Title Insurance

The problem posed by the occasional imperfect land title obviously suggests risk spreading through insurance, and in much of the United States title insurance is common. Usually, a metropolitan area is served by a single title insurance company, which can — within whatever state regulatory limits are enforced — extract monopoly profits, especially by keeping good files but charging for searches when the same house changes hands repeatedly. Title insurance companies have a way of becoming part of the fabric of local government, in part because comfortable relations with courthouse employees are useful to those whose work depends heavily on official records.

◆ SLATE v. BOONE COUNTY ABSTRACT CO.
432 S.W.2d 305 (Mo. 1968)

CONNETT, Jr., Special Judge. This is a suit for damages in the amount of $16,200 brought by the buyers of land against an abstract company. The buyers, Donald and Adelia Slate, allege in their petition that they were damaged as a result of the Boone County Abstract Company's negligent failure to include a utility easement in an abstract of title for a tract of land prepared and certified by the abstracter and delivered by it to the buyers at the request of the sellers of the land. Defendant abstracter contended in a motion to dismiss plaintiffs' petition that the contract to prepare and certify the abstract was between it and the seller of the land, and because there was no privity of contract between it and the buyers, it is not liable to them. This motion was sustained by the Circuit Court and the buyers appealed to this Court.

Appellants ask the Court to abrogate the requirement of privity in suits on contracts such as these. Their argument is that the rule requiring privity before one can sue on a contract is based upon a necessity of protecting a promisor from unlimited liability to an unlimited number of people, and also from obligations and liabilities to others which the parties would not voluntarily assume. But when the end and aim of the contract between promisee and promisor was the performance of a service for the benefit of a known third party the rule has been abrogated.

The respondent cites as authority for its contention that a lack of privity between plaintiff and itself relieves it from any liability to plaintiff, the case of Anderson versus this same defendant, Anderson v. Boone County Abstract Company, Mo., 418 S.W.2d 123, decided last year by this Court. In that case plaintiff sought damages for defendant's negligent omission of a recorded restrictive covenant in an abstract of title to land prepared at the request of one Powell, who sold the land to Wulff, who in turn sold to Fristoe, who in turn sold to the plaintiff, Anderson. The abstract was not recertified at each sale and each buyer relied on the abstract and certificate originally requested by Powell for the sale to Wulff. In that case we denied recovery on the grounds there was no privity between the abstract company and Anderson, the third buyer. We declined to abrogate the requirement of privity between

POLICY OF TITLE INSURANCE

issued by

The Title Guarantee Company

BALTIMORE, MARYLAND 21202

SUBJECT TO THE EXCLUSIONS FROM COVERAGE, THE EXCEPTIONS CONTAINED IN SCHEDULE B AND THE PROVISIONS OF THE CONDITIONS AND STIPULATIONS HEREOF, THE TITLE GUARANTEE COMPANY, a Maryland corporation, herein called the Company, insures, as of Date of Policy shown in Schedule A, against loss or damage, not exceeding the amount of insurance stated in Schedule A, and costs, attorneys' fees and expenses which the Company may become obligated to pay hereunder, sustained or incurred by the insured by reason of:

1. Title to the estate or interest described in Schedule A being vested otherwise than as stated therein;

2. Any defect in or lien or encumbrance on such title;

3. Lack of a right of access to and from the land; or

4. Unmarketability of such title.

EXCLUSIONS FROM COVERAGE

The following matters are expressly excluded from the coverage of this policy:

1. Any law, ordinance or governmental regulation (including but not limited to building and zoning ordinances) restricting or regulating or prohibiting the occupancy, use or enjoyment of the land, or regulating the character, dimensions or location of any improvement now or hereafter erected on the land, or prohibiting a separation in ownership or a reduction in the dimensions or area of the land, or the effect of any violation of any such law, ordinance or governmental regulation.

2. Rights of eminent domain or governmental rights of police power unless notice of the exercise of such rights appears in the public records at Date of Policy.

3. Defects, liens, encumbrances, adverse claims, or other matters (a) created, suffered, assumed or agreed to by the insured claimant; (b) not known to the Company and not shown by the public records but known to the insured claimant either at Date of Policy or at the date such claimant acquired an estate or interest insured by this policy and not disclosed in writing by the insured claimant to the Company prior to the date such insured claimant became an insured hereunder; (c) resulting in no loss or damage to the insured claimant; (d) attaching or created subsequent to Date of Policy; or (e) resulting in loss or damage which would not have been sustained if the insured claimant had paid value for the estate or interest insured by this policy.

IN WITNESS WHEREOF, the Company has caused this policy to be signed and sealed, to become valid when countersigned by a validating officer or agent of the Company, all in accordance with its By-Laws.

The Title Guarantee Company

By _Frederick R. Buck_
                                                      President

ATTEST: _Hammond D. Jackson_
                                                      Secretary

(Seal: INCORPORATED THE TITLE GUARANTEE COMPANY MARYLAND)

This policy valid only if Schedules A and B are attached.

SAMPLE DOCUMENT 17-6
Title Insurance Policy

CONDITIONS AND STIPULATIONS

1. Definition of Terms

The following terms when used in this policy mean:

(a) "insured": the insured named in Schedule A, and, subject to any rights or defenses the Company may have had against the named insured, those who succeed to the interest of such insured by operation of law as distinguished from purchase including, but not limited to, heirs, distributees, devisees, survivors, personal representatives, next of kin, or corporate or fiduciary successors.

(b) "insured claimant": an insured claiming loss or damage hereunder.

(c) "knowledge": actual knowledge, not constructive knowledge or notice which may be imputed to an insured by reason of any public records.

(d) "land": the land described, specifically or by reference in Schedule A, and improvements affixed thereto which by law constitute real property; provided, however, the term "land" does not include any property beyond the lines of the area specifically described or referred to in Schedule A, nor any right, title, interest, estate or easement in abutting streets, roads, avenues, alleys, lanes, ways or waterways, but nothing herein shall modify or limit the extent to which a right of access to and from the land is insured by this policy.

(e) "mortgage": mortgage, deed of trust, trust deed, or other security instrument.

(f) "public records": those records which by law impart constructive notice of matters relating to said land.

2. Continuation of Insurance after Conveyance of Title

The coverage of this policy shall continue in force as of Date of Policy in favor of an insured so long as such insured retains an estate or interest in the land, or holds an indebtedness secured by a purchase money mortgage given by a purchaser from such insured, or so long as such insured shall have liability by reason of covenants of warranty made by such insured in any transfer or conveyance of such estate or interest; provided, however, this policy shall not continue in force in favor of any purchaser from such insured of either said estate or interest or the indebtedness secured by a purchase money mortgage given to such insured.

3. Defense and Prosecution of Actions—Notice of Claim to be given by an Insured Claimant

(a) The Company, at its own cost and without undue delay, shall provide for the defense of an insured in all litigation consisting of actions or proceedings commenced against such insured, or a defense interposed against an insured in an action to enforce a contract for a sale of the estate or interest in said land, to the extent that such litigation is founded upon an alleged defect, lien, encumbrance, or other matter insured against by this policy.

(b) The insured shall notify the Company promptly in writing (i) in case any action or proceeding is begun or defense is interposed as set forth in (a) above, (ii) in case knowledge shall come to an insured hereunder of any claim of title or interest which is adverse to the title to the estate or interest as insured, and which might cause loss or damage for which the Company may be liable by virtue of this policy, or (iii) if title to the estate or interest, as insured, is rejected as unmarketable. If such prompt notice shall not be given to the Company, then as to such insured all liability of the Company shall cease and terminate in regard to the matter or matters for which such prompt notice is required; provided, however, that failure to notify shall in no case prejudice the rights of any such insured under this policy unless the Company shall be prejudiced by such failure and then only to the extent of such prejudice.

(c) The Company shall have the right at its own cost to institute and without undue delay prosecute any action or proceeding or to do any other act which in its opinion may be necessary or desirable to establish the title to the estate or interest as insured, and the Company may take any appropriate action under the terms of this policy, whether or not it shall be liable thereunder, and shall not thereby concede liability or waive any provision of this policy.

(d) Whenever the Company shall have brought any action or interposed a defense as required or permitted by the provisions of this policy, the Company may pursue any such litigation to final determination by a court of competent jurisdiction and expressly reserves the right, in its sole discretion, to appeal from any adverse judgment or order.

(e) In all cases where this policy permits or requires the Company to prosecute or provide for the defense of any action or proceeding, the insured hereunder shall secure to the Company the right to so prosecute or provide defense in such action or proceeding, and all appeals therein, and permit the Company to use, at its option, the name of such insured for such purpose. Whenever requested by the Company, such insured shall give the Company all reasonable aid in any such action or proceeding, in effecting settlement, securing evidence, obtaining witnesses, or prosecuting or defending such action or proceeding, and the Company shall reimburse such insured for any expense so incurred.

4. Notice of Loss—Limitation of Action

In addition to the notices required under paragraph 3(b) of these Conditions and Stipulations, a statement in writing of any loss or damage for which it is claimed the Company is liable under this policy shall be furnished to the Company within 90 days after such loss or damage shall have been determined and no right of action shall accrue to an insured claimant until 30 days after such statement shall have been furnished. Failure to furnish such statement of loss or damage shall terminate any liability of the Company under this policy as to such loss or damage.

5. Options to Pay or Otherwise Settle Claims

The Company shall have the option to pay or otherwise settle for or in the name of an insured claimant any claim insured against or to terminate all liability and obligations of the Company hereunder by paying or tendering payment of the amount of insurance under this policy together with any costs, attorneys' fees and expenses incurred up to the time of such payment or tender of payment, by the insured claimant and authorized by the Company.

6. Determination and Payment of Loss

(a) The liability of the Company under this policy shall in no case exceed the least of:

(i) the actual loss of the insured claimant; or

(ii) the amount of insurance stated in Schedule A.

(b) The Company will pay, in addition to any loss insured against by this policy, all costs imposed upon an insured in litigation carried on by the Company for such insured, and all costs, attorneys' fees and expenses in litigation carried on by such insured with the written authorization of the Company.

(c) When liability has been definitely fixed in accordance with the conditions of this policy, the loss or damage shall be payable within 30 days thereafter.

7. Limitation of Liability

No claim shall arise or be maintainable under this policy (a) if the Company, after having received notice of an alleged defect, lien or encumbrance insured against hereunder, by litigation or otherwise, removes such defect, lien or encumbrance or establishes the title, as insured, within a reasonable time after receipt of such notice; (b) in the event of litigation until there has been a final determination by a court of competent jurisdiction, and disposition of all appeals therefrom, adverse to the title, as insured, as provided in paragraph 3 hereof; or (c) for liability voluntarily assumed by an insured in settling any claim or suit without prior written consent of the Company.

8. Reduction of Liability

All payments under this policy, except payments made for costs, attorneys' fees and expenses, shall reduce the amount of the insurance pro tanto. No payment shall be made without producing this policy for endorsement of such payment unless the policy be lost or destroyed, in which case proof of such loss or destruction shall be furnished to the satisfaction of the Company.

SAMPLE DOCUMENT 17-6
(continued)

plaintiff and defendant in that case. A distinguishing factor between the Anderson case and the instant case is that in this case it is alleged that the abstract company knew that the abstract was to be used and relied upon by these plaintiffs.

An analysis of this case discloses it to be a third party beneficiary contract, i.e., a contract in which the promisor engages to the promisee to render some performance to a third person. In instances where the promisee owes a duty or obligation to a third party, which would be satisfied by the promisor's performance, the third party is sometimes called a third party creditor beneficiary. In the instant case according to the allegations of the petition the sellers of the land were to furnish the buyers with a certified abstract of title to the land. The abstracter promised the seller for a consideration to prepare such an abstract and to deliver it to the buyers. The plaintiffs as buyers were the beneficiaries of this promise. The certified abstract of title was furnished for the sole use of the buyer. It was of no value or use to the seller, other than to fulfill their obligation to the buyers to supply such an abstract.

It has long been the law in Missouri that a third party may sue upon a contract between two other parties, based upon valid consideration and made for the benefit of such third party, although the third party furnished none of the consideration. See Rogers v. Gosnell, 58 Mo. 589, wherein a real estate broker was permitted to recover upon a promise made by the buyer of land to the seller to pay one-half of broker's commission. . . . Thus we see that a third party beneficiary may sue the promisor in a contract made for the benefit of the third party whether it be on a theory that a third party beneficiary is in privity with the promisor, or that privity is not necessary to permit the third party beneficiary to sue the promisor.

Therefore, we decide that plaintiffs as third party beneficiaries of the contract between the defendant abstracter and the sellers of the land, may bring suit against the defendant for its alleged negligent omission to include an easement in the certified abstract of title to the land. . . .

The judgment is reversed and the case is remanded.

Sometimes the *Slate* result is reached on a tort "duty of reasonable care" rationale, rather than a "third party beneficiary" theory. See, e.g., Chun v. Park, 51 Haw. 462, 462 P.2d 905 (1969). But most jurisdictions retain the requirement of privity. See, e.g., Colonial Savings & Loan Association v. Redwood Empire Title Co., 236 Cal. App. 2d 186, 46 Cal. Rptr. 16 (1965). Among exceptions to the majority rule are fraud, recklessness, and collusion by the abstractor. Some states require bonding of abstractors, and extend liability beyond the contractual relationship.

Problems

1. The *A*'s buy their house, and insure the title with Chicago Title and Trust Co. Five years later, when the property has risen in value to $125,000, the *A*'s' title to a portion of the backyard, stipulated to be then worth $10,000, fails. The title insurance policy was for $100,000. How much should the *A*'s recover? Lawyers Title Insurance Co. v. McKee, 354 S.W.2d 401 (Tex. Civ. App. 1962), held that the damage recoverable for partial failure of the title was the difference between the purchase price and the price the land would have brought at the time of sale had the parties known of the encumbrance. What result in McKee if the title insurance policy had carried a face amount $10,000 less than the sale price?

2. The *A*'s secure a title insurance policy that provides for automatic conversion to a warrantor's policy if they sell the property. Before selling, the *A*'s learn of an easement that reduces the sale price. After the sale, the *A*'s sue for the loss. The company defends on the ground that the *A*'s never gave them the opportunity to clear the title by negotiating with the owner of the easement. For a decision in favor of the title insurer on this issue, see Stewart Title Guaranty Co. v. Lunt Land Corp., 162 Tex. 435, 347 S.W.2d 584 (1961).

Note

Plaintiffs alleged that they had authorized defendant savings and loan companies to purchase title insurance for them, that it was always obtained from Chicago Title & Trust Co., and that defendants then received from Chicago Title 10 percent of the premiums. A U.S. Court of Appeals held that such an alleged "kickback" would not violate the federal antitrust laws. Freeman v. Chicago Title & Trust Co., 505 F.2d 527 (7th Cir. 1974). What other theories would you suggest to plaintiffs, based on the materials in this book?

2. Marketable Title Acts

◆ REED v. FAIN
145 So. 2d 858 (Fla. 1962)

THORNAL, Justice. By petition for writ of *certiorari* we are requested to review a decision of the District Court of Appeal, Second District, appearing at 122 So. 2d 322, because of an alleged conflict on the same point of law with prior decisions of this Court.

Our judgment turns on the interpretation and application of Section 95.23, Florida Statutes, F.S.A., which applies to certain instruments which have been on record for 20 years or more. . . .

In 1930, J. M. Reed, joined by his wife, Stella, conveyed his homestead to his son the petitioner, George V. Reed. George immediately reconveyed the property to J. M. and his wife in order to create an estate by the entirety. Title originally was held by J. M. alone. Both conveyances were without consideration. In 1951, the father and mother conveyed the property to their son George, reserving to themselves a life estate with survivorship. The 1951 conveyance had no effect upon the outcome of this litigation because at the time of its execution, J. M. Reed lacked the mental capacity to execute the document. The factual statement of the district court then contains the observation "Stella M. Reed conveyed her *life estate* to George in 1955." She died within a year. In 1957, respondent Vivian Reed Fain, daughter of J. M. and Stella Reed, filed this suit in equity to obtain cancellation of the deeds above mentioned. She alleged fraud and undue influence, lack of consideration and the violation of her rights under the Florida Homestead Laws. The defendants in the trial court, who are the petitioners here, filed an answer in which they relied upon Section 95.23, Florida Statutes, in view of the fact that the 1930 conveyance to J. M. and Stella Reed had been of record without adverse claim for more than twenty years. To give the subject statute the effect contended for by the plaintiffs below, the chancellor concluded that when J. M. Reed died in 1954, he held title to the property as a homestead, that it inured to his widow as a life estate and then to his two children in fee as tenants in common. He held that the 1957 deed from Stella to her son George, conveyed only her life estate because in his view she had nothing else to convey. The chancellor reached this conclusion by holding the 1930 transaction between the Reeds and their son George, as being an ineffective attempt to alienate the homestead without consideration. . . .

Section 95.23, Florida Statutes, F.S.A., provides as follows:

Limitations where deed or will of record for twenty years or more. — After the lapse of twenty years from the record of any deed or the probate of any will purporting to convey lands no person shall assert any claim to said lands as against the claimants under such deed or will, or their successors in title.

After the lapse of twenty years all such deeds or wills shall be deemed valid and effectual for conveying the lands therein described, as against all persons who have not asserted by competent record title an adverse claim.

The majority of the court of appeal had the view that the twenty year period prescribed by this statute begins to run from the date of record of a deed or probate of a will. Unless something is read into the statute which is not apparent from the clear language thereof, this conclusion is the correct one.

The judge writing the minority view of the district court on this subject makes reference to an article by Dr. James W. Day, entitled "Curative Acts and Limitations Acts Designed to Remedy Defects in Florida Land Titles — IV.," IX U. of Fla. L. Rev. 145. As expressed in the cited article it is the view of Dr. Day and Judge Shannon of the district court that Section 95.23, *supra*, is in the nature of "a curative act with a limitation provision." In this view, the twenty year provision of Section 95.23, *supra*, does not begin to run until a cause of action accrues in favor of the party asserting the adverse claim against the recorded instrument. This view stems from the contention that if applied otherwise, the act would be unconstitutional for the reason that the twenty year period could run before the accrual of a right of action adverse to the recorded instrument. Those of us who sat at the knee of Professor Day in the University of Florida College of Law, regard his views on any subject, and particularly real property, with tremendous respect. We would not lightly lay aside the opinions and advice of one who has contributed so much to the development of the law and lawyers in Florida. We think it unnecessary, however, in this case to take issue with the analysis of the statute expressed in the opinion of Judge Shannon, except to conclude that in the instant case it was not applicable.

The property here involved was a homestead. The Florida Constitution, Article X, Section 4, F.S.A., and the Florida Statutes, Section 731.27, F.S.A., obviously recognize the homestead and the interests of the family in the title thereto as a very special kind of property right that enjoys the fullest measure of protection against improper encroachment and illegal alienation. The point that recurs is that Mrs. Fain could have proceeded to protect her interests during the running of the twenty year period from the date in 1930 when the deed was recorded. We think she could have done so by an appropriate proceeding in equity to establish the property as a homestead at the time of the 1930 transaction, as well as to adjudicate the effectiveness of the alienation that was attempted at that time. We have said that a deed to homestead between husband and wife, where there is a child or children living "is prima facie ineffective to convey legal title to such homestead, insofar as the vested interest of the children are concerned." Church v. Lee, 102 Fla. 478, 136 So. 242, 247. This Court had earlier committed itself to the proposition that "the 'heirs' of the homestead owner, as well as the owner and his wife, if he has one, have an interest that can be 'alienated' only as provided in the Constitution. If the requirements of the constitution and the statutes are not complied with in 'alienating' homestead real estate the attempt is a nullity as to the 'heirs' of the homestead owner and also as to the husband and wife."

In view of the decisions of this Court which have consistently been extended to protect the interest of the heirs of a homestead owner, we have the view that in the event that there is an attempted alienation which is illegal or otherwise ineffective against the heirs, then they may immediately enter a court of equity to establish their interest in the subject matter. By following this application of the rule, Section 95.23, *supra*, is saved against the constitutional impediment suggested by Professor Day and Judge Shannon and permits the application of the statute just as it was writen by the Legislature. . . .

Because of conflicts hereinabove pointed out, the decision of the district court is quashed and the cause is remanded to that court for the entry of a judgment consistent herewith.

DREW, Justice (dissenting). . . . I revert to the main contention of Professor Day that the existence of a cause of action is a prerequisite to the operation of a limitations act. As I construe the opinion of the majority, they apparently concede this to be correct when they state in summary that Mrs. Fain, the objecting daughter, could have instituted these proceedings to question the validity of the subject conveyance at any time during the twenty-year period. I think the majority are wrong in their conclusion in this respect because the head of the family was living during this period of time. This fact would preclude the daughter, in my opinion, from maintaining an action because, as pointed out by Professor Day, under the statutes of this state the lineal descendants who inherit an interest in a homestead are those in being at the death of the owner. To put it another way, during the lifetime of the father (during which the twenty-year statute was running) the daughter had no interest which would entitle her to maintain any cause of action in the courts of this State. I assume it could be argued that the effect of the majority opinion is to hold that such a cause of action did in fact exist in the daughter. I don't believe this point is properly before us in these proceedings. Even if it were, I could not agree that the children of the head of a family, during the lifetime of the head of the family, could maintain an action in any court to contest the validity of a deed of the homestead premises. This is particularly true where, as here, the head of the family continued in possession.

There can be no doubt that the deed involved in this litigation was void. In the Blocker case this Court held that this statute did not embrace a forged deed and, in the opinion, this Court drew no distinction between a forged deed and a void deed. The authorities cited by the Court . . . did not distinguish between void deeds and forged deeds. They seemed to deal with them in the same breath and applied the same rules.

ON REHEARING

HOBSON, Justice. After a lengthy and careful consideration of the controlling question in this case and the decisions which deal with it, we are convinced that no truer words were ever spoken than those appearing in Mr. Justice Drew's dissent. He states: "This indeed is an involved and highly important question. Some of the cases *confuse rather than clarify the issues.*"

We do not mean to be unduly critical of the initial majority opinion prepared by Mr. Justice Thornal. . . .

The real question in this case is not: "When did the 20 year period set forth in Section 95.23 F.S. begin to run?" but rather: "Were the provisions of Section 95.23 F.S. intended to be applicable to a 'void' deed, or are they, in any event, applicable in this equitable suit under the facts disclosed by the record herein?" We answer both segments of this bipartite query in the negative. . . .

Homestead property is a special kind of species of property. It is so treated in our Constitution and in our statutes. The Legislature originally would have normally and specifically included homestead property had it intended such type of property to be embraced by Section F.S. 95.23. . . . Moreover, the legislators, many of whom are lawyers, are presumed, as is everyone, to know the law. Consequently, had it been their intention to place homestead property within the purview of F.S. Section 95.23, they would have expressly done so, because it is well established that equity is not necessarily bound by a statute of limitations. The legislators might have intentionally omitted "homestead property" from F.S. Section 95.23, because they may have envisaged the probability of the statute being declared unconstitutional. . . .

The entire transaction between the parents and their son was a nullity because it was violative of the constitutional inhibitions regarding the alienation of homestead property. Were this not so, it nevertheless without doubt is true insofar as the "inchoate" interest in the homestead property of the "heir" (Mrs. Fain) is concerned. Such interest is guaranteed to her and protected by the Florida Constitution, as such sections have been construed by the Supreme Court of this State. The artifice employed by the Reeds and their son was also ineffectual as to the "inchoate" interest of George as well as the interest of Stella Reed as the "widow" of the homestead owner. It matters not that neither George Reed nor his mother has ever complained of the conspiratorial, fraudulent and invalid (void) transaction in which each was *particeps criminis.* . . .

Assuming that 1951 was the year in which Mrs. Fain learned about the attempt to destroy her constitutionally created interest in the homestead property, she has not been guilty, under the facts disclosed by the record, of unreasonable or inexcusable delay which resulted in prejudice to any (fancied) rights of her brother George. No normal child would even question or investigate the propriety or legality of his parents' action much less bring a suit against them, at any time, especially during the evening tide of life, and take the chance of disrupting or destroying the cordial parent and child relationship which should ever remain inviolate. The biblical admonition to "Honour thy father and thy mother" would be sufficient justification for the adoption of a Fabian policy.

Summarizing, we hold that F.S. Section 95.23, is not applicable in this case because, first, the critical deed is void, second, if not void *ab initio*, it was and is void as to Mrs. Fain's "inchoate" interest in the homestead which became "vested" upon the death of her father; third, the Legislature did not intend F.S. Section 95.23, to be applicable to deeds or wills conveying or devising "homestead property"; fourth, F.S. Section 95.23, F.S.A., is unconstitutional if it be construed in such manner as to breathe life into an instrument made and executed in contravention of *constitutional* inhibitions.

◆ L. SIMES & C. TAYLOR, THE IMPROVEMENT OF CONVEYANCING BY LEGISLATION
6-9 (1960)

MODEL MARKETABLE TITLE ACT

SECTION 1. MARKETABLE RECORD TITLE

Any person having the legal capacity to own land in this state, who has an unbroken chain of title of record to any interest in land for forty years or more, shall be deemed to have a marketable record title to such interest as defined in Section 8, subject only to the matters stated in Section 2 hereof. A person shall be deemed to have such an unbroken chain of title when the official public records disclose a conveyance or other title transaction, of record not less than forty years at the time the marketability is to be determined, which said conveyance or other title transaction purports to create such interest, either in

(a) the person claiming such interest, or

(b) some other person from whom, by one or more conveyances or other title transactions of record, such purported interest has become vested in the person claiming such interest;

with nothing appearing of record, in either case, purporting to divest such claimant of such purported interest.

SECTION 2. MATTERS TO WHICH MARKETABLE TITLE IS SUBJECT

Such marketable record title shall be subject to:

(a) All interests and defects which are inherent in the muniments of which such chain of record title is formed; *provided*, however, that a general reference in such muniments, or any of them, to easements, use restrictions or other interests created prior to the root of title shall not be sufficient to preserve them, unless specific identification be made therein of a recorded title transaction which creates such easement, use restriction or other interest.

(b)   All interests preserved by the filing of proper notice or by possession by the same owner continuously for a period of forty years or more, in accordance with Section 4 hereof.

(c)   The rights of any person arising from a period of adverse possession or user, which was in whole or in part subsequent to the effective date of the root of title.

(d)   Any interest arising out of a title transaction which has been recorded subsequent to the effective date of the root of title from which the unbroken chain of title of record is started; *provided*, however, that such recording shall not revive or give validity to any interest which has been extinguished prior to the time of the recording by the operation of Section 3 hereof.

SECTION 3.   INTERESTS EXTINGUISHED BY MARKETABLE TITLE

[S]uch marketable record title shall be held . . . free and clear of all interests . . . the existence of which depends upon any act, transaction, event or omission that occurred prior to the effective date of the root of title. All such interests . . . are hereby declared to be null and void.

SECTION 4.   EFFECT OF FILING NOTICE OR THE EQUIVALENT

(a) Any person claiming an interest in land may preserve and keep effective such interest by filing for record during the forty-year period immediately following the effective date of the root of title of the person whose record title would otherwise be marketable, a notice in writing, duly verified by oath, setting forth the nature of the claim. No disability or lack of knowledge of any kind on the part of anyone shall suspend the running of said forty-year period. Such notice may be filed for record by the claimant or by any other person acting on behalf of any claimant who is

(1)   under a disability,

(2)   unable to assert a claim on his own behalf, or

(3)   one of a class, but whose identity cannot be established or is uncertain at the time of filing such notice of claim for record.

(b) If the same record owner of any possessory interest in land has been in possession of such land continuously for a period of forty years or more, during which period no title transaction with respect to such interest appears of record in his chain of title, and no notice has been filed by him or on his behalf as provided in Subsection (a), and such possession continues to the time when marketability is being determined, such period of possession shall be deemed equivalent to the filing of the notice immediately preceding the termination of the forty-year period described in Subsection (a).

SECTION 5. CONTENTS OF NOTICE: RECORDING AND INDEXING

To be effective and to be entitled to record the notice above referred to shall contain an accurate and full description of all land affected by such notice which description shall be set forth in particular terms and not by general inclusions, but if said claim is founded upon a recorded instrument, then the description in such notice may be the same as that contained in such recorded instrument. Such notice shall be filed for record in the registry of deeds of the county or counties where the land described therein is situated. The recorder of each county shall accept all such notices presented to him which describe land located in the county in which he serves and shall enter and record full copies thereof in the same way that deeds and other instruments are recorded and each recorder shall be entitled to charge the same fees for the recording thereof as are charged for recording deeds. In indexing such notices in his office each recorder shall enter such notices under the grantee indexes of deeds under the names of the claimants appearing in such notices. Such notices shall also be indexed under the description of the real estate involved in a book set apart for that purpose to be known as the "Notice Index."

SECTION 6. INTERESTS NOT BARRED BY ACT

This Act shall not be applied to bar any lessor or his successor as a reversioner of his right to possession on the expiration of any lease; or to bar or extinguish any easement or interest in the nature of an easement, the existence of which is clearly observable by physical evidence of its use; or to bar any right, title or interest of the United States, by reason of failure to file the notice herein required.

3. Registration

◆ STATE v. JOHNSON
278 N.C. 126, 179 S.E.2d 371 (1971)

HUSKINS, Justice. . . . What is the status of title as between the defendants? Appellants contend that the Torrens registration of 1916 was invalid for failure to comply with statutory requirements as to publication. Chapter 128 of the 1915 Public Laws amended the Torrens Act to require eight weeks publication instead of four. A publisher's affidavit shows that publication lasted only four weeks. Appellants say this defect is jurisdictional and therefore the lower court erred in finding as a fact and concluding as a matter of law that the property in question was duly registered under the Torrens system from 1916 to 1966, at which time it was removed by judicial decree. This requires examination of the

Torrens Act and its application to the facts appearing of record in this case.

The judicial system of registering titles to land was enacted in North Carolina by Chapter 90 of the 1913 Public Laws, now codified as Chapter 43 of the General Statutes. It is known generally as the Torrens Law. "The principle of the 'Torrens System' is conveyance by registration and certificate instead of by deed, and assimilates the transfer of land to the transfer of stocks in corporations." . . .

The Torrens Law authorizes any person in the peaceable possession of land in North Carolina who claims an estate of inheritance therein to "prosecute a special proceeding *in rem* against all the world in the superior court for the county in which such land is situate, to establish his title thereto, to determine all adverse claims and have the title registered."

Such proceeding for the registration of title is commenced "by a petition to the court by the persons claiming, singly or collectively, to own or have the power of appointing or disposing of an estate in fee simple in any land, whether subject to liens or not." The petition must be signed and verified by each petitioner, must contain a full description of the land to be registered together with a plot of same by metes and bounds, must show when, how and from whom it was acquired, list all known liens, interests, equities and claims, adverse or otherwise, vested or contingent, and give full names and addresses, if known, of all persons who may be interested by marriage or otherwise, including adjoining owners and occupants.

When such petition is filed the clerk is required to issue a summons directed to the sheriff of every county in which named interested persons reside, naming them as defendants. The summons is returnable as in other cases of special proceedings, "except that the return shall be at least sixty days from the date of summons." It must be served at least ten days before the return thereof and the return recorded in the same manner as in other special proceedings.

The clerk is required, at the time of issuing the summons, to publish a notice of filing of the petition in some secular newspaper published in the county wherein the land is situate, once a week for eight issues of such paper. The notice shall be addressed "To whom it may concern" and shall set forth the title of the proceeding, the relief demanded, and state the return day of the summons.

> The provisions of this section, in respect to the issuing and service of summons and the publication of the notice, shall be mandatory and essential to the jurisdiction of the court to proceed in the cause: Provided, that the recital of the service of summons and publication in the decree or in the final judgment in the cause, and in the certificate issued to the petitioner as hereinafter provided, shall be conclusive evidence thereof.

The petition is then set for hearing upon the pleadings and exhibits filed. If any person files an answer claiming an interest in the land described in the petition, the matter is referred to the "examiner of titles" who hears the cause on such parol or documentary evidence as may be offered, makes such independent examination of the title as may be necessary, and files with the clerk a report of his conclusions of law and fact, setting forth the state of the title, together with an abstract of title to the lands. Any party to the proceeding may file exceptions to said report, whereupon the clerk must transmit the record to the judge of superior court for his determination. If title is found to be in the petitioner, "the judge shall enter a decree to that effect, ascertaining all limitations, liens, etc., declaring the land entitled to registration accordingly, and the same, together with the record, shall be docketed by the clerk of the court as in other cases, and a copy of the decree certified to the register of deeds of the county for registration as hereinafter provided."

Judgment by default is not permitted. The court must require an examination of the title in every instance except as to parties who, by proper pleadings, admit petitioner's claim. If no answer is filed, the clerk must refer the matter to the examiner of titles anyway. If title is found in the petitioner, then the clerk enters a decree to that effect, declares the land entitled to registration, and certifies it for registration after approval by the judge of the superior court.

> Every decree rendered as hereinbefore provided shall bind the land and bar all persons and corporations claiming title thereto or interest therein; quiet the title thereto, and shall be forever binding and conclusive upon and against all persons and corporations, whether mentioned by name in the order of publication, or included under the general description, "to whom it may concern"; and every such decree so rendered . . . shall be conclusive evidence that such person or corporation is the owner of the land therein described, and no other evidence shall be required in any court of this State of his or its right or title thereto. [G.S. §43-12.]

The county commissioners are required to furnish a book to the register of deeds, to be called "Registration of Titles," in which the register shall enroll, register and index (1) the decree of title mentioned in G.S. §43-11(c) and (d), (2) the copy of the plot contained in the petition, (3) all subsequent transfers of title, and (4) all voluntary transactions in any wise affecting the title to the land, authorized to be entered thereon. Upon the registration of such decree, the register of deeds is directed to issue an "owner's certificate of title," the form of which is prescribed, bearing a number which is retained as long as the boundaries of the land remain unchanged.

Every registered owner of land brought under the Torrens System (with certain exceptions not pertinent here) holds the land free from any and all adverse claims, rights or encumbrances not noted on the certificate of title. And "[n]o title to nor right or interest in registered land in derogation of that of the registered owner shall be acquired by prescription or adverse possession."

The only way to transfer or affect the title to registered land is by registration of the writing, instrument or document by which such transfer is accomplished. Thus no voluntary or involuntary transaction affects the title to registered lands until registered, *and the registration of titles book is the sole and conclusive legal evidence of title.* . . .

Any person claiming any right, title or interest in registered land adverse to the registered owner, arising after the date of the original decree of registration, may file with the register of deeds of the county in which such decree .was rendered or certificate of title thereon was issued, a verified written statement setting forth fully the right, title or interest claimed, how or from whom it was acquired, referring to the number, book and page of the certificate of title of the registered owner, together with a metes and bounds description of the land, and containing the adverse claimant's address and place of residence, and such statement must be noted and filed by the register of deeds. An action to enforce such claim may then be maintained provided it is commenced within six months of the filing of the statement. If action is not timely commenced as required, the register of deeds must make a memorandum notation to that effect and cancel upon the registry the adverse claim so asserted.

The sale and transfer, in whole or in part, of registered land is accomplished by the execution and acknowledgment of a paperwriting in the form set out in G.S. §43-31, which paperwriting has the full force and effect of a deed in fee simple. This paperwriting must be presented to the register of deeds together with the seller's certificate of title, and the transaction is then duly noted and registered in accordance with the provisions of the Torrens Law.

This summary of the pertinent parts of the Torrens Act shows that it

> not only manifests a purpose on the part of the General Assembly to establish a title in the registered owner, impregnable against attack at the time of the decree, but also to protect him against all claims or demands not noted on the book for the registration of titles, and to make that book a complete record and the only conclusive evidence of the title. . . .

When viewed in light of the stated purpose of the Torrens Act, it is clear the proviso in G.S. §43-10 [specifying eight weeks' publication] is intended to cure any jurisdictional defect with respect to issuance and service of summons and the publication of notice so as to foreclose all jurisdictional attacks on a Torrens title. . . .

We therefore hold that the recital in the final Torrens decree of registration that "publication of notice has been duly made" is conclusive evidence of the fact, and that any attack on the 1916 degree is foreclosed. . . .

COMMENT, "YES VIRGINIA — THERE IS A TORRENS ACT," 9 U. Rich. L. Rev. 301, 318 n.130 (1975): The main argument advanced in opposition to the Torrens Act is that the cost of registering a title would be so enormous as to make the procedure economically prohibitive for the "ordinary" conveyance transaction. In fact, when the cost estimate for registration is determined on the basis of the administrative fees involved, the cost is comparable to that required for the recordation of a deed. The fees to be charged for the registration of a title are enumerated in §88 of the Virginia Torrens Act. For a registration involving a parcel of land valued at $50,000, the cost would be as follows:

1. For docketing, indexing and filing the
   original petition $2.00
2. Publishing and mailing notices of the petition postage
3. Entry of the original certificate and issuance
   of the duplicate certificate $2.00
4. Fee for examiner's report to the court,
   including the examination of title and
   findings of fact (one-tenth of one percent of
   the value of the land) $50.00
5. For report of sheriff as to occupants on the
   registered land $1.00
6. For the docketing, indexing or filing of any
   other paper submitted during the proceeding $1.00

The cost would be increased by any required court costs, an order of publication, if needed, and by any other fees allowed by law for administrative services in other cases but not specifically enumerated in the Act. The unknown factor in this cost estimate is the attorney's fee. If the attorney is familiar with the procedures of the Torrens Act, the time required to register a title would be no more than that required to record a deed and handle the closing. If the attorney has to educate himself with respect to the particulars of the Act, the fee would naturally be greater as the time required on the part of the attorney to register the title would have increased substantially. If an adverse interest has been asserted, the cost of either litigating the issue or seeking a settlement would be the same under either system, assuming of course that the vendee-client still desires the property. The only comparable fee not found under the record system which would be required under the Torrens Act is that charged for the time spent by the attorney before the court of land registration. But, when one considers that the result of these efforts is the declaration of a title absolutely indefeasible and that the necessity of obtaining costly title insurance has been avoided, the additional cost is well worth the expense.

◆ BUTLER v. HALEY GREYSTONE CORP.
347 Mass. 478, 198 N.E.2d 635 (1964)

SPIEGEL, Justice. This is a bill of complaint brought to determine the rights of the plaintiffs and the defendants in a parcel of beach property in Marblehead. The case was originally entered in the Superior Court and was subsequently transferred to the Land Court. A judge of that court entered a final decree from which the plaintiffs and the two corporate defendants appealed. The evidence is reported and all of the exhibits are before us.

The judge made findings, which we herewith summarize. In 1925, Sterling Realty Company (Sterling) took title by recorded deed to two tracts of land in Marblehead. "One parcel [Section No. 1] was a tract of seashore land situated on the southeasterly side of Atlantic Avenue together 'with all rocks, beaches, and flats hereto belonging.' The other parcel [Section No. 2] was situated on the northwestern side of Atlantic Avenue opposite the first parcel." Sterling subdivided Section No. 1 into house lots, roads, ways, and a beach reservation. A plan of the subdivision that included the location of the beach area known as Sandy Beach Reservation was filed with the registry of deeds in 1926, other subdivision plans were filed at later dates.

Section No. 1 "was developed by laying out the lots, building roads and ways and putting in utilities. Sterling . . . printed sales literature, and commenced to sell the lots." Louis Gutterman (Gutterman), Sterling's principal stockholder, was active "in promoting the development and sale of the lots from 1926 until his death in 1954. He talked with the prospective buyers, showed them the lots, discussed the prices of the lots, the conditions and restrictions which were to be imposed on the lots for the benefit of the development and took part in the preparation of sales agreements and the deeds." He informed prospective purchasers that "he would permit only those persons owning property in Section No. 1 or guests of such owners to use . . . [Sandy Beach Reservation]." In 1926, a lot in Section No. 1 was conveyed by deed to one Hannah Sweet. Title to the lot was conveyed "together with the right to use 'Sandy Beach Reservation,' . . . for recreation in common with the grantor, its successors, grantees and assigns, and subject to such rules and regulations as the grantor may establish or adopt." The conveyance was made subject to certain restrictions and conditions, to remain in force until January 1, 1956, one of which was that "[n]o use shall be made of the 'Beach Reservation' . . . except for recreation." The grantor reserved the right "to construct, lay and maintain in, through, over and upon . . . [Hannah Sweet's land] for the benefit of . . . [Section No. 2] sewers, water pipes and culverts and mains for conveying both fresh and salt or ocean water. . . ." The deed to Hannah Sweet "is incorporated by reference in the subsequent deeds of the remaining lots in Section No. 1."

Although prior to Gutterman's death only one lot was sold out of Section No. 2, "he described to interested persons the proposed development of that area. It was the intention of Sterling to drain this area and lay out lots and roads, and to build thereon a salt-water lagoon for swimming and bathing purposes, and to pipe salt water from the ocean to this lagoon. [As noted above, a]n easement for the laying of these pipes was put on Section No. 1." The one conveyance out of Section No. 2 during Gutterman's lifetime, in 1947, was made by a deed that stated in part: "Said premises are conveyed with the provision, restriction or reservation that no right is conveyed, and the grantee and those claiming under him shall have no right to, in any way, use any portion of Sandy Beach Reservation located in Section No. 1. . . ." In June, 1955, Sterling conveyed by deeds to John H. Procter Sandy Beach Reservation and the remainder of Section No. 2 "with all rights appurtenant thereto." Procter had been "well acquainted" with Gutterman and had also bought lots in Section No. 1, some of which he held for resale purposes. After Procter took title to Section No. 2,

> he subdivided . . . [it] into lots some of which he sold. He granted in his deeds an appurtenant right to these lots to use the beach reservation. . . . Procter, in 1959, conveyed all of Section No. 2 to which he then held title, together with the beach reservation to the defendant Haley Greystone Corporation [Haley]. . . . On July 9, 1959 the said Haley granted to one of the lots in Section No. 2 an appurtenant easement to use the beach reservation. . . . Haley advertised in newspapers that it had for sale lots with beach rights and that it proposed to erect a beach club on the beach reservation for the benefit of the buyers of the lots.

While Gutterman was alive, Sterling strictly enforced compliance with the conditions on which lots in Section No. 1 had been conveyed. Policemen were hired "to prevent the use of the beach by unauthorized persons. . . . In recent years the beach itself has been used on week days on the average by thirty people, and on week-ends on the average by forty people." It appears, nevertheless, that despite Gutterman's efforts at enforcement of beach rights,

> [o]ver the years . . . the beach . . . would be used intermittently by unauthorized persons without complaint by the lot owners in Section No. 1. . . . Shortly after the death of . . . Gutterman in 1954, the lot owners in Section No. 1 found it necessary to form a voluntary unincorporated asso-

ciation for the purpose of maintaining the beach reservation and in policing the area to keep unauthorized persons from using the beach. Dues
were . . . [collected] which were used to pay the expenses of hiring a
policeman and also for the cost of repairs and maintenance work on the
beach reservation.

Until 1959, lot owners in Section No. 2 were freely permitted to use the
beach and some of them were members of the association. However,
when apprised of the plan to build the beach club and a proposal by
Haley to sell 100 house lots in Section No. 2 and "give to each lot an
appurtenant right to use the beach reservation," several owners in Section No. 1 decided to bring the present suit. Dues to owners in Section
No. 2 were returned.

Both Gutterman and Procter told prospective purchasers of lots in
Section No. 1 that "nothing was to be built on the reservation so that the
water view from adjacent lots would not be restricted or limited." In a
1930 agreement of sale covering a lot in section No. 1, to which Sterling
and one Joseph W. Worthen were parties, it was stated that "no structures shall be erected . . . on the beach reservation except seats, shelters
or other similar structures."

"Sterling registered its title to . . . 'Sandy Beach Reservation.' " The
decree of the Land Court is dated February 9, 1931, and contains the
following language, "The land hereby registered is subject to the restrictions, rights and easements heretobefore granted or imposed by deeds
and which may hereafter be so granted or imposed by the petitioner
[Sterling] and its successors in title. . . ."

> An examination of the abstract and papers in Registration Case No. 14481
> [the 1931 registration of Sandy Beach Reservation] discloses that in para-
> graph three of the petition, it was alleged that the land was affected by an
> encumbrance described as "the right of grantees of the petitioner's
> [Sterling's] other land to use the land described for recreation in common
> with the petitioner [Sterling], its successors, grantees and assigns, subject
> to such rules and regulations as the petitioner [Sterling] may establish or
> adopt." In the abstract in the case . . . are shown plans of the subdivision
> of Section No. 1 into lots. There is no reference to Section No. 2 being the
> "other land" referred to in the petition.

In addition to the facts summarized above the judge stated:

> I find that the specific reference to the beach rights as set out in the deed
> from Sterling to Procter of lots in Section No. 1 . . . ; that the failure to
> mention beach rights in the deed from Sterling to Procter of the land in
> Section No. 2 . . . ; that the specific denial of beach rights to the parcel
> conveyed out of Section No. 2 to Sullivan [the 1947 conveyance] . . . ; that
> the statement[s] and conduct of Gutterman acting for Sterling, and those

statements of Procter show an intent to confine the beach rights to the lots in Section No. 1. I find further that the bill was filed within a reasonable time and that there are no laches. I find further that . . . the development of . . . Section No. 1 was under a general building scheme; that no structures other than seats, shelters, or other similar structures were to be erected on . . . Sandy Beach Reservation . . . ; that the appurtenant easement to use the "Sandy Beach Reservation" was not limited or dismissed by the restrictive covenants expiring January 1, 1956. I find . . . that the defendant Haley . . . and . . . Procter do not and did not have the right to grant as appurtenant to the land in Section No. 2 . . . the right to use Sandy Beach Reservation. . . .

A final decree was entered in which Haley was enjoined "from granting to any grantee or grantees . . . [of land in Section No. 2] any appurtenant right to use Sandy Beach Reservation . . . for recreation; . . . from erecting or building . . . [thereon] any structures other than seats, shelters or similar structures; . . . [which must not] interfere with the plaintiff's easement to use . . . Sandy Beach Reservation for recreation. . . ." The bill was dismissed as to the other defendants, who are described in the plaintiff's bill of complaint as "owners of . . . lots in Section 2 . . . that also purportedly received from their grantor easements appurtenant thereto consisting, *inter alia*, of the right to use said Sandy Beach Reservation for recreational purposes in common with others."

General Laws c.185, §47, provides that when land is registered, the decree of registration "shall set forth . . . in such manner as to show their relative priority . . . all *particular* . . . easements . . . to which the land or the owner's estate is subject" (emphasis supplied). Under G.L. c.185, §45, "[s]uch decree shall not be opened . . . by any proceeding at law or in equity for reserving judgments or decrees." General Laws c.185, §46, states: "Every petitioner receiving a certificate of title in pursuance of a decree of registration, and every subsequent purchaser of registered land taking a certificate of title for value and in good faith, shall hold the same free from all encumbrances except those noted on the certificate." If, as Haley contends, the present suit is actually a "collateral attack" on the 1931 registration decree, there is grave doubt as to whether the plaintiffs are entitled to maintain it.

"The purpose of registration law is to bind the land and to quiet title to it. Registration is conclusive upon every one, with a few exceptions . . . , and the rights of innocent purchasers for value are given special protection." . . . As the judge noted the decree of registration refers to easements which were imposed by deed and which would thereafter be imposed. But the language of the decree does not supply the requirement of the statute that "particular . . . easements" be set forth. The judge stated that the petition for the 1931 decree refers to the "right of the grantees of the petitioner's [Sterling's] other land" to use the registered land for recreation. General Laws c.185, §47, provides that the "decree shall be stated in a form convenient for transcription upon the certificates of title hereinafter mentioned." This provision lends emphasis to the view that a decree of registration is to be a reasonably self-contained document. In light of both §47 and previous decisions of this court, we are not inclined to the opinion that the petition for registration constitutes part of such a decree.

However, even if *arguendo* we treat the petition as part of the decree, we are not satisfied that with regard to the easements claimed for all the lots in Section No. 1, the requirement of particularity is met. A prospective purchaser of registered land, learning that such land is subject to an easement for the benefit of "the petitioner's [Sterling's] other land," would hardly be enlightened as to the extent or nature of the easements or as to the persons who are benefited thereby. Nor would such a purchaser be certain that the easement would be for the benefit of land which the petitioner (Sterling) had conveyed prior to entry of the decree. A decree of registration is "a definitive judgment that binds the parties, even though it does not conform to the evidence or the findings. . . ." If the failure to make the decree so conform was error, it could have been corrected only upon some seasonable and legally recognized proceeding for appellate or other review.

The 1931 decree does not show that particular easements had been granted to any of the plaintiffs. In these circumstances, pursuant to G.L. c.185, §46, it may be that the only valid easements to use Sandy Beach Reservation are those "noted on the certificate [of title]." If the deeds containing the easements noted on the certificate expressly state that only owners of lots in Section No. 1 are entitled to use Sandy Beach Reservation, neither Procter nor Haley had authority to grant any other owners an appurtenant easement to use this land. We are of opinion that neither the incorporation by reference of Hannah Sweet's deed into the deeds noted on the certificate nor any of the other circumstances referred to by the judge was sufficient to show that any easements so noted were particularly limited to owners in Section No. 1.

[W]e think that if at the time Haley purchased Sandy Beach Reservation it knew of easements exclusive or otherwise, previously granted by deed, these easements will be enforceable to the extent of Haley's knowledge even if not appearing on the decree of registration or the certificate of title. The same rule of enforceability applies to each purchaser of lots in Section No. 2 who by deed has been granted easements to use Sandy Beach Reservation. The judge's findings do not show whether Haley or any other purchaser knew of the easements claimed by owners in Section No. 1. Accordingly, the decree is reversed, and the case is remanded to the Land Court for further proceedings consistent with this opinion.

Does the final paragraph in *Butler* explain why North Carolina has a race-type recording system? Isn't Torrens *plus* a race statute the solution to endless litigation over land ownership? Or are the issues of fairness, reflected both by a hostility to takers with notice and by Reed v. Fain, so compelling that we should pay a price in simplicity and efficiency in order to respond to them?

McDOUGAL, TITLE REGISTRATION AND LAND LAW REFORM: A REPLY, 8 U. Chi. L. Rev. 63, 65-69, 77 (1940): To a foreign anthropologist land transfer in the United States would probably look, as one of my former students forcefully put it, much like an aboriginal, ritualistic clambake. Like most other subjects of "property," land is transferred by symbols, pieces of paper; but, unlike many of the other symbols, these particular symbols do not pass freely from hand to hand — their circulation is accompanied by much dilatory, costly, and extra-necessitous behavior of wise men. Transfer is normally effected by a double-barrelled ceremony requiring both a "contract" and a "deed" and culminating in "recordation" of at least the latter. Why the two symbols of contract and deed? Why a period of time between "agreement" and final "transfer"? Largely because of "title" difficulties, of "insecurities" in the public recording system. The vendor must have opportunity to prove and the vendee to determine that the vendor has what he says he has. This requires either an elaborate search of the alphabetically-indexed public records against every former owner of the land, begining with a good "root" of title at a date so distant that adverse possession must have cured all prior defects, or else resort to the owners of some private title plant who have kept all the entries in the public records up to date with a better index. To the danger that something may be missed in this search must be added the doctrine of *caveat emptor* and the fact that at the present time a multitude of interests are not even required to be evidenced in the public records. It is, hence, not unnatural that on the closing date, when the deed is to be delivered and the price paid or secured, a dispute not infrequently arises as to what the vendor actually has; it is notoriously a poor lawyer who cannot find something wrong, or apparently wrong, with a title as old as most titles are in this country. Such a dispute may force the vendor to bring suit either to quiet his title against the allegedly interested parties or to get a court to declare, as against the vendee, that his title is "marketable," despite possible defects. Eventually accepting or being forced to accept the proffered deed and land, the vendee still has no assurance that he will be able to keep the land or even be reimbursed if he loses the land. When some ghostly defect does materialize and a claimant "prior" to his vendor takes the land, what is his recourse? He can go back on his vendor only if he extracted a "warranty" deed and his vendor is still "available, solvent, and unable to escape through some of the loopholes in the highly technical judicial doctrines about covenants." He can go back on his lawyer or his abstracter only if he can prove "negligence." He can recover from a title insurance company only if he has made the extra payment for such protection and probably only if he has obtained a policy, *rara avis*, which does something more than guarantee a careful search by the abstracter. Such are but minimum indications of the difficulties and absurdities of the system. . . .

To assume the merits of an alternative system — thoroughly tried over a long period of time in Europe, England, the British Dominions, and several of our own states — which offers an expeditious mode of getting rid of stale claims, which by its tract index and constant posting of the books eliminates the tedious, costly search and the necessity of paying monopoly prices, which by making the records for all practical purposes conclusive insures that the bona fide purchaser will really get the land, which at negligible cost offers adequate recourse to anybody injured by the operation of the system, and which greatly shortens and cheapens the whole process of land transfer, would seem to be no great intellectual crime. Such broad claims for title registration are not in fact "assumed"; they are not the vain, visionary hopes of Utopian reformers, but are based on the actual results of the practical operation of the system in places as nearby as Massachusetts, Illinois, and Minnesota. Yet Professor Bordwell [at 7 U. Chi. L. Rev. 470 (1940)] relies heavily upon "experience" in this country and England to discredit registration. His error is a simple one: it lies in failing to make a distinction between the preliminary difficulties of getting a registration system adopted and in actual use, and the operation of such a system after it is in use. The only thing that "experience" in this country or England shows, beyond the beneficent results of actual operation indicated above, is that a voluntary system with a costly initial registration (i.e., a "lawsuit"), and without adequate provisions for transition from the old to the new, cannot hope quickly to overcome public ignorance and inertia and professional opposition. There is, however, no insuperable reason why a simple change in the keeping of the public books about a piece of land should have to be initiated by an expensive action to quiet title, or why a voluntary system should not be given the small public subsidy which would enable it to compete with interests vested in the chaos of the recording system, or even why registration should not be made compulsory with transition provisions — requiring registration only on any new sale or mortgage when the title must be searched anyway — which would reduce the strain on public personnel and private pocketbook. Surely Professor Bordwell knows that it is not any proved demerit of registration which has precluded its wide popular acceptance in this country. It is, of course, easy to take the frequent castigations of title lawyers and companies, to puff them at a high level of abstraction into a "Satanic interpretation of history," and then to ridicule that interpretation. It is quite another thing to establish relative demerits of title registration, as compared with recording, and to get rid of the well-known tangible, and bitter professional opposition to registration. . . .

The problem of land transfer, insoluble by obsessive reiteration of ancient bromides about individualism or by making the eagle scream with far-fetched analogies, is rightly nothing more than a question of organizational efficiency and of cost and protection to the consumer. From such a perspective, despite General MacChesney's and Professor Bordwell's insistence that "it can't happen here," the day for title registration in this country is just beginning to dawn: it has no need of "resurrection"; it is far from dead; it is big with all the life of the swelling contemporary demands of millions of people for livable homes, in a livable environment, at an approachable price and of other millions for some kind of farm security; it may not "save" these millions for some far-flung millennium; but it is an indispensable, if perhaps minor, element in a comprehensive program for the rehabilitation of a substantial part of their lives.

SCLAR, from THE LEGISLATURES: MINNESOTA SIMPLIFIES LAND REGISTRATION, 11 Real Est. L.J. 258, 258-262 (1982): A recently enacted Minnesota Law, Minn. Stat. Ann. §§502A.01-508A.85, establishes a procedure that has the potential for greatly simplifying the means by which owners of real property can establish their fee simple titles. The first of its kind, this law enables an owner whose title is uncontested to secure, at reasonable cost and speed, a certificate of possessory title (CPT). Thereafter, the owner and every subsequent bona fide purchaser of the property as to which a CPT has been issued holds the property free from all encumbrances and adverse claims except those that are memorialized on the CPT and those that are listed in the statute.

Establishing title by CPT is an alternative to establishing title under either the recording system or the Torrens registration system. Once title by CPT is established, however, the land becomes registered land and is forever withdrawn from the recording system. The land becomes eligible to enter the Torrens registration system after the expiration of five years from the issuance of the CPT. As land leaves the recording system and enters the Torrens registration system, it thereafter is unnecessary to search and evaluate the land records to determine whether interests arising out of prior transactions are clouds on the title. This reduces the kinds of risks that need be insured against by title insurance. The ultimate result, therefore, should be greater security of titles at substantially lower costs. . . .

Minnesota, particularly in the counties in the Minneapolis-St. Paul metropolitan area, is an exception to the lack of interest in Torrens registration. The office of the Hennepin County Title Examiner estimates that between 40 and 45 percent of all titles in that area are under the Torrens system. This level of utilization may well be attributable to the high degree of confidence a Minnesota property owner can have in a registered title. Except in rare instances, the Minnesota courts have upheld the conclusiveness of Torrens titles. Mistakes in registration and transfer proceedings are rare; in Hennepin County only one claim has been made against the assurance fund since its creation in 1901. The Minnesota statute creating the CPT registration system has the potential for removing the remaining disincentive for Torrens registration — the high cost of registering uncontested titles by judicial proceeding.

In virtually every respect the statute is identical to the Torrens statute. The major difference is that a judicial proceeding is unnecessary if the title is uncontested. A possessory estate in land may be registered under a CPT. This is defined as

> a fee simple estate held by an owner who (1) has been found on examination by the examiner of titles . . . to be the record owner of the land described; (2) has satisfied the examiner of titles that he and his predecessors in title have had actual or constructive possession . . . for a period of not less than 15 consecutive years . . . ; and (3) has paid the taxes on the land described for at least five years during the 15 year period.

The major cost of CPT registration is the title search required in order to comply with the requirement that the application state the names of all persons who appear of record or are known to the applicant to have an interest in the property. This is, however, precisely the same search that ordinarily is made whenever property is sold or encumbered. Since CPT title is more conclusive than record title, it would be in the interest of a prospective purchaser or encumbrancer to require, as part of the agreement with the owner, that the CPT registration process be initiated. The cost of CPT registration, which should not be significantly greater than the costs of the title search, could be borne by the same party who otherwise would have borne the title related costs.

DUNHAM, LAND PARCEL IDENTIFIERS AND THE UNIFORM LAND TRANSACTIONS ACT, 43 U. Cinn. L. Rev. 469, 481-483 (1974): The Reporters are proposing something similar to the "block" system in use in New York City. In that system there is a separate index page for each block. If there are many documents within the block, they may be alphabetized; but if there are few, they may be entered in a chronological fashion. The Reporters' proposal is to establish a "locator" system aggregating all of the documents within a subarea so as to exclude all of those dealing with another area but within the subarea entering the reference to transactions on an alphabetical and chronological basis. Instead of a "block" which is currently an uncertainly used term, the Reporters are considering squares of 50 by 50 (meters or feet) shown on a map to which is assigned a locator number. All references to legal parcels within that square will be aggregated against that number. If a searcher's call for a locator square results in documents referring to other parcels also being retrieved, the searcher must analyze the documents or the other indicators in the index to determine whether it concerns the critical parcel. If the legal parcel falls in more than one square, the document will be retrievable by reference to all of the squares in which the parcel falls. By calling for the locator number for several squares, the searcher can obtain information not only as to all of the parcels in question but as to the title history of parcels which allegedly abut the critical parcel. Again the title examiner must by perusal or use of other signals or indicators exclude the irrelevant documents.

In short, the proposal of the Reporters rejects the idea that the recording office must index the documents with reference to a number permanently assigned to each parcel. The locator square is a physical fact of the earth so that changes in parcel boundary lines — enlargement or contraction — will be reflected automatically by a contraction or enlargement of the number of squares into which the parcel falls by reason of its legal description.

This system avoids the problem of the absence of precise and accurate maps. The searcher or the person initiating recording can enter the locator into as many locator squares as he thinks the parcel falls and this will change as the parcel size varies.

This system must be judged not only in terms of its usability for retrieval of chains of title but also in relation to other proposals which will tend to reduce the information required by a good conveyancer. Among the proposals in ULTA which affect the utility of this system are the following:

(a) A reduction of the amount of information related to an owner which affects all parcels of the owner wherever situated. An attempt is made to require any involuntary claims such as a judgment lien to be converted to a specific lien attaching only to described property as soon as seems appropriate.

(b) A reduction in the time during which a non-possessory claim remains valid by a rigorous "marketable record title" provision to the effect that claims which antedate a good root of title at least 30 years old, lapse unless they have been re-recorded.

(c) An increase in the instances in which an apparent possessory owner may "overreach" interests by conveying to a bona fide purchaser whose only "notice" of the claim exists by reason of the record.

(d) By reducing the number of offices (e.g., probate, tax and recorder) where title information is available.

Thus the proposal is a very modest one. It increases the utility of the grantor-grantee index system by creating small sub-recording areas so that information for the whole district need not be searched in grantor-grantee indexes for the whole district. While Cook County, Illinois may have 3,000,000 parcels of land and may also have 1,000,000 documents each year concerning these parcels, a square containing a portion of the University of Chicago and portions of 2 or 3 faculty houses may have only 3 or 4 entries a year speedily retrievable because the locator system automatically separates the remaining 999,995 transactions from concern.

G. TRANSFERRING TITLE

Once Mr. and Ms. Ambitious are satisfied that Mr. Bailout's ownership is adequate, they are ready to *take title*, which occurs at the *closing*. This event, surrounded by a modicum of ceremony, usually takes place at the registry office (so that the buyers and their lender can be certain no last minute claims have been recorded against the land) or at the office of the bank or savings and loan that is providing the mortgage money. When the closing takes place away from the registry, the lender's lawyer will go immediately to record the transaction, or may be in contact by telephone with an agent at the registry who immediately records.

At closing, the buyer receives a *deed* from the seller. The deed is the document that transfers the remaining incidents of ownership from Mr. Bailout to Mr. and Ms. *A*. It names the grantor and grantee, recites the consideration paid, describes the property being conveyed, states the interest being granted (e.g., fee simple) and any restrictions on that interest, and sets forth whatever warranties are being made to the grantee by the grantor.

Sellers of real estate may give one of three sorts of warranties. A seller may *warrant generally*, meaning that he or she assumes responsibility for any defects in the title he or she is undertaking to convey. Or he or she may only *warrant specially*, meaning that he or she promises that there are no defects that have arisen during his ownership, but takes no responsibility for competing title claims that owe their origin to some predecessor in the chain of title. Or a seller may give a *quitclaim deed*, which transfers ownership he or she has, but makes no promises as to the extent of, or possible exceptions to, his rights.

Sample Document 17-7: Deed

This Deed, Made this first day of July, in the year one thousand nine hundred and sixty-three, by and between Harry L. Burkheimer and Doris W. Burkheimer, Grantor and The Howard Research and Development Corporation, a body corporate of the State of Maryland, Grantee.

Witnesseth: that in consideration of the sum of Five Dollars, and other valuable considerations, the receipt whereof is hereby acknowledged, the said Grantor does hereby grant, convey, and assign unto The Howard Research and Development Corporation, a body corporate as aforesaid, its successors and assigns, in fee simple, all that piece or parcel of land situate in the Fifth Election District of Howard County in the State of Maryland, and described as follows, that is to say: and which according to a survey made by Purdum and Jeachke, Professional Engineers and Land Surveyors on October 18, 1963, is more particularly described as follows:

BEGINNING for the same at a point on the centerline of Cedar Lane as laid out and now existing, said point being at the end of the First or South 3° 30' East 71½ perch line of the First Parcel of that land which by deed dated August 3, 1942 and recorded among the Land Records of Howard County, Maryland in Liber B.M. Jr. 176 at Folio 20 was granted and conveyed by Harrison Dorsey Worthington and Gladys Worthington, his wife, John Thomas Worthington, Jr. and Neville Lee Worthington, his wife, Napoleon A. Worthington and Dorothy J. Worthington, his wife, and Mary Posey and Walter Posey, her husband, Matilda W. Hutton and Joseph J. Hutton, her husband, and Charles Tyson Worthington, unmarried, to Harry L. Burkheimer and Doris W. Burkheimer, his wife, and running thence binding along the centerline of the abovementioned Cedar Lane and reversely along said First line of said First Parcel and continuing the same course binding reversely along the Fourth or South 1° 15' East 34 perch line of the Third Parcel described in the abovementioned deed from Harrison Dorsey Worthington, et al., to Harry L. Burkheimer, and wife, as now surveyed two (2) following courses and distances, as follows:

East 123.66 feet and; (2) North 01° 54' 40" East 1630.53 feet thence leaving said Cedar Lane and binding reversely along the Third line of the Third Parcel of the abovementioned deed North 80° 56' 24" East 997.55 feet, thence binding reversely along the First line of the Third Parcel and continuing the same course binding reversely along the Sixth line of the First Parcel of the abovementioned deed as now surveyed South 33° 54' 56" East 1137.89 feet to an iron pipe, thence binding reversely along the Fifth, Fourth,

Third and Second lines of said First Parcel the four (4) following courses and distances as now surveyed, viz.: (1) South 04° 24' 12" West 1766.10 feet as to a stone; (2) South 79° 06' 21" West 1031.25 feet; (3) North 03° 25' 32" East 814.52 feet and; (4) North 72° 57' 20" West 602.76 feet to the place of beginning, containing 84.556 acres of land more or less.

BEING the First and Third parcels of that land which by deed dated August 3, 1942 and recorded among the Land Records of Howard County, Maryland in Liber B.M. Jr. 176 at Folio 20 were granted and conveyed by Harrison Dorsey Worthington and Gladys Worthington, his wife, John Thomas Worthington, Jr. and Neville Lee Worthington, his wife, Napoleon A. Worthington and Dorothy J. Worthington, his wife, Mary E. Posey and Walter Posey, her husband, Matilda W. Hutton and Joseph J. Hutton, her husband and Charles Tyson Worthington, unmarried to Harry L. Burkheimer and Doris W. Burkheimer, his wife.

Together with the buildings and improvements thereupon; and the rights, alleys, ways, waters, privileges, appurtenances and advantages to the same belonging or in anywise appertaining.

To have and to hold the said described lot(s) of ground and premises unto and to the use of the said The Howard Research and Development Corporation, a body corporate of the State of Maryland, its successors and assigns.

And the said Grantor covenants to warrant specially the property hereby granted and conveyed, and to execute such further assurances of said land as may be requisite.

Whenever used, the singular number shall include the plural, the plural the singular, and the use of any gender shall be applicable to all genders.

Witness the hand(s) and seal(s) of the said Grantor(s):

WITNESS: _____ [Seal]

_____   *Harry L. Burkheimer*

                                                _____ [Seal]

_____   *Doris W. Burkheimer*

State of Maryland, COUNTY OF HOWARD, TO WIT:

I HEREBY CERTIFY, that on this _____ day of _____ 1963 before me, a Notary Public of the State aforesaid, person-

ally Harry L. Burkheimer and Doris W. Burkheimer, his wife
_____ known to me (or satisfactorily proven) to be
the person(s) whose name(s) is/are subscribed to the within instrument, who signed the same in my presence, and acknowledged
that he/they executed the same for the purposes therein contained.

WITNESS my hand and Notarial Seal

_____

Notary Public
My commission expires: May 3, 1963

The Burkheimer property is subject to the following encumbrances:

(a) The reservation of the Dorsey Family graveyard with right of
ingress and egress thereto as contained in a deed dated February 28, 1930 and recorded among the land records of Howard
County in Liber H.S.K. 138, folio 228, from John T. Worthington and wife to Clarence T. Bond and wife;

(b) The provisions regarding said graveyard contained in a deed
dated August 3, 1942 and recorded among the land records of
Howard County in Liber B.M.J. 176, folio 20, from Harrison
Dorsey Worthington and wife, et al. to Harry L. Burkheimer
and wife.

(c) The provisions of an agreement regarding poles, wires, etc.,
dated August 11, 1945 and recorded among the land records of
Howard County in Liber B.M.J. 186, folio 301, between Harry
L. Burkheimer and wife and The Consolidated Gas and Electric
Light and Power Company of Baltimore.

Problems

1. Why is the consideration recited as five dollars?
2. Note that the conveyance is "in fee simple." Why not "and his
heirs"? Does this mean there are no restrictions on the property, such as
covenants and easements? If there are, are they applicable against the
new grantee if they are not recited in either the contract or the deed?
3. See the reference to an iron pipe on p.748 *supra*. What happens if
someone removes it?
4. Must the property be described in such detail? What is the relevance of such descriptions to our system of title searching, and especially to grantor-grantee indices?
5. Why the reference on p.748 *supra* to prior deeds? What if the
description in this deed does not match that in the prior deed?

6. Why the phrase "to the use of" Howard Development?

7. Is this a quitclaim, a special warranty, or a general warranty deed? See Md. Real Property Code §2-106 (1974):

> A covenant by a grantor in a deed, "that he will warrant specially the property hereby granted" has the same effect as if the grantor had covenanted that he will warrant forever and defend the property to the grantee, against any lawful claim and demand of the grantor and every person claiming or to claim by, through, or under him.

8. Suppose that Mr. Bailout had told the A's that the land on which his house was erected was original soil and undisturbed terrain. In fact, the area had been a swamp, and the house was built on unstable landfill. The A's then incurred $4,000 in damages due to uneven settling, but were still told that the property was essentially worthless. Assuming that the As' deed was similar to the one Howard R & D got from the Burkheimers, do they have a cause of action? For an extreme result, see Buist v. C. Dudley DeVelbiss, 182 Cal. App. 2d 325, 6 Cal. Rptr. 259 (1960), where buyers received as damages the entire purchase price plus the cost of improvements they had made and were permitted to keep the house and land.

1. Merger

◆ REED v. HASSELL
340 A.2d 157 (Del. Super. 1975)

CHRISTIE, Judge. By contract dated August 16, 1969, the plaintiffs, Thomas J. Reed and Sally Reed, his wife, agreed to purchase from Andrew Hassell (who died before the transaction was completed) and Loretta Hassell, his wife, Lots 82 and 83, Second Addition, Bay View Park, Baltimore Hundred, Sussex County, Delaware.

The printed contract form used by the parties provided that the title was to be "good and merchantable, free of liens and encumbrances except . . . publicly recorded easements for public utilities and other easements which may be observed by the inspection of the property."

By deed dated February 4, 1970, Loretta Hassell (the surviving seller and the defendant in this action) conveyed the lots to plaintiffs pursuant to the contract using a special warranty deed as required by the contract.

At the time of the contract and at the time of the conveyance, there was an existing road known as Hassell Avenue which (contrary to the information on the recorded plot plan) seriously encroached upon Lot 82 so as to deprive that lot of about 25 percent of its square footage. This encroachment reduced the lot to a relatively small, inconvenient lot which will be difficult to build upon in view of zoning requirements which include set-back and side line restrictions.

By this suit, plaintiffs seek damages on account of the encroachment. There is no evidence that defendant knew that the road constituted an encroachment at the time of settlement and, of course, the plaintiffs were unaware of the encroachment at the time of settlement.

The evidence indicates that the intention of the seller was to convey building lots essentially as they were shown on the lot plan, and the intention of the buyers was to buy such lots because they were of such size and shape as to be suitable for the construction of houses. Although there was an exception in the contract as to easements observable by inspection of the property, it is clear that the agreement would never have been entered into if it had been known that there was a major encroachment which severely limited the usefulness of the lot. Indeed, the seller made an innocent and unknowing representation to the buyers to the effect that she was able to convey such lots essentially as shown on the plot plan. This the seller was unable to do.

At the time of settlement there was heavy and tall growth on the lots which made it impossible to inspect the boundaries of the land or to measure the lots without costly or time-consuming work to cut down portions of the growth. During the two summers after settlement, the plaintiffs personally cleared the land. In October, 1973, the land had been cleared to the extent that a survey could be conducted and then, for the first time, it was discovered by a professional surveyor that the road was so located as to constitute a major encroachment on Lot 82.

Plaintiffs seek damages based upon alleged "misrepresentation, deceit and fraud" and, by informal amendment of the complaint, they, in the alternative, seek damages on account of an alleged breach of the covenant of warrant contained in the deed. At the hearing, plaintiffs failed to establish a factual basis for recovery on account of "misrepresentation, deceit and fraud" as such, but it was clearly established that the road constituted a breach of the covenant of special warranty of fee simple title free of encumbrances which the law reads into deeds such as the deed issued by the seller to the buyers in this case.

Thus, the question to be resolved by the Court is whether a major encroachment not known to be an encroachment by either the seller or the buyers at the time of settlement gives rise to an action for damages after such encroachment is discovered by the buyers many months after the deed had been accepted by the buyers. Resolution of this issue, in turn, depending in part upon the effect or lack of effect which is given to the provision in the sales contract which excepted from the title guarantees contained in such contract "easements which may be observed by an inspection of the property." . . .

Plaintiffs . . . contend that, in any event, the contract "merged" with the deed at time of settlement and, at that time, the contract became void as a separate document. Plaintiffs say the effect of this "merger" is that the seller is now held to the terms of the special warranty of title which the law attaches to a deed and seller is deprived of any benefit from the less exacting terms of the contract pursuant to which the special warranty deed was issued.

We come at last to the real crux of the case: Does a savings clause in the real estate sales contract survive the issuance of a special warranty deed so as to protect the grantor from liability for an encumbrance which was unrecognized by the parties but was in fact in basic derogation of the title the deed purported to convey?

The solution to the problem lies in the application of the merger rule under which the law is generally deemed to provide that a deed makes full execution of a contract of sale and constitutes the overriding contract between the parties as to what the seller conveyed to the buyer thereby rendering ineffective or obsolete any inconsistent terms of the prior contract. . . .

[T]he merger rule is subject to exceptions and *the intent of the parties is controlling* the question being one of construction.

The difficulty with the merger rule as applied to the case at bar is that it does not appear to have been developed to resolve the type of problem here posed. The merger rule appears to have been developed to resolve issues raised where a seller of real property undertook certain obligations in a contract of sale and then delivered something less than he promised as, for example, when seller delivered a deed not carrying out all the contract promises or a lot with certain encumbrances or containing a lesser acreage than contracted for. . . .

Under the merger rule, a deed is often deemed to supersede promises contained in the sales contract and, if the purchaser accepts the deed as compliance with the sales contract, he cannot seek additional rights he formerly had under the contract unless those additional rights survived the acceptance of the deed because they fell within one of the numerous exceptions to merger rule. Is the converse true? That is, does an unconditional special warranty deed supersede the lesser undertakings or escape clauses contained in the sales contract so that the seller must make good on the warranties of the deed even though the seller was expressly excused from such undertaking in the sales contract?

I think, under the circumstances here present, the merger rule should be applied and the seller should be held to the warranties contained in the deed because the obvious intent of the parties from the very beginning was that the seller would convey and the buyers would receive the two building lots essentially as shown on the plot plan. . . .

The merger rule is deemed to apply here because it serves to carry out the basic intent of the parties. The warranties in the deed are deemed to be binding on the seller under the circumstances.

◆ KNUDSON v. WEEKS
394 F. Supp. 963 (W.D. Okla. 1975)

DAUGHERTY, Chief Judge. In the Spring of 1970 Plaintiff, Eleanor Gray Knudson, came to Oklahoma City, Oklahoma, for the purpose of purchasing a home. She had been employed at the University of California and had accepted employment at the University of Oklahoma as Dean of the College of Nursing. She employed a local real estate agent, Frank Kelley, to assist her. Through Kelley she located a home known as 6008 Queens Gate which is more specifically described as Lot 5, Block 4 of the Lansbrook Addition to Oklahoma City, Oklahoma. On May 10, 1970 Plaintiff contracted to purchase the house from its builder, Defendant Donald W. Weeks. Kelley contacted the Glenn Justice Mortgage Company (Glenn Justice) to obtain a loan for Plaintiff. Glenn Justice found a lender in the Kingfisher Savings and Loan Association (Kingfisher) who was willing to advance a mortgage loan at an agreeable interest rate. Kingfisher in its dealings with Glenn Justice requested a survey of the property. Accordingly Glenn Justice contacted the Hughes Engineering Company (Hughes) and ordered a survey. The order was made on May 26, 1970. On June 3, 1970 a survey of the subject property was made by Hughes. An error was made in the survey as it failed to disclose that the house at 6008 Queens Gate encroached over the rear lot line of Lot 5, Block 4 of Lansbrook Addition. The certificate of encroachments in the survey failed to note this defect. The certificate was delivered to Kingfisher. Hughes was paid for his work by Kingfisher. The cost of the survey was passed on to Plaintiff as an itemized loan closing cost. Plaintiff paid this charge when the loan closed. The sale of the house from Defendant Weeks to Plaintiff was consummated on June 16, 1970.

In August 1970, R. N. Coyle, President of the Lansbrook Association, informed Plaintiff that her house was over its back lot line. Plaintiff then owned and was occupying the property. Coyle stated that the encroachment was into a community owned greenbelt area and that he would take care of the problem. Coyle had learned of the encroachment from Defendants Weeks who had learned of it from a builder who was working on the house next door. The corrective action promised by Coyle was a quitclaim deed from the Lansbrook Association. It was not realized at the time that the encroachment was into a utilities easement which had been dedicated to the City of Oklahoma City. Thus, the community owned greenbelt area at the location here involved was burdened with the utilities easement. The promised quitclaim deed was not executed until April 11, 1972.

In April, 1973 Plaintiff contracted to sell the subject property to one Edward Caston. The contract price was substantially higher than the price for which Plaintiff had purchased the property. The sale to Caston fell through when Caston's mortgage lender ordered a loan survey and discovered the encroachment into the utilities easement and that the title defect had not been fully cured by the quitclaim deed from the Lansbrook Association. Caston's lender declined to advance a mortgage on the property with this defect in its title. In an effort to save the sale Plaintiff asked Weeks to escrow the estimated cost of curing the title defect, $7,500.00. Weeks refused to take this action. The contract between plaintiff and Caston called for closing on or before May 1, 1973. Several extensions were made, the last one being until May 29, 1973. However, Plaintiff was unable to cure her title defect in this period of time and the sale to Caston was lost.

After the Caston sale failed the title defect was cured at Weeks' expense. On June 14, 1973 Weeks sent a letter to Plaintiff's attorney waiving any statute of limitations concerning any cause of action Plaintiff might have against him. The letter was not supported by consideration. The utilities easement was vacated where the house extended over it. Utility lines were dug up and rerouted and the area was resodded. It developed during this time that the air conditioner pad for the house had been laid over a manhole cover of the sewer which ran behind the house. During the period of time it took to correct these defects economic conditions in the United States changed. Interest rates soared and loans became difficult to obtain. Consequently Plaintiff experienced much difficulty in selling her house after the title defect was cured. When she finally did obtain a buyer she received a much lower price than she would have obtained if the sale to Caston had been consummated. . . .

It is Plaintiff's theory that she is entitled to recover damages from Defendants Weeks for their failure to convey to her merchantable title to the subject property. On May 10, 1970 Plaintiff and Weeks entered into a real estate purchase contract whereby Plaintiff agreed to buy and Weeks agreed to sell the subject property. The contract called for the conveyance of merchantable title by the seller. On June 16, 1970 Weeks and his wife executed a warranty deed conveying the subject property to Plaintiff in performance of the contract. Subsequently it developed that the deed had failed to convey merchantable title. Plaintiff alleges this failure cost her the Caston sale. After the sale fell through Weeks caused the title defect in the subject property to be corrected.

Plaintiff contends Defendants Weeks are liable to her for the damages she sustained by her loss of the Caston sale in that they failed to convey merchantable title as was called for in the May 10, 1970 purchase contract. Defendants Weeks do not deny the contract or breach thereof. It is, however, their position that the May 10, 1970 purchase contract was merged into their June 16 warranty deed, that Plaintiff is only entitled under the law to recover under the warranties of said deed, that recovery under the warranties is limited to the cost of curing the title defect and that they have already cured the defect and paid the cost thereof. . . .

The facts of this case do not show fraud or the type of mistake which has been held to prevent merger. Moreover, the burden of proof is on Plaintiff to show that the parties did not intend that the contract merge into the deed. Plaintiff has wholly failed to submit any evidence whatsoever which would overcome the presumption that she intended the contract to merge into the deed. Therefore, the May 10, 1970 contract merged into the deed and Plaintiff is limited to her remedies on the warranties of the deed.

Defendants Weeks conveyed the subject property to Plaintiff by a statutory warranty deed. The statutory covenants of the title under the Oklahoma law are seizin, right to convey, against incumbrances, quiet possession, and warranty. Plaintiff has not addressed the question of which of these covenants may have been broken by the Weeks' conveyance, or what damages may be recoverable thereunder. Defendants Weeks admit that they have broken either the covenant of seizin or right to convey, which are synonymous in Oklahoma, or the covenant against incumbrances, but contend that in either event, under the circumstances of this case, the Plaintiff is not entitled to further recovery.

There are two Oklahoma Statutes delineating the damages recoverable by a grantee for a grantor's breach of covenant in the execution of a warranty deed. 23 Oklahoma Statutes §26 provides the measure of damages for the breach of the covenant against incumbrances and 23 Oklahoma Statutes §25 provides the measure of damages for the breach of any of the other statutory covenants. It does not appear that the covenant against incumbrances was breached by the Defendants Weeks herein. In general, the covenant against incumbrances extends to adverse claims or liens on the estate conveyed whereby it may be defeated wholly or in part. An incumbrance may be defined as any right to, or interest in, land which may subsist in another to the diminution of its value, but consistent with the passing of the fee. Black's Law Dictionary, Fourth Edition. The subject house extended over the back lot line and into an adjacent common greenbelt area burdened with a utilities easement. The Lansbrook Association did not have an incumbrance against said Lot 5, Block 4 as a result of the encroachment of the house on said lot onto the greenbelt. An easement is a liberty, privilege or advantage without profit which the owner of one parcel of land may have in the lands of another.

An easement is an incorporal hereditament, it does not confer title to land or create a lien thereon. It appears from the plat of the Lansbrook Addition that the subject utilities easement is appurtenant to Lot 5, Block 4, the commons or greenbelt area being the servient estate. Thus the warranty deed from the Defendants Weeks to the Plaintiff did not pass title to the land or the dominant utilities easement over both of which the house encroached. As the title to the land and the dominant utilities easement on which the house encroached did not pass by Defendants Weeks' Warranty Deed, it cannot be said that this defect in title constituted an incumbrance within the abovementioned definitions. Therefore, reliance on 23 Oklahoma Statutes §26 would be misplaced and if a covenant of title was breached, the measure of damages is provided by 23 Oklahoma Statutes §25.

As has been previously mentioned the covenants of seizin or right to convey are synonymous in Oklahoma. The covenant of seizin is that the covenantor has the estate he purports to convey. It is apparent that the Defendants Weeks purported to convey both the subject house and the ground upon which it stood. This they failed to do as they had no title to the ground in the greenbelt burdened with the utilities easement upon which part of the house encroached. Therefore, their covenants of seizin and right to convey were breached when the deed was executed. The measure of damages provided by 23 Oklahoma Statutes §25 for such a breach is as follows:

> The detriment caused by the breach of a covenant of seizin, of right to convey, of warranty, or of quiet enjoyment, in a grant of an estate in real property, is deemed to be:
> 1. The price paid to the grantor, or, if the breach is partial only, such proportion of the price as the value of the property affected by the breach bore, at the time of the grant, to the value of the whole property.
> 2. Interest thereon for the time during which the grantee derived no benefit from the property, not exceeding six years; and,
> 3. Any expenses properly incurred by the covenantee in defending his possession.

The applicable measure of damages under this statute in this case is such proportion of the purchase price of the subject house paid by the Plaintiff to the Defendants Weeks as the value of the property affected by the breach (area of encroachment) bore, at the time of the grant, to the value of the whole property. What then is the value of the property affected by the breach? In the case of unimproved land of uniform unit value, the measure of damages under this statute for a grantor's partial breach of covenant of seizin, such as is the case herein, could be ascertained by determining the unit value (square foot, acre) of the property, and multiplying that value times the number of units which the grantor purported to convey but failed to convey. In this case, however, the value of the property affected by Defendants Weeks' breach of covenant of seizin goes beyond such a simple solution. The breach of covenant of seizin herein (the encroachment) affected the value of Plaintiff's entire house. As a result of the encroachment part of Plaintiff's house was on land on which she had no right to maintain it. The effect of the breach was that Plaintiff had either to move her house off the easement, cut off the part of the house which was over the easement, or to acquire the land upon which the encroachment rested and vacate the easement and move the utilities lines. The cost of performing one of these acts is the true measure of the value of the property affected by Defendants' breach of covenant herein. Defendants Weeks have already sustained the cost of acquiring the needed land, vacating and re-routing the easement and moving the utilities lines. Plaintiff has accepted their curative efforts. Thus in effect Defendants Weeks have already tendered damages for their breach of covenant of seizin and Plaintiff has accepted the tender. Defendants Weeks have satisfied the statutory measure of damages applicable in this case. Therefore, further recovery by Plaintiff is precluded.

Note

Express warranties of the fitness of the swimming pool, septic system, and air conditioning, made in a contract to sell house and land, did not merge into the deed because they were "collateral agreements in the contract where the deed is only a partial execution of that contract." This is true even though the warranties had been inserted by the real estate broker in a form purchase agreement supplied by him. Oral representations by the seller to the buyer before entry of the contract cannot be the basis for a cause of action; their use is barred by the parol evidence rule. Rouse v. Brooks, 66 Ill. App. 3d 107, 383 N.E.2d 666 (1978).

2. Sellers' Liabilities

a. Present Covenants

◆ McGUCKIN v. MILBANK
152 N.Y. 297, 46 N.E. 490 (1897)

Appeal from an order of the General Term of the Supreme Court in the first judicial department, entered February 6, 1895, which sustained defendants' exceptions ordered to be heard in the first instance at General Term, set aside a verdict in favor of plaintiff directed by the court and granted a new trial.

This action was brought to recover damages for an alleged breach of a covenant against incumbrances in a conveyance.

One Davies, prior to March, 1887, was the owner of lots numbers 59, 61, 63, 65, 67 and 69 East One Hundred and Twentieth street, New York city.

March 9, 1887, he executed and delivered to William A. Cauldwell a mortgage on each of said lots, each of which was given to secure $5,000, or such part as should be advanced toward improving the premises. June 27th following, Davies made a further mortgage to George N.

Manchester, covering the six lots, which mortgage contained a clause immediately following the description of the property, providing that the mortgage was in trust to secure the payment, to various individuals therein named, of certain sums aggregating $5,000. Cauldwell subsequently foreclosed his mortgages, and in the actions of foreclosure made George N. Manchester a party, naming him individually and not as trustee. Decrees were entered in all these foreclosure suits; subsequently the properties were bought by Cauldwell at the foreclosure, who afterwards sold all of the lots to this plaintiff and conveyed them by deed containing a covenant against incumbrances. Plaintiff made no objection to taking the title on the ground that Manchester had been named individually as a defendant in the foreclosure suits, and it does not appear that either of the parties to the conveyance was aware that there was any basis for a claim that Manchester's mortgage had not been cut off by the foreclosure.

After plaintiff had obtained title he made an application to the Metropolitan Life Insurance Company for a loan of $10,500 upon each of the lots. The loan was made and thereafter plaintiff sold four of the lots, and as to them there is no controversy. In 1890 the Metropolitan Life Insurance Company commenced suits to foreclose its mortgages on No. 65 and 69, which resulted in judgments of foreclosure and sale, bearing date the 28th day of May of that year, the referee's report of sale being dated October 20, 1890. It does not appear that at the sales the attention of any one was called to the fact that George N. Manchester was made a party defendant individually, and not as trustee in the Cauldwell foreclosures, and so far as we are advised by the record, it does not appear that such fact was taken into consideration, or that it in any wise affected the bidding for the properties. After the commencement of such foreclosure suits one Cain, to whom the plaintiff had conveyed lot 65, made a contract for its sale to one Wittkowski, who subsequently refused performance on the ground that the Davies mortgage was an incumbrance upon the property. Subsequent to the sale of the lots pursuant to the judgment of May 28, 1890, by which plaintiff was divested of title, a suit was commenced by George N. Manchester, as trustee, to foreclose the mortgage complained of, in which action all subsequent parties in interest were made defendants, including the plaintiff and each of the persons who were *cestuis que trust* under the Davies mortgage to Manchester. It resulted in a judgment dismissing the complaint, adjudging that the sale under the six several judgments of foreclosure obtained on the foreclosure of the Cauldwell mortgages did actually divest the lien of the mortgage executed by Davies and wife to George N. Manchester as trustee.

The premises conveyed by Cauldwell to the plaintiff consisted of a plot of ground 100 feet on East 120th Street, upon which, at the time of the conveyance, six houses were in the course of erection, one on each of the lots into which the plot was divided. They were afterwards completed by the plaintiff, and when completed each house and lot had cost him $14,700. Before the commencement of the foreclosure action on the mortgage to the Metropolitan Life Insurance Company the plaintiff had sold and conveyed five of the six to different persons; but it does not appear that the deeds of conveyance contained any covenants of warranty or that they were made subject to the Manchester mortgage, or that they were sold with any reference to that mortgage as an outstanding incumbrance.

The trial judge ruled that the Manchester mortgage was not cut off by the foreclosure of the Cauldwell mortgage, and directed a verdict in favor of the plaintiff for $1,666.66, one-third of the principal of that mortgage, on the theory that that was the sum properly apportionable to the two lots, 65 and 69, and apparently upon the further assumption that the plaintiff was the owner of these two lots at the time his title was divested under the judgment and foreclosure of the mortgage to the Metropolitan Life Insurance Company. The General Term sustained the exceptions of the defendants taken on the trial and set aside the verdict and ordered a new trial, from which order the plaintiff appealed to this court, giving the usual stipulation.

ANDREWS, Ch. J. Unless upon the evidence the plaintiff was in any event entitled to recover at least the sum for which the verdict was directed, the direction was erroneous and the order of the General Term must be affirmed, although a case was or might have been made for the recovery of damages to some amount for the breach of the covenant against incumbrances contained in the deed of Cauldwell. The action was brought upon the theory that the Manchester mortgage had not been cut off by the foreclosure of the mortgage under which Cauldwell acquired title, although it was a subsequent lien, and Manchester was made a party defendant to those foreclosures. The defendants, while insisting that the lien of the Manchester mortgage was extinguished by the foreclosures, further contend that although it may have been an outstanding and valid incumbrance on the property at the time of the conveyance by Cauldwell to the plaintiff, and constituted a breach of the covenant against incumbrances contained in Cauldwell's deed, no case was made for the recovery of more than nominal damages. The plaintiff was neither evicted under the Manchester mortgage, nor has he paid the mortgage or any part of it. It is the general rule that a grantee under a deed containing a covenant against incumbrances, who has not been disturbed in his possession and who has not paid the mortgage or other money lien on the land, is not entitled in an action for the breach of the covenant to recover more than nominal damages. The principle of the decision is that a covenant against incumbrances is treated as a contract of indemnity, and although broken as soon as made, if broken at all, nevertheless a recovery (beyond nominal damages) is confined to the actual loss sustained by the covenantee by reason of the payment or enforcement of the incumbrance against the property. He is not permitted to recover the amount of the outstanding incumbrance, before payment or loss of the property, although its existence may be an embarrassment to his title and subject him to inconvenience. . . .

The inference from the facts proved is that neither the grantor nor the grantees in these deeds supposed at the time the conveyances were made that the Manchester mortgage was a lien on the premises. All the parties assumed that it was divested by the foreclosure of the Cauldwell mortgages. It does not appear, therefore, that the plaintiff suffered any injury as to the five lots by reason of the existence of the Manchester mortgage, and he was not entitled to any damages as to those lots. The plaintiff, upon the proofs, was not bound to indemnify his grantees, and the benefit of the covenant did not pass to them by the conveyances from the plaintiff. In respect to the one lot, the title to which remained in the plaintiff up to the time of the foreclosure, a different question is presented. If there was evidence that the sum bid for that lot on the sale was affected by the fact of the incumbrance of the Manchester mortgage, which (if a lien) was paramount to the lien of the mortgages of the Metropolitan Life Insurance Company, under which the sale was made, and the lot on that account brought less than it otherwise would, then a reasonable basis for the award of substantial damages would have been established, provided, as we assume for the purposes of this case, the Manchester mortgage was an existing incumbrance. . . . But the infirmity of the plaintiff's case is that the evidence fails to show that the Manchester mortgage was a factor which entered into the sale, or was in contemplation of the purchasers on the foreclosure. The Metropolitan Life Insurance Company had accepted the title when it took its mortgages. No reference was made to the Manchester mortgage at the foreclosure sale. In fact the inference is very strong that the bids were made on the assumption that the Metropolitan Insurance Company mortgages were the first and paramount liens on the property. There is no evidence of the value of the lot owned by the plaintiff at the time of the sale or that such value exceeded the sum for which it was sold. The lot sold for a sum nearly equal to what the property had cost the plaintiff. The plaintiff was entitled to recover a sum equal to any actual injury he had suffered in respect to the one lot from a breach of the covenant, but it was not shown that such injury was equal to the one-third part of the Manchester mortgage. His legal injury under the evidence could not exceed the loss he sustained on the one lot to which alone he had title at the time of the foreclosure, and not to two lots which the trial judge seems to have assumed he owned at that time.

We think the trial court erred in directing a verdict for any specific sum, and that the order of the General Term properly granted a new trial.

◆ HILLIKER v. RUEGER
228 N.Y. 11, 126 N.E. 266 (1920)

McLaughlin, J. On the 1st of May, 1905, the defendants, Rueger's testator and his wife, conveyed to the plaintiff and his wife (now deceased), as tenants by the entirety, certain real property situate in the city of New York. The consideration was $7,000, of which $500 was paid down and the balance secured by a purchase-money mortgage. The grantors in the deed of conveyance covenanted that they were "seised of the said premises in fee simple and have good right to convey the same." Subsequent to the conveyance the grantees entered into a contract with one Schaefer to convey the premises to him for $8,500, of which $500 was paid on the execution of the contract and the balance agreed to be paid or secured when the title passed. Schaefer thereafter refused to complete the contract, on the ground that the title tendered was unmarketable, and he demanded that the $500 paid be returned to him. The demand not being complied with, he brought an action to recover the same. It was finally determined in that action that the grantees did not have a marketable title to a part of the premises conveyed [which title was in the City of New York, as owner of a long-abandoned Dutch road, the Newton and Bushwick turnpike, see Schaefer v. Hilliker, 140 App. Div. 173 (1910), aff'd, 206 N.Y. 708 (1911)], for which reason plaintiff was entitled to recover the amount paid at the time the contract was executed, with interest, expenses, etc. The defendants in the present action had notice of that action, and were afforded an opportunity to defend it, which they neglected and refused to do. After Hilliker had paid the judgment recovered by Schaefer he brought this action to recover the damages alleged to have been sustained by reason of the breach of the covenant of seizin, to which reference has been made. The trial court found there was a breach of the covenant of seizin, in that the defendants' testator did not have title to a part of the premises conveyed, and by reason thereof plaintiff had sustained damage to the amount of $1,200, being the difference between $7,000, the consideration paid, and $5,800, the proportionate value of the part of the premises of which the grantors had title at the time of the conveyance, with interest on the $1,200 for six years immediately prior to the commencement of the action; also for $1,500, the amount expended by the plaintiff for counsel and attorney's fees in defending the action brought by Schaefer against him, with interest, and an extra allowance of 5 per cent, as costs on the amount recovered.

If a covenant of seizin be broken at all, it is at the time of the delivery of the conveyance. It is not essential in an action to recover damages for the breach of such a covenant that the grantee should be evicted. . . . Possession does not satisfy a covenant of seizin. Such covenant means that the grantor, at the time of the conveyance, was lawfully seized of a good, absolute, and indefeasible estate of inheritance in fee simple, and had power to convey the same. If the covenant be broken by the failure of title then an action can at once be maintained to recover the damages sustained as the direct result of the breach.

The trial court found, as indicated, that the grantors in the deed to the plaintiff did not have title to a part of the land conveyed. That finding has been unanimously affirmed. There was therefore a breach of the covenant of seizin which entitled plaintiff to whatever damages he had sustained by reason of it. The trial court also found that he had sustained damages to the extent of $1,200. I am of the opinion, however, that the judgment is erroneous in so far as it permitted the plaintiff to recover the $1,500, attorney's and counsel fees paid in defending the action brought against him by Schaefer. The rule seems well established that costs and expenses, including counsel fees, can only be allowed when a direct attack is made upon the title. The grantee, when sued, of course can defend his title and possession, or take such steps as may be necessary to obtain possession. Whatever it costs him to do this, if the title fail — not exceeding the consideration paid for the part or portion of the premises involved, together with the necessary costs and disbursements — may be recovered of the grantor.

The Schaefer action was not a direct attack upon the title. It was that the title was not marketable. The fact that it was not marketable did not establish that the title was bad, or that there was a breach of the covenant of seizin.

The judgment appealed from, therefore, should be modified by striking out the item of $1,500 and interest thereon, and the extra allowance of costs is reduced proportionately, and as thus modified affirmed, without costs to either party.

Problem

In 1953, Palliser applied for permission to build 15 apartment buildings consisting of 217 units on his 10-acre tract now located in Columbia. The zoning ordinance then in effect permitted apartments to be built at one unit per 675 square feet. Subsequently, a new comprehensive zoning ordinance was passed, limiting such construction to one unit per 3,000 square feet. The Palliser development was permitted, however, under a "grandfather" clause in the new ordinance.

The development was built in such a way as to leave about 3½ acres undeveloped. After selling the apartment buildings and the 6½ acres of land under them, Palliser conveyed the 3½ acres of undeveloped land to Finn in a deed containing, *inter alia*, the following language:

And the said parties of the first part hereby covenant that they have not done or suffered to be done any act, matter, or thing whatsoever to encumber the property hereby conveyed; that they will warrant specially the property granted and that they will execute such further assurances of the same as may be requisite.

Finn has been unsuccessful in obtaining permission to build on his 3½ acres, since under the terms of the new ordinance the entire building capacity for the 10-acre plot has been filled. Finn now files suit against Palliser for violation of the covenant. What result? Does the result turn on whether Finn had notice of the zoning ordinance when he bought?

See Marathon Builders, Inc. v. Polinger, 263 Md. 410, 283 A.2d 617 (1971), where the court held that zoning ordinances and land use statutes do not constitute encumbrances and so cannot occasion a breach of a covenant against encumbrances. The purchaser is deemed to have contracted with knowledge of the applicable zoning restrictions.

Notes

1. On July 15, 1960, Hines conveyed to Brewster 145 acres of land with "covenants of general warranty of title." Brewster paid Hines the full consideration at that time. By 1967 Brewster had spent a considerable sum preparing the land for the purpose of cutting and selling timber. On advice of his attorney, Brewster at that time had a title search done, and was advised that Holway was holder in fee simple of the title to all 145 acres.

On August 21, 1967, Brewster filed a complaint against Hines claiming breach of warranty. While this action was pending, Brewster filed suit against Holway to quiet title. Holway defended on the ground that he was owner of the property "in fee simple absolute." Notice of the suit against Holway was given to Hines.

Hines now contends that Brewster has no cause of action, because he was never "actually or constructively evicted from the real estate": He brought trouble on himself by — in effect — waking up Holway. For a decision against Hines on these facts, see Brewster v. Hines, 155 W. Va. 302, 185 S.E.2d 513 (1971).

2. Plaintiffs bought 80 acres in Montgomery County, Illinois, from William and Faith Bost in 1957, receiving a statutory warranty deed. They went into possession and recorded. In 1974, they granted an option to Consolidated Coal Co. for coal rights on the land for $6,000. In 1970, plaintiffs "discovered" that they owned only 1/3 of the coal rights, because of a reservation by a prior owner in 1947. Plaintiffs sued the Bosts for $4,000.

Held: The Bosts' covenant of seisin was broken if at all in 1957, and any action based on that covenant is barred by the 10-year statute of limitations. The covenant of quiet enjoyment, on the other hand, is breached only when there is an actual or constructive eviction by the paramount titleholder. Thus, the statute of limitations has not run, but plaintiffs have no cause of action because they have not been ousted. Brown v. Lober, 75 Ill. 2d 547, 389 N.E.2d 1188 (1979).

3. Selling real property with knowledge that it violates building codes does not violate the covenant of seisin, the covenant against encumbrances, or the covenant of quiet enjoyment. Monti v. Tangora, 99 Ill. App. 3d 575, 425 N.E.2d 597 (1981).

b. Damages to Remote Grantees

◆ TAYLOR v. WALLACE
20 Colo. 211, 37 P. 963 (1894)

GODDARD, J. The court below, upon the evidence introduced on the trial of the cause, found the issues in favor of plaintiff, and further found that, by the judgment of the Indiana court, the title to the land in question was settled, and that the title warranted by defendants had been overthrown, and that defendants were liable upon their warranty, but held that as there was no evidence of the amount of the consideration paid by plaintiff to Sharp [Wallace's Grantee] he was entitled to recover only nominal damage, and thereupon entered judgment in his favor for one dollar and costs. The sole question, therefore, presented for our consideration by the assignments of error, is whether the court below adopted the correct measure of damages. It held that in this character of action, where the assignee of a covenantee sues the original covenantor, the amount of the recovery is the consideration paid by him to his immediate grantor, with interest not exceeding the consideration paid for the original conveyance. Counsel for plaintiff in error strenuously insist that the measure of recovery is the value of the land at the time of the conveyance by the original covenantor to the covenantee, and that that value is conclusively fixed by the consideration then paid. . . .

It is now well settled by the great weight of authority that by the covenant for quiet enjoyment and of general warranty, the grantor binds himself to pay his immediate grantee, in case of failure of title and eviction, the value of the land when conveyed; and this value is determined by the price paid, and that sum, with interest, is the limit of the measure of damages recovered by such grantee; that these covenants run with the land, and any subsequent grantee, upon eviction, may sue for the breach. To hold otherwise is to construe the covenant as one of indemnity, — a view that was rejected in the earlier cases, with few exceptions. In the case of Staats v. Ten Eyck's Ex'rs, 3 Caines, 111, it was held, in analogy with the rule applied in the common-law action of *warrantia chartae*, that the value of the land at the time of the conveyance was the criterion of damages, and not the enhanced value of the land at the time of eviction, whether owing to increase from natural causes or by improvements made by the grantee. There are rules that may reduce the amount of recovery within this limit. Interest is allowed for the time that the grantee is liable to the true owner for mesne profits; and when, by the statute of limitations, mesne profits are recoverable only for a certain number of years, interest will not be allowed for any longer time; and where by the payment of a judgment which is an incumbrance, or where the defect of title is remedied by purchase, the amount of recovery is limited to the amount that was fairly and reasonably paid for that purpose. If, therefore, the measure of damages may be diminished by the disallowance of interest when the profits are equivalent thereto, and a deduction of the principal allowed in the case of a *pro tanto* eviction in an action by the immediate grantee, it is difficult to perceive why the same rule should not apply as to a remote grantee, and his recovery be limited to this actual damage. . . .

A remote grantee may simultaneously sue his immediate grantor and all previous covenantors, and recover several judgments against each of them, although entitled to but one satisfaction; and the amount of recovery against each can in no event exceed the consideration received by him. Under the rule contended for by counsel for plaintiff in error, it would follow that his recovery would be in such an event as variable as the various amounts received by each covenantor; and in case the consideration paid by him to his immediate grantee is less than the consideration received by the original covenantor, his recovery would be less against such grantee than it would be in an action against the original covenantor; while, under the rule that the amount of his recovery is the amount of consideration actually paid by him for the land, not exceeding the original purchase price, the recovery in both cases would be the same. The rule limiting the measure of damages in a case like this, where the remote grantee elects to sue the original covenantor, to the actual loss sustained by him, seems to us not only equitable, but is in principle analogous to the doctrine that applies in an action by the original covenantee. Compensation for his loss is all that any evicted grantee can reasonably ask; and when this can be obtained by the recovery of the consideration paid, with interest, the ends of justice are attained. We think, therefore, that the court below adopted the correct rule of damages, and the judgment is accordingly affirmed.

◆ SOLBERG. v. ROBINSON
34 S.D. 55, 147 N.W. 87 (1914)

POLLEY, J. On the 27th day of January, 1906, one C. C. Robinson and wife executed and delivered to W. J. and J. L. Smith a certain warranty deed, purporting to convey to said Smiths, with other property, a quarter section of land in Hughes County. On the 9th day of January, 1907, said Smiths executed and delivered to plaintiffs a warranty deed, purporting to convey said land to plaintiffs, but neither the Robinsons nor the Smiths were ever in the actual possession of the land. Thereafter, one Vesey commenced an action against plaintiffs for the purpose of quieting title to said premises and to enjoin the plaintiffs in this action from asserting further claim thereto. Said action was defended by plaintiffs but, on the trial, it developed that, from a time long prior to the attempted conveyance from the Robinsons to the Smiths and down to the time of the trial, said Vesey was the absolute owner in fee of the land in question; that, while Robinson's title appeared to come through Vesey, the deed which purported to divest him of his title proved to be a forgery, and he had judgment as prayed for. Upon appeal to this court, said judgment was affirmed. Vesey v. Solberg, 27 S.D. 618, 132 N.W. 254. In the deed from Robinson to the Smiths, Robinson and wife covenanted with the Smiths, "their heirs and assigns, that they are well seised in fee of the lands and premises aforesaid, and have good right to sell and convey the same in manner and form aforesaid," and that "the above-bargained and granted lands and premises in quiet and peaceable possession of the said parties of the second part, their heirs and assigns, and against all persons lawfully claiming or to claim the whole or any part thereof, the said parties of the first part will warrant and forever defend." The deed from the Smiths to plaintiffs contained covenants of similar import.

After the affirmance of the judgment quieting title to the said premises in Vesey, plaintiffs commenced this action against the defendant, as administrator of the estate of the said C. C. Robinson, who had died in the meantime, for the purpose of recovering on the above-quoted covenants in the Robinson deed of January 27, 1906. During all of this time the land in question was vacant and unoccupied. The Smiths were named as defendants in the summons; but only one of them was ever served, and, as to him, the action was dismissed. Plaintiff seeks to recover the amount Robinson had received for the land, with interest, together with the expenses necessarily incurred in defending the Vesey case in the circuit court, upon appeal to this court, and upon motion for rehearing, including attorney's fees for conducting all of these proceedings. Plaintiffs had judgment in the circuit court for $1,183.98. From this judgment, and the order denying a new trial, defendant appeals.

It is contended by appellant that, as Robinson had neither possession nor right of possession at the time he executed the deed to the Smiths, the covenants sued upon were broken as soon as made, and therefore did not run with the land nor inure to the benefit of his remote grantees. As to the covenant of seizin, this contention is undoubtedly correct. Our statute (section 1139, Civ. Code) enumerates certain covenants as those which run with the land; but no mention is made of the covenant of seizin, and this covenant does not run with the land. Under a statute like ours it would appear that it is only the immediate grantee of the covenantor who can recover on this covenant. Plaintiffs could have recovered from the Smiths upon the breach of this covenant, and they, in turn, could have recovered from defendant, provided they bought their action within the period of the statute of limitations. But there was no such privity of contract between plaintiffs and defendant's intestate as would entitle them to recover against defendant.

The other covenant set out in plaintiffs' complaint (that of quiet enjoyment) presents a different proposition. By express statute, this covenant does run with the land. This covenant is made for the benefit of remote as well as immediate grantees, and, unless there is something in the facts connected with this case to relieve appellant from liability on the covenant, the plaintiff is entitled to recover, and the judgment should be affirmed. This is conceded by appellant, but, to avoid liability, he contends that, because his intestate had no estate whatever in the premises at the time of making the covenant, and because his intestate's grantees did not go into possession of the land, there was nothing to which the covenant could attach to carry it to the covenantor's remote grantees. He also contends that, the covenantor having neither possession nor right of possession at the time he made the covenant, a constructive eviction took place at once, and that the covenant immediately ripened into a cause of action in favor of his covenantee that neither ran with the land nor passed to his covenantee's grantee, and that, in any event, more than six years had elapsed since the breach of the covenant, and plaintiffs' action is barred by the six-year statute of limitations. In other words, that in this particular case the effect of both covenants is exactly the same, and plaintiffs are not entitled to recover on either. If appellant's position is correct, the covenant for quiet enjoyment contained in the Robinson deed could never, under the facts in this case, become the basis for a recovery by any one except his immediate grantee. Although the deed purporting to divest Vesey of his title was a forgery, and conveyed no title in fact, it appeared upon its face to be a valid conveyance, and the apparent chain of title from Vesey to plaintiffs was perfect. For aught plaintiffs knew or could know until Vesey asserted his title, they were the absolute owners of the fee and could have gone into the physical possession of the land at any time. Supposing plaintiffs had taken possession and afterward had learned the facts relative to the title to the land, and, before they had been disturbed by

Vesey, had brought this suit against defendant for breach of the covenant for quiet enjoyment, he could have said: "You have not been disturbed in your rightful possession of the land, and you may never be disturbed. While your deed may not be good, it is yet color of title, and, if you are not disturbed by Vesey within the time for bringing an action for that purpose, your present title, although defective, will ripen into a title that can never be disturbed by any one. In other words, you have no cause of action until you have been actually ousted by a decree of court." This would be a complete defense to plaintiffs' demand, or the most they could recover would be nominal damages only.

That the proposition that covenants found in deeds purporting to convey title to land do not run with the land unless the covenantor was possessed of some estate in the land to which the covenant could attach is supported by many, if not the great weight of, judicial decisions, is not questioned. . . .

The covenants usually found in deeds of conveyance of real property are the subject of legislative enactment in many of the states. Our statute (section 1138, Rev. Civ. Code) reads as follows: "Every covenant contained in a grant of an estate in real property, which is made for the direct benefit of the property, or some part of it then in existence, runs with the land." Section 1139: "The last section includes covenants of warranty, for quiet enjoyment, or for further assurance, on the part of a grantor. . . ." But these statutes do not seem to have changed the rule that, in order that the covenant will run with the land so as to inure to the benefit of a remote grantee, the covenantee must have received some estate in the land to which the covenant could attach.

It seems to be generally held that, where the covenantor delivers the possession of the land to his grantee, and he, in turn, puts his grantee in possession, this constitutes a privity of estate sufficient to carry the covenant with the land. And it may be taken as true that the reason for the rule originated at a time when physical possession of land was the chief muniment of title thereto. But this reason no longer exists. A person who has a grant of land from the owner of the fee becomes the absolute owner thereof, and is entitled to all the benefits that can be derived therefrom, even though neither of them was ever in the actual possession thereof. This being the case, why should it be necessary that actual, as distinguished from constructive, possession should be delivered in order to carry a covenant with the land when the covenantor was without title? It is for the purpose of protecting the covenantee and his grantees in their right of possession of the land, and to protect them against defective title thereto, that the covenant is made. The right of quiet enjoyment of a piece of land is its most valuable attribute, and a covenant from a grantor that this grantee shall be protected in the quiet enjoyment thereof adds materially to the value of the land itself, and a material portion of the consideration paid for the grant may be, and as a rule is, paid because of the covenantee's expectation of the right of quiet enjoyment of the demised premises. If a perfect title is passed to the grantee, then he *need* never avail himself of the covenant in his deed; while, on the other hand, if it should develop that the covenantor had no estate whatever in the premises attempted to be conveyed, the grantee could not, except as against his immediate covenantor, avail himself of the covenant. This, at least, is the logical conclusion to be drawn from the decisions holding that a remote grantee cannot recover upon a covenant, unless the covenantor had some estate in the land when the covenant was made. . . .

But, again, since it is held that a delivery of the possession of the disputed premises is necessary in order that the covenant of a grantor without title may inure to the benefit of his remote grantees, then the constructive possession of the grantee ought to be sufficient to carry the covenant. In this case, while the Smiths acquired no title to the land by virtue of their deed from the Robinsons, still they had the apparent title even as against Vesey himself. The county records showed they had a perfect chain of title, and therefore the Smiths and their grantees (plaintiffs in this action), as against the defendant, should be held to have had constructive possession of the granted premises, and that plaintiffs are entitled to recover against the defendant because of the eviction by Vesey. This, of course, involves the doctrine of estoppel by deed, and we believe this to be a proper case for the application of this doctrine. . . .

Where a grantor represents himself as the owner of the fee to a piece of land, and agrees that he will protect his grantee and assigns in their peaceful possession thereof, and it afterward develops that he was not the owner of the fee and cannot defend his grantees in their possession of the land, and they call upon him to respond to damages, why should he not be estopped from saying that he did not have, and convey the constructive possession of the land as he represented he had and for which he had received a valuable consideration, and that, therefore, his covenant did not pass beyond his immediate grantee and that he is not liable to the party who has suffered by his broken covenant? And why should the rule just quoted not apply? . . .

The trial court awarded respondent the amount paid for the Robinson deed, with interest thereon for a period of six years. This is urged as error. Section 2296, Rev. Civ. Code, fixes the measure of damages for breach of the covenant involved at the price paid to the grantor, with interest thereon during the time the grantee derived no benefit from the property, not exceeding six years. Appellant bases his contention upon the ground that there is no evidence in the record to show that the respondents derived no benefit from the land involved; that they were entitled to possession of the land until they were evicted, and therefore are presumed to have derived benefit therefrom. In this contention, appellant is right in part only. Having already held that the appellant is estopped from denying that respondent was in the constructive possession of the land, and allowed respondent to recover on the covenant upon the theory that respondents and their immediate grantors, believing themselves to be the absolute owners of the land, were in the constructive possession thereof, it would be inconsistent and illogical to allow respondent to recover interest on the purchase price upon the ground that they were not in possession of the land, and therefore derived no benefit therefrom. As against appellant, respondents' constructive possession continued so long as they believed themselves to be entitled to the actual possession. When they received notice of Vesey's title, their constructive possession terminated, and it is from the date of receiving such notice that interest on the purchase price should be computed. So far as appears from this record, respondents were first notified of Vesey's ownership by the commencement of his action against them, and interest should be allowed from that date only.

The trial court also awarded respondents costs and expenses, including witness fees, incurred by them in defending their supposed title in the circuit court and the Supreme Court, and attorney's fees paid by them in that action. The allowance of these two items is assigned as error. By the provisions of section 2296, Rev. Civ. Code, the respondents are entitled to recover, not only the consideration paid for the land and interest thereon, but any expenses incurred by them in defending their possession. The objection to the allowance of these items is based upon the fact that appellant was not notified of the commencement of the suit by Vesey and required to come in and defend in that action. These expenses were properly incurred by respondents in defending their possession, and are within the meaning of section 2296, and, unless a condition is read into that section that was not placed there by its authors, respondents are entitled to recover these expenses. . . .

The judgment should be modified in regard to the amount of interest allowed respondents as herein indicated, and as so modified it is affirmed.

Problem

By deed containing a covenant for seisin, A conveys land to B for $10,000. In turn, B conveys to C for $8,000. C then is ousted from possession by O, who holds good title.

(1) If the deed from B to C is a quitclaim deed, is B entitled to recover from A for breach of the covenant for seisin? If so, how much?

(2) If the deed from B to C contains a covenant for seisin, but C has not brought any suit against B for breach of his covenant, is B entitled to recover from A for breach of the covenant? If so, how much?

(3) Again, if the deed from B to C contains a covenant for seisin, but

this time C sues B for breach of the covenant of seisin and recovers $8,000, is B entitled to recover from A for breach of the covenant for seisin? If so, how much?

Note

The law concerning covenants of title was much litigated in the nineteenth century, and certain arbitrary limits on recovery by dispossessed grantees were created by courts. The limits seemed essential to protect earlier sellers, in a time of rapidly inflating land values and imperfect title records. See Horwitz, The Transformation in the Conception of Property in American Law 1780-1860, 40 U. Chi. L. Rev. 248, 285-288 (1973).

Keep in mind that covenants for title were a rare exception to the general policy of *caveat emptor* in real estate transactions. Covenants may become less important as the real estate business feels the effects of general movements for the protection of consumers.

c. Implied Warranty of Habitability

◆ McDONALD v. MIANECKI
79 N.J. 275, 398 A.2d 1283 (1979)

PASHMAN, J. In this case we are called upon to decide whether an implied warranty of workmanship and habitability arises upon the sale of a home by a builder-vendor, and, if so, whether potability of the water supply is included within the realm of warranted items. For the reasons given herein, we conclude that both questions must be answered in the affirmative. A further issue is raised regarding the plaintiff's duty to mitigate damages. . . .

In 1972, Joseph Mianecki, one of the defendants herein, placed a newspaper advertisement in which he offered to build a house on a certain piece of property now identified as 7 Dolores Place, Mine Hill Township. Plaintiffs Mr. and Mrs. Henry McDonald, desirous of purchasing a new home, responded to this advertisement and in July 1972 met with Mianecki at the proposed site and discussed the type of house they wished to have constructed. At that meeting the McDonalds were informed that Mianecki had built two other houses in the area. Although Mianecki was also employed as a construction project engineer by a large commercial contractor, by the start of the present litigation he classified his occupation as that of "builder."

The parties reached agreement as to the dwelling to be erected which was formalized in a written contract dated July 17, 1972. The purchase price was $44,500. The contract provided, *inter alia*, that the house would be serviced by water from a well to be constructed by Mianecki, and that the well system would be guaranteed for a one-year period. The McDonalds had never before had a house built for them nor had they lived in a home serviced by well water.

During the early stages of the construction process, the McDonalds frequently visited the property to do some painting and perform other odd jobs. At first they cleaned their hands and brushes at a nearby barn as their water supply had not yet been connected. Later, as the house neared completion, the water began to flow and the McDonalds washed up inside the home. They soon noticed that the sinks and toilet fixtures were becoming discolored and that standing water in the fixtures had a "chocolate brown" tint. The McDonalds apprised Mianecki of the situation and were told that inasmuch as the well was newly dug there might be some impurities still present. A commercial stain-remover, "Rust-Raze," was supplied to Mrs. McDonald, who cleaned the discolored fixtures. The stains, however, shortly returned.

Due to the continuing discoloration problem, Mianecki arranged to have the water tested. This test was, in any event, a prerequisite to the obtaining of a certificate of occupancy. The test, performed by third-party defendant Duncan Medical Laboratory, indicated an unacceptably high iron content. Mianecki attempted to rectify this situation through the installation of a water softener/conditioner, manufactured and installed by third-party defendant Deran Sales, Inc. A test performed after the installation of the unit indicated that the water was acceptable and, based upon its results, a certificate of occupancy was granted. Closing of title occurred on November 15, 1972, and two days later the McDonalds settled into their new home.

The problems with the water continued after the McDonalds moved in. Although water tests conducted before March 1973 showed that the water, after passing through the conditioner, met State standards, there was sufficient evidence from which a jury could have determined that the water was non-potable. It is clear that the raw water — i.e., water before it passed through the conditioner — never satisfied State standards of potability. There was testimony that, among other things, the staining of the fixtures continued; the water had a bad odor and taste; when left standing the water fizzled like "Alka-Seltzer," gave off a vapor and turned colors; clothes washed in the washing machine became stained, as did dishware and utensils when washed in the dishwasher, and coffee would turn deep black and sugar would not dissolve. Furthermore, according to expert testimony, after March 1973 even the treated water continuously failed to meet State standards of potability.

According to plaintiffs, Mianecki was continuously informed about the condition of the water. A number of unsuccessful attempts were made to alleviate the problem. These included replacement of the heating coils, alteration of the back-flushing cycle on the water conditioner, and the installation of a venting system designed to eliminate gas in the water pipes. By the spring of 1973 the relationship between the parties had deteriorated and no further repairs were attempted. Alternative sources of water were suggested, but, due to a variety of circumstances, no viable solution was adopted. Although each party alleged that these failures were due to the other's fault, there is sufficient evidence upon which a jury could have found that plaintiffs did not act unreasonably in their attempts to ameliorate the condition.

On March 25, 1974 the plaintiffs instituted the instant suit for damages against Mianecki. . . .

The jury returned an award in favor of plaintiffs in the amount of $32,000. . . .

Prior to the mid-1950's the ancient maxim of *caveat emptor* ("let the buyer beware") long ruled the law relating to the sale of real property. Thought to have originated in late sixteenth-century English trade society, the doctrine was especially prevalent during the early 1800's when judges looked upon purchasing land as a "game of chance." Hamilton, "The Ancient Maxim Caveat Emptor," 40 Yale L.J. 1133, 1187 (1931). The maxim, derived from the then contemporary political philosophy of *laissez faire*, held that a "buyer deserved whatever he got if he relied on his own inspection of the merchandise and did not extract an express warranty from the seller." . . .

In light of this modern day change in home buying practices, it is not surprising that increased pressure developed to abandon or modify the ancient doctrine. A host of commentators began to advocate the recognition of implied warranties in the sale of new houses. . . .

A further catalyst to change derived from the evolving doctrine of implied warranties in the sale of personal property. . . .

As a result of these pressures, the law began to change. As of today, a growing number of jurisdictions have applied some form of implied warranty of habitability to the sale of new homes. . . .

Finally, we would be remiss if we did not note our own Legislature's commendable program of protecting homeowners. It has recently enacted The New Home Warranty and Builders' Registration Act, N.J.S.A. 46:3B-1 *et seq.*, which provides for the registration of all builders of new homes . . . and authorizes the Commissioner of the Department of Community Affairs to establish certain new home warranties. . . . Claims for breach may be satisfied out of a home warranty security fund after notice and hearing. . . . The statute specifically states that the protection it offers does not affect other rights and remedies available to the owner, although an election of remedies is required. . . . The implied warranty which we today find exists in a contract for the sale of a new home thus complements the act and is, in our opinion, fully in accord with the legislative policy there evinced.

The reasoning underlying the abandonment of *caveat emptor* in the area of home construction is not difficult to fathom. Tribunals have come to recognize that "[t]he purchase of a new home is not an everyday transaction for the average family[;] . . . in many instances [it] is the most important transaction of a lifetime."

Courts have also come to realize that the two parties involved in this important transaction generally do not bargain as equals. The average buyer lacks the skill and expertise necessary to make an adequate inspection.

Furthermore, most defects are undetectable to even the most observant layman and the expense of expert advice is often prohibitive. The purchaser therefore ordinarily relies heavily upon the greater expertise of the vendor to ensure a suitable product.

Aside from superior knowledge, the builder-vendor is also in a better position to prevent the *occurrence* of major problems. . . .

[We] hold that builder-vendors do impliedly warrant that a house which they construct will be of reasonable workmanship and habitability. An implicit understanding of the parties to a construction contract is that the agreed price is tendered as consideration for a home that is reasonably fit for the purpose for which it was built — i.e., habitation. Illusory value is a poor substitute for quality. The consumer-purchaser should not be subjected to harassment caused by structural defects. He deserves both the focus and concern of the law. Any other result would be intolerable and unjust.

Further, we hold that such a warranty arises whenever a consumer purchases from an individual who holds himself out as a builder-vendor of new homes — regardless of whether he can be labeled a "mass producer." Whether the builder be large or small, the purchaser relies upon his superior knowledge and skill, and he impliedly represents that he is qualified to erect a habitable dwelling. He is also in a better position to prevent the existence of major defects. Whether or not engaged in mass production, builders utilize standard form contracts, and hence the opportunity to bargain for protective clauses is by and large nonexistent. Finally, it is the builder who has introduced the article into the stream of commerce. Should defects materialize, he — as opposed to the consumer-purchaser — is the less innocent party.

We need not here decide whether an implied warranty of habitability applies to every sale of a new home. This is not a case, for example, where an individual builds a house for his own use and later decides to sell. The sale here was "commercial in nature, not casual or personal." . . . Mr. Mianecki placed a general advertisement evidencing his willingness to construct a home on a particular plot of land. He had previously built two homes in the same general neighborhood and so informed plaintiffs. By the time of trial he declared his profession to be that of "builder." Although he was also employed as a construction engineer, he was nevertheless in "business" as a builder, albeit on a part-time basis. Under these circumstances, we have no hesitation in finding that the doctrine of implied warranty applies.

Defendants maintain that they should not be held responsible for the lack of potable water inasmuch as the defect was not due to any substandard construction on their part. Although we concede that the considerations in favor of an implied warranty do not weigh as strongly in a case such as this, nevertheless we are convinced that of the two parties the burden should fall on the less innocent defendant. . . .

Notes

1. For extensive discussion of the reasons for implying a warranty of habitability in cases involving the sale of new homes by a builder-vendor, see Petersen v. Hubschman Construction Co., 76 Ill. 2d 31, 389 N.E.2d 1154 (1979).

But see Witty v. Schramm, 62 Ill. App. 3d 185, 379 N.E.2d 333 (1978), finding no warranty of fitness as to sales of unimproved land:

> To hold otherwise could well lead to the opening of Pandora's box and the escape of the evils contained therein. Should a vendor of a vacant lot by implication be charged with warranty that there is no sub-surface water, or that there is a certain amount of subsurface water, or that the soil is of a certain texture or consistency? We believe not, for what may be a defect in one instance may be a desirable feature or benefit in another.

See also Conyers v. Molloy, 50 Ill. App. 3d 17, 364 N.E.2d 986 (1977), holding that a contract disclaimer of the warranty of habitability as to a new house ("there are no warranties . . .") gave insufficient notice to the purchasers. The court asked, "Where an implied warranty is recognized, can the disclaimer be far behind?" But the court said that public policy does not prohibit disclaimers of the warranty if the disclaimer is sufficiently specific to give adequate notice to the buyer.

2. For warranties of habitability on condominium sales, see Herlihy v. Dunbar Builders Corp., 92 Ill. App. 3d 310, 415 N.E.2d 1224 (1980), and on cooperative sales, see Suarez v. Rivercross Tenants' Corp., 107 Misc. 2d 135, 438 N.Y.S.2d 164 (Sup. Ct. 1981).

3. Sellers advertised "lg. single house, converted to 8 lovely, 2 completely furn. (includ. TV and china) apts. 8 baths." Kannavos, a self-employed hairdresser, read the ad, "wanted to acquire some income real estate," responded to Foote Realty, executed a purchase agreement, and took title. Kannavos had not obtained counsel; papers had been drawn by the mortgagee's lawyer.

Several months after Kannavos took title, he received a registered letter from the city, advising him that the multi-family use violated the building code and zoning ordinance. The property was worth much less for single-family use than for multi-family occupancy.

The Massachusetts Supreme Judicial Court reaffirmed the proposition that the seller had no obligation to inform Kannavos of defects in the property, but held that the "8 apts." advertisement was an implied misrepresentation that the use was lawful. Therefore Kannavos was entitled to rescind. Kannavos v. Annino, 356 Mass. 42, 247 N.E.2d 708 (1969).

Can the Kannavos court's approval of silent sales survive the following two provisions?

Mass. Gen. Laws Ann. ch. 93A §9(1) (1975):

> Any person who purchases or leases goods, services or property, real or personal, primarily for personal, family or household purposes and thereby suffers any loss of money or property . . . as a result of the use or employment by another person of an unfair or deceptive practice declared unlawful . . . by any rule or regulation issued [by the Attorney General] may . . . bring an action in the superior court for damages. . . .

Attorney General of Massachusetts, Chapter 93A Rules and Regulations §XV (1975):

> . . . an act or practice is a violation of Chapter 93A, Section 2 if:
> B. Any person or other legal entity subject to this act fails to disclose to a buyer or prospective buyer any fact, the disclosure of which may have influenced the buyer or prospective buyer not to enter into the transaction.

Mass. Gen. Laws Ann. §93A was applied to impose liability on a seller who told a buyer that certain land was dry and had good drainage, when after the closing the lot turned out to have "a drainage problem." Heller v. Silverbranch Construction Corp., 376 Mass. 621, 382 N.E.2d 1065 (1978). But see Nei v. Burley, 388 Mass. 307, 446 N.E.2d 674 (1983), holding that a one-time seller of real estate had no obligation to disclose the existence of a seasonal watercourse on the lands; and Security Title and Guaranty Co. v. Mid-Cape Realty, Inc., 723 F.2d 150 (1st Cir. 1983), holding that a vendor need not disclose a known colorable claim that the vendor has no title.

Indiana has extended its protection against economic loss due to latent defects in a home to cover not only the initial purchaser but subsequent purchasers as well. See Barnes v. MacBrown & Co. 264 Ind. 227, 342 N.E.2d 619 (1976).

Notice that the burdens stemming from increased public concern with the social impact of land and housing do not fall only on sellers. See Mass. Gen. Laws Ann. ch. 111 §197 (1975):

Whenever a child or children under six years of age resides in any residential premises in which any paint, plaster or other accessible materials contain dangerous levels of lead . . . , the owner shall remove or cover said paint, plaster or other material so as to make it inaccessible to children under six years of age. Whenever any such residential premises containing said dangerous levels of lead undergoes a change of ownership and as a result thereof, a child or children under six years of age will become a resident therein, the new owner shall remove or cover said paint, plaster or other material so as to make it inaccessible to such children.

What do you advise the A's if (1) Mr. Bailout's house was built 20 years ago, and so probably contains several layers of lead-based paint; (2) removing the paint can cost up to $1,000 per room; and (3) the A's may have children?

4. Reed v. King, 145 Cal. App. 3d 261, 193 Cal. Rptr. 130 (1983), held that the vendor must inform the buyer that a house was the site of a multiple murder. Buyer had learned of the infamous occurrence from a neighbor after purchasing the house and had sued for rescission and damages. The complaint said seller had represented that the premises were in good condition and fit for an elderly lady living alone. It also said that buyer had paid $76,000, but the house was only worth $65,000 because of its past.

H. COST OF THE REAL ESTATE TRANSACTION

In recent years the high costs of real estate transactions have been a subject of analysis and controversy. See, e.g., the FHA-VA Report on Mortgage Settlement Costs (1972), a study made pursuant to the Emergency Home Finance Act of 1970, 84 Stat. 461 (1970), which led HUD and the VA to publish (but, in a storm of criticism, not to put into effect) proposed maximum settlement costs for six geographic areas. 37 Fed. Reg. 13186 (1972) (HUD); 37 Fed. Reg. 17425 (1972) (VA). HUD's own conclusion is that "big-city conveyancing is a subsystem of local politics," and that "to maintain [the] local consensus, . . . questions are seldom raised." HUD suggests that "the first step . . . is to isolate those costs, paid ultimately by consumers — the buyers and builders of homes — which keep the system running, greased and oiled, but do not benefit buyers or consumers." Department of HUD, Real Estate Settlement Process and Its Costs (1971).

In 1974 Congress moved to reduce the cost of real estate transfers. The Real Estate Settlement Procedures Act, 88 Stat. 1724 (1974), imposed a standard form for the itemization of costs; required lenders to give this form to buyers and sellers at least 12 days before the closing; required lenders to discover and inform buyers of the previous "arms-length" selling price of the house; and barred kickbacks in real estate transactions involving a federally related mortgage loan. By 1975, the real estate industry was able to obtain major modification of the 1974 act, convincing Congress that compliance had proved oppressive and expensive. See Real Estate Settlement Procedures Act Amendments of 1975, P.L. 94-205, 89 Stat. 1157 (1975). Now the form need only be presented "at or before" the closing, and buyers can waive the right to receive a form at all; the requirement that the prior selling price be disclosed has been deleted; and the anti-kickback provisions have been "clarified" to "make it clear that cooperative brokerage and referral arrangements of real estate agents are exempt. . . ." See House Report No. 94-6674, 2 U.S. Code Cong. & Adm. News 2448, 2454 (1975).

Even had the 1974 Act not been weakened, do you think it would have affected the true causes behind the expense of selling and buying real estate?

But public dissatisfaction with the costs and details of land-transfer continues, much of it blaming the legal profession for the present system. Consider the words of Chief Justice Burger, in a speech to the American Law Institute, May 21, 1974:

> [T]he basic system of real estate titles and transfers and the related matters concerning financing and purchase of homes cries out for reexamination and simplification. In a country that transfers not only expensive automobiles but multi-million dollar airplanes with a few relatively simple pieces of paper covering liens and all, I believe that if American lawyers will put their ingenuity and inventiveness to work on this subject they will be able to devise simpler methods than we now have.

18 ◆ FINANCING THE LAND TRANSACTION

A. MORTGAGES

When the A's "close" with Mr. Bailout, purchasing the house from him, they will have to pay him a large amount of cash. Some, a "down payment," they may have saved, or may obtain from parents, friends, or employers. The larger part probably comes from a savings and loan association, a bank, or some other lending institution, which takes in return a mortgage. This only means that the lender obtains a security interest in the house and land that will allow it to take over and sell the property, subject to certain legal controls, should the A's fail to pay interest and principal when due or violate a major promise or covenant. Thus, at the closing, the lending bank gives money to Mr. and Ms. A, who add their down payment and pass the entire amount to Mr. Bailout, who probably passes a substantial portion to *his* lender, to redeem the mortgage he had given when he bought the house.

At common law a mortgage was a conveyance of legal title from the borrowing owner (mortgagor) to the lender (mortgagee) with a defeasance clause. This clause allowed for voiding of the deed and return of title to the mortgagor when all of the conditions subsequent were met (debt and interest paid).

The word "mortgage" comes from the two words for "dead" and "pledge." See, e.g., Coke on Littleton 205:

> It seemeth that the cause why it is called mortgage is, for that it is doubtful whether the Feoffor will pay at the day limited such summe or not, & if he doth not pay, then the Land which is put in pledge upon condition for the payment of the money, is taken from him for ever, and so dead to him upon condition, etc. And if he doth pay the money, then the pledge is dead as to the Tenant, etc.

781

As the quotation from Coke suggests, with default the mortgagor's legal right to the property ended. This could be an extremely harsh result, particularly when the property was worth more than the outstanding debt. To avoid such forfeitures, equity courts came to recognize that, although legal title had passed to the mortgagee, the mortgator retained an interest; over time this interest developed into the "equity of redemption." Under this doctrine the mortgagor was allowed to redeem his property if he was willing and able to tender the outstanding debt and interest to the mortgagee. It is this equitable right of the mortgagor to avoid forfeiture through redemption that distinguishes the mortgage from other loans and makes it a preferable form for the borrower.

Mere recognition of a mortgagor's right to redeem did not achieve a satisfactory reconciliation of the interests of borrowers and lenders. At some point the mortgagee needed clear title, so that he could dispose of the property to a buyer who would be spared risk of redemption. Courts and statutes set a fixed period after default during which the mortgagor could redeem but after which he was barred. This process is known as strict foreclosure.

The second important means of foreclosure is by a foreclosure sale. Once the redemption period has expired, a court supervises a foreclosure sale — usually an auction — of the property. The outstanding debt is satisfied out of the proceeds of the sale and any surplus is paid to the mortgagor. Foreclosure by sale thus offers some consolation to the mortgagor when the property is more valuable than the outstanding debt. Conversely, when the property would sell for less than the value of the outstanding debt, the mortgagor may have some leverage to renegotiate the mortgage terms or gain time to find the money for past-due payments.

The common law and its variations thus reflect a "title" theory of mortgages: title passes from the borrower to the lender. The title theory is subscribed to by most states east of the Mississippi, with some exceptions, notably New York. In the West, states subscribe to a "lien" theory whereby both legal and equitable title remain with the mortgagor but the mortgagee takes a lien on the property that becomes possessory upon default and foreclosure. Whether a state calls itself a title theory or a lien theory state makes no difference in practical application, and little emphasis is now placed on the distinction.

Sample Document 18-1: Note

September 30, 1965

FOR VALUE RECEIVED, the undersigned Chatham Associates, Inc., a New York corporation, promises to pay to Oxford

Associates, Inc., a New York corporation, or order, the principal sum of $235,000, with interest on the unpaid principal balance from the date of this note, until paid at the rate of five and one-half percent per annum. The principal and interest shall be payable at 405 Lexington Avenue, New York City, or such other place as the holder hereof may designate in writing, in consecutive monthly installments, until the entire indebtedness evidenced hereby is fully paid.

The undersigned shall have the right to prepay the principal amount outstanding in whole or in part, provided that the holder hereof may require that any partial prepayment shall be made on the date monthly installments are due and shall be in the amount of that part of one or more installments which would be applicable to principal.

Presentment, notice of dishonor, and protest are hereby waived.

The indebtedness evidenced by this Note is secured by a mortgage, dated of even date herewith, and reference is made thereto for rights as to acceleration of the indebtedness evidenced by this note.

CHATHAM ASSOCIATES, INC.
By:

As you read the following sample mortgage, consider the case for simplification of legal language. New York General Obligations Law §5-702, enacted in 1978, says that every written agreement for a lease or mortgage involving less than $50,000 must be written in a "clear and coherent manner using words with common and everyday meanings."

Sample Document 18-2: Mortgage

THIS MORTGAGE, made the 30th day of September, nineteen hundred and sixty-five, BETWEEN CHATHAM ASSOCIATES, INC., a New York corporation, having its principal office at 405 Lexington Avenue, Borough of Manhattan, City of New York,   ,
the mortgagor, and OXFORD ASSOCIATES, Inc., a New York corporation, having its principal office at 405 Lexington Avenue, Borough of Manhattan, City of New York,
                                                          , the mortgagee, WITNESSETH, that to secure the payment of an indebted-

ness in the sum of Two hundred thirty-five thousand and 00/100 ($235,000.00) dollars, lawful money of the United States, to be paid on demand   with interest thereon to be computed from the date hereof, at the rate of 5½% per centum per annum, and to be paid on demand   according to a certain bond, note or obligation bearing even date herewith, the mortgagor hereby mortgages to the mortgagee ALL that certain plot, piece or parcel of land, with the buildings and improvements thereon erected, situate lying and being in the Borough of Manhattan, City and County of New York, bounded and described as follows:

[Description excised]

TOGETHER with all right, title and interest of the mortgagor in and to the land lying in the streets and roads in front of and adjoining said premises;

TOGETHER with all fixtures, chattels and articles of personal property now or hereafter attached to or used in connection with said premises;

TOGETHER with all fixtures, chattels and articles of personal property now or hereafter attached to or used in connection with said premises, including but not limited to furnaces, boilers, oil burners, radiators and piping, coal stokers, plumbing and bathroom fixtures, refrigeration, air conditioning and sprinkler systems, wash-tubs, sinks, gas and electric fixtures, stoves, ranges, awnings, screens, window shades, elevators, motors, dynamos, refrigerators, kitchen cabinets, incinerators, plants and shrubbery and all other equipment and machinery, appliances, fittings, and fixtures of every kind in or used in the operation of the buildings standing on said premises, together with any and all replacements thereof and additions thereto;

TOGETHER with all awards heretofore and hereafter made to the mortgagor for taking by eminent domain the whole or any part of said premises or any easement therein, including any awards for changes of grade of streets, which said awards are hereby assigned to the mortgagee, who is hereby authorized to collect and receive the proceeds of such awards and to give proper receipts and acquittances therefor, and to apply the same toward the payment of the mortgage debt, notwithstanding the fact that the amount owing thereon may not then be due and payable; and the said mortgagor hereby agrees, upon request, to make, execute and deliver any and all assignments and other instruments sufficient for the purpose of assigning said awards to the mortgagee, free, clear and discharged of any encumbrances of any kind or nature whatsoever.

AND the mortgagor covenants with the mortgagee as follows:

1. That the mortgagor will pay the indebtedness as hereinbefore provided.

2. That the mortgagor will keep the buildings on the premises insured against loss by fire for the benefit of the mortgagee; that he will assign and deliver the policies to the mortgagee; and that he will reimburse the mortgagee for any premiums paid for insurance made by the mortgagee on the mortgagor's default in so insuring the buildings or in so assigning and delivering the policies.

3. That no building on the premises shall be altered, removed or demolished without the consent of the mortgagee.

4. That the whole of said principal sum and interest shall become due at the option of the mortgagee: after default in the payment of any instalment of principal or of interest for ten days; or after default in the payment of any tax, water rate, sewer rent or assessment for thirty days or after default after notice and demand either in assigning and delivering the policies insuring the buildings against loss by fire or reimbursing the mortgagee for premiums paid on such insurance, as hereinbefore provided; or after default upon request in furnishing a statement of the amount due on the mortgage and whether any offsets or defenses exist against the mortgage debt, as hereinafter provided. An assessment which has been made payable in instalments at the application of the mortgagor or lessee of the premises shall nevertheless, for the purpose of this paragraph, be deemed due and payable in its entirety on the day the first instalment becomes due or payable or a lien.

5. That the holder of this mortgage, in any action to foreclose it, shall be entitled to the appointment of a receiver.

6. That the mortgagor will pay all taxes, assessments, sewer rents or water rates, and in default thereof, the mortgagee may pay the same.

7. That the mortgagor within five days upon request in person or within ten days upon request by mail will furnish a written statement duly acknowledged of the amount due on this mortgage and whether any offsets or defenses exist against the mortgage debt.

8. That notice and demand or request may be in writing and may be served in person or by mail.

9. That the mortgagor warrants the title to the premises.

10. That the fire insurance policies required by paragraph No. 2 above shall contain the usual extended coverage endorsement; that in addition thereto the mortgagor, within thirty days after notice and demand, will keep the premises insured against war risk and any other hazard that may reasonably be required by the

mortgagee. All of the provisions of paragraphs No. 2 and No. 4 above relating to fire insurance and the provisions of Section 254 of the Real Property Law construing the same shall apply to the additional insurance required by this paragraph.

11. That in case of a foreclosure sale, said premises, or so much thereof as may be affected by this mortgage, may be sold in one parcel.

12. That if any action or proceeding be commenced (except an action to foreclose this mortgage or to collect the debt secured thereby) to which action or proceeding the mortgagee is made a party, or in which it becomes necessary to defend or uphold the lien of this mortgage, all sums paid by the mortgagee for the expense of any litigation to prosecute or defend the rights and lien created by this mortgage (including reasonable counsel fees), shall be paid by the mortgagor, together with interest thereon at the rate of six percent per annum and any such sum and the interest thereon shall be a lien on said premises, prior to any right, or title to, interest in or claim upon said premises attaching or accruing subsequent to the lien of this mortgage, and shall be deemed to be accrued by this mortgage. In any action or proceeding to foreclose this mortgage, or to recover or collect the debt secured thereby, the provisions of law respecting the recovering of costs, disbursements and allowances shall prevail unaffected by this covenant.

13. That the mortgagor hereby assigns to the mortgagee the rents, issues and profits of the premises as further security for the payment of said indebtedness, and the mortgagor grants to the mortgagee the right to enter upon and to take possession of the premises for the purpose of collecting the same and to let the premises or any part thereof, and to apply the rents, issues and profits, after payment of all necessary charges and expenses, on account of said indebtedness. This assignment and grant shall continue in effect until this mortgage is paid. The mortgagee hereby waives the right to enter upon and to take possession of said premises for the purpose of collecting said rents, issues and profits, and the mortgagor shall be entitled to collect and receive said rents, issues and profits until default under any of the covenants, conditions or agreements contained in this mortgage, and agrees to use such rents, issues and profits in payment of principal and interest becoming due on this mortgage and in payment of taxes, assessments, sewer rents, water rates and carrying charges becoming due against said premises, but such right of the mortgagor may be revoked by the mortgagee upon any default on five days' written notice. The mortgagor will not, without the written consent of the mortgagee, receive or collect rent from any tenant of said premises or any part thereof for a period of more than one month in advance, and in the event of any default under this mortgage will pay

monthly in advance to the mortgagee, or to any receiver appointed to collect said rents, issues and profits, the fair and reasonable rental value for the use and occupation of said premises or of such part thereof as may be in the possession of the mortgagor, and upon default in any such payment will vacate and surrender the possession of said premises to the mortgagee or to such receiver, and in default thereof may be evicted by summary proceedings.

14. That the whole of said principal sum and the interest shall become due at the option of the mortgagee: (a) after failure to exhibit to the mortgagee, within ten days after demand, receipts showing payment of all taxes, water rates, sewer rents and assessments; or (b) after the actual or threatened alteration, demolition or removal of any building on the premises without the written consent of the mortgagee; or (c) after the assignment of the rents of the premises or any part thereof without the written consent of the mortgagee; or (d) if the buildings on said premises are not maintained in reasonably good repair; or (e) after failure to comply with any requirement or order or notice of violation of law or ordinance issued by any governmental department claiming jurisdiction over the premises within three months from the issuance thereof; or (f) if on application of the mortgagee two or more fire insurance companies lawfully doing business in the State of New York refuse to issue policies insuring the buildings on the premises; or (g) in the event of the removal, demolition or destruction in whole or in part of any of the fixtures, chattels or articles of personal property covered hereby, unless the same are promptly replaced by similar fixtures, chattels and articles of personal property at least equal in quality and condition to those replaced, free from chattel mortgages or other encumbrances thereon and free from any reservation of title thereto; or (h) after thirty days' notice to the mortgagor, in the event of the passage of any law deducting from the value of land for the purposes of taxation any lien thereon, or changing in any way the taxation of mortgages or debts accrued thereby for state or local purposes; or (i) if the mortgagor fails to keep, observe and perform any of the other covenants, conditions or agreements contained in this mortgage; or (j) if the mortgagor fails to keep, observe and perform any of the covenants, conditions or agreements contained in any prior mortgage or fails to repay to the mortgagee the amount of any instalment of principal or interest which the mortgagee may have paid on such mortgage with interest thereon as provided in paragraph 16 of this mortgage.

15. That the mortgagor will, in compliance with Section 13 of the Lien Law, receive the advances accrued hereby and will hold the right to receive such advances as a trust fund to be applied first for the purpose of paying the cost of the improvement and will apply the same first to the payment of the cost of the improvement

before using any part of the total of the same for any other purpose.

16. If the mortgagor fails to pay any instalment of principal or interest on any prior mortgage when the same becomes due, the mortgagee may pay the same, and the mortgagor on demand will repay the amount so paid with interest thereon at the legal rate and the same shall be added to the mortgage indebtedness and be secured by this mortgage.

17. That the execution of this mortgage has been duly authorized by the board of directors of the mortgagor.

18. This mortgage is subject and subordinate to a consolidated mortgage held by the Comptroller of the State of New York, as trustee of NEW YORK STATE EMPLOYEES RETIREMENT SYSTEM and a mortgage to HANOVER EQUITIES CORPORATION.

19. The mortgagor shall not modify, change or vary any of the terms, of any prior mortgage without first obtaining the written consent of the holder of this mortgage. Failure to comply with this provision shall constitute a default hereunder and the principal balance and accrued interest shall immediately become due and payable.

This mortgage may not be changed or terminated orally. The covenants contained in this mortgage shall run with the land and bind the mortgagor, the heirs, personal representatives, successors and assigns of the mortgagor and all subsequent owners, encumbrances, tenants and subtenants of the premises, and shall enure to the benefit of the mortgagee, the personal representatives, successors and assigns of the mortgagee and all subsequent holders of this mortgage. The word "mortgagor" shall be construed as if it read "mortgagors" and the word "mortgagee" shall be construed as if it read "mortgagees" whenever the sense of this mortgage so requires.

IN WITNESS WHEREOF, Chatham Associates, Inc., has executed this mortgage as of the date set forth herein above.

CHATHAM ASSOCIATES, INC.
By:

◆ MID-STATE INVESTMENT CORP. v. O'STEEN
133 So. 2d 455 (Fla. App.), *cert. denied*, 136 So. 2d 349 (Fla. 1961)

CARROLL, Chief Judge. The defendant has filed this appeal from a final judgment entered against it by the Civil Court of Record for Duval

County, based upon a directed verdict on the issue of liability and a jury verdict on the issue of damages.

The evidence at the trial was rather nebulous as to the exact nature of the parties' transactions, but the following facts seem to be established by the evidence, and the trial court undoubtedly so construed the evidence in directing its verdict on the issue of liability: The plaintiffs, who are husband and wife, on April 4, 1958, purchased a house and paid for it with money which they borrowed from the defendant, an investment corporation. As part of this loan transaction, the plaintiffs apparently assigned to the defendant their deed to the land and took back an unrecorded contract for deed, which was conditioned upon the monthly payment of $55.22 plus six percent interest until the indebtedness of $3,312 was paid. This contract contained the following provision:

> And in case of failure of the said parties of the second part to make either of the payments or any part thereof, or to perform any of the covenants on their part hereby made and entered into, this contract shall, at the option of the party of the first part, be forfeited and terminated, and the party of the second part shall forfeit all payments made by them on this contract; and such payments shall be retained by the said party of the first part in full satisfaction and liquidation of all damages by them sustained, and said party of the first part shall have the right to re-enter and take possession of the premises aforesaid without being liable to any action therefor.

These payments were due on the 15th day of each month beginning on May 15, 1958. The plaintiffs apparently seldom made these payments on time and were usually one or two months behind. For several months the defendant accepted these late payments, but on April 24, 1959, when the plaintiffs were two months behind in their payments, the defendant elected to repossess the house in accordance with the above-quoted provision of the contract. One more payment of $55.20 was tendered by the plaintiffs and accepted by the defendant on April 28, 1959, four days after the repossession. In February of 1959 the plaintiffs had left Jacksonville and moved to Apopka, Florida, where the plaintiff husband had secured employment. They had closed their house in Jacksonville and left their furniture, two washing machines, some tools and clothes, and other personal belongings locked inside the house. They were in Apopka on April 28, 1959, when they received a telegram from the defendant advising that their house had been repossessed.

On April 24, 1959, one West, an agent of the defendant, went to the plaintiffs' house, entered it through a window, and took possession of the premises, both the realty and the mentioned personalty. Most of the furniture and one of the washing machines were subject to a purchase money mortgage executed by the plaintiffs to a certain local store. West called the store and asked that it send its representatives to pick up the property on which it had a claim, which they did. Some of the tools were given by the defendant to a next-door neighbor to hold for the plaintiffs in case they should return, and the rest of the plaintiffs' personal effects were lost, except for a box of rags and the second washing machine, which were left in the house. The defendant almost immediately sold the house to the half-brother of the next-door neighbor.

The plaintiffs filed this action against the defendant, seeking damages for the trespass to their real property and for the conversion of their personal property. The defendant answered by denying liability and affirmatively alleging that it had legally taken possession of the property under the above-quoted provision of the contract. This affirmative defense was stricken by the trial court upon a motion by the plaintiffs. At the close of the evidence the trial court directed a verdict for the plaintiffs on the issue of liability and submitted the issue of damages to the jury. The jury returned a verdict of $2,750 for the plaintiffs. After the defendant's motion for a new trial was denied by the trial court, this appeal followed.

The defendant-appellant raises several points on this appeal, but its main argument seems to revolve around the question of the validity of the above-quoted repossession provision in the contract.

We think, and we hold, that the contract involved in this appeal falls within the ken of the provisions of Section 697.01, Florida Statutes, F.S.A., which reads in pertinent part:

> 697.01 Instruments deemed mortgages
> "All conveyances, obligations conditioned or defeasible, bills of sale or other instruments of writing conveying or selling property, either real or personal, for the purpose or with the intention of securing the payment of money, whether such instrument be from the debtor to the creditor or from the debtor to some third person in trust for the creditor, shall be deemed and held mortgages, and shall be subject to the same rules of foreclosure and to the same regulations, restraints and forms as are prescribed in relation to mortgages.

In our opinion the contract before us was clearly intended to secure the payment of money and must be deemed and held to be a mortgage, subject to the same rules of foreclosure and to the same regulations, restraints, and forms as are prescribed in relation to mortgages, to use the words of the statute. This being so, the defendant had only a naked legal title as security for the indebtedness, had no legal right to repossess the real or personal property, and had no such right to trespass upon the real property or exercise dominion over the personal property. The courts of this state have many times applied the principle of the quoted statute to instruments of writing in circumstances analogous to those on this appeal.

In the state of the evidence at the close of the trial, which evidence we think permitted no reasonable inference other than that the defendant was liable in trespass and conversion as charged, the trial court correctly directed the verdict against the defendant on the issue of liability and properly submitted the question of damages to the jury. . . . [T]he general rule established in Florida . . . is that the correct measure of damages is the difference in value of the property trespassed upon before and after the trespass is committed. . . . The plaintiffs have not been deprived permanently of their possession or ownership of the land. They have not been ousted, nor will the effects of the trespass continue indefinitely. As we held earlier in this opinion, the defendant had nothing more than a mortgage lien when it sought to repossess. The defendant's clear equitable remedy was a foreclosure of this lien. Its deed of the land to the neighbor's brother-in-law was obviously a *nudum pactum* and passed no title to the land. . . .

◆ FIDELITY FEDERAL SAVINGS & LOAN
ASSOCIATION v. DE LA CUESTA
458 U.S. 141 (1982)

Justice BLACKMUN delivered the opinion of the Court.
At issue in this case is the pre-emptive effect of a regulation, issued by the Federal Home Loan Bank Board (Board), permitting federal savings and loan associations to use "due-on-sale" clauses in their mortgage contracts. Appellees dispute both the Board's intent and its statutory authority to displace restrictions imposed by the California Supreme Court on the exercise of these clauses.
The Federal Home Loan Bank Board, an independent federal regulatory agency, was formed in 1932 and thereafter was vested with plenary authority to administer the Home Owners' Loan Act of 1933 (HOLA), 48 Stat. 128, as amended, 12 U.S.C. §1461 et seq. (1976 ed. and Supp. IV). Section 5(a) of the HOLA . . . empowers the Board, "under such rules and regulations as it may prescribe, to provide for the organization, incorporation, examination, operation, and regulation of associations to be known as 'Federal Savings and Loan Associations.' " Pursuant to this authorization, the Board has promulgated regulations governing "the powers and operations of every Federal savings and loan association from its cradle to its corporate grave."
In 1976, the Board became concerned about the increasing controversy as to the authority of a federal savings and loan association to exercise a "due-on-sale" clause — a contractual provision that permits the lender to declare the entire balance of a loan immediately due and payable if the property securing the loan is sold or otherwise trans-

ferred.[2] Specifically, the Board felt that restrictions on a savings and loan's ability to accelerate a loan upon transfer of the security would have a number of adverse effects: (1) that "the financial security and stability of Federal associations would be endangered if . . . the security property is transferred to a person whose ability to repay the loan and properly maintain the property is inadequate"; (2) that "elimination of the due on sale clause will cause a substantial reduction of the cash flow and net income of Federal associations, and that to offset such losses it is likely that the associations will be forced to charge higher interest rates and loan charges on home loans generally"; and (3) that "elimination of the due on sale clause will restrict and impair the ability of Federal associations to sell their home loans in the secondary mortgage market, by making such loans unsalable or causing them to be sold at reduced prices, thereby reducing the flow of new funds for residential loans, which otherwise would be available." . . . The Board concluded that "elimination of the due-on-sale clause will benefit only a limited number of home sellers, but generally will cause economic hardship to the majority of home buyers and potential home buyers."

Accordingly, the Board issued a regulation, effective July 31, 1976, governing due-on-sale clauses. The regulation, now 12 CFR §545.8-3(f) (1982), provides in relevant part:

> [A federal savings and loan] association continues to have the power to include, as a matter of contract between it and the borrower, a provision

---

2. The due-on-sale clause used in many loan instruments is ¶17 of the uniform mortgage instrument developed by the Federal Home Loan Mortgage Corporation and the Federal National Mortgage Association. Paragraph 17 appears in two of the deeds of trust at issue in this case and reads:

17. Transfer of the Property; Assumption. If all or any part of the Property or an interest therein is sold or transferred by Borrower without Lender's prior written consent, excluding (a) the creation of a lien or encumbrance subordinate to this Deed of Trust, (b) the creation of a purchase money security interest for household appliances, (c) a transfer by devise, descent or by operation of law upon the death of a joint tenant or (d) the grant of any leasehold interest of three years or less not containing an option to purchase, *Lender may, at Lender's option, declare all the sums secured by this Deed of Trust to be immediately due and payable.* Lender shall have waived such option to accelerate if, prior to the sale or transfer, Lender and the person to whom the Property is to be sold or transferred reach agreement in writing that the credit of such person is satisfactory to Lender and that the interest payable on the sums secured by this Deed of Trust shall be at such rate as Lender shall request. If Lender has waived the option to accelerate provided in this paragraph 17 and if Borrower's successor in interest has executed a written assumption agreement accepted in writing by Lender, Lender shall release Borrower from all obligations under this Deed of Trust and the Note.

If Lender exercises such option to accelerate, Lender shall mail Borrower notice of acceleration in accordance with paragraph 14 hereof. Such notice shall provide a period of not less than 30 days from the date the notice is mailed within which Borrower may pay the sums declared due. If Borrower fails to pay such sums prior to the expiration of such period, Lender may, without further notice or demand on Borrower, invoke any remedies permitted by paragraph 18 hereof.

in its loan instrument whereby the association may, at its option, declare immediately due and payable sums secured by the association's security instrument if all or any part of the real property securing the loan is sold or transferred by the borrower without the association's prior written consent. Except as [otherwise] provided in . . . this section . . . , exercise by the association of such option (hereafter called a due-on-sale clause) shall be exclusively governed by the terms of the loan contract, and all rights and remedies of the association and borrower shall be fixed and governed by that contract.

In the preamble accompanying final publication of the due-on-sale regulation, the Board explained its intent that the due-on-sale practices of federal savings and loans be governed "exclusively by Federal law." The Board emphasized that "[f]ederal associations shall not be bound by or subject to any conflicting State law which imposes different . . . due-on-sale requirements."

Appellant Fidelity Federal Savings and Loan Association (Fidelity) is a private mutual savings and loan association chartered by the Board pursuant to §5(a) of the HOLA. Fidelity's principal place of business is in Glendale, Cal. Appellees, de la Cuesta, Moore, and Whitcombe, each made a purchase of California real property from one who had borrowed money from Fidelity. As security for the loan, the borrower had given Fidelity a deed of trust on the property. Each deed of trust contained a due-on-sale clause. Two of the deeds also included a provision, identified as ¶15, which stated that the deed "shall be governed by the law of the jurisdiction in which the Property is located."

Fidelity was not notified prior to each appellee's purchase of property; when it did learn of the transfer, it gave notice of its intent to enforce the due-on-sale clause. Fidelity expressed a willingness to consent to the transfer, however, if the appellee agreed to increase the interest rate on the loan secured by the property to the then-prevailing market rate. Each appellee refused to accept this condition; Fidelity then exercised its option to accelerate the loan. When the loan was not paid, Fidelity instituted a nonjudicial foreclosure proceeding.

In response, each appellee filed suit in the Superior Court of California for Orange County. Each asserted that, under the principles announced by the California Supreme Court in Wellenkamp v. Bank of America, 21 Cal. 3d 943, 148 Cal. Rptr. 379, 582 P.2d 970 (1978), Fidelity's exercise of the due-on-sale clause violated California's prohibition of unreasonable restraints on alienation, Cal. Civ. Code Ann. §711 (West) (1954), "unless the lender can demonstrate that enforcement is reasonably necessasry to protect against impairment to its security or the risk of default." . . . Each complaint sought (1) a judicial declaration that the due-on-sale clause was not enforceable unless Fidelity first showed that the transfer had harmed its security interest, (2) an injunction against any foreclosure procedures based on the clause, and (3) compensatory and punitive damages. . . .

As even the Court of Appeal recognized, the Board's intent to pre-empt the *Wellenkamp* doctrine is unambiguous. . . .

The question remains whether the Board acted within its statutory authority in issuing the pre-emptive due-on-sale regulation. The language and history of the HOLA convince us that Congress delegated to the Board ample authority to regulate the lending practices of federal savings and loans so as to further the Act's purposes, and that §545.8-3(f) is consistent with those purposes.

Congress delegated power to the Board expressly for the purpose of creating and regulating federal savings and loans so as to ensure that they would remain financially sound institutions able to supply financing for home construction and purchase. . . .

The due-on-sale regulation was promulgated with these purposes in mind. The Board has determined that due-on-sale clauses are "a valuable and often an indispensable source of protection for the financial soundness of Federal associations and for their continued ability to fund new home loan commitments." . . . Specifically, the Board has concluded that the due-on-sale clause is "an important part of the mortgage contract" and that its elimination "will have an adverse [e]ffect on the earning power and financial stability of Federal associations, will impair the ability of Federal associations to sell their loans in the secondary markets, will reduce the amount of home-financing funds available to potential home buyers, and generally will cause a rise in home loan interest rates."

The Board's analysis proceeds as follows: It observes that the federal associations' practice of borrowing short and lending long — obtaining funds on a short-term basis and investing them in long-term real estate loans, which typically have a 25- to 30-year term — combined with rising interest rates, has increased the cost of funds to these institutions and reduced their income. Exercising due-on-sale clauses enables savings and loans to alleviate this problem by replacing long-term, low-yield loans with loans at the prevailing interest rates and thereby to avoid increasing interest rates across the board. . . . Moreover, the Board has determined that restrictions like the *Wellenkamp* doctrine lengthen the expected maturity date of a lender's mortgages, thus reducing their marketability in the secondary mortgage market. As a result, the Board fears, "the financial stability of Federal associations in California will be eroded and the flow of home loan funds into California will be reduced."

Admittedly, the wisdom of the Board's policy decision is not uncontroverted. But neither is it arbitrary or capricious. As judges, it is neither our function, nor within our expertise, to evaluate the economic soundness of the Board's approach. In promulgating the due-on-sale regulation, the Board reasonably exercised the authority, given it by Congress, so as to ensure the financial stability of "local mutual thrift institutions in which people . . . invest their funds and . . . [which] provide for the financing of homes." . . . By so doing, the Board intended to pre-empt conflicting state restrictions on due-on-sale practices like the California Supreme Court's *Wellenkamp* doctrine.

Our inquiry ends there. Accordingly, we hold that the Board's due-on-sale regulation bars application of the *Wellenkamp* rule to federal savings and loan associations. The judgment of the Court of Appeal is reversed.

It is so ordered. . . .

Justice REHNQUIST, with whom Justice STEVENS joins, dissenting.

Section 5(a) of the HOLA . . . unquestionably grants broad authority to the Board to regulate the mortgage lending practices of federal savings and loans. In order to perform this role, the Board may take into account state property and contract law which governs real estate transactions in general and the enforceability and interpretation of mortgage lending instruments in particular. Thus, it would be within the Board's power to determine that it constitutes an unsafe lending practice for a federal savings and loan to conclude a real property mortgage without a fully enforceable due-on-sale clause. It would be within the authority delegated to it by Congress for the Board to conclude that a due-on-sale clause must be included in a mortgage instrument as a means of enabling a federal savings and loan to remove unprofitable loans from its portfolio.

Such a regulation would be entirely consistent with the approach taken by Congress in regulating the savings and loan industry. . . . Thus, there is no indication in the FHLBA that the Board may, by promulgating regulations, preempt those state laws that are deemed to be economically unsound. Instead, if the Board concludes that California's limitations upon the enforceability of due-on-sale clauses endangers the soundness of the system established by the HOLA and the FHLBA, then the response contemplated by Congress is for the Board to "withhold or limit the operation" of the system in California.

In declaring the due-on-sale clause enforceable as a matter of federal law, however, the Board has departed from the approach contemplated by Congress. Although Congress has authorized the Board to regulate the lending activities of federal savings and loan associations, there is no indication in the HOLA itself, or in its legislative history, that Congress has empowered the Board to determine whether and when federal law shall govern the enforceability of particular provisions contained in mortgages concluded by federal savings and loan associations. If anything, §8 of the FHLBA indicates that it was Congress' understanding in 1932 that the enforceability of provisions in mortgages is a matter of state law. Contract and real property law are traditionally the domain of state law. In the HOLA, Congress did not intend to create a federal common law of mortgages.

Notes

1. What are the implications of the doctrine of equity of redemption for the notion of private property? To what extent does the Constitution limit the state's power to define (and redefine) what property is? The Minnesota Mortgage Moratorium Law, enacted during the depression, provided relief against mortgage foreclosures and execution sales. County courts were permitted to extend the period of redemption from foreclosures sales "for such additional time as the court may deem just and equitable." When mortgagees sued, the United States Supreme Court, by a 5 to 4 vote, upheld the constitutionality of the law. Chief Justice Hughes wrote:

> [T]here has been a growing appreciation of public needs and of the necessity of finding ground for a rational compromise between individual rights and public welfare. The settlement and consequent contraction of the public domain, the pressure of a constantly increasing density of population, the interrelation of the activities of our people and the complexity of our economic interests, have inevitably led to an increased use of the organization of society in order to protect the very bases of individual opportunity. . . . [T]he question is no longer merely that of one party to contract as against another, but of the use of reasonable means to safeguard the economic structure upon which the good of all depends.

In a lengthy dissent, Justice Sutherland was able to show that the contract clause had been included in the Constitution at the behest of creditor interests concerned to prevent just the sort of debtor-relief legislation Minnesota had enacted. He said:

> A provision of the Constitution . . . does not mean one thing at one time and an entirely different thing at another time. . . . If the provisions of the Constitution be not upheld when they pinch as well as when they comfort, they may as well be abandoned. . . . He simply closes his eyes to the necessary implications of the decision who fails to see in it the potentiality of future gradual but ever-advancing encroachments upon the sanctity of private and public contracts. [Home Bldg. & Loan Association v. Blaisdell, 290 U.S. 398 (1934).]

2. Suppose the A's have paid $10,000 down at the closing, and have given a purchase-money mortgage to Mr. Bailout to secure payment of an additional $90,000. The A's then convey to Mr. and Ms. C, who "assume the mortgage." The C's convey to Mr. and Ms. D, "subject to

the mortgage." Still later, the *D*'s convey to Horace *E*, who "assumes the mortgage." The mortgage is now in default. Who has what legal rights?

3. Suppose the *A*'s pay $10,000 in cash at the closing, obtain $60,000 from the Columbia Savings Bank on a first mortgage, and give Mr. Bailout a second mortgage for $80,000. Both mortgages are properly recorded. Now Bailout's mortgage is in default, and he brings foreclosure proceedings against the *A*'s. Bailout joins the Columbia Savings Bank in his lawsuit. What should the bank do?

4. *Failure to Include Acceleration Clauses:* Bailout is the holder of a promissory note from the *A*'s, secured by a mortgage. The note provides that the indebtedness is to be paid in monthly installments over a period of five years. Neither the note nor the mortgage contains an acceleration clause. The *A*'s fail to make three consecutive payments during the first year. Bailout wishes to foreclose the mortgage. What problems will he encounter? Compare Rains v. Mann, 68 Ill. 264 (1873) (mortgagee may foreclose only on sums then due), with Blazey v. Delius, 74 Ill. 299 (1874) (upon foreclosure, the court may direct that the entire mortgaged premises be sold, if doing so will do justice among the equitable rights of the parties, even though only a part of the mortgage debt is due).

5. *Conflict between Note and Mortgage:* Oxford Associates is the holder of a promissory note given by the *A*'s and secured by a mortgage encumbering property owned by them. The note provides for the principal amount plus interest to be paid in ten annual installments. The mortgage contains a provision that if the sum secured thereby or any part thereof is not paid when due, the entire principal sum plus interest thereon shall become due and payable immediately. The note contains no such clause. The *A*'s default on the first payment. In an action to foreclose the mortgage, can Oxford Associates also sue on the note for a deficiency judgment in the event the proceeds of the foreclosure sale are less than the debt?

Compare Boyette v. Carden, 347 So. 2d 759 (Fla. App. 1977) (when other instruments are executed contemporaneously with a mortgage and are part of the same transaction, the mortgage may be modified by the other instruments and all the documents are to be read together to determine and give effect to the intention of the parties), with Lincoln Park West v. American National Bank & Trust Co., 88 Ill. App. 3d 660, 410 N.E.2d 990 (1980) (mortgage and note are separate contracts, and any provision in the mortgage as to payment of the debt not contained in the note relates solely to the security pledged and not to the personal obligation of the maker of the note). Cf. Starkman v. Signond, 184 N.J. Super. 600, 446 A.2d 1249 (1982) (when acceleration provisions of a note and mortgage are in an irreconcilable conflict, the note will prevail).

6. *Usury:* Columbia Savings Bank holds a two-year promissory note at 9 percent interest from Chatham Associates, a corporate borrower. The note is secured by a mortgage encumbering Chatham's property.

Both the note and the mortgage contain clauses providing that upon default in any installment payment of principal or interest by Chatham, Columbia Savings Bank can declare the entire unpaid balance to be due immediately. The face amount of the note, $290,000, is $5,800 more than Chatham actually received at the loan closing because the bank had withheld $5,800 from the loan proceeds as a "commitment fee."

What is the effect of this "fee" if Chatham defaults and CSB exercises its right to accelerate? In St. Petersburg Bank & Trust Co. v. Hamm, 414 So. 2d 1071 (Fla. 1982), the Florida Supreme Court said the calculation should be done this way:

1. The spreading of any such advance or forbearance for the purpose of computing the rate of interest shall be calculated by first computing the advance or forbearance as a percentage of the total stated amount of the loan.
   a) Advance of $5,800.00.
   b) $5,800.00/$290,000.00 = 2% of total stated amount.
2. This percentage rate shall then be divided by the number of years, and fractions thereof, of the loan according to its stated maturity date, without regard to early maturity in the event of default.
   a) Two year term.
   b) 2% spread over two years is 1% annual percentage rate.
3. The resulting annual percentage rate shall then be added to the stated annual percentage rate of interest to produce the effective rate of interest for purposes of this chapter.
   a) The resulting annual percentage rate from paragraph 2(b) above is 1% per year.
   b) The stated annual rate on the note is 9% per year.
   c) The effective rate of interest is 9% + 1% = 10%.

Since the usury limit at the time was 10 percent, the loan was not usurious.

The court below had concluded that the loan was usurious by, in effect, figuring the percentages based on the amount the borrower had received — the $290,000 minus the $5,800 "commitment fee."

See also Abromowitz v. Barnett Bank, 394 So. 2d 1033 (Fla. App. 1981) (where a "service fee" deducted from face amount of a loan as "hidden interest" and added to "actual interest" in determining whether loan is usurious was held usurious).

7. *Waiver and Estoppel:* Columbia Savings Bank holds a promissory note from A that is secured by a mortgage encumbering property owned by A. Both the note and the mortgage contain acceleration clauses giving the bank the right to declare the entire indebtedness due and payable immediately upon default in any payment by A. During the first year of the loan period, A makes substantial improvements to the property, but he is unable to make the first annual mortgage payment at the end of the year. Two months later, Columbia Savings Bank begins a foreclosure

action against *A* based on the acceleration clause. *A* then tenders the amount due to the bank, which refuses to accept it. What result? See Strong v. Stoneham Co-operative Bank, 357 Mass. 662, 260 N.E.2d 646 (1970) (foreclosure ordered). Assume Columbia Saving Bank had accepted partial payment of the overdue balance, but had continued foreclosure proceedings. See U.S. Savings Bank v. Continental Arms. Inc., 338 A.2d 579 (Del. Super. 1975) (foreclosure ordered). What if Columbia Savings Bank had accepted full payment and had continued foreclosure proceedings? See Petti v. Putignano, 393 N.E.2d 935 (Mass. App. 1979) (foreclosure ordered). What if Columbia Savings Bank had received *A*'s payment only a few days late and had refused it and returned it? See Ciavarelli v. Zimmerman, 122 Ariz. 143, 593 P.2d 697 (1979) (foreclosure ordered).

Assume Columbia Savings Bank had informed *A* of its intent to accelerate the payment of its loan but had not yet started foreclosure proceedings. When *A* tenders and the bank refuses to accept, what result? See Campbell v. Werner, 232 So. 2d 252 (Fla. App. 1970) (foreclosure ordered). What if *A* had tendered payment after being in default but before Columbia Savings Bank had elected to accelerate? See Walker Bank & Trust Co. v. Nerlson, 26 Utah 2d 383, 490 P.2d 328 (1971) (foreclosure precluded). Assume that Columbia Savings Bank had not elected to accelerate until 11 months after *A*'s default, during which time *A* had continued to make substantial improvements on the property, but on receipt of notice of the bank's election to accelerate, *A* tendered payment. See Koschorek v. Fischer, 145 So. 2d 755 (Fla. App. 1962) (whether mortgagee is estopped by its delay, and whether foreclosure would be unconscionable, are questions of fact). But cf. Whalen v. Etheridge, 428 S.W.2d 824 (Tex. Civ. App. 1968) (permitting default for many months is not a waiver of right to elect to accelerate).

Assume *A*'s payment on the first installment had been accepted late by Columbia Saving Bank. Upon *A*'s default on the second payment, the bank elected to foreclose. What result? See Motlong v. World Savings & Loan Association, 168 Colo. 540, 452 P.2d 384 (1969) (acceptance of first payment not a waiver of acceleration clause; foreclosure ordered).

Assume this loan has been transacted in a jurisdiction that has a statute allowing a mortgagee to "cure" a default and avoid foreclosure once in five years, even after the mortgagor has begun foreclosure proceedings. Assume that after *A* had defaulted and Columbia Savings Bank had begun foreclosure proceedings, *A* cured the default through the use of the statute with the bank voluntarily dismissing the suit. Two years later, *A* again defaults and attempts to use the statute to cure, claiming it had not used the statute the first time because the bank had voluntarily dismissed the suit. What result? See State Farm Life Insurance Co. v. Town & Country Association, 85 Ill. App. 3d 319, 406 N.E.2d 923 (1980) (foreclosure ordered).

8. In November of 1980, Colorado voters had the opportunity to rid

themselves of the infamous "due-on-sale" clause. Proposition 4 on the state ballot pitted real estate brokers against land developers against attorneys, with would-be home buyers watching somewhat bewilderedly from the sidelines. The commercial airwaves jingled with advertising: "Four is fair, and fair is for you!" vied with "Don't be fooled by Four!" and other similarly sophisticated statements for or against the proposition.

Proposition 4, which sought to end due-on-sale clauses, was defeated.

9. In 1978 the California Supreme Court ruled that lender enforcement of a due-on-sale clause constitutes an "unreasonable restraint on alienation." Justice Clark, dissenting, said:

> We have thus come full circle. In attempting to take away contractual rights of lenders in order to assist borrowers in selling encumbered properties, the majority opinion has devised a scheme which affords yesterday's borrower a clear advantage over today's seller who comes to the marketplace with his property free from encumbrance. But our beneficence may be shortsighted. For in attempting to assist the Wellenkamps, the majority opinion must necessarily restrict if not dry up mortgage funds otherwise available to the next generation of borrowers.

Wellenkamp v. Bank of America, 21 Cal. 3d 943, 582 P.2d 970, 148 Cal. Rptr. 379 (1978).

Dawn Investment Co. v. Superior Court, 116 Cal. App. 3d 439, 172 Cal. Rptr. 142 (1982), refused to extend *Wellenkamp* to the situation of a noninstitutional seller of commercial real estate who held a second deed of trust securing a promissory note for part of the purchase price.

10. See the anti-redline laws, formally the Home Mortgage Disclosure Act of 1975 and the Community Reinvestment Act of 1977, 12 U.S.C. §§2801-2811 (1980).

◆ CONNOR v. GREAT WESTERN SAVINGS & LOAN ASSOCIATION
69 Cal. 2d 850, 447 P.2d 609, 73 Cal. Rptr. 369 (1968)

TRAYNOR, Chief Justice. These consolidated appeals are from a judgment of nonsuit in favor of defendant Great Western Savings and Loan Association in two actions consolidated for trial.

Plaintiffs in each action purchased single-family homes in a residential tract development known as Weathersfield, located on tracts 1158, 1159, and 1160 in Ventura County. Thereafter their homes suffered serious damage from cracking caused by ill-designed foundations that could not withstand the expansion and contraction of adobe soil. Plaintiffs accordingly sought rescission or damages from the various parties involved in the tract development.

Holders of promissory notes secured by second deeds of trust on the homes filed cross-complaints, alleging that their security had been impaired by the damage to the homes. They sought to impose liens on any recovery plaintiffs might obtain from other defendants.

There was abundant evidence that defendant Conejo Valley Development Company, which built and sold the homes, negligently constructed them without regard to soil conditions prevalent at the site. Specifically, it laid slab foundations on adobe soil without taking proper precautions recommended to it by soil engineers. When the adobe soil expanded during rainstorms two years later, the foundations cracked and their movement generated further damage.

In addition to seeking damages from Conejo, plaintiffs sought to hold Great Western liable, either on the ground that its participation in the tract development brought it into a joint venture or a joint enterprise with Conejo, which served to make it vicariously liable, or on the ground that it breached an independent duty of care to plaintiffs. . . .

The Weathersfield project originated in December 1958, when Harris Goldberg, president of South Gate Development Company, undertook negotiations to purchase for South Gate 547 acres of the McRea ranch, a parcel of approximately 1,600 acres of undeveloped real property in the Conejo Valley, which was then undergoing the beginnings of large-scale development. Goldberg and Keith Brown together owned and controlled South Gate Development Company. They planned to develop the property with the goal of creating a community of approximately 2,000 homes.

Neither Goldberg nor Brown had any significant experience in large-scale construction of tract housing. Goldberg had left the men's apparel business in 1955 to begin a career in real estate. He subsequently established a number of companies that engaged principally in subdividing raw acreage. In 1958 he undertook the construction of a 31-home development called Waverly Manor; when 15 or 20 homes had been partially completed under the supervision of a South Gate employee, he engaged Brown to supervise completion of the job. This task was Brown's first experience with tract construction, although he had been licensed as a general contractor in 1950 and had built approximately 50 . . . dwellings on an individual custom basis before 1958.

In January 1959 South Gate signed an agreement to purchase 100 acres of the McRea ranch for $340,000 within 120 days, and a conditional sales agreement to purchase 447 adjoining acres for $2,500 per acre over a 10-year period. Neither South Gate nor Goldberg had the financial resources to perform these agreements, and in March Goldberg approached Great Western for the necessary funds to purchase the 100-acre parcel on which Weathersfield was to be constructed.

Great Western processed between 8,000 and 9,000 loans each year, amounting to more than $100,000,000, but had not previously made loans in Ventura County. It expressed an interest to Goldberg in developing a volume of new construction loan business and in providing long-term financing in the form of first trust deeds to the buyers of the homes to be built. By the end of April, the general outlines of an agreement with Goldberg had been developed, and they were recorded in the minutes of Great Western's Loan Committee.

During the ensuing four months the parties and their lawyers worked out the details of a transaction whereby Great Western would supply the funds necessary to enable Goldberg to purchase the 100-acre parcel and construct homes thereon. In return, Great Western was given the right to make construction loans on the homes to be built and the right of first refusal to make long-term loans to the buyers of the homes. Before agreeing to provide money for the purchase of the land, Great Western also demanded and received a "gentleman's agreement" that it would have the right of first refusal to make construction loans on the homes to be built on the adjoining 477-acre parcel.

Great Western employed a geologist to determine whether an adequate quantity and quality of water would be available in the area. As a result of the geologist's report and its own investigations, Great Western further demanded and received a guarantee from South Gate, Goldberg, and Mr. and Mrs. Brown that if Great Western held title to the 100-acre parcel in September 1960, adequate water service lines from a new or existing public utility would be available at the property line for consumer use.

In July, Great Western provided the necessary funds for the purchase of the Weathersfield tract. Goldberg had deposited $190,000 of the $340,000 purchase price with the escrow agent on behalf of South Gate. He apparently obtained the money by draining assets from his corporations, leaving a combined net worth in those enterprises of $36,000 as of July 31.

Goldberg, by amended escrow instructions, substituted Conejo Development Company in place of South Gate as purchaser of the land from the McReas, and all funds deposited theretofore by South Gate were credited to Conejo. Conejo had been incorporated several months earlier, though with only $15,000 capital to handle the tract development.

Great Western deposited the remaining $150,000 of the purchase price in a second escrow opened between Conejo as seller and Great Western as buyer, took title to the land from Conejo, and granted South Gate a one-year option to repurchase the land in three parcels for a total of $180,000. South Gate, Goldberg, and Mr. and Mrs. Brown agreed to repurchase the property from Great Western on demand for $200,000 if the option were not exercised and adequate water facilities were not available by September 1960.

The arrangement for the purchase of the land by Great Western was an early example of what has come to be known as "land warehousing." Under such an arrangement, a financial institution holds land for a developer until he is ready to use it. Unlike a normal bailee of personal property, however, the institution retains title to the property as well as the right to possession.

At the outset Great Western confronted the problem that it could not lend Goldberg $150,000 outright and still retain the land as security, for section 7155 of the Financial Code prohibited it from lending more than 33⅓ percent of the appraised value of unimproved property. It therefore sought to circumvent the specific statutory prohibition by disguising what was in substance admittedly a loan as the kind of investment in real property that was sanctioned by section 6705 of the Financial Code.

Great Western agreed to make the necessary construction loans to Conejo only after assuring itself that the homes could be successfully built and sold. During the negotiations on the terms of the contemplated construction loans to Conejo and the long-term loans to be offered to the buyers of homes in the proposed development, Great Western investigated Goldberg's financial condition and learned that it was weak. Moreover, Great Western received, without comment or inquiry, an August 1959 financial statement from Conejo that set forth capital of $325,000, of which $320,000 was accounted for as estimated profits from the sales of homes when the sales transactions, then in escrow, were completed. Such an entry was far outside the bounds of generally accepted accounting principles. The estimated profits, representing 64/65 of the total purported capital, were not only hypothetical, but were hypothesized on the basis of houses that had not yet been constructed.

Great Western delved no deeper into the proposed foundations of the houses than into the conjectural bases of Conejo's capital. It did require Conejo to submit plans and specifications for the various models of homes to be built, cost breakdowns, a list of proposed subcontractors and the type of work each was to perform, and a schedule of proposed prices. Conejo, which at no time employed an architect, purchased plans and specifications from a Mr. L. C. Majors that he had prepared for other developments, and submitted them to Great Western.

Great Western departed from its normal procedure of reviewing and approving plans and specifications before making a commitment to provide construction funds. It did not examine the foundation plans and did not make any recommendations as to the design or construction of the houses. It was preoccupied with selling prices and sales. It suggested increases in Goldberg's proposed selling prices, which he accepted. It also refused any formal commitment of funds to Conejo until a specified number of houses were pre-sold, namely, sold before they were constructed.

Prospective buyers reserved lots after inspecting three landscaped and furnished model homes standing on 1.6 acres of the otherwise barren tract. The model homesites as well as a 60-foot wide access road had been granted by the McReas directly to Conejo "without consideration and as an accommodation" two weeks before the close of the land-purchase escrows.

When Conejo sold the lots, its sales agents informed the buyers that Great Western was willing to make long-term loans secured by first trust deeds to approved persons, and obtained credit information for later submission to Great Western. This procedure was dictated by the right of first refusal that Conejo agreed to give Great Western to obtain the construction loans. If an approved buyer wished to obtain a long-term loan elsewhere, Great Western had 10 days to meet the terms of the proposed financing; if it met the terms and the loan was not placed with Great Western, Goldberg, Brown, and South Gate were required to pay Great Western the fees and interest obtained by the other lender in connection with the loan. Most of the buyers of homes in the Weathersfield tract applied to Great Western for loans. They obtained approximately 80 percent of the purchase price in the form of 24-year loans from Great Western at 6.6 percent interest secured by first trust deeds. Great Western charged Conejo a 1 percent fee for loans made to qualified buyers, and a 1½ percent fee for loans made to Conejo on behalf of buyers who, in Great Western's opinion, were poor risks.

By September, the specified number of houses had been reserved by buyers, and Great Western accordingly made approximately $3,000,000 in construction loans to Conejo. Conejo agreed to pay Great Western a 5 percent construction loan fee and 6.6 percent interest on the construction loans as disbursed for six months and thereafter on the entire amount. Great Western had originally demanded 6.6 percent interest on the entire amount without regard to the disbursement of the funds, and its 5 percent loan fee was higher than normal because it assessed the loan as one involving a substantial risk. When the construction loans were recorded, Conejo became entitled to advances on the loans and to "land draws," lump sums calculated as a percentage of the value of the land. Conejo received advances on the construction loans and land draws in the sum of $148,200. It turned this sum together with $31,800 over to South Gate, which in turn paid the total of $180,000 back to Great Western in the exercise of its option to repurchase the 100-acre tract from Great Western. South Gate simultaneously transferred the land to Conejo.

Conejo accepted notes secured by the second trust deeds from the buyers of homes for the balance of the purchase price that was not provided by Great Western. Goldberg planned to discount the notes at 50 percent of their face value and to use the proceeds to pay the interest and fees to Great Western and provide a profit to Conejo. The evidence indicates, however, that in his enthusiasm to develop the first 100 acres of his projected community, Goldberg pared estimated profits to the dangerously thin margin of $500 per house, and that he exceeded his depth in expertise and finances, with a resulting deterioration in his financial position as construction progressed. Conejo ultimately pledged the notes as security for a $300,000 loan, 43 percent of their face value, forfeiting profits in the urgent need for liquid capital. This loan was obtained from cross-complainants Meyer Pritkin et al. seven business acquaintances of Goldberg who at his suggestion organized a joint venture in December 1959 to purchase 382 acres of land in the Conejo Valley.

A subcontractor employed by Conejo began grading the property before Great Western made a final commitment to provide construction loan funds, and while Great Western still nominally owned the land. During the course of construction, Great Western's inspectors visited the property weekly to verify that the pre-packaged plans were being followed and that money was disbursed only for work completed. Under the loan agreement, if construction work did not conform to plans and specifications, Great Western had the right to withhold disbursement of funds until the work was satisfactorily performed; failure to correct a nonconformity within 15 days constituted a default. Representatives of Great Western remained in constant communication with the developers of the Weathersfield tract until all the houses were completed and sold in mid-1960. . . .

Even though Great Western is not vicariously liable as a joint venturer for the negligence of Conejo, there remains the question of its liability for its own negligence. Great Western voluntarily undertook business relationships with South Gate and Conejo to develop the Weathersfield tract and to develop a market for the tract houses in which prospective buyers would be directed to Great Western for their financing. In undertaking these relationships, Great Western became much more than a lender content to lend money at interest on the security of real property. It became an active participant in a home construction enterprise. It had the right to exercise extensive control of the enterprise. Its financing, which made the enterprise possible, took on ramifications beyond the domain of the usual money lender. It received not only interest on its construction loans, but also substantial fees for making them, a 20 percent capital gain for "warehousing" the land, and protection from loss of profits in the event individual home buyers sought permanent financing elsewhere.

Since the value of the security for the construction loans and thereafter the security for the permanent financing loans depended on the construction of sound homes, Great Western was clearly under a duty of care to its shareholders to exercise its powers of control over the enterprise to prevent the construction of defective homes. Judged by the standards governing nonsuits, it negligently failed to discharge that duty. It knew or should have known that the developers were inexperienced, undercapitalized, and operating on a dangerously thin capitalization. It therefore knew or should have known that damage from attempts to cut corners in construction was a risk reasonably to be foreseen. It knew or should have known of the expansive soil problems, and yet it failed to require soil tests, to examine foundation plans, to recommend changes in the prepackaged plans and specifications, or to recommend changes in the foundations during construction. It made no attempt to discover gross structural defects that it could have discovered by reasonable inspection and that it would have required Conejo to remedy. It relied for protection solely upon building inspectors with whom it had had no experience to enforce a building code with the provisions of which it was ignorant. The crucial question remains whether Great Western also owed a duty to the home buyers in the Weathersfield tract and was therefore also negligent toward them.

The fact that Great Western was not in privity of contract with any of the plaintiffs except as a lender does not absolve it of liability for its own negligence in creating an unreasonable risk of harm to them. "Privity of contract is not necessary to establish the existence of a duty to exercise ordinary care not to injure another, but such duty may arise out of a voluntarily assumed relationship if public policy dictates the existence of such a duty." . . .

By all the foregoing tests, Great Western had a duty to exercise reasonable care to prevent the construction and sale of seriously defective homes to plaintiffs. The countervailing considerations invoked by Great Western and *amici curiae* are that the imposition of the duty in question upon a lender will increase housing costs, drive marginal builders out of business, and decrease total housing at a time of great need. These are conjectural claims. In any event, there is no enduring social utility in fostering the construction of seriously defective homes. If reliable construction is the norm, the recognition of a duty on the part of tract financiers to home buyers should not materially increase the cost of housing or drive small builders out of business. If existing sanctions are inadequate, imposition of a duty at the point of effective financial control of tract building will insure responsible building practices. Moreover, in either event the losses of family savings invested in seriously defective homes would be devastating economic blows if no redress were available. . . .

Mosk, Justice (dissenting). I dissent.

The evidence is overwhelming, and the majority concede, that as between the lender of funds and the tract developer there was no agency, no joint venture, no joint enterprise. It is clear there was merely a lender-borrower relationship. Nevertheless, the majority here hold the lender of funds vicariously liable to third parties for the negligence of the borrower. This result is (a) unsupported by statute or precedent; (b) inconsistent with accepted principles of tort law; (c) likely to be productive of untoward social consequences.

At the threshold, it would be helpful to review some elementary economic factors and relationships that appear to be involved in this proceeding.

The function of the entrepreneur in a free market is to discern what goods or services are in apparent demand and to gather and arrange the factors of production in order to supply to the consumer, at a profit, the goods and services desired. In so doing, the entrepreneur undertakes a number of risks. The demand may be less than he calculated; the costs of production may be greater. He is not only in danger of losing his own capital investment but he incurs obligations to the suppliers of land, materials, labor and capital, and he stands liable under now-accepted principles of law for harm and loss caused by defects in his products to those persons injured thereby.

The entrepreneur undertakes these calculated risks in the hope of an ultimate substantial monetary reward resulting from the return over and above his costs, which include not only land, materials and labor but the charges incurred in obtaining capital. Indeed, "profit" has been commonly understood to be the return above expenses to innovators or entrepreneurs as the reward for their innovation and enterprise. The upper limit of the entrepreneur's profit is determined by his success in the market, and this results from his skill in assessing the demand for his product and his minimizing losses through skillful production.

Conejo Valley Development Company and associated parties were entrepreneurs.

The role of the supplier of capital is entirely different. The lender, as a supplier of capital, is to receive by contract a fixed return or price for his investment. He owns no right to participate in the profits of the enterprise no matter how great they may be. On the other hand, he is insulated from the risk of loss of capital and interest in return for making his money available, other than the risk of nonpayment of the contract obligations. Indeed, it is elementary that the owner of money lends it to an entrepreneur and receives only a fixed return, rather than obtaining the gain from using the money himself as an entrepreneur, on the condition that he be relieved of risk. The basic, underlying risk in mortgage lending is that the lender might not get back what is owed to him in principal and interest.

It seems abundantly clear, both legally and logically, that if the lender has no opportunity to share in the profits or gains beyond the fixed return for his supplying of capital, i.e., if he has no chance of reaping the entrepreneur's reward and exercises no control over the entrepreneur's business, elementary fairness requires that he should not be subjected to the entrepreneur's risks.

Great Western Savings and Loan Association was a lender, a supplier of capital.

By imposing the entrepreneur's risks upon the supplier of capital, even though the latter has bargained away the opportunity of participating in the entrepreneurial gain on his capital by lending it at a fixed fee, the majority have effected a drastic restructuring of traditional economic relationships. The results may reverberate throughout the economy of our state, and may seriously affect the money and investment market, the construction industry, and regulatory schemes of financial institutions, all without the faintest hint in either statutory or case authority that such a draconian result is compelled. . . .

There appear to be adequate remedies both in law and in equity for victims of negligent builders. But if home purchasers are not sufficiently protected today in their available remedies for latent constructional defects, legislative bodies can take appropriate action to revamp building codes, give more power to regulatory agencies, make licensing requirements more strict, compel bonding of home builders, provide for industry-wide insurance. The answer does not lie in a judicially created cause of action that will compel lending institutions to assume a supervisory role in home construction. Such a requirement will raise interest rates and the cost of money and thus increase the cost of home construction. More significantly, it will place supervisory responsibility on institutions which are limited by law to financing operations and therefore ill-equipped with the skilled scientific, mechanical and engineering personnel necessary to perform a supervisory function effectively.

For all of the foregoing reasons, I would affirm the judgment.

Notes

1. *Connor* was overturned, at least in very substantial degree, the year after it was decided. Cal. Civ. Code §3434 (West 1970).

2. Junior creditor said first mortgagee had violated a duty to exercise due diligence to foreclose and that in the intervening time the junior creditor lost its security. *Held:* First mortgagee owes no such duty. Seppala & Aho Construction Co. v. Petersen, 373 Mass. 316, 367 N.E.2d 613 (1977).

3. Block v. Neal, 460 U.S. 289 (1983), discussed the possible liability of the federal Farmers Home Administration for negligent inspection of respondent's prefabricated house. The house, subsidized through a government program, had major construction defects, and the Supreme Court allowed a federal Tort Claims Act suit to go forward on the basis approved by the court of appeals: "that one who undertakes to act, even though gratuitously, is required to act carefully and with the exercise of due care and will be liable for injuries proximately caused by failure to use such care."

M. WOLF, SHARED APPRECIATION MORTGAGES: PERILS OF THE RESIDENTIAL JOINT VENTURE, LINCOLN INSTITUTE OF LAND POLICY ROUNDTABLE, Basic Concept Series No. 104 at 5-10 (1983): There is no more telling measure of the distance between FDR's New Deal and the Reagan Administration's New Beginning than in the contrast between each program's approach to a national housing crisis. Five decades ago, the answers to a home ownership and construction nightmare lay in a four-pronged federal legislative approach: (1) the institution of deposit insurance; (2) the segregation of banking from speculative investment functions; (3) the advent and institutionalization of long-term, fixed-rate home financing; and (4) the creation of a government-sponsored secondary mortgage market.

The danger signs are all around today — a devastated homebuilding industry, thrift institutions stretched on a rack between paying higher returns and collecting inadequate interest from pre-rampant-inflation mortgages, delinquencies and foreclosures on the rise. And on the most difficult, the personal, level, many Americans are seriously questioning whether they will ever be able to own a home.

Yet far from heeding and extending the programs of the past, there have been marked departures in the direction of non-insured money market funds; investment company forays into banking services (best typified by the *New York Times* headline: "The National Bank of Merrill Lynch"); and a new system of innovative, and often haphazard, financing arrangements that baffle the newly-privatized secondary mortgage market. . . .

. . . While a mere ten to fifteen percent of all home transactions involved new financing devices a few years ago, the proportion now stands closer to seventy-five percent. In some areas it is virtually impossible to find a conventional lender willing to extend an FRM, even if one could handle the monthly payments on a sixteen to eighteen percent loan.

Included among the Adjustables is the most popular form of creative financing, the Variable Rate Mortgage (VRM), which ties increases and decreases in the interest rate to a verifiable index. It was only natural that American lenders in the late 1970s and early 1980s would turn to the practice of indexation already quite prevalent in South America and other countries beset by inflation. While this instrument protects lenders from steady increases in [the] costs of funds, it does little to help the borrower whose income fails to keep up with a skyrocketing index.

The Graduated Payment Mortgage, or GPM, provides some relief from inordinate interest rates by establishing a sliding scale of scheduled increases in monthly payments. By the end of the loan period, the interest rate will exceed market levels. In exchange for the early interest break, the mortgagor may delay the process of paying off the principal of the loan — a condition labeled negative amortization. The GPM lender's great fear, therefore, is that somewhere down the line the mortgagor will realize she has less to lose by failing to keep up her non-equity payments than from paying off a mounting obligation. And, while the increases are predictable for the life of the GPM, there is still some risk, as with the VRM, that the mortgagor will be unable to keep up with her commitment. . . .

Another group of creative financing techniques seeks to formalize just this desire for a "rich uncle" investor. Unlike the first set of instruments, primarily designed to offset the negative effects of inflation, equity sharing seeks to distribute a distinct *benefit* of inflation: appreciation in hosuing values. In contrast to RAMs and other post-mortgage Equity Liberators, Equity Sharers strive to take advantage of increased housing values from the beginning of the lending period.

The typical shared equity arrangement is a scaled down version of a commercial joint venture. An investor, either a relative, friend, or increasingly an outside party, will put up one-half or more of the downpayment for the property and share the conventional mortgage payments with the homeowner. In exchange for this capital, the investor receives, upon sale or refinancing, a piece of the equity in the home and capital gains treatment (assuming the property is held long enough). Recent Congressional action even allows investors to take the full range of tax shelter benefits including interest and depreciation deductions.

Shared Appreciation Mortgages

While, as with other alternative financing forms, the specific terms of a SAM may vary, the FHLBB's proposed regulations of September 30, 1980, furnish the most useful paradigm for study and comparison:

> For purposes of this section, a shared appreciation mortgage loan is a loan bearing (1) interest at a fixed rate below the prevailing market rate for similar loans over the term of the loan and (2) contingent interest not to exceed 40 percent of the net appreciated value of the security property payable upon the earlier of maturity or payment in full of the loan or sale or transfer of the security property.

The duration and termination of the mortgage deviates from "normal" instruments as well:

> The term of the loan shall not exceed 10 years, with guaranteed refinancing at maturity as provided in paragraph (d) of this section. The loan must be repayable in equal monthly installments of principal and fixed interest during the loan term in an amount sufficient to retire a debt with the same principal and fixed interest rate over a period not exceeding

40 years, with the unamortized principal and contingent interest payable on the earlier of maturity or payment in full of the loan or sale or transfer of the security property. . . .

In actual practice, SAMs have differed, sometimes markedly, from the Bank Board's recommendations. The best publicized program was organized and administered in the summer of 1980 by Advance Mortgage Corporation, an affiliate of Oppenheimer & Company. In exchange for one third of the profit realized upon sale, exchange, prepayment, or expiration of the loan term, Advance's lenders in five markets — Atlanta, Phoenix, Denver, Sarasota, and Washington, D.C. — offered ten million dollars worth of mortgages with interest rates set at levels one third below prevailing rates. . . .

The advantages of the SAM are straightforward enough: the borrower qualifies today as a homeowner at a discounted rate and is assured that the monthly payments will not vary during the life of the loan; the lender, while foregoing some income today, can make up or exceed the difference through the contingent interest payment upon sale, exchange, maturity, or other termination of the SAM.

As for the negative side, the ever-growing literature on SAMs is replete with caveats concerning the administration, enforceability, and desirability of these unique equity-sharing instruments. . . .

B. MONEY AND TAXES

For Mr. and Ms. Ambitious, their house purchase is probably the largest financial transaction in which they will ever participate. Many aspects of it will be murky to them, and will seem arbitrary, even if their lawyer provides reasonable guidance. For example, the interest rate, over which they have virtually no influence, will determine how costly the house will be to them over the years of their mortgage commitment.

Consider, for example, certain possible borrowing arrangements that Mr. and Ms. A might make if they purchased the house for $45,000.

	Amount	Interest Rate	Term	Monthly Payment	Total Payment
1st Mortgage	$33,500	9%	20 Years	$301.41	$72,338.40
1st Mortgage	$33,500	7¼%	20 Years	$264.78	$63,547.20

Bank will charge less interest if Mr. and Ms. A only borrow 70 percent of the purchase price and get the rest elsewhere.

	Amount	Interest Rate	Term	Monthly Payment	Total Payment
1st Mortgage	$31,500	7%	20 Years	$244.22	$58,612.80
2nd Mortgage	$ 2,000	12%	5 Years	$ 44.45	$ 2,667.00
				$288.67	$61,279.80

In other words, by paying $23.89 more for the first five years, the A's can cut their total cost by $2,267.40.

The Internal Revenue Code is important to the A's calculations. For example, it lets them deduct that part of their mortgage payments which is interest (in the early years, interest comprises most of the payments), and everything they pay in real estate taxes. If they were still renting an apartment, much of their rent would go (through the landlord's hands) for interest and real estate taxes, but the A's would get no income tax deduction. Also, the A's are likely to build substantial capital value in their house, through inflation, but to avoid tax on that increase in their net worth until they sell, and even then to be able to postpone taxes if they buy another, larger house soon after.

But if the money market and the Internal Revenue Code are factors of considerable significance for the A's, for large real estate developers — the individuals and firms that commission and manage most of America's new housing stock — they are even more important. We present in this chapter in the context of a single interesting apartment house "deal," an introduction to some of the vital issues of real estate finance and taxation.

1. Developers

Who are real estate developers? In general they are simply business people who have (or think they have) some competence in developing property, or who are attracted to real estate investment for tax reasons. At the outset, it is easiest to think of the developer as one person who arranges the financing, puts up cash, takes the risk, and enjoys the tax treatment of the investment. Usually, however, more than one person is involved in the transaction. The developer may arrange a package (for a fee or as a participant) and attract others to join him or her. The pooling of risk, return, tax advantage, and liability can be arranged in several ways. Usually the investors will become "limited patners" in a partnership set up to "do" the transaction; this means they are taxed directly,*

---

* If the business were incorporated (instead of being carried on as a partnership) the corporation would be taxed as an entity, and its distributions of profits to its owners would be taxed again ("double taxation") as their personal income. Also, shareholders cannot deduct annual losses, whereas partners can take advantage of what may be "paper" losses resulting largely from favorable depreciation formulas permitted by the Internal Revenue Code.

bear no personal liability beyond their cash investment, and do not participate in the management of the business. Investors may also get together to form a real estate investment trust, another arrangement for distributing risk, taxes, liability, and return. Some recent experience with both partnership syndicates and investment trusts has been disastrous, primarily because the arrangements were so attractive and successful that eager investors bid up prices on real assets over the level at which a reasonable return could be expected; many of the arrangements failed.

2. Borrowed Money

Large real estate developers may invest their own cash in new acquisitions. More commonly, however, developers (and other purchasers of real estate) have plans that exceed their own resources, or have other good reasons, such as tax advantages, to borrow money. The search fo·a source of money on good terms is a major concern for developers.

Size of Down Payment. Down payment (or "equity") is the cash the borrower must put up to begin the transaction; the rest is provided by the lender. Obviously, the larger the down payment, the fewer the borrowers with the necessary cash and the less risk taken by the lender. Before the advent of government-insured mortgages, the minimum down payment was roughly one-third of the value of the mortgaged asset. Under the Federal Housing Administration and the Veterans Administration, mortgages have much higher loan-to-value ratios; both programs have at times gravitated toward the 100 percent mortgage. See C. Haar, Federal Credit and Private Housing 61 (1960):

[A low down payment increases] the possibility of buying [property] and the long-term burden of the operation as well. The lower the down payment, the higher (other things being equal) the monthly installment, and the larger the total interest cost to the purchaser.

It is claimed that a low down payment enables an individual to invest his free capital more profitably elsewhere. [A homeowner (for example) who makes a large down payment] is forced into compulsory saving. But this saving takes the form of equity which yields no interest; had this money been invested elsewhere, it might have brought a greater return than the interest cost of the mortgage. This conclusion, however, in turn depends on whether the purchaser is the kind of person who (1) does not need the whiplash of compulsory savings and (2) also has available to him opportunities for investment at a rate of return more profitable than the interest cost on the mortgage. However, investment opportunity may be rare. In practice many put down more than the minimum payment asked of them. Low down payments have not escaped the moral criterion: is the individual who has been unwilling to exercise prudence or self-restraint in accumulating a small sum of money entitled to legislative pampering to enable him to purchase a home [or other property]?

Length of Mortgage Term. Over the period of the mortgage, the borrower makes payments to the lender to pay off the mortgage. Interest on the amount borrowed has always been payable as it is incurred by the borrower. However, if only interest were paid throughout the term, the borrower would have to repay the amount borrowed (principal) in a lump at the end. Since most borrowers cannot do that, mortgages are now self-amortizing — that is, the borrower's periodic payments include both part of principal ("amortization" payments) and the interest on the remaining unpaid principal.

A typical developer is more interested in the amount of money to be paid to the lender each month than in the term of the mortgage. This is because many developers plan to dispose of the asset before the full term has expired, transferring the mortgage to another or paying it off. Also, given the mobility of Americans, the homeowner with a mortgage obtained when interest rates were lower would like the right to transfer the mortgage to a buyer, while all owners desire the opportunity to "prepay" when interest rates fall.

See Haar, *ibid.*:

> On the other hand, there are potent arguments which attempt to save the borrower from himself against a greatly extended mortgage term. In the first place, it increases the total amount of interest that must be paid. This viewpoint is often put forward by the savings and loan associations, whose conventional loans are normally of shorter maturity than those insured or guaranteed by the government. Second, the longer the period of amortization the greater the possibility of some type of misfortune halting the borrower's income. Although over the extended period each payment is smaller, some borrowers may suddenly face a cessation of income; had the period been shorter, the property might have been fully paid for before the difficulty arose.
>
> A third objection to the longer maturity term is that the rate of amortization under the mortgage may be so slow that physical depreciation may outdistance repayment. Fourth, a slow rate of repayment means a reduced turnover of capital and less money available for relending to other mortgagors. Finally, potential lenders who for statutory or business reasons cannot commit themselves for long periods might be discouraged from participation.
>
> In spite of the merit of these arguments, in particular the increased total interest cost, the fact remains that a low monthly charge proves a definite attraction, and is decisive for many home purchasers of the lower income group. And in the last resort the consumer or investor must be allowed to judge the wisdom of his individual commitment.

Rate of Interest. The rate of interest is the factor concerning credit that most vitally affects the cost of a real estate investment. But it also —

and this is a large factor — directly determines the amount of capital which investors are willing to commit to financing mortgages. When money is so tight that lenders cannot meet all credit demands, mortgages must compete with other types of investments (e.g., corporations investing in new plant equipment) for the available borrowable money. If lenders can earn a higher return on other investments, mortgages will not be given — or their interest rates will rise. Thus, while rate of interest is important to the developer, it is also the variable over which he is least likely to exercise individual control.

Rate of Amortization. As we have seen above, mortgages are usually self-amortizing. The amortization may be paid off according to different formulas, however. The total amount paid each month by the borrower is called the "debt service." This amount usually includes both amortiza-

TABLE 18-1
Level Payment Debt Service

$33,500 Mortgage at 7¼% Interest (Term: 20 years)

Month	Installment	Interest	Principal	Principal Balance After Monthly Payment
1	$ 264.78	$ 202.40	$ 62.38	$33,437.62
2	264.78	202.02	62.76	33,374.86
3	264.78	201.64	63.14	33,311.72
.	.	.	.	.
.	.	.	.	.
.	.	.	.	.
240	264.78			0.00
Total Payment	$63,547.20	$30,047.20	$33,500.00	

tion and interest payments, the proportions determined by the formula elected by the borrower and lender when the mortgage was drafted. With a "constant amortization" mortgage, the borrower pays the same amount of amortization each month; since this decreases the amount of principal owed to the lender over time, the interest payable each month also decreases over time, as does the monthly debt service.

The most common form of mortgage, however, provides for "level payment" debt service — the same total amount is paid to the lender each month. Normally each installment is applied first to the payment of interest on the unpaid balance with the remaining sum applied to principal reduction (amortization). A little reflection will reveal that under this arrangement the ratio of interest to amortization for each monthly payment will decline over time. That is, the first payment will take a tiny chip off the unpaid principal and include a large interest payment; the next payment will include a little less interest (reflecting the previously decreased principal) and a little more amortization; the last payment at the end of term will be mostly amortization. Table 18-1 on the previous page illustrates this.

A mortgage that is not fully self-amortizing — which has unpaid principal after the last debt service payment at the end of the term — is said to have a "balloon." Balloon mortgages may be written to require interest payments only, or, more frequently, to provide only partial amortization. For the developer, this has the advantage of costing less (in cash) during the term of the mortgage. But when the mortgage matures, the developer must be able either to procure the "balloon" cash or to refinance the unpaid balance.

3. Leverage

"Leverage" is a general term used to describe the advantage enjoyed by investors who increase the return on their cash by investing borrowed money as well as their own. The proper use of mortgages produces leverage, and is an important element of successful real estate development. As will be explained later, the tax laws provide further leverage.

To illustrate how leverage works, consider an investor who buys an apartment building for $1,000,000 and gets a cash income from it of $100,000 annually after expenses (ignore taxes at this point). If the developer paid for the building completely in cash, the return on the investment is 10 percent annually.

However, assume instead that the developer borrows part of the purchase price and can get mortgage terms of 6 percent with a 20-year term and level payments. Look at the rate of return, on the accompanying table, if varying amounts are borrowed:

$500,000 Equity, $500,000 Mortgage

Cash income before debt service	$100,000
Less debt service	−43,020
Net cash return	$ 56,980
Percent return on equity	11.4

$100,000 Equity, $900,000 Mortgage

Cash income before debt service	$100,000
Less debt service	−77,436
Net cash return	$ 22,564
Percent return on equity	22.56

You should notice two things. First, leverage will not work unless the "points" are less than the rate of "free-and-clear" return. Points are the percentage of debt service, expressed in terms of dollars per thousand borrowed. With the mortgage terms used above, the points were 86.04 ($43,020 debt service on $500,000 mortgage, or $77,436 debt service on $900,000 mortgage). The free-and-clear return is the net income as a percentage of the *total* dollar investment, *disregarding* any mortgage payments (the return "free-and-clear" of financing costs). Here the free-and-clear return is 10 percent, or 100 points. Note that if the mortgage terms get tougher, the points get higher and leveraging becomes more difficult.

Second, given the proper points, it seems a borrower could leverage himself into absurdly high returns. This is unlikely, however. Lenders will not make mortgages with very low down payments because of the risks noted earlier. Also, the developer should be aware of his own risk. The "net cash return" to him gets smaller as the leverage increases. This net cash return is the developer's margin of solvency. If rent income falls or expenses increase, he may slip into the red, and the red is closer as the leverage increases and the margin of solvency is honed down. Clearly, as leverage increases so does risk. History records more than one real estate empire that was leveraged into oblivion.

4. Taxation

a. Overview of Federal Income Taxation

Sophisticated structuring of real estate transactions can produce tax advantages for developers that often are more important to them than are normal business profits. Indeed, transactions where the sole rationale is tax benefit are common; an investment may be attractive for a high-income taxpayer even though the investment itself yields a substantial pretax loss.

The first step in calculating federal income tax liability is to determine "gross income," defined in the tax statutes as "all income from whatever source derived." This broad definition includes items such as wages and salaries, return on investments (e.g., rents from property), gains from the sale of an asset, and business income. Recovery of the principal of a loan, receipt of borrowed funds, or return of invested capital is not "gross income" since these are just changes in the form of property (e.g., an enforceable debt into a repaid debt). Congress has also provided by statute for some exclusions from gross income, including gifts, inheritances, scholarships, and interest on municipal securities.

The next step in calculating tax is to subtract certain items from gross income to find "adjusted gross income." The deductions that yield AGI are mostly for business-related expenses. The rationale for allowing these deductions is that the profit of a business or business activity should be taxed, not its gross receipts. Profit is the correct indicator of benefit to the recipient; taxing "benefit" is really the idea behind the income tax.

From AGI, a few more items are deducted to yield "taxable income." These items generally relate to personal expenses. Most personal expenses (as distinguished from business expenses) are *not* deductible; otherwise, the income tax would be a tax on personal savings. But Congress has allowed a few personal deductions: medical expenses and charitable contributions are two familiar ones. These usually do not concern a developer or investor.

Most of the complexities that concern (or delight) the real estate developer arise in connection with business deductions. For instance, if a real estate developer buys an apartment building for cash, how should the transaction be treated? Is the amount completely deductible as a business expense in the year of purchase? Or should it be spread over many years?

In justifying the business deduction above, we relied on the observation that a true depiction of a business transaction to determine the income (profit) derived from it requires the deduction of related business expenses. How does the purchase of an apartment building fit into this observation? The purchase is an expense of earning income. But is the expense "used up" when the building is purchased? When the developer makes the purchase, he or she pays out cash, but obtains the ownership of an asset (the building and land) of presumably equal value. The "expense" incurred, then, is in his or her bank account (or wherever the developer keeps cash) but not in his or her overall "worth." And it is changes in this "worth" category, and not the narrower category of cash assets, that reflect income.

A more concrete way of looking at this issue is to consider what the business accounts would look like if the purchase price were taken as a current (i.e., immediate) expense and deducted. The first year would show a huge loss; succeeding years, during which rental income would be collected, would show income not offset by the cost of the building. Surely this would not be an accurate picture of how the business was "really" doing.

There are two problems. One is the "paper" problem of making the business accounts reflect real expenses rather than cash expenses. The accounting methods that solve this problem are outlined below. The second problem is estimating noncash expenses when it is difficult to tell just what they really are because it is unclear how fast an asset is being used up. The tax laws deal with this problem by allowing deductions for "depreciation" based on certain criteria. Depreciation is also discussed below.

Another problem raised tangentially in figuring deductions deals not with the amount and timing of expense deductions, but rather with the recognition of certain income as a "capital gain." In our case, the developer might sell his building at some point and make money on it (i.e., get more than he or she paid for it); this amount under some circumstances would qualify as a long-term capital gain. Capital gains are taxed at a lower rate than so-called "ordinary" income, in part to provide an incentive for capital investment and in part because a large capital gain in a single year, if taxed at regular rates, could put a taxpayer in a much higher "bracket," which might be thought unfair if the gain actually reflects gradual increase in the asset's value over many years.

·Questions

1. Assuming a developer wants to pay as little tax as legally possible, can you identify what kind of tax treatment he or she will look for regarding the various items of typical real estate transactions? For instance, is it "better" to treat a purchase as a current deduction, or as depreciable? Is it better to depreciate an asset quickly or slowly?

2. Can you see some interaction between depreciation and capital gains treatment for the developer who buys, operates, and then sells a building? If the taxation of capital gains is based on the amount realized from the buying and selling of an asset, should factors enter into this computation other than the purchase and selling prices? For instance, should some account be taken of the depreciation ("tax write-off") the developer has taken while holding the building?

3. Would depreciation be a good way to calculate expenses from the purchase of *services* under a long-term contract? Why or why not? What might be the difference between expenditures for "capital assets" and other expenses?

b.   Accrual Accounting

Modern "accrual accounting," which is used by most businesses, allows representations of business operations more accurate than would be achieved by simple notations of when cash came in or went out. Accrual accounting is really just a set of standards for manipulating figures so that, during a given period (e.g., taxable year), the "real" expenses and income of a business operation are counted in determining profit or loss. The accountant essentially ignores (for most purposes) whether cash has changed hands or not, and looks instead at the practical questions of whether income was earned and expenses used up during the accounting period.

Suppose for instance that a tenant occupies a building and pays rent during one year. It is clear that the rental transaction should be recognized by the landlord during that year, since he has performed his obligation and been paid. But suppose alternatively that the tenant prepays the rent a year early. The landlord should not recognize this transaction in the earlier year; he has not yet performed, or earned the income. Recognition of the income should be deferred. This is done by creating special bookkeeping accounts that in essence delay recognition until the proper period. When the proper period arrives (the year of the rental), the landlord's accountant will include the income in the "income statement" (which shows profit and loss) for the year. Similarly, if the tenant pays late, recognition can be speeded up on paper.

Expenses can be treated in the same way. For example, if a heating fuel bill is paid before the fuel is used up, recognition can be deferred until the use. The purchase and use of a major asset such as a building is treated according to the same principle. We have seen that periodic deductions for the expense of the building itself (as distinguished, e.g., from upkeep expenses) are called "depreciation." We saw that depreciation is supposed to reflect the amount by which a capital asset (e.g., a building) is "used up" over a year while producing income. But this decline in value is hard to assess; the asset may even appreciate in value. If the true or market value of the building could be accurately assessed each year and reported for tax purposes, perhaps the yearly recognition of this expense (or gain) would not be difficult. But this is not the case. To substitute for yearly appraisal, two general rules apply. First, deductions are taken in the form of depreciation, usually according to a formula rather than according to any individual assessment of how much the asset is used up. It is generally conceded that in most cases depreciation exceeds any reasonable estimate of the actual loss in value of the asset to the taxpayer. Second, to the extent that the asset in fact is either used up or appreciates differently than the depreciation formula reflects, this difference is not realized for tax purposes until the asset is sold (i.e., in one sense cash and not accrual accounting is used here). The result is a double benefit to the taxpayer: (1) usually unrealistically high depreciation deductions now, and (2) postponement of adjustments until sale of the asset, and then often adjustments at lower (capital gains) rates.

c. Depreciation and Deductions

As noted above, the taxpayer is allowed to deduct business expenses, including depreciation, to reflect the purported decline in the value of an asset as it is used up in business. If an asset is completely used up in one year, the issue of depreciation does not arise; the deduction is taken in whole for that year ("expensed"). On the other hand, for assets that are used up slowly, recognition of depreciation over a number of years is clearly proper under accrual accounting, both for financial and tax purposes. Some items may not be easily identified as depreciable assets (which must be "capitalized" and depreciated) or deductible expenses. Consider, for instance, repairs to a building: Should the expenditure be capitalized and depreciated, or taken immediately? Often there is no clear answer to this question, so a tax statute will set a maximum figure for repairs that may be expensed during the year; beyond this they must be capitalized.

Depreciation poses more difficult problems than deductions because it is usually unclear just how fast an asset is declining in value. To deal with this problem, the tax statutes allow depreciation deductions according to set formulas that may bear little if any relationship to the "real" decline (if any) in value of an asset. The set formulas are used primarily for administrative convenience and certainty, and also to favor business investment. Property must be capable of "wear, tear, and exhaustion" to be depreciable. This means that land (and some other assets, such as art) cannot be depreciated.

Question

If a developer buys land and a building for a total price, but will be able to depreciate only the value of the building, how will an allocation of the total price be made? Will the buyer want a high or low proportion of the price allocated to the building? Does the seller have an opposite interest — so that the tax commissioner can rely on a private agreement to make the allocation fairly?

Intuitively, it is not hard to see how depreciation might be computed. If we are looking for an annual estimate of decline in value, we would estimate the life of the asset and the total value of the decline, and divide to find an annual figure. In tax language, we would determine the "basis": the amount paid for the asset, plus capital improvements; the expected decline would be the basis apportioned equally over the years of life. Depreciation calculated this way is said to be done by the "straight line" method.

However, the statute allows departures from the intuitive approach that are generally beneficial to the taxpayer. For instance, rather than requiring an estimation of useful life, the statute establishes 5 classes of property, including a "18-year real property" class.* Thus, real property

* Prior to the Tax Reform Act of 1984, the depreciation period for this class of property was 15 years. The fifteen-year period continues to apply to low-income housing, property placed in service prior to March 15, 1984, and certain property that the taxpayer was under

is fully depreciable over 18 years (even though its "real" depreciation might be over a much longer period). In addition, the 175 percent declining balance method of depreciation is allowed (200 percent declining balance method for low-income housing), thus allowing a larger-than-proportionate deduction to be taken in the early years. This is known as "Accelerated Cost Recovery System" (ACRS).

Under this method of depreciation, the first year's deduction is 1¾ the straight line amount. For the next year, the previous deduction is subtracted from the basis and the remainder depreciated according to the 175 percent rate. For example, assume a depreciable asset has a basis of $18,000 and comes within the class of 18-year real property.

1. The straight line depreciation would be $1,000 per year (basis divided by the class life of the asset). The depreciation rate is 5.56 percent.

2. Under 175 percent declining balance depreciation, 1¾ times the straight line rate, or (roughly) 9.7 percent, is used. However, it is not necessary calculate the deduction for each of the 18 years since the IRS has provided a table of percentages of the original basis that constitute the depreciation rate for each of the 18 years. (Although these percentages are only approximations of the exact rates, the IRS allows their use for simplicity.) Thus, the deductions are as follows:

Year	Percentage	Deduction
1	9%	$1620
2	9	1620
3	8	1440
4	7	1260
5	7	1260
6	6	1080
7	5	900
8	5	900
9	5	900
10	5	900
11	5	900
12	5	900
13	4	720
14	4	720
15	4	720
16	4	720
17	4	720
18	4	720

a binding contract to construct or acquire on March 15, 1984, or the construction of which was commenced on or before that date. Such "transitional" property must be placed in service prior to January 1, 1987, to qualify for 15-year depreciation.

Note that after the 7th year, the straight line depreciation rate is higher than the 175 percent declining balance rate (the 175 percent declining balance depreciation amount would be $854 in our example, as opposed to the $900 allowed by the table, which is approximately the straight line amount). To allow complete depreciation at relatively high rates, the tax law permits taxpayers to switch to straight line depreciation, which the IRS table does after year 6. In addition, the statute gives the taxpayer the option of depreciating based on the straight line method over 18, 35 or 45 years.

ACRS was instituted in 1981. Prior to that system, the statute included the Asset Depreciation Range (ADR), which allowed depreciation based on the useful life of an asset, with "class lives" for many different categories of assets (as opposed to the 5 fixed classes of ACRS). While ADR was more beneficial to taxpayers than straight line depreciation, ACRS is even more advantageous.

Questions

1. If the amount of depreciation depends in part on the basis of the asset, can a taxpayer fully depreciate an asset whose purchase he or she has financed with borrowed money? In other words, can the taxpayer get a tax advantage from borrowed money? The answer is yes: The taxpayer can get full depreciation of a million-dollar asset even if all the money for it was borrowed and even if there was no personal liability on the mortgage.

As to whether this is reasonable, consider the rationale for allowing depreciation as a business expense deduction and whether this rationale is a sham if the taxpayer has no personal liability on his or her obligation to the lender. If the taxpayer were not allowed to depreciate, should the lender be? Would this differ much from a leasing transaction?

It should be obvious that allowance of depreciation of borrowed assets is an instance of tremendous leverage, in this instance due to the tax laws.

2. If each purchaser of an asset can claim 175 percent declining balance depreciation, which is of greatest value in the early years of ownership, doesn't this encourage frequent disposition and acquisition of assets, to get as much early and large depreciation as possible? The answer is yes: Each new owner can depreciate the asset according to his or her own basis — what was paid for it — and according to the class of assets into which it fits. This is true even if the previous owner *fully depreciated* the asset.

3. Does this tremendous advantage of very large deductions in the early years suggest a way in which investors in apartment buildings could maximize their profits? Investors who build or purchase buildings

and rent out apartments in the first few years can take advantage of the tax losses generated by the large depreciation deductions. In later years, when amortization exceeds depreciation and these tax losses disappear, the building owners can convert to condominiums and sell the units individually. In effect, ACRS could make investment in rental property profitable once again.

d.   Capital Gains Treatment

A developer may simply hold on to property he or she has bought or built, taking depreciation over the years until it runs out. At some point, however, it is more likely that he or she will sell — because the depreciation does run out, or because newer property would be more quickly depreciable. The sale of an asset will yield gain or loss, each of which will have tax consequences.

For determining tax liability, only 40 percent of long-term capital gains are added to other income received during the year. In effect, therefore, long-term capital gains are taxed at 40 percent the rate of other income. Thus, a taxpayer who normally pays taxes of 50 percent on income pays only 50 percent of the 40 percent inclusion, or only 20 percent of capital gains. To qualify, an asset must be sold or exchanged; it must have been held for at least one year; and it must be either a "capital asset" or "property used in the trade or business." Losses from the sale or exchange of business-related assets can usually be subtracted from capital gains, so that only net gain is taxed. Net losses can be carried forward to offset future gains for a limited number of years.

Questions

Can you foresee under what conditions a taxpayer would want a transaction treated as involving a capital asset, and when the taxpayer would not want this? Why is it better that a business-related asset involved in a loss transaction *not* qualify for capital asset treatment? The answer is that a loss offset against ordinary income is a full-rate deduction. A loss offset against capital gains brings tax benefits at a lower rate.

Once it has been determined how a transaction will be treated, the figures must then be plugged in. The beginning point is the basis, the same as that used in calculating depreciation. The basis is usually the price of acquisition or market value of the asset. To this, subsequent capital expenditures (e.g., nondeducted renovations on a building) are added. Depreciation is subtracted, yielding the "adjusted basis."

The adjusted basis is essentially the amount the developer invested. When this is subtracted from the amount realized on the sale of the asset, the gain (or loss, if the amount is negative) results.

It is important to understand why depreciation is subtracted from basis, as indicated above. Note that the effect of subtracting depreciation is to raise the tax. If depreciation were not subtracted, the basis would be much higher and the gain much less; hence the tax would be lower. The depreciation deductions taken by the taxpayer while using the asset were supposed to reflect the decline in value of the asset, and recognize this decline for tax purposes. When the asset is sold, should this earlier tax recognition of (and taxpayer benefit from) the purported decline in value of the asset be ignored? Obviously not; otherwise the taxpayer would get a double benefit: depreciation deductions *and* a decline in the value of the asset between acquisition and disposition, which will lower the capital gain (or increase the loss). For instance, suppose a taxpayer bought an asset for $1,000 and fully depreciated it — i.e., took $1,000 of depreciation deductions. If the taxpayer then sold the asset for $600, it would show that the asset had *not* been all used up. The subtraction of depreciation from basis ensures that this "phony depreciation" — here, $600 worth — will not escape taxation. However, the taxpayer nevertheless achieves an important saving. The annual deduction for depreciation is taken against ordinary income, thus providing a benefit at ordinary income rates; however, when the taxpayer sells the asset, he or she pays tax only at capital gains rates on the phony depreciation.

This final income tax advantage — "loophole" — from depreciating real estate has been substantially diminished. The tax "reform" statutes of 1969, 1976, 1981, and 1984 have provided for "recapture" of excess depreciation; this means that the taxpayer must pay at ordinary income rates when he or she sells the property for that part of the gain that is a return of excess depreciation taken while he or she owned the property. However, the recapture provisions do not apply if the straight line method of depreciation has been used. In such a case, all gain will be taxed at the capital gains rate. In addition, there is no recapture of excess depreciation on "low-income housing" held for more than 17 years; between 8 and 16 years there is partial recapture on low-income housing. (This provision applies to a great deal of the housing built under federal and state subsidy programs that is inhabited by persons well above the median income.)

One additional interesting aspect of the tax law with regard to the preceding material is the 25 percent tax credit allowed for qualified rehabilitation expenditures on any certified historic structure. This means that the amount of taxes owed by the building's owner can be reduced by 25 percent of the rehabilitation expenditure, which can result in a large savings when this type of investment has been substantial.

e.   Tax Policy

In evaluating the consequences and propriety of the tax rules presented
above, consider the following report of the Treasury Department.

U.S. TREASURY DEPT. TAX REFORM STUDIES AND PROPOSALS,
HOUSE WAYS AND MEANS COMMITTEE AND SENATE FINANCE
COMMITTEE, 91st Cong., 1st Sess. at 441-445 (1969): Looking at the
accelerated depreciation provisions by themselves, it is evident that
where allowable tax depreciation exceeds the actual rate at which buildings are used up and become obsolescent, income tax liabilities are deferred resulting in revenue reductions. It is estimated that this involves a
current revenue cost of about $750 million, of which $250 million relates
to rental residential investments and some $500 million to other kinds of
real estate, including industrial and commercial buildings, hotels and
motels, shopping plazas, and the like.

In view of the Nation's concern with housing construction goals, it
seems worthwhile to examine in more detail the rough estimates of the
breakdown of the $750 million revenue cost or "tax expenditure" by
destination:

> Some $500 million as just indicated is used for tax advantages for
> motels, office buildings, shopping centers, and commercial and industrial
> construction of all kinds.
> As much as another $100 million is used for continued tax advantages
> for older housing which is undergoing its second, third, or fourth round of
> depreciation writeoffs at rates above straight line.
> Probably another $100 million goes for relatively recent housing con-
> struction in the semiluxury or luxury highrise category.
> Only about $50 million feeds directly into the process of rewarding
> investors who currently or recently have made commitments increasing
> the low- and moderate-income housing supply. . . .

It is virtually impossible in the present state of the economic art to
reach reliable quantitative estimates of the effect of the present preferential tax provisions on construction and housing supply. Lacking quantitative measures of these effects of the millions of "tax expenditure"
dollars now being spent to assist building generally and housing in
particular, what are the qualitative effects?

In broad outline, the effects of the Federal income tax assistance
seem to show the following pattern:

> The tax assistance provided, through accelerated depreciation and
> capital gain treatment, for building investors generally and landlords, pre-
> sumably tends to encourage construction and rental housing supply in the
> aggregate but by unknown amounts; the *a priori* effect one would logically

expect — after all, millions of tax dollars are being provided annually — cannot be reliably measured either in terms of building in the aggregate, housing generally, or low-income housing.

In the housing field the tax stimuli are probably more effective for luxury and moderate-income rental housing where profitability and appreciation prospects relative to risk are inherently more attractive than in lower income housing.

The "trickle down" supply effect for the lower income rental housing market is apparently slow and uncertain in a growing general housing market.

Capital and other resource demands engendered by the existing tax stimuli probably tend to expand luxury housing, . . . and other forms of more glamorous investment, squeezing out lower income housing.

The investor tax stimuli depend on and are sensitive to favorable financial leverage and interest rates relative to rents, so that they are turned on and off abruptly with abrupt changes in monetary policy; as a consequence, investors apparently rank loan-term factors high and ahead of taxes in deciding whether to invest.

The tax benefits are not focused on new construction but are spread over repeated turnover of older properties; this may support the market and prices for older housing, but the beneficial feedback to new construction incentive is probably not proportionate to the revenue cost.

The present treatment seems to create a tax environment favorable to frequent turnover which tends to discourage long-range "stewardship" and adequate maintenance; it also encourages thin equities and unsound financial structures which could topple if the market for real estate and rental housing weakened.

The tax stimuli probably aid new construction more than improvement or remodeling of existing housing since it appears that remodeling of risky low-income projects cannot be conventionally financed as well as new housing. . . .

To sum up on the effects of the present system of accelerated depreciation and related tax treatment of real estate operators and investors — the real estate tax shelter — the system —

> is costly and inefficient as a means of getting more housing or other construction;
> offers no assurance that construction resources are directed to priority needs; indeed — it may be surmised — it diverts promotional talent, capital, and other resources into forms of building which are less essential than many basic housing needs;
> is basically incompatible with the operation of a fair tax system and the important objectives of tax reform; and
> is also incompatible with budgetary responsibility since it involves substantial tax-expenditure commitments via the revenue side of the

budget which escape the tests and controls of sound modern budgetary procedures.

5. Tax Shelters

a. The Concept

Conceptually, the elements of a tax shelter can be grouped into four categories:

(1) *Tax Deferral:* the time when tax is paid is postponed. ACRS is the example discussed above: overestimated depreciation is not taxed until sale of an asset. The result is an interest-free loan to the taxpayer for the intervening period.

(2) *Rate Shifts:* when tax is paid, it is at a lower rate. Payment of overestimated depreciation at capital gains rates, when the deductions were against ordinary income, is the example discussed above. The recapture provision partially closes this loophole.

(3) Leverage: the taxpayer gets tax benefits from money he or she has borrowed as well as his or her own money. The allowance of taxpayer depreciation of a lender-financed asset is the example discussed above.

(4) *Overt Subsidies:* in the real estate field, federally assisted housing programs involve certain subsidies. These are not treated in detail here.

It remains to plug in some figures to see how the advantages work.

b. The Elements: Depreciation versus Mortgage Amortization

Assume a developer in a 50 percent tax bracket buys a building free and clear for $900,000. Revenues for the first year total $225,000; all currently deductible operating expenses are $110,000. The building is depreciated over 18 years using the straight-line method. The developer's account appears as follows:

Tax		Cash	
Revenues	$225,00	Revenues	$225,000
Less expenses	−110,000	Less expenses	−110,000
deprec.	− 50,000		
Taxable income	$ 65,000	Cash income	$115,000

What does this mean? The taxpayer has $65,000 of taxable income, plus another $50,000 that is not taxed. The after-tax income is $82,500 ($65,000 at 50 percent plus $50,000), so the return is a little more than nine percent of initial investment. Had the developer taken accelerated depreciation, the proportion of untaxed income would rise, as would the after-tax return (to over 10 percent with 175 percent declining balance depreciation).

Can the developer do better? Remember leverage. Assume the developer has an 18-year, 10 percent mortgage with constant yearly amortization, for half the price of the building. Then:

Tax			*Cash*	
Revenues	$225,000		Revenues	$225,000
Less expenses	− 110,000		Less expenses	− 110,000
deprec.	− 50,000		interest	− 45,000
interest	− 45,000		amort.	− 25,000
Taxable income	$ 20,000		Cash income	$ 45,000

The after-tax income is $35,000 ($20,000 taxable income at 50 percent tax, plus $25,000 tax-free), and the return on the $450,000 of the taxpayer's own money is only about 8 percent in the first year. The developer does worse with the mortgage. Do you see why?

Consider the following variation. Assume now that the developer uses a higher depreciation rate — the 175 percent declining balance method. Then:

Tax			*Cash*	
Revenues	$225,000		Revenues	$225,000
Less expenses	− 110,000		Less expenses	− 110,000
deprec.	− 81,000		interest	− 45,000
interest	− 45,000		amort.	− 25,000
Taxable income	$(11,000)		Cash income	$ 45,000

The figures now show a tax *loss* of $11,000, with cash income unchanged. What is the benefit to the taxpayer? The developer gets the $45,000 untaxed cash income ("cash flow"), plus the opportunity to offset the tax loss against other taxable income (from another project, salary, or wages, etc.). If $11,000 of other income is offset, the benefit is the tax saved on the amount: in the 50 percent bracket, $5,500. The after-tax benefit is $50,500. This shows that a tax loss can coexist with real cash income. Bonanza (for the taxpayer)!

Careful comparison of the tables above shows that all the items in the "tax" and "cash" accounts match, except one: the depreciation-amortization pair. (Make sure you see this. Do you see why this is so,

given the tax laws?) This means that WHENEVER DEPRECIATION EX-
CEEDS AMORTIZATION, TAX SHELTER BENEFITS RESULT. This is
the basic key to the real estate tax shelter. And it should be evident that
the higher the taxpayer's bracket, the more the tax shelter is worth.

Questions

Does this mean that the higher the taxpayer's bracket, the easier it is
to enter an investment? Think of this in terms of the government under-
writing part of the risk. Is this fair to poorer developers? Is this why the
rich get richer? Consider, though, that to the extent the government
underwrites an investment, it presumably will get more of the income
because of the higher bracket.

c. Dangers of Collapse

While those of you in high tax brackets may be ready to fire your investment advisers and buy real estate, it should be evident that there are
risks and problems involved in these investments. Consider, for a moment, what can happen if a very natural event occurs: You misjudge the
market and can only fill half your apartments. Typically many expenses
will remain constant (e.g., real estate tax). If the mortgage terms are the
same as in the last example, but revenues drop to $100,000:

Tax		*Cash*	
Revenues	$100,000	Revenues	$100,000
Less expenses	− 75,000	Less expenses	− 75,000
deprec. (SL)	− 50,000	interest	− 45,000
interest	− 45,000	amort.	− 25,000
Tax loss	$(70,000)	Cash loss	$(45,000)

No doubt you have sheltered a healthy portion of your loss. But there
still *is* a cash loss that must be paid. And supposing this taxpayer has
been unlucky "all over" and has no other income, or just a little income,
against which to offset the tax loss? No more benefit from the tax shelter.
These are the elements of imminent bankruptcy.

Leveraging can aggravate the situation. Suppose in the above situation accelerated depreciation and a larger mortgage were combined to
make a highly leveraged package. The tax shelter might remain the same
or might be higher, but so would both the tax loss and cash loss in
absolute terms. A taxpayer facing liquidity problems (which might be

expected here, since less personal cash and more bank money initially was put up) would be in more serious trouble.

The taxpayer using tax shelters can die a slow death as well as a sudden one. You will recall that the continued success of a deal using leverage (as almost all do) depends on depreciation exceeding amortization. Were straight line depreciation to be used while amortization is constant, the tax shelter would continue until the asset was used up (assuming depreciation starts out higher than amortization). But this arrangement is seldom used, since the high early yields from the 175 percent declining balance method of depreciation are so inviting and the initial payments of a constant amortization mortgage may be onerous. If the initially attractive alternative is taken, however, what happens? The amount of depreciation decreases each year while (with constant payment mortgage) amortization increases each year. Either alone, or both in combination, yield a formula leading to a collision. Depreciation will not stay higher than amortization forever. Consider a $900,000 asset depreciated over 18 years with 175 percent declining balance depreciation subject to an 18-year, $450,000 mortgage with constant amortization. Amortization and depreciation will be:

Year	Depreciation	Amortization
1	81,000	54,000
2	81,000	54,000
3	72,000	54,000
4	63,000	54,000
5	63,000	54,000
6	54,000	54,000
7	45,000	54,000

After the sixth year, the tax shelter runs out. A taxpayer faced with an evaporated tax shelter, and hence with more taxable income than cash income, should consider three options:

(1) Sell or exchange the property. As noted earlier in this chapter, this will involve capital gains considerations. But more practically, no one may be willing to buy the property.

(2) Switch from declining balance depreciation to straight line depreciation. This will at least postpone the evaporation of the tax shelter, and may prevent it altogether if the constant straight line depreciation exceeds constant mortgage amortization. Thus, the tax shelter will typically be much less advantageous than it was in earlier years. In the example above, the IRS rate table switches to straight line depreciation; the tax shelter still disappears.

(3) Refinance the mortgage to decrease amortization payments.

> This can be done by obtaining a longer mortgage, so the proportion of principal due each year is smaller. But again, this option may confront practical difficulties. The mortgage market may be tight or the banks unwilling to take the new risk. Prepayment of the old mortgage may be impossible or expensive.

In short, the developer has to plan ahead to meet these risks as best he or she can.

To put together all these elements of a tax shelter, study the Sutton Townhouse case discussed below. It presents a problem in the factual context faced by a developer.

Keep in mind that when comparing the figures of various investment alternatives, an investor will want to look at the after-tax return on his original investment. To make all the figures correspond, the value of benefits or liabilities that arise in the future should be reduced to present value, or compounded to value at some common time in the future.

C. APPLYING THE CONCEPTS: THE SUTTON TOWNHOUSE CASE

◆ ADAPTED FROM PHILIP DAVID, URBAN LAND DEVELOPMENT
20, 23-26 (1970)

In June 1965, Mr. James Channing was considering the purchase of the Sutton Townhouse, a 13-story-plus penthouse luxury building on the "fashionable" East Side of Manhattan between 1st Avenue and Sutton Place. The brick and concrete structure, completed October 1961, has 171 centrally air conditioned rental apartments: 67 2½-room apartments; 27 3-room apartments; 31 3½-room apartments; 20 4-room apartments; 24 4½-room apartments; and 2 5-room apartments, for a total of 555 rooms. The building also has a 56-car garage, which is leased to a garage operator for five more years at a net annual rental of $20,000.

The building is situated on an irregular plot of 200 × 102 × 88, or approximately 18,970 square feet of land. Although the assessed value of the land for real estate tax purposes is $488,000, the actual cost of land in this area is over $60 per square foot, or $948,500, almost double the assessed valuation.

This building, with a gross rent roll of $537,960, was being offered for sale at $1,200,000 cash above the $2,400,000 balance of the first mortgage. The real estate broker assured Mr. Channing that the property

PHOTOGRAPH 18-1
Sutton Townhouse (1976)

could be acquired for $1,000,000 cash. The set-up projected a net cash flow of $121,089 before state and federal tax and before vacancies, repairs, and management expense, but after repayment or amortization of mortgage debt.

Mr. Channing felt that the location was excellent and would become even more valuable in the future, since the number of available sites for new apartment buildings in this area was rapidly dwindling while the demand for luxury, "walk to work" apartments located in a residential area was growing. In addition, the recent change in the New York City zoning laws requiring more costly "set backs" for new construction was expected to discourage new building in the near future. Any new buildings constructed would require higher rentals to justify the added construction cost.

The price of $3,400,000 ($1,000,000 cash plus assuming the $2,400,000 mortgage) at which he felt he could acquire this property should result in an increase in the assessed value of the property for real estate tax purposes. Since property in New York City was generally assessed at 80 percent of the actual value, the assessment should increase to $2,720,000, or $170,000 above the old assessment. At the prevailing tax rate of $4.52 per $100 of assessed value in New York City, the result would probably be a $7,700 increase in the real estate tax.

Mr. Channing provided the following recalculation of the expected cash flow:

Gross rental & income	$538,000
Less concessions, vacancies, and renting expenses	21,300
Net rental income	$516,700
Less operating expenses (fuel, payroll, real estate tax, etc.)	202,400
Less management expense	10,500
Less repairs and maintenance	25,000
Less additional real estate tax	7,700
Cash Flow	$271,100
Less principal payment	72,500
Less interest	142,000
Net:	$ 56,600

While a 5.6 percent cash flow on his $1,000,000 investment did not seem to justify even considering the property, Channing nevertheless felt that purchasing this high-grade property in a quality location at a yield of approximately 8 percent on a free and clear basis (before financing) was quite attractive. The 8 percent free and clear figure is the return on the full investment as though there were no mortgage. It was unlikely that he would be permitted to refinance the property before August 1, 1972 under the terms of the mortgage, but he was almost certain, on the basis of his experience, that after that date he could easily capture the entire amount of the amortization payments made on the mortgage, or about $800,000 (the original $2.6 million balance of the mortgage, less the $1.8 million balance on August 1, 1972), less a $54,000 prepayment penalty.

He also felt the high interest rate of 6 percent reflected the unknown nature and high risk of the property at the time the mortgage commitment was obtained, which was before construction on the building had begun. If the mortgage were repayable at this time, Mr. Channing felt a new mortgage with better terms would be available, probably with constant debt service of about 7 percent (interest rate plus principal amortization). This would allow the positive use of leverage, since the free and clear return was about 8 percent.

However, under the present mortgage the constant debt service was over 8 percent ($214,500 on $2,600,000 or 8.25 percent). In this case, of course, leverage had a negative effect on the return on equity. Channing's best estimate was that when he was permitted to refinance the mortgage under its terms in 1972, he would be able to arrange mortgage terms at no higher than constant payment of 7.5 percent with interest at 5.5 percent, or an annual debt service of $195,000 on a mortgage of $2,600,000. Obtaining a new mortgage for this amount in 1972 would mean that Mr. Channing would receive his prior amortization payments back; if the terms were better this would also increase the property's income and hence its sale value.

Figuring the income tax was not difficult. Mr. Channing took the estimated cash income, added back in amortization of the mortgage debt (a nondeductible expense) and subtracted depreciation (a noncash but deductible expense). The amortization portion of the $214,500 debt service the first year was $72,500, and would increase steadily as a decreasing portion of the debt service went toward interest payments.

The $3,400,000 cost of the property was divided between building — a depreciable asset — and land — a nondepreciable asset. For depreciation purposes, the division used by assessors for real estate tax purposes is normally employed. The $488,000 for the land represents only 19 percent of the total assessment of $2,550,000 for land and building, allowing Channing to depreciate the 81 percent or $2,750,000 of his purchase price that has been assigned as the cost of the building. The depreciation is figured over 15 years, as this property falls within the tax law's "15-Year Real Property" class, with the 175 percent declining balance method of depreciation, allowing a deduction of $330,000 for the first year ($2,750,000 × 12%).

The statement of income for tax purposes would be as follows:

Estimated Cash Income	$ 56,000
Plus: amortization of mortgage debt	72,500
Total Income	128,500
Less depreciation deduction (175 percent)	330,000
Tax Loss	($201,500)
Other Income Offset (for a 50% taxpayer)	$100,750

Of course, as the depreciation deduction declines and amortization payments increase over the years, a smaller tax loss will result, leading eventually to a tax liability.

Thus, the depreciation deduction exceeds the amortization expense through the thirteenth year, and therefore either creates a tax loss or shields part of the cash income from taxes through this period. In the fourteenth and fifteenth years, the income tax is payable on not only the cash income estimated at $56,000, but also on the excess of the amortization over depreciation.

Mr. Channing also expected the rental income per room to increase about 16 percent by 1972. Although expenses could also be expected to increase by about the same percentage, income was higher than expenses in dollar value, so the net effect would be an increasing cash flow generated by the property. Mr. Channing estimated this increase at about $8,000 per year, although he was aware this was somewhat conjectural. Six years of increases would provide a cash flow of $104,000 in the seventh year.

Channing was thinking of selling the property after the seventh year, primarily because decreasing depreciation would be cutting into tax benefits by then. The best indicator of the cash price Channing could get was the "capitalized" value of the income coming from the asset. (A prospective purchaser would judge how much to pay for the asset by taking the return in dollars and projecting — capitalizing — what the total price should be for a given desired return on investment. Note that this assumes that the purchaser would be interested in the mortgage and how much it had been paid off *only* as this affected debt service, and not as representing equity in the asset. Does this make sense?) Capitalized at 8 percent, and assuming a cash flow of $104,000 per year, Channing calculated a cash sale price of $1,300,000 for the asset, plus assumption of the mortgage. A broker's fee of $75,000 would have to be deducted from this.

Even better than just selling the building with its existing mortgage after seven years would be refinancing (retiring the old mortgage and getting a new one) and then selling. Refinancing would have two benefits.

(1) Channing thought he could get a new mortgage in 1972 for the same amount as the old one ($2,600,000). By 1972, he would have paid about $605,000 amortization on the old mortgage; retiring the old mortgage principal ($1,795,000) and receiving proceeds of $2,600,000 from a new mortgage would allow him to recover more than the amortization he had paid. Channing thought it would not be difficult to persuade a bank to give a new mortgage as large as the old one, since the building was kept in good condition.

(2) As mentioned above, Channing thought he could get a mortgage with better terms in 1972. The better terms would mean a smaller annual debt service — estimated at $19,500 per year less, which would increase cash flow by the same amount. With a larger cash flow of $123,500 (the $104,000 projected 1972 cash flow plus added benefit from

the better mortgage terms) capitalized at 8 percent, Channing calculated a cash sale price of $1,543,750 for the asset, plus assumption of the (new) mortgage. The broker's fee of $75,000 and prepayment penalty of three percent of unretired principal would have to be deducted.

Under either the sale or refinance-sale options, capital gains taxes would have to be paid at the time of sale. (This was before the enactment of the recapture provisions.)

You should note the risks involved in this transaction as revealed with the actual passage of time. For instance, how would today's high interest rates, high fuel costs, or enactment of the recapture provisions affect the investment?

Notes

1. Ignored in the Sutton Townhouse case is attention to the people who live there. The case focuses on the building only as a vehicle for investor income, but of course the justification (if there is one) for the various public subsidies of Channing is that the supply of housing is increased. Yet most of the apartments in Sutton Townhouse carried rents above $4,000 per year in the late 1960s. Subsidizing Channing provides housing for persons below the national median income only on some version of a "trickle-down" theory, which would allege that the Sutton residents vacate other premises into which move aspiring Suttonites, and so forth.

Of course federal, state, and local government intervenes in the housing market in various other ways. You saw some of them in Parts 2 and 3. Also, a large amount of residential construction is financed with mortgages insured by the Federal Housing Administration or the Veterans Administration. The terms and conditions of these programs had a great deal to do with the nature of the suburbanization phenomenon that dominated American life in the quarter century after World War II. In particular FHA and the VA were at best neutral, and often hostile, toward racial and economic integration and toward housing for nonwhites generally. Early editions of the FHA Appraisers' Handbook forbade integration, and demanded that mortgage institutions follow suit.

More recently, the government has at certain times been willing to lower the price of new housing by lending money at interest rates lower than that at which it borrows. Finally, Section 8 of the Housing and Community Development Act of 1974 sought to direct federal housing benefits at the poor through two major components: programs using *existing housing* under which a local public agency issued certificates of eligibility to low-income families who "spent" the certificates on housing units of their choice; and *new construction or substantial rehabilitation* programs, under which a private developer received a contract commitment from Housing and Urban Development (HUD) to provide a subsidy for up to twenty years. Common to both were the following elements: a family was certified as eligible based on family size and income, including an imputed income from assets owned (minus depreciation); eligibility limits were established based on the median income in the area; maximum rent limits were set; the assistance the family received equaled the difference between the rent for the unit and the contribution the family was required to pay. This payment could not exceed 25 percent of their adjusted income and, in cases of very low-income families, 15 percent. Eligibility was recertified annually, and the subsidy payment adapted to reflect changes in the family's income. Finally, to receive assistance, a family had to sign a lease and the unit had to meet minimum standards.

The programs did not avoid major criticisms. The chief objections — aside from federal budgetary input and the usual red tape of endless bureaucratic review — were aimed at the inability of section 8 to produce new housing, primarily due to the separation of long-term financing from the subsidy. Note, too, that there were no tenants too poor for section 8 housing. Currently, Section 8 is being phased our in favor of a cash voucher scheme recommended by the President's Commission on Housing. In November 1983 Congress authorized such a program, but limited it initially to serve no more than 15,000 households.

2. G. Nelson and D. Whitman, Cases and Materials on Real Estate Finance and Development 545 (1976):

> We have generally subsidized poor families in newly constructed, rather costly housing built especially for the poor. Aside from the obvious political appeal of this approach to the homebuilders' lobby, construction unions, and associated groups, it does have some substantive advantages. It adds to the aggregate supply of housing, thus tending to avoid the inflationary impact which might be felt if poor families were given augmented purchasing power for housing but no additional housing were built. It arguably permits the deconcentration of central-city poverty as new subsidized housing is built in suburban areas (although suburbs frequently resist such housing, and there is little evidence that, even when built, it draws significant numbers of poverty families from the central urban core). Moreover, new construction has the capacity to produce a dramatic upgrading of older neighborhoods, especially when coupled with appropriate rehabilitation of existing housing there.
>
> On the other hand, tying subsidies to new housing units has a number of disadvantages. The most obvious is that new housing is more costly than existing housing; this fact will be reflected either in the form of higher costs to the government or as a limitation on the number of fortunate recipients of subsidized housing. Part of the higher cost of new housing will be recovered in the form of lower maintenance costs during the early years of its life, but not all will be. In addition, building enclaves of new housing for poor people has negative social consequences, both for the

residents (who find themselves surrounded by other families with economic and social problems similar to their own, and thus are unlikely to
learn much that will help them improve their lot), and for the neighbors of
the project (who are likely to resist construction of a "gilded ghetto" which
they suspect will destroy their property values and educational system
while raising their property taxes to pay for additional municipal services).

D.   APPLYING THE CONCEPTS: THE LIMITED PARTNERSHIP

The Sutton Townhouse situation shows some of the elements relevant
to a developer considering a real estate investment. As the story illustrates, Channing creates, and then holds among his bundle of ownership interests, a valuable commodity called a "tax shelter." Channing
himself, if he has several such shelter deals and does not have other
large sources of income, cannot take full advantage of these deductions.
He is this encouraged to *syndicate:* to find persons in need of tax deductions (often professionals with a large annual income from salary or fees)
and sell them the shelter ("a piece of the action"), which is worth more
to them than to him. These individuals have little interest in being in the
real estate business. They would be happy to purchase shares of corporate stock. But except in special circumstances the tax code does not
permit a corporate shareholder to take annual losses against his or her
other income. Thus, a hybrid form has developed, combining corporate
and partnership features, which is now frequently used for real estate
syndications. The arrangement is called a *limited partnership.* It requires a
general partner, one or more individuals who manage the enterprise and
are personally liable for its responsibilities, and one or more *limited
partners* who are investors without the power to manage and who assume no liability beyond their initial commitment. (To keep personal
liability to a minimum, the general partner can even be a corporation!)
As the *Bassan* case suggests, there has developed a complicated syn-
thetic creature, as individualized a social animal as any of the feudal
property structures discussed in Parts 2 and 4, yet one apparently (for
the moment) appropriate to the needs of investors, managers, and the
IRS.

♦ BASSAN v. INVESTMENT EXCHANGE CORP.
83 Wash. 2d 922, 524 P.2d 233 (1974)

UTTER, Associate Justice. The appellants are limited partners in Auburn
West Associates, and the respondent Investment Exchange Corporation

is the sole general partner. This action was brought for an accounting and dissolution upon the theory that the general partner had, in purchasing land and selling it to Auburn West Associates, derived profits without the consent of the limited partners in breach of its fiduciary relationship. The cause was tried to the court which dismissed the action after hearing the evidence.

The controlling issue in this case is whether the partners consented to the profit made by the general partner in the sale of the Murakami property to the partnership. We find an absence of such consent in the record and reverse the trial court.

In 1964 Investment Exchange Corporation, a Washington corporation, formed Auburn West Associates as a limited partnership. The purpose of the partnership as stated in the articles of partnership was "[to] initially acquire, for investment, improve and hold for lease or resale, a tract of real property. The General Partner presently is the owner of interests in said real property. To additionally acquire from the General Partner such other adjacent and contiguous tracts as, in the sole determination of the General Partner, will enhance the Partnership properties and objectives."

The general partner was given broad discretion in the articles to manage the affairs of the partnership and they acknowledged the right of all partners, including the general partner, to engage in "and/or possess an interest in other business ventures of every nature, and description, independently or with others, including but not limited to the ownership, financing, leasing, operation, management, syndication, brokerage and/or development of real property; . . . " They also gave the general partner the right to have an interest in or be employed by another business which might deal with the partnership.

The articles provided that the general partner might devote such of its time as in its discretion is deemed necessary to the partnership affairs and business, and that it should be reimbursed by the partnership for all the costs and expenses which it incurred in connection therewith, in addition to its respective share of the profits of the partnership.

The partnership articles provided that 100 units of the partnership, consisting of 40 units as general partner and 60 units as limited partner totaling $100,000, should be given to the general partner as partial payment of the purchase price of the original piece of real property, the purchase price being $593,000. That price was greater than the acquisition cost to the general partner.

Each of the appellants owned one or more limited partnership units. The remaining 29 limited partners did not elect to join in the action.

The general partner annually mailed out a financial statement to the limited partners. These financial statements advised the limited partners of the price the partnership paid for the real estate purchased from the general partner. The limited partners were represented at the partnership council meetings by plaintiff Milton Grout and others.

The last transaction upon which the appellants claimed a right to receive the benefit of the profit made by the general partner was the Murakami property. All claims by the limited partners except that one were held barred by the statute of limitations.

The general partner had formed a real estate subsidiary and informed the limited partnership it intended to utilize this corporation as sales and purchase agent for partnership property. The court found the articles of limited partnership and prospectus had authorized the real estate subsidiary to retain commissions on sales and purchases. This subsidiary received a $24,500 commission from Murakami in the sale of the property in addition to the markup of $167,500 by the general partner.

The court found that in the issuance of the prospectus, the publication of financial statements and in its dealings with the appellant and its conduct of partnership affairs, the general partner made no false or fraudulent representations and did not engage in any improper conduct. It found no breach in its fiduciary obligations to the limited partners inasmuch as the price charged for the Murakami parcel was fair and the amount of profit made by the general partner was reasonable. There is no substantial dispute regarding the facts in this case and all of the claims prior to the Murakami transaction are barred by the statute of limitations. The validity of this transaction is our only concern in this appeal.

Under the Washington Uniform Limited Partnership Act, the general partner has all the rights and powers, and is subject to all the restrictions and liabilities, of a partner in a partnership without limited partners. He is therefore accountable to the limited partners as a fiduciary. The Washington Uniform Partnership Act requires every partner to "account to the partnership for any benefit, and hold as trustee for it any profits derived by him without the consent of the other partners from any transaction connected with the . . . conduct . . . of the partnership. . . ."

The partnership agreement does not provide consent by the limited partners to the general partner for a profit on the sale of the Murakami property to the partnership. The articles contain no provision setting forth the price to be paid for this property nor any method for determining such a price. Partners may include in the partnership articles practically any agreement they wish and if the asserted self-dealing was actually contemplated and specifically authorized with a method for determining, in advance, the amount of the profit it would not, ipso facto, be impermissible and deemed wrongful. Here, however, the partnership agreement is silent as to any formula to determine the general partner's profit.

The prospectus, from which it could be argued most earlier purchases by the partnership from the general partner were contemplated, does not mention the Murakami piece. It also fails to set forth a formula to determine the general partner's profit in either the anticipated purchases or in any future transactions by the general partner on behalf of the partnership. The articles of limited partnership merely state that five parcels, the Henack, Nelson, Coast No. 2, Belus and Coast No. 1 were to be acquired at a cost of $593,000 from the general partner. The prospectus disclosed that the general partner intended, as well, to acquire the Davis parcel for $50,000 but the articles and prospectus do not specifically describe any other anticipated acquisitions.

Neither the articles nor prospectus disclose the actual amount of the profit to be made by Investment Exchange Corporation in their resale of properties to the Auburn West Associates partnership. The only source of information to the limited partners on the profits by the general partner was an accounting footnote in the 1964 partnership financial statement issued after the limited partners had invested funds in the partnership, indicating that property acquired by Auburn West Associates for $642,342 had previously cost the general partner $459,000.

The only other report indicating the amount of profit to the general partner was found in a prospectus required by the Securities and Exchange Commission. This indicated that from May 1964 through December 1965, prior to the Murakami purchase, Auburn West Associates had acquired eight parcels of property from Investment Exchange Corporation for $749,250 which property had cost Investment Exchange Corporation $488,221.

An investigation of the separate transactions prior to the Murakami purchase showed no consistent percentage of profit taken by the general partner on these transactions. Of those parcels described in the prospectus to be acquired by the general partner, the highest profit received was $67,000 on a piece sold for $182,000 (the Henack parcel). The smallest was a $20,000 profit on a piece sold for $180,000 to the partnership (the Belus parcel). Of those properties not described in the prospectus, and purchased subsequent to those described in the prospectus, the highest profit was $80,000 on a piece sold for $108,750 to the partnership (the Layos parcel) and the lowest was $24,000 on a piece sold to the partnership for $50,000 (the Davis parcel).

The trial court found an understanding did exist that the general partner would acquire property and sell it to the partnership at a fair price and would realize a profit on the transaction. It did not and could not find that a formula existed or was agreed upon explicitly or inferentially that established a basis upon which the exact amount of this profit was to be determined. The limited partners, therefore, could only consent after the fact to whatever profit the general partner determined it should have as to a particular transaction. Because of this, although the limited partners may have consented after the fact to specific profits taken on previous transactions, this could not imply consent to the Murakami transaction because the limited partners could not know what the profit to Investment Exchange Corporation was until after the sale closed.

No consent may be implied from the conduct of the limited partners regarding Murakami after they were informed of the profit. The formal action of Investment Exchange Corporation adopting the $167,500 profit was on November 15, 1969, and suit was brought on November 26, 1969 by appellants.

Where consent is lacking, the general partner is held under RCW 25.04.210, as a trustee, to account to the partnership for any profits derived by it. That standard, by the terms of the statute, is not whether the general partner acted fairly and reasonably, but whether it acted as a fiduciary.

The benefit of this standard is nowhere more apparent than in a limited partnership of this nature. The articles give the general partner the authority to conduct "any and all of the business of the Partnership. . . ." Once the limited partner has joined the partnership he has no effective voice in the decision-making process. He must, then, be able to rely on the highest standard of conduct from the general partner. Any deviation from this must be clearly stated in terms that would give the limited partner the option of deciding whether or not, in the first instance, to join the partnership.

The duty of loyalty resulting from a partner's fiduciary position is such that the severity of a partner's breach will not be questioned. The question is only whether there has been any breach at all.

This is to be distinguished from questions related to the use of business judgment of a partner in partnership affairs. Here the degree of care required is one of reasonableness, or in some jurisdictions, of good faith. This is the standard the trial court apparently applied.

This case does not involve the issue of whether the general partner is entitled to make a profit for use of its expertise. Compensation may be provided for the general partner by specific consent of the parties. There is also no issue about the general partner's right to be reimbursed for its expenses. Article 8, section 2 of the partnership articles provides that the general partner shall be reimbursed for all the costs and expenses it incurs in the devotion of its time to the partnership business.

Investment Exchange Corporation did not act in a fiduciary capacity regarding the profits it obtained in the Murakami transaction. Consent was not given by the appellants as to the profit taken in that transaction and Investment Exchange Corporation should be held accountable to the partnership for the profits it there realized. This will result in the establishment of a common fund for the benefit of the partnership. The expense of legal services, including counsel fees, is a proper charge against the common fund so preserved or protected.

The judgment is reversed and remanded to the trial court to determine counsel fees.

ROSELLINI, Associate Justice (dissenting). The majority in this case has overturned the finding of the trial court that it was the understanding and agreement of the parties to the limited partnership agreement that the general partner would buy land and would resell it to the partnership at a reasonable profit to itself. In doing so, it has not made so bold as to assert that there was no substantial evidence to support this finding. The trial court found that this agreement, while not expressed in the articles of limited partnership, was established by the evidence showing the course of dealing between the general partner and the limited partners over a period of years. . . .

The agreement which the trial court found to exist in this case is not an extraordinary one. It is generally the rule that, where there is an otherwise enforceable contract to purchase property and the price is not agreed upon, the court will determine the price upon the basis of the fair value of the property. . . .

It is not denied by the majority that the articles of partnership provided no method of compensating the general partner for its expertise and efforts in acquiring the properties for the partnership, and that unless the general partner could make a profit on the sale of properties to the partnership, its services would be bestowed gratuitously. It suggests no reason why the general partner would have been willing to give the partnership the benefit of these services without compensation.

It is true that the general partner was entitled to a share of the profits of the partnership as owner of 100 units of the partnership. However, those profits were attributable to its investment and not to its services, which the trial court found to have been of considerable value. It appears that the services of the general partner were necessary to achieve the partnership purposes.

◆ HAYES & HARLAN, CAVEAT EMPTOR IN REAL
ESTATE EQUITIES
50 Harv. Bus. Rev. No. 2, at 86, 92-93 (March-April 1972)

In the course of studying real estate development and financing for several years, we have interviewed dozens of business executives, entrepreneurs, and Wall Street financiers. Our conclusion is that many corporate developers and individual investors are insufficiently aware of all the ramifications of their real estate decisions.

The main reason for their shortsightedness is the emphasis that the real estate industry and Wall Street place on the tax-shield benefits of investment in this field. Unless the responsible industry leaders and investment advisers rededicate themselves to selling the genuine elements of value in projects rather than selling the often-illusory tax shields, a collapse of confidence in real estate investment similar to that of the 1950s is in the offing. This will, in turn, speed the exodus of important corporate and personal financing resources from the field. . . .

Obviously, both the seller and buyer have a vital stake not only in the final price but also in the terms of a real estate transaction. While every deal should, of course, be subjected to . . . analysis, . . . it is not always certain just who, if anyone, is doing it. Let us consider each participant:

The investor — Our investigation indicates that investors are not usually doing it for themselves; most of the new wave of investors are relatively unsophisticated in real estate. But even if they were analyzing each property, in many deals the investors are too numerous and too dispersed to exert much influence on the complex development of the project proposal. They are limited to simply accepting or rejecting the finished package.

Moreover, investors tend to infer a stamp of approval on a proposal which bears the name of a well-known developer, lender, or packager. Our interviews with a large sample of investors indicate that the more recognizable the name of the "sponsor," the more sophisticated the financial analysis they assume he has made.

The developer — He is not always doing a detailed analysis either. He often relies on the first-mortgage lender to signal the attractiveness of a proposed project by his decision on whether to advance the mortgage money and, if he decides to, by the amount as related to the project cost. Further, the developer is more frequently "leaning on" the financial packager to indicate to him the amount for which the finished project can be resold. On the basis of these assurances from lender and packager, the developer may feel he has eliminated most of his market risk and with this "closed transaction" can dispense with further economic and market analysis.

This may be shortsighted, however, because even if the loan is granted and the packager successfully syndicates the deal, the developer is likely to remain economically tied up in the project after the "sale" in one or more of the forms we mentioned earlier. At the very least, his reputation is riding on the outcome.

The lender — If the basis for developing the project is the approval of the capital sources, is the prospective lender doing the analysis? Our interviews indicate he is doing *an* analysis, but it is not one an investor should act on since it seldom identifies for the equity investor what *his* risks are. The lender focuses on the prospective operating performance of the business, against which he measures the exposure of his first-mortgage money.

But the lender's and the investors' occupancy break-even points are not the same; the former's is perhaps 75 percent to 80 percent of capacity and the latter's is perhaps 90 percent of capacity where seller financing has been employed. Equity investors must carefully examine their own break-even points and exposure to the variability of the cash flows available to service their requirements. These variations are a function of the additional layers of financing burden beyond the first-mortgage lender's exposure.

Incidentally, since lenders are increasingly taking equity positions in conjunction with their mortgage loan extensions, they too should be analyzing the equity investors' financing risks. Their frequent failure to do it may be attributable to the notion that equity participation is a "free ride," so detailed risk analysis of that additional position is unnecessary.

The packager — If neither the developer nor the lender typically analyzes the project from the investors' viewpoint, is the financial packager performing this service? This should, of course, be his first step. Conscientious analysis would position him to negotiate with the seller on firm ground — instead of reacting to the price and other terms established by the developer. If he did the analysis, he would serve the investors' interest as well as his own.

However, the incentives, the economic environment, and human nature combine to influence the packager to act merely as a broker between investors and developer, thus earning his immediate commission. For the packager with questionable integrity, the great current interest in real estate tax shelter is ideal. The nature of the investment delays adequate assessment of the quality of a project for two to four years. This creates ripe conditions for packagers to exploit the investor euphoria, make their money, and leave the business — to be replaced by a new wave of middlemen.

Unlike the stock market, where "performance" is quickly measured, real estate requires time for the project to be constructed (12 to 18 months), rented (6 to 12 months), and then stabilized. During this period a packager motivated strictly by the commission dollars (typically received when the outside investors contribute their cash) can often operate very profitably without being called to account. Few packagers remain tied to the project over the life of the investment.

E. APPLYING THE CONCEPTS: THE UDC

Much of the syndication industry in the early 1970s used state housing finance agencies as instrumentalities. Such agencies were "the only game in town" during that period of mortgage capital famine. State agencies were also a partial answer to the acknowledged inability of the federal government to address itself, by means of a broad national program, to the diverse and differing needs and markets of the nation's urban areas. The most famous such agency was New York's Urban Development Corporation (UDC). It issued tax-exempt bonds secured by the "moral obligation" of the state. The corporation was also empowered to receive federal subsidies and to lend money to developers, including first mortgages for up to 95 percent of total project cost. In addition, UDC could obtain land by compulsory process, could override local zoning and building codes, could grant exemptions from local real estate taxes, and could develop industrial estates, commercial properties, and new communities. Underlying this vast sweep was UDC's distinctive ability to initiate projects on its own, when and where it chose, rather than responding to proposals by private developers.

UDC's "basic purpose," as stated in the prospectus it issued when it sold $200 million of 6 percent general revenue bonds in 1973, was

> to deal more effectively with problems of physical deterioration, economic stagnation, unemployment, shortage of housing and lack of civic facilities that confront the State, its municipalities and its citizens. Rather than being limited to any single area of need, such as housing or community facilities, UDC's purpose encompasses a broad range of problems. It can plan and carry out projects to supply housing for low, moderate and middle income families; to redevelop blighted areas; to assist industrial and commercial development in areas of unemployment and blight; to provide needed educational, cultural, community and other civic facilities; and, though a combination of these activities, to develop new communities.

It was also "a fundamental principle of UDC, enunciated in the Act, to encourage maximum participation of the private sector of the economy and the use of private financing in developments which it sponsors."

As of May 1973, UDC had 13 projects under construction on sites to which it had not yet gained title. Moreover, two parcels (with a total development value of $11,300,000) were on land acquired from the Penn-Central just before the railroad entered reorganization proceedings. The prospectus acknowledged that federal subsidies "are essential to the economic feasibility of most UDC residential projects":

> Interest subsidies generally have been made available to UDC in accordance with the following procedure. An application for such assistance for each UDC project is submitted by UDC to HUD and processed by HUD to determine whether the project for which assistance is requested meets various statutory and administrative requirements ("preconditions for assistance"). These preconditions for assistance relate principally to environ-

mental conditions in the area of the project, the comparability of the subsidy cost per unit of the UDC project to the subsidy cost per unit of "comparable" projects on which mortgages are insured by HUD, the marketability of the project and the impact of the project on housing opportunities for minority groups. During the course of this processing HUD determines whether to make subsidy funds available for the project and, if the determination is affirmative, issues administrative reservations or allocations for the required subsidy funds. Such reservations or allocations, referred to herein as administrative assurances of fund availability, are not contractual commitments, and in the event that such an administrative assurance is issued prior to a determination by HUD that all preconditions for assistance have been satisfied, such preconditions must be satisfied before a binding subsidy contract is signed. . . .

The Federal government in January 1973 announced a temporary moratorium on new commitments for Federal housing assistance, and indicated that existing Federal housing assistance programs will be reexamined during the period of the moratorium and may be substantially revised, replaced by new programs or conceivably terminated. UDC has administrative assurances of interest reduction subsidies covering some of its residential projects which may start construction in calendar 1973. Except for such projects, UDC is not presently in a position to determine reliably how the moratorium will in the immediate future affect the availability of Federal subsidies needed for its low and moderate income residential projects now in planning that require such assistance for feasibility. Neither can UDC at this time reliably predict the nature and scale of future Federal housing assistance programs, if any, and the longer range effect of such programs on the availability of Federal assistance for UDC's future housing program.

EXCERPTS FROM THE LIMITED PARTNERSHIP AGREEMENT OF HARBORVIEW ASSOCIATES: [The Harborview partnership was formed by a developer and his investors to construct a large apartment complex in downtown Buffalo. In addition to the rights among the partners, as set out in the *Bassan* case, modified to meet the special situation of constructing subsidized housing, there are other provisions that deal with the special relation with UDC, within whose overall scheme this project must be set.

As you read the materials, consider the following:

a) Who owns Harborview Houses?

b) How are the risks and profits allocated as between the public and private sectors?

c) What did the State of New York gain from participating in this project? The United States? At what cost?]

ARTICLE I: DEFINED TERMS

. . . "Annual Distribution" means an amount equal to six percent of Private Investment Funds during the Supervisory Period. . . . [T]he

Annual Distribution will be the maximum amount of Cash Flow which may be distributed annually to the Partners. . . .

"Estimated Project Cost" means $7,147,368. . . .

"Supervisory Period" means . . . continuing until the later of (a) repayment of principal of, and interest and other charges on, the Mortgage or (b) the 20th anniversary of the Construction Completion Date. . . .

ARTICLE IV: PARTNERS; CAPITAL

. . . No Limited Partner shall be liable for any debts, liabilities, contracts or obligations of the Partnership. A Limited Partner shall only be liable to make payments of his Capital Contribution as and when the same are due hereunder. . . .

The aggregate Capital Contributions of all Limited Partners shall be 1,100,000 Dollars. . . .

ARTICLE VI: GENERAL PARTNERS

In order to assure the fulfillment of its responsibility to UDC, as set forth in Section 4.1 of the Equity and Regulatory Agreement, the Housing Company, throughout the Supervisory Period, shall retain the right and shall have the duty to UDC, solely upon the direction of UDC, to take over and assume all powers, rights and authorities of the Managing General Partner with respect to the development, construction, manage-

PHOTOGRAPH 18-2
Harborview Apartments (1976)

PHOTOGRAPH 18-3
Harborview Apartments against the Buffalo skyline

ment, operation and maintenance of the Project and, thereafter, to act as the Managing General Partner in accordance with instructions from UDC, provided that UDC may direct the Housing Company to take such action only upon 20 days' notice (which notice may run concurrently with any period of time required to perfect any Event of Default, as defined in the Equity and Regulatory Agreement) to the Housing Company and to the Managing General Partner. . . .

. . . For administrative services . . . the Partnership shall be required to pay a salary of $100,000 to the Managing General Partners [and] a total fee equal to the Capital Contributions of the Limited Partners less [certain contingencies plus $218,684]. [There was also a Developer's Fee of $131,202.]

ARTICLE X: PROFITS AND LOSSES

All profits and losses . . . shall be allocated 95% to the Limited Partners and 5% to the General Partners. . . .

ARTICLE XII: ACCOUNTING

. . . [T]he Partnership shall elect to use . . . accelerated depreciation methods. . . .

Note

In February 1975, the unthinkable happened: The UDC ran out of funds and for a few days actually defaulted on $135 million worth of debt to the big New York banks. "It is absolutely essential," said the executive vice-president of Morgan Guaranty, "that the state take responsibility and admit paternity" for $1.1 billion of UDC "moral obligation" bonds. It did. Had the New York legislature not acted, what would have been the consequences for the limited partners of Harborview Associates? For the general partner? For residents of Harborview Houses?

VI ◆ SHARED USE

What is property?

Blackstone could conceive of a landowner whose domain was complete within its boundaries and up to the heavens. He thus defined property as a "sole and despotic dominion." But, as the materials in Part 1 show, even in Blackstone's day the definition was false. During the nineteenth century, the idea of sole dominion came gradually to seem quite absurd. For example, statutory acknowledgment of the wife's partial control of family property — which occurred first in the nineteenth century, but has been the subject of important recent developments — denied the husband's absolute dominion and instead gave him a share of a legal construct called a concurrent estate.

Also, as living conditions became more dense, landowners realized that they could only make full use of their portion of the earth if they could receive assurances about the compatible use of neighboring land. To obtain such assurances, owners were willing to give commitments regarding their property. Gradually, the common law barriers to such agreements had to give way, usually through legal artifice and technical distinction, but sometimes by honest rejection of archaic doctrine. The array of legal devices for enforcible private restriction of land use — easements, licenses, covenants, conditions, servitudes — is considered in this part.

In the twentieth century, institutions of government have found it necessary or desirable to pursue majority preferences by limiting through zoning and land use planning the ways in which land can be exploited by individual owners. Here too legal imagination has been required in the search for procedures that give adequate incentive to the private owner while reflecting relevant technical and democratic values through mechanisms of public choice.

Concurrent estates, private contractual restrictions, and zoning are now vital areas of legal practice and legal change, as our increasing interdependence makes shared use a dominant ingredient in the very nature of property. In this part, you can wrestle with the remnants of outdated doctrine and, more interestingly, observe some of the unexpected consequences of recent reform.

The policy questions faced by attorneys involve crucial public issues: the nature of the family, racial and economic integration, environmental protection, planned growth. Underlying these immediate issues are standard conceptual and ideological considerations: evaluating the strengths and weaknesses of the economic market; devising processes for fair and efficient democratic decision; the role of experts and the place of technology; the appropriate pace of social change; and, overriding all else, the extent of our commitment to equal justice and how that commitment is to be fulfilled. Part 6 raises these issues and explores some of them in depth.

19 ◆ CONCURRENT ESTATES

A. JOINT TENANCIES AND TENANCIES IN COMMON

When John and Mary Ambitious bought their house, they might have sought to write a contract detailing the rights and obligations of each with respect to the premises. Instead, as people usually do, they took title together, probably unaware that they were placing themselves in a concurrent estate — one of several categories gradually worked out at common law to govern the relations of persons who share the possession of real estate.

Joint tenants hold undivided shares in an entire parcel of land. Their possession is said to be "undivided" because each has a right to use the whole. Traditionally, creation of a joint tenancy has required "unity" of time, title, interest, and possession, meaning that the tenants must take the same type and duration of interest at the same moment from the same instrument and that each must have a right to the use of the whole. If any of the four unities is destroyed, *partition* occurs: sale of the property, and distribution of the proceeds among the former joint tenants. If one of the tenants dies during the course of the tenancy, the other has rights of *survivorship,* and becomes sole owner of the property. If there are three joint tenants and one dies, the other two then own as joint tenants.

Tenants in common also hold undivided shares in land, but only one unity is required, that of possession. Thus tenants in common can take different interests in the same property at different times from different sources. Like a joint tenant, a tenant in common can force partition. However, there is no right of survivorship, so that when one tenant in common dies, his or her share passes to his or her heirs or devisees, who take over the decedent's place in the shared possession.

does not go to other tenants

At common law, two or more persons who bought land together without specifying the terms of their occupancy became joint tenants. Modern statutes in virtually every jurisdiction have reversed the presumption, so that parties who do not express their desires now become tenants in common.

Consider New York Estates, Powers and Trusts Law §6-2.2 (1976):

"(a) A disposition of property to two or more persons creates in them a tenancy in common, unless expressly declared to be a joint tenancy. . . .

"(e) Property passing in intestacy to two or more persons is taken by them as tenants in common."

◆ McKNIGHT v. BASILIDES
19 Wash. 2d 391, 143 P.2d 307 (1943)

SIMPSON, Chief Justice. In the year 1901 appellant married Alice King in the city of Chicago. At the time of her marriage to appellant, Mrs. King had two children by a former marriage, Alice, now Alice McKnight, and Fred W. King. Defendant Ruth Allison is the child of appellant and his wife Alice. During the year 1907 the family moved to Seattle, where appellant engaged in business and acquired two pieces of real property, one known in the evidence as the "little house," located at 326 West Forty-first Street, and the other, known as the "big house," located at 5203 First Avenue Northwest, both in the city of Seattle.

Alice Basilides died intestate, November 20, 1929, and the estate has never been probated. Appellant has been in possession of both pieces of property since the death of his wife, and has paid all the taxes and assessments levied against the property. In addition, he made certain improvements upon the real estate. He rented the "little house" and occupied the "big house" as his home. During the time from the death of his wife, Alice, until a few days prior to the beginning of this action, appellant never made any claim to respondents that he was the sole owner of the property, nor did respondents make any claim to the property during the same period of time. . . .

Appellant contends that the evidence shows him to have been in actual, uninterrupted, open, notorious, hostile and exclusive possession of the property under claim of right since November 20, 1929, and for that reason he has acquired title by adverse possession.

The general rule relative to securing title to property owned in common by adverse possession is found in the following comprehensive statements:

Since acts of ownership which, in case of a stranger, would be deemed adverse and per se a disseisin, are, in cases of tenancies in common, susceptible of explanation consistently with the real title, they are not necessarily inconsistent with the unity of possession existing under a cotenancy. For this reason, whether the acts of ownership will be such as to break and dissolve the unity of possession, constitute an adverse possession as against the cotenants, and amount to a disseisin, depends upon the intent with which they are done, and upon their notoriety and essential character. Accordingly, it is a general rule that the entry of a cotenant on the common property, even if he takes the rents, cultivates the land, or cuts the wood and timber without accounting or paying for any share of it, will not ordinarily be considered as adverse to his cotenants and an ouster of them. Rather, such acts will be construed in support of the common title. Mere exclusive possession, accompanied by no act that can amount to an ouster of the other cotenant, or give notice to him that such possession is adverse, will not be held to amount to a disseisin of such cotenant. Mere intention, unannounced, is not sufficient to support a claim of adverse title. Although the exclusive taking of the profits by one tenant in common for a long period of time, with the knowledge of the other cotenant and without any claim of right by him, may raise a natural presumption of ouster upon which the jury may find the fact to exist, if it satisfies their minds, yet the law will not, from this fact, merely raise a presumption of such ouster. . . .

1 Am. Jur., Adverse Possession, §54. . . .

. . . We therefore hold that the evidence in this case was not sufficient to establish the claim that appellant made any adverse claim to the property, and that the facts indicate that his actions in living in the "big house" and collecting rents from the "little house" were not such outward acts as would amount to adverse possession. . . .

The trial court compelled appellant to make an accounting. In so doing, appellant was given credit for repairs, improvements, taxes and insurance in the amount of $4,753.46. He was then charged for the use of the properties between November 20, 1929, and May, 1943, in the total sum of $8,001. Respondents were given a judgment in the sum of $1,083.18 for their share of the rental use of the two properties, and the judgment was made a lien upon the interest that appellant owned in the properties. A portion of the income received consisted of rentals for the "little house," which was sold April 1, 1938, on a partial payment sales contract. Since the date of the sale, appellant was charged a reasonable value for its use. The charge for the use of the "big house" was fixed at an amount which the court found from testimony to be the reasonable rental value thereof. The record discloses that the income was at all times sufficient to pay the taxes and other expenses. The improvements were of a minor nature and did not to any appreciable extent enhance the rental or sales value of the property. Appellant was responsible for and was properly held to an accounting of the rents he received from the "little house."

The charge for the occupancy of the "big house" and the reasonable rental value of the "little house" subsequent to its sale presents a more difficult problem. . . .

The last expression of this court upon the question under discussion is found in In re Foster's Estate, 139 Wash. 224, 246 P. 290. The facts in that case were that one John Foster was the owner of an undivided one-half interest in real estate upon which he made his home. The other half was owned by his children. After the death of his wife, Foster remarried and subsequently died. The surviving spouse brought an action against the children for taxes, insurance, and improvements made upon the property. The evidence showed that the taxes and insurance had been paid by Foster, and that his widow had made a number of improvements on the property. The trial court denied the right to show the rental value of the use of the premises occupied by the widow from the time of the death of Foster. This court reversed the case and in so doing stated:

> Objection is also made that the court refused to allow recovery for the rental value of the premises occupied by Adeline Foster from the time of decedent's death. If it is sought to render a money judgment in favor of Adeline Foster for improvements made from her separate funds, there should be offset against this one-half of the reasonable rental value of the premises from the time of decedent's death. The court was of the opinion that the claim for rent should be filed in the matter of the estate. But the occupancy by Adeline Foster of the premises in question was not an occupancy as administratrix. It was personal. As to the one-half belonging to the estate she may be required at the time of her final account as administratrix to render an account as to its rental value if the circumstances justify, but, as to the one-half belonging to the other cotenant, her use is a personal one, which can be offset against any claim that she has against the cotenants.
>
> The cause is reversed, with instructions (1) to ascertain if the improvements made upon the premises were necessary, or to what extent they enhanced the value thereof; (2) to ascertain the reasonable value of the rental of the premises, and allow recovery for one-half of that amount. . . .

No practical or reasonable argument can be advanced for allowing one in possession to reap a financial benefit by occupying property owned in common without paying for his personal use of that part of the property owned by his cotenants. The fairest method in cases in which the cotenant occupies and uses common property, instead of renting it out, is to charge him with its reasonable rental value. Of course there would be an exception to this holding in cases where the income resulted from improvements placed upon the property by the cotenant in possession. Appellant used the "big house" as a home for many years, and it was proper that he be charged with the reasonable rental value of that use and made to account to his cotenants for their share of that rental value. However, appellant should not be charged with the rental value of the "little house" after its sale, for the reason that he did not receive any rent, nor did he occupy or use it in any way.

MALLERY, Justice (dissenting). "The generally accepted rule is that at common law one tenant in common who occupies all or more than his proportionate share of the common premises is not liable, because of such occupancy alone, to his cotenant or cotenants for rent or for use and occupation." 62 C.J. Tenancy in Common, P. 446, Sec. 64.

This rule accords well with the rule that in the absence of an ouster the cotenant's possession is not adverse. In the face of the presumption of permission, the hostile character of the possession must fail. Therefore the majority opinion rightly holds that appellant's claim to title by adverse possession cannot prevail.

By the same token, since the adverse possession failed by reason of the permissive nature of his possession, he cannot be held liable for rent for the use of the "big house." His cotenants deliberately let him "carry the burden" during the depression years. They cannot now deny their permission without establishing his hostile possession. Of course, the rentals for the "little house" were received in trust for his cotenants.

Appellant has been charged in the accounting with his share of $8,001 of the rental value on the "big house" for the period beginning November 20, 1929, and ending May, 1943, which is over thirteen years.

Rem. Rev. Stat, §157 limits an action for the rents and profits or for the use and occupation of real estate to a period of six years. He should have been charged nothing. Even a stranger to the title could have been held for only six years. I dissent.

Notes

1. In 1959 Minnie Johnson and her husband, George, purchased, in joint tenancy, a two-flat building in Chicago. In 1966, George, without telling Minnie, quit-claimed his interest in the building to his attorney, who then reconveyed it in joint tenancy to George and Rosie Johnson, George's daughter by a previous marriage. George died in 1967. Who now owns the building?

When George conveyed to his lawyer, he forced partition, making the lawyer and Minnie tenants in common. When the lawyer's share was then conveyed to George and Rosie, the four unities of time, title, interest and possession were preserved, allowing them to hold as joint tenants an undivided one-half interest in the realty. By right of survivorship incident to a joint tenancy, Rosie became sole holder of that interest on George's death. The other undivided one-half interest had remained in Minnie after partition, leaving Minnie and Rosie as tenants in common. Johnson v. Johnson, 11 Ill. App. 3d 681, 297 N.E.2d 285 (1973).

Observe that a direct conveyance from George to himself and Rosie would have destroyed unity of time, and that the resulting tenancy in common would have meant that upon George's death, his share in the tenancy in common with Rosie would have passed through his estate. By playing the complicated game with his lawyer, George got the property out of his estate and to Rosie as surviving joint tenant. Thirty years ago, intricate legal requirements comparable to those that necessitated this fancy paperwork were struck down by the New Hampshire Supreme Court as "incomprehensible to laymen and in the twentieth century difficult of justification by the legal profession," and as "mak[ing] a fetish out of form." In so doing, the court noted, "It has been many years since the technicalities of real estate conveyancing have been much regarded here. Given an instrument signed and under seal, all the rest is determined according to the manifest intent of the parties . . . without regard to rules or titles coming down from feudal times." Therrien v. Therrien 94 N.H. 66, 46 A.2d 538 (1946), quoting from Newmarket Mfg. v. Town of Nottingham, 86 N.H. 321, 168 A. 892 (1933).

2. When a husband killed his wife, he effected a severance of their joint tenancy, and so husband became tenant in common with heirs of his wife other than himself. Maine Savings Bank v. Bridges, 431 A.2d 633 (Maine 1981).

3. When two adjacent lots are owned separately but spanned by a single building, can the owner of one lot maintain partition? *Held:* No, in Burford v. Burford, 396 N.E.2d 394 (Ind. App. 1979). But one of four tenants in common of one of the parcels can force a sale of that parcel, and achieve his share of whatever that sale will bring.

4. Harms v. Sprague, 119 Ill. App. 3d 503, 456 N.E.2d 976 (1983), held that a joint tenancy was not severed by the attempt of one joint tenant to give a mortgage, although, of course, the surviving joint tenant's ownership was unencumbered by the mortgage lien that the deceased joint tenant had given.

5. Minonk State Bank v. Grassman, 103 Ill. App. 3d 1106, 432 N.E.2d 386 (1982), held that the unilateral action by one joint tenant conveying her interest from herself as a joint tenant to herself as a tenant in common was effective to sever the joint tenancy.

6. Spitalnik v. Springer, 59 N.Y.2d 112, 450 N.E.2d 670, 463 N.Y.S.2d 750 (1983), held that when a rental building converted to cooperative ownership, neither of two joint tenants could purchase acting alone, and so the right to buy shares in the cooperative corporation could only be exercised by the two joint tenants acting together.

◆ KLEINBERG v. HELLER
45 A.D.2d 514, 360 N.Y.S.2d 422 (1974)

LUPIANO, Justice. In this discovery proceeding commenced by the Executor of the Estate of Jessie Lang against Harriet Heller, survivor-tenant of a joint savings account, the survivor-tenant appeals from so much of the decree of the Surrogate's Court, Bronx County, entered April 24, 1974, which adjudged and decreed that Harriet Heller pay to the executor money she withdrew from the joint savings account in excess of her moiety during the lifetime of the decedent Jessie Lang.

The Surrogate observed as follows:

> Decedent died on March 31, 1972 at the age of 91. Until October, 1968, she occupied an apartment jointly with her daughter. In that month her daughter died and decedent continued to occupy the apartment alone until August 20, 1970. . . . From August 20, 1970 until her death decedent was a resident of a nursing home. . . . At a date which was never definitively established by either party at the hearing, decedent opened a savings account at the Bankers Trust Company with the respondent niece [Harriet Heller] as a joint tenant with right of survivorship. The testimony does suggest that this account was opened at sometime during 1969. Respondent [Harriet Heller] conceded that on August 31, 1970, she withdrew $1,094.90 from this joint account. . . . Respondent further conceded that in March, 1971, she withdrew the sum of $5,469.89, the then entire balance in the Bankers Trust Company account, and transferred it to an account in the name of herself and her husband, as joint tenants. All of the funds in the joint account were deposited therein by the decedent. Absolutely no evidence was adduced at the hearing to in any way impugn the presumption in favor of respondent's joint tenancy created by section 675 of the Banking Law.

The crucial issue in this proceeding is the effect of the withdrawal of more than one-half of the funds in a joint savings account during the lifetime of both joint tenants upon the surviving tenant who withdrew such funds. The well-reasoned and comprehensive analysis by Surrogate Sobel in Matter of Filfiley, 63 Misc. 2d 824, 313 N.Y.S.2d 793, is dispositive of this issue. In that case, it is declared:

> [t]here are no circumstances in which the survivor will be entitled to less than the whole fund where one of the tenants has withdrawn more than his moiety *and* the right of survivorship has vested in either one of them since a withdrawing joint tenant can only suffer a forfeiture to a survivor in whom that right has vested. In short, after a right of survivorship has vested, there should in legal theory never be a recovery of half the fund or the excess over the moiety. *The survivor must take all.* Only while both joint

tenants are still living may the recovery be for the excess over the moiety withdrawn.

Since more than a moiety is unilaterally inalienable by either joint tenant, withdrawal of the whole fund is a nullity. . . .

Accordingly, the statutory provision for a joint tenancy relationship in respect of joint bank deposits impels the conclusion that the surviving joint tenant, Harriet Heller, did not effect a termination of the joint tenancy in respect of the excess of her moiety. The decree should be reversed on the law, without costs of disbursements, and the petition dismissed.

◆ KLEINBERG v. HELLER
38 N.Y.2d 836, 345 N.E.2d 592, 382 N.Y.S.2d 49 (1976)

Order reversed with costs. . . .

FUCHSBERG, J., concurs in the following opinion. The phrase "joint tenancy," when applied to joint bank accounts, has different meanings in different jurisdictions, depending in part on whether its creation and consequences are regulated by common-law principles alone or are subject to particular statutes as well. Such accounts were intended, among other things, to make it easier to effect the transfer of property without the strictures attached to testamentary dispositions. It was intended also to limit the need to comply with technical common law and statutory requisites for gifts, trusts, joint tenancies or contracts. However, that quest for simplicity and certainty turned out to be elusive.

In New York which was the first State to pass a law authorizing payment to the survivor of funds deposited in a joint account, the controlling legislation ended up providing only some, not all, of the characteristics of such an account. One of these, created by the legislation itself, is that the opening of an account in the names of two people in facial form "to be paid or delivered to either, or the survivor of them" evinces an intention to create a "joint tenancy," thereby placing the burden of refutation on anyone who challenges it. That does not prevent a joint account from being attacked for fraud, undue influence or lack of capacity, all of which go to its inception, but the burden of proving such a claim still rests on the shoulders of whoever asserts it. In the present case, despite decedent's advanced age, no such claims were pressed, nor was any attempt made to overcome the prima facie evidence of intention to create such a tenancy.

Also spelled out by the statute itself is a right of survivorship. Though such right is inchoate, some decisions, followed by the majority below, have talked of it in terms of absolute inviolability. However, they overlook the uniquely hybrid genesis of the law applicable to joint tenancies in bank accounts, the fact that the maturing of the rights of survivorship which accompany them is subject to the contingency of the death of one of the tenants, and the fact that the analogy with joint tenancies in real property, the source of the law of joint tenancies, is more a convenient fiction than a fact, real property hardly having the physically separable character of money.

Experience indicates that most people who open such accounts, though lacking legal or business sophistication, do understand and intend some ultimate survivorship incident to a joint tenancy, at least with regard to funds remaining in such an account at the time of death. But they do not usually intend the perhaps more crucial fact that, from the moment of the creation of a joint account, a present unconditional property interest in an undivided one half of the moneys deposited devolves upon each tenant. Even when one of them is the sole donor of the fund, once such a moiety comes into existence it cannot be canceled unilaterally. That consequence is not directly stated in the statute. It results from an application of common-law principles of which most laymen are unaware. It follows that when the aunt opened the account here, the niece, *ipso facto*, gained title to half the fund. The niece's half interest was not merely a "presumed" one, as the Surrogate here suggested. It was as much hers as the remaining half was the aunt's, the latter's being no greater because she was the donor.

Since half of the account was her property, the niece had the right and power to alienate it. For either tenant had the right, during the lifetime of the other, to effectuate such an alienation by withdrawing up to the full amount of her moiety. And, if that is all she had withdrawn, the balance remaining in the account, though it represented the moiety of the aunt, would have remained subject to the niece's inchoate right of survivorship, despite the fact that the withdrawal of the niece's own moiety served to destroy her aunt's right of survivorship in it.

Recognition that such survivorship is destroyed is the product of case law. The statute itself makes no attempt to deal directly with such an event. And, the only way the aunt could have avoided the one-sidedness of the partial obliteration of her inchoate right of survivorship in the niece's moiety was by withdrawing her own half and, by so destroying what was left of the *res*, eliminating the niece's remaining right of survivorship as well.

It is also well established, again by judicial decree in the absence of statutory proviso, that, where a joint tenant withdraws more than his or her moiety, as was the case here, there is an absolute right in the other tenant, during the lifetime of both, to recover such excess. There is no proof the aunt made any effort to do so here; had she done so and recovered, the excess would have come into her possession as her personal property and not that of the joint tenancy. Then, unless she had decided to redeposit it in the original account, hardly likely under such circumstances, so much of her moiety as she had recouped would have been solely hers, free and clear of any inchoate right of survivorship in the niece. And when the aunt predeceased the niece, it is unquestioned that, like all the rest of the property of which she died possessed, it would have become part of the aunt's estate.

But suppose the aunt, during her lifetime, though reducing her claim against the niece to judgment, had not yet executed upon it or otherwise exercised a possessory right to the amount withdrawn? Should the result be any different? I think not. . . . Instead, the right of survivorship should be regarded as affected to the extent of the entire withdrawal and, without more, unavailable after the aunt's death as a ground for divesting her estate of its right to recover the amount of the excess withdrawal from the niece.

But that does not end the matter. The niece could successfully have resisted the turnover had the aunt consented to the withdrawal. In that event, she would have been acting in the aunt's right; the aunt's moiety would then, in effect, have to be regarded as withdrawn by the aunt herself. Such consent need not have been given in advance; it could have come by way of ratification. It need not have been express; it could have been implied. In short, agreement to the withdrawal could be found to have come about in any number of ways, though most often in such cases it is to be divined from circumstantial evidence of the intent of the one whose moiety was invaded. That intent, it should be made clear, however, speaks to the time of the invasion of the fund, not to the time of the creation of the account, though some of the relevant circumstances may very well be common to both events. . . .

Other factors which, absent more direct proof, appear to be among those available for consideration in such cases to determine whether the excess withdrawer's burden of proving consent has been met, are the duration, nature and closeness of the business, social or familial relationship between the tenants; the presence or absence of a habit of freely commingling their funds; significant revelations, if any, in the tenant's testamentary dispositions; the generosity, or lack of it, manifested by the survivor in his other *inter vivos* dealing with the decedent; the amounts involved; the pattern of withdrawals; their purpose and timing; the age and physical and mental condition of each at the time of the withdrawal; the source of the funds; the circumstances in which possession of the bankbook came into the hands of the survivor at the time of the withdrawal; decedent's ignorance or knowledge of the withdrawal and, if the latter, the length of time during which it existed; the protest or lack of protest against the withdrawal; the efforts, if any, to effect its return, considering of course, the absence or presence of opportunity to do so; and, highly important, whether the survivor was the donor.

There are those who prefer not to resort to such indices of agreement for the determination of such cases, favoring instead the supposed greater certainty of a rule under which inviolability of the right of survivorship to all funds withdrawn in excess of tenant's own moiety is maintained by the legal fiction of regarding the withdrawal as though never made and, therefore, a nullity. Under such a rule, followed here by the majority in the Appellate Division, death would serve to ratify a survivor's most excessive withdrawals, no matter how unconscionable. Whatever the appropriateness of a "survivor must take all" rule in the context of other types of joint tenants, its force is lost when applied to bank accounts created under section 675. It is preferable, I think, to leave open the area of indicated factfinding at least as to excess withdrawal cases such as the one before us here. Since, as already indicated, so many of these accounts are created as a kind of testamentary substitute, it is highly appropriate that we retain the greater flexibility which a rule directed to the ascertainment of intent provides, rather than a rule whose rigidity makes it more difficult to avoid harsh results. . . .

So tested, the case before us was not without its own factual texture. One of the two withdrawals involved had taken place when the aunt was 89, the other when she was 90. She did not appear to know of the latter one, which was by far the greater, until about a week before her death, when her accountant discovered it. That withdrawal was not shown to have been made in contemplation of death. In fact, it had been made about a year earlier. It was not made for the aunt's benefit, but solely to create a new account for the niece and her husband. Significantly, the niece's testimony before the Surrogate to the effect that the first withdrawal had been used to pay the nursing home for the benefit of the decedent did not find support in the information furnished by the home itself. It is also worth noting that the aunt's will, under which she bequeathed substantial assets to charity and designated another relative's husband as executor, made no mention of the niece at all.

These circumstances were sufficient for a factual determination as to whether the niece had sustained her burden of proof that the excess withdrawal was with the direct or implied consent of the aunt or had been ratified by her. Though the Surrogate found she had not met that burden, the Appellate Division's reversal was based solely on the law. Accordingly, on the foregoing analysis, the order of the Appellate Division should be reversed and the matter remitted for a review of the facts.

B. ESTATES BETWEEN SPOUSES

1. At Common Law

The common law presumed that married couples who took possession of real estate should not hold by either a tenancy in common or a joint tenancy. They took as *tenants by the entireties*.

[A]t common law a devise or conveyance to husband and wife created a tenancy by the entireties. The four unities of time, title, interest and possession necessary for a joint tenancy were also required for a tenancy by the entireties. In addition, a valid marriage had to be in existence at the time of the transfer. If all of these five requirements were met, a tenancy by the entireties arose unless the transferor manifested an intent that the grantees should hold as joint tenants or tenants in common.

Tenants by the entireties hold, it is said, *per tout et non per my*: individual interests in the estate are not recognized, in contrast with the joint tenancy. The estate can be severed and converted into a tenancy in common by divorce. It can be terminated by (1) transfer of each spouse's interest to a third party; (2) transfer of the interest of either spouse to the other; or (3) death of one spouse, in which case the survivor owns the entire undivided interest.

At common law, entireties property was under the exclusive control of the husband. He had the sole privilege of occupancy; he was entitled to all of the income; he could alienate these rights without his wife's consent; and his creditors could levy against them. As a practical matter, only the wife's right of survivorship was hers absolutely and free of unilateral disposition by her husband. This result was consistent with the other property incidents of the common law marital relationship — in fact, it was almost identical to the husband's right of *jure uxoris* in his wife's separate realty. [Johnston, Sex and Property: The Common Law Tradition, The Law School Curriculum, and Developments Toward Equity, 47 N.Y.U.L. Rev. 1033 (1972).]

The theoretical cornerstone for the wife's property rights (or absence thereof) was the relationship described as coverture: that the husband and wife were one person.

By marriage, the husband and wife are one person in law; that is, the very being or legal existence of the woman is suspended during the marriage, or at least is incorporated and consolidated into that of the husband; under whose wing, protection, and cover, she performs everything; and is therefore called in our law-french a *femecovert, foemina viro co-operta*; is said to be covert-baron, or under the protection and influence of her husband, her baron, or lord; and her condition during her marriage is called her coverture. [Blackstone, Commentaries on the Law of England 442 (1765).]

The explanations for this fictional unity range from biblical notions that husband and wife become "one flesh" (Genesis 2:24) to a kind of guardianship that arose upon utterance of the marriage vows, regardless of the actual capacities of the two parties. Whatever the explanation, the consequence was clear:

Substantively, she lost control and management of her real property to her husband; he did not have to account to her for the rents and profits, although he could not alienate them. In respect to her leasehold interests, she suffered an even worse fate; not only did her husband gain control of them upon marriage, but he could alienate them and keep the proceeds for himself. All of her chattels she owned at the time of marriage and those she acquired later became her husband's absolutely. . . .

In addition, as a result of her marriage a woman lost her power to transfer her own real property by an ordinary conveyance and, except in certain special cases, to contract with either her husband or third parties. . . .

At the same time, marriage did not represent a matter of all economic gain and no loss, for the husband. For one thing, the wife immediately upon marriage, became entitled to inherit a life estate in one-third of all lands of which her husband was seised at any time during the marriage and which her issue might have inherited. Though this was the right of inheritance, it vested in the wife upon marriage and thus reduced the husband's estate; it also tended to restrict the alienability of the husband's property during his lifetime, potential purchasers normally insisting upon the wife's relinquishment of her dower rights, as they were called. Moreover, the husband upon marriage acquired the obligation to support his wife and family. While this duty may have arisen partly in consideration of the wife's property acquired by the husband upon marriage, it was also in keeping with the concept of the husband's role as head and master of the family. [L. Kanowitz, Women and the Law 36-37 (1969).]

While legal scholars may have subscribed to Blackstone's reasoning that "even the disabilities which the wife lies under are for the most part intended for her protection and benefit: so great a favourite is the female sex of the laws of England," at least one contemporary author took a more realistic view: "It must be remembered that the point of honour which decrees that a man must not under any circumstances accept money from a woman with whom he is on certain terms, is of very modern growth, and is still tempered by the proviso that he may take as much as he likes or can get from his wife." Preface to Henry Fielding's Tom Jones. A century later, Ernestine Rose, an active member of the nascent American women's rights movement, provided a bitterly reasoned view of the legal status of married women:

At marriage she loses her entire identity, and her being is said to have become merged in her husband. Has nature thus merged it? Has she ceased to exist and feel pleasure and pain? When she violates the laws of her being, does her husband pay the penalty? When she breaks the moral laws, does he suffer the punishment? When he supplies his wants, is it enough to satisfy her nature? And when at his nightly orgies, in the grog-shop and the oyster-cellar, or at the gaming-table, he squanders the means she helped, by her co-operation and economy, to accumulate, and she awakens to penury and destitution, will it supply the wants of her children to tell them that, owing to the superiority of man she had no redress by law, and that as her being was merged in his, so also ought theirs to be? What an inconsistency, that from the moment she enters that compact, in which she assumes the high responsibility of wife and mother, she ceases legally to exist, and becomes a purely submissive being. Blind submission in woman is considered a virtue, while submission to wrong is itself wrong, and resistance to wrong is virtue, alike in woman as in man.

But it will be said that the husband provides for the wife, or in other words, he feeds, clothes, and shelters her! I wish I had the power to make every one before me fully realize the degradation contained in that idea. Yes! he *keeps* her, and so he does a favorite horse; by law they are both considered his property. Both may, when the cruelty of the owner compels them to run away, be brought back by the strong arm of the law, and according to a still extant law of England, both may be led by the halter to the market-place and sold. This is humiliating indeed, but nevertheless true; and the sooner these things are known and understood, the better for humanity. It is no fancy sketch. I know that some endeavor to throw the mantle of romance over the subject, and treat woman like some ideal existence, not liable to the ills of life. Let those deal in fancy, that have nothing better to deal in; we have to do with sober, sad realities, with stubborn facts. [E. Rose, On Legal Discrimination (1851), quoted in Up from the Pedestal 225 (A. Kraditor ed. 1970).]

◆ CARLISLE v. PARKER

38 Del. 83, 188 A. 67 (Super. Ct. 1936)

RODNEY, Judge, delivering the opinion of the Court: The land was held by the husband and wife as tenants by the entirety. A joint mortgage was given by them and subsequently foreclosed, the mortgage paid and the balance of the proceeds is now deposited in this court.

The first question to be determined is whether the same estate or interest exists in the proceeds of sale as had existed in the real estate prior to sale; in other words, whether the fund represented by the proceeds of sale has attached to it those peculiar attributes of an estate by entireties which had existed prior to the conversion of the land into money. In Leet v. Miller, 6 Pa. Dist. R. 725, the answer to the question was assumed from the statement that estate by entireties could exist in personal property. To us it seems that an affirmative answer to the question is shown from a joint consideration of the law governing estates by entireties and that governing executions. . . .

We know of no rule of law which would destroy an estate by entireties in a surplus arising from a foreclosure of a mortgage on an entirety estate. Both parties are now living and every unity of person, of time and estate which ever existed exists now.

It is not necessary here to discuss the effect that the Married Women's Act had on estates by entireties. It had been held in many jurisdictions before the passage of the Married Women's Act that as the husband had a life interest in all real estate belonging to his wife, that such right gave the husband full power to manage, control and encumber the estate by entireties — but only for his life and not affecting the right of survivorship. This, however, has been changed by the Acts giving to the married woman full and free control of her own property, and at no time did this control of the husband flow as an attribute of an estate by entireties, but simply from the law regulating husband and wife.

From the Delaware cases, certain principles governing estates by entirety seem reasonably clear:

1.   That estates by entirety were not abolished by Married Women's Act.
2.   That the interest of the wife in the estate is her "separate property."
3.   That neither the entirety estate nor the interest of either spouse can be sold during their joint lives, except with the consent of both husband and wife.
4.   That no judgment against one tenant by the entirety is a lien on the entirety property or any interest therein during the joint lives of both husband and wife. . . .

We shall not pause to consider in detail the cases which hold that during the joint lives of husband and wife the interest of one alone may be subjected to some sort of a lien, which while not destroying the right of survivorship, may attach for some purposes. The estate of one spouse in an estate by entireties has been likened to an estate for life or to a defeasible or contingent estate, to a contingent remainder, to a "contingent expectant estate." No definition is apt nor can it be precisely defined unless such definition include all its attributes. . . .

The interest of a wife in an estate by entireties is her separate property which she may hold free of her husband's debts. One of the incidents of the estate is the power to sell it with her husband's consent. It is for this reason, the denial of her right of alienation, which makes invalid during their joint lives any deed or mortgage executed by the husband alone, ↓ ∞ that a judgment against the husband is ineffective.

A wife, as tenant by the entirety, has a right to obtain her husband's consent to a sale of property, which would terminate the estate. Any deed, mortgage, lien, including lien on expectancy, would be an impairment of her right and so would subject her property to her husband's debt. . . .

If, as we have held, the surplus of the proceeds of the foreclosure sale are to be considered in this case as the land itself, we see no reason why said fund is not to be governed or disposed of by the husband and wife, acting jointly, to the same degree or extent as they could have disposed of the real estate itself, just prior to the sale.

The prayer of the petition of the husband and wife that the fund be paid to them jointly, less the costs of this proceeding, is granted, and the prayer of the petition of the First National Bank & Trust Company, of Milford, the judgment creditor of the husband alone, is denied.

Note

Carlisle v. Parker refers to the Married Women's Acts, a nineteenth-century effort at legislative reform of common law restraints on property disposition by wives. In the decades after Mississippi's reform of 1839, most states (and Victorian England) passed what were usually known as Married Women's Property Acts. Basically the married woman was given a degree of control over her own property, whether she acquired it before or during marriage, along with protection for her separate property from her husband's creditors. The actual wording and subsequent interpretation of the statutes varied greatly among the states, reflecting the conflicting motives that lay behind passage of the acts. The growing struggle for women's rights played a role in passage in some states; in others, support came from wealthy fathers, who felt the need for ways to protect married daughters' inheritances from profligate husbands, and from well-to-do husbands, who sought schemes for avoiding creditors' claims by insulating assets as their wives' separate unattachable property.

◆ ROBINSON v. TROUSDALE COUNTY
516 S.W.2d 626 (Tenn. 1974)

HENRY, Justice. This is an inverse condemnation suit involving the nature of the estate of tenancy by the entireties under Tennessee law and the common law disability of coverture.

Petitioners, husband and wife, sued Trousdale County for damages for the taking of certain real estate owned by them as tenants by the entirety, for the purpose of widening a public road adjacent to their property, and for incidental damages.

The answer of Trousdale County, among other defenses, asserts that petitioners are barred from seeking compensation and damages by virtue of a deed, executed by the husband alone, conveying the property involved to Trousdale County, in fee simple. . . .

The trial judge held that the husband was estopped to claim any damage because of the deed; that there were no incidental damages, and allowed the wife Five Hundred Thirty Dollars ($530.00) as actual damages for the value of the land taken.

All parties prayed and perfected appeals to the Court of Appeals.

That court affirmed the judgment of the trial court in all respects except as to the ownership and disposition of the money ($530.00), representing the value of the land. The court directed (1) that this sum be held by the Clerk of the trial court and invested by him during the joint married lives of petitioners; (2) that should the husband die first, the entire recovery would be paid to the wife; (3) that should the wife die first the entire recovery would be paid to Trousdale County, and (4) in the event of a divorce, it would be distributed equally between the wife and Trousdale County. . . .

All parties have petitioned this Court for *certiorari*. We granted the petition of the wife with argument limited to the disposition of the recovery. . . .

Our investigation leads us to the conclusion that the decisional law of Tennessee, not only is nebulous and confusing, but is in substantial conflict and out of harmony with justice, reason and logic.

We, therefore, propose to clarify the law by a clear, comprehensive and definitive opinion. . . .

In *In re Guardianship, Plowman*, the Court held that a husband was not obligated to account to the wife for rents and profits collected by him from real property owned as tenants by the entirety. . . .

The Court makes this unusual observation:

> To permit the wife to demand an accounting of rents collected by her husband on property owned by them as tenants by the entirety by suit at law would disrupt and injure the marriage relationship and would be of little, if any, benefit to the wife. It would, no doubt, bring an end to the relationship. [217 Tenn. 487, 398 S.W.2d 721 (1966)]

We are constrained to doubt that any such dire and disastrous consequences would ensue if the wife were accorded equal legal status as opposed to being made legally subservient and subordinate to her husband. This is but a judicially decreed recognition of the traditional pattern of married women being forced into a subservient and supportive role that is inherently unequal, patently unfair, and at variance with the concept of equality mandated by contemporary standards of justice. . . .

We do not believe that the common law disability of coverture has any sanction in our jurisprudence or any relevance in our society. At best it is outmoded; at worst oppressive and degrading. . . .

To put the present law in proper perspective, let us assume that a husband and wife, having no other assets whatsoever, simultaneously inherit the sum of $250,000.00 each and that they pool their inheritances and purchase an apartment house, taking title as tenants by the entirety. The rental income starts coming in. The husband, the dominant tenant, appropriates all rental income and expends it in accordance with his desires, without the consent of the wife and over her protest. Short of resorting to the divorce courts, she has no legal remedy. One does not have to be a "Women's Libber" or even have an educated conscience, or anything beyond an elemental sense of justice to grasp the patent unfairness of such a situation. It is not only archaic; it is gross and unconscionable. . . .

We abolish the last vestige of the common law disability of coverture in Tennessee.

We do not abolish the estate of tenancy by the entirety, but we strip it of the artificial and archaic rules and restrictions imposed at the common law, and we fully deterge it of its deprivations and detriments to women and fully emancipate them from its burdens.

From this date forward each tenant shall have a joint right to the use, control, incomes, rents, profits, usufructs and possession of property so held, and neither may sell, encumber, alienate or dispose of any portion thereof except his or her right of survivorship, without the consent of the other. Any unilateral attempt will be wholly and utterly void at the instance of the aggrieved tenant and any prospective purchaser, transferee, lessee, mortgagee, and the like will act at his peril.

Lastly we reach the matter of the ownership of the fund now in the Registry of the Court. The husband conveyed his right of expectancy. The County has acquired the needed land for the public road. The result is that all parties in this case have received their just deserts except Mrs. Robinson. She gets the money.

HENRY (Justice), concurring: I wrote the main opinion to reflect the unanimous views of the Court.

While I am in full accord with the conclusions we have reached on the common law disability of coverture and share with my colleagues a sense of pride in this progressive action, I am convinced that we should have based our decision to a substantial extent, on constitutional grounds. . . .

I would hold that the application of the common law disability of coverture is violative of Section 1 of the Fourteenth Amendment to the Constitution of the United States in that married women are "citizens" of the United States and the application of this doctrine deprives them of their property without due process of law, and denies them the equal protection of the law. Moreover, said doctrine is an invidious and "suspect" classification based upon sex and marital status, and is predicated on no rational basis, and abridges their right to acquire, enjoy, lease, hold, own and benefit from their own property.

I would hold, for the same reasons, that the application of this doctrine is violative of Article 1, Section 8, of the Constitution of the State of Tennessee in that it operates to deprive married women of their property and abridges their rights and privileges as citizens of the State, contrary to the law of the land.

Notes

1. In Hardy v. Hardy, 235 F. Supp. 208 (D.D.C. 1964), the plaintiff had given his wife weekly sums to cover household expenses over a period of years, and she invested excesses of these funds in securities, in her own name. He denied any knowledge of such activities until the year they filed for divorce, when he sued to impress a trust on her stock portfolio. The court, unswayed by her claim that the surplus was a product of her household management, including having discharged the maid and doing the cooking and cleaning herself, found for the husband:

> The court recognizes that such household allowances generally comprehend expenditures by the wife for personal needs such as clothes, entertainment and transportation. Such expenses are within the obligation of the husband to support and maintain his wife. Acquiescence in these expenditures does not indicate an acquiescence in the use of such funds for the creation of a portfolio of securities for the wife's sole account. To hold otherwise would be to invite disruptive influences in the home.

2. *Ending the estate:* As long as a marriage continues, tenants by the entireties have no right of partition. When one spouse dies, the surviving spouse automatically becomes sole owner, without the property passing through the estate and the relevant matrix of wills, taxes, dower, curtesy, and statutory shares considered in Part 4. Upon divorce, however, the courts often play a role in the distribution of marital property, including the partition of estates by the entireties.

Historically, state divorce laws have encompassed a wide range of solutions, varying in the weight given to such factors as fault and economic contribution of the spouses, but generally allowing wide judicial discretion. The Uniform Marriage and Divorce Act, a reform proposal from the National Conference of Commissioners on Uniform State Laws approved by the American Bar Association in 1974 and adopted in several states, incorporates novel concepts of no-fault divorce, marital property, and contributions by the homemaker, although in enumerating the relevant factors for judges to consider, it falls short of the equal distribution of property urged by the National Organization of Women and other groups.

UNIFORM MARRIAGE AND DIVORCE ACT §307 (Disposition of Property) (1977):

(a) In a proceeding for dissolution of a marriage, legal separation, or disposition of property following a decree of dissolution of marriage or legal separation by a court which lacked personal jurisdiction over the absent spouse or lacked jurisdiction to dispose of the property, the court, without regard to marital misconduct, shall, and in a proceeding for legal separation may, finally equitably apportion between the parties the property and assets belonging to either or both however and whenever acquired, and whether the title thereto is in the name of the husband or wife or both. In making apportionment the court shall consider the duration of the marriage, any prior marriage of either party, antenuptial agreement of the parties, the age, health, station, occupation, amount and sources of income, vocational skills, employability, estate, liabilities, and needs of each of the parties, custodial provisions, whether the apportionment is in lieu of or in addition to maintenance, and the opportunity of each for future acquisition of capital assets and income. The court shall also consider the contribution or dissipation of each party in the acquisition, preservation, depreciation, or appreciation in value of the respective estates, and the contribution of a spouse as a homemaker or to the family unit.

(b) In a proceeding, the court may protect and promote the best interests of the children by setting aside a portion of the jointly and separately held estates of the parties in a separate fund or trust for the support, maintenance, education, and general welfare of any minor, dependent, or incompetent children of the parties.

For a comprehensive treatment of the problems of the nonworking spouse at divorce, see Kulzer, Law and the Housewife: Property, Divorce, and Death, 28 U. Fla. L. Rev. 1 (1975).

3. In July 1983, the National Conference of Commissioners on Uniform State Laws adopted the Uniform Marital Property Act. The fundamental principle of the act, derived from the community property system, is that ownership of all economic gains from the personal efforts of each spouse during the marriage is vested and equal. The proposition that this sharing mode is an ownership right already in place at the end of a marriage — at divorce or death — obviates the reliance on adversary division by a court or statutory transfer of property. The interest is legally defined and enforceable. The concepts at the root of the act also include the separation of the management and control of marital property from its ownership, the accommodation of full contractual freedom between the spouses with respect to the marital property, and the denial to premarital creditors of a windfall from the marriage.

4. For an interplay among rules familiar and unfamiliar, consider this conveyance, which was scrutinized by the court in Bails v. Davis, 241 Ill. 536, 89 N.E. 706 (1909): Jonas Nye "conveyed the premises by a statutory quitclaim deed 'to Joseph Kretzer and Mora Kretzer, his wife, during their natural lives and after their death to the heirs of said Joseph Kretzer.' "

After divorce, Mora Kretzer had conveyed her interest to Joseph

Kretzer. The Illinois Supreme Court applied the Rule in Shelley's Case, "one of the most firmly established rules of property and . . . unshaken in this state," and found there to be a fee simple in appellants, who had purchased from Joseph Kretzer. Would the same result have been reached if Joseph Kretzer and Mora Kretzer were still married?

5. A husband and wife held parcels of farmland as joint tenants. Upon divorce, the wife sought partition. The Illinois Partition Act provides for distribution "to the persons entitled thereto, according to their interests." Ill. Rev. Stat., 1975, ch. 106, ¶62. The husband had borrowed and spent a considerable sum to maintain and improve the property. The wife had refused to contribute from her salary and had refused to work on the farm. "She told me she was liberated," the husband testified. *Held:* Each party had a one-half interest, "irrespective of the contributions made by each in the acquisition of the land. There is ordinarily a strong presumption that a gift is being made, . . . when one spouse makes improvements. . . ." But after the divorce, improvements "were no longer intended as gifts to [wife]." The Illinois Marriage and Dissolution of Marriage Act, providing that marital property be divided "in just proportions," would call for the same result. Capogreco v. Capogreco, 61 Ill. App. 3d 512, 378 N.E.2d 279 (1978).

6. The Illinois Marriage and Dissolution of Marriage Act of 1977 provides that "all property acquired by either spouse after the marriage . . . is presumed to be marital property, regardless of whether title is held individually or by the spouses in some form of co-ownership." *Held:* The act is based on the Uniform Marriage and Divorce Act. It has exemptions, *inter alia,* for property held by one spouse at the time of marriage. It affects distribution of property upon divorce, but does not alter rights during marriage. Application of this provision to property obtained before 1977 is not unconstitutional as a taking of property or as an infringement of contract: "[E]ven under the preexisting law, as regards his spouse, plaintiff did not have an absolute right to his property upon termination of his marriage. . . . On balance . . . the State interest to be promoted by applying the section retrospectively greatly outweighs the asserted property interest. . . ." Kujawinski v. Kujawinski, 71 Ill. 2d 563, 376 N.E.2d 1382 (1978).

7. A husband and wife were both physicians, but she was also an heiress. Upon divorce, he sought alimony and a share in three homes, an art collection, and a $60,000 wine cellar held by her. Two hours before their marriage, he and she had signed an agreement providing that in the event of divorce, neither would have claims to property of the other or alimony.

The Massachusetts Supreme Judicial Court upheld the agreement and rejected the husband's claims. Osborne v. Osborne, 384 Mass. 591, 428 N.E.2d 810 (1981).

8. *Held:* Husband's master's degree in business administration, ob-

tained while his wife was working as an airline stewardess and providing 70 percent of the couple's income, was not "property" subject to division under the Uniform Dissolution of Marriage Act. "An educational degree . . . does not have an exchange value on an open market. It is personal to the holder. It terminates on the death of the holder and is not inheritable. It cannot be assigned, sold, transferred, conveyed, or pledged." But the wife's contribution to the husband's education would be relevant to a decision on alimony, which this wife did not seek. At trial, the M.B.A. had been valued at $82,836, and the wife was awarded $33,134, payable in monthly installments of $100. In re Marriage of Graham, 194 Colo. 429, 574 P.2d 75 (1978) (4-3).

◆ WEST v. FIRST AGRICULTURAL BANK
382 Mass. 534, 419 N.E.2d 262 (1981)

KAPLAN, Justice. For convenience, we discuss in one opinion two cases in which the respective plaintiff wives sought to present constitutional challenges to the Massachusetts form of tenancy by the entirety as it existed before its reformulation by legislation that became effective in 1980. Invoked by the plaintiff Ruby West was the equal protection clause of the Fourteenth Amendment, and by both plaintiffs, art. 1, of the Massachusetts Declaration of Rights, as amended by Art. 106 of the Articles of Amendment, effective November 2, 1976, which states in part, "Equality under the law shall not be denied or abridged because of sex . . ." (hereafter E.R.A., the Equal Rights Amendment).

We shall conclude by giving effect to the older form of the tenancy as to the pre-1980 transactions at bar in both cases. That form encounters some constitutional problems which we recognize and analyze. But the retroactive alteration of incidents of the tenancy which are sought in these cases, and which would apply in many like cases, is not required and would be undesirable. The Legislature has provided for the present and future.

West case. The defendant First Agricultural Bank on August 7, 1979, recovered a deficiency judgment of $36,179.52 upon a mortgage foreclosure against Ernest L. West, the plaintiff's husband. On September 15, 1979, the bank caused execution to be levied under the judgment on three parcels of land in which the husband had ownership interests, and notice was given of a sheriff's sale to occur on December 21, 1979. One of these properties was an improved parcel on Lafayette Street, Pittsfield, which had been held by the husband and the present plaintiff Ruby West as tenants by the entirety since 1954, and evidently was their residence.

On December 7, 1979, the plaintiff commenced her action in Superior Court to enjoin the sale of the husband's interest in the Lafayette Street property. That interest, under the classic form of tenancy by the entirety prevailing in Massachusetts, would consist of his exclusive right of control, possession, and income during the joint lives, together with an "indestructible" right to a remainder if he survived his wife; and the interest could be reached by the husband's individual creditors. The wife's interest consisted only of a corresponding right of survivorship, but this was not subject to levy by her creditors (or her husband's).[4] The wife in the *West* case was asserting that the Massachusetts tenancy as described was unconstitutionally discriminatory as based on sex; therefore she must be accorded some (not clearly expressed) rights of control, possession, and income in association (not clearly defined) with those of the husband, only joint obligations of both spouses being leviable by creditors, and then (presumably) against the entire estate. The court, rejecting the wife's contention, allowed the defendant bank's motion to dismiss the complaint for failure to state a claim, and we allowed an application for direct appellate review.

McDougall case. These were the facts, as found by a master, with some amplification by the judge. The plaintiff Joan McDougall and her husband Duncan became tenants by the entirety of the property 615-631 Dutton Street, Lowell, on March 4, 1974. Before that date the premises were occupied by several businesses owned or controlled by the husband, including a corporation, S & S of New Eng., Inc. (hereafter New England). Just before the date of purchase, according to the master, New England was a tenant at will of the entire premises, paying rent to the prior owner, and allowing the other McDougall businesses to share occupancy with it. After March 4, 1974, the date of purchase, there was no agreement for payment of rent and no rent was paid; the husband simply withdrew from the businesses monthly the $1,500 needed to meet the mortgage requirements.

In May, 1976, the defendant corporation S & S of N.E., Inc. (hereafter S & S), acquired the assets and assumed the obligations of New England. The husband owned 700 of S & S's 1,000 shares; the plaintiff McDougall, one John Finnegan, and Doris Finnegan (his wife), each owned 100 shares. S & S remained an occupant of the premises. Still

---

4. The survivorship right in either spouse was indestructible in the sense that partition was not (and continues not to be) available to a tenant by the entirety. See G.L. c.241, §1 (which has not been amended). But, as indicated, the husband in the classical tenancy could dispose alone of his survivorship right, while the wife could not so dispose of her survivorship.

Both spouses, acting together could convey the estate, destroying both survivorships. Upon divorce the tenancy dissolved and became a tenancy in common (unless the parties intended or agreed otherwise).

By way of contrast: a "joint" tenant has a right to the remainder if he survives the other, but the joint tenancy is destroyed if he aliens his interest, or creditors levy on his interest, or he partitions under G.L. c.241, §1.

Tenants in common have no survivorship rights; at death the interest of a tenant descends to his heirs or passes to his devisees.

there was no agreement as to payment of rent by any occupant, and no rent was paid.

On May 12, 1977, the plaintiff and her husband, advised by the husband's attorney, executed a deed transferring the property to the plaintiff as an individual, and the plaintiff, in turn, executed a deed transferring the property back to the plaintiff and her husband as tenants by the entirety. The former deed was recorded on May 17, 1977. The latter deed was not recorded. It was left in the custody of the attorney. The husband later obtained the deed, and sometime in spring, 1978, tore it into pieces, and handed the pieces to the plaintiff. She produced the pieces (taped together to form the entire deed) at the master's hearing.

On September 9, 1977, the husband sold his 700 shares in S & S to John Finnegan for $20,000. The purchase agreement stated that S & S "occupied" as tenant at will. At that time Finnegan asked the husband about future rent, but the husband refused to discuss the question and never thereafter raised the question. Finnegan had no discussion at the time with the plaintiff about rent.

On the September, 1977, date of the sale of stock to Finnegan, the plaintiff and her husband had been separated for over a month, and the husband sued for divorce on November 9, 1977. In early November the plaintiff approached Finnegan about rent. He gave her two checks totalling $300 but then declined to pay any more. On November 5, 1977, the plaintiff served on S & S a fourteen-day notice under G.L. c.186, §12, to vacate for nonpayment of rent.

On February 14, 1978, the plaintiff commenced the present action against S & S for rent from June 1, 1977. On February 17, 1978, the husband brought his separate action against S & S for rent for the same period. On March 1, 1978, the Union National Bank took possession of the Dutton Street property upon foreclosure of a mortgage held by it which had been given by Joan and Duncan McDougall when they acquired the property in 1974. . . .

In neither case has it been argued that the 1980 legislation is operative, and we accept for purposes of these cases that it is not operative. Then in the *West* case, the wife's claim that creditors could levy only for defaulted joint obligations of the spouses seeks and is predicated upon changes in fixed rules of property on constitutional grounds.

As to the *McDougall* case, a constitutional issue would not arise if the reconveyance could be considered ineffective, leaving the whole fee in the plaintiff wife. . . .

[A]n unrecorded deed conveying "an estate in fee simple . . . shall not be valid as against any person, except the grantor . . . and persons having actual notice of it. . . ." The plaintiff was the grantor. She has argued that the object of the statute was only to protect subsequent purchasers against prior unrecorded conveyances. That might be the statute's primary purpose, but it may rule also against a grantor's taking unfair advantage of a recording system to deny a deed she executed but did not record.[11] The plaintiff has also argued that the tearing up of the second deed in effect reinstated the first. But that second deed had previously been delivered through its being placed and remaining in the possession of the attorney, and its destruction, even by the husband as one of the grantees, would not produce the result of reviving the first, whatever might be the force of an argument of estoppel as between a grantor and a grantee who later tore up the dispositive instrument. . . . The plaintiffs contend that, before its 1980 statutory modification, our local form of tenancy by the entirety, preserving precisely the ancient estate,[14] was sex-biased and presented features which were offensive to the standard of the equal protection clause and (*a fortiori*) to that of the E.R.A. On a surface view, the tenancy appeared to be a reflection of discredited stereotypes. The male was assumed competent, and thus was to have full control of the property and returns from it during his lifetime and could alien or lose all his interest in it including his survivorship right. The female was thought incompetent, and so was given no rights in the property during her husband's lifetime, and must abide his ideas of proper management, but was protected in her survivorship right against her creditors (and even against her husband and his creditors).

The theoretical support for the tenancy was the concept of the legal unity of the husband and wife, and if it turned out that in that unity the husband was dominant, this was perhaps because the stereotypes mentioned had determined the shape of the concept. . . .

This question of the constitutionality of the Massachusetts tenancy has not previously come before this court, but it has reached Federal courts in this locality. We digest in the margin the cases of Klein v. Mayo, 367 F. Supp. 583 (D. Mass. 1973) (three-judge court), *aff'd without op.*, 416 U.S. 953, 94 S. Ct. 1964, 40 L. Ed. 2d 303 (1974); D'Ercole v. D'Ercole, 407 F. Supp. 1377 (D. Mass. 1976); Friedman v. Harold, 638 F.2d 262 (1st Cir. 1981). The decisions do not overlook the aridity of the "unity" concept and its probable original basis in the contemporary ideas about the capacities of men and women. However it was suggested, particularly in the D'Ercole case, *supra*, that the parties seeking to attack the various aspects of the tenancy could not show final State

---

11. The master found that Doris Finnegan typed both the first and second deeds for Duncan McDougall. Thus there were at least intimations that S & S was on "actual notice" of the unrecorded deed.

14. Of the twenty-odd States in which tenancies by the entirety still exist, only Massachusetts, North Carolina, and Michigan preserved into modern times the tenancy's traditional husband oriented form.

Michigan amended the tenancy in 1975, but North Carolina, to this date, apparently has not.

responsibility for the deprivations claimed. This was because the parties to the tenancy had voluntarily selected that form of land holding; the State had not compelled them. There was, indeed, no form of estate in land, readily available for selection, that replicated the tenancy by the entirety but reversed the roles therein of husband and wife, although we supposed draftsmanship might achieve the substantive result, or something approximating it, by the use of a trust with "spendthrift" provisions. Still the joint and common tenancies, with indubitably equal rights, were available; and in any event, in the absence of proved coercion, misrepresentation, or ignorance guilefully manipulated, the parties entering on a tenancy by the entirety were making a choice of their own (and were in a position to revise the initial choice by mutual agreement thereafter).

The reality of the choice is fortified by the fact that — regardless of historical origins and claims about stereotypes — tenancy by the entirety was suitable to the requirements of many married couples, and could have been and, no doubt, often was recommended to them on a quite reasonable basis. It made sense in common situations where there was no particular concern about division of management rights, and the couple wanted assurance that the surviving spouse would take the property free and clear of any debts (including tort judgments) of the deceased spouse. The wife had an advantage in that her survivorship could not be reached even by her own creditors. For some years the tenancy had State inheritance tax advantages, and on passage of the property upon death of either spouse probate might be avoided if the estate was otherwise small. . . . In fairness we should add that the existence of a category of estate associated with the husband-wife relation might lead to some unthinking or mechanical use of that form in conveyances to married couples and until 1973 there was an evidential presumption that a conveyance to husband and wife was to them as tenants by the entirety (but the presumption could be overcome by proper language in the conveyance).

With regard to *McDougall*, the element of voluntary choice on the given facts might be thought so real as to shut off constitutional demands, whatever position was taken on the general class of cases. Here the entire fee of business property was in Mrs. McDougall by force of the transfer to her individually and she then by her deed elected the tenancy *in haec verba* by which she may be taken to have relinquished willingly to her husband the current control of the property, including the matter of rental. *West's* case has the appearance of a tenancy of the more usual sort, not out of keeping with a standard situation. The tenancy was entered into in 1954 and generated about it a web of relationships. The wife is not prepared to relinquish her survivorship or the immunity of the tenancy from her debts, but balks at another incident, the burdening of the current tenancy by the husband's obligations. She argues for an equality retrospectively imposed, but equalization could very rationally take a form that would not relieve the husband's interest of levy by his creditors, but would rather subject the wife's interest to her own creditors.

But the question of possible relief should be considered more broadly. As noted, the parties make no claim that the 1980 legislation applies (retroactively) to their cases. That legislation covers conveyances from and after February 11, 1980. It amended G.L. c.209, §1, to provide: "A husband and wife shall be equally entitled to the rents, products, income or profits and to the control, management and possession of property held by them as tenants by the entirety." And further: "The interest of a debtor spouse in property held as tenants by the entirety shall not be subject to seizure or execution by a creditor of such debtor spouse so long as such property is the principal residence of the non-debtor spouse" (with a proviso regarding liability of the spouses for necessaries). From these provisions the whole shape of the new tenancy will be extrapolated.

Any "equalization" of the rights of spouses by decision of this court as to conveyances antedating February 11, 1980, would pose formidable problems as to the starting date. It is not clear that selection of the date of the E.R.A. would be anything more than arbitrary in view of equal protection claims. In delineating the changed rights, the court would be faced with choosing among multiple patterns of equalization that have been attempted around the country in modifying tenancies by the entirety (it is a notable fact that the statutory changes have generally been wholly prospective). The very variety of the patterns, as indicated in the margin, suggests that the process of selection is more suitably done by the Legislature than by a court. . . .

The further, grave objection to going backward to tenancies created by past conveyances is that it would upset expectations and defeat reliances based on a long established form of conveyance used in thousands of transactions, not all of which were of the family type, as the record in *McDougall* shows. There would be other aspects of unfairness. The retroactive "equalization" of rights could amount to forcing a party to make a never intended and quite possibly unmerited gift to another. Retroactive alteration of the law is strongly contraindicated when the subject is settled rules of property.

Thus we conclude that a decision by us on constitutional grounds would be prospective and would affect only tenancies created after the issuance of our decision; and relief would be denied in both our cases. In fact the 1980 legislation has come in ahead of a decision on those lines, and has brought in changes from February 11, 1980, but not such as to cover the instant cases.

The judgment in the *West* case will be affirmed, and any outstanding stay vacated. The *McDougall* appeal will be dismissed.

◆ WROTH v. TYLER
[1973] 2 W.L.R. 405 (Ch.)

MEGARRY, J. The plaintiffs, for whom Mr. Blackburne appeared, are a young married couple who, while still engaged, were seeking to buy a home. The defendant, for whom Mr. Lyndon-Stanford appeared, is a married man aged 62 who wished to retire from his Civil Service employment. The plaintiffs and the defendant are all on modest means. The premises concerned are a bungalow in Ashford, formerly in Middlesex but now in Surrey; and the defendant lives there with his wife and grown-up daughter. His title to the bungalow is registered as absolute at the Land Registry.

In or about March 1971 the defendant decided to sell the bungalow and purchase a bungalow being built (or about to be built) in Norfolk. He had already disestablished himself in the Civil Service, and had taken his gratuity; but although he is still employed as a civil servant this is on an unestablished basis, and he can retire at any time. The principal attraction of the move was that he could sell his Ashford bungalow for over £2,000 more than he would have to pay for the Norfolk bungalow, and this would suffice to discharge the amount due under the existing mortgage on the Ashford bungalow, some £1,250, and cover the moving and incidental expenses. He would thus begin his retirement in a state of financial freedom.

The defendant put his bungalow in the hands of agents, and very soon the plaintiffs came to see it. This was their first purchase of a house. Their initial visit was on March 6, 1971, and the next day they returned. On this visit, among other things, the defendant's wife explained to the plaintiffs the working of the cooker, gas drier, extractor fan and other articles that would go with the bungalow. Two days later the first plaintiff (the husband) visited the bungalow alone. The price asked by the defendant was £6,050, a figure which included £50 for the various fittings and chattels that would go with the bungalow. The first plaintiff saw the defendant, telling him that they could not afford £6,050, and trying to persuade him to reduce the price by £200. The plaintiffs were expecting to be able to raise £4,600 on mortgage, and they had £950 of their own. The defendant would not reduce his price, and the first plaintiff went away. He then discussed matters with the second plaintiff, and they agreed to pay the £6,050. The next day he informed the agents and put down a deposit of £25.

Some weeks later the plaintiffs made two more visits to the bungalow; and although the discussions were in the main with the defendant, the defendant's wife may at least have been in the bungalow on one or more of these visits. Finally, after the defendant had begun to press for a contract to be signed, contracts for the sale of the bungalow by the defendant to the plaintiffs were exchanged on May 27, 1971, in a form which incorporated the current edition of the National Conditions of Sale, with modifications. Neither side, I may say, has relied on any provision in those conditions. The sale was by the defendant as beneficial owner, and the property was sold with vacant possession. Completion was to take place "on or before" October 31, 1971, that being the date by which the defendant expected the Norfolk bungalow to be ready for him. The price was £6,050, with a deposit of £605 which was duly paid to the defendant's solicitors as stakeholders. The plaintiffs and the defendant each had solicitors acting for them on the sale. On the same day, the defendant entered into a contract for the purchase of the Norfolk bungalow. I have not seen this contract, but on the defendant's evidence the price was about £3,800 and he paid a deposit of £100.

Thus far, the transaction was wholly unremarkable, with nothing to distinguish it from thousands of other transactions. However, the next day, on May 28, 1971, the event occurred from which all the difficulty stems. The defendant's wife, no doubt acting through solicitors, caused the entry in the charges register against the defendant's title at the Land Registry of a notice of her rights of occupation under the Matrimonial Homes Act 1967. I have heard evidence from both the plaintiffs and the defendant, but not from the defendant's wife, so that what I say must be taken subject to that qualification. I should say at once that the evidence given by the plaintiffs and by the defendant was given frankly and openly, and I accept all three as witnesses of truth. There was, indeed, very little conflict of evidence.

On the evidence before me, it is perfectly plain that the defendant's wife had never given any indication whatever to the plaintiffs that she was not willing to move out of the bungalow. Indeed, by explaining to them the working of the apparatus in the kitchen, she had given them the justifiable impression that she was concurring in the proposed move. Within the home, she had shown no enthusiasm for the move. The defendant said that his wife and daughter were very close to each other, and the attitude of both of them to the sale of the bungalow was "very cool." The defendant had discussed the sale of the bungalow and the move to Norfolk before he had put the bungalow into the hands of the agents, and they, though very cool about the move, had in some sort of way agreed to it. On this, the defendant had proceeded with his plan; and he had thought that they would have come with him when he moved. On the evidence as it stands, the picture is one of reluctance but not of any open opposition to the move. The defendant's wife and daughter had lived with him in the area since 1949, and in this particular bungalow since 1963; and they understandably did not want to be uprooted from their friends, and in the case of the daughter, from her employment. The wife, I may say, is 52 and the daughter is 25.

The registration of the notice was not disclosed to the defendant.

His wife said nothing about it to him; and for nearly three weeks she continued her life with the defendant without his having any knowledge or suspicion of what she had done. One can only speculate on the wife's thoughts as she lived her daily life with the defendant, with this unrevealed secret in her mind. During this time the solicitors were proceeding with the necessary conveyancing steps; the requisitions on title were duly delivered and answered; and the defendant's solicitors returned the draft transfer duly approved. Subject to the one question of the rights of the defendant's wife, Mr. Blackburne told me that the defendant's title to the bungalow was accepted. However, on June 11, 1971, the building society to which the bungalow was mortgaged wrote to the defendant's solicitors enclosing a notice of the wife's rights of occupation which had been received by the society from the Land Registry. . . .

. . . The defendant had gone to Norfolk to get the dimensions of the windows of the new bungalow for curtaining, and so on. It is not without significance that his wife and daughter had never been to see the district in Norfolk in which they were to live when they moved. The defendant left home for work the next day, Friday, June 18, 1971, before the arrival of a letter from his solicitors telling him of his wife's registration of the notice. He found this letter on his return that evening. Its contents came as a complete surprise to him.

That evening there was a row about the notice between the defendant and his wife, after which he decided to withdraw from both transactions. The next day, Saturday, June 19, he telephoned the Norfolk vendors to say that he would not be buying the Norfolk property, and he wrote to his solicitors asking them to cancel the Norfolk purchase and also the sale of his bungalow. That day he and his wife hardly spoke to each other. The next day, Sunday, there was a worse row between the defendant and his wife about the cost to the defendant of breaking his contracts. It ended with the defendant slapping his wife, who thereupon sent for the police and called for a doctor. In addition to these two rows, the defendant made some further attempts to persuade his wife to withdraw her notice, though he could not recall the details beyond saying that he did it when she seemed to be in an amiable mood; but she was adamant. . . .

[To this soap-opera story was applied a late piece of legislative reform, the Matrimonial Homes Act 1967.] As is well known, the Act was passed after the House of Lords had held in National Provincial Bank Ltd. v. Hastings Car Mart Ltd. [1965] A.C. 1175 that there was no such thing as the so-called deserted wife's equity. Over the previous 10 or 15 years there had been much controversy about this alleged equity. The idea that a husband might desert his wife and then sell the former matrimonial home over her head, leaving her homeless, was obviously repugnant to the ideas of any civilised society, and plainly ought to be made impossible. One difficulty of the courts dealing with the matter was that any doctrine evolved by the courts was likely to take many years, and much litigation involving heavy costs, before a workable doctrine emerged in an established and fully-fledged form; and there was much uncertainty about many of the features of the equity. Did the equity arise only on desertion, or did it subsist throughout the marriage? Did it apply to constructive desertion, where the wife had been driven out by her husband? Was it dependent upon desertion, or would it arise when there was some other matrimonial offence, such as adultery or cruelty? Was there a deserted husband's equity? Above all, how far were purchasers, mortgagees and others obliged to investigate the state of the marriage in order to be protected? It would have been intolerable if, when an overdraft was secured on the husband's house, the bank had to make inquiries as to the husband's matrimonial behaviour before honouring his cheques.

Statute could avoid all the difficulties, expenses and delays of a doctrine evolved by the courts by laying down a complete system *uno ictu*. In truth, the institution of what might amount to a new right of property, however badly needed, is a reform which the courts are ill-equipped to make. The Act of 1967 could thus have brought certainty and clarity into what was a confused and contentious field. Whether in fact it has done so is another matter.

The Act is in far wider terms than the alleged equity ever was. It is in no way confined to desertion or any other matrimonial offence, but confers all the rights that it gives forthwith upon marriage. It is not confined to wives, but applies to husbands as well; and it is not confined to one house, but applies to all dwelling houses owned by either spouse, except "a dwelling house which has at no time been a matrimonial home of the spouses in question": section 1(8). The mainsprings of the Act for the purposes of this case are section 1(1) and section 2(1). Section 1(1) provides as follows:

> Where one spouse is entitled to occupy a dwelling house by virtue of any estate or interest or contract or by virtue of any enactment giving him or her the right to remain in occupation, and the other spouse is not so entitled, then, subject to the provisions of this Act, the spouse not so entitled shall have the following rights (in this Act referred to as "rights of occupation"): — (a) if in occupation, a right not to be evicted or excluded from the dwelling house or any part thereof by the other spouse except with the leave of the court given by an order under this section; (b) if not in occupation, a right with the leave of the court so given to enter into and occupy the dwelling house.

I pause there to say that in relation to the present case the right that the defendant's wife has is "a right not to be evicted or excluded" from the bungalow or any part of it by the defendant. Despite the statutory phrase "rights of occupation," an occupying wife is given no positive right of occupation; the Act works by giving her a shield against eviction or exclusion by her husband. . . .

In the present case the defendant has endeavoured to persuade his wife to concur in the sale, but has failed. It is true that after the failure of his initial attempt on the Friday night he then instructed his solicitors to withdraw from both the sale and his Norfolk purchase; but he again tried to persuade his wife on the Sunday, and there is some evidence of later attempts. As the evidence stands, I think that the defendant has sufficiently attempted to obtain her consent, short of litigation. The mere fact that he sought to withdraw from the contract before he had made all his attempts does not seem to me to make much difference; if a later attempt had succeeded, he could still have completed at the date fixed for completion.

Persuasion having failed, I think that the court should be slow to grant a decree of specific performance that would require an unwilling husband to make an application to the court under section 1(2) of the Act of 1967, particularly as the decision of the court depends upon the application of phrases such as "just and reasonable" under section 1(3). In any case, the court would be reluctant to make an order which requires a husband to take legal proceedings against his wife, especially while they are still living together. Accordingly, although this is a contract of a type which the court is normally ready to enforce by a decree of specific performance, in my judgment it would, in Lord Redesdale L.C.'s phrase, be "highly unreasonable" to make such a decree if there is any other form of order that could do justice; and that I must consider in due course. Let me add that I would certainly not regard proceedings under the Act by the defendant against his wife as being without prospect of success. As the evidence stands (and of course I have not heard the defendant's wife) there is at least a real prospect of success for the defendant. He does not in any way seek to deprive his wife of a home; the difference between them is a difference as to where the matrimonial home is to be. In that, the conduct of the wife towards the plaintiffs and the defendant must play a substantial part. . . .

In my judgment, therefore, if under Lord Cairns' Act damages are awarded in substitution for specific performance, the court has jurisdiction to award such damages as will put the plaintiffs into as good a position as if the contract had been performed, even if to do so means awarding damages assessed by reference to a period subsequent to the date of the breach. This seems to me to be consonant with the nature of specific performance, which is a continuing remedy, designed to secure (*inter alia*) that the purchaser receives in fact what is his in equity as soon as the contract is made, subject to the vendor's right to the money, and so on. On the one hand, a decree may be sought before any breach of contract has occurred, and so before any action lies for common law damages; and on the other hand the right to a decree may continue long after the breach has occurred. On the facts of this case, the damages that may be awarded are not limited to the £1,500 that is appropriate to the date of the breach but extend to the £5,500 that is appropriate at the present day, when they are being awarded in substitution for specific performance. . . .

That brings me to a subsidiary point which Mr. Lyndon-Stanford urged upon me. He contended that an award of damages of the order of £5,500 was precluded by the operation of what is often called the "second rule" in Hadley v. Baxendale (1854) 9 Exch. 341, relating to what was in the contemplation of the parties. . . . It was beyond question that a rise in the price of houses was in the contemplation of the parties when the contract was made in this case. But Mr. Lyndon-Stanford took it further. He contended that what a plaintiff must establish is not merely a contemplation of a particular head of damage, but also of the quantum under that head. Here, the parties contemplated a rise in house prices, but not a rise of an amount approaching that which in fact took place. A rise which nearly doubled the market price of the property was, as the evidence showed, outside the contemplation of the parties, and so it could not be recovered. Thus ran the argument.

I do not think that this can be right. On principle, it seems to me to be quite wrong to limit damages flowing from a contemplated state of affairs to the amount that the parties can be shown to have had in contemplation, for to do this would require evidence of the calculation in advance of what is often incalculable until after the event. The function of the so-called "second rule" in Hadley v. Baxendale, 9 Exch. 341, seems to me to be not so much to add to the damages recoverable as to exclude from them any liability for any type or kind of loss which could not have been foreseen when the contract was made. . . .

The conclusion that I have reached, therefore, is that as matters stand I ought to award damages to the plaintiffs of the order of £5,500, in substitution for decreeing specific performance, with all the doubts and difficulties and probably undesirable consequences that a decree in either form would produce. An award of damages on this scale, I accept, will bear hardly on the defendant. Though able in one way or another to raise £1,500 without selling his bungalow, £5,500 is another matter; in all probability he could not raise that sum without selling the bungalow with vacant possession, and he has no power to do this. If, however, he becomes bankrupt, then his trustee in bankruptcy can sell the bungalow free from the wife's rights, even though they are registered: see section 2(5) of the Act of 1967. With the money so raised, the trustee in bankruptcy will then be able to pay the plaintiffs their damages, one hopes in full; or it may be possible for the plaintiffs to take the bungalow in satisfaction of their claim. This is a dismal prospect for the defendant, but if the plaintiffs obtain neither a decree of specific performance nor

£5,500 by way of damages, theirs also is a dismal prospect. Having made a binding contract to purchase for £6,000 a bungalow now worth £11,500, they would recover neither the bungalow nor damages that would enable them to purchase anything like its equivalent. It is the plaintiffs who are wholly blameless. Nothing whatever can be said against them, or has been, save as to the contention that delay barred them from a decree of specific performance; and that I have rejected. Nor do I think that there was any delay on their part that could affect the measure of damages. . . .

In these circumstances, I think that what I ought to do is to make no order today, but, subject to what counsel may have to say, to adjourn the case until the first day of next term. In ordinary circumstances, I would adjourn the case for only a week, but unfortunately the impending vacation makes this impossible. During the adjournment I hope that the defendant and his wife will take advice, separately or together. When I resume the hearing, it may be that the defendant's wife will not have changed her mind about her charge. In that case, I shall award the plaintiffs damages against the defendant of the order of £5,500, even though the probable consequence will be the bankruptcy of the defendant and the sale of the bungalow with vacant possession by his trustee in bankruptcy, free from the wife's rights. On the other hand, the defendant's wife may by then have changed her mind, and rather than force her husband into bankruptcy without avoiding having to vacate the bungalow, she may have taken effective steps to enable the defendant to convey the bungalow to the plaintiffs free from her rights. In that case I shall decree specific performance of the contract. In this way the plaintiffs will obtain either the bungalow that they bought or else an amount of damages which will enable them to purchase its equivalent. I may add that of course I give each side liberty to apply in the meantime; and I should say that I shall be available until 4 p.m. today. As I have indicated, I feel much sympathy for the defendant as well as for the plaintiffs at being embroiled in this way. Yet as between the two sides both the law and the merits seem to me to point to the plaintiffs as being the parties who should be as little hurt as possible; and they have already suffered considerably, not least in relation to their temporary accommodation pending these proceedings. Counsel will no doubt assist me with any submissions that they may have on this proposed adjournment, which was not mooted during the argument.

There [is another matter] that I should mention. [T]his case is a potent illustration of the need for the Act of 1967 and its operation to be given urgent reconsideration, whether by the Law Commission or otherwise. What has happened to the plaintiffs in this case might happen to any purchaser of any house from a married man or woman. The Act can be used to involve purchasers in matrimonial disputes about where the spouses shall live. The Act can be used by spouses who are not in the smallest peril of being deprived of a matrimonial home. "Spite" registrations may easily be made. Despite the example of the years of litigation that were necessary to clarify the nature of a statutory tenancy under the Rent Acts, litigation which was in large part conducted at the expense of those who could ill afford it, the legislature has created a new "charge" with scant information as to the nature and effect of the charge. There is now a companion in obloquy for what in Keeves v. Dean (1923) 93 L.J. K.B. 203, 207, Scrutton L.J. stigmatised as *monstrum horrendum informe ingens.* Millions of spouses who need no protection at present, but may possibly need it in the future, can secure that protection (and by some are encouraged to secure it) by cluttering up the Land Registry with millions of entries, most of which will never do anyone any good. As may be seen by comparing this case with Miles v. Bull [1969] 1 Q.B. 258, and Miles v. Bull (*No.* 2) [1969] 3 All E.R. 1585, the Act is one which sometimes does too much and sometimes does too little. For these and many other reasons that I need not specify it seems to me to be a matter of some urgency that the scope and operation of the Act of 1967 be reconsidered so as to evolve some means of protecting those who need protection without the cumbersome uncertainties that the Act of 1967 has produced, to the peril of all, and not least of those of modest means. One must not under-estimate the difficulties; but something better than the Act of 1967 — much better — must be possible. I have done my best to see how the Act could and should work, but after prolonged consideration and much assistance from counsel, many serious difficulties remain. The Act certainly changed the law; but not every change is reform. . . .

January 11, 1973. The defendant's wife refused to remove the notice. Damages of £5,500 assessed as at January 11, 1973, were awarded in lieu of specific performance, with costs.

Order accordingly.

Notes

1. Kiralfy, The English Law, in Comparative Law of Matrimonial Property, 188-189 (A. Kiralfy ed. 1972):

> The position of the two spouses differed where the occupation of the matrimonial home was concerned. A deserted husband could not insist on remaining in a dwelling belonging to his wife, and was guilty of trespass if he did so. On the other hand the husband's duty to support his wife required him to find her accommodation, and a deserted wife was entitled, as against her husband, to remain in possession until he found her

other accommodation. This right was based on the matrimonial law and not the law of property and did not affect third parties. At the end of the Second World War there was an acute housing shortage and a large number of war-time marriages were breaking down. The husband usually had the legal title, enabling him to sell the home over the wife's head, at a time when it was often impossible for her to find any suitable alternative place in which to live. The courts tried to shield wives who had been wrongfully deserted by their husbands by maintaining them in possession as against the husband's creditors and trustee in bankruptcy, and as against persons acting in bad faith, such as a friend of the husband pretending to buy the house at a gross undervalue. But this invasion of property law brought great inconveniences, for example, a bank could not safely permit a husband to overdraw his bank account and rely on the security of his house, in case he had in fact deserted his wife. The position of bona fide purchasers in general was also somewhat unclear and hazardous. Ultimately the House of Lords decided that a wife had no property right which could be set up against third parties. . . .

However, there was a storm of criticism of this decision as overtechnical and inhumane, although it was equally recognised that some means of protecting honest third parties had also to be worked out, which would relieve them of having to enquire into intimate problems of marital relations. . . .

The new law is contained in the Matrimonial Homes Act of 1967. . . .

2. Mass. Gen. Laws Ann. Ch. 208, §34B (1976):

Any court having jurisdiction of actions for divorce, or for nullity of marriage or of separate support or maintenance, may, upon commencement of such action and during the pendency thereof, order the husband or wife to vacate forthwith the marital home for a period of time not exceeding ninety days, and upon further motion for such additional certain period of time, as the court deems necessary or appropriate if the court finds, after a hearing, that the health, safety or welfare of the moving party or any minor children residing with the parties would be endangered or substantially impaired by a failure to enter such an order. The opposing party shall be given at least three days' notice of such hearing and may appear and be heard either in person or by his attorney. If the moving party demonstrates a substantial likelihood of immediate danger to his or her health, safety or welfare or to that of such minor children from the opposing party, the court may enter a temporary order without notice, and shall immediately thereafter notify said opposing party and give him or her an opportunity to be heard as soon as possible but not later than five days after such order is entered on the question of continuing such temporary order. The court may issue an order to vacate although the opposing party does not reside in the marital home at the time of its issuance, or if the moving party has left such home and has not returned there because of fear for his or her safety or for that of any minor children.

2.   Community Property

◆ YOUNGER, COMMUNITY PROPERTY, WOMEN
AND THE LAW SCHOOL CURRICULUM
48 N.Y.U.L. Rev. 211, 214-223 (1973)

The notion of marital community is much older than common law principles. Its sources are the Code of Hammurabi, the Twelve Tables of Gortyn and the Fuero Juzgo, or Visigothic Code. Stemming from a way of life said to be classless and democratic and spread, incidentally, by people said to be barbaric, the community property system would seem to have been well-suited to the American frontier. Had it survived in England until the first landings at Jamestown and Plymouth the predominant American pattern might have been different. However, the English rejected the marital community in the thirteenth century; it arrived in the New World, therefore, as part of the civil law systems of the Spanish and the French. At one time it enjoyed fairly wide recognition in America, existing "in every one of the southern tier of states" as well as a number of those northern ones which formed part of the Northwest Territory. In lasting impact, however, the civil law community was no match for the English common law. In some jurisdictions it was viewed as a transplanted but rootless "exotic" and was soon displaced. In others — Louisiana, Texas and California — it was retained despite the omnipresence of the rival system in other areas of law. In still other states — Nevada, New Mexico, Arizona, Washington and Idaho — it was adopted anew after a test of married life under common law property rules. In Louisiana the civil law governed not only marital property but everthing else as well; in Texas it applied to marital property, land and civil procedure; and in California, Nevada, New Mexico, Arizona, Washington, and Idaho, it governed marital property only. The common law was the source of all other rules.

It is not always clear why the states rejected, retained or adopted the marital community. Of the retaining states, Louisiana was the first to take a firm stand by prohibiting acceptance of the common law as a unit in the Constitution of 1812. Texas formally retained the marital community in 1840 and California followed suit in 1850; together the two influenced its adoption in the other five community states. Only in California, however, does the record show that the relative merits of common law and community systems were actually discussed. The occasion was the California Constitutional Convention of 1849; the focal point was the proposed inclusion in the state constitution of a provision defining the wife's separate estate. One delegate made his personal preferences crystal clear: he saw the constitutional definition and the community system as a way to attract wives. Calling on all fellow bachelors at the Convention to vote accordingly, he anticipated the migration of rich, marriageable women to California. Another delegate lent his support for a less selfish reason: the common law "annihilated" married women. While he himself could "stand" the system, he entreated the Convention not to impose its "despotic provisions" on wives. The advocates of the common law rallied to its defense. To this group there was nothing more natural than the notion of woman's inferior place. Delegate Lippit, citing the sad example of France, described its capital as a "spectacle of domestic disunion" where, he assured the Convention, two-thirds of the married couples were living apart. Civil law principles caused such disorder by "setting the wife up as an equal, in everything whatever, to the husband" and "raising her from the condition of head clerk to partner." Delegate Botts was even more emphatic. In his eyes, common law marital rules were "beautiful," "admirable" and "beneficial"; husbands were better protectors of wives than the law; the opposition's plan "to make the wife independent of the husband" was contrary to "nature" and "wisdom"; and the "doctrine of woman's rights" was the doctrine of "those mental hermaphrodites, Abby Folsom, Fanny Wright, and the rest of that tribe."

Both factions were overreacting, for the community system, as it ultimately developed in this country, offered nothing for married women to celebrate or married men to fear. Basically, it created a community. The members, of course, were husband and wife. Community property, or "common" property as it was called in early American statutes, included everything acquired by either spouse after marriage, except for gifts and inheritances. Common property was said to belong to both spouses as partners in marriage. In theory, it followed, the wife's interest in the common property was that of a full "partner" — a startling contrast to the common law in which all was vested in the husband. In practice, however, the two systems had like effect. The wife was a decidedly inferior partner; in fact, her partnership interest began at the partnership's end. While the marriage and the community lasted, the husband was vested with the sole management and control of its assets, generally enjoying the same power of disposition over them as he had over his separate estate. Until dissolution of the marriage and the community, the wife's interest seemed suspended. As the Louisiana Code frankly provided, she had "no sort of right" in community assets "until her husband be dead." She was then entitled to sue his heirs if she could prove he had fraudulently sold community assets in order to injure her. The exact nature of the wife's interest gave rise to much discussion, since courts then, as now, felt the need to match theory and practice so as to justify the law's preference for husbands. Some were forthright: the husband, they said, was made manager of the community because the community property was really his. According to others, the husband was given control of the community not because he was its exclusive owner, but because someone must manage it and the law chose him. Of course, both spouses might have been designated joint managers of community assets, or management responsibilities might have been apportioned between them. Neither of these schemes, however, was part of early American law.

The other aspect of the community system which differed theoretically from the common law was its clear recognition of wife's separate estate. . . .

Thus, by the turn of the century, the stage was set for forty-two common law and eight community property states; and so it remained except for short-lived conversions to community property by the then territory of Hawaii and the states of Michigan, Nebraska, Oklahoma, Oregon and Pennsylvania. These departures were motivated by the hope of securing tax advantages for married residents, not by legislative concern for women's rights. Static in terms of the number of jurisdictions embracing it, the community system has nevertheless undergone significant substantive change since its American reception. The first modification, now completely effective, has been the freeing of wives via Married Women's Property Acts to manage, control and otherwise deal with their separate estates. The second, not yet effected in all eight states but equally important in terms of women's rights, has been a discernible trend toward revesting wives with their full "partnership" interest in community assets, including the right during marriage to manage and control them.

◆ BEAM v. BANK OF AMERICA
   6 Cal. 3d 12, 490 P.2d 257, 98 Cal. Rptr. 137 (1971)

TOBRINER, Associate Justice. Mrs. Mary Beam, defendant in this divorce action, appeals from an interlocutory judgment awarding a divorce to both husband and wife on grounds of extreme cruelty. The trial court determined that the only community property existing at the time of trial was a promissory note for $38,000, and, upon the husband's stipulation, awarded this note to the wife; the court found all other property to be the separate property of the party possessing it. The court additionally awarded Mrs. Beam $1,500 per month as alimony and granted custody of the Beams' two minor children to both parents, instructing the husband to pay $250 per month for the support of each child so long as the child remained within the wife's care.

On this appeal, Mrs. Beam attacks the judgment primarily on the grounds that the trial court (1) failed adequately to compensate the community for income attributable to the husband's skill, efforts and labors expended in the handling of his sizable separate estate during the marriage, and (2) erred in suggesting that community living expenses, paid from the income of the husband's separate estate, should be charged against community income in determining the balance of community funds. In addition, the wife challenges the court's categorization of several specific assets as separate property of her husband. For the reasons discussed below, we have concluded that substantial precedent and evidence support the various conclusions under attack; thus we conclude that the judgment must be affirmed.

Mr. and Mrs. Beam were married on January 31, 1939; the instant divorce was granted in 1968, after 29 years of marriage. Prior to and during the early years of the marriage, Mr. Beam inherited a total of $1,629,129 in cash and securities, and, except for brief and insignificant intervals in the early 1940's, he was not employed at all during the marriage but instead devoted his time to handling his separate estate and engaging in private ventures with his own capital. Mr. Beam spent the major part of his time studying the stock market and actively trading in stocks and bonds; he also undertook several real estate ventures, including the construction of two hotel resorts, Cabana Holiday I at Piercy, California, and Cabana Holiday II at Prunedale, California. Apparently, Mr. Beam was not particularly successful in these efforts, however, for, according to Mrs. Beam's own calculations, over the lengthy marriage her husband's total estate enjoyed only a very modest increase to $1,850,507.33.

Evidence introduced at trial clearly demonstrated that the only moneys received and spent by the parties during their marriage were derived from the husband's separate estate; throughout the 29 years of marriage Mrs. Beam's sole occupation was that of housewife and mother (the Beams have four children). According to the testimony of both parties, the ordinary living expenses of the family throughout the marriage amounted to $2,000 per month and, in addition, after 1960, the family incurred extraordinary expenses (for travel, weddings, gifts) of $22,000 per year. Since the family's income derived solely from Mr. Beam's separate estate, all of these household and extraordinary expenses were naturally paid from that source.

During the greater part of the marriage (1946 to 1963) the Beams resided in a home on Spencer Lane in Atherton, California. In 1963 the family sold the Spencer Lane house and acquired a smaller residence in Atherton, on Selby Lane. This home was sold in 1966 for a cash down payment, which was apparently divided between the parties, and for a promissory note in the sum of $38,000, payable in monthly installments of $262.56. The trial court concluded that this note was community property but, upon Mr. Beam's stipulation, awarded the entire proceeds of the note to the wife.

On this appeal, Mrs. Beam of course does not question the disposition of the promissory note, but does attack the trial court's conclusion that this asset was the only community property existing at the time of the divorce. Initially, and most importantly, the wife contends that the trial court erred in failing to find any community property resulting from the industry, efforts and skill expended by her husband over the 29 years of marriage. We address this issue first.

Section 5108 of the Civil Code provides generally that the profits accruing from a husband's separate property are also separate property. Nevertheless, long ago our courts recognized that, since income arising from the husband's skill, efforts and industry is community property, the community should receive a fair share of the profits which derive from the husband's devotion of more than minimal time and effort to the handling of his separate property. . . .

Over the years our courts have evolved two quite distinct, alternative approaches to allocating earnings between separate and community income in such cases. One method of apportionment, commonly referred to as the *Pereira* [v. Pereira, 156 Cal. 1, 103 P. 488 (1909)] approach, "is to allocate a fair return on the [husband's separate property] investment [as separate income] and to allocate any excess to the community property as arising from the husband's efforts." The alternative apportionment approach, which traces its derivation to Van Camp v. Van Camp [53 Cal. App. 17, 199 P. 885 (1921)], is "to determine the reasonable value of the husband's services . . . , allocate that amount as community property, and treat the balance as separate property attributable to the normal earnings of the [separate estate].". . .

The trial court in the instant case was well aware of these apportionment formulas and concluded from all the circumstances that the *Pereira* approach should be utilized. As stated above, under the *Pereira* test, community income is defined as the amount by which the actual income of the separate estate exceeds the return which the initial capital investment could have been expected to earn absent the spouse's personal management. In applying the *Pereira* formula the trial court adopted the legal interest rate of 7 percent simple interest as the "reasonable rate of return" on Mr. Beam's separate property. . . .

Testimony at trial indicated that, based upon this 7 percent simple interest growth factor, Mr. Beam's separate property would have been worth approximately 4.2 million dollars at the time of trial if no expenditures had been made during the marriage. Since Mrs. Beam's own calculations indicate that the present estate, plus all expenditures during marriage, would not amount to even 4 million dollars, it appears that, under *Pereira*, the entire increase in the estate's value over the 29-year period would be attributable to the normal growth factor of the property itself, and, thus, using this formula, all income would be designated as separate property. . . .

Under the *Van Camp* test community income is determined by designating a reasonable value to the services performed by the husband in connection with his separate property. At trial Mrs. Beam introduced evidence that a professional investment manager, performing similar functions as those undertaken by Mr. Beam during the marriage, would have charged an annual fee of 1 percent of the corpus of the funds he was managing; Mrs. Beam contends that such a fee would amount to $17,000 per year (1 percent of the 1.7 million dollar corpus) and that, computed over the full term of their marriage, this annual "salary" would amount to $357,000 of community income. Mrs. Beam asserts that under the *Van Camp* approach she is now entitled to one-half of this $357,000.

Value of husband [handwritten margin note]

Mrs. Beam's contention, however, overlooks the fundamental distinction between the total community *income* of the marriage, i.e., the figure derived from the *Van Camp* formula, and the community *estate* existing at the dissolution of the marriage. The resulting community estate is not equivalent to total community income so long as there are any community *expenditures* to be charged against the community income. A long line of California decisions has established that "it is presumed that the expenses of the family are paid from community rather than separate funds [citations] [and] thus, in the absence of any evidence showing a different practice the community earnings are chargeable with these expenses." . . .

If the "family expense" presumption is applied in the present case, clearly no part of the remaining estate can be considered to be community property. Both parties testified at trial that the family's *normal* living expenses were $2,000 per month, or $24,000 per year, and if those expenditures are charged against the annual community income, $17,000 under the *Van Camp* accounting approach, quite obviously there was never any positive balance of community property which could have been built up throughout the marriage.

> When a husband devotes his services to and invests his separate property in an economic enterprise, the part of the profits or increment in value attributable to the husband's services must be apportioned to the community. If the amount apportioned to the community is less than the amount expended for family purposes and if the presumption that family expenses are paid from community funds applied, all assets traceable to the investment are deemed to be the husband's separate property. . . .

Mrs. Beam contends that the evidence clearly establishes that her husband transmuted the two resort business enterprises, Cabana Holiday I and Cabana Holiday II, concededly financed with his separate property, into community property, and thus that the trial court erred in concluding that the enterprises remained her husband's separate property. We believe that sufficient evidence in the record supports the trial court's characterization of the business as separate property.

Mrs. Beam testified at trial that in 1959, when the plans for the resorts were first initiated, her husband gathered the family together and presented the idea of the Cabana projects as a "family project," in which husband and wife were to be "partners." Thereafter, Mrs. Beam stated, she assisted in the plans for the resorts' construction and helped with the management of the project; she declared at trial that she believed these resorts were to be a "community project."

At trial Mr. Beam did not deny that his wife did expend some effort in connection with these resort projects, but he did dispute her claim that he intended to transmute the Cabana Holiday enterprises, worth almost one-half million dollars, into community property. The husband testified that at various times throughout the marriage he and his wife discussed the manner in which title was to be held on his property and, while his wife wanted some property held in joint tenancy, he consistently stated that he desired to keep his separate property in his name alone. The evidence reveals that whereas the family's residences were held in the names of both husband and wife, the Cabana properties remained in Mr. Beam's name alone. . . .

Examining the instant record as a whole, we find that substantial evidence supports the trial court's conclusion. Mr. Beam testified that he entertained no intention of changing the status of the Cabana properties from separate to community property. Although he did not contradict the wife's declaration that some casual references to the enterprises as "family projects" had occurred, he did establish that the formal title of the property continued to be held in his name alone. The court heard testimony as to the total history of the family finances and could conclude, on the basis of the above evidence, that no transmutation of the resort properties occurred.

Notes

1. *Beam* illustrates the problems of distribution of community property when the marriage is ended by divorce; similar pitfalls may await a surviving spouse after the other's death:

> If the wife owns half of the community during marriage, she should also have the right to leave it by will. This rule is followed in every community property state except New Mexico, where her interest expires at her death and the whole community goes to her husband. On his death, however, he has full testamentary powers over his share.
>
> A different inequity exists in the law of California. There the husband has continuing power over his wife's share of the community pending administration of her estate. He need not transfer it to her personal representative except to the extent necessary to carry her will into effect. He is free, in the interim, to change its form, though not its status. When the

wife's personal representative needs the property for distribution under the wife's will, he may demand it from her husband. Before then, however, he may have substantial difficulty in establishing either its status as community property or its value. It remains, though the wife has willed it, subject to her husband's debts. Similarly, when the husband dies, under either New Mexico or California law, the entire community is first subject to his separate debts. Only after his creditors get their share does the wife get hers. No justification for these niggling but nevetheless damaging distinctions has been offered and none can be convincingly made. They are created by statute and linger as unpleasant remnants of the husband's lifetime managerial powers.

Still another distinction persists, though not supported by statute. Husbands in community property states can dispose of the entire community by will, including the wife's share, and leave her something else instead. If a husband clearly intends his wife to take one or the other but not both, she must elect between her share of the community and the alternate gift in the will. This, of course, is a carryover from the common law election between dower rights or statutory forced shares and alternate provisions in wills. Such an election seems particularly inappropriate in the case of community property since the wife's interest is not described as inchoate during her husband's life but as present, equal and existing. How then can the husband dispose of it or require her to elect whether to keep it? [Younger, Community Property, Women and the Law School Curriculum, 48 N.Y.U.L. Rev. 211 (1973).]

See also, Comment, Never Marry A Rich Man: The Lesson of Beam v. Bank of America, 13 Santa Clara Lawyer 121 (1972).

CALIF. CIV. CODE §5127 (1970): [T]he husband has the management and control of the community real property, but the wife . . . must join with him in executing any instrument by which such community real property or any interest therein is leased for a longer period than one year, or is sold. . . .

CALIF. CIV. CODE §5127 (West Supp. 1975): [E]ither spouse has the management and control of the community real property, whether acquired prior to or on or after January 1, 1975, but both spouses . . . must join in executing any instrument by which such community real property or any interest therein is leased for a longer period than one year, or is sold. . . .

Is the retroactive effect of the new §5127 constitutional? See Reppy, Retroactivity of the 1975 California Community Property Reforms, 48 So. Calif. L. Rev. 977 (1975).

2. A California court, applying community property doctrines upon divorce, said that the husband should pay the wife, each month, half of his military pension. The U.S. Supreme Court reversed, holding that the federal military retirement statutes bar the state from awarding

rights in the pension to the wife. Yet, as Justice Rehnquist's vigorous dissent said, the Court could point to no explicit federal statutory language requiring the result and relied only on "vague implications from tangentially related enactments or Congress' *failure* to act." McCarty v. McCarty, 453 U.S. 210 (1981).

3.   *Contract*

◆ MARVIN v. MARVIN
18 Cal. 3d 660, 557 P.2d 106, 134 Cal. Rpt. 815 (1976)

TOBRINER, J. During the past 15 years, there has been a substantial increase in the number of couples living together without marrying. Such nonmarital relationships lead to legal controversy when one partner dies or the couple separates. Courts of Appeal, faced with the task of determining property rights in such cases, have arrived at conflicting positions: two cases hold that the Family Law Act requires division of the property according to community property principles, and one decision has rejected that holding. We take this opportunity to resolve that controversy and to declare the principles which should govern distribution of property acquired in a nonmarital relationship. . . .

Since the trial court rendered judgment for defendant on the pleadings, we must accept the allegations of plaintiff's complaint as true, determining whether such allegations state, or can be amended to state, a cause of action.

Plaintiff avers that in October of 1964 she and defendant "entered into an oral agreement" that while "the parties lived together they would combine their efforts and earnings and would share equally any and all property accumulated as a result of their efforts whether individual or combined." Furthermore, they agreed to "hold themselves out to the general public as husband and wife" and that "plaintiff would further render her services as a companion, homemaker, housekeeper and cook to . . . defendant."

Shortly thereafter plaintiff agreed to "give up her lucrative career as an entertainer [and] singer" in order to "devote her full time to defendant . . . as a companion, homemaker, housekeeper and cook;" in return defendant agreed to "provide for all of plaintiff's financial support and needs for the rest of her life."

Plaintiff alleges that she lived with defendant from October of 1964 through May of 1970 and fulfilled her obligations under the agreement. During this period the parties as a result of their efforts and earnings acquired in defendant's name substantial real and personal property, including motion picture rights worth over $1 million. In May of 1970, however, defendant compelled plaintiff to leave his household. He continued to support plaintiff until November of 1971, but thereafter refused to provide further support.

On the basis of these allegations plaintiff asserts two causes of action. The first, for declaratory relief, asks the court to determine her contract and property rights; the second seeks to impose a constructive trust upon one half of the property acquired during the course of the relationship. . . .

In Trutalli v. Meraviglia (1932) 215 Cal. 698, 12 P.2d 430 we established the principle that nonmarital partners may lawfully contract concerning the ownership of property acquired during the relationship. We reaffirmed this principle in Vallera v. Vallera (1943) 21 Cal. 2d 681, 685, 134 P.2d 761, 763, stating that "If a man and woman [who are not married] live together as husband and wife under an agreement to pool their earnings and share equally in their joint accumulations, equity will protect the interests of each in such property."

In the case before us plaintiff, basing her cause of action in contract upon these precedents, maintains that the trial court erred in denying her a trial on the merits of her contention. Although that court did not specify the ground for its conclusion that plaintiff's contractual allegations stated no cause of action, defendant offers some four theories to sustain the ruling; we proceed to examine them.

Defendant first and principally relies on the contention that the alleged contract is so closely related to the supposed "immoral" character of the relationship between plaintiff and himself that the enforcement of the contract would violate public policy. He points to cases asserting that a contract between nonmarital partners is unenforceable if it is "involved in" an illicit relationship. A review of the numerous California decisions concerning contracts between nonmarital partners, however, reveals that the courts have not employed such broad and uncertain standards to strike down contracts. The decisions instead disclose a narrower and more precise standard: a contract between nonmarital partners is unenforceable only *to the extent* that it *explicitly* rests upon the immoral and illicit consideration of meretricious sexual services. . . .

Defendant also contends that the contract was illegal because it contemplated a violation of former Penal Code section 269a, which prohibited living "in a state of cohabitation and adultery." Defendant's standing to raise the issue is questionable because he alone was married and thus guilty of violating section 269a. Plaintiff, being unmarried could neither be convicted of adulterous cohabitation nor of aiding and abetting defendant's violation. . . .

The numerous cases discussing the contractual rights of unmarried couples have drawn no distinction between illegal relationships and lawful nonmarital relationships. Moreover, even if we were to draw such a distinction — a largely academic endeavor in view of the repeal of section 269a — defendant probably would not benefit; his relationship with plaintiff continued long after his divorce became final, and plaintiff sought to amend her complaint to assert that the parties reaffirmed their contract after the divorce.

Although the past decisions hover over the issue in the somewhat wispy form of the figures of a Chagall painting, we can abstract from those decisions a clear and simple rule. The fact that a man and woman live together without marriage, and engage in a sexual relationship, does not in itself invalidate agreements between them relating to their earnings, property, or expenses. Neither is such an agreement invalid merely because the parties may have contemplated the creation or continuation of a nonmarital relationship when they entered into it. Agreements between nonmarital partners fail only to the extent that they rest upon a consideration of meretricious sexual services. Thus the rule asserted by defendant, that a contract fails if it is "involved in" or made "in contemplation" of a nonmarital relationship, cannot be reconciled with the decisions. . . .

[I]n the present case a standard which inquires whether an agreement is "involved" in or "contemplates" a nonmarital relationship is vague and unworkable. Virtually all agreements between nonmarital partners can be said to be "involved" in some sense in the fact of their mutual sexual relationship, or to "contemplate" the existence of that relationship. Thus defendant's proposed standards, if taken literally, might invalidate all agreements between nonmarital partners, a result no one favors. Moreover, those standards offer no basis to distinguish between valid and invalid agreements. By looking not to such uncertain tests, but only to the consideration underlying the agreement, we provide the parties and the courts with a practical guide to determine when an agreement between nonmarital partners should be enforced. . . .

In summary, we base our opinion on the principle that adults who voluntarily live together and engage in sexual relations are nonetheless as competent as any other persons to contract respecting their earnings and property rights. Of course, they cannot lawfully contract to pay for the performance of sexual services, for such a contract is, in essence, an agreement for prostitution and unlawful for that reason. But they may agree to pool their earnings and to hold all property acquired during the relationship in accord with the law governing community property; conversely they may agree that each partner's earnings and the property acquired from those earnings remains the separate property of the earning partner.[10] So long as the agreement does not rest upon illicit meretricious consideration, the parties may order their economic affairs as they

---

10. A great variety of other arrangements are possible. The parties might keep their earnings and property separate, but agree to compensate one party for services which benefit the other. They may choose to pool only part of their earnings and property, to form a partnership or joint venture, or to hold property acquired as joint tenants or tenants in common, or agree to any other such arrangement.

choose, and no policy precludes the courts from enforcing such agreements. . . .

As we have noted, both causes of action in plaintiff's complaint allege an express contract; neither asserts any basis for relief independent from the contract. In In re Marriage of Cary 34 Cal. App. 3d 345, 109 Cal. Rptr. 862, however, the Court of Appeal held that, in view of the policy of the Family Law Act, property accumulated by nonmarital partners in an actual family relationship should be divided equally. Upon examining the Cary opinion, the parties to the present case realized that plaintiff's alleged relationship with defendant might arguably support a cause of action independent of any express contract between the parties. The parties have therefore briefed and discussed the issue of the property rights of a nonmarital partner in the absence of an express contract. Although our conclusion that plaintiff's complaint states a cause of action based on an express contract alone compels us to reverse the judgment for defendant, resolution of the Cary issue will serve both to guide the parties upon retrial and to resolve a conflict presently manifest in published Court of Appeal decisions. . . .

The principal reason why the pre-Cary decisions result in an unfair distribution of property inheres in the court's refusal to permit a nonmarital partner to assert rights based upon accepted principles of implied contract or equity. We have examined the reasons advanced to justify this denial of relief, and find that none have merit.

In summary, we believe that the prevalence of nonmarital relationships in modern society and the social acceptance of them, marks this as a time when our courts should by no means apply the doctrine of the unlawfulness of the so-called meretricious relationship to the instant case. As we have explained, the nonenforceability of agreements expressly providing for meretricious conduct rested upon the fact that such conduct, as the word suggests, pertained to and encompassed prostitution. To equate the nonmarital relationship of today to such a subject matter is to do violence to an accepted and wholly different practice.

We are aware that many young couples live together without the solemnization of marriage, in order to make sure that they can successfully later undertake marriage. This trial period, preliminary to marriage, serves as some assurance that the marriage will not subsequently end in dissolution to the harm of both parties. We are aware, as we have stated, of the pervasiveness of nonmarital relationships in other situations.

The mores of the society have indeed changed so radically in regard to cohabitation that we cannot impose a standard based on alleged moral considerations that have apparently been so widely abandoned by so many. Lest we be misunderstood, however, we take this occasion to point out that the structure of society itself largely depends upon the institution of marriage, and nothing we have said in this opinion should be taken to derogate from that institution. The joining of the man and woman in marriage is at once the most socially productive and individually fulfilling relationship that one can enjoy in the course of a lifetime.

We conclude that the judicial barriers that may stand in the way of a policy based upon the fulfillment of the reasonable expectations of the parties to a nonmarital relationship should be removed. As we have explained, the courts now hold that express agreements will be enforced unless they rest on an unlawful meretricious consideration. We add that in the absence of an express agreement, the courts may look to a variety of other remedies in order to protect the parties' lawful expectations.[24]

The courts may inquire into the conduct of the parties to determine whether that conduct demonstrates an implied contract or implied agreement of partnership or joint venture or some other tacit understanding between the parties. The courts may, when appropriate, employ principles of constructive trust. Finally, a nonmarital partner may recover in *quantum meruit* for the reasonable value of household services rendered less the reasonable value of support received if he can show that he rendered services with the expectation of monetary reward. Since we have determined that plaintiff's complaint states a cause of action for breach of an express contract, and, as we have explained, can be amended to state a cause of action independent of allegations of express contract, we must conclude that the trial court erred in granting defendant a judgment on the pleadings.

The judgment is reversed and the cause remanded for further proceedings consistent with the views expressed herein.

Notes

1. After a 3-month trial, the judge awarded Michelle Triola Marvin "$104,000, to be used by her primarily for her economic rehabilitation." The award was reversed as outside the pleadings in Marvin v. Marvin, 122 Cal. App. 3d 871, 176 Cal. Rptr. 555 (1981). The trial court had found that plaintiff benefited economically from her relationship with defendant, and that the facts showed that the defendant had no express or implied contractual obligation to share his earnings or wealth with plaintiff.

2. Contra Marvin v. Marvin (i.e., no money for woman who lived for 15 years with man in unmarried, family-like relationship to which

---

24. We do not seek to resurrect the doctrine of common law marriage, which was abolished in California by statute in 1895. Thus we do not hold that plaintiff and defendant were "married," nor do we extend to plaintiff the rights which the Family Law Act grants valid or putative spouses; we hold only that she has the same rights to enforce contracts and to assert her equitable interest in property acquired through her effort as does any other unmarried person.

three children were born, because claim contravened implicit public policies) is Hewitt v. Hewitt, 77 Ill. 2d 49, 394 N.E.2d 1204 (1979).

3. New York's version of Marvin v. Marvin "declined to recognize a contract which is implied from the rendition and acceptance of services" but "required the explicit and structured understanding of an express contract." The contract can be oral, but illicit sexual relations cannot be "part of the consideration." Morone v. Morone, 50 N.Y.2d 481, 413 N.E.2d 1154, 429 N.Y.S.2d 592 (1980).

4. Miss Cooke met Mr. Head. "He was in a good way of business in Bexhill. He was a married man. He had a wife and two children. He took Miss Cooke out in his car to give her driving lessons. An attachment grew up between them. . . ." Hoping Mrs. Head would divorce him, Mr. Head bought land (in his own name), and Mr. Head and Miss Cooke together built a bungalow on it.

> Mr. Head, before the judge, disputed the amount of work she had done. He said that she had only gone up there as a spectator, and played with a blue cat. The judge . . . accepted the evidence of Miss Cooke herself, and . . . was satisfied that Miss Cooke did quite an unusual amount of work for a woman. She used a sledgehammer. . . .

When the bungalow neared completion, the couple separated. Mr. Head sold the bungalow and realized £1,946 above the mortgage.

> If this case had come up 20 or 30 years ago, I do not suppose that Miss Cooke would have had any claim to a share. It would be said that, when she did all the work on the house there was no contract to pay her anything for it. And when she put these moneys into the money box, Mr. Head made no contract to repay it. So it was a gift. But that has all been altered now. . . . [T]he courts may impose or impute a constructive or resulting trust.

Miss Cooke got one-third of the proceeds. Cooke v. Head, [1971] 2 All E.R. 38 (C.A.) (Lord Denning, M.R.).

4. Comparative Notes

♦ KULZER, LAW AND THE HOUSEWIFE: PROPERTY, DIVORCE AND DEATH
28 U. Fla. L. Rev. 1, 51-52 (1975)

There are growing indications that marriage is moving from status to contract. To the extent that this becomes a reality there will be a theoretical and actual basis for equality within marriage. The gradual disengagement of the state from the marital relationship is one indication that this relationship is becoming a matter for individual determination, although, so far, one that is weighted in favor of the husband. As wives achieve some property, and with it equality of bargaining power, the movement toward contract will be furthered. Even now, however, contract as a basis for marriage or indeed, as a substitute for it, is receiving considerable public and scholarly attention.

Antenuptial and postnuptial contracts have not been an uncommon means of settling on property distributions in the event of divorce or death among well-advised and wealthy spouses. Statutes in many states recognize their validity at least insofar as property provisions for these two contingencies are concerned. Recent proposals, however, go well beyond the traditional sort of settlement and contemplate the division of labor, standard of living, number and education of children, methods and responsibility for contraception, and other details of married life as proper subjects for individualized contracts.

It had been thought that contracts attending the status of marriage were unenforceable, at least to the degree that they attempted to alter legally prescribed responsibilities derived from and resulting in the husband's supremacy. Proponents of contract as a component of, or substitute for, marriage now challenge this view. If they are correct, as they would seem to be, then contract as a meaningful alternative may well emerge. Whether that alternative will be available to significant numbers of persons, however, is open to question. This depends on the continued movement of women toward more education and employment opportunities. Women who have little choice but marriage will scarcely be in a position to negotiate a reasonable contract; indeed, they may not wish to do so. There is still considerable pressure to socialize young girls toward domestic goals, and as a result, many of them will seek no other occupation than marriage. For the growing ranks of women who are, or who seek to be, financially independent, however, the individualized contract may well be worthy of consideration. To be sure, traditions of romance, love and self-sacrifice conflict violently with the notion of sitting down and hammering out a marriage contract, but there is ample precedent. For different reasons, the marriage contract is an ideal whose time has come again. Perhaps this has been precipitated by the torpid — indeed, almost imperceptible — response of marital and property laws to the propertyless condition of women.

◆ MARKOVITS, MARRIAGE AND THE STATE:
A COMPARATIVE LOOK AT EAST AND WEST
GERMAN FAMILY LAW
24 Stan. L. Rev. 116, 118-123, 151-155 (1971)

Up to the present, West German courts have approached marriage as a form of moral possession, a viewpoint based on the Civil Code of 1900. In its original version, the code treated marriage as a contractual relationship performing primarily financial functions: of the 265 sections regulating the relationship between husband and wife, 200 concerned matrimonial property rights. Although the wife's legal position in this contractual relationship was designed to be considerably weaker than the husband's, the Civil Code showed some awareness of the wife's financial interests. While it treated her as dependent upon her husband as the provider, it also safeguarded her right to be provided for. Marriage appeared above all as an exchange relationship in which the wife paid for her financial security by granting the husband the right to manage and use the property brought by her into marriage — thus the standard, though not compulsory matrimonial property rules changed only by the Equal Rights Law in 1957. The most striking reflection of this approach is Civil Code section 1300, still in force today, which grants a right to financial indemnity to a woman of "good character" who allows her fiancé cohabitation in the expectation of marriage if the engagement later breaks up through no fault of her own. The drafters of the Civil Code justified this claim on the ground that the woman's loss of virginity "destroyed or at least impaired her chances to be provided for" in the future. . . .

Despite social changes since the turn of the century, much of this approach has been preserved in West German family law. Particularly with respect to the wife, marriage is still viewed as a kind of personal insurance, safeguarded by the threat of financial claims against eventual violation. However, a significant change of emphasis has occurred: While the architects of the Civil Code intended to protect the monetary security offered by matrimony, West German courts have used its provisions to protect the social and moral status of "being married." For example, despite constant criticism of the so-called "defloration" claim of Civil Code section 1300, the majority of West German courts have continued to grant deserted brides financial damages for intercourse with their former fiancés, not, however, because their prospects for finding another husband as provider had been impaired — courts generally agreed that this probably is no longer the case — but because their "female dignity" had been violated. In present-day West German case law, being married is not any longer seen primarily as a financially advantageous bilateral arrangement but as an absolute moral possession. . . .

In East Germany, the possessive approach to marriage has been rejected from the very beginning. Even before the first independent East German family law legislation of 1955 and thus at a time when the Civil Code and the Marriage Statute of the Allied Control Council were in force in the GDR as well as in the Federal Republic, all notions that marriage gave the marriage partners a financial or moral property right were attacked in both case law and literature. Under socialist conditions "the institution of marriage degraded by bourgeois morals" was to be "lifted to those heights where it belonged according to the principles of socialist ethics." These principles had been spelled out by the classics of Marxism, which analyzed bourgeois marriage as an arrangement serving the interests of private property, both by preserving capitalist class control over property through safeguarding its transmission to legitimate heirs and by allowing the suppression and exploitation of woman by man. Since the fulfillment of these functions did not depend on the emotional viability of the actual marriage relationship, bourgeois legal doctrine, according to the Marxist analysis, indeed had reason to stress the importance of marriage as a legally protected status relationship regardless of its personal contents. Under socialism, on the other hand, the property-preserving functions of marriage would be obliterated. The abolition of private property would do away with marriage's role in the legitimation of property transfer through inheritance. Complete integration of women into the production process and the public takeover of former household functions would liberate wives from their domestic servitude and put them on an equal footing with their husbands. With husband and wife thus financially and socially independent equals, marriage would lose all economic aspects and would be placed on the only moral foundation possible: "reciprocal love." . . .

At present, East and West German matrimonial property law are more alike than any other area of the two states' family law. Although technically the property rules offered in the West German Civil Code and the East German Family Code are quite different, their primary aim — a fair adjustment of the financial interest of the individual spouse on the one hand and the marriage community on the other — is the same, and the results are accordingly fairly similar. . . .

In East Germany legal equality with respect to matrimonial property was realized a little earlier than in West Germany: while in the Federal Republic, the Civil Code's old system of management and use of the wife's estate by the husband was declared to be abolished only as of April 1, 1953, the date on which according to article 117 of the Basic Law the constitutional principle of equality came into force regardless of its implementation through statute, in the GDR the husband's management and usufruct was struck down by the East German constitution of October 7, 1949. In both parts of Germany the courts, for lack of new provisions, were thus left with the task of developing a new matrimonial property law, and in both parts they decided on a system of complete separation of assets as the only truly equal matrimonial régime. However, this system, although legally equal, fostered factual inequities in the vast majority of cases where the husband was the only breadwinner while the wife, having no income of her own, was left at the termination of marriage without any money, despite the fact that her housekeeping contributed indirectly to her husband's earnings. In the GDR, therefore, courts very soon developed the concept of a compensation claim for the wife. Based on the assumption that her domestic services were as important for the family's income as the husband's outside work, the courts granted the wife at divorce a monetary compensation which could run as high as 50 percent of the assets accumulated by the couple during marriage.

In West Germany, a very similar system was adopted in 1957, when the Gleichberechtigungsgesetz (Equal Rights Law) introduced the "community of increase" as the statutory *régime matrimonial*. Under the new system, all assets of the spouses remain separate during coverture. There is thus no communal property of the couple, although the common household is somewhat protected by the requirement that transactions concerning household objects or the capital of one spouse in its entirety need the consent of the other partner. At the termination of the marriage, however, the increase in capital obtained by both partners during marriage is equally divided between the spouses. In the average case where husband and wife began marriage on an equal financial footing, then distributed functions during marriage according to the traditional pattern of housekeeping for the wife and moneymaking for the husband, the wife at divorce thus has a financial compensation claim against her husband entitling her to the value of one half of his unconsumed capital.

In East Germany, the Family Code of 1965 rejected this system in favor of the "community of acquests," a system under which objects and assets acquired with the couple's earnings become common property during marriage and as such are equally divided at the termination of the marriage. The somewhat ambivalent wording of Family Code section 13 ("things, assets, and savings acquired through work or with the help of income from work") has caused some debate in the GDR as to whether the spouses' wages themselves were part of the couple's common property. The majority opinion and the quasi-official Family Code Commentary consider wages to be the spouses' personal property, a solution which . . . leaves the ordinary wage-earner's most important financial asset at least partly to his individual disposal. Given the very severe restrictions under which private enterprise has to operate in the GDR, however, individual spending as a rule finds no outlet in entrepreneurial investments but is largely limited to individual consumption, and is therefore less threatening to the other spouse's interests. Most cases litigated in the GDR involve disputes about the earnings of self-employed craftsmen or owners of privately operated enterprises or stores that, having been brought into marriage or later inherited by one of the spouses, have remained this spouse's individual property. . . .

The most remarkable similarity between the matrimonial property system of the West German Equal Rights Law and the East German Family Code, however, lies in the fact that in this area the Family Code does not discriminate against the wife who resigns herself to the traditional role of housewife. On the contrary, the code protects her financial participation in the husband's earnings by accepting her domestic services as sufficient contribution to the family income to warrant common property in all purchases made during marriage, regardless of who made them. This position runs counter to the socialist principle of protecting a worker's "material interest" in his own productivity; it lowers the husband's incentive to work. Moreover, the principle of common property in all earnings is out of line with other attempts made in East German family law, particularly in maintenance law, to force the housewife through financial disadvantages into productive labor. Financial discrimination against housewives in property matters as well would, from an ideological viewpoint, have been the more consistent solution. However, in addition to creating hardship for the divorced spouse, it would have interfered to a far greater extent than the East German maintenance provisions with a couple's individual notions of how to distribute functions within marriage. The East German legislature's tolerance of marital self-determination in this area is a realistic response to persisting social behavior patterns, reflecting an awareness that the family as the "smallest cell" even of a socialist society cannot be manipulated at will.

◆ M. MEIJER, MARRIAGE LAW AND POLICY IN THE CHINESE PEOPLE'S REPUBLIC
201, 237 (1971)

According to Article 10 [of the 1950 Marriage Law] "Both husband and wife have equal rights in the possession and management of the family property." The term translated by "possession," so-yu-ch'üan, actually means property right.

The family is thus endowed with property. It may be a subject of rights. The family property consists of the following categories:

1. The property owned by the spouses at the time of concluding the marriage.
2. The property acquired during the period of common life in marriage by the spouses, meaning:
    (a) property acquired by labour; the labour of the wife in the household is considered to be of the same value as the labour of the husband to procure the means of livelihood;
    (b) property inherited by one of the spouses during this time;
    (c) property belonging to minor children like land, or other property acquired during the land reform.

3.   Property acquired as a gift by either of the spouses during marriage. . . .

Very scant material has been found on the way of handling the family property since the establishment of the communes. As land is collectively owned by the members of the commune, it cannot also be part of the family property; since then disputes at divorce about family property must be confined to houses, fruit-trees, movables, savings, and personal effects. The personal property before marriage may still consist of the fruits of the labour of the individual parties, gifts or inherited property, or of the dowry the woman brought along.

20 ◆ LAND USE REGULATION BY PRIVATE AGREEMENT

Concurrent estates are only one way in which several individuals can have rights in particular real estate at the same time. In situations where people live close together — adjacent farms along a river, single-family houses on a suburban street, or apartments in the same building with common hallways and elevators — sharing is desirable and sometimes essential. You have already considered nuisance law, which is one body of doctrine for regulating the impact that the use of one parcel inevitably has on surrounding land. We referred then to the possibility that individuals could by negotiation and agreement alter the allocation of rights to decide the use of land that would otherwise be imposed by statute, common law doctrine, or individual will. We now consider the rules that have developed to formalize, channel, and sometimes bar such agreements.

Two facts should be recognized at the outset. First, this is not an area of land law in which the common law performance deserves admiration. Rather it is one where rigid categories, silly distinctions, and unreconciled conflicts over basic values have often led to unhappy results for landowners. Second, it is an area of tremendous importance. As living arrangements become more dense, the need for agreements among neighbors increases. And if the public continues to be dissatisfied with the primary alternative regulatory scheme, governmental zoning, private use agreements will remain significant.

The Columbia problem that follows shows a business context in which shared use arrangements seem appropriate. Imagine who would like rights in what land. Can the different interests be reconciled? Reconsider the Columbia problem after you examine the standard doctrinal categories of consensual ownership-sharing. Do the traditional rules permit what Columbia needs? How? To the extent that they make Columbia's program difficult, should they therefore be changed?

Problem

The Columbia Town Center is a group of office buildings, shops, and restaurants located along the shore of the lake in downtown Columbia. Development plans call for the town center to be built in stages, as the Columbia population grows. A major problem is the provision of adequate parking.

A minimum requirement of parking spaces around retail and office buildings is set forth in the Howard County Zoning Ordinance (section 23). But the ordinance merely says what must be provided, not how it is to be assured. The latter point is of the utmost importance to the developers who will construct the buildings and to the lenders who will finance them, since inadequate parking facilities have a major impact on the attractiveness of the buildings to potential tenants, and thus on the rental income the buildings will be able to generate.

Commonly, adequate parking would be assured by a series of easements that would burden each parcel in the development for the benefit of all other parcels. This is a nonexclusive parking easement in that the spaces on any given parcel may not be claimed for the exclusive use of the tenant of that parcel; rather, they are available for use by all tenants in the development. When the entire project is planned at once, the owner of each parcel can be clear as to both the number of spaces that will be required on his parcel and the total number of spaces that will be available in the development.

However, it should be clear that no such assurance can be given when a nonexclusive parking easement is applied to a staged development. The easement is designed to assure the tenant of each parcel that there will be sufficient parking for the project as a whole. In our case, the total demand for parking spaces cannot be known in advance, since it depends on the type and density of development in future stages (e.g., retail space requires 3.75 parking spaces per 1,000 square feet, and office space only 2.5 spaces per 1,000 square feet).

Clearly, no developer or lender participating in the first stage will want to take the risk that uses in a later stage will result in inadequate parking for his building or a need to place more spaces on his land than was originally thought to be necessary. Such an easement would be a major cloud on the title to the parcel.

One possible solution would tie the number of spaces required on any given parcel to the size and use of the building on that parcel. But this is inflexible. The proper emphasis is on the total parking needs of the total development; for example, an office building and a theater can use the same parking spaces, the former in the day and the latter in the evening. The above proposal would require that each have sufficient spaces to meet its total needs.

Any acceptable solution would seem to require that one party have the responsibility for providing sufficient parking in the town center. Since Rouse will control the staged development, he would seem to be the logical one. For designing a solution, remember that Rouse wants to remain as flexible as possible; the fewer commitments he has to make that a particular piece of ground will *always* be a parking lot, the happier he will be. On the other hand, consider how important adequate parking would be to you if you represented a lending institution. Note that you are as concerned with the positioning of spaces as you are with the number of spaces. Would it be possible to require each developer to waive his rights under the easement so long as a stated number of spaces is provided adjacent to his premises? If so, would Rouse have to guarantee to meet the overall parking requirement? How? What are the problems with this?

Think through possible arrangements for meeting the economic needs of Rouse, lenders, merchants, and customers. Keep this problem in mind as you investigate some of the common law doctrines that have grown up around similar arrangements.

Note

See Mutual of Omaha Life Insurance Co. v. Executive Plaza, Inc., 99 Ill. App. 3d 190, 425 N.E.2d 503 (1981), holding that lease language, giving lessee and its employees and customers rights in common with other occupants to use parking spaces, created an easement appurtenant. Tenants obtained an injunction against assignment of certain spaces to one tenant, even though they could not show that the assignment would deprive them of sufficient spaces or that it would disrupt their business.

See also J. Weingarten, Inc. v. Northgate Mall, Inc., 390 So. 2d 527 (La. App. 1980), *rev'd*, 404 So. 2d 896 (La. 1981). There, a lease gave a tenant a nonexclusive easement to six parking spaces for every 1,000 feet of floor area. When the landlord breached the contract by constructing a $4 million addition that reduced the parking ratio, the tenant sought an injunction for removal of about 40,000 feet of construction. The court of appeal ordered removal, but the Louisiana Supreme Court held that money damages were the appropriate remedy.

And see the court's holding in Madigan Brothers, Inc. v. Melrose Shopping Center Co., 123 Ill. App. 3d 851, 463 N.E.2d 824 (1984):

> [T]he intent of the parties was to grant the shopping center tenants an easement in the parking area for ingress, egress and parking as set out in the plat. It is the law in Illinois that where no reservation by the landlord of the right to alter the common area is made in the lease and where the site plan attached to the lease accurately and precisely delineates the common

areas, the tenant has an easement to the particular configuration of common space delineated by the lease and attached plats. In order to make a tenant's easement over the common areas moveable, the lease must expressly and specifically grant the landlord the right to change the arrangement of the common areas. No such right is granted to the landlord in the instant case. Certain provisions in the lease contemplate enlargements of the shopping center, but these merely specify plaintiff's rights in such circumstances and do not specifically grant the landlord the right to rearrange the parking areas. . . .

It is therefore clear that the provisions of the lease gave plaintiff a non-exclusive easement to the parking areas as they are shown in the plat attached to the lease, and that the lease contains no provisions which can be construed to make this easement moveable. We therefore find that the trial court did not err in enjoining the construction of the restaurant in the shopping center parking area without plaintiff's consent.

A. THE TRADITIONAL DOCTRINES

1. Easements

THE LAW RELATING TO EASEMENTS, 113 The Law Journal 607 (Eng. 1963): The true nature of an easement has for long baffled the layman. To those with a desire for enlightenment there is nothing inherently difficult in the concept that property may include not only the kind of right which enables a man to say, "I own Blackacre" but also the kind of right which entitles him to say, "I have a right of way over Whiteacre." Further progress on the road to comprehension, however, is rendered more difficult by the illogical classification and terminology designed for us by our legal ancestors. . . .

An easement is a right enforceable against the land of another. It approximates to what the Roman lawyers called a praedial servitude. The Roman concept of servitudes stipulated a right *in rem*, vested in one person or annexed to one piece of land but extending over the land of another and operating in restriction of the enjoyment of that other land. Such rights were divided into personal and praedial servitudes and in the case of a praedial servitude the burden imposed on one property (*praedium serviens*) had to be related to a benefit attached to another property (*praedium dominans*). This principle is echoed by English law and the requirement that the right claimed must accommodate the dominant tenement is one of the distinguishing characteristics of the easement.

English law recognizes two classes of servitudes, easements and profits. A profit was defined most succinctly by Lindley, L.J., in Duke of Sutherland v. Heathcote ([1892] 1 Ch., at p.484), where he said that a profit "is a right to take something off another's land."

An easement, however, is a privilege without a profit such as the right to walk over the land of another but not to take anything from it.

Easements may be positive or negative. A positive easement confers a right to do something on the land of another, for example to walk over it, drive cattle across it, or deposit rubbish on it. A negative easement, however, simply imposes a restriction on the use which the owner of the servient tenement may make of his land. Thus in the case of a right to light, the servient owner may not build on his land in such a way as to obstruct the light flowing to the dominant tenement. Similarly, in the case of an easement of support the servient owner may not carry out operations on his own land which would have the effect of causing the dominant land to settle.

(+)
(-)

An easement is an interest in land that entitles its holder to some limited use or enjoyment of land possessed by another. There are two types: easements in gross and easements appurtenant. If the easement is established to benefit the owner personally and not his land, it is said to be in gross. But if the owner of the easement possesses other land that normally adjoins the land burdened by the easement, and the easement is created to benefit the owner's use of his land, then the easement is appurtenant to that other land.

(1)

(2)

Suppose Whiteacre and Blackacre are adjoining parcels. A owns Whiteacre and B owns Blackacre. If B conveys to A an easement in gross to walk over Blackacre to reach Whiteacre, then the right is A's regardless of whether A continues to own Whiteacre. If on the other hand an easement appurtenant is conveyed, and then A conveys his interest in Whiteacre to C, C now has the ownership rights that A had. It is as if Whiteacre has rights against Blackacre. Whiteacre is called the dominant tenement, and Blackacre the servient tenement.

In the Common Law 297-299 (1881; 1968 ed.), Holmes examined this concept:

> . . . In the first Lecture of this course the thought with which we have to deal was shown in its theological stage, to borrow Comte's well-known phraseology, as where an axe was made the object of criminal process; and also in the metaphysical stage, where the language of personification alone survived, but survived to cause confusion of reasoning. The case put seems to be an illustration of the latter. The language of the law of easements was built up out of similes drawn from persons at a time when the *noxæ deditio* was still familiar; and then, as often happens, language reacted upon thought, so that conclusions were drawn as to the rights themselves from the terms in which they happened to be expressed. When one estate was said to be enslaved to another, or a right of way was said to be a quality or incident of a neighboring piece of land, men's minds were not alert to see that these phrases were only so many personifying

metaphors, which explained nothing unless the figure of speech was true. . . .

All that can be said is, that the metaphors and similes employed naturally led to the rule which has prevailed, and that, as this rule was just as good as any other, or at least was unobjectionable, it was drawn from the figures of speech without attracting attention, and before any one had seen that they were only figures, which proved nothing and justified no conclusion.

As easements were said to belong to the dominant estate, it followed that whoever possessed the land had a right of the same degree over what was incidental to it. If the true meaning had been that a way or other easement admits of possession, and is taken possession of with the land to which it runs, and that its enjoyment is protected on the same grounds as possession in other cases, the thought could have been understood. But that was not the meaning of the Roman law, and, as has been shown, it is not the doctrine of ours. We must take it that easements have become an incident of land by an unconscious and unreasoned assumption that a piece of land can have rights. It need not be said that this is absurd, although the rules of law which are based upon it are not so.

◆ CUSHMAN VIRGINIA CORP. v. BARNES
204 Va. 245, 129 S.E.2d 633 (1963)

CARRICO, Justice. Cushman Virginia Corporation, hereinafter referred to as Cushman, filed a bill of complaint against Donald C. Barnes, hereinafter referred to as Barnes, praying that an adjudication be made that there was appurtenant to the land of Cushman a right of way over the land of Barnes. The bill also prayed that Barnes be enjoined from interfering with Cushman's use of the right of way. The trustees and beneficiaries under deeds of trust on the Cushman land were also made parties complainant, but their presence as such is not of concern on this appeal.

Barnes filed an answer to the bill denying that Cushman had any right of way over his property. The answer further alleged that if such a right of way had ever existed, it had been extinguished by "cessation of purpose" or abandonment. Barnes prayed for such relief "as may be appropriate." . . .

The evidence shows that the lands of Cushman and Barnes were originally parts of a large farm known as "Midway," containing approximately 955 acres, in Albemarle County. In 1895, "Midway" was divided among three heirs in a partition proceeding.

Lot 1, containing 410¾ acres which abutted on the public road, was conveyed to W. O. Durrette. The other two lots did not abut on the public road but lot 2, containing 255 acres, was conveyed to J. Frank

Durrette, "together with the right of way by the present road through *easement* Lot No. 1 to the County road." Lot 3, containing 289¾ acres, "together with the right of way by the present road through Lots Nos. 2 and 1 to the County road," was conveyed to Mary M. Durrette (who later married G. Norris Watson), "her heirs and assigns."

The road thus established, and which is in controversy here, became known as the Durrette road. . . .

In 1930, Mary Durrette Watson acquired a portion of lot 2 of "Midway," containing 9.2 acres. This tract adjoined Mrs. Watson's lot 3 in the area near her home and was traversed by a portion of the Durrette road.

Cushman acquired its land, totalling 126.67 acres, all a part of lot 3 *Lot 2+3* of "Midway," from Mrs. Watson and her husband by two deeds. The first deed, in 1943, conveyed 123 acres together with a right of way thirty feet wide, running from the 123 acre tract through the 9.2 acre portion of lot 2, "to the center of the *Durrett* Road," and also a right of way 30 feet wide, running from the 123 acre tract through the remaining portion of lot 3, "to the center of the branch in line of Farmington, Inc." The second deed, in 1944, conveyed tracts of 1.77 acres and 1.9 acres. No mention was made in the deeds of the right of way through lots 1 and 2 of "Midway" other than the reference to the termination of the thirty foot right of way in "the center of the *Durrett* Road."

Barnes acquired his land, totalling approximately 335 acres, made *Lots 1,2,3* up of portions of lots 1, 2 and 3 of "Midway," by two deeds. The first deed, in 1947, conveyed 234.9 acres, being the major portion of lot 2 and traversed by the Durrette road, and 12.4 acres, being a portion of lot 3 but not so traversed. The second deed, in 1952, conveyed 88.4 acres, being a portion of lot 1 and traversed by the road. Each of these conveyances was made subject to the right of way established in the Durrette partition. . . .

In 1929, the Watsons had acquired a new right of way from their property through the lands of Farmington, Inc., and they ceased using the Durrette road as a means of access. A fence was erected across the road between the Watson land and that now owned by Barnes, although sliding bars were installed to permit the passage of members of the *abandoned* Farmington Hunt Club. A portion of the road on lot 2, near the Watson property, became overgrown with trees and brush.

However, occasional use was made of the old road on Barnes' land after 1929 by horseback riders, by a farmer hauling corn from the Cushman land and by one person who drove an automobile over it. And Mr. and Mrs. Watson, in 1942, conveyed a tract of 1.96 acres to George H. Barkley with, "a right of way along the old right of way out to the old Ivy Road created" in the Durrette partition. In 1949, they conveyed to J. Deering Danielson a tract of 32.7 acres, together with a right of way over the old road.

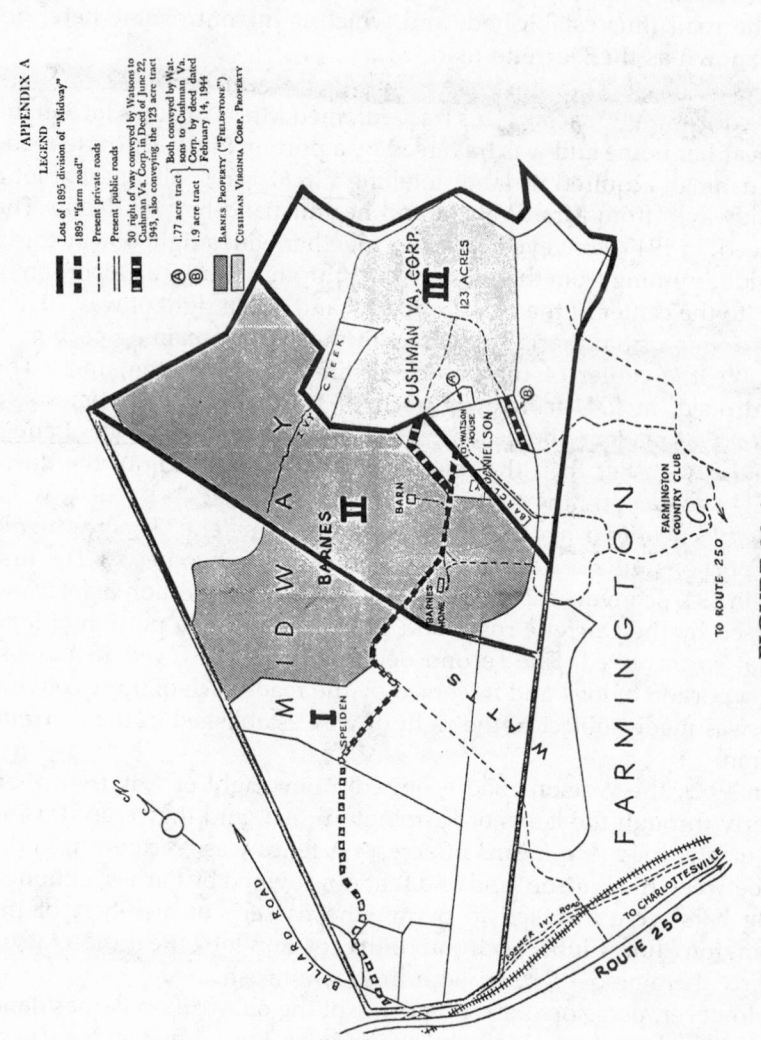

APPENDIX A

LEGEND

Lots of 1895 division of "Midway"

1895 "farm road"

Present private roads

Present public roads

30 right of way conveyed by Watsons to Cushman Va. Corp. in Deed of June 22, 1943, also conveying the 123 acre tract

Ⓐ 1.77 acre tract Both conveyed by Watsons to Cushman Va.
Ⓑ 1.9 acre tract   Corp. by deed dated February 14, 1944

BARNES PROPERTY ("FIELDSTONE")

CUSHMAN VIRGINIA CORP. PROPERTY

FIGURE 20-1

Map from the official report of *Cushman*

The present controversy arose when Cushman advised Barnes of its intention to subdivide the 126.67 acre tract and to use the Durrette road in connection therewith.

At the hearing before the chancellor, there was no direct evidence of the width of the right of way or the scope of its use immediately after its establishment in 1895. There was testimony dating back to 1907 that the road served the three farms along its route to carry buggies, hay wagons, threshing machines, trucks and other farm equipment. One witness said that, "two people could pass most everywhere on that road except when you got out there on the mountain some places." However, there was other testimony that there was only, "a one track road, you could pass if you were to drive out in the field;" that the road, "in narrow places would give a buggy about six inches on each side;" that the road was 8 or 10 feet wide, and that there were gates across the road in seven or more different places, each being 10 to 12 feet wide. . . .

Did the chancellor err in finding that there was a right of way over Barnes' land appurtenant to the Cushman tract? This question arises from Barnes' contention that the deed of the 123 acre tract from Watson to Cushman in 1943 did not convey a right of way over the Durrette road. He also argues that since the 30 foot right of way granted to Cushman terminated in "the center of the *Durrett* Road," there was an expressed intention not to convey any rights beyond that point.

We think there is no merit in Barnes' contention in this respect. Code, §55-50 provides as follows:

"*Appurtenances, etc., included in deed of land.* — Every deed conveying land shall, unless an exception be made therein, be constructed to include all buildings, privileges and appurtenances of every kind belonging to the lands therein embraced."

The right of way over lots 1 and 2, established in the partition proceedings for the benefit of lot 3 of "Midway," was an appurtenance belonging to the latter lot, and to every portion thereof. When a portion of that lot was conveyed by the Watsons, it carried with it the use of the right of way, if accessible to it, unless an exception thereto was made in the deed. . . .

The next question is, did the court err in determining that the right of way, "does not exceed the width of the farm road existing in 1895, the travelled portion being limited to a single track, not exceeding 10 feet and the outside width, including cuts, fills, ditches, embankments, etc., at no point exceeding 15 feet"?

We think the chancellor did not err in this ruling. . . .

Cushman contends that since the deeds were silent as to the width of the right of way, it will be presumed that the parties intended that 30 feet would be its width. The basis for this presumption, Cushman says, is the fact that at the time the right of way was established all public roads in Virginia were 30 feet wide.

The Durrette road is not, nor has it ever been, a public road. Even Cushman does not now urge that it be so declared.

The testimony of the witnesses who had been familiar with the road since 1907; the technical evidence and expert testimony of the surveyor, Bailey; the photographic exhibits which displayed facts to which time has given testimony, and which cannot be refuted, all lead to but one conclusion — the Durrette heirs never intended, and did not establish, the right of way to be 30 feet wide. Instead, this evidence, all of which was credible, supports the chancellor's determination of its width.

The next question is, did the chancellor err in determining,

> that such right of way may not be used for the purpose of developing or serving the residential or commercial subdivision of the 126.67 acre tract and such right of way is accordingly limited to normal farm or residential use of not more than two single family dwellings together with any servant or tenant houses used solely for housing of the occupant employees of such dwellings located on any part of the 126.67 acre tract, regardless of the number of any future off conveyances or subdivisions of the 126.67 acre tract?

We are of opinion that the chancellor did err in this respect. His ruling unreasonably restricts Cushman's rights in the use of the right of way.

When a right of way is granted over land, the servient estate, for the benefit of other land, the dominant estate, and the instrument creating the easement does not limit the use to be made thereof, it may be used for any purpose to which the dominant estate may then, or in the future, reasonably be devoted. This rule is subject to the qualification that no use may be made of the right of way, different from that established at the time of its creation, which imposes an additional burden upon the servient estate. And, as has been seen, the right to the use of the easement is an appurtenance of the dominant estate and of every portion thereof. When a portion of the dominant estate is conveyed away, without excepting the right of way, the owner of such portion has the right, in connection with the reasonable use of his land, to make use of the easement if his land is accessible thereto. The fact that the dominant estate is divided and a portion or portions conveyed away does not, in and of itself, mean that an additional burden is imposed upon the servient estate. The result may be that the degree of burden is increased, but that is not sufficient to deny use of the right of way to an owner of a portion so conveyed.

In the case before us, the deeds creating the right of way contained no terms of limitation upon its use. Mary Durrette Watson, the owner of lot 3 of "Midway," provided she devoted her land to a reasonable purpose which did not impose an additional burden upon lots 1 and 2, was entitled to make such use of the right of way as its narrow width permitted. That same right, subject to the same conditions, passed to Cushman as an appurtenance of the 126.67 acre tract acquired from Mrs. Watson. The final decree improperly limits Cushman's rights. . . .

To support Barnes' theory that the right of way had been abandoned, there was testimony that after the Watsons had acquired the new right of way through Farmington in 1929, they abandoned the right of way over the Durrette road, erected a fence across it and never used it thereafter; that a "No Passin" sign was erected on the right of way between lots 1 and 2 when Barnes purchased his land, and that the right of way was permitted to become overgrown with trees and bushes.

To support Cushman's theory that the right of way had not been abandoned, there was testimony that occasional use had been made of the road since 1929, and that after the Watsons were supposed to have abandoned the right of way they made conveyances of portions of their land in which they granted the right to use the easement.

Thus, there was presented to the chancellor conflicting evidence upon this issue. He has determined to accept that version of the evidence which supports the theory of no abandonment. That version was credible and persuasive and he was justified in accepting it. Under these circumstances, we will not disturb his ruling.

Notes

1. A 1912 deed had established a reciprocal easement between two lots, creating a "right of way in common, forever, over and through an alley three feet wide." The District of Columbia Court of Appeals, relying on *Cushman*, affirmed the lower court's imposition of a series of time and use restrictions on the ingress and egress of workers, supplies, and equipment being used by one lot owner to construct another building. The court emphasized that the right of way could not be used "in a manner that would burden the servient estate to a greater extent than was contemplated or intended at the time of the grant." Moreover, the court held that, despite the lack of restrictions in the grant, "the easement is not one of unlimited use, but one of unlimited *reasonable* use." Wheeler v. Lynch, 445 A.2d 646 (D.C. 1982) (emphasis in original).

2. Plaintiff's predecessor had obtained in 1892 an easement in a 12-foot alley "as an inlet and outlet" to his own lot. The Virginia court, following *Cushman*, said this did not permit him to install underground water and gas lines in the alley, because "no use may be made . . . different from that established at the time of its creation, which imposes an additional burden on the servient estate." Gordon v. Hoy, 211 Va. 539, 178 S.E.2d 495 (1971).

Easements are acquired by grant, by prescription, by implication, and sometimes by eminent domain.

Compulsory government taking of easements has become an important device for protecting environmental amenities at less cost to taxpayers than would be required for purchase of the entire fee. See D. Gregory, The Easement as a Conservation Technique 19 (1972):

> The basic idea of conservation easements is very simple and has the characteristics of a negative easement in gross. The private property owner relinquishes his right to use his land or a portion of it in a certain specified manner which, it is thought, would derogate from its natural qualities. The holder of the easement, who ordinarily would not own nearby land, does not, of course, acquire the right relinquished but instead obtains the power to enforce the restriction against the landowner, subsequent title-holders, and even strangers. The transfer of an easement can be accomplished by gift, negotiated sale, or expropriation. While the principal hope of this arrangement has been directed toward preserving open space, the possible variants of the basic idea may well be innumerable.

Termination of Easements

Release. An easement may be terminated by a written release complying with the Statute of Frauds.

Its Own Terms. An express easement may expire by its own terms, as when A grants B a right of way over Whiteacre for ten years.

Unity of Title. An easement terminates when title to the easement and servient tenement come to the same person. Example: A, owner of Whiteacre, grants Blackacre a right of way over Whiteacre. B, who owns Blackacre, purchases Whiteacre from A. Unity of title now exists, and if C purchases Blackacre, he will have no easement over Whiteacre unless expressly granted, or unless a new easement is found through implication or prescription.

Prescription. If the owner of the servient tenement uses his land in a manner adversely to the owner of the easement for the time required for acquisition of prescriptive rights, the easement will terminate.

Abandonment. An easement may be extinguished by nonuse with acts or words indicating an intent never to use the easement again.

Estoppel. An easement is extinguished if, in reasonable reliance on the conduct of the owner of the easement, the servient tenant uses the servient tenement in a manner inconsistent with the existence of the easement, and it would be inequitable to restore the privilege of use authorized by the easement. Example: A grants B a right of way over Whiteacre. B indicates to A his intent to abandon. In reasonable reliance, A spends a substantial sum in constructing a fence where the easement allowed B to pass. B will be estopped from using the easement.

NATIONAL CONFERENCE OF COMMISSIONERS ON UNIFORM STATE LAWS, UNIFORM CONSERVATION EASEMENT ACT (1982):

§1.

(1) "Conservation easement" means a nonpossessory interest of a holder in real property imposing limitations or affirmative obligations the purposes of which include retaining or protecting natural, scenic, or open-space values of real property, assuring its availability for agricultural, forest, recreational, or open-space use, protecting natural resources, maintaining or enhancing air or water quality, or preserving the historical, architectural, archaeological, or cultural aspects of real property. . . .

§2.

(a) Except as otherwise provided in this Act, a conservation easement may be created, conveyed, recorded, assigned, released, modified, terminated, or otherwise altered or affected in the same manner as other easements.

(b) No right or duty in favor of or against a holder and no right in favor of a person having a third-party right of enforcement arises under a conservation easement before its acceptance by the holder and a recordation of the acceptance.

(c) Except as provided in Section 3(b), a conservation easement is unlimited in duration unless the instrument creating it otherwise provides.

(d) An interest in real property in existence at the time a conservation easement is created is not impaired by it unless the owner of the interest is a party to the conservation easement or consents to it.

§3.

(a) An action affecting a conservation easement may be brought by:
(1) an owner of an interest in the real property burdened by the easement;
(2) a holder of the easement;
(3) a person having a third-party right of enforcement; or
(4) a person authorized by other law.

(b) This Act does not affect the power of a court to modify or terminate a conservation easement in accordance with the principles of law and equity.

§4.

A conservation easement is valid even though:
(1) it is not appurtenant to an interest in real property;
(2) it can be or has been assigned to another holder;
(3) it is not of a character that has been recognized traditionally at common law;

(4)   it imposes a negative burden;

(5)   it imposes affirmative obligations upon the owner of an interest in the burdened property or upon the holder;

(6)   the benefit does not touch or concern real property; or

(7)   there is no privity of estate or of contract.

§5.

(a)   This Act applies to any interest created after its effective date
which complies with this Act, whether designated as a conservation easement or as a covenant, equitable servitude, restriction, easement, or otherwise.

(b)   This Act applies to any interest created before its effective date
if it would have been enforceable had it been created after its
effective date unless retroactive application contravenes the
constitution or laws of this State or the United States.

(c)   This Act does not invalidate any interest, whether designated
as a conservation or preservation easement or as a covenant,
equitable servitude, restriction, easement, or otherwise, that is
enforceable under other law of this State.

§6.

This Act shall be applied and construed to effectuate its general
purpose to make uniform the laws with respect to the subject of the Act
among states enacting it.

CONARD, EASEMENT NOVELTIES, 30 Calif. L. Rev. 125, 126-127, 150
(1942): An elementary idea about what may be the subject of an easement is the thought that the conduct which an easement authorizes
must be the same kind of conduct which some past easement has authorized. This may be expressed in a mere list of permissible varieties, as
in an English writer's pronouncement that "nothing can amount to a
valid easement unless the subject matter of the claim is capable of being
referred to one or other of six definite heads — air, light, support, water,
ways and fences." Another Englishman, in his treatise upon easements,
thought it more accurate to say that "the law will not permit a landowner to create easements of a novel kind and annex them to the soil.
. . ." In accordance with ideas of this sort, it has been argued that there
can be no easement of walking for pleasure, of boating for pleasure, of
withdrawing from land its subjacent support, of maintaining trees
whose limbs cross a boundary, of opening sluices of a reservoir when its
level rises dangerously or of maintaining bathhouses, either because
such an easement does not conform to the prevailing conception of any
of the listed varieties, or simply because it is novel. In the course of the
opinion in the boating case, Baron Martin declared, "None of the cases
cited are at all analogous [to] this, and some authority must be produced
before we can hold that such a right can be created." The learned Baron

went on to warn of the consequences of sustaining an easement without precedent; it "would lead to the creation of an infinite variety of estates in land." In this prediction he was no doubt correct. That servitudes are infinite in variety had been acknowledged with complete composure by [Bracton].

Efforts to stem the tide of legal progress by enumerating the limits of its past advances have a familiar ring. Constitutional lawyers recall how the United States Supreme Court of the 1920's sought to limit businesses "clothed with a public interest" to those franchised by, or granted to the public, and also to "certain occupations . . . recognized from the earliest times" such as inns, cabs and grist mills. Tort lawyers remember how Judge Sanborn sought to salvage remnants of Winterbottom v. Wright by restricting departures from it to three exceptions "well defined and settled." No lawyer will be surprised to learn that easements, like manufacturers' liabilities and enterprises affected with a public interest, broke the bounds that were set for them. . . .

[An examination of the cases shows that an] easement may authorize acts which have not been authorized before and acts whose effects and functions have not been authorized before. It may differ in many legal incidents from previously known easements.

Yet there are limits. An interest so extensive that it amounts to an estate is not an easement. An interest too vague for judicial administration is not an easement. An interest too slight to merit judicial recognition is not an easement. Particular incidents which serve no useful purpose will not be judicially enforced, although they will not prevent the other incidents from being sanctioned.

But in the main, landowners may create in others an unlimited variety of privileges, and attendant rights, to make non-possessory uses of the land. It was wisely said a century ago by the first English writers on easements that, "The number and modifications of rights of this kind may be infinite both in their extent and mode of enjoyment, as the convenience of man in using his property requires."

◆ KELLY v. IVLER
187 Conn. 31, 450 A.2d 817 (1982)

HEALEY, Associate Justice. This matter arises out of a dispute over the use of and interference with certain easements existing across both parties' properties in Stamford. The plaintiffs brought an action seeking damages and an injunction in an attempt to force the defendants to remove certain improvements from an easement which runs across the southerly portion of the defendants' property and to enjoin them from interfering with their use of that easement. The defendants counterclaimed and alleged that the plaintiffs had no easement across the defendants' property and also that the plaintiffs have interfered with easements of the defendants which run across the westerly and southerly portions of the plaintiffs' property. The trial court found certain issues for both parties from which the defendants appealed and the plaintiffs cross appealed.

The plaintiffs are owners of two parcels of land, each with a house situated thereon, located in the Shippan area of Stamford. [See Figure 20-2.] Each parcel fronts on a 29.58 foot strip of land, owned in fee by the plaintiffs, which extends northerly from Ocean Drive East and which has been designated as the "right of way." The parties and the trial court have designated these parcels as Lots 1 and 2 with Lot 1 being to the north of Lot 2. Directly to the east of Lot 1 and abutting the same is another lot with a house situated thereon, designated as Lot 3, which the defendants own. Lot 3 is bounded on the east by Long Island Sound. Neither of the plaintiffs' properties has any direct access to Long Island Sound. The plaintiffs do, however, claim an easement, reserved in a deed by a predecessor in title, of six feet in width along the southerly boundary of the defendants' Lot 3 to the waters of Long Island Sound (hereinafter "the Long Island Sound easement").

The defendants, on the other hand, have no direct access to Ocean Drive East or to the plaintiffs' 29.58 foot right of way which extends to its north. The plaintiffs concede, however, that the defendants' access to Ocean Drive East is by way of the 29.58 foot right of way described above. Also conceded is the fact that access to the defendants' property from the 29.58 foot right of way is by way of an easement, nine feet in width, running from west to east along the southerly boundary of the plaintiffs' Lot 2 ("the nine foot easement") and by another connecting easement, six feet in width, running from south to north along the easterly boundary of the same lot ("the six foot easement"). Both parties agree that the six foot and nine foot easements, as they exist today, are represented by a driveway leading from Ocean Drive East to the defendants' house on Lot 3. Additionally, the defendants have title to a parking space located within the 29.58 foot right of way, the use of which is in dispute, as well as the right to park other vehicles within the right of way.

The defendants have erected a fence along the southerly boundary of their property allegedly encroaching upon the plaintiffs' Long Island Sound easement. The defendants have installed a catch basin at the westerly boundary of that easement and, in the process, removed a step from a stone stairway which had previously existed. The defendants also installed drainage pipes which empty into that easement thereby changing the flow of surface water on their property. This has caused excess water to flow into the Long Island Sound easement greatly increasing the erosion thereon. Within the nine and six foot easements, the defendants have installed, and the plaintiffs have removed, mush-

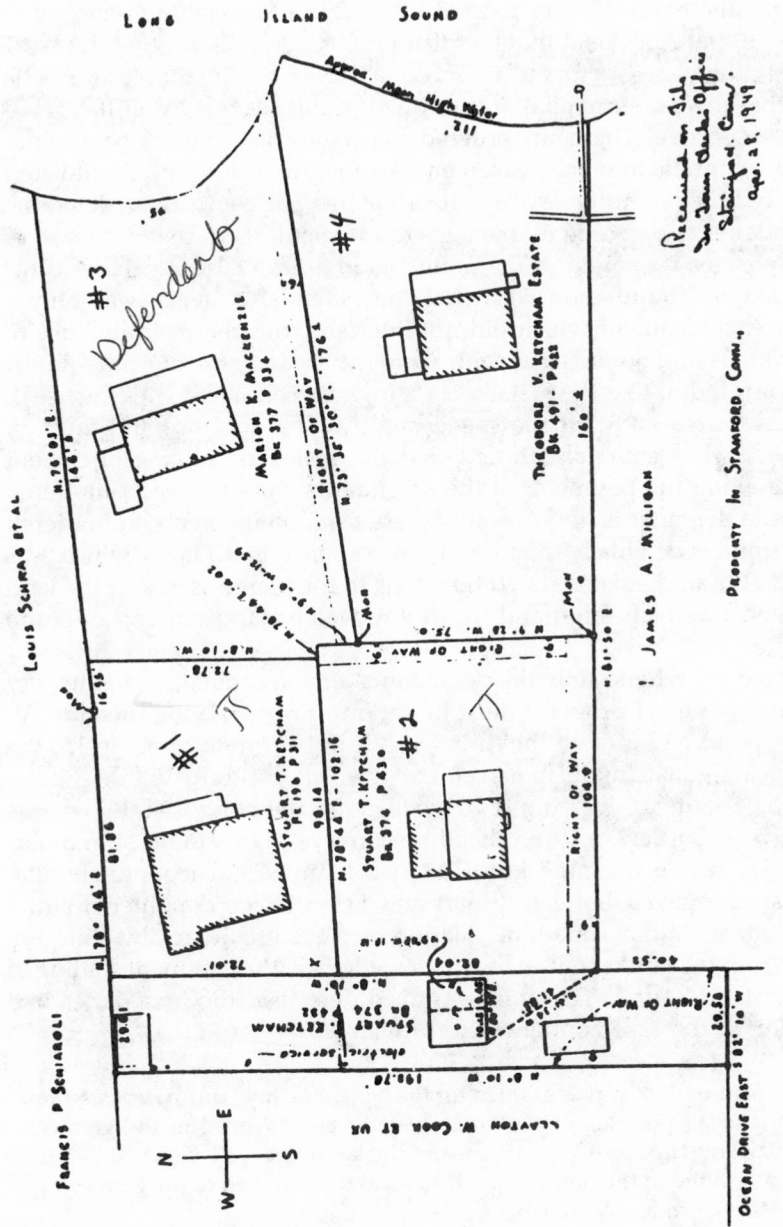

FIGURE 20-2

Map from the Appendix to the official report of *Kelly*

925

room-type lights, apparently to make the driveway safer for nighttime travel. The plaintiffs, meanwhile, have built a speed bump in the nine foot easement and have placed cement blocks along the perimeter of the defendants' parking space located in the 29.58 foot right of way.

The trial court held that the plaintiffs had established that the Long Island Sound easement was reserved in a deed by a predecessor in title and that it was permanent and ran with the land in favor of the plaintiffs' properties. The court ordered the removal of the drainage pipes which emptied into that easement because they interfered with and impaired the plaintiffs' use of that easement. The court also ordered the defendants to pay $500 in damages to the plaintiffs to cover the cost of the damages sustained in the Long Island Sound easement. The court additionally found, however, that the defendants' fence was only a slight encroachment which did not interfere with the plaintiffs' use of the Long Island Sound easement. As to the six and nine foot easements, the court found that the installed lighting was consistent with the use of the easements and that the speed bump was a nuisance and must be removed. The court also found that the plaintiffs' placing of cement blocks along the perimeter of the defendants' parking space interfered with the defendants' ingress and egress from their vehicle and ordered them removed. Finally, apparently in response to a matter which was raised at trial, the court stated that "[a]s to the plaintiffs' use of the land between the mean high and mean low water marks, there can be no dispute." . . .

To comprehend fully the defendants' first argument, a brief history of these pieces of property must be set out. Prior to 1916, Theodore V. Ketcham owned each of the three parcels of land now belonging to the parties along with a fourth parcel (Lot 4) which is directly to the south of the defendants' property and which also has the Long Island Sound as its easterly border. In 1916, Theodore conveyed Lot 1 to his son, Stuart Ketcham, while retaining Lots 2, 3 and 4. In 1929, Theodore simultaneously conveyed Lot 2 to Stuart and Lot 3 to his daughter, Marion MacKenzie. At the same time, Marion conveyed to Stuart, by quitclaim deed from the land about to be conveyed to her, the easement leading to Long Island Sound. The quitclaim deed described the boundaries and location of the easement and also provided:

> Said right of way is granted for the benefit of any [sic] appurtenant to any and all portions of the land about to be conveyed to the grantee [Stuart] by Theodore V. Ketcham and the land [Lot 1] now owned by the grantee lying to the north of the land so to be conveyed to the grantee by the said Theodore V. Ketcham.
>
> To have and to hold the premises, with all the privileges and appurtenances, unto said releasee [Stuart] his heirs and assigns forever, so that neither I [Marion] the said releasor nor my heirs, nor any person under me or them shall hereafter have any claim, right or title in or to the premises,

or any part thereof, but therefrom I am and they are by these presents forever barred and secluded except my fee simple ownership thereof.

The defendants have conceded, and correctly so, that this 1929 deed created and granted a permanent easement (i.e., "the Long Island Sound easement") to the owners of Lots 1 and 2.

The situation remained unchanged until 1953 when two transactions occurred. On April 24, Stuart quitclaimed his interest in Lot 3 for one dollar to Marion. One minute later, Marion conveyed her entire interest in Lot 3 to Orestes LaPolla by warranty deed. In the April 24, 1953 quitclaim deed from Stuart to Marion, the following appeared:

> reserving, however, to me the said releasor [Stuart] as appurtentant to my other land shown on said map a right of way and easement of use for any and all purposes in, over, and upon a strip of land six (6) feet in width designated as "Right of Way" . . . and lying along the southerly boundary line of [Lot 3].

The resolution of this first issue turns on the interpretation accorded to this reservation clause. The plaintiffs became the owners of Lot 1 in 1959 and of Lot 2 in 1960. The defendants became the owners of Lot 3 in 1976 after the property had changed hands twice in the interim. Stuart died in 1955.

The defendants claim that the above quoted language from the 1953 quitclaim deed operated to convert the undisputed permanent Long Island Sound easement, granted in the 1929 deed, into a mere personal right of way in Stuart which terminated with his death in 1955. The defendants point out that since there were no words of limitation such as "to my heirs and assigns," the easement reserved was personal to the grantor and, therefore, the plaintiffs have no right to use the Long Island Sound easement running along the southerly portion of the defendants' property. Additionally, the defendants allege that the "surrounding circumstances" existing at the time the 1953 deed was executed do not demonstrate an intention to create anything other than a reservation of a personal right of way. The trial court rejected these arguments and found this issue for the plaintiffs and we affirm that decision.

Since the defendants have conceded that the 1929 quitclaim deed from Marion to Stuart created a permanent appurtenant easement in the owners of Lots 1 and 2, the major focus of this issue becomes whether the reservation clause contained in the 1953 deed from Stuart to Marion reduced the appurtenant easement to an easement in gross. "The meaning and effect of the reservation are to be determined, not by the actual intent of the parties, but by the intent expressed in the deed, considering all its relevant provisions and reading it in the light of the surrounding circumstances; and its interpretation presented a question of law."

It is well settled that "[i]f the easement makes no mention of the heirs and assigns of the grantee, a presumption is created that the intent of the parties was that merely a personal right of way was reserved. This presumption, however, is not conclusive. A reservation will be interpreted as creating a permanent easement if, from all the surrounding circumstances, it appears that that was the intention of the parties." Since the 1953 reservation clause does not contain words of limitation, i.e., heirs and assigns, we would ordinarily presume that a mere easement in gross was reserved thereby supporting the defendants' argument. When the "surrounding circumstances" are examined, however, it is apparent that the intentions of Stuart and Marion were to reserve a permanent easement. . . .

. . . It is true that if the only intent were to continue Stuart's permanent easement across Lot 3 after its sale, no additional deed would have been necessary to accomplish this. It is precisely this fact, however, which leads us to conclude, along with the "surrounding circumstances," that more than that was intended and accomplished by this 1953 deed. Notwithstanding the defendants' argument, it is a fair inference that the purpose of this transaction between brother and sister must have been to purge Stuart of any interest he may have had in Lot 3 in order to allow Marion to pass a clear title to her purchaser in this first out-of-the-family transfer involving these lots. Viewed in this light, it made perfect sense for Stuart to include the reservation clause in the 1953 deed not merely to affirm his permanent easement but . . . to avoid extinguishing or releasing the permanent easement. . . .

. . . There was also testimony demonstrating that at least one of the defendants knew, before the property was purchased, that people, including the plaintiffs, used the Long Island Sound easement to gain access to the beach area. Florence Carberry, the sister of one of the plaintiffs, testified that she had used the easement for nineteen years without anyone preventing her from doing so. The defendants have countered this evidence with testimony of a predecessor in title of Lot 3 from 1970 to 1973, Charles Bennett Norman, in which he stated that, on two separate occasions during his ownership, he prevented Florence Carberry from using the Long Island Sound easement. However, merely two interruptions during the nineteen year period of the plaintiffs' use of the easement is not sufficient to overcome the significance of the recognition by the servient estates' predecessors in title, as well as those of the defendants themselves, both in their deeds and in their actions, of the plaintiffs' right to use the Long Island South easement. . . .

We next address the defendants' claim that the trial court erred in awarding $500 to the plaintiffs for damages sustained to the Long Island Sound easement. "The law is settled that the obligation of the owner of the servient estate, as regards an easement, is not to maintain it, but to refrain from doing or suffering something to be done which results in an impairment of it. . . ."

The record discloses that the plaintiffs failed to prove any amount of damage as to the diminution in value of their property; or as to the cost of repairs to return the easement to its original state; or as to the difference in the value of the easement just before the interference and the value immediately after the obstruction was completed. This being the case, the plaintiffs were entitled to no more than nominal damages.

We now turn to the issues raised by the plaintiffs' cross appeal. The plaintiffs first argue that the trial court erred in finding that there was no interference with the plaintiffs' use of the Long Island Sound easement even though the defendants' fence encroached upon that easement. The plaintiffs claim that the court should have ordered the removal of the fence because it constituted a nuisance. . . .

In the present case, the court found, after viewing the premises, that the fence "slightly" encroached on the easement but that it did not interfere with the use of the easement by the owners of the dominant estate. The evidence disclosed that the fence did encroach on the boundary line of the Long Island Sound easement by 0.6 feet or 7¼ inches. It is important to note, however, that the sole purpose of this easement was to provide the owners of Lots 1 and 2 with a means by which they could walk to the beach. We cannot say, after viewing the photographs included as exhibits and in light of the use of the easement, that the fence materially or substantially interferes with pedestrian passage over the easement. This was a question of fact for the trial court whose decision we will not set aside unless clearly erroneous . . .

There is error in part, the judgment with respect to damages is set aside and the case is remanded with direction to render a judgment for the plaintiffs for $1 damages. The judgment is affirmed in all other respects.

Notes

1. Plaintiff owned Monterey Farm, including a strip of land called Cann Road. Defendant, who owned the land adjacent to the road, had used the road over many years to reach distant parts of her farm. The vice-chancellor held that her uses had been without permission and of sufficient frequency to put the owner on notice of the claimed right thereto, so that she had acquired a prescriptive easement. But since her uses were agricultural, she could not now employ the road for access by persons living in houses on her subdivided farm. Biggs v. Wolfe, 40 Del. Ch. 212, 178 A.2d 482 (1962).

2. Whittier Extension Co. constructed a permanent gravel roadway through its land, for access to its lemon and avocado fields. When it sold one piece of its land to Fristoe, the deed said Whittier could use the part of the road on Fristoe's land, but said nothing about Fristoe using the

part over Whittier's land. The court held that the road was essential for Fristoe's farming, and so she has "an easement *by implied grant.*" And her easement is not limited to agricultural use, since "intent [is] the criterion" and "we cannot say as a matter of law that the use of the road for purposes connected with a private residence was not within the contemplation of the parties." Fristoe v. Drapeau, 35 Cal. 2d 5, 215 P.2d 729 (1950).

3. For over forty years a country club had used a certain strip of land adjacent to its golf course as a rough for the sixth fairway. Club members had regularly entered the adjacent land to retrieve misdirected golf balls, with the landowner's knowledge. The country club was held to have acquired a prescriptive easement over the adjacent land. Mac-Donald Properties, Inc. v. Bel-Air Country Club, 72 Cal. App. 3d 693, 140 Cal. Rptr. 367 (1977).

2. Licenses

CONARD, AN ANALYSIS OF LICENSES IN LAND, 42 Colum. L. Rev. 809 (1942): Chancellor Kent was puzzled by easements and licenses, and he admitted it. "This distinction," Kent wrote, "between a privilege or easement carrying an interest in land, and requiring a writing . . . to support it, and a license which may be by parol, is quite subtle, and it becomes difficult in some of the cases, to discern a substantial difference between them." What was difficult for the great Chancellor was no easier for other men of the law; many of them were content to cite the Commentaries and concede that the distinction was "difficult of discernment." With even greater emphasis, one puzzled jurist lamented, "The distinction between an easement and a license is often so metaphysical, subtle and shadowy as to elude analysis."

According to Lord Chief Justice Vaughan, in perhaps the most frequently quoted definition, a license "passeth no interest, nor alters or transfers property in any thing, but only makes an action lawful, which without it, had been unlawful. As a license . . . to hunt in a man's park, to come into his house, are only actions, which without license, had been unlawful." Thomas v. Sorrel, Vaugh. 330, 351, 124 Eng. Rep. 1098 (C.P. 1673).

3 Tiffany, Law of Real Property §829 (1939) explains that:

> The distinction between such an easement and a license privilege lies primarily in the fact that the licensee has a privilege and nothing more, while the holder of an easement has not only a privilege but also rights against the members of the community in general, including the owner of

the land, that they refrain from interference with the exercise or enjoyment of the privilege. That a licensee, as such, has no right of action
against a third person obstructing his exercise of the license privilege is, it
is conceived, beyond question, in spite of occasional decisions to the contrary. That he has no right of action against the landowner himself by
reason of such an obstruction by the latter follows from the doctrine that a
license is revocable and may be revoked by an act on the part of the
licensor indicating an intention to revoke.

Licenses are also distinguished from easements in that they require
no formal writing to make them effective. Thus an attempted easement
lacking formality may be declared to be a license by a formalistic court,
upsetting the parties' intentions and expectations.

If a license were never more than a revocable privilege, its nature
would be clear. However, if a license is always and immediately revocable, considerable injustice could result when the licensee has purchased
the license at substantial cost in reliance on indications it would not be
revoked, or has expended labor in reliance on its continuance. Where
justice requires, a court may declare a license to be irrevocable; in such a
circumstance, the practical distinction between easement and license
may well be "metaphysical, subtle, and shadowy."

One more term should be considered: The "license coupled with
interest." The Restatement explains that "A license coupled with an
interest is one which is incidental to the ownership of an interest in a
chattel personal located on the land with respect to which the license
exists" (§513) and gives the following example:

> A, the owner and possessor of Whiteacre, sells to B a car of coal already
> mined and standing on Whiteacre, which is owned and possessed by A. If
> there is an effective sale of the coal, B has a license coupled with an interest
> to go on Whiteacre to remove the coal.

The license coupled with an interest is irrevocable for a reasonable
period of time.

◆ BASEBALL PUBLISHING CO. v. BRUTON
302 Mass. 54, 18 N.E.2d 362 (1938)

LUMMUS, Justice. The plaintiff, engaged in the business of controlling
locations for billboards and signs and contracting with advertisers for
the exhibition of their placards and posters, obtained from the defendant on October 9, 1934, a writing signed but not sealed by the defendant whereby the defendant "in consideration of twenty-five dollars . . .
agrees to give" the plaintiff "the exclusive right and privilege to main-

tain advertising sign one ten feet by twenty-five feet on wall of building 3003 Washington Street" in Boston, owned by the defendant, "for a period of one year with the privilege of renewal from year to year for four years more at the same consideration." It was provided that "all signs placed on the premises remain the personal property of the" plaintiff. The writing was headed "Lease No. — ." It was not to be effective until accepted by the plaintiff.

It was accepted in writing on November 10, 1934, when the plaintiff sent the defendant a check for $25, the agreed consideration for the first year. The defendant returned the check. The plaintiff nevertheless erected the contemplated sign, and maintained it until February 23, 1937, sending the defendant early in November of the years 1935 and 1936 checks for $25 which were returned. On February 23, 1937, the defendant caused the sign to be removed. On February 26, 1937, the plaintiff brought this bill for specific performance, contending that the writing was a lease. The judge ruled that the writing was a contract to give a license, but on November 2, 1937, entered a final decree for specific performance, with damages and costs. The defendant appealed. It is stipulated that on November 3, 1937, the plaintiff tendered $25 for the renewal of its right for another year beginning November 10, 1937, but the defendant refused the money.

The distinction between a lease and a license is plain, although at times it is hard to classify a particular instrument. A lease of land conveys an interest in land, requires a writing to comply with the statute of frauds though not always a seal, and transfers possession. A license merely excuses acts done by one on land in possession of another that without the license would be trespasses, conveys no interest in land, and may be contracted for or given orally. A lease of a roof or a wall for advertising purposes is possible. The writing in question, however, giving the plaintiff the "exclusive right and privilege to maintain advertising sign . . . on wall of building," but leaving the wall in the possession of the owner with the right to use it for all purposes not forbidden by the contract and with all the responsibilities of ownership and control, is not a lease. The fact that in one corner of the writing are found the words, "Lease No. — ," does not convert it into a lease. Those words are merely a misdescription of the writing.

Subject to the right of a licensee to be on the land of another for a reasonable time after the revocation of a license, for the purpose of removing his chattels, it is of the essence of a license that it is revocable at the will of the possessor of the land. The revocation of a license may constitute a breach of contract, and give rise to an action for damages. But it is none the less effective to deprive the licensee of all justification for entering or remaining upon the land. . . .

The writing in the present case, however, seems to us to go beyond a mere license. It purports to give "the exclusive right and privilege to maintain" a certain sign on the defendant's wall. So far as the law permits, it should be so construed as to vest in the plaintiff the right which it purports to give. That right is in the nature of an easement in gross, which, whatever may be the law elsewhere, is recognized in Massachusetts. We see no objection to treating the writing as a grant for one year and a contract to grant for four more years an easement in gross thus limited to five years.

An easement, being inconsistent with seisin in the person owning it, always lay in grant and could not be created by livery of seisin. It is an interest in land within the statute of frauds and, apart from prescription, requires a writing for its creation. But in equity a seal is not necessary to the creation of an easement. Since equity treats an act as done where there is a duty to do it enforceable in equity, or, as more tersely phrased, equity treats that as done which ought to be done, an enforceable unsealed contract such as the writing in this case, providing for the creation of an easement, actually creates an easement in equity.

There is no error in the final decree granting specific performance. The affirmance of this decree will not prevent an assessment of the damages as of the date of the final decree after rescript.

Notes

1. A landowner granted to an oil company the right to "lay pipes for the transportation of petroleum, and operate the same on, over and through his lands. . . ." The oil company laid two parallel pipe lines pursuant to this grant. Some years later, when it attempted to lay a third line, the landowner objected and physically threatened the company's workers as they sought to lay the line. In holding that the grant was "something more than an easement," the court stated:

> Nor is [the grant], in its essential nature a license, nor can it be reduced in its nature in that respect. It by its terms granted a permanent right to lay the pipe, to maintain the same, and to remove the same. It gave an interest in the land quite as positive and as permanent as that in which a deed is given granting the right to lay a line of water pipes or to erect a line of telephone poles across the grantor's land, where the circumstances indicate that the work done thereunder was to be permanent. [Standard Oil Co. v. Buchi, 72 N.J. Eq. (2 Buch.) 492, 66 A. 427 (1907).]

2. Defendants purchased a parcel of land from plaintiff. As part of the sale transaction, the parties had executed an "Agreement for Easement" for defendants' ingress and egress across plaintiff's adjacent land. This agreement had a number of conditions attached; one said that plaintiff could revoke if defendants interfered with plaintiff's "activities

and operations" on his property. Based on this clause, the court held that the agreement was a revocable license, not an easement, and enjoined defendants from the use of any rights upon or across plaintiff's land. Jabout v. Toppino, 293 So. 2d 123 (Fla. App. 1974).

3. A received a letter from B's lawyer, on which B had written "right of way ok" referring to a certain road passing across B's property. When B later objected to A's use of the road, A failed in an attempt to enjoin B from interfering with his use of the road. The court said that B had granted "at best, a license which was revocable." Davenport v. Broadhurst, 406 N.E.2d 1030 (Mass. App. 1980).

3. Covenants

a. The Common Law Background

A. W. B. SIMPSON, AN INTRODUCTION TO THE HISTORY OF THE LAND LAW 109-111 (1961): Covenants which affect land have a close affinity with easements, and there are obvious resemblances between the law which governs them. Historically, however, the two are quite distinct. Easements from a very early period rank as a form of property, and the law which governs land itself is extended to them through the medium of the assize of nuisance, which is an extension of the assize of novel disseisin. The law of covenants affecting land is an extension of the medieval law of contract, which grew up around the action of covenant. The model for this extension was the ancient law of warranty. Upon a subinfeudation by feoffment (the normal mode of conveyance before Quia Emptores (1290)) it was normal for the feoffor to warrant the land to the feoffee, and even if he did not do so an obligation to warrant arose by implication on the receipt of homage; this is an illustration of the feudal notion that a lord has a duty to protect his tenants. The obligation to warrant, which was the consequence of the tenure created by the grant, descended to the heirs of the feoffor, and the benefit passed down to the heirs of the feoffee, thus it provided an example of an obligation which passed down like real property. In the course of time the reliance upon implied warranties gave way to a reliance upon express warranties; partially this was the result of Quia Emptores (1290), which limited subinfeudation to estates other than the fee simple. Express warranties in a charter could be sued upon as covenants in the action of covenant; by being inserted in charters they automatically became promises under seal. Naturally enough they were treated as covenants annexed to the estate of the covenantee, they guaranteed the actual estate granted, and by an extension of the normal rules governing the action of covenant they could be relied upon by persons other than the original covenantee, so long as he had the estate to which the benefit of the covenant had been originally attached. The recognition of the rule that the benefit of an express warranty would run with the estate to which it was annexed for the purposes of the writ of covenant merely copied the same rule which applied for the purposes of the writ of *warrantia cartae* (the special writ for enforcing warranties), for voucher, and for rebutting a claim to the land. In the fourteenth century it was settled in Pakenham's Case (1369) that the benefit of other sorts of the covenant could be annexed to the estate of the covenantee; the covenant enforced in that case was held to bind the defendant to celebrate divine service in the chapel of the plaintiff, who was a successor in title of the original covenantee. Thus the power of running with the estate in land of the covenantee was extended outside the original context of warranties. This breach of the ordinary rule of privity of contract was limited to the benefit of covenants affecting land.

On the running of the burden of covenants there is little known of the medieval law, but we can perhaps guess what a medieval lawyer would have said by looking at the law of warranty. The obligation to warrant descended upon the heirs of the warrantor; it could not be annexed to land, for on an alienation the land passed to the alienee who took the benefit. By the thirteenth century it was settled that it was not possible to alter this rule about the obligation to warrant by making contrary provision in a deed. Though there is an absence of authority upon whether upon a feoffment, a burden (such as a *duty* to say divine service) could be annexed to the land of the feoffee by mere covenant the probability is that this could not be done, by analogy with the law of warranty.

Thus it was the rule that the benefit of a covenant could be annexed to the estate in land of the covenantee, but it is unlikely that a burden could be imposed. It must be noted that the medieval law on this point does not depend upon the existence of privity of estate between the parties to an action on the covenant, for this does not exist between grantor and grantee of an estate in fee simple. The rules which govern the landlord and tenant relationship, where there is privity, do not develop until the sixteenth century. It seems probable, however, that the benefits of covenants in a lease ran with the land at common law in the medieval period, by analogy with the decision in Pakenham's Case. At the same time it is not likely, though there is little authority on the matter, that covenants could in medieval law be annexed to a reversion. Certainly this was not established until after the medieval period.

BERGER, A POLICY ANALYSIS OF PROMISES RESPECTING THE USE OF LAND, 55 Minn. L. Rev. 167, 172 (1970): The most important case historically in the development of a system of running burdens and benefits is Spencer's Case [5 Co. Rep. 16a, 77 Eng. Rep. 72 (K.B. 1583)]. Plaintiff Spencer, the landlord, had leased realty to a tenant, the latter covenanting for himself, his executors and administrators that he, his executors, administrators or *assigns* would build a brick wall on a part of the leased land. The tenant assigned his interest to *J* who assigned to defendant. The defendant refused to build the wall and plaintiff land-lord brought an action of covenant against defendant. The court held for defendant and in a broad series of dicta laid down general principles for the resolution of the issue of when a burden shall run with the land. First, the court said, when the covenant extends to a thing in being ("in esse"), the burden of the covenant shall run with the land and bind the assignee even if there are no express words in the instrument purport-ing to bind a later assignee. Second, and on the other hand, if the covenant has to do with a thing not in being, there must be express words evincing an intent to bind the assignee. Third, the covenant will run and bind the assignee only if it "touches and concerns" the lease property and is not merely "collateral." And fourth, the covenant will run and bind only those in privity of estate with the lessor and lessee.

Apparently on the basis of the fact that the tenant covenanted for himself, his executors and administrators and did not in the very first instance mention the word "assigns," the court held the covenant was not binding on the defendant, as the wall was not in being.

♦ WHEELER v. SCHAD
   7 Nev. 204 (1871)

By the Court, Lewis, C.J.: On the fifth day of June, a.d. 1862, M. S. Hurd, Ferdinand Dunker and Peter Bossell, being the owners and in possession of a certain mill-site and water privilege, regularly conveyed to Charles Doscher, Charles Itgen, Charles D. McWilliams and William C. Duval a portion thereof, together with the privilege connected there-with. The grantees entered into possession and erected a quartz mill on the premises thus conveyed. The stream was first conducted to the mill of Hurd and associates, and thence to that of their grantees. On the eleventh day of the same month, the respective parties entered into an agreement which, after reciting the necessity of constructing a dam across the river and a flume to conduct the water to their several mills, provided that the dam and flume should be constructed at their joint expense, Hurd and his associates, however, agreeing to pay five hun-dred dollars more than one-half the cost, and the other parties the bal-ance; the dam and flume, when completed, to be owned and enjoyed jointly in equal shares. It was also agreed that they should be kept in good order and repair at the joint and equal expense of the respective parties. Some time after the construction of these works, Wheeler suc-ceeded to the interest of Bossell, and he, together with Hurd and Dun-ker, continued in the ownership and remained in possession of the first mill, known as the Eureka.

Doscher and his associates having mortgaged their mill some time between January and March, 1868, put the assignee of the mortgage (defendant) in possession, who continued to hold the property under the mortgage until he obtained the absolute title by virtue of foreclosure and sale under his mortgage, which occurred in October, A.D. 1868. Early in the year 1868, while the defendant was in possession under the mortgage, the dam and flume were damaged to such an extent that it became necessary to make extensive repairs upon them. Before proceeding with the work, the plaintiffs notified the defendant of their damaged condition, and requested him to unite with them in making the proper repairs. The defendant agreed that the work should proceed, and requested the plaintiff Wheeler to superintend it and "take charge of the workmen." The repairs were made in due time, at an expense of three thousand five hundred dollars, one-half of which is now sought to be recovered. Judgment for defendant; plaintiffs appeal; and it is argued on their behalf: first, that the defendant is liable on the agreement entered into between the defendant's grantors and the plaintiffs; and secondly, if not, that he is so upon his own agreement with the plaintiffs, authorizing the work to be done.

To maintain the first point, it is contended that the deed of conveyance of the mill-site to the grantors of the defendant, and the agreement referred to, should be held to be one instrument; that the stipulations of the latter should be engrafted upon the deed and held to be covenants running with the land. But nothing is clearer than that the two instruments are utterly disconnected, as completely independent of each other as they possibly could be. The deed was executed on the fifth day of June, at which time it does not appear that there was any thought of an agreement to construct or keep in repair any dam or flume. There is no evidence that such a project was in contemplation even by any of the parties, much less that any agreement of this character was in view. It was not, in fact, executed until six days afterwards, and there can be no presumption other than that it was not contemplated until such time. Had it entered into the transaction; had it been understood between the parties at the time of the conveyance that such contract should be executed, there might be some ground for the claim that the agreement and deed constituted but one transaction, and therefore should be construed as one instrument; but unfortunately for the appellants, there is no such showing in the case. If, in fact, the agreement did not enter into the conveyance, or was not contemplated at the time, it is of no consequence how soon afterwards it may have been executed; a day or an hour would as completely separate the instruments and make them independent of each other, as a year. It is impossible, under the evidence in this case, to merge the deed and agreement into one instru- ment, and construe them as if executed simultaneously.

Unless they constituted one instrument or transaction, it cannot be claimed that the covenants of the agreement run with the land so as to charge the grantee of the covenantor. To make a covenant run with the land, it is necessary, first, that it should relate to and concern the land; and secondly, a covenant imposing a burden on the land can only be created where there is privity of estate between the covenantor and covenantee. Whether a covenant for the benefit of land can be created where there is no privity is still questioned by some authorities; but it was held in Packenham's case, determined as early as the time of Edward III, that a stranger might covenant with the owner in such manner as to attach the benefit of a covenant to the land and have it run in favor of the assignees of the covenantee; and the rule there established has since been frequently recognized as law, although questioned by text writers, and the broad doctrine sought to be maintained that privity of estate is absolutely essential in all cases, to give one man a right of action against another upon a covenant, when there is no privity of contract.

Whether the rule announced in Packenham's case be law or not, is not necessary to determine here, for all the courts hold that the _burden_ of a covenant can only be imposed upon land so as to run with it when there is privity of estate between the covenantor and covenantee. It was said by Lord Kenyon, in Webb v. Russell, 3 Term. 393, that "it is not sufficient that a covenant is concerning the land, but in order to make it run with the land there must be a privity of estate between the covenanting parties." That was the law long prior to the time of Kenyon, and has never been doubted, although perhaps cases may be found where an erroneous application of the rule has been made. To render a covenant binding on the assignee of the covenantor, it must therefore not only be meant to bind his estate as well as his person, but the relation between the parties must be such as to render the intention effectual — that is, there must be privity of estate between the covenanting parties. To constitute such relation, they must both have an interest in the land sought to be charged by the covenant. It is said their position must be such as would formerly have given rise to the relation of tenure. A covenant real is, and can only be, an incident to land. It cannot pass independent of it. It adheres to the land, is maintained by it, is in fact a legal parasite, created out of and deriving life from the land to which it adheres. It follows, that the person in whose favor a covenant is made must have an interest in the land charged with it; for he can only get the covenant through, and as an incident to, the land to which it is attached. Says Coke, 385, (a): "A seized of the Mannor of D, whereof a Chappell was parcell, a prior with the assent of his covent covenanteth by deed indented with A and his heires to celebrate divine service in his said Chappell weekely, for the lord of the said Mannor and his servants, &c. In this case the assignees shall have an action of covenant, albeit they are not named, for that the remedie by covenant doth runne with the land, to give damages to the partie grieved, and was in a manner appurtenant to the Mannor. But if the covenant had beene with a stranger to celebrate divine service in the Chappell of *A*, and his heirs, there the assignee shall not have an action of covenant; for the covenant cannot be annexed to the Mannor because the covenantee was not seized of the Mannor." So it is manifest this interest in the land sought to be charged with the covenant must exist at the time the covenant is made. It needs no argument to show that an interest acquired afterwards would not avail the covenantee.

Did the plaintiffs in this case have any estate in the land owned by the defendant at the time this agreement was entered into? It is not even claimed they had. Nor did the agreement itself create any such interest. There is no attempt in it to convey any estate to them, nor a word of grant in the whole instrument. It is a mere contract for the erection of a dam, which does not appear to be on the premises either of the plaintiffs or defendant, and a flume to conduct water to their respective mills, and to maintain them in good order. Suppose the grantors of the defendant had entered into an agreement binding themselves to build the dam and flume for the benefit of the plaintiffs, for a stipulated sum of money; will it be claimed that such an agreement could be held a covenant running with land owned by such grantors, and which was entirely distinct from that upon which the work was to be performed? We apprehend not. Where the distinction, as to its capacity to run with the land, between such a covenant and that entered into here, where instead of compensation in money the defendant's grantors were to receive a benefit from the improvement itself? . . . The judgment below must be affirmed.

◆ MORSE v. ALDRICH
   36 Mass. (19 Pick.) 449 (1837)

This was an action of covenant. The cause was tried before PUTNAM, J.

In 1794, Stephen Cook, the defendants' ancestor, conveyed to William Hull, in fee, a tract of land in Watertown, containing about thirteen acres; with the privilege of using and improving the land and mill pond west of the same tract, for the purpose of fish ponds, baths, &c. within certain bounds described, including a portion of the grantor's mill pond; and the "full liberty of ingress, egress, and regress to and from any part of the said described land and water, to dig out and carry away the whole or any part of the soil, &c.; to build such causeways and dams as may be necessary to divide the same into six separate and distinct fish ponds."

Hull conveyed the same premises to the plaintiff.

Afterward, in November 1809, an agreement under seal was made by and between Cook and the plaintiff, in which, in consideration of the covenants on the part of the plaintiff, Cook covenants with the plaintiff, his heirs and assigns, "that he will draw off his said pond when thereto requested by said Morse, in the months of August and September, not exceeding six working days in the whole, in each year, for the purpose of giving said Morse an opportunity of digging and carrying out mud, &c. as long as there may be mud in said pond, and no longer." It was upon this clause that the present action was brought. In the same agreement are other covenants, some concerning Morse's land and Cook's mill pond, and some concerning the discontinuance and costs of certain actions then pending between Cook and Morse. Cook does not covenant, in express terms, for his heirs or assigns.

It was contended by the plaintiff, that the covenant above recited was a covenant running with the land, and therefore binding upon the defendants, who derive their title to their estate as heirs of Cook, as to four fifths thereof, and as assignees by quitclaim, of one of his heirs, as to the other fifth. And this construction was supported at the trial, against the objection of the defendant. The plaintiff claimed the right to take the mud, &c. for the purpose of manuring his land.

The plaintiff requested the defendants to draw off the pond in September 1835, in order that he might get out the mud, but the defendants refused.

The plaintiff claimed a right to dig and carry out the mud in and from every part of the pond; but the defendants contended that he was limited to the line of his own land, which runs through the pond, the plaintiff owning the land on one side and the defendants owning the land on the other side of this line. The judge ruled the point in favor of the plaintiff.

While Cook was in the occupation of the pond, the plaintiff enjoyed the privilege of taking the mud, and afterwards, whenever he requested to have the pond drawn off, until 1835. Cook died in 1833.

It was proved that the defendants made a lease of their estate, subject to the plaintiff's right to have the pond drawn off and to take the mud, according to the covenant, and that they afterwards permitted the lessee to keep up the pond, contrary to the covenant, in consideration that the lessee would permit them to have the ice which should be made on the pond.

The plaintiff proved that there was a great quantity of mud in the pond; and the jury were directed to inquire particularly whether the damage would have been more or less if the plaintiff had been restrained to dig on his own land under the pond, for the year 1835. The jury found a verdict for the plaintiff for $25, as the damages sustained in 1835; and they found that there was so great a quantity of mud upon his own land, that it would have made no difference that year, whether he had been restricted to his own land, or had taken mud from any other part of the pond. . . .

WILDE, J. afterward drew up the opinion of the Court. The defendants are charged as the heirs of Stephen Cook, their ancestor, with the breach of a covenant made by him with the plaintiff, and the question submitted to the Court is, whether this covenant is such as is binding upon the heirs of the covenantor? And the decision of this question depends on another, namely, whether the covenant is a real covenant, running with the land, which the defendants inherit from their ancestor, the covenantor?

It is generally true, as has been argued by the defendants' counsel, that, by the principles of the common law, the heir is not bound by the covenant of his ancestor, unless it be stipulated by the terms of the covenant, that it shall be performed by the heir; and unless assets descend to him from his ancestor sufficient to answer the charge. If therefore the heir be not named in the covenant, it will be binding only on the covenantor, his executors and administrators, although the heir may take by descent from the covenantor assets sufficient to answer the claim.

But this principle is not to be applied to real covenants running with the land granted or demised, and to which the covenants are attached for the purpose of securing to the one party the full benefit of the grant or demise, or to the other party the consideration on which the grant or demise was made. Such covenants are said to be inherent in the land, and will bind the heir or the assignee though not named. For as he is entitled to all the advantages arising from the grant or demise, it is but reasonable that he should sustain all such burdens as are annexed to the land.

When a covenant is said to run with the land, it is obviously implied that he who holds the land, whether by descent from the covenantor, or by his express assignment, shall be bound by the covenant. The heir may be charged as an assignee, for he is an assignee in law, and so an executor may be charged as the assignee of the testator. And a devisee may be charged in the like manner, and is entitled to the benefit of any covenant running with the land.

If then the covenant in question runs with the land, it is clear that the defendants are liable; and it is immaterial whether the heirs and assigns of the covenantor are named in the covenant, or not, *quia transit terra cum onere.*

To create a covenant which will run with the land, it is necessary that there should be a privity of estate between the covenantor and covenantee. . . . In these cases, and in most of the cases on the same subject, the covenants were between lessors and lessees; but the same privity exists between the grantor and grantee, where a grant is made of any subordinate interest in land; the reversion or residue of the estate being reserved by the grantor, all covenants in support of the grant, or in relation to the beneficial enjoyment of it, are real covenants and will bind the assignee.

This principle is decisive of the present action. It appears by the deed of Stephen Cook, the defendants' ancestor, to William Hull, that the former conveyed to the latter a tract of land adjoining the mill pond in question, "with the full and free privilege of using and improving the said mill pond within certain limits, with the full liberty of ingress and egress, to dig out and carry away the whole or any part of the soil in said pond, and to divide the same pond, as described in the deed, into six separate and distinct fish ponds."

William Hull conveyed the premises to the plaintiff; after which, disputes arose between Cook and the plaintiff relative to their respective rights, and for settling the same they entered into sundry covenants in relation to said grant, and qualifying the same; for the breach of one of which this action was brought. At the time these covenants were made, there was a privity of estate between the parties in that part of the mill pond described in the grant to Hull. The covenant in question was made in reference to the plaintiff's right and interest under that grant, and was manifestly intended to confirm it, and to secure the plaintiff in the enjoyment thereof. This covenant therefore, upon the principles stated, is a real covenant, running with the land, and is binding on the heirs of the covenantor.

Judgment on the verdict.

A, owner of Whiteacre, and *B*, owner of Blackacre, wish to agree that Blackacre will only be used for residential purposes. They are likely to decide they want an agreement that will *run with the land*, so that:

If *A* sells to *C*, *C* may enforce the covenant against *B*, even though *C* was not originally a party to it. The _benefit_ thus runs with the land.

If *B* sells to *D*, *A* can enforce the convenant against *D*, although *D* was not originally a party to it. The _burden_ runs with the land.

Traditionally, three requirements had to be fulfilled to enable a covenant to run with the land *at law*. (Equity is discussed at pp. 958-970 *infra*.)

Ⓝ *Intention.* Obviously, a covenant could not run with the land unless the parties who made it intended that it should do so. But what was required to make that intention clear? A written instrument satisfying the Statute of Frauds was necessary (although we will see certain exceptions later). The court in Spencer's Case distinguished between covenants concerning things in being ("in esse"), which ran at law without express words binding later assignees, and covenants concerning things not in being, which required the use of express words binding assignees. This distinction has generally been ignored over the years, and only a small minority of courts hold to it today. The modern approach is to determine intent based upon an examination of the instrument as a whole.

Ⓨ *Touch and Concern.* Berger, A Policy Analysis of Promises Respecting the Use of Land, 55 Minn. L. Rev. 167, 208-209 (1970):

The touch and concern requirement is a method of restricting kinds of promises that may devolve to remote parties. It is as if the law were saying, "It is not every kind of promise contained in a lease or deed which will run with the land to assignees of the original parties. Only those which 'touch and concern' the land itself will run to these subsequent holders." Why should the law take certain kinds of promises and say these shall run, while these others shall not? Perhaps the use of an extreme example will help to explain the underlying policies. Suppose L leases Blackacre to T and T agrees in the written instrument to (1) pay rent of $1,000 per year; (2) keep the premises in good repair; and (3) buy L's horse, Dobbin, for $10,000. Suppose further, that T assigns the lease to A, who refuses to perform any of the agreements in the lease. L now sues A to recover for breach of the three covenants. It is apparent that there is a difference in the nature of these undertakings. This can best be shown by thinking of the problem from A's point of view. When A studies the lease before taking the assignment, he is likely to assume that covenants (1) and (2) will be binding upon him because they have to do with the tenancy relationship and the duties of T as a tenant, and he is also likely to assume that covenant (3) is not binding upon him for the reverse reason that the promise of T to buy L's horse bound T not as a tenant but as an individual. That promise had nothing to do with the lease at all and could just as well have been in a different instrument. The law says that covenants (1) and (2) touch and concern the land and run and that covenant (3) is collateral or personal and does not run. Therefore, A will be liable to perform (1) and (2) but not (3).

On the other hand, if one fact were changed in the above hypothetical, the situation takes on an entirely different cast. Assume that L is leasing a racing stable to T and that as a part of the deal, L is selling Dobbin to T. In that case, A in taking the assignment might well expect that the agreement concerning Dobbin would accompany what really is in effect the purchase of a racing stable enterprise. Thus, A should be liable on that promise as well. The real policy, then, is to give effect to the intent that most people would probably have if they thought about the issue and thereby protect subsequent parties against unexpected and unexpectable liability. Touch and concern is a device for intent effectuation, through which the law conforms itself to the normal, usual or probable understandings of the community.

C. Clark, Real Covenants and Other Interests Which "Run With Land" 96-100 (2d ed. 1947):

The requirement as to the nature of the promise, . . . like the requirement of privity of estate, operates to limit the covenants permissible as encumbrances on title, and in effect the requirements seem sometimes to overlap. Spencer's Case settled the rule as to covenants with leaseholds — that only such covenants as touched or concerned the land might run — and the same rule has since been applied to covenants with fees. It has been found impossible to state any absolute tests to determine what covenants touch and concern land and what do not. The question is one for the court to determine in the exercise of its best judgment upon the facts of each case. Professor Bigelow has, however, . . . set forth a scientific method of approach to the problem which seems to afford the most practical working tests for the court to employ. The method he states is to ascertain the exact effect of the covenant upon the legal relations of the parties. In effect it is a measuring of the legal relations of the parties with and without the covenant. If the promisor's legal relations in respect to the land in question are lessened — his legal interest as owner rendered less valuable by the promise — the burden of the covenant touches or concerns that land; if the promisee's legal relations in respect to that land are increased — his legal interest as owner rendered more valuable by the promise — the benefit of the covenant touches or concerns that land. It is necessary that this effect should be had upon the legal relations of the parties as owners of the land in question, and not merely as members of the community in general, such as taxpayers, or owners of other land, in order that the covenant may run. Thus, an agreement by the lessee to leave part of the leased land unploughed each year restricts the lessee's privilege of user, while it gives a right benefiting the lessor in his reversion in the land by securing a crop rotation; hence both right and duty should run. So a power in the lessor to terminate the lease under certain conditions is a beneficial power to the lessor as such and a burdensome liability to the lessee, and both benefit and burden run. But an agreement by the lessee to pay taxes for the lessor on other than the leased premises calls for the duty of making a money payment unconnected with the leased premises and a right for the benefit of the lessor not in his capacity of reversioner, and neither right nor duty should run.

Though some decisions seem to show a different tendency there would seem to be no reason for applying the rule of touching and concerning in an overtechnical manner, which is unreal from the standpoint of the parties themselves. Where the parties, as laymen and not as lawyers, would naturally regard the covenant as intimately bound up with the land, aiding the promisee as landowner or hampering the promisor in similar capacity, the requirement should be held fulfilled. On this basis covenants to pay taxes or assessments on the land in question, covenants to insure, options to purchase contained in leases, and similar covenants about which controversy has arisen, should be considered capable of running.

Privity. Privity requirements are complex. In attempting to understand them, it is necessary to distinguish between "vertical privity" and "horizontal privity."

For the _burden_ of a covenant to run at law, there had to be horizontal privity between covenantor and covenantee and vertical privity between covenantor and assignee. Example: A, owner of Whiteacre, covenants with B, owner of Blackacre, that an apartment complex will not be built upon Blackacre. B sells to C, who wishes to build the apartment complex. A may enforce only if there was a horizontal privity between A and B, and vertical privity between B and C.

For the *benefit* of a covenant to run at law, there had to be vertical privity between covenantee and assignee; courts differed on whether horizontal privity (between covenantor and covenantee) was necessary. The Restatement §548 said that it should not be required. Example: In the above hypothetical, suppose A sells to D. For D to enforce the covenant at law against B or C, there must have been vertical privity between A and D, and courts differed as to whether horizontal privity between A and B was necessary.

But what are vertical and horizontal privity? The vertical privity requirement was that the party suing or being sued have succeeded to the same estate as the original covenantee or covenantor. For example, if the covenantor, B, owns Blackacre in fee simple, and conveys a life estate to C, B and C are not in vertical privity of estate; for there to be vertical privity, B must convey to C in fee simple. Similarly, if C gains his title by adverse possession, B and C are not in vertical privity.

The concept of horizontal privity has been given different meanings in different states and at different times. One interpretation, borrowed from England, was that A and B could make a covenant that would run with the land only if A and B were in a tenurial relationship, as landlord-tenant or reversioner-life tenant, for example. Thus A could not impose a covenant that would run with the land when he sold to B, and A and B could not bind their land if they were merely adjoining owners in fee simple.

A second interpretation, only slightly less restrictive, was the Massachusetts, or "simultaneous interest," rule. The rule required that covenantor and covenantee have a continuous and simultaneous interest in the same property. The required privity existed when there was a tenurial relationship between A and B, or when A conveyed to B an easement or reserved an easement in a conveyance to B.

Another interpretation of horizontal privity required either that a continuing tenurial relationship exist or that the parties impose the covenant while the land is being conveyed from A to B. The latter criterion could be satisfied with a complicated transaction (which also generated large legal fees). Thus, if A and B, neighbors, wished to impose a running covenant, B could convey his land to A who would convey back to B with a deed imposing the covenant.

See the discussion of privity written by the leading academic scholar on the subject, Dean Clark of the Yale Law School, after he had become a circuit judge. 165 Broadway Building, Inc. v. City Investing Co., 120 F.2d 813, 816 (2d Cir.), *cert. denied*, 314 U.S. 682 (1941):

> As to the requirement of "privity of estate," . . . [t]his particular requirement is probably the greatest source of confusion in the subject, because an understandable policy against title encumbrances (carried, however, to an unreal extreme in these days of modern community land developments) has been buttressed by privity doctrines of seemingly au-

thentic, but actually dubious, historicity. That the parties to an action to enforce a covenant, if not themselves makers of the contract, must each have succeeded by privity to the estate of one of such makers is good enough sense; it is why we say a covenant runs with such estate. But to go further and require that there must be some such succession between the covenanting parties themselves — that there must have been a grant or conveyance between them at the time of the covenant or possibly some continuing interest of tenure, easement, or otherwise — is supported neither by ancient land law nor by modern policy. As to the former, the idea goes back no further than a dubious and unsupported statement by Lord Kenyon in Webb v. Russell, 3 T.R. 393 (K.B. 1789); as to the latter, it is, at best, only an irresponsible way of eliminating running covenants quite by chance, where the parties have not understood the doctrinal significance of pure form and no conveyancer has warned them of the safeguard to their plans which the mere exchange of cross deeds may afford. Holmes, The Common Law, 371-409. That a requirement so anomalous should exist at all is therefore doubtful; the authorities tend to show that, if it is not to be rejected altogether, it is not applicable in any event to the running of the benefit of covenants, as here.

b.   Reform

◆ NEPONSIT PROPERTY OWNERS' ASSOCIATION v. EMIGRANT INDUSTRIAL SAVINGS BANK
278 N.Y. 248, 15 N.E.2d 793 (1938)

LEHMAN, J. The plaintiff, as assignee of Neponsit Realty Company, has brought this action to foreclose a lien upon land which the defendant owns. The lien, it is alleged, arises from a covenant, condition or charge contained in a deed of conveyance of the land from Neponsit Realty Company to a predecessor in title of the defendant. The defendant purchased the land at a judicial sale. The referee's deed to the defendant and every deed in the defendant's chain of title since the conveyance of the land by Neponsit Realty Company purports to convey the property subject to the covenant, condition, or charge contained in the original deed. . . .

It appears that in January, 1911, Neponsit Realty Company, as owner of a tract of land in Queens county, caused to be filed in the office of the clerk of the county a map of the land. The tract was developed for a strictly residential community, and Neponsit Realty Company conveyed lots in the tract to purchasers, describing such lots by reference to the filed map and to roads and streets shown thereon. In 1917, Neponsit Realty Company conveyed the land now owned by the defendant to Robert Oldner Deyer and his wife by deed which contained the covenant upon which the plaintiff's cause of action is based.

That covenant provides:

> And the party of the second part for the party of the second part and the
> heirs, successors and assigns of the party of the second part further cove-
> nants that the property conveyed by this deed shall be subject to an annual
> charge in such an amount as will be fixed by the party of the first part, its
> successors and assigns, not, however exceeding in any year the sum of
> four ($4.00) dollars per lot 20 x 100 feet. The assigns of the party of the first
> part may include a Property Owners' Association which may hereafter be
> organized for the purposes referred to in this paragraph, and in case such
> association is organized the sums in this paragraph provided for shall be
> payable to such association. The party of the second part for the party of
> the second part and the heirs, successors and assigns of the party of the
> second part covenants that they will pay this charge to the party of the first
> part, its successors and assigns on the first day of May in each and every
> year, and further covenants that said charge shall on said date in each year
> become a lien on the land and shall continue to be such lien until fully
> paid. Such charge shall be payable to the party of the first part or its
> successors or assigns, and shall be devoted to the maintenance of the
> roads, paths, parks, beach, sewers and such other public purposes as shall
> from time to time be determined by the party of the first part, its succes-
> sors or assigns. And the party of the second part by the acceptance of this
> deed hereby expressly vests in the party of the first part, its successors and
> assigns, the right and power to bring all actions against the owner of the
> premises hereby conveyed or any part thereof for the collection of such
> charge and to enforce the aforesaid lien therefor.
>
> These covenants shall run with the land and shall be construed as real
> covenants running with the land until January 31, 1940, when they shall
> cease and determine.

Every subsequent deed of conveyance of the property in the defendant's chain of title, including the deed from the referee to the defendant, contained, as we have said, a provision that they were made
subject to covenants and restrictions of former deeds of record.

There can be no doubt that Neponsit Realty Company intended that
the covenant should run with the land and should be enforceable by a
property owners association against every owner of property in the
residential tract which the realty company was then developing. The
language of the covenant admits of no other construction. Regardless of
the intention of the parties, a covenant will run with the land and will be
enforceable against a subsequent purchaser of the land at the suit of one
who claims the benefit of the covenant, only if the covenant complies
with certain legal requirements. These requirements rest upon ancient
rules and precedents. The age-old essentials of a real covenant, aside
from the form of the covenant, may be summarily formulated as follows:
(1) it must appear that grantor and grantee intended that the covenant
should run with the land; (2) it must appear that the covenant is one

"touching" or "concerning" the land with which it runs; (3) it must appear that there is "privity of estate" between the promisee or party claiming the benefit of the covenant and the right to enforce it, and the promisor or party who rests under the burden of the covenant. Although the deeds of Neponsit Realty Company conveying lots in the tract it developed "contained a provision to the effect that the covenants ran with the land, such provision in the absence of the other legal requirements is insufficient to accomplish such a purpose."

The covenant in this case is intended to create a charge or obligation to pay a fixed sum of money to be "devoted to the maintenance of the roads, paths, parks, beach, sewers and such other public purposes as shall from time to time be determined by the party of the first part [the grantor], its successors or assigns." It is an affirmative covenant to pay money for use in connection with, but not upon, the land which it is said is subject to the burden of the covenant. Does such a covenant "touch" or "concern" the land? These terms are not part of a statutory definition, a limitation placed by the State upon the power of the courts to enforce covenants *intended* to run with the land by the parties who entered into the covenants. Rather they are words used by courts in England in old cases to describe a limitation which the courts themselves created or to formulate a test which the courts have devised and which the courts voluntarily apply. In truth the test so formulated is too vague to be of much assistance and judges and academic scholars alike have struggled, not with entire success, to formulate a test at once more satisfactory and more accurate. "It has been found impossible to state any absolute tests to determine what covenants touch and concern land and what do not. The question is one for the court to determine in the exercise of its best judgment upon the facts of each case."

Even though that be true, a determination by a court in one case upon particular facts will often serve to point the way to correct decision in other cases upon analogous facts. Such guideposts may not be disregarded. It has been often said that a covenant to pay a sum of money is a personal affirmative covenant which usually does not concern or touch the land. Such statements are based upon English decisions which hold in effect that only covenants, which compel the covenanter to submit to some *restriction on the use* of his property, touch or concern the land, and that the burden of a covenant which requires the covenanter to do an affirmative act, even on his own land, for the benefit of the owner of a "dominant" estate, does not run with his land. . . . We have not abandoned the historic distinction drawn by the English courts. So this court has recently said:

> Subject to a few exceptions not important at this time, there is now in this
> State a settled rule of law that a covenant to do an affirmative act, as

distinguished from a covenant merely negative in effect, does not run with the land so as to charge the burden of performance on a subsequent grantee [citing cases]. This is so though the burden of such a covenant is laid upon the very parcel which is the subject-matter of the conveyance. [Guaranty Trust Co. v. N.Y. & Queens County Ry. Co., 253 N.Y. 190, 204, opinion by Cardozo, Ch. J.]

Both in that case and in the case of Miller v. Clary the court pointed out that there were some exceptions or limitations in the application of the general rule. Some promises to pay money have been enforced, as covenants running with the land, against subsequent holders of the land who took with notice of the covenant. It may be difficult to classify these exceptions or to formulate a test of whether a particular covenant to pay money or to perform some other act falls within the general rule that ordinarily an affirmative covenant is a personal and not a real covenant, or falls outside the limitations placed upon the general rule. At least it must "touch" or "concern" the land in a substantial degree, and though it may be inexpedient and perhaps impossible to formulate a rigid test or definition which will be entirely satisfactory or which can be applied mechanically in all cases, we should at least be able to state the problem and find a reasonable method of approach to it. It has been suggested that a covenant which runs with the land must affect the legal relations — the advantages and the burdens — of the parties to the covenant, as owners of particular parcels of land and not merely as members of the community in general, such as taxpayers or owners of other land. That method of approach has the merit of realism. The test is based on the effect of the covenant rather than on technical distinctions. Does the covenant impose, on the one hand, a burden upon an interest in land, which on the other hand increases the value of a different interest in the same or related land?

Even though we accept that approach and test, it still remains true that whether a particular covenant is sufficiently connected with the use of land to run with the land, must be in many cases a question of degree. A promise to pay for something to be done in connection with the promisor's land does not differ essentially from a promise by the promisor to do the thing himself, and both promises constitute, in a substantial sense, a restriction upon the owner's right to use the land, and a burden upon the legal interest of the owner. On the other hand, a covenant to perform or pay for the performance of an affirmative act disconnected with the use of the land cannot ordinarily touch or concern the land in any substantial degree. Thus, unless we exalt technical form over substance, the distinction between covenants which run with land and covenants which are personal, must depend upon the effect of the covenant on the legal rights which otherwise would flow from ownership of land and which are connected with the land. The problem then is: Does the covenant in purpose and effect *substantially* alter these rights? . . .

Looking at the problem presented in this case and stressing the intent and substantial effect of the covenant rather than its form, it seems clear that the covenant may properly be said to touch and concern the land of the defendant and its burden should run with the land. True, it calls for payment of a sum of money to be expended for "public purposes" upon land other than the land conveyed by Neponsit Realty Company to plaintiff's predecessor in title. By that conveyance the grantee, however, obtained not only title to particular lots, but an easement or right of common enjoyment with other property owners in roads, beaches, public parks or spaces and improvements in the same tract. For full enjoyment in common by the defendant and other property owners of these easements or rights, the roads and public places must be maintained. In order that the burden of maintaining public improvements should rest upon the land benefited by the improvements, the grantor exacted from the grantee of the land with its appurtenant easement or right of enjoyment a covenant that the burden of paying the cost should be inseparably attached to the land which enjoys the benefit. It is plain that any distinction or definition which would exclude such a covenant from the classification of covenants which "touch" or "concern" the land would be based on form and not on substance.

Another difficulty remains. Though between the grantor and the grantee there was privity of estate, the covenant provides that its benefit shall run to the assigns of the grantor who "may include a Property Owners Association which may hereafter be organized for the purposes referred to in this paragraph." The plaintiff has been organized to receive the sums payable by the property owners and to expend them for the benefit of such owners. Various definitions have been formulated of "privity of estate" in connection with covenants that run with the land, but none of such definitions seems to cover the relationship between the plaintiff and the defendant in this case. The plaintiff has not succeeded to the ownership of any property of the grantor. It does not appear that it ever had title to the streets or public places upon which charges which are payable to it must be expended. It does not appear that it owns any other property in the residential tract to which any easement or right of enjoyment in such property is appurtenant. It is created solely to act as the assignee of the benefit of the covenant, and it has no interest of its own in the enforcement of the covenant.

The arguments that under such circumstances the plaintiff has no right of action to enforce a covenant running with the land are all based upon a distinction between the corporate property owners association and the property owners for whose benefit the association has been formed. If that distinction may be ignored, then the basis of the arguments is destroyed. How far privity of estate in technical form is necessary to enforce in equity a restrictive covenant upon the use of land, presents an interesting question. Enforcement of such covenants rests upon equitable principles, and at times, at least, the violation "of the restrictive covenant may be restrained at the suit of one who owns property, or for whose benefit the restriction was established, irrespective of whether there were privity either of estate or of contract between the parties, or whether an action at law were maintainable." The covenant in this case does not fall exactly within any classification of "restrictive" covenants, which have been enforced in this State, and no right to enforce even a restrictive covenant has been sustained in this State where the plaintiff did not own property which would benefit by such enforcement so that some of the elements of an equitable servitude are present. In some jurisdictions it has been held that no action may be maintained without such elements. We do not attempt to decide now how far the rule will be carried, or to formulate a definite rule as to when, or even whether, covenants in a deed will be enforced, upon equitable principles, against subsequent purchasers with notice, at the suit of a party without privity of contract or estate. (Cf. Equitable Rights and Liabilities of Strangers to a Contract, by Harlan F. Stone, 18 Colum. L. Rev. 291.) There is no need to resort to such a rule if the courts may look behind the corporate form of the plaintiff.

The corporate plaintiff has been formed as a convenient instrument by which the property owners may advance their common interests. We do not ignore the corporate form when we recognize that the Neponsit Property Owners Association, Inc., is acting as the agent or representative of the Neponsit property owners. As we have said in another case: when Neponsit Property Owners Association, Inc., "was formed, the property owners were expected to, and have looked to that organization as the medium through which enjoyment of their common right might be preserved equally for all." Under the conditions thus presented we said: "it may be difficult, or even impossible, to classify into recognized categories the nature of the interest of the membership corporation and its members in the land. The corporate entity cannot be disregarded, nor can the separate interests of the members of the corporation." Only blind adherence to an ancient formula devised to meet entirely different conditions could constrain the court to hold that a corporation formed as a medium for the enjoyment of common rights of property owners owns no property which would benefit by enforcement of common rights and has no cause of action in equity to enforce the covenant upon which such common rights depend. Every reason which in other circumstances may justify the ancient formula may be urged in support of the conclusion that the formula should not be applied in this case. In substance if not in form the covenant is a restrictive covenant which touches and concerns the defendant's land, and in substance, if not in form, there is privity of estate between the plaintiff and the defendant.

◆ NICHOLSON v. 300 BROADWAY REALTY CORP.
7 N.Y.2d 240, 164 N.E.2d 832, 196 N.Y.S.2d 945 (1959)

FULD, J. On this appeal, here by our permission, the plaintiffs seek a reversal of an order dismissing their complaint. The action was brought for specific performance of an agreement, made some 30 years ago by The Embossing Company, the defendant's predecessor in title, to furnish heat to the building on the land belonging to the plaintiffs, and for damages resulting from the defendant's failure to perform that agreement. The plaintiffs recently sold their property to the defendant and, while this renders impossible a decree of specific performance, it does not render the appeal moot or academic, since there still remains the possibility of damages stemming from breach of the agreement.

The facts to be gleaned from the complaint, which, of course, we read in a light most favorable to the plaintiffs, date from 1929. In that year, The Embossing Company, desiring to build a switch branch track from its factory, located on Church Street in Albany, to the main track of the railroad owned and operated by the Delaware & Hudson Company, applied to that company and to the City of Albany for permission to do so. To accomplish this, it was also necessary for Embossing to obtain the consent of Aaron Nicholson who owned the adjoining premises. As a condition to give his consent, Nicholson insisted upon a contract whereby Embossing agreed "to furnish steam heat" to the building on his property and "to furnish and maintain all necessary steam pipes and return pipes for that purpose" and, in consideration, Nicholson agreed to pay $50 a year. The agreement, dated October 7, 1929, expressly provided that it "applies to and is binding upon the heirs, executors, administrators and assignees of the parties." Embossing's application was granted and the branch track was constructed. In fulfillment of its covenant, Embossing set up the necessary steam pipes and return pipes, undertook to furnish steam heat to the adjoining building and for some 27 years, from 1929 until 1956, continued to carry out its agreement and to furnish heat to the plaintiffs' premises in return for the stipulated fee of $50.

The defendant purchased Embossing's property in 1956, and it was this sale which precipitated the present lawsuit.

More particularly, and we continue to cull from the complaint, in March of 1956, Embossing entered into a contract with one Jack Spitzer to sell the property to him. In making this contract, Spitzer "intended that title to said premises would be conveyed to the defendant, 300 Broadway Realty Corporation, and was acting for and on behalf of [said] defendant . . . , then or about to be organized and incorporated by the said Spitzer." And Spitzer, on behalf of himself and his assignees, "agreed upon the conveyance of said premises . . . to perform" Embossing's obligation under the 1929 agreement. Then, on April 25, 1956, Spitzer, still "acting for and on behalf of the defendant," assigned the contract to Betty Thompson who was also "acting solely as the [defendant's] agent . . . and on its behalf" and, on the same day, Embossing, at Spitzer's request, executed a deed of the property to her. This deed, signed and acknowledged by Thompson as grantee, recited that the premises "are conveyed subject to the terms of [Embossing's 1929] agreement . . . pertaining to the heating" of the premises and that the grantee, by her execution of the instrument, "agrees to perform" those terms. And, more or less contemporaneously, Thompson executed another deed, conveying the premises to the defendant, but this one made no reference to the 1929 agreement.

The complaint goes on to charge that the defendant, having "actual, as well as constructive, notice and knowledge" of the 1929 agreement, adopted the procedure outlined solely "for the purposes of attempting to avoid performance of the obligation of supplying steam heat." And, finally, after characterizing the obligation as "a covenant running with the land," the complaint recites that the plaintiffs made demands upon the defendant to furnish the heat, that the latter refused to do so and that the plaintiffs were damaged thereby.

As noted above, the complaint was dismissed on the ground that it fails to state a cause of action. Reasoning that a covenant to furnish heat, being affirmative in nature, is not one which may run with the land, the courts below concluded that Embossing's obligation was not enforceable against the defendant as a subsequent grantee, and that frames one of the questions for decision: does the affirmative character of the covenant exclude it from the classification of covenants which "touch" or "concern" the land? . . .

If, as our decision in *Neponsit* makes clear, the test as to whether a covenant touches or concerns the land is "based upon substance rather than upon form," on "the [covenant's] effect . . . rather than on technical distinctions," it would seem that the covenant here under consideration does touch and concern the land of the defendant. As is evident, it affected the legal relations of the parties to the covenant as owners of particular parcels of land. More particularly, the covenant gave to the covenantee Nicholson a right, not possessed by other landowners, of having heat supplied to his building, as long as it stood, and it imposed upon the covenantor Embossing, so long as the heat-producing facilities remained on its land, the burden, not cast upon other landowners, of furnishing heat to premises adjoining its own. The fear expressed that the covenant imposes an undue restriction on alienation or an onerous burden in perpetuity is dispelled by the fact that by its terms it may run with the land only as long as both buildings are standing and in use.

The complaint before us may thus be sustained upon the theory that Embossing's covenant runs with the land and is, therefore, enforceable against the defendant as a subsequent grantee. However, the complaint may also be upheld upon the simpler and equally compelling ground that it spells out a cause of action for breach of contract. Accordingly, we briefly recapitulate its allegations insofar as they reflect such cause of action. By the 1929 agreement, Embossing promised to furnish steam heat, as specified, so long as the promisee should continue to make payments of $50 a year. Under the "heirs and assigns" clause of that agreement, the plaintiffs are the successors in right of the original promisee, Aaron Nicholson, and entitled to enforce their rights under the agreement not only against Embossing, but also against any other party who expressly assumed Embossing's contract duty to the plaintiffs. What, then, is the legal effect of the purchase transaction which resulted in the April 25, 1956 conveyances by Embossing to Thompson and by Thompson to the defendant?

If the defendant had merely taken conveyance of the property, without expressly assuming performance of the contract duty owed by Embossing to the plaintiffs under the 1929 contract, the plaintiffs would have had no contractual claim against the defendant. But the complaint here alleges that the defendant, initially through its agent Spitzer and then through its agent Thompson, expressly assumed the performance of Embossing's contract duty to furnish steam heat to the plaintiffs' building.

Although Embossing could not relieve itself of its obligation on the covenant in the absence of a complete novation, it may be inferred from the complaint that Embossing would not have sold its property on the terms fixed had it not been assured that the grantee, the real grantee, of its property would assume its obligation to furnish heat. The complaint alleges that the conveyance procedure employed by the defendant was designed solely to enable it "to avoid performance of [its] obligation." If such was the defendant's purpose, it must be condemned; to approve what was here attempted would be to sanction an evasion which offends against concepts of fair dealing and falls far below permissible standards of business morality. Be this as it may, though, any purpose or intent that the defendant may have had to avoid performance of the obligation will be wholly ineffectual if the plaintiffs are able to prove their allegations of agency and express assumption of duty.

Accepting, as on this appeal we must, the truth of the allegations that the express provisions of assumption were actually made by Spitzer and Thompson, as agents, "acting for and on behalf of the defendant," there can be no doubt that the plaintiffs have a direct right of action against the latter to enforce the contract duty explicitly assumed by it through agents. The assumption agreement between Embossing and the defendant is supported by manifest consideration and constitutes a creditor beneficiary contract in which Embossing is promisee, the defendant is promisor and the plaintiffs are third-party beneficiaries. . . .

Chief Judge Conway and Judges Desmond, Froessel and Burke concur with Judge Fuld; Judge Van Voorhis concurs in the following memorandum in which Judge Dye concurs: In Guaranty Trust Co. v. New York & Queens County Ry. Co., it was said in the opinion by Cardozo, Ch. J.: "Subject to a few exceptions not important at this time, there is now in this State a settled rule of law that a covenant to do an affirmative act, as distinguished from a covenant merely negative in effect, does not run with the land so as to charge the burden of performance on a subsequent grantee." In *Neponsit*, this statement was quoted in the opinion by Judge Lehman, coupled with the statement in relation thereto: "We have not abandoned the historic distinction drawn by the English courts." Insofar as the instant case deals with this question, I concur in holding that this covenant to supply heat runs with the land for so long as both buildings remain standing and in use. In thus voting, however, I do so on the assumption that the rule above stated is not being overruled but remains in force subject to this and a few other exceptions.

DUNHAM, PROMISES RESPECTING THE USE OF LAND, 8 J. Law & Econ. 133, 164-165 (1965): There remains the more general policy question: why should not any legal person be able to bargain according to ordinary contract rules whereby he promises for himself and further agrees that any subsequent owner of a described parcel of land then owned by the promisor is also bound on the promise? To make the question concrete: why should not a mortgagor, when he is promising to pay a debt and agreeing that his land is subject to a mortgage to secure performance of the promise, be able to promise that any subsequent owner of the mortgaged land is personally obligated to pay the mortgage debt? Two explanations of the restriction on running of the personal obligation are traditionally offered. One is said to be the policy favoring free transferability of interests in land; and the other is said to be the risks or dangers involved in permitting a person to be sued as a promisor upon a promise which he has not made. In reality this is, or should be, a civil liberties argument. It is an interference with a person's liberty to contract or not to contract to impose on him an obligation which he did not make. When one considers the instances where encumbrances on land are recognized it is clear that the freedom of alienation policy argument has no more than stare decisis to commend it. The civil liberties argument has more merit. Perhaps it is too onerous a burden to impose on an individual the choice of not owning an object of real scarcity, land, as the only means of avoiding the personal obligation of a promise made by a predecessor. While many of the technical rules concerning promises have been relaxed or eliminated there seems to be no urge to make all promises run with land. The basic requirement which should remain is that the promise should be one adjusting the dependency of land uses. If a promise respecting the use of land is an aspect of an attempt by a firm or by neighboring individual owners to maximize satisfactions from land use by agreeing to appropriate locations and provision of services, it should be able to run with the land.

Notes

1. When a subdivider sold to a lot purchaser, he granted a covenant that "the party of the first part shall supply to the party of the second part, seasonally from May 1st to October 1st, of each year, water for domestic use only, from the well located on other property of the party of the first part" for $35 per year. The New York Court of Appeals, purporting to apply the standard set out in *Neponsit*, held that because the covenant in question did not substantially affect the ownership interest of the landowner, it did not "touch and concern" the land. The court went on to give an "additional reason" against enforcement:

> The affirmative covenant is disfavored in the law because of the fear that this type of obligation imposes an "undue restriction on alienation or an onerous burden in perpetuity.". . . In *Nicholson*, the covenant to supply heat was not interdicted by this concern because it was conditioned upon the continued existence of the buildings on both the promisor's and the promisee's properties. Similarly, in *Neponsit*, the original 1917 deed containing the covenant to pay an annual charge for the maintenance of public areas expressly provided for its own lapse in 1940. Here no outside limitation has been placed on the obligation to purchase water from appellant. Thus, the covenant falls prey to the criticism that it creates a burden in perpetuity, and purports to bind all future owners, regardless of the use to which the land is put. Such a result militates strongly against its enforcement. [Eagle Enterprises, Inc. v. Gross, 39 N.Y.2d 505, 349 N.E.2d 816, 384 N.Y.S.2d 717 (1976).]

2. Does a covenant not to compete "touch and concern" the land? In Norcross v. James, 140 Mass. 188, 2 N.E. 946 (1885), Justice Holmes, writing for the Supreme Judicial Court of Massachusetts, held that such a covenant did not "touch and concern" the land, reasoning that the covenant conferred no "direct physical advantage in the occupation of the dominant estate." Holmes applied his own analysis — worked out in The Common Law at 371-409 (1881) — of a distinction between promises making the use of the dominant estate more convenient and, on the other hand, promises simply tending indirectly to increase the value of that estate.

However, in Whitinsville Plaza, Inc. v. Kotseas, 378 Mass. 85, 390

N.E.2d 243 (1979), the Supreme Judicial Court reversed *Norcross,* and concluded that plaintiff had stated a cause of action for defendant's violation of an anticompetition agreement, holding that the covenant did "touch and concern" the land. The court stated:

> Massachusetts has been practically alone in its position that covenants not to compete do not run with the land to which they relate. Reasonable anticompetitive covenants are enforceable in the great majority of States where the issue has arisen. Modern judicial analysis of cases like the one at bar appears to concentrate on the effects of particular covenants on competition and to avoid the esoteric convolutions of the law of real covenants.
>
> In addition to the doctrinal questions about the *Norcross* rule and the preference of most authorities for a more flexible approach, we may note the unfairness that would result from applying that rule to the facts of this case. In what appears to have been an arm's-length transaction, Kotseas agreed in 1968 not to use retained land in competition with the Trust. We may assume (a) that Kotseas received compensation for thus giving up part of his ownership rights by limiting the uses he could make of the retained land, and (b) that freedom from destructive, next-door competition was part of the inducement for the Trust's purchase and of the price paid by the Trust. Plaza, a closely associated business entity, succeeded to the Trust's interest in 1975. One of these entities established a business, presumably at great cost to itself and in reliance on the contractually obtained limitation of competition on its own narrow market area. Notwithstanding the promise not to do so, Kotseas proceeded to lease land to CVS for the purpose of carrying on the business that it knew would, at least in part, compete with Plaza and divert customers from Plaza's premises. Acting with full knowledge of the 1968 arrangement, CVS participated in this inequitable conduct by Kotseas. If we assume for the moment that the 1968 covenants are reasonable in their application to the present facts, we cannot condone the conduct of Kotseas and CVS. Yet, if *Norcross* remains the law, we are powerless to prevent Kotseas and CVS from indirectly destroying or diminishing the value of Plaza's investment in its business.
>
> We think the time has come to acknowledge the infirmities and inequities of *Norcross.* . . .
>
> [R]easonable covenants against competition may be considered to run with the land when they serve a purpose of facilitating orderly and harmonious development for commercial use. To the extent they are inconsistent with this statement, *Norcross* [and other cases] are hereby expressly overruled.

3. Section 1951(2) of the New York Real Property Actions and Proceedings Law authorizes a court to extinguish a restrictive covenant if

> the restriction is of no actual and substantial benefit to the persons seeking its enforcement . . . either because the purpose of the restriction has already been accomplished, or by reason of changed conditions or other causes, its purpose is not capable of accomplishment, or for any other reason.

The statute's legislative history explains that restrictions that "purport to prohibit virtually any use whatever . . . would be void on the ground that they were repugnant to the estate granted, or contrary to public policy, or unreasonable."

Relying on this authority, the New York Court of Appeals extinguished a covenant that had restricted use of a parcel of land along the Neversink River exclusively to hydroelectric purposes, finding that New York City's condemnation of riparian rights subsequent to imposition of the restrictions had left the land unusable and thus within §1951(2). The court lifted the restrictive covenant despite its findings that the covenant ran with and touched and concerned the land, and that there was privity of estate. Orange & Rockville Utilities, Inc. v. Philwold Estates, 52 N.Y.2d 253, 418 N.E.2d 1310, 437 N.Y.S.2d 291 (1981).

4. Equitable Servitudes

In England, because horizontal privity could exist only when covenantor and covenantee were in a tenurial relationship, the running of covenants at law was severely limited. But this difficulty was partly resolved by the more flexible equity courts that often ignored the rule. These decisions led to a new category of restrictions: equitable servitudes.

◆ TULK v. MOXHAY
2 Ph. 774, 41 Eng. Rep. 1143 (Ch. 1848)

In the year 1808 the Plaintiff, being then the owner in fee of the vacant piece of ground in Leicester Square, as well as of several of the houses forming the Square, sold the piece of ground by the description of "Leicester Square garden or pleasure ground, with the equestrian statue then standing in the centre thereof, and the iron railing and stone work round the same," to one Elms in fee: and the deed of conveyance contained a covenant by Elms, for himself, his heirs, and assigns, with the Plaintiff, his heirs, executors, and administrators,

> that Elms, his heirs, and assigns should, and would from time to time, and at all times thereafter at his and their own costs and charges, keep and maintain the said piece of ground and square garden, and the iron railing round the same in its then form, and in sufficient and proper repair as a square garden and pleasure ground, in an open state, uncovered with any buildings, in neat and ornamental order; and that it should be lawful for the inhabitants of Leicester Square, tenants of the Plaintiff, on payment of a reasonable rent for the same, to have keys at their own expense and the privilege of admission therewith at any time or times into the said square garden and pleasure ground.

The piece of land so conveyed passed by divers mesne conveyances into the hands of the Defendant, whose purchase deed contained no similar covenant with his vendor; but he admitted that he had purchased with notice of the covenant in the deed of 1808.

The Defendant having manifested an intention to alter the character of the square garden, and asserted a right, if he thought fit, to build upon it, the Plaintiff, who still remained owner of several houses in the square, filed this bill for an injunction; and an injunction was granted by the Master of the Rolls to restrain the Defendant from converting or using the piece of ground and square garden, and the iron railing round the same, to or for any other purpose than as a square garden and pleasure ground in an open state, and uncovered with buildings. . . .

Mr. R. Palmer, for the Defendant, contended that the covenant did not run with the land, so as to be binding at law upon a purchaser from the covenantor, and he relied on the dictum of Lord Brougham C. in Keppell v. Bayley (2 M. & K. 547), to the effect that notice of such a covenant did not give a Court of Equity jurisdiction to enforce it by injunction against such purchaser, inasmuch as "the knowledge by an assignee of an estate, that his assignor had assumed to bind others than the law authorised him to affect by his contract — had attempted to create a burthen upon property which was inconsistent with the nature of that property, and unknown to the principles of the law — could not bind such assignee by affecting his conscience." In applying that doctrine to the present case, he drew a distinction between a formal covenant as this was, and a contract existing in mere agreement, and requiring some further act to carry it into effect; contending that executory contracts of the latter description were alone such as were binding in equity upon purchasers with notice; for that where the contract between the parties was executed in the form of a covenant, their mutual rights and liabilities were determined by the legal operation of that instrument, and that if a Court of Equity were to give a more extended operation to such covenant, it would be giving the party that for which he had never contracted. . . .

The LORD CHANCELLOR [COTTENHAM], (without calling upon the other side). That this Court has jurisdiction to enforce a contract between the owner of land and his neighbour purchasing a part of it, that the latter shall either use or abstain from using the land purchased in a particular way, is what I never knew disputed. Here there is no question about the contract; the owner of certain houses in the square sells the land adjoining, with a covenant from the purchaser not to use it for any other purpose than as a square garden. And it is now contended, not that the vendee could violate that contract, but that he might sell the piece of land, and that the purchaser from him may violate it without this Court having any power to interfere. If that were so, it would be impossible for an owner of land to sell part of it without incurring the risk of rendering what he retains worthless. It is said that, the covenant being one which does not run with the land, this Court cannot enforce it: but the question is, not whether the covenant runs with the land, but whether a party shall be permitted to use the land in a manner inconsistent with the contract entered into by his vendor, and with notice of which he purchased. Of course, the price would be affected by the covenant, and nothing could be more inequitable than that the original purchaser should be able to sell the property the next day for a greater price, in consideration of the assignee being allowed to escape from the liability which he had himself undertaken.

That the question does not depend upon whether the covenant runs with the land is evident from this, that if there was a mere agreement and no covenant, this Court would enforce it against a party purchasing with notice of it; for if an equity is attached to the property by the owner, no one purchasing with notice of that equity can stand in a different situation from the party from whom he purchased. . . .

With respect to the observations of Lord Brougham in Keppell v. Bayley, he never could have meant to lay down that this Court would not enforce an equity attached to land by the owner, unless under such circumstances as would maintain an action at law. If that be the result of his observations, I can only say that I cannot coincide with it.

I think the cases cited before the Vice Chancellor and this decision of the Master of the Rolls perfectly right, and, therefore, that this motion must be refused, with costs.

Z. CHAFEE, JR. AND S. SIMPSON, CASES ON EQUITY 704-706, 710-711 (1934): In the middle of the seventeenth century the Earl of Leicester laid out Leicester Square and built Leicester House on its north side. . . . The basin [in the center] was replaced in 1748 by a gilded equestrian statue, in metal, of George I by Van Nost. [The property descended to two married Sidney sisters. The share of one sister was sold to James S. Tulk in 1772. Later, the Sidney trustee filed a bill of partition against the Tulks, and the houses were divided between the two families.] Meanwhile, the social status of Leicester Square had declined, and since the division of ownership the central garden had fallen on evil days. . . . The enclosure became a wilderness, a receptacle for rubbish, and a last resting place for dead cats. King George lost an arm and his horse a leg.

Both Tulk and Moxhay died in 1849. In 1851 (the year of the first International Exposition, at the Crystal Palace) Wyld, a geographer, purchased the garden from Moxhay's widow for the purpose of erecting thereon a building to contain a large model of the earth. As the Tulk family objected, Wyld made an agreement with them, which refers to the very ruinous and dilapidated condition of the garden and the iron railings, and in which Wyld was licensed to erect a globe for ten years in return for an option to the Tulks to purchase an undivided half of the garden at the end of that time for £500. The owners of the former Sidney houses on the north side of the Square refused to participate in this agreement. A vast domed structure known as "Wyld's Globe" was then erected and used for geographical and historical lectures and exhibits. In 1861 John A. Tulk, the grandson of Charles, exercised the option, so that he and Wyld became co-tenants of the garden. The Globe was taken down and the battered statue again set up, to be treated to the jokes of Punch and the pranks of idlers, who on October 17, 1866, painted the horse white with black spots and put a foolscap on the head of King George.

By this time the public authorities had become active. In 1863 a bill was introduced in Parliament for a public market in the Square, which was successfully opposed. In 1865 the Metropolitan Board of Works took possession of the garden under the Town Gardens Protection Act of 1863 (26 Vict. c.13), which empowered the Board to take charge of any grounds which had been set apart for the use of the inhabitants of a surrounding square, when the body appointed for the care of the same had neglected to keep it in proper order. John A. Tulk at once brought an action of trespass *quare clausum fregit* against the Board and won a decision that Leicester Square was not within the statute. Tulk v. Metropolitan Board of Works, L.R. 3 Q.B. 682 (1868), *aff'g* id. 94 (1867). Thus Tulk succeeded in keeping the Square in its desolate condition. Tulk hoped to convert the garden into building land, as Moxhay had formerly tried to do. The maintenance of billboards around the enclosure was prevented by another equity decree (unreported), probably at the suit of the north side owners. While an appeal was pending, the Metropolitan Board of Works obtained compulsory powers of acquisition by the Leicester Square Act, 1874 (37 & 38 Vict. c.10).

Before condemnation took place, Albert Grant, M.P., purchased Tulk's rights, opened negotiations with the other owners, took possession of the garden, and offered it free of cost to the Board of Works for public enjoyment. The unfortunate horse was removed in February, 1874 and replaced by a statue of Shakespeare, while the four corners of the garden were ornamented with statues of former residents of Leicester Square — Reynolds, Newton, Hogarth, and Dr. John Hunter. After Mr. Grant had laid out the park in its present form at a total expenditure of £28,000, it was handed over to the public on July 2, 1874.

RENO, THE ENFORCEMENT OF EQUITABLE SERVITUDES IN LAND, 28 Va. L. Rev. 951, 970-973 (1942): With the growth of cities and their suburban real estate developments for residential purposes, there arose a demand for some legal machinery whereby the residential character of these developments could be preserved. To induce the expenditure of large sums of money in erecting residences in cities, there must be some legal machinery available for the purpose of protecting the investment from depreciation through the infiltration of businesses and undesirable structures into the subdivision. The types of incorporeal interests developed at law were insufficient for this purpose. We have found a marked antagonism of the law courts toward extending the doctrine of negative easements to include new forms of restrictions. Unless the desired building restrictions fall within the clearly recognized types of negative easements, they are not enforceable as such. Furthermore in the formulation of a residential building plan in a subdivision, it may be desirable to impose affirmative as well as negative duties upon the purchasers of lots. As has been shown, outside of the few "spurious easements" which have been recognized, easements cannot create any affirmative duties upon the servient landowner which will run with the land to subsequent owners.

Although by means of covenants running with the land it is possible to create new types of either affirmative or negative duties in purchasers of lots in the subdivision, yet the running of these duties to subsequent owners is hedged in by the rules relating to privity of estate. We have found that the burden in such covenants attaches, not to the land itself so as to pass to all possessors or users of the land, but to the estate of the covenantor, so as not to be enforceable against subsequent possessors and users who have not taken by transfer the legal interest of the covenantor. Likewise, the fact that the original covenantor always remains liable under privity of contract for breach of the covenant, even after he has transferred his entire estate, will act as a strong deterrent to the use of this legal device as a means of creating a restricted real estate development. In addition, refusal of the English courts to recognize the running of the burdens of covenants, except as between landlord and tenant, totally prevents their use as a device for creating a restricted development in England and in those American states which have followed the lead of these English cases.

It was for these reasons that equity developed the doctrine of equitable servitudes, or what is often called "the doctrine of Tulk v. Moxhay." In that case the English court laid down the principle that where an owner of land enters into a contract that he will use or abstain from using his land in a particular way or manner, equity will enforce the agreement against any purchaser or possessor with notice who attempts to use the land in violation of its terms, irrespective of whether the agreement creates a valid covenant running with the land at law or not. Lord Cottenham in his opinion seemed to base the doctrine upon two different bases: first, that since the conscience of a purchaser with notice should be bound by the agreement, equity will not permit him to profit through its violation, and second, that an equity has attached to the land so as to bind the land in the hands of purchasers with notice. Whichever theory is followed, it is apparent that the fundamental basis for the doctrine is the inability of the subsequent possessor or user of the land to set up the defense at law of purchaser without notice. For this reason many of the courts have referred to the running of the burden in equity as the doctrine of "notice."

Although several of the early English cases did enforce in equity against purchasers with notice agreements creating affirmative duties, yet it was finally settled in England that only negative agreements were enforceable under this doctrine. Whether this refusal to enforce affirmative agreements against subsequent purchasers with notice was due to the difficulty of supervising the performance of such agreements or because of their analogy to legal easements, where affirmative duties cannot exist, does not appear from the cases. However, in several English cases affirmative agreements have been enforced by the issuance of a negative injunction against doing a particular act which would constitute a breach of the affirmative duties. This would seem to indicate that the refusal to enforce affirmative agreements rests upon the difficulty of supervising performance by a mandatory injunction, rather than any policy of equity against the running of affirmative duties to purchasers with notice. Although several American equity courts have likewise refused to enforce affirmative agreements against subsequent purchasers with notice, the decided weight of authority favors their enforcement without reference to whether the duties created by the agreement are negative or affirmative.

Although the doctrine of equitable servitudes has now received wide acceptance in this country, there is no substantial agreement among the courts as to the theoretical basis for enforcing the burden of an agreement respecting land against subsequent possessors or users with notice. A few early cases intimated that equity was merely extending the doctrine of covenants running with the land. However, this is clearly not the basis since lack of privity of estate, either between the promisor and promisee or between the promisor and the present possessor of the land, has been no deterrent to the enforcement of the agreement. Enforcement has been granted upon the basis of notice against an underlessee, a mere occupant of the land, and even against an adverse possessor. A relationship between the parties to the suit, an element which courts of law required in covenants running with the land and found in the concept of privity of estate, seems never to have been considered necessary in equity if the defendant is charged with notice. One writer has described the necessary relationship as merely the "equitable principle of privity of conscience."

Most discussions of the theoretical basis for the doctrine center around one or the other of two widely different theories: one, that the doctrine of Tulk v. Moxhay, is merely an application by equity of its principle of specific performance of contracts concerning land, and the other, that it is the recognition of the existence in equity of equitable easements not recognized and enforceable at law. Under the first theory the enforcement rests on a contractual obligation only, and under the second it is based on a property interest in the burdened land in many respects similar to legal easements.

◆ RILEY v. BEAR CREEK PLANNING COMMITTEE
17 Cal. 3d 500, 551 P.2d 1213, 131 Cal. Rptr. 381 (1976)

BY THE COURT. In this proceeding, arising out of an effort by defendants Bear Creek Planning Committee and some of its members to enforce certain building restrictions alleged to control the construction of improvements on plaintiffs' real property, defendants appeal from a judgment quieting title in plaintiffs. After decision by the Court of Appeal, Third Appellate District, affirming the judgment, we granted a hearing in this court for the purpose of giving further consideration to the issues raised. Having made a thorough examination of the cause, we have concluded that the opinion of the Court of Appeal prepared by Presiding Justice Puglia and concurred in by Justices Janes and Evans correctly treats and disposes of the issues involved, and we may adopt such opinion as and for the opinion of this court. Such opinion (with appropriate deletions and additions) is as follows:

Central to the disposition of this appeal is the question whether or not plaintiffs' property is burdened by an equitable servitude for the benefit of other lots in the tract of which plaintiffs' property is a part.

On February 26, 1964, Alpine Slopes Development Company (hereinafter "grantor"), a limited partnership, by grant deed conveyed Lot 101 in Alpine Meadows Estates Subdivision No. 3, located in Placer County, to Ernest H. and Jewel Riley, husband and wife. The deed, recorded March 13, 1964, contains no restrictions upon the use of the plaintiffs' property nor is there any reference therein to any instrument purporting to impose restrictions upon Lot 101. In fact, at the time of the conveyance there was no document of record purporting to restrict the use of Lot 101.

On November 25, 1964, exactly nine months after the conveyance to plaintiffs, the grantor caused to be recorded with the Placer County Recorder a document entitled "Declaration of Covenants, Conditions, Restrictions and Reservations on Lots 72 through 116 of Alpine Meadows Estates Unit No. 3" (referred to hereinafter as "declaration"). The declaration was executed by an agent of the grantor and by him acknowledged on November 20, 1964. Preliminarily the declaration recites that grantor is the owner and subdivider of Lots 72 through 116 inclusive (which are particularly described therein by reference to a recorded map); that

> it [grantor] has established and does hereby establish a general plan for the improvement and development of said property and does hereby establish

restrictions, easements, conditions, covenants and reservations upon and subject to which all of the aforementioned lots and parcels of said real property shall be improved and sold or conveyed by it as such owner, each and all of which is or are for the benefit of the [grantor] and the owner of any part or parcel of said property or interest therein and shall apply to and bind the respective successors in interest of the owner or owners thereof and are, and each thereof is, imposed upon said property as a servitude in favor of each subsequent declarant and of each and every parcel of land therein as a dominant tenement or tenements. . . .

There follow 26 numbered paragraphs in which restrictions, covenants and conditions common to subdivision developments of the type here involved are spelled out which are to remain in full force and effect until January 1, 1983.

It is the plaintiffs' alleged violation of the provisions of paragraph 6 of the declaration that precipitated the instant controversy. Insofar as relevant, paragraph 6 provides:

No dwelling, garage, building, fence, wall, retaining wall or other structure or excavation therefor shall be moved onto, commenced, erected or maintained on said lots, nor shall any addition to, change, or alteration therein, be made until the plans and specifications for same have been submitted to the Bear Creek Planning Committee and the approval of said Committee has been secured. . . .[2]

At a time not established by the record, the plaintiffs constructed a snow tunnel on their lot. In reaction thereto, on January 12, 1972, the committee recorded a "Notice of Violation of Covenants, Conditions and Restrictions." Referring specifically to Lot 101 and the declaration recorded November 25, 1964, the notice recited the "probable violation" of the provisions of the declaration in that "A covered walkway has been constructed on said lot 101 without prior compliance with Paragraph 6 of the above described recorded restrictions."

Thereafter plaintiffs filed their complaint to quiet title and for damages for slander of title and defendants cross-complained for declaratory relief. The resulting judgment quieted plaintiffs' title to Lot 101 against all claims of defendants and found for plaintiffs and against defendants on the latter's cross-complaint for declaratory relief.

Inasmuch as there is no privity of contract between defendants and plaintiffs, [defendants'] right to enforce use restrictions against plaintiffs

---

2. The record shows only that the Bear Creek Planning Committee is an unincorporated association, in existence at least since 1962, and purporting to exercise architectural control over structures erected in the tract containing plaintiff's lot. Otherwise, considering that the committee claims control over the erection, placement or alteration of any building in the tract area, the record is remarkably silent concerning the origin, organization, operation and, of primary importance, source of jurisdiction of the committee.

depends upon whether or not the restrictions sought to be enforced are comprehended within mutually enforceable equitable servitudes for the benefit of the tract. . . . The issue thus framed, [defendants'] claim founders upon the rule announced in Werner v. Graham (1919) 181 Cal. 174, at pages 183-185, 183 P. 945, at page 949:

> It is undoubted that when the owner of a subdivided tract conveys the various parcels in the tract by deeds containing appropriate language imposing restrictions on each parcel as part of a general plan of restrictions common to all parcels and designed for their mutual benefit, mutual equitable servitudes are thereby created in favor of each parcel as against all the others. The agreement between the grantor and each grantee in such a case as expressed in the instruments between them is both that the parcel conveyed shall be subject to restrictions in accordance with the plan for the benefit of all the other parcels and also that all other parcels shall be subject to such restrictions for its benefit. In such a case the mutual servitudes spring into existence as between the first parcel conveyed and the balance of the parcels at the time of the first conveyance. As each conveyance follows, the burden and the benefit of the mutual restrictions imposed by preceding conveyances as between the particular parcel conveyed and those previously conveyed pass as an incident of the ownership of the parcel, and similar restrictions are created by the conveyance as between the lot conveyed and the lots still retained by the original owner.
>
> . . . [H]ere there is no language in the instruments between the parties, that is, the deeds, which refers to a common plan of restrictions or which expresses or in any way indicates any agreement between grantor and grantee that the lot conveyed is taken subject to any such plan.
>
> . . . The intent of the common grantor — the original owner — is clear enough. He had a general plan of restrictions in mind. But it is not his intent that governs. It is the joint intent of himself and his grantees, and as between him and each of his grantees the instrument or instruments between them, in this case the deed, constitute the final and exclusive memorial of such intent. It is also apparent that each deed must be construed as of the time it is given. It cannot be construed as of a later date, and in particular, its construction and effect cannot be varied because of deeds which the grantor may subsequently give to other parties. . . . Whatever rights were created by the deed were created and vested [when it was given], and the fact that it later appears that [the grantor] was pursuing a general plan common to all the lots in the tract cannot vary those rights. The same is true of each deed as it was given. Nor does it make any difference that, as claimed by the defendants, [the grantor] gave each grantee to understand, and each grantee did understand, that the restrictions were exacted as part of a general scheme. Such understanding was not incorporated in the deeds, and as we have said, the deeds in this case constitute the final and exclusive memorials of the understandings between the parties. Any understanding not incorporated in them is

wholly immaterial in the absence of a reformation. . . . This whole discussion may in fact be summed up in the simple statement that, if the parties desire to create mutual rights in real property of the character of those claimed here, they must say so, and must say it in the only place where it can be given legal effect, namely, in the written instruments exchanged between them which constitute the final expression of their understanding.[4]

From the recordation of the first deed which effectively imposes restrictions on the land conveyed and that retained by the common grantor, the restrictions are binding upon all subsequent grantees of parcels so affected who take with notice thereof notwithstanding that similar clauses have been omitted from their deeds. Neither proof nor contention is made that plaintiffs are grantees subsequent to the recordation of such a deed with notice thereof and, quite apart from the rule of Werner v. Graham, it is manifest that acknowledgement and recordation of a declaration of restrictions by the grantor after the conveyance to plaintiffs cannot affect property in which the grantor no longer has any interest.

To surmount the obstacle erected by the rule of Werner v. Graham, defendants postulate an analysis of the pertinent law dependent upon the following premises: parol evidence is admissible to explain the terms of a deed to the same extent as with contracts generally; the rule of Werner v. Graham is a function of and predictated upon the parol evidence rule; the modification of the parol evidence rule accomplished by Masterson v. Sine (1968) 68 Cal. 2d 222, 65 Cal. Rptr. 545, 436 P.2d 561, therefore operated in effect to overrule Werner v. Graham *sub silentio.* Accordingly, defendants conclude, extrinsic evidence is admissible to establish the mutual intention of the parties to the conveyance to plaintiffs that it be subject to restrictions identical to those contained in the declaration recorded subsequently by the grantor and specifically in paragraph 6 thereof.

In furtherance of this theory, defendants at trial offered extrinsic evidence of the understanding of the plaintiffs and their grantor. The evidence was received provisionally, subject to the trial court's later ruling on plaintiffs' continuing objection thereto and motion to strike

---

4. Murry v. Lovell, 132 Cal. App. 2d 30, 281 P.2d 316 (1955), a leading authority in the *Werner* line, makes clear that even if the restrictions here in question had been recorded prior to the issuance of plaintiffs' deed, no equitable servitude would have been created absent the inclusion of such restrictions, by recitation or incorporation, in the deed. Compare Martin v. Holm (1925) 197 Cal. 733, 242 P. 718, wherein the deed to defendants contained no restrictions but they took with record notice of a prior deed establishing reciprocal servitudes binding upon their grantor.

based both on the parol evidence rule and the principle that the evidence was irrelevant as the deed is conclusive of the parties' intention with respect to mutually restrictive covenants. In summary, the challenged evidence tended to prove that the grantor intended to convey and plaintiffs intended to purchase a parcel which both parties assumed to be governed by building restrictions; that prior to purchase plaintiffs' attention had been directed to the existence of the assumed restrictions and for the first several years of their occupancy of the lot, they conducted themselves in compliance with what they understood to be binding controls upon the use of the property. The trial court, regarding Werner v. Graham as controlling, granted plaintiffs' motion to strike all extrinsic evidence of the intention of the parties. Defendants assign the ruling as reversible error. . . .

In contrast to the rationale of the rule barring parol evidence, the "Purpose of the statute of frauds is to prevent fraud and perjury with respect to certain agreements by requiring for enforcement the more reliable evidence of some writing signed by the party to be charged. . . ."

Thus the statute of frauds excludes proof of certain types of agreements which are not sufficiently evidenced by a writing. . . . Every material term of an agreement within the statute of frauds must be reduced to writing. No essential element of a writing so required can be supplied by parol evidence. . . . Among the types of agreement to which the statute of frauds applies are contracts for the sale of real property or an interest therein . . . and agreements which by their terms are not to be performed within a year.

In Masterson v. Sine, *supra*, 68 Cal. 2d 222, 65 Cal. Rptr. 545, 436 P.2d 561, [this court] abandoned the rule that evidence of oral agreements collateral to an agreement in writing must be excluded where the instrument on its face appears to be an integration. Rather, the court held that credible extrinsic evidence of a collateral oral agreement is admissible if, considering the circumstances of the parties, the agreement is one which " 'might naturally be made as a separate agreement.' ". . . Defendants contend that under the rule announced in *Masterson*, the extrinsic evidence which was stricken by the court was credible evidence admissible to show the collateral oral understanding of plaintiffs and their grantor that Lot 101 be subject to the restrictions which defendants seek here to enforce.

Although certain language in our *Werner* case was susceptible of the conclusion that the principle there announced had its roots in the parol evidence rule, our decision four years later in McBride v. Freeman (1923) 191 Cal. 152, 215 P. 678, made it clear that other considerations were of greater importance. There, in strongly reaffirming our adherence to *Werner* in the face of a vigorous frontal attack upon it, we stated: "Any other rule would make important questions of the title to real estate largely dependent upon the uncertain recollection and testimony of interested witnesses. The rule of the *Werner* case is supported by every consideration of sound public policy which has led to the enactment and enforcement of statutes of frauds in every English-speaking commonwealth." . . .

We recognize that a deed poll such as used here and commonly throughout California does not satisfy the requirement of the statute of frauds that the written memorandum be subscribed by the party to be charged [when that party is the grantee.] Notwithstanding the lack of complete congruity of common conveyancing practice in the creation of so-called negative easements to the requirements of the statute of frauds, we are of the view that the doctrine of Werner v. Graham, though undoubtedly a function in part of the parol evidence rule, is not exclusively so; that independently therefrom it derives vitality from the policies underlying and implemented by the statute of frauds; that as a consequence, it remains a viable "rule of property" unimpaired and unaffected by subsequent modifications of the parol evidence rule.

Moreover, there is a practical consideration favoring the rule of Werner v. Graham. The grantee of property subject to mutually enforceable restrictions takes not just a servient tenement but, as owner of a dominant tenement, acquires a property interest in all other lots similarly burdened for the benefit of his property. That fact significantly affects the expectations of the parties and inevitably enters into the exchange of consideration between grantor and grantee. Even though the grantor omits to include the mutual restrictions in deeds to parcels thereafter severed from the servient tenement, those who take such property with notice, actual or constructive, of the restrictions are bound thereby. . . . Thus, the recording statutes operate to protect the expectations of the grantee and secure to him the full benefit of the exchange for which he bargained. . . . Where, however, mutually enforceable equitable servitudes are sought to be created outside the recording statutes, the vindication of the expectations of the original grantee, and for that matter succeeding grantees, is hostage not only to the good faith of the grantor, but, even assuming good faith, to the vagaries of proof by extrinsic evidence of actual notice on the part of grantees who thereafter take a part of the servient tenement either from the common grantor or as successors in interest to his grantees. The uncertainty thus introduced into subdivision development would in many cases circumvent any plan for the orderly and harmonious development of such properties and result in a crazy-quilt pattern of uses frustrating the bargained-for expectations of lot owners in the tract. . . .

The trial court correctly struck extrinsic evidence of the intention of plaintiffs and their grantor.

TOBRINER, Justice (dissenting). I dissent.

I cannot subscribe to the majority's conclusion that a buyer of a subdivision lot, who takes his deed with actual knowledge of a general plan of mutual restrictions applicable to the entire subdivision and who conducts himself for many years in a manner which demonstrates his belief that such restrictions apply to his property, may therafter violate all such restrictions with impunity simply because the restrictions were inadvertently omitted from his individual deed. Contrary to the majority's suggestion, we need not decree this inequitable result in order to prevent fraud to maintain security in land titles; the very antithesis — a ruling that a buyer with *actual knowledge* of restrictions is thereby bound — ensures fairness and promotes security in land transactions; it implements the intention of both the buyer and the seller. As I shall explain, the majority can sustain their forced result only by ignoring a host of recent decisions of this court which have abandoned the antiquated rule that "property rights" can be ascertained only within the "four corners of a deed."

The majority's holding will permit plaintiffs in this case to ignore restrictions designed to preserve natural beauty and property values in a carefully planned residential community. Although the use of all other lots in the community will continue to be restricted, plaintiffs will be free to subdivide their land into any number of small building sites, construct apartments or rent commercial space, ignore building lines and obstruct views from neighboring lots, raise livestock, and strip the land by removing trees and shrubs.

Common sense and substantive justice dictates that the plaintiffs should not be free to violate such restrictions. At the time of purchase plaintiffs had actual knowledge of those restrictions; the restrictions formed a part of the consideration exchanged by the parties. The restrictions continue to enhance the value of plaintiffs' individual lot because all other property owners in the subdivision are bound thereby. As I shall explain, the intent of the parties should govern, and the rule of Werner v. Graham (1919) 181 Cal. 174, 183 P. 945, which forbids proof of intent by extrinsic evidence should be rejected, as indeed it has been by virtually every other state.

In the present case, defendants offered proof to establish that (1) prior to their purchase of the lot, plaintiffs received copies of the written restrictions, the by-law of defendant committee and the real estate commissioner's public report, which stated that the subdivision lots were subject to building restrictions; (2) because of a mistake by the title company, plaintiffs' deed did not contain the restrictions and was recorded prior to recording of the declaration of restrictions; and (3) despite the mistakes of the title company, plaintiffs conducted themselves in accordance with the restrictions for a number of years, seeking defendant committee's approval for the construction of a home and the removal of a tree on their lot. Thus the evidence offered by defendants would demonstrate that plaintiffs took their deed with the understanding that the lot was subject to valid restrictions. . . .

5. *Reforming the Structure of Private Use Restrictions*

◆ REICHMAN, TOWARD A UNIFIED CONCEPT OF SERVITUDES
55 So. Calif. L. Rev. 1179, 1179-1182, 1228-1230 (1982)

"Privity of estate" is necessary for the "running" of covenant obligations, but is inapplicable to [easements and to equitable servitudes]. No servitudes, other than easements, can be acquired by prescription or held "in gross." Rights acquired according to a "general scheme," however, can usually only be enforced under a theory of equitable servitudes. Once created, covenants "run" with the promisor's estate (vertical privity), whereas easements and equitable servitudes are "attached to land" and seem to be enforceable even against a person who acquired title by adverse possession. Only equitable servitudes are enforceable against a subsequent owner who had no notice of the restriction, provided that no value was given for the land. In some cases, an action for breach of covenant can be maintained by the original promisee against the original promisor, notwithstanding the fact that the land was transferred prior to the violation. No such remedy is available to the owner of an easement or an equitable servitude. The doctrine of "change in circumstances" applies to equitable servitudes, and perhaps to covenants, but not to easements. Other defenses, like laches, hardship, and unclean hands, are traditionally only associated with equitable servitudes.

The above rules reflect what seems to be the majority view, but the subject is so marred with disagreement that contradictory authority can be found to refute almost all of the above propositions. In some jurisdictions, differences also exist as to the effect of eminent domain procedures and tax sales on existing servitudes.

Since different rules seemingly apply to each form of servitude, distinguishing between the servitudes is important. According to the Restatement of Property, easements are "executed transactions" which convey "property rights"; covenants are "promises respecting the use of land" which create "property interests"; and equitable servitudes result "solely from the enforceability in equity of a promise respecting the use of land." Unfortunately, very little substance lies behind these phrases and using such definitions to distinguish between the forms is virtually impossible.

The only sensible way to distinguish between the three rights would be to identify each of them with a particular type of land use regulation. In American law however, unlike the English system, the forms of servitudes historically were never entirely identified with subject matter distinctions. The most widely used servitudes are those aimed at restricting land uses. In this country such burdens have been simultaneously classified as "negative easements," covenants, and equitable servitudes. When examining restrictive servitudes, then, the courts were able to use the forms as interchangeable concepts. Free to frame each right as belonging to one category or another, the desired result often dictated the classification. Much the same was true of affirmative obligations, i.e., the duties of one owner to perform some activity on his own land to benefit his neighbor. These duties were generally regarded as covenants, but some older decisions analyzed such obligations as "spurious easements," and modern case law tends to treat them as equitable servitudes. . . .

The thesis of this Article is that the three forms of servitudes should be considered as one concept. The normative distinctions indicated above would therefore almost entirely disappear. It is unimportant whether the unified concept is entitled a servitude, a land obligation, or any other term. The importance is in understanding that only a single concept is necessary — a concept which primarily partakes the qualities of what is presently described as an easement. In fact, the proposed approach accords with today's practices. All servitudes appear in the same documents and substantially serve the same function. By clarifying the subject, the problems mentioned above will be alleviated and private land use planning will gain greater flexibility. In most jurisdictions the reform called for could be implemented by the judiciary without the need to resort to legislation. The proposed model would dispense with empty labels without affecting the bulk of the rules governing servitudes. . . .

The only significant difference between equitable servitudes and real covenants is the privity of estate rule. Elimination of that rule would have caused equitable servitudes to be merged with the broader concept of real covenants. Both equitable servitudes and real covenants appeared in America at the same time and both were initially based on contract theory. Each treated the problem of notice in a different way and each had its own practical limitations; they were kept alive as separate forms to complement each other. The shift away from the contractual approach made these two forms very similar to easements. Today, the cycle is complete: the conceptual basis of all three forms is the same.

Clark correctly observed that easements and equitable servitudes should be one category; he failed, however, to include real covenants in that category. From its inception the theory of real covenants was not truly contractual. This is apparent if one ignores phraseology used at the time, and instead examines the substantive rules involved. A comparison between mortgage and real covenants illustrates this point. A mortgagor's transferee is not personally obligated to pay his transferor's debt unless he assumes it. But even in a situation where an assumption takes place, the mortgagor could be made to pay the debt. The results are different under real covenants law. The obligation binds the transferee upon transfer of title. Not only is an assumption unnecessary, but even an express release by the transferor would not exempt the transferee from the duty to perform the covenant. In this sense, real covenants have always been interests in land similar to other rights in the land of another. . . .

The "touch and concern" test is another important distinction between real covenants and covenants in leases. Pursuing the analogy to leases, one might have concluded that a covenant is binding whenever a promise is made to perform some activity on the encumbered land. The benefit could thus personally inure to the promisee, his assignees, or heirs. Such an approach would have enabled real covenants to accomplish ends that have nothing to do with land use regulation.

Such was not the course adopted by the courts. The "touch and concern" rule was given a different definition in the real covenants context. To qualify as a "running" covenant, the promised activity not only had to be carried out on the promisor's land, but also had to benefit the promisee's land. That development introduced to real covenants law the dominant-servient estate relationship derived from the law of easements. Equitable servitudes were similarly affected by this development. Real covenants law approached easements law only indirectly when it embraced the "touch and concern" test in Spencer's Case; however, this does not obscure the result.

Since the institutional differences between courts of law and equity have disappeared, real covenants are usually specifically enforced. Of course, the administration of specific performance does not magically transform a real covenant into an equitable servitude. American courts no longer require the inclusion of the word "assigns," and now openly recognize real covenants as interests in land. Thus, a writing is necessary to create such rights; once created, they are clearly within the scope of the recording acts.

Covenants operate as grants. Unlike contractual obligations, even a substantial breach by the plaintiff will not exempt the promisor. The only exception to the rule is a previous violation of a substantially identical restriction by the suing promisee. The Restatement of Property points out that only injunctions could be withheld due to "change of conditions," but damages should still be available. Rarely, however, do courts award damages in such a case. Indeed, although not openly admitted by courts, a change in neighborhood conditions will terminate real covenants. When a "change of circumstances" occurs, injunctions are refused because that remedy rests with the discretion of the court; damages are refused because the implied intent of the parties was that the promise not be enforced upon a drastic change of circumstances. Although both explanations are conceptually inadequate, it is important to point out that the latter is not employed in contract law.

In conclusion, the three forms of servitudes have merged. Very little remains of the contractual nature of real covenants, and, indeed, contract law is no longer necessary to justify the recognition of affirmative duties as servitudes. The privity rule, although of little practical importance, remains the last differentiating factor. Until it is abolished, students of property law will continue to memorize the nonexistent differences between easements, real covenants, and equitable servitudes, admiring their professors who draw privity diagrams on the blackboard and seriously explain that real covenants run with estates as a "bird rides on a wagon." It is strange indeed how long we have succumbed to fetishism of legal forms.

◆ BERGER, UNIFICATION OF THE LAW OF SERVITUDES
55 So. Calif. L. Rev. 1339 (1982)

At first blush, the notion of unifying the law of servitudes into one coherent whole sounds both attractive and superficially plausible. After all, easements, equitable servitudes, and real covenants all involve the limited rights of one person in the land of another. Specifically, they are respectively rights to use or to control the use of another's land or at least to insist that he perform some land-related affirmative duty. So why not have one body of law to govern them? The answer, I suppose, is that it really does not matter whether one labels the structure as one, two, or three bodies of law. The real issues are whether the rules in the structure make good policy sense and whether they are unnecessarily inconsistent. I say this because it is absolutely clear that the law about the various servitudes cannot be "unified" in the sense that the same rules should always apply to each of them. The rules are different and many of the variances make good sense.

Let me give a number of examples of what I mean. Affirmative easements may be created by prescription. If A wrongfully crosses B's land throughout the statutory period for adverse possession, and A's acts meet the various requirements of being open, notorious, uninterrupted, hostile, and so on, the courts give A a prescriptive easement by analogy to the statutory rules of adverse possession. The theory, of course, is that A is committing a trespass for which B has a cause of action, and if he does not bring a suit within the period of the adverse possession statute, he is barred from doing so later and A's trespass ripens into a permanent legal right. In the United States no analogous rule applies to so-called negative easements or equitable servitudes. For example, if C, as owner of Blackacre, receives air and light from across D's adjacent unimproved land, C cannot get a prescriptive right to have the air and light continue. Analytically, the reason for this is that D has no cause of action against C for receiving the air and light. There is, therefore, no lawsuit that C can claim is barred by the passage of time, and C's receipt of the air and light does not ripen into a prescriptive right. And in policy it should not. No act of C calls D's attention to the fact that D must sue or lose a right to build on his own property. Rights to do acts on someone else's land can be acquired by prescription by actually doing them. Rights that a neighbor not do something on his own land by their nature cannot and should not be so acquired.

A second illustration also relates to the difference between easements and the other servitudes. If E, as owner of Whiteacre, conveys to F an inner portion thereof in such a way that the granted land is landlocked, the law implies that F also receives a right of way over E's retained land to a public road. This is known as an easement by necessity. A closely related device is known as an easement by implication. Assume G owns Greenacre, on which a drainage ditch on the west half drains water off the east half. It is said that this is a quasi-easement, with the east half the dominant tenement and the west half the servient tenement. If G then sells H the dominant portion, and the quasi-easement is characterized as apparent, permanent, and important for the enjoyment of the conveyed parcel, H receives an easement by implication to drain his lands through G's ditch. Both easements by necessity and easements by implication arise by operation of law without any express intent to create them.

There are really no analogous doctrines in the law of real covenants or equitable servitudes. Suppose that J owns a large parcel of land with a house on one end, and that the value and pleasurable use of the house depend upon the fact that the other part of the land is vacant, allowing a lovely view of the lake nearby. If J sells the house to K, there is no implied covenant that J will not build an apartment house on the retained vacant land. There are probably two reasons for this difference in approach between easements and the other servitudes. First, courts create easements by necessity or implication only where the need for them is great. That occurs when the very use of certain land depends upon a concomitant right to use the neighboring land as well. Courts do not create covenants by implication in analogous cases because the necessity is not as compelling when it is a claim that the use of certain land depends upon a concomitant right that neighboring land not be used in an inconsistent way. One's need for access to land or drainage from it is ordinarily much greater than his need to be free from a conflicting neighboring activity. . . .

One more illustration of difference in treatment will suffice to show the difficulty of thoroughly integrating all the rules concerning servitudes. This concerns the continuing liability of the originally burdened person after he no longer has an interest in the property. Suppose L conveys an easement over his land to M and later sells the fee simple to N. Thereafter if N tries to interfere with M's right to cross, L is not responsible for his grantee's wrongful act. The same rule is true of restrictive covenants. For example, a promisor-former owner is not liable for his grantee's breach of a covenant against construction of commercial property. Only the breaching party is liable in damages or injunction.

The law is more complex, however, with respect to affirmative covenants at law. On the one hand a tenant who assigns his leasehold interest in land to an assignee is still bound on his promise to pay rent and if the assignee fails to pay, the tenant-assignor must make good, although he has an action over against the assignee. On the other hand, a person buying in fee simple and promising to pay a monthly assessment to an association for maintenance of common areas is not liable for obligations accruing after he sells the property to another. The reason for the difference is clear. In the landlord-tenant situation when the landlord rents the property, he is relying upon the credit of the tenant for the entire lease period, and the tenant should not be able to escape that liability just by assigning the lease. With a fee simple, however, it is well understood that the first buyer will not own the property forever, and it is contemplated that he will pay the assessments only as long as he is an owner. Further, unlike the lease, the assessment is a potentially infinite obligation which, if it were held to bind the original promisor forever, would render the assessment device useless. Nobody would buy property subject to such an onerous personal obligation. The rules on original party liability are not uniform as to the different servitudes, nor should they be. The differences in legal result make good sense. They stem from the fact that, although servitudes of different types may be similar and related to each other, there are enough differences in their origin, economic function, and community expectation concerning them that opposing, yet sound rules about them can appropriately evolve.

That is not to say that some streamlining and simplification of the rules on servitudes is not desireable. [I]t would undoubtedly serve a useful purpose to get rid of most of the privity of estate requirements as to covenants at law and thereby integrate those rules about servitudes. In general, the possessor of land ought to be responsible for breach of a duty created by servitude whether in the form of a restrictive covenant, affirmative covenant, or affirmative easement. However, even there complete uniformity is not possible. For it is clear that, although a tenant should not be allowed to violate a restrictive covenant agreed to by his landlord (for example, not to operate a commercial establishment), he should not, unless he consents, be personally liable to perform his landlord's affirmative promises (e.g., to pay maintenance association dues). . . .

In conclusion, I would agree that the law of servitudes should be "unified" (however that word is defined) where that would mean the elimination of unnecessary or irrational differences in the rules (as in privity of estate at law) but the variances should be maintained in those many areas where the law, as it has evolved, is supported by sound policy and community expectation.

6. Condominiums

Easements, licenses, covenants, and servitudes are weapons in the arsenal of twentieth century land lawyers. Suburban developers and central city redevelopers are able to pick and choose from among the standard arrangements, and to establish arrangements that attract and then safeguard invested capital. Later material in this part looks more deeply at some of these arrangements, and especially at some of their exclusionary consequences.

Meanwhile, however, the last 20 years have seen the adoption, the extensive employment, and thus the sophisticated legal development of a new arrangement that now belongs on the list of standard land-use devices for sharing ownership: the condominium.

Density — urban growth, transportation costs, expensive land, violent crime, "swinging singles," and couples whose children are grown — created a market for high- and low-rise multiple dwellings. An apartment complex must have common facilities: elevators, furnaces, tennis courts, parking lots, landscaping, lobbies. These facilities require more complicated substantive and procedural rules than neighboring single-family houses. Also, the fact that ownership units are arranged vertically — that houses are stacked on top of each other — seems to suggest different ownership arrangements than are appropriate for horizontal neighbors. As Part 2 showed, rental arrangements are at least as old as the working-class areas of industrializing London. But the 1970s needed something different. A renter accumulates no capital share. The part of his rent that pays mortgage interest and real estate taxes is not deductible for federal income tax purposes. His participation in decisions about facilities and neighbors is limited. He is not an owner. Similarly, the developer who becomes a landlord is tied to his investment for a long time, and may have to accept the consequences of tenant behavior affected by an absence of long-term commitment.

One solution is the *cooperative:* a building owned by a corporation, with residents owning both stock in the corporation and a lease on a particular apartment. A second arrangement, discovered by U.S. lawyers in Puerto Rico, where it had apparently been derived from civil law precedents, is the *condominium,* in which each resident owns an apartment in fee simple (even if it is 23 floors above the ground), and also owns stock in the corporation that controls common areas and that contracts to provide services to individual apartments. Cooperatives are a significant fact, especially in New York City. But condominiums are a far greater fact, apparently because financing is easier when a bank can lend against a wholly-owned residential unit (although, of course, the value of that unit is intimately related to the surrounding structure). Some authorities assert that half the new housing built in America in the 1990s will be condominiums. (One-quarter may be mobile homes, but that is another story.)

In a sense, the condominium is only an imaginative assembly of earlier legal devices: a fee simple in the apartment, a license for the tennis court, an easement across the lobby, a covenant to pay a landscaping charge, and so forth. But the device is so prevalent, and the law surrounding it so sophisticated, that it is now sensible to consider the condominium an estate, and to observe legislatures and courts working out a standardized law of high-rise condominium relationships.

BERGER, CONDOMINIUM: SHELTER ON A STATUTORY FOUNDATION, 63 Colum. L. Rev. 987, 989-994 (1963): What is this condominium that has aroused such sudden interest? According to its Latin meaning, condominium is co-ownership; however, co-ownership is not today its primary feature. The most common modern instance of condominium is a multi-unit dwelling each of whose residents enjoys exclusive ownership of his individual apartment. With "title" to an apartment goes a cotenant's undivided interest in the common facilities — the land, the hallways, the heating plant, etc. Remarkably flexible, condominium is susceptible of an endless variety of legal formulations and can be adapted to a multiplicity of land uses or project designs. But in all of its forms its principal goal remains constant: to enable occupants of a multi-unit project to achieve more concomitants of ownership than are now available either to renters or to cooperators. The realization of this goal depends mainly on whether the individual units will gain independent dignity as mortgage security and as a basis for property taxation.

. . . Of the previously attempted unions [of home ownership and apartment occupancy], the stock cooperative is best known. In this kind of venture, the apartment project is owned by a corporation; each cooperator is a shareholder; and stock ownership carries with it a proprietary lease for one unit, so that the corporation becomes, in effect, the landlord and the stockholders the tenants. Because a cooperator in good standing may automatically renew his lease at fixed intervals, he acquires a paper security of occupancy greater than the rental tenant can obtain. Instead of "rent," which some regard as a sign of inferior social status, the cooperator pays a periodic "assessment," his *pro rata* share of the project's taxes, debt service, capital outlays, and operating costs. The Internal Revenue Code allows him, as it does the home-owner, to deduct that part of the assessment earmarked for mortgage interest and property taxes; and for the upper-bracket taxpayer, this may be the decisive factor in the choice between a rental or cooperative apartment. The cooperator may, if he wishes, participate in the management of the venture's affairs. Also, the absence of a profit-seeking landlord tends to lower costs below those for comparable rental units.[23]

Although the stock-cooperative has been popular in New York City, where state and local programs have provided the stimulant of partial subsidy, elsewhere it is fairly uncommon and designed chiefly for the more affluent consumer. . . .

The enthusiasts of the stock-cooperative are messianic in their ardor; but its failure to cut a broader swath betrays a basic limitation: the stock-cooperative fashions a rather skimpy bundle of "ownership" rights. This shortcoming would be partly remedied if its proponents would view cooperation as an experience in capitalism rather than fellowship. Curbs on resale price detract from many cooperatives' attractiveness as a capital investment; in some ventures the selling cooperator may recover only his down payment; in others he must offer his interest to the cooperative at "book value." A still greater disadvantage is that, for purposes of mortgage financing and property taxation, the cooperator's stock-lease "estate" lacks sufficient personality to support an individual obligation. As a result the entire cooperative structure is burdened by a blanket mortgage and a single tax assessment. By saddling the venture with overall liens, the stock-cooperative imposes upon the tenants the duty of meeting collectively the tax and debt service obligations as they fall due; frequently the two items exceed two-thirds of the monthly assessment.

Even if the risk of financial interdependence has been overdrawn, the blanket mortgage scheme imposes serious disadvantages upon the cooperator. He lacks the flexibility with regard to debt reduction, refinancing, or resale that the home owner enjoys. He cannot shift his assets or take advantage of earnings peaks or asset increments to reduce or eliminate the mortgage affecting his unit. Refinancing, which is often needed to effect modernization, modify debt service charges, "borrow against one's equity," or facilitate resale, is not possible unless the cooperator can persuade his fellow stockholders to refinance the blanket debt. . . .

By enabling the unit owner to undertake an individual financing program, the condominium offers a major and perhaps critical advantage over the present-day cooperative. Yet the condominium relinquishes none of the ownership benefits afforded by stock-cooperatives

---

23. . . . Professor Haar questions whether the cooperative spokesmen have established that rental housing is inherently more expensive for the consumer. He suggests that many cost savings attributed to cooperation are the results of economies of large scale development or more attractive government-insured financing, advantages that can be made available to any form of multi-family venture. The absence of an owner's profit, reduced somewhat by the earning power of the cooperator's cash investment, may be the one cost savings peculiar to the cooperative. Haar, Middle-Income Housing: The Cooperative Snare?, 20 Land Econ. 289 (1953).

— voice in its management, permanence of tenure, avoidance of profit to the landlord, and tax savings.

SENATOR WILLIAM PROXMIRE, 120 Cong. Rec. 32704 (1974): The condominium boom, once confined to vacation spots, is now hitting our Nation's cities with epidemic force. A study of 25 metropolitan areas showed that in 1972, 40.3 percent of the new units for sale were condominiums. The figures for individual cities ran far higher. In Milwaukee, for example, 45 percent of the new housing was condominiums; in Cleveland it was 57 percent, in Bridgeport, Conn. an astonishing 83 percent.

All indications are that the condominium craze is growing rapidly and changing the face of the housing market. The National Association of Homebuilders estimates that condominiums accounted for 8 percent of total housing starts in 1972, 10.8 percent in 1973 and up to 14.3 percent this year.

Furthermore, these figures just take into account new condominium construction. The total is in fact much larger because of the huge number of apartment buildings that are being converted from rental to condominium units, thus feeding the ownership market at the expense of the rental market.

What does the condominium buyer get in his purchase? He becomes the owner of one unit in a multi-family housing complex, which may be an apartment in a high-rise or low-rise structure or a townhouse, and may be located in the city's center, in the suburbs, or in a resort area. Along with his unit, the buyer also acquires an undivided share in the project's common areas and facilities, which can range from the lobby, grounds, and electrical and mechanical systems to extensive recreational facilities such as swimming pools and tennis courts.

The price of a condominium can range from $20,000 or less to over $100,000. The purchaser makes monthly payments on the mortgage on his unit and takes the same tax deductions for mortgage interest and property taxes as does the owner of a single-family home. In addition, the condominium owner pays a monthly condominium fee, for operating and maintenance and any common costs shared by the project's owners as a whole; this is not tax deductible. Other fees may be charged on top of that, such as recreation fees.

CAUSES OF THE "CONDOMINIUM CRAZE"

What are the causes of the condominium craze? The basic answer is cost. Inflation in real estate prices has pushed the price of the standard single-family house beyond the reach of many potential homebuyers. Soaring land and construction costs, sewer moratoriums and other anti-growth policies have placed further pressures on the supply and price of housing, leading even to some predictions that the single-family detached house may become obsolete.

Another side of the picture is that rental housing has become an increasingly less attractive investment. Costs of maintenance and utilities have risen rapidly, as have real estate taxes, and imposition of rent controls in many cities has cut into landlords' profit margins. Thus the incentive is to turn the building over to a developer, who takes his tax breaks, does some renovation, then sells the units at an inflated price and gets his money out fast. As for building new rental housing, costs of construction make projected rents prohibitively high, and here again, the developer sees an advantage in getting his money out quickly and turning responsibility for running the building over to the residents.

BRIGHT PROMISES, SAD REALITIES

So developers and real estate agents are heralding the condominium as the wave of the future. Open the real estate pages of any metropolitan area newspaper and you will be bombarded with advertisements that promise your dreams will come true when you buy your own condominium. Prospective buyers are told that they will have all the advantages of homeownership, without the headaches of maintenance and repair. They are lured with visions of swimming pools and tennis courts — country club living at apartment prices.

Certainly condominiums do represent an attractive housing choice for many people. They offer homeownership and its accompanying tax benefits to people whose incomes are too low to afford conventional housing.

But too often bright promises fade in the face of sad realities, and the condominium owner finds himself faced with unanticipated problems and unexpected expenses.

The monthly condominium fee charged for maintaining common areas and other building expenses doubles or triples, because the developer understated the expenses in the promotional material.

The swimming pool he thought he had bought along with the house turns out to belong instead to the developer, who rents it out to the condominium owners at an exorbitant fee.

The project's owners are locked into a long-term contract with a management company, often one in which the developer has an interest, so they are not free to select the management and negotiate the rates.

In older buildings converted to condominiums, owners are often saddled with expensive repairs, as long-neglected electrical and mechanical systems left untouched by cosmetic renovation fall apart completely.

The owner may find himself paying as much or more for his condominium as he would have to pay for a house. He is disappointed and frustrated; he feels he has been misinformed and misled. And yet willy-nilly he is the owner of his condominium castle, and the law holds that he is responsible for whatever befalls him in it.

◆ POINT EAST MANAGEMENT CORP. v. POINT EAST ONE CONDOMINIUM CORP.
282 So. 2d 628 (Fla. 1973), *cert. denied*, 415 U.S. 921 (1974)

ADKINS, Justice: . . . Petitioner is the original developers of the Point East condominium project, a management corporation contracted to manage the project for a period of 25 years, and lessors of a recreation facility to the condominium association on a 99-year lease. The various identities of petitioner simply represent different stages of the developers' involvement with the project. Petitioner developed the condominium project and, subsequent to the formation of the condominium associations, contracted with itself for management of the condominiums and for the lease.

Respondents are the condominium associations — as presently constituted by individual condominium unit owners — who brought suit for rescission of the lease and management contract, for damages in fraud, for damages for breach of a fiduciary duty, and for damages for breach of contract. All relief sought was denied by the trial court except for invalidation of the management contract, and the District Court of Appeal, Third District, affirmed.

Petitioner seeks a reversal of the District Court of Appeal on the invalidation of the management contract, and respondents, by cross-petition, seek reversals of the District Court of Appeal on the affirmance of all other holdings of the trial court.

We have carefully reviewed those issues raised by the cross-petition and find them to be without merit. However, we have determined that the point raised by petitioner is meritorious, and the District Court of Appeal must be reversed on its invalidation of the management contracts.

The District Court of Appeal recognized that rescission of the management contract would not lie merely because it arose from the dealings of the developers with themselves while they constituted all of the members of the condominium associations and of the management corporation.

However, the District Court of Appeal held that the 25-year management contract is void because it violates the provisions of the Condominium Act in wresting the control of the management of the condominiums away from the associations. This interpretation is based on three sections of the Condominium Act.

First, Fla. Stat. §711.03(2) defines the association as "the entity responsible for the operation of a condominium." Fla. Stat. §711.03(12) then defines operation of the condominium as including "the administration and management" of the property. Finally, the District Court of Appeal relies upon Fla. Stat. §711.12(1) which provides:

> The operation of the condominium shall be by the association, the name of which shall be stated in the declaration.
> The District Court of Appeal then, in effect, rescinded the contracts complained of, holding them to be invalid because they . . . divest from the association in a material or substantial degree the power and privilege granted it by the statute to operate the condominium. . . .

We cannot agree with the District Court of Appeal that the Legislature, by placing in the condominium associations the power and duty to manage the condominium properties, intended to restrict the ability of the associations to contract for the management of the associations. The fact that the contract is of long duration does not make the contract any more objectionable, and the fact that the developers of the condominiums contracted with themselves for the management contract does not invalidate it.

The Legislature has chosen to allow the owners of condominium units to cancel initial management contracts by a vote of 75 percent of the owners of the individual units. Accordingly, it must be assumed that the Legislature recognized the existence of and chose not to abolish such contracts. It is impossible, therefore, to discover a legislative prohibition against a management contract.

The fact of the contract and its terms were made known — or at least available — to all who bought or considered buying condominium units, and the contracts of sale included affirmation of the management contract. Admittedly, a prospective purchaser had no option as to the management contract, but he knew or should have known that the contract was part of the purchase price of his condominium unit. Considered in that light, enforcement of the contract cannot be said to work a hardship on the present condominium owners. . . .

ERVIN, Justice (dissenting): . . .

As is stated in the majority opinion, the petitioner, as developer of the condominium, contracted with itself for management of the condominium and for the lease. Thus, the management contracts were executed by the developers while they controlled the condominium associates prior to their present makeup of individual condominium apartment owners. The resulting lopsided character of these "agreements" are best evidenced by an examination of the provisions contained therein. The contracts extend for periods of up to twenty-five years with no right of termination by the condominium associates except for cause after sixty days notice of default. The manager "to the exclusion of all persons including the Association and its members [presently, the apartment owners]" is given, in part, the following powers:

1) The right to hire, supervise, and fire, "in its absolute discretion" such persons as are required to fulfill its duties under the management agreement.

2) The power to collect all assessments from the associations' members and to take such action in the name of the associations as is needed to collect payment — to include "foreclosing the association lien therefore, or by way of other legal process as may be required. . . ."

3) The power to carry on "normal" maintenance and repair work except that no one item of repair is to exceed $30,000.00 unless authorized by the associations.

4) The right to purchase "equipment, tools, vehicles, appliances," etc. as are "reasonably necessary" to perform its duties.

5) The right to maintain all books and records subject only to the right of the associations to conduct an independent audit at their own expense.

6) The right to deposit funds collected from the associations either in a special bank account or to commingle the monies with similar funds "as the manager shall determine."

7) The right to "retain and employ attorneys-at-law, tax consultants, certified public accountants, health consultants, and such other experts and professionals whose services the Manager may reasonably require. . . ." (The result of this provision is that the apartment owners are paying the costs sustained by both parties in the present suit.)

8) The power to insure that payments received from assessments or other revenue are sufficient to pay the costs of all services and to adequately fund reserves. Failure of the associations to increase the monthly assessments as requested by the manager "within a reasonable time may, at the option of the manager, be construed as a breach of this agreement."

The above provisions are only a sampling of the terms of the "Management Agreement" that was before the trial court together with voluminous testimony attesting to the impotency of the associations to have the benefits and to function autonomously under the Condominium Act when saddled by the terms of what amount to adhesion contracts together with details of the resultant excessive and overreaching extractions mulched from the unit owners. . . .

The long duration of the contracts herein makes them statutorily objectionable because it serves to undercut the legislative mandate of autonomy for the unit owners. That problem is further compounded in the present case because the associations (i.e., the developers) were of an entirely different composition when the contracts were negotiated.

As is stated in petitioner's brief and may be taken as an admission against interest:

> At the time the Management Agreements and the Community Facilities Lease were made, no interests of any purchasers or other third parties were involved. No apartment units had been sold. The developer . . . was the sole owner of all apartment units and the entire condominium property and the developer was the only member of the associations. No interests of anyone other than the developer were in anywise affected by the Management Agreements and the Community Facilities Leases.

Petitioner then asserts, as does the majority, that no harm resulted from this blatant attempt to circumvent the intent and mandate of the Condominium Act because "the apartments were sold and purchased with full disclosure and complete knowledge of the contents of the Management Agreements and Community Facilities Leases. . . ." Such rationalization not only ignores the statutory provision for association automony, but completely ignores the reality of unequal bargaining positions between individual apartment purchasers and a multimillion dollar corporation intent on foisting long-term management contracts of adhesion upon them, contrary to regulatory law.

The fact that the Legislature has more recently taken further steps to insure that such unconscionable contracts can be terminated by a vote of seventy-five percent of the apartment unit owners does not have the secondary effect of rendering Respondents remediless in this litigation because the subject contracts were entered into prior to the effective date of that legislation.

The fact that the Legislature became more acutely aware of this problem and further acted three years ago to bolster remedies against future injustice, does not mean that the courts are powerless to strike down an illegal contract that is clearly violative of other provisions, in effect at the time the contracts were signed. . . .

I should like to reiterate a portion of my dissent in Fountainview Association, Inc. v. Bell, 214 So. 2d at 609, 613-614 (Fla. 1968), that has relevance to the cause instanter:

> A condominium association does not involve an arm's length relationship as in the case of an outright sale of a dwelling between two strangers. It contemplates cooperative ownership of several apartment units in association with others and long continued, prudent management of the apartment building and the individual units as an integrated whole. If the project has been subjected to promotional fraud in its inception or overreaching in its management, its ability to be successful as a viable, cooperative project over a long period of time will be jeopardized. The

association and its membership have a vital and continuing interest in seeing that its management is free of conflicts of interest and fraud. . . .

One of the primary purposes of our condominium law is to give the association members legal status similar to corporate stockholders so they may require, if necessary, that the condominium project be operated free of fraud and conflicts of interest. . . .

FLORIDA CONDOMINIUM ACT, Fla. Rev. Stat. ch. 718 (1983 Supp.), created by Laws 1976, ch. 76-222, §3:

§718.106

(2) There shall pass with a unit, as appurtenances thereto:

    (a) An undivided share in the common elements and common surplus.

    (b) The exclusive right to use such portion of the common elements as may be provided by the declaration.

    (c) An exclusive easement for the use of the airspace occupied by the unit as it exists at any particular time and as the unit may lawfully be altered or reconstructed from time to time. . . .

§718.111

(1) The operation of the condominium shall be by the association, which must be a corporation for profit or a corporation not for profit. . . . The owners of units shall be shareholders or members of the association. The officers and directors of the association have a fiduciary relationship to the unit owners. . . .

§718.112

    (f) The board of administration shall mail a meeting notice and copies of the proposed annual budget of common expenses to the unit owners. . . . If an adopted budget requires assessment against the unit owners in any fiscal or calendar year exceeding 115 percent of the assessments for the preceding year, the board . . . shall call a special meeting of the unit owners . . . At the special meeting, unit owners shall consider and enact a budget. . . .

§718.202

(1) If a developer contracts to sell a condominium parcel and the construction . . . has not been substantially completed . . . , the developer shall pay into an escrow account . . . all payments up to 10 percent of the sale price received by the developer from the buyer towards the sale price. . . .

§718.203

(1) The developer shall be deemed to have granted to the purchaser of each unit an implied warranty of fitness and merchantability for the purpose or uses intended as follows:

(a) As to each unit, a warranty for 3 years commencing with the completion of the building containing the unit.

§718.301

(1) When unit owners other than the developer own 15 percent or more of the units . . . , the unit owners other than the developer shall be entitled to elect not less than one-third of the members of the board of administration of the association. Unit owners other than the developers are entitled to elect not less than a majority. . . .

(a) Three years after 50 percent of the units . . . have been conveyed to purchasers;

(b) Three months after 90 percent of the units . . . have been conveyed . . .

§718.302

(1) Any grant or reservation . . . and any contract made by an association prior to assumption of control of the association by unit owners other than the developer that provides for operation, maintenance, or management . . . shall be fair and reasonable, and may be canceled by unit owners other than the developers:

(a) . . . by concurrence of the owners of not less than 75 percent of the units other than the units owned by the developers. . . .

(4) It is declared that the public policy of this state prohibits the inclusion or enforcement of escalation clauses in management contracts for condominiums . . . [A]n escalation clause is any clause . . . which provides that the fee under the contract shall increase at the same percentage rate as any nationally recognized and conveniently available commodity or consumer price index.

NATIONAL CONFERENCE OF COMMISSIONERS ON UNIFORM STATE LAWS, UNIFORM CONDOMINIUM ACT (1980):

§2-108. [Allocation of Common Element Interests, Votes, and Common Expense Liabilities]

(a) The declaration shall allocate a fraction or percentage of undivided interests in the common elements and in the common expenses of the association, and a portion of the votes in the association, to each unit and state the formulas used to establish those allocations. . . .

(c) The number of votes allocated to each unit must be equal, proportionate to that unit's common expense liability, or proportionate to that unit's common element interest. If the declaration allocates an equal number of votes in the association to each unit, each unit that may be subdivided or converted by the declarant into 2 or more units, common elements, or both (Section 2-115), must be allocated a number of votes in the association proportionate to the relative size of that unit compared to the aggregate size of all units, and the remaining votes in the association must be allocated equally to the other units. The declaration may provide that different allocations of votes shall be made to the units on particular matters specified in the declaration.

Note

Does anything remain of the Florida Supreme Court's holding in *Point East?* See Avila South Condominium Association, Inc. v. Kappa Corp., 347 So. 2d 599 (Fla. 1977), where the court "reaffirm[ed the] decision in *Point East,* that self-dealing by officers and directors of a condominium association, without more, is not actionable . . . ," over the dissent's urging "not [to] waste words trying to explain the continued validity of the court's decision in the *Point East* case. I would simply concede that it has been overruled and adopt the dissenting views expressed in that case by Justice Ervin."

NOTE, CONDOMINIUM REGULATION: BEYOND DISCLOSURE, 123 U. Pa. L. Rev. 639, 642, 646 (1975): The condominium developer can expose the purchaser to two general classes of risks: misleading or fraudulent advertising, and the more sophisticated arrangements that, although not misrepresentations, may still ensure exorbitant returns to the developer at the expense of the purchaser. Generally speaking, both federal and state regulation has been aimed at the first risk, requiring "full disclosure" of all terms prior to sale. But it is the second class of risks, those that may be disclosed but whose significance is only recognized by the sophisticated analyst, that have resulted in more serious consequences to the condominium purchaser. For those subject to such risks, current federal and state regulation offers little in the way of protection or remedy.

Five examples of this second class of risk . . . are the use of deposits, sweetheart leases, management contracts, extended control, and liability for shares of unsold unit expenses. Each of these practices may be technically lawful under the "full disclosure" regulation now applied by the federal and most state governments. So long as the terms of sale permitting such abuses are disclosed, the purchaser has little recourse against the unscrupulous developer for the abuses.

Many developers must secure a minimum number of preconstruction subscriptions before a lender will commit itself to financing the project. This external pressure may lead to hasty sales programs which describe, through colorful and enticing literature, the future appearance of what, at that point, is most likely a totally unimproved or only partially excavated parcel of land. Deposits are collected from the subscribed purchasers. Most of the state statutes make no provision for the use or ultimate disposition of the deposit receipts, which are, at this early stage, high risk money. There is often no direct or indirect prohibition against using the money to defray construction costs of that particular project or, in fact, of any other of the developer's projects. Purchasers generally acquire no lien or other priority against the property, and they may ultimately be left with nothing but a worthless general claim if the project fails and the developer becomes bankrupt. With respect to the safety of his deposits, the purchaser's lack of remedy creates a substantial risk factor in most investments in a condominium under construction. For this reason New York requires the developer to include a warning for depositors which reads, *"[i]f this offering is not consummated for any reason you may lose all or part of your investment."*

Another area of abuse is the so-called "sweetheart lease" agreement. Here the developer keeps title to the land and leases it to the condominium owners at exorbitant rates. According to some courts, the developer owes no fiduciary duty to the purchaser to guarantee fairness in the terms of these rental arrangements. A related practice is the "sweetheart" recreation lease, under which the developer conveys the unit in fee but retains title to certain of the recreational common facilities and leases them back to the development at inflated values and excessively long tenancies. This developer self-dealing is accomplished prior to the sale of the first unit, when the sponsor is in complete control. During this time, there is no actual or implied duty to future purchasers. Thus, for the most part, developers may profiteer without legal restraint.

Developers have also been able, under most state statutes, to enter into lengthy management contracts with the condominium association, which they control, at inflated rates of compensation. Here also, the courts have been unwilling to interfere with the agreements. The courts have consistently failed to imply any quasi-fiduciary relationship between seller and buyer.

Condominium documents are often drafted so that control effectively remains with the developer for longer periods of time than the state statutes had envisioned. For example, although most state statutes tie voting rights in the association to the percentage interest in common elements, they do not expressly require that these rights vest immediately. Many developers will include a provision in the master plan or by-laws which prevents exercise of the franchise for a period of five years or until the *last* unit is sold. During this time, the developer may act in his own self interest.

Finally, developers might refuse to pay their allocable share of monthly assessments as "owners" of the unsold "units." The condominium documents will limit the description of a unit to a narrow, technically defined concept rather than to the broader definition suggested by the underlying statutes. A "unit," for example, may not exist for purposes of paying monthly assessments until a certificate of occupancy is issued — an event which will not occur, according to the documents, until after sale and settlement.

Note

Is there a possible antitrust problem with the type of agreement entered into between the developer and each condominium purchaser in *Point East*, which incorporated the management contract into each sale? Could this constitute a "tying agreement" in restraint of trade under the Sherman Anti-Trust Act §1, 15 U.S.C. §1? See, e.g., Miller v. Granados, 529 F.2d 393 (5th Cir. 1976).

◆ CHATEAU VILLAGE NORTH CONDOMINIUM v. JORDAN
643 P.2d 791 (Colo. App. 1982)

TURSI, Judge. Pamela S. Jordan appeals the judgment of the trial court granting the Chateau Village North Condominium Association (Association) a permanent injunction enjoining her from maintaining pets in her condominium unit. We reverse.

Jordan is the owner of a condominium unit in Chateau Village North Condominiums. The condominium declaration provides that the Association may by rules or regulations prohibit or limit the keeping of animals in any unit or on the common elements of the condominium complex. The administrative rules and regulations appended to the by-laws of the Association provide in pertinent part: "No cats, dogs, or other animal . . . shall be kept, maintained, or harbored in the development unless the same in each instance is expressly permitted in writing by the Managing Agent, or, if there is no Managing Agent, then by the Board of Managers."

Pursuant to this rule Jordan applied to the board of managers for permission to keep two cats in her unit, and at a board meeting she presented a petition signed by residents of the condominium which requested the board to grant the application. The board denied the application on the basis of their policy to allow no pets in the condominium units other than those that they referred to as being "grandfathered in." Jordan was notified by letter of the board's decision, but refused to remove her cats from the premises. The Association then instituted this action seeking a mandatory injunction to enjoin and restrain Jordan from continuing to harbor cats in her unit. The Association also requested the awarding of reasonable attorney's fees. . . .

We do agree with Jordan's contentions that the trial court erred in ruling that the Association did not act arbitrarily and capriciously in denying her request for permission to keep a pet. The rules and regulations adopted pursuant to the by-laws and the recorded condominium declaration were not a blanket prohibition on pets but rather a limitation which provided that pets could be kept in the development if permission to do so was granted by the Association. However, the board adopted a blanket policy against keeping pets, and denied this petition based solely upon that policy. In so doing, it exceeded its authority.

In Rhue v. Cheyenne Homes, Inc., 168 Colo. 6, 449 P.2d 361 (1969), at issue was a restrictive covenant which, in substance, prohibited the construction or placing of a building on a lot unless the proposed construction was first approved by an architectural control committee, but which contained no specific standards governing the committee's determination. The court held that specific standards were not required provided that the intention of the covenant was clear and that the architectural control committee exercised its discretion in a reasonable and good faith manner, and in a manner which was not arbitrary or capricious.

The rule adopted by the Association here pursuant to the declaration is analogous to the restrictive covenants discussed in *Rhue*, . . . and, therefore, the "reasonable and good faith standard" of *Rhue* applies. Since, under the rule, Jordan had the right to apply for permission to keep pets in her condominium unit, the Association had the duty to consider her application and apply its discretion in a reasonable and good faith manner. Rather than considering the facts of Jordan's individual application, the board of managers merely relied upon its own policy prohibiting all pets in the complex. Because the board did not act in a reasonable and good faith manner in denying Jordan's application, the granting of injunctive relief and attorney's fees in favor of the Association was error.

The judgment of the trial court granting a permanent injunction and attorney's fees is reversed, and the cause is remanded with instructions to dismiss the complaint.

Notes

1. Hidden Harbour Condominium Association had the power "to make and amend reasonable rules and regulations respecting the use of the condominium property." Two association members objected to a rule prohibiting use of alcoholic beverages in the club house. The trial judge held that the association could not bar lawful private activity

unless it constituted a nuisance. "With all due respect to the veteran trial judge," the court of appeals reversed. "[I]nherent in the condominium concept is the principle that to promote the . . . peace of mind of the majority of the unit owners since they are living in such close proximity . . . , each unit owner must give up a certain degree of freedom of choice. . . ." Hidden Harbour Estates, Inc. v. Norman, 309 So. 2d 180 (Fla. App. 1975).

2. Rules requiring owners of cooperative or condominium apartments to obtain permission before selling or to offer the unit on "first refusal" to the association are normally upheld. See, e.g., Mowatt v. 1540 Lake Shore Drive Corp., 385 F.2d 135 (7th Cir. 1967); Chianese v. Culley, 397 F. Supp. 1344 (S.D. Fla. 1975).

3. The board of directors of a cooperative apartment house adopts the following rule:

> The playing of musical instruments shall be prohibited except during the following hours:
>
> a) Between 10 a.m. and 8 p.m. weekdays
> b) Between 11 a.m. and 8 p.m. weekends
>
> Playing in excess of 1½ hours per day by one person is prohibited.

Defendants' two daughters are a violinist and a flutist who need to practice 3½ hours per day. Defendants moved in (in 1959) after being assured their daughters could practice. On April 29, 1965, following tenant complaints, especially about the loud, piercing flute, the board adopted the above rule. What result? See Justice Court Mutual Housing Cooperative, Inc. v. Sandow, 50 Misc. 2d 541, 270 N.Y.S.2d 829 (Sup. Ct. 1966), holding that the rules were "arbitrary and unreasonable."

4. An owner of a condominium unit tripped over a water sprinkler negligently maintained by the association in a common area. The association defended with the argument that the negligence of each member must be imputed to each other member, and therefore plaintiff is barred from tort recovery because of its responsibility for the location of the sprinkler. The court disagreed, finding that "the condominium project and the condominium association must be considered separate legal entities from its owners and association members." The opinion quoted from the "condominium plan" that plaintiff had been given: "In case management is not to your satisfaction, you may have no recourse." White v. Cox, 17 Cal. App. 3d 824, 95 Cal. Rptr. 259 (1971).

If a deliveryman were hurt in the common area and recovered a judgment, should he be able to levy on the property of each condominium member? Would you advise a condominium to incorporate its common areas?

5. Plaintiff Ritchey, owner of a condominium in Villa Nueva, had

leased his unit to a woman with two children. The condominium association brought suit against Ritchey and his lessee to remove lessee from the unit, based upon a violation of a bylaw restricting occupancy to persons 18 or older. The complaint was dismissed when the lessee moved out, but Ritchey sought injunctive and declaratory relief, challenging the validity of the bylaw.

The trial judge granted the association's motion for summary judgment, and the court of appeals affirmed, holding that the authority of a condominium association includes the power to issue reasonable regulations governing an owner's use of his unit, including restrictions on occupancy. Ritchey v. Villa Nueva Condominium Association, 81 Cal. App. 3d 688, 146 Cal. Rptr. 695 (1978).

6. Defendant transferred a one-half interest in his unit to his brother. Plaintiff challenged the transfer on two grounds: 1) the brother had children below age twelve in violation of the bylaws, and 2) dual ownership violated the "single family residence" requirement. The circuit court ruled for plaintiffs, but the district court of appeal reversed. The Florida Supreme Court held: 1) that, while the age restriction involved here is reasonable, as enforced against defendant and his brother, it was selective and arbitrary, as there were at least six other children under age twelve living in the complex unchallenged, thus estopping plaintiff from enforcing the restriction; and 2) that dual ownership involving alternating use of the unit did not violate the "single family residence" requirement. White Egret Condominium, Inc. v. Franklin, 379 So. 2d 346 (Fla. 1979).

7. When condominium owners run short of funds, two creditors will often compete to claim the apartment: the condominium association, which is owed maintenance payments; and the mortgagee, who loaned the funds with which the unit was purchased. Damen Savings & Loan Association v. Johnson, 126 Ill. App. 3d 940, 467 N.E.2d 1139 (1984), sorted out conflicting Illinois statutes and held that the foreclosing mortgagee took title to the apartment free of the association's claims.

7. Time-Sharing

◆ LAGUNA ROYALE OWNERS ASSOCIATION v. DARGER
119 Cal. App. 3d 670, 174 Cal. Rptr. 136 (1981)

KAUFMAN, Associate Justice. Defendants Stanford P. Darger and Darlene B. Darger (the Dargers) were the owners of a leasehold condominium in Laguna Royale, a 78-unit community apartment complex on the ocean front in South Laguna Beach. The Dargers purported to assign three one-quarter undivided interests in the property to three other couples: Wendall P. Paxton and Daila D. Paxton, Keith I. Gustaveson and Elsie Gustaveson, and Keith C. Brown and Geneva B. Brown (collectively the other defendants) without the approval of Laguna Royale Owners Association (Association). Association instituted this action to obtain a declaration that the assignments from the Dargers to defendants were invalid because they were made in violation of a provision of the instrument by which the Dargers acquired the property, prohibiting assignment or transfer of interests in the property without the consent and approval of Association's predecessor in interest. Following trial to the court judgment was rendered in favor of Association invalidating the assignments from the Dargers to the other defendants. Defendants appeal.

The Laguna Royale development is built on land leased by the developer from the landowner in a 99-year ground lease executed in 1961. As the units were completed, the developer sold each one by executing a Subassignment and Occupancy Agreement with the purchaser. This document conveyed an undivided 1/78 interest in the leasehold estate for a term of 99 years, a right to exclusive use of a designated unit and one or more garage spaces and a right to joint use of common areas and facilities; it also contained certain restrictions. The restriction pertinent to this action is paragraph 7, which provides in relevant part: "7. Subassignee [the purchaser] shall not assign or otherwise transfer this agreement, . . . nor shall subassignee sublet . . . without the consent of and approval of Lessee. . . ."

Upon the sale of all units and completion of the project, the developer entered into an "Assignment Agreement" with the Association, transferring and assigning to the Association all the developer's rights, powers and duties under the Subassignment and Occupancy Agreements, including *inter alia* the "right to approve or disapprove assignments or transfers of interests in Laguna Royale pursuant to Paragraph 7 of the Subassignment and Occupancy Agreements."

In 1965, Ramona G. Sutton acquired unit 41, consisting of some 3,000 square feet, by a Subassignment and Occupancy Agreement with the developer. In 1973 the Dargers purchased unit 41 from the executrix of Mrs. Sutton's estate. As owner of a unit in the project, the Dargers automatically became members of the Association and were bound by the Association's bylaws.

The Dargers reside in Salt Lake City, Utah, where Mr. Darger became a vice president of a large banking chain not long after the Dargers acquired their unit at Laguna Royale. The responsibilities of Mr. Darger's new position made it difficult for them to get away, and they attempted unsuccessfully to lease their unit through real estate agents in Laguna Beach. On October 30, 1973, Mr. Darger wrote to Mr. Yount, then chairman of the board of governors of the Association, in which he stated in part:

It has been suggested that we might sell shares in our apartment to two or three other couples here. These associates would be aware of the restrictions regarding children under 16 living there, as well as the restrictions regarding pets, and would submit themselves to the regular investigation of the Board given prospective purchasers and lessees. I would expect that the apartment will remain vacant most of the time, as now, and not more than one of the families will occupy the apartment at one time.

By letter dated November 12, 1973, Mr. Yount responded in relevant part:

Following receipt of your letter of October 30, 1973 regarding the possibility of selling shares in your apartment #41, we discussed the matter at the regular meeting of the Board of Governors held on November 10, 1973. Prior to the meeting we had referred the letter to our attorney, Mr. James Ralston Smith, for Laguna Royale Owner's Association for his opinion. We received his opinion prior to the meeting and this is quoted as follows: "As to the request of Mr. Darger, as owner of apartment #41, to sell undivided interests in that apartment to other parties, it is my opinion that if such other parties otherwise qualified and indicate no intended use of the apartment other than single family owner's use, there would be no legal basis to refuse such transfers. However, State law restricts more than four (4) transfers of undivided interests, without qualifying as a subdivision."

The letter then indicated that a number of members of the board of governors had voiced some objections to multiple ownership of a unit and then stated:

The Board of Governors is quite sympathetic with your problem of being unable to lease your apartment; however, because of the reasons given above, it is our opinion that the multiple ownership would not be beneficial to the other unit owners. We believe that our opinion is shared by the majority of the unit owners of Laguna Royale. Even in view of the Board's opinion, we would have no alternative except to approve the transfer which you suggested, providing you would comply with the legal opinion of Mr. Smith. . . .

After consultation with legal counsel the Dargers proceeded nevertheless, and on June 11 they executed instruments purporting to assign undivided one-fourth interests in the property to themselves and the other three couples.

After unsuccessfully demanding that the other defendants retransfer their purported interests to the Dargers, the Association filed this action.

We reject Association's contention that its right to give or withhold approval or consent is absolute. We likewise reject defendants' contention that the claimed right to approve or disapprove transfers is an invalid restraint on alienation because it is repugnant to the conveyance of a fee. We hold that in exercising its power to approve or disapprove transfers or assignments Association must act reasonably, exercising its power in a fair and nondiscriminatory manner and withholding approval only for a reason or reasons rationally related to the protection, preservation and proper operation of the property and the purposes of Association as set forth in its governing instruments. We hold that the restriction on transfer contained in paragraph 7 of the Subassignment and Occupancy Agreement (hereafter simply paragraph 7), thus limited, does not violate defendants' constitutional rights of association and is not invalid as an unreasonable restraint on alienation. However, we conclude that in view of the present provisions of Association's bylaws, its refusal to consent to the transfers to defendants was unreasonable as a matter of law. Accordingly, we reverse the judgment with directions to enter judgment for defendants. . . .

We reject the extreme contentions of both parties; the rules of law they propose, borrowed from the law of landlord and tenant developed during the feudal period in English history, are entirely inappropriate tools for use in affecting an accommodation of the competing interests involved in the use and transfer of a condominium. Even assuming the continued vitality of the rule that a lessor may arbitrarily withhold consent to a sublease, there is little or no similarity in the relationship between a condominium owner and his fellow owners and that between lessor and lessee or sublessor and sublessee. Even when the right to the underlying land is no more than an undivided interest in a ground lease or sublease, ownership of a condominium constitutes a statutorily recognized estate in real property, and in our society the right freely to use and dispose of one's property is a valued and protected right. Ownership and use of condominiums is an increasingly significant form of "home ownership" which has evolved in recent years to meet the desire of our people to own their own dwelling place, in the face of heavy concentrations of population in urban areas, the limited availability of housing, and, thus, the impossibly inflated cost of individual homes in such areas.

On the other hand condominium living involves a certain closeness to and with one's neighbors, and, as stated in Hidden Harbour Estates, Inc. v. Norman (Fla. App. 1975) 309 So. 2d 180, 181-182:

> [I]nherent in the condominium concept is the principle that to promote the health, happiness, and peace of mind of the majority of the unit owners since they are living in such close proximity and using facilities in common, each unit owner must give up a certain degree of freedom of choice which he might otherwise enjoy in separate, privately owned property.

Thus, it is essential to successful condominium living and the maintenance of the value of these increasingly significant property interests that the owners as a group have the authority to regulate reasonably the use and alienation of the condominiums.

Happily, there is no impediment to our adoption of such a rule; indeed, the existing law suggests such a rule. In the only California appellate decision of which we are aware dealing with the problem of restraints on alienation of a condominium, Ritchey v. Villa Nueva Condominium Assn., 81 Cal. App. 3d 688, 146 Cal. Rptr. 695 (1978), the court upheld as a reasonable restriction on an owner's right to sell his unit to families with children, a duly adopted amendment to the condominium bylaws restricting occupancy to persons 18 years and over. And, of course, Civil Code section 1355 pertaining to condominiums expressly authorizes the recordation of a declaration of project restrictions and subsequent amendments thereto, "which restrictions shall be enforceable equitable servitudes where reasonable, and shall inure to and bind all owners of condominiums in the project."

Reasonable restrictions on the alienation of condominiums are entirely consistent with Civil Code section 711 in which the California law on unlawful restraints on alienation has its origins. The day has long since passed when the rule in California was that all restraints on alienation were unlawful under the statute; it is now the settled law in this jurisdiction that only unreasonable restraints on alienation are invalid. . . .

Insofar as approval was withheld based on multiple ownership alone, Association's action was clearly unreasonable. In the first place, multiple ownership has no necessary connection to intensive use. Twenty, yea a hundred, persons could own undivided interests in a condominium for investment purposes and lease the condominium on a long-term basis to a single occupant whose use of the premises would probably be less intense in every respect than that considered "normal and usual." Secondly, the Association bylaws specifically contemplate multiple ownership; in Section 7 of Article III, dealing with voting at meetings, it is stated: "Where there is more than one record owner of a unit, any or all of the record owners may attend [the meeting] but only one vote will be permitted for said unit. In the event of disagreement among the record owners of a unit, the vote for that unit shall be cast by a majority of the record owners." Finally, the evidence is uncontroverted that a number of units are owned by several unrelated persons. Although those owners at the time of trial used their units "as a family," there is nothing in the governing instruments as they presently exist that would prevent them from changing the character of their use.

We turn to the assertion that the use of the premises proposed by defendants would be in violation of section 1 of article VIII of the bylaws which provides: "All apartment unit uses are restricted and limited to single family residential use and shall not be used or occupied for any other purpose" and paragraph 4 of the Subassignment and Occupation Agreement which provides: "The premises covered hereby shall be used solely for residential purposes. . . ." The term "single family residential use" is not otherwise defined, and if there is any ambiguity or uncertainty in the meaning of the term it must be resolved most favorably to free alienation. Actually, there is no evidence that the defendants proposed to use the property other than for single family residential purposes. It is uncontroverted that they planned to and did use the property one family at a time for residential purposes. Thus, the proposed use was not in violation of the restriction to single family residential use. . . .

Under these circumstances we are constrained to hold that Board's refusal to approve the transfers to the other defendants on the basis of the prospect of intensified use was unreasonable as a matter of law.

GARDNER, Presiding Justice, dissenting. Stripped to its essentials, this is a case in which the other owners of a condominium are attempting to stop the owner of one unit from embarking on a time sharing enterprise. The majority properly conclude that the owners as a group have the authority to regulate reasonably the use and alienation of the units. The majority then conclude that the Board's refusal to approve this transfer was unreasonable as a matter of law. To the contrary, I would find it to be entirely reasonable and would affirm the judgment of the trial court.

The use of a unit on a time sharing basis is inconsistent with the quiet enjoyment of the premises by the other occupants. Time sharing is a remarkable gimmick. P. T. Barnum would have loved it. It ordinarily brings enormous profits to the seller and in this case would bring chaos to the other residents. Here we have only four occupants but if this transfer is permitted there is nothing to stop a more greedy occupant of a unit from conveying to 52 or 365 other occupants.

If as an occupant of a condominium I must anticipate that my neighbors are going to change with clocklike regularity I might just as well move into a hotel — and get room service.

Rising construction and development costs have, in many cases, priced conventional resort condominiums out of the reach of the average potential second-home buyer. Recently, however, developers have captured the strong demand for affordable vacation homes through a mechanism called time-sharing. Time-sharing divides ownership of a condominium property temporally into a number of fixed time periods, usually weeks or months, during which each purchaser has the exclusive right of use and occupancy of the condominium property. It results in a lower purchase price and maintenance costs because the owner only buys the portion of the condominium he or she will use. Prices vary according to season, and time-shares are generally alienable. Developers sometimes offer exchange programs through which owners can trade occupancy periods with owners in other states or countries.

Legally, the time-share may be defined in several ways. The Uniform Condominium Act (1977) defines the time-share estate as either a time-span estate (U.C.A. §4-103(a)(2)) or an interval estate (U.C.A. §4-103(a)(1)). A time-span estate consists of an undivided tenancy in common in a unit, together with the exclusive right of occupancy of the unit for a designated recurring time period. An interval estate is an estate for years in a unit, during which title to the unit rotates among the owners thereof, vesting in each for a designated recurring time period, coupled with a vested individual fee simple in the remainder. The Uniform Real Estate Time-Sharing Act (1979) defines a time-share estate (§1-102(14)) and a time-share license (§1-102(18)). A time-share estate under the URETSA is the right to occupy a unit during five or more separated time periods over a period of at least five years coupled with a freehold estate or estate for years in the property. A time-share license embodies the right of occupancy defined above but is not coupled with a freehold estate or estate for years.

Since the time-sharing idea is still quite new, little relevant case law yet exists. However, the concept can be legally complex, and future litigation is likely. Potential issues include: (1) regulation of the creation of time-share interests in a condominium development by individual unit owners (see Laguna Royale Owners Association v. Darger, *supra*); (2) the legal nature of the time-share estate (see Cal-Am Corp. v. Department of Real Estate, 104 Cal. App. 3d 453, 163 Cal. Rptr. 729 (1980)) and of the declaration of covenants, conditions, and restrictions designating use periods; (3) whether the property may be sold to satisfy outstanding tax assessment against one tenant in common; (4) allocation of assessments and voting rights among time-share owners (see URETSA §2-103); (5) whether time-share interests are subject to state subdivision regulations.

UNIFORM LAW COMMISSIONERS, MODEL REAL ESTATE TIME-SHARE ACT (1980):

§1-103. [Status and Taxation of Time-Share Estates]

(a) Except as expressly modified by this Act and notwithstanding any contrary rule of common law, a grant of an estate in a unit conferring the right of possession during a potentially infinite number of separated time periods creates an estate in fee simple having the character and incidents of such an estate at common law, and a grant of an estate in a unit conferring the right of possession during [5] or more separated time periods over a finite number of years equal to [5] or more, including renewal options, creates an estate for years having the character and incidents of such an estate at common law.

(b) Each time-share estate constitutes for all purposes a separate estate in real property. Each time-share estate [other than a time-share estate for years] must [not] be separately assessed and taxed. [Notices of assessments and bills for taxes must be furnished to the managing entity, if any, or otherwise to each time-share owner, but the managing entity is not liable for the taxes as a result thereof.]

(c) A document transferring or encumbering a time-share estate may not be rejected for recordation because of the nature or duration of that estate.

§2-103. [Allocation of Time-Share Expense Liability and Voting Rights]

(a) The time-share instrument must state the amount of or formula used to determine any time-share expense liability allocated to each time share.

(b) If the time-share instrument provides for voting, it must allocate votes to each time-share unit and to each time-share estate and may allocate votes to any time-share license. It may not allocate any votes to any other property or to any person who is not a time-share owner. The number of votes allocated to each time share must be equal for all time shares or proportionate to each time share's value as estimated by the developer, time-share expense liability, or unit size. The time-share instrument may specify some matters as to which the votes must be equal and others as to which they must be proportionate.

(c) Except as otherwise provided pursuant to Section 2-102(a)(5), the votes and time-share expense liability allocated to a time share may not be altered without the unanimous consent of all time-share owners entitled to vote and voting at a meeting in which at least [80] percent, or in an initiative or referendum in which at least [80] percent, of the votes allocated to time shares are cast.

(d) Except for minor variations due to rounding, the sum of the time-share expense liabilities assigned to all time shares must equal one if stated as fractions or 100 percent if stated as percentages. In the event of discrepancy between the time-share liability or votes allocated to a time share and the result derived from the application of the formulas, the allocated time-share expense liability or vote prevails.

Note

Royal Aloha Partners v. Real Estate Division, 59 Or. App. 564, 651 P.2d 1350 (1982), held that the Oregon regulatory agency did not have statutory authority to insist on disclosure before purchasers bought "rights to use" apartments in a vacation club. Royal Aloha Vacation Club avoided regulation by conveying only the short-term rights to use, and not conveying fee ownership.

8. Example: A Modern System of Private Land Use Restrictions.

You have now seen the array of legal arrangements available to those wishing to restrict the use of land, whether developers planning a subdivision or neighbors seeking to share a driveway. What agreements of this sort should we permit? Entered into by whom? Enforceable by whom? Is this private government, and should it be bound by the constitutional rules we apply to public actions? When do such arrangements intrude unacceptably on individual privacy? How long should such agreements last? Should they become null if circumstances change? And, throughout, what role should we assign to courts in managing this privately ordered regime? These issues arise under all types of restraints: easements, covenants, servitudes, conditions, and condominiums.

As background for the doctrinal material, consider the land use rules imposed on residents of Columbia, Maryland, the "new town" whose legal creation was discussed in Part 5.

◆ DECLARATION OF COVENANTS FOR COLUMBIA, MARYLAND

Deed, Agreement and Declaration of Covenants, Easements, Charges and Liens

THIS DEED, AGREEMENT AND DECLARATION, made this _____ day of December, 1966, by and between THE COLUMBIA PARK AND RECREATION ASSOCIATION, INC., a Maryland nonprofit membership corporation (hereinafter referred to as "CPRA"), Grantor, and C. AILEEN AMES, unmarried, a resident of Howard County, Maryland (hereinafter referred to as the "Declarant"), Grantee.

WHEREAS, THE HOWARD RESEARCH AND DEVELOPMENT CORPORATION, a Maryland corporation (hereinafter referred to as "HRD"), has heretofore acquired the fee interest or leasehold interest in those certain tracts or parcels of land containing, in the aggregate, 13,690.118 acres of land, more or less, situated, lying and being in the Second, Fifth and Sixth Election Districts of Howard County, Maryland, and more particularly described in Exhibit A annexed hereto and made a part hereof;

WHEREAS, HRD intends to develop a new town (to be known as "Columbia") on the land included in the "Property", as hereinafter defined, affording well-planned residential, commercial, industrial, recreational, institutional and open space uses, buildings, facilities and areas;

PHOTOGRAPH 20-3
Columbia town center

WHEREAS, HRD desires to subject the Property (whether owned by it or by others) to the covenants, easements, charges and liens imposed hereby in order (i) to provide funds for use as specified in Article IV hereof, and (ii) to grant rights, easements and privileges relating to the use of certain facilities, subject to the conditions set forth herein;

WHEREAS, HRD has caused CPRA to be formed for the purpose of providing a non-profit civic organization to serve as the representative of the Owners and Residents with respect to: the assessment, collection and application of all charges imposed hereunder; the enforcement of all covenants contained herein and all liens created hereby; and the creation, operation, management and maintenance of the facilities and services referred to hereafter;

WHEREAS, the within instrument is the "Declaration" referred to in the Articles of Incorporation of CPRA; and

WHEREAS, in order to cause said covenants, easements, charges and liens to run with, burden and bind the Property, HRD has, by deed of even date, conveyed the Property to CPRA upon condition that CPRA execute the within instrument, and CPRA, by this instrument, hereby conveys the Property to the Declarant upon condition that Declarant covenant and declare as herein provided and forthwith reconvey the Property to HRD subject to, and burdened and bound by, all covenants, easements, charges and liens imposed hereby.

NOW, THEREFORE, THIS DEED, AGREEMENT AND DECLARATION, WITNESSETH: that for and in consideration of the premises and the sum of Five Dollars ($5.00), paid by each party to the other, the receipt and sufficiency whereof being hereby mutually acknowledged, the parties hereto do hereby grant, covenant and declare as follows:

CPRA does hereby GRANT, CONVEY, AND ASSIGN unto the Declarant, the Property, subject, however, to the covenants, easements, charges and liens hereinafter set forth.

TOGETHER with any and all rights and appurtenances thereunto belonging or in anywise appertaining.

To HAVE AND TO HOLD the above granted Property unto the Declarant, her heirs and assigns, forever, in fee simple with respect to those properties conveyed in fee simple to CPRA by the aforesaid deed from HRD, and for the terms of years unexpired with respect to the leasehold estates assigned and conveyed to CPRA by the aforesaid deed from HRD, subject, however, to the following covenants, easements, charges and liens, which it is hereby covenanted and agreed shall be binding upon (i) CPRA, its successors and assigns, (ii) the Declarant, her heirs, executors, administrators and assigns, and (iii) the Property, to the end that such covenants, easements, charges and liens shall run with, bind and burden the Property, in perpetuity with respect to the fee simple estates conveyed hereby and for the remainder of the unexpired terms of the leasehold estates assigned and conveyed hereby.

AND the parties hereto further covenant, agree and declare as follows: . . .

ARTICLE II.   ASSESSMENT OF ANNUAL CHARGE

Section 2.01. For the purpose of providing funds for use as specified in Article IV hereof, the Board shall in each year, commencing with the year 1966, assess against the Assessable Property a charge (which shall be uniform with respect to all Assessable Property) equal to a specified number of cents (not in excess of seventy-five cents) for each One Hundred Dollars ($100) of the then current "Assessed Valuation", as hereinafter defined, of the Assessable Property. In making each such assessment, the Board shall separately assess each Lot based upon its Assessed Valuation, and each such Lot shall be charged with and subject to a lien for the amount of such separate assessment which shall be deemed the "Annual Charge" with respect to such Lot. . . .

Section 2.04. If the Owner of any Lot shall fail to pay the Annual Charge within ninety (90) days following receipt of the bill referred to in Section 2.03 hereof, in addition to the right to sue the Owner for a personal judgment, CPRA shall have the right to enforce the lien hereinafter imposed to the same extent, including a foreclosure sale and deficiency decree, and (to the extent the appropriate court will accept jurisdiction) subject to the same procedures, as in the case of mortgages under applicable law, and the amount due by such Owner shall include the Annual Charge, as well as the cost of such proceedings, including a reasonable attorney's fee, and the aforesaid interest. If in any case the appropriate court refuses jurisdiction of the enforcement of said lien, then CPRA shall have the right to sell the property at public or private sale after giving notice to the Owner (by registered mail or by publication in a newspaper of general circulation in Howard County) at least 30 days prior to such sale. . . .

ARTICLE III.   IMPOSITION OF CHARGE AND LIEN UPON PROPERTY

Section 3.01. Declarant, for herself, her heirs, executors, administrators and assigns, hereby covenants and agrees (in perpetuity with respect to the fee simple estates conveyed hereby, and for the remainder of the unexpired terms of the leasehold estates assigned and conveyed hereby):

(i) that she will pay to CPRA the Annual Charge assessed by CPRA in each year against the Assessable Property; and

(ii) that the Annual Charge, both prior to and after the assessment thereof in each year, together with the continuing obligation to pay all future Annual Charges assessed in all future years, shall be and remain a first charge against, and a continuing first lien upon, (a) the Assessable Property, and (b) all Exempt Property to the extent that any change of ownership may result in any portion of the same becoming Assessable Property, to the end that said charge and lien shall be superior to any and all other charges, liens or encumbrances which may hereafter in any manner arise or be imposed upon the Assessable Property (or the Exempt Property to the extent that the same may later become Assessable Property) whether arising from or imposed by judgment or decree or by any agreement, contract, mortgage or other instrument, saving and excepting only such liens for taxes or other public charges as are by applicable law made superior. . . .

ARTICLE IV.   USE OF FUNDS

Section 4.01. CPRA shall apply all funds received by it pursuant to these Restrictions . . . to the following, *pro tanto* and in the order stated:

   (i)   the payment of all principal and interest, when due, on all loans borrowed by CPRA, to the extent required under any agreement with Note Holders referred to [herein];

  (ii)   the costs and expenses of CPRA; and

 (iii)   for the benefit of the Property, Owners and Residents by devoting the same to the acquisition, construction, reconstruction, conduct, alteration, enlargement, laying, renewal, replacement, repair, maintenance, operation and subsidizing of such of the following as the Board, in its discretion, may from time to time establish or provide:

any or all projects, services, facilities, studies, programs, systems and properties relating to: parks, recreational facilities or services; drainage systems; streets, roads, highways, walkways, curbing, gutters, sidewalks, trees, flowers and landscaping, fountains, benches, shelters, directional and informational signs, walkways, and bridges, and street, road and highway lighting facilities; facilities for the collection, treatment and disposal of garbage and refuse, mass transit systems, stations and terminals, airfields, airports, air terminals and associated facilities; facilities for the fighting and preventing of fires; public utility systems, including plants, systems, facilities or properties used or useful in connection with the manufacture, production, distribution, delivery and storage of electric power and manufacture of natural gas or any other power source, and any integral part thereof, utility lines, poles, surface and underground ducts, relay stations, cables, pipes, pipelines, valves, meters and equipment and appurtenances, and all properties, rights, easements and franchises, relating thereto; communication systems and facilities, including all buildings, systems, facilities and properties used or useful in connection with the operation of communication networks and facilities, stations, towers, relay systems and facilities, cables, underground and surface ducts, lines, poles, receiving, transmitting and relay equipment, and appurtenances and all properties, rights, easements and franchises relating thereto; auditoriums, galleries, halls, amphitheaters, theaters, arenas and stadiums, educational buildings and facilities, including equipment, supplies and accessories in connection therewith, office buildings, buildings, storage and maintenance yards, garages and other buildings and facilities deemed necessary or desirable by the Board in connection with the administration, management, control and operation of CPRA; libraries, including equipment, books, supplies and accessories in connection therewith; hospitals and clinics, including equipment, medicines, supplies and accessories in connection therewith; traffic engineering programs and parking facilities; facilities for animal rescue and shelter; lakes, dams, parks, golf courses, tennis courts, zoos, playgrounds, boat basins and marinas, equestrian centers and facilities; skeet ranges, bowling alleys, and other unrelated recreational facilities; and any and all other improvements, facilities and services that the Board shall find to be necessary, desirable or beneficial to the interest of the Property, Owners and Residents. . . .

ARTICLE V. RIGHTS OF ENJOYMENT IN COMMUNITY FACILITIES

Section 5.01. It is intended that HRD will convey to CPRA, subsequent to the recordation of this Declaration, a certain tract of land within the Property for park and recreational purposes. Said tract, together with such other parts of CPRA Land as the Board, in its absolute discretion, may by resolution from time to time hereafter designate for use by Owners and Residents are hereinafter collectively referred to as "Community Facilities". Upon designation of any part of CPRA Land as a Community Facility, as herein provided, the Board shall cause a declaration to be executed and recorded among the Land Records of Howard County, which declaration shall include a description of the land so designated and shall state that such land has been designated as a Community Facility for purposes of this Section 5.01. No CPRA Land, or any part thereof, shall be a Community Facility subject to the rights and easements of enjoyment and privileges hereinafter granted unless and until the same shall have been so designated and the above described declaration filed in accordance with the procedure provided herein.

Every Owner, by reason of such ownership, shall have a right and easement of enjoyment in and to all Community Facilities, and such easement shall be appurtenant to and shall pass with every Lot upon transfer. All Residents shall have a non-transferable privilege to use and enjoy all Community Facilities for so long as they are Residents within the previously defined meaning of that term. All such rights, easements, and privileges, however, shall be subject to the right of CPRA to adopt and promulgate reasonable rules and regulations pertaining to the use of Community Facilities which shall enhance the preservation of such facilities, the safety and convenience of the users thereof, or which, in the discretion of the Board, shall serve to promote the best interests of the Owners and Residents, including the making available of certain Community Facilities to school children, with or without charge. CPRA shall have the right to charge Owners and Residents reasonable admission and other fees in connection with the use of any Community Facility. In establishing such admission and other fees, the Board may, in its absolute discretion, establish reasonable classifications of Owners and of Residents; such admission and other fees must be uniform within each such class but need not be uniform from class to class. CPRA shall have the right to borrow money for the purpose of improving any Community Facility and in aid thereof, to mortgage the same and the rights of any such mortgagee shall be superior to the easements herein granted and assured. . . .

ARTICLE VI. DURATION, AMENDMENT, AND SUPPLEMENTS

Section 6.01. All Restrictions set forth or provided for in this Declaration shall be deemed covenants running with the land and/or charges and liens upon the land and any and every conveyance of any part of the Property shall be absolutely subject to said Restrictions whether or not it shall be so expressed in the deed, lease or other conveyance thereof. The said Restrictions shall continue with full force and effect until December 31, 2065. From and after December 31, 2065, the Restrictions as set forth herein shall continue in full force and effect in perpetuity, amended, however, so as to limit the maximum amount of the Annual Charge in each year thereafter to that amount found by the Board to be necessary to produce sufficient revenue to operate, maintain, renew, replace and repair (including such sums as may be necessary to defray the costs and expenses of CPRA in connection with such operation, maintenance, renewal, replacement and repair) such facilities authorized by Section 4.01 as may be in existence on December 31, 2065, subject, nevertheless, to the maximum number of cents per $100 of Assessed Valuation applicable to the Annual Charges as specified in Section 2.01 hereof.

Section 6.02. The size of the Property may be increased, from time to time, by the filing among the Land Records of Howard County of supplements to this Declaration signed by CPRA and the Owner of the additional property described in such supplement, provided that such additional property is expressly subjected to the Restrictions imposed hereby.

ARTICLE VII. MISCELLANEOUS

Section 7.01. No change of conditions or circumstances shall operate to extinguish, terminate, or modify any of the provisions of this Declaration. . . .

Section 7.03. CPRA shall have the right to construe and interpret the provisions of this Declaration, and in absence of an adjudication by a court of competent jurisdiction to the contrary, its construction or interpretation shall be final and binding as to all persons or property benefited or bound by the provisions hereof.

Section 7.04. CPRA shall be empowered to assign its rights hereunder to any successor non-profit membership corporation (hereinafter referred to as the "Successor Corporation") and, upon such assignment the Successor Corporation shall have all the rights and be subject to all the duties of CPRA hereunder and shall be deemed to have agreed to be bound by all provisions hereof, to the same extent as if the Successor Corporation had been an original party instead of CPRA and all references herein to the "Board" shall refer to the Board of Directors of such Successor Corporation. Any such assignment shall be accepted by the Successor Corporation under a written agreement pursuant to which the Successor Corporation expressly assumes all duties and obligations of CPRA hereunder. If for any reason CPRA shall cease to exist without having first assigned its rights hereunder to a Successor Corporation, the covenants, easements, charges and liens imposed hereunder shall nevertheless continue and any Owner may petition a court of competent jurisdiction to have a trustee appointed for the purpose of organizing a non-profit membership corporation and assigning the rights of CPRA hereunder with the same force and effect, and subject to the same conditions, as provided in this Section 7.04 with respect to an assignment and delegation by CPRA to a Successor Corporation. . . .

[The following statement of specific purposes of the association comes from CPRA's Articles of Incorporation:]

. . . For the general purpose aforesaid, and limited to that purpose (hereinafter sometimes referred to as the "Purpose"), the Corporation shall have the following specific purposes:

(1) To aid, promote, and provide for the establishment, advancement and perpetuation of any and all utilities, systems, services and facilities within Columbia which tend to promote the general welfare of its people with regard to health, safety, education, culture, recreation, comfort or convenience to the extent and in the manner deemed desirable by the Board of Directors;

(2) To exercise all the rights, powers and privileges and to perform all of the duties and obligations of the Corporation as set forth and undertaken in the Declaration and Agreement of Covenants, Conditions and Restrictions (the "Declaration") applicable to The Property, which

shall hereafter be executed by and between THE HOWARD RESEARCH AND DEVELOPMENT CORPORATION, or any other person, firm, corporation or entity having principal title to any part of The Property and this Corporation and the trustees mentioned therein, which is to be filed among the Land Records of Howard County, Maryland, and as the same may be modified or supplemented from time to time as therein provided;

(3) To operate and maintain, or provide for the operation and maintenance of, any properties which may from time to time be designated or conveyed to the Corporation for operation and maintenance as areas serving the general welfare of Columbia and the people thereof with regard to health, safety, education, culture, recreation, comfort and convenience, all pursuant to the Declaration and subject to the provisions thereof;

(4) To enforce all covenants, restrictions, reservations, servitudes, profits, licenses, conditions, agreements, easements, and liens provided in the Declaration, and to assess, collect, and disburse the charges created under such Declaration and to use the proceeds of such charges for the promotion of any and all of the purposes heretofore mentioned in any lawful manner determined by the Board of Directors, pursuant to and subject to the provisions of the Declaration; and

(5) To do any and all lawful things and acts that the Corporation may from time to time, in its discretion, deem to be for the benefit of Columbia and the inhabitants thereof or advisable, proper or convenient for the promotion of the interests of said inhabitants with regard to health, safety, education, culture, recreation, comfort or convenience. . . .

In addition to the covenants imposed by the CPRA deed, another set was imposed on each village within Columbia. The CPRA covenants are concerned with the Annual Assessment and the uses to which funds generated by it may be put; the village covenants deal with architectural control and other restrictions on the way people may use their property.

◆ WILDE LAKE VILLAGE COVENANTS

DEED, AGREEMENT AND DECLARATION

THIS DEED, AGREEMENT AND DECLARATION, made this _____ day of _____, 1967, by and between THE HOWARD RESEARCH AND DEVELOPMENT CORPORATION, a Maryland corporation (hereinafter referred to as "HRD"), Grantor, and C. AILEEN AMES, unmarried, a resident of Baltimore City, Maryland (hereinafter referred to as the "Declarant"), Grantee, and THE COLUM-

BIA PARK AND RECREATION ASSOCIATION, INC., a Maryland non-profit membership corporation (hereinafter referred to as "CPRA").

WHEREAS, HRD has heretofore acquired the fee simple interest in the land described in Exhibit A annexed hereto and made a part hereof, said land in its entirety being hereinafter referred to as the "Property";

WHEREAS, the Property, together with certain other property, was heretofore subjected to those certain covenants, easements, charges and liens set forth in that certain Deed, Agreement and Declaration of Covenants, Easements, Charges and Liens dated the 15th day of December, 1966, by and between CPRA and Declarant and recorded among the Land Records of Howard County in Liber W.H.H. 463, folio 158, et seq., all said covenants, easements, charges and liens so imposed being hereinafter referred to as the "CPRA Restrictions";

WHEREAS, HRD has subdivided the Property and desires to subject the same to those certain additional covenants, agreements, easements, restrictions, charges and liens (hereinafter referred to collectively as the "Wilde Lake Restrictions") as hereinafter set forth;

WHEREAS, CPRA is a non-profit civic organization formed for the purposes described in its Charter and in the CPRA Restrictions and for the purposes described herein;

WHEREAS, Wilde Lake Community Association, Inc., is a Maryland non-profit membership corporation (hereinafter referred to as the "Association") formed for the purposes described in its Charter and herein;

WHEREAS, CPRA has approved the Association for the purposes stated in Article Seventh of the CPRA Charter; and

WHEREAS, in order to cause the Wilde Lake Restrictions to run with, burden and bind the Property, HRD does, by this deed, convey the Property to the Declarant upon condition that Declarant covenant and declare as herein provided and forthwith reconvey the Property to HRD subject to, and burdened and bound by, the Wilde Lake Restrictions.

NOW, THEREFORE, THIS DEED, AGREEMENT AND DECLARATION, WITNESSETH: that for and in consideration of the premises and the sum of Five Dollars ($5.00), paid by each party to the other, the receipt and sufficiency whereof being hereby mutually acknowledged, the parties hereto do hereby grant, covenant and declare as follows:

HRD does hereby GRANT, CONVEY AND ASSIGN unto the Declarant, the Property, subject, however, to the Wilde Lake Restrictions imposed hereby.

TOGETHER with any and all improvements thereon and all rights and appurtenances thereunto belonging or in anywise appertaining.

To HAVE AND To HOLD the above granted property unto the Declarant, her heirs, executors, administrators and assigns, forever, in fee simple, subject, however, to the Wilde Lake Restrictions which it is hereby covenanted and agreed shall be binding upon (i) the Declarant, her heirs, executors, administrators and assigns, and (ii) the Property, to the end that the Wilde Lake Restrictions shall run with, bind and burden the Property, for and during the period of time specified hereafter.

AND the parties hereto further covenant and declare as follows: . . .

ARTICLE VI.   COVENANTS FOR MAINTENANCE

Section 6.01. Each Owner shall keep all Lots owned by him, and all improvements therein or thereon, in good order and repair, including but not limited to, the seeding, watering and mowing of all lawns, the pruning and cutting of all trees and shrubbery and the painting (or other appropriate external care) of all buildings and other improvements, all in a manner and with such frequency as is consistent with good property management. If, in the opinion of the "Architectural Committee", as hereinafter defined, any Owner fails to perform the duties imposed by the preceding sentence, HRD, CPRA or the Association, after approval by a two-thirds (⅔) decision of the Association Board, and after fifteen (15) days' written notice to Owner to remedy the condition in question, shall have the right, through its agents and employees, to enter upon the Lot in question and to repair, maintain, repaint and restore the Lot or such improvement and the cost thereof shall be a binding, personal obligation of such Owner as well as a lien (enforceable in the same manner as a mortgage) upon the Lot in question.

Section 6.02. The lien provided in Section 6.01 hereof shall not be valid as against a bona fide purchaser (or bona fide mortgagee) of the Lot in question unless a suit to enforce said lien shall have been filed in a court of record in Howard County prior to the recordation among the Land Records of Howard County of the deed (or mortgage) conveying the Lot in question to such purchaser (or subjecting the same to such mortgage).

ARTICLE VII.   ARCHITECTURAL COMMITTEE;
ARCHITECTURAL CONTROL

Section 7.01. The "Architectural Committee" shall be composed of those three or more individuals so designated from time to time (i) by HRD during the Development Period and (ii) by CPRA and the Association after the Development Period, CPRA being entitled at all times after the Development Period to appoint a majority thereof. Except as hereinafter provided, the affirmative vote of a majority of the membership of the Architectural Committee shall be required in order to adopt or promulgate any rule or regulation, or to make any findings, determinations, ruling or order, or to issue any permit, authorization or approval pursuant to directives or authorizations contained herein. With regard to review of plans and specifications as set forth in this Article VII, however, and with regard to all other specific matters (other than the promulgation of rules and regulations) as may be specified by resolution of the entire Architectural Committee, each individual member of the Architectural Committee shall be authorized to exercise the full authority granted herein to the Architectural Committee. Any approval by one such member of any plans and specifications submitted under this Article VII, or the granting of any approval, permit or authorization by one such member in accordance with the terms hereof, shall be final and binding. Any disapproval, or approval based upon modification or specified conditions by one such member shall also be final and binding, provided, however, that in any such case, any applicant for such approval, permit or authorization may, within ten (10) days after receipt of notice of any such adverse decision, file a written request to have the matter in question reviewed by the entire Architectural Committee. Upon the filing of any such request, the matter with respect to which such request was filed shall be submitted to and reviewed as soon as possible by the entire Architectural Committee. Thereafter, the decision of a majority of the members of the Architectural Committee with respect to such matter shall be final and binding.

Section 7.02. No structure shall be commenced, erected, placed, moved on to or permitted to remain on any Lot, nor shall any existing Structure upon any Lot be altered in any way which materially changes the exterior appearance thereof, nor shall any new use be commenced on any Lot, unless plans and specifications (including a description of any proposed new use) therefor shall have been submitted to and approved in writing by the Architectural Committee. Such plans and specifications shall be in such form and shall contain such information, as may be required by the Architectural Committee, but in any event shall include (i) a site plan of the Lot showing the nature, exterior color scheme, kind, shape, height, materials and location with respect to the particular Lot (including proposed front, rear and side set-backs and free spaces, if any are proposed) of all Structures, the location thereof with reference to Structures on adjoining portions of the Property, and the number and location of all parking spaces and driveways on the Lot; and (ii) a grading plan for the particular Lot.

Section 7.03. The Architectural Committee shall have the right to disapprove any plans and specifications submitted hereunder because of any of the following:

(a) failure to comply with any of the Wilde Lake Restrictions;
(b) failure to include information in such plans and specifications as may have been reasonably requested;
(c) objection to the exterior design, appearance or materials of any proposed Structure;
(d) incompatibility of any proposed Structure or use with existing Structures or uses upon other Lots in the vicinity;

(e) objection to the location of any Structure upon any Lot or with reference to other Lots in the vicinity;

(f) objection to the grading plan for any Lot;

(g) objection to the color scheme, finish, proportions, style of architecture, height, bulk or appropriateness of any proposed Structure;

(h) objection to parking areas proposed for any Lot on the grounds of (i) incompatibility to proposed uses and Structures on such Lot or (ii) the insufficiency of the size of parking areas in relation to the proposed use of the Lot; or

(i) any other matter which, in the judgment of the Architectural Committee, would render the proposed Structure, Structures or uses inharmonious with the general plan of improvement of the Property or with Structures or uses located upon other Lots in the vicinity.

In any case where the Architectural Committee shall disapprove any plans and specifications submitted hereunder, or shall approve the same only as modified or upon specified conditions, such disapproval or qualified approval shall be accompanied by a statement of the grounds upon which such action was based. In any such case the Architectural Committee shall, if requested, make reasonable efforts to assist and advise the applicant in order that an acceptable proposal can be prepared and submitted for approval. . . .

ARTICLE VIII. GENERAL COVENANTS AND RESTRICTIONS

Section 8.01. Without the prior written approval of the Architectural Committee:

(a) No previously approved Structure shall be used for any purpose other than that for which it was originally designed;

(b) No Lot shall be split, divided, or subdivided for sale, resale, gift, transfer or otherwise;

(c) No facilities, including poles and wires, for the transmission of electricity, telephone messages and the like shall be placed or maintained above the surface of the ground on any Lot, and no external or outside antennas of any kind shall be maintained; and

(d) No boat, boat trailer, house trailer, trailer or any similar items shall be stored in the open on any Lot.

Section 8.02. No tree having a diameter of six (6) inches or more (measured from a point two feet above ground level) shall be removed from any Lot without the express written authorization of CPRA. CPRA, in its discretion, may adopt and promulgate rules and regulations regarding the preservation of trees and other natural resources and wildlife upon the Property. If it shall deem it appropriate, CPRA may mark certain trees, regardless of size, as not removable without written authorization. In carrying out the provisions of this Section 8.02, CPRA and the Architectural Committee and the respective agents of each may come upon any Lot during reasonable hours for the purpose of inspecting or marking trees or in relation to the enforcement and administration of any rules and regulations adopted and promulgated pursuant to the provisions hereof. Neither CPRA nor the Architectural Committee, nor their respective agents shall be deemed to have committed a trespass or wrongful act by reason of any such entry or inspection.

Section 8.03. No birds, animals or insects shall be kept or maintained on any Lot except for domestic purposes. Under no circumstances shall any commercial or business enterprise involving the use of animals be conducted on the Property without the express written consent of the Architectural Committee. The Architectural Committee may, from time to time, publish and impose reasonable regulations setting forth the type and number of animals that may be kept on any Lot.

Section 8.04. No sign or other advertising device of any nature shall be placed upon any Lot except as provided herein. The Architectural Committee may, in its discretion, adopt and promulgate rules and regulations relating to signs which may be employed. Signs and other advertising devices may be erected and maintained upon any portion of the Property zoned for industrial or commercial uses if approved by the Architectural Committee, as to color, location, nature, size and other characteristics of such signs or devices.

Section 8.05. No temporary building, trailer, garage or building in the course of construction or other Structure shall be used, temporarily, or permanently, as a residence on any Lot.

Section 8.06. No lumber, metals, bulk materials, refuse or trash shall be kept, stored, or allowed to accumulate on any Lot, except building materials during the course of construction of any approved Structure. If trash or other refuse is to be disposed of by being picked up and carried away on a regular and recurring basis, containers may be placed in the open, on any day that a pick-up is to be made, at such place on the Lot so as to provide access to persons making such pick-up. At all other times such containers shall be stored in such a manner so that they cannot be seen from adjacent and surrounding property. The Architectural Committee, in its discretion, may adopt and promulgate reasonable rules and regulations relating to the size, shape, color and type of containers permitted and the manner of storage of the same on the Property.

Section 8.07. No water pipe, gas pipe, sewer pipe or drainage pipe shall be installed or maintained on any Lot above the surface of the ground, except hoses and movable pipes used for irrigation purposes. No Lot shall be used for the purpose of boring, mining, quarrying, exploring for or removing oil or other hydrocarbons, minerals, gravel or earth.

Section 8.08. HRD, CPRA and the Association shall have the right to enter upon any Lot and trim or prune, at the expense of the Owner, any hedge or other planting which in the opinion of HRD, CPRA or the Association, by reason of its location upon the Lot or the height to which it is permitted to grow, is unreasonably detrimental to the adjoining property or obscures the view of street traffic or is unattractive in appearance; provided, however, that the Owner shall be given fifteen (15) days prior written notice of such action. . . .

ARTICLE XI. RESIDENTIAL PROTECTIVE COVENANTS AND RESTRICTIONS

Section 11.01. The provisions of this Article XI shall relate solely to Lots zoned for residential purposes.

Section 11.02. No profession or home industry shall be conducted in or on any part of a Lot or in any improvement thereon on the Property without the specific written approval of the Architectural Committee. The Architectural Committee, in its discretion, upon consideration of the circumstances in each case, and particularly the effect on surrounding property, may permit a Lot or any improvement thereon to be used in whole or in part for the conduct of a profession or home industry. No such profession or home industry shall be permitted, however, unless it is considered, by the Architectural Committee, to be compatible with a high quality residential neighborhood. The following activities, without limitation, may be permitted by the Architectural Committee in its discretion: music, art and dancing classes; day nurseries and schools; medical and dental offices; fraternal or social club meeting place; seamstress services.

Section 11.03. All else herein notwithstanding, with the written approval of the Architectural Committee, any Lot may be used for a model home or for a real estate office during the Development Period.

Section 11.04. No clothing or any other household fabrics shall be hung in the open on any Lot unless the same are hung from an umbrella or retractable clothes hanging device which is removed from view when not in use or unless the same are enclosed by a fence or other enclosure at least six inches higher than such hanging articles, provided such fence or other enclosure is approved by the Architectural Committee. No machinery shall be placed or operate upon any Lot except such machinery as is usual in maintenance of a private residence.

Section 11.05. Notwithstanding other provisions herein, the Architectural Committee may authorize any Owner with respect to his Lot to:

(a) temporarily use a single family dwelling house for more than one family;
(b) maintain a sign other than as expressly permitted herein;
(c) locate structures other than the principal dwelling house within set-back areas; or
(d) use Structures other than the principal dwelling house for residence purposes on a temporary basis.

Notes

1. Judicial enforcement of restrictive covenants is based on a balancing of the competing interests of the property owner in the free use of his property and of the community in a degree of certainty regarding future uses of surrounding land. Consider the tremendous discretion given to the Architectural Committee by the covenants (for example, §7.03 (e)-(g)). How does this weigh in assuring that future land uses will be predictable? Is a covenant that spells out its restrictions more desirable? Or is a flexible approach preferable because it can take into account future changes in circumstances?

Note that the developer controls the Architectural Committee for the first seven years, during the Development Period (§7.01). What standards should a court impose in reviewing decisions of the committee? For whose benefit was it established? Should members of the committee (either during or after the time developer maintains control) be held personally liable for economic injury that results from their decisions?

Should the committee's decisions be based on "objective" or "subjective" criteria? For example, should review of a proposed structure be based on design principles, or on the reaction of neighboring property owners? What does "incompatibility of any proposed Structure or use with existing Structures or uses" mean (§7.03(d))? On what basis may one object to a "style of architecture" (§7.03(g))? Should the committee insist that a given neighborhood be all "colonial," or all "split level"?

In creating such a detailed scheme, and maintaining control of it during most of the initial building, it seems clear that the developer has some "grand scheme" in mind, some picture of how Columbia should look. If he were to build the entire city himself, keep title to the fee, and give only leases to residents, we would have no trouble in saying that he should be able to do what he wants (within zoning limitations, of course). Tenants will know what they have gotten themselves into, and will be able to get out (with relative ease) when they want. Is the same thing true when the developer sells the fee? Certainly, the purchaser still knows what he is getting into, but how easy is it for him to get out? Aren't his rights to use the property free from restrictions related to the risk he has taken by purchasing it? And since the Architectural Committee will ultimately be controlled by his neighbors, who will change with the years, can't it be said that he really cannot know what the future restrictions on his property will be, and on what basis they will be imposed?

2. In Van Dusen v. Bussman, 343 Mo. 1096, 125 S.W.2d 1 (1939), the agreement provided that "all or any of the foregoing . . . restrictions may be modified, amended, released or extinguished" by owners of 75 percent of the frontage involved. An attempt to exclude apartment houses, originally allowed in the subdivision, was held not within this language. See Bessette v. Guarino, 85 R.I. 188, 128 A.2d 839 (1957) (restrictions to remain in effect for eleven and one-half years, then subject to change but only with consent of two-thirds of lot owners). Fox Point, Wisconsin, Restrictions (1956) provided in article 7 that an architectural control committee "shall be organized in such a manner as may be directed by the Senior Judge of the Circuit Court of Milwaukee County, upon a petition or application therefor made to him by an interested party."

3. In reading the materials that follow, keep in mind the issues posed by the following statement: Deed restrictions "are an individualistic approach to the problem of preserving a desired condition for a limited time in a limited area. They lack the compulsion of a public law enforced by public officials who may impose a rigid pattern of integrated supervision upon everyone concerned." Reeve, Recent Developments in the Law of Property, in The Metropolis in Modern Life 188 (Fisher ed. 1955).

4. A large firm is interested in locating a major manufacturing plant in Columbia. In addition to the sale price of the land, Rouse stands to benefit in at least two other ways: the plant will "establish" Columbia as a prime industrial location; the large work force the plant will require will generate increased demand for housing and will have a ripple effect on commercial demand. There is one hitch, though. The permanent improvements that the firm will build will be very expensive; they will have a much higher value land coverage ratio than any other property in Columbia. This fact will be reflected in a very high assessment by CPRA — since the assessment is uniform and is on top of other property taxes, the resulting expense would put the plant at a competitive disadvantage. Thus, the firm is not willing to come to Columbia unless the assessment covenant can be removed from the property it intends to purchase.

Two issues face Rouse in attempting to remove the covenants: first, is there any way they can be lifted? Second, if so, what form of legal action should be used and who are the necessary parties? Consider the difficulty of joining the owners of all property that benefits from the covenants. It is clear from the Declaration of Covenants that CPRA has the right to enforce the covenants. Is it possible to argue that this right is exclusive to CPRA? Would your answer be different if we were dealing with negative rather than affirmative covenants? Who is *directly* benefitted by enforcement of the covenants? How do property owners derive their benefit from enforcement? Does this affect the "touch and concern" requirement for covenants that run with the land? If CPRA's right of enforcement is exclusive, does this mean that CPRA's board has absolute discretion? If not, how can property owners insure that the covenants are fairly enforced for the purposes recited in the Articles and Declaration? Is their ability to do this a prerequisite to any enforcement of the covenants at all?

Rouse is considering adding a new tract to the restricted property at the same time the industrial site is removed. This new tract would have a greater assessed valuation than the old. Would such a plan serve the *policy* behind enforcement of covenants in favor of benefitted property? If so, would such an addition be necessary before property could be removed from the covenants? Or would even this be insufficient — does the interest of the benefitted property run to the specific property burdened rather than some seemingly similar property? (Note that the developed value of the new tract will likely be less than the developed value of the proposed industrial tract. Does it matter that the latter tract probably won't be developed at all unless the restrictions are lifted, or do the owners of the benefitted property have an absolute right to take that gamble?)

B. THE JUDICIAL ROLE IN ADMINISTERING A SYSTEM OF PRIVATE RESTRICTIONS

1. *Flexibility in Classification*

◆ WALDROP v. TOWN OF BREVARD
233 N.C. 26, 62 S.E.2d 512 (1950)

This is an action in which the plaintiffs seek to have abated as a private and public nuisance the presently maintained garbage dump of the Town of Brevard, and to recover special damages resulting from its operation since October 1, 1946.

In 1938 the Town of Brevard purchased from I. F. Shipman and wife a tract of land, consisting of five acres, for a garbage dump. The land purchased was near the middle of a 120-acre tract owned by the grantors. At the time the appellees purchased this land, only the grantors and one other family lived on the Shipman lands.

The duly recorded deed from Shipman and wife to the Town of Brevard, in addition to conveying the five-acre tract of land, contains the following provisions:

> Together with a right of way across the lands of the parties of the first part 16 feet in width, extending from the road from Rocky Hill to Camp Illahee along the present road leading from said road to the property herein described. With the right to construct, reconstruct, repair or maintain said road in any manner which the party of the second part may see fit.
>
> It is understood and agreed that the party of the second part is purchasing the property hereinabove described for use as a dumping ground for garbage, waste, trash, refuse, and other materials and products which the party of the second part desires to dispose of. And as a part of this conveyance the parties of the first part do hereby grant and convey unto the said party of the second part, its successors and assigns, the right, without limit as to time and quantity, to use the lands hereinabove described as a dumping ground for the Town of Brevard for garbage, waste, trash, refuse and other materials and products of any and every kind which the said party of the second part desires to dispose of by dumping on said lands and burning or leaving thereon, and the said parties of the first part do hereby release, discharge, waive and convey unto the said party of the second part, its successors or assigns, any or all rights of action, either legal or equitable which they have or ever might or may have by reason of any action of the party of the second part in using the lands hereinabove described as a dumping ground for the Town of Brevard, or by reason of any fumes, odors, vapors, smoke or other discharges into the atmosphere by reason of such location and use of a dumping ground on the lands hereinabove described.
>
> The agreements and waiver hereinabove set out shall be covenants running with the remainder of the lands owned by the parties of the first part, and binding on said parties as the owners of said lands, and their heirs and assigns, and anyone claiming under them, or any of them, as owners or occupants thereof.

After the Town of Brevard began using the land referred to herein as a garbage dump, I. F. Shipman and wife began selling other portions of the original 120-acre tract. Now some 35 or 40 families live in the neighborhood.

In 1939 Van R. Tinsley and wife purchased a lot from I. F. Shipman and wife, the lot being a portion of the original 120-acre tract and situate approximately 300 yards or more from the land used by the defendant as a garbage dump. The Tinsleys constructed a house on the lot and conveyed the property to the plaintiffs in 1940. They have owned and resided on the premises since that time.

The plaintiffs offered evidence which they contend supports the allegations of their complaint, to the effect that the garbage dump as maintained by the defendant is a public and private nuisance, and that they have suffered special damages as a result thereof. . . .

DENNY, Justice. If it be conceded that the normal operation of the defendant's garbage dump in a reasonably careful and prudent manner constitutes a nuisance, in our opinion these plaintiffs are estopped from asserting any claim for damages or for other relief by reason thereof, in view of the grant and covenants contained in the conveyance from I. F. Shipman and wife to the Town of Brevard.

It was stated in the conveyance to the Town of Brevard, that the property was to be used as a garbage dump, and I. F. Shipman and wife expressly granted to it the right, without limit as to time and quantity, to use the premises conveyed as a dumping ground for the Town of Brevard, for garbage, waste, etc., and for themselves, their heirs and assigns, they released, discharged and waived any or all rights of action, either legal or equitable which they have or might have by reason of any action of the Town of Brevard in using the lands conveyed to it as a dumping ground for said town, or by reason of any fumes, odors, vapors, smoke or other discharges into the atmosphere by reason of the use of the premises as a garbage dumping ground. The parties further stipulated that the agreements and waiver set forth in the deed shall be covenants running with the remainder of the lands owned by the grantors and binding on them "as the owners of said lands, and their heirs and assigns, and anyone claiming under them, as owners or occupants thereof."

"A covenant or agreement may operate as a grant of an easement if it is necessary to give it that effect in order to carry out the manifest intention of the parties." 17 Am. Jur., Sec. 27, p. 940.

The grant and release or waiver contained in the deed from I. F. Shipman and wife to the Town of Brevard, in our opinion, created a right in the nature of an easement in favor of the Town of Brevard, upon the remainder of the lands owned by the grantors. And the waiver or release of any right to make a future claim for damages or other relief, resulting from the use of the premises conveyed to the defendant as a garbage dump, constitutes a covenant not to sue and is binding on the grantors, their heirs and assigns.

"If the owner of property has charged it with a servitude as to the matter complained of, a subsequent grantee cannot recover damages therefor."

The appellants contend they are not bound by the covenants in the deed from I. F. Shipman and wife to the Town of Brevard, because (1) the Town of Brevard is not plaintiffs' predecessor in title; (2) no deed in plaintiffs' chain of title contains or refers to the covenants contained in the defendant's deed; and (3) there has been such a change in the neighborhood it would be unconscionable and inequitable, and against public policy to enforce the covenants in the defendant's deed.

The plaintiffs are relying on the case of Turner v. Glenn, 220 N.C. 620, 18 S.E.2d 197, as authority for their position that since no deed in their chain of title contains or refers to the covenants set forth in the Shipman deed to the defendant, they are not bound thereby. This position might be well taken if we were dealing with restrictive covenants instead of an easement and a waiver and release of any and all claims for damages incident to the exercise of the easement granted. Grantees take title to lands subject to duly recorded easements which have been granted by their predecessors in title. . . .

The plaintiffs' contention that conditions have changed to such an extent, in the neighborhood adjacent to the defendant's garbage dump, that the covenants in the defendant's deed should not be enforced, is without merit. Changed conditions may, under certain circumstances, justify the non-enforcement of restrictive covenants, but a change, such as that suggested by the plaintiffs here, will not in any manner affect a duly recorded easement previously granted.

We do not construe the plaintiffs' complaint to allege that the nuisance complained of was the result of negligent conduct on the part of the defendant, its agents or employees. Therefore, in view of the interpretation we have given to the provisions contained in the defendant's conveyance from I. F. Shipman and wife, plaintiffs' predecessors in title, the judgment as of nonsuit entered below should be upheld.

Affirmed.

C. CLARK, REAL COVENANTS AND OTHER INTERESTS WHICH "RUN WITH LAND" 5, 96-100 (2d ed. 1947): In addition to the confusion in terms and that resulting from diverse views of history, the narrow lines of demarcation between the interests have occasioned difficulty. Why should not a covenant pass as does an easement, and why should not an equitable servitude be transferable as either easement or covenant? The reasons lie in history. The various interests developed differently. Thus an easement or a profit might arise either by grant or prescription and pass with "the land" itself even as against disseisors. On the other hand, a covenant was created only by a formal agreement and could pass only upon a transfer of an estate in land. The equitable restriction or servitude was a later development of equity. It was created by agreement or by estoppel and passed to all takers with notice.

Confusion results from the fact that essentially the same interest may be treated under some circumstances as any one of these things. Thus a formal agreement not to build a store upon Blackacre might be in effect an easement, or a covenant, or an equitable servitude. If, however, it is claimed by prescription it must be treated as an easement; if it is couched in terms of formal promise it cannot, under some authorities, be an easement; and if it is contained in a general neighborhood plan for residential development, it can only be made fully effective as an equitable restriction. It is clear, therefore, that the various interests overlap each other, and that the distinctions between them often break down.

◆ WOLF v. HALLENBECK
  109 Colo. 70, 123 P.2d 412 (1942)

Mr. Justice BAKKE delivered the opinion of the court.

. . . Hallenbeck brought this action against . . . Wolf and others to "remove cloud from title" to certain lots in the city of Denver. He had judgment for title, possession and costs. Wolf, alone, seeks reversal of the holding on a writ of error.

It appears from the record that November 7, 1935, Hallenbeck conveyed the property in question to one Lewis by warranty deed in which it was recited, *inter alia*:

> As a part of the consideration for this conveyance, the grantee covenants that on or before Dec. 1, 1937, he will cause to be erected on the property a house with a minimum cost of $7,500.00, and in the event the grantee fails to cause such a house to be constructed, the title to said property shall revert to C. V. Hallenbeck and the amount paid therefor of $525.00 shall be forfeited to C. V. Hallenbeck as liquidated damages.

This deed was recorded February 26, 1937.

November 10, 1936, Lewis conveyed the property to Wolf. . . .

Wolf . . . admits that no building was erected upon the property at any time, but asserts that the action is barred by section 154, chapter 40, '35 C.S.A.

Said section 154 is as follows:

> No action shall be commenced or maintained to recover possession of real property or to enforce the terms of any restriction concerning real property, or to compel the removal of any building or improvement on land because of the violation of any of the terms of any restriction, unless said action be commenced within one year from the date of violation for which the action is sought to be brought or maintained.

It is admitted that this action was not instituted until twenty-one months after December 1, 1937.

Hallenbeck contends that the provision in the deed requiring the construction of a $7,500.00 house on the premises before December 1, 1937, is a condition subsequent, and therefore not covered by said section 154, which, under a proper interpretation, he says is limited to building restrictions, as such, technically construed as in section 372(f), p.359, 18 C.J., and in section 141(f), p.474, 26 C.J.S. We seriously doubt that the word "restriction," as used in said section 154, should be given such a limited meaning. We have held that the provisions of the act, of which section 154 is a part, should be harmoniously construed. Section 153, immediately preceding, refers to "building restrictions *and all restrictions as to the use* or occupancy *of real property*" and "restrictions which provide for the forfeiture or defeasance of title," and section 154, as already noted, includes the words "the terms of any restriction." (Italics are ours.) It must be conceded, we think, that this language is sufficiently broad to include this "condition subsequent," as Hallenbeck interprets the restrictive clause in the deed. In fact, one of the instruments upon which he relies refers to it as a "restriction." A covenant of this kind is included in article 8, page 48 under the heading, "Restrictions as to the Use of Land," Thompson on Real Property (Permanent ed.), vol. 7, p.70, §3583 (3378). . . .

As already indicated, we believe, and so hold, that the special covenant used here is a "restriction concerning real property" within the meaning of said section 154. We also are of the opinion that although this action is entitled "To Remove Cloud from Title," it, nevertheless, is an action to enforce the terms of a restriction. It is to be remembered that Wolf is the record title owner; by which we mean that any person desiring to ascertain the status of the fee title would find upon examination of the public records that such fee was in him. Assuming that the language used in the deed from Hallenbeck to Lewis is a "condition subsequent," the breach of the condition does not cause the title to automatically revert to Hallenbeck. He must take some action to make the reversion effective. "On the occurrence of the event which constitutes a breach of a condition subsequent annexed to an estate in fee simple defeasible, the estate does not terminate . . . unless and until the power of termination is exercised." Restatement of the Law — Property — Introduction — Freehold Estates, p.196, §57.

We do not suggest how this power of termination should be exercised, but where, as here, the grantor seeks to do so by judicial proceedings, it would seem he is bound by the time limitation fixed by statute which by its terms is to be liberally construed to the end that the record title may be relied upon. This being true, we believe the conclusion inescapable that this is an action to enforce the "defeasance of title" in Wolf. Section 306, Berry, Restrictions on use of Real Property, begins as follows: "Equity will enforce covenants . . . in regard to the use of the property," which would indicate that the word "enforce," as used in said section 154, applies to the present action.

We therefore conclude that this action is barred by said section 154, and accordingly the judgment is reversed and the cause remanded with instructions to dismiss the complaint.

2. Consumer Non-protection

◆ HOLLIDAY v. SPHAR
262 Ky. 45, 89 S.W.2d 327 (1935)

RICHARDSON, Justice. A. H. Hampton, on October 22, 1919, conveyed to W. F. Randolph 45 acres of land on the west side of Boone avenue fronting South Belmont street, in Winchester, Clark county, Ky. It was a part of Hampton's farm. Its four boundary lines are of unequal length and angles. About one-third of it was within the city limits. It was conveyed "as an addition to the city" and later called Hampton's Court. The recited consideration for the tract was $45,000 cash, "and the further consideration of the agreements and covenants" set out in the deed, to "run with the land." The covenants of the deed required streets of certain widths to be laid off and dedicated for street purposes, and that: "No dwelling house shall be built in any part of said addition, when laid off into streets, lots and alleys, closer than 25 feet to the pavement line, and no residence shall be built on Boone avenue or Belmont street, which is now known as the Colbyville Pike, costing less than thirty-five hundred ($3,500.00) dollars, and no part of the property herein sold shall ever be sold or leased to any person of African descent." "No dwelling house shall be built on the new street next to the orchard at any point closer than four hundred (400) feet to Boone avenue which costs less than thirty-five hundred ($3,500.00) dollars."

Hampton owned a gas line on and under the land. He reserved it, with certain rights respecting it.

On October 29, 1919, Randolph subdivided the 45 acres into lots, each with 25 feet front. On a plat of the subdivision he wrote, signed, and acknowledged, and caused to be recorded in the county clerk's office of Clark county, the office in which Hampton's deed to him was recorded, this statement: "No dwelling house shall be built in any part of said addition, when laid off into streets, lots and alleys closer than twenty-five (25) feet to the pavement line." On the plat a red line is drawn 25 feet from the front of each lot, indicating the 25 feet referred to in the statement indorsed on the plat.

The corporate limits of the city of Winchester at that time was in the form of a circle, 1 mile in diameter. Its area, therefore, was 502.6560 acres. The city's population was 8,333. Soon after Randolph acquired the title, he advertised and sold the lots at public auction. The advertisement of the sale contained these statements:

> All the lots in this beautiful new subdivision absolutely without reserve — your opportunity has arrived when you can buy that home site right where you want it, where the people of Winchester have been trying to buy for years. No one has built a home in Winchester in recent years

without first trying to buy a site from Mr. Hampton. Drive out and look this place over and if you ever expect to build that permanent home in Winchester you will certainly buy a lot in Hampton Court on Wednesday, October 29th.

For a long time your city has been growing more than any other city in the section — a steady growth — now we find nearly all desirable places for building high class residence property has been used up. People are trying to come to Winchester. It is impossible for them to locate when they can find no homes. On Wednesday, October 29th, an opportunity will be given to the people to buy the very choicest building lots that have been offered in Winchester, when Hampton Court lots will be sold at public auction.

W. M. Holliday, on the 9th day of May, 1935, acquired title to lots Nos. 1, 2, 3, 4, and 5 in block A of this subdivision. His deed carried the restrictions contained in the deed of Hampton to Randolph. His lots lie at the southwest corner of the intersection of Boone avenue and Belmont street, as located on the plat. On Holliday declaring his intention to construct a service station on his lots for the conduct of business thereat, W. R. Sphar, who owned lots Nos. 6 and 7 in block A, adjoining Holliday's, filed this action for injunction relief to prevent his erecting the station and engaging thereat in business. The circuit court granted the relief sought. Holliday appeals.

A number of witnesses testified as to their knowledge and understanding of the intention of Hampton and Randolph to restrict the use of the lots for residences only, and as to their knowledge of the effect and influence on the use and vendible value of the lots, if and when the service station were erected and business conducted thereat. Others deposed that such station would not be injurious to either. Sphar insists that Hampton's deed to Randolph restricts the use of all of the lots into which the 45 acres were divided to residences only. Holliday contends contrariwise. The duty devolves upon us to determine the issue thus presented.

In such case the rule is that restrictions on the use of property should be given that effect which the expressed language of the instrument containing the same authorizes, when considered in connection with the circumstances surrounding the transaction and the object which the parties had in view at the time they executed it. . . .

The vendor's oral representation, or his advertisement of the sale of lots, that the land is to be wholly devoted to one purpose is not operative as an estoppel to use a portion of it for a nonrestrictive purpose. Such is merely to be considered as a circumstance in ascertaining from the language used in the deed the intention of the parties to the deed containing the restrictions. A dotted or other line on a plat showing the distance buildings are to be erected from the street is also a mere circumstance to be considered for like purpose. . . . Under the general rule governing the interpretation of written instruments, it is permissible for the expositor to place himself as nearly as possible in the position of the maker of such instrument, and to this extent parol evidence is admissible to show the facts and circumstances surrounding the maker at the time the instrument was executed. . . .

Restrictive covenants cannot be established by such evidence or otherwise save a recordable instrument employing adequate words so unequivocally evincing the party's or parties' intention to limit the free use of the land that its ascertainment is not dependent on inference, implication, or doubtful construction.

Analyzing, testing, and measuring the words of Hampton's deed to Randolph by these principles, it is very plain that they entirely fail to restrict the use of the lots of Holliday only to residential purposes. They deal with, and relate to, only, the minimum cost of the residences which owners may choose to erect, and fix the distance from the street the same may be built. Indeed, the language employed does not expressly or impliedly require, nor forbid, the use of the land for any purpose. The essence of the restrictions is, if the owner erects a residence thereon, the same shall cost not less than the sum designated in the deed, and not nearer the street fronting the same than the distance fixed in it. At most, such are no more than limited "building restrictions," and not a limitation on the free use of the land. . . .

[Sphar] argues that "the restriction not to erect a dwelling closer than 25 feet of the street was intended to protect residents and dwellings." Continuing, he asserts:

> No one would want to build a handsome residence anywhere in this addition if it were not restricted, and his neighbor would open a junk yard next to him or place on the adjoining lot any kind of cheap business house that would be a blemish on the landscape. It was the clear intent of the parties to guard against such conditions even as to residences, for they had to be set back twenty-five feet from the pavement line and to cost a sum sufficient to guarantee a substantial class of homes. . . . When it is remembered that these covenants were made by the grantor to run with the land and to be a part of the consideration for the deed, no construction should be arrived at that renders these restrictions futile and abortive.

To accept this argument and accordingly construe the restrictions would be the equivalent to enlarging or extending the same by construction which we are forbidden to do, however much we might wish the parties could accomplish what it might have been thought they were acquiring by the deed of Hampton to Randolph and what those who have since purchased lots in the subdivision expected and desired at the time they acquired their title.

It seems to be conceded that Holliday in locating the station desired to be constructed by him has recognized and intends to comply with the requirement of the restriction as to the 25 feet limit from the street. Therefore, we express no opinion as to the enforceability of this restriction as to buildings erected for any purpose other than residential.

3. Common Plan

◆ BUFFALO ACADEMY OF THE SACRED HEART v.
BOEHM BROTHERS, INC.
267 N.Y. 242, 196 N.E. 42 (1935)

FINCH, J. This controversy, submitted pursuant to the provisions of the Civil Practice Act, §§546-548, presents for determination the question whether title to certain real estate is marketable. The plaintiff agreed to discharge an indebtedness to the defendant by conveying to it good and marketable title to certain realty, the contract further providing that if title should prove unmarketable the plaintiff would pay the defendant $60,000 in cash. The plaintiff has tendered defendant a deed to the property in question and the defendant has refused to accept, on the ground that title is unmarketable.

It bases its refusal on the following grounds:

1. That the subdivision "University Terrace," in which the lots are situated, is subject to a uniform building plan which restricts the use of each and every lot in said subdivision to the erection of buildings for residential purposes only.

2. That a deed conveying four lots in said subdivision to the Kendall Refining Company prohibited the erection and operation of gasoline filling stations and the sale of motor oil and fuel on any lots in the subdivision other than the four so conveyed to the Kendall Refining Company.

The Appellate Division decided against the defendant on the first point, finding that there was no uniform building plan, but granted judgment for the defendant on the ground that the property was subject to a restrictive covenant prohibiting the erection or operation of gasoline filling stations. Defendant, therefore, had judgment in the sum of $60,000.

Taking up the question of a uniform building plan, it is clear that the Appellate Division was correct in deciding that the property was not subject to the restriction of a plan limiting the use of the property to residential purposes. The plaintiff's grantor set up two adjoining subdivisions. They were called "University Terrace, Part One" and "University Terrace, Part Two." Surveys were made, streets and lots laid out, maps prepared and filed in the county clerk's office. No plan or declaration of a purpose to restrict any particular portion of the subdivisions or lots thereon to residential or other specific purposes was included or indicated in the maps filed, nor do any of the deeds contain covenants on the part of the grantor that the remainder of the tract should be subject to restriction. The plaintiff's grantor in selling the lots did not follow a uniform policy of development pursuant to which restrictions either for or against the grantees in the various deeds were established. Some lots were restricted to the erection of two-family houses; others to one-family houses. Stores were permitted on some lots, provided no gasoline or oil business should be conducted. In a great number of deeds a "saving clause" was inserted, providing that the grantee obtained no rights in other lots of the subdivision by reason of the restrictive provisions of the deeds. Many deeds contained no restrictions. It is apparent that restrictions were made whenever the grantor thought them necessary or advisable to bring about and maintain the desirability and salability of the property. Clearly he was not following a fixed plan of restricting the use of the lots sold and did not intend to bind himself or his remaining lots by the covenants contained in the deeds which he gave. The defendant emphasizes the "saving clause" found in many of the deeds and seeks to deduce from this that the earlier deeds were in accordance with a plan which restricted the plaintiff's grantor and that, therefore, the clause was inserted to prevent later deeds from carrying the benefit of the covenants already made. The argument cuts both ways. It is equally potent as showing that no general plan to restrict all lots ever was contemplated. If the grantor had in fact restricted all his property in the subdivisions, of what use was the denial of the benefits under the covenants to the later purchasers, when sixty-two prior purchasers already possessed the power to enforce such restrictions? Thus we are brought to the conclusion that no uniform building plan ever came into being.

The defendant next urges that the deed given by the plaintiff's predecessor to the Kendall Refining Company prohibited the erection and operation of a gas filling station upon all the other lots in the subdivision; that, although no mention of such restriction is made in the deed or chain of title to the plaintiff, it is binding on the property deeded to him; and that, therefore, the title offered to the defendant is not marketable.

The clause in the deed to the Kendall Company reads as follows:

> This conveyance is made and accepted subject to the following restrictions, which shall be covenants running with the land:
> First: So long as the said premises shall be used as a gasoline or motor fuel distributing station, the party of the second part or its assigns or successors agree: (a) That any grease pit or pits must and shall be level with the ground. (b) That there shall not be more than 8 pump housings for the distribution of motor oils and fuels. (c) That there shall not be more than one building for the sale or distribution of motor fuels.

Second: That at no time will the said premises be used for what is known as industrial or factory purposes. And the party of the first part covenants that he will not sell, or cause or permit to be sold, gasoline or lubricating oils, or motor fuels, nor erect, or cause to be erected, or permit to be erected, any other gasoline, lubricating oils or motor fuels distributing or sale station or stations upon the entire tracts of land known as University Terrace Number (or Part) 1 and University Terrace Number (or Part) 2; and that in the event that the party of the first part acquires the tract of land adjoining the said University Terrace tracts on the east, or any interest therein, the foregoing restrictive covenants to apply thereto to equal force and effect.

Upon the face of the foregoing deed, the only covenants which expressly are made to run with the land are those imposing obligations upon the Kendall Company, namely, pits must be level with the ground, the number of pump housings and buildings limited and the premises never used for industrial or factory purposes. When the grantor comes to covenanting on his part, he starts covenanting anew and omits, apparently purposely, to provide that such covenant shall run with the land, although having so provided expressly with reference to the covenant on the part of the grantee, less than a dozen lines back in the same instrument. That the covenant on the part of the grantor only purports to be a personal undertaking is strengthened by the fact that the grantor binds himself alone and does not, either expressly or by legal implication, attempt to bind his heirs, grantees, or assigns. The grantor's covenant was that he would not sell gasoline and oil or erect filling stations on his remaining lots, but he avoided sedulously any covenant that his grantee would not do these things. Taking the restrictions in the order in which they appear in the deed, we find that those expressly intended to run with the land are the restrictions upon the use of the land conveyed, which are applicable only to it, namely, those limiting the extent and nature of the structures upon the land. The remainder of the covenant is nothing more than an agreement prohibiting the grantor personally from becoming a competitor of the grantee in the filling station business. Nowhere do we find any provision extending such prohibition to the assigns of the grantor.

Thus, the covenant is personal to the grantor and cannot by implication be impressed upon future owners of other premises. The grantor could have made his covenant an obligation upon the lots of the plaintiff by inserting a covenant in the deed prohibiting a gasoline station upon such lots, but the grantor did not do so but gave a deed to the plaintiffs free of any such covenant. Therefore, his obligation under this covenant stopped at himself and never attached to the lots later transferred to the plaintiff. . . .

Assuming, however, that the deed embodies a restrictive covenant running with the land, intended to bind not only the grantor but in addition all the property in the subdivision owned by the grantor, for the defendant to succeed it is necessary also to find that this will bind land in the subdivision subsequently sold by deeds which make no mention of the covenant and which transfer property to grantees who are unaware of the existence of the covenant. The defendant claims that the mere fact that this one deed contains a restrictive convenant furnished constructive notice to all subsequent purchasers of property from the same grantor. To so claim goes contrary to the well-settled principle that a purchaser takes with notice from the record only of incumbrances in his direct chain of title. In the absence of actual notice before or at the time of his purchase or of other exceptional circumstances, an owner of land is only bound by restrictions if they appear in some deed of record in the conveyance to himself or his direct predecessors in title. This rule would seem to be implicit in the acts providing for the recording of conveyances. Recording constitutes notice only of instruments in the chain of title of the parcel granted. To have to search each chain of title from a common grantor lest notice be imputed would seem to negative the beneficent purposes of the recording acts.

In several states it has been held that a purchaser of a lot which formed part of a larger tract is not charged with notice of restrictive covenants contained in a prior deed from the same grantor to any other lot or parcel of the same general tract, although the deed is recorded and by its terms applies to all other lots.

It is true that in some other states it has been held that the recording of such a deed by a common grantor affords notice to all his subsequent grantees. In New York no authorities in the Court of Appeals have been brought to our attention which prescribe the principle to be followed. In the Appellate Division there is an instance where a covenant in one deed has been held to affect property subsequently deeded by the common grantor free from the covenant. In that case, however, the covenant in the prior deed sought to establish a front line for adjacent houses. From the facts and circumstances it was held that the defendant had notice of the restrictive covenant in the earlier deed. Any one building in a residential section who projects his house farther into the street line than the adjacent house might be said to be put on notice as to whether he is restricted from so doing, either by a general plan of building or by some right or easement which his adjacent neighbor may have acquired.

In the absence of exceptional circumstances, the consideration of which we may well leave until they arise, New York should follow the general well-settled principle that a purchaser takes with notice from the record only of incumbrances in his direct chain of title.

The judgment should be reversed and judgment directed in accordance with this opinion, with costs.

4.   Judicial Review of Arbitrariness

◆ BERGER v. VAN SWERINGEN CO.
6 Ohio St. 2d 100, 216 N.E.2d 54 (1966)

Plaintiffs, homeowners in the village of Beachwood (now a city), brought suit on behalf of themselves and others similarly situated seeking a permanent injunction against the use by defendants Levin and Visconsi of an 80-acre parcel of land owned by them, for any purpose other than single-family residences.

The property is located in Beachwood in an exclusive residential neighborhood, in which are located homes valued at from $40,000 to $90,000. This parcel of land is bounded on the east by Ohio State Route No. 1, a four-lane interstate highway, on the north by Shaker Boulevard, a four-lane divided highway, on the west by Richmond Road, a 100-foot roadway, and on the south by South Woodland Road, also a 100-foot roadway.

The Council of the village of Beachwood, upon application by the defendants Levin and Visconsi, rezoned this parcel from a residential classification to a shopping-center classification.

The validity of this change in zoning classification was before this court in Willott v. Village of Beachwood, 175 Ohio St. 557, 197 N.E.2d 201.

The questions presented by this appeal were not decided by this court in that case.

The property is restricted to residential use, except for a certain small parcel. These restrictions were imposed by the Van Sweringen Company, which developed the whole area originally.

In 1959, the Van Sweringen Foundation, a corporation not for profit, was organized for the purpose of acquiring, owning and holding substantially all the stock of the Sweringen Company. This corporation was to be operated exclusively for the benefit of the communities of Shaker Heights, Beachwood and Pepper Pike. The trustees of the foundation are the mayors of the respective communities or their appointees. The directors of the company are elected by the trustees of the foundation.

In January 1960, the board of directors adopted a resolution of intent to change the restrictions on the 80-acre parcel with which we are concerned in this case, if and when Beachwood rezoned such parcel to permit it to be used for commercial purposes. . . .

At the March meeting in 1961, the board of directors of the company, acting upon an application by the defendants, voted two to one *not* to waive such restrictions. In August 1961, a new director from Shaker Heights was appointed. Subsequently, the board of directors voted two to one to waive the restrictions upon the 80 acres to permit the construction of a shopping center.

At the trial of this case, there was sharply conflicting testimony upon almost all pertinent points. These conflicts were resolved by the trial court in favor of plaintiffs, and a decree was granted to the plaintiffs in accordance with the prayer of the petition. . . .

O'NEILL, Judge. The first question to be determined is whether plaintiffs are entitled to enforce the restrictive covenants covering defendants' land against the defendants.

It is defendants' contention that only owners of property within a subdivision or allotment may enforce such covenants against other owners within the same subdivision or allotment, and that, since defendants' land has never been subdivided, plaintiffs are not within the same subdivision and are, therefore, not entitled to enforce such covenants. . . . [T]he answer lies not in the ascertainment of artificial and arbitrary lines drawn upon a plat book but in the determination of the intention of the parties to be gained from the language of the instrument and the surrounding circumstances. The question to be asked is: For whose benefit was the restriction imposed? . . .

In the instant case, plaintiffs, while they are not within an allotment or subdivision in which defendants' property lies, are adjacent property owners and as such will be affected by the shopping center proposed by defendants. Restrictions were imposed upon at least a part of defendants' land by the same instruments imposing restrictions upon the lands of several of the plaintiffs.

Likewise, an intent that the surrounding property owners are to be the beneficiaries of such restrictions is shown by the following paragraph from the instruments imposing restrictions. While there are slight variations among such instruments they are not here material. Paragraph 18 of those instruments provides:

> The herein enumerated restrictions, rights, reservations, limitations, agreements, covenants and conditions shall be deemed as covenants and not as conditions hereof, and shall run with the land, and shall bind the owner until the first day of May, 2026, in any event, and continuously thereafter, unless and until any proposed change shall have been approved in writing by *the owners of the legal title to all the land on both sides of the highway within the block in which is located the property,* the use of which is sought to be altered by said proposed change.

At least some of the plaintiffs own land across the highway from this parcel within the block in which a portion of this parcel is located.

In the above-quoted paragraph it is to be noted that the owner is absolutely bound by the covenants until 2026 and, after that time, may secure a release of those covenants only by obtaining the consent of surrounding property owners. The fact that such property owners are given eventual control over such change of use indicates that they were intended to benefit from the covenants restricting the use of defendants' property.

The factual question whether the restrictive covenants in question are part of a uniform plan of development and were imposed with the intention of benefiting plaintiffs was determined by the courts below in favor of plaintiffs, and there is sufficient evidence to support such finding. It is the opinion of this court that the plaintiffs are proper persons to bring this action.

The next question to be decided is whether the courts below erred in finding that the company's release of restrictions covering the 80-acre parcel was illegal and void and in conflict with its obligations to plaintiffs.

The several instruments imposing restrictions upon defendants' property provide for certain conditions under which the Van Sweringen Company may release restrictions upon property which it has sold.

Paragraph 17 of the instruments imposing restrictions provides, with minor variations among the several instruments, as follows:

> The Van Sweringen Company reserves the right to waive, change or cancel any and all of the restrictions contained in this instrument or in any other instrument given by the Van Sweringen Company in respect to lots or parcels within the Van Sweringen Company's subdivisions, or elsewhere *if, in its judgment, the development warrants the same or if, in its judgment, the ends or purposes of said subdivisions would be better* served. . . .

Paragraph 17 gives the company the right to waive, change or cancel the restrictions only if the above conditions are met. This paragraph places great power in the hands of the company to control the development of property previously sold by it, and such control continues today even though the company no longer has any property to develop. The company has discretion to act, but it must not abuse that discretion and must exercise its sound judgment in determining that restrictions should be waived, changed or cancelled.

The trial court found that the company had acted in conflict with its obligations to plaintiffs, and that its actions were *ultra vires*. The court said:

> To now permit the Van Sweringen Company through its trustees to negate the bond made with these purchasers in order to permit more recent purchasers to build and operate any type of commercial establishment, even though such an installation might benefit other persons many blocks away taxwise, must certainly "shock the conscience of the chancellor" to such an extent that it cannot be allowed. . . .

The Court of Appeals further stated:

> We are met with what we believe to be the vital question. Is there anything shown by the record that this tract cannot be developed according to the original intention of the purchasers of these valuable homes and The Van Sweringen Company in keeping with the relationship formed contractually between these parties, who in good faith sold and acquired these properties over the years? In answer to the question posed, it must be said that the record does not. But on the contrary, there is credible evidence in the record which shows that now, since the Hilltop sewer project has been completed, this parcel can, in a reasonably short time, be developed with single-family residences comparable to those that presently surround this area.

There is sufficient evidence in the record to support such findings.

The obvious purpose of paragraph 17 was to provide a means whereby one who bought property in good faith could escape the burden of the restrictions if it was found to be impossible to continue the development as planned, and still provide protection for the property of surrounding owners who had bought on the strength of the restrictions.

As this court stated in Wallace v. Clifton Land Co., 92 Ohio St. 349, 359, 110 N.E. 940, 942:

> These restrictions were not imposed for the benefit of the original proprietor, further than the fact that the general and uniform plan of restricting the allotment to resident purposes might contribute to a readier sale of the lots. *The real purpose of the restrictions was to guarantee to the purchasers a quiet residence locality. . . . The great majority of these purchasers undoubtedly bought with this idea in view.* Their grantor kept faith and imposed like restrictions upon all the lots in this allotment that were similarly located. . . .

◆ KENNEY v. MORGAN
22 Md. App. 698, 325 A.2d 419 (Ct. Spec. App. 1974)

MENCHINE, J. George L. Morgan, Jr. and Edwina C. Morgan, his wife, (Morgans) are the owners, by virtue of a deed in fee simple, of a lot and dwelling in a development in Anne Arundel County known as "Turnbull Estates." Their title was aquired from Thomas T. Kenney and Margaret B. Kenney, his wife, (Kenneys) who reside in that development but are also its developers and the owners of more than 100 unsold, unimproved lots within it. The Morgans, acting for themselves and on behalf on 13 of 17 residents of Turnbull Estates, filed a bill for declaratory judgment and injunctive relief against the Kenneys and others in the Circuit Court for Anne Arundel County. Prior to the actual development of Turnbull Estates, the Kenneys had recorded among the land records of Anne Arundel County a declaration of covenants and restrictions to be applicable to all lots within the development. All subsequent lot sales were made subject to that declaration. The bill sought: (a) to have those covenants and restrictions declared to be illegal and unenforceable; and (b) to have the bylaws of The Turnbull Homes Association, Inc. (a corporation to be formed under provisions of the recorded declaration) declared to be void, with required adoption of new bylaws under voting procedures to be fixed by court decree. . . .

COVENANTS J AND K

J. None of the property subject to this Declaration shall be occupied, leased, demised, rented, conveyed or otherwise alienated, except by way of a Mortgage or Deed of Trust and sale for default thereunder, nor shall the title or possession thereof be transferred, without the consent in writing had and obtained from The Turnbull Company, except that The Turnbull Company may not withhold such consent, if written request has been made to it to permit such occupation, leasing, renting, conveying, or alienation, signed by a majority of the owners of the lots which are subject to this Declaration, and which adjoin or face said lot upon both sides of the street, or streets, and within a distance of five lots from the side lines thereof.

K. In order to facilitate operation of Covenant J above, the owners of property subject to this Declaration covenant for themselves, their heirs and assigns, that in the event at any time they shall desire to lease, rent or sell said property they will appoint The Turnbull Company agent for such purpose. . . .

Covenant J imposed a restriction upon alienation. The limitation imposed by Covenant K conjunctively was attached to that restriction. Accordingly the two covenants will stand or fall together. The trial court concluded, properly we think, that Covenants J and K imposed unlawful restrictions repugnant to the inherent nature and quality of a fee simple estate. . . .

COVENANT C

C. No building shall be located on any Building Site less than Fifty Feet from the front lot line for all sites covered by these Covenants, nor less than Twenty-five Feet from any side street line. No building shall be located less than Ten Feet from any side lot line. *The Turnbull Company may waive minor violations of these provisions.*

The decree of the trial court struck down the italicized portion of covenant C. We find no invalidity in the provision.

Appellees suggest that the Turnbull Company is a non-existent entity. The record shows that the Kenneys functioned under the firm name of The Turnbull Company. The recorded document plainly authorized them to do so.

The right of a developer of property to retain a power to waive restrictions is clearly recognized in this State. . . .

There is not a scintilla of evidence to demonstrate any arbitrary or capricious abuse of the reserved power. In Jones v. Real Estate Co., 149 Md. 271, 131 A. 446, it was said:

> There is some discussion in the brief of the appellants as to whether the provision in the tenth covenant, giving the appellee the right to waive many, if not all, of the restrictions in any particular case, does not destroy the theory of a general plan of development, and render the covenants unenforceable on the ground of lack of mutuality. We would have to consider this in a suit brought by one lot owner against another, but we do not consider it necessary to pass upon it in this suit, because we are here dealing with an original grantor, who still owns a considerable part of the land, and the assignees of an original purchaser, and, as the deed specifically states that the covenants are to bind "the grantees, their heirs and assigns," there would seem to be no question, under the authorities of the grantor's right to enforce the covenants, if they are otherwise valid.

Covenant N

> N. The owner of each Building Site shall be entitled to one membership in The Association and to participate in all of the affairs of the Association in accordance with the By-laws of the Association. *Each Building Site,* from the date of its purchase from The Developers, *shall be subject to the payment of an annual charge of Eighteen ($18.00) Dollars,* which shall be payable to the Association on the first day of January of each year and shall be applied as dues for said membership. Said annual charge due the first day of January of each year, if not paid on or before the first day of March of that year, shall bear interest from said last-mentioned date at the rate of six per centum per annum.

It will be observed that this covenant incorporates by reference those sections of the declaration wherein "Building Site" and "Association" had been defined as follows:

"Building Site" shall mean any lot, or any portion thereof, or any two or more contiguous lots, or a parcel of land of record and in unity of title, *upon which a dwelling may be erected* in conformance with the Covenants herein.

"Association" shall mean a non-profit, non-stock association or corporation to be organized under the laws of the State of Maryland by the property owners of lots as shown on the Plat aforesaid, or upon any further Plats of Turnbull Estates, in the tract of land hereinbefore mentioned or adjacent thereto, to be known as The Turnbull *Homes* Association.

A non-profit, non-stock corporation known as Turnbull Estates Homes Association, Inc. (The Association) was formed in conformity with the provisions of the recorded declaration.

The dispute between the Kenneys and the Morgans with respect to covenant N has been restricted to its interpretation. Its alleged invalidity was not pressed at trial. The Kenneys contend that the covenant operates to grant to them, as owners of more than one hundred unsold and undeveloped lots, one vote in The Association for each such lot. The Morgans contend that voting membership in The Association is limited to those residents of the development (currently 17 in number including the Kenneys) who are the owners of a building site upon which a dwelling has been erected.

The decree of the trial court thus resolved this dispute:

> Covenant N is interpreted as meaning that the owner of each building site purchased from the developers is entitled to one membership in "The Association". More specifically, Thomas T. Kenney and Margaret B. Kenney, his wife, are not entitled to a membership for each lot that they own. The Eighteen Dollar ($18.00) annual charge recited in covenant N attaches to each building site as of the day it is sold by the developers and the money goes to the "Association" as opposed to the developer and/or Thomas T. Kenney and Margaret B. Kenney, his wife. . . .

Inclusion of the defined words "Building Site" and "Association" within the language of covenant N would reasonably indicate to purchasers from the Kenneys: (a) that each such purchaser would thereby become a member of an association formed or to be formed for their benefit; and (b) that the annual charge of $18.00 required to be paid by each such member would be utilized by that association under voting procedures granting to each resident in the development a single vote. The record shows that the Kenneys paid only one annual charge for each of the years since formation of the corporation. This course of action by them is inconsistent with their present contention. A contractual interpretation given by parties by their acts and conduct may be considered in cases where ambiguity exists.

The name chosen for the corporation in the recorded declaration, namely, "The Turnbull *Homes* Association" (emphasis added) lends added weight in persuasion that the corporation proposed to be formed was intended as a vehicle to benefit the resident home owners, rather than the developer or other lot owners.

Similarly, the use of the words "upon which a dwelling may be erected" in the definition of "Building Site" within the recorded declaration strengthens the conclusion that proper interpretation of the covenant is that made by the trial judge. The use of the word "may" in the document adds further persuasion. Although the word has a variety of meanings, one of them given in the American Heritage Dictionary of the English Language (1973) defines the word to mean "obligation or function, with the force of *must* or *shall* in statutes, deeds and other legal documents."

The interpretation of covenant N was correct. The covenant will be construed most strongly against the Kenneys, who prepared it. . . .

Bylaws of the Association

Although, as previously stated, the trial court found that Association to be a *de jure* corporation created in accordance with the record declaration, its decree in effect struck down the bylaws of that corporation in their entirety. For reasons hereafter stated we find only Article 3 of the bylaws, relating to voting rights of members of The Association to be invalid, with all other Articles thereof validly adopted and presently subsisting. . . .

The record shows that the bylaws of The Association were adopted by the directors named in the corporate charter. The right to do so is plainly authorized by statute. No action has been taken to repeal or amend them. The exercise of the power thus conferred is not unlimited. The provisions of corporate bylaws must be consistent with law.

Article 3 of the corporate bylaws reads as follows:

ARTICLE 3 — Voting Rights:

Section 1 — In all matters which shall come before the members of this Corporation, and in all corporate matters, the voting power of the members of this Corporation shall be unequal, according to the following rules:

(a) — Except as provided in (d) of this section, each member of this Corporation shall have at least one vote.

(b) — Except as provided in (d) of this section, each member of this Corporation owning of record one or more building sites shall have the right to the number of votes equal to the total number of building sites of which he is the owner of record.

(c) — Except as provided in (d) of this section, each purchaser who is a resident on a building site and is purchasing it under a contract or agreement of purchase shall be entitled to one vote.

(d) — When a building site is owned of record in joint tenancy or tenancy in common, or when two or more residents are purchasing a building site under a contract or agreement of purchase and residing thereon, the several owners or purchasers of said building site shall collectively be entitled to one vote only therefor.

(e) — Voting rights may be exercised only when all dues and obligations set out in the Protective Covenants and By-Laws have been complied with in full.

In Fletcher Cyclopedia Corporations, Permanent Edition (1966) §4188, it is said:

"It is settled law that a corporation has no power to adopt bylaws which impair or destroy the obligations of contracts or rights thereunder or vested rights, and that bylaws which have that effect are invalid and unenforceable against a person whose rights are impaired or destroyed thereby."

Article 3 of the subject bylaws would destroy the vested right of the appellees to a voice of equal strength to other persons similarly situated in the management of The Association granted in the recorded declaration. This could not lawfully be done.

Notes

1. A land developer had reserved to its agent, the Architectural Control Committee, the right to amend or annul restrictions at the agent's sole discretion. Subsequently, the committee had sought to abolish the restrictions with regard to one lot in order to permit the property to be used for business purposes. The Alabama Supreme Court reversed the lower court approval of the action, concluding that the declaration of covenants was intended to create a "general scheme or plan of development with restrictions benefiting all owners of land." The court held that reservation of the right to annul could only be exercised "in a reasonable manner consistent with that general scheme or plan of development." It found that the committee's actions were not in keeping with a general scheme. Wright v. Cypress Shores Development Co., 413 So. 2d 1115 (Ala. 1982).

2. But what determines whether a decision pursuant to reserved authority is "reasonable and made in good faith, and not arbitrary or capricious"? A Colorado court said that an architectural review committee should seek "to protect present and future property values in the subdivision." With that implied standard read in, the court found the reserved power sufficiently specific to avoid arbitrary decision. Snowmass American Corp. v. Schoenheit, 524 P.2d 645 (Colo. App. 1974).

3. Japanese Gardens, developer of a mobile home park with 370 lots, obtained covenants from lot purchasers to pay $8.75 per month maintenance. In addition, "such monthly assessment for all lots can be raised . . . by a majority vote of the owners of any and all lots." When 162 lots had been sold, a majority vote raised the assessment to $12.90, with Japanese Gardens casting votes for the 208 unsold lots. The court said that "owner" does not mean "purchaser"; thus Japanese Gardens was correct in voting its unsold lots. But it remanded for judicial determination of whether the increase was "reasonably necessary and

proper" for maintenance of the development. Japanese Gardens Mobile Estates, Inc. v. Hunt, 261 So. 2d 193 (Fla. App. 1972).

5. Democratic Theory

◆ REICHMAN, RESIDENTIAL PRIVATE GOVERNMENTS: AN INTRODUCTORY SURVEY
43 U. Chi. L. Rev. 253, 260-264, 268-269, 273-274, 286-291 (1976)

The nature of modern housing developments has virtually dictated the establishment of residential private governments. Commonly-owned facilities need management, on-going financing and permanent regulation. Without them, such projects could easily fall into decay. Furthermore, the character of the new developments required the provision of certain services (such as complex indoor services in a multi-unit apartment house) that local governments furnish inadequately, if at all. The developer who intends to sell, rather than lease, the residential units will typically be interested in terminating his ties with the project as soon as possible in order to avoid tying up his resources on a completed project, collecting recurrent assessments, setting a permissible margin of profits, and satisfying the community's demands for service. The soundest and easiest way for the developer to solve managerial problems is to charge the owners themselves with the responsibility and let them operate as a nonprofit association to reduce costs. The structure of such an arrangement, however, must be formulated early enough to assure the first purchasers that the operation will be run efficiently and without serious friction after the developer turns over control.

Yet the residential private government is structured in a way that serves the developer's more immediate interests as well. Several years are usually required to complete a project of, say, a few hundred units. During that time, stringent controls must be imposed on the independent builders working on individual lots and on the new residents of the emerging community to prevent them from damaging the rest of the project. To attract potential home buyers, various recreational facilities, designed to serve the entire community, are completed along with the first residential structures. To ensure that at least part of the operating costs of these facilities are covered, the infant private government scheme must allow the developer to levy assessments on the project's first residents. Even though the developer naturally fears interference with his long-range plan, the arrangements cannot be made too one-sided: total domination by the developer could cause serious friction that might be costly in terms of litigation, work postponement and adverse publicity. Thus the system must allow the residents of the development to participate to a certain extent in the decision-making process by providing a mechanism for representation through which dissent may be expressed and compromises reached. Finally, the developer must also build into the private government scheme enough flexibility to enable him to modify plans and standards to meet unforeseen contingencies. . . .

Could the homeowners' association, which was intended to sail on the waters of conformity, bring about social change? Although the entrepreneurs who created them certainly did not intend to produce such a result, the structure of the homeowners' association could unwittingly provide a mechanism for reversing the anticommunity trends of the last century. Although the days of self-sufficient units are long over, community organization centered around the home, largely independent of general production-consumption lines, still seems feasible. The homeowners' association, focusing on the total residential environment rather than nationwide interests, could provide a vehicle for this type of development. Residents may be expected to participate in the regular and extraordinary meetings of the residential private government out of basic self-interest: the decisions reached in each association meeting may affect each individual owner financially as well as by determining the standard of services to be supplied and the rules of behavior to be enforced. . . .

Having said all this, a few words of caution must be interjected. First, the movement toward residential private governments is not likely to reach the people who might benefit from it the most: the indigent and alienated segments of the population. Second, the hypothesis that innovative legal arrangements can improve social relationships is not substantiated by any relevant comparative research. Finally, even when the tools of cooperation are made available, human factors might frustrate the entire scheme: apathy could plague the organization, and culture differences could prove to be unbridgeable. . . .

Beyond [the] explicit regulations set forth in the homeowners' covenants or articles of association, there is the ever-present possibility of new regulation. So far as the legal instruments of residential private governments are concerned, the owner's privileges are merely conditional. Ownership and life in the community are totally subordinated to whatever rules are proclaimed by the homeowners' organization. Unlike local municipal governments, which are restricted by federal and state laws, constitutional standards and administrative norms from impairing private ownership beyond a certain point, the laws of the private residential government rarely include any substantive criteria to limit future "legislation." The only safeguards provided are procedural in nature: all decisions must be made by a majority and a "supermajority" is required on some matters. The only restrictions within the system may be found in the articles of association, and they are broadly drafted. The promotion of health, safety, the common good and social welfare is almost always declared as the primary objective, suggesting that the home-owners' organization claims to possess at least the same powers that municipalities have — without the concomitant limitations of public law. Adjusted as they are to a climate of regulated living, it would not be surprising if the majority opted for further regulation, whether in the form of explicit prohibitions or further enlargement of discretionary powers. Thus, given the existing and potential encroachments on own-ership rights, it is clear that the concept of ownership under residential private government rule deviates significantly from the theoretical model of traditional property rights. . . .

The covenants and bylaws of the typical homeowners' association are aimed at securing absolute control for the developer until a substan-tial part of the project is sold. Various private government schemes are used to achieve this purpose. The model forms, proposed by the Urban Land Institute, recommend a harsh, yet straightforward technique, sug-gesting that the developer be given three votes per unit, while the own-ers have only one vote each. The entrepreneur thereby enjoys a majority vote in the homeowners' association until 75 percent of the lots have been sold. The right to amend the articles during this development period is specifically prohibited. The developer's control over the private government is thus assured and undesired controversies are theoreti-cally avoided.

The same approach has been adopted by virtually all of the large-scale horizontal developments, although with varying degrees of liberal-ism and sophistication. In Reston, Virginia, for example, a system of one unit-one vote prevails and gives the developer a majority up to the day he disposes of 50 percent of his plots. Thereafter a minimum of one-third of the votes is secured to him until a given date or until 80 percent of the lots are sold, whichever is later. The developer is protected, how-ever, by "supermajority" provisions that allow 10 percent of the votes to veto fundamental changes and require approval by seven-ninths of the entire board of directors and 50 percent of the voters to amend other clauses. Since the developer chooses the directors who serve for the first five years, and may later enlarge his voting power by adding land to the original development, it seems clear that he will be able to forestall any amendment of the servitudes and will enjoy "political" control over the development for as long as he deems necessary.

Federally-sponsored new towns employ a somewhat different scheme. According to HUD's guidelines, the right to vote in the associa-tion must be granted to owners and renters alike. Perhaps fearful that a system that does not endorse the principle of "one man-one vote" might be held unconstitutional, HUD also insisted that the developer have only one vote in the private organization. This requirement does not, however, prevent the entrepreneurs from keeping control. As is often done in corporations, the device of special voting classifications is used to maintain minority control. At the outset, the developer, who is referred to as a "class B" member, has the power to choose the entire board of directors except for one, who is elected by and from the members of the association (class A). Thereafter, whenever a certain number of dwelling units are occupied, class A members gain the right to elect one more class B director. In this way the system provides for the gradual transfer of power to the residents. In several of these projects, the developer also has the right to veto any amendments to the original charter until the project is substantially completed. Other projects permit the modification of all the servitudes, with no power vested in the class B members to prevent it, if two-thirds of the residents and the Secretary of HUD approve. The entrepreneurs in these projects seem to enjoy tremendous powers, notwithstanding their negligible voting rights. The servitudes provide the associations' directors and the architectural control committees (the majority of the members of which are also appointed to a fixed term by the developer) with farreaching discretionary powers. Furthermore, in several ventures it is provided that only the *directors* have the power to formulate and amend the associations' bylaws. . . .

There has been some literature on the possibility of curtailing the developer's domination to cure these abuses. Proponents of government intervention advocate employing social planners and establishing a "board of overseers" with the power to intervene in the affairs of the residential private government. Other critics argue that the internal structure of the organization should be modified. It is suggested, for example, that compelling a gradual transfer of power to the residents, as is done in federally-sponsored new communities, would suffice. Other commentators contend that the residents' political power should be upgraded by early incorporation and the formation of homeowners' associations independent of the developer, by the even earlier transfer of some planning responsibilities and the disclosure of all relevant economic data to the residents, and by the maintenance of continued, steady financial support for community activities.

There are several factors that must be considered when boundaries are set and abuses defined in the context of the balance of power in residential private governments. First, it seems clear that the developer's ability to carry out his building plans, which were approved by public authorities, should not be hampered by the residents. But this conclusion does not require the total rejection of cooperation. Developers may argue that residents often fail to consider the interests of the community as a whole and tend to react in an extreme manner. Yet even if this is true, input from the residents is crucial both as an end in itself and as a means of gaining valuable knowledge about the community's needs and desires for services, facilities, and planning.

Second, the residential private government scheme must provide for a gradual transfer of power so that a vacuum is not created by the developer's departure. Recent research has indicated that condominium and townhouse owners who are disenchanted with the operation of their homeowners' associations generally blame the developer for such failures; his abrupt departure, without an organized transfer of responsibility and a period of training, is the reason usually given. The importance of having a residential private government scheme that will provide for local participation without tying the developer's hands and will establish a method for transferring control should not be minimized; these organizational factors are no less significant than compliance with building codes or zoning restrictions on building density. Since local, municipal and county governments are already in the business of granting permits and inspecting developments, they should also be empowered to review the homeowners' association rules to insist on minimum citizen participation and a reasonable scheme for the transfer of power in developments over a certain size. . . .

In recent years the courts have assumed a growing part of the task of resolving the disputes referred to above. Cases involving discretionary servitudes have replaced the bulk of traditional litigation regarding servitudes. In considering these cases, the judiciary has already been instrumental in laying down boundary lines and acting against certain abuses. Today, the developer's powers are checked and controlled by the courts. Still, doctrines are but slowly formulated and most of the legal remedies are as yet ad hoc situations; the precedents therefore provide unsatisfactory guidelines for the behavior of all homeowners' associations.

◆ HYATT, CONDOMINIUM AND HOME OWNER
ASSOCIATIONS: FORMATION AND DEVELOPMENT
24 Emory L.J. 977, 982-984, 1006-1008 (1975)

In the condominium context, state law ordains the creation of the association; in both forms of development, moreover, the creating documents are filed with and enforced through the state courts. In most cases, the association provides for its members' utility services, road maintenance, street and common area lighting, and refuse removal; in many cases, it also provides security services and various forms of communication within the community. There exists, therefore, a clear analogy to the municipality's police and public safety functions; moreover, these functions are financed through assessments, or taxes, levied upon the members of the community association. The governmental role which creates a special concern for strict observance of the dictates of due process of law is made more acute by the power of the association through its rule-making authority and through its assessment authority to regulate the use and enjoyment of property. This "power of levy" is a distinctive characteristic of the association and removes it from a mere voluntary neighborhood civic group. The declaration, which must be strictly construed and obeyed, establishes a variety of use restrictions including, for example, restrictions upon sale and leasing, exterior alterations, use of the common area, parking, and even limitations upon the nature of uses to which the interior of the unit may be placed. In addition, a typical declaration will empower the board of directors to make rules and to establish penalties for violations thereof. The imposition of penalties, whether fines collected as a lien upon the property or a denial of the use of facilities enforced by injunction, certainly represents a quasi-judicial power to affect an individual's property rights.

The possession and exercise of such power has substantial consequences with clear constitutional implications. The Supreme Court has found a basis for requiring compliance with constitutional procedures in the context of a company town and in the practices of political parties; the association's mandatory nature, created and enforced by and through state law and action and its authority to affect property rights make compelling the conclusion that the association's actions are "public" in a constitutional sense requiring at least minimal observance of due process and equal protection principles. The courts have not yet considered a direct constitutional challenge to an association's action; however, the possible contexts for such an attack are most interesting. For example, at annual association meetings, at which as little as 10 percent of the membership may constitute a quorum in accordance with many declarations, the agenda often includes votes permitting special assessments or major expenditures of common funds, limiting the use of common areas, or delegating authority to the board of directors to take such action. Further, board meetings are often closed, a fact which raises an interesting question of the applicability of the so-called Sunshine Laws requiring open meetings. At such meetings, open or closed, the directors transact association business which involves contractual, economic, and personnel decisions and make and enforce rules. Whether contracting with a roofer, drafting a pet restriction, or imposing a fine for violation of a rule, the board is acting in a governmental capacity in relation to its constituency of mandatory members. . . .

[It has been] argued strongly that directors may not ignore the duties with which they are charged without accepting liability for injuries caused by their neglect. As noted above, officers and directors have a fiduciary duty to those whom they represent, and they must act in a manner reasonably related to the exercise of that duty. Failing to do so will result in liability, not only for the association, but also for the individuals themselves. There is much law yet to be developed in this area, and one who is dealing with problems of formation and development of an association must be mindful of the principles which flow from the association's dual role. . . .

It is no solution, moreover, to say as many developers have, that association developments are obsolete. The economic times, the flagrant abuses in some portions of the condominium market, and the ravenous appetite of the developers and lenders to build thousands of condominiums before they or their market are educated to the peculiarities of the concept have admittedly hurt sales in condominiums and in landed homes associations. The fact remains, however, that the realities of land use and economic planning necessitate that a substantial portion of the nation's housing be one form of multi-family ownership or another. The association serves many functions necessary to society, for "[t]he explosive growth of our cities, their trend to giantism, and the high mobility of their residents are rapidly destroying a sense of community among individuals in urban America." The association is a grass roots counterweight to this trend and brings to many who have never had it a sense of pride in a community and a great share of the responsibility for developing and maintaining that community. The association-oriented multi-family form for ownership of property is also a tremendous boon to lower income groups and makes available, for the first time, a means of affording good quality construction, ample amenities, and pleasant surroundings in home ownership. Condominiums and home associations are not dead, and developers will find that with more sophistication and more planning this form is ideally tailored to many geographic, demographic, and economic groups and areas. It is, however, an area that all who would be involved, from the developer to the ultimate purchaser, must understand and appreciate.

♦ ELLICKSON, CITIES AND HOMEOWNERS ASSOCIATIONS

130 U. Pa. L. Rev. 1519, 1519-1520, 1526-1532, 1534-1536, 1543-1544 (1982)

In his recent article, The City as a Legal Concept, [93 Harv. L. Rev. 1059 (1980)], Professor Gerald Frug compared the city and the business corporation as possible vehicles for the exercise of decentralized power. In the course of his analysis, Frug asserted that American law is deeply biased against the emergence of powerful cities and, by implication, is less restrictive on corporate power. Joining the circle of critical legal scholars who want to "rethink" and "restructure" American society, Frug suggested as a modest first step that cities be empowered to engage in banking and insurance operations. Frug believes that if cities were to manage enterprises of this sort, individuals would be better able to influence the decisions that affect their lives. According to Frug, citizen control through participatory democracy leads to "public freedom," a form of human fulfillment that the critical legal scholars think an impersonal market economy suppresses.

Despite his prodigious research, Frug never directed his attention at a third candidate for the exercise of decentralized power: the private homeowners association. The association, not the business corporation, is the obvious private alternative to the city. Like a city, an association enables households that have clustered their activities in a territorially defined area to enforce rules of conduct, to provide "public goods" (such as open space), and to pursue other common goals they could not achieve without some form of potentially coercive central authority. Although they were relatively exotic as recently as twenty years ago, homeowners associations now outnumber cities. Developers create thousands of new associations each year to govern their subdivisions, condominiums, and planned communities.

American law currently treats the city and the homeowners association dramatically differently. One is "public"; the other, "private.". . .

Both cities and homeowners associations regulate the conduct of residents. Both may have rules requiring that dogs be kept on leashes, that residential structures be built in a Colonial style, or that external noise from social gatherings cease at 8:00 p.m. Nevertheless, courts rightly use different standards in reviewing the substantive validity of public and private rules.

In the case of public rules, the basic federal constitutional constraints arise from the due process and equal protection clauses of the fourteenth amendment. More often than not, the constitutional issue is whether the contested regulation is rationally related to a legitimate state interest. In the hands of most state and federal courts, this test now usually proves undemanding.

Because the fourteenth amendment only applies when state action is present, one might expect even greater judicial deference to the substantive validity of private regulations. In fact, however, courts are more vigorous in their examination of the validity of certain types of private regulations. Prevailing common-law and statutory rules ask courts to scrutinize the "reasonableness" of private regulations — an apparent invitation to Lochnerian activism. This active judicial review is inappropriate when the provisions contained in an association's original governing documents are at issue, but it is fully appropriate when litigants challenge amendments to those documents.

The initial members of a homeowners association, by their voluntary acts of joining, unanimously consent to the provisions in the association's original governing documents. . . .

External legal norms of course constrain the contracting process, and in some instances should lead to the judicial invalidation of offensive "constitutional" provisions, such as those that would regulate the racial characteristics of association members. Nevertheless, because original membership in an association is more voluntary than original membership in a city, an association's constitution should be allowed to contain substantive restrictions not permissible in a city charter. For example, if a group of orthodox Jews set up a condominium and stipulated by original covenant that males were required to wear yarmulkes in common areas on holy days, a court should enforce that original covenant in deference to the unanimous wishes of the original members. An identical "public" regulation would, of course, violate the first amendment's ban on the establishment of religion, and perhaps a number of other constitutional guarantees.

The pattern of judicial decisions tends to honor the suggested principle of greater private associational autonomy. Although the Supreme Court has recently held that age is not a suspect classification, lower courts perceive municipal zoning by age as posing serious constitutional questions. By contrast, homeowners-association regulations that limit the age of dwelling occupants have tended to survive legal challenge. As a second example, private associations have successfully defended design controls (dealing with exterior paint colors and so on) whose public counterparts would make city attorneys squirm. . . .

When courts are asked to rule on the validity of an association's actions to flesh out and apply its original constitution, they currently apply the previously mentioned test of "reasonableness." The association's governing documents or a state statute may call for application of the reasonableness standard; if not, courts imply the standard as a matter of law into the original constitution. The reasonableness standard applies to several types of association actions. It constrains all administrative actions — for example, an association's decision to expel a member, to veto the transfer of a membership, or to deny approval of architectural plans. In addition, it constrains the substance of all "legislation" that an association adopts by procedures less cumbersome than the association's procedures for a constitutional amendment. "Legislation" would include, for example, house rules that a board of directors might adopt under an express grant of authority in the original declaration.

"Reasonable," the most ubiquitous legal adjective, is not selfdefining. In reviewing an association's legislative or administrative decisions, many judges have viewed the "reasonableness" standard as entitling them to undertake an independent cost-benefit analysis of the decision under review and to invalidate association decisions that are not cost-justified by general societal standards. This variant of reasonableness review ignores the contractarian underpinnings of the private association. As some courts have recognized, respect for private ordering requires a court applying the reasonableness standard to comb the association's original documents to find the association's collective purposes, and then to determine whether the association's actions have been consonant with those purposes. To illustrate, the reasonableness of a board rule banning alcoholic beverages from the swimming pool area cannot be determined in the abstract for all associations. So long as the rule at issue does not violate fundamental external norms that constrain the contracting process, the rule's validity should not be tested according to external values, for example, the precise package of values that would constrain a comparable action by a public organization. Rather, the validity of the rule should be judged according to the enacting association's own original purposes. . . .

Before the member knew what specific amendments would later be considered, the member plausibly would want an amendment process that would minimize the sum of the present value of three different types of costs: (1) the opportunity costs the member would incur when amendment procedures prevented an association from adopting amendments that would benefit the member; (2) the losses the member would suffer from harmful amendments adopted over the member's dissent ("victimization costs"); and (3) the member's share of the administrative costs of the amendment procedure. . . .

Even if his association had an express taking clause promising compensation of objective losers from an amendment, an entrant in his *ex ante* calculation probably would still want to require amendment approval by extraordinary majority. To avoid reliance on victims' self-interested testimony about losses, legal damages are usually measured by diminutions in market value. This measure of damages can be unfair to victims with atypical tastes. For example, if most elderly people dislike the presence of dogs, an amendment banning dogs in a retirees' condominium association where dogs had originally been explicitly allowed would probably raise the market value of all units. However, a member who loved dogs might nevertheless suffer a deep subjective loss and be skeptical of the adequacy of damage remedies. In his *ex ante* calculation, this member might therefore favor supplementing the taking clause with an extraordinary-majority rule for constitutional amendments.

Although an entrant into an association would be chary of a rule requiring unanimous member approval of wealth-creating amendments, he would also fear being regularly on the losing end of the amendment process. A taking clause in the original constitution that entitled losers from amendments to compensation would appear to be an attractive way to resolve the entrant's dilemma. If an amendment would indeed be wealth-enhancing, then the gainers would still favor it even if they had to compensate the losers. A policy of full compensation of losers also ensures the Pareto superiority of amendments.

There is, of course, a catch: the potentially high administrative costs of rendering accurate compensation. Administrative-cost considerations may explain why, to my knowledge, drafters of association constitutions have never included express taking clauses, and why condominium statutes do not impose a taking clause as a matter of law. Nor have courts and commentators discussed the compensation possibility; they seem to perceive the only alternative to be property-rule protection of either the majority or minority.

Private taking clauses nevertheless have great promise in reconciling majoritarian flexibility and minority rights. As I would apply it, a private taking clause would give any objective loser from an amendment a *prima facie* entitlement to compensation. An association would be freed from liability only if it could make out a defense derived from the Michelman fairness test. This defense would place on the association the burden of proving both (1) that the challenged amendment was indeed wealth-enhancing, that is, that it met the Kaldor-Hicks criterion; and (2) that the losers should be able to see why the failure to compensate would fit into a consistent compensation practice that would be in their own long-run self-interest (for example, by lowering otherwise insuperable administrative-cost hurdles to the adoption of wealth-enhancing amendments). To reduce adjudication costs, an express taking clause included in a private constitution could specify that taking disputes between associations and members were to be decided by compulsory arbitration. . . .

Although there are thousands of private homeowners associations, I know of none with an electoral structure that comports with the one-resident/one-vote principle. As in business corporations, voting rights in community associations tend to be apportioned according to share ownership, a rough approximation of economic stake. State statutes governing condominium associations sometimes provide that voting rights *must* be allocated according to a particular formula, such as one vote per unit, or in proportion to floor area. Most statutes, however, allocate votes according to the ownership interests set out in the original declaration, a system that gives developers some initial flexibility. The statutory intent seems to be that a unit purchaser should be able to know at the time of purchase what fraction of total voting power attaches to his unit. A one-resident/one-vote rule would violate this statutory intent because relative voting power would fluctuate with the vagaries of household composition. Thus almost all state condominium statutes forbid the voting system that the Supreme Court required in *Avery.*

A consumer would presumably be willing to pay more to purchase a condominium in an association with a "better" political system than competing associations have. If the condominium statutes were preventing developers from maximizing profits, one might expect developers to seek passage of statutory amendments authorizing voting by residency in private associations. I am aware of no evidence that either developers or entrants into new private communities are unhappy with the prevailing system of voting by economic stake. This is a clue that one-resident/one-vote does not have much consumer appeal as a *private* voting system.

Regardless of the precise formula used, in virtually all condominium associations, absentee landlords can vote, but their tenants cannot. The owner of multiple units can cast multiple votes (assuming votes are allocated one per unit). Professor Krasnowiecki's influential model legal documents go even farther. To prevent early purchasers from taking control before the developer has marketed most of the units, Professor Krasnowiecki would effectively grant the developer *three* votes for every unsold unit during the initial stages of a development. Could one flout the principle of one-resident/one-vote any more openly?

Voting systems in private associations seem primarily designed to advance efficiency goals, not the redistributive goals the Supreme Court was arguably pursuing in the *Avery* line of cases. Because the intensity of a voter's interest in a community matter is likely to be positively correlated with the voter's economic stake in the community, voting by economic stake appears to be a surer route to allocate efficiency than voting by residency would be. If so, efficiency-minded entrants into an association would prefer one-unit/one-vote to one-resident/one-vote. Moreover, members of a homeowners association can be expected to prefer that the association *not* engage in coercive redistributive programs. If political power were to be allocated in proportion to economic stake, there would likely be less redistribution than there would be if political power were allocated more progressively. The current private voting rules also seem to reflect members' interests in minimizing administrative costs. The economic stake of an owner depends on the *current* market value of his unit (not its value at its creation), and also on any subjective surplus value he might have in the unit. Tenants, especially those who value their units at above contract rent, also have some economic stake. Association voting formulas almost never reflect these nuances, but instead opt for rules that are easier to administer — such as one-unit/one-vote. . . .

◆ FRUG, CITIES AND HOMEOWNERS
ASSOCIATIONS: A REPLY
130 U. Pa. L. Rev. 1589, 1595-1596 (1982)

I oppose Professor Ellickson's attack on the democratic franchise in both of its proposed forms. The stringent taking clause he advocates would reallocate wealth by defining as property expectations not previously protected by law. Although Professor Ellickson's definition of property is so open that a prediction as to the effect of such a reallocation is impossible, the Supreme Court's recent preference for protecting "investment-based" expectations over other kinds of expectations demonstrates how such a clause can be used to protect the rich — those with money to invest — in preference to the poor. Moreover, a stringent taking clause prevents collective decisionmaking by requiring compensation whenever a change in social organization is proposed. "Government hardly could go on," Justice Holmes said, "if to some extent values incident to property could not be diminished without paying for every such change in the general law." It seems that Professor Ellickson's taking clause is designed precisely to prevent government — that is, the collective choice of the residents of the homeowners association — from going on. The taking clause thus by itself attempts to limit the role of democracy.

My objections to Professor Ellickson's proposals to restrict the franchise to property owners are the same as my objections to his taking clause proposals. Indeed, the similarity of my objections demonstrates the similarity of his two proposals. First, . . . a restriction on the franchise is itself a transfer of wealth, a transfer likely to be from the poor to the rich. Secondly, the restriction on the franchise will prevent all non-property owners (as Professor Ellickson defines them) from engaging in collective decisionmaking over their future. Indeed, if one takes seriously Professor Ellickson's claim (in his taking clause section) that a voting right, once allocated, is a property right that cannot be diluted without compensation, the result of his two proposals, taken together, would be not only to restrict the franchise to property owners, but to deter the reestablishment of a fully democratic franchise by requiring compensation before the exclusive voting rights of property owners could be changed.

6. Aesthetics and Architectural Control

◆ RHUE v. CHEYENNE HOMES, INC.
  168 Colo. 6, 449 P.2d 361 (1969)

PRINGLE, Justice. In the trial court, Cheyenne Homes, Inc., obtained an injunction prohibiting Leonard Rhue and Family Homes, Inc., hereinafter referred to as plaintiffs in error, from moving a thirty year old Spanish style house into a new subdivision which was about 80 percent improved and which contained only modern ranch style or split level homes.

At the time that the subdivision in which the plaintiffs in error seek to locate this house was platted, the owner placed upon the entire area certain restrictive covenants contained in a "Declaration of Protective Covenants," which was duly recorded. As recited in the document, these protective covenants were for the purpose of "protecting the present and future values of the properties located" in the subdivision. Admittedly, the house which the plaintiffs in error wish to put in the subdivision does not violate any of the few specific restrictions contained in the protective covenants. However, paragraph C-2 of the record protective covenants contains the following declaration:

"C-2 No building shall be erected, placed or altered on any lot until the construction plans and specifications and a plan showing the location of the structure shall have been approved by the architectural control committee. . . ."

Plaintiffs in error failed to submit their plans to the architectural control committee, and the trial court, in entering its injunction, held (1) that such failure constituted a breach of the restrictive covenants, and (2) that the placing of the house would not be in harmony with the existing neighborhood and would depreciate property values in the area.

Plaintiffs in error contend that restriction C-2 is not enforceable because no specific standards are contained therein to guide the committee in determining the approval or disapproval of plans when submitted. We disagree.

It is no secret that housing today is developed by subdividers who, through the use of restrictive covenants, guarantee to the purchaser that his house will be protected against adjacent construction which will impair its value, and that a general plan of construction will be followed. Modern legal authority recognizes this reality and recognizes also that the approval of plans by an architectural control committee is one method by which guarantees of value and general plan of construction can be accomplished and maintained.

So long as the intention of the covenant is clear (and in the present case it is clearly to protect present and future property values in the subdivision), covenants such as the one before us have been upheld against the contention that they lacked specific restrictions providing a framework within which the architectural committee must act. . . .

We have recognized in Colorado that restrictive covenants placed on land for the benefit of purchasers within a subdivision are valid and not against public policy, and are enforceable in equity against all purchasers. While we have here enunciated the proposition that the covenant requiring approval of the architectural committee before erection of a house in the subdivision is enforceable, we point out that there is a corollary to that proposition which affords protection and due process of law to a purchaser of a lot in the subdivision, namely, that a refusal to approve plans must be reasonable and made in good faith and must not be arbitrary or capricious.

Since two of the three committee members testified that they would disapprove the plans if they were presented to them, we examine the evidence to determine if such refusal is warranted under the rules we have laid down. There was testimony that the house was about thirty years old, and that the other houses were no older than two years. The house of plaintiffs in error has a stucco exterior and a red tile roof. The other houses are commonly known as ranch style or split level, and are predominantly of brick construction with asphalt shingle roofs. There was further testimony that the style of the house would devalue the surrounding properties because it was "not compatible" with the houses already in place.

One member of the committee expressed concern that the house of plaintiffs in error would devalue surrounding property. The other added that he thought the covenant gave the architectural committee the authority to refuse approval to plans for property which would seriously affect the market value of other homes in the area. Clearly, a judgment of disapproval of the plans by the committee is reasonable and in good faith and in harmony with the purposes declared in the covenant.

◆ DAVIS v. HUEY
620 S.W.2d 561 (Tex. 1981)

WALLACE, Justice. Petitioners Tom H. Davis and Hattie Davis, husband and wife, appealed from a permanent injunction entered by the District Court ordering them to remove a portion of their residence built in a residential subdivision without approval of the developer pursuant to restrictive covenants of record. The Court of Civil Appeals affirmed the trial court judgment. . . . We reverse the judgment of the Court of Civil Appeals and render judgment that Respondents, Robert M. and Mary Paige Huey, take nothing. . . .

Northwest Hills, Section 7, a residential subdivision in Austin, Texas, was developed by the Austin Corporation. In 1965, prior to the sale of any lots in the subdivision, the Austin Corporation filed in the Deed Records of Travis County certain restrictive covenants applicable to the subdivision. These covenants are contained in ten paragraphs, numbers 7 and 8 being the ones primarily at issue in this cause. Paragraph 7 establishes the setback, front-line, side-line and rear-line limits of the lot in question. Paragraph 7 provides:

> 7.   *Set-Back, Front Line, Side Line and Rear Line*
>
> No structure shall be located or erected on any lot nearer to the front plot line than twenty-five (25) feet, nor nearer than five (5) feet to any side plot line except that the total combined setback from both sides shall in no event be less than fifteen (15) feet, nor nearer than fifteen (15) feet to the rear plot line.

Paragraph 8 provides that prior to the commencement of construction on a lot, the lot owner is required to submit the construction plans to the developer or an architectural committee for approval. Paragraph 8 provides:

8.   Architectural Control and Building Plans

For the purpose of insuring the development of the subdivision as a residential area of high standards, the Developers, or in the alternative an Architectural committee appointed at intervals of not more than five years by the then owners of a majority of the lots in Northwest Hills Section Seven Addition, reserve the right to regulate and control the buildings or structures or other improvements placed on each lot. No building, wall or other structure shall be placed upon such lot until the plan therefor and the plot plan have been approved in writing by the Developers. Refusal of approval of plans and specifications by the Developers, or by the said Architectural Committee, may be based on any ground, including purely aesthetic grounds, which in the sole and uncontrolled discretion of the Developers or Architectural Committee shall seem sufficient. No alterations in the exterior appearance of any building of structure shall be made without like approval. No house or other structure shall remain unfinished for more than two years after the same has been commenced.

The Davises' lot adjoins the Huey lot on the canyon rim in an area located within Section 7 of Northwest Hills. The Davises purchased their lot in May, 1976. The record is not precise on this point, but the Hueys apparently purchased their lot in late 1973 or early 1974. The Davises originally proposed to build a house on their lot to be situated twenty-five feet from the rear plot line. It is undisputed that the proposed placement of the house complied with the set-back restrictions in Paragraph 7. However, the developer, Austin Corporation, acting through David B. Barrow, Jr., refused to approve the Davises' plans on the basis that the proposed placement of the house on the lot was inconsistent with the general plan of the subdivision. In refusing approval, Barrow relied on the general authority of Paragraph 8 to refuse approval of a plan "on any ground, including purely aesthetic grounds, which in the sole and uncontrolled discretion" of the developer shall seem sufficient. After negotiations between the parties regarding placement of the house proved fruitless, the Davises began construction despite the lack of approval of their plans. Thereafter, the Hueys instituted proceedings, in which Barrow and Austin Corporation, intervened seeking to halt construction on the grounds that the disapproval of the plans was a reasonable, good faith exercise of the authority granted by Paragraph 8; that the completion of the house would reduce the value of the surrounding property because of its size and placement; and, the proposed construction would block the views of the Hueys and other neighbors.

The trial court rendered judgment permanently enjoining the Davises from further construction on their lot until the plans had been approved by the Austin Corporation and ordering them to remove a part of the house already constructed. The court of civil appeals affirmed holding *inter alia* that a covenant requiring written approval of building plans by the developer prior to any placement of any structure on a lot in a subdivision was valid and enforceable when exercised reasonably and pursuant to a general plan or scheme; that evidence supported the findings that there was a general plan or scheme created by the developer; and, that the developer acted reasonably in disapproving Davises' plans. . . .

It has been stated that housing today is ordinarily developed by subdividers, who, through the use of restrictive covenants, guarantee to the homeowner that his house will be protected against adjacent construction which will impair its value, and that a general plan of construction will be followed. Restrictions enhance the value of the subdivision property and form an inducement for purchasers to buy lots within the subdivision. A covenant requiring submission of plans and prior approval before construction is one method by which guarantees of value and of adherence to a general scheme of development can be accomplished and maintained.

Although covenants restricting the free use of property are not favored, when restrictions are confined to a lawful purpose and are within reasonable bounds and the language employed is clear, such covenants will be enforced. . . . However, a purchaser is bound by only those restrictive covenants attaching to the property of which he has actual or constructive notice. One who purchases for value and without notice takes the land free from the restriction. . . .

We find that the better reasoned view is that covenants requiring submission of plans and prior consent before construction are valid insofar as they furnish adequate notice to the property owner of the specific restriction sought to be enforced. Therefore, the question before this Court is whether the approval clause set out in Paragraph 8 of the restrictions placed the Davises on notice that their lot was subject to more stringent building site restrictions than those set out in the specific restriction governing set-back and side-lines, Paragraph 7. We hold that as a matter of law Paragraph 8 failed to provide the Davises with notice of the placement restrictions sought to be enforced and therefore the developer's refusal to approve the plans exceeded the authority granted by the restrictive covenants and was void. . . .

It is undisputed that Austin Corporation, by impressing upon all lots in Section 7 a uniform set of restrictive covenants, intended to establish a scheme or plan to insure the development of a "residential area of high standards." There is also little dispute that the developer has implemented in the subdivision a general scheme or plan which has resulted in a residential area of high standards. David B. Barrow, Jr., who, acting on behalf of Austin Corporation, refused to approve the Davises' plans testified that his disapproval was in furtherance of an intention to maintain Section 7 as a residential area of high standards. Barrow testified that his refusal to approve the Davises' plans was essentially based on the placement of the house on the lot because, in his view, the proposed construction was incompatible with the houses in the surrounding area. He stated that in the area of the Davises' lot all the houses are located roughly equidistant from the street, have a rear area or back yard, have only minor variations in size, and are located on their lots so as to avoid interference with neighbors' views. Barrow stated that the Davises' house was incompatible with the surrounding houses because of its larger dimensions, its placement near the rear of the lot, and its obstruction of the views from neighboring houses. However, it is to be emphasized that Barrow also acknowledged that "in the abstract," the Davises' house would not detract from and was not inconsistent with a residential area of high standards. Thus, it is apparent that in the view of Barrow, the Davises' plans were consistent with a residential area of high standards but were incompatible with a general plan or scheme involving the placement of houses on lots in Section 7.

However, there is nothing in the record which will support a holding that a general plan or scheme had been adopted by the developer with respect to placement so as to place the Davises on notice of such restrictions. Barrow testified that at the time the restrictions were filed, the developers had no definite intentions concerning the regulation of placement under Paragraph 8. In addition, other than the specific restrictions on building site and size, there is no language in any of the covenants, particularly in Paragraph 8, which would place a purchaser on notice that his lot was subject to the placement limitation sought to be enforced. . . . Even more significant is the following testimony of Barrow:

Q: All right. Now, it is true, as I recall it, sir, that you made your decision on where you were going to allow someone to build on Lot 22 at a later date after some other people chose to build their houses up near the fronts of their lots?

A: Yes, sir. . . .

Q: So the Hueys' choice, you are letting influence what the Davises do, rather than the restrictive covenants, isn't that true?

A: The — yes, sir, all the homes along the street in that area influenced the decision.

Based on the language of the restrictive covenants and Barrow's testimony, it is clear that a general scheme regarding the placement of houses on lots in Section 7 did not exist at the time the restrictions were filed but that the placement restrictions sought to be imposed were in response to developing conditions in the subdivision. Thus, the limitations on the Davises' free use of their property were not based on the restrictive covenants but rather on the voluntary decisions of neighboring lot owners who had the good fortune to construct their houses prior to the Davises. The personal decisions of adjoining lot owners do not appear in the Davises' chain of title or in any other instrument of record. Therefore, the Davises did not purchase with notice of the limitation sought to be imposed and their lot is not burdened by the placement restriction. . . .

A contrary holding would be inconsistent with the basic concept underlying the use of restrictive covenants that each purchaser in a restricted subdivision is subjected to the burden and entitled to the benefit of the covenant. In the instant case, under the theory advanced by the developer, lot owners who built their houses early in the development of the subdivision had a relatively free hand in deciding on placement of their houses on their lots, limited only by the specific restrictions. However, once these houses were constructed the surrounding undeveloped lots were burdened to the extent that placement of houses on these lots could not be inconsistent with the developed lots as determined by the approving authority in the subdivision. Thus, lot owners who built their houses early in the development of the subdivision received the benefits of the covenants but not the burdens. In contrast, the Davises were burdened by the restrictions but essentially will receive no benefits because their house was constructed after other lot owners had decided on placement of their houses. . . . Thus, the placement restriction sought to be enforced in this cause clearly lacks the mutuality of obligation central to the purpose of restrictive covenants.

Accordingly, we hold that the refusal of the developer to approve the Davises' plans exceeded his authority under the restrictive covenants and was void.

Accordingly, we reverse the judgments of the courts below and render judgment that the Hueys take nothing.

Notes

1. The managing committee of the community association denied homeowners' request for permission to build a second-story addition to their existing one-story home. Homeowners sought declaratory and injunctive relief. They claimed that because they had not received notice of the committee's policy to disapprove requests for second-story additions at the time they purchased their lots, the committee could not now enforce such a policy against them, despite the homeowners' agreement to abide by covenants requiring committee approval of remodeling. The court upheld enforcement of the restriction. McNamee v. Bishop Trust Co., 62 Hawaii 397, 616 P.2d 205 (1980).

2. Subdivision homeowners had received approval from the architectural control committee to erect a barn on their property. Neighbors sought an injunction against use of the barn, alleging that it did not comply with paragraph 2 of the applicable restrictive covenants, which

required buildings other than homes to be "concealed from general view to the extent possible." The trial court awarded damages for breach of covenant. On appeal, the court reversed and held that the issue was the reasonableness and good faith of the committee's approval of the homeowners' plans. Thus, "the trial court's determination of a breach of covenant, without a determination that the architectural control committee acted unreasonably or in bad faith, was in error." Norris v. Phillips, 626 P.2d 717 (Colo. App. 1981).

7.   Change in Circumstances

◆ LOEB v. WATKINS
428 Pa. 480, 240 A.2d 513 (1968)

Musmanno, Justice. The problem in this case is simply one of reading the English language, and importing meaning, plus enforceability, to its simple and plain words.

On March 18, 1922, a six-block tract of land in Philadelphia was divided by court decree into 31 parcels, numbered 1 to 31 inclusive. The owners entered into a restrictive agreement, duly recorded in the office of the Recorder of Deeds, which said, *inter alia:*

". . . there should not at any time hereafter be erected or built on any of the thirty-one (31) lots or pieces of ground as shown by the said plan more than two (2) detached private dwelling houses. . . ."

Jerome Balka, owner of one-third of Lot No. 27 erected on it, the land belonging to him, a private dwelling. The defendants in this case, Thomas H. Watkins, Louise Watkins, Artis T. Ray, Jr., and Vivian D. Ray, owners of another one-third of Lot 27, made it known that they were about to construct on their land two additional houses. The plaintiffs in this case, William S. Loeb, Nancy A. Loeb, Jerome Blum, Marilyn K. Blum, Aloysius F. Kurtz, and Marie J. Kurtz, adjoining landowners, who had taken title to their land with the same building restriction sought to be imposed on the defendants, notified, through their attorneys, the defendants that only one house could be erected on their land. The defendants did no building for three years and then resumed their project of erecting two additional homes on Lot 27. The plaintiffs, again through their attorneys, notified the defendants that such action would violate the restriction contained in their deeds.

When the defendants ignored this notice and proceeded to advance their building project, the plaintiffs filed a Complaint in Equity to enjoin construction of more than one house on Lot 27. The Court of Common Pleas of Philadelphia County, after hearing, dismissed the Complaint and the plaintiffs appealed.

The lower court held that the restriction propounded by the defendants expired 25 years after its original promulgation, namely, in 1947. The court came to this conclusion because of a statement in the original restrictive agreement that the owners agreed, each with the other

> that there shall not be for the period of twenty-five years from the date hereof erected or built upon any part of the hereinbefore described lots of ground any buildings or building improvements or improvements designed for use or to be used for other than strictly private or residential purposes without abridging or restricting in any way the general language used it is understood that the words strictly private residential purposes shall not include hotel apartment house or flat purposes nor shall any building hereafter to be erected thereon during said restricted period of twenty-five years be converted from strictly residential to other purposes or uses. . . .

This part of the restrictive covenant obviously describes the type of construction permitted on the land and specifically excludes hotel apartment houses and flats. However, immediately following the 25-year proviso, there appears this plate-glass-clear language: "ALSO that there shall not at any time hereafter be erected or built on any of the thirty-one lots or pieces of ground as shown by the said plan more than two detached private dwelling houses. . . ."

Attention is specifically directed to the capital letters ALSO. The parties emphasized by the use of ALSO that the two-dwelling house interdiction was *in addition* to the 25-year no hotel or flat provision. Thus, the 25-year limitation can by no interpretation of language be considered a modification of the binding restriction that "there shall not *at any time* hereafter" (emphasis supplied) be erected more than two detached private dwelling houses on one lot. *At any time hereafter* certainly denotes a time beyond 25 years. *At any time hereafter* is ominous in its infinity but this is what the owners, one with the other, agreed to. They undoubtedly desired to enjoy plenty of space about their respective dwellings, and wished to exclude any beehive appearance to their community of houses. It is not for the Courts to interfere with this freedom of landowners to use their land as they wish.

The learned Chancellor erred in reducing infinity to 25 years. He erred further in his conclusion that equitable relief should be denied the plaintiffs because they did not show that upholding of the restriction would result in any substantial benefit to them. Who is to say that it will not result in damage to them if the antecedents in title believed a greater enjoyment would be theirs if the tract of land was restricted to 62 private dwellings? Who should say they did not have the right to limit the building operations to that extent? If a covenant running with land proclaims that a lake ornamenting the land must never be destroyed, no successor in title would have the right to argue that the lake is not pretty, the water muddy and no good for fishing, and, therefore, should be drained. Where a man's land is concerned, he may impose, in so far as the imposition does not violate any law or public policy, any restriction he pleases.

Restrictive covenants are enforceable without the necessity of showing that the enforcement would work a substantial gain to the legal beneficiary of the covenant. The plaintiffs' rights here to enforce the restrictive covenant is absolute, regardless of proof that they do or do not suffer damage as a result of the breach of the covenant. . . .

O'BRIEN, Justice (concurring). I concur in the result reached by the majority, but disagree with the view that equity should grant relief even in the absence of any substantial benefit to plaintiffs.

However, I disagree with the dissent's view that no substantial benefit has been shown. The dissent takes the approach that since commercial and apartment uses are now possible, the covenant limiting a lot to two dwelling houses is useless. Such is not the case. While cases are legion holding that a change of neighborhood will preclude enforcement of a covenant, I can find no case that deprives a landowner of his contractual right because of the mere *possibility* of a change of neighborhood. On the contrary, there is authority to the effect that even a continuing pattern of change of neighborhood does not preclude relief where some part of the residential neighborhood still remains. . . .

COHEN, Justice (dissenting). The majority opinion prostitutes equity jurisdiction. As a general rule, equity will not enforce a restrictive covenant which is of no benefit to the dominant tenement or is an absurd, futile, and ineffective attempt to achieve a desired end. . . .

Furthermore, equity will deny relief to a party seeking enforcement of a restrictive covenant "if the harm done by granting the injunction will be disproportionate to the benefit secured thereby." Restatement of Property, §563 (1944). It is important to note that these equitable principles evolved from the legal maxim that restrictions on the use of land are not favored by the law because they constitute an interference with the free use and alienability of real property. . . .

Here the enforcement of the restrictive covenant would result in no benefit, economic or otherwise, to the parties seeking its enforcement. It would be an anachronism to interpose equitable relief in support of a restriction which on the one hand prohibits more than two detached dwelling houses, while at the same time permits every other conceivable use of the property. (The apparent interpretation of the restrictive covenant now permits the property to be utilized for apartment complexes and/or commercial or industrial purposes.)

Assuming *arguendo* that such an absurd result actually was intended by the contracting parties, equity, nevertheless, should not support the enforcement of a covenant which, now, due to the expiration of the other use restrictions, makes little, if any, sense, involves no benefit to the property owner seeking its enforcement, and only serves to seriously hamper a reasonable use of the property. When the twenty-five year period expired eliminating the other use restrictions, the usefulness and benefit of the proviso prohibiting more than two detached private dwellings likewise expired. The fact that a technical violation of the agreement may be committed is not sufficient under this covenant to warrant a court of equity to enjoin such a violation.

Notes

1. A 1952 deed restriction barred any "trailer house, secondhand cars [or] junk yard." Defendant installed a $4,100 mobile home on a steel foundation. The court said: "Whether injunctive relief will be granted to restrain the violation of restrictions is a matter within the sound discretion of the trial court to be determined in the light of all the facts and circumstances." It recognized the existence of "numerous violations of the restrictive covenants — used, secondhand or previously constructed houses and buildings . . . property . . . used for business purposes; and other trailer houses and secondhand cars. . . ." Concluding that enforcement of the restriction against defendants would be "inequitable and without appreciable benefit to property in the restricted area," and that "in relation to other houses in the neighborhood, [the mobile home's] attractiveness cannot be disputed," the court affirmed denial of an injunction against the mobile home. The dissenting justice found the asserted violations of the covenants to be "puny," and demanded enforcement of "the plain and unambiguous restriction." Hecht v. Stephens, 204 Kan. 559, 464 P.2d 258 (1970).

2. In 1912, a rectangular tract of approximately eight continuous blocks was subdivided and laid out for residential purposes. Known as Wellington Square, and situated about five miles from the heart of Los Angeles, the property was divided into 397 lots. Covenants were inserted in all deeds, prohibiting until the year 1960 the construction of any structures but residences.

Defendant, who purchased Lot 27 in 1920, conceded the validity of the restrictive covenants but claimed that the character of the surrounding neighborhood had changed. Lot 27 is a border lot, abutting West Adams Street and facing an unrestricted area. At the time of purchase, there was a large Chinese vegetable garden across the street, on unrestricted property. During the year preceding the trial, however, business buildings had been erected in place of the garden. The California Supreme Court affirmed refusal of an injunction preventing defendant from completing his store building. Justice Richards, dissenting, emphasized that the defendant's sole excuse for his breach of the express conditions, covenants, and restrictions of his grant is that the lands and lots of an adjoining tract across the street from one side of this restricted area, and which constitutes an unrestricted area, are being devoted in part to business purposes. There is no evidence in the case showing that the other three sides of this restricted subdivision have been invaded by business or are other than residential in character, nor is there any evidence that the unrestricted tract on Adams Street opposite the defendant's lot has been wholly devoted to business establishments. In fact, the evidence is to the contrary. We have the condition as shown by the practically undisputed evidence wherein the defendant, because some places of business have been erected in an unrestricted area across the street from him, claims the right to put a store upon his lot within the restricted area, in violation of the covenants and restrictions of his deed, the effect of which, if permitted, will inevitably be to open the way to such an invasion of Wellington Square by stores, garages, service stations, apartment and lodging houses and other forbidden structures and uses as would ere long entirely destroy the restrictive covenants upon which residential owners of property within this area purchased and have improved and enjoyed their restrictive holding therein. [Downs v. Kroeger, 200 Cal. 743, 254 P. 1101 (1927).]

3. In the case of a large subdivision, who should be entrusted with administration of the common plan? Increasingly, the choice has turned toward the community association. This arrangement raises questions of enforcement by an institution that does not have an interest in land, and of pre-emption by the association of all enforcement rights so as to foreclose individual suits. Is Columbia Park and Recreation Association, Inc., conceived of as an organization that would serve as representative and protector of the interests of the people of Columbia even though residents have so little power over the corporation? Compare the operations of such an association with those of a city council. Does the association become government by contract? Do some kinds of private property rights become the equivalent of the right to govern? Should exercise of such power be subject to constitutional limitations? Is the method of enforcing decisions the chief distinction between public and private land-use control authority?

◆ BLAKELEY v. GORIN
365 Mass. 590, 313 N.E.2d 903 (1974)

HENNESSEY, Justice. . . . The petitioners, owners of a parcel of land subject to certain restrictions known as the Commonwealth Restrictions, seek a determination and declaration that the restrictions are obsolete and unenforceable. . . .

The Commonwealth Restrictions date from the middle of the last century. By 1850 the condition of the tidal flats which composed the area now known as the Back Bay had become a nuisance, largely due to drainage problems. The Commonwealth determined to fill in the area and sell lots for dwellings, subject to restrictions in conformity with a comprehensive land use plan.

With some exceptions and minor variations the same stipulations and agreements were inserted into all the deeds to land in the Back Bay district, from the Commonwealth as grantor to various private grantees, beginning in 1857.

General Laws c.184, §30, on which the petitioners rely, provides that no restriction shall be enforced or declared to be enforceable unless it is determined that the restriction is, at the time of the proceeding, of actual and substantial benefit to a person claiming rights of enforcement. Further, even if a restriction is found to be of such benefit, it shall not be enforced except by award of money damages if any of several enumerated conditions are found to exist.[2]

The facts are as follows. The petitioners are the owners of two parcels of land separated by Public Alley No. 437; the first is known as 2, 4, 6, 8 and 10 Commonwealth Avenue and the second as 13-15 Arlington Street and 1, 3, and 5 Newbury Street. The former is presently a vacant lot; the latter is the site of the Ritz-Carlton Hotel. Both are subject to various of the Commonwealth Restrictions. The petitioners plan to build on the former lot a 285 foot high hotel-apartment building, with a twelve-story structure as a bridge over the alley, connecting it with the Ritz-Carlton. Plans call for the new building to contain such restaurant and shopping facilities as are usually incidental to the running of a large hotel, and an underground garage for off-street parking as required by the Boston Zoning Code.

The respondents are the owners of 12-14 Commonwealth Avenue, a parcel which is adjacent to the petitioners' vacant lot and backs on the

2. Those conditions are as follows:
(1) changes in the character of the properties affected or their neighborhood, in available construction materials or techniques, in access, services or facilities, in applicable public controls of land use or construction, or in any other conditions or circumstances, which reduce materially the need for the restriction or the likelihood of the restriction accomplishing its original purposes or render it obsolete or inequitable to enforce except by award of money damages, or (2) conduct of persons from time to time entitled to enforce the restriction has rendered it inequitable to enforce except by award of money damages, or (3) in case of a common scheme the land of the person claiming rights of enforcement is for any reason no longer subject to the restriction or the parcel against which rights of enforcement are claimed is not in a group of parcels still subject to the restriction and appropriate for accomplishment of its purposes, or (4) continuation of the restriction on the parcel against which enforcement is claimed or on parcels remaining in a common scheme with it or subject to like restrictions would impede reasonable use of land for purposes for which it is most suitable, and would tend to impair the growth of the neighborhood or municipality in a manner inconsistent with the public interest or to contribute to deterioration of properties or to result in decadent or substandard areas or blighted open areas, or (5) enforcement, except by award of money damages, is for any other reason inequitable or not in the public interest.

PHOTOGRAPH 20-4
Ritz Hotel on left, site for addition on right (1977)

PHOTOGRAPH 20-5
Ritz Hotel and addition (1984)

same alley. This property contains an eight-story building with eight apartments on each floor except the first, half facing Commonwealth Avenue and half the alley in back, half (the corner apartments) being of two rooms and half efficiency apartments. The thirty-two rear apartments derive their principal light and air from one window in each apartment on the alley.

Among the restrictions contained in the original deeds to the parcel numbered 4, 6, 8 and 10 Commonwealth Avenue are the following:

[a] That a passageway, sixteen feet wide, is to be laid out in the rear of the premises, the same to be filled in by the Commonwealth, and to be kept open and maintained by the abutters in common . . . [b] That any building erected on the premises . . . shall not in any event be used . . . for any . . . mercantile . . . purposes . . . [c] That any building erected on the premises . . . shall not in any event be used for a stable . . . [d] That no cellar or lower floor of any building shall be placed more than four feet below the level of the Mill Dam, as fixed by the top surface of the hammered stone at the Southeasterly corner of the emptying sluices. [e] That the front wall [of any building erected on the premises] . . . shall be set back twenty feet . . . provided that steps, windows, porticoes, and other usual projections appurtenant thereto, are to be allowed in said reserved space of twenty feet.

Among the restrictions contained in the original deed to the parcel numbered 2 Commonwealth Avenue are the same restrictions as those applicable to the parcel numbered 4, 6, 8, and 10 Commonwealth Avenue except that any building constructed thereon shall be set back from Commonwealth Avenue twenty-two feet, rather than twenty feet as stipulated for 4, 6, 8, and 10 Commonwealth Avenue. Among the restrictions contained in the original deeds to the parcels numbered 13-15 Arlington Street and 1, 3, and 5 Newbury Street is the following: "That a passageway, Sixteen feet wide, is to be laid out in the rear of the premises, the same to be filled in by the Commonwealth, and to be kept open and maintained by the abutters in common. . . ."

We have found no error in the judge's decision that none of these restrictions shall be enforced, except in so far as he found that no damages shall be awarded. We note that the most difficult aspect of this case concerns the passageway. There will be no obstruction to the movements of persons or vehicles, since the bridge between the Ritz-Carlton building and the new building will start at a point thirteen feet above the ground. Nevertheless, the bridge will occupy most of the space between the two buildings for a height of twelve stories, with consequent effect on light and air. For this reason we have determined, as discussed later in this opinion, that damages are to be awarded for loss of light and air. . . .

The respondents argue briefly, almost without discussion, that G.L.

c. 184, §30, is unconstitutional or has been unconstitutionally applied. The dissenting Justices in this case conclude that the statute is unconstitutional. We believe that the statute is constitutional and was constitutionally applied here. . . .

Equity does not invariably and automatically grant specific enforcement of such restrictions on the use of land. While the usual grounds for denying such enforcement in a case involving real property is laches, or other inequitable conduct by the party seeking to enforce the restriction, this need not always be the case. The Restatement: Property, §563 (1944), would deny enforcement, apparently without compensation, if the "harm done by granting the injunction will be disproportionate to the benefit secured thereby." The official comments, while suggesting that the standard be a "disproportion . . . of considerable magnitude," do not even consider the possibility that such a limitation of remedies could conflict with the constitutional mandate of the taking clause.

The United States Supreme Court has never considered that every government regulation impinging directly or indirectly on property rights would constitute a "taking" of property in the constitutional sense. As long ago as 1885 Mr. Justice Gray stated in Head v. Amoskeag Mfg. Co., 113 U.S. 9, 21 (1885), that "[w]hen property, in which several persons have a common interest, cannot be fully and beneficially enjoyed in its existing condition, the law often provides a way in which they may compel one another to submit to measures necessary to secure its beneficial enjoyment, making equitable compensation to any whose control of or interest in the property is thereby modified." While the court there dealt with conflicting water rights and the opinion used partition of a joint tenancy as an example, the language is equally apposite to the situation in the present case. See also Euclid v. Ambler Realty Co., 272 U.S. 365 (1926) (zoning constitutional although it greatly decreases value of land). Just this year, in another zoning case, the Supreme Court restated the proposition of Mr. Justice Holmes that "property rights may be cut down, and to that extent taken, without pay." Belle Terre v. Boraas, 416 U.S. 1 (1974), quoting Block v. Hirsh, 256 U.S. 135 (1921).

To rule that G.L. c.184, §30, is unconstitutional would raise to a constitutional right the ordinary rule of equity that property interests may be enforced by a decree of specific performance. This result, by removing the discretion inherent in courts of equity to determine whether to grant specific performance, would reverse legal precedents even older than the Commonwealth Restrictions themselves. . . .

Changes in law and circumstances since the time of the creation of the Commonwealth Restrictions militate in favor of adopting the view that the statute circumscribes remedies rather than "takes" land. With the advent of zoning and the growth of numerous public regulatory bodies, the use of land has been controlled for the most part by public law rather than private restrictions. . . .

Even assuming that c.184, §30, is viewed as allowing a taking of property in this case, we believe the taking would be constitutional. . . .

The statute in question here was clearly passed to promote the "reasonable use of land for purposes for which it is most suitable," as well as to increase the marketability of real estate which may be impaired by obsolete restrictions. These are proper purposes, of great benefit and utility to the public, which justify the taking of property interests of the kind at issue here. The parcel of land in question here has been vacant for over a decade. By the operation of this statute a large apartment-hotel complex may be built upon it, providing numerous benefits to the general public, not the least being its effect on the tax base. That the owner of the land may also benefit as a private party is irrelevant. If this situation constitutes a taking we cannot say it was accomplished for a purely private purpose. . . .

As to the restriction against mercantile uses, we conclude that the proposed hotel would not violate the restriction against use for "mechanical, mercantile or manufacturing purposes." The judge's finding to the contrary was plainly wrong. In a case analyzing the identical phrases in another deed we held that mercantile use was limited to buying and selling commercial commodities for a profit, and did not include the operation of a private hospital. As the hotel and apartment use is permissible, the incidental use of a small portion of the building for shops would not in any case be deemed to create a violation of the restriction. We need not consider the petitioners' further argument that the major changes that have occurred in the neighborhood largely destroy the utility of the restriction against mercantile uses.

The final restriction is that mandating that the passageway behind the petitioners' lot, now Public Alley No. 437, shall "be kept open." The judge found, on evidence which clearly supports his findings, that the respondents have an actual and substantial benefit in the enforcement of this restriction and that the proposed building would violate it. However, his further findings that the restriction is obsolete and that the respondents are entitled to only nominal damages are plainly wrong. We nevertheless hold that, even though it is not obsolete, the restriction shall not be specifically enforced. . . . In lieu of specific enforcement, damages are to be awarded.

Considerable and conflicting evidence was adduced at trial as to the potential effect that bridging the alley would have on the light and air available to the apartments in the rear of the respondents' building. It appears that all parties are in agreement that the "bridge" would decrease the direct sunlight available to the apartments; the dispute is as to the magnitude of the decrease. The testimony on ambient light and on available air was conflicting as to whether there would be an increase or a decrease. Clearly there would be some effect on the property. There was testimony to support a finding that the effect would not be *de minimis* but would be substantial. . . .

Applying [the criteria of c.184, §30], we observe that the evidence shows, *inter alia*, that the properties and the neighborhood have drastically changed. Single-family residences have been replaced by moderately high-rise buildings for apartments and institutional use. We have found that the passageway restriction is of an actual and substantial benefit in its effect on light and air, but the proposed bridge will have only a modest impact in view of the drastic changes which have already occurred. In particular, an occupant of the respondents' building, in looking out a rear window of that structure, would see to his immediate left and across the passageway the high-rise Ritz-Carlton building. As to the petitioners' unused land to that viewer's immediate left, on the same side of the passageway, it seems inevitable that, even if the bridge were not permitted, a building higher than the respondents' building would at some time be constructed on it.

Further, since this restriction was first imposed, public controls have been imposed which tend to preempt the restriction in a manner contemplated by §30. At least three different public authorities have been given control over the basic design structure of buildings on premises subject to the restrictions. Also, a public commission of the city has been given authority, with the approval of the mayor, to permit bridging over public alleys. Additionally, at least three zoning variances will have to be procured before the entire structure can be completed.

The record also clearly supports a conclusion that continued enforcement of the restriction would tend to impede reasonable use of the land for purposes for which it is most suitable. The uncontradicted evidence was that a free standing tower is economically unfeasible presumably because of the small size of the parcel, and that the plaintiffs' proposal for an apartment-hotel complex connected to the adjacent Ritz-Carlton is the most suitable use of the land.

The evidence supports a conclusion that the proposed bridge is not an arbitrary and unnecessarily large intrusion. The twelve stories of the bridge relate to twelve of the lower floors of the new building which are to be used as a hotel; above those floors there will be apartments. The hotel floors are feasible only if connected to the hotel services of the Ritz Carlton. Therefore, all considerations of equity, and the most suitable use of the property, support the planned bridge construction in size as well as purpose.

Weighing and comparing the interests of the parties and the public in accordance with the several provisions of §30 brings us almost inevitably to the conclusion that there should be no specific enforcement. In the words of provision (5) of the statute, which unquestionably confers the broadest discretion on the court, enforcement here would be inequitable and not in the public interest. The magnitude of the harm to the petitioners in specific enforcement of the restriction far exceeds that to the respondents in its denial. Moreover we are mandated by the statute to have due regard for the public interest in determining the manner of enforcement of a restriction. The land in question has been vacant for over a decade. We take judicial notice of the exceedingly high property tax rates current in the city of Boston and the beneficial effect on the tax base of the petitioners' plan to construct a multimillion dollar project of public usefulness on presently unutilized land. In the circumstances both the balance of equities between the parties and a consideration of the public interest require that the respondents accept money damages by way of enforcement of this restriction. . . .

QUIRICO, Justice (dissenting, with whom REARDON, J. joins). I am unable to agree with the decision of the court. I disagree principally with the decision that G.L. c.184, §30, inserted by St. 1961, c.448, §1, is constitutional as applied in this case and that in this proceeding, which is brought under the terms of such statute, the respondents may be deprived of valuable property rights and be required or permitted to accept money damages in lieu thereof. I also disagree with certain factual conclusions reached by the court in its opinion. . . .

It appears that, as originally conceived, the set-back restriction was primarily intended to insure the continued existence and enjoyment of unobstructed open spaces between the Commonwealth Avenue street lines and the fronts of buildings along the street. . . .

. . . In upholding the constitutionality of G.L. c.184, §30, in this case I believe the court has placed in the hands of private persons, in this instance the petitioners, the power to take from their neighbors an interest in real estate without the latter's consent, not for any public use or purpose but solely for the petitioners' own private gain and profit. . . .

In reaching this conclusion, I am not, as the court implies, exalting "the discretionary remedy" of specific performance "into a constitutional right," and thereby limiting or removing the traditional and inherent discretion of the equity court. I, of course, recognize that specific enforcement is not a remedy that is "invariably and automatically" granted and, in particular, I do not mean to suggest that the Commonwealth Restrictions must be enforced in perpetuity against all lots in the Back Bay area to which they were made applicable more than a century ago. Even before the passage of G.L. c.184, §30, equitable restrictions found to be of no continuing value because of changed conditions would not be specifically enforced. But c.184, §30, presents a very different situation. The statute explicitly prohibits the granting of specific enforcement even as to a restriction which is of actual and substantial value to a person claiming its benefit when any one of a broad range of factors is found to exist. It is the statute itself which is setting new limits on the sound discretion of the trial judge as well as effecting a radical — and to my mind, unconstitutional — change in the substantive law of property.

Note

The Cogliano brothers sought to be relieved of a covenant restricting use of their land to uses that had been permitted by the city zoning bylaws when the property was purchased. They pointed to a number of industrial developments on unrestricted land nearby, claiming that the character of the neighborhood had changed substantially in the 17 years since their purchase of the property. The Massachusetts Supreme Judicial Court declined to remove the restrictions. The court noted that there was evidence that the Coglianos were considering selling their land and that its value would be enhanced through removal of the restrictions. Further, the court concluded:

> By the decree [of the lower court dismissing the petition] the Coglianos were asked to do no more that live up to covenants they voluntarily undertook and which figured to reduce the price they paid for the land. On this land they were living and doing a profitable business. There was no stringency existing or in immediate prospect that would make continuance of the current restriction unfair to them. And there was a public interest in keeping the locus residential even though some industrial uses were allowed nearby. [Cogliano v. Lyman, 370 Mass. 508, 348 N.E.2d 765, (1976).]

C.   CONTROLLING CONTRACTUAL DISCRIMINATION

◆ SHELLEY v. KRAEMER
334 U.S. 1 (1948)

Mr. Chief Justice VINSON delivered the opinion of the Court. These cases present for our consideration questions relating to the validity of court enforcement of private agreements, generally described as restrictive covenants, which have as their purpose the exclusion of persons of designated race or color from the ownership or occupancy or real property. Basic constitutional issues of obvious importance have been raised.

The first of these cases comes to this Court on *certiorari* to the Supreme Court of Missouri. On February 16, 1911, thirty out of a total of thirty-nine owners of property fronting both sides of Labadie Avenue between Taylor Avenue and Cora Avenue in the city of St. Louis, signed an agreement, which was subsequently recorded, providing in part:

> . . . the said property is hereby restricted to the use and occupancy for the term of Fifty (50) years from this date, so that it shall be a condition all the time and whether recited and referred to as [*sic*] not in subsequent conveyances and shall attach to the land as a condition precedent to the

sale of the same, that hereafter no part of said property or any portion thereof shall be, for said term of Fifty-years, occupied by any person not of the Caucasian race, it being intended hereby to restrict the use of said property for said period of time against the occupancy as owners or tenants of any portion of said property for resident or other purpose by people of the Negro or Mongolian Race.

The entire district described in the agreement included fifty-seven parcels of land. The thirty owners who signed the agreement held title to forty-seven parcels, including the particular parcel involved in this case. At the time the agreement was signed, five of the parcels in the district were owned by Negroes. One of those had been occupied by Negro families since 1882, nearly thirty years before the restrictive agreement was executed. The trial court found that owners of seven out of nine homes on the south side of Labadie Avenue, within the restricted district and "in the immediate vicinity" of the premises in question, had failed to sign the restrictive agreement in 1911. At the time this action was brought, four of the premises were occupied by Negroes, and had been so occupied for periods ranging from twenty-three to sixty-three years. A fifth parcel had been occupied by Negroes until a year before this suit was instituted.

On August 11, 1945, pursuant to a contract of sale, petitioners Shelley, who are Negroes, for valuable consideration received from one Fitzgerald a warranty deed to the parcel in question.[1] The trial court found that petitioners had no actual knowledge of the restrictive agreement at the time of the purchase.

On October 9, 1945, respondents, as owners of other property subject to the terms of the restrictive covenant, brought suit in the Circuit Court of the city of St. Louis praying that petitioners Shelley be restrained from taking possession of the property and that judgment be entered divesting title out of petitioners Shelley and revesting title in the immediate grantor or in such other person as the court should direct. The trial court denied the requested relief on the ground that the restrictive agreement, upon which respondents based their action, had never become final and complete because it was the intention of the parties to that agreement that it was not to become effective until signed by all property owners in the district, and signatures of all the owners had never been obtained.

The Supreme Court of Missouri sitting *en banc* reversed and directed the trial court to grant the relief for which respondents had prayed. That court held the agreement effective and concluded that enforcement of its

1. The trial court found that title to the property which petitioners Shelley sought to purchase was held by one Bishop, a real estate dealer, who placed the property in the name of Josephine Fitzgerald. Bishop, who acted as agent for petitioners in the purchase, concealed the fact of his ownership.

provisions violated no rights guaranteed to petitioners by the Federal Constitution. At the time the court rendered its decision, petitioners were occupying the property in question. . . .

It cannot be doubted that among the civil rights intended to be protected from discriminatory state action by the Fourteenth Amendment are the rights to acquire, enjoy, own and dispose of property. Equality in the enjoyment of property rights was regarded by the framers of that Amendment as an essential pre-condition to the realization of other basic civil rights and liberties which the Amendment was intended to guarantee. Thus, §1978 of the Revised Statutes, derived from §1 of the Civil Rights Act of 1866 which was enacted by Congress while the Fourteenth Amendment was also under consideration, provides: "All citizens of the United States shall have the same right, in every State and Territory, as is enjoyed by white citizens thereof to inherit, purchase, lease, sell, hold, and convey real and personal property." This Court has given specific recognition to the same principle. Buchanan v. Warley, 245 U.S. 60 (1917).

It is likewise clear that restrictions on the right of occupancy of the sort sought to be created by the private agreements in these cases could not be squared with the requirements of the Fourteenth Amendment if imposed by state statute or local ordinance. We do not understand respondents to urge the contrary. In the case of Buchanan v. Warley, *supra*, a unanimous Court declared unconstitutional the provisions of a city ordinance which denied to colored persons the right to occupy houses in blocks in which the greater number of houses were occupied by white persons, and imposed similar restrictions on white persons with respect to blocks in which the greater number of houses were occupied by colored persons. During the course of the opinion in that case, this Court stated: "The Fourteenth Amendment and these statutes enacted in furtherance of its purpose operate to qualify and entitle a colored man to acquire property without state legislation discriminating against him solely because of color." . . .

Since the decision of this Court in the Civil Rights Cases, 109 U.S. 3 (1883), the principle has become firmly embedded in our constitutional law that the action inhibited by the first section of the Fourteenth Amendment is only such action as may fairly be said to be that of the States. That Amendment erects no shield against merely private conduct, however discriminatory or wrongful.

We conclude, therefore, that the restrictive agreements standing alone cannot be regarded as violative of any rights guaranteed to petitioners by the Fourteenth Amendment. So long as the purposes of those agreements are effectuated by voluntary adherence to their terms, it would appear clear that there has been no action by the State and the provisions of the Amendment have not been violated.

But here there was more. These are cases in which the purposes of the agreements were secured only by judicial enforcement by state courts of the restrictive terms of the agreements. The respondents urge that judicial enforcement of private agreements does not amount to state action; or, in any event, the participation of the State is so attenuated in character as not to amount to state action within the meaning of the Fourteenth Amendment. . . .

We have no doubt that there has been state action in these cases in the full and complete sense of the phrase. The undisputed facts disclose that petitioners were willing purchasers of properties upon which they desired to establish homes. The owners of the properties were willing sellers; and contracts of sale were accordingly consummated. It is clear that but for the active intervention of the state courts, supported by the full panoply of state power, petitioners would have been free to occupy the properties in question without restraint.

These are not cases, as has been suggested, in which the States have merely abstained from action, leaving private individuals free to impose such discriminations as they see fit. Rather, these are cases in which the States have made available to such individuals the full coercive power of government to deny to petitioners, on the grounds of race or color, the enjoyment of property rights in premises which petitioners are willing and financially able to acquire and which the grantors are willing to sell. The difference between judicial enforcement and the nonenforcement of the restrictive covenants is the difference to petitioners between being denied rights of property available to other members of the community and being accorded full enjoyment of those rights on an equal footing. . . .

Respondents urge, however, that since the state courts stand ready to enforce restrictive covenants excluding white persons from the ownership or occupancy of property covered by such agreements, enforcement of covenants excluding colored persons may not be deemed a denial of equal protection of the laws to the colored persons who are thereby affected. This contention does not bear scrutiny. The parties have directed our attention to no case in which a court, state or federal, has been called upon to enforce a covenant excluding members of the white majority from ownership or occupancy of real property on grounds of race or color. But there are more fundamental considerations. The rights created by the first section of the Fourteenth Amendment are, by its terms, guaranteed to the individual. The rights established are personal rights. It is, therefore, no answer to these petitioners to say that the courts may also be induced to deny white persons rights of ownership and occupancy on grounds of race or color. Equal protection of the laws is not achieved through indiscriminate imposition of inequalities. . . .

For the reasons stated, the judgment of the Supreme Court of Missouri . . . must be reversed.

Mr. Justice Reed, Mr. Justice Jackson, and Mr. Justice Rutledge took no part in the consideration or decision of these cases.

Notes

1. In Northwest Real Estate Co. v. Serio, 156 Md. 229, 144 A. 245 (1929), the challenged covenant read:

> And for the purpose of maintaining the property hereby conveyed and the surrounding property as a desirable high class residential section for themselves their successors, heirs, executors, administrators and assigns that until January 1, 1932, no owner of the land hereby conveyed shall have the right to sell or rent the same without written consent of the grantor herein which shall have the right to pass upon the character desirability and other qualifications of the proposed purchaser or occupant of the property. . . .

The majority held it void. In his dissenting opinion, Bond, C.J., stated:

> The restraint upon alienation included in the deed . . . seems clearly enough to be one intended merely to give the developer of a suburban area of land power to control the character of the development for a time long enough to secure a return of his capital outlay, and to give early purchasers of lots and buildings some security in their own outlay. In those objects there is nothing against the public interest. We can hardly hold that the modern method of developing city or suburban areas as single large enterprises is detrimental to the public. On the contrary, it seems to be often the only method by which such areas can be conveniently and economically opened, so that houses may be provided upon convenient terms, with all the neighborhood necessities of streets, sewers, and the like ready at the outset. The venture of capital for this purpose appears to be distinctly a public benefit rather than a detriment, one which it is to the public advantage to encourage and promote rather than to hinder. But we know that there are real, substantial dangers to be feared in such ventures, and that, under the modern conditions of rapid city growth and rapid shifts of city populations, one of the most important risks is probably that which comes from the chance of invasion into the new neighborhood of an element of the population which the people to whom the developer must look for the return of his outlay will regard as out of harmony with them. However fanciful may be the aversions which give rise to it, and however deplorable they may be, to the developer they and their consequences must be as real as destructive physical forces. And, if it is to the public interest that this method of development be encouraged rather than hindered, then practically there must be a public gain in removal or diminution of this deterring danger. And the temporary restraint on alienation which the parties here involved have adopted to that end must, I think, be viewed as in point of fact reasonable, and from the

standpoint of the public interest actually desirable. And, if this is true, then I venture to think there is no substantial reason why the law should interfere with it, denying the parties the right to agree as they have agreed, or denying their agreement full validity.

2. In holding void a covenant reading "Land not to be sold to Jews or persons of objectionable nationality," the court in Re Drummond Wren, [1945] Ont. 778, [1945] 4 D.L.R. 674, after quoting from the Atlantic Charter, the United Nations Charter, and statements of Roosevelt, Churchill, and DeGaulle, concluded:

> How far this is obnoxious to public policy can only be ascertained by projecting the coverage of the covenant with respect both to the classes of persons whom it may adversely affect, and to the lots or subdivisions of land to which it may be attached. So considered, the consequences of judicial approbation of such a covenant are portentous. If sale of a piece of land can be prohibited to Jews, it can equally be prohibited to Protestants, Catholics or other groups or denominations. If the sale of one piece of land can be so prohibited, the sale of other pieces of land can likewise be prohibited. In my opinion, nothing could be more calculated to create or deepen divisions between existing religions and ethnic groups in this province, or in this country, than the sanction of a method of land transfer which would permit the segregation and confinement of particular groups to particular business or residential areas. . . . The unlikelihood of such a policy as a legislative measure is evident from the contrary intention of the recently enacted Racial Discrimination Act, and the judicial branch of government must take full cognizance of such factors.
>
> Ontario, and Canada too, may well be termed a province, and a country, of minorities in regard to the religious and ethnic groups which live therein. It appears to me to be a moral duty, at least, to lend aid to all forces of cohesion, and similarly to repel all fissiparous tendencies which would imperil national unity. The common law courts have, by their actions over the years, obviated the need for rigid constitutional guarantees in our policy by their wise use of the doctrine of public policy as an active agent in the promotion of the public weal. While courts and eminent judges have, in view of the powers of our legislatures, warned against inventing new heads of public policy, I do not conceive that I would be breaking new ground were I to hold the restrictive covenant impugned in this proceeding to be void as against public policy. Rather would I be applying well recognized principles of public policy to a set of facts requiring their invocation in the interest of the public good. . . . If the common law of treason encompasses the stirring up of hatred between different classes of His Majesty's subjects, the common law of public policy is surely adequate to void the restrictive covenant which is here attacked.
>
> My conclusion therefore is that the covenant is void because offensive to the public policy of this jurisdiction. This conclusion is reinforced, if reinforcement is necessary, by the wide official acceptance of international

policies and declarations frowning on the type of discrimination which the covenant would seem to perpetuate.

3. Racial covenants prohibiting the sale of real estate to minority groups, or its occupancy by them, were only sporadic before the great migration of blacks to the cities in both the North and the South in the 1920s. The only case decided prior to 1915 was Gandolfo v. Hartman, 49 Fed. 181 (C.C.S.D. Cal. 1892); a covenant restricting use to other than "Chinamen" was invalidated because it violated the Fourteenth Amendment and, alternatively, because it was contrary to the treaty with China. But this decision was ignored in subsequent cases. Prior to Shelley v. Kraemer the problem had been presented to the courts of 20 states and the District of Columbia. The arguments proposed were as varied as those used in the Canadian courts: repugnant to a fee, void under the rule against perpetuities, against public policy, and lacking in equity. But the width of the attack seemed like a Don Quixote tilting at the windmill: The courts generally rejected these arguments. Covenants against use and occupancy were upheld almost universally, while those against alienation were deemed valid by most courts.

In the companion case to *Shelley*, Hurd v. Hodge, 334 U.S. 24 (1948), the *Shelley* doctrine was extended to the District of Columbia, based on the Civil Rights Act, 14 Stat. 27 (1866), and on the contention that the enforcement of these covenants was against the public policy of the United States. In view of the Canadian courts' efforts (and Mr. Justice Frankfurter's concurring opinion in Hurd v. Hodge), why was "policy" not employed as the ground for decision in *Shelley*?

Shelley had specifically not declared restrictive covenants illegal. ("We conclude, therefore, that the restrictive agreements standing alone cannot be regarded as violative of any rights guaranteed to petitioners by the Fourteenth Amendment." 334 U.S. at 13.) The supreme courts of Missouri and Oklahoma held that an award of damages for breach of a racial restrictive covenant did not violate any constitutional right. A federal district court in Michigan reached the opposite conclusion. Barrows v. Jackson, 346 U.S. 249 (1953), ended the possibility of recovery; it held that such a covenant could not be enforced at law for damages. Chief Justice Vinson dissented on the ground that the rights of the person discriminated against were not involved.

4. Homeowners' association sued, alleging that use of a leased dwelling to house eight severely retarded adults violated single-family covenants. The court of appeals said that such a use was not single-family use, but that the covenant could not be enforced in equity because "to do so would contravene a long-standing public policy favoring . . . such residences." Crane Neck Association, Inc. v. New York City/ Long Island County Services Group, 61 N.Y.2d 154, 460 N.E.2d 1336, 472 N.Y.S.2d 901 (1984).

◆ JONES v. ALFRED H. MAYER CO.
392 U.S. 409 (1968)

Mr. Justice STEWART delivered the opinion of the Court. In this case we are called upon to determine the scope and constitutionality of an Act of Congress, 42 U.S.C. §1982, which provides that: "All citizens of the United States shall have the same right, in every State and Territory, as is enjoyed by white citizens thereof to inherit, purchase, lease, sell, hold, and convey real and personal property."

On September 2, 1965, the petitioners filed a complaint in the District Court for the Eastern District of Missouri, alleging that the respondents had refused to sell them a home in the Paddock Woods community of St. Louis County for the sole reason that petitioner Joseph Lee Jones is a Negro. Relying in part upon §1982, the petitioners sought injunctive and other relief. The District Court sustained the respondents' motion to dismiss the complaint, and the Court of Appeals for the Eighth Circuit affirmed, concluding that §1982 applies only to state action and does not reach private refusals to sell. We granted *certiorari* to consider the questions thus presented. For the reasons that follow, we reverse the judgment of the Court of Appeals. We hold that §1982 bars *all* racial discrimination, private as well as public, in the sale or rental of property, and that the statute, thus construed, is a valid exercise of the power of Congress to enforce the Thirteenth Amendment.

At the outset, it is important to make clear precisely what this case does *not* involve. Whatever else it may be, 42 U.S.C. §1982 is not a comprehensive open housing law. In sharp contrast to the Fair Housing Title (Title VIII) of the Civil Rights Act of 1968, Pub. L. 90-284, 82 Stat. 81, the statute in this case deals only with racial discrimination and does not address itself to discrimination on grounds of religion or national origin. It does not deal specifically with discrimination in the provision of services or facilities in connection with the sale or rental of a dwelling. It does not prohibit advertising or other representations that indicate discriminatory preferences. It does not refer explicitly to discrimination in financing arrangements or in the provision of brokerage services. It does not empower a federal administrative agency to assist aggrieved parties. It makes no provision for intervention by the Attorney General. And, although it can be enforced by injunction, it contains no provision expressly authorizing a federal court to order the payment of damages. . . .

We begin with the language of the statute itself. In plain and unambiguous terms, §1982 grants to all citizens, without regard to race or color, "the same right" to purchase and lease property "as is enjoyed by white citizens." As the Court of Appeals in this case evidently recognized, that right can be impaired as effectively by "those who place property on the market" as by the State itself. For, even if the State and its agents lend no support to those who wish to exclude persons from their communities on racial grounds, the fact remains that, whenever property "is placed on the market for whites only, whites have a right denied to Negroes." So long as a Negro citizen who wants to buy or rent a home can be turned away simply because he is not white, he cannot be said to enjoy "the *same* right . . . as is enjoyed by white citizens . . . to . . . purchase [and] lease . . . real and personal property." 42 U.S.C. §1982. (Emphasis added.)

On its face, therefore, §1982 appears to prohibit *all* discrimination against Negroes in the sale or rental of property. . . .

Stressing what they consider to be the revolutionary implications of so literal a reading of §1982, the respondents argue that Congress cannot possibly have intended any such result. Our examination of the relevant history, however, persuades us that Congress meant exactly what it said. . . .

The remaining question is whether Congress has power under the Constitution to do what §1982 purports to do: to prohibit all racial discrimination, private and public, in the sale and rental of property. Our starting point is the Thirteeth Amendment, for it was pursuant to that constitutional provision that Congress originally enacted what is now §1982. The Amendment consists of two parts. Section 1 states: "Neither slavery nor involuntary servitude, except as a punishment for crime whereby the party shall have been duly convicted, shall exist within the United States, or any place subject to their jurisdiction." Section 2 provides: "Congress shall have power to enforce this article by appropriate legislation."

As its text reveals, the Thirteenth Amendment "is not a mere prohibition of state laws establishing or upholding slavery, but an absolute declaration that slavery or involuntary servitude shall not exist in any part of the United States." Civil Rights Cases, 109 U.S. 3, 20. . . . It has never been doubted, therefore, "that the power vested in Congress to enforce the article by appropriate legislation," ibid., includes the power to enact laws "direct and primary, operating upon the acts of individuals, whether sanctioned by state legislation or not." Id., at 23. . . .

Thus, the fact that §1982 operates upon the unofficial acts of private individuals, whether or not sanctioned by state law, presents no constitutional problem. If Congress has power under the Thirteenth Amendment to eradicate conditions that prevent Negroes from buying and renting property because of their race or color, then no federal statute calculated to achieve that objective can be thought to exceed the constitutional power of Congress simply because it reaches beyond state action to regulate the conduct of private individuals. The constitutional question in this case, therefore, comes to this: Does the authority of Congress to enforce the Thirteenth Amendment "by appropriate legislation" include the power to eliminate all racial barriers to the acquisition of real and personal property? We think the answer to that question is plainly yes.

"By its own unaided force and effect," the Thirteenth Amendment "abolished slavery, and established universal freedom." Civil Rights Cases, 109 U.S. 3, 20. . . . Whether or not the Amendment *itself* did any more than that — a question not involved in this case — it is at least clear that the Enabling Clause of that Amendment empowered Congress to do much more. For that clause clothed "Congress with power to pass *all laws necessary and proper for abolishing all badges and incidents of slavery in the United States*." . . . Surely Congress has the power under the Thirteenth Amendment rationally to determine what are the badges and the incidents of slavery, and the authority to translate that determination into effective legislation. Nor can we say that the determination Congress has made is an irrational one. For this Court recognized long ago that, whatever else they may have encompassed, the badges and incidents of slavery — its "burdens and disabilities" — included restraints upon "those fundamental rights which are the essence of civil freedom, namely, the same right . . . to inherit, purchase, lease, sell and convey property, as is enjoyed by white citizens." Civil Rights Cases, 109 U.S. 3, 22. . . . Just as the Black Codes, enacted after the Civil War to restrict the free exercise of those rights, were substitutes for the slave system, so the exclusion of Negroes from white communities became a substitute for the Black Codes. And when racial discrimination herds men into ghettos and makes their ability to buy property turn on the color of their skin, then it too is a relic of slavery.

Negro citizens, North and South, who saw in the Thirteenth Amendment a promise of freedom — freedom to "go and come at pleasure" and to "buy and sell when they please" — would be left with "a mere paper guarantee" if Congress were powerless to assure that a dollar in the hands of a Negro will purchase the same thing as a dollar in the hands of a white man. At the very least, the freedom that Congress is empowered to secure under the Thirteenth Amendment includes the freedom to buy whatever a white man can buy, the right to live wherever a white man can live. If Congress cannot say that being a free man means at least this much, then the Thirteenth Amendment made a promise the Nation cannot keep. . . .

The judgment is reversed.

Mr. Justice HARLAN, whom Mr. Justice WHITE joins, dissenting. The decision in this case appears to me to be most ill-considered and ill-advised. . . . For me, there is an inherent ambiguity in the term "right," as used in §1982. The "right" referred to may either be a right to equal status under the law, in which case the statute operates only against state-sanctioned discrimination, or it may be an "absolute" right enforceable against private individuals. To me, the words of the statute, taken alone, suggest the former interpretation, not the latter. . . . [An] analysis of the language, structure, and legislative history of the 1866 Civil Rights Act shows, I believe, that the Court's thesis that the Act was meant to extend to purely private action is open to the most serious doubt, if indeed it does not render that thesis wholly untenable. Another, albeit less tangible, consideration points in the same direction. Many of the legislators who took part in the congressional debates inevitably must have shared the individualistic ethic of their time, which emphasized personal freedom and embodied a distaste for governmental interference which was soon to culminate in the era of laissez-faire. It seems to me that most of these men would have regarded it as a great intrusion on individual liberty for the Government to take from a man the power to refuse for personal reasons to enter into a purely private transaction involving the disposition of property, albeit those personal reasons might reflect racial bias. It should be remembered that racial prejudice was not uncommon in 1866, even outside the South. Although Massachusetts had recently enacted the Nation's first law prohibiting racial discrimination in public accommodations, Negroes could not ride within Philadelphia streetcars or attend public schools with white children in New York City. Only five States accorded equal voting rights to Negroes, and it appears that Negroes were allowed to serve on juries only in Massachusetts. Residential segregation was the prevailing pattern almost everywhere in the North. There were no state "fair housing" laws in 1866, and it appears that none had ever been proposed. In this historical context, I cannot conceive that a bill thought to prohibit purely private discrimination not only in the sale or rental of housing but in all property transactions would not have received a great deal of criticism explicitly directed to this feature. The fact that the 1866 Act received no criticism of this kind is for me strong evidence that it was not regarded as extending so far.

In sum, the most which can be said with assurance about the intended impact of the 1866 Civil Rights Act upon purely private discrimination is that the Act probably was envisioned by most members of Congress as prohibiting official, community-sanctioned discrimination in the South, engaged in pursuant to local "customs" which in the recent time of slavery probably were embodied in laws or regulations. . . . In holding that the Thirteenth Amendment is sufficient constitutional authority for §1982 as interpreted, the Court also decides a question of great importance. . . . After mature reflection, however, I have concluded that this is one of those rare instances in which an event which occurs after the hearing of argument so diminishes a case's public significance, when viewed in light of the difficulty of the questions presented, as to justify this Court in dismissing the writ as improvidently granted.

The occurrence to which I refer is the recent enactment of the Civil Rights Act of 1968. Title VIII of that Act contains comprehensive "fair housing" provisions, which by the terms of §803 will become applicable on January 1, 1969, to persons who, like the petitioners, attempt to buy houses from developers. Under those provisions, such persons will be entitled to injunctive relief and damages from developers who refuse to sell to them on account of race or color, unless the parties are able to resolve their dispute by other means. Thus, the type of relief which the petitioners seek will be available within seven months' time under the terms of a presumptively constitutional Act of Congress. In these circumstances, it seems obvious that the case has lost most of its public importance, and I believe that it would be much the wiser course for this Court to refrain from deciding it. I think it particularly unfortunate for the Court to persist in deciding this case on the basis of a highly questionable interpretation of a sweeping, century-old statute which, as the Court acknowledges, contains none of the exemptions which the Congress of our own time found it necessary to include in a statute regulating relationships so personal in nature. . . .

◆ CIVIL RIGHTS ACT OF 1968
42 U.S.C.A. §3601 (1977)

TITLE VIII — FAIR HOUSING

§3601. It is the policy of the United States to provide, within constitutional limitations, for fair housing throughout the United States. . . .
   §3603. . . .
   (b) Nothing in [this title] shall apply to —
   (1) any single-family house sold or rented by an owner: *Provided,* That such private individual owner does not own more than three such single-family houses at any one time: . . . *Provided further,* That after December 31, 1969, the sale or rental of any such single-family house shall be excepted from the application of this sub-chapter only if such house is sold or rented (A) without the use in any manner of the sales or rental facilities or the sales or rental services of any real estate broker, agent, or salesman, or of such facilities or services of any person in the business of selling or renting dwellings, or of any employee or agent of any such broker, agent, salesman, or person and (B) without the publication, posting or mailing, after notice, of any advertisement or written notice. . . .
   §3604. [I]t shall be unlawful —
   (a) To refuse to sell or rent after the making of a bona fide offer, or to refuse to negotiate for the sale or rental of, or otherwise make unavailable or deny, a dwelling to any person because of race, color, religion, sex, or national origin.
   (b) To discriminate against any person in the terms, conditions, or privileges of sale or rental of a dwelling, or in the provision of services or

facilities in connection therewith, because of race, color, religion, sex, or national origin.

(c) To make, print, or publish, or cause to be made, printed, or published any notice, statement, or advertisement, with respect to the sale or rental of a dwelling that indicates any preference, limitation, or discrimination based on race, color, religion, sex, or national origin, or an intention to make any such preference, limitation, or discrimination.

(d) To represent to any person because of race, color, religion, sex, or national origin that any dwelling is not available for inspection, sale, or rental when such dwelling is in fact so available.

(e) For profit, to induce or attempt to induce any person to sell or rent any dwelling by representations regarding the entry or prospective entry into the neighborhood of a person or persons of a particular race, color, religion, sex, or national origin. . . .

§3610. (a) Any person who claims to have been injured by a discriminatory housing practice or who believes that he will be irrevocably injured by a discriminatory housing practice that is about to occur . . . may file a complaint with the Secretary [of HUD]. . . .

(d) If within thirty days after a complaint is filed with the Secretary or within thirty days after expiration of any period of reference . . . the Secretary has been unable to obtain voluntary compliance with this title, the person aggrieved may, within thirty days thereafter, commence a civil action in any appropriate United States district court, against the respondent named in the complaint, to enforce the rights granted or protected by this title, insofar as such rights relate to the subject of the complaint: *Provided,* That no such civil action may be brought in any United States district court if the person aggrieved has a judicial remedy under a State or local fair housing law which provides rights and remedies for alleged discriminatory housing practices which are substantially equivalent to the rights and remedies provided in this title. . . .

(e) In any proceeding brought pursuant to this section, the burden of proof shall be on the complainant. . . .

§3612. (a) The rights granted by [this Title] may be enforced by civil action in appropriate United States district courts without regard to the amount in controversy and in appropriate State or local courts of general jurisdiction. A civil action shall be commenced within one hundred and eighty days after the alleged discriminatory housing practice occurred. . . .

(c) The court may grant as relief, as it deems appropriate, any permanent or temporary injunction, temporary restraining order, or other order, and may award to the plaintiff actual damages and not more than $1,000 punitive damages, together with court costs and reasonable attorney fees in the case of a prevailing plaintiff: *Provided,* That the said plaintiff in the opinion of the court is not financially able to assume said attorney's fees.

§3613. Whenever the Attorney General has reasonable cause to believe that any person or group of persons is engaged in a pattern or practice of resistance to the full enjoyment of any of the rights granted by this title, or that any group of persons has been denied any of the rights granted by this title and such denial raises an issue of general public importance, he may bring a civil action in any appropriate United States district court by filing with it a complaint setting forth the facts and requesting such preventive relief, including an application for a permanent or temporary injunction, restraining order, or other order against the person or persons responsible for such pattern or practice or denial of rights, as he deems necessary to insure the full enjoyment of the rights granted by this sub-chapter. . . .

Note

Havens Realty Corp. v. Coleman, 455 U.S. 363 (1982), addressed the issue of the standing to sue under the 1968 Civil Rights Act of "testers" — whites and blacks who pose as apartment hunters in an effort to develop evidence of racial discrimination. The case also brought into consideration the question of whether the act is violated by real estate brokers who "steer" blacks to particular neighborhoods to seek apartments. The Court found that black testers — who had been falsely told by landlords that no apartments were available — had suffered specific injury in fact, while white testers — who had been accurately told that apartments were available — suffered no such injury.

The Court also held that members of Housing Opportunities Made Equal (HOME) in Richmond and adjoining Henrico County, Virginia, should have an opportunity for a trial on their assertion that they have standing to sue because of their legitimate concern with the "important social, professional, business and economic, political and aesthetic benefits of interracial associations that arise from living in integrated communities free from discriminatory housing practices."

◆ WEST HILL BAPTIST CHURCH v. ABBATE
24 Ohio Misc. 66, 261 N.E.2d 196 (C.P. 1969)

CRAMER, J. The plaintiff seeks a declaratory judgment declaring that certain restrictive covenants appearing in the chain of title of its real estate be declared invalid and unenforceable. United in interest with the plaintiff and seeking the same relief as does plaintiff but seeking it by way of cross-petitions and joined as defendants here are Adath Israel Anshe Sfard (hereinafter referred to as Anshe Sfard) and the Maronite

Club of Akron, Ohio. These latter defendants are owners of land in the area involved, each seeking to erect houses of worship thereon. . . .

The pleadings and the evidence raise the issue as to whether the plaintiff, The Maronite Club and Anshe Sfard as property owners and religious organizations, have the right to construct and operate their respective churches and synagogue thereon notwithstanding the existence of two sets of restrictive covenants which prohibit the use of their property for other than single family residence purposes. . . .

Zoning is the exercise of police power regulating and controlling the uses of real property. Restrictive covenants, with which we are here dealing, and which, of course, purport to control the use of real property are in the nature of private zoning or zoning by contract.

Restrictive covenants do not supersede or in any way affect the requirements of a zoning ordinance. They may be less restrictive than the ordinance and, if so, the ordinance prevails; and if the restrictive covenant is more restrictive than the ordinance the covenant prevails but, in either case, the ordinance is enforceable. The ordinance cannot abrogate or impair or enlarge the effect of a restrictive covenant and a valid covenant is not terminated or nullified by the enactment of a zoning ordinance nor is the validity of a restriction thereby affected.

It would follow, however, that if a zoning ordinance is in its operation, unconstitutional, a restrictive covenant in the same area having the same effect would likewise be unconstitutional.

In Shelley v. Kraemer, 334 U.S. 1, the Court declared: "That the action of state courts and of judicial officers in their capacities is to be regarded as action of the State within the meaning of the Fourteenth Amendment. . . ."

Therefore, if this Court were to enforce (by declaratory judgment) the restrictive covenants here we would be engaging in state action.

In a majority of the states, churches cannot be wholly excluded from residential districts (through zoning legislation) because the courts have held that, under the circumstances, such exclusion amounts to unfair discrimination and, in any event, is contrary to the public welfare as a general rule thus being an arbitrary and unauthorized exercise of the police power by the local authorities.

The courts have considered that the private enjoyment of surrounding property and maintenance of its economic value are not considered important enough to require exclusion of religious uses.

It has also been held that a zoning ordinance which prohibits the use of certain residential land for church purposes does not bear any relation to public health, safety, morals and general welfare and, therefore, is violative of constitutional rights.

Thus, it seems to us, that covenants such as these here in issue, which seek to limit an area to residential use only, thereby barring churches, would be unconstitutional as to houses of worship if they were in the form of zoning ordinances or resolutions rather than covenants. . . .

It is conceivable that to relegate houses of worship to areas other than those here in question thereby excluding them from residential districts not as fully populated would result in imposing a burden on the free right to worship and could conceivably result in prohibiting altogether the exercise of that right.

In the case of Cantwell v. State of Connecticut, 310 U.S. 296, it was stated that: "It cannot be left to the uncontrolled discretion of any public official as to when, where and under what conditions a religious organization may build a church or maintain a place of assembly." It has also been said that although the Supreme Court of the United States has been strict in its prohibition of prior restraint, on the exercise of freedom of religion, it has been held that reasonable regulations of time and place for the exercise of such freedoms are valid.

Here, these restrictive covenants came as a result of the "uncontrolled discretion" of private individuals thus resulting in their unreasonable regulation of "time and place" for the exercise of religion by those coming into the area affected by the restrictions.

While it is true, of course, that when the effect of such a covenant upon the exercise of one's freedom of religion is small and the public interest to be protected is substantial such freedom is to give way to the public interest, that situation does not here exist. The private interests of the individuals, parties to the restrictive covenants, as distinguished from the public interest, were their chief and perhaps only concern. It is claimed the evidence shows that the excessive noise and increased traffic hazards engendered by the erection of three additional places of religious worship will occur, so that the public interest and welfare must be balanced against the freedom. We do not find that the evidence discloses that such results will take place to the extent claimed. . . .

It is our conclusion that the enforcement of these covenants which would result in prohibiting the use by the plaintiff and the crosspetitioners of their property for the erection thereon of houses of worship, would constitute state action (through this Court) violative of the free exercise of religion provision of the First Amendment of the Constitution of the United States and of comparable provisions of the Constitution of Ohio and against public policy, and that such action bears no reasonable relationship to the public health, safety, morals and general welfare.

We, therefore, declare that such restrictive covenants are not enforceable, so as to prevent the use of the properties of plaintiff and crosspetitioners to which they seek to put them, namely, the erection and maintenance of churches and a synagogue and all structures necessary to be used in connection therewith.

Notes

1. Compare Evangelical Lutheran Church of the Ascension v. Sahlem, 254 N.Y. 161, 172 N.E. 455 (1930) (Cardozo, C.J.):

Neither at law nor in equity is it written that a license has been granted to religious corporations, by reason of the high purpose of their being, to set covenants at naught. Indeed, if in such matters there can be degrees of obligation, one would suppose that a more sensitive adherence to the demands of plighted faith might be expected of them than would be looked for of the world at large.

2. In Ginsberg v. Yeshiva, 45 A.D.2d 334, 358 N.Y.S.2d 477, aff'd mem., 364 N.Y.2d 706, 325 N.E.2d 876, 366 N.Y.S.2d 418 (1976), the court enforced a covenant similar to the covenant that the Abbate court had declined to enforce, and enjoined operation of a religious school on the lot in question. The court refused to extend Shelley v. Kramer beyond racially discriminatory covenants. Virtually every other court to pass on this issue has enjoined the religious institution from violating the restrictive covenant. See Note, Restrictive Covenants and Religious Uses: The Constitutional Interplay, 29 Syracuse L. Rev. 993 (1978).

3. Defendants purchased a lot in the Enchanted Acres Subdivision, a mobile home subdivision consisting of 39 lots. A Declaration of Restrictions included the provision, "restricted to persons 21 years of age and older." The restriction was enforced, the court distinguishing Shelley v. Kraemer by arguing that children, unlike blacks, are not a suspect classification for Equal Protection Clause purposes. The court found no relevance in Arizona Rev. Stat. §33-303, first enacted in 1921, which makes criminal the refusal "to rent . . . a place . . . to be used for a dwelling for the reason that the other person has a child or children . . ." Riley v. Stoves, 22 Ariz. App. 223, 526 P.2d 747 (1974).

See also Travolio, Suffer the Little Children — But Not in My Neighborhood: A Constitutional View of Age-Restrictive Housing, 40 Ohio St. L.J. 295 (1979); Note, Judicial Enforcement of Restrictive Covenants Against Children: An Equal Protection Analysis, 17 Ariz. L. Rev. 717 (1975); Note, Housing Discrimination against Children: The Legal Status of a Growing Social Problem, 16 J. Fam. L. 559 (1977-1978).

4. Can a court order a homeowner to take down an outdoor citizens band radio antenna on the grounds that it violates a covenant prohibiting outdoor antennas? A California court rejected a homeowner's argument that he had a first amendment right to free speech that was violated by court enforcement of the covenant. Conard v. Dunn, 92 Cal. App. 3d 236, 154 Cal. Rptr. 726 (1979).

5. In Girard v. 94th Street & Fifth Avenue Corp., 530 F.2d 66 (2d

Cir.), *cert. denied,* 425 U.S. 974 (1976), plaintiff alleged that when she separated from her husband and they attempted to transfer the lease of their cooperative apartment to her, the board of directors refused permission because of a policy forbidding possession by single female tenants. The district judge held that there was no state action, so no violation of the federal civil rights statutes. But see *Hudsonview Properties,* p.411 *supra.*

21 ◆ LAND USE REGULATION BY GOVERNMENT

Regulation of land use by agreement has evolved into sophisticated schemes of private governance. Nevertheless, contractual use control suffers inherent limitations: the difficulty of persuading all to be bound, or all to pay, in a bargaining environment where a free ride is worth a holdout; the inflexibility of specific rules once negotiated; the burden of archaic (or — and this can be worse — uncertain) legal doctrines, in the many unreformed jurisdictions. Although Houston (alone among major cities) still controls its land use solely by agreement, the transaction costs of making, amending, and rescinding contracts are apparently very great.

The alternative is zoning: land use control by government decree rather than by private consent; by majority instead of by unanimity; under constitutional and statutory delegation rather than within the old doctrines of easement and covenant. Constitutionally validated only 60 years ago, zoning is now a central task of local government, a major consumer of a property lawyer's energy, and an important force in shaping our physical environment, our income distribution, and our politics.

This chapter considers three sorts of legal protests against land use regulation by local majority decision: the complaint of the developer, whose parcel has been reduced in value; the objection of the residents, whose liberty has been impaired; and the protest of the person residing elsewhere, denied possible housing by a zoning decision in which he could not participate. Have we developed comprehensible doctrines for considering each (or any) of these challenges?

The chapter also considers cases that illustrate the inevitable consequence of comprehensive zoning: the permission to build as a major stick in the owner's "bundle" of interests, one readily contested between landlord and tenant, as well as between "owner" and municipality.

A.   THE NATURE OF ZONING

◆ VILLAGE OF EUCLID v. AMBLER REALTY CO.
272 U.S. 365 (1926)

Mr. Newton D. Baker, with whom Mr. Robert M. Morgan was on the brief, for the appellee.

The recent industrial development of the City of Cleveland, following the railroad lines, has already reached the Village and to some extent extends over into it. In its obvious course, this industrial expansion will soon absorb the area in the Village for industrial enterprises. It is in restraint of this prospect that the ordinance seeks to operate. In effect it erects a dam to hold back the flood of industrial development and thus to preserve a rural character in portions of the Village which, under the operation of natural economic laws, would be devoted most profitably to industrial undertakings. This, the evidence shows, destroys value without compensation to the owners of lands who have acquired and are holding them for industrial uses.

Since the industrial development of a great city will go on, the effect of this attempted action necessarily is to divert industry to other less suited sites, with a consequent rise in value thereof; so that the loss sustained by the proprietors of land who cannot so use their land is gained by proprietors of land elsewhere. In other words, the property, or value, which is taken away from one set of people, is, by this law, bestowed upon another set of people, imposing an uncompensated loss on the one hand and a gain which is arbitrary and unnatural on the other hand, since it results, not from the operation of economic laws, but from arbitrary considerations of taste enacted into hard and fast legislation. Such legislation also tends to monopolize business and factory sites. . . .

That municipalities have power to regulate the height of buildings, area of occupation, strengths of building materials, modes of construction, and density of use, in the interest of the public safety, health, morals, and welfare, are propositions long since established; that a rational use of this power may be made by dividing a municipality into districts or zones, and varying the requirements according to the characteristics of the districts, is, of course, equally well established. We believe it, however, to be the law that these powers must be reasonably exercised, and that a municipality may not, under the guise of the police power, arbitrarily divert property from its appropriate and most economical uses, or diminish its value, by imposing restrictions which have no other basis than the momentary taste of the public authorities. Nor can police regulations be used to effect the arbitrary desire to have a municipality resist the operation of economic laws and remain rural, exclusive and aesthetic, when its land is needed to be otherwise devel-

oped by that larger public good and public welfare, which takes into
consideration the extent to which the prosperity of the country depends
upon the economic development of its business and industrial enterprises.

The municipal limits of the Village of Euclid are, after all, arbitrary
and accidental political lines. The metropolitan City of Cleveland is one
of the great industrial centers of the United States. If the Village may
lawfully prefer to remain rural and restrict the normal industrial and
business development of its land, each of the other municipalities, cir-
cumadjacent to the City of Cleveland, may pursue a like course. Thus
the areas available for the expanding industrial needs of the metropolitan city will be restricted, the value of such land as is left available
artificially enhanced, and industry driven to less advantageous sites. All
this would be done at the expense of those land owners whose lands,
being most advantageously located from an industrial point of view,
have as a part of their right of property, which the constitutions of the
Nation and the States undertake to protect, the expectation of value due
to their superior availability for industrial development. . . .

Mr. Justice SUTHERLAND delivered the opinion of the Court. The
Village of Euclid is an Ohio municipal corporation. It adjoins and practically is a suburb of the City of Cleveland. Its estimated population is
between 5,000 and 10,000, and its area from twelve to fourteen square
miles, the greater part of which is farm lands or unimproved acreage. It
lies, roughly, in the form of a parallelogram measuring approximately
three and one-half miles each way. East and west it is traversed by three
principal highways: Euclid Avenue, through the southerly border, St.
Clair Avenue, through the central portion, and Lake Shore Boulevard,
through the northerly border in close proximity to the shore of Lake
Erie. The Nickel Plate railroad lies from 1,500 to 1,800 feet north of
Euclid Avenue, and the Lake Shore railroad 1,600 feet farther to the
north. The three highways and the two railroads are substantially parallel.

Appellee is the owner of a tract of land containing 68 acres, situated
in the westerly end of the village, abutting on Euclid Avenue to the
south and the Nickel Plate railroad to the north. Adjoining this tract,
both on the east and on the west, there have been laid out restricted
residential plats upon which residences have been erected.

On November 13, 1922, an ordinance was adopted by the Village
Council, establishing a comprehensive zoning plan for regulating and
restricting the location of trades, industries, apartment houses, two-
family houses, single family houses, etc., the lot area to be built upon,
the size and height of buildings, etc.

The entire area of the village is divided by the ordinance into six
classes of use districts, denominated U-1 to U-6, inclusive; three classes
of height districts, denominated H-1 to H-3, inclusive; and four classes

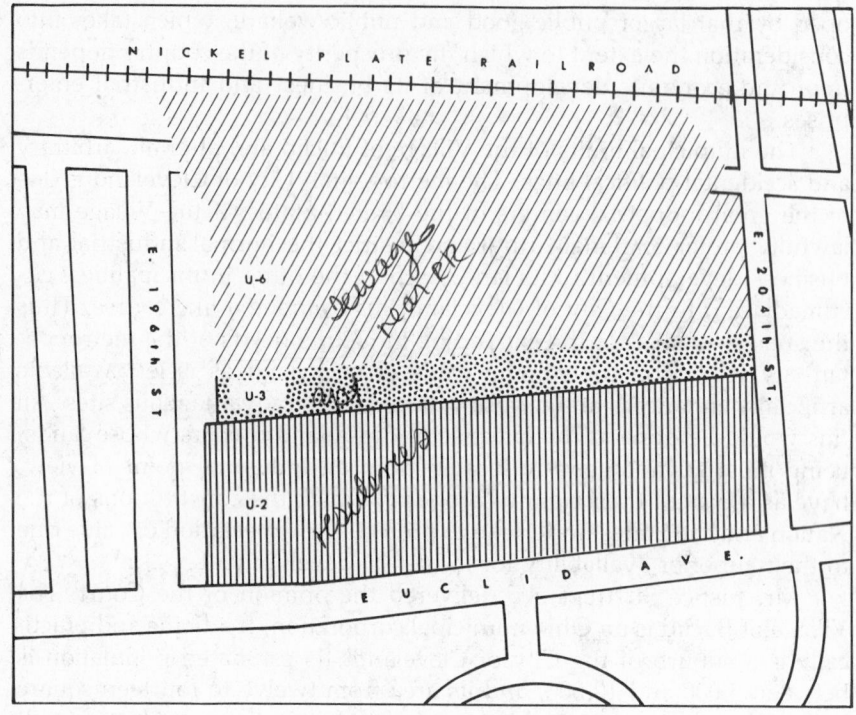

FIGURE 21-1
The Ambler Realty site

of area districts, denominated A-1 to A-4, inclusive. The use districts are classified in respect of the buildings which may be erected within their respective limits, as follows: U-1 is restricted to single family dwellings, public parks, water towers and reservoirs, suburban and interurban electric railway passenger stations and rights of way, and farming noncommercial greenhouse nurseries and truck gardening; U-2 is extended to include two-family dwellings; U-3 is further extended to include apartment houses, hotels, churches, schools, public libraries, museums, private clubs, community center buildings, hospitals, sanitariums, public playgrounds and recreation buildings, and a city hall and courthouse; U-4 is further extended to include banks, offices, studios, telephone exchanges, fire and police stations, restaurants, theatres and moving picture shows, retail stores and shops, sales offices, sample rooms, wholesale stores for hardware, drugs and groceries, stations for gasoline and oil (not exceeding 1,000 gallons storage) and for ice delivery, skating rinks and dance halls, electric substations, job and newspaper printing, public garages for motor vehicles, stables and wagon sheds (not exceeding five horses, wagons or motor trucks) and distributing stations for central store and commercial enterprises; U-5 is further extended to include billboards and advertising signs (if permitted), warehouses, ice and ice cream manufacturing and cold storage plants, bottling works, milk bottling and central distribution stations, laundries, carpet cleaning, dry cleaning and dyeing establishments, blacksmith, horseshoeing, wagon and motor vehicle repair shops, freight stations, street car barns, stables and wagon sheds (for more than five horses, wagons or motor trucks), and wholesale produce markets and salesrooms; U-6 is further extended to include plants for sewage disposal and for producing gas, garbage and refuse incineration, scrap iron, junk, scrap paper and rag storage, aviation fields, cemeteries, crematories, penal and correctional institutions, insane and feeble minded institutions, storage of oil and gasoline (not to exceed 25,000 gallons), and manufacturing and industrial operations of any kind other than, and any public utility not included in, a class U-1, U-2, U-3, U-4 or U-5 use. There is a seventh class of uses which is prohibited altogether. . . .

The ordinance is assailed on the grounds that it is in derogation of §1 of the Fourteenth Amendment to the Federal Constitution in that it deprives appellee of liberty and property without due process of law and denies it the equal protection of the law, and that it offends against certain provisions of the Constitution of the State of Ohio. The prayer of the bill is for an injunction restraining the enforcement of the ordinance and all attempts to impose or maintain as to appellee's property any of the restrictions, limitations or conditions. The court below held the ordinance to be unconstitutional and void, and enjoined its enforcement.

Before proceeding to a consideration of the case, it is necessary to determine the scope of the inquiry. The bill alleges that the tract of land in question is vacant and has been held for years for the purpose of selling and developing it for industrial uses, for which it is especially adapted, being immediately in the path of progressive industrial development; that for such uses it has a market value of about $10,000 per acre, but if the use be limited to residential purposes the market value is not in excess of $2,500 per acre; that the first 200 feet of the parcel back from Euclid Avenue, if unrestricted in respect of use, has a value of $150 per front foot, but if limited to residential uses, and ordinary mercantile business be excluded therefrom, its value is not in excess of $50 per front foot. . . .

Building zone laws are of modern origin. They began in this country about twenty-five years ago. Until recent years, urban life was comparatively simple; but with the great increase and concentration of population, problems have developed, and constantly are developing, which require, and will continue to require, additional restrictions in respect of the use and occupation of private lands in urban communities. Regulations, the wisdom, necessity and validity of which, as applied to existing conditions, are so apparent that they are now uniformly sustained, a century ago, or even half a century ago, probably would have been rejected as arbitrary and oppressive. Such regulations are sustained, under the complex conditions of our day, for reasons analogous to those which justify traffic regulations, which, before the advent of automobiles and rapid transit street railways, would have been condemned as fatally arbitrary and unreasonable. And in this there is no inconsistency, for while the meaning of constitutional guaranties never varies, the scope of their application must expand or contract to meet the new and different conditions which are constantly coming within the field of their operation. In a changing world, it is impossible that it should be otherwise. But although a degree of elasticity is thus imparted, not to the *meaning*, but to the *application* of constitutional principles, statutes and ordinances, which, after giving due weight to the new conditions, are found clearly not to conform to the Constitution, of course, must fall.

The ordinance now under review, and all similar laws and regulations, must find their justification in some aspect of the police power, asserted for the public welfare. The line which in this field separates the legitimate from the illegitimate assumption of power is not capable of precise delimitation. It varies with circumstances and conditions. A regulatory zoning ordinance, which would be clearly valid as applied to the great cities, might be clearly invalid as applied to rural communities. In solving doubts, the maxim *sic utere tuo ut alienum non laedas,* which lies at the foundation of so much of the common law of nuisances, ordinarily will furnish a fairly helpful clew. And the law of nuisances, likewise, may be consulted, not for the purpose of controlling, but for the helpful aid of its analogies in the process of ascertaining the scope of, the power. Thus the question whether the power exists to forbid the erection of a building of a particular kind or for a particular use, like the question whether a particular thing is a nuisance, is to be determined, not by an abstract consideration of the building or of the thing considered apart, but by considering it in connection with the circumstances and the locality. A nuisance may be merely a right thing in the wrong place — like a pig in the parlor instead of the barnyard. If the validity of the legislative classification for zoning purposes be fairly debatable, the legislative judgment must be allowed to control.

There is no serious difference of opinion in respect of the validity of laws and regulations fixing the height of buildings within reasonable limits, the character of materials and methods of construction, and the adjoining area which must be left open, in order to minimize the danger of fire or collapse, the evils of overcrowding, and the like, and excluding from residential sections offensive trades, industries and structures likely to create nuisances.

Here, however, the exclusion is in general terms of all industrial establishments, and it may thereby happen that not only offensive or dangerous industries will be excluded, but those which are neither offensive nor dangerous will share the same fate. But this is no more than happens in respect of many practice-forbidding laws which this Court has upheld although drawn in general terms so as to include individual cases that may turn out to be innocuous in themselves. The inclusion of a reasonable margin to insure effective enforcement will not put upon a law, otherwise valid, the stamp of invalidity. Such laws may also find their justification in the fact that, in some fields, the bad fades into the good by such insensible degrees that the two are not capable of being readily distinguished and separated in terms of legislation. In the light of these considerations, we are not prepared to say that the end in view was not sufficient to justify the general rule of the ordinance, although some industries of an innocent character might fall within the proscribed class. It can not be said that the ordinance in this respect "passes the bounds of reason and assumes the character of a merely arbitrary fiat." Moreover, the restrictive provisions of the ordinance in this particular may be sustained upon the principles applicable to the broader exclusion from residential districts of all business and trade structures, presently to be discussed.

It is said that the Village of Euclid is a mere suburb of the City of Cleveland; that the industrial development of that city has now reached and in some degree extended into the village and, in the obvious course of things, will soon absorb the entire area for industrial enterprises; that the effect of the ordinance is to divert this natural development elsewhere with the consequent loss of increased values to the owners of the lands within the village borders. But the village, though physically a suburb of Cleveland, is politically a separate municipality, with powers of its own and authority to govern itself as it sees fit within the limits of the organic law of its creation and the State and Federal Constitutions. Its governing authorities, presumably representing a majority of its inhabitants and voicing their will, have determined, not that industrial development shall cease at its boundaries, but that the course of such development shall proceed within definitely fixed lines. If it be a proper exercise of the police power to relegate industrial establishments to localities separated from residential sections, it is not easy to find a sufficient reason for denying the power because the effect of its exercise is to divert an industrial flow from the course which it would follow, to the injury of the residential public if left alone, to another course where such injury will be obviated. It is not meant by this, however, to exclude the possibility of cases where the general public interest would so far outweigh the interest of the municipality that the municipality would not be allowed to stand in the way.

We find no difficulty in sustaining restrictions of the kind thus far reviewed. The serious question in the case arises over the provisions of the ordinance excluding from residential districts, apartment houses, business houses, retail stores and shops, and other like establishments.

This question involves the validity of what is really the crux of the more recent zoning legislation, namely, the creation and maintenance of residential districts, from which business and trade of every sort, including hotels and apartment houses, are excluded. Upon that question this Court has not thus far spoken. . . .

The matter of zoning has received much attention at the hands of commissions and experts, and the results of their investigations have been set forth in comprehensive reports. These reports, which bear every evidence of painstaking consideration, concur in the view that the segregation of residential, business, and industrial buildings will make it easier to provide fire apparatus suitable for the character and intensity of the development in each section; that it will increase the safety and security of home life; greatly tend to prevent street accidents, especially to children, by reducing the traffic and resulting confusion in residential sections; decrease noise and other conditions which produce or intensify nervous disorders; preserve a more favorable environment in which to rear children, etc. With particular reference to apartment houses, it is pointed out that the development of detached house sections is greatly retarded by the coming of apartment houses, which has sometimes resulted in destroying the entire section for private house purposes; that in such sections very often the apartment house is a mere parasite, constructed in order to take advantage of the open spaces and attractive surroundings created by the residential character of the district. Moreover, the coming of one apartment house is followed by others, interfering by their height and bulk with the free circulation of air and monopolizing the rays of the sun which otherwise would fall upon the smaller homes, and bringing, as their necessary accompaniments, the disturbing noises incident to increased traffic and business, and the occupation, by means of moving and parked automobiles, of larger portions of the streets, thus detracting from their safety and depriving children of the privilege of quiet and open spaces for play, enjoyed by those in more favored localities, — until, finally, the residential character of the neighborhood and its desirability as a place of detached residences are utterly destroyed. Under these circumstances, apartment houses, which in a different environment would be not only entirely unobjectionable but highly desirable, come very near to being nuisances.

If these reasons, thus summarized, do not demonstrate the wisdom or sound policy in all respects of those restrictions which we have indicated as pertinent to the inquiry, at least, the reasons are sufficiently cogent to preclude us from saying, as it must be said before the ordinance can be declared unconstitutional, that such provisions are clearly arbitrary and unreasonable, having no substantial relation to the public health, safety, morals, or general welfare.

It is true that when, if ever, the provisions set forth in the ordinance in tedious and minute detail, come to be concretely applied to particular premises, including those of the appellee, or to particular conditions, or to be considered in connection with specific complaints, some of them, or even many of them, may be found to be clearly arbitrary and unreasonable. But where the equitable remedy of injunction is sought, as it is here, not upon the ground of a present infringement or denial of a specific right, or of a particular injury in process of actual execution, but upon the broad ground that the mere existence and threatened enforcement of the ordinance, by materially and adversely affecting values and curtailing the opportunities of the market, constitute a present and irreparable injury, the court will not scrutinize its provisions, sentence by sentence, to ascertain by a process of piecemeal dissection whether there may be, here and there, provisions of a minor character, or relating to matters of administration, or not shown to contribute to the injury complained of, which, if attacked separately, might not withstand the test of constitutionality. In respect of such provisions, of which specific complaint is not made, it cannot be said that the land owner has suffered or is threatened with an injury which entitles him to challenge their constitutionality. . . .

Decree reversed.

Mr. Justice VAN DEVANTER, Mr. Justice MCREYNOLDS and Mr. Justice BUTLER, dissent.

Notes

1. McCormack, A Law Clerk's Recollections, 46 Colum. L. Rev. 710, 712 (1946):

> Justice Sutherland, for instance, was writing an opinion for the majority in Village of Euclid v. Ambler Realty Co., holding the zoning ordinance unconstitutional, when talks with his dissenting brethren (principally Stone, I believe) shook his convictions and led him to request a reargument, after which he changed his mind and the ordinance was upheld.

Having seen the light, does Justice Sutherland adequately answer Mr. Baker's argument?

2. See Ambler Realty Co. v. Village of Euclid, 297 F. 307 (N.D. Ohio 1924):

> The plain truth is that the true object of the ordinance in question is to place all the property in an undeveloped area of 16 square miles in a straitjacket. The purpose to be accomplished is really to regulate the mode of living of persons who may hereafter inhabit it. In the last analysis, the result to be accomplished is to classify the population and segregate them according to their income or situation in life. The true reason why some

persons live in a mansion and others in a shack, why some live in a single-family dwelling and others in a double-family dwelling, why some live in a two-family dwelling and others in an apartment, or why some live in a well-kept apartment and others in a tenement, is primarily economic. It is a matter of income and wealth, plus the labor and difficulty of procuring adequate domestic service. Aside from contributing to these results and furthering such class tendencies, the ordinance has also an esthetic purpose; that is to say, to make this village develop into a city along lines now conceived by the village council to be attractive and beautiful. The assertion that this ordinance may tend to prevent congestion, and thereby contribute to the health and safety, would be more substantial if provision had been or could be made for adequate east and west and north and south street highways. Whether these purposes and objects would justify the taking of plaintiff's property as and for a public use need not be considered. It is sufficient to say that, in our opinion, and as applied to plaintiff's property, it may not be done without compensation under the guise of exercising the police power.

3. The property at issue in the *Euclid* case is now owned by General Motors, used as a Fisher Body Plant, and zoned industrial.

4. In Nectow v. City of Cambridge, 227 U.S. 183 (1928), the Supreme Court held that, as applied to petitioner's property, the Cambridge zoning ordinance violated the Fourteenth Amendment by depriving petitioner of his property without due process of law. The City of Cambridge had been divided into three kinds of districts, with petitioner's land in a district that excluded business and industry. The Court explained that the zoning power of a government is not unlimited, and may be imposed only when the restriction bears a substantial relation to the health, safety, morals, and welfare of the community. In this case, the master's findings of fact stated the restriction on petitioner's land allowed him to make no practical use of his land and in fact led to a lost sale. Further, the restriction did not promote the health, safety, morals, or welfare of the community. Thus, the city's interference with petitioner's use of his land was unjustified. The principal distinction drawn from *Euclid* was that in *Nectow* the loss was tangible and real, while the loss in *Euclid* was speculative.

5. Appellants acquired five acres of unimproved land in Tiburon, California. Then the city modified its zoning ordinance, placing the property in a residential planned development and open space zone, permitting no more than five single-family residences on the tract. Appellants said that their land, with "magnificent views of San Francisco Bay," was among the most valuable parcels in all of California, and that the rezoning had reduced the value of the land by $2 million. The Supreme Court rejected an attack on the rezoning, agreeing with the California Supreme Court that the valid public purpose was to discourage the "premature and unnecessary conversion of open-space land to

urban uses," and "to protect the residents of Tiburon from the ill-effects of urbanization." Agins v. City of Tiburon, 447 U.S. 255 (1980).

6. After finding the existing zoning ordinance of the city of Worthington, Ohio, unconstitutional as applied to plaintiff's land, the trial judge, rather than leaving the property "unzoned" and thereby affording the owner complete freedom of choice as to future use, had ordered the property in question rezoned to a certain classification. The Ohio Supreme Court reversed the lower court's order, holding that it had "exceeded its proper judicial role in zoning matters. . . ." Rather, the trial court should have given notice

> to the zoning authorities that, within a reasonably certain time, it may, at its option, rezone the land. Further notice should be given that, if the property is not rezoned within such period of time, the court will authorize the property owner to proceed with the proposed use if, on the basis of the evidence before it, the court determines the proposed use to be reasonable. [Union Oil Co. v. City of Worthington, 62 Ohio St. 2d 263, 405 N.E.2d 277 (1980).]

7. Zoning ordinances spread rapidly once they received Supreme Court approval. Led by Secretary Herbert Hoover, the U.S. Department of Commerce prepared and promulgated a Standard State Zoning Enabling Act in 1928; most of the states quickly fell into line with variations of the Standard Act. By 1931, every state had authorized zoning to some degree, and more than 1,000 municipalities had land use ordinances. The Standard Act set out the basic decision-making structure that has become common:

> *Sec. 6. Zoning Commission*
> . . . [S]uch legislative body shall appoint a . . . zoning commission, to recommend the boundaries of the various original districts and appropriate regulations to be enforced therein. . . . Where a city plan commission already exists, it may be appointed as the zoning commission.
>
> *Sec. 7. Board of Adjustment*
> Such local legislative body may provide for the appointment of a board of adjustment, and . . . may provide that the said board of adjustment may, in appropriate cases and subject to appropriate conditions and safeguards, make special exceptions to the terms of the ordinance in harmony with its general purpose and intent.

Thus the key actors in the zoning process are the local legislative body; any group to which it may delegate the task of creating a long-range land use plan for the community; a zoning board, which initially adopts (or recommends) a zoning ordinance, and is similarly responsible for changes; and a board of adjustment or appeal, which deals in a quasi-judicial way with cases of alleged individual hardship. Of course there is no clear line between the jurisdiction of the plan and that of the zoning ordinance, or between generally applicable changes in the ordinance and particular exceptions to it. These murky borderlands give rise to dispute and litigation.

8. For a brief extract from a sample zoning ordinance, see National Institute of Municipal Law Officers, Model Zoning Ordinance (1953):

Sec. 11-212. A-2. One-Family Districts
(a) Permitted Buildings and Uses. In a one-family district the following buildings and uses and their accessory buildings and uses are permitted:

    (1) Dwelling houses, each occupied by not more than one family and not more than two roomers or boarders.

    (2) One two-family dwelling on a corner lot only.

    (3) Playground; Parks.

    (4) The extension of existing cemeteries. . . .

    (10) The following buildings and uses if approved by the Board of Appeals after public notice and public hearing and if adequate yard spaces and other safeguards to preserve the character of the neighborhood are provided, and if in the judgment of said Board such buildings and uses are appropriately located and designed and will meet a community need without adversely affecting the neighborhood.

        (10a) A temporary or permanent use of a building by a nonprofit organization for a dormitory, fraternity, or sorority house, for the accommodation of those enrolled in or employed by an educational institution permitted in the district.

        (10b) Fire stations; police stations.

The NIMLO model ordinance suggests that there be one-family districts, two-family, and multi-family, as well as districts called neighborhood business, general business, central business, and industrial. It is common for districts to be assigned minimum lot sizes, percentages of the lot area that can be covered by a structure, maximum heights, setback distances from the street, and minimum provisions for parking.

9. Is zoning desirable? See Ellickson, Alternatives to Zoning: Covenants, Nuisance Rules, and Fines as Land Use Controls, 40 U. Chi. L. Rev. 681, 723 (1973):

    . . . Assume, for example, that there is a grocery in the Santa Monica Mountains, the only external harm to the neighbors is added noise, and administrative costs are zero. The Coase theorem states that if the cost to the grocer of going out of business is less than his neighbors' gains from the reduction in noise resulting from the termination of his enterprise, the grocer will shut down regardless of the initial distribution of rights. If homeowners have the right to recover for injury caused by the noise, the grocer will choose to absorb the smaller loss of going out of business rather than pay for the damage he causes by staying open. If the law does not require the grocer to compensate the homeowners for noise, the homeowners will combine to pay the grocer to close. The grocer will agree if the bounty is larger than his losses from closing, and the homeowners will be willing to offer more than the amount of his loss if their total damage exceeds that amount.

On the other hand, when the cost to the grocer of closing exceeds the resulting benefit to the homeowners, the grocer will continue to operate. If the homeowners have the right to recover, the grocer will pay damages rather than absorb the larger costs of terminating his business. If the grocer need not pay damages, the homeowners will not pay him to adopt a more neighborly course of action, because the minimum payment he would insist on to shut down exceeds the value of the damage they are currently suffering. In brief, the Coase theorem states that private bargaining will tend to reduce the sum of nuisance and prevention costs over time, regardless of assignment of rights.

10. Reich, The Law of the Planned Society, 75 Yale L.J. 1227, 1244-1247 (1966):

. . . Our constitutional plan is based upon fear of concentrated power. Hence the division of power between nation and states, the doctrine of enumerated and limited powers, the system of checks and balances, and the Bill of Rights. But where are these to be found in a planned society? The existence of a planned economy tends to undermine these concepts. Can there be effective separation of powers when government engages in planning? Since Congress does not really set standards and the courts do not really review, all power is necessarily concentrated in the planning and allocation agencies. And the agencies are not only free of the separation of powers; they are also free of traditional limitations upon the areas of legitimate governmental concern. In planning and allocation the agency may with some logic take almost any factor (no matter how local or personal) into consideration in making its decision; the enumerated powers of the constitution are turned into a general welfare clause that can readily penetrate into the private lives of citizens. This is especially serious because in planning and allocation the interests of the community are in the forefront of the planner's consciousness, and hence the factors of individual liberty and privacy tend not to be weighed so heavily. Under the balancing theory, the public interest becomes equivalent to the majority interest, and this "outweighs" any "individual" interest in liberty or privacy. Moreover, planning by its very nature is hard to confine within fixed boundaries, and this runs counter to any concept of the rule of law. Planning means discretion. How shall we object to a decision that puts a superhighway through a park? Can there be a "law" against it? Perhaps. But the trend to a rule of discretion is unmistakable.

Discretion can be benevolent, but it can also be oppressive. It is an unfortunate fact that a large portion of the official corruption that mars American political life occurs in those agencies which engage in planning and allocation and therefore have discretion to grant or deny licenses, contracts, franchises, and other favors. In addition, discretion can readily be used unfairly or arbitrarily, so as to discriminate against some groups or individuals. Scandals involving liquor licenses, highway contracts, building codes and farm subsidies show that the discretion that accompanies planning and allocation is an almost unbearable temptation to human nature's less admirable side.

How does planning comport with the . . . constitutional ideal of equality? The more comprehensive the system of planning, the more it is true that every inequality is the responsibility of government, not a mere fortuity. In the unplanned society, men who are situated differently can only blame the spin of the wheel or the inscrutable will of fate. But the more actively government plans, the more it becomes responsible for the consequences. . . .

The more basic problem of value choosing is whether expertise can ever substitute for individual choices. In an unplanned society we have a multiple sovereignty of private property and every owner engages in value choosing. Planning is based upon the theory that such multiple choosing becomes impractical in a crowded world. Therefore government must make some choices that will govern us all. We are invited to look ahead to a scientific society in which values will be chosen on a rational basis. Unfortunately, science is not yet able to encompass the many different values that human beings choose if left to their own individual idiosyncrasies. As yet, science knows very little about what makes people happy or what adds to the richness and satisfaction of life.

B. THE ZONING PROCESS

1. The Comprehensive Plan

◆ FASANO v. BOARD OF COUNTY COMMISSIONERS
264 Ore. 574, 507 P.2d 23 (1973)

HOWELL, Justice. The plaintiffs, homeowners in Washington county, unsuccessfully opposed a zone change before the Board of County Commissioners of Washington County. . . .

The defendants are the Board of County Commissioners and A.G.S. Development Company. A.G.S., the owner of 32 acres which had been zoned R-7 (Single Family Residential), applied for a zone change to P-R (Planned Residential), which allows for the construction of a mobile home park. The change failed to receive a majority vote of the Planning Commission. The Board of County Commissioners approved the change and found, among other matters, that the change allows for "increased densities and different types of housing to meet the needs of urbanization over that allowed by the existing zoning.". . .

According to the briefs, the comprehensive plan of development for Washington county was adopted in 1959 and included classifications in the county for residential, neighborhood commercial, retail commercial, general commercial, industrial park and light industry, general and heavy industry, and agricultural areas.

The land in question, which was designated "residential" by the comprehensive plan, was zoned R-7, Single Family Residential.

Subsequent to the time the comprehensive plan was adopted, Washington county established a Planned Residential (P-R) zoning classification in 1963. The P-R classification was adopted by ordinance and provided that a planned residential unit development could be established and should include open space for utilities, access, and recreation; should not be less than 10 acres in size; and should be located in or adjacent to a residential zone. The P-R zone adopted by the 1963 ordinance is of the type known as a "floating zone," so-called because the ordinance creates a zone classification authorized for future use but not placed on the zoning map until its use at a particular location is approved by the governing body. The R-7 classification for the 32 acres continued until April 1970 when the classification was changed to P-R to permit the defendant A.G.S. to construct the mobile home park on the 32 acres involved.

The defendants argue that (1) the action of the county commissioners approving the change is presumptively valid, requiring plaintiffs to show that the commissioners acted arbitrarily in approving the zone change; (2) it was not necessary to show a change of conditions in the area before a zone change could be accomplished; and (3) the change from R-7 to P-R was in accordance with the Washington county comprehensive plan.

We granted review in this case to consider the questions — by what standards does a county commission exercise its authority in zoning matters; who has the burden of meeting those standards when a request for change of zone is made; and what is the scope of court review of such actions?

Any meaningful decision as to the proper scope of judicial review of a zoning decision must start with a characterization of the nature of that decision. The majority of jurisdictions state that a zoning ordinance is a legislative act and is thereby entitled to presumptive validity. . . .

At this juncture we feel we would be ignoring reality to rigidly view all zoning decisions by local governing bodies as legislative acts to be accorded a full presumption of validity and shielded from less than constitutional scrutiny by the theory of separation of powers. Local and small decision groups are simply not the equivalent in all respects of state and national legislatures. . . .

Ordinances laying down general policies without regard to a specific piece of property are usually an exercise of legislative authority, are subject to limited review, and may only be attacked upon constitutional grounds for an arbitrary abuse of authority. On the other hand, a determination whether the permissible use of a specific piece of property should be changed is usually an exercise of judicial authority and its propriety is subject to an altogether different test. An illustration of an exercise of legislative authority is the passage of the ordinance by the Washington County Commission in 1963 which provided for the formation of a planned residential classification to be located in or adjacent to any residential zone. An exercise of judicial authority is the county commissioners' determination in this particular matter to change the classification of A.G.S. Development Company's specific piece of property. . . .

We reject the proposition that judicial review of the county commissioners' determination to change the zoning of the particular property in question is limited to a determination whether the change was arbitrary and capricious.

In order to establish a standard of review, it is necessary to delineate certain basic principles relating to land use regulation.

The basic instrument for county or municipal land use planning is the "comprehensive plan." Haar, In Accordance with a Comprehensive Plan, 68 Harv. L. Rev. 1154 (1955).

The plan has been described as a general plan to control and direct the use and development of property in a municipality.

In Oregon the county planning commission is required by ORS 215.050 to adopt a comprehensive plan for the use of some or all of the land in the county. Under ORS 215.110(1), after the comprehensive plan has been adopted, the planning commission recommends to the governing body of the county the ordinances necessary to "carry out" the comprehensive plan. The purpose of the zoning ordinances, both under our statute and the general law of land use regulation, is to "carry out" or implement the comprehensive plan. Although we are aware of the analytical distinction between zoning and planning, it is clear that under our statutes the plan adopted by the planning commission and the zoning ordinances enacted by the county governing body are closely related; both are intended to be parts of a single integrated procedure for land use control. The plan embodies policy determinations and guiding principles; the zoning ordinances provide the detailed means of giving effect to those principles. . . .

We believe that the state legislature has conditioned the county's power to zone upon the prerequisite that the zoning attempt to further the general welfare of the community through consciousness, in a prospective sense, of the factors mentioned above. In other words, except as noted later in this opinion, it must be proved that the change is in conformance with the comprehensive plan.

In proving that the change is in conformance with the comprehensive plan in this case, the proof, at a minimum, should show (1) there is a public need for a change of the kind in question, and (2) that need will be best served by changing the classification of the particular piece of property in question as compared with other available property.

In the instant case the trial court and the Court of Appeals interpreted prior decisions of this court as requiring the county commissioners to show a change of conditions within the immediate neighborhood in which the change was sought since the enactment of the comprehensive plan, or a mistake in the comprehensive plan as a condition precedent to the zone change. . . .

However, [these cases] should not be interpreted as establishing a rule that a physical change of circumstances within the rezoned neighborhood is the only justification for rezoning. The county governing body is directed by ORS 215.055 to consider a number of other factors when enacting zoning ordinances, and the list there does not purport to be exclusive. The important issues . . . are compliance with the statutory directive and consideration of the proposed change in light of the comprehensive plan.

Because the action of the commission in this instance is an exercise of judicial authority, the burden of proof should be placed, as is usual in judicial proceedings, upon the one seeking change. The more drastic the change, the greater will be the burden of showing that it is in conformance with the comprehensive plan as implemented by the ordinance, that there is a public need for the kind of change in question, and that the need is best met by the proposal under consideration. As the degree of change increases, the burden of showing that the potential impact upon the area in question was carefully considered and weighed will also increase. If other areas have previously been designated for the particular type of development, it must be shown why it is necessary to introduce it into an area not previously contemplated and why the property owners there should bear the burden of the departure.

Although we have said that zoning changes may be justified without a showing of a mistake in the original plan or ordinance, or of changes in the physical characteristics of an affected area, any of these factors which are present in a particular case would, of course, be relevant. Their importance would depend upon the nature of the precise change under consideration.

By treating the exercise of authority by the commission in this case as the exercise of judicial rather than of legislative authority and thus enlarging the scope of review on appeal, and by placing the burden of the above level of proof upon the one seeking change, we may lay the court open to criticism by legal scholars who think it desirable that planning authorities be vested with the ability to adjust more freely to changed conditions. However, having weighed the dangers of making desirable change more difficult against the dangers of the almost irresistible pressures that can be asserted by private economic interests on local government, we believe that the latter dangers are more to be feared. . . .

When we apply the standards we have adopted to the present case, we find that the burden was not sustained before the commission. The record now before us is insufficient to ascertain whether there was a justifiable basis for the decision. The only evidence in the record, that of the staff report of the Washington County Planning Department, is too conclusory and superficial to support the zoning change. It merely states:

> The staff finds that the requested use does conform to the residential designation of the Plan of Development. It further finds that the proposed use reflects the urbanization of the County and the necessity to provide increased densities and different types of housing to meet the needs of urbanization over that allowed by the existing zoning. . . .

Such generalizations and conclusions, without any statement of the facts on which they are based, are insufficient to justify a change of use. Moreover, no portions of the comprehensive plan of Washington County are before us, and we feel it would be improper for us to take judicial notice of the plan without at least some reference to its specifics by counsel.

As there has not been an adequate showing that the change was in accord with the plan, or that the factors listed in ORS 215.055 were given proper consideration, the judgment is affirmed.

Bryson, Justice (specially concurring). The basic facts in this case exemplify the prohibitive cost and extended uncertainty to a homeowner when a governmental body decides to change or modify a zoning ordinance or comprehensive plan affecting such owner's real property.

This controversy has proceeded through the following steps:

1. The respondent opposed the zone change before the Washington County Planning Department and Planning Commission.
2. The County Commission, after a hearing, allowed the change.
3. The trial court reversed (disallowed the change).
4. The Court of Appeals affirmed the trial court.
5. We ordered reargument and additional briefs.
6. This court affirmed.

The principal respondent in this case, Fasano, happens to be an attorney at law, and his residence is near the proposed mobile home park of the petitioner A.G.S. No average homeowner or small business enterprise can afford a judicial process such as described above nor can a judicial system cope with or endure such a process in achieving justice. The number of such controversies is ascending.

In this case the majority opinion, in which I concur, adopts some sound rules to enable county and municipal planning commissions and governing bodies, as well as trial courts, to reach finality in decision. However, the procedure is no panacea and it is still burdensome.

It is solely within the domain of the legislative branch of government to devise a new and simplified statutory procedure to expedite finality of decision.

Note

The California Supreme Court has rejected the view expressed in *Fasano* that in some instances a zoning ordinance is an adjudicative decision. Instead, the court has held that the label of a land use regulatory change determines whether it is legislative or adjudicative in character, so that, regardless of the size of the subject parcel or the number of landowners affected, a rezoning is legislative while a permit or variance is adjudicative. Arnell Development Co. v. City of Costa Mesa, 28 Cal. 3d 511, 620 P.2d 565, 169 Cal. Rptr. 904 (1980). On remand, the court of appeal overturned the local initiative ordinance as arbitrary and discriminatory. 126 Cal. App. 3d 330, 178 Cal. Rptr. 723 (1981).

◆ AMERICAN LAW INSTITUTE, A MODEL LAND DEVELOPMENT CODE
(1975)

SECTION 3-102. PURPOSES OF PREPARING A LOCAL LAND DEVELOPMENT PLAN

The purposes of preparing a Local Land Development Plan are:

(1) to initiate comprehensive studies of factors relevant to development;

(2) to recognize and state major problems and opportunities concerning development and the environmental, social and economic effects of development;

(3) to set forth the desired sequence, patterns, and characteristics of future development and its probable environmental, economic and social consequences;

(4) to provide a statement of programs to obtain the desired sequence, patterns, and characteristics of development; and

(5) to determine the probable environmental, economic and social consequences of the desired development and the proposed programs.

Section 3-103.   Planning Studies

(1) A Local Land Development Plan shall be based on all of the following studies unless the Plan specifies that particular studies are unneeded in the community and states the reasons therefor;

   (a) population and population distribution, which may include analyses by age, educational level, income, employment, race, or other appropriate characteristics;

   (b) amount, type, intensity, and general location of commerce and industry;

   (c) amount, type, quality, and general location of housing;

   (d) general location and extent of existing or currently planned major transportation, utility, and community facilities;

   (e) amount, general location, and interrelationship of different categories of land use;

   (f) extent and general location of blighted or deteriorated areas and factors related thereto;

   (g) areas, sites, or structures of historical, archeological, architectural, or scenic significance;

   (h) natural resources, including air, water, open spaces, forests, soils, rivers and other waters, shorelines, fisheries, wildlife, and minerals;

   (i) present and prospective availability of financial resources needed to undertake development proposed in the plan; and

   (j) any other matter found to be important to future development.

Section 3-104.   Statements of Trends, Objectives, Policies and Standards

(1) The Local Land Development Plan shall contain statements identifying the present conditions and major problems relating to development, physical deterioration, and the location of land uses and the social and economic effects thereof, and may show the projected nature and rate of change in present conditions for the reasonably foreseeable future based on a projection of current trends, and may forecast probable environmental, social and economic consequences which will result from such changes.

(2) The Plan shall include statements of objectives, policies and standards regarding proposed or foreseeable changes in present conditions and problems and regarding any other matters of governmental concern. The Plan shall analyze the probable social and economic consequences of its objectives, policies and standards, and shall evaluate, to the extent feasible, alternative objectives, policies and standards with respect to probable environmental, social and economic consequences.

(3) The Plan may include statements regarding the coordination of the Plan's objectives, policies and standards.

2. *Zoning Flexibility: From Nonconforming Uses to Planned Unit Developments*

D. HAGMAN, URBAN PLANNING AND LAND DEVELOPMENT CONTROL LAW 190 (1971): When a property owner wishes to use property in a manner that would be improper as presently zoned, there may be more than one way by which he can obtain permission. He might seek a legislative change through a textual or zone map amendment; he might proceed administratively and seek a variance or a special permit; he might proceed judicially and seek a declaration that the land is zoned improperly or unconstitutionally; or he might seek to qualify the property for an exception or as a nonconforming use.

More than one route to permission may be appropriate, or none may be appropriate, and there are peculiarities to each, so that the routes may be analogized as "zoning forms of action." As with common law forms of action, the choice of a form may or will dictate the allegations to be made, decision makers involved, subject matter jurisdiction of the decision makers, evidence to be presented, parties who have standing to be proponents or opponents, scope of relief and routes of appeal. *Res judicata*-like effects may differ, as will opportunities to merge or split "causes of action" or to "plead in the alternative," what advocates can be used (for example, lawyers or laymen) and so forth. Depending on the needs of the property owner, one zoning form of action may be preferable over another where alternative forms are available.

MANDELKER, DELEGATION OF POWER AND FUNCTION IN ZONING ADMINISTRATION, 1963 Wash. U.L.Q. 60, 61-63: As elsewhere in public administration, the basic problem in zoning is to achieve as clear a differentiation as possible between policy-making and policy-application. On this score the Standard State Zoning Enabling Act, on which a majority of the state statutes are modeled, failed to make tenable distinctions. Policy-making was confided to the governing body of the locality, which was given the authority to adopt the zoning ordinance. Administration was given to the zoning administrator, often the building inspector, who has the power to issue zoning permits. But ambiguity comes in the introduction of two agencies, the plan commission and the board of adjustment, known also as the board of zoning appeals. Both the commission and the board exercise functions that are partly legislative and partly administrative.

The plan commission is to advise on the enactment and amendment of the original ordinance. In theory, zoning amendments [often called rezoning] are to be made in response to substantial changes in environmental conditions or in other instances in which a policy change is indicated. Instead, amendments have often been employed to take care of limited changes in use, usually confined to one lot, a technique that has disapprovingly been called "spot zoning." Spot zoning for one parcel, vigorously opposed by adjacent neighbors, takes on adversary characteristics that give it a distinctly adjudicative cast.

The agency originally intended to provide a safety valve from the zoning ordinance is the board of adjustment. This board was authorized to grant both variances and exceptions. Confusion about the role of exceptions and variances is endemic to zoning, reflecting the confusion over underlying purposes, and shows little sign of being resolved. The variance is an administratively-authorized departure from the terms of the zoning ordinance, granted in cases of unique and individual hardship, in which a strict application of the terms of the ordinance would be unconstitutional. The grant of the variance is meant to avoid an unfavorable holding on constitutionality.

By way of contrast, an exception [often called a special exception or special permit] is a use permitted by the ordinance in a district in which it is not necessarily incompatible, but where it might cause harm if not watched. Exceptions are authorized under conditions which will insure their compatibility with surrounding uses. Typically, a use which is the subject of a special exception demands a large amount of land, may be public or semi-public in character and might often be noxious or offensive. . . .

As originally conceived, the administrative structure merely supplied the supporting cast for the zoning ordinance, which sought to legislate policy by dividing the community into districts based on the principle of compatibility. If this organizing device had worked, the ambiguities inherent in the administrative structure might not have become critical. But the division of a community into districts presupposes that generalized differentiations of land use can successfully be applied to a multiplicity of individual ownerships. This expectation has not been realized, largely because an increasingly complex urban environment requires delicate adjustments among competing land uses. These adjustments cannot always be made before the fact.

◆ HARBISON v. CITY OF BUFFALO
4 N.Y.2d 553, 152 N.E.2d 42, 176 N.Y.S.2d 598 (1958)

FROESSEL, J. Petitioner Andrew Harbison, Sr., purchased certain real property located at 35 Cumberland Avenue in the City of Buffalo on January 5, 1924. Shortly thereafter he erected a 30- by 40-foot frame building thereon, and commenced operating a cooperage business, which, with his son, he has continued to date. The building has not been enlarged, and the volume of petitioners' business is stated to be the same now as then. The only difference is that, whereas petitioners formerly dealt mainly with wooden barrels, they now recondition, clean and paint "used" steel drums or barrels. No issue of that difference is made here. These drums, or barrels, are stacked to a height of about 10 feet in the yard, and on an average day about 600 or 700 barrels are stored there.

When petitioner Andrew Harbison, Sr., established his business in 1924, the street upon which it was located was an unpaved extension of an existing street, the city operated a dump in the area, and there was a glue factory in the vicinity. At the present time, the glue factory has gone, and there are residences adjoining both sides of petitioners' property and across the street. The change in the surrounding area is reflected by the fact that in 1924 the land was unzoned, but since 1926 (except for the period between 1949 and 1953, when it was zoned for business), the land has been zoned for residential use; and it is presently in an "R3" dwelling district.

Thus it is clear that at the time of the enactment of the first zoning ordinance affecting the premises, petitioners had an existing nonconforming use, that is, the conduct of a cooperage business in a residential zone. In 1936, under an ordinance which included the operations of petitioners in a definition of "junk dealers," petitioners applied for and received a license to carry on their business. Licenses were obtained by petitioners every year from 1936 through the fiscal year of 1956.

However, the ordinances of the City of Buffalo were amended, effective as of July 30, 1953, so as to state in chapter LXX (§18):

> 1. Continuing existing uses: Except as provided in this section, any non-conforming use of any building, structure, land or premises may be continued. Provided, however, that on premises situate in any "R" district each use which is not a conforming use in the "R5" district and which falls into one of the categories hereinafter enumerated shall cease or shall be changed to a conforming use within 3 years from the effective date of this amended chapter. The requirements of this subdivision for the termination of non-conforming uses shall apply in each of the following cases: .... (d) Any junkyard. ....

On this appeal, the City of Buffalo argues (1) that petitioners did not have a *lawful* nonconforming use when the zoning ordinance was enacted in 1926, since at that time they had not complied with an ordinance enacted in 1892 requiring the licensing of wholesale junk dealers; (2) that petitioners are not entitled to the peremptory grant of a license since they have not enclosed their premises with a solid wood or sheet metal fence or masonry wall not less than 6 feet high, as required by section 194 of article XIII of chapter V of the ordinance, and (3) that the ordinance, held invalid by the courts below, is a valid exercise of the police power.

The first point need not detain us long. The ordinance of 1892, upon which the city relies, related to "the business of purchasing or selling old silver, iron, brass, copper scraps or other secondhand or partially ruined or damaged materials, [or] carry[ing] on . . . a junk shop." It is argued that this ordinance does not clearly encompass petitioners' business of repairing and reconditioning barrels. In any event, I might note that petitioners operated a *licensed* wholesale junk business from 1936 to 1956, and the city never raised the foregoing objection on any of the applications for renewal of the license. Hence this argument has no merit.

Nor does the second point appear to be a sound ground for refusal to issue a license here. If, as appears, petitioners have not complied with the letter of the ordinance since their property is enclosed by a picket fence rather than one of solid wood or metal, an order directing the issuance of a license could readily be conditioned upon compliance with such provisions inasmuch as petitioners are quite willing to comply with this requirement. It may be noted that this defense was not interposed until the close of the hearings.

In the major point involved on this appeal, the city argues that the ordinance requiring the termination of petitioners' nonconforming use of the premises as a junk yard within three years of the date of said ordinance is a valid exercise of its police power. Its claim is not based on the theory of nuisance, and indeed this record contains little evidence as to the manner of operation of petitioners' business and the nature of the surrounding neighborhood. Rather, in this case, the city bases its claim largely on out-of-State decisions which have sustained ordinances requiring the termination of nonconforming uses or structures after a period of permitted continuance, where such "amortization" period was held reasonable.

When zoning ordinances are initially adopted to limit permissible uses of property, or when property is rezoned so as to prevent uses of property previously allowed, a degree of protection is constitutionally required to be given owners of property then using their premises in a manner forbidden by the ordinance. Thus we have held that, where substantial expenditures were made in the commencement of the erection of a building, a zoning ordinance may not deprive the owner of the "vested right" to complete the structure. So, where the owner already has structures on the premises, he cannot be directed to cease using them, . . . just as he has the right to continue a prior business carried on there.

However, where the benefit to the public has been deemed of greater moment than the detriment to the property owner, we have sustained the prohibition of continuation of prior nonconforming uses.

These cases involved the prior use of property for parking lots. We have also upheld the restriction of projected uses of the property where, at the time of passage of the ordinance, there had been no substantial investment in the nonconforming use. In these cases, there is no doubt that the property owners incurred a loss in the value of their property and otherwise as a result of the fact that they were unable to carry out their prospective uses; but we held that such a deprivation was not violative of the owners' constitutional rights. . . .

The development of the policy that nonconforming uses should be protected and their existence preserved at the stage of development existing at the time of passage of the ordinance seems to have been based upon the assumption that the ultimate ends of zoning would be accomplished as the nonconforming use terminated with time. But this has not proven to be the case, as commentators have noted that the tendency of many of these uses is to flourish, capitalizing on the fact that no new use of that nature could be begun in the area. Because of this situation, communities have sought new forms of ordinances restricting nonconforming uses, and in particular have turned to provisions which require termination after a given period of time. . . .

Leaving aside eminent domain and nuisance, we have often stated in our decisions that the owner of land devoted to a prior nonconforming use, or on which a prior nonconforming structure exists (or has been substantially commenced), has the right to continue such use, but we have never held that this right may continue virtually in perpetuity. Now that we are for the first time squarely faced with the problem as to whether or not this right may be terminated after a reasonable period, during which the owner may have a fair opportunity to amortize his investment and to make future plans, we conclude that it may be, in accordance with the overwhelming weight of authority found in the courts of our sister States, as well as with the textwriters and commentators who have expressed themselves upon the subject. . . .

If, therefore, a zoning ordinance provides a sufficient period of permitted nonconformity, it may further provide that at the end of such period the use must cease. This rule is analogous to that with respect to nonconforming structures. In ascertaining the reasonable period during which an owner of property must be allowed to continue a nonconforming use, a balance must be found between social harm and private injury. We cannot say that a legislative body may not in any case, after consideration of the factors involved, conclude that the termination of a use after a period of time sufficient to allow a property owner an opportunity to amortize his investment and make other plans is a valid method of solving the problem.

To enunciate a contrary rule would mean that the use of land for such purposes as a tennis court, an open air skating rink, a junk yard or a parking lot — readily transferable to another site — at the date of the enactment of a zoning ordinance vests the owner thereof with the right to utilize the land in that manner in perpetuity, regardless of the changes in the neighborhood over the course of time. In the light of our ever expanding urban communities, such a rule appears to us to constitute an unwarranted restriction upon the Legislature in dealing with what has been described as "One of the major problems in effective administration of modern zoning ordinances." When the termination provisions are reasonable in the light of the nature of the business of the property owner, the improvements erected on the land, the character of the neighborhood, and the detriment caused the property owner, we may not hold them constitutionally invalid. . . .

Material triable issues of fact thus remain, and a further hearing should adduce evidence relating to the nature of the surrounding neighborhood, the value and condition of the improvements on the premises, . . . the cost of . . . relocation. . . . It is only upon such evidence that it may be ascertained whether . . . the ordinance would be unconstitutional as applied to . . . this case.

VAN VOORHIS, J. (dissenting). The decision which is about to be rendered marks, in my view, the beginning of the end of the constitutional protection of property rights in this State in pre-existing nonconforming uses under zoning ordinances. Special Term and the Appellate Division unanimously followed the existing law in holding this amendment to the zoning ordinance of the City of Buffalo to be unconstitutional. In my view the traditional rule is right, and should not be abrogated. . . .

The circumstance that this is a cooperage establishment or junk yard ought not to obscure that the principle of the decision applies to any kind of business which, due to lapse of time, has been overtaken by changes in the neighborhood. The principle of the decision applies equally to stores, shops or service organizations which are retroactively legislated out of existence by the abolition of prior nonconforming uses. If petitioners' establishment is not secure against this kind of invasion, no one else's business is better protected. The neighbors or the officials of a municipality in one year may look askance at a junk or cooperage yard, and in another year may frown upon the conduct in a particular locality of any other type of commerce or industry. The people who moved into petitioners' vicinity and now find their business offensive may not be aware that the principle of this decision unsettles their own property rights, and that it may suddenly be used against them in unexpected ways if agitation arises to legislate them out of business by a similar procedure. It makes little difference what the nature of their businesses may be. The smaller they are the more vulnerable they become to this kind of attack, which is based on the misfortune of unpopularity. Democracy depends upon respect for the individual as well as upon majority rule. The relaxation of constitutional safeguards protecting commonly accepted personal and property rights, goes hand in hand with the multiplication of pressure groups. People should not be obliged to organize to preserve rights the safeguarding of which is the proper function of law. The small manufacturer or merchant feels this acutely, since he ordinarily finds it more difficult to succeed in wielding organized power for his own protection when property rights depend upon the discretion of legislative bodies. No question is raised here concerning the good faith of the enactment or administration of this ordinance. Nevertheless petitioners find themselves confronted by the organized civil power of the municipality, set in motion by the complaints of their neighbors who wish to eliminate them from the locality in which petitioners settled first. If this part of the city is to be redeveloped, it should be done through the enactment of a statute similar in principle to slum clearance acts, whereby just compensation can be paid for private property that is confiscated for a public use. Petitioners have well-recognized legal property rights which ought to be protected in court. . . .

The lack of any principle in applying the novel theory of "amortization" betrays a fundamental weakness in the theory. Zoning, like other public programs, is not always best administered at the hands of its enthusiasts. The existence of nonconforming uses has spoiled the symmetry in the minds of zoning experts. It has bulked so large in this context that, desirable as the elimination of nonconforming uses may be, it has sometimes been presented as though it were more important than ordinary property rights.

Many means of eliminating and controlling nonconforming uses have been proposed and tried. Among these means are retroactive zoning, amortization of nonconforming uses, abatement of nonconforming uses as nuisances, public purchase and eminent domain, prohibition of the resumption of a nonconforming use after a period of discontinuance, and refusal to provide governmental services to nonconforming users. (1951 Wis. L. Rev. 687.)

This Wisconsin Law Review article points out how most of these different proposals have been tried and found wanting, particularly the method of exercising the power of eminent domain which is said to have been discarded mainly for the reason that it is too expensive. The same is said at page 93 of Volume 102 of the Pennsylvania Law Review. The fault found with eminent domain is that it failed to achieve the object of destroying the owner's right in his property without paying for it. Consequently the most promising legal theory at the moment is known as "amortization." . . . "Amortization" is explained [in the Pennsylvania Law Review article] as follows: "'The only positive method of getting rid of nonconforming uses yet devised is to amortize a nonconforming building. That is, to determine the normal useful remaining life of the building and prohibit the owner from maintaining it after the expiration of that time.'" The opinion in City of Los Angeles v. Gage adds: "The length of time given the owner to eliminate his nonconforming use or building varies with the city and with the type of structure."

This theory to justify extinguishing nonconforming uses means less the more one thinks about it. . . . In the first place, the periods of time vary so widely in the cases which have been cited from different States where it has been tried, and have so little relation to the useful lives of the structures, that this theory cannot be used to reconcile these discordant decisions. Moreover the term "amortization," as thus employed, has not the same meaning which it carries in law or accounting. It is not even used by analogy. It is just a catch phrase.

There could be no presumption that all junk yards, all auto wrecking or dismantling establishments, and all improvements assessed for tax purposes at not more than $500 will or have any tendency to depreciate to zero in three years. This shows that the ordinance in suit could not possibly have been based on the amortization theory.

Moreover this theory, if it were seriously advanced, would imply that the owner should not keep up his property by making necessary replacements to restore against the ravages of time. Such replacements would be money thrown away. The amortization theory would thus encourage owners of nonconforming uses to allow them to decay and become slums.

Notes

1. Other courts have approved the application of ordinances requiring amortization of nonconforming uses. See, e.g., the elaborate balancing test in City of Los Angeles v. Gage, 127 Cal. App. 2d 442, 274 P.2d 34 (1954):

> . . . The distinction between an ordinance restricting future uses and one requiring the termination of present uses within a reasonable period of time is merely one of degree, and constitutionality depends on the relative importance to be given to the public gain and to the private loss. Zoning as it affects every piece of property is to some extent retroactive in that it applies to property already owned at the time of the effective date of the ordinance. The elimination of existing uses within a reasonable time does not amount to a taking of property nor does it necessarily restrict the use of property so that it cannot be used for any reasonable purpose. Use of a reasonable amortization scheme provides an equitable means of reconciliation of the conflicting interests in satisfaction of due process requirements. As a method of eliminating existing nonconforming uses it allows the owner of the nonconforming use, by affording an opportunity to make

new plans, at least partially to offset any loss he might suffer. The loss he suffers, if any, is spread out over a period of years, and he enjoys a monopolistic position by virtue of the zoning ordinance as long as he remains. If the amortization period is reasonable the loss to the owner may be small when compared with the benefit to the public. Nonconforming uses will eventually be eliminated. A legislative body may well conclude that the beneficial effect on the community of the eventual elimination of all nonconforming uses by a reasonable amortization plan more than offsets individual losses.

The ordinance in question provides, according to a graduated periodic schedule, for the gradual and ultimate elimination of all commercial and industrial uses in residential zones. These provisions require the discontinuance of nonconforming uses of land within a five-year period, and the discontinuance of nonconforming commercial and industrial uses of residential buildings in the "R" zones within the same five-year period. These provisions are the only ones pertinent to the decision in this case. However, it may be noted that other provisions of the ordinance require the discontinuance of nonconforming billboards and, in residential zones, the discontinuance of nonconforming buildings and of nonconforming uses of nonconforming buildings, within specified periods running from 20 to 40 years according to the type of building construction.

We have no doubt that Ordinance 90,500, in compelling the discontinuance of the use of defendants' property for a wholesale and retail plumbing and plumbing supply business, and for the open storage of plumbing supplies within five years after its passage, is a valid exercise of the police power. Lots 220 and 221 are several blocks from a business center and it appears that they are not within any reasonable or logical extension of such a center. The ordinance does not prevent the operation of defendants' business; it merely restricts its location. Discontinuance of the nonconforming use requires only that Gage move his plumbing business to property that is zoned for it. Such property can be found within a half mile of Gage's property. The cost of moving is $5,000, or less than 1% of Gage's minimum gross business for five years, or less than half of 1% of the mean of his gross business for five years. He has had eight years within which to move. The property is usable for residential purpose. Since 1930 lot 221 has been used for residential purposes. All of the land within 500 feet of Gage's property is now improved and used for such purposes. Lot 220, now unimproved, can be improved for the same purposes.

We think it apparent that none of the agreed facts and none of the ultimate facts found by the court justify the conclusion that Ordinance 90,500, as applied to Gage's property, is clearly arbitrary or unreasonable, or has no substantial relation to the public's health, safety, morals, or general welfare, or that it is an unconstitutional impairment of his property rights. . . .

2. The following was proposed as an amendment to a state enabling act:

Any nonconforming use or structure existing at the time of passage of an ordinance may be continued upon the lot or in the building so occupied. But reasonable provisions may be adopted for the gradual elimination of such nonconforming uses or structures, including but in no way limited to, reasonable provisions for:

    a. amortization over a period of time;

    b. elimination of nonconforming uses of unimproved land;

    c. elimination of nonconformances upon termination of the rental period of the person in possession;

    d. elimination of nonconforming uses located in structures adaptable to conforming uses;

    e. elimination of nonconformances upon discontinuance, abandonment or destruction.

3. The neighborhood around the intersection of Park Avenue and 75th Street on Manhattan's Upper East Side was zoned for residential use, but the flower shop on the northeast corner had been issued a nonconforming use permit. When it was closed down and its owners were criminally convicted of drug trafficking and arranging to bomb a rival florist, Kyu-Song Choi, a Korean immigrant, signed a 10-year lease and proposed to open a 24-hour delicatessen.

Some neighbors immediately protested to city building, zoning, and landmark officials and began passing out leaflets opposing Mr. Choi's plans. The leader of the protesters claimed that the delicatessen would draw "a generally undesirable type of person that we are not accustomed to." Mr. Choi immediately corrected technical violations found by city inspectors and agreed to many of the changes desired by the protesters — including calling it a "gourmet and health food" store rather than a deli, removing his coffee urn so that he would not be serving "take-out" food, and limiting his business hours. Mr. Choi opened for business in March 1984 despite the furor caused by his presence on Park Avenue. Could much of the misunderstanding have been avoided if the city zoning classifications had been more refined in establishing classes of commercial uses? Is there a significant difference between a flower (and heroin) shop and a delicatessen (with or without take-out food)? See N.Y. Times, Feb. 20, 1985.

◆ MacDONALD v. BOARD OF COUNTY
COMMISSIONERS
238 Md. 549, 210 A.2d 325 (1965)

OPPENHEIMER, J. Adjacent property owners appeal from an order of the Circuit Court for Prince George's County affirming a zoning action of the Board of County Commissioners for Prince George's County, sitting as a District Council for the Prince George's portion of the Maryland-

Washington Regional District (the Council). The Council had approved applications of the Isle of Thye Land Company, one of the appellees (the Land Company), to reclassify three tracts of land all zoned R-R (Rural Residential). Two tracts of approximately nine and three acres respectively were rezoned to C-2 (General Commercial) and the third, of about 29 acres, to R-H (Multiple Family, High Rise Residential).

The three tracts are part of a larger area of 655 acres owned by the Land Company, called Tantallon on the Potomac, located in the southwestern portion of the County, on Swan Creek, which empties into the Potomac. The Woodrow Wilson Bridge and the Capital Beltway are four or five miles to the north. Fort Washington National Park, a 341 acre reservation, is adjacent to the area on the south and Mount Vernon is across the Potomac River to the west. . . .

The technical staff of the Planning Commission recommended denial of all three applications. Its amended report stated, in part:

> The staff, in its review of this application, concludes that the granting of any zone on this property other than the existing R-R Zone, would be spot zoning. The development which has occurred in the area has been that of single family dwellings on larger than minimum lot size standards, and, the changes which have occurred in this area, the Tantallon community included, are a continuation and solidification of this pattern. . . .

The Planning Board recommended denial of the R-H rezoning for the reasons given by its technical staff. . . .

At the hearing before the Council, the expert witnesses of the Land Company offered voluminous and plausible testimony as to the attractive nature of the plans for the area which it owns. It claimed but offered no evidence to support a mistake in the Master Zoning Map. It relied, instead, upon claimed substantial changes in the area since the adoption of the comprehensive zoning map. The nature of the alleged changes will be considered hereafter. The Chief Engineer of the Planning Commission elaborated upon the reports of the technical staff, and testified that the changes that had occurred in the area of the Land Company's property were oriented towards low density, single family development. Neighboring and adjacent property owners, including the appellants, presented testimony in opposition to the reclassifications, with letters from other protestants, including Secretary of the Interior Udall.

The Council, one of the Commissioners dissenting, approved all three of the Land Company's applications for rezoning. The formal notice of the Council gave no reasons for its decision. The only statement in the nature of reasons is contained in what appears to be a press release on behalf of the Council. This release, apart from some extraneous remarks, contained the following statements:

Commissioner Brooke, in making his motion, pointed out that the several proposed 20-story apartments would be 3400 feet back from the river, "in a natural valley which would keep them screened from view from the river and the Virginia shore."

He also noted expanded highway development in the general area and that neither the Board of Education nor the National Capital Planning Commission opposed the planned community. . . .

It was also stated that the Chairman of the Council, who votes only in case of tie, had declared himself in sympathy with the zoning request. Commissioner Gladys Spellman, who dissented, in a separate announcement, said in part:

The changes which have taken place in the area are not sufficient to warrant rezoning from a low density, single family category. . . . No need has been established for high density apartments in the middle of an area of extremely low density, other than that of remunerative return for the applicant. . . . No proof of error in the original zoning was presented.

The Isle of Thye Land Company plans high rise apartments on approximately 29 acres, and accordingly requests a change to R-H zoning. However, the use of this zone category in a low-density setting is *totally at variance* with the *purpose* of R-H zoning as set forth in the text of the classification. . . . We must recognize that the District Council is concerned for the County as a whole and not merely 650 acres of the county. It is certainly not reasonable to assume that because a community is well-planned and well-balanced, it may be set down at any point in the County without doing violence to the surrounding areas. Planning must extend beyond the borders of individual communities and encompass the larger areas of the County in order that communities may complement each other rather than inflict harm upon one another.

There was a hearing on the Petition for Review of the Council's order before Judge Loveless. In his opinion affirming the order, the Judge pointed out that the Land Company had not contended there had been a mistake in the original zoning, and that the court had no alternative other than to say that no mistake had been shown. Judge Loveless referred to the 14 items relied upon by the Land Company as changes in the area since the original zoning was made and held they were sufficient evidence to justify a reclassification if the Council, in its legislative discretion, so decided. He held, further, that the issues were fairly debatable, and that the Board's action in approving the applications was not arbitrary or capricious. We disagree in respect of the Board's order granting the application to rezone the 29 acres for high-rise apartments.

We have repeatedly held that there is a strong presumption of the correctness of original zoning, and that to sustain a piecemeal change therefrom, there must be strong evidence of mistake in the original zoning or else of a substantial change in conditions. The Land Company contends that here comprehensive rezoning is involved, because of the extent of its entire acreage and the nature of its plans for the development of that acreage. However, as Commissioner Spellman points out in her dissent from the Council's order, it is not the proposed treatment of a particular tract within the broad territory encompassed by the original zoning plan which governs; the impingement of the proposed rezoning upon the general plan is the criterion. We hold that, in this case, it is proposed piecemeal rezoning which is involved and that the strong presumption of the correctness of the original comprehensive zoning prevails.

The majority of the Council, in effect, gave no reasons for its order. The alleged changes of conditions in the immediate area adduced by the Land Company to support their application to rezone the 29 acres for high-rise apartments, in our opinion, do not constitute evidence sufficient to make the facts fairly debatable. A number of these changes have taken place, or are contemplated, within the Tantallon tract itself. The building of a golf course, the dredging of Swan Creek, the reservation of a school site within the tract, and the authorization of public utility services for the Tantallon enterprise are as consistent with increased rural residential development as they are with the building of high-rise apartments. The characterization by the appellants of these alleged changes as "bootstrap" arguments, in our opinion, is appropriate. The report of the technical staff of the Planning Commission states that the development which has occurred within the area, including the Tantallon tract, has been a continuation and solidification of the single family dwelling pattern, with lots larger than the minimum standard, and this statement was not contradicted. The road improvements referred to by the Land Company do not change the character of the neighborhood; as the technical staff pointed out, "[t]he character of the surrounding area is reflected in the road network which consists of generally narrow, winding two-lane pavements designed to serve traffic volumes generated by low density, large lot development." The completion of the Woodrow Wilson Bridge and Anacostia Freeway listed as additional changes presumably were envisaged in the comprehensive zoning plan, adopted by the legislative body only a little less than five years before the Land Company's application. In any event, the Bridge and Freeway are some miles away.

The Planning Board, as well as its technical staff, recommended that the applications for the high-rise apartment rezoning be denied. The majority of the Council refused to accept the Board's recommendations, without substantive evidence to support its actions. In similar circumstances, although on varying facts, we have held that an order of the lower court affirming the Board's action must be reversed. . . .

The Land Company does not contend that denial of the application would preclude the use of its property for any purpose to which it is reasonably adapted. On the contrary, it admitted it would be practical, although from its point of view not as satisfactory, to continue the development of Tantallon without high-rise apartments. The developer's desire to make additional profits is a legitimate motive, but not sufficient to justify a rezoning.

BARNES, J. (dissenting). In my opinion, the majority has not only gone astray in its application of the law of zoning to the facts of the case, but has applied principles and standards that I believe are inapposite to the factual situation present in this appeal. In either event the time has come when the soundness of the foundations upon which those principles and standards rest should be reexamined. . . .

In my opinion, the physical changes alone would support a finding by the District Council and by the lower court that there had been a "change of conditions" within the meaning of the Maryland Rule, if applicable. The physical changes are substantial ones relating to the public roads which form the southern, eastern and part of the northern boundaries of the Tantallon development, the increased accommodation of traffic from the District of Columbia to the area, the rearrangement of areas for parks, the providing of utilities for the area and the provisions for school facilities by the Board of Education. Swan Creek, with the approval of the proper governmental officers, has been dredged as contemplated by the master plan of Tantallon. The subdivision plats are based on the master plan of Tantallon which includes the five high-rise apartments. This master plan is known to, and there is no objection to it from, the National Capital Planning Commission. If these physical changes in the neighborhood are not sufficient to justify the District Council in believing that there had been a "change in conditions," it is difficult for me to visualize a case in which the change of conditions rule could apply. . . .

[T]he majority's statement that the population boom, together with the new highways and bridges some miles away "presumably were envisaged in the comprehensive plan," does not seem justified to me. There is no evidence that they were so envisaged and the probabilities are strong that they were not. The situation in Prince George's County is too volatile to attribute such prophetic powers to those who prepared the "comprehensive" plan. It should be kept in mind that the Tantallon area was virgin territory and, with most of such territory in this area, was all put in the R-R area in order to cover this area with this general type of zoning restriction. The plan was "comprehensive" only in that it covered all areas in the County. There have been no detailed plans in this area promulgated by the County; the only detailed plan is the October 1961 development plan of Tantallon prepared by Mr. Robinson. Then too, what physical changes occurring after the promulgation of the "comprehensive" plan in 1957 by the County might not be said to have been "presumably envisaged" in that plan and thus be made to disappear, as it were, from consideration as subsequent changes? There is far too much room here for the operation of subjective considerations. . . .

Commissioner Gladys Spellman, the single Councilman who failed to concur in the granting of the R-H rezoning request, based her dissent largely on the basis of the presumed effect of the proposed apartments on the Potomac shoreline and skyline, and the deleterious effect upon the view from Mount Vernon and Fort Washington. Secretary of the Interior Udall also expressed these sentiments in a letter to the Council which prophesied that the apartments might become "dominant." The appellant MacDonald, a historian by profession, voiced his fear that the apartments would be "shockingly visible." But opposed to these opinions was an overwhelming mass of evidence to the effect that Secretary Udall's fears had little chance of materializing. It was testified that the proposed luxury apartments would be some 3400 feet back from the Potomac, on the south side of Swan Creek, approximately in the center of the 650-acre parcel of land. Indeed Councilman Sutphin stated he would have opposed R-H rezoning had they not been. The apartments would be screened from view by trees, already in place, 60 feet in height, surrounded by a high ridge on the south, southwest, and southeast. . . .

The majority states, in effect, that rezoning can only be sustained when there is "strong evidence of mistake" in the original zoning or where there is "a substantial change in conditions" in the neighborhood. This "mistake-change in conditions" rule came into the Maryland law by way of dicta of our predecessors and in a rather oblique way. . . . *doctrine* It was entirely judicially conceived and delivered. It had no legislative assistance. It has had a rapid and, to my mind, unhealthy growth in the Maryland law. The formulae have become talismanic phrases now applied with Draconian severity to the rezoning efforts of the local legislative bodies, with unfortunate results. In my opinion, the time to reexamine the entire doctrine and its premises is long overdue. As it is entirely "judge-made," a change in, or broadening of, the doctrine would operate only prospectively and it would in no way impair vested rights, inasmuch as it is not a rule of property. Under these circumstances, the doctrine of *stare decisis* is not a substantial obstacle in effecting a much-needed change. If my Brethren are reluctant to overrule or modify the "mistake-change" doctrine, I suggest with great respect, that the Legislative Council and ultimately the General Assembly give serious thought to a change by appropriate legislation.

Let us examine the syllogisms upon which this "change-or-mistake" rule rests. As I see them they are:

Major premise: The comprehensive zoning plan was a good plan when enacted; the plan is good today, if physical conditions have not changed.

Minor premise: Physical conditions have not changed.

Conclusion: The plan is good today.

The "mistake" part of the "change-or-mistake" rule is founded on another such syllogism, equally grim, which goes like this:

Major premise: Today's plan is a good plan, but differs from the original plan; if physical conditions have not changed, the original plan must have been bad.

Minor premise: Physical conditions have not changed.

Conclusion: The original plan must have been bad.

The difficulty lies in the dependence upon the terms "good" — "bad" — "conditions," and the interpretation to be placed on each. Or, to put the matter a different way, the defect may lie in confining the term "conditions" to the connotation of "physical conditions." As a cursory glance at the Index to Legal Periodicals and to other compilations of journal topics will show, the ideas of planning and zoning, for the modern urban complex, have come a long way since that day in 1926 when Euclid, Ohio v. Ambler Realty Company first upheld the idea and practical application of zoning.

The "change-or-mistake" rule derived from the syllogisms above set forth is rendered erroneous by the simple truth: "Ideas change."

In my opinion, the correct rule in considering the validity of rezoning ordinances is whether or not the ordinance is unreasonable, arbitrary or capricious. . . .

There is a strong presumption in favor of the reasonableness of a zoning ordinance, but we have indicated that this presumption of reasonableness does not apply with the same weight or "with as great force" to a rezoning ordinance. . . . In my opinion, the presumption of reasonableness is just as strong in support of the rezoning ordinance as it was in support of the original zoning ordinance. This seems to be the general rule. . . .

It is also clear that if there is a mistake in the original zoning or if there has been a change in the physical conditions in the neighborhood of the area affected by the rezoning ordinance, its reasonable relationship to the police power is obviously "fairly debatable" and the ordinance must be sustained. But the "mistake-change in physical condition" rule should not be an *exclusive* test. While, of course, an amendment is often predicated upon the recognition of changing conditions or of a mistake in original zoning, such factors, while relevant, are not controlling, and are among many circumstances for the Council to weigh and evaluate. Similarly, reviewing courts should consider the presence or absence of such factors merely as *some evidence* tending to show whether or not the action of the Council, in granting or denying a proposed reclassification, was arbitrary, unreasonable, or capricious. The majority has now made the rule the exclusive test and has confined the "change in conditions" portion of the rule to a change in *physical* conditions. Herein lies the error. As above indicated, ideas change.

They particularly change in considering zoning reclassifications in a volatile situation and particularly in an area of rural virgin territory in the process of change to urban or suburban development. The syllogisms of the "mistake-change in condition" rule applied by the majority give no place to these new ideas. As I see the matter, it is entirely possible that the original zoning viewed in the light of conditions existing at the time of the formulation of the original comprehensive plan might have been proper and in accordance with the then recognized zoning concepts, and, with no change in physical conditions in the meantime, a new subdivision, prepared in accordance with more modern and more enlightened zoning ideas, be proper a relatively short time later. If we broadened our perspective and raised our sights in the "change in conditions" portion of the rule to include changes in zoning concepts and philosophy and did not limit it to a change in physical conditions merely, the problem would be largely solved. The people's representatives would then be free to give effect to the new ideas and concepts; they would arise from the present Procrustean bed upon which we have placed them, with renewed vigor, to advance the public interest. The case at bar is an excellent example of the unfortunate effect of the presently restricted rule. . . .

Note

When the zoning problem stalled Tantallon, the developers found themselves in litigation with the estate of an individual who had sold them land in return for an interest in the project. See Isle of Thye Land Co. v. Whisman, 262 Md. 682, 279 A.2d 484 (1971).

Immediately after *MacDonald*, a new attempt was made to obtain multi-family high density residential zoning for part of Tantallon. Preswick, Inc. filed a rezoning application on July 1, 1966. The planning commission recommended approval but the district council rejected the application. The circuit court reversed, concluding that there had been a mistake in the 1957 comprehensive zoning, and also that there had been substantial change in the character of the neighborhood. The court of appeals reversed, reinstating the district council's rejection of the application. Prince George's County Council v. Preswick, Inc., 263 Md. 217, 282 A.2d 491 (1971).

◆ LIFE OF THE LAND, INC. v. CITY COUNCIL
   61 Hawaii 390, 606 P.2d 866 (1980)

MARUMOTO, Justice. This case arose in connection with a project, known as The Admiral Thomas, for the development by The Victoria Partnership and The Admiral Thomas Venture (the Developers), of a parcel of land in Honolulu, owned by the First United Methodist Church, under a development agreement executed by the Church and the Developers on August 22, 1975.

The Victoria Partnership is a Hawaii limited partnership, and The Admiral Thomas Venture is a Hawaii joint venture. The latter is the general partner of the former. In all business dealings, the Developers are represented by Sheridan Ing as their agent.

The case is before us on an appeal by plaintiffs from a judgment of the First Circuit Court dismissing their complaint and from an order of that court denying their motion for relief from the judgment. The circuit court entered its judgment pursuant to its denying plaintiffs' motion for partial summary judgment and granting the motion of defendants and intervening defendants for summary judgment.

On this appeal, our function is to resolve questions of law applicable to the facts which appear in the record. There is no genuine issue regarding the facts contained in the record. Only questions of law are set forth by plaintiffs, as well as by defendants and intervening defendants, in their statements of questions presented on appeal required by our rules.

The Admiral Thomas project contemplates construction of a highrise building containing residential apartments, and off-street automobile parking stalls, to be sold as condominiums, and a two-story administration and classroom building to be used by the Church, on the project site. There is a sanctuary on the site, which will not be disturbed by the project.

Construction of the two-story building and retention of the sanctuary are not in controversy. Controversy exists only with respect to the construction of the highrise building.

The project site is located on the easterly side of Victoria Street, between Kinau Street and Beretania Street, directly across Honolulu Academy of Arts and cater corner from Thomas Square. It is rectangular in shape, slopes about 11 feet from Kinau Street to Beretania Street, and contains an area of 2.07 acres, or 90,053 square feet.

Thomas Square and the Academy are designated for preservation on the State and National registers because of their historical significance. . . .

Plaintiffs are organizations and individuals interested in the preservation and enhancement of the historical, cultural, and scenic values of the Academy and Thomas Square and opposed to the construction of a highrise building of the nature contemplated in the project in the immediate vicinity of the Academy and Thomas Square. Neither the Academy nor any of its directors or officers is among the plaintiffs who filed the complaint.

EXHIBIT I.

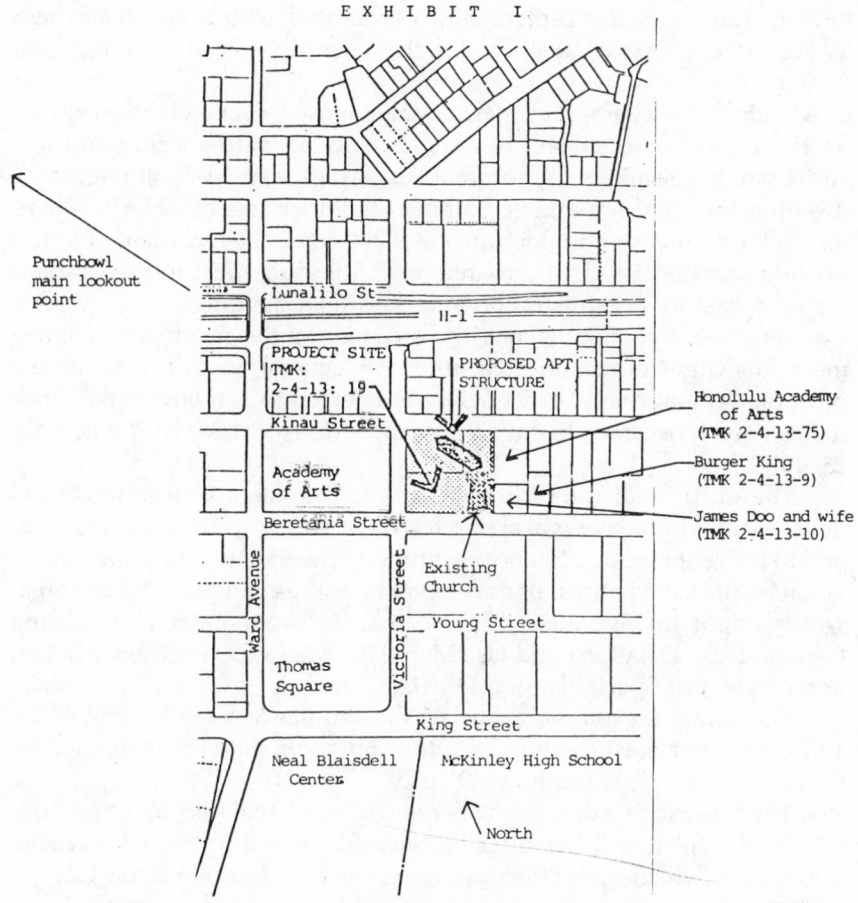

Punchbowl
main lookout
point

Lunalilo St

II-1

PROJECT SITE
TMK:
2-4-13: 19

Kinau Street

Academy
of Arts

Beretania Street

PROPOSED APT
STRUCTURE

Honolulu Academy
of Arts
(TMK 2-4-13-75)

Burger King
(TMK 2-4-13-9)

James Doo and wife
(TMK 2-4-13-10)

Ward Avenue

Victoria Street

Existing
Church

Young Street

Thomas
Square

King Street

Neal Blaisdell
Center

McKinley High School

North

FIGURE 21-2
Map from the Appendix to the official report of *Life of the Land*

In their complaint, plaintiffs named the members of the City Council of the City and county of Honolulu, the Mayor, and the Directors of the Department of Land Utilization (DLU) and the Building Department, as defendants, and sought a judgment declaring the invalidity of the action taken by the City Council on September 21, 1977, as amended on November 10, 1977, with respect to the construction of the buildings contemplated in the project.

The Church and the Developers are parties in this case as intervening defendants by leave of court, obtained over plaintiffs' objection.

At the time the Church and the Developers executed their development agreement on August 22, 1975, and at all subsequent times pertinent to this case, the project site was located within an area zoned as Apartment District A-4, under the Comprehensive Zoning Code (CZC). . . .

Under such zoning, it is permissible for the Developers to construct on the project site, subject to requirements for yard-spacing and off-street parking facilities for automobiles, a high density multiple-family dwelling 350 feet high and containing total floor area of 309,476 square feet, after deducting the floor area of 9,200 square feet contained in the existing sanctuary and a floor area of 17,313 square feet in the contemplated two-story administration and classroom building.

However, five months after the execution of the development agreement, the City Council enacted, under its general police and homerule powers, Ordinance No. 4551, hereafter referred to as the Kaakako Ordinance, which became effective upon approval by the Mayor on January 23, 1976.

The purpose of the ordinance was to provide a vehicle to control development in the general area referred to therein as the Kakaako area, and to prevent race of diligence by property owners, pending the formulation by the City Council of development polices and plans for the area, which might involve amendments to CZC, amendments to existing General Plan, Detailed Land Use Map (DLUM), and Development Plan, and creation of Special Design District. . . .

The original expiration date of the ordinance was November 26, 1976, but, after mesne extensions, the expiration date was extended by Ordinance No. 77-113 to June 30, 1979.

The Kakaako Ordinance was repealed and replaced by Ordinance No 78-64, which will hereafter be referred to as the Revised Kakaako Ordinance, which took effect upon approval by the Mayor on July 12, 1978. . . .

On July 11, 1977, almost two years after the date of the development agreement, and one year and six months after the enactment of the Kaakako Ordinance, the Developers filed their application for variance or modification, as provided in section IV-A of the Kaakako Ordinance. . . .

The project for which variance or modification was sought by the Developers included a high density multiple-family dwelling, 206 feet wide on the broad side; 59 feet wide on the narrow side; with a height of 350 feet, plus a mechanical penthouse 20 feet high; containing 177 one-bedroom and two-bedroom units on 35 apartment floors over four levels of off-street automobile parking facilities; set back 95 feet from Victoria Street; with the narrower dimension of the building oriented toward the Punchbowl main lookout platform, as shown [in Figure 21-2].

At the time the developers filed their application, construction of such building was permissible under CZC, but the Kaakako Ordinance blocked the obtaining of necessary building permit. . . .

The Planning Commission held a public hearing on the proposed ordinance on February 18, 1976, at which it received written evidence and heard oral testimony. Thereafter, on April 27, 1976, it submitted its report to the City Council, recommending rejection of the proposed ordinance. . . .

At its meeting on September 21, 1977, the City Council approved the Developers' application, with . . . three conditions [for unobtrusive materials and landscaping]. . . .

The action of the City Council generated considerable community criticism, including editorials in the Honolulu Advertiser and the Honolulu Star-Bulletin.

The criticism centered on the bulk and height of the proposed apartment building, characterized by some opponents of the project as "the massive highrise monster towering over the historic Academy and Thomas Square."

In the light of such criticism, City Councilman Kaapu spearheaded the formation of an ad hoc committee chaired by Rev. Olin Pendleton, former chairman of the Council of Presidents. . . .

On November 3, 1977, the Developers, through Sheridan Ing, offered the following changes in the proposed apartment building, subject to approval of the Church:

(a) decrease the height of the building from the maximum of 350 feet, permissible under CZC, to an average of 299 feet, with a staggered roofline 288 feet high on the Academy side and the elevated portion to be on the side farthest away from the Academy and Thomas Square;

(b) maintain a setback of 95 feet from the property line on the Academy side, compared to the CZC setback requirement of 20 feet, with the setback area landscaped in an attractive manner as open space, not available for automobile parking, to blend with the parklike environment of the immediate area;

(c) decrease the number of apartment units in the building to approximately 150 units from the proposed 177 units; and

(d) decrease the bulk of the building 46 percent from its original design. . . .

October 25, 1978. The City Council adopted PZC Committee Report No. 2074 recommending that the application for the Admiral Thomas project be reported out to the Council for favorable action in consideration of:

Communication from Sheridan Ing, requesting favorable consideration on the Admiral Thomas project so that they can secure the building permit and proceed with construction; and

> Verbal opinion of Deputy City Counsel Nakamoto that the City Council can exercise its discretion concerning compliance of the conditions contained in Committee of the Whole Report No. 174.

The voting on the adoption of the committee report was seven votes in the affirmative, with Chairman Bornhorst and City Councilman Clement casting negative votes. . . .

The City Council approval of the Developers' application was a non-legislative act because it administered a law already in existence, the law already in existence being section IV-A of the Kakaako Ordinance.

Under RHC, section 5-104(1), the veto power of the Mayor extends to ordinances, resolutions authorizing proceedings in eminent domain, and resolutions adopting or amending the General Plan.

Treating the Developers' application as a non-legislative matter, the City Council approved the same at its meeting on September 21, 1977, upon the motion of City Councilman Pacarro, seconded by City Councilman Koga, and amended the September 21, 1977 approval at its meeting on November 10, 1977, upon the motion of City Councilman Kaapu, seconded by City Councilman Loo.

The City Council actions of September 21, 1977, and November 10, 1977, were not subject to the veto power of the Mayor because they were not ordinances, resolutions authorizing proceedings in eminent domain, or resolutions adopting or amending the General Plan.

In taking those actions, the City Council did not violate the principle of checks and balances, because it did so in accordance with the procedure authorized in the second sentence of RHC, section 3-201, and not with any intent to circumvent the veto power of the Mayor. . . .

Spot zoning is an arbitrary zoning action by which a small area within a large area is singled out and specially zoned for a use classification different from and inconsistent with the classification of the surrounding area and not in accord with comprehensive plan. . . .

The City Council actions on the Developers' application did not single out the project site for a use classification different from and inconsistent with the CZC classification of the surrounding area, which was Apartment District A-4.

The Kakaako Ordinance did not disturb the underlying zoning of the area embraced therein. It merely prohibited the Building Department from accepting applications for permits for construction within the interim development control area, except in those cases where the City Council approved applications for variance or modification.

The function of the City Council actions of September 21, 1977, and November 10, 1977, was to permit the Building Department to accept the Developers' application for a building permit within the ambit of

EXHIBIT III

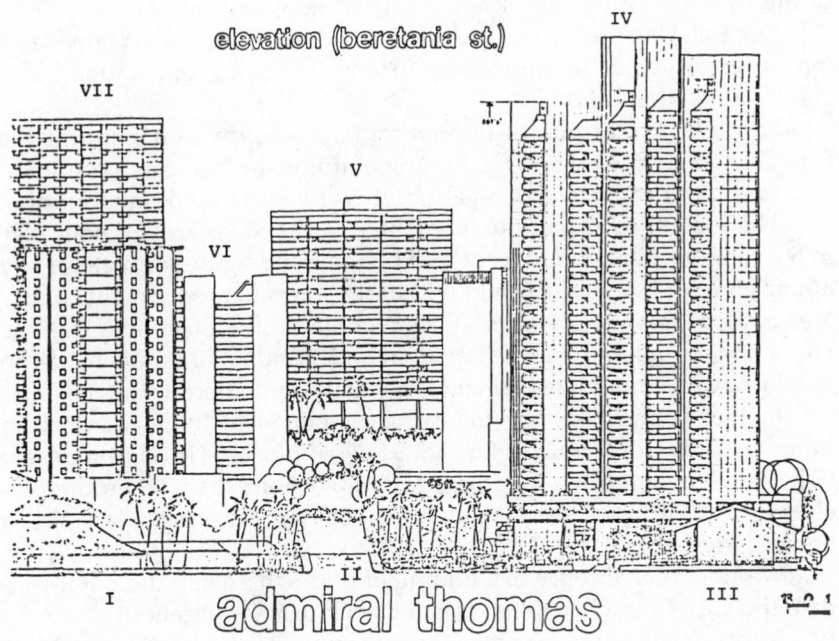

LEGEND

I	Honolulu Academy of Arts
II	Victoria Street
III	Existing sanctuary
IV	Proposed apartment building
V	Existing apartment building
VI	Existing apartment building
VII	Existing apartment building

FIGURE 21-3
Illustration from the Appendix to the official report of *Life of the Land*

those actions. The ambit of the City council actions was within the ambit of the CZC provisions applicable to Apartment District 4-A. . . .

The Kakaako Ordinance included section IV-A among its provisions "in order to avoid the imposition of any inequities and undue hardships" in its application.

However, the ordinance did not contain any provision requiring the City Council to make a specific finding of undue hardship as a condition precedent to its approval of an application for variance or modification.

The inequities and undue hardships in the Kakaako Ordinance lay in the total prohibition of acceptance by the Building Department of any application for a permit to build within the interim development control area covered in the ordinance. In that situation, the existence of undue hardship would have been self-evident and a finding of undue hardship would have been a mere formality, a ritual incantation of the obvious.

In that connection, the following statement of Judge Cardozo in Wood v. Duff-Gordon, 222 N.Y. 88, 91, 118 N.E. 214 (1917) is apposite: "The law has outgrown its primitive stage of formalism when the precise word was the sovereign talisman, and every slip was fatal. It takes a broader view today."

We hold that absence of a finding of undue hardship did not invalidate the City Council actions on the Developers' application.

In concluding this opinion, the statement of the late Robert Maynard Hutchins in one of his lectures that "Utopia thrives on controversy" is apposite. Hutchins was chairman and director of the Center for the Study of Democratic Institutions at the time of his death, had previously served as chancellor of the University of Chicago and dean of Yale Law School, and was a controversial figure himself.

As a result of the controversy, the building which could have been 350 feet high, containing 275 apartments occupying 309,476 square feet of floor area, ended up with a building of an average height of 299 feet, containing 150 apartments occupying 178,416 square feet of floor area.

In a controversy such as this, which involves amorphous concepts such as historical, cultural, and scenic values, the issues are neither all white nor all black, and they could have been resolved only by accommodation, not in the cynical sense of the statement of Artemus Ward, "My pollertics, like my religion, being of an exceedin' accommodatin' character," but in the sense of accommodation by the willingness of the Church and the Developers, who had direct financial stakes in the project, to respond not only to the concern of the Academy but to the concern of the public sector, and by the effort of nine conscientious elected representatives of the people to find a viable middle ground in the public interest. Among those elected representatives of the people is included City Councilman Clement, as to whose negative votes in the November 10, 1977, actions, Chairman Bornhorst said, "I respect your feelings."

The outcome of the controversy left the Developers with 131,060 square feet of floor area less to sell, and the Church with 131,060 square feet of floor area less to lease and derive income to carry on its activities.

The Developers and the Church took such reduction voluntarily, albeit in response to the concerns of the Academy and the public sector.

In the circumstance, we cannot say that the Developers and the Church acted in bad faith in any manner in connection with the Admiral Thomas project.

Also the City Council was justified in determining that the plan it approved was consistent with the spirit of the amendments to CZC, General Plan, DLUM, and Development Plan, and with the health, safety, morals, and general welfare of the City and County of Honolulu.

Affirmed.

Notes

1. Block 197 in Dumont, N.J., was zoned for residential use. The amendment under review changed Block 197 to a business district. The Boroughs of Creskill and Demarest border Block 197 across Knickerbocker Road. The Borough of Haworth borders it across Massachusetts Avenue. Creskill, Demarest, and Haworth were all zoned almost exclusively for single-family residences. A New Jersey superior court prohibited the amendment, saying that residences in Dumont, Creskill, Demarest, and Haworth had been built "in reliance upon" the prior zoning of Block 197, and that therefore the change "does not promote the public welfare; it is not in accordance with any comprehensive plan; it does not promote any of the statutory purposes relating to zoning. A business conducted in Block 197 would constitute both a public and a private nuisance per se." In discussing the "vested rights" of residents of neighboring towns in the original Dumont zoning, the court quoted from Fearne upon Contingent Remainders: "A 'vested right' is . . . 'an immediate, fixed right of present or future enjoyment.'" Borough of Creskill v. Borough of Dumont, 28 N.J. Super. 26, 100 A.2d 182 (Law Div. 1953). (See Figure 21-4.)

2. Plaintiff spent substantial amounts of money in the development of low density condominiums on property zoned for low density residential development. Subsequently, the property was rezoned general forest, and plaintiff challenged that classification, claiming, inter alia, that it constituted spot zoning since surrounding property similar to his was zoned less restrictively. The trial court dismissed the complaint. The court of appeal stated that

> Spot zoning occurs where a small parcel is restricted and given lesser rights than the surrounding property, as where a lot in the center of a

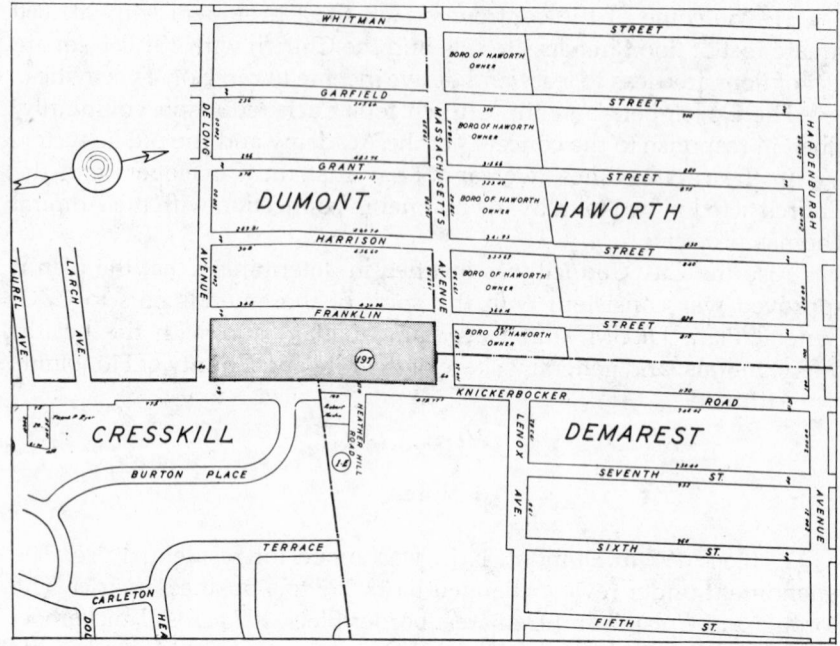

FIGURE 21-4
The Dumont site

business or commercial district is limited to uses for residential purposes
thereby creating an "island" in the middle of a larger area devoted to other
uses. Usually spot zoning involves a small parcel of land, the larger the
property the more difficult it is to sustain an allegation of spot zoning. . . .
Likewise, where the "spot" is not an island but is connected on some sides
to a like zone the allegation of spot zoning is more difficult to establish
since lines must be drawn at some point. . . . Even where a small island is
created in the midst of less restrictive zoning, the zoning may be upheld
where rational reason in the public benefit exists for such a classification.

The court concluded that the complaint stated a cause of action for
declaratory and injunctive relief from spot zoning, noting that "[w]hile
allegations that zoning is invalid due to discriminatory effect or spot
zoning may be difficult to prove, it is not the function of a demurrer to
try the action." Viso v. State, 92 Cal. App. 3d 15, 154 Cal. Rptr. 580
(1979).

   3. See New York Daily News, April, 22, 1977:

Ten months after his death, the world's richest man has still to find a last
resting place. . . . The trouble is that Malibu [California] zoning laws are in

conflict with the last will and testament of [J. Paul Getty]. . . . Getty's executors thought there would be no trouble getting approval [for the $50,000 mausoleum specified in the will] from Los Angeles City Council. After all, the billionaire had given the city the [Getty Museum] and its priceless collections of Greek and Roman antiques. But the zoning laws are explicit. Malibu is for single family residences only. . . . Hearings [on the request by the executors for a zoning variance] should begin soon, perhaps by summer.

4. The San Francisco Department of City Planning has promoted a policy of "[f]oster[ing] sculpturing of building form, less overpowering buildings and more interesting building tops." To that end, the department proposed the following:

> The bulk controls would establish basic restrictions on building mass, but would not, of themselves, achieve the desired treatment. As a further control, all buildings would be required to be massed, within the limits of the height and bulk controls, to create distinctive building tops. "Distinctive building tops" refers to complex, decorative, intricate means of articulating the building mass to create a visually distinctive termination of the building facade. Examples of types of treatments would include cornices, stepped parapets, hip roofs, mansard roofs, stepped terraces, domes, and other forms of multi-faceted sculptured tops. The intent is to return to the complex visual imagery of the surrounding hillsides and to the complex architectural qualities of older San Francisco buildings. However, direct mimicry and replication of historical detailing would be discouraged. What is desired is the evolution of a San Francisco imagery that departs from the austere, flat top box — a facade cut off in space. [San Francisco Department of City Planning, The Downtown Plan (1983).]

◆ CHENEY v. VILLAGE 2 AT NEW HOPE, INC.
429 Pa. 626, 241 A.2d 81 (1968)

Opinion by Mr. Justice ROBERTS.

Under traditional concepts of zoning the task of determining the type, density and placement of buildings which should exist within any given zoning district devolves upon the local legislative body. In order that this body might have to speak only infrequently on the issue of municipal planning and zoning, the local legislature usually enacts detailed requirements for the type, size and location of buildings within each given zoning district, and leaves the ministerial task of enforcing these regulations to an appointed zoning administrator, with another administrative body, the zoning board of adjustment, passing on individual deviations from the strict district requirements, deviations known commonly as variances and special exceptions. At the same time, the overall rules governing the dimensions, placement, etc., of primarily public additions to ground, e.g., streets, sewers, playgrounds, are formulated by the local legislature through the passage of subdivision regulations. These regulations are enforced and applied to individual lots by an administrative body usually known as the planning commission.

This general approach to zoning fares reasonably well so long as development takes place on a lot-by-lot basis, and so long as no one cares that the overall appearance of the municipality resembles the design achieved by using a cookie cutter on a sheet of dough. However, with the increasing popularity of large scale residential developments, particularly in suburban areas, it has become apparent to many local municipalities that land can be more efficiently used, and developments more aesthetically pleasing, if zoning regulations focus on density requirements rather than on specific rules for each individual lot. Under density zoning, the legislature determines what percentage of a particular district must be devoted to open space, for example, and what percentage used for dwelling units. The task of filling in the particular district with real houses and real open spaces then falls upon the planning commission usually working in conjunction with an individual large scale developer.

. . . The ultimate goal of this so-called density or cluster concept of zoning is achieved when an entire self-contained little community is permitted to be built within a zoning district, with the rules of density controlling not only the relation of private dwellings to open space, but also the relation of homes to commercial establishments such as theaters, hotels, restaurants, and quasi-commercial uses such as schools and churches. The present controversy before this Court involves a frontal attack upon one of these zoning districts, known in the trade as a Planned Unit Development (hereinafter PUD).

Spurred by the desire of appellant developer to construct a Planned Unit Development in the Borough of New Hope, in December of 1964 borough council began considering the passage of a new zoning ordinance to establish a PUD district in New Hope. After extensive consultation with appellant, council referred the matter to the New Hope Planning Commission for further study. This body, approximately six months after the project idea was first proposed, formally recommended to council that a PUD district be created. Council consulted with members of the Bucks County Planning Commission on the text of the proposed ordinance, held public hearings, and finally on June 14, 1965 enacted ordinance 160 which created the PUD district, and ordinance 161 which amended the borough zoning map, rezoning a large tract of land known as the Rauch farm from low density residential to PUD. Pursuant to the procedural requirements of ordinance 160, appellant presented plans for a Planned Unit Development on the Rauch tract to the borough planning commission. These plans were approved on November 8, 1965, and accordingly four days later two building permits, known as zoning permits 68 and 69, were issued to appellant. Subsequently, permit number 75 was issued. Appellees, all neighboring property owners opposing the issuance of these permits, appealed to the zoning board of adjustment. The board, after taking extensive testimony, upheld ordinances 160 and 161 and accordingly affirmed the issuance of the permits. Appellees then appealed to the Court of Common Pleas of Bucks County. That tribunal took no additional testimony, but reversed the board, holding the ordinances invalid for failure to conform to a comprehensive plan and for vesting too much discretion in the New Hope Planning Commission. This Court granted *certiorari* under Supreme Court Rule 68½. . . .

Approximately one year before the PUD seed was planted in New Hope, borough council had approved the New Hope Comprehensive Plan. This detailed land use projection clearly envisioned the Rauch tract as containing only single family dwellings of low density. The court below therefore concluded that the enactment of ordinance 160, and more specifically the placing of a PUD district on the Rauch tract by ordinance 161 was not "in accordance with a comprehensive plan," as required by the Act of February 1, 1966, P.L. (1965) 1656, §3203, 53 P.S. §48203.

The fallacy in the court's reasoning lies in its mistaken belief that a comprehensive plan, once established, is forever binding on the municipality and can never be amended. Cases subsequent to *Eves* [Eves v. Zoning Board of Adjustment, 401 Pa. 211, 164 A.2d 7 (1960)] have made it clear, however, that these plans may be changed by the passage of new zoning ordinances, provided the local legislature passes the new ordinance with some demonstration of sensitivity to the community as a whole, and the impact that the new ordinance will have on this community. As Mr. Chief Justice Bell so artfully stated in Furniss v. Lower Merion Twp., 412 Pa. 404, 406, 194 A.2d 926, 927 (1963):

> It is a matter of common sense and reality that a comprehensive plan is not like the law of the Medes and the Persians; it must be subject to reasonable change from time to time as conditions in an area or a township or a large neighborhood change. . . .

Given this rule of law allowing post-plan zoning changes, and the presumption in favor of an ordinance's validity, we are not in a position, having reviewed the record in the present case, to say that the zoning board committed an abuse of discretion or an error of law when it concluded that ordinances 160 and 161 were properly passed. Presented as it was with evidence that the PUD district had been under consideration by council for over six months and had been specifically recommended by the borough planning commission, a body specially equipped to view proposed ordinances as they relate to the rest of the community, we hold that the board, within its sound discretion, could have concluded that council passed the ordinances with the proper overall considerations in mind. The PUD district established by ordinance 160 is not the type of use which by its very nature could have no place in the middle of a predominantly residential borough. It is not a steel mill, a fat rendering plant, or a desiccated egg factory. It is, in fact, nothing more than a miniature residential community.

Closely tied to the comprehensive plan issue is the argument raised by appellees that ordinances 160 and 161 constitute spot zoning outlawed by *Eves, supra.* Given the fact situation in *Eves,* however, as well as the post-*Eves* cases, we do not believe that there is any spot zoning here. In *Eves,* the municipality created a limited industrial district, F-1, which, by explicit legislative pronouncement, was not to be applied to any particular tract until the individual landowner requested that his own tract be so rezoned. The obvious evil in this procedure did *not* lie in the fact that a limited industrial district might be placed in an area previously zoned, for example, residential. The evil was the *preordained* uncertainty as to where the F-1 districts would crop up. The ordinance all but invited spot zoning where the legislature could respond to private entreaties from landowners and rezone tracts F-1 without regard to the surrounding community. In *Eves,* it was almost impossible for the F-1 districts to conform to a comprehensive plan since tracts would be rezoned on a strictly ad hoc basis.

Quite to the contrary, no such "floating zone" exists in the present case. On the very day that the PUD district was created by ordinance 160, it was brought to earth by ordinance 161; and, as discussed *supra,* this *was* done "in accordance with a comprehensive plan." Speaking of a similar procedure in Donahue v. Zoning Bd. of Adjustment, 412 Pa. 332, 194 A.2d 610 (1963), this Court faced squarely an attack based upon *Eves* and responded thusly:

> It was this case by case review [in *Eves*] which demonstrated the absence of a comprehensive plan and which sought to enable the board of supervisors [the local legislative body] to exercise powers they did not statutorily possess.
>
> In the instant case, the new classification was established and the zoning map amended within a very short period of time [in the case at bar, on the same day]. Under the rules of statutory construction which are likewise applicable to ordinances, these ordinances should be read together as one enactment.
>
> So construed, ordinances 151 [creating new zone] and 155 [amending zoning map] do not create the "floating zone," anchored only upon case by case application by landowners, which we struck down in *Eves.* While it is true that the change here was made upon request of a particular landowner, this does not necessarily create the evils held invalid in *Eves* where the defects were specifically created by the very terms of the ordinances. It

is not unusual for a zoning change to be made on request of a landowner, and such change is not invalid if made in accordance with a comprehensive plan.

We think *Donahue* is completely controlling on the issue of alleged spot zoning and compels the conclusion that ordinances 160 and 161 do not fall on that ground.

The court below next concluded that even if the two ordinances were properly *passed*, they must fall as vesting authority in the planning commission greater than that permitted under Pennsylvania's zoning enabling legislation. More specifically, it is now contended by appellees that complete project approval by the planning commission under ordinance 160 requires that commission to encroach upon legislative territory whenever it decides where, within a particular PUD district, specific types of buildings should be placed.

In order to appreciate fully the arguments of counsel on both sides it is necessary to explain in some detail exactly what is permitted within a PUD district, and who decides whether a particular landowner has complied with these requirements. Admittedly the range of permissible uses within the PUD district is greater than that normally found in a traditional zoning district. Within a New Hope PUD district there may be: single family attached or detached dwellings; apartments; accessory private garages; public or private parks and recreation areas including golf courses, swimming pools, ski slopes, etc. (so long as these facilities do not produce noise, glare, odor, air pollution, etc., detrimental to existing or prospective adjacent structures); a municipal building; a school; churches; art galleries; professional offices; certain types of signs; a theatre (but not a drive-in); motels and hotels; and a restaurant. The ordinance then sets certain overall density requirements. The PUD district may have a maximum of 80 percent of the land devoted to residential uses, a maximum of 20 percent for the permitted commercial uses and enclosed recreational facilities, and must have a minimum of 20 percent for open spaces. The residential density shall not exceed 10 units per acre, nor shall any such unit contain more than two bedrooms. All structures within the district must not exceed maximum height standards set out in the ordinance. Finally, although there are no traditional "set back" and "side yard" requirements, ordinance 160 does require that there be 24 feet between structures, and that no townhouse structure contain more than 12 dwelling units.

The procedure to be followed by the aspiring developer reduces itself to presenting a detailed plan for his planned unit development to the planning commission, obtaining that body's approval and then securing building permits. Of course, the planning commission may not approve any development that fails to meet the requirements set forth in the ordinance as outlined above.

We begin with the observation that there is nothing in the borough zoning enabling act which would prohibit council from creating a zoning district with this many permissible uses. . . .

Given such broad power to zone, we cannot say that New Hope Borough Council abrogated its legislative function by creating a PUD district permitting the mixture of uses outlined *supra*, especially given the density requirements. . . .

There is no doubt that it would be statutorily permissible for council itself to pass a PUD ordinance and simultaneous zoning map amendment so specific that no details would be left for any administrator. The ordinance could specify where each building should be placed, how large it should be, where the open spaces are located, etc. But what would be the practical effect of such an ordinance? One of the most attractive features of Planned Unit Development is its flexibility; the chance for the builder and the municipality to sit down together and tailor a development to meet the specific needs of the community and the requirements of the land on which it is to be built. But all this would be lost if the Legislature let the planning cement set before any developer could happen upon the scene to scratch his own initials in that cement. . . .

The remaining two municipal bodies which could oversee the shaping of specific Planned Unit Developments are both administrative agencies, the zoning board of adjustment and the planning commission. As this Court views both reality and zoning enabling act, the zoning board of adjustment is not the proper body. . . . [Its] powers in no way encompass the authority to review and approve the plan for an entire development when such plan is neither at variance with the existing ordinance nor is a special exception to it; . . .

Moreover, from a practical standpoint, a zoning board of adjustment is, of the three bodies here under discussion, the one least equipped to handle the problem of PUD approval. Zoning boards are accustomed to focusing on one lot at a time. They traditionally examine hardship cases and unique uses proposed by landowners. As Professor Krasnowiecki has noted: "To suggest that the board is intended, or competent, to handle large scale planning and design decisions is, I think, far fetched." We agree.

Thus, the borough planning commission remains the only other body both qualified and statutorily permitted to approve PUD. Of course, we realize that a planning commission is not authorized to engage in actual rezoning of the land. But merely because the commission here has the power to approve more than one type of building for a particular lot within the PUD district does not mean that the commission is usurping the zoning function. Indeed, it is acting in strict *accordance* with the applicable zoning ordinance, for that ordinance, No. 160, *permits* more than one type of building for a particular lot. . . .

Nor is this Court sympathetic to appellees' argument that ordinance

160 permits the planning commission to grant variances and special exceptions. We fail to see how a development such as appellant's that meets every single requirement of the applicable zoning ordinance can be said to be the product of a variance or a special exception. The very essence of variances and special exceptions lies in their *departure* from ordinance requirements, not in their compliance with them. We therefore conclude that the New Hope Planning Commission has the power to approve development plans submitted to it under ordinance 160.

◆ CITY OF EASTLAKE v. FOREST CITY ENTERPRISES, INC.
426 U.S. 668 (1976)

Mr. Chief Justice BURGER delivered the opinion of the Court. The question in this case is whether a city charter provision requiring proposed land use changes to be ratified by 55 percent of the voters violates the due process rights of a landowner who applies for a zoning change.

The city of Eastlake, Ohio, a suburb of Cleveland, has a comprehensive zoning plan codified in a municipal ordinance. Respondent, a real estate developer, acquired an eight-acre parcel of real estate in Eastlake zoned for "light industrial" uses at the time of purchase.

In May 1971, respondent applied to the City Planning Commission for a zoning change to permit construction of a multi-family, high-rise apartment building. The Planning Commission recommended the proposed change to the City Council, which under Eastlake's procedures could either accept or reject the Planning Commission's recommendation. Meanwhile, by popular vote, the voters of Eastlake amended the City Charter to require that any changes in land use agreed to by the Council be approved by a 55 percent vote in a referendum.[1] The City Council approved the Planning Commission's recommendation for reclassification of respondent's property to permit the proposed project. Respondent then applied to the Planning Commission for "parking and yard" approval for the proposed building. The Commission rejected the

---

1. As adopted by the voters, Art. VII, §3, of the Eastlake City Charter provides in pertinent part:

That any change to the existing land uses or any change whatsoever to any ordinance cannot be approved unless and until it shall have been submitted to the Planning Commission, for approval or disapproval. That in the event the city council should approve any of the preceding changes, or enactments, whether approved or disapproved by the Planning Commission it shall not be approved or passed by the declaration of an emergency, and it shall not be effective, but it shall be mandatory that the same be approved by a 55 percent favorable vote of all votes cast of the qualified electors of the City of Eastlake at the next regular municipal election, if one shall occur not less than sixty (60) or more than one hundred and twenty (120) days after its passage, otherwise at a special election falling on the generally established day of the primary election. . . .

application, on the ground that the City Council's rezoning action had not yet been submitted to the voters for ratification.

Respondent then filed an action in state court, seeking a judgment declaring the charter provision invalid as an unconstitutional delegation of legislative power to the people.[2] While the case was pending, the City Council's action was submitted to a referendum, but the proposed zoning change was not approved by the requisite 55 percent margin. Following the election, the Court of Common Pleas and the Ohio Court of Appeals sustained the charter provision.[3]

The Ohio Supreme Court reversed. Concluding that enactment of zoning and rezoning provisions is a legislative function, the court held that a popular referendum requirement, lacking standards to guide the decision of the voters, permitted the police power to be exercised in a standardless, hence arbitrary and capricious manner. . . .

The conclusion that Eastlake's procedure violates federal constitutional guarantees rests upon the proposition that a zoning referendum involves a delegation of legislative power. A referendum cannot, however, be characterized as a delegation of power. Under our constitutional assumptions, all power derives from the people, who can delegate it to representative instruments which they create. See, e.g., Federalist Papers, No. 39. In establishing legislative bodies, the people can reserve to themselves power to deal directly with matters which might otherwise be assigned to the legislature.

The reservation of such power is the basis for the town meeting, a tradition which continues to this day in some States as both a practical and symbolic part of our democratic processes. The referendum, similarly, is a means for direct political participation, allowing the people the final decision, amounting to a veto power, over enactments of representative bodies. The practice is designed to "give citizens a voice on questions of public policy."

In framing a state constitution, the people of Ohio specifically reserved the power of referendum to the people of each municipality within the State. . . .

To be subject to Ohio's referendum procedure, the question must be one within the scope of legislative power. The Ohio Supreme Court expressly found that the City Council's action in rezoning respondent's eight acres from light industrial to high-density residential use was legis-

---

2. Respondent also contended that the charter amendment could not apply to its rezoning application since the application was pending at the time the amendment was adopted. The Court of Common Pleas rejected the argument. Respondent neither appealed this point nor argued it in the Court of Appeals or the Ohio Supreme Court; the issue is therefore not before us.

3. The Court of Common Pleas, however, invalidated the charter provision requiring assessment of election costs against the affected property owner. In affirming, the Court of Appeals also upheld that portion of the trial court's judgment. No appeal was taken to the Ohio Supreme Court on this issue. The question was, accordingly, not passed on by the state supreme court, and is therefore not before us.

lative in nature. Distinguishing between administrative and legislative acts, the court separated the power to zone or rezone, by passage or amendment of a zoning ordinance, from the power to grant relief from unnecessary hardship.[8] The former function was found to be legislative in nature.[9]

The Ohio Supreme Court further concluded that the amendment to the City Charter constituted a "delegation" of power violative of federal constitutional guarantees because the voters were given no standards to guide their decision. Under Eastlake's procedure, the Ohio Supreme Court reasoned, no mechanism existed, nor indeed could exist, to assure that the voters would act rationally in passing upon a proposed zoning change. This meant that "appropriate legislative action [would] be made dependent upon the potentially arbitrary and unreasonable whims of the voting public." The potential for arbitrariness in the process, the court concluded, violated due process.

Courts have frequently held in other contexts that a congressional delegation of power to a regulatory entity must be accompanied by discernible standards, so that the delegatee's action can be measured for its fidelity to the legislative will.

Assuming, arguendo, their relevance to state governmental functions, these cases involved a delegation of power by the legislature to regulatory bodies, which are not directly responsible to the people; this doctrine is inapplicable where, as here, rather than a delegation of power, we deal with a power reserved by the people to themselves.[10] . . .

8. By its nature, zoning "interferes" significantly with owners' uses of property. It is hornbook law that "[m]ere diminution of market value or interference with the property owner's personal plans and desires relative to his property is insufficient to invalidate a zoning ordinance or to entitle him to a variance or rezoning." There is, of course, no contention in this case that the existing zoning classification renders respondent's property valueless or otherwise diminishes its value below the value when respondent acquired it.

9. The power of initiative or referendum may be reserved or conferred "with respect to any matter, legislative or administrative, within the realm of local affairs. . . ." 5 McQuillan, Municipal Corporations, §16.54, at 208. However, the Ohio Supreme Court concluded that only land use changes granted by the City Council when acting in a *legislative* capacity were subject to the referendum process. Under the court's binding interpretation of state law, a property owner seeking relief from unnecessary hardship occasioned by zoning restrictions would not be subject to Eastlake's referendum procedure. For example, if unforeseeable future changes give rise to hardship on the owner, the holding of the Ohio Supreme Court provides avenues of administrative relief not subject to the referendum process.

10. The Ohio Supreme Court's analysis of the requirements for standards flowing from the Fourteenth Amendment also sweeps too broadly. Except as a legislative history informs an analysis of legislative action, there is no more advance assurance that a legislative body will act by conscientiously applying consistent standards than there is with respect to voters. For example, there is no certainty that the City Council in this case would act on the basis of "standards" explicit or otherwise in Eastlake's comprehensive zoning ordinance. Nor is there any assurance that townspeople assembling in a town meeting, as the people of Eastlake could do, will act according to consistent standards. The critical constitutional inquiry, rather, is whether the zoning restriction produces arbitrary or capricious results.

Nothing in our cases is inconsistent with this conclusion. Two decisions of this Court were relied on by the Ohio Supreme Court in invalidating Eastlake's procedure. The thread common to both decisions is the delegation of legislative power, originally given by the people to a legislative body, and in turn delegated by the legislature to a *narrow segment* of the community, not to the people at large. In Eubank v. City of Richmond, 226 U.S. 137 (1912), the Court invalidated a city ordinance which conferred the power to establish building setback lines upon the owners of two-thirds of the property abutting any street. Similarly, in Washington ex rel. Seattle Title Trust Co. v. Roberge, 278 U.S. 116 (1928), the Court struck down an ordinance which permitted the establishment of philanthropic homes for the aged in residential areas, but only upon the written consent of the owners of two-thirds of the property within 400 feet of the proposed facility.[12]

Neither *Eubank* nor *Roberge* involved a referendum procedure such as we have in this case; the standardless delegation of power to a limited group of property owners condemned by the court in *Eubank* and *Roberge* is not to be equated with decisionmaking by the people through the referendum process. The Court of Appeals for the Ninth Circuit put it this way:

> A referendum, however, is far more than an expression of ambiguously founded neighborhood preference. It is the city itself legislating through its votes — an exercise by the voters of their traditional right through direct legislation to override the views of their elected representatives as to what serves the public interest. [Southern Alameda Spanish Speaking Organization v. City of Union City, California, 424 F.2d 291, 294 (CA9 1970).]

Our decision in James v. Valtierra, 402 U.S. 137 (1971), upholding California's mandatory referendum requirement, confirms this view. Mr Justice Black, speaking for the Court in that case, said: "This procedure ensures that *all the people* of a community will have a voice in a decision which may lead to large expenditures of local governmental funds for increased public services. . . ."

---

12. The Ohio Supreme Court also treated this Court's decision in Thomas Cusack Co. v. Chicago, 242 U.S. 526 (1917). In contrast to *Eubank* and *Roberge, the Cusack* Court *upheld* a neighborhood consent provision which permitted property owners to waive a municipal restriction prohibiting the construction of billboards. This Court in *Cusack* distinguished *Eubank* in the following way:

"[The ordinance in *Eubank*] left the establishment of the building line untouched until the lot owners should act and then . . . gave to it the effect of law. The ordinance in the case at bar absolutely prohibits the erection of any billboads . . . but permits this prohibition to be modified with the consent of the persons who are to be most affected by such modification."

Since the property owners could simply waive an otherwise applicable legislative limitation, the Court in *Cusack* determined that the provision did not delegate legislative power at all.

Mr. Justice Black went on to say that the referendum procedure at issue here is a classic demonstration of "devotion to democracy. . . ." As a basic instrument of democratic government, the referendum process does not, in itself, violate the Due Process Clause of the Fourteenth Amendment when applied to a rezoning ordinance.[13] Since the rezoning decision in this case was properly reserved to the People of Eastlake under the Ohio Constitution, the Ohio Supreme Court erred in holding invalid, on federal constitutional grounds, the charter amendment permitting the voters to decide whether the zoned use of respondent's property could be altered.

The judgment of the Ohio Supreme Court is reversed and the case is remanded for further proceedings not inconsistent with this opinion.

Mr. Justice POWELL, dissenting. There can be no doubt as to the propriety and legality of submitting generally applicable legislative questions, including zoning provisions, to a popular referendum. But here the only issue concerned the status of a single small parcel owned by a single "person." This procedure, affording no realistic opportunity for the affected person to be heard, even by the electorate, is fundamentally unfair. The "spot" referendum technique appears to open disquieting opportunities for local government bodies to by-pass normal protective procedures for resolving issues affecting individual rights.

Mr. Justice STEVENS, with whom Mr. Justice BRENNAN joins, dissenting.

The city's reliance on the town meeting process of decisionmaking tends to obfuscate the two critical issues in this case. These issues are (1) whether the procedure which a city employs in deciding to grant or to deny a property owner's request for a change in the zoning of his property must comply with the Due Process Clause of the Fourteenth Amendment; and (2) if so, whether the procedure employed by the city of Eastlake is fundamentally fair? . . .

We might rule in favor of the city on the theory that the referendum requirement did not deprive respondent of any interest in property and therefore the Due Process Clause is wholly inapplicable. After all, when respondent bought this parcel, it was zoned for light industrial use and it still retains that classification. The court does not adopt any such

---

13. The fears expressed in dissent rest on the proposition that the procedure at issue here is "fundamentally unfair" to landowners; this fails to take into account the mechanisms for relief potentially available to property owners whose desired land use changes are rejected by the voters. First, if hardship is occasioned by zoning restrictions, *administrative* relief is potentially available. Indeed, the very purpose of "variances" allowed by zoning officials is to avoid "practical difficulties and unnecessary hardship."

The situation presented in this case is not one of a zoning action denigrating the use or depreciating the value of land; instead, it involves an effort to *change* a reasonable zoning restriction. No existing rights are being impaired; new use rights are being sought from the City Council. Thus, this case involves an owner seeking approval of a new use free from the restrictions attached to the land when it was acquired.

rationale; nor, indeed, does the city even advance that argument. On the contrary, throughout this litigation everyone has assumed, without discussing the problem, that the Due Process Clause does apply. Both reason and authority support that assumption.

Subject to limitations imposed by the common law of nuisance and zoning restrictions, the owner of real property has the right to develop his land to his own economic advantage. As land continues to become more scarce, and as land use planning constantly becomes more sophisticated, the needs and the opportunities for unforeseen uses of specific parcels of real estate continually increase. For that reason, no matter how comprehensive a zoning plan may be, it regularly contains some mechanism for granting variances, amendments, or exemptions for specific uses of specific pieces of property.[3] No responsibly prepared plan could wholly deny the need for presently unforeseeable future change.[4]

A zoning code is unlike other legislation affecting the use of property. The deprivation caused by a zoning code is customarily qualified by recognizing the property owner's right to apply for an amendment or variance to accommodate his individual needs. The expectancy that particular changes consistent with the basic zoning plan will be allowed frequently and on their merits is a normal incident of property ownership. When the governing body offers the owner the opportunity to seek such a change — whether that opportunity is denominated a privilege or a right — it is affording protection to the owner's interest in making legitimate use of his property.

3. "Zoning maps are constantly being changed, for various reasons; and the question is, under what circumstances are such changes justified. . . . The problem is then to develop criteria for distinguishing valid from invalid zoning changes; . . ." Williams, American Land Planning Law (1975), Vol. 1, p.6.

Legally, all zoning enabling acts contemplate the possibility of dezoning, the power to amend zoning ordinances serving that purpose. The provisions do not show on their face whether they are intended to remedy particular errors or hardships or whether they contemplate readjustments called for by the changing character of neighborhoods; undoubtedly, however, they may be made available for either purpose.

Freund, Some Inadequately Discussed Problems of the Law of City Planning and Zoning, 24 Ill. L. Rev. 135, 145 (1929).

For most communities, zoning as long range planning based on generalized legislative facts without regard to the individual facts has proved to be a theoretician's dream, soon dissolved in a series of zoning map amendments, exceptions and variances — reflecting, generally, decisions made on individual grounds — brought about by unanticipated and often unforeseeable events: social and political changes, ecological necessity, location and availability of roads and utilities, economic facts (especially costs of construction and financing), governmental needs, and, as important as any, market and consumer choice.

Kropf v. City of Sterling Heights, 391 Mich. 139, 168, 215 N.W.2d 179, 191-192 (1974).
4. "Zoning is a means by which a governmental body can plan for the future — it may not be used as a means to deny the future." National Land & Investment Co. v. Kohn, 419 Pa. 504, 527-528, 215 A.2d 597, 610 (1965).

The fact that an individual owner (like any other petitioner or plaintiff) may not have a legal right to the relief he seeks does not mean that he has no right to fair procedure in the consideration of the merits of his application. The fact that codes regularly provide a procedure for granting individual exceptions or changes, the fact that such changes are granted in individual cases with great frequency, and the fact that the particular code in the record before us contemplates that changes consistent with the basic plan will be allowed, all support my opinion that the opportunity to apply for an amendment is an aspect of property ownership protected by the Due Process Clause of the Fourteenth Amendment. . . .

Although this Court has decided only a handful of zoning cases, literally thousands of zoning disputes have been resolved by state courts. Those courts have repeatedly identified the obvious difference between the adoption of a comprehensive citywide plan by legislative action and the decision of particular issues involving specific uses of specific parcels. In the former situation there is generally great deference to the judgment of the legislature; in the latter situation state courts have not hesitated to correct manifest injustice. . . .

. . . [The Ohio] Supreme Court held that the mandatory referendum was "clearly invalid" insofar as it purported to apply to a change in land use approved by the City Council "in an administrative capacity." Without explaining when the Council's action is properly characterized as legislative instead of administrative, the Court then held that even though its approval in this case was legislative, the entire referendum requirement was invalid. The Court reasoned:

> Due process of law requires that procedures for the exercise of municipal power be structured such that fundamental choices among competing municipal policies are resolved by a responsible organ of government. It also requires that a municipality protect individuals against the arbitrary exercise of municipal power, by assuring that fundamental policy choices underlying the exercise of that power are articulated by some responsible organ of municipal government. The Eastlake charter provision ignored these concepts and blatantly delegated legislative authority, with no assurance that the result reached thereby would be reasonable or rational. For these reasons, the provision clearly violates the due process clause of the Fourteenth Amendment.

The concurring opinion expressed additional reasons for regarding the referendum requirement as arbitrary. Speaking for four members of the Ohio Supreme Court, Justice Stern stated:

> There can be little doubt of the true purpose of Eastlake's charter provision — it is to obstruct change in land use, by rendering such change so burdensome as to be prohibitive. The charter provision was apparently adopted specifically, to prevent multi-family housing, and indeed was

adopted while Forest City's application for rezoning to permit a multi-family housing project was pending before the City Planning Commission and City Council. The restrictive purpose of the provision is crudely apparent on its face. Any zoning change, regardless of how minor, and regardless of its approval by the Planning Commission and the City Council, must be approved by a city-wide referendum. The proposed change must receive, rather than a simple majority, at least a 55 percent affirmative vote. Finally, the owner of the property affected is required to pay the cost of the election, although the provision gives no hint as to exactly which costs would be billed to a property owner.

There is no subtlety to this; it is simply an attempt to render change difficult and expensive under the guise of popular democracy.

Even stripped of its harsher provisions the charter provision poses serious problems. A mandatory, city-wide referendum which applies to any zoning change must, of necessity, submit decisions that affect one person's use of his property to thousands of voters with no interest whatever in that property. We need only imagine the adoption of this same provision in a city such as Cleveland. By such a provision, rezoning for a corner gasoline station would require the approval of hundreds of thousands of voters, most of them living miles away, and few of them with the slightest interest in the matter. This would be government by caprice, and would seriously dilute the right of private ownership of property. The law recognizes that the use a person makes of his property must inevitably affect his neighbors and, in some cases, the surrounding community. These real interests are entitled to be balanced against the rights of a property owner; but a law which requires a property owner, who proposes a wholly benign use of his property, to obtain the assent of thousands of persons with no such interest, goes beyond any reasonable public purpose. . . .

The essence of fair procedure is that the interested parties be given a reasonable opportunity to have their dispute resolved on the merits by reference to articulable rules. If a dispute involves only the conflicting rights of private litigants, it is elementary that the decision-maker must be impartial and qualified to understand and to apply the controlling rules.

I have no doubt about the validity of the initiative or the referendum as an appropriate method of deciding questions of community policy. I think it is equally clear that the popular vote is not an acceptable method of adjudicating the rights of individual litigants. The problem presented by this case is unique, because it may involve a three-sided controversy, in which there is at least potential conflict between the rights of the property owner and the rights of his neighbors, and also potential conflict with the public interest in preserving the city's basic zoning plan. If the latter aspect of the controversy were predominant, the referendum would be an acceptable procedure. On the other hand, when the record indicates without contradiction that there is no threat to the general public interest in preserving the city's plan — as it does in this case, since respondent's proposal was approved by both the Planning Commission and the City Council and there has been no allegation that the use of this eight-acre parcel for apartments rather than light industry would adversely affect the community or raise any policy issue of city-wide concern — I think the case should be treated as one in which it is essential that the private property owner be given a fair opportunity to have his claim determined on its merits.

As Justice Stern points out in his concurring opinion, it would be absurd to use a referendum to decide whether a gasoline station could be operated on a particular corner in the city of Cleveland. The case before us is not that clear because we are told that there are only 20,000 people in the city of Eastlake. Conceivably, an eight-acre development could be sufficiently dramatic to arouse the legitimate interest of the entire community; it is also conceivable that most of the voters would be indifferent and uninformed about the wisdom of building apartments rather than a warehouse or factory on these eight acres. The record is silent on which of these alternatives is the more probable. Since the ordinance places a manifestly unreasonable obstacle in the path of every property owner seeking any zoning change, since it provides no standards or procedures for exempting particular parcels or claims from the referendum requirement, and since the record contains no justification for the use of the procedure in this case, I am persuaded that we should respect the state judiciary's appraisal of the fundamental fairness of this decisionmaking process in this case.

I therefore conclude that the Ohio Supreme Court correctly held that Art. VIII, §3 of the Eastlake Charter violates the Due Process Clause of the Fourteenth Amendment, and that its judgment should be affirmed.

Note

A developer had purchased land in the Nukolii area of the Hawaiian island of Kauai, and had successfully sought amendments to both the county general plan and the comprehensive zoning code to change the zoning designation from "open space/agriculture" to "resort." When the developer began building the resort, the Committee to Save Nukolii circulated a petition calling for repeal of the rezoning and eventually collected enough signatures to place a referendum question on the 1980 general election ballot. The committee finally won voter approval — by a 2 to 1 margin — to repeal the zoning ordinance. In the interim, however, the developer, not having been required by the courts to halt construction, had completed 150 condominium units (priced at $185,000 each) and had begun work on a 350-room hotel. A total of $50 million had been sunk into the project.

Kauai County filed a lawsuit to determine the rights of the parties involved. The circuit court ruled that, because the zoning ordinance had not been suspended, the building permits had been validly issued. The developer had acquired "vested rights" by the time of the election and the county was equitably estopped from prohibiting the developer from completing the project.

The Hawaii Supreme Court reversed, ruling that the developer had acquired "vested rights" only if final discretionary action on the project had taken place before the referendum petition was certified. The court then reasoned that because the referendum itself constituted a development approval, the vesting of rights had not occurred. The court restrained further construction and instructed the trial court to order the building permits revoked. County of Kauai v. Pacific Standard Life Insurance Co., 65 Haw. 318, 653 P.2d 766 (1982), *appeal dismissed sub nom.* Pacific Standard Life Insurance Co. v. Committee to Save Nukolii, 460 U.S. 1077 (1983).

In February 1984 a special election, $50,000 of the cost of which was paid for by the resort developer, was held on Kauai to decide whether to allow completion of the Nukolii project. This time the voters chose to restore resort zoning to the development site, allowing the developer to complete construction of the project. N.Y. Times, Feb. 6, 1984.

Note on Zoning and Nuisance

Regarding New York's statutory authorization for "any three taxpayers" to proceed against a zoning violation if town authorities fail to do so, N.Y. Town Law §268, ¶2, see Little Joseph Realty, Inc. v. Town of Babylon, 41 N.Y.2d 738, 363 N.E.2d 1163, 395 N.Y.S.2d 428 (1977). The court of appeals reversed a judge who refused to enjoin a profitable zoning activity and merely awarded damages. The court of appeals found Boomer v. Atlantic Cement Co., 26 N.Y.2d 219, 257 N.E.2d 870, 309 N.Y.S.2d 219 (1970), inapposite:

> First and foremost, it should be noted that no zoning violation, or for that matter, the violation of any other statute, was involved in that case. The action there was one to enjoin the continued commission of a nuisance in the operation of a cement plant which apparently offended no statutory edict, but tortiously imposed upon the plaintiff's property.
>
> The law of nuisance and that of zoning both relate to the use of property, but they each protect a different interest. So a use which fully complies with a zoning ordinance may still be enjoined as a nuisance, albeit "the plaintiff assumes a heavy burden of proof."

Nuisance is based upon the maxim that "a man shall not use his property so as to harm another." It is traditionally required that, after a balancing of risk-utility considerations, the gravity of the harm to a plaintiff be found to outweigh the social usefulness of a defendant's activity. On that basis, it was logical in *Boomer*, where the adverse economic effects of a permanent injunction far outweighed the loss plaintiffs there would suffer, to limit the relief to monetary damages as compensation for the "servitude" which had been imposed upon them.

Zoning is far more comprehensive. Its design is, on a planned basis, to serve as "a vital tool for maintaining a civilized form of existence" for the benefit and welfare of an entire community. Its provisions must be enforced with these goals in mind. It follows that, when a continuing use flies in the face of a valid zoning restriction, it must, subject to the existence of any appropriate equitable defenses, be enjoined unconditionally.

Consequently, however appropriate the remedy fashioned by the Appellate Division might be in resolving a private nuisance case, it is inappropriate here. In private nuisance, there is frequently a need to resolve a dispute between a plaintiff and a defendant over conflicting though valid uses of land. In such a case, the remedial options delineated in *Boomer* provide means by which courts can adjust such competing uses with a view towards maximizing the social value of each.

On the other hand, when it has been established that a defendant violates a valid zoning ordinance, there is no need for judicial accommodation of the defendant's use to that of the plaintiff. For a court to do so would be for it to usurp the legislative function. Specifically, in the case now before us, if the defendants can continue the unlawful use of the property after complying with the relief granted on remand, the trial court's judgment would have worked to rezone the land with conditions notwithstanding the fact that the power to do so is reserved to the town board alone.

This is not to say that risk-utility considerations have not entered into the adoption of a zoning law's restriction on use. It is rather that presumptively they have already been weighed and disposed of by the Legislature which enacted them.

◆ NEWPORT ASSOCIATES, INC. v. SOLOW
30 N.Y.2d 263, 283 N.E.2d 600, 332 N.Y.S.2d 617 (1972), *cert. denied*, 410 U.S. 931 (1973)

SCILEPPI, J. This is an action to compel a determination of a claim to real property pursuant to article 15 of the Real Property Actions and Proceedings Law. There is no dispute as to the operative facts. Plaintiff is the owner in fee of a parcel of New York City land, improved by a building, known as 4 West 58th Street and defendant is in possession thereof pursuant to a long-term lease which, by the exercise of certain options, will not expire until 2052. In addition to his leasehold interest in the subject property, defendant is the fee owner of two adjoining parcels: 10-40 West 58th Street and 9-25 West 57th Street. These parcels are contiguous with the leased premises and defendant is in the process of constructing a 45-story office building on its fee property. As an incident to this construction, defendant filed plans with the New York City Buildings Department and secured a building permit. The controversy between the parties centers upon this building permit and its effect on plaintiff's property rights.

The New York City Zoning Resolution sets certain limits on the quantum of floor space that a particular building may have. These limits, called floor area ratios, consist of the total floor area on a zoning lot divided by the lot area of that zoning lot (Zoning Resolution, §12-10). The existing building on the leasehold property does not represent a complete utilization of the floor area ratio for that building and hence there is surplus air space which is apparently buildable. Since defendant's fee property is contiguous to that which he leases, the municipal authorities, issuing the building permits, allowed defendant to incorporate the unused air space on the leased property in computing the maximum floor space for the building now being constructed on the fee property.

In this litigation, plaintiff has contended that the lease did not pass air space rights and that defendant's construction represents a diminution in the value of its reversionary interest; defendant has counterclaimed for a judgment sanctioning its construction. Both sides moved for summary judgment and Special Term, rejecting plaintiff's arguments, adopted the position that, under the applicable zoning ordinance, defendant was the owner of one zoning lot consisting of that which he held in fee and that which he leased; as such, the construction project was authorized. Additionally, the court concluded that plaintiff's damages, if any, were remote and speculative and that the construction was not violative of the lease. A judgment and order was entered granting defendant's motion for summary judgment, denying plaintiff's cross motion and declaring that defendant was authorized to use, in its construction, the unexpended and unused floor area ratio permissible and attributable to plaintiff's property. On appeal, the Appellate Division reversed and granted summary judgment to the plaintiff on the basis of section 4.03 of the lease which reads as follows:

> Lessee may make such additions, alterations and changes to the Premises as will suit Lessee's convenience and requirements of its business, and the business of any tenants to whom Lessee may lease portions of the Building, provided that such addition, change or alteration will not change the character of the Building and provided further that no structural addition, alteration or change, the estimated cost of which is in excess of $25,000 will be made without prior approval of Lessor, which Lessor covenants shall not be unreasonably withheld.

Inasmuch as defendant was utilizing the unused part of the floor area ratio for the leased premises on its fee property, the construction was not an alteration within the meaning of section 4.03. On the contrary, the court viewed it as an elimination of a valuable property right not vested in defendant by the lease. We reverse and reinstate the order and judgment of Special Term.

Although we agree that section 4.03, limited as it is to alterations of the leased building, should not be deemed a source of power authorizing defendant's utilization of unused air space in the construction of the office building on its property, we conclude that the court below has erroneously treated the section as dispositive of the litigation at bar.

The rather limited question presented in this appeal is whether defendant's construction of the office building on his fee property constitutes a wrong to plaintiff for which it may be given redress in this action. As previously stated, floor area ratios are computed on the basis of the size of a particular zoning lot. In section 12-10 of the Zoning Resolution a zoning lot is defined in the following manner:

> (a) A lot of record existing on the effective date of this resolution or any applicable subsequent amendment thereto, or (b) A tract of land, either unsubdivided or consisting of two or more contiguous lots of record, located within a single *block*, which on the effective date of this resolution or any applicable amendment thereto, was in single ownership, or (c) A tract of land, located within a single *block*, which at the time of filing for a building permit (or, if no building permit is required, at the time of filing for a certificate of occupancy), is designated by its owner or developer as a tract all of which is to be used, *developed*, or built upon as a unit under single ownership. A *zoning lot* therefore may or may not coincide with a lot as shown on the official tax maps of the City of New York, or on any recorded subdivision plat or deed.

Thus, where several contiguous lots are in single ownership, they may be lumped together and treated as a "zoning lot" for the purpose of the floor area ratio computation. Ownership is defined to include long-term leasehold interests: "For the purposes of this definition, ownership of a *zoning lot* shall be deemed to include a lease of not less than 50 years duration, with an option to renew such lease so as to provide a total lease of not less than 75 years duration." (Id.) Though defendant's lease, executed in 1953, had a minimum term of 21 years with options to renew for additional periods until the year 2052, it would appear that in issuing the building permit, the municipal authorities found that the lease satisfied the requirements of section 12-10. Defendant was, therefore, the owner of contiguous lots under the Zoning Resolution and as such was entitled to full utilization of air space rights. Inasmuch as there is no provision in the lease which precludes defendant's exercise of rights under the Zoning Resolution, it cannot be said that he has wronged plaintiff.

It is, of course, plaintiff's argument that with the 45-story building on the defendant's fee property, a valuable asset is destroyed since it loses the right to sell its air rights to owners of parcels adjoining the other side of the leased property. But this overlooks the fact that, in view of defendant's ownership of the adjoining building, his lease from plaintiff and the Zoning Resolution itself, plaintiff possesses no such right of sale. There is nothing in the ordinance which treats its reversionary interest as ownership for the purpose of floor area ratios or air space rights. In other words, whatever rights that plaintiff may otherwise have had were not lost by any act of the defendant, but rather as a result of the operation of the ordinance. Since defendant did not violate any of the provisions of the lease, plaintiff is not entitled to relief.

Notes

1. The landlord was permitted to transfer air rights, and the long-term tenant refused power to block the transfer, in Macmillan, Inc. v. C. F. Lex Assoc., 56 N.Y.2d 386, 437 N.E.2d 1134, 452 N.Y.S.2d 377 (1982). *Newport Associates* was not cited.

2. Percentage depletion allowances are available to lessees of underground coal, even though they are subject to termination on 30 days' notice. United States v. Swank, 451 U.S. 571 (1981).

◆ FRED F. FRENCH INVESTMENT CO. v. CITY OF NEW YORK
39 N.Y.2d 587, 350 N.E.2d 381, 385 N.Y.S.2d (1976), *appeal dismissed and cert. denied*, 429 U.S. 990 (1977)

BREITEL, C.J. . . . The issue is whether the rezoning of buildable private parks exclusively as parks open to the public, thereby prohibiting all reasonable income productive or other private use of the property, constitutes a deprivation of property rights without due process of law in violation of constitutional limitations. . . .

Tudor City is a four-acre residential complex built on an elevated level above East 42nd Street, across First Avenue from the United Nations in mid-town Manhattan. Planned and developed as a residential community, Tudor City consists of 10 large apartment buildings housing approximately 8,000 people, a hotel, four brownstone buildings, and two 15,000 square-foot private parks. The parks, covering about 18½ percent of the area of the complex, are elevated from grade and located on the north and south sides of East 42nd Street, with a connecting viaduct.

On September 30, 1970, plaintiff sold the Tudor City complex to defendant Ramsgate Properties for $36,000,000. In addition to cash, plaintiff took back eight purchase money mortgages, two of which covered in part the two parks. Payment of the mortgage interest for three years was personally guaranteed by defendant Helmsley. Ramsgate thereafter conveyed, subject to plaintiff's mortgages, properties including the north and south parks to defendants, North Assemblage Co. and South Assemblage Co. Each of the mortgages secured in part by the parks has been in default since December 7, 1972.

Soon after acquiring the Tudor City property, the new owner announced plans to erect a building, said to be a 50-story tower, over East 42nd Street between First and Second Avenues. This plan would have required New York City Planning Commission approval of a shifting of development rights from the parks to the proposed adjoining site and a corresponding zoning change. Alternatively, the owner proposed to erect on each of the Tudor City park sites a building of maximum size permitted by the existing zoning regulations.

There was immediately an adverse public reaction to the owner's proposals, especially from Tudor City residents. After public hearings, the City Planning Commission recommended, over the dissent of one commissioner, and on December 7, 1972 the Board of Estimate approved, an amendment to the zoning resolution establishing Special Park District "P." By contemporaneous amendment to the zoning map, the two Tudor City parks were included within Special Park District "P."

Under the zoning amendment, "only passive recreational uses are permitted" in the Special Park District and improvements are limited to "structures incidental to passive recreational use." When the Special Park District would be mapped, the parks are required to be open daily to the public between 6:00 a.m. and 10:00 p.m.

The zoning amendment permits the transfer of development rights from a privately owned lot zoned as a Special Park District, denominated a "granting lot," to other areas in midtown Manhattan, bounded by 60th Street, Third Avenue, 38th Street and Eighth Avenue, denominated "receiving lots." Lots eligible to be receiving lots are those with a minimum lot size of 30,000 square feet and zoned to permit development at the maximum commercial density. The owner of a granting lot would be permitted to transfer part of his development rights to any eligible receiving lot, thereby increasing its maximum floor area up to 10%. Further increase in the receiving lot's floor area, limited to 20% of the maximum commercial density, is contingent upon a public hearing and approval by the City Planning Commission and the Board of Estimate. Development rights may be transferred by the owner directly to a receiving lot or to an individual or organization for later disposition to a receiving lot. Before development rights may be transferred, however, the Chairman of the City Planning Commission must certify the suitability of a plan for the continuing maintenance, at the owner's expense, of the granting lot as a park open to the public.

It is notable that the private parks become open to the public upon mapping of the Special Park District, and the opening does not depend upon the relocation and effective utilization of the transferable development rights. Indeed, the mapping occurred on December 7, 1972, and the development rights have never been marked or used.

Plaintiff contends that the rezoning of the parks constitutes a compensable "taking" within the meaning of constitutional limitations.

The power of the State over private property extends from the regulation of its use under the police power to the actual taking of an easement or all or part of the fee under the eminent domain power. The distinction, although definable, between a compensable taking and a noncompensable regulation is not always susceptible of precise demarcation. . . .

In the present case, while there was a significant diminution in the value of the property, there was no actual appropriation or taking of the parks by title or governmental occupation. The amendment was declared void at Special Term a little over a year after its adoption. There was no physical invasion of the owner's property; nor was there an assumption by the city of the control or management of the parks. Indeed, the parks served the same function as before the amendment, except that they were now also open to the public. Absent factors of governmental displacement of private ownership, occupation or management, there was no "taking" within the meaning of constitutional limitations. There was, therefore, no right to compensation as for a taking in eminent domain.

Since there was no taking within the meaning of constitutional limitations, plaintiff's remedy, at this stage of the litigation, would be a declaration of the amendment's invalidity, if that be the case. Thus, it is necessary to determine whether the zoning amendment was a valid exercise of the police power under the due process clauses of the State and Federal Constitutions. . . .

A zoning ordinance is unreasonable, under traditional police power and due process analysis, if it encroaches on the exercise of private property rights without substantial relation to a legitimate governmental purpose. A legitimate governmental purpose is, of course, one which furthers the public health, safety, morals or general welfare.

. . . Moreover, a zoning ordinance, on similar police power analysis, is unreasonable if it is arbitrary, that is, if there is no reasonable relation between the end sought to be achieved by the regulation and the means used to achieve that end.

Finally, and it is at this point that the confusion between the police power and the exercise of eminent domain most often occurs, a zoning ordinance is unreasonable if it frustrates the owner in the use of his property, that is, if it renders the property unsuitable for any reasonable

income productive or other private use for which it is adapted and thus destroys its economic value, or all but a bare residue of its value.

The ultimate evil of a deprivation of property, or better, a frustration of property rights, under the guise of an exercise of the police power is that it forces the owner to assume the cost of providing a benefit to the public without recoupment. There is no attempt to share the cost of the benefit among those benefited, that is, society at large. Instead, the accident of ownership determines who shall bear the cost initially. Of course, as further consequence, the ultimate economic cost of providing the benefit is hidden from those who in a democratic society are given the power of deciding whether or not they wish to obtain the benefit despite the ultimate economic cost, however initially distributed. In other words, the removal from productive use of private property has an ultimate social cost more easily concealed by imposing the cost on the owner alone. When successfully concealed, the public is not likely to have any objection to the "cost-free" benefit.

In this case, the zoning amendment is unreasonable and, therefore, unconstitutional because, without due process of law, it deprives the owner of all his property rights, except the bare title and a dubious future reversion of full use. The amendment renders the park property unsuitable for any reasonable income productive or other private use for which it is adapted and thus destroys its economic value and deprives plaintiff of its security for its mortgages.

It is recognized that the "value" of property is not a concrete or tangible attribute but an abstraction derived from the economic uses to which the property may be put. Thus, the development rights are an essential component of the value of the underlying property because they constitute some of the economic uses to which the property may be put. As such, they are a potentially valuable and even a transferable commodity and may not be disregarded in determining whether the ordinance has destroyed the economic value of the underlying property.

Of course, the development rights of the parks were not nullified by the city's action. In an attempt to preserve the rights they were severed from the real property and made transferable to another section of mid-Manhattan, in the city, but not to any particular parcel or place. There was thus created floating development rights, utterly unusable until they could be attached to some accommodating real property, available by happenstance of prior ownership, or by grant, purchase, or devise, and subject to the contingent approvals of administrative agencies. In such case, the development rights, disembodied abstractions of man's ingenuity, float in a limbo until restored to reality by reattachment to tangible real property. Put another way, it is a tolerable abstraction to consider development rights apart from the solid land from which as a matter of zoning law they derive. But severed, the development rights are a double abstraction until they are actually attached to a receiving parcel, yet to be identified, acquired, and subject to the contingent future approvals of administrative agencies, events which may never happen because of the exigencies of the market and the contingencies and exigencies of administrative action. The acceptance of this contingency-ridden arrangement, however, was mandatory under the amendment.

The problem with this arrangement, as Mr. Justice Waltemade so wisely observed at Special Term, is that it fails to assure preservation of the very real economic value of the development rights as they existed when still attached to the underlying property. By compelling the owner to enter an unpredictable real estate market to find a suitable receiving lot for the rights, or a purchaser who would then share the same interest in using additional development rights, the amendment renders uncertain and thus severely impairs the value of the development rights before they were severed. Hence, when viewed in relation to both the value of the private parks after the amendment, and the value of the development rights detached from the private parks, the amendment destroyed the economic value of the property. It thus constituted a deprivation of property without due process of law.

None of this discussion of the effort to accomplish the highly beneficial purposes of creating additional park land in the teeming city bears any relation to other schemes, variously described as a "development bank" or the "Chicago Plan" (see Costonis, The Chicago Plan: Incentive Zoning and the Preservation of Urban Landmarks, 85 Harv. L. Rev. 574; Costonis, Development Rights Transfer: An Exploratory Essay, 83 Yale L.J. 75, 86-87). For under such schemes or variations of them, the owner of the granting parcel may be allowed just compensation for his development rights, instantly and in money, and the acquired development rights are then placed in a "bank" from which enterprises may for a price purchase development rights to use on land owned by them. Insofar as the owner of the granting parcel is concerned, his development rights are taken by the State, straightforwardly, and he is paid just compensation for them in eminent domain. The appropriating governmental entity recoups its disbursements, when, as, and if it obtains a purchaser for those rights. In contrast, the 1972 zoning amendment short-circuits the double-tracked compensation scheme but to do this leaves the granting parcel's owner's development rights in limbo until the day of salvation, if ever it comes. . . .

It would be a misreading of the discussion above to conclude that the court is insensitive to the inescapable need for government to devise methods, other than by outright appropriation of the fee, to meet urgent environmental needs of a densely concentrated urban population. It would be equally simplistic to ignore modern recognition of the principle that no property has value except as the community contributes to that value. The obverse of this principle is, therefore, of first significance: no property is an economic island, free from contributing to the welfare of the whole of which it is but a dependent part. The limits are that unfair or disproportionate burdens may not, constitutionally, be placed on single properties or their owners. The possible solutions undoubtedly lie somewhere in the areas of general taxation, assessments for public benefit (but with an expansion of the traditional views with respect to what are assessable public benefits), horizontal eminent domain illustrated by a true "taking" of development rights with corresponding compensation, development banks, and other devices which will insure rudimentary fairness in the allocation of economic burdens.

Solutions must be reached for the problems of modern zoning, urban and rural conservation, and last but not least landmark preservations, whether by particular buildings or historical districts. Unfortunately, the land planners are now only at the beginning of the path to solution. In the process of traversing that path further, new ideas and new standards of constitutional tolerance must and will evolve. It is enough to say that the loose-ended transferable development rights in this case fall short of achieving a fair allocation of economic burden. Even though the development rights have not been nullified, their severance has rendered their value so uncertain and contingent, as to deprive the property owner of their practical usefulness, except under rare and perhaps coincidental circumstances.

The legislative and administrative efforts to solve the zoning and landmark problem in modern society demonstrate the presence of ingenuity. That ingenuity further pursued will in all likelihood achieve the goals without placing an impossible or unsuitable burden on the individual property owner, the public fisc, or the general taxpayer. These efforts are entitled to and will undoubtedly receive every encouragement. The task is difficult but not beyond management. The end is essential but the means must nevertheless conform to constitutional standards.

Note

Consider the comments of Judge Breitel, quoted in Urban Land Institute, Environmental Comment, April 1978, at 8:

In the *Fred F. French* case, the owner at one point had been offered a tremendous price for those development rights somewhere else in mid-Manhattan. But by the time the case was decided, mid-Manhattan was terribly overbuilt and the value of the TDRs had dropped. That really isn't an accidental circumstance. This is the nature of our economy. This is the reason why the TDR transfers were found insufficient in *Fred F. French* and why, on the other hand, we found them of some value in *Penn Central*.

C. REASONABLE MEANS AND LEGITIMATE PURPOSES

1. *Preservation*

◆ JUST v. MARINETTE COUNTY
56 Wis. 2d 7, 201 N.W.2d 761 (1972)

HALLOWS, Chief Justice. Marinette County's Shoreland Zoning Ordinance Number 24 was adopted September 19, 1967, became effective
October 9, 1967, and follows a model ordinance published by the Wisconsin Department of Resource Development in July of 1967. The ordinance was designed to meet standards and criteria for shoreland
regulation which the legislature required to be promulgated by the department of natural resources under sec. 144.26, Stats.

Shorelands for the purpose of ordinances are defined as lands
within 1,000 feet of the normal high-water elevation of navigable lakes,
ponds, or flowages and 300 feet from a navigable river or stream or the
landward side of the flood plain, whichever distance is greater. The state
shoreland program is unique. All county shoreland zoning ordinances
must be approved by the department of natural resources prior to their
becoming effective. If a county does not enact a shoreland zoning ordinance which complies with the state's standards, the department of
natural resources may enact such an ordinance for the county.

There can be no disagreement over the public purpose sought to be
obtained by the ordinance. Its basic purpose is to protect navigable
waters and the public rights therein from the degradation and deterioration which results from uncontrolled use and development of shorelands. In the Navigable Waters Protection Act, the purpose of the state's
shoreland regulation program is stated as being to "aid in the fulfillment
of the state's role as trustee of its navigable waters and to promote public
health, safety, convenience and general welfare." The Marinette County
shoreland zoning ordinance in secs. 1.2 and 1.3 states the uncontrolled
use of shorelands and pollution of navigable waters of Marinette County
adversely affect public health, safety, convenience, and general welfare
and impair the tax base.

The shoreland zoning ordinance divides the shorelands of Marinette County into general purpose districts, general recreation districts,
and conservancy districts. A "conservancy" district is required by the
statutory minimum standards and is defined in sec. 3.4 of the ordinance
to include "all shorelands designated as swamps or marshes on the
United States Geological Survey maps which have been designated as
the Shoreland Zoning Map of Marinette County, Wisconsin, or on the
detailed Insert Shoreland Zoning Maps." The ordinance provides for
permitted uses and conditional uses. One of the conditional uses requir-

ing a permit is the filling, drainage or dredging of wetlands according to the provisions of sec. 5 of the ordinance. "Wetlands" are defined as "[a]reas where ground water is at or near the surface much of the year or where any segment of plant cover is deemed an aquatic according to N.C. Fassett's 'Manual of Aquatic Plants.' " Section 5.42(2) of the ordinance requires a conditional-use permit for any filling or grading

> [o]f any area which is within three hundred feet horizontal distance of a navigable water and which has surface drainage toward the water and on which there is: (a) Filling of more than five hundred square feet of any wetland which is contiguous to the water . . . (d) Filling or grading of more than 2,000 square feet on slopes of twelve per cent or less.

In April of 1961, several years prior to the passage of this ordinance, the Justs purchased 36.4 acres of land in the town of Lake along the south shore of Lake Noquebay, a navigable lake in Marinette County. This land had a frontage of 1,266.7 feet on the lake and was purchased partially for personal use and partially for resale. During the years 1964, 1966, and 1967, the Justs made five sales of parcels having frontage and extending back from the lake some 600 feet, leaving the property involved in these suits. This property has a frontage of 366.7 feet and the south one half contains a stand of cedar, pine, various hard woods, birch and red maple. The north one half, closer to the lake, is barren of trees except immediately along the shore. The south three fourths of this north one half is populated with various plant grasses and vegetation including some plants which N.C. Fassett in his manual of aquatic plants has classified as "aquatic." There are also non-aquatic plants which grow upon the land. Along the shoreline there is a belt of trees. The shoreline is from one foot to 3.2 feet higher than the lake level and there is a narrow belt of higher land along the shore known as a "pressure ridge" or "ice heave," varying in width from one to three feet. South of this point, the natural level of the land ranges one to two feet above lake level. The land slopes generally toward the lake but has a slope less than twelve percent. No water flows onto the land from the lake, but there is some surface water which collects on land and stands in pools.

The land owned by the Justs is designated as swamps and marshes on the United States Geological Survey map and is located within 1,000 feet of the normal high-water elevation of the lake. Thus, the property is included in a conservancy district and, by sec. 2.29 of the ordinance, classified as "wetlands." Consequently, in order to place more than 500 square feet of fill on this property, the Justs were required to obtain a conditional-use permit from the zoning administrator of the county and pay a fee of $20 or incur a forfeiture of $10 to $200 for each day of violation.

In February and March of 1968, six months after the ordinance became effective, Ronald Just, without securing a conditional-use permit, hauled 1,040 square yards of sand onto this property and filled an area approximately 20 feet wide commencing at the southwest corner and extending almost 600 feet north to the northwest corner near the shoreline, then easterly along the shoreline almost to the lot line. He stayed back from the pressure ridge about 20 feet. More than 500 square feet of this fill was upon wetlands located contiguous to the water and which had surface drainage toward the lake. The fill within 300 feet of the lake also was more than 2,000 square feet on a slope less than 12 percent. It is not seriously contended that the Justs did not violate the ordinance and the trial court correctly found a violation.

The real issue is whether the conservancy district provisions and the wetlands-filling restrictions are unconstitutional because they amount to a constructive taking of the Justs' land without compensation. Marinette County and the state of Wisconsin argue the restrictions of the conservancy district and wetlands provisions constitute a proper exercise of the police power of the state and do not so severely limit the use or depreciate the value of the land as to constitute a taking without compensation.

To state the issue in more meaningful terms, it is a conflict between the public interest in stopping the despoliation of natural resources, which our citizens until recently have taken as inevitable and for granted, and an owner's asserted right to use his property as he wishes. The protection of public rights may be accomplished by the exercise of the police power unless the damage to the property owner is too great and amounts to a confiscation. The securing or taking of a benefit not presently enjoyed by the public for its use is obtained by the government through its power of eminent domain. The distinction between the exercise of the police power and condemnation has been said to be a matter of degree of damage to the property owner. In the valid exercise of the police power reasonably restricting the use of property, the damage suffered by the owner is said to be incidental. However, where the restriction is so great the landowner ought not to bear such a burden for the public good, the restriction has been held to be a constructive taking even though the actual use or forbidden use has not been transferred to the government so as to be a taking in the traditional sense. Whether a taking has occurred depends upon whether "the restriction practically or substantially renders the land useless for all reasonable purposes."

The loss caused the individual must be weighed to determine if it is more than he should bear. As this court stated in Stefan Auto Body v. State Highway Comm., 21 Wis. 2d 363, 369-370, 124 N.W.2d 319, 323 (1963),

> . . . if the damage is such as to be suffered by many similarly situated and is in the nature of a restriction on the use to which land may be put and

ought to be borne by the individual as a member of society for the good of the public safety, health or general welfare, it is said to be a reasonable exercise of the police power, but if the damage is so great to the individual that he ought not to bear it under contemporary standards, then courts are inclined to treat it as a "taking" of the property or an unreasonable exercise of the police power. . . .

This case causes us to re-examine the concepts of public benefit in contrast to public harm and the scope of an owner's right to use of his property. In the instant case we have a restriction on the use of a citizen's property, not to secure a benefit for the public, but to prevent a harm from the change in the natural character of the citizens' property. We start with the premise that lakes and rivers in their natural state are unpolluted and the pollution which now exists is man made. The state of Wisconsin under the trust doctrine has a duty to eradicate the present pollution and to prevent further pollution in its navigable waters. This is not, in a legal sense, a gain or a securing of a benefit by the maintaining of the natural status quo of the environment. What makes this case different from most condemnation or police power zoning cases is the interrelationship of the wetlands, the swamps and the natural environment of shorelands to the purity of the water and to such natural resources as navigation, fishing, and scenic beauty. Swamps and wetlands were once considered wasteland, undesirable, and not picturesque. But as the people became more sophisticated, an appreciation was acquired that swamps and wetlands serve a vital role in nature, are part of the balance of nature and are essential to the purity of the water in our lakes and streams. Swamps and wetlands are a necessary part of the ecological creation and now, even to the uninitiated, possess their own beauty in nature.

Is the ownership of a parcel of land so absolute that man can change its nature to suit any of his purposes? The great forests of our state were stripped on the theory man's ownership was unlimited. But in forestry, the land at least was used naturally, only the natural fruit of the land (the trees) were taken. The despoilage was in the failure to look to the future and provide for the reforestation of the land. An owner of land has no absolute and unlimited right to change the essential natural character of his land so as to use it for a purpose for which it was unsuited in its natural state and which injures the rights of others. The exercise of the police power in zoning must be reasonable and we think it is not an unreasonable exercise of that power to prevent harm to public rights by limiting the use of private property to its natural uses.

This is not a case where an owner is prevented from using his land for natural and indigenous uses. The uses consistent with the nature of the land are allowed and other uses recognized and still others permitted by special permit. The shoreland zoning ordinance prevents to some extent the changing of the natural character of the land within

1,000 feet of a navigable lake and 300 feet of a navigable river because of such land's interrelation to the contiguous water. The changing of wetlands and swamps to the damage of the general public by upsetting the natural environment and the natural relationship is not a reasonable use of that land which is protected from police power regulation. Changes and filling to some extent are permitted because the extent of such changes and fillings does not cause harm. We realize no case in Wisconsin has yet dealt with shoreland regulations and there are several cases in other states which seem to hold such regulations unconstitutional; but nothing this court has said or held in prior cases indicate that destroying the natural character of a swamp or a wetland so as to make that location available for human habitation is a reasonable use of that land when the new use, although of a more economical value to the owner, causes a harm to the general public. . . .

The Justs argue their property has been severely depreciated in value. But this depreciation of value is not based on the use of the land in its natural state but on what the land would be worth if it could be filled and used for the location of a dwelling. While loss of value is to be  considered in determining whether a restriction is a constructive taking, value based upon changing the character of the land at the expense of harm to public rights is not an essential factor or controlling.

Notes

1. Bumper sticker seen often in Wisconsin: "What God Giveth/ DNR [Department of Natural Resources] Taketh Away"

2. Jordahl, Conservation and Scenic Easements: An Experience Resumé, 39 Land Econ. 343, 354 (1963):

> The Wisconsin Highway Commission has been acquiring easements along the Great River Road in western Wisconsin adjacent to the Mississippi River since 1952. This road is a part of the Great River Road system extending from the Gulf of Mexico to Canada. States are cooperating with each other and with the National Park Service and the Bureau of Public Roads in developing the road to parkway standards and in preserving scenic beauty.
>
> Although many states have improved the physical quality of their portion of the road, the Wisconsin Highway Commission has led in protecting adjacent beauty through the use of scenic easements. By 1961 Wisconsin had acquired easements adjacent to 55 miles of highway at an average cost of $650.64 per mile. The average cost per acre had been $20.66 in contrast to a fee simple cost of lands acquired [by eminent domain] for roadway purposes at the same time of $41.29. The scenic easement, which is negative, prohibits dumping of any refuse, erection of billboards, destruction of trees and shrubs, fur farms, erection of or alteration of buildings, and commercial and industrial uses of lands and buildings. The

control zone is usually 350 feet from the center line. A standard easement form was used in all instances. Of the 234 parcels acquired, only 43 were condemned [by eminent domain]. The basis for the condemnation was price and not necessity for the taking.

◆ CALIFORNIA PUBLIC RESOURCES CODE
(West 1977; Supp. 1984)

§30001. LEGISLATIVE FINDINGS AND DECLARATIONS;
ECOLOGICAL BALANCE

The Legislature hereby finds and declares:

(a) That the California coastal zone is a distinct and valuable natural resource of vital and enduring interest to all the people and exists as a delicately balanced ecosystem.

(b) That the permanent protection of the state's natural and scenic resources is a paramount concern to present and future residents of the state and nation.

(c) That to promote the public safety, health, and welfare, and to protect public and private property, wildlife, marine fisheries, and other ocean resources, and the natural environment, it is necessary to protect the ecological balance of the coastal zone and prevent its deterioration and destruction. . . .

(d) That existing developed uses, and future developments that are carefully planned and developed consistent with the policies of this division, are essential to the economic and social well-being of the people of this state and especially to working persons employed within the coastal zone.

§30001.2 LEGISLATIVE FINDINGS AND DECLARATIONS;
ECONOMIC DEVELOPMENT

The Legislature further finds and declares that, notwithstanding the fact electrical generating facilities, refineries, and coastal-dependent developments, including ports and commercial fishing facilities, offshore petroleum and gas development, and liquefied natural gas facilities, may have significant adverse effects on coastal resources or coastal access, it may be necessary to locate such developments in the coastal zone in order to ensure that inland as well as coastal resources are preserved and that orderly economic development proceeds within the state. . . .

§30001.5 LEGISLATIVE FINDINGS AND DECLARATIONS;
GOALS

The Legislature further finds and declares that the basic goals of the state for the coastal zone are to:

(a) Protect, maintain, and, where feasible, enhance and restore the overall quality of the coastal zone environment and its natural and artificial resources.

(b) Assure orderly, balanced utilization and conservation of coastal zone resources taking into account the social and economic needs of the people of the state.

(c) Maximize public access to and along the coast and maximize public recreational opportunities in the coastal zone consistent with sound resources conservation principles and constitutionally protected rights of private property owners.

(d) Assure priority for coastal-dependent and coastal-related development over other development on the coast.

(e) Encourage state and local initiatives and cooperation in preparing procedures to implement coordinated planning and development for mutually beneficial uses, including educational uses, in the coastal zone. . . .

§30010. COMPENSATION FOR TAKING OF PRIVATE PROPERTY; LEGISLATIVE DECLARATION

The Legislature hereby finds and declares that this [law] is not intended, and shall not be construed as authorizing the regional commission, the commission, port governing body, or local government acting pursuant to this [law] to exercise their power to grant or deny a permit in a manner which will take or damage private property for public use, without the payment of just compensation therefor. This section is not intended to increase or decrease the rights of any owner of property under the Constitution of the State of California or the United States. . . .

§30240. ENVIRONMENTALLY SENSITIVE HABITAT AREAS; ADJACENT DEVELOPMENTS

(a) Environmentally sensitive habitat areas shall be protected against any significant disruption of habitat values, and only uses dependent on such resources shall be allowed within such areas. . . .

§30301. MEMBERSHIP

The commission shall consist of the following 15 members:

(a) The Secretary of the Resources Agency.

(b) The Secretary of the Business and Transportation Agency.

(c) The Chairperson of the State Lands Commission.

(d) Six representatives of the public, who shall not be members of any regional commission, from the state at large. The Governor, the

Senate Rules Committee, and the Speaker of the Assembly shall each appoint two of such members.

(e) Six representatives from the regional commissions, selected by each regional commission from among its members. . . .

§30600.   COASTAL DEVELOPMENT PERMIT; LOCAL GOVERNMENT

(a) In addition to obtaining any other permit required by law from any local government or from any state, regional, or local agency, on or after January 1, 1977, any person wishing to perform or undertake any development in the coastal zone, other than a [power] facility, shall obtain a coastal development permit. . . .

§30604.   COASTAL DEVELOPMENT PERMIT; ISSUANCE; FINDING

(c) Every coastal development permit issued for any development between the nearest public road and the sea or the shoreline of any body of water located within the coastal zone shall include a specific finding that such development is in conformity with the public access and public recreation policies of [California law]. . . .

§30608.   VESTED RIGHTS; PRIOR PERMITS; CONDITIONS

(a) No person who has obtained a vested right in a development prior to the effective date of this [law] or who has obtained a permit from the California Coastal Zone Conservation Commission pursuant to the California Coastal Zone Conservation Act of 1972 shall be required to secure approval for the development pursuant to this [law]; provided, however, that no substantial change may be made in any such development without prior approval having been obtained under this [law]. . . .

◆ PENN CENTRAL TRANSPORTATION CO. v. NEW YORK CITY
438 U.S. 104 (1978)

Mr. Justice BRENNAN delivered the opinion of the Court. The question presented is whether a city may, as part of a comprehensive program to preserve historic landmarks and historic districts, place restrictions on the development of individual historic landmarks — in addition to those imposed by applicable zoning ordinances — without effecting a "taking" requiring the payment of "just compensation." Specifically, we must decide whether the application of New York City's Landmarks

Preservation Law to the parcel of land occupied by Grand Central Terminal has "taken" its owners' property in violation of the Fifth and Fourteenth Amendments.

Over the past 50 years, all 50 States and over 500 municipalities have enacted laws to encourage or require the preservation of buildings and areas with historic or aesthetic importance. These nationwide legislative effects have been precipitated by two concerns. The first is recognition that, in recent years, large numbers of historic structures, landmarks, and areas have been destroyed without adequate consideration of either the values represented therein or the possibility of preserving the destroyed properties for use in economically productive ways. The second is a widely shared belief that structures with special historic, cultural, or architectural significance enhance the quality of life for all. Not only do these buildings and their workmanship represent the lessons of the past and embody precious features of our heritage, they serve as examples of quality for today. "[H]istoric conservation is but one aspect of the much larger problem, basically an environmental one, of enhancing — or perhaps developing for the first time — the quality of life for people."

New York City, responding to similar concerns and acting pursuant to a New York State enabling Act, adopted its Landmarks Preservation Law in 1965. The city acted from the conviction that "the standing of [New York City] as a world-wide tourist center and world capital of business, culture and government" would be threatened if legislation were not enacted to protect historic landmarks and neighborhoods from precipitate decisions to destroy or fundamentally alter their character. The city believed that comprehensive measures to safeguard desirable features of the existing urban fabric would benefit its citizens in a variety of ways: e.g., fostering "civic pride in the beauty and noble accomplishments of the past"; protecting and enhancing "the city's attractions to tourists and visitors"; "support[ing] and stimul[ating] business and industry"; "strengthen[ing] the economy of the city"; and promoting "the use of historic districts, landmarks, interior landmarks and scenic landmarks for the education, pleasure and welfare of the people of the city."

The New York City law is typical of many urban landmark laws in that its primary method of achieving its goals is not by acquisitions of historic properties, but rather by involving public entities in land-use decisions affecting these properties and providing services, standards, controls, and incentives that will encourage preservation by private owners and users. While the law does place special restrictions on landmark properties as a necessary feature to the attainment of its larger objectives, the major theme of the law is to ensure the owners of any such properties both a "reasonable return" on their investments and maximum latitude to use their parcels for purposes not inconsistent with the preservation goals.

The operation of the law can be briefly summarized. The primary responsibility for administering the law is vested in the Landmarks Preservation Commission (Commission), a broad based, 11-member agency assisted by a technical staff. The Commission first performs the function, critical to any landmark preservation effort, of identifying properties and areas that have "a special character or special historical or aesthetic interest or value as part of the development, heritage or cultural characteristics of the city, state or nation." If the Commission determines, after giving all interested parties an opportunity to be heard, that a building or area satisfies the ordinance's criteria, it will designate a building to be a "landmark," situated on a particular "landmark site," or will designate an area to be a "historic district." After the Commission makes a designation, New York City's Board of Estimate, after considering the relationship of the designated property "to the master plan, the zoning resolution, projected public improvements and any plans for the renewal of the area involved," may modify or disapprove the designation, and the owner may seek judicial review of the final designation decision. Thus far, 31 historic districts and over 400 individual landmarks have been finally designated, and the process is a continuing one.

Final designation as a landmark results in restrictions upon the property owner's options concerning use of the landmark site. First, the law imposes a duty upon the owner to keep the exterior features of the building "in good repair" to assure that the law's objectives not be defeated by the landmark's falling into a state of irremediable disrepair. Second, the Commission must approve in advance any proposal to alter the exterior architectural features of the landmark or to construct any exterior improvement on the landmark site, thus ensuring that decisions concerning construction on the landmark site are made with due consideration of both the public interest in the maintenance of the structure and the landowner's interest in use of the property.

In the event an owner wishes to alter a landmark site, three separate procedures are available through which administrative approval may be obtained. First, the owner may apply to the Commission for a "certificate of no effect on protected architectural features": that is, for an order approving the improvement or alteration on the ground that it will not change or affect any architectural feature of the landmark and will be in harmony therewith. Denial of the certificate is subject to judicial review.

Second, the owner may apply to the Commission for a certificate of "appropriateness." Such certificates will be granted if the Commission concludes — focusing upon aesthetic, historical, and architectural values — that the proposed construction on the landmark site would not unduly hinder the protection, enhancement, perpetuation, and use of the landmark. Again, denial of the certificate is subject to judicial review. Moreover, the owner who is denied either a certificate of no exterior effect or a certificate of appropriateness may submit an alternative or modified plan for approval. The final procedure — seeking a certificate of appropriateness on the ground of "insufficient return," provides special mechanisms, which vary depending on whether or not the landmark enjoys a tax exemption, to ensure that designation does not cause economic hardship.

Although the designation of a landmark and landmark site restricts the owner's control over the parcel, designation also enhances the economic position of the landmark owner in one significant respect. Under New York City's zoning laws, owners of real property who have not developed their property to the full extent permitted by the applicable zoning laws are allowed to transfer development rights to contiguous parcels on the same city block. A 1968 ordinance gave the owners of landmark sites additional opportunities to transfer development rights to other parcels. Subject to a restriction that the floor area of the transferee lot may not be increased by more than 20% above its authorized level, the ordinance permitted transfers from a landmark parcel to property across the street or across a street intersection. In 1969, the law governing the conditions under which transfers from landmark parcels could occur was liberalized, apparently to ensure that the Landmarks Law would not unduly restrict the development options of the owners of Grand Central Terminal. The class of recipient lots was expanded to include lots "across a street and opposite to another lot or lots which except for the intervention of streets or street intersections f[or]m a series extending to the lot occupied by the landmark building [, provided that] all lots [are] in the same ownership." In addition, the 1969 amendment permits, in highly commercialized areas like midtown Manhattan, the transfer of all unused development rights to a single parcel.

This case involves the application of New York City's Landmarks Preservation Law to Grand Central Terminal. The Terminal, which is owned by the Penn Central Transportation Co. and its affiliates, is one of New York City's most famous buildings. Opened in 1913, it is regarded not only as providing an ingenious engineering solution to the problems presented by urban railroad stations, but also as a magnificent example of the French beaux-arts style. . . .

On August 2, 1967, following a public hearing, the Commission designated the Terminal a "landmark" and designated the "city tax block" it occupies a "landmark site." . . .

On January 22, 1968, appellant Penn Central, to increase its income, entered into a renewable 50-year lease and sublease agreement with appellant UGP Properties, Inc. (UGP), a wholly owned subsidiary of Union General Properties, Ltd., a United Kingdom corporation. Under the terms of the agreement, UGP was to construct a multistory office building above the Terminal. UGP promised to pay Penn Central $1 million annually during construction and at least $3 million annually thereafter. The rentals would be offset in part by a loss of some $700,000 to $1 million in net rentals presently received from concessionaires displaced by the new building.

Appellants UGP and Penn Central then applied to the Commission for permission to construct an office building atop the Terminal. Two separate plans, both designed by architect Marcel Breuer and both apparently satisfying the terms of the applicable zoning ordinance, were submitted to the Commission for approval. The first, Breuer I, provided for the construction of a 55-story office building, to be cantilevered above the existing facade and to rest on the roof of the Terminal. The second, Breuer II Revised, called for tearing down a portion of the Terminal that included the 42d Street facade, stripping off some of the remaining features of the Terminal's facade, and constructing a 53-story office building. The Commission denied a certificate of no exterior effect on September 20, 1968. Appellants then applied for a certificate of "appropriateness" as to both proposals. After four days of hearings at which over 80 witnesses testified, the Commission denied this application as to both proposals. . . .

[A]ppellants filed suit in New York Supreme Court, Trial Term, claiming, *inter alia*, that the application of the Landmarks Preservation Law had "taken" their property without just compensation in violation of the Fifth and Fourteenth Amendments and arbitrarily deprived them of their property without due process of law in violation of the Fourteenth Amendment. Appellants sought a declaratory judgment, injunctive relief barring the city from using the Landmarks Law to impede the construction of any structure that might otherwise lawfully be constructed on the Terminal site, and damages for the "temporary taking" that occurred between August 2, 1967, the designation date, and the date when the restrictions arising from the Landmarks Law would be lifted. . . .

[W]e have frequently observed that whether a particular restriction will be rendered invalid by the government's failure to pay for any losses proximately caused by it depends largely "upon the particular circumstances [in that] case." . . .

In engaging in these essentially ad hoc, factual inquiries, the Court's decisions have identified several factors that have particular significance. The economic impact of the regulation on the claimant and, particularly, the extent to which the regulation has interfered with distinct investment-backed expectations are, of course, relevant considerations. . . . So, too, is the character of the governmental action. A "taking" may more readily be found when the interference with property can be characterized as a physical invasion by government . . . than when interference arises from some public program adjusting the benefits and burdens of economic life to promote the common good. . . .

Apart from our own disagreement with appellants' characterization of the effect of the New York City law, the submission that appellants may establish a "taking" simply by showing that they have been denied the ability to exploit a property interest that they heretofore had believed was available for development is quite simply untenable. Were this the rule, this Court would have erred not only in upholding laws restricting the development of air rights, but also in approving those prohibiting both the subjacent, and the lateral development of particular parcels. "Taking" jurisprudence does not divide a single parcel into discrete segments and attempt to determine whether rights in a particular segment have been entirely abrogated. In deciding whether a particular governmental action has effected a taking, this Court focuses rather both on the character of the action and on the nature and extent of the interference with rights in the parcel as a whole — here, the city tax block designated as the "landmark site." . . .

Stated baldly, appellants' position appears to be that the only means of ensuring that selected owners are not singled out to endure financial hardship for no reason is to hold that any restriction imposed on individual landmarks pursuant to the New York City scheme is a "taking" requiring the payment of "just compensation." Agreement with this argument would, of course, invalidate not just New York City's law, but all comparable landmark legislation in the Nation. We find no merit in it.

It is true, as appellants emphasize, that both historic-district legislation and zoning laws regulate all properties within given physical communities whereas landmark laws apply only to selected parcels. But, contrary to appellants' suggestion, landmark laws are not like discriminatory, or "reverse spot," zoning: that is, a land-use decision which arbitrarily singles out a particular parcel for different, less favorable treatment than the neighboring ones. . . . In contrast to discriminatory zoning, which is the antithesis of land-use control as part of some comprehensive plan, the New York City law embodies a comprehensive plan to preserve structures of historic or aesthetic interest wherever they might be found in the city, and as noted, over 400 landmarks and 31 historic districts have been designated pursuant to this plan.

Equally without merit is the related argument that the decision to designate a structure as a landmark "is inevitably arbitrary or at least subjective, because it is basically a matter of taste," thus unavoidably singling out individual landowners for disparate and unfair treatment. The argument has a particularly hollow ring in this case. For appellants not only did not seek judicial review of either the designation or of the denials of the certificates of appropriateness and of no exterior effect, but do not even now suggest that the Commissioner's decisions concerning the Terminal were in any sense arbitrary or unprincipled. But, in any event, a landmark owner has a right to judicial review of any Commission decision, and, quite simply, there is a no basis whatsoever for a conclusion that courts will have any greater difficulty identifying arbitrary or discriminatory action in the context of landmark regulation than in the context of classic zoning or indeed in any other context.

Next, appellants observe that New York City's law differs from zoning laws and historic-district ordinances in that the Landmarks Law does not impose identical or similar restrictions on all structures located in particular physical communities. It follows, they argue, that New York City's law is inherently incapable of producing the fair and equitable distribution of benefits and burdens of governmental action which is characteristic of zoning laws and historic-district legislation and which they maintain is a constitutional requirement if "just compensation" is not to be afforded. It is, of course, true that the Landmarks Law has a more severe impact on some landowners than on others, but that in itself does not mean that the law effects a "taking." Legislation designed to promote the general welfare commonly burdens some more than others. The owners of the brickyard in *Hadacheck,* of the cedar trees in Miller v. Schoene, and of the gravel and sand mine in Goldblatt v. Hempstead, were uniquely burdened by the legislation sustained in those cases. Similarly, zoning laws often affect some property owners more severely than others but have not been held to be invalid on that account. For example, the property owner in *Euclid* who wished to use its property for industrial purposes was affected far more severely by the ordinance than its neighbors who wished to use their land for residences.

In any event, appellants' repeated suggestions that they are solely burdened and unbenefited is factually inaccurate. This contention overlooks the fact that the New York City law applies to vast numbers of structures in the city in addition to the Terminal — all the structures contained in the 31 historic districts and over 400 individual landmarks, many of which are close to the Terminal. Unless we are to reject the judgment of the New York City Council that the preservation of landmarks benefits all New York citizens and all structures, both economically and by improving the quality of life in the city as a whole — which we are unwilling to do — we cannot conclude that the owners of the Terminal have in no sense been benefited by the Landmarks Law. Doubtless appellants believe they are more burdened than benefited by the law, but that must have been true, too, of the property owners in *Miller, Hadacheck, Euclid,* and *Goldblatt.*

Appellants' final broad-based attack would have us treat the law as an instance, like that in United States v. Causby, in which government, acting in an enterprise capacity, has appropriated part of their property for some strictly governmental purpose. Apart from the fact that *Causby* was a case of invasion of airspace that destroyed the use of the farm beneath and this New York City law has in nowise impaired the present use of the Terminal, the Landmarks Law neither exploits appellants' parcel for city purposes nor facilitates nor arises from any entrepreneurial operations of the city. The situation is not remotely like that in *Causby* where the airspace above the property was in the flight pattern for military aircraft. The Landmarks Law's effect is simply to prohibit appellants or anyone else from occupying portions of the airspace above the Terminal, while permitting appellants to use the remainder of the parcel in a gainful fashion. This is no more an appropriation of property by government for its own uses than is a zoning law prohibiting, for "aesthetic" reasons, two or more adult theaters within a specified area, see Young v. American Mini Theatres, Inc., 427 U.S. 50 (1976), or a safety regulation prohibiting excavations below a certain level. . . .

Unlike the governmental acts in *Goldblatt, Miller, Causby, Griggs,* and *Hadacheck,* the New York City law does not interfere in any way with the present uses of the Terminal. Its designation as a landmark not only permits but contemplates that appellants may continue to use the property precisely as it has been used for the past 65 years: as a railroad terminal containing office space and concessions. So the law does not interfere with what must be regarded as Penn Central's primary expectation concerning the use of the parcel. More importantly, on this record, we must regard the New York City law as permitting Penn Central not only to profit from the Terminal but also to obtain a "reasonable return" on its investment. . . .

Second, to the extent appellants have been denied the right to build above the Terminal, it is not literally accurate to say that they have been denied *all* use of even those pre-existing air rights. Their ability to use these rights has not been abrogated; they are made transferable to at least eight parcels in the vicinity of the Terminal, one or two of which have been found suitable for the construction of new office buildings. Although appellants and others have argued that New York City's transferable development-rights program is far from ideal, the New York courts here supportably found that, at least in the case of the Terminal, the rights afforded are valuable. While these rights may well not have constituted "just compensation" if a "taking" had occurred, the rights nevertheless undoubtedly mitigate whatever financial burdens the law has imposed on appellants and, for that reason, are to be taken into account in considering the impact of regulation.

On this record, we conclude that the application of New York City's Landmarks Law has not effected a "taking" of appellants' property. The restrictions imposed are substantially related to the promotion of the general welfare and not only permit reasonable beneficial use of the landmark site but also afford appellants opportunities further to enhance not only the Terminal site proper but also other properties.

Mr. Justice REHNQUIST, with whom THE CHIEF JUSTICE and Mr. Justice STEVENS join, dissenting. Of the over one million buildings and structures in the city of New York, appellees have singled out 400 for designation as official landmarks. The owner of a building might initially be pleased that his property has been chosen by a distinguished committee of architects, historians, and city planners for such a singular distinction. But he may well discover, as appellant Penn Central Transportation Co. did here, that the landmark designation imposes upon him a substantial cost, with little or no offsetting benefit except for the honor of the designation. The question in this case is whether the cost associated with the city of New York's desire to preserve a limited number of "landmarks" within its borders must be borne by all of its taxpayers or whether it can instead be imposed entirely on the owners of the individual properties. . . .

Appellees . . . would argue that a taking only occurs where a property owner is denied *all* reasonable value of his property. The Court has frequently held that even where a destruction of property rights would not *otherwise* constitute a taking, the inability of the owner to make a reasonable return on his property requires compensation under the Fifth Amendment. But the converse is not true. A taking does not become a noncompensable exercise of police power simply because the government in its grace allows the owner to make some "reasonable use of his property." "[I]t is the character of the invasion, not the amount of damage resulting from it, so long as the damage is substantial, that determines the question whether it is a taking." United States v. Cress, 243 U.S. 316, 328 (1917); United States v. Causby, 328 U.S., at 266. See also Goldblatt v. Hempstead, 369 U.S., at 594.

Appellees, apparently recognizing that the constraints imposed on a landmark site constitute a taking for Fifth Amendment purposes, do not leave the property owner empty-handed. As the Court notes, the property owner may theoretically "transfer" his previous right to develop the landmark property to adjacent properties if they are under his control. Appellees have coined this system "Transfer Development Rights," or TDR's.

Of all the terms used in the Taking Clause, "just compensation" has the strictest meaning. The Fifth Amendment does not allow simply an approximate compensation but requires "a full and perfect equivalent for the property taken." Monongahela Navigation Co. v. United States, 148 U.S., at 326.

> [I]f the adjective "just" had been omitted, and the provision was simply that property should not be taken without compensation, the natural import of the language would be that the compensation should be the equivalent of the property. And this is made emphatic by the adjective "just." There can, in view of the combination of those two words, be no doubt that the compensation must be a full and perfect equivalent for the property taken. [Ibid.]

. . . And the determination of whether a "full and perfect equivalent" has been awarded is a "judicial function." . . . The fact that *appellees* may believe that TDR's provide full compensation is irrelevant.

> The legislature may determine what private property is needed for public purposes — that is a question of a political and legislative character; but when the taking has been ordered, then the question of compensation is judicial. It does not rest with the public, taking the property, through Congress or the legislature, its representative, to say what compensation shall be paid, or even what shall be the rule of compensation. The Constitution has declared that just compensation shall be paid, and the ascertainment of that is a judicial inquiry. [Monongahela Navigation Co. v. United States, 148 U.S. 312, 327 (1893).]

Appellees contend that, even if they have "taken" appellants' property, TDR's constitute "just compensation." Appellants, of course, argue that TDR's are highly imperfect compensation. Because the lower courts held that there was no "taking," they did not have to reach the question of whether or not just compensation has already been awarded. The New York Court of Appeals' discussion of TDR's gives some support to appellants: "The many defects in New York City's program for development rights transfers have been detailed elsewhere. . . . The area to which transfer is permitted is severely limited [and] complex procedures are required to obtain a transfer permit." And in other cases the Court of Appeals has noted that TDR's have an "uncertain and contingent market value" and do "not adequately preserve" the value lost when a building is declared to be a landmark. . . . On the other hand, there is evidence in the record that Penn Central has been offered substantial amounts for its TDR's. Because the record on appeal is relatively slim, I would remand to the Court of Appeals for a determination of whether TDR's constitute a "full and perfect equivalent for the property taken."[14]

Over 50 years ago, Mr. Justice Holmes, speaking for the Court,

---

14. The Court suggests that if appellees are held to have "taken" property rights of landmark owners, not only the New York City Landmarks Preservation Law, but "all comparable landmark legislation in the Nation," must fall. This assumes, of course, that TDR's are not "just compensation" for the property rights destroyed. It also ignores the fact that many States and cities in the Nation have chosen to preserve landmarks by purchasing or condemning restrictive easements over the facades of the landmarks and are apparently quite satisfied with the results. See, e.g., Ore. Rev. Stat. §§271.710, 271.720 (1977); Md. Ann. Code, Art 41, §181A (1978); Va. Code §§10-145.1 and 10-138(e) (1978); Richmond, Va., City Code §17-23 et seq. (1975). The British National Trust has effectively used restrictive easements to preserve landmarks since 1937. See National Trust Act, 1937, 1 Edw. 8 and 1 Geo. 6 ch. lvii, §§4 and 8. Other States and cities have found that tax incentives are also an effective means of encouraging the private preservation of landmark sites. See, e.g., Conn. Gen. Stat. §12-127a (1977); Ill. Rev. Stat., ch. 24, §11-48.2-6 (1976); Va. Code §10-139 (1978). The New York City Landmarks Preservation Law departs drastically from these traditional, and constitutional, means of preserving landmarks.

warned that the courts were "in danger of forgetting that a strong public desire to improve the public condition is not enough to warrant achieving the desire by a shorter cut than the constitutional way of paying for the change." . . . The Court's opinion in this case demonstrates that the danger thus foreseen has not abated. The city of New York is in a precarious financial state, and some may believe that the costs of landmark preservation will be more easily borne by corporations such as Penn Central than the overburdened individual taxpayers of New York. But these concerns do not allow us to ignore past precedents construing the Eminent Domain Clause to the end that the desire to improve the public condition is, indeed, achieved by a shorter cut than the constitutional way of paying for the change.

PENN CENTRAL TRANSPORTATION CO. v. CITY OF NEW YORK, 42 N.Y.2d 324, 366 N.E.2d 1271, 397 N.Y.S.2d 914 (1977): [In the New York Court of Appeals opinion affirmed by the Supreme Court in *Penn Central*, Chief Judge Breitel had written as follows:]

In broad terms, the problem in this case is determining the scope of governmental power, within the Constitution, to preserve, without resorting to eminent domain, irreplaceable landmarks deemed to be of inestimable social or cultural significance. In controversy is the constitutionality of regulation which would prohibit appellants, owner and proposed developer of the air rights above Grand Central Terminal, from constructing an office building atop the terminal. . . .

Plaintiffs, Penn Central Transportation Company and its affiliates, who have a fee interest in Grand Central Terminal, and UGP Properties, Inc., lessee of the development rights over the terminal, seek a declaration that the landmark preservation provisions of the Administrative Code of the City of New York, as applied to the terminal property, are unconstitutional. They also seek to enjoin defendants, the City of New York and the City Landmarks Preservation Commission, from enforcing those provisions against the subject property. Trial Term granted the requested relief, but a divided Appellate Division reversed and granted judgment to defendants. Plaintiffs appeal.

The order of the Appellate Division should be affirmed. Although government regulation is invalid if it denies a property owner all reasonable return, there is no constitutional imperative that the return embrace all attributes, incidental influences, or contributing external factors derived from the social complex in which the property rests. So many of these attributes are not the result of private effort or investment but of opportunities for the utilization or exploitation which an organized society offers to any private enterprise, especially to a public utility, favored by government and the public. These, too, constitute a background of massive social and governmental investment in the organized community without which the private enterprise could neither exist nor prosper. It is enough, for the limited purposes of a landmarking statute, albeit it is also essential, that the privately created ingredient of property receive a reasonable return. It is that privately created and privately managed ingredient which is the property on which the reasonable return is to be based. All else is society's contribution by the sweat of its brow and the expenditure of its funds. To that extent society is also entitled to its due.

Moreover, in this case, the challenged regulation provides Penn Central with transferable above-the-surface development rights which, because they may be attached to specific parcels of property, some already owned by Penn Central or its affiliates, may be considered as part of the owner's return on the terminal property.

Thus, the regulation does not deprive plaintiffs of property without due process of law, and should be upheld as a valid exercise of the police power. . . .

Grand Central Terminal is no ordinary landmark. It may be true that no property has economic value in the absence of the society around it, but how much more true it is of a railroad terminal, set amid a metropolitan population, and entirely dependent on a heavy traffic of travelers to make it an economically feasible operation. Without people Grand Central would never have been a successful railroad terminal, and without the terminal, a major transportation center, the proposed building site would be much less desirable for an office building.

Of course it may be argued that had Grand Central Terminal never been built, the area would not have developed as it has. Thus, the argument runs, construction of the terminal triggered growth of the area, and created much of the terminal property's current value. Indeed, the argument has some validity. But, in reality, it is of little moment which comes first, the terminal or the travelers. For it is the interaction of economic influences in the greatest megalopolis of the western hemisphere — the terminal initially drawing people to the area, and the society developing the area with shops, hotels, office buildings, and unmatched civil services — that has made the property so valuable. Neither factor alone accounts for the increase in the property's value; both, in tandem, have contributed to the increase.

Of primary significance, however, is that society as an organized entity, especially through its government, rather than as a mere conglomerate of individuals, has created much of the value of the terminal property. Although recent financial troubles and consequent governmental assistance make the fact more apparent, railroads have always been a franchised and regulated public utility, favored monopolies at public expense, subsidy, and with limited powers of eminent domain, without which their existence and character would not have been possible.

Even in the best of times, railroads were dependent on government-granted monopolies for their rights of way, government grants for their land, and government assistance for such projects as grade crossing eliminations. Railroads were given franchises to use city streets without charge, often to the detriment of neighboring residents and often without leaving the city power to terminate the franchise. . . . Through the years, Penn Central and its predecessors have benefited mightily from this assistance. Today, government influence is even more pervasive, extending even to the real estate tax exemption enjoyed by Grand Central Terminal itself. . . .

Government has aided the terminal in less direct ways, as well. It is no accident that much of the city's mass transportation system converges on Grand Central. Numerous subways and bus routes pass through or near the terminal. Without the assistance of the city's transit system, now municipally owned and subsidized, the property, with or without a towering office structure atop it, would be of considerably decreased value. It is true that most city property benefits to some extent from public transportation, but the benefit is peculiarly concentrated and great in the area surrounding Grand Central Terminal.

Absent this heavy public governmental investment in the terminal, the railroads, and connecting transportation, it is indisputable that the terminal property would be worth but a fraction of its current economic value. Plaintiffs may not now frustrate legitimate and important social objectives by complaining, in essence, that government regulation deprives them of a return on so much of the investment made not by private interests but by the people of the city and State through their government. Instead, to prevail, plaintiffs must establish that there was no possibility of earning a reasonable return on the privately contributed ingredient of the property's value.

To put the matter another way, the massive and indistinguishable public, governmental, and private contributions to a landmark like the Grand Central Terminal are inseparably joint, and for most of its existence, made both the terminal and the railroads of which it was an integral part, a great financial success for generations of stockholders and bondholders. Their investment has long been eliminated or impaired by the recent vicissitudes of the Penn Central complex. It is exceedingly difficult but imperative, nevertheless, to sort out the merged ingredients and to assess the rights and responsibilities of owner and society. A fair return is to be accorded the owner, but society is to receive its due for its share in the making of a once great railroad. The historical, cultural, and architectural resource that remains was neither created solely by the private owner nor solely by the society in which it was permitted to evolve.

Plaintiffs contend that the terminal currently operates at a loss. Even if that be true, it is not of critical importance. What is significant, instead, is whether the property, managed efficiently, is capable of producing a reasonable return. If the courts were forced to look to the property as it is, rather than as it could be, any inadequacy of managers of property could frustrate any land use restrictions.

Perhaps of greater importance, the property may be capable of producing a reasonable return for its owners even if it can never operate at a profit. For it should be evident that plaintiff's heavy real estate holdings in the Grand Central area, including hotels and office buildings, would lose considerable value and deprive plaintiffs of much income, were the terminal not in operation. Some of this income must, realistically, be imputed to the terminal. . . .

Development rights, once transferrred, may not be equivalent in value to development rights on the original site. But that, alone, does not mean that the substitution of rights amounts to a deprivation of property without due process of law. Land use regulation often diminishes the value of the property to the landowner. Constitutional standards, however, are offended only when that diminution leaves the owner with no reasonable use of the property. The situation with transferable development rights is analogous. If the substitute rights received provide reasonable compensation for a landowner forced to relinquish development rights on a landmark site, there has been no deprivation of due process. The compensation need not be the "just" compensation required in eminent domain, for there has been no attempt to take property. . . .

Notes

1. Before the *Penn Central* decision, New York's Landmarks Preservation Commission had been "circumspect in its designation of privately owned structures." After *Penn Central*, however, the commission became bolder and more active; as of early 1984, it had designated 44 historic districts containing more than 16,000 buildings, 690 individual landmarks, and 45 interior or scenic landmarks. Of late, the commission has been charged with "overstepp[ing] its role by becoming involved in land use matters that should properly be addressed by the City Planning Commission," and with assisting "community activists" in "neighborhood preservation and the obstruction of unwanted development." A critic of the commission points to the 1981 "historic district" designation of a large portion of Manhattan's Upper East Side as

[t]he most egregious example of trespass on planning and zoning matters. . . . In one vote the Commission gave blanket protection to 60 city blocks containing 1,044 buildings on some of New York's most valuable real estate, thereby freezing development in one of the city's most vital areas. . . . Even Beverly Moss Spatt, a former LPC chairman known for her aggressive preservationist views, voted against the designation because

she felt the Commission was "usurping the City Planning Commission's powers to prevent demolition, to prevent development and change" in an area that was not "a unified historic district in terms of architectural style or historicity." [Rose, Landmarks Preservation in New York, The Public Interest No. 74, at 132 (1984).]

2. *Penn Central* requires that a constitutionally satisfactory reasonable economic return be available to the owner (if Chief Judge Breitel is right, only when the railroad is well managed). What if the owner is a nonprofit charity? The court of appeals posed the test as "whether the impact on the Society [for Ethical Culture] and its charitable activities is so severe that the restrictions become confiscatory."

Compare Society for Ethical Culture v. Spatt, 51 N.Y.2d 449, 415 N.E.2d 922, 434 N.Y.S.2d 932 (1980) (prevention of demolition and reconstruction — including for-rent commercial development — upheld), *with* Lutheran Church in America v. City of New York, 35 N.Y.2d 121, 316 N.E.2d 305, 359 N.Y.S.2d 7 (1974), (landmark structure hopelessly inadequate to church's needs, so designation without compensation a "naked taking").

3. St. Bartholomew's Episcopal Church is a Romanesque stone structure built in 1918 on midtown Manhattan's Park Avenue. The architect was Bertram Goodhue. The church's proposal to construct a 59-story office building on the site of its adjacent community house sparked a challenge under New York's Landmarks Preservation Law. A sharp debate over the constitutionality of the law, the role of the First Amendment, and the architectural, aesthetic, and historic merits of the proposal created what has been called "one of the most important landmarks struggles of the decade." The view of the church is that it has a right, protected under the First Amendment, to use its land as it sees fit; and that the millions of dollars in office rents will finance charitable work that is an essential obligation of the congregation. The rector said, "There are many people in this city who could care less, but the commitment to theology is at the heart of this matter." A lawyer for opponents of the plan replied: "There is no first amendment right to construct office buildings. I know of no faith whose major tenet is to construct office buildings." See N.Y. Times, Dec. 21, 1984.

2. *Human Rights*

◆ VILLAGE OF BELLE TERRE v. BORAAS
416 U.S. 1 (1974)

Mr. Justice DOUGLAS delivered the opinion of the Court.
Belle Terre is a village on Long Island's north shore of about 220

homes inhabited by 700 people. Its total land area is less than one square mile. It has restricted land use to one-family dwellings excluding lodging houses, boarding houses, fraternity houses, or multiple-dwelling houses. The word "family" as used in the ordinance means, "[o]ne or more persons related by blood, adoption, or marriage, living and cooking together as a single housekeeping unit, exclusive of household servants. A number of persons but not exceeding two (2) living and cooking together as a single housekeeping unit though not related by blood, adoption, or marriage shall be deemed to constitute a family."

Appellees the Dickmans are owners of a house in the village and leased it in December 1971 for a term of 18 months to Michael Truman. Later Bruce Boraas became a colessee. Then Anne Parish moved into the house along with three others. These six are students at nearby State University at Stony Brook and none is related to the other by blood, adoption, or marriage. When the village served the Dickmans with an "Order to Remedy Violations" of the ordinance, the owners plus three tenants thereupon brought this action under 42 U.S.C. §1983 for an injunction and a judgment declaring the ordinance unconstitutional. The District Court held the ordinance constitutional, and the Court of Appeals reversed, one judge dissenting, . . .

The present ordinance is challenged on several grounds: that it interferes with a person's right to travel; that it interferes with the right to migrate to and settle within a State; that it bars people who are uncongenial to the present residents; that it expresses the social preferences of the residents for groups that will be congenial to them; that social homogeneity is not a legitimate interest of government; that the restriction of those whom the neighbors do not like trenches on the newcomers' rights of privacy; that it is of no rightful concern to villagers whether the residents are married or unmarried; that the ordinance is antithetical to the Nation's experience, ideology, and self-perception as an open, egalitarian, and integrated society.[4]

We find none of these reasons in the record before us. It is not aimed at transients. It involves no procedural disparity inflicted on some but not on others. It involves no "fundamental" right guaranteed by the Constitution, such as voting, the right of association, the right of access to the courts, or any rights of privacy. We deal with economic and social legislation where legislatures have historically drawn lines which we respect against the charge of violation of the Equal Protection Clause if the law be "reasonable, not arbitrary" and bears "a rational relationship to a [permissible] state objective."

It is said, however, that if two unmarried people can constitute a "family," there is no reason why three or four may not. But every line

4. Many references in the development of this thesis are made to F. Turner, The Frontier in American History (1920), with emphasis on his theory that "democracy [is] born of free land."

drawn by a legislature leaves some out that might well have been included.[5] That exercise of discretion, however, is a legislative, not a judicial, function.

It is said that the Belle Terre ordinance reeks with an animosity to unmarried couples who live together.[6] There is no evidence to support it; and the provision of the ordinance bringing within the definition of a "family" two unmarried people belies the charge.

The ordinance places no ban on other forms of association, for a "family" may, so far as the ordinance is concerned, entertain whomever it likes.

The regimes of boarding houses, fraternity houses, and the like present urban problems. More people occupy a given space; more cars rather continuously pass by; more cars are parked; noise travels with crowds.

A quiet place where yards are wide, people few, and motor vehicles restricted are legitimate guidelines in a land-use project addressed to family needs. This goal is a permissible one, . . . The police power is not confined to elimination of filth, stench, and unhealthy places. It is ample to lay out zones where family values, youth values, and the blessings of quiet seclusion and clean air make the area a sanctuary for people. . . .

When Mr. Justice Holmes said for the Court in Block v. Hirsh, 256 U.S. 135, 155, "property rights may be cut down, and to that extent taken, without pay," he stated the issue here. As is true in most zoning cases, the precise impact on value may, at the threshold of litigation over validity, not yet be known.

Reversed.

Mr. Justice MARSHALL dissenting. . . . In my view, the disputed classification burdens the students' fundamental rights of association and privacy guaranteed by the First and Fourteenth Amendments. Because the application of strict equal protection scrutiny is therefore required, I am at odds with my Brethren's conclusion that the ordinance may be sustained on a showing that it bears a rational relationship to the accomplishment of legitimate governmental objectives.

---

5. Mr. Justice Holmes made the point a half century ago.

When a legal distinction is determined, as no one doubts that it may be, between night and day, childhood and maturity, or any other extremes, a point has to be fixed or a line has to be drawn, or gradually picked out by successive decision, to mark where the change takes place. Looked at by itself without regard to the necessity behind it the line or point seems arbitrary. It might as well or nearly as well be a little more to one side or the other. But when it is seen that a line or point there must be, and that there is no mathematical or logical way of fixing it precisely, the decision of the legislature must be accepted unless we can say that it is very wide of any reasonable mark.

Louisville Gas Co. v. Coleman, 277 U.S. 32, 41 (dissenting opinion).

6. U.S. Dept. of Agriculture v. Moreno, 413 U.S. 528, is therefore inapt as there a household containing anyone unrelated to the rest was denied food stamps.

I am in full agreement with the majority that zoning is a complex and important function of the State. It may indeed be the most essential function performed by local government, for it is one of the primary means by which we protect that sometimes difficult to define concept of quality of life. I therefore continue to adhere to the principle of Euclid v. Ambler Realty Co., that deference should be given to governmental judgments concerning proper land-use allocation. That deference is a principle which has served this Court well and which is necessary for the continued development of effective zoning and land-use control mechanisms. Had the owners alone brought this suit alleging that the restrictive ordinance deprived them of their property or was an irrational legislative classification, I would agree that the ordinance would have to be sustained. Our role is not and should not be to sit as a zoning board of appeals.

I would also agree with the majority that local zoning authorities may properly act in furtherance of the objectives asserted to be served by the ordinance at issue here: restricting uncontrolled growth, solving traffic problems, keeping rental costs at a reasonable level, and making the community attractive to families. The police power which provides the justification for zoning is not narrowly confined. And, it is appropriate that we afford zoning authorities considerable latitude in choosing the means by which to implement such purposes. But deference does not mean abdication. This Court has an obligation to ensure that zoning ordinances, even when adopted in furtherance of such legitimate aims, do not infringe upon fundamental constitutional rights. . . .

The instant ordinance discriminates on the basis of just such a personal lifestyle choice as to household companions. It permits any number of persons related by blood or marriage, be it two or twenty, to live in a single household, but it limits to two the number of unrelated persons bound by profession, love, friendship, religious or political affiliation, or mere economics who can occupy a single home. Belle Terre imposes upon those who deviate from the community norm in their choice of living companions significantly greater restrictions than are applied to residential groups who are related by blood or marriage, and compose the established order within the community. The village has, in effect, acted to fence out those individuals whose choice of lifestyle differs from that of its current residents.

This is not a case where the Court is being asked to nullify a township's sincere efforts to maintain its residential character by preventing the operation of rooming houses, fraternity houses, or other commercial or high-density residential uses. Unquestionably, a town is free to restrict such uses. Moreover, as a general proposition, I see no constitutional infirmity in a town's limiting the density of use in residential areas by zoning regulations which do not discriminate on the basis of constitutionally suspect criteria. This ordinance, however, limits the density of occupany of only those homes occupied by unrelated persons. It thus reaches beyond control of the use of land or the density of population, and undertakes to regulate the way people choose to associate with each other within the privacy of their own homes. . . .

There are some 220 residences in Belle Terre occupied by about 700 persons. The density is therefore just above three per household. The village is justifiably concerned with density of population and the related problems of noise, traffic, and the like. It could deal with those problems by limiting each household to a specified number of adults, two or three perhaps, without limitation on the number of dependent children. The burden of such an ordinance would fall equally upon all segments of the community. It would surely be better tailored to the goals asserted by the village than the ordinance before us today, for it would more realistically restrict population density and growth and their attendant environmental costs. Various other statutory mechanisms also suggest themselves as solutions to Belle Terre's problems — rent control, limits on the number of vehicles per household, and so forth, but, of course, such schemes are matters of legislative judgment and not for this Court. Appellants also refer to the necessity of maintaining the family character of the village. There is not a shred of evidence in the record indicating that if Belle Terre permitted a limited number of unrelated persons to live together, the residential, familial character of the community would be fundamentally affected.

Notes

1. Can *Belle Terre* be squared with Demiragh v. DeVos, 476 F.2d 403 (2d Cir. 1973), holding unconstitutional a Stamford, Connecticut, ordinance "declaring it a health hazard when vacancy rate falls below 2 percent" and stating that any person becoming a Stamford resident during the existence of such a hazard is ineligible for welfare benefits?

2. See City of White Plains v. Ferraioli, 34 N.Y.2d 300, 313 N.E.2d 756, 357 N.Y.S.2d 449 (1974), holding that a home consisting of a couple and their two children and ten foster children could be maintained in a single-family district.

3. See also Stoner v. Miller, 377 F. Supp. 177 (E.D.N.Y. 1974), declaring that the constitutional rights to travel and to privacy were violated by a Long Beach, Long Island, ordinance requiring that hotels in the city not register persons requiring continuous medical or psychiatric services. Long Beach was attempting to prevent conversion of beach hotels into facilities for "halfway house" treatment of mental patients.

4. The city of Detroit sought to disperse "adult" movie theaters by amending its "anti-skid row" zoning ordinance to provide that no adult theater could be located within 1,000 feet of any two other "regulated

uses" including "adult" book stores, cabarets, bars, hotels, pawnshops, pool halls, rooming houses and second-hand stores. The Supreme Court, by a 5 to 4 vote, found no constitutional violation. Writing for the majority, Justice Stevens concluded:

> The mere fact that the commercial exploitation of material protected by the First Amendment is subject to zoning and other licensing requirements is not a sufficient reason for invalidating these ordinances. . . . Since what is ultimately at stake is nothing more than a limitation on the place where adult films may be exhibited, . . . we conclude that the city's interest in the present and future character of its neighborhoods adequately supports its classification of motion pictures.

The opinion also noted the limited First Amendment protection afforded "erotic materials":

> Whether political oratory or philosophical discussion moves us to applaud or to despise what is said, every schoolchild can understand why our duty to defend the right to speak remains the same. But few of us would march our sons and daughters off to war to preserve the citizen's right to see "Specified Sexual Activities" exhibited in the theaters of our choice. [Young v. American Mini Theatres, Inc., 427 U.S. 50 (1976).]

◆ MOORE v. CITY OF EAST CLEVELAND
431 U.S. 494 (1977)

Mr. Justice POWELL announced the judgment of the Court, and delivered an opinion in which Mr. Justice BRENNAN, Mr. Justice MARSHALL, and Mr. Justice BLACKMUN joined. . . .

Appellant, Mrs. Inez Moore, lives in her East Cleveland home together with her son, Dale Moore, Sr., and her two grandsons, Dale, Jr., and John Moore, Jr. The two boys are first cousins rather than brothers; we are told that John came to live with his grandmother and with the elder and younger Dale Moores after his mother's death.

In early 1973, Mrs. Moore received a notice of violation from the city, stating that John was an "illegal occupant" and directing her to comply with the ordinance. When she failed to remove him from her home, the city filed a criminal charge. Mrs. Moore moved to dismiss, claiming that the ordinance was constitutionally invalid on its face. Her motion was overruled, and upon conviction she was sentenced to five days in jail and a $25 fine. The Ohio Court of Appeals affirmed after giving full consideration to her constitutional claims, and the Ohio Supreme Court denied review. We noted probable jurisdiction of her appeal.

The city argues that our decision in Village of Belle Terre v. Boraas requires us to sustain the ordinance attacked here. Belle Terre, like East Cleveland, imposed limits on the types of groups that could occupy a single dwelling unit. Applying the constitutional standard announced in this Court's leading land-use case, Euclid v. Ambler Realty Co., we sustained the Belle Terre ordinance on the ground that it bore a rational relationship to permissible state objectives.

But one overriding factor sets this case apart from *Belle Terre*. The ordinance there affected only *unrelated* individuals. It expressly allowed all who were related by "blood, adoption, or marriage" to live together, and in sustaining the ordinance we were careful to note that it promoted "family needs" and "family values." East Cleveland, in contrast, has chosen to regulate the occupancy of its housing by slicing deeply into the family itself. This is no mere incidental result of the ordinance. On its face it selects certain categories of relatives who may live together and declares that others may not. In particular, it makes a crime of a grandmother's choice to live with her grandson in circumstances like those presented here.

When a city undertakes such intrusive regulation of the family, neither *Belle Terre* nor *Euclid* governs; the usual judicial deference to the legislature is inappropriate. "This Court has long recognized that freedom of personal choice in matters of marriage and family life is one of the liberties protected by the Due Process Clause of the Fourteenth Amendment." Of course, the family is not beyond regulation. But when the government intrudes on choices concerning family living arrangements, this Court must examine carefully the importance of the governmental interests advanced and the extent to which they are served by the challenged regulation.

When thus examined, this ordinance cannot survive. The city seeks to justify it as a means of preventing overcrowding, minimizing traffic and parking congestion, and avoiding an undue financial burden on East Cleveland's school system. Although these are legitimate goals, the ordinance before us serves them marginally, at best. For example, the ordinance permits any family consisting only of husband, wife, and unmarried children to live together, even if the family contains a half dozen licensed drivers, each with his or her own car. At the same time it forbids an adult brother and sister to share a household, even if both faithfully use public transportation. The ordinance would permit a grandmother to live with a single dependent son and children, even if his school-age children number a dozen, yet it forces Mrs. Moore to find another dwelling for her grandson John, simply because of the presence of his uncle and cousin in the same household. We need not labor the point. Section 1341.08 has but a tenuous relation to alleviation of the conditions mentioned by the city. . . .

Substantive due process has at times been a treacherous field for this Court. There *are* risks when the judicial branch gives enhanced protection to certain substantive liberties without the guidance of the more specific provisions of the Bill of Rights. As the history of the *Lochner* era demonstrates, there is reason for concern lest the only limits to such judicial intervention become the predilections of those who happen at the time to be Members of this Court. That history counsels caution and restraint. But it does not counsel abandonment, nor does it require what the city urges here: cutting off any protection of family rights at the first convenient, if arbitrary boundary — the boundary of the nuclear family. . . .

Whether or not such a household is established because of personal tragedy, the choice of relatives in this degree of kinship to live together may not lightly be denied by the State. *Pierce* struck down an Oregon law requiring all children to attend the State's public schools, holding that the Constitution "excludes any general power of the State to standardize its children by forcing them to accept instruction from public teachers only." By the same token the Constitution prevents East Cleveland from standardizing its children — and its adults — by forcing all to live in certain narrowly defined family patterns.

Mr. Justice STEVENS, concurring in the judgment.

. . . The state decisions have upheld zoning ordinances which regulated the identity, as opposed to the number, of persons who may compose a household only to the extent that the ordinances require such households to remain nontransient, single-housekeeping units.

There appears to be no precedent for an ordinance which excludes any of an owner's relatives from the group of persons who may occupy his residence on a permanent basis. Nor does there appear to be any justification for such a restriction on an owner's use of his property. . . .

[Chief Justice Burger and Justices Stewart, White, and Rehnquist dissented on various grounds.]

Notes

1. Santa Barbara, California, barred groups of more than 5 ("excluding servants") from sharing a dwelling unit. A group of 12 adults, sharing a 24-room house, sued and won. The California Supreme Court rested its decision on the state's constitutional protection for privacy, which was added by referendum in 1972. City of Santa Barbara v. Adamson, 27 Cal. 3d 123, 610 P.2d 436, 164 Cal. Rptr. 539 (1980).

2. See also Village of Carpentersville v. Fiala, 98 Ill. App. 3d 1005, 425 N.E.2d 33 (1981), upholding a zoning ordinance that forbids keeping more than two adult dogs in and around a single-family residence.

3. Recent Ohio cases have held that a foster home is not a "one family residential dwelling unit" within the meaning of a zoning ordi-

nance, Carroll v. Washington Township Zoning Commission, 63 Ohio St. 2d 249, 408 N.E.2d 191 (1980), and that the state is not exempt from local zoning when it seeks to locate a halfway house, Brownfield v. State, 63 Ohio St. 2d 282, 407 N.E.2d 1365 (1980); Garcia v. Siffrin Residential Association, 63 Ohio St. 2d 259, 407 N.E.2d 1369 (1980), *cert. denied*, 450 U.S. 911 (1981).

But a Massachusetts case held that a community residence for former mental patients could be opened, notwithstanding local zoning, because of a statutory zoning exemption for uses that have a "public educational purpose." Fitchburg Housing Authority v. Board of Zoning Appeals, 380 Mass. 869, 406 N.E.2d 1006 (1980).

◆ SCHAD v. BOROUGH OF MOUNT EPHRAIM
452 U.S. 61 (1981)

Justice WHITE delivered the opinion of the Court.

In 1973, appellants began operating an adult bookstore in the commercial zone in the Borough of Mount Ephraim in Camden County, N.J. The store sold adult books, magazines and films. Amusement licenses shortly issued permitting the store to install coin-operated devices by virtue of which a customer could sit in a booth, insert a coin and watch an adult film. In 1976, the store introduced an additional coin-operated mechanism permitting the customer to watch a live dancer, usually nude, performing behind a glass panel. Complaints were soon filed against appellants charging that the bookstore's exhibition of live dancing violated §99-15B of Mount Ephraim's zoning ordinance, which described the permitted uses in a commercial zone,[1] in which the store was located, as follows:

B. Principal permitted uses on the land and in buildings.

(1) Offices and banks; taverns; restaurants and luncheonettes for sit-down dinners only and with no drive-in facilities; automobile sales; retail stores, such as but not limited to food, wearing apparel, millinery, fabrics, hardware, lumber, jewelry, paint, wallpaper, appliances, flowers, gifts, books, stationery, pharmacy, liquors, cleaners, novelties, hobbies and toys; repair shops for shoes, jewels, clothes and appliances; barbershops and beauty salons; cleaners and laundries; pet stores, and nurseries. Offices may, in addition, be permitted to a group of four (4) stores or more

---

1. The zoning ordinance establishes three types of zones. The "R-1" residential district is zoned for single-family dwellings. The "R-2" residential district is zoned for single-family dwellings, townhouses, and garden apartments. The "C" district is zoned for commercial use, as specified in §99-15 of the Mount Ephraim Code.

without additional parking, provided the offices do not exceed the equivalent of twenty percent (20%) of the gross floor area of the stores.
(2) Motels.[2]

Section 99-4 of the Borough's code provided that "[a]ll uses not expressly permitted in this chapter are prohibited."

Appellants were found guilty in the municipal court and fines were imposed. . . .

As the Mount Ephraim code has been construed by the New Jersey courts — a construction that is binding upon us — "live entertainment," including nude dancing, is "not a permitted use in any establishment" in the Borough of Mount Ephraim. . . . By excluding live entertainment throughout the Borough, the Mount Ephraim ordinance prohibits a wide range of expression that has long been held to be within the protections of the First and Fourteenth Amendments. Entertainment, as well as political and ideological speech, is protected; motion pictures, programs broadcast by radio and television and live entertainment, such as musical and dramatic works fall within the First Amendment guarantee. Nor may an entertainment program be prohibited solely because it displays the nude human figure. "Nudity alone" does not place otherwise protected material outside the mantle of the First Amendment. Furthermore, as the state courts in this case recognized, nude dancing is not without its First Amendment protections from official regulation. . . .

The power of local governments to zone and control land use is undoubtedly broad and its proper exercise is an essential aspect of achieving a satisfactory quality of life in both urban and rural communities. But the zoning power is not infinite and unchallengeable; it "must be exercised within constitutional limits." Accordingly, it is subject to judicial review; and as is most often the case, the standard of review is determined by the nature of the right assertedly threatened or violated rather than by the power being exercised or the specific limitation imposed. . . .

As an initial matter, this case is not controlled by Young v. American Mini Theatres, Inc., 427 U.S. 50 (1976), the decision relied upon by the Camden County Court. Although the Court there stated that a zon-

---

2. Section 99-15A states the purpose of the commercial zone:

A. Purpose. The purpose of this district is to provide areas for local and regional commercial operations. The zone district pattern recognizes the strip commercial pattern which exists along Kings Highway and the Black Horse Pike. It is intended, however, to encourage such existing uses and any new uses or redevelopment to improve upon the zoning districts of greater depth, by encouraging shopping center-type development with buildings related to each other in design, landscaping and site planning, and by requiring off-street parking, controlled ingress and egress, greater building set-backs, buffer areas along property lines adjacent to residential uses, and a concentration of commercial uses into fewer locations to eliminate the strip pattern.

ing ordinance is not invalid merely because it regulates activity protected under the First Amendment, it emphasized that the challenged restriction on the location of adult movie theaters imposed a minimal burden on protected speech. The restriction did not affect the number of adult movie theaters that could operate in the city; it merely dispersed them. The Court did not imply that a municipality could ban all adult theaters — much less all live entertainment or all nude dancing — from its commercial districts citywide. Moreover, it was emphasized in that case that the evidence presented to the Detroit Common Council indicated that the concentration of adult movie theaters in limited areas led to deterioration of surrounding neighborhoods, and it was concluded that the city had justified the incidental burden on First Amendment interests resulting from merely dispersing, but not excluding, adult theaters.

In this case, however, Mount Ephraim has not adequately justified its substantial restriction of protected activity. None of the justifications asserted in this court was articulated by the state courts and none of them withstands scrutiny. First, the Borough contends that permitting live entertainment would conflict with its plan to create a commercial area that caters only to the "immediate needs" of its residents and that would enable them to purchase at local stores the few items they occasionally forgot to buy outside the Borough. No evidence was introduced below to support this assertion, and it is difficult to reconcile this characterization of the Borough's commercial zones with the provisions of the ordinance. Section 99-15A expressly states that the purpose of creating commercial zones was to provide areas for "local and *regional* commercial operations." (Emphasis added.) The range of permitted uses goes far beyond providing for the "immediate needs" of the residents. Motels, hardware stores, lumber stores, banks, offices, and car showrooms are permitted in commercial zones. The list of permitted "retail stores" is nonexclusive, and it includes such services as beauty salons, barber shops, cleaners, and restaurants. Virtually the only item or service that may not be sold in a commercial zone is entertainment, or at least live entertainment. The Borough's first justification is patently insufficient.

Second, Mount Ephraim contends that it may selectively exclude commercial live entertainment from the broad range of commercial uses permitted in the Borough for reasons normally associated with zoning in commercial districts, that is, to avoid the problems that may be associated with live entertainment, such as parking, trash, police protection, and medical facilities. The Borough has presented no evidence, and it is not immediately apparent as a matter of experience, that live entertainment poses problems of this nature more significant than those associated with various permitted uses; nor does it appear that the Borough's zoning authority has arrived at a defensible conclusion that unusual problems are presented by live entertainment. We do not find it self-evident that a theater, for example, would create greater parking problems than would a restaurant. Even less apparent is what unique problems would be posed by exhibiting live nude dancing in connection with the sale of adult books and films, particularly since the bookstore is licensed to exhibit nude dancing on films. It may be that some forms of live entertainment would create problems that are not associated with the commercial uses presently permitted in Mount Ephraim. Yet this ordinance is not narrowly drawn to respond to what might be the distinctive problems arising from certain types of live entertainment, and it is not clear that a more selective approach would fail to address those unique problems if any there are. The Borough has not established that its interests could not be met by restrictions that are less intrusive on protected forms of expression.

The Borough also suggests that §99-15B is a reasonable "time, place and manner" restriction; yet it does not identify the municipal interests making it reasonable to exclude all commercial live entertainment but to allow a variety of other commercial uses in the Borough. . . .

To be reasonable, time, place and manner restrictions not only must serve significant state interests but also must leave open adequate alternative channels of communication.

Here, the Borough totally excludes all live entertainment, including nonobscene nude dancing that is otherwise protected by the First Amendment. . . .

The Borough nevertheless contends that live entertainment in general and nude dancing in particular are amply available in close-by areas outside the limits of the Borough. Its position suggests the argument that if there were countywide zoning, it would be quite legal to allow live entertainment in only selected areas of the county and to exclude it from primarily residential communities, such as the Borough of Mount Ephraim. This may very well be true, but the Borough cannot avail itself of that argument in this case. There is no countywide zoning in Camden County, and Mount Ephraim is free under state law to impose its own zoning restrictions, within constitutional limits. Furthermore, there is no evidence in this record to support the proposition that the kind of entertainment appellants wish to provide is available in reasonably nearby areas. The courts below made no such findings; and at least in their absence, the ordinance excluding live entertainment from the commercial zone cannot constitutionally be applied to appellants so as to criminalize the activities for which they have been fined. "[O]ne is not to have the exercise of his liberty of expression in appropriate places abridged on the plea that it may be exercised in some other place."

Accordingly, the convictions of these appellants are infirm and the judgment of the Appellate Division of the Superior Court of New Jersey is reversed and the case is remanded for further proceedings not inconsistent with this opinion.

So ordered.

Notes

1. In Metromedia v. City of San Diego, 453 U.S. 490 (1981), the Supreme Court struck down San Diego's regulation of billboards. Four justices said that both traffic safety and aesthetics are legitimate grounds for limitation of this medium of communication. While the justices said further that the city is allowed to permit onsite advertising while banning offsite billboards, they concluded that the ordinance invalidly infringed on constitutionally protected free speech rights when it permitted certain commercial advertisements while banning noncommercial messages at the same locations. Two other justices found the traffic safety and aesthetic justifications insufficient for any billboard ban.

2. Cleveland Heights, Ohio, had used the zoning power to prevent Donna S. Reid from building a one-story modern house in a neighborhood of multi-story traditional structures. The city's action was upheld against the charge that it invalidly restricted Ms. Reid's right to freedom of expression. Reid v. Architectural Board of Review, 119 Ohio App. 67, 192 N.E.2d 74 (1963). The architectural board had said that the proposed house "does not maintain the high character of community development in that it does not conform to the character of the houses in the area." The court said that other houses nearby "are, in the main, dignified, stately and conventional structures, two and one-half stories high." The proposed house was "a flat-roofed complex of twenty modules, each of which is ten feet high, twelve feet square and arranged in a loosely formed 'U' which winds its way through a grove of trees."

3. Defendants, long-time residents of Rye, New York, hung old clothes and rags on a clothesline in their front yard as a form of "peaceful protest" against high local taxes. For five years, they added an additional clothesline each year. Finally, the city banned clotheslines in yards abutting a street except where there is "a practical difficulty or unnecessary hardship in drying clothes elsewhere on the premises."

Defendants were convicted of a criminal offense. Their appeal said the ordinance unconstitutionally restricted free speech. The court of appeals upheld the law as "an attempt to preserve the residential appearance of the city." Judge Van Voorhis, dissenting, said that

> to direct by ordinance that all buildings erected in a certain area should be one-story ranch houses would scarcely go beyond the present ruling as a question of power, or to lay down the law that they should be all of the

same color, or of different colors, or that each should be of one or two or more color tones as might suit the aesthetic predilections of the city councillors or zoning boards of appeal. [People v. Stover, 12 N.Y.2d 462, 191 N.E.2d 272, 240 N.Y.S.2d 734, *appeal dismissed,* 375 U.S. 42 (1963).]

4. The City of Brockton, Massachusetts, had denied Caswell a license for 75 coin-operated video games at his entertainment center, on the authority of a state statute authorizing city licensing commissions to grant, suspend, or revoke "a license to keep and operate an automatic amusement device for hire, gain or reward. . . ." Caswell asserted that the statute was an unconstitutional violation of his right to free expression. The court dismissed the complaint and Caswell appealed. The Supreme Judicial Court refused to hold that video games are protected speech under the First Amendment:

> Although the affidavit indicates that video games might involve the element of communication that is the *sine qua non* of First Amendment protection — for example, a player may strive to shoot down invaders — this showing is insufficient to demonstrate protected expression. . . . [H]e has failed to demonstrate that video games import sufficient communicative, expressive or informative elements to constitute expression protected under the First Amendment to the United States Constitution. . . . From the record before us, it appears that any communication or expression of ideas that occurs during the playing of a video game is purely inconsequential. Caswell has succeeded in establishing only that video games are more technologically advanced games than pinball or chess. That technological advancement alone, however, does not impart First Amendment status to what is an otherwise unprotected game. Hence, we determine that on this record protected expression has not been shown. [Caswell v. Licensing Commission, 387 Mass. 864, 444 N.E.2d 922 (1983).]

See also Marshfield Family Skateland, Inc. v. Marshfield, 389 Mass. 436, 450 N.E.2d 605 (1983):

> . . . The merchants in this case, in an attempt to demonstrate that video games contain sufficient communicative elements to be entitled to constitutional protection, prepared a videotape demonstration of parts of the audiovisual work of five different video games, together with a written explanation of the videotape. The videotape and explanation, however, do not demonstrate any more communicative aspects of these video games than were demonstrated by the plaintiff in *Caswell.* We recognize that in the future video games which contain sufficient communicative and expressive elements may be created. We are not prepared in this case, however, to hold that these video games, which are, in essence, only technologically advanced pinball machines, are entitled to constitutional protection.

And see America's Best Family Showplace Corp. v. City of New York, 536 F. Supp. 170 (E.D.N.Y. 1982):

> In no sense can it be said that video games are meant to inform. Rather, a video game, like a pinball game, a game of chess, or a game of baseball, is pure entertainment with no informational element. That some of these games "talk" to the participant, play music, or have written instructions does not provide the missing element of "information." I find, therefore, that although video game programs may be copyrighted, they "contain so little in the way of particularized form of expression" that video games cannot be fairly characterized as a form of speech protected by the First Amendment.

5. In 1976, Southborough, Massachusetts, adopted a zoning bylaw amendment classifying an "abortion clinic" as a "prohibited use" throughout the town. The Massachusetts Supreme Judicial Court, relying on a woman's fundamental right of privacy to terminate a pregnancy during the first trimester, as expounded by the U.S. Supreme Court in Roe v. Wade, 410 U.S. 113 (1973), held the bylaw amendment invalid. Framingham Clinic, Inc. v. Board of Selectmen, 373 Mass. 279, 367 N.E.2d 606 (1977).

D. "EXCLUSIONARY" ZONING

1. *Economic Zoning*

◆ BILBAR CONSTRUCTION CO. v. EASTTOWN TOWNSHIP BOARD
393 Pa. 62, 141 A.2d 851 (1958)

Opinion by Mr. Chief Justice JONES: Tredyffrin Construction Co. and its grantee, Bilbar Construction Company, have separately appealed from the order of the court below sustaining the action of the Zoning Board of Adjustment of Easttown Township, Chester County, which, in turn, had affirmed the Zoning Officer's refusal of Tredyffrin Construction Co.'s application for a building permit. The applicant sought permission to erect a dwelling on a specified lot of a subdivision which it proposed to lay out from a portion of its 50-acre tract of unimproved land in Easttown Township. The refusal of the permit was based on the fact that the lot upon which the proposed dwelling was to be built was patently deficient in area, as well as frontage, under the provisions of the township's zoning ordinance. . . .

As shown by the maps attached to and made part of the ordinance, property fronting on Greenlawn Road in Easttown Township is classified "A" residential. In such a district a single-family dwelling, *inter alia*, is a permissible structure on a lot of a minimum area of not less than 43,560 square feet (an acre) and having a frontage of 150 feet. For less restricted districts, the minimum lot areas and frontages are scaled downward by the ordinance and its incorporated maps. Greenlawn Road, which runs in a generally east-west direction, constitutes part of the northern boundary of Easttown Township and its center line is the division line between Tredyffrin Township on the north and Easttown Township on the south. . . .

In other jurisdictions, which have considered the problem of zoned lot sizes, minimum areas of approximately an acre or greater have been upheld as bearing a reasonable relation to the problem of public health, safety, morals or general welfare. . . . In the few instances where minimum lot areas have been invalidated . . . the rationale of the decisions was that the prescribed area was excessive in view of the properties already developed in the same zoning jurisdiction on considerably less area per lot. And, of course, minimum lot areas may not be ordained so large as to be exclusionary in effect and, thereby, serve a private rather than the public interest. Certainly a residence lot area of one acre in a rural and agricultural locality such as Easttown Township cannot justifiably be adjudged zoning for exclusiveness.

Our decision in Medinger Appeal, 377 Pa. 217, 104 A.2d 118, which the appellants cite, has no pertinency to the question involved in the instant case. Basically, *Medinger* was an attempt by municipal authorities to prescribe floor areas in rooms inside private dwellings — an exertion of zoning power which could hardly be thought to promote public health, safety, morals or welfare. There is no logical relation between "a minimum habitable floor area" inside a dwelling and a minimum lot area outside. It is the latter which comes peculiarly within zoning's competency.

The only thing which the applicant asserted in the way of suggested hardship was that dwellings built on half-acre lots would be more readily salable than dwellings built on acre lots and that, as a consequence, the development of half-acre lots would prove relatively *more* profitable. There was neither allegation nor proof that houses built on acre lots would entail a loss to the owner or developer. In any event, both Tredyffrin Construction Co. and Bilbar Construction Company entered into the development project fully aware, or at least bound with knowledge, of the existing zoning regulations affecting the property in question. The Board of Adjustment found, and the conclusion has not been seriously questioned either below or here, that "The district of which the lot here in question is a part can be developed under the present requirements of the Easttown Township Zoning Ordinance of 1939 and would be, if so developed, a creditable development."

The order of the court below is affirmed at appellants' costs.

Dissenting opinion by Mr. Justice BELL: . . . Today a majority of this Court . . . hold that the Ordinance is constitutional. This relatively simple case has attained monumental stature because, in order to reach its conclusion, the three present members of this Court (1) have had to repudiate and by necessary implication overrule myriad decisions of this Court, and (2) to predicate their conclusion on the doctrine of *unlimited* police power — a doctrine which is repugnant to our birthright of Liberty, our traditions, our Constitution, and our American Way of Life. . . .

. . . [T]he Commissioners contended that even though 5000 minimum square feet, 8500 minimum square feet, 14,000 minimum square feet, and 21,000 minimum square feet, satisfied the requirements of public health, safety and morals and general welfare of these residential districts, still this particular residential district (which adjoined them) was required to have a minimum lot area of one acre — 43,560 square feet. This one acre was required, they contended, because any less area would (a) substantially increase taxes, and (b) eventually necessitate additional police, a new fire engine, and an addition to or the construction of a new school, and (c) create a density of population which would be injurious to safety in the event of an atomic attack. Of course these contentions are absolutely devoid of merit. These contentions would be even more applicable to every residential district in that township which required a minimum lot area of ½ or ¼ or ⅛ of what is required in this particular district, and if these were essential requirements for one acre in order to comply with health or safety or general welfare, the ordinance in its application to the other residential districts in this Township was obviously unconstitutional. Moreover, such an unconstitutional concept and application of the police power would likewise apply to *every* suburban area, district, township and county and would stifle and in reality effectually block the expansion of our country's rapidly growing population into any suburban township or county, or would herd the poor and medium income people into specified areas and effectually and intentionally limit parts or all of a county to the rich or well-to-do. Such an intentional and exclusionary interdiction is contrary to our constitutional guarantees and to the American Way of Life. It is clear that the aforesaid theories and contentions of the zoning authorities, even if supported by testimony — which they were not — (1) are for the benefit of only the rich or well-to-do and are not for the general welfare, and (2) have no substantial relation to and are not reasonably and clearly necessary for the health, safety or morals of the residential district involved.

The majority opinion in this case . . . base their decision in the last analysis upon the proposition of *unlimited* police power and its derivative, general welfare. I believe this is the most pernicious doctrine ever enunciated in Pennsylvania. . . .

The present case is a concrete local example of the cry for land and homes which, because of the rapidly increasing and expanding population, is worldwide. In this case the fight has taken the form of a battle between the State, which is constantly attempting to expand the power of Government, and the rights of individuals to own, enjoy, use and protect their own property in any way they desire, so long as it does not interfere with their neighbor's property — an ageless, everlasting struggle which began before Magna Charta and is now intensely vexing peoples and governments all over the world.

The people of this Country long before and ever since we became a Nation have constantly fought against a curtailment (a) of their unalienable Rights of Liberty which were proudly proclaimed in the Declaration of Independence, and (b) of private property, which were ordained and guaranteed in the Constitution of the United States.

Nearly every property owner objects to down-grading the residential neighborhood of which he is a part, or allowing anything which would change its quiet, peaceful, exclusive tone. But we sometimes forget that the Constitution is not "a fair weather friend" — a Rock of Gibraltar when it guarantees what we presently desire to do or believe in, and "a scrap of paper" when it restrains or prohibits what we presently desire to do or believe in.

An owner of land may constitutionally make his property as large and as private or secluded or exclusive as he desires and his purse can afford. He may, for example, singly or with his neighbors, purchase sufficient neighboring land to protect and preserve by restriction in deeds or by covenants *inter se*, the privacy, a minimum acreage, the quiet, peaceful atmosphere and the tone and character of the community which existed when he or they moved there. But Government, as such, or through any of its local agencies, possesses no such right. It cannot constitutionally restrict or burden or use land, except under a *Legitimate* exercise of the police power; it can take land for a proper public use by purchase or by eminent domain proceedings and then only by *paying* just compensation therefor as required by the Constitution. The present Ordinance is obviously and intentionally intended to exclude from this area the poor and medium income people. It has no substantial or clear and necessary relationship to health or safety or morals, and it is obviously for the welfare of the few and not for the public, and for these reasons it is obviously, under the evidence in this case, unconstitutional.

Unlimited police power or its derivative, unlimited "general welfare," never has been and never must be adopted in this Country. We all know that every civilized Government must have police power, otherwise there would be anarchy. The police power exists for the general welfare of the People — not for the welfare of special or private interests — and is presumptively always exercised for their general welfare. *The Great Divide* that separates us from totalitarian governments is that in our Country neither police power nor general welfare is *unlimited*. The right of each individual to basic human freedom — freedom of religion, freedom of the press, freedom of speech, freedom of thought, the rights of private property, the right of contract, the rights of a person accused of crime, and due process — although constantly and insidiously attacked with sugar-coated slogans or heart-warming titles, cannot, under our Constitution, be ignored, erased, obliterated or destroyed.

2. Zoning as Discrimination

◆ NATIONAL LAND & INVESTMENT CO. v. EASTTOWN TOWNSHIP BOARD
419 Pa. 504, 215 A.2d 597 (1965)

Opinion by Mr. Justice ROBERTS: . . . Easttown Township has an area of 8.2 square miles devoted almost exclusively to residential use. It is traversed in the north by the Main Line of the Pennsylvania Railroad as well as by U.S. Route 30, a heavily traveled highway which emanates in Philadelphia, 20 miles to the east, and heads west to Lancaster and eventually to the West Coast. It is along this strip that the township's sole commercial activity is conducted and where its two small industrial concerns are located.

— The township finds itself in the path of a population expansion approaching from two directions. From the east, suburbs closer to the center of Philadelphia are reaching capacity and residential development is extending further west to Easttown. In addition, a market for residential sites is being generated by the fast growing industrial-commercial complex in the King of Prussia-Valley Forge area to the north of Easttown Township.

Easttown's vital statistics provide a good indication of its character. At present, about 60 percent of the township's population resides in an area of about 20 percent of the township. The remaining 40 percent of the population occupies the balance of about 80 percent of its area. Privately imposed restrictions limit lot areas to four, five and ten acre-minimums on approximately 10 percent of the total area of the township, consisting of land located in the southern and western sections. Of the total 5,157 acres in the township, some 898, or about 17 percent, have been restricted by the new zoning ordinance to minimum lots of two acres. Approximately 1,565 acres composing about 30 percent of the township are restricted by the zoning ordinance to lots of four acres minimum area. About 5 percent of the population live in the areas zoned for two and four acre sites which together constitute about 47 percent of the township. Some 1,835 acres, representing about 35 percent of the township, remain unaffected by the new zoning and continue, under the township's original zoning classification, to be zoned for building sites with a minimum area of one acre.

Before 1959 most of the northeast quadrant of the township, as well as various other areas, had either been built up or prepared for development. In 1959 sporadic developments occurred in the south and central parts of the township, followed by several others in the south and southeast portions in 1960. In 1961 other developments occurred in the northeast and southwest sections, followed by lesser numbers in smaller areas of the north and central sections in 1962 and 1963.

U.S. Census figures show that Easttown's population grew from 2,307 in 1920 to 6,907 in 1960. As of April, 1963, the population estimate was 8,400. Public school population through the sixth grade grew from 498 in the school year 1955-1956 to 1,052 in the school year 1963-1964 and, as projected, will be about 1,680 in 1969-1970.

New residential construction from 1951 through the first eight months of 1963, a twelve-year period, consisted of 1,149 units at an estimated cost of about $21,000,000, with an average of 100 building permits annually. At this rate of growth, allowing four persons per housing unit in Easttown, its population, related to new residences, would grow under the previous one acre minimum zoning at the rate of about 400 persons per annum.

Despite the growth and development of Easttown Township, much of the land in the central, southern and western sections continues to be held in parcels of considerable acreage. "Sweetbriar," located on the southern boundary of the township, is one of these large parcels. There is discussion in the briefs as to whether the township, and particularly those sections zoned for four acres, is rural. Such semantic disputes are of little relevance in zoning cases since realities, rather than the label which, for convenience sake, is applied to them, are determinative of the issue. However, if a catch-all designation is to be applied, "semi-rural" or "estate rural" probably best describes the portions of the township zoned for minimum lots of four acres.

The task of considering the Easttown Township zoning ordinance and passing upon the constitutionality of its four acre minimum area requirement as applied to appellees' property is not an easy one. In the span of years since 1926 when zoning received its judicial blessing, the art and science of land planning has grown increasingly complex and sophisticated. The days are fast disappearing when the judiciary can look at a zoning ordinance, and, with nearly as much confidence as a professional zoning expert, decide upon the merits of a zoning plan and

PP Lochner

its contribution to the health, safety, morals or general welfare of the community. This Court has become increasingly aware that it is neither a super board of adjustment nor a planning commission of last resort. Instead, the Court acts as a judicial overseer, drawing the limits beyond which local regulation may not go, but loathing to interfere, within those limits, with the discretion of local governing bodies.

The zoning power is one of the tools of government which, in order to be effective, must not be subjected to judicial interference unless clearly necessary. For this reason, a presumption of validity attaches to a zoning ordinance which imposes the burden to prove its invalidity upon the one who challenges it. While recognizing this presumption, we must also appreciate the fact that zoning involves governmental restrictions upon a landowner's constitutionally guaranteed right to use his property, unfettered, except in very specific instances, by governmental restrictions. The time must never come when, because of frustration with concepts foreign to their legal training, courts abdicate their judicial responsibility to protect the constitutional rights of individual citizens. Thus, the burden of proof imposed upon one who challenges the validity of a zoning regulation must never be made so onerous as to foreclose, for all practical purposes, a landowner's avenue of redress against the infringement of constitutionally protected rights. . . .

The relative advantages of a one acre lot over a one-half acre lot are easy to comprehend. Similarly, a two acre lot has advantages over a one acre lot and three acres may be preferred over two acres or ten acres over three. The greater the amount of land, the more room for children, the less congestion, the easier to handle water supply and sewage, and the fewer municipal services which must be provided. At some point along the spectrum, however, the size of lots ceases to be a concern requiring public regulation and becomes simply a matter of private preference. The point at which legitimate public interest ceases is not a constant one, but one which varies with the land involved and the circumstances of each case.

We turn, then, to the question of the constitutionality of a four acre minimum in the factual context of the instant case. Quite obviously, appellees will be deprived of part of the value of their property if they are limited in the use of it to four acre lots. When divided into one acre lots as originally planned, the value of "Sweetbriar" for residential building was approximately $260,000. When the four acre restriction was imposed, the number of available building sites in "Sweetbriar" was reduced by 75 percent and the value of the land, under the most optimistic appraisal, fell to $175,000. The four acre minimum greatly restricts the marketability of this tract because, with fewer potential lots, the cost of improvements such as curbing, streets and other facilities is thus greater on each lot. In addition, each building lot being larger, the cost per lot is automatically increased. The desire of many buyers not to be burdened with the upkeep of a four acre lot also makes "Sweetbriar," so restricted, less desirable. Although there was some evidence in the record that lots of four acres or more could eventually be sold, it is clear that there is not a readily available market for such offerings.

Against this deprivation of value, the alleged public purposes cited as justification for the imposition of a four acre minimum area requirement upon appellees' land must be examined. Appellants contend that the four acre minimum is necessary to insure proper sewage disposal in the township and to protect township water from pollution. At present, only a very small portion of the township in the densely populated northern section is served by a sewage system. The remainder of the lots in the township utilize on-site sewage disposal. With regard to water supply, the evidence was fairly conclusive that the Philadelphia Suburban Water Company serves most, if not all, of the township and that it would furnish water to a development in "Sweetbriar." . . .

It can be seen, therefore, that the restriction to four acre lots, so far as traffic is concerned, is based upon possible future conditions. Zoning is a tool in the hands of governmental bodies which enables them to more effectively meet the demands of evolving and growing communities. It must not and can not be used by those officials as an instrument by which they may shirk their responsibilities. Zoning is a means by which a governmental body can plan for the future — it may not be used as a means to deny the future. The evidence on the record indicates that for the present and the immediate future the road system of Easttown Township is adequate to handle the traffic load. It is also quite convincing that the roads will become increasingly inadequate as time goes by and that improvements and additions will eventually have to be made. Zoning provisions may not be used, however, to avoid the increased responsibilities and economic burdens which time and natural growth invariably bring.

It is not difficult to envision the tremendous hardship, as well as the chaotic conditions, which would result if all the townships in this area decided to deny to a growing population sites for residential development within the means of at least a significant segment of the people.

The third justification for rezoning, and one urged upon us most assiduously, deals with the preservation of the "character" of this area. The photographic exhibits placed in the record by appellants attest to the fact that this is an area of great beauty containing old homes surrounded by beautiful pasture, farm and woodland. It is a very desirable and attractive place in which to live.

Involved in preserving Easttown's "character" are four aspects of concern which the township gives for desiring four acre minimum zoning. First, they cite the preservation of open space and the creation of a "greenbelt" which, as most present day commentators impress upon us, are worthy goals. While in full agreement with these goals, we are convinced that four acre minimum zoning does not achieve the creation of a greenbelt in its technical sense and, to the limited extent that open space is so preserved, such zoning as is here involved is not a permissible means to that end.

By suggesting that the creation of a greenbelt is a purpose behind this zoning, appellants betray their argument that there is a ready market for four acre plots. Only if there is no market for four acre lots will the land continue to be open and undeveloped and a greenbelt created. This, however, would amount to confiscation of the property of Easttown landowners for which they must be compensated. . . .

There is no doubt that many of the residents of this area are highly desirous of keeping it the way it is, preferring, quite naturally, to look out upon land in its natural state rather than on other homes. These desires, however, do not rise to the level of public welfare. This is purely a matter of private desire which zoning regulations may not be employed to effectuate.

Appellants make some attempt to impose upon this area an aura of historic significance which deserves the protection of the township. Of course, the fact that these houses are old makes them architecturally and historically interesting. But it does not justify the creation of a special setting for them. They are all privately owned; most are already surrounded by substantial land holdings which, if their owners so desire, serve as protection against being "fenced in" by new residential development. In addition, there is nothing about south Easttown which differentiates it from any other area in the southeastern section of Pennsylvania. Surely, no one would seriously maintain that the entire southeast corner of the state should be declared immune from further development on areas of less than four acres simply because there are many old homes located there.

The fourth argument advanced by appellants, and one closely analogous to the preceding one, is that the rural character of the area must be preserved. If the township were developed on the basis of this zoning, however, it could not be seriously contended that the land would retain its rural character — it would simply be dotted with larger homes on larger lots. . . .

The township's brief raises (but, unfortunately, does not attempt to answer) the interesting issue of the township's responsibility to those who do not yet live in the township but who are part, or may become part, of the population expansion to the suburbs. Four acre zoning represents Easttown's position that it does not desire to accommodate those who are pressing for admittance to the township unless such admittance will not create any additional burdens upon governmental functions and services. The question posed is whether the township can stand in the way of the natural forces which send our growing population into hitherto undeveloped areas in search of a comfortable place to live. We have concluded not. A zoning ordinance whose primary purpose is to prevent the entrance of newcomers in order to avoid future burdens, economic and otherwise, upon the administration of public services and facilities can not be held valid. Of course, we do not mean to imply that a governmental body may not utilize its zoning power in order to insure that the municipal services which the community requires are provided in an orderly and rational manner.

The brief of the appellant-intervenors creates less of a problem but points up the factors which sometime lurk behind the espoused motives for zoning. What basically appears to bother intervenors is that a small number of lovely old homes will have to start keeping company with a growing number of smaller, less expensive, more densely located houses. It is clear, however, that the general welfare is not fostered or promoted by a zoning ordinance designed to be exclusive and exclusionary. But this does not mean that individual action is foreclosed.

> An owner of land may constitutionally make his property as large and as private or secluded or exclusive as he desires and his purse can afford. He may, for example, singly or with his neighbors, purchase sufficient neighboring land to protect and preserve by restrictions in deeds or by covenants *inter se*, the privacy, a minimum acreage, the quiet, peaceful atmosphere and the tone and character of the community which existed when he or they moved there. [Bilbar Construction Co. v. Easttown Twp. Bd. of Adjustment, 393 Pa. 62, 94, 141 A.2d 851, 867 (1958) (dissenting opinion).]

In light of the foregoing, therefore, we are compelled to conclude that the board of adjustment committed an error of law in upholding the constitutionality of the Easttown Township four acre minimum requirement as applied to appellees' property.

COHEN, Justice (dissenting). . . . The majority recognizes that "The task of considering the Easttown Township zoning ordinance and passing upon the constitutionality of its four acre minimum area requirement as applied to appellees' property is not an easy one." To me it becomes very easy to uphold the constitutionality when one recognizes, as the record discloses, that the legislative authority of Easttown Township gave the overall planning of the township considerable study. The four acre restriction was not applied to the entire township, but was only one part of a three part class "A" residential zoning enactment — one of four acres, one of two acres, and one of one acre. This zoning determination for type "A" residential properties included 3,297 acres of the 5,157 acre township and included 2,468 acres of undeveloped property for which no public sewage was available and which also included areas of poor natural drainage and varied stream pollution. It seems a reasonable and proper exercise of the legislative function for the township commissioners to take what is comparatively a small area (3,297 acres), divide it into residential zones and restrict a certain number of the residential zones to four acre lots — some to two and some to one.

_____

For 12 years after the *National Land* decision, the Pennsylvania courts attempted to distinguish those minimum residential lot area requirements that "bear no reasonable relationship to the public health, safety or welfare" from those having "an exclusionary effect." For example, in Concord Township Appeal, 439 Pa. 466, 268 A.2d 765 (1970), the supreme court invalidated a two-acre and three-acre minimum lot ordinance, but held that an area requirement is not unreasonable per se. In 1977, Surrick v. Zoning Hearing Board, 476 Pa. 182, 382 A.2d 105 (1977), adopted the "fair share" approach to exclusionary zoning ordinances, similar to the New Jersey Supreme Court's approach in *Mt. Laurel I*, p.1206 *infra*. The Pennsylvania Supreme Court adopted a three part test to be utilized in determining whether a zoning ordinance is unconstitutionally exclusive: (1) whether the community in question is a logical area for development and growth; (2) the present level of development in the community; and (3) whether the challenged zoning scheme effects an exclusionary result or manifests an exclusionary intent to zone out natural growth.

However, since *Surrick*, the Pennsylvania courts have been hesitant to find a challenged ordinance exclusionary. See, e.g., In re Appeal of M. A. Kravitz Co., 501 Pa. 200, 460 A.2d 1075 (1983) (considering township's distance from major employment centers, lack of major highway links, and projected population growth, the township properly determined that it was not a logical place for rapid growth, despite the fact that only 40 of the township's 6,491 acres were zoned for multi-family housing); In re Appeal of Elocin, Inc., 501 Pa. 348, 461 A.2d 771 (1983) (the fact that a municipality's zoning ordinance has zoned 12 percent of its land for two-family houses and "apartment houses" with a four-unit maximum is sufficient to repel constitutional attack, despite its total exclusion of townhouses and mid- and high-rise apartments); Fernley v. Board of Supervisors, 464 A.2d 587 (Pa. Commw. 1983) (zoning ordinance prohibiting multiple dwellings upheld because township not a logical area for growth and development); Hostetter v. North Londonderry, 63 Pa. Commw. 122, 437 A.2d 806 (1981) (township that zoned 2.6 percent of its total land for multi-family dwellings has met its fair share obligation in a rural and agricultural area). But see, e.g., Environmental Communities of Pennsylvania, Inc. v. North Coventry Township, 49 Pa. Commw. 167, 412 A.2d 650 (1980) (township's zoning of 1.37 percent of its total acreage for mobile homes, with 80 percent zoned for one-acre minimum lots does not provide a fair share of the township's acreage for mobile home land use); Lower Gwynedd Township v. Provincial Investment Co., 39 Pa. Commw. 546, 395 A.2d 1055 (1979) (zoning ordinance that failed to provide for townhouse development as a matter of right was unconstitutionally exclusionary).

Note

Stull, Community Environment, Zoning, and the Market Value of Single-Family Homes, 18 J. of L. & Econ. 535, 551 (1975):

> [T]he data seem to reveal that in the study area households were fairly sensitive to the land use environments of the communities in which they purchased homes. They discriminated not only between single-family and nonsingle-family uses but also among various categories of nonsingle-family use. Moreover, the nature of the discrimination revealed was generally what one would expect. Homeowners attached the highest value to communities which were predominantly single-family but which also contained a small amount of commercial activity. Homes in communities with large amounts of multiple-family, commercial, industrial or vacant land sold at a discount, other things equal.

◆ SOUTHERN BURLINGTON COUNTY NAACP v. TOWNSHIP OF MT. LAUREL
67 N.J. 151, 336 A.2d 713, *appeal dismissed and cert. denied*, 423 U.S. 808 (1975)

HALL, J. This case attacks the system of land use regulation by defendant Township of Mount Laurel on the ground that low and moderate income families are thereby unlawfully excluded from the municipality. The trial court so found and declared the township zoning ordinance totally invalid. Its judgment went on, in line with the requests for affirmative relief, to order the municipality to make studies of the housing needs of low and moderate income persons presently or formerly residing in the community in substandard housing, as well as those in such income classifications presently employed in the township and living elsewhere or reasonably expected to be employed therein in the future, and to present a plan of affirmative public action designed "to enable and encourage the satisfaction of the indicated needs." Jurisdiction was retained for judicial consideration and approval of such a plan and for the entry of a final order requiring its implementation. . . .

The implications of the issue presented are indeed broad and far-reaching, extending much beyond these particular plaintiffs and the boundaries of this particular municipality.

There is not the slightest doubt that New Jersey has been, and continues to be, faced with a desperate need for housing, especially of decent living accommodations economically suitable for low and moderate income families.[2] The situation was characterized as a "crisis" and fully explored and documented by Governor Cahill in two special messages to the Legislature.

Plaintiffs represent the minority group poor (black and Hispanic) seeking such quarters. But they are not the only category of persons barred from so many municipalities by reason of restrictive land use regulations. We have reference to young and elderly couples, single persons and large, growing families not in the poverty class, but who still cannot afford the only kinds of housing realistically permitted in most places — relatively high-priced, single-family detached dwellings on sizeable lots and, in some municipalities, expensive apartments. We will, therefore, consider the case from the wider viewpoint that the effect of Mount Laurel's land use regulation has been to prevent various categories of persons from living in the township because of the limited extent of their income and resources. In this connection, we accept the representation of the municipality's counsel at oral argument that the regulatory scheme was not adopted with any desire or intent to exclude prospective residents on the obviously illegal bases of race, origin or believed social incompatibility. . . .

Mount Laurel is a flat, sprawling township, 22 square miles, or about 14,000 acres, in area, on the west central edge of Burlington County. It is roughly triangular in shape, with its base, approximately eight miles long, extending in a northeasterly-southwesterly direction roughly parallel with and a few miles east of the Delaware River. Part of its southerly side abuts Cherry Hill in Camden County. That section of the township is about seven miles from the boundary line of the city of Camden and not more than 10 miles from the Benjamin Franklin Bridge crossing the river to Philadelphia.

In 1950, the township had a population of 2,817, only about 600 more people than it had in 1940. It was then, as it had been for decades, primarily a rural agricultural area with no sizeable settlements or commercial or industrial enterprises. The populace generally lived in individual houses scattered along country roads. There were several pockets of poverty, with deteriorating or dilapidated housing (apparently 300 or so units of which remain today in equally poor condition). After 1950, as in so many other municipalities similarly situated, residential develop-

2. "Low income" was used in this case to refer to those persons or families eligible, by virtue of limited income, for occupancy in public housing units or units receiving rent supplement subsidies according to formulas therefor in effect in the area. "Moderate income" was similarly used to refer to those eligible for occupancy in housing units receiving so-called Section 235 or 236 or like subsidies. In another case, the figures of income up to $7,000 a year for the first category and up to $10,000-$12,000 for the second were projected. While the formula figures vary depending on family size, the dollar amounts mentioned are close enough to represent the top income in each classification for present purposes. "Middle income" and "upper income" are the designations of higher income categories.

ment and some commerce and industry began to come in. By 1960 the population had almost doubled to 5,249 and by 1970 had more than doubled again to 11,221. These new residents were, of course, "outsiders" from the nearby central cities and older suburbs or from more distant places drawn here by reason of employment in the region. The township is now definitely a part of the outer ring of the South Jersey metropolitan area, which area we define as those portions of Camden, Burlington and Gloucester Counties within a semicircle having a radius of 20 miles or so from the heart of Camden city. And 65 percent of the township is still vacant land or in agricultural use. . . .

The location and nature of development has been, as usual, controlled by the local zoning enactments. The general ordinance presently in force, which was declared invalid by the trial court, was adopted in 1964. We understand that earlier enactments provided, however, basically the same scheme but were less restrictive as to residential development. The growth pattern dictated by the ordinance is typical.

Under the present ordinance, 29.2 percent of all the land in the township, or 4,121 acres, is zoned for industry. This amounts to 2,800 more acres than were so zoned by the 1954 ordinance. The industrial districts comprise most of the land on both sides of the turnpike and routes I-295, 73 and 38. Only industry meeting specified performance standards is permitted. The effect is to limit the use substantially to light manufacturing, research, distribution of goods, offices and the like. Some non-industrial uses, such as agriculture, farm dwellings, motels, a harness racetrack, and certain retail sales and service establishments, are permitted in this zone. At the time of trial no more than 100 acres, mostly in the southwesterly corner along route 73 adjacent to the turnpike and I-295 interchanges, were actually occupied by industrial uses. They had been constructed in recent years, mostly in several industrial parks, and involved tax ratables of about 16 million dollars. The rest of the land so zoned has remained undeveloped. If it were fully utilized, the testimony was that about 43,500 industrial jobs would be created, but it appeared clear that, as happens in the case of so many municipalities, much more land has been so zoned than the reasonable potential for industrial movement or expansion warrants. At the same time, however, the land cannot be used for residential development under the general ordinance.

The amount of land zoned for retail business use under the general ordinance is relatively small — 169 acres, or 1.2 percent of the total. Some of it is near the turnpike interchange; most of the rest is allocated to a handful of neighborhood commercial districts. While the greater part of the land so zoned appears to be in use, there is no major shopping center or concentrated retail commercial area — "downtown" — in the township.

The balance of the land area, almost 10,000 acres, has been developed until recently in the conventional form of major subdivisions. The general ordinance provides for four residential zones, designated R-1, R-1D, R-2 and R-3. All permit only single-family, detached dwellings, one house per lot — the usual form of grid development. Attached town-houses, apartments (except on farms for agricultural workers) and mobile homes are not allowed anywhere in the township under the general ordinance. This dwelling development, resulting in the previ-ously mentioned quadrupling of the population, has been largely con-fined to the R-1 and R-2 districts in two sections — the northeasterly and southwesterly corners adjacent to the turnpike and other major high-ways. The result has been quite intensive development of these sec-tions, but at a low density. The dwellings are substantial; the average value in 1971 was $32,500 and is undoubtedly much higher today.

The general ordinance requirements, while not as restrictive as those in many similar municipalities, nonetheless realistically allow only homes within the financial reach of persons of at least middle income. The R-1 zone requires a minimum lot area of 9,375 square feet, a minimum lot width of 75 feet at the building line, and a minimum dwelling floor area of 1,100 square feet if a one-story building and 1,300 square feet if one and one-half stories or higher. Originally this zone comprised about 2,500 acres. Most of the subdivisions have been constructed within it so that only a few hundred acres remain (the testimony was at variance as to the exact amount). The R-2 zone, com-prising a single district of 141 acres in the northeasterly corner, has been completely developed. While it only required a minimum floor area of 900 square feet for a one-story dwelling, the minimum lot size was 11,000 square feet; otherwise the requisites were the same as in the R-1 zone.

The general ordinance places the remainder of the township . . . in the R-3 zone. This zone comprises over 7,000 acres — slightly more than half of the total municipal area — practically all of which is located in the central part of the township extending southeasterly to the apex of the triangle. The testimony was that about 4,600 acres of it then remained available for housing development. Ordinance requirements are sub-stantially higher, however, in that the minimum lot size is increased to about one-half acre (20,000 square feet). (We understand that sewer and water utilities have not generally been installed, but, of course, they can be.) Lot width at the building line must be 100 feet. Minimum dwelling floor area is as in the R-1 zone. Presently this section is primarily in agricultural use; it contains as well most of the municipality's substan-dard housing. . . .

A variation from conventional development has recently occurred in some parts of Mount Laurel, as in a number of other similar munici-palities, by use of the land use regulation device known as "planned unit development" (PUD). This scheme differs from the traditional in that the type, density and placement of land uses and buildings, instead of being detailed and confined to specified districts by local legislation in advance, is determined by contract, or "deal," as to each development between the developer and the municipal administrative authority, under broad guidelines laid down by state enabling legislation and an implementing local ordinance. The stress is on regulation of density and permitted mixture of uses within the same area, including various kinds of living accommodations with or without commercial and industrial enterprises. The idea may be basically thought of as the creation of "new towns" in virgin territory, full-blown or in miniature, although most frequently the concept has been limited in practice, as in Mount Laurel, to residential developments of various sizes having some variety of housing and perhaps some retail establishments to serve the inhabitants.

New Jersey passed such enabling legislation in 1967, and Mount Laurel adopted the implementing enactment as a supplement to its general zoning ordinance in December of that year. While the ordinance was repealed early in 1971, the township governing body in the interim had approved four PUD projects, which were specifically saved from extinction by the repealer.

These projects, three in the southwesterly sector and one in the northeasterly sector, are very substantial and involve at least 10,000 sale and rental housing units of various types to be erected over a period of years. Their bounds were created by agreement rather than legislative specification on the zoning map. . . . If completed as planned, they will in themselves ultimately quadruple the 1970 township population, but still leave a good part of the township undeveloped. . . .

While multi-family housing in the form of rental garden, medium rise and high rise apartments and attached townhouses is for the first time provided for, as well as single-family detached dwellings for sale, it is not designed to accommodate and is beyond the financial reach of low and moderate income families, especially those with young children. The aim is quite the contrary; as with the single-family homes in the older conventional subdivisions, only persons of medium and upper income are sought as residents. . . .

All this affirmative action for the benefit of certain segments of the population is in sharp contrast to the lack of action, and indeed hostility, with respect to affording any opportunity for decent housing for the township's own poor living in substandard accommodations, found largely in the section known as Springville (R-3 zone). The 1969 Master Plan Report recognized it and recommended positive action. The continuous official reaction has been rather a negative policy of waiting for dilapidated premises to be vacated and then forbidding further occupancy. An earlier non-governmental effort to improve conditions had been effectively thwarted. In 1968 a private non-profit association sought to build subsidized, multi-family housing in the Springville section with funds to be granted by a higher level governmental agency. Advance municipal approval of the project was required. The Township Committee responded with a purportedly approving resolution, which found a need for "moderate" income housing in the area, but went on to specify that such housing must be constructed subject to all zoning, planning, building and other applicable ordinances and codes. This meant single-family detached dwellings on 20,000 square foot lots. (Fear was also expressed that such housing would attract low income families from outside the township.) Needless to say, such requirements killed realistic housing for this group of low and moderate income families.

The record thoroughly substantiates the findings of the trial court that over the years Mount Laurel "has acted affirmatively to control development and to attract a selective type of growth" and that "through its zoning ordinances has exhibited economic discrimination in that the poor have been deprived of adequate housing and the opportunity to secure the construction of subsidized housing, and has used federal, state, county and local finances and resources solely for the betterment of middle and upper-income persons."

There cannot be the slightest doubt that the reason for this course of conduct has been to keep down local taxes on *property* (Mount Laurel is not a high tax municipality) and that the policy was carried out without regard for non-fiscal considerations with respect to *people*, either within or without its boundaries. This conclusion is demonstrated not only by what was done and what happened, as we have related, but also by innumerable direct statements of municipal officials at public meetings over the years. . . .

. . . This pattern of land use regulation has been adopted for the same purpose in developing municipality after developing municipality. Almost every one acts solely in its own selfish and parochial interest and in effect builds a wall around itself to keep out those people or entities not adding favorably to the tax base, despite the location of the municipality or the demand for varied kinds of housing. There has been no effective intermunicipal or area planning or land use regulation. . . . One incongruous result is the picture of developing municipalities rendering it impossible for lower paid employees of industries they have eagerly sought and welcomed with open arms (and, in Mount Laurel's case, even some of its own lower paid municipal employees) to live in the community where they work.

The other end of the spectrum should also be mentioned because it shows the source of some of the demand for cheaper housing than the developing municipalities have permitted. Core cities were originally the location of most commerce and industry. Many of those facilities furnished employment for the unskilled and semi-skilled. These employees lived relatively near their work, so sections of cities always have housed the majority of people of low and moderate income, generally in old and deteriorating housing. Despite the municipally confined tax structure, commercial and industrial ratables generally used to supply enough revenue to provide and maintain municipal services equal or superior to those furnished in most suburban and rural areas.

The situation has become exactly the opposite since the end of World War II. Much industry and retail business, and even the professions, have left the cities. Camden is a typical example. The testimonial and documentary evidence in this case as to what has happened to that city is depressing indeed. For various reasons, it lost thousands of jobs between 1950 and 1970, including more than half of its manufacturing jobs (a reduction from 43,267 to 20,671, while all jobs in the entire area labor market increased from 94,507 to 197,037). A large segment of retail business faded away with the erection of large suburban shopping centers. The economically better situated city residents helped fill up the miles of sprawling new housing developments, not fully served by public transit. In a society which came to depend more and more on expensive individual motor vehicle transportation for all purposes, low income employees very frequently could not afford to reach outlying places of suitable employment and they certainly could not afford the permissible housing near such locations. These people have great difficulty in obtaining work and have been forced to remain in housing which is overcrowded, and has become more and more substandard and less and less tax productive. There has been a consequent critical erosion of the city tax base and inability to provide the amount and quality of those governmental services — education, health, police, fire, housing and the like — so necessary to the very existence of safe and decent city life. This category of city dwellers desperately needs much better housing and living conditions than is available to them now, both in a rehabilitated city and in outlying municipalities. They make up, along with the other classes of persons earlier mentioned who also cannot afford the only generally permitted housing in the developing municipalities, the acknowledged great demand for low and moderate income housing.

The legal question before us, as earlier indicated, is whether a developing municipality like Mount Laurel may validly, by a system of land use regulation, make it physically and economically impossible to provide low and moderate income housing in the municipality for the various categories of persons who need and want it and thereby, as Mount Laurel has, exclude such people from living within its confines because of the limited extent of their income and resources. Necessarily implicated are the broader questions of the right of such municipalities to limit the kinds of available housing and of any obligation to make possible a variety and choice of types of living accommodations. We conclude that every such municipality must, by its land use regulations, presumptively make realistically possible an appropriate variety and choice of housing. More specifically, presumptively it cannot foreclose the opportunity of the classes of people mentioned for low and moderate income housing and in its regulations must affirmatively afford that opportunity, at least to the extent of the municipality's fair share of the present and prospective regional need therefore. These obligations must be met unless the particular municipality can sustain the heavy burden of demonstrating peculiar circumstances which dictate that it should not be required so to do.

We reach this conclusion under state law and so do not find it necessary to consider federal constitutional grounds urged by plaintiffs . . . It is required that, affirmatively, a zoning regulation, like any police power enactment, must promote public health, safety, morals or the general welfare. . . . Conversely, a zoning enactment which is contrary to the general welfare is invalid. . . . Indeed, these considerations are specifically set forth in the zoning enabling act . . . N.J.S.A. 40:55-32. . . . If a zoning regulation violates the enabling act in this respect, it is also theoretically invalid under the state constitution. We say "theoretically" because, as a matter of policy, we do not treat the validity of most land use ordinance provisions as involving matters of constitutional dimension; that classification is confined to major questions of fundamental import. . . . We consider the basic importance of housing and local regulations restricting its availability to substantial segments of the population to fall within the latter category. . . .

Frequently the decisions in this state, . . . have spoken only in terms of the interest of the enacting municipality, so that it has been thought, at least in some quarters, that such was the only welfare requiring consideration. It is, of course, true that many cases have dealt only with regulations having little, if any, outside impact where the local decision is ordinarily entitled to prevail. However, it is fundamental and not to be forgotten that the zoning power is a police power of the state and the local authority is acting only as a delegate of that power and is restricted in the same manner as is the state. So, when regulation does have a substantial external impact, the welfare of the state's citizens beyond the borders of the particular municipality cannot be disregarded and must be recognized and served. . . .

This brings us to the relation of housing to the concept of general welfare just discussed and the result in terms of land use regulation which that relationship mandates. There cannot be the slightest doubt that shelter, along with food, are the most basic human needs. "The question of whether a citizenry has adequate and sufficient housing is certainly one of the prime considerations in assessing the general health and welfare of that body." . . . The same thought is implicit in the legislative findings of an extreme, long-time need in this state for decent low and moderate income housing, set forth in the numerous statutes providing for various agencies and methods at both state and local levels designed to aid in alleviation of the need. . . .

It is plain beyond dispute that proper provision for adequate housing of all categories of people is certainly an absolute essential in promotion of the general welfare required in all local land use regulation. Further the universal and constant need for such housing is so important and of such broad public interest that the general welfare which developing municipalities like Mount Laurel must consider extends beyond their boundaries and cannot be parochially confined to the claimed good of the particular municipality. It has to follow that, broadly speaking, the presumptive obligation arises for each such municipality affirmatively to plan and provide, by its land use regulations, the reasonable opportunity for an appropriate variety and choice of housing, including, of course, low and moderate cost housing, to meet the needs, desires and resources of all categories of people who may desire to live within its boundaries. Negatively, it may not adopt regulations or policies which thwart or preclude that opportunity. . . .

Without further elaboration at this point, our opinion is that Mount Laurel's zoning ordinance is presumptively contrary to the general welfare and ouside the intended scope of the zoning power in the particulars mentioned. A facial showing of invalidity is thus established, shifting to the municipality the burden of establishing valid superseding reasons for its action and non-action. We now examine the reasons it advances. . . .

By way of summary, what we have said comes down to this. As a developing municipality, Mount Laurel must, by its land use regulations, make realistically possible the opportunity for an appropriate variety and choice of housing for all categories of people who may desire to live there, of course including those of low and moderate income. It must permit multi-family housing, without bedroom or similar restrictions, as well as small dwellings on very small lots, low cost housing of other types and, in general, high density zoning, without artificial and unjustifiable minimum requirements as to lot size, building size and the like, to meet the full panoply of these needs. Certainly when a municipality zones for industry and commerce for local tax benefit purposes, it without question must zone to permit adequate housing within the means of the employees involved in such uses. (If planned unit developments are authorized, one would assume that each must include a reasonable amount of low and moderate income housing in its residential "mix," unless opportunity for such housing has already been realistically provided for elsewhere in the municipality.) The amount of land removed from residential use by allocation to industrial and commercial purposes must be reasonably related to the present and future potential for such purposes. [S]uch municipalities must zone primarily for the living welfare of people and not for the benefit of the local tax rate.

We have earlier stated that a developing municipality's obligation to afford the opportunity for decent and adequate low and moderate income housing extends at least to ". . . the municipality's fair share of the present and prospective regional need therefore." Some comment on that concusion is in order at this point. Frequently it might be sounder to have more of such housing, like some specialized land uses, in one municipality in a region than in another, because of greater availability of suitable land, location of employment, accessibility of public transportation or some other significant reason. But, under present New Jersey legislation, zoning must be on an individual municipal basis, rather than regionally. So long as that situation persists under the present tax structure, or in the absence of some kind of binding agreement among all the municipalities of a region, we feel that every municipality therein must bear its fair share of the regional burden. (In this respect our holding is broader than that of the trial court, which was limited to Mount Laurel-related low and moderate income housing needs.) . . .

We are not at all sure what the trial judge had in mind as ultimate action with reference to the approval of a plan for affirmative public action concerning the satisfaction of indicated housing needs and the entry of a final order requiring implementation thereof. Courts do not build housing nor do municipalities. That function is performed by private builders, various kinds of associations, or, for public housing, by special agencies created for that purpose at various levels of government. The municipal function is initially to provide the opportunity through appropriate land use regulations and we have spelled out what Mount Laurel must do in that regard. It is not appropriate at this time, particularly in view of the advanced view of zoning law as applied to housing laid down by this opinion, to deal with the matter of the further extent of judicial power in the field or to exercise any such power. The municipality should first have full opportunity to itself act without judicial supervision. We trust it will do so in the spirit we have suggested, both by appropriate zoning ordinance amendments and whatever additional action encouraging the fulfillment of its fair share of the regional need for low and moderate income housing may be indicated as necessary and advisable. (We have in mind that there is at least a moral obligation in a municipality to establish a local housing agency pursuant to state law to provide housing for its resident poor now living in dilapidated, unhealthy quarters.) The portion of the trial court's judgment ordering the preparation and submission of the aforesaid study, report and plan to it for further action is therefore vacated as at least premature. Should Mount Laurel not perform as we expect, further judicial action may be sought by supplemental pleading in this cause. . . .

MOUNTAIN, J. (concurring). I agree with the conclusions reached in the Court's opinion and essentially with the opinion itself. In one important respect, however, I disagree. The Court rests its decision upon a ground of State constitutional law. I reach the same result by concluding that the term, "general welfare," appearing in N.J.S.A. 40:55-32, can and should properly be interpreted with the same amplitude attributed to that phrase in the opinion of the Court, as well as otherwise in the manner there set forth. I therefore would rest the conclusions we here announce upon an interpretation of the statute, and not upon the State constitution.

Accordingly, since I read the statute — without resort to the Constitution — to justify, if not compel, our decision, I find it unnecessary to express any view as to the merits of the constitutional argument set forth in the Court's opinion.

PASHMAN, J. (concurring). With this decision, the Court begins to cope with the dark side of municipal land use regulation — the use of the zoning power to advance the parochial interests of the municipality at the expense of the surrounding region and to establish and perpetuate social and economic segregation.

The problem is not a new one. Early opponents of zoning advanced the possibility of such abuse as an argument against allowing municipalities the power to zone. Later, even those sympathetic to the goals and methods of zoning began to express concern. . . .

The misuse of the municipal zoning power at issue in this case, generically described as "exclusionary zoning," see, e.g., Brooks, Exclusionary Zoning 3 (Am. Soc. of Planning Officials 1970), involves two distinct but interrelated practices: (1) the use of the zoning power by municipalities to take advantage of the benefits of regional development without having to bear the burdens of such development; and (2) the use of the zoning power by municipalities to maintain themselves as enclaves of affluence or of social homogeneity.

Both of these practices are improper and to be strongly condemned. They are violative of the requirement, found both in the Constitution of 1947 and the zoning enabling statute itself, that municipal zoning ordinances further the general welfare. They are inconsistent with the fundamental premise of the New Jersey zoning legislation that zoning is concerned with the physical condition of the municipality not its social condition. In a deeper sense, they are repugnant to the ideals of the pluralistic democracy which America has become. . . .

The majority has chosen not to explore in this case either the extent of the affirmative obligations upon developing municipalities or the role of the courts in enforcing those obligations. It has also chosen not to consider the degree to which the principles applicable to developing municipalities are also applicable to rural ones and to largely developed ones. The facts set out above seem to me to demonstrate that exclusionary zoning is a problem of such magnitude and depth as to require that the Court extend these principles to all municipalities in the State, recognizing, of course, that they may have different implications for municipal conduct when applied in different areas, and that the Court establish a policy of active judicial enforcement, not only of the negative obligations imposed upon municipalities by this decision but also of the affirmative obligations. . . .

A municipality need not exercise at all the powers permitted it by the zoning and planning statutes. Once, however, it chooses to enter the field of land use regulation it assumes a duty — one of constitutional dimension — to act affirmatively to provide its fair share of the low and moderate income housing necessary to meet the regional housing needs. . . .

There is little hope that the private housing construction industry will be able to satisfy the State's housing needs in the foreseeable future, even if all exclusionary barriers are removed. To meet these needs, State or federal assistance will be required. This fact has been recognized by both the State Legislature and Congress in a lengthy series of statutes providing governmental subsidies for private construction and ownership of low and moderate income housing. . . . Developing municipalities have a duty to make all reasonable efforts to encourage and facilitate private efforts to take advantage of these programs. . . .

Since conflicting decisions within a given region would be highly undesirable, all municipalities in the region should be joined as parties at the earliest practical point in the proceedings, if not at the instance of one of the parties, then on the motion of the court. . . .

It is not the business of this Court or any member of it to instruct the municipalities of the State of New Jersey on the good life. Nevertheless, I cannot help but note that many suburban communities have accepted at face value the traditional canard whispered by the "blockbuster": "When low income families move into your neighborhood, it will cease being a decent place to live." But as there is no difference between the love of low income mothers and fathers and those of high income for their children, so there is no difference between the desire for a decent community felt by one group and that felt by the other. Many low income families have learned from necessity the desirability of community involvement and improvement. At least as well as persons with higher incomes, they have learned that one cannot simply leave the fate of the community in the hands of the government, that things do not run themselves, but simply run down.

Equally important, many suburban communities have failed to learn the lesson of cultural pluralism. A homogeneous community, one exhibiting almost total similarities of taste, habit, custom and behavior is culturally dead, aside from being downright boring. New and different life styles, habits and customs are the lifeblood of America. They are its strength, its growth force. Just as diversity strengthens and enriches the country as a whole, so will it strengthen and enrich a suburban community. Like animal species that over-specialize and breed out diversity and so perish in the course of evolution, communities, too, need racial, cultural, social and economic diversity to cope with our rapidly changing times.

Finally, many suburban communities have failed to recognize to whom the environment actually belongs. By environment, I mean not just land or housing, but air and water, flowers and green trees. There is a real sense in which clean air belongs to everyone, a sense in which green trees and flowers are everyone's right to see and smell. The right to enjoy these is connected to a citizen's right to life, to pursue his own happiness as he sees fit provided his pursuit does not infringe another's rights.

The people of New Jersey should welcome the result reached by the Court in this case, not merely because it is required by our laws, but, more fundamentally, because the result is right and true to the highest American ideals.

◆ SOUTHERN BURLINGTON COUNTY NAACP v. TOWNSHIP OF MT. LAUREL
92 N.J. 158, 456 A.2d 390 (1983)

Wilentz, C.J. This is the return, eight years later, of Southern Burlington County NAACP v. Township of Mount Laurel (*Mount Laurel I*). We set forth in that case, for the first time, the doctrine requiring that municipalities' land use regulations provide a realistic opportunity for low and moderate income housing. The doctrine has become famous. The *Mount Laurel* case itself threatens to become infamous. After all this time, ten years after the trial court's initial order invalidating its zoning ordinance, Mount Laurel remains afflicted with a blatantly exclusionary ordinance. Papered over with studies, rationalized by hired experts, the ordinance at its core is true to nothing but Mount Laurel's determination to exclude the poor. Mount Laurel is not alone; we believe that there is widespread non-compliance with the constitutional mandate of our original opinion in this case.

To the best of our ability, we shall not allow it to continue. This Court is more firmly committed to the original *Mount Laurel* doctrine than ever, and we are determined, within appropriate judicial bounds, to make it work. The obligation is to provide a realistic opportunity for housing, not litigation. We have learned from experience, however, that unless a strong judicial hand is used, *Mount Laurel* will not result in housing, but in paper, process, witnesses, trials and appeals. We intend by this decision to strengthen it, clarify it, and make it easier for public officials, including judges, to apply it.

This case is accompanied by five others, heard together and decided in this opinion. All involve questions arising from the *Mount Laurel* doctrine. They demonstrate the need to put some steel into that doctrine. The deficiencies in its application range from uncertainty and inconsistency at the trial level to inflexible review criteria at the appellate level. The waste of judicial energy involved at every level is substantial and is matched only by the often needless expenditure of talent on the part of lawyers and experts. The length and complexity of trials is often outrageous, and the expense of litigation is so high that a real question develops whether the municipality can afford to defend or the plaintiffs can afford to sue.

There is another side to the story. We believe, both through the representations of counsel and from our own research and experience, that the doctrine has done some good, indeed, perhaps substantial good. We have tried to make the doctrine clearer for we believe that most municipal officials will in good faith strive to fulfill their constitutional duty. There are a number of municipalities around the State that have responded to our decisions by amending their zoning ordinances to provide realistic opportunities for the construction of low and moderate income housing. Further, many other municipalities have at least recognized their obligation to provide such opportunities in their ordinances and master plans. Finally, state and county government agencies have responded by preparing regional housing plans that help both the courts and municipalities themselves carry out the *Mount Laurel* mandate. Still, we are far from where we had hoped to be and nowhere near where we should be with regard to the administration of the doctrine in our courts.

These six cases not only afford the opportunity for, but demonstrate the necessity of reexamining the *Mount Laurel* doctrine. We do so here. The doctrine is right but its administration has been ineffective.

A brief statement of the cases may be helpful at this point. *Mount Laurel II* results from the remand by this Court of the original *Mount Laurel* case. The municipality rezoned, purportedly pursuant to our instructions, a plenary trial was held, and the trial court found that the rezoning constituted a bona fide attempt by Mount Laurel to provide a realistic opportunity for the construction of its fair share of the regional lower income housing need. Reading our cases at that time (1978) as requiring no more, the trial court dismissed the complaint of the NAACP and other plaintiffs but granted relief in the form of a builder's remedy, to a developer-intervenor who had attacked the total prohibition against mobile homes. Plaintiffs' appeal of the trial court's ruling sustaining the ordinance in all other respects was directly certified by this Court, as ultimately was defendant's appeal from the grant of a builder's remedy allowing construction of mobile homes. We reverse and remand to determine Mount Laurel's fair share of the regional need and for further proceedings to revise its ordinance; we affirm the grant of the builder's remedy. . . .

Our rulings today have several purposes. First, we intend to encourage voluntary compliance with the constitutional obligation by defining it more clearly. We believe that the use of the State Development Guide Plan and the confinement of all *Mount Laurel* litigation to a small group of judges, selected by the Chief Justice with the approval of the Court, will tend to serve that purpose. Second, we hope to simplify litigation in this area. While we are not overly optimistic, we think that the remedial use of the SDGP may achieve that purpose, given the significance accorded it in this opinion. Third, the decisions are intended to increase substantially the effectiveness of the judicial remedy. In most cases, upon determination that the municipality has not fulfilled its constitutional obligation, the trial court will retain jurisdiction, order an immediate revision of the ordinance (including, if necessary, supervision of the revision through a court appointed master), and require the use of effective affirmative planning and zoning devices. The long delays of interminable appellate review will be discouraged, if not completely ended, and the opportunity for low and moderate income housing found in the new ordinance will be as realistic as judicial remedies can make it. We hope to achieve all of these purposes while preserving the fundamental legitimate control of municipalities over their own zoning and, indeed, their destiny.

The following is a summary of the more significant rulings of these cases:

(1) *Every* municipality's land use regulations should provide a realistic opportunity for decent housing for at least some part of its resident poor who now occupy dilapidated housing. The zoning power is no more abused by keeping out the region's poor than by forcing out the resident poor. In other words, each municipality must provide a realistic opportunity for decent housing for its indigenous poor except where they represent a disproportionately large segment of the population as compared with the rest of the region. This is the case in many of our urban areas.

(2) The existence of a municipal obligation to provide a realistic opportunity for a fair share of the region's present and prospective low and moderate income housing need will no longer be determined by whether or not a municipality is "developing." The obligation extends, instead, to every municipality, any portion of which is designated by the State, through the SDGP as a "growth area." This obligation, imposed as a remedial measure, does not extend to those areas where the SDGP discourages growth — namely, open spaces, rural areas, prime farmland, conservation areas, limited growth areas, parts of the Pinelands and certain Coastal Zone areas. The SDGP represents the conscious

determination of the State, through the executive and legislative branches, on how best to plan its future. It appropriately serves as a judicial remedial tool. The obligation to encourage lower income housing, therefore, will hereafter depend on rational long-range land use planning (incorporated into the SDGP) rather than upon the sheer economic forces that have dictated whether a municipality is "developing." Moreover, the fact that a municipality is fully developed does not eliminate this obligation although, obviously, it may affect the extent of the obligation and the timing of its satisfaction. The remedial obligation of municipalities that consist of both "growth areas" and other areas may be reduced, based on many factors, as compared to a municipality completely within a "growth area."

There shall be a heavy burden on any party seeking to vary the foregoing remedial consequences of the SDGP designations.

(3) *Mount Laurel* litigation will ordinarily include proof of the municipality's fair share of low and moderate income housing in terms of the number of units needed immediately, as well as the number needed for a reasonable period of time in the future. "Numberless" resolution of the issue based upon a conclusion that the ordinance provides a realistic opportunity for *some* low and moderate income housing will be insufficient. Plaintiffs, however, will still be able to prove a *prima facie* case, without proving the precise fair share of the municipality, by proving that the zoning ordinance is substantially affected by restrictive devices, that proof creating a presumption that the ordinance is invalid.

The municipal obligation to provide a realistic opportunity for low and moderate income housing is not satisfied by a good faith attempt. The housing opportunity provided must, in fact, be the substantial equivalent of the fair share.

(4) Any future *Mount Laurel* litigation shall be assigned only to those judges selected by the Chief Justice with the approval of the Supreme Court. The initial group shall consist of three judges, the number to be increased or decreased hereafter by the Chief Justice with the Court's approval. The Chief Justice shall define the area of the State for which each of the three judges is responsible: any *Mount Laurel* case challenging the land use ordinance of a municipality included in that area shall be assigned to that judge.

Since the same judge will hear and decide all *Mount Laurel* cases within a particular area and only three judges will do so in the entire state, we believe that over a period of time a consistent pattern of regions will emerge. Consistency is more likely as well in determinations of regional housing needs and allocations of fair share to municipalities within the region. Along with this consistency will come the predictability needed to give full effect to the *Mount Laurel* doctrine. While determinations of region and regional housing need will not be conclusive as to any municipality not a party to the litigation, they shall be given presumptive validity in subsequent litigation involving any municipality included in a previously determined region.

The Chief Justice will analyze all pending *Mount Laurel* litigation to determine which, if any, should be transferred to one of the three *Mount Laurel* judges. As for the cases pending before us, given the knowledge acquired by the judges of the particular facts of the case, each will be remanded to the judge who heard the matter below with the exception of Round Valley, Inc. v. Clinton and Urban League of Greater New Brunswick v. Carteret, since neither of the judges who determined those matters remains on the trial bench.

(5) The municipal obligations to provide a realistic opportunity for the construction of its fair share of low and moderate income housing may require more than the elimination of unnecessary cost-producing requirements and restrictions. Affirmative governmental devices should be used to make that opportunity realistic, including lower-income density bonuses and mandatory set-asides. Furthermore the municipality should cooperate with the developer's attempts to obtain federal subsidies. For instance, where federal subsidies depend on the municipality providing certain municipal tax treatment allowed by state statutes for lower income housing, the municipality should make a good faith effort to provide it. Mobile homes may not be prohibited, unless there is solid proof that sound planning in a particular municipality requires such prohibition.

(6) The lower income regional housing need is comprised of both low and moderate income housing. A municipality's fair share should include both in such proportion as reflects consideration of all relevant factors, including the proportion of low and moderate income housing that make up the regional need.

(7) Providing a realistic opportunity for the construction of least-cost housing will satisfy a municipality's *Mount Laurel* obligation if, and only if, it cannot otherwise be satisfied. In other words, it is only after *all* alternatives have been explored, *all* affirmative devices considered, including, where appropriate, a reasonable period of time to determine whether low and moderate income housing is produced, only when everything has been considered and tried in order to produce a realistic opportunity for low and moderate income housing that least-cost housing will provide an adequate substitute. Least-cost housing means what it says, namely, housing that can be produced at the lowest possible price consistent with minimal standards of health and safety.

(8) Builder's remedies will be afforded to plaintiffs in *Mount Laurel* litigation where appropriate, on a case-by-case basis. Where the plaintiff has acted in good faith, attempted to obtain relief without litigation, and thereafter vindicates the constitutional obligation in *Mount Laurel*-type litigation, ordinarily a builder's remedy will be granted, provided that the proposed project includes an appropriate portion of low and moderate income housing, and provided further that it is located and designed

in accordance with sound zoning and planning concepts, including its environmental impact.

(9) The judiciary should manage *Mount Laurel* litigation to dispose of a case in all of its aspects with one trial and one appeal, unless substantial considerations indicate some other course. This means that in most cases after a determination of invalidity, and prior to final judgment and possible appeal, the municipality will be required to rezone, preserving its contention that the trial court's adjudication was incorrect. If an appeal is taken, all facets of the litigation will be considered by the appellate court including both the correctness of the lower court's determination of invalidity, the scope of remedies imposed on the municipality, and the validity of the ordinance adopted after the judgment of invalidity. The grant or denial of a stay will depend upon the circumstances of each case. The trial court will appoint a master to assist in formulating and implementing a proper remedy whenever that course seems desirable.

(10) The *Mount Laurel* obligation to meet the prospective lower income housing need of the region is, by definition, one that is met year after year in the future, throughout the years of the particular projection used in calculating prospective need. In this sense the affirmative obligation to provide a realistic opportunity to construct a fair share of lower income housing is met by a "phase-in" over those years; it need not be provided immediately. Nevertheless, there may be circumstances in which the obligation requires zoning that will provide an immediate opportunity — for instance, zoning to meet the region's present lower income housing need. In some cases, the provision of such a realistic opportunity might result in the immediate construction of lower income housing in such quantity as would radically transform the municipality overnight. Trial courts shall have the discretion, under those circumstances, to moderate the impact of such housing by allowing even the present need to be phased in over a period of years. Such power, however, should be exercised sparingly. The same power may be exercised in the satisfaction of prospective need, equally sparingly, and with special care to assure that such further postponement will not significantly dilute the *Mount Laurel* obligation.

We reassure all concerned that *Mount Laurel* is not designed to sweep away all land use restrictions or leave our open spaces and natural resources prey to speculators. Municipalities consisting largely of conservation, agricultural, or environmentally sensitive areas will not be required to grow because of *Mount Laurel*. No forests or small towns need be paved over and covered with high-rise apartments as a result of today's decision.

As for those municipalities that may have to make adjustments in their lifestyles to provide for their fair share of low and moderate income housing, they should remember that they are not being required to provide more than their *fair* share. No one community need be concerned that it will be radically transformed by a deluge of low and moderate income developments. Nor should any community conclude that its residents will move to other suburbs as a result of this decision, for those "other suburbs" may very well be required to do their part to provide the same housing. Finally, once a community has satisfied its fair share obligation, the *Mount Laurel* doctrine will not restrict other measures, including large-lot and open area zoning, that would maintain its beauty and communal character.

Many of these points will be discussed later in this opinion. We mention them now only to reassure all concerned that any changes brought about by this opinion need not be drastic or destructive. Our scenic and rural areas will remain essentially scenic and rural, and our suburban communities will retain their basic suburban character. But there will be *some* change, as there must be if the constitutional rights of our lower income citizens are ever to be protected. That change will be much less painful for us than the status quo has been for them.

In Oakwood v. Madison, this Court held that it was sufficient in *Mount Laurel* litigation for courts to look to the "substance" of challenged zoning ordinances and to the existence of *"bona fide efforts"* by municipalities to meet their obligations. It was hoped that this test would adequately protect the constitutional rights of lower income persons while at the same time minimizing the role of the courts in this area. Unfortunately, experience has taught us that this formulation is too vague to provide adequate guidance for either trial courts or municipalities. As the *Mount Laurel II* and *Mahwah* cases demonstrate, the *Madison* test does not ensure sufficient judicial scrutiny of zoning ordinances. Even those that plainly fail to meet the requisites of the *Mount Laurel* doctrine may pass the test of *Madison*.

Therefore, proof of a municipality's bona fide attempt to provide a realistic opportunity to construct its fair share of lower income housing shall no longer suffice. Satisfaction of the *Mount Laurel* obligation shall be determined solely on an objective basis: if the municipality has *in fact* provided a realistic opportunity for the construction of its fair share of low and moderate income housing, it has met the *Mount Laurel* obligation to satisfy the constitutional requirement; if it has not, then it has failed to satisfy it.[8] Further, whether the opportunity is "realistic" will

8. "Moderate income families" are those whose incomes are no greater than 80 percent and no less than 50 percent of the median income of the area, with adjustments for smaller and larger families. "Low income families" are those whose incomes do not exceed 50 percent of the median income of the area, with adjustments for smaller and larger families.

When we refer in this opinion to housing being "affordable" by lower income families ("lower" meaning "low and moderate") we mean that the family pays no more than 25 percent of its income for such housing, the 25 percent figure being widely accepted in the relevant literature.

depend on whether there is in fact a likelihood — to the extent economic conditions allow — that the lower income housing will actually be constructed. Plaintiff's case will ordinarily include proof of the municipality's fair share of the regional need and defendant's proof of its satisfaction. Good or bad faith, at least on this issue, will be irrelevant. The numberless approach encouraged in *Madison*, where neither plaintiffs nor defendants are required to prove a fair share number, is no longer acceptable.

In order to meet their *Mount Laurel* obligations, municipalities, at the very least, must remove all municipally created barriers to the construction of their fair share of lower income housing. Thus, to the extent necessary to meet their prospective fair share and provide for their indigenous poor (and, in some cases, a portion of the region's poor), municipalities must remove zoning and subdivision restrictions and exactions that are not necessary to protect health and safety. . . .

Once a municipality has revised its land use regulations and taken other steps affirmatively to provide a realistic opportunity for the construction of its fair share of lower income housing, the *Mount Laurel* doctrine requires it to do no more. For instance, a municipality having thus complied, the fact that its land use regulations contain restrictive provisions incompatible with lower income housing, such as bedroom restrictions, large lot zoning, prohibition against mobile homes, and the like, does not render those provisions invalid under *Mount Laurel*. Obviously, if they are otherwise invalid — for instance if they bear no reasonable relationship to any legitimate governmental goal — they may be declared void on those other grounds. But they are not void because of *Mount Laurel* under those circumstances. *Mount Laurel* is not an indiscriminate broom designed to sweep away all distinctions in the use of land. Municipalities may continue to reserve areas for upper income housing, may continue to require certain community amenities in certain areas, may continue to zone with some regard to their fiscal obligations: they may do all of this, provided that they have otherwise complied with their *Mount Laurel* obligations.

Despite the emphasis in *Mount Laurel I* on the *affirmative* nature of the fair share obligation, the obligation has been sometimes construed (after *Madison*) as requiring in effect no more than a theoretical, rather than realistic, opportunity. As noted later, the alleged realistic opportunity for lower income housing in *Mount Laurel II* is provided through three zones owned entirely by three individuals. There is absolutely no assurance that there is anything realistic in this "opportunity": the individuals may, for many different reasons, simply not desire to build lower income housing. They may not want to build any housing at all, they may want to use the land for industry, for business, or just leave it vacant. It was never intended in *Mount Laurel I* that this awesome constitutional obligation, designed to give the poor a fair chance for housing, be satisfied by meaningless amendments to zoning or other ordinances. "Affirmative," in the *Mount Laurel* rule, suggests that the *municipality* is going to do something, and "realistic opportunity" suggests that what it is going to do will make it *realistically* possible for lower income housing to be built. Satisfaction of the *Mount Laurel* doctrine cannot depend on the inclination of developers to help the poor. It has to depend on affirmative inducements to make the opportunity real.

It is equally unrealistic, even where the land is owned by a developer eager to build, simply to rezone that land to permit the construction of lower income housing if the construction of other housing is permitted on the same land and the latter is more profitable than lower income housing. One of the new zones in Mount Laurel provides a good example. The developer there intends to build housing out of the reach of the lower income group. After creation of the new zone, he still is allowed to build such housing but now has the "opportunity" to build lower income housing to the extent of 10 percent of the units. There is absolutely no reason why he should take advantage of this opportunity if, as seems apparent, his present housing plans will result in a higher profit. There is simply no inducement, no reason, nothing affirmative, that makes this opportunity "realistic." For an opportunity to be "realistic" it must be one that is at least sensible for someone to use.

Therefore, unless removal of restrictive barriers will, without more, afford a realistic opportunity for the construction of the municipality's fair share of the region's lower income housing need, affirmative measures will be required.

There are two basic types of affirmative measures that a municipality can use to make the opportunity for lower income housing realistic: (1) encouraging or requiring the use of available state or federal housing subsidies, and (2) providing incentives for or requiring private developers to set aside a portion of their developments for lower income housing. Which, if either, of these devices will be necessary in any particular municipality to assure compliance with the constitutional mandate will be initially up to the municipality itself. Where necessary, the trial court overseeing compliance may require their use. We note again that least-cost housing will not ordinarily satisfy a municipality's fair share obligation to provide low and moderate income housing unless and until it has attempted the inclusionary devices outlined below or otherwise has proven the futility of the attempt. . . .

There are several inclusionary zoning techniques that municipalities must use if they cannot otherwise assure the construction of their fair share of lower income housing. Although we will discuss some of them here, we in no way intend our list to be exhaustive; municipalities and trial courts are encouraged to create other devices and methods for meeting fair share obligations.

The most commonly used inclusionary zoning techniques are incentive zoning and mandatory set-asides. The former involves offering economic incentives to a developer through the relaxation of various restrictions of an ordinance (typically density limits) in exchange for the construction of certain amounts of low and moderate income units. The latter, a mandatory set-aside, is basically a requirement that developers include a minimum amount of lower income housing in their projects. . . .

It is nonsense to single out inclusionary zoning (providing a realistic opportunity for the construction of lower income housing) and label it "socio-economic" if that is meant to imply that other aspects of zoning are not. Detached single family residential zones, high-rise multi-family zones of any kind, factory zones, "clean" research and development zones, recreational, open space, conservation, and agricultural zones, regional shopping mall zones, indeed practically any significant kind of zoning now used, has a substantial socio-economic impact and, in some cases, a socio-economic motivation. It would be ironic if inclusionary zoning to encourage the construction of lower income housing were ruled beyond the power of a municipality because it is "socio-economic" when its need has arisen from the socio-economic zoning of the past that excluded it.

Looked at somewhat differently, having concluded that the constitutional obligation can sometimes be satisfied only through the use of these inclusionary devices, it would take a clear contrary constitutional provision to lead us to conclude that that which is necessary to achieve the constitutional mandate is prohibited by the same Constitution. In other words, we would find it difficult to conclude that our Constitution both requires and prohibits these measures.

We find the distinction between the exercise of the zoning power that is "directly tied to the physical use of the property," and its exercise tied to the income level of those who use the property artificial in connection with the *Mount Laurel* obligation, although it obviously troubled us in *Madison*. The prohibition of this kind of affirmative device seems unfair when we have for so long allowed large lot single family residence districts, a form of zoning keyed, in effect, to income levels. The constitutional obligation itself is not to build three bedroom units, or single family residences on very small lots, or high-rise multi-family apartments, but rather to provide through the zoning ordinance a realistic opportunity to construct *lower income housing*. All of the physical uses are simply a means to this end. We see no reason why the municipality cannot exercise its zoning power to achieve that end directly rather than through a mass of detailed regulations governing the "physical use" of land, the sole purpose of which is to provide housing within the reach of lower income families. We know of no governmental purpose relating to zoning that is served by requiring a municipality to ingeniously design detailed land use regulations, purporting to be "directly tied to the physical use of the property," but actually aimed at accommodating lower income families, while not allowing it directly to require developers to construct lower income units. Indirection of this kind has no more virtue where its goal is to achieve that which is permitted — indeed, constitutionally mandated — than it has in achieving that which is prohibited. . . . Insofar as the *Mount Laurel* doctrine is concerned, whether mobile homes must be permitted as an affirmative device will depend upon the overall effectiveness of the municipality's attempts to comply: if compliance can be just as effectively assured without allowing mobile homes, *Mount Laurel* does not command them; if not, then assuming a suitable site is available, they must be allowed. . . .

If within the time allotted by the trial court a revised zoning ordinance is submitted by the defendant municipality that meets the municipality's *Mount Laurel* obligations, the trial court shall issue a judgment of compliance. If the revised ordinance does not meet the constitutional requirements, or if no revised ordinance is submitted within the time allotted, the trial court may issue such orders as are appropriate, including any one or more of the following:

(1) that the municipality adopt such resolutions and ordinances, including particular amendments to its zoning ordinance, and other land use regulations, as will enable it to meet its *Mount Laurel* obligations;

(2) that certain types of projects or construction as may be specified by the trial court be delayed within the municipality until its ordinance is satisfactorily revised, or until all or part of its fair share of lower income housing is constructed and/or firm commitments for its construction have been made by responsible developers;

(3) that the zoning ordinance and other land use regulations of the municipality be deemed void in whole or in part so as to relax or eliminate building and use restrictions in all or selected portions of the municipality (the court may condition this remedy upon failure of the municipality to adopt resolutions or ordinances mentioned in (1) above); and

(4) that particular applications to construct housing that includes lower income units be approved by the municipality, or any officer, board, agency, authority (independent or otherwise) or division thereof.

In determining remedies for non-compliance, the trial court may use the assistance and advice of a master subject to the guidelines set forth above. . . .

In short, there being a constitutional obligation, we are not willing to allow it to be disregarded and rendered meaningless by declaring that we are powerless to apply any remedies other than those conventionally used. We intend no discourse on the history of judicial remedies, but suspect that that which we deem "conventional" was devised because it seemed perfectly adequate in view of the obligation it addressed. We suspect that the same history would show that as obligations were recognized that could not be satisfied through such conventional remedies, the courts devised further remedies, and indeed the history of Chancery is as much a history of remedy as it is of obligation. The process of remedial development has not yet been frozen.

Notes

1. According to a newspaper article written more than one year after *Mt. Laurel II*, there has been progress in building low- and moderate-income housing in suburban New Jersey. In fact, the article asserted that "[j]udges, municipal planners, zoning experts and lawyers say scores of towns over the next decade will either agree voluntarily or be forced by judicial decree to accept housing and the consequent recasting of their social and political fabric." Some Jersey Towns, Yielding to Courts, Let in Modest Homes, N.Y. Times, Feb. 29, 1984.

2. See Rose, The *Mt. Laurel II* Decision: Is It Based on Wishful Thinking?, 12 Real Est. L.J. 115 (1983):

> The *Mount Laurel II* decision is a strong and determined statement by the New Jersey Supreme Court of its belief in the fundamental principle protected by the state constitution, that every person has the right to move freely within the state and to live where he believes opportunities of employment, safety, and the pursuit of happiness exist. This constitutionally protected right may not be frustrated by land-use regulations that make housing prohibitively expensive or by the failure of municipalities to take affirmative measures to make housing available for low-income persons.
>
> These are noble ideals and cannot be faulted. The weakness of the decision may emerge in time, not from its ethical principles, but from the economic and political assumptions on which it rests. It remains to be seen whether *new* housing can be built that meets minimum standards of safety and health, and is affordable by low income persons; it remains to be seen whether there is any realistic prospect of a sufficient commitment by the American people of a portion of our national resources for anything more than a token amount of subsidized low-income housing; it remains to be seen whether the net effect of the decision will result in anything more than an acceleration of the movement of upwardly mobile middle-income families from the central cities to the suburbs, creating an even greater exacerbation of the problem of the deteriorating central cities; it remains to be seen whether municipal officials representing embattled suburban citizens seeking to protect their own quest for safety, security, and happiness will accede to the authority of the three judges and their appointed "masters": it remains to be seen whether the principles of sound state land-use planning will prevail against the political forces directed by a fearful and threatened suburban citizenry. Until these questions can be answered

with some certainty, it may be fair to continue to ask whether the underlying goals and remedial measures of the *Mount Laurel II* decision are presently achievable or whether they are "based upon the wistful hopes of an idealistic but credulous court."

3. The Coastal Area Facility Review Act, N.J.S.A. 13:9A, empowers the New Jersey Department of Environmental Protection to approve any "development" in coastal areas. CAFRA's primary purpose is to protect the fragile coastal zones, but it is also intended to protect the "social, economic, aesthetic and recreational interests of all the people of the State," and to dedicate coastal areas "to those kinds of land use which promote the public health, safety and welfare. . . ." When Egg Harbor Associates, developers, sought a permit for a large waterfront development near Atlantic City that would include more than 1,500 housing units, the DEP granted it on the condition that 10 percent low-income and 10 percent moderate-income housing units be included. The New Jersey Supreme Court affirmed the granting of the conditional permit, reasoning that the legislature should use land use regulation to promote the general welfare, and that it may delegate this power to state agencies. Furthermore, relying on *Mt. Laurel II*, the court held that promotion of the general welfare permits the use of inclusionary zoning through mandatory set-asides. In light of a finding that 50 percent of the region's housing needs would be for low- and moderate-income units, the DEP's requirements were not arbitrary, capricious, or unreasonable. In re Egg Harbor Association (Bayshore Centre): Imposition of Conditions of Coastal Area Facility Permit #CA 79-0231-5, 94 N.J. 358, 464 A.2d 1115 (1983).

4. See American Law Institute, Model Land Development Code §7-305 (1976):

> [N]o Land Development Agency shall grant a permit for Development of Regional Impact that will create more than [100] opportunities for full-time employees that did not previously exist within the jurisdiction of the local government, unless the Land Development Agency also finds that
>
> (1) adequate and reasonably accessible housing for prospective employees is available within or without the jurisdiction of the local government; or
> (2) the local government has adopted a Land Development Plan designed to make available adequate and reasonably accessible housing within a reasonable time; or
> (3) a State Land Development Plan shows that the proposed location is a desirable location for the proposed employment source.

LEVY, EXCLUSIONARY ZONING: AFTER THE WALLS COME DOWN, from LAND USE CONTROLS: PRESENT PROBLEMS AND FUTURE REFORM 179-181 (D. Listokin, ed. 1974): Assume that restrictive zoning is eliminated from a large part of the land area of a major metropolitan area through judicial action, the removal of zoning powers to higher levels of government, or any other mechanism. Assume further, that this happens rapidly and in the near future. Large areas which were formerly zoned exclusively for single family houses on large lots are now rezoned for single family houses on small lots, garden apartments, row houses, and high rise apartments.

These areas are not in the older, close-in suburbs, but in what is often termed "exurbia." In Westchester County, New York, for example, those municipalities considered to be in the "middle ring" by the area's regional planning agencies contain little land zoned for lots greater than one half acre in area and no land zoned for lots larger than one acre. In addition, there is relatively little undeveloped land available for and suitable to residential development in these municipalities regardless of zoning category.

By contrast, in the municipalities in the "outer ring" of the county, approximately 69 per cent of the total land area, much of it presently undeveloped, is zoned for single family houses on lots of one acre or larger. Minimum lot sizes range up to four acres.

Consider two alternative outcomes:

Outcome A (Best Case). Private builders and public agencies formerly blocked by local zoning ordinances move into the exurban areas to produce a rapid expansion of the housing stock. Consequently there is a large migration of low- and middle-income people, many of them black, from the central city. Access to suburban jobs enables these migrants to make major improvement in their own economic status and at the same time they prove a boon to suburban industry. Numerous black and other minority group children who had formerly attended largely non-white central city schools are now enrolled in predominantly white suburban schools. The result is a rapid increase in their educational progress with all that that implies.

Those members of the central city's population who remain behind also benefit. As some members of the central city's labor force move to suburbia and exchange their city jobs for suburban jobs, pressure is put on the city's labor market forcing wages up and unemployment rates down. (That this effect is at least a possibility is suggested by the fact that suburban unemployment rates are often significantly lower than those of the central city.) Many members of the working poor are able to better their circumstances and some city residents who had dropped out of the labor force in discouragement return to it. These changes reduce the demands on the city for a variety of poverty-related services, thus permitting the city to deal more effectively with other problems and provide a generally higher level of municipal services.

When all is said and done, both those central city residents who moved and those who stayed behind have benefited. The original suburban residents, if nothing else, at least have the satisfaction that any distress they may have suffered has been for a useful purpose and that society as a whole has been well served by their involuntary sacrifices.

Outcome B (Worst Case). As the barriers of exclusionary zoning drop, a large supply of housing is constructed in the affected areas. But it soon becomes apparent that the main customers for this housing are middle class whites who have wanted to leave the central city for some time but were not able to find suitable suburban housing at acceptable prices. The less affluent central city whites and most central city blacks can no more afford $40,000 houses on quarter-acre lots than they previously could have afforded $50,000 houses on one-acre lots. Nor can they afford row houses at $30,000 and upwards or garden apartments renting at $250 a month or more. The necessity for an automobile in the "outer ring" areas due to the inadequacy of public transportation is a further obstacle to the migration of lower income families to these areas.

The loss of a significant portion of the central city's remaining white middle class proves to be a severe blow. The impact is particularly great on the public school system, since the out-migration of white families is concentrated among those with school age children. This is hardly surprising, for it is through the schools that many families most acutely feel the pains of class and race conflict. As the percentage of white students in the city school system falls, it becomes impossible to achieve any meaningful degree of integration in the school system. . . .

Financial demands on the city for poverty-related services rise at the same time that the city's tax base is shrinking. The city becomes poorer and progressively less able to cope with its problems and maintain adequate levels of municipal services. The only beneficiaries of the process are the middle class whites who have moved out. The urban blacks find themselves more segregated and in economically more difficult circumstances than before. Their choice of housing is greater than before due to vacancies created by the departure of their more prosperous neighbors, but this is their only gain. . . .

But one fundamental fact strongly suggests that if events are allowed to take their natural course, the elimination of exclusionary zoning will more often tend to favor outcome B than outcome A. This fact is the relationship of white to non-white family income in central cities. The 1969 census figures showed that the median income nationally for black families in central cities was estimated at $6,794 while for white families in central cities the comparable figure was $9,797. The $10,000 to $14,999 range contained 27.3 per cent of all white families but only 17.1 per cent of all black families. The $10,000 to $11,999 range contained 13.2 per cent of all white families and 9.2 per cent of all black families.

Assume that the $10,000 to $15,000 group will accelerate the migration to suburbia because of the elimination of exclusionary zoning.

Those below the $10,000 line will have great difficulty making the move without assistance while those over $15,000 would be able to move under existing conditions if they so chose.

If the above assumption is valid, then for financial reasons alone the white out-migration attributable to the elimination of exclusionary zoning will be higher than its percentage of the central city population as a whole. Non-financial factors such as discriminatory practices by suburban realtors may increase the ratio of white out-migration to non-white out-migration still further.

3. Inclusionary Zoning

Mt. Laurel II requires that municipalities that cannot otherwise assure construction of low-income housing take "affirmative measures" to increase the supply of such housing, specifically through inclusionary zoning devices such as incentive zoning and mandatory set-asides. The court said that this requirement is the one significant method by which to avoid the charge that the Mt. Laurel doctrine "embodies rights in a vacuum, existing only on paper."

Density bonus zoning, a voluntary incentive program, offers developers economic incentives, such as relaxation of zoning ordinance density limits, in exchange for construction of specific amounts of low- and moderate-income housing. In theory, by being allowed to construct more units than otherwise permitted by zoning regulations, the developer can save on enough land costs to absorb the losses incurred from the lower income units and retain a reasonable return on investment.

A mandatory set-aside program requires a developer to build a mandatory percentage of lower income housing within a subdivision. Some ordinances hinge the requirement on the availability of government subsidies; others require the mandatory set-aside regardless of a subsidy.

Both of these types of programs have been criticized. For instance, studies have found that developers are reluctant to participate in a voluntary program, even in the case of relatively generous density bonuses. See Fox and Davis, Density Bonus Zoning to Provide Low and Moderate Cost Housing, 3 Hastings Const. L.Q. 1015 (1976). With regard to mandatory set-asides, one commentator has asserted:

> [M]ost "inclusionary" programs are ironically titled. These programs are essentially taxes on the production of new housing. The programs will usually increase general housing prices, a result which further limits the housing opportunities of moderate-income families. In short, despite the assertions of inclusionary zoning proponents, most inclusionary ordi-

nances are just another form of exclusionary practice. [Ellickson, The Irony of "Inclusionary Zoning," 54 S. Cal. L. Rev. 1167 (1981).]

In addition, a mandatory set-aside requirement may constitute an unconstitutional taking without just compensation. See Parker, Inclusionary Zoning — A Proper Police Power or a Constitutional Anathema?, 9 Western St. U.L. Rev. 175 (1982).

The *Mt. Laurel II* court recognized such problems as being inherent in both of these approaches to inclusionary zoning. However, when the two approaches are combined, the result is favorable. A study conducted at the Stanford University Graduate School of Business Administration analyzed by computer a variety of density bonus policies that offered a developer a 20 to 40 percent increase in unit density per acre coupled with a significant set-aside percentage for lower income housing. The results were that all of the density bonus policies studied provided a developer with a greater profit per unit than could have been obtained by building market-priced units without a bonus. The results of the study are abstracted in Fox and Davis, *supra*. In addition, it has been argued that the combination of the two incentive zoning devices would withstand constitutional attack. Comment, Inclusionary Zoning: An Alternative for Connecticut Municipalities, 14 Conn. L. Rev. 789 (1982).

4. Planning

◆ GOLDEN v. PLANNING BOARD OF RAMAPO
30 N.Y.2d 359, 285 N.E.2d 291, 334 N.Y.S.2d 138, *appeal dismissed*, 409 U.S. 1003 (1972)

SCILEPPI, J. . . . Experiencing the pressures of an increase in population and the ancillary problem of providing municipal facilities and services,[1] the Town of Ramapo, as early as 1964, made application for a grant under section 801 of the Housing Act of 1964 to develop a master plan.

1. The Town's allegations that present facilities are inadequate to service increasing demands goes uncontested. We must assume, therefore, that the proposed improvements, both as to their nature and extent, reflect legitimate community needs and are not veiled efforts at exclusion. In the period 1940-1968 population in the unincorporated areas of the Town increased 285.9 percent. Between the years of 1950-1960 the increase, again in unincorporated areas, was 130.8 percent; from 1960-1966 some 78.5 percent; and from the years 1966-1969 20.4 percent. In terms of real numbers, population figures compare at 58,626 as of 1966, with the largest increment of growth since the decennial census occurring in the undeveloped areas. Projected figures, assuming current land use and zoning trends, approximate a total Town population of 120,000 by 1985. Growth is expected to be heaviest in the currently undeveloped western and northern tiers of the Town, predominantly in the form of subdivision development with some apartment construction. A growth rate of some 1,000 residential units per annum has been experienced in the unincorporated areas of the Town.

The plan's preparation included a four-volume study of the existing land uses, public facilities, transportation, industry, commerce, housing needs and projected population trends. The proposals appearing in the studies were subsequently adopted pursuant to the Town Law in July, 1966 and implemented by way of a master plan. The master plan was followed by the adoption of a comprehensive zoning ordinance. Additional sewage district and drainage studies were undertaken which culminated in the adoption of a capital budget, providing for the development of the improvements specified in the master plan within the next six years. Pursuant to the Town Law, authorizing comprehensive planning, and as a supplement to the capital budget, the Town Board adopted a capital program which provides for the location and sequence of additional capital improvements for the 12 years following the life of the capital budget. The two plans, covering a period of 18 years, detail the capital improvements projected for maximum development and conform to the specifications set forth in the master plan, the official map and drainage plan.

Based upon these criteria, the Town subsequently adopted the subject amendments for the alleged purpose of eliminating premature subdivision and urban sprawl. Residential development is to proceed according to the provision of adequate municipal facilities and services, with the assurance that any concomitant restraint upon property use is to be of a "temporary" nature and that other private uses, including the construction of individual housing, are authorized.

The amendments did not rezone or reclassify any land into different residential or use districts,[2] but, for the purposes of implementing the proposals appearing in the comprehensive plan, consist, in the main, of additions to the definitional sections of the ordinance, section 46-3, and the adoption of a new class of "Special Permit Uses," designated "Residential Development Use." "Residential Development Use" is defined as "The erection or construction of dwellings [on] any vacant plots, lots

2. As of July, 1966, the only available figures, six residential zoning districts with varying lot size and density requirements accounted for in excess of nine-tenths of the Town's unincorporated land area. Of these the RR classification (80,000 square feet minimum lot area) plus R-35 zone (35,000 square feet minimum lot area) comprise over one-half of all zoned areas. The subject sites are presently zoned RR-50 (50,000 square feet minimum lot area). The reasonableness of these minimum lot requirements are not presently controverted, though we are referred to no compelling need in their behalf. Under present zoning regulations, the population of the unincorporated areas could be increased by about 14,600 families (3.5 people) when all suitable vacant land is occupied. Housing values as of 1960 in the unincorporated areas range from a modest $15,000 (approximately 30 percent) to higher than $25,000 (25 percent), with the undeveloped western tier of Town showing the highest percentage of values in excess of $25,000 (41 percent). Significantly, for the same year only about one-half of one percent of all housing units were occupied by non-white families. Efforts at adjusting this disparity are reflected in the creation of a public housing authority and the authority's proposal to construct biracial low-income family housing.

or parcels of land"; and, any person who acts so as to come within that definition, "shall be deemed to be engaged in a residential development which shall be a separate use classification under this ordinance and subject to the requirement of obtaining a special permit from the Town Board."

The standards for the issuance of special permits are framed in terms of the availability to the proposed subdivision plat of five essential facilities or services: specifically (1) public sanitary sewers or approved substitutes; (2) drainage facilities; (3) improved public parks or recreation facilities, including public schools; (4) State, county or town roads — major, secondary or collector; and, (5) firehouses. No special permit shall issue unless the proposed residential development has accumulated 15 development points, to be computed on a sliding scale of values assigned to the specified improvements under the statute. Subdivision is thus a function of immediate availability to the proposed plat of certain municipal improvements; the avowed purpose of the amendments being to phase residential development to the Town's ability to provide the above facilities or services.

Certain savings and remedial provisions are designed to relieve of potentially unreasonable restrictions. Thus, the board may issue special permits vesting a present right to proceed with residential development in such year as the development meets the required point minimum, but in no event later than the final year of the 18-year capital plan. The approved special use permit is fully assignable, and improvements scheduled for completion within one year from the date of an application are to be credited as though existing on the date of the application. A prospective developer may advance the date of subdivision approval by agreeing to provide those improvements which will bring the proposed plat within the number of development points required by the amendments. And applications are authorized to the "Development Easement Acquisition Commission" for a reduction of the assessed valuation. Finally, upon application to the Town Board, the development point requirements may be varied should the board determine that such a variance or modification is consistent with the on-going development plan.

The undisputed effect of these integrated efforts in land use planning and development is to provide an over-all program of orderly growth and adequate facilities through a sequential development policy commensurate with progressing availability and capacity of public facilities. While its goals are clear and its purposes undisputably laudatory, serious questions are raised as to the manner in which these ends are to be effected, not the least of which relates to their legal viability under present zoning enabling legislation, particularly sections 261 and 263 of the Town Law. The owners of the subject premises argue, and the Appellate Division has sustained the proposition, that the primary purpose of the amending ordinance is to control or regulate population growth within the Town and as such is not within the authorized objectives of the zoning enabling legislation. We disagree.

In enacting the challenged amendments, the Town Board has sought to control subdivision in all residential districts, pending the provision (public or private) at some future date of various services. . . . [C]onsidering the activities enumerated by the Town Law, and relating those powers to the authorized purposes, the challenged amendments are proper zoning techniques, exercised for legitimate zoning purposes. The power to restrict and regulate includes within its grant, by way of necessary implication, the authority to direct the growth of population for the purposes indicated, within the confines of the township. It is the matrix of land use restrictions, common to each of the enumerated powers and sanctioned goals, a necessary concomitant to the municipalities' recognized authority to determine the lines along which local development shall proceed, though it may divert it from its natural course. . . .

There is . . . something inherently suspect in a scheme which, apart from its professed purposes, effects a restriction upon the free mobility of a people until sometime in the future when projected facilities are available to meet increased demands. Although zoning must include schemes designed to allow municipalities to more effectively contend with the increased demands of evolving and growing communities, under its guise, townships have been wont to try their hand at an array of exclusionary devices in the hope of avoiding the very burden which growth must inevitably bring. Though the conflict engendered by such tactics is certainly real, and its implications vast, accumulated evidence, scientific and social, points circumspectly at the hazards of undirected growth and the naive, somewhat nostalgic imperative that egalitarianism is a function of growth.

Of course, these problems cannot be solved by Ramapo or any single municipality, but depend upon the accommodation of widely disparate interests for their ultimate resolution. To that end, State-wide or regional control of planning would insure that interests broader than that of the municipality underlie various land use policies. Nevertheless, that should not be the only context in which growth devices such as these, aimed at population assimilation, not exclusion, will be sustained; especially where, as here, we would have no alternative but to strike the provision down in the wistful hope that the efforts of the State Office of Planning Coordination and the American Law Institute will soon bear fruit.

Hence, unless we are to ignore the plain meaning of the statutory delegation, this much is clear: phased growth is well within the ambit of existing enabling legislation. . . . The evolution of more sophisticated efforts to contend with the increasing complexities of urban and suburban growth has been met by a corresponding reluctance upon the part of the judiciary to substitute its judgment as to the plan's over-all effectiveness for the considered deliberations of its progenitors. Implicit in such a philosophy of judicial self-restraint is the growing awareness that matters of land use and development are peculiarly within the expertise of students of city and suburban planning, and thus well within the legislative prerogative, not lightly to be impeded. . . . It is the nature of all land use and development regulations to circumscribe the course of growth within a particular town or district and to that extent such restrictions invariably impede the forces of natural growth. . . . What segregates permissible from impermissible restrictions, depends in the final analysis upon the purpose of the restrictions and their impact in terms of both the community and general public interest. The line of delineation between the two is not a constant, but will be found to vary with prevailing circumstances and conditions (see, e.g., Euclid v. Ambler Co., 272 U.S. 365, 387, 47 S. Ct. 114, 71 L. Ed. 303; Rodgers v. Village of Tarrytown, 302 N.Y. 115, 96 N.E.2d 731). What we will not countenance, then, under any guise, is community efforts at immunization or exclusion. But, far from being exclusionary, the present amendments merely seek, by the implementation of sequential development and timed growth, to provide a balanced cohesive community dedicated to the efficient utilization of land. The restrictions conform to the community's considered land use policies as expressed in its comprehensive plan and represent a bona fide effort to maximize population density consistent with orderly growth. True other alternatives, such as requiring off-site improvements as a prerequisite to subdivision, may be available, but the choice as how best to proceed, in view of the difficulties attending such exactions, cannot be faulted.

Perhaps even more importantly, timed growth, unlike the minimum lot requirements recently struck down by the Pennsylvania Supreme Court as exclusionary, does not impose permanent restrictions upon land use. . . .

. . . In sum, Ramapo asks not that it be left alone, but only that it be allowed to prevent the kind of deterioration that has transformed well-ordered and thriving residential communities into blighted ghettos with attendant hazards to health, security and social stability — a danger not without substantial basis in fact.

We only require that communities confront the challenge of population growth with open doors. Where in grappling with that problem, the community undertakes, by imposing temporary restrictions upon development, to provide required municipal services in a rational manner, courts are rightfully reluctant to strike down such schemes. . . .

Accordingly, the order appealed from should be reversed and the actions remitted to Special Term for entry of a judgment declaring section 46-13.1 of the Town Ordinance constitutional.

Breitel, J. (dissenting). The limited powers of district zoning and subdivision regulation delegated to a municipality do not include the power to impose a moratorium on land development. Such conclusion is dictated by settled doctrine that a municipality has only those powers, and especially land use powers, delegated or necessarily implied.

But there is more involved in these cases than the arrogation of undelegated powers. Raised are vital constitutional issues, and, most important, policy issues trenching on grave domestic problems of our time, without the benefit of a legislative determination which would reflect the interests of the entire State. The policy issues relate to needed housing, planned land development under government control, and the exclusion in effect or by motive, of walled-in urban populations of the middle class and the poor. The issues are raised by a town ordinance, which, as one of the Appellate Division Justices noted below, reflects a parochial stance without regard to its impact on the region or the State, especially if it becomes a valid model for many other towns similarly situated. . . .

It is not necessary now to confront the serious constitutional issues raised by mandatory delayed development. The crux of the matter in these cases is that before wrestling with the constitutional issues the Ramapo ordinance is destroyed at the threshold. It lacks statutory authorization and this despite the fact that its reach is more ambitious than any before essayed even with enabling legislation.

Notes

1. When the price of oil skyrocketed after 1973, commuting to Ramapo was no longer so attractive and demand for development slackened.

"Ramapo's problem now is too little growth. Fred Rella, township supervisor, says, 'We want more growth, but growth that's compatible with our country-like atmosphere.' " The city repealed its growth limitations. Wall Street Journal, Aug. 31, 1983.

2. Testimony of James Rouse before the House Committee on Banking and Currency, March 25, 1966:

. . . The simple fact is that, with the powers and processes that now exist in local government and in the homebuilding industry, it is impossible to provide, in an orderly and intelligent way, for the metropolitan growth which we know lies just ahead.

Our cities grow by accident — by whim of the private developer and public agencies. A farm is sold and begins raising houses instead of potatoes — then another farm; forests are cut; valleys are filled; streams are buried in storm sewers; kids overflow the schools — here a new school is built — there a church. Then more schools and churches. Traffic grows; roads are widened; service stations, Tasty Freeze, hamburger stands pockmark the highway. Traffic strangles. An expressway is cut through the landscape — brings clover leaves — which bring shopping centers, office buildings, high rise apartments. Relentlessly, the bits and pieces of a city are splattered across the landscape.

By this irrational process, noncommunities are born — formless places without order, beauty or reason; with no visible respect for people or the land. Thousands of small, separate decisions — made with little or no relationship to one another, nor to their composite impact — produce a major decision about the future of our cities and our civilization — a decision we have come to label "suburban sprawl."

Sprawl is dreadfully inefficient. It stretches out the distances people must travel to work, to shop, to worship, to play. It fails to relate those activities in ways that strengthen each and thus, it suppresses values that orderly relationships and concentration of uses would stimulate.

Sprawl is ugly, oppressive, massively dull. It squanders the resources of nature — forests, streams, hillsides — and produces vast, monotonous armies of housing and graceless tasteless clutter. But worst of all, sprawl is inhuman. It is antihuman. The vast, formless spread of housing, pierced by the unrelated spotting of schools, churches, stores, creates areas so huge and irrational that they are out of scale with people — beyond their grasp and comprehension — too big for people to feel a part of, responsible for, important in.

The richness of real community — in both its support and its demand — is largely voided. Variety and choice are reduced to a sort of prepackaged brandname selection of recreation, culture, and education. The individual is immersed in the mass.

What nonsense this is. What reckless, irresponsible dissipation of nature's endowment and man's hopes for dignity, beauty, and growth.

We face the addition of 70 million people to our cities over the next 20 years — a new Toledo each month or a Denver, a Dallas and an Atlanta each year. Yet not one single metropolitan area in the United States has plans to match the growth it knows it must face; and if it had the plans it would lack the power and processes to execute them. This is the state of our nation and the prospect of our civilization as we convert over 1 million acres of land each year from agricultural to urban use; as we move forward to produce over the next ten years in our urban centers the equivalent of everything we have built in our cities and suburbs since Plymouth Rock.

Urban growth should be our opportunity, not our enemy. It invites us to correct the past; to build new places that are infused with nature and stimulating to man's creative sense of beauty; places that are in scale with people and so formed as to encourage and give strength to real community which will enrich life; build character and personality; promote concern, friendship, brotherhood.

This is the purpose of our civilization — the only valid, ultimate purpose of any civilization — to grow better people; more creative, more productive, more inspired, more loving people.

3. Chilmark, a town on Martha's Vineyard, Massachusetts, severely restricted subdivision and development of its land, but the town

wanted to permit children of long-time year-round residents to stay in the town. Thus, a bylaw permitted the sale of undersized lots for development by individuals under 30 years of age who had resided in the town for 8 consecutive years. A challenge to the ordinance failed in Sturges v. Town of Chilmark, 380 Mass. 246, 402 N.E.2d 1346 (1980).

◆ CONSTRUCTION INDUSTRY ASSOCIATION v.
CITY OF PETALUMA
522 F.2d 897 (9th Cir. 1975), *cert. denied*, 424 U.S. 934

CHOY, Circuit Judge. The City of Petaluma (the City) appeals from a district court decision voiding as unconstitutional certain aspects of its five-year housing and zoning plan. We reverse.

The City is located in southern Sonoma County, about 40 miles north of San Francisco. In the 1950's and 1960's, Petaluma was a relatively self-sufficient town. It experienced a steady population growth from 10,315 in 1950 to 24,870 in 1970. Eventually, the City was drawn into the Bay Area metropolitan housing market as people working in San Francisco and San Rafael became willing to commute longer distances to secure relatively inexpensive housing available there. By November 1972, according to unofficial figures, Petaluma's population was at 30,500, a dramatic increase of almost 25 percent in little over two years.

The increase in the City's population, not surprisingly, is reflected in the increase in the number of its housing units. From 1964 to 1971, the following number of residential housing units were completed:

1964	270
1965	440
1966	321
1967	234
1968	379
1969	358
1970	591
1971	891

In 1970 and 1971, the years of the most rapid growth, demand for housing in the City was even greater than above indicated. Taking 1970 and 1971 together, builders won approval of a total of 2000 permits although only 1482 were actually completed by the end of 1971.

Alarmed by the accelerated rate of growth in 1970 and 1971, the demand for even more housing, and the sprawl of the City eastward, the City adopted a temporary freeze on development in early 1971. The construction and zoning change moratorium was intended to give the

City Council and the City planners an opportunity to study the housing and zoning situation and to develop short and long range plans. The Council made specific findings with respect to housing patterns and availability in Petaluma, including the following: That from 1960-1970 housing had been in almost unvarying 6000 square-foot lots laid out in regular grid patterns; that there was a density of approximately 4.5 housing units per acre in the single-family home areas; that during 1960-1970, 88 percent of housing permits issued were for single-family detached homes; that in 1970, 83 percent of Petaluma's housing was single-family dwellings; that the bulk of recent development (largely single-family homes) occurred in the eastern portion of the City, causing a large deficiency in moderately priced multi-family and apartment units on the east side.

To correct the imbalance between single-family and multi-family dwellings, curb the sprawl of the City on the east, and retard the accelerating growth of the City, the Council in 1972 adopted several resolutions, which collectively are called the "Petaluma Plan" (the Plan).

The Plan, on its face limited to a five-year period (1972-1977), fixes a housing development growth rate not to exceed 500 dwelling units per year. Each dwelling unit represents approximately three people. The 500-unit figure is somewhat misleading, however, because it applies only to housing units (hereinafter referred to as "development-units") that are part of projects involving five units or more. Thus, the 500-unit figure does not reflect any housing and population growth due to construction of single-family homes or even four-unit apartment buildings not part of any larger project.

The Plan also positions a 200 foot wide "greenbelt" around the City, to serve as a boundary for urban expansion for at least five years, and with respect to the east and north sides of the City, for perhaps ten to fifteen years. One of the most innovative features of the Plan is the Residential Development Control System which provides procedures and criteria for the award of the annual 500 development-unit permits. At the heart of the allocation procedure is an intricate point system, whereby a builder accumulates points for conformity by his projects with the City's general plan and environmental design plans, for good architectural design, and for providing low and moderate income dwelling units and various recreational facilities. The Plan further directs that allocations of building permits are to be divided as evenly as feasible between the west and east sections of the City and between single-family dwellings and multiple residential units (including rental units), that the sections of the City closest to the center are to be developed first in order to cause "infilling" of vacant area, and that 8 to 12 percent of the housing units approved be for low and moderate income persons.

In a provision of the Plan, intended to maintain the close-in rural space outside and surrounding Petaluma, the City solicited Sonoma

County to establish stringent subdivision and appropriate acreage parcel controls for the areas outside the urban extension line of the City and to limit severely further residential infilling.

The purpose of the Plan is much disputed in this case. According to general statements in the Plan itself, the Plan was devised to ensure that "development in the next five years, will take place in a reasonable, orderly, attractive manner, rather than in a completely haphazard and unattractive manner." The controversial 500-unit limitation on residential development-units was adopted by the City "[i]n order to protect its small town character and surrounding open space." The other features of the Plan were designed to encourage an east-west balance in development, to provide for variety in densities and building types and wide ranges in prices and rents, to ensure infilling of close-in vacant areas, and to prevent the sprawl of the city to the east and north. The Construction Industry Association of Sonoma County (the Association) argues and the district court found, however, that the Plan was primarily enacted "to limit Petaluma's demographic and market growth rate in housing and in the immigration of new residents." . . .

According to undisputed expert testimony at trial, if the Plan (limiting housing starts to approximately 6 percent of existing housing stock each year) were to be adopted by municipalities throughout the region, the impact on the housing market would be substantial. For the decade 1970 to 1980, the shortfall in needed housing in the region would be about 105,000 units (or 25 percent of the units needed). Further, the aggregate effect of a proliferation of the Plan throughout the San Francisco region would be a decline in regional housing stock quality, a loss of the mobility of current and prospective residents and a deterioration in the quality and choice of housing available to income earners with real incomes of $14,000 per year or less. If, however, the Plan were considered by itself and with respect to Petaluma only, there is no evidence to suggest that there would be a deterioration in the quality and choice of housing available there to persons in the lower and middle income brackets. Actually, the Plan increases the availability of multi-family units (owner-occupied and rental units) and low-income units which were rarely constructed in the pre-Plan days. . . .

The City also challenges the standing of the Association and the Landowners to maintain the suit. The standing requirement raises the threshold question in every federal case whether plaintiff has made out a "case or controversy" between himself and the defendant within the meaning of Article III of the Constitution. In order to satisfy the constitutional requirement that courts decide only cases or controversies and to ensure the requisite concreteness of facts and adverseness of parties, plaintiff must show that he has a "personal stake in the outcome of the controversy," or that he has suffered "some threatened or actual injury resulting from the putatively illegal action." Further, the plaintiff must satisfy the additional court-imposed standing requirement that the "interest sought to be protected by the complainant is arguably within the zone of interests to be protected or regulated by the statute or constitutional guarantee in question." A corollary to the "zone of interest" requirement is the well-recognized general rule that "even when the plaintiff has alleged injury sufficient to meet the 'case or controversy' requirement, . . . the plaintiff generally must assert his own legal rights and interests, and cannot rest his claim to relief on the legal rights or interests of third parties." Warth v. Seldin, 422 U.S. 490, 499, 95 S. Ct. 2197, 2205 (1975). Appellees easily satisfy the "injury in fact" standing requirement. The Association alleges it has suffered in its own right monetary damages due to lost revenues. Sonoma County builders contribute dues to the Association in a sum proportionate to the amount of business the builders do in the area. Thus, in a very real sense a restriction on building in Petaluma causes economic injury to the Association.

The two Landowners also have already suffered or are threatened with a direct injury. It is their position that the Petaluma Plan operated, of itself, to adversely affect the value and marketability of their land for residential uses, and such an allegation is sufficient to show that they have a personal stake in the outcome of the controversy.

Although appellees have suffered or are threatened with direct personal injury, the "zone of interest" requirement poses a huge stumbling block to their attempt to show standing. The primary federal claim upon which this suit is based — the right to travel or migrate — is a claim asserted not on the appellees' own behalf, but on behalf of a group of unknown third parties allegedly excluded from living in Petaluma. Although individual builders, the Association, and the Landowners are admittedly adversely affected by the Petaluma Plan, their economic interests are undisputedly outside the zone of interest to be protected by any purported constitutional right to travel. Accordingly, appellees' right to travel claim "falls squarely within the prudential standing rule that normally bars litigants from asserting the rights or legal interests of others in order to obtain relief from injury to themselves." Warth v. Seldin, 422 U.S. at 509, 95 S. Ct. at 2210. . . .

Although we conclude that appellees lack standing to assert the rights of third parties, they nonetheless have standing to maintain claims based on violations of rights personal to them. Accordingly, appellees have standing to challenge the Petaluma Plan on the grounds asserted in their complaint that the Plan is arbitrary and thus violative of their due process rights guaranteed by the Fourteenth Amendment and that the Plan poses an unreasonable burden on interstate commerce. . . .

Although we assume that some persons desirous of living in Petaluma will be excluded under the housing permit limitation and that, thus, the Plan may frustrate some legitimate regional housing needs, the Plan is not arbitrary or unreasonable. We agree with appellees that unlike the situation in the past most municipalities today are neither isolated nor wholly independent from neighboring municipalities and that, consequently, unilateral land use decisions by one local entity affect the needs and resources of an entire region. It does not necessarily follow, however, that the *due process* rights of builders and landowners are violated merely because a local entity exercises in its own self-interest the police power lawfully delegated to it by the state. If the present system of delegated zoning power does not effectively serve the state interest in furthering the general welfare of the region or entire state, it is the state legislature's and not the federal courts' role to intervene and adjust the system. As stated *supra*, the federal court is not a super zoning board and should not be called on to mark the point at which legitimate local interests in promoting the welfare of the community are outweighed by legitimate regional interests.

We conclude therefore that under *Belle Terre* . . . the concept of the public welfare is sufficiently broad to uphold Petaluma's desire to preserve its small town character, its open spaces and low density of population, and to grow at an orderly and deliberate pace.

Notes

1. As the *Petaluma* opinion suggests, all litigation in this area is now burdened by the holding in Warth v. Seldin, 422 U.S. 490 (1975) (5-4), that nonresidents of Penfield, New York, did not have standing to allege that the town's denial of permission for a low-income housing project unconstitutionally denied them the opportunity to obtain an apartment. The Court also denied standing to Rochester taxpayers (Penfield is a suburb of Rochester) who had alleged that Penfield's exclusionary policies forced Rochester to accommodate poor residents who would otherwise live in Penfield. And it refused to permit current Penfield residents to assert a constitutional right to the benefits of living in an integrated community.

2. All citizens have "the same right . . . as is enjoyed by white citizens . . . to . . . purchase . . . real . . . property," 42 U.S.C. §1982 (the 1866 Civil Rights Act). Because of housing discrimination there is a "dual housing market," and blacks must pay more than whites for physically equivalent housing. *Held*: black purchasers state a cause of action for discrimination when they allege a dual housing market in a suit for damages against builders and land companies from whom they purchased. Clark v. Universal Builders, Inc., 501 F.2d 324 (7th Cir.), *cert. denied*, 419 U.S. 1070 (1974). After a trial on the merits, the district court found and the court of appeals affirmed that plaintiffs had failed to meet their burden of proof concerning the alleged discrimination. Clark v. Universal Builders, Inc., 706 F.2d 204 (7th Cir. 1983).

3. The Town of Raymond, New Hampshire, in response to a 64 percent increase in its population from 1970 to 1977, had passed a "slow-growth" amendment to its zoning ordinance limiting the availability of residential building permits. Plaintiff, a developer, after having applied for five permits and having been granted only four, challenged the ordinance in court. While the New Hampshire Supreme Court ruled in his favor on narrow statutory grounds, the court upheld the validity of the slow-growth ordinance "as a temporary emergency measure to allow the town two years at most to develop a master or comprehensive plan for phasing in growth and providing therefor." However, the court stated further:

> This zoning ordinance as a *permanent* enactment is of doubtful validity. It is not based on any study, and is not part of a comprehensive plan. Its apparent primary purpose is to prevent the entrance of newcomers in order to avoid burdens upon the public services and facilities. This alone is not a valid public purpose. Moreover the great bulk of such expenses as sewer and water lines and streets are usually forced upon the developer and in turn upon the ultimate homeowners.
>
> Towns may not refuse to confront the future by building a moat around themselves and pulling up the drawbridge. They must develop plans to insure that municipal services, which normal growth will require, will be provided for in an orderly and rational manner. Any limitations on expansion must not unreasonably restrict normal growth. This is not to say that some reasonable limitations on growth based upon the use of master or comprehensive planning are barred.

Beck v. Town of Raymond, 118 N.H. 793, 394 A.2d 847 (1978).

4. On the same day on which *Town of Raymond* was decided, the New Hampshire Supreme Court also ruled invalid the slow-growth ordinance of the Town of Pembroke, which prohibited a landowner from subdividing land into more than five building lots in one calendar year. In rejecting the town's reliance on a statute empowering towns to pass bylaws "for making and ordering their prudential affairs," the court noted: "We are cognizant of the problems facing communities throughout the State caused by the rapid increase in population. This court, however, is not the appropriate governmental branch to accommodate those concerns by interpreting a legislative mandate in a strained manner." Stoney-Brooke Development Corp. v. Town of Pembroke, 118 N.H. 791, 394 A.2d 853 (1978).

5. A year after *Town of Raymond* and *Town of Pembroke*, the New Hampshire legislature substantially codified their holdings in N.H. Rev. Stat. Ann. 31:62-b (Supp. 1983), which provides the following: "In unusual circumstances requiring prompt attention and for the purpose of developing or altering a growth management process . . . or a master plan or capital improvement program, a city or town may adopt an

ordinance imposing interim regulations upon development." The statute allows an interim regulation to remain in effect for one year. For a
discussion of the statute's effects, see Conway v. Town of Stratham, 120
N.H. 257, 414 A.2d 539 (1980).

◆ ASSOCIATED HOME BUILDERS v. CITY OF
WALNUT CREEK

4 Cal. 3d 633, 484 P.2d 606, 94 Cal. Rptr. 630, *appeal dismissed*, 404
U.S. 878 (1971)

Mosk, Justice. Section 11546 of the Business and Professions Code authorizes the governing body of a city or county to require that a subdivider must, as a condition to the approval of a subdivision map,
dedicate land or pay fees in lieu thereof for park or recreational purposes. In this class action for declaratory and injunctive relief, Associated Home Builders of the Greater East Bay, Incorporated (hereinafter
called Associated) challenges the constitutionality of section 11546 as
well as legislation passed by the City of Walnut Creek to implement the
section. It is also asserted that the city's enactments do not comply with
the requirements set forth in the section. The trial court found in favor of
the city, and Associated appeals from the ensuing judgment. . . .

Section 10-1.516 of the Walnut Creek Municipal Code, which will be
discussed *infra*, refers to a general park and recreational plan adopted by
the city. It provides that if a park or recreational facility indicated on the
general plan falls within a proposed subdivision the land must be dedicated for park use by the subdivider in a ratio (set forth in a resolution)
determined by the type of residence built and the number of future
occupants. Pursuant to the ratio, two and one-half acres of park or
recreation land must be provided for each 1,000 new residents. If, however, no park is designated on the master plan and the subdivision is
within three-fourths of a mile radius of a park or a proposed park, or the
dedication of land is not feasible, the subdivider must pay a fee equal to
the value of the land which he would have been required to dedicate
under the formula. . . .

If a subdivision does not contain land designated on the master plan
as a recreation area, the subdivider pays a fee which is to be used for
providing park or recreational facilities to serve the subdivision. One
purpose of requiring payment of a fee in lieu of dedication is to avoid
penalizing the subdivider who owns land containing an area designated
as park land on the master plan. It would, of course, be patently unfair
and perhaps discriminatory to require such a property owner to dedicate
land, while exacting no contribution from a subdivider in precisely the
same position except for the fortuitous circumstance that his land does
not contain an area which has been designated as park land on the plan.

Associated's primary contention is that section 11546 violates the equal protection and due process clauses of the federal and state Constitutions in that it deprives a subdivider of his property without just compensation. It is asserted that the state is avoiding the obligation of compensation by the device of requiring the subdivider to dedicate land or pay a fee for park or recreational purposes, that such contributions are used to pay for public facilities enjoyed by all citizens of the city and only incidentally by subdivision residents, and that all taxpayers should share in the cost of these public facilities. Thus, it is asserted, the future residents of the subdivision, who will ultimately bear the burden imposed on the subdivider, will be required to pay for recreational facilities the need for which stems not from the development of any one subdivision but from the needs of the community as a whole.

In order to avoid these constitutional pitfalls, claims Associated, a dedication requirement is justified only if it can be shown that the need for additional park and recreational facilities is attributable to the increase in population stimulated by the new subdivision alone and the validity of the section may not be upheld upon the theory that all subdivisions to be built in the future will create the need for such facilities.

In Ayres v. City Council of City of Los Angeles (1949), 34 Cal. 2d 31, 207 P.2d 1, we rejected similar arguments. In that case, a city imposed upon a subdivider certain conditions for the development of a residential tract, including a requirement that he dedicate a strip of land abutting a major thoroughfare bordering one side of the subdivision but from which there was no access into the subdivision. The subdivider insisted that he could be compelled to dedicate land only for streets within the subdivision to expedite the traffic flow therein and that no dedication could be required for additions to existing streets and highways. Moreover, he asserted, the city had been contemplating condemning the property for the purposes indicated in any event, the benefit to the lot owners in the tract would be relatively small compared to the benefit to the city at large, and the dedication requirement amounted, therefore, to the exercise of the power of eminent domain under the guise of subdivision map proceedings.

We held that the city was not acting in eminent domain but, rather, that a subdivider who was seeking to acquire the advantages of subdivision had the duty to comply with reasonable conditions for dedication so as to conform to the welfare of the lot owners and the general public. We held, further, that the conditions were not improper because their fulfillment would incidentally benefit the city as a whole or because future as well as immediate needs were taken into consideration and that potential as well as present population factors affecting the neighborhood could be considered in formulating the conditions imposed upon the subdivider. We do not find in *Ayres* support for the principle urged by Associated that a dedication requirement may be upheld only if the particular subdivision creates the need for dedication. . . .

We see no persuasive reason in the face of these urgent needs caused by present and anticipated future population growth on the one hand and the disappearance of open land on the other to hold that a statute requiring the dedication of land by a subdivider may be justified only upon the ground that the particular subdivider upon whom an exaction has been imposed will, solely by the development of his subdivision, increase the need for recreational facilities to such an extent that additional land for such facilities will be required. . . .

Associated next poses as an eventuality that, if the requirements of section 11546 are upheld as a valid exercise of the police power on the theory that new residents of the subdivision must pay the cost of park land needs engendered by their entry into the community, a city or county could also require contributions from a subdivider for such services as added costs of fire and police protection, the construction of a new city hall, or even a general contribution to defray the additional cost of all types of governmental services necessitated by the entry of the new residents.

This proposition overlooks the unique problem involved in utilization of raw land. Undeveloped land in a community is a limited resource which is difficult to conserve in a period of increased population pressure. The development of a new subdivision in and of itself has the counterproductive effect of consuming a substantial supply of this precious commodity, while at the same time increasing the need for park and recreational land. In terms of economics, subdivisions diminish supply and increase demand. Another answer to Associated's assertion is found in the provisions of section 11546 itself. As we have seen, the section requires that land dedicated or in-lieu fees are to be used for the recreational needs of the subdivision which renders the exaction. Since the increase in residents creates the need for additional park land and the land or fees are used for facilities for the new residents, although not to the exclusion of others, the circumstances may be distinguished from a more general or diffuse need created for such areawide services as fire and police protection.

D. MANDELKER, THE ROLE OF ZONING IN HOUSING AND METROPOLITAN DEVELOPMENT, IN PAPERS SUBMITTED TO THE SUBCOMM. ON HOUSING OF THE HOUSE COMM. ON BANKING AND CURRENCY, 92nd Cong., 1st Sess. at 785, 786-787 (1971): [T]he early zoning was defensive, a better word than the usual characterization of the early zoning ordinances as negative. That is, zoning ordinances as they were first conceived were aimed at preventing the worst in conflicting mixtures of land uses which were considered harmful to the urban environment.

It is certainly true that this legal approach to zoning regulation was legally well-contrived. At the time zoning was initially adopted, legal restrictions on the free use of land in the name of a larger public interest were suspect. Perplexing and difficult constitutional problems were avoided by fastening the zoning technique on ancient and well-accepted legal notions which arose out of the law of nuisance. Long before the first zoning ordinances were passed, courts had been willing to issue prohibitory decrees at the request of private landowners either prohibiting or restricting offending land uses in areas in which they were considered incompatible. For example, courts had long issued decrees which had the effect of keeping nonresidential land uses out of residential areas. In doing so, they necessarily had to adopt a judicial position toward the neighborhood, and even the city, which they sought to protect. Judicial zoning was the result. Courts would inquire into the character of neighborhoods which were under review, and would or would not issue court orders prohibiting intruding and offending uses depending on how they characterized the area into which the use sought entry.

Zoning merely codified this long-established judicial function. It did this by means of a local ordinance which set, in advance and by preregulation, the various districts in which uses of different kinds were or were not to be allowed. Two important aspects of the zoning function emerge from this early history: 1) zoning was based on preregulation, avoiding legal objections of unfairness and illegality in the distribution of land uses by allocating areas of competing land uses comprehensively and in advance of development; 2) possible legal objections to restrictions on the private right of land development were avoided by fastening zoning on well-established legal notions of frictional land use incompatibilities. Zoning thus did not pretend to make more ambitious land use decisions with the larger objectives of community and regional development in mind.

It is obvious to most observers of the urban scene that, on both counts, the original nature of the zoning process has been completely turned around. Preregulation of land uses has not worked in developing and urbanizing areas, and the original and limited objectives of separating frictional land uses has been displaced by more ambitious objectives related to larger and more comprehensive planning purposes. Some comment on both of these points is in order. Preregulation of land use simply did not work on the fast-growing urban fringe. Not only were there legal objections to the prezoning of undeveloped land in which land use patterns had not been fixed, but the pace of development in urbanizing areas often outstripped and outdated earlier planning and zoning determinations. Other factors probably played a part. Zoning was (and is) a gross tool at best. Fairly crude legal distinctions could be made among types of land uses, but zoning administrators were interested in more control. Often who the developer was turned out to be more important than what he actually proposed to do with his land. As a result, zoning was gradually converted from a system which preregulated land uses to a system of administrative control in which individual applications for development were considered ad hoc as applications for zoning changes of various kinds came before zoning administrators. This change in the basic decision making function inherent in the zoning process came about through the adaptation of existing legal powers rather than through their formal legal reconstruction. Tensions in the use of the zoning power have therefore resulted which continue to remain both troublesome and unresolved.

These changes in the purpose of zoning largely came about with changes in methods of land development. While development in the early decades of the century took place piecemeal, on small lots, changes in building methods stimulated by the greater accessibility induced by the automobile led to newer development techniques in which urban development came to occur on large aggregates of land especially assembled for development purposes. The large subdivision or apartment complex replaced the single home on the individual lot. Extensive regional shopping centers replaced the corner store. Where these massive developments would go would have important effects on the shape and character of urban areas. Moreover, the coming of the automobile and the high-speed expressway significantly widened the area in which new development could occur. Control over the location of major developments in largely open territory came to be an important zoning problem. No longer could the exercise of zoning controls be justified in the name of preventing narrower land use incompatibilities. Zoning was increasingly used as a method of implementing larger objectives based on a comprehensive plan.

Notes

1. In giving a developer permission to subdivide and to establish a "mobile-home park," Cook County imposed conditions designed to reduce the burden on the public school system: only 25 percent of the sites for families with children, and a cash contribution to the schools of $43,000. The Illinois Supreme Court found that the first condition violated public policy and that the second was beyond the powers available "under the guise of zoning authority." Was it relevant that Ill. Rev. Stat. Ch. 80, §§37, 38 (1977), prohibited leasing of property on condition that the lessee have no children under the age of 14? Duggan v. County of Cook, 60 Ill. 2d 107, 324 N.E.2d 406 (1975).

2. By statute, New York permitted the Museum of Modern Art to build an extension that included condominium apartments on top, with the owners of the apartments paying to the museum what would otherwise be their municipal real estate taxes. *Held:* Not unconstitutional as

special legislation applicable only to a single enterprise. Hotel Dorset Co. v. Trust for Cultural Resources, 46 N.Y.2d 358, 385 N.E.2d 1284, 413 N.Y.S.2d 357 (1978).

◆ VILLAGE OF ARLINGTON HEIGHTS v.
METROPOLITAN HOUSING DEVELOPMENT
CORP.
429 U.S. 252 (1977)

Mr. Justice POWELL delivered the opinion of the Court.

In 1971 respondent Metropolitan Housing Development Corporation (MHDC) applied to petitioner, the Village of Arlington Heights, Ill., for the rezoning of a 15-acre parcel from single-family to multiple-family classification. Using federal financial assistance, MHDC planned to build 190 clustered townhouse units for low and moderate income tenants. The Village denied the rezoning request. MHDC, joined by other plaintiffs who are also respondents here, brought suit in the United States District Court for the Northern District of Illinois. They alleged that the denial was racially discriminatory and that it violated, *inter alia*, the Fourteenth Amendment and the Fair Housing Act of 1968, 42 U.S.C. §3601 et seq. . . .

Arlington Heights is a suburb of Chicago, located about 26 miles northwest of the downtown Loop area. Most of the land in Arlington Heights is zoned for detached signle-family homes, and this is in fact the prevailing land use. The Village experienced substantial growth during the 1960s, but, like other communities in northwest Cook County, its population of racial minority groups remained quite low. According to the 1970 census, only 27 of the Village's 64,000 residents were black.

The Clerics of St. Viator, a religious order (the Order), own an 80-acre parcel just east of the center of Arlington Heights. Part of the site is occupied by the Viatorian high school, and part by the Order's three-story novitiate building, which houses dormitories and a Montessori school. Much of the site, however, remains vacant. Since 1959, when the Village first adopted a zoning ordinance, all the land surrounding the Viatorian property has been zoned R-3, a single-family specification with relatively small minimum lot size requirements. On three sides of the Viatorian land there are single-family homes just across a street; to the east the Viatorian property directly adjoins the back yards of other single-family homes.

The Order decided in 1970 to devote some of its land to low and moderate income housing. Investigation revealed that the most expeditious way to build such housing was to work through a nonprofit developer experienced in the use of federal housing subsidies under §236 of the National Housing Act, 12 U.S.C. §1715z-1.[2]

MHDC is such a developer. It was organized in 1968 by several prominent Chicago citizens for the purpose of building low and moderate income housing throughout the Chicago area. In 1970 MHDC was in the process of building one §236 development near Arlington Heights and already had provided some federally assisted housing on a smaller scale in other parts of the Chicago area.

After some negotiation, MHDC and the Order entered into a 99-year lease and an accompanying agreement of sale covering a 15-acre site in the southeast corner of the Viatorian property. MHDC became the lessee immediately but the sale agreement was contingent upon MHDC's securing zoning clearances from the Village and §236 housing assistance from the Federal Government. If MHDC proved unsuccessful in securing either, both the lease and the contract of sale would lapse. The agreement established a bargain purchase price of $300,000, low enough to comply with federal limitations governing land acquisition costs for §236 housing.

MHDC engaged an architect and proceeded with the project, to be known as Lincoln Green. The plans called for 20 two-story buildings with a total of 190 units, each unit having its own private entrance from the outside. One hundred of the units would have a single bedroom, thought likely to attract elderly citizens. The remainder would have two, three or four bedrooms. A large portion of the site would remain open, with shrubs and trees to screen the homes abutting the property to the east.

The planned development did not conform to the Village's zoning ordinance and could not be built unless Arlington Heights rezoned the parcel to R-5, its multiple-family housing classification. Accordingly, MHDC filed with the Village Plan Commission a petition for rezoning, accompanied by supporting materials describing the development and specifying that it would be subsidized under §236. The materials made

---

2. Section 236 provides for "interest reduction payments" to owners of rental housing projects which meet the Act's requirements, if the savings are passed on to the tenants in accordance with a rather complex formula. Qualifying owners effectively pay one percent interest on money borrowed to construct, rehabilitate or purchase their properties.

New commitments under §236 were suspended in 1973 by executive decision, and they have not been revived. Projects which formerly could claim §236 assistance, however, will now generally be eligible for aid under §8 of the Housing and Community Development Act of 1974, 42 U.S.C. §1437f (1970 ed., Supp. V). Under the §8 program, the Department of Housing and Urban Development contracts to pay the owner of the housing units a sum which will make up the difference between a fair market rent for the area and the amount contributed by the low-income tenant. The eligible tenant family pays between 15 and 25 percent of its gross income for rent. Respondents indicated at oral argument that, despite the demise of the §236 program, construction of the MHDC project could proceed under §8 if zoning clearance is now granted.

clear that one requirement under §236 is an affirmative marketing plan designed to assure that a subsidized development is racially integrated. MHDC also submitted studies demonstrating the need for housing of this type and analyzing the probable impact of the development. To prepare for the hearings before the Plan Commission and to assure compliance with the Village building code, fire regulations, and related requirements, MHDC consulted with the Village staff for preliminary review of the development. The parties have stipulated that every change recommended during such consultation was incorporated into the plans.

During the Spring of 1971, the Plan Commission considered the proposal at a series of three public meetings, which drew large crowds. Although many of those attending were quite vocal and demonstrative in opposition to Lincoln Green, a number of individuals and representatives of community groups spoke in support of rezoning. Some of the comments, both from opponents and supporters, addressed what was referred to as the "social issue" — the desirability or undesirability of introducing at this location in Arlington Heights low and moderate income housing, housing that would probably be racially integrated.

Many of the opponents, however, focused on the zoning aspects of the petition, stressing two arguments. First, the area always had been zoned single-family, and the neighboring citizens had built or purchased there in reliance on that classification. Rezoning threatened to cause a measurable drop in property value for neighboring sites. Second, the Village's apartment policy, adopted by the Village Board in 1962 and amended in 1970, called for R-5 zoning primarily to serve as a buffer between single-family development and land uses thought incompatible, such as commercial or manufacturing districts. Lincoln Green did not meet this requirement, as it adjoined no commercial or manufacturing district.

At the close of the third meeting, the Plan Commission adopted a motion to recommend to the Village's Board of Trustees that it deny the request. The motion stated: "While the need for low and moderate income housing may exist in Arlington Heights or its environs, the Plan Commission would be derelict in recommending it at the proposed location." Two members voted against the motion and submitted a minority report, stressing that in their view the change to accommodate Lincoln Green represented "good zoning." The Village Board met on September 28, 1971, to consider MHDC's request and the recommendation of the Plan Commission. After a public hearing, the board denied the rezoning by a 6-1 vote.

The following June MHDC and three Negro individuals filed this lawsuit against the Village, seeking declaratory and injunctive relief. A second nonprofit corporation and an individual of Mexican-American descent intervened as plaintiffs. The trial resulted in a judgment for petitioners. Assuming that MHDC had standing to bring the suit, the District Court held that the petitioners were not motivated by racial discrimination or intent to discriminate against low income groups when they denied rezoning, but rather by a desire "to protect property values and the integrity of the Village's zoning plan." The District Court concluded also that the denial would not have a racially discriminatory effect.

A divided Court of Appeals reversed. . . . [I]t ruled that the denial of the Lincoln Green proposal had racially discriminatory effects and could be tolerated only if it served compelling interests. Neither the buffer policy nor the desire to protect property values met this exacting standard. The court therefore concluded that the denial violated the Equal Protection Clause of the Fourteenth Amendment. . . .

Clearly MHDC has met the constitutional requirements [for standing], and it therefore has standing to assert its own rights. Foremost among them is MHDC's right to be free of arbitrary or irrational zoning actions. See Euclid v. Ambler Realty Co., 272 U.S. 365 (1926); Nectow v. Cambridge, 277 U.S. 183 (1928); Village of Belle Terre v. Boraas, 416 U.S. 1 (1974). But the heart of this litigation has never been the claim that the Village's decision fails the generous *Euclid* test, recently reaffirmed in *Belle Terre*. Instead it has been the claim that the Village's refusal to rezone discriminates against racial minorities in violation of the Fourteenth Amendment. . . .

Our decision last Term in Washington v. Davis, 426 U.S. 229 (1976), made it clear that official action will not be held unconstitutional solely because it results in a racially disproportionate impact. "Disproportionate impact is not irrelevant, but it is not the sole touchstone of an invidious racial discrimination." Id., at 242. Proof of racially discriminatory intent or purpose is required to show a violation of the Equal Protection Clause. Although some contrary indications may be drawn from some of our cases, the holding in *Davis* reaffirmed a principle well established in a variety of contexts.

Davis does not require a plaintiff to prove that the challenged action rested solely on racially discriminatory purposes. Rarely can it be said that a legislature or administrative body operating under a broad mandate made a decision motivated solely by a single concern, or even that a particular purpose was the "dominant" or "primary" one. In fact, it is because legislators and administrators are properly concerned with balancing numerous competing considerations that courts refrain from reviewing the merits of their decisions, absent a showing of arbitrariness or irrationality. But racial discrimination is not just another competing consideration. When there is a proof that a discriminatory purpose has been a motivating factor in the decision, this judicial deference is no longer justified. . . .

[T]he Court of Appeals focused primarily on respondents' claim that the Village's buffer policy had not been consistently applied and was being invoked with a strictness here that could only demonstrate some other underlying motive. The court concluded that the buffer policy, though not always applied with perfect consistency, had on several occasions formed the basis for the board's decision to deny other rezoning proposals. "The evidence does not necessitate a finding that Arlington Heights administered this policy in a discriminatory manner." The Court of Appeals therefore approved the District Court's findings concerning the Village's purposes in denying rezoning to MHDC.

. . . The impact of the Village's decision does arguably bear more heavily on racial minorities. Minorities comprise 18 percent of the Chicago area population, and 40 percent of the income groups said to be eligible for Lincoln Green. But there is little about the sequence of events leading up to the decision that would spark suspicion. The area around the Viatorian property has been zoned R-3 since 1959, the year when Arlington Heights first adopted a zoning map. Single-family homes surround the 80-acre site, and the Village is undeniably committed to single-family homes as its dominant residential land use. The rezoning request progressed according to the usual procedures. The Plan Commission even scheduled two additional hearings, at least in part to accommodate MHDC and permit it to supplement its presentation with answers to questions generated at the first hearing.

The statements by the Plan Commission and Village Board members, as reflected in the official minutes, focused almost exclusively on the zoning aspects of the MHDC petition, and the zoning factors on which they relied are not novel criteria in the Village's rezoning decisions. There is no reason to doubt that there has been reliance by some neighboring property owners on the maintenance of single-family zoning in the vicinity. The Village originally adopted its buffer policy long before MHDC entered the picture and has applied the policy too consistently for us to infer discriminatory purpose from its application in this case. Finally, MHDC called one member of the Village Board to the stand at trial. Nothing in her testimony supports an inference of invidious purpose.

In sum, the evidence does not warrant overturning the concurrent findings of both courts below. Respondents simply failed to carry their burden of proving that discriminatory purpose was a motivating factor in the Village's decision.[21] This conclusion ends the constitutional in-

21. Proof that the decision by the Village was motivated in part by a racially discriminatory purpose would not necessarily have required invalidation of the challenged decision. Such proof would, however, have shifted to the Village the burden of establishing that the same decision would have resulted even had the impermissible purpose not been considered. If this were established, the complaining party in a case of this kind no longer fairly could attribute the injury complained of to improper consideration of a discriminatory purpose. In such circumstances, there would be no justification for judicial interference with the challenged decision. But in this case respondents failed to make the required threshold showing.

quiry. The Court of Appeals' further finding that the Village's decision carried a discriminatory "ultimate effect" is without independent constitutional significance. Respondents' complaint also alleged that the refusal to rezone violated the Fair Housing Act, 42 U.S.C. §§3601 et seq. They continue to urge here that a zoning decision made by a public body may, and that petitioners' action did, violate §3604 or §3617. The Court of Appeals, however, proceeding in a somewhat unorthodox fashion, did not decide the statutory question. We remand the case for further consideration of respondents' statutory claims.

Reversed and remanded.

Notes

1. Is there another approach for plaintiffs? Consider the court's holding in Metropolitan Housing Development Corp. v. Village of Arlington Heights, 558 F.2d 1283 (7th Cir. 1977):

> We therefore hold that at least under some circumstances a violation of section 3604(a) [of the Fair Housing Act] can be established by a showing of discriminatory effect without a showing of discriminatory intent. A number of courts have agreed. . . .
>
> Plaintiffs contend that once a racially discriminatory effect is shown a violation of section 3604(a) is necessarily established. We decline to extend the reach of the Fair Housing Act this far. Although we agree that a showing of discriminatory intent is not required under section 3604(a), we refuse to conclude that every action which produces discriminatory effects is illegal. Such a per se rule would go beyond the intent of Congress and would lead courts into untenable results in specific cases. See Brest, Foreword, 90 Harv. L. Rev. at 29. Rather, the courts must use their discretion in deciding whether, given the particular circumstances of each case, relief should be granted under the statute.
>
> We turn now to determining under what circumstances conduct that produces a discriminatory impact but which was taken without discriminatory intent will violate section 3604(a). Four critical factors are discernible from previous cases. They are: (1) how strong is the plaintiff's showing of discriminatory effect; (2) is there some evidence of discriminatory intent, though not enough to satisfy the constitutional standard of Washington v. Davis; (3) what is the defendant's interest in taking the action complained of; and (4) does the plaintiff seek to compel the defendant to affirmatively provide housing for members of minority groups or merely to restrain the defendant from interfering with individual property owners who wish to provide such housing.

2. After the seventh circuit found that Arlington Heights had violated the Fair Housing Act in its refusal to rezone the Viator's property, MHDC and Arlington Heights agreed on a new site for low- and moderate-income housing. It was located on the border of Arlington Heights

and the Village of Mount Prospect. Mount Prospect challenged the suitability of the site in Metropolitan Housing Development Corp. v. Village of Arlington Heights, 616 F.2d 1006 (7th Cir. 1980), questioning the effect of low-income housing on *its* residential neighborhoods. The court of appeals rejected Mount Prospect's challenge and approved the site. In the court's view, national and local interests had merged at the site:

> In the present posture of this case, there is no longer an issue of the interest of a state or its municipality versus the national interest; the local and national governmental interests are now aligned together against the alleged rights of individual neighboring landowners and of an adjoining village. The changed alignment of interests from that formerly existing requires us to analyze the various interests and the policies they represent in terms of national policies supporting open housing, state and local policies supporting the actions required of Arlington Heights by the consent decree, and the policies supporting the use of consent decrees which effectuate the amalgam of the national and local interests in housing cases such as this.

> Congress has declared in the Fair Housing Act that "[i]t is the policy of the United States to provide, within constitutional limitations, for fair housing throughout the United States." 42 U.S.C. §3601. Section 3604(a) of the Act provides in part that "it shall be unlawful . . . [t]o . . . make unavailable or deny, a dwelling to any person because of race, color, religion, sex, or national origin." . . .

> The language of the Fair Housing Act is "broad and inclusive," subject to "generous construction," and "complaints by private persons are the primary method of obtaining compliance with the Act." Trafficante v. Metropolitan Life Ins. Co., 409 U.S. 205, 209, 212, 93 S. Ct. 364, 366, 34 L. Ed. 2d 415 (1972). Generally, and particularly in a fair housing situation, the existence of a federal statutory right implies the existence of all measures necessary and appropriate to protect federal rights and implement federal policies. Sullivan v. Little Hunting Park, Inc., 396 U.S. 229, 239, 90 S. Ct. 400, 405, 24 L. Ed. 2d 386 (1969).

> The courts of appeals, recognizing these policies, regularly have provided relief from exclusionary zoning (or its equivalent by refusal to permit tying into city's water and sewer systems through denial of annexation or issuance of permit) under the Fair Housing Act. . . .

> The relief normally granted by both federal and state courts in exclusionary zoning cases is what has become known as "site-specific relief," that is, the opening up of a particular parcel to low- or moderate-income multiple housing on a case-by-case basis. Developments in the Law — Zoning, 91 Harv. L. Rev. 1427, 1695-99 (1978). Such relief ordinarily runs counter to local zoning or other local legislation, but given the national open housing policy established by Congress, acting under the Civil War Amendments, the state or local legislation must yield to the paramount national policy. . . .

> The often diverse interests of national policy and local zoning have

merged here in the consent decree, which carries, in addition, its own presumption of regularity and is subject to approval by the trial court after hearing proffered objections.

3. For a case finding that Parma, Ohio, had systematically excluded subsidized housing so as to keep out blacks, see United States v. City of Parma, 661 F.2d 562 (6th Cir. 1981), *cert. denied*, 456 U.S. 926 (1982). (In the 1970 census, Parma, the largest suburb of Cleveland, had a population of 100,216, of whom 50 were black.) Broad remedial relief was ordered. Judge Merritt, dissenting in part, found first amendment problems with the item in the relief order that directed the Parma City Council to adopt an ordinance welcoming blacks to the city and to undertake an advertising campaign aimed at changing the city's exclusionary image.

◆ THE BRITISH GOVERNMENT'S *WHITE PAPER — LAND*
CMD No. 5730 (1974)

1. Of all the resources available in these islands, land is the one resource that cannot be increased. By trading with other nations we can obtain more food, more oil, or more iron ore, in exchange for those commodities or goods that we have in abundance. But with land the supply is fixed. We live in a small densely populated country, so the supply of land is not only fixed, it is also scarce. This makes it doubly important that we should plan to use our land well. . . .

3. It is not generally disputed that the community itself must control the development of land, and the planning system that has evolved has often been a potent force in preventing development that is harmful to the community. But our system of planning control is largely a negative one. The community, via its elected local authority and, in the final analysis, central Government, can veto proposals for development, but the initiative is left largely in private hands. The community does not at present have sufficient power always to plan positively, to decide where and when particular developments should take place. Public ownership of development land is designed to give this power to its rightful owner, the community.

4. Side by side with the need to secure positive planning, the nation has to deal with another problem, that of land prices and betterment. "The growth in value, more especially of urban sites, is due to no expenditure of capital or thought on the part of the ground owner, but entirely owing to the energy and enterprise of the community. . . . It is undoubtedly one of the worst evils of our present system of land tenure that instead of reaping the benefit of the common endeavour of

its citizens a community has always to pay a heavy penalty to its ground landlords for putting up the value of their land." (Rt. Hon. David Lloyd George — Official Report, April 29, 1909, Vol. IV, col. 532). [T]he public ownership of development land will secure these increments for the community that has created them. . . .

16. Some of the problems standing in the way of an effective planning system are still with us. Accordingly, the Government reiterate that their objectives are to establish a permanent means:

a.   to enable the community to control the development of land in accordance with its needs and priorities; and
b.   to restore to the community the increase in value of land arising from its efforts.

17. Every physical development comprises two actions; at the same time that something new is created, what previously existed is destroyed. One of the principal aims of planning, therefore, must be to see that what is created is better attuned to the requirements of society than what is extinguished. The existence of any planning system constitutes an acceptance of the principle that the market will not, of itself, inevitably arrive at a satisfactory conclusion as to how our land should be used.

18. Our existing negative planning control provides a valuable check on the market, and would at first sight seem capable of safeguarding our heritage and resolving the conflict between private interests and the public good. But the difficulties inherent in a patchwork quilt of land ownership, and the overwhelming financial problems associated with acquiring land, mean that the best use of land is not always achieved.

19. This is not to deny that plan-making is a very valuable function of our local authorities; it is rather to point out that the existing powers to implement their plans are restricted by the price that the market puts on some land, and by the fact that the planners' resource is in the hands of private owners rather than at the disposal of the community.

20. Public ownership of development land puts control of our scarcest resource in the hands of the community, and enables it thereby to take an overall perspective. In addition, by having this land available at the value of its current use, rather than at a value based on speculation as to its possible development, the community will be able to provide, in the places that it needs them, the public facilities it needs, but cannot now afford because of the inflated price it has to pay to the private owner.

21. Market forces encourage concentration of commercial development in areas that seem to offer special advantages to particular firms; but what the market does not consider are the side effects — the breakdown of old-established communities and the increasing desertion of

city centres — and their implications, not the least being the effect on the transport system of requiring people to live so far from their workplaces. There are costs involved — the cost of providing more roads, more trains and buses for example; and there are stresses, too, on the individual who has to spend time and money, probably in crowded conditions, travelling to and from work. These costs and stresses are not taken into account by the market, but they should be by the planning authorities. It is important that they are, and this is why planning must be strengthened, and why the community should buy the land and benefit from the development values created. . . .

27. Subject to the permanent exemptions from acquisition in paragraphs 34 and 35, and to the important transitional arrangements set out in paragraphs 36-45, it is the Government's intention to lay a duty on local authorities to acquire all land required for private development. From the date that the duty is brought in, no development will be allowed to begin save on land owned by a public authority, or made available by them for this purpose. Local authorities will therefore buy land which in their opinion is suitable for development and will also be required to buy where the need for development (e.g. as indicated in a planning application) is accepted even though it may be a departure from the plan. The general vesting declaration procedure set out in the Town and Country Planning Act 1968 can apply to such acquisitions to secure speedy disposal for development. . . .

55. The terms on which local authorities dispose of land acquired under these arrangements will need in general to ensure that the local community retains a share of future increases in value. The disposal of land for commercial or industrial development therefore will be on a leasehold basis with provision for rent revisions. In general disposals, whether on a freehold or a leasehold basis, will be at the market value at the time.

56. The Government have made it clear that their public ownership proposals do not seek to affect the provision of land on which houses can be built for owner-occupation. Land for housing can be disposed of in a variety of ways. Local authorities will be encouraged to offer it to builders on licence, with the plots being conveyed direct to the house purchasers. Plots for owner-occupation will also be made available freehold. . . .

59. The effect of these proposals will be that the community will enjoy the full value created when land is developed. The community in general, i.e. the taxpayer, will have made a contribution towards the acquisition of land and the Government propose therefore that the benefits from the scheme should be shared between central and local government. The major part of the benefit will accrue to the taxpayer in general through the Exchequer; but a part will remain with the local community and a part will be distributed amongst local authorities to

help equalise the benefits of the scheme between ratepayers at large. The Government will consult with the local authority associations in order to arrive at a rational distribution of benefits. It is the Government's intention that those buying their first homes should share in the benefits of the scheme. It must be recognised that because of the timelag between acquisition and disposal it will be some time before benefits accrue generally.

VII ♦ PUBLIC PROPERTY

What is property?

Certainly it is both substance and process: the claims that the society declares valid and also the procedures established for asserting and defending those claims. Substance and procedure interweave, together creating the expectations we call property. For example, individuals commit money, labor, and emotion in reliance on their predictions that the sun will rise and warm crops, that the zoning board will act by majority vote, and that the courts and the police will expel trespassers. The social and economic order depends on shared beliefs that what will happen in the future can be predicted, based on what has happened in the past. But every such prediction is not a property right. Rather, the concept of property identifies the subset of economic expectations that carries the legitimacy of public acknowledgment — express or implied — that an individual's reliance will be honored. The sources of this acknowledgment are varied and sometimes inconsistent: tradition, efficiency, fairness, equality, progress. Whatever our standards for according the special status of property, the concept is necessarily Janus-faced: looking back at the expectations with which society purchased reliance in the past, and forward to the conduct sought to be induced with today's promises.

The notion of property as the promises that the society must keep to its members is implemented institutionally in the United States through the constitutional guarantees against being "deprived of . . . property, without due process of law," and against having "private property . . . taken for public use, without just compensation." Judges have had to give meaning to these provisions, and so have had to determine the extent to which an individual's expectations are safe from legislative or administrative disappointment. This judicial task has taken on new significance recently with the awareness that property, in our time, means both more and less than land and buildings. The kinds of interests that give a person status, wealth, and security now extend to jobs, pensions, and welfare benefits. At the same time, landownership itself is now so qualified — because of recognition of the consequences, for neighbors and for the larger community, of an individual's use of his or her land — that owners purchase with an expectation of the likelihood of regulation. The courts, and particularly the Supreme Court, have thus been required to devise a new conceptual framework within which to approach issues of constitutional property. That framework is not fully fashioned, but its outline can be seen and is sketched in this Part.

22 ◆ OLD PROPERTY

A. THE IDEA OF A "TAKING"

1. *Police Power*

◆ MILLER v. SCHOENE — ~~possession~~ *public nuisance*
  276 U.S. 272 (1928)

Mr. Justice STONE delivered the opinion of the Court. Acting under the
Cedar Rust Act of Virginia, now embodied in Va. Code (1924) as §§885 to
893, defendant in error, the state entomologist, ordered the plaintiffs in
error to cut down a large number of ornamental red cedar trees growing
on their property, as a means of preventing the communication of a rust
or plant disease with which they were infected to the apple orchards in
the vicinity. The plaintiffs in error appealed from the order to the Circuit
Court of Shenandoah county which, after a hearing and a consideration
of evidence, affirmed the order and allowed to plaintiffs in error $100 to
cover the expense of removal of the cedars. Neither the judgment of the
court nor the statute as interpreted allows compensation for the value of
the standing cedars or the decrease in the market value of the realty
caused by their destruction whether considered as ornamental trees or
otherwise. But they save to plaintiffs in error the privilege of using the
trees when felled. . . .

The Virginia statute presents a comprehensive scheme for the condemnation and destruction of red cedar trees infected by cedar rust. By
§1 it is declared to be unlawful for any person to "own, plant or keep
alive and standing" on his premises any red cedar tree which is or may
be the source of "host plant" of the communicable plant disease known
as cedar rust, and any such tree growing within a certain radius of any
apple orchard is declared to be a public nuisance, subject to destruction.
Section 2 makes it the duty of the state entomologist,

1265

upon the request in writing of ten or more reputable free-holders of any county or magisterial district, to make a preliminary investigation of the locality . . . to ascertain if any cedar tree or trees . . . are the source of, harbor or constitute the host plant for the said disease . . . and constitute a menace to the health of any apple orchard in said locality, and that said cedar tree or trees exist within a radius of two miles of an apple orchard in said locality.

If affirmative findings are so made, he is required to direct the owner in writing to destroy the trees and, in his notice, to furnish a statement of the "fact found to exist whereby it is deemed necessary or proper to destroy" the trees and to call attention to the law under which it is proposed to destroy them. Section 5 authorizes the state entomologist to destroy the trees if the owner, after being notified, fails to do so. Section 7 furnishes a mode of appealing from the order of the entomologist to the circuit court of the county, which is authorized to "hear the objections" and "pass upon all questions involved," the procedure followed in the present case.

As shown by the evidence and as recognized in other cases involving the validity of this statute, cedar rust is an infectious plant disease in the form of a fungoid organism which is destructive of the fruit and foliage of the apple, but without effect on the value of the cedar. Its life cycle has two phases which are passed alternately as a growth on red cedar and on apple trees. It is communicated by spores from one to the other over a radius of at least two miles. It appears not to be communicable between trees of the same species but only from one species to the other, and other plants seem not to be appreciably affected by it. The only practicable method of controlling the disease and protecting apple trees from its ravages is the destruction of all red cedar trees, subject to the infection, located within two miles of apple orchards.

The red cedar, aside from its ornamental use, has occasional use and value as lumber. It is indigenous to Virginia, is not cultivated or dealt in commercially on any substantial scale, and its value throughout the state is shown to be small as compared with that of the apple orchards of the state. Apple growing is one of the principal agricultural pursuits in Virginia. The apple is used there and exported in large quantities. Many millions of dollars are invested in the orchards, which furnish employment for a large portion of the population, and have induced the development of attendant railroad and cold storage facilities.

On the evidence we may accept the conclusion of the Supreme Court of Appeals that the state was under the necessity of making a choice between the preservation of one class of property and that of the other whenever both existed in dangerous proximity. It would have been none the less a choice if, instead of enacting the present statute, the state, by doing nothing, had permitted serious injury to the apple orchards within its borders to go on unchecked. When forced to such a choice the state does not exceed its constitutional powers by deciding upon the destruction of one class of property in order to save another which, in the judgment of the legislature, is of greater value to the public. It will not do to say that the case is merely one of a conflict of two private interests and that the misfortune of apple growers may not be shifted to cedar owners by ordering the destruction of their property; for it is obvious that there may be, and that here there is, a preponderant public concern in the preservation of one interest over the other.

And where the public interest is involved, preferment of that interest over the property interest of the individual, to the extent even of its destruction, is one of the distinguishing characteristics of every exercise of the police power which affects property.

We need not weigh with nicety the question whether the infected cedars constitute a nuisance according to the common law; or whether they may be so declared by statute. For where, as here, the choice is unavoidable, we cannot say that its exercise, controlled by considerations of social policy which are not unreasonable, involves any denial of due process.

◆ PENNSYLVANIA COAL CO. v. MAHON—Dim in value
260 U.S. 393 (1922)

Mr. Justice HOLMES delivered the opinion of the Court. This is a bill in equity brought by the defendants in error to prevent the Pennsylvania Coal Company from mining under their property in such way as to remove the supports and cause a subsidence of the surface and of their house. The bill set out a deed executed by the Coal Company in 1878, under which the plaintiffs claim. The deed conveys the surface, but in express terms reserves the right to remove all the coal under the same, and the grantee takes the premises with the risk, and waives all claim for damages that may arise from mining out the coal. But the plaintiffs say that whatever may have been the Coal Company's rights, they were taken away by an Act of Pennsylvania, approved May 27, 1921, P.L. 1198, commonly known there as the Kohler Act. The Court of Common Pleas found that if not restrained the defendant would cause the damage to prevent which the bill was brought, but denied an injunction, holding that the statute if applied to this case would be unconstitutional. On appeal the Supreme Court of the State agreed that the defendant had contract and property rights protected by the Constitution of the United States, but held that the statute was a legitimate exercise of the police power and directed a decree for the plaintiffs. A writ of error was granted bringing the case to this Court.

The statute forbids the mining of anthracite coal in such a way as to cause the subsidence of, among other things, any structure used as a human habitation, with certain exceptions, including among them land where the surface is owned by the owner of the underlying coal and is distant more than one hundred and fifty feet from any improved property belonging to any other person. As applied to this case the statute is admitted to destroy previously existing rights of property and contract. The question is whether the police power can be stretched so far.

Government hardly could go on if to some extent values incident to property could not be diminished without paying for every such change in the general law. As long recognized, some values are enjoyed under an implied limitation and must yield to the police power. But obviously the implied limitation must have its limits, or the contract and due process clauses are gone. One fact for consideration in determining such limits is the extent of the diminution. When it reaches a certain magnitude, in most if not in all cases there must be an exercise of eminent domain and compensation to sustain the act. So the question depends upon the particular facts. The greatest weight is given to the judgment of the legislature, but it always is open to interested parties to contend that the legislature has gone beyond its constitutional power.

This is the case of a single private house. No doubt there is a public interest even in this, as there is in every purchase and sale and in all that happens within the commonwealth. Some existing rights may be modified even in such a case. But usually in ordinary private affairs the public interest does not warrant much of this kind of interference. A source of damage to such a house is not a public nuisance even if similar damage is inflicted on others in different places. The damage is not common or public. The extent of the public interest is shown by the statute to be limited, since the statute ordinarily does not apply to land when the surface is owned by the owner of the coal. Furthermore, it is not justified as a protection of personal safety. That could be provided for by notice. Indeed the very foundation of this bill is that the defendant gave timely notice of its intent to mine under the house. On the other hand the extent of the taking is great. It purports to abolish what is recognized in Pennsylvania as an estate in land — a very valuable estate — and what is declared by the Court below to be a contract hitherto binding the plaintiffs. If we were called upon to deal with the plaintiffs' position alone, we should think it clear that the statute does not disclose a public interest sufficient to warrant so extensive a destruction of the defendant's constitutionally protected rights.

But the case has been treated as one in which the general validity of the act should be discussed. The Attorney General of the State, the City of Scranton, and the representatives of other extensive interests were allowed to take part in the argument below and have submitted their contentions here. It seems, therefore, to be our duty to go farther in the

PHOTOGRAPH 22-1
Oliver Wendell Holmes

statement of our opinion, in order that it may be known at once, and that further suits should not be brought in vain.

It is our opinion that the act cannot be sustained as an exercise of the police power, so far as it affects the mining of coal under streets or cities in places where the right to mine such coal has been reserved. As said in a Pennsylvania case, "For practical purposes, the right to coal consists in the right to mine it." What makes the right to mine coal valuable is that it can be exercised with profit. To make it commercially impracticable to mine certain coal has very nearly the same effect for constitutional purposes as appropriating or destroying it. This we think that we are warranted in assuming that the statute does.

It is true that in Plymouth Coal Co. v. Pennsylvania, 232 U.S. 531, it was held competent for the legislature to require a pillar of coal to be left along the line of adjoining property, that, with the pillar on the other side of the line, would be a barrier sufficient for the safety of the employees of either mine in case the other should be abandoned and allowed to fill with water. But that was a requirement for the safety of employees invited into the mine, and secured an average reciprocity of advantage that has been recognized as a justification of various laws.

The rights of the public in a street purchased or laid out by eminent domain are those that it has paid for. If in any case its representatives have been so short sighted as to acquire only surface rights without the right of support, we see no more authority for supplying the latter without compensation than there was for taking the right of way in the first place and refusing to pay for it because the public wanted it very much. The protection of private property in the Fifth Amendment presupposes that it is wanted for public use, but provides that it shall not be taken for such use without compensation. A similar assumption is made in the decisions upon the Fourteenth Amendment. When this seemingly absolute protection is found to be qualified by the police power, the natural tendency of human nature is to extend the qualification more and more until at last private property disappears. But that cannot be accomplished in this way under the Constitution of the United States.

The general rule at least is, that while property may be regulated to a certain extent, if regulation goes too far it will be recognized as a taking. It may be doubted how far exceptional cases, like the blowing up of a house to stop a conflagration, go — and if they go beyond the general rule, whether they do not stand as much upon tradition as upon principle. In general it is not plain that a man's misfortunes or necessities will justify his shifting the damages to his neighbor's shoulders. We are in danger of forgetting that a strong public desire to improve the public condition is not enough to warrant achieving the desire by a shorter cut than the constitutional way of paying for the change. As we already have said, this is a question of degree — and therefore cannot be disposed of by general propositions. But we regard this as going beyond any of the cases decided by this Court. The late decisions upon laws dealing with the congestion of Washington and New York, caused by the war, dealt with laws intended to meet a temporary emergency and providing for compensation determined to be reasonable by an impartial board. They went to the verge of the law but fell far short of the present act. Block v. Hirsh, 256 U.S. 135.

We assume, of course, that the statute was passed upon the conviction that an exigency existed that would warrant it, and we asume that an exigency exists that would warrant the exercise of eminent domain. But the question at bottom is upon whom the loss of the changes desired should fall. So far as private persons or communities have seen fit to take the risk of acquiring only surface rights, we cannot see that the fact that their risk has become a danger warrants the giving to them greater rights than they bought.

Decree reversed.

Mr. Justice BRANDEIS, dissenting. The Kohler Act prohibits, under certain conditions, the mining of anthracite coal within the limits of a city in such a manner or to such an extent "as to cause the . . . subsidence of any dwelling or other structure used as a human habitation, or any factory, store, or other industrial or mercantile establishment in which human labor is employed." Coal in place is land; and the right of the owner to use his land is not absolute. He may not so use it as to create a public nuisance; and uses, once harmless, may, owing to changed conditions, seriously threaten the public welfare. Whenever they do, the legislature has power to prohibit such uses without paying compensation; and the power to prohibit extends alike to the manner, the character and the purpose of the use. Are we justified in declaring that the Legislature of Pennsylvania has, in restricting the right to mine anthracite, exercised this power so arbitrarily as to violate the Fourteenth Amendment?

Every restriction upon the use of property imposed in the exercise of the police power deprives the owner of some right theretofore enjoyed, and is, in that sense, an abridgment by the State of rights in property without making compensation. But restriction imposed to protect the public health, safety or morals from dangers threatened is not a taking. The restriction here in question is merely the prohibition of a noxious use. The property so restricted remains in the possession of its owner. The State does not appropriate it or make any use of it. The State merely prevents the owner from making a use which interferes with paramount rights of the public. Whenever the use prohibited ceases to be noxious, — as it may because of further change in local or social conditions, — the restriction will have to be removed and the owner will again be free to enjoy his property as heretofore.

The restriction upon the use of this property can not, of course, be lawfully imposed, unless its purpose is to protect the public. But the purpose of a restriction does not cease to be public, because incidentally some private persons may thereby receive gratuitously valuable special benefits. Thus, owners of low buildings may obtain, through statutory restrictions upon the height of neighboring structures, benefits equivalent to an easement of light and air. Furthermore, a restriction, though imposed for a public purpose, will not be lawful, unless the restriction is an appropriate means to the public end. But to keep coal in place is surely an appropriate means of preventing subsidence of the surface; and ordinarily it is the only available means. Restriction upon use does not become inappropriate as a means, merely because it deprives the owner of the only use to which the property can then be profitably put. Nor is a restriction imposed through exercise of the police power inappropriate as a means, merely because the same end might be effected through exercise of the power of eminent domain, or otherwise at public expense. Every restriction upon the height of buildings might be secured through acquiring by eminent domain the right of each owner to build above the limiting height; but it is settled that the State need not resort to that power. If by mining anthracite coal the owner would necessarily unloose poisonous gasses, I suppose no one would doubt the power of the State to prevent the mining, without buying his coal fields. And why may not the State, likewise, without paying compensation, prohibit one from digging so deep or excavating so near the surface, as to expose the community to like dangers? In the latter case, as in the former, carrying on the business would be a public nuisance.

It is said that one fact for consideration in determining whether the limits of the police powers have been exceeded is the extent of the resulting diminution in value; and that here the restriction destroys existing rights of property and contract. But values are relative. If we are to consider the value of the coal kept in place by the restrictions, we should compare it with the value of all other parts of the land. That is, with the value not of the coal alone, but with the value of the whole property. The rights of an owner as against the public are not increased by dividing the interests in his property into surface and subsoil. The sum of the rights in the parts can not be greater than the rights in the whole. The estate of an owner in land is grandiloquently described as extending *ab orco usque ad coelum*. But I suppose no one would contend that by selling his interest above one hundred feet from the surface he could prevent the State from limiting, by the police power, the height of structures in a city. And why should a sale of underground rights bar the State's power? For aught that appears the value of the coal kept in place by the restriction may be negligible as compared with the value of the whole property, or even as compared with that part of it which is represented by the coal remaining in place and which may be extracted despite the statute. . . .

A prohibition of mining which causes subsidence of [public] structures and facilities is obviously enacted for a public purpose; and it seems, likewise, clear that mere notice of intention to mine would not in this connection secure the public safety. Yet it is said that these provisions of the act cannot be sustained as an exercise of the police power where the right to mine such coal has been reserved. The conclusion seems to rest upon the assumption that in order to justify such exercise of the police power there must be "an average reciprocity of advantage" as between the owner of the property restricted and the rest of the community; and that here such reciprocity is absent. Reciprocity of advantage is an important consideration, and may even be an essential, where the State's power is exercised for the purpose of conferring benefits upon the property of a neighborhood, as in drainage projects, or upon adjoining owners, as by party wall provisions. But where the police power is exercised, not to confer benefits upon property owners, but to protect the public from detriment and danger, there is, in my opinion, no room for considering reciprocity of advantage. There was no reciprocal advantage to the owner prohibited from using his oil tanks in 248 U.S. 498; his brickyard, in 239 U.S. 394; his livery stable, in 237 U.S. 171; his billiard hall, in 225 U.S. 623; his oleomargarine factory, in 127 U.S. 678; his brewery, in 123 U.S. 623; unless it be the advantage of living and doing business in a civilized community. That reciprocal advantage is given by the act to the coal operators.

Note

Writing to Laski, Holmes called *Pennsylvania Coal*

a question of degree, upon which people naturally differ but the lads were with me except B. If you read the document you will see that I do not, as he suggests, rely upon average reciprocity of advantage as a general ground, but only to explain a certain class of cases. [Letter of December 14, 1922, 1 Holmes-Laski Letters 462 (Howe ed. 1953).]

A month later, Holmes was still writing about the case:

I fear that I am out of accord for the moment with my public-minded friends. . . . Frankfurter generally writes to me about any important opinions of mine and he has been silent as to the one I sent you in which Brandeis dissented; probably feeling an unnecessary delicacy about saying that he disagrees. . . . I always have thought that old Harlan's decision in Mugler v. Kansas was pretty fishy. But I am not going to reargue the matter now. I was not greatly impressed by Atcheson's [sic: he meant Dean Acheson, law clerk to Brandeis during the 1919 Term] support of his former boss in the New Republic except for the admirable politeness with which he expressed his difference. He thought B's view more statesman-like — which is an effective word but needs caution in using it. . . . [Letter of January 13, 1923, 1 ibid. at 473-474.]

SAX, TAKINGS AND THE POLICE POWER, 74 YALE L.J. 36, 36-41 (1964): If the government wants to convert a private house into a post office, or run a new highway through a farm, or build a dam which will flood nearby land, it is going to have to compensate the losses sustained as a result of these activities. In such cases courts uniformly hold that property has been taken by the government, thus bringing into operation the constitutional mandate that private property may not be taken for public use without just compensation. But if government prohibits the continuance of a business which has been established for a long time, or outlaws certain businesses altogether, or prohibits the use of land for any of the purposes which give it substantial economic value it may not have to pay a penny. In cases of this type, where the government is engaged in zoning, nuisance abatement, conservation, business regulation, or a host of other functions, courts will usually decide that the economic loss suffered by the private citizen was a mere incident of the lawful exercise of the "police power,"[6] and thus not compensable.

Though all agree that compensation is required only for a governmental "taking" of property and not for losses occasioned by mere "regulation," the generality of the theory thus formulated is of little help in deciding any given case. In some specific instances it has become clear that the compensation clause of the fifth amendment predictably will or will not be held applicable. Nevertheless, the predominant characteristic of this area of law is a welter of confusing and apparently incompatible results. The principle upon which the cases can be rationalized is yet to be discovered by the bench: what commentators have called the "crazy-quilt pattern of Supreme Court doctrine" has effectively been acknowledged by the Court itself, which has developed the habit of introducing

---

6. The term "police power" has no exact definition. Berman v. Parker, 348 U.S. 26, 32 (1954). It is used by the courts to identify those state and local governmental restrictions and prohibitions which are valid and which may be invoked without payment of compensation. In its best known and most traditional uses, the police power is employed to protect the health, safety, and morals of the community in the form of such things as fire regulations [Munn v. Illinois, 94 U.S. 113, 146 (1876) (Field, J., dissenting)], garbage disposal control [Gardner v. Michigan, 199 U.S. 325 (1905)], and restrictions upon prostitution [L'Hote v. City of New Orleans, 177 U.S. 587 (1900)] and liquor [Boston Beer Co. v. Massachusetts, 97 U.S. 25 (1878)]. But it has never been thought that government authority under the police power was limited to those narrow uses. Munn v. Illinois, 94 U.S. 113 (1876) (price control). See generally Barbier v. Connolly, 113 U.S. 27, 31 (1885); Mugler v. Kansas, 123 U.S. 623, 662 (1887); Chicago & A.R.R. v. Tranbarger, 238 U.S. 67, 76-77 (1915).

Most of the federal regulation which will be discussed here arises not under a police power but under the authority to regulate interstate commerce. But a parallel conflict exists between the asserted authority to regulate without paying compensation and the demands of the fifth amendment. See e.g., United States v. Kansas City Life Ins. Co., 339 U.S. 799, 808 (1950). Where federal regulation of water is involved, the compensation question is complicated by the presence of the so-called navigation servitude. See generally Morreale, Federal Powers in Western Waters: The Navigation Power and the Rule of No Compensation, 3 Nat. Res. J. 1 (1963).

its uniformly unsatisfactory opinions in this area with the understatement that "no rigid rules" or "set formula" are available to determine where regulation ends and taking begins. . . .

[In Mugler v. Kansas, 123 U.S. 623 (1887), plaintiff was a brewery aggrieved by the state's enactment of prohibition. Justice Harlan] proposed two corollary theories. First, he said, this regulation was not in any sense a "taking" because it involved no appropriation of property for the public benefit but merely a limitation upon use by the owner for certain purposes declared to be injurious to the community. This theory Harlan apparently derived from the literal language of the fifth amendment, which deals only with the "taking" of property. . . .

The second Harlan theory looks not to the role of the government (whether proprietor or mere prohibitor) but to the quality of the property owner's activity which calls forth government action. Harlan distinguished innocent from noxious uses. Thus, the operation of a fertilizer factory in the midst of a city is a noxious use which the government can abate without having to make compensation, no matter how great the economic loss involved. The rationale is that no one can obtain a vested right to injure or endanger the public. Thus the abatement of a noxious use is not a taking of property, since uses in contravention of the public interest are not property. Conversely, if the government interferes with "unoffending property," compensation is required. . . .

What was unique and truly original about Holmes' contribution was that he saw the issue not in conceptual or formal terms, but as a manifestation of social conflict. Established economic interests were engaged in a battle for survival against the forces of social change; to Holmes it was constitutionally irrelevant whether the battle was at any given time being waged in a desirable fashion. For him it was sufficient that interests on both sides had some claims of legitimacy, and the struggle was in any event "inevitable, unless the fundamental axioms of society and even the fundamental conditions of life, are to be changed." The job of the law was, as Holmes saw it, not to fashion otherworldly conceptualisms but to assure that the battle of conflicting interests is "carried on in a fair and equal way."

In seeking a test of fairness Holmes found the Harlan approach lacking; while he never seems to have discussed or specifically rejected the proprietary interest, invasion, or noxious use tests, his own decisions rest upon entirely different grounds. Holmes saw no qualitative difference between traditional takings and traditional exercises of the police power, but only a continuum in which established property interests were asked to yield more or less to the pressures of public demands.

Fairness, as Holmes finally formulated it, required some restraint on the part of all parties. The owner of private property must concede that the "constitutional requirements of compensation when property is taken cannot be pressed to its grammatical extreme; that property rights may be taken for public purposes without pay if you do not take too much; that some play must be allowed to the joints if the machine is to work." And on the other hand those who would promote change must recognize that the "play" in the machine "must have its limits or the contract and due process clauses are gone" and "private property disappears."

The specific point on which Holmes seems to have chosen to focus the constitutional question was the extensiveness of the economic harm inflicted by the regulation. While he never flatly stated that degree of economic harm was *the* critical factor in his theory, a reading of his opinions leaves little doubt that this was indeed the theory he devised. "[T]he question narrows itself," he once said, "to the magnitude of the burden imposed. . . ." And in [Hudson County Water Co. v. McCarter, 209 U.S. 349, 355 (1908)], he said that while government may properly diminish values somewhat under the police power, if the exercise of that power makes the affected property "wholly useless, the right of property would prevail over the other public interest, and the police power would fail." When he upheld a regulation against a claim that compensation was required, it was usually upon the ground that it involved only a "comparatively insignificant taking" or "the infliction of some fractional and relatively small losses."

MICHELMAN, PROPERTY, UTILITY AND FAIRNESS: COMMENTS ON THE ETHICAL FOUNDATIONS OF "JUST COMPENSATION" LAW, 80 Harv. L. Rev. 1165, 1214-1215 (1967): A strictly utilitarian argument leading to the specific identification of "compensable" occasions would have a quasi-mathematical structure. Let us define three quantities to be known as "efficiency gains," "demoralization costs," and "settlement costs." "Efficiency gains" we define as the excess of benefits produced by a measure over losses inflicted by it, where benefits are measured by the total number of dollars which prospective gainers would be willing to pay to secure adoption, and losses are measured by the total number of dollars which prospective losers would insist on as the price of agreeing to adoption. "Demoralization costs" are defined as the total of (1) the dollar value necessary to offset disutilities which accrue to losers and their sympathizers specifically from the realization that no compensation is offered, and (2) the present capitalized dollar value of lost future production (reflecting either impaired incentives or social unrest) caused by demoralization of uncompensated losers, their sympathizers, and other observers disturbed by the thought that they themselves may be subjected to similar treatment on some other occasion. "Settlement costs" are measured by the dollar value of the time, effort, and resources which would be required in order to reach compensation settlements adequate to avoid demoralization costs. Included are the costs of settling not only the particular compensation claims presented, but also those of all persons so affected by the measure in question or similar measures as to have claims not obviously distinguishable by the available settlement apparatus.

A measure attended by positive efficiency gains is, under utilitarian ethics, *prima facie* desirable. But felicific calculation under the definition given for efficiency gains is imperfect because it takes no account of demoralization costs caused by a capricious redistribution, or alternatively, of the settlement costs necessary to avoid such demoralization costs. When pursuit of efficiency gains entails capricious redistribution, either demoralization costs or settlement costs must be incurred. It follows that if, for any measure, both demoralization costs and settlement costs (whichever were chosen) would exceed efficiency gains, the measure is to be rejected; but that otherwise, since either demoralization costs or settlement costs must be paid, it is the lower of these two costs which should be paid. The compensation rule which then clearly emerges is that compensation is to be paid whenever settlement costs are lower than both demoralization costs and efficiency gains. But if settlement costs, while lower than demoralization costs, exceed efficiency gains, then the measure is improper regardless of whether compensation is paid. The correct utilitarian statement, then, insofar as *the issue of compensability* is concerned, is that compensation is due whenever demoralization costs exceed settlement costs, and not otherwise.

Notes

1. These issues are discussed with great sophistication and imagination in B. Ackerman, Private Property and the Constitution (1977).
2. Compare the Constitution of the People's Republic of China (Foreign Languages Press, Peking 1975):

> Article 6. All mineral resources and waters as well as the forests, underdeveloped land and other resources owned by the state are the property of the whole people.
> The state may requisition by purchase, take over for use, or nationalize urban and rural land as well as other means of production under conditions prescribed by law.
> Article 8. Socialist public property shall be inviolable. The state shall ensure the consolidation and development of the socialist economy and prohibit any person from undermining the socialist economy and the public interest in any way whatsoever.

3. Compare also Constitution (Basic Law) of the Union of Soviet Socialist Republics (1936, as amended since):

Article 4. The socialist system of economy and socialist ownership of the instruments and means of production established as a result of the liquidation of the capitalist system of economy, the abolition of private ownership of the instruments and means of production, and the annihilation of the exploitation of man by man, shall constitute the economic foundation of the USSR.

Article 5. Socialist ownership in the USSR shall have either the form of state ownership (the wealth of the whole people) or the form of cooperative and collective-farm ownership (ownership on the part of individual collective farms, ownership on the part of cooperative units).

Article 6. The land, its minerals, waters, forests, mills, factories, mines, quarries, rail, water, and air transport, banks, means of communications, large state-organized agricultural enterprises (state farms, machine-tractor stations, etc.), as well as municipal enterprises and the bulk of the housing in the cities and at industrial sites, shall constitute state ownership, that is, the wealth of the whole people.

Article 7. Social enterprises in collective farms and cooperative organizations, with their livestock and implements, goods produced by collective farms and cooperative organizations, and also their common buildings, shall constitute social, socialist ownership on the part of collective farms and cooperative organizations.

Each collective-farm household, in addition to its basic income from the social collective-farm economy, shall have for personal use a small plot of household land and in personal ownership a subsidiary husbandry on the household plot, a dwelling house, livestock, poultry, and minor agricultural implements. . . .

Article 8. The land occupied by collective farms shall be secured to them for their use free of charge and for an unlimited time, that is, in perpetuity.

Article 9. Alongside the socialist system of economy, constituting the predominant form of economy in the USSR, the law shall permit the small-scale private economy of individual peasants and handicraftsmen based on personal labor and precluding the exploitation of the labor of others.

Article 10. The right of personal ownership on the part of citizens in the income and savings from their labor, in a dwelling house and subsidiary household economy, in household articles, and in articles of personal use and convenience, as well as the right to inherit [objects of] personal ownership of citizens, shall be protected by law.

4. The original Indian constitution, adopted after independence, included "private property" among the seven enumerated fundamental freedoms. State acquisition of private property was permitted only for a public purpose and with compensation. After judicial invalidation of government compensation awards, however, the Fourth Amendment in 1955 declared that the adequacy of compensation should not be liable to be questioned in court.

The Supreme Court and the government continued to spar over the proper judicial role in takings cases. At one point the constitution was amended to immunize 188 particular enactments from judicial scrutiny as infringements of private property, and also to authorize uncompensated agricultural land reform. The Supreme Court responded by holding that judicial review is an essential feature of the Indian constitution that cannot be altered even by constitutional amendment.

Finally, in 1978, the government (controlled by the Janata Party after the electorate rejected Indira Gandhi) enacted the 44th Amendment, eliminating altogether the right of property from the list of fundamental rights. The constitution now addresses private property only in article 31(1): "No person shall be deprived of his property save by authority of law."

The leading commentary on the Indian constitution makes pointed reference to the fact that the U.S.S.R.'s and the People's Republic of China's constitutions give private property greater protections than does India currently. Durga Das Basu, Introduction to the Constitution of India 112-117 (10th ed. 1983).

◆ LORETTO v. TELEPROMPTER MANHATTAN CATV CORP.
458 U.S. 419 (1982)

Justice MARSHALL delivered the opinion of the Court.

This case presents the question whether a minor but permanent physical occupation of an owner's property authorized by government constitutes a "taking" of property for which just compensation is due under the Fifth and Fourteenth Amendments of the Constitution. New York law provides that a landlord must permit a cable television company to install its cable facilities upon his property. In this case, the cable installation occupied portions of appellant's roof and the side of her building. The New York Court of Appeals ruled that this appropriation does not amount to a taking. Because we conclude that such a physical occupation of property is a taking, we reverse.

Appellant Jean Loretto purchased a five-story apartment building located at 303 West 105th Street, New York, in 1971. The previous owner had granted appellees Teleprompter Corporation, and Teleprompter Manhattan CATV ("Teleprompter") permission to install a cable on the building and the exclusive privilege of furnishing cable television ("CATV") services to the tenants. The New York Court of Appeals described the installation as follows:

On June 1, 1970 TelePrompter installed a cable slightly less than one-half inch in diameter and of approximately 30 feet in length along the length of the building about 18 inches above the roof top, and directional taps, approximately 4 inches by 4 inches by 4 inches, on the front and rear of the

roof. By June 8, 1970 the cable had been run from the directional taps to
the adjoining building at 305 West 105th Street.

Teleprompter also installed two large silver boxes along the roof cables.
The cables are attached by screws or nails penetrating the masonry at
approximately two foot intervals, and other equipment is installed by
bolts.

Initially, Teleprompter's roof cables did not service appellant's
building. They were part of what could be described as a cable "highway" circumnavigating the city block, with service cables periodically
dropped over the front or back of a building in which a tenant desired
service. Crucial to such a network is the use of so-called "crossovers" —
cable lines extending from one building to another in order to reach a
new group of tenants. Two years after appellant purchased the building,
Teleprompter connected a "noncrossover" line — i.e., one that provided CATV service to appellant's own tenants — by dropping a line to
the first floor down the front of appellant's building.

Prior to 1973, Teleprompter routinely obtained authorization for its
installations from property owners along the cable's route, compensating the owners at the standard rate of 5% of the gross revenues that
Teleprompter realized from the particular property. To facilitate tenant
access to CATV, the State of New York enacted §828 of the Executive
Law, effective January 1, 1973. Section 828 provides that a landlord may
not "interfere with the installation of cable television facilities upon his
property or premises," and may not demand payment from any tenant
for permitting CATV, or demand payment from any CATV company "in
excess of any amount which the [State Commission on Cable Television]
shall, by regulation, determine to be reasonable." The landlord may,
however, require the CATV company or the tenant to bear the cost of
installation, and to indemnify for any damage caused by the installation.
Pursuant to §828(1)(b), the State Commission has ruled that a one-time
$1 payment is the normal fee to which a landlord is entitled. The Com-
mission ruled that this nominal fee, which the Commission concluded
was equivalent to what the landlord would receive if the property were
condemned pursuant to New York's Transportation Corporations Law,
satisfied constitutional requirements "in the absence of a special showing of greater damages attributable to the taking."

The Court of Appeals determined that §828 serves the legitimate
public purpose of "rapid development of and maximum penetration by
a means of communication which has important educational and community aspects," and thus is within the State's police power. We have
no reason to question that determination. It is a separate question, however, whether an otherwise valid regulation so frustrates property rights
that compensation must be paid. . . . We conclude that a permanent

physical occupation authorized by government is a taking without regard to the public interests that it may serve. Our constitutional history
confirms the rule, recent cases do not question it, and the purposes of
the Takings Clause compel its retention. As *Penn Central* affirms, the
Court has often upheld substantial regulation of an owner's use of his
own property where deemed necessary to promote the public interest.
At the same time, we have long considered a physical intrusion by
government to be a property restriction of an unusually serious character for purposes of the Takings Clause. Our cases further establish that
when the physical intrusion reaches the extreme form of a permanent
physical occupation, a taking has occurred. In such a case, "the character of the government action" not only is an important factor in resolving whether the action works a taking but is determinative.

When faced with a constitutional challenge to a permanent physical
occupation of real property, this Court has invariably found a taking. . . .

The historical rule that a permanent physical occupation of another's property is a taking has more than tradition to commend it. Such
an appropriation is perhaps the most serious form of invasion of an
owner's property interests. To borrow a metaphor, the government
does not simply take a single "strand" from the "bundle" of property
rights: it chops through the bundle, taking a slice of every strand.

Property rights in a physical thing have been described as the rights
"to possess, use and dispose of it." . . . To the extent that the government permanently occupies physical property, it effectively destroys
each of these rights. First, the owner has no right to possess the occupied
space himself, and also has no power to exclude the occupier from
possession and use of the space. The power to exclude has traditionally
been considered one of the most treasured strands in an owner's bundle
of property rights. Second, the permanent physical occupation of property forever denies the owner any power to control the use of the
property; he not only cannot exclude others, but can make no non-
possessory use of the property. Although deprivation of the right to use
and obtain a profit from property is not, in every case, independently
sufficient to establish a taking, it is clearly relevant. Finally, even though
the owner may retain the bare legal right to dispose of the occupied
space by transfer or sale, the permanent occupation of that space by a
stranger will ordinarily empty the right of any value, since the purchaser
will also be unable to make any use of the property.

Moreover, an owner suffers a special kind of injury when a *stranger*
directly invades and occupies the owner's property. [P]roperty law has
long protected an owner's expectation that he will be relatively undisturbed at least in the possession of his property. To require, as well, that
the owner permit another to exercise complete dominion literally adds
insult to injury. Furthermore, such an occupation is qualitatively more

severe than a regulation of the *use* of property, even a regulation that imposes affirmative duties on the owner, since the owner may have no control over the timing, extent, or nature of the invasion.

The traditional rule also avoids otherwise difficult line-drawing problems. Few would disagree that if the State required landlords to permit third parties to install swimming pools on the landlords' rooftops for the convenience of the tenants, the requirement would be a taking. If the cable installation here occupied as much space, again, few would disagree that the occupation would be a taking. But constitutional protection for the rights of private property cannot be made to depend on the size of the area permanently occupied. Indeed, it is possible that in the future, additional cable installations that more significantly restrict a landlord's use of the roof of his building will be made. Section 828 requires a landlord to permit such multiple installations.

Finally, whether a permanent physical occupation has occurred presents relatively few problems of proof. The placement of a fixed structure on land or real property is an obvious fact that will rarely be subject to dispute. Once the fact of occupation is shown, of course, a court should consider the *extent* of the occupation as one relevant factor in determining the compensation due. For that reason, moreover, there is less need to consider the extent of the occupation in determining whether there is a taking in the first instance. . . .

In light of our analysis, we find no constitutional difference between a crossover and a noncrossover installation. The portions of the installation necessary for both crossovers and noncrossovers permanently appropriate appellant's property. Accordingly, each type of installation is a taking.

Appellees raise a series of objections to application of the traditional rule here. Teleprompter notes that the law applies only to buildings used as rental property, and draws the conclusion that the law is simply a permissible regulation of the use of real property. We fail to see, however, why a physical occupation of one type of property but not another type is any less a physical occupation. Insofar as Teleprompter means to suggest that this is not a permanent physical invasion, we must differ. So long as the property remains residential and a CATV company wishes to retain the installation, the landlord must permit it.

Teleprompter also asserts the related argument that the State has effectively granted a tenant the property right to have a CATV installation placed on the roof of his building, as an appurtenance to the tenant's leasehold. The short answer is that §828(1)(a) does not purport to give the *tenant* any enforceable property rights with respect to CATV installation, and the lower courts did not rest their decisions on this ground. Of course, Teleprompter, not appellant's tenants, actually owns the installation. Moreover, the government does not have unlimited power to redefine property rights.

Finally, we do not agree with appellees that application of the physical occupation rule will have dire consequences for the government's power to adjust landlord-tenant relationships. This Court has consistently affirmed that States have broad power to regulate housing conditions in general and the landlord-tenant relationship in particular without paying compensation for all economic injuries that such regulation entails. . . . In none of these cases, however, did the government authorize the permanent occupation of the landlord's property by a third party. Consequently, our holding today in no way alters the analysis governing the State's power to require landlords to comply with building codes and provide utility connections, mailboxes, smoke detectors, fire extinguishers, and the like in the common area of a building. So long as these regulations do not require the landlord to suffer the physical occupation of a portion of his building by a third party, they will be analyzed under the multi-factor inquiry generally applicable to nonpossessory governmental activity. . . .

The judgment of the New York Court of Appeals is reversed and the case is remanded for further proceedings not inconsistent with this opinion. . . .

Justice BLACKMUN, with whom Justice BRENNAN and Justice WHITE join, dissenting.

. . . The Court's recent Takings Clause decisions teach that *nonphysical* government intrusions on private property, such as zoning ordinances and other land-use restrictions, have become the rule rather than the exception. Modern government regulation exudes intangible "externalities" that may diminish the value of private property far more than minor physical touchings. Nevertheless, as the Court recognizes, it has "often upheld substantial regulation of an owner's use of his own property where deemed necessary to promote the public interest."

Precisely because the extent to which the government may injure private interests now depends so little on whether or not it has authorized a "physical contact," the Court has avoided per se takings rules resting on outmoded distinctions between physical and nonphysical intrusions. As one commentator has observed, a takings rule based on such a distinction is inherently suspect because "its capacity to distinguish, even crudely, between significant and insignificant losses is too puny to be taken seriously." Michelman, Property, Utility, and Fairness: Comments on the Ethical Foundations of "Just Compensation" Law, 80 Harv. L. Rev. 1165, 1227 (1967).

Surprisingly, the Court draws an even finer distinction today — between "temporary physical invasions" and "permanent physical occupations." When the government authorizes the latter type of intrusion, the Court would find "a taking without regard to the public interests" the regulation may serve. Yet an examination of each of the three words in the Court's "permanent physical occupation" formula illustrates that the newly-created distinction is even less substantial than the distinction between physical and nonphysical intrusions that the Court already has rejected.

First, what does the Court mean by "permanent"? Since all "temporary limitations on the right to exclude" remain "subject to a more complex balancing process to determine whether they are a taking," . . . the Court presumably describes a government intrusion that lasts forever. But as the Court itself concedes, §828 does not require appellant to permit the cable installation forever, but only "[s]o long as the property remains residential and a CATV company wishes to retain the installation." This is far from "permanent."

The Court reaffirms that "States have broad power to regulate housing conditions in general and the landlord-tenant relationship in particular without paying compensation for all economic injuries that such regulation entails." Thus, §828 merely defines one of the many statutory responsibilities that a New Yorker accepts when she enters the rental business. If appellant occupies her own building, or converts it into a commercial property, she becomes perfectly free to exclude Teleprompter from her one-eighth cubic foot of roof space. But once appellant chooses to use her property for rental purposes, she must comply with all reasonable government statutes regulating the landlord-tenant relationship. If §828 authorizes a "permanent" occupation, and thus works a taking "without regard to the public interests that it may serve," then all other New York statutes that require a landlord to make physical attachments to his rental property also must constitute takings, even if they serve indisputably valid public interests in tenant protection and safety.

The Court denies that its theory invalidates these statutes, because they "do not require the landlord to suffer the physical occupation of a portion of his building by a third party." But surely this factor cannot be determinative, since the Court simultaneously recognizes that temporary invasions by third parties are not subject to a per se rule. Nor can the qualitative difference arise from the incidental fact that, under §828, Teleprompter, rather than appellant or her tenants, owns the cable installation. If anything, §828 leaves appellant better off than do other housing statutes, since it ensures that her property will not be damaged aesthetically or physically, without burdening her with the cost of buying or maintaining the cable. . . .

Third, the Court's talismanic distinction between a continuous "occupation" and a transient "invasion" finds no basis in either economic logic or Takings Clause precedent. In the landlord-tenant context, the Court has upheld against takings challenges rent control statutes permitting "temporary" physical invasions of considerable economic magnitude. See, e.g., Block v. Hirsh, 256 U.S. 135 (1921). . . .

In sum, history teaches that takings claims are properly evaluated under a multifactor balancing test. By directing that all "permanent physical occupations" automatically are compensable, "without regard to whether the action achieves an important public benefit or has only minimal economic impact on the owner," the Court does not further equity so much as it encourages litigants to manipulate their factual allegations to gain the benefit of its *per se* rule. I do not relish the prospect of distinguishing the inevitable flow of *certiorari* petitions attempting to shoehorn insubstantial takings claims into today's "set formula." . . .

In the end, what troubles me most about today's decision is that it represents an archaic judicial response to a modern social problem. Cable television is a new and growing, but somewhat controversial, communications medium. The New York Legislature not only recognized, but responded to, this technological advance by enacting a statute that sought carefully to balance the interests of all private parties. New York's courts in this litigation, with only one jurist in dissent, unanimously upheld the constitutionality of that considered legislative judgment.

This Court now reaches back in time for a per se rule that disrupts that legislative determination. Like Justice Black, I believe that "the solution of the problems precipitated by . . . technological advances and new ways of living cannot come about through the application of rigid constitutional restraints formulated and enforced by the courts." I would affirm the judgment and uphold the reasoning of the New York Court of Appeals.

Note

On remand, the New York Court of Appeals upheld the statutory scheme that empowered the Cable Television Commission to set $1 as the proper compensation for the "taking" that the U.S. Supreme Court said had occurred. Loretto v. TelePrompter Manhattan CATV Corp., 58 N.Y.2d 143, 446 N.E.2d 428, 439 N.Y.S.2d 743 (1983).

The commission then determined that $1 was adequate because cable wiring would usually increase the value of the building. N.Y. Times, May 9, 1983.

◆ DEPARTMENT FOR NATURAL RESOURCES & ENVIRONMENTAL PROTECTION v. NO. 8 LIMITED OF VIRGINIA
528 S.W.2d 684 (Ky. 1975)

LUKOWSKY, Justice. This is an appeal from a judgment of the Franklin Circuit Court which declared KRS 350.060(8) to be unconstitutional and granted appropriate ancillary injunctive relief. We affirm.

The declared purpose of Chapter 350 of the Kentucky Revised Statutes is to provide such regulation and control of the strip mining of coal as to minimize or prevent its injurious effects on the people and resources of the commonwealth. KRS 350.020.

The apposite portions of KRS 350.060 are as follows:

(1) No operator shall engage in strip mining without having first obtained from the department a permit. . . .

(8) Each application shall also be accompanied by a statement of consent to have strip mining conducted upon the area of land described in the application for a permit. The statement of consent shall be signed by each holder of a freehold interest in such land. Each signature shall be notarized. No permit shall be issued if the application therefor is not accompanied by the statement of consent. . . .

The source of subsection 8 is section 2 of Chapter 373 of the 1974 Acts of the General Assembly. Section 1 of that chapter, which is not codified in the Kentucky Revised Statutes, is as follows:

It is the intent of the General Assembly in this Act to declare that the notarized statement of consent required by Section 2 of this Act is a perfectly legitimate, right, and proper requirement to protect the public safety and welfare as it pertains to the broad form deed. It is also the intent of the General Assembly that this Act does not affect any other form of contract in any manner, nor affect underground mining in any manner.

It is immediately apparent that subsection 8 does not apply to situations in which the owner of the mineral rights also owns the surface rights to the land or in which the owner of the mineral rights was granted specific authority to conduct strip mining in the deed which conveyed the mineral rights to him. It is an obvious retrospective diminution of rights granted by a specific form of contract bare of any attempt to control the noxious aspects of the strip mining operation. It is equally apparent that subsection 8 does not involve the construction and validity of broad form deeds.

[T]he Constitution of the United States and the Constitution of the Commonwealth of Kentucky provide that the legislature may not impair the obligations of a contract and that private property may not be taken for a public use without just compensation. However, government could hardly go on if, to some extent, values incident to property could not be diminished without paying for every such change in the general law. As long recognized, some values are enjoyed under an implied limitation, and must yield to the police power. But obviously the implied limitation must have its limits or the contract and due process clauses are emasculated.

The limits are that the police power may be used so as to invade private rights only if the legislation bears a real and substantial relation to the public health, safety, morality or some other phase of the general welfare.

This dissection exposes the "gut issue" here. May subsection 8 be justified as a legitimate exercise of the police power?

In order to be justified it must stand as an environmental conservation measure. It may well be that the General Assembly, in the exercise of its legislative wisdom, might strike a balance between the "energy crunch" and the necessity to conserve the environment which, for example, would prohibit strip mining entirely, prohibit strip mining which would remove tillable soil from production, limit strip mining to areas which have less than a given percentage of grade, require extensive restoration and reforestation of land to be stripped, limit the activity in areas where the watershed and wildlife might be adversely affected and even protect aesthetic beauty.

But that is not this case. Here the legislation is ineffective as an environmental conservation measure. It does no more than delegate to an individual, a privy of a party to the contract which severed the mineral, a veto over the use of land by the other party to the contract. It puts the surface owner in a position to be paid again for what he or his predecessor in title has already received compensation.

In Martin v. Kentucky Oak Mining Co., 429 S.W.2d 395, 397 (1968), we demonstrated that the consent of the surface owner bears no rational relationship to environmental conservation.

> The court is fully aware of the great public concern with the conservation problems attendant upon strip and auger mining, and the urgent necessity to protect the soil and the water courses from destruction and pollution. However, counsel for the landowners, and for those amicus curiae who side with them in arguing that the broad form deed does not permit strip or auger mining, frankly concede that a decision of this court upholding their contention as to the construction of the deed will not stop strip or auger mining. They admit that in Pennsylvania and West Virginia, where the courts have held that the broad form deed does not authorize strip or auger mining, that type of mining is even more prevalent than in eastern Kentucky. And of course it is common knowledge that strip mining has been done on a large scale in western Kentucky where the broad form deed was not commonly used.

Subsection 8 delegates to countless private individuals who own interests in surface estates from which the mineral has been severed the right to undo whatever environmental conservation purpose the legislation may have by granting their consent, for a consideration, to surface mining on their land. It is beyond cavil that the primary purpose and effect of subsection 8 is to change the relative legal rights and economic bargaining positions of many private parties under their contracts rather than achieve any public purpose. It is, therefore, axiomatic that subsection 8 is unconstitutional.

The judgment is affirmed.

All concur.

Notes

1. The Surface Mining Control and Regulation Act of 1977, 30 U.S.C. §§1201-1328 (Supp. 1983), requires strip miners to reclaim mined areas and return them to their "approximate original contours." A group of Virginia miners, seeking declaratory and injunctive relief, challenged this requirement on a number of grounds. The federal district court held that the statute violated the Tenth Amendment to the U.S. Constitution, as unjustified federal interference with the state's traditional control of land use. Virginia had argued that the federal controls requiring that the land be returned to its "approximate original contours" were not in the state's best interests. Rather, Virginia said, strip mining can be economically desirable because it levels the land, increasing its value for "schools, airports, industries, recreational areas, shopping centers, and agriculture." The state asserted that some land is worth $5 to $75 per acre before stripping and "a minimum of $5,000 and . . . as much as $300,000 an acre" afterwards. The federal law that Virginia opposed requires return of the land to the lower value.

The district court also held that the reclamation requirement effected an unconstitutional taking without just compensation. The court argued that the effect of imposing the environmental restrictions was for land values to be "diminished to practically nothing." In addition, the act's prohibition against mining in certain locations would "clearly prevent a person from mining his own land or having it mined," thus depriving the owner of "any use of [his] land, not only the most profitable."

On a direct appeal, the Supreme Court reversed and upheld the act. The Court rejected the tenth amendment argument, finding adequate federal authority for regulation of environmental consequences of strip mining. The Court concluded that the taking issue was not ripe for judicial review, holding that "mere enactment" of a statute does not constitute a taking since it does not deprive an owner of "economically viable use of [the] property." However, the Court left open the possibility of a future attempt to show that "as applied to particular parcels of land, the Act and the Secretary's regulations effect a taking." Hodel v. Virginia Surface Mining & Reclamation Association, 452 U.S. 264 (1981).

2. The same statute, 30 U.S.C. §1304 (Supp. 1983), tells the secretary of the interior not to lease Federal coal deposits "until the surface owner has given written consent to enter and commence surface mining

operations. . . ." See also id. §1304(f): "This section shall not apply to Indian lands."

3. San Diego Gas & Electric Co. bought land in San Diego as a possible site for a nuclear power plant. The city rezoned the land, reducing the industrial acreage and assigning some of the land to an open space zone. The city also sought to purchase some of the property for a park, but the voters turned down the necessary bond issue. The company said it had been the victim of "inverse condemnation": that the city, by regulation, had effected an uncompensated transfer of the land to public use. The California courts appeared to hold that the only remedy for a landowner making such a claim is *mandamus* or declaratory relief, invalidating the offending regulatory action. Thus, the landowner could not get money damages even if he established that the regulation exceeded police power limits. The U.S. Supreme Court dismissed the company's appeal, concluding that no final California judgment was before it. But four justices said, and at least one other seemed ready to say, that if a constitutionally invalid regulation is in force for a period of time, the landowner has a right to money damages for his lost value. See San Diego Gas & Electric Co. v. City of San Diego, 450 U.S. 621 (1981).

Lower courts have been taking their cue from the dissenting opinion of Justice Brennan in *San Diego Gas*, which was joined by three other justices and with which Justice Rehnquist expressed sympathy. For example, in Hernandez v. City of Lafayette, 643 F.2d 1188 (5th Cir. 1981), the court held that a municipality is not entitled to absolute immunity from liability in damages under 42 U.S.C. §1983 for actions taken by it in its legislative capacity. In support of this holding, the court cited the reasoning of Justice Brennan's *San Diego Gas* dissent and stated that

> . . . an action will lie under §1983 in favor of any person whose property is taken for public use without just compensation by a municipality through a zoning regulation that denies the owner any economically viable use thereof. The measure of damages in such a case will be an amount equal to just compensation for the value of the property during the period of the taking

In Burrows v. City of Keene, 121 N.H. 590, 432 A.2d 15 (1981), the Supreme Court of New Hampshire "agree[d] with Justice Brennan" that damages can be collected for an inverse condemnation and held that the city's amendment of its zoning ordinance, which had the effect of including in a conservation district a substantial parcel of land that the plaintiff had planned to subdivide, constituted inverse condemnation entitling plaintiff to damages. The court rejected "out of hand" the approach of "cases such as Agins v. Tiburon, 24 Cal. 3d 266, 598 P.2d 25, 157 Cal. Rptr. 373 (1979), *aff'd on other grounds*, 447 U.S. 255 (1980) [see p.1098 *supra*] which hold that a landowner . . . may not recover damages for inverse condemnation. . . ."

Other courts have also accepted Justice Brennan's dissenting opinion as the view of a majority of the justices. See Pratt v. State Department of Natural Resources, 309 N.W.2d 767 (Minn. 1981); Ripley v. City of Lincoln, 330 N.W.2d 505 (N.D. 1983); Martino v. Santa Clara Valley Water District, 703 F.2d 1141 (9th Cir. 1983), *cert. denied*, 104 S. Ct. 151 (1983).

2. *Private Property, Public Access*

◆ LLOYD CORP. v. TANNER
407 U.S. 551 (1972)

Mr. Justice POWELL delivered the opinion of the Court. This case presents the question reserved by the Court in Amalgamated Food Employees Union Local 590 v. Logan Valley Plaza, Inc., 391 U.S. 308 (1968), as to the right of a privately owned shopping center to prohibit the distribution of handbills on its property when the handbilling is unrelated to the shopping center's operations. . . .

Lloyd Corp., Ltd. owns a large, modern retail shopping center in Portland, Oregon. Lloyd Center embraces altogether about 50 acres, including some 20 acres of open and covered parking facilities which accommodate more than 1,000 automobiles. It has a perimeter of almost one and one-half miles, bounded by four public streets. It is crossed in varying degrees by several other public streets, all of which have adjacent public sidewalks. Lloyd owns all land and buildings within the Center, except these public streets and sidewalks. There are some 60 commercial tenants, including small shops and several major department stores.

The Center embodies a relatively new concept in shopping center design. The stores are all located within a single large, multi-level building complex sometimes referred to as the "Mall." Within this complex, in addition to the stores, there are parking facilities, malls, private sidewalks, stairways, escalators, gardens, an auditorium, and a skating rink. Some of the stores open directly on the outside public sidewalks, but most open on the interior privately owned malls. Some stores open on both. There are no public streets or public sidewalks within the building complex, which is enclosed and entirely covered except for the landscaped portions of some of the interior malls.

The distribution of the handbills occurred in the malls. They are a distinctive feature of the Center, serving both utilitarian and esthetic functions. Essentially, they are private, interior promenades with 10-foot sidewalks serving the stores, and with a center strip 30 feet wide in which flowers and shrubs are planted, and statuary, fountains, benches, and other amenities are located. There is no vehicular traffic on the malls. An architectural expert described the purpose of the malls as follows:

> In order to make shopping easy and pleasant, and to help realize the goal of maximum sales [for the Center], the shops are grouped about special pedestrian ways or malls. Here the shopper is isolated from the noise, fumes, confusion and distraction which he normally finds along city streets, and a controlled, carefree environment is provided. . . .

Although the stores close at customary hours, the malls are not physically closed, as pedestrian window shopping is encouraged within reasonable hours. Lloyd employs 12 security guards, who are commissioned as such by the city of Portland. The guards have police authority within the Center, wear uniforms similar to those worn by city police, and are licensed to carry handguns. They are employed by and subject to the control of Lloyd. Their duties are the customary ones, including shoplifting surveillance and general security.

At a few places within the Center small signs are embedded in the sidewalk which state:

"NOTICE — Areas in Lloyd Center Used By The Public Are Not Public Ways But Are For The Use Of Lloyd Center Tenants And The Public Transacting Business With Them. Permission To Use Said Areas May Be Revoked At Any Time. Lloyd Corporation, Ltd."

The Center is open generally to the public, with a considerable effort being made to attract shoppers and prospective shoppers, and to create "customer motivation" as well as customer goodwill in the community. In this respect the Center pursues policies comparable to those of major stores and shopping centers across the country, although the Center affords superior facilities for these purposes. Groups and organizations are permitted, by invitation and advance arrangement, to use the auditorium and other facilities. Rent is charged for use of the auditorium except with respect to certain civic and charitable organizations, such as the Cancer Society and Boy and Girl Scouts. The Center also allows limited use of the malls by the American Legion to sell poppies for disabled veterans, and by the Salvation Army and Volunteers of America to solicit Christmas contributions. It has denied similar use to other civic and charitable organizations. Political use is also forbidden, except that presidential candidates of both parties have been allowed to speak in the auditorium.

The Center had been in operation for some eight years when this litigation commenced. Throughout this period it had a policy, strictly enforced, against the distribution of handbills within the building complex and its malls. No exceptions were made with respect to handbilling, which was considered likely to annoy customers, to create litter, potentially to create disorders, and generally to be incompatible with the purpose of the Center and the atmosphere sought to be preserved.

On November 14, 1968, the respondents in this case distributed within the Center handbill invitations to a meeting of the "Resistance Community" to protest the draft and the Vietnam war. The distribution, made in several different places on the mall walkways by five young people, was quiet and orderly, and there was no littering. There was a complaint from one customer. Security guards informed the respondents that they were trespassing and would be arrested unless they stopped distributing the handbills within the Center. The guards suggested that respondents distribute their literature on the public streets and sidewalks adjacent to but outside of the Center complex. Respondents left the premises as requested "to avoid arrest" and continued the handbilling outside. Subsequently this suit was instituted in the District Court seeking declaratory and injunctive relief.

The District Court, emphasizing that the Center "is open to the general public," found that it is "the functional equivalent of a public business district." That court then held that Lloyd's "rule prohibiting the distribution of handbills within the Mall violates . . . First Amendment rights." In a per curiam opinion, the Court of Appeals held that it was bound by the "factual determination" as to the character of the Center, and concluded that the decisions of this Court in Marsh v. Alabama, 326 U.S. 501 (1946), and Amalgamated Food Employees Union v. Logan Valley Plaza, 391 U.S. 308 (1968), compelled affirmance. . . .

The courts below considered the critical inquiry to be whether Lloyd Center was "the functional equivalent of a public business district." This phrase was first used in *Logan Valley*, but its genesis was in *Marsh*. It is well to consider what *Marsh* actually decided. As noted above, it involved an economic anomaly of the past, "the company town." One must have seen such towns to understand that "functionally" they were no different from municipalities of comparable size. They developed primarily in the Deep South to meet economic conditions, especially those which existed following the Civil War. Impoverished States, and especially backward areas thereof, needed an influx of industry and capital. Corporations attracted to the area by natural resources and abundant labor were willing to assume the role of local government. Quite literally, towns were built and operated by private capital with all of the customary services and utilities normally afforded by a municipal or state government: there were streets, sidewalks, sewers, public lighting, police and fire protection, business and residential areas, churches, postal facilities, and sometimes schools. In short, as Mr. Justice Black said, Chickasaw, Alabama, had "all the characteristics of any other American town." The Court simply held that where private interests were substituting for and performing the customary functions of government, First Amendment freedoms could not be denied where exercised in the customary manner on the town's sidewalks and streets. Indeed, as title to the entire town was held privately, there were no publicly owned streets, sidewalks, or parks where such rights could be exercised.

Logan Valley extended *Marsh* to a shopping center situation in a different context from the company town setting, but it did so only in a context where the First Amendment activity was related to the shopping center's operations. There is some language in *Logan Valley*, unnecessary to the decision, suggesting that the key focus of *Marsh* was upon the "business district," and that whenever a privately owned business district serves the public generally its sidewalks and streets become the functional equivalents of similar public facilities. . . .

The holding in *Logan Valley* was not dependent upon the suggestion that the privately owned streets and sidewalks of a business district or a shopping center are the equivalent, for First Amendment purposes, of municipally owned streets and sidewalks. No such expansive reading of the opinion of the Court is necessary or appropriate. The opinion was carefully phrased to limit its holding to the picketing involved, where the picketing was "directly related in its purpose to the use to which the shopping center property was being put," and where the store was located in the center of a large private enclave with the consequence that no other reasonable opportunities for the pickets to convey their message to their intended audience were available.

Neither of these elements is present in the case now before the Court.

The handbilling by respondents in the malls of Lloyd Center had no relation to any purpose for which the center was built and being used. It is nevertheless argued by respondents that, since the Center is open to the public, the private owner cannot enforce a restriction against handbilling on the premises. The thrust of this argument is considerably broader than the rationale of *Logan Valley*. It requires no relationship, direct or indirect, between the purpose of the expressive activity and the business of the shopping center. The message sought to be conveyed by respondents was directed to all members of the public, not solely to patrons of Lloyd Center or of any of its operations. Respondents could have distributed these handbills on any public street, on any public sidewalk, in any public park, or in any public building in the city of Portland.

Respondents' argument, even if otherwise meritorious, misapprehends the scope of the invitation extended to the public. The invitation is to come to the Center to do business with the tenants. It is true that facilities at the Center are used for certain meetings and for various promotional activities. The obvious purpose, recognized widely as legitimate and responsible business activity, is to bring potential shoppers to the Center, to create a favorable impression, and to generate goodwill. There is no open-ended invitation to the public to use the Center for any and all purposes, however incompatible with the interests of both the stores and the shoppers whom they serve. . . .

It is noteworthy that respondents' argument based on the Center's being "open to the public" would apply in varying degrees to most retail stores and service establishments across the country. They are all open to the public in the sense that customers and potential customers are invited and encouraged to enter. In terms of being open to the public, there are differences only of degree — not of principle — between a free-standing store and one located in a shopping center, between a small store and a large one, between a single store with some malls and open areas designed to attract customers and Lloyd Center with its elaborate malls and interior landscaping. . . .

The basic issue in this case is whether respondents, in the exercise of asserted First Amendment rights, may distribute handbills on Lloyd's private property contrary to its wishes and contrary to a policy enforced against *all* handbilling. In addressing this issue, it must be remembered that the First and Fourteenth Amendments safeguard the rights of free speech and assembly by limitations on *state* action, not on action by the owner of private property used nondiscriminatorily for private purposes only. The Due Process Clauses of the Fifth and Fourteenth Amendments are also relevant to this case. They provide that "[n]o person shall . . . be deprived of life, liberty, or property, without due process of law." There is the further proscription in the Fifth Amendment against the taking of "private property . . . for public use, without just compensation."

Although accommodations between the values protected by these three Amendments are sometimes necessary, and the courts properly have shown a special solicitude for the guarantees of the First Amendment, this Court has never held that a trespasser or an uninvited guest may exercise general rights of free speech on property privately owned and used nondiscriminatorily for private purposes only. Even where public property is involved, the Court has recognized that it is not necessarily available for speaking, picketing, or other communicative activities. . . .

Respondents contend, however, that the property of a large shopping center is "open to the public," serves the same purposes as a "business district" of a municipality, and therefore has been dedicated to certain types of public use. The argument is that such a center has sidewalks, streets, and parking areas which are functionally similar to facilities customarily provided by municipalities. It is then asserted that all members of the public, whether invited as customers or not, have the same right of free speech as they would have on the similar public facilities in the streets of a city or town.

The argument reaches too far. The Constitution by no means requires such an attenuated doctrine of dedication of private property to public use. The closest decision in theory, Marsh v. Alabama, involved the assumption by a private enterprise of all of the attributes of a state-created municipality and the exercise by that enterprise of semi-official municipal functions as a delegate of the State. In effect, the owner of the company town was performing the full spectrum of municipal powers and stood in the shoes of the State. In the instant case there is no comparable assumption or exercise of municipal functions or power.

Nor does property lose its private character merely because the public is generally invited to use it for designated purposes. Few would argue that a free-standing store, with abutting parking space for customers, assumes significant public attributes merely because the public is invited to shop there. Nor is size alone the controlling factor. The essential private character of a store and its privately owned abutting property does not change by virtue of being large or clustered with other stores in a modern shopping center. This is not to say that no differences may exist with respect to government regulation or rights of citizens arising by virtue of the size and diversity of activities carried on within a privately owned facility serving the public. There will be, for example, problems with respect to public health and safety which vary in degree and in the appropriate government response, depending upon the size and character of a shopping center, an office building, a sports arena, or other large facility serving the public for commercial purposes. We do say that the Fifth and Fourteenth Amendment rights of private property owners, as well as the First Amendment rights of all citizens, must be respected and protected. The Framers of the Constitution certainly did not think these fundamental rights of a free society are incompatible with each other. There may be situations where accommodations between them, and the drawing of lines to assure due protection of both, are not easy. But on the facts presented in this case, the answer is clear.

We hold that there has been no such dedication of Lloyd's privately owned and operated shopping center to public use as to entitle respondents to exercise therein the asserted First Amendment rights. Accordingly, we reverse the judgment and remand the case to the Court of Appeals with directions to vacate the injunction.

Judgment reversed and case remanded.

[Justice Marshall dissented in an opinion joined by Justices Douglas, Brennan, and Stewart.]

◆ PRUNEYARD SHOPPING CENTER v. ROBBINS
447 U.S. 74 (1980)

Mr. Justice REHNQUIST delivered the opinion of the Court.

. . . Appellant PruneYard is a privately owned shopping center in the city of Campbell, Cal. It covers approximately 21 acres — 5 devoted to parking and 16 occupied by walkways, plazas, sidewalks, and buildings that contain more than 65 specialty shops, 10 restaurants, and a movie theater. The PruneYard is open to the public for the purpose of encouraging the patronizing of its commercial establishments. It has a policy not to permit any visitor or tenant to engage in any publicly expressive activity, including the circulation of petitions, that is not directly related to its commercial purposes. This policy has been strictly enforced in a nondiscriminatory fashion. The PruneYard is owned by appellant Fred Sahadi.

Appelles are high school students who sought to solicit support for their opposition to a United Nations resolution against "Zionism." On a Saturday afternoon they set up a card table in a corner of PruneYard's central courtyard. They distributed pamphlets and asked passersby to sign petitions, which were to be sent to the President and Members of Congress. Their activity was peaceful and orderly and so far as the record indicates was not objected to by PruneYard's patrons.

Soon after appellees had begun soliciting signatures, a security guard informed them that they would have to leave because their activity violated PruneYard regulations. The guard suggested that they move to the public sidewalk at the PruneYard's perimeter. Appellees immediately left the premises and later filed this lawsuit in the California Superior Court of Santa Clara County. They sought to enjoin appellants from denying them access to the PruneYard for the purpose of circulating their petitions.

The Superior Court held that appellees were not entitled under either the Federal or California Constitution to exercise their asserted rights on the shopping center property. . . . It concluded that there were "adequate, effective channels of communication for [appellees] other than soliciting on the private property of the [PruneYard]." The California Court of Appeal affirmed.

The California Supreme Court reversed, holding that the California Constitution protects "speech and petitioning, reasonably exercised, in shopping centers even when the centers are privately owned." It concluded that appellees were entitled to conduct their activity on Prune-Yard property. . . .

. . . Before this Court, appellants contend that their constitutionally established rights under the Fourteenth Amendment to exclude appellees from adverse use of appellants' private property cannot be denied by invocation of a state constitutional provision or by judicial reconstruction of a State's laws of private property. . . .

We now affirm. . . .

Appellants first contend that Lloyd Corp. v. Tanner, 407 U.S. 551 (1972), prevents the State from requiring a private shopping center owner to provide access to persons exercising their state constitutional rights of free speech and petition when adequate alternative avenues of communication are available. . . . We stated that property does not "lose its private character merely because the public is generally invited to use it for designated purposes," and that "[t]he essential private character of a store and its privately owned abutting property does not change by virtue of being large or clustered with other stores in a modern shopping center."

Our reasoning in *Lloyd*, however, does not *ex proprio vigore* limit the authority of the State to exercise its police power or its sovereign right to adopt in its own Constitution individual liberties more expansive than those conferred by the Federal Constitution. . . . In *Lloyd*, there was no state constitutional or statutory provision that had been construed to create rights to the use of private property by strangers, comparable to those found to exist by the California Supreme Court here. It is, of course, well established that a State in the exercise of its police power may adopt reasonable restrictions on private property so long as the restrictions do not amount to a taking without just compensation or contravene any other federal constitutional provision. *Lloyd* held that when a shopping center owner opens his private property to the public for the purpose of shopping, the First Amendment to the United States Constitution does not thereby create individual rights in expression beyond those already existing under applicable law.

Appellants next contend that a right to exclude others underlies the Fifth Amendment guarantee against the taking of property without just compensation and the Fourteenth Amendment guarantee against the deprivation of property without due process of law.

It is true that one of the essential sticks in the bundle of property rights is the right to exclude others. And here there has literally been a "taking" of that right to the extent that the California Supreme Court has interpreted the State Constitution to entitle its citizens to exercise free expression and petition rights on shopping center property. But it is well established that "not every destruction or injury to property by governmental action has been held to be a 'taking' in the constitutional sense." Rather, the determination whether a state law unlawfully infringes a landowner's property in violation of the Taking Clause requires an examination of whether the restriction on private property "forc[es] some people alone to bear public burdens which, in all fairness and justice, should be borne by the public as a whole." This examination entails inquiry into such factors as the character of the governmental action, its economic impact, and its interference with reasonable investment-backed expectations. When "regulation goes too far it will be recognized as a taking."

Here the requirement that appellants permit appellees to exercise state-protected rights of free expression and petition on shopping center property clearly does not amount to an unconstitutional infringement of appellants' property rights under the Taking Clause. There is nothing to suggest that preventing appellants from prohibiting this sort of activity will unreasonably impair the value or use of their property as a shopping center. The PruneYard is a large commercial complex that covers several city blocks, contains numerous separate business establishments, and is open to the public at large. The decision of the California Supreme Court makes it clear that the PruneYard may restrict expressive activity by adopting time, place, and manner regulations that will minimize any interference with its commercial functions. Appellees were orderly, and they limited their activity to the common areas of the shopping center. In these circumstances, the fact that they may have "physically invaded" appellants' property cannot be viewed as determinative.

This case is quite different from Kaiser Aetna v. United States. *Kaiser Aetna* was a case in which the owners of a private pond had invested substantial amounts of money in dredging the pond, developing it into an exclusive marina, and building a surrounding marina community. . . .

The Government's attempt to create a public right of access to the improved pond interfered with Kaiser Aetna's "reasonable investment backed expectations." We held that it went "so far beyond ordinary regulation or improvement for navigation as to amount to a taking. . . ." Nor as a general proposition is the United States, as opposed to the several States, possessed of residual authority that enables it to define "property" in the first instance. A State is, of course, bound by the Just Compensation Clause of the Fifth Amendment, but here appellants have failed to demonstrate that the "right to exclude others" is so essential to the use or economic value of their property that the state-authorized limitation of it amounted to a "taking."

We concude that neither appellants' federally recognized property rights nor their First Amendment rights have been infringed by the California Supreme Court's decision recognizing a right of appellees to exercise state-protected rights of expression and petition on appellants' property. The judgment of the Supreme Court of California is therefore affirmed.

Mr. Justice BLACKMUN joins the opinion of the Court except that sentence thereof which reads: "Nor as a general proposition is the United States, as opposed to the several States, possessed of residual authority that enables it to define 'property' in the first instance."

Notes

1. In State v. Shack, 58 N.J. 297, 277 A.2d 369 (1971), a fieldworker for the Southwest Citizens Organization for Poverty Elimination and a

staff attorney of Camden Regional Legal Services had been convicted of trespassing for an attempt to visit migrant farm workers housed at a camp on complainant's farm. Reversing their convictions, the court held that under New Jersey law, "the ownership of real property does not include the right to bar access to governmental services available to migrant workers and hence there was no trespass within the meaning of the penal statute."

The court rejected the idea of

> trying to decide upon a conventional category and then forcing the present subject into it. That approach would be artificial and distorting. The quest is for a fair adjustment of the competing needs of the parties, in the light of the realities of the relationship between the migrant worker and the operator of the housing facility.

The court also quoted from 5 Powell, Real Property §746 (Rohan ed. 1970):

> As one looks back along the historic road traversed by the law of land in England and in America, one sees a change from the viewpoint that he who owns may do as he pleases with what he owns, to a position which hesitatingly embodies an ingredient of stewardship; which grudgingly, but steadily, broadens the recognized scope of social interests in the utilization of things. . . .
>
> To one seeing history through the glasses of religion, these changes may seem to evidence increasing embodiments of the golden rule. To one thinking in terms of political and economic ideologies, they are likely to be labeled evidences of "social enlightenment," or of "creeping socialism" or even of "communistic infiltration," according to the individual's assumed definitions and retained or acquired prejudices. With slight attention to words or labels, time marches on toward new adjustments between individualism and the social interests.

2. California's Labor Relations Board adopted a regulation requiring farm owners to permit union organizers to go onto the farm to speak with workers. The California Supreme Court said this was not an unconstitutional taking of the owner's property. Agricultural Labor Relations Board v. Superior Court, 16 Cal. 3d 392, 546 P.2d 687, 128 Cal. Rptr. 183, *app. dismissed sub nom.* Pandol v. Agricultural Labor Relations Board, 429 U.S. 802 (1976).

3. Cape Cod Nursing Home Council v. Rambling Rose Rest Home, 667 F.2d 238 (1st Cir. 1981), refused to extend the company town and shopping center analogies to permit organizations to enter nursing homes in order to inform residents of the services the organizations provide.

3.   *Public Use*

♦ BERMAN v. PARKER
348 U.S. 26 (1954)

Mr. Justice DOUGLAS delivered the opinion of the Court.

This is an appeal from the judgment of a three-judge District Court which dismissed a complaint seeking to enjoin the condemnation of appellants' property under the District of Columbia Redevelopment Act of 1945, 60 Stat. 790, D.C. Code 1951, §§5-701 to 5-719. The challenge was to the constitutionality of the Act, particularly as applied to the taking of appellants' property. The District Court sustained the constitutionality of the Act. . . .

By §2 of the Act, Congress made a "legislative determination" that

> owing to technological and sociological changes, obsolete lay-out, and other factors, conditions existing in the District of Columbia with respect to substandard housing and blighted areas, including the use of buildings in alleys as dwellings for human habitation, are injuries to the public health, safety, morals, and welfare, and it is hereby declared to be the policy of the United States to protect and promote the welfare of the inhabitants of the seat of the Government by eliminating all such injurious conditions by employing all means necessary and appropriate for the purpose.

Section 2 goes on to declare that acquisition of property is necessary to eliminate these housing conditions.

Congress further finds in §2 that these ends cannot be attained "by the ordinary operations of private enterprise alone without public participation"; that "the sound replanning and redevelopment of an obsolescent or obsolescing portion" of the District "cannot be accomplished unless it be done in the light of comprehensive and coordinated planning of the whole of the territory of the District of Columbia and its environs"; and that "the acquisition and the assembly of real property and the leasing or sale thereof for redevelopment pursuant to a project area redevelopment plan . . . is hereby declared to be a public use."

Section 4 creates the District of Columbia Redevelopment Land Agency (hereinafter called the Agency), composed of five members, which is granted power by §5(a) to acquire and assemble, by eminent domain and otherwise, real property for "the redevelopment of blighted territory in the District of Columbia and the prevention, reduction, or elimination of blighting factors or causes of blight."

Section 6(a) of the Act directs the National Capital Planning Commission (hereinafter called the Planning Commission) to make and develop "a comprehensive or general plan" of the District, including "a land-use plan" which designates land for use for "housing, business, industry, recreation, education, public buildings, public reservations, and other general categories of public and private uses of the land." Section 6(b) authorizes the Planning Commission to adopt redevelopment plans for specific project areas. These plans are subject to the approval of the District Commissioners after a public hearing; and they prescribe the various public and private land uses for the respective areas, the "standards of population density and building intensity", and "the amount or character or class of any low-rent housing."

Once the Planning Commission adopts a plan and that plan is approved by the Commissioners, the Planning Commission certifies it to the Agency. . . . At that point, the Agency is authorized to acquire and assemble the real property in the area.

After the real estate has been assembled, the Agency is authorized to transfer to public agencies the land to be devoted to such public purposes as streets, utilities, recreational facilities, and schools, and to lease or sell the remainder as an entirety or in parts to a redevelopment company, individual, or partnership. The leases or sales must provide that the lessees or purchasers will carry out the redevelopment plan and that "no use shall be made of any land or real property included in the lease or sale nor any building or structure erected thereon" which does not conform to the plan. Preference is to be given to private enterprise over public agencies in executing the redevelopment plan.

The first project undertaken under the Act relates to Project Area B in Southwest Washington, D.C. In 1950 the Planning Commission prepared and published a comprehensive plan for the District. Surveys revealed that in Area B, 64.3% of the dwellings were beyond repair, 18.4% needed major repairs, only 17.3% were satisfactory; 57.8% of the dwellings had outside toilets, 60.3% had no baths, 29.3% lacked electricity, 82.2% had no wash basins or laundry tubs, 83.8% lacked central heating. In the judgment of the District's Director of Health it was necessary to redevelop Area B in the interests of public health. The population of Area B amounted to 5,012 persons, of whom 97.5% were Negroes.

The plan for Area B specifies the boundaries and allocates the use of the land for various purposes. It makes detailed provisions for types of dwelling units and provides that at least one-third of them are to be low-rent housing with a maximum rental of $17 per room per month.

After a public hearing, the Commissioners approved the plan and the Planning Commission certified it to the Agency for execution. The Agency undertook the preliminary steps for redevelopment of the areas when this suit was brought.

Appellants own property in Area B at 712 Fourth Street, S.W. It is not used as a dwelling or place of habitation. A department store is located on it. Appellants object to the appropriation of this property for the purposes of the project. They claim that their property may not be taken constitutionally for this project. It is commercial, not residential property; it is not slum housing; it will be put into the project under the management of a private, not a public, agency and redeveloped for private, not public, use. That is the argument; and the contention is that appellants' private property is being taken contrary to two mandates of the Fifth Amendment — (1) "No person shall . . . be deprived of . . . property, without due process of law"; (2) "nor shall private property be taken for public use, without just compensation." To take for the purpose of ridding the area of slums is one thing; it is quite another, the argument goes, to take a man's property merely to develop a better balanced, more attractive community. The District Court, while agreeing in general with that argument, saved the Act by construing it to mean that the Agency could condemn property only for the reasonable necessities of slum clearance and prevention, its concept of "slum" being the existence of conditions "injurious to the public health, safety, morals and welfare." The power of Congress over the District of Columbia includes all the legislative powers which a state may exercise over its affairs.

. . .We deal, in other words, with what traditionally has been known as the police power. An attempt to define its reach or trace its outer limits is fruitless, for each case must turn on its own facts. The definition is essentially the product of legislative determinations addressed to the purposes of government, purposes neither abstractly nor historically capable of complete definition. Subject to specific constitutional limitations, when the legislature has spoken, the public interest has been declared in terms well-nigh conclusive. In such cases the legislature, not the judiciary, is the main guardian of the public needs to be served by social legislation, whether it be Congress legislating concerning the District of Columbia, or the states legislating concerning local affairs. This principle admits of no exception merely because the power of eminent domain is involved. The role of the judiciary in determining whether that power is being exercised for a public purpose is an extremely narrow one.

Public safety, public health, morality, peace and quiet, law and order — these are some of the more conspicuous examples of the traditional application of the police power to municipal affairs. Yet they merely illustrate the scope of the power and do not delimit it. Miserable and disreputable housing conditions may do more than spread disease and crime and immorality. They may also suffocate the spirit by reducing the people who live there to the status of cattle. They may indeed make living an almost insufferable burden. They may also be an ugly sore, a blight on the community which robs it of charm, which makes it a place from which men turn. The misery of housing may despoil a community as an open sewer may ruin a river.

We do not sit to determine whether a particular housing project is or is not desirable. The concept of the public welfare is broad and inclusive. The values it represents are spiritual as well as physical, aesthetic as well as monetary. It is within the power of the legislature to determine that the community should be beautiful as well as healthy, spacious as well as clean, well-balanced as well as carefully patrolled. In the present case, the Congress and its authorized agencies have made determinations that take into account a wide variety of values. It is not for us to reappraise them. If those who govern the District of Columbia decide that the Nation's Capital should be beautiful as well as sanitary, there is nothing in the Fifth Amendment that stands in the way.

Once the object is within the authority of Congress, the right to realize it through the exercise of eminent domain is clear. For the power of eminent domain is merely the means to the end. Once the object is within the authority of Congress, the means by which it will be attained is also for Congress to determine. Here one of the means chosen is the use of private enterprise for redevelopment of the area. Appellants argue that this makes the project a taking from one businessman for the benefit of another businessman. But the means of executing the project are for Congress and Congress alone to determine, once the public purpose has been established. . . . The public end may be as well or better served through an agency of private enterprise than through a department of government — or so the Congress might conclude. We cannot say that public ownership is the sole method of promoting the public purposes of community redevelopment projects. What we have said also disposes of any contention concerning the fact that certain property owners in the area may be permitted to repurchase their properties for redevelopment in harmony with the overall plan. That, too, is a legitimate means which Congress and its agencies may adopt, if they choose.

In the present case, Congress and its authorized agencies attack the problem of the blighted parts of the community on an area rather than on a structure-by-structure basis. That, too, is opposed by appellants. They maintain that since their building does not imperil health or safety nor contribute to the making of a slum or a blighted area, it cannot be swept into a redevelopment plan by the mere dictum of the Planning Commission or the Commissioners. The particular uses to be made of the land in the project were determined with regard to the needs of the particular community. The experts concluded that if the community were to be healthy, if it were not to revert again to a blighted or slum area, as though possessed of a congenital disease, the area must be planned as a whole. It was not enough, they believed, to remove existing buildings that were insanitary or unsightly. It was important to redesign the whole area so as to eliminate the conditions that cause slums — the overcrowding of dwellings, the lack of parks, the lack of adequate streets and alleys, the absence of recreational areas, the lack of light and air, the presence of outmoded street patterns. It was believed that the piecemeal approach, the removal of individual structures that were offensive, would be only a palliative. The entire area needed redesigning so that a balanced, integrated plan could be developed for the region, including not only new homes but also schools, churches, parks, streets, and shopping centers. In this way it was hoped that the cycle of decay of the area could be controlled and the birth of future slums prevented. Such diversification in future use is plainly relevant to the maintenance of the desired housing standards and therefore within congressional power.

The District Court below suggested that, if such a broad scope were intended for the statute, the standards contained in the Act would not be sufficiently definite to sustain the delegation of authority. . . . We do not agree. We think the standards prescribed were adequate for executing the plan to eliminate not only slums as narrowly defined by the District Court but also the blighted areas that tend to produce slums. Property may of course be taken for this redevelopment which, standing by itself, is innocuous and unoffending. But we have said enough to indicate that it is the need of the area as a whole which Congress and its agencies are evaluating. If owner after owner were permitted to resist these redevelopment programs on the ground that his particular property was not being used against the public interest, integrated plans for redevelopment would suffer greatly. The argument pressed on us is, indeed, a plea to substitute the landowner's standard of the public need for the standard prescribed by Congress. But as we have already stated, Community redevelopment programs need not, by force of the Constitution, be on a piecemeal basis — lot by lot, building by building.

It is not for the courts to oversee the choice of the boundary line nor to sit in review on the size of a particular project area. Once the question of the public purpose has been decided, the amount and character of land to be taken for the project and the need for a particular tract to complete the integrated plan rests in the discretion of the legislative branch.

The District Court indicated grave doubts concerning the Agency's right to take full title to the land as distinguished from the objectionable buildings located on it. We do not share those doubts. If the Agency considers it necessary in carrying out the redevelopment project to take full title to the real property involved, it may do so. It is not for the courts to determine whether it is necessary for successful consummation of the project that unsafe, unsightly, or insanitary buildings alone be taken or whether title to the land be included, any more than it is the function of the courts to sort and choose among the various parcels selected for condemnation.

The rights of these property owners are satisfied when they receive that just compensation which the Fifth Amendment exacts as the price of the taking.

The judgment of the District Court, as modified by this opinion, is affirmed.

◆ POLETOWN NEIGHBORHOOD COUNCIL v. CITY
OF DETROIT
410 Mich. 616, 304 N.W.2d 455 (1981)

PER CURIAM. This case arises out of a plan by the Detroit Economic Development Corporation to acquire, by condemnation if necessary, a large tract of land to be conveyed to General Motors Corporation as a site for construction of an assembly plant. The plaintiffs, a neighborhood association and several individual residents of the affected area, brought suit in Wayne Circuit Court to challenge the project on a number of grounds, not all of which have been argued to this Court. Defendants' motions for summary judgment were denied pending trial on a single question of fact: whether the city abused its discretion in determining that condemnation of plaintiffs' property was necessary to complete the project.

The trial lasted 10 days and resulted in a judgment for defendants and an order on December 9, 1980, dismissing plaintiffs' complaint. . . .

Does the use of eminent domain in this case constitute a taking of private property for private use and, therefore, contravene Const. 1963, Art. 10, §2?

Did the court below err in ruling that cultural, social and historical institutions were not protected by the Michigan Environmental Protection Act?

We conclude that these questions must be answered in the negative and affirm the trial court's decision.

This case raises a question of paramount importance to the future welfare of this state and its residents: Can a municipality use the power of eminent domain granted to it by the Economic Development Corporations Act, to condemn property for transfer to a private corporation to build a plant to promote industry and commerce, thereby adding jobs and taxes to the economic base of the municipality and state?

Const. 1963, Art. 10, §2, states in pertinent part that "[p]rivate property shall not be taken for public use without just compensation therefor being first made or secured in a manner prescribed by law." Art. 10, §2 has been interpreted as requiring that the power of eminent domain not be invoked except to further a public use or purpose. Plaintiffs-appellants urge us to distinguish between the terms "use" and "purpose", asserting they are not synonymous and have been distinguished in the law of eminent domain. We are persuaded the terms have been used interchangeably in Michigan statutes and decisions in an effort to describe the protean concept of public benefit. The term "public use" has not received a narrow or inelastic definition by this Court in prior cases. Indeed, this Court has stated that "[a] public use changes with changing conditions of society" and that "[t]he right of the public to receive and enjoy the benefit of the use determines whether the use is public or private". . . .

There is no dispute about the law. All agree that condemnation for a public use or purpose is permitted. All agree that condemnation for a private use or purpose is forbidden. Similarly, condemnation for a private use cannot be authorized whatever its incidental public benefit and condemnation for a public purpose cannot be forbidden whatever the incidental private gain. The heart of this dispute is whether the proposed condemnation is for the primary benefit of the public or the private user.

The Legislature has determined that governmental action of the type contemplated here meets a public need and serves an essential public purpose. The Court's role after such a determination is made is limited. . . .

The power of eminent domain is to be used in this instance primarily to accomplish the essential public purposes of alleviating unemployment and revitalizing the economic base of the community. The benefit to a private interest is merely incidental.

Our determination that this project falls within the public purpose, as stated by the Legislature, does not mean that every condemnation proposed by an economic development corporation will meet with similar acceptance simply because it may provide some jobs or add to the industrial or commercial base. If the public benefit was not so clear and significant, we would hesitate to sanction approval of such a project. The power of eminent domain is restricted to furthering public uses and purposes and is not to be exercised without substantial proof that the public is primarily to be benefited. Where, as here, the condemnation power is exercised in a way that benefits specific and identifiable private interests, a court inspects with heightened scrutiny the claim that the public interest is the predominant interest being advanced. Such public benefit cannot be speculative or marginal but must be clear and significant if it is to be within the legitimate purpose as stated by the Legislature. We hold this project is warranted on the basis that its significance for the people of Detroit and the state has been demonstrated. . . .

The decision of the trial court is affirmed.

FITZGERALD, Justice (dissenting). This Court today decides that the power of eminent domain permits the taking of private property with the object of transferring it to another private party for the purpose of constructing and operating a factory, on the ground that the employment and other economic benefits of this privately operated industrial facility are such as to satisfy the "public use" requirement for the exercise of eminent domain power. Because I believe the proposed condemnation clearly exceeds the government's authority to take private property through the power of eminent domain, I dissent.

In the spring of 1980, General Motors Corporation informed the City of Detroit that it would close its Cadillac and Fisher Body plants located within the city in 1983. General Motors offered to build an assembly complex in the city, if a suitable site could be found. General Motors set four criteria for the approval of a site: an area of between 450 and 500 acres; a rectangular shape (¾ mile by 1 mile); access to a long-haul railroad line; and access to the freeway system. The city evaluated a number of potential sites and eventually made an in-depth study of nine sites. Eight of the sites were found not to be feasible, and the ninth, with which we are concerned, was recommended. It occupies approximately 465 acres in the cities of Detroit and Hamtramck. A plan was developed to acquire the site, labeled the Central Industrial Park, under the Economic Development Corporations Act, 1974 PA 338. As authorized by the statute, the project plan contemplated the use of condemnation to acquire at least some of the property within the site.

This action was brought by several residents faced with the loss of their property to condemnation as part of the project. After an expedited trial on the merits, the circuit court entered judgment for the defendants, the effect of which is to allow the pending condemnation actions under the Michigan "quick take" statute, 1980 PA 87, to proceed. . . .

The majority relies on the principle that the concept of public use is an evolving one; however, I cannot believe that this evolution has eroded our historic protection against the taking of private property for private use to the degree sanctioned by this Court's decision today. The decision that the prospect of increased employment, tax revenue, and general economic stimulation makes a taking of private property for transfer to another private party sufficiently "public" to authorize the use of the power of eminent domain means that there is virtually no limit to the use of condemnation to aid private businesses. Any business enterprise produces benefits to society at large. Now that we have authorized local legislative bodies to decide that a different commercial or industrial use of property will produce greater public benefits than its present use, no homeowner's, merchant's or manufacturer's property, however productive or valuable to its owner, is immune from condemnation for the benefit of other private interests that will put it to a "higher" use. . . .

The condemnation contemplated in the present action goes beyond the scope of the power of eminent domain in that it takes private property for private use. I would reverse the judgment of the circuit court.

RYAN, Justice (dissenting). This is an extraordinary case.

The reverberating clang of its economic, sociological, political, and jurisprudential impact is likely to be heard and felt for generations. By its decision, the Court has altered the law of eminent domain in this state in a most significant way and, in my view, seriously jeopardized the security of all private property ownership.

This case will stand, above all else, despite the sound intentions of the majority, for judicial approval of municipal condemnation of private property for private use. This is more than an example of a hard case making bad law — it is, in the last analysis, good faith but unwarranted judicial imprimatur upon government action taken under the policy of the end justifying the means.

My separate views are set down some days after the Court's 5-to-2 decision has been made and announced and the controlling and dissenting opinions of my colleagues released. I take this unusual step for a number of reasons:

— The speed with which this case was submitted, argued, considered and decided has meant preparation of opinions which, in my view, do not adequately address the constitutional issues involved.

— The ever-broadening audience for which we write may profit from a longer and more detailed analysis of the unique facts which generated this litigation in order to appreciate the economic, social, and political context in which, in my view, our constitutional precedents have been disregarded.

— Because this case so remarkably alters our jurisprudence, it is worthwhile to trace our precedent from the beginning and to note with care where and how, from this dissenting perspective, the Court departed from it.

— Finally, it seems important to describe in detail for the bench and bar who may address a comparable issue on a similarly stormy day, how easily government, in all of its branches, caught up in the frenzy of perceived economic crisis, can disregard the rights of the few in allegiance to the always disastrous philosophy that the end justifies the means. . . .

It was, of course, evident to all interested observers that the removal by General Motors of its Cadillac manufacturing operations to a more favorable economic climate would mean the loss to Detroit of at least 6,000 jobs as well as the concomitant loss of literally thousands of allied and supporting automotive design, manufacture and sales functions. There would necessarily follow, as a result, the loss of millions of dollars in real estate and income tax revenues. The darkening picture was made even bleaker by the operation of other forces best explained by the social sciences, including the city's continuing loss of its industrial base and the decline of its population.

Thus it was to a city with its economic back to the wall that General Motors presented its highly detailed "proposal" for construction of a new plant in a "green field" location in the City of Detroit. In addition to the fact that Detroit had virtually no "green fields", the requirements of the "proposal" were such that it was clear that no existing location would be suitable unless the city acquired the requisite land one way or another and did so within the General Motors declared time schedule. The corporation told the city that it must find or assemble a parcel 450 to 500 acres in size with access to long-haul railroad lines and a freeway system with railroad marshalling yards within the plant site. As both General Motors and the city knew at the outset, no such "green field" existed. Unquestionably cognizant of its immense political and economic power, General Motors also insisted that it must receive title to the assembled parcel by May 1, 1981.

In a most impressive demonstration of governmental efficiency, the City of Detroit set about its task of meeting General Motors' specifications. Nine possible sites were identified and suggested to General Motors. Only one was found adequate — a parcel consisting of 465 acres straddling the Detroit-Hamtramck border that has come to be known as Central Industrial Park (CIP).

In July, 1980, the general outlines of the proposal to condemn property to meet General Motors' demands were submitted to the Detroit Common Council, which promptly approved the boundaries of CIP. The city had already begun to purchase property in contemplation of CIP's establishment. Approval of the CIP boundaries by the Common Council set in motion other activities: surveying in the area was begun, appraisals of the affected properties were made, and two major documents were prepared: "Project Plan: Central Industrial Park" and "Draft Environmental Impact Statement: Central Industrial Park, The Cities of Detroit and Hamtramck, Michigan" (EIS). On September 30, 1980, the completed project plan was approved by the Detroit Economic Development Corporation. Two weeks later a public hearing was held on the then proposed CIP and the next day, October 15, 1980, the Environmental Impact Statement was issued. On October 29, 1980 the Detroit Community and Economic Development Department, pursuant to the mandate of §9 of 1974 PA 338, sent a letter to the Detroit Common Council recommending that the council approve the project plan with suggested amendments for the CIP. Two days later, the council followed the recommendation, passed a resolution approving the project plan with minor modifications, and declared in the resolution "that said project constitutes a public purpose" and "is hereby determined to be for the use and benefit of the public." On November 3, 1980 the mayor of the City of Detroit signed the resolution.

Behind the frenzy of official activity was the unmistakable guiding and sustaining, indeed controlling, hand of the General Motors Corporation. The city administration and General Motors worked in close contact during the summer and autumn of 1980 negotiating the specifics for the new plant site. . . .

The evidence then is that what General Motors wanted, General

Motors got. The corporation conceived the project, determined the cost, allocated the financial burdens, selected the site, established the mode of financing, imposed specific deadlines for clearance of the property and taking title, and even demanded 12 years of tax concessions.

It is easy to underestimate the overwhelming psychological pressure which was brought to bear upon property owners in the affected area, especially the generally elderly, mostly retired and largely Polish-American residents of the neighborhood which has come to be called Poletown. As the new plant site plans were developed and announced, the property condemnation proceedings under the "quick-take" statute begun and the demolitionist's iron ball razed neighboring commercial properties such as the already abandoned Chrysler Dodge Main plant, a crescendo of supportive applause sustained the city and General Motors and their purpose. Labor leaders, bankers, and businessmen, including those for whom a new GM plant would mean new economic life, were joined by radio, television, newspaper and political opinion-makers in extolling the virtues of the bold and innovative fashion in which, almost overnight, a new and modern plant would rise from a little known inner-city neighborhood of minimal tax base significance. The promise of new tax revenues, retention of a mighty GM manufacturing facility in the heart of Detroit, new opportunities for satellite businesses, retention of 6,000 or more jobs, and concomitant reduction of unemployment, all fostered a community-wide chorus of support for the project. It was in such an atmosphere that the plaintiffs sued to enjoin the condemnation of their homes.

The judiciary, cognizant of General Motors' May 1 deadline for the city's taking title to all of the property, moved at flank speed. The circuit court conducted a trial on defendants' motion to dismiss plaintiffs' complaint from November 17 to December 2, 1980, and the decision to dismiss the complaint was made on December 9, 1980. Application for leave to appeal prior to decisions by the Court of Appeals was received in this Court on December 15, 1980. However, the trial transcript was not received by us until January 5, 1981. We promptly convened, conferred, and granted leave to appeal on January 29, 1981. The case was argued on March 3, 1981.

In less than two weeks, the lead opinions were filed by this Court and released. It is in such circumstances that we were asked to decide, and did decide, an important constitutional issue having towering implications both for the individual plaintiff property owners and for the City of Detroit and the state alike, to say nothing of the impact upon our jurisprudence. . . .

The production of automobiles certainly entails public benefits. Nevertheless, it could hardly be contended that the existence of the automotive industry or the construction of a new General Motors assembly plant requires the use of eminent domain.

Instead, what defendants are really claiming is that eminent domain is required for the existence of a new General Motors assembly plant within the city limits of Detroit *in order to comply with the specifications of General Motors.* This is an altogether different argument, acceptance of which would vitiate the requirements of "necessity of the extreme sort" and significantly alter the balance between governmental power and private property rights struck by the people and embodied in the taking clause. Just as ominously, it would work a fundamental shift in the relative force between private corporate power and individual property rights having the sanction of the state. . . .

One of the reasons advanced by the defendants as justification of the taking in this case, and adopted by the majority, is the claim of alleviation of unemployment. Even assuming, *arguendo,* that employment per se is a "necessity of the extreme sort", there are no guarantees from General Motors about employment levels at the new assembly plant. General Motors has made *representations* about the number of employees who will work at the new plant, and I certainly do not doubt the good faith of those representations. But the fact of the matter is that once CIP is sold to General Motors, there will be no public control whatsoever over the management, or operation, or conduct of the plant to be built there. General Motors will be accountable not to the public, but to its stockholders. Who knows what the automotive industry will look like in 20 years, or even 10? For that matter, who knows what cars will look like then? For all that can be known now, in light of present trends, the plant could be fully automated in 10 years. Amid these uncertainties, however, one thing is certain. The level of employment at the new GM plant will be determined by private corporate managers primarily with reference, not to the rate of regional unemployment, but to profit.

By permitting the condemnation in this case, this Court has allowed the use of the public power of eminent domain without concomitant public accountability. . . .

Eminent domain is an attribute of sovereignty. When individual citizens are forced to suffer great social dislocation to permit private corporations to construct plants where they deem it most profitable, one is left to wonder who the sovereign is.

The sudden and fundamental change in established law effected by the Court in this case, entailing such a significant diminution of constitutional rights, cannot be justified as a function of judicial construction; the only proper vehicle for change of this dimension is a constitutional amendment. What has been done in this case can be explained by the overwhelming sense of inevitability that has attended this litigation from the beginning; a sense attributable to the combination and coincidence of the interests of a desperate city administration and a giant corporation willing and able to take advantage of the opportunity that presented itself. The justification for it, like the inevitability of it, has been made to seem more acceptable by the "team spirit" chorus of approval of the project which has been supplied by the voices of labor, business, industry, government, finance, and even the news media. Virtually the only discordant sounds of dissent have come from the minuscule minority of citizens most profoundly affected by this case, the Poletown residents whose neighborhood has been destroyed.

With this case the Court has subordinated a constitutional right to private corporate interests. As demolition of existing structures on the future plant site goes forward, the best that can be hoped for, jurisprudentially, is that the precedential value of this case will be lost in the accumulating rubble.

Notes

1. New York Times columnist William Safire wrote a column headlined "Poletown Wrecker's Ball" that included the following:

> Not long ago I spared the tears for elderly residents of Miami Beach who wanted to misuse historic-preservation laws to prevent hotel developers from tearing down Art Deco neighborhoods. The property belongs to the owners, not the renting residents. In the same way, the property in Detroit's Poletown belongs to the owners, many of whom happen to be residents, and must not be snatched by government to give to another private owner, no matter what wonderful things the new owner promises to do with it. . . . At a time when we are encouraging the Poles in Poland to turn toward capitalism, it is ironic to have Americans in Poletown facing expropriation of their property. [N.Y. Times, April 30, 1981.]

2. Michelman, Property as a Constitutional Right, 38 Wash. & Lee L. Rev. 1097 (1981):

> It is obvious from their conduct that the Poletowners cannot be made whole by monetary just compensation. After all, an eminent domain taking of their homes and neighborhood, to be accompanied by compensation payments, is exactly what they are resisting. In these circumstances, we can easily see that property may represent more than money because it may represent things that money itself can't buy — place, position, relationship, roots, community, solidarity, status — yes, and security too, but security in a sense different and perhaps deeper than that of the Kaiser Aetna Corporation's "reasonable investment-backed expectations." In the Poletown case either property and security must yield, or police power and general welfare must yield. Compensation cannot mediate the conflict. And so we are finally up against the question: What can we make the Constitution tell us about *the substance, the content,* of the property rights it purports to protect?

My suggestion is to seek a *rapprochement* of property and popular sovereignty in the idea that rights under a political constitution, including property rights, are first of all to be regarded as political rights. They are precisely such, I suggest, because and insofar as they are rights affecting the individual's participation in popular sovereignty itself. In this view it is a mistake to see property — as I gather William Safire sees it — as something categorically apart from — beyond the reach of — political action. Rather one regards property as "an essential component of individual competence in social and political life," as a "material foundation" for "self-determination and self-expression," in sum, as "an indispensable ingredient in the constitution of the individual as a participant in the life of the society, including not least the society's processes for collectively regulating the conditions of an ineluctably social existence."

Just consider, if you will, how the obliteration of Poletown and the rupture of its society, with or without payments of money to the former inhabitants, may bear on their identity and efficacy as participants in the politics of Detroit, of Michigan, of the United States, in which are constantly being forged the conditions in which their, and our, future identity and efficacy will be determined. From these considerations I do not travel directly to the conclusion that the Michigan Supreme Court should have held invalid the city's exercise of eminent domain power in Poletown. I am just trying to explain my sense that what is happening in Poletown is constitutionally disquieting.

For a full explication of Professor Michelman's argument, see Michelman, Mr. Justice Brennan: A Property Teacher's Appreciation, 15 Harv. Civ. Rts. – Civ. Lib. L. Rev. 296 (1980).

3. Seattle sought to acquire land downtown near a monorail terminal by eminent domain. Its goals were to revitalize trade; to establish a public park, public pedestrian space, and parking space; and to build a new building for the Seattle Art Museum. The city was to invest $17.8 million from a general obligation bond issue and federal Urban Development Action Grant funds.

The Washington Supreme Court found the necessary takings statutorily and constitutionally unsupported, because the heart of the project was a retail shopping center to be built and owned by private developers. "It may be conceded that the Westlake Project is in 'the public interest.' However, the fact that the public interest may require it is insufficient if the use is not really public. . . . [T]o forestall 'flight to the suburbs' " may be a valid public purpose but does not constitute "public use" of the land to be taken. Justice Utter, dissenting, said "municipalities need flexibility," and asked, "Are we now to deny municipalities the opportunity to integrate private and public energies to serve the good of the public in our urban centers?" Petition of the City of Seattle, 96 Wash. 2d 616, 638 P.2d 549 (1981).

4. When the Oakland Raiders of the National Football League moved from Oakland to Los Angeles in 1980, the City of Oakland in-

stituted an action to acquire the franchise by eminent domain. The trial court granted summary judgment for the Raiders and dismissed the action, but the California Supreme Court reversed. The court held that the Raiders' professional football franchise, although consisting of a "network of intangible contractual rights," may be acquired by a municipality through eminent domain proceedings, and acquiring and operating a sports franchise may constitute a "public use," despite the fact that the city planned to sell the franchise to a private party soon after acquiring it. The court remanded the case for trial to allow the city to prove the existence of a public use.

Chief Justice Bird, concurring and dissenting, expressed concern over "one unexplored aspect" of the court's decision: "If a small business that rents a storefront on land originally taken by the city for a redevelopment project decides to move to another city in order to expand, may the city take the business and force it to stay at its original location?" She further warned that the "court should proceed most cautiously before placing a constitutional imprimatur upon this aspect of creeping statism." City of Oakland v. Oakland Raiders, 31 Cal. 3d 656, 646 P.2d 835, 183 Cal. Rptr. 673 (1982).

◆ HAWAII HOUSING AUTHORITY v. MIDKIFF
104 S. Ct. 2321 (1984)

Justice O'CONNOR delivered the opinion of the Court.

The Fifth Amendment of the United States Constitution provides, in pertinent part, that "private property [shall not] be taken for public use, without just compensation." These cases present the question whether the Public Use Clause of that Amendment, made applicable to the States through the Fourteenth Amendment, prohibits the State of Hawaii from taking, with just compensation, title in real property from lessors and transferring it to lessees in order to reduce the concentration of ownership of fees simple in the State. We conclude that it does not.

The Hawaiian Islands were originally settled by Polynesian immigrants from the eastern Pacific. These settlers developed an economy around a feudal land tenure system in which one island high chief, the ali'i nui, controlled the land and assigned it for development to certain subchiefs. The subchiefs would then reassign the land to other lower ranking chiefs, who would administer the land and govern the farmers and other tenants working it. All land was held at the will of the ali'i nui and eventually had to be returned to his trust. There was no private ownership of land.

Beginning in the early 1800's, Hawaiian leaders and American settlers repeatedly attempted to divide the lands of the kingdom among the crown, the chiefs, and the common people. These efforts proved largely unsuccessful, however, and the land remained in the hands of a few. In the mid-1960's, after extensive hearings, the Hawaii Legislature discovered that, while the State and Federal Governments owned almost 49% of the State's land, another 47% was in the hands of only 72 private landowners. The legislature further found that 18 landholders, with tracts of 21,000 acres or more, owned more than 40% of this land and that, on Oahu, the most urbanized of the islands, 22 landowners owned 72.5% of the fee simple titles. The legislature concluded that concentrated land ownership was responsible for skewing the State's residential fee simple market, inflating land prices, and injuring the public tranquility and welfare.

To redress these problems, the legislature decided to compel the large landowners to break up their estates. The legislature considered requiring large landowners to sell lands which they were leasing to homeowners. However, the landowners strongly resisted this scheme, pointing out the significant federal tax liabilities they would incur. Indeed, the landowners claimed that the federal tax laws were the primary reason they previously had chosen to lease, and not sell, their lands. Therefore, to accommodate the needs of both lessors and lessees, the Hawaii Legislature enacted the Land Reform Act of 1967 (Act), Haw. Rev. Stat., ch. 516, which created a mechanism for condemning residential tracts and for transferring ownership of the condemned fees simple to existing lessees. By condemning the land in question, the Hawaii Legislature intended to make the land sales involuntary, thereby making the federal tax consequences less severe while still facilitating the redistribution of fees simple.

Under the Act's condemnation scheme, tenants living on single-family residential lots within developmental tracts at least five acres in size are entitled to ask the Hawaii Housing Authority (HHA) to condemn the property on which they live. When 25 eligible tenants,[1] or tenants on half the lots in the tract, whichever is less, file appropriate applications, the Act authorizes HHA to hold a public hearing to determine whether acquisition by the State of all or part of the tract will "effectuate the public purposes" of the Act. If HHA finds that these public purposes will be served, it is authorized to designate some or all of the lots in the tract for acquisition. It then acquires, at prices set either by condemnation trial or by negotiation between lessors and lessees, the former fee owners' full "right, title, and interest" in the land.

After compensation has been set, HHA may sell the land titles to tenants who have applied for fee simple ownership. HHA is authorized to lend these tenants up to 90% of the purchase price, and it may condi-

1. An eligible tenant is one who, among other things, owns a house on the lot, has a bona fide intent to live on the lot or be a resident of the State, shows proof of ability to pay for a fee interest in it, and does not own residential land elsewhere nearby.

tion final transfer òn a right of first refusal for the first 10 years following sale. If HHA does not sell the lot to the tenant residing there, it may lease the lot or sell it to someone else, provided that public notice has been given. However, HHA may not sell to any one purchaser, or lease to any one tenant, more than one lot, and it may not operate for profit. In practice, funds to satisfy the condemnation awards have been supplied entirely by lessees. While the Act authorizes HHA to issue bonds and appropriate funds for acquisition, no bonds have issued and HHA has not supplied any funds for condemned lots. . . .

The starting point for our analysis of the Act's constitutionality is the Court's decision in Berman v. Parker, 348 U.S. 26 (1954). In *Berman*, the Court held constitutional the District of Columbia Redevelopment Act of 1945. That Act provided both for the comprehensive use of the eminent domain power to redevelop slum areas and for the possible sale or lease of the condemned lands to private interests. The "public use" requirement is thus coterminous with the scope of a sovereign's police powers.

There is, of course, a role for courts to play in reviewing a legislature's judgment of what constitutes a public use, even when the eminent domain power is equated with the police power. But the Court in *Berman* made clear that it is "an extremely narrow" one. . . .

To be sure, the Court's cases have repeatedly stated that "one person's property may not be taken for the benefit of another private person without a justifying public purpose, even though compensation be paid." . . .

But where the exercise of the eminent domain power is rationally related to a conceivable public purpose, the Court has never held a compensated taking to be proscribed by the Public Use Clause.

On this basis, we have no trouble concluding that the Hawaii Act is constitutional. The people of Hawaii have attempted, much as the settlers of the original 13 Colonies did,[5] to reduce the perceived social and economic evils of a land oligopoly traceable to their monarchs. The land oligopoly has, according to the Hawaii Legislature, created artificial deterrents to the normal functioning of the State's residential land market and forced thousands of individual homeowners to lease, rather than buy, the land underneath their homes. Regulating oligopoly and the evils associated with it is a classic exercise of a State's police powers. We cannot disapprove of Hawaii's exercise of this power.

Nor can we condemn as irrational the Act's approach to correcting the land oligopoly problem. The Act presumes that when a sufficiently large number of persons declare that they are willing but unable to buy

---

5. After the American Revolution, the colonists in several states took steps to eradicate the feudal incidents with which large proprietors had encumbered land in the colonies.

lots at fair prices the land market is malfunctioning. When such a malfunction is signalled, the Act authorizes HHA to condemn lots in the relevant tract. The Act limits the number of lots any one tenant can purchase and authorizes HHA to use public funds to ensure that the market dilution goals will be achieved. This is a comprehensive and rational approach to identifying and correcting market failure.

Of course, this Act, like any other, may not be successful in achieving its intended goals. But "whether *in fact* the provision will accomplish its objectives is not the question: the [constitutional requirement] is satisfied if . . . the . . . [state] Legislature *rationally could have believed* that the [Act] would promote its objective."

When the legislature's purpose is legitimate and its means are not irrational, our cases make clear that empirical debates over the wisdom of takings — no less than debates over the wisdom of other kinds of socioeconomic legislation — are not to be carried out in the federal courts. Redistribution of fees simple to correct deficiencies in the market determined by the state legislature to be attributable to land oligopoly is a rational exercise of the eminent domain power. Therefore, the Hawaii statute must pass the scrutiny of the Public Use Clause.

The Court of Appeals read our cases to stand for a much narrower proposition. First, it read our "public use" cases, especially *Berman*, as requiring that government possess and use property at some point during a taking. Since Hawaiian lessees retain possession of the property for private use throughout the condemnation process, the court found that the Act exacted takings for private use. Second, it determined that these cases involved only "the review of . . . *congressional* determination[s] that there was a public use, *not* the review of . . . state legislative determination[s]." Because state legislative determinations are involved in the instant cases, the Court of Appeals decided that more rigorous judicial scrutiny of the public use determinations was appropriate. The court concluded that the Hawaii Legislature's professed purposes were mere "statutory rationalizations." We disagree with the Court of Appeals' analysis.

The State of Hawaii has never denied that the Constitution forbids even a compensated taking of property when executed for no reason other than to confer a private benefit on a particular private party. A purely private taking could not withstand the scrutiny of the public use requirement; it would serve no legitimate purpose of government and would thus be void. But no purely private taking is involved in this case. The Hawaii Legislature enacted its Land Reform Act not to benefit a particular class of identifiable individuals but to attack certain perceived evils of concentrated property ownership in Hawaii — a legitimate public purpose. Use of the condemnation power to achieve this purpose is not irrational. Since we assume for purposes of this appeal that the weighty demand of just compensation has been met, the requirements of the Fifth and Fourteenth Amendments have been satisfied. Accordingly, we reverse the judgment of the Court of Appeals, and remand these cases for further proceedings in conformity with this opinion.

The mere fact that property taken outright by eminent domain is transferred in the first instance to private beneficiaries does not condemn that taking as having only a private purpose. The Court long ago rejected any literal requirement that condemned property be put into use for the general public. . . . "[W]hat in its immediate aspect [is] only a private transaction may . . . be raised by its class or character to a public affair." Block v. Hirsh, 256 U.S., at 155. As the unique way titles were held in Hawaii skewed the land market, exercise of the power of eminent domain was justified. The Act advances its purposes without the State taking actual possession of the land. In such cases, government does not itself have to use property to legitimate the taking; it is only the taking's purpose, and not its mechanics, that must pass scrutiny under the Public Use Clause.

Similarly, the fact that a state legislature, and not the Congress, made the public use determination does not mean that judicial deference is less appropriate.[7] Judicial deference is required because, in our system of government, legislatures are better able to assess what public purposes should be advanced by an exercise of the taking power. State legislatures are as capable as Congress of making such determinations within their respective spheres of authority. Thus, if a legislature, state or federal, determines there are substantial reasons for an exercise of the taking power, courts must defer to its determination that the taking will serve a public use.

4. Just Compensation

◆ ALMOTA FARMERS ELEVATOR & WAREHOUSE CO. v. UNITED STATES
409 U.S. 470 (1973)

Mr. Justice STEWART delivered the opinion of the Court. Since 1919 the petitioner, Almota Farmers Elevator and Warehouse Company, has conducted grain elevator operations on land adjacent to the tracks of the Oregon-Washington Railroad and Navigation Company in the State of Washington. It has occupied the land under a series of successive leases from the railroad. In 1967, the Government instituted this eminent do-

---

7. It is worth noting that the Fourteenth Amendment does not itself contain an independent "public use" requirement. Rather, that requirement is made binding on the states only by incorporation of the Fifth Amendment's Eminent Domain Clause through the Fourteenth Amendment's Due Process Clause. It would be ironic to find that state legislation is subject to greater scrutiny under the incorporated "public use" requirement than is congressional legislation under the express mandate of the Fifth Amendment.

main proceeding to acquire the petitioner's property interest by condemnation. At that time there were extensive buildings and other
improvements that had been erected on the land by the petitioner, and
the then current lease had 7½ years to run.

In the District Court the Government contended that just compensation for the leasehold interest, including the structures, should be "the
fair market value of the legal rights possessed by the defendant by virtue
of the lease as of the date of taking," and that no consideration should
be given to any additional value based on the expectation that the lease
might be renewed. The petitioner urged that, rather than this technical
"legal rights theory," just compensation should be measured by what a
willing buyer would pay in an open market for the petitioner's leasehold.

As a practical matter the controversy centered upon the valuation to
be placed upon the structures and their appurtenances. The parties
stipulated that the Government had no need for these improvements
and that the petitioner had a right to remove them. But that stipulation
afforded the petitioner only what scant salvage value the buildings
might bring. The Government offered compensation for the loss of the
use and occupancy of the buildings only over the remaining term of the
lease. The petitioner contended that this limitation upon compensation
for the use of the structures would fail to award what a willing buyer
would have paid for the lease with the improvements, since such a
buyer would expect to have the lease renewed and to continue to use the
improvements in place. The value of the buildings, machinery, and
equipment in place would be substantially greater than their salvage
value at the end of the lease term, and a purchaser in an open market
would pay for the anticipated use of the buildings and for the savings he
would realize from not having to construct new improvements himself.
In sum, the dispute concerned whether Almota would have to be
satisfied with its right to remove the structures with their consequent
salvage value or whether it was entitled to an award reflecting the value
of the improvements in place beyond the lease term. . . .

In view of [a] conflict in the circuits, we granted *certiorari* to decide
an important question of eminent domain law: "Whether, upon condemnation of a leasehold, a lessee with no right of renewal is entitled to
receive as compensation the market value of its improvements without
regard to the remaining term of its lease, because of the expectancy that
the lease would have been renewed."[1] . . .

The Fifth Amendment provides that private property shall not be

___

1. This was the statement of the question presented by the Government in opposing
the grant of the petition for *certiorari*. As the petitioner phrased the question, the Court
was asked to decide: "In awarding just compensation to a tenant in the condemnation of a
leasehold interest in real property, including tenant owned building improvements and
fixtures situated thereon, *may an element of great inherent value in the improvements be excluded
merely because it does not, by itself, rise to the status of a legal property right.*"

taken for public use without "just compensation." "And 'just compensation' means the full monetary equivalent of the property taken. The owner is to be put in the same position monetarily as he would have occupied if his property had not been taken." . . . To determine such monetary equivalence, the Court early established the concept of "market value": the owner is entitled to the fair market value of his property at the time of the taking. . . . And this value is normally to be ascertained from "what a willing buyer would pay in cash to a willing seller." . . .

By failing to value the improvements in place over their useful life — taking into account the possibility that the lease would be renewed as well as the possibility that it might not — the Court of Appeals in this case failed to recognize what a willing buyer would have paid for the improvements. If there had been no condemnation, Almota would have continued to use the improvements during a renewed lease term, or if it sold the improvements to the fee owner or to a new lessee at the end of the lease term, it would have been compensated for the buyer's ability to use the improvements in place over their useful life. As Judge Friendly wrote for the Court of Appeals for the Second Circuit:

> Lessors do desire, after all, to keep their properties leased, and an existing tenant usually has the inside track to a renewal for all kinds of reasons — avoidance of costly alterations, saving of brokerage commissions, perhaps even ordinary decency on the part of landlords. Thus, even when the lease has expired, the condemnation will often force the tenant to remove or abandon the fixtures long before he would otherwise have had to, as well as deprive him of the opportunity to deal with the landlord or a new tenant — the only two people for whom the fixtures would have a value unaffected by the heavy costs of disassembly and reassembly. The condemnor is not entitled to the benefit of assumptions, contrary to common experience, that the fixtures would be removed at the expiration of the stated term. [United States v. Certain Property, Borough of Manhattan, 388 F.2d 596, 601-602.]

It seems particularly likely in this case that Almota could have sold the leasehold at a price which would have reflected the continued ability of the buyer to use the improvements over their useful life. Almota had an unbroken succession of leases since 1919, and it was in the interest of the railroad, as fee owner, to continue leasing the property, with its grain elevator facilities, in order to promote grain shipments over its lines. In a free market, Almota would hardly have sold the leasehold to a purchaser who paid only for the use of the facilities over the remainder of the lease term, with Almota retaining the right thereafter to remove the facilities — in effect, the right of salvage. . . .[2]

2. The compensation to which Almota is entitled is hardly "totally set free from [its] property interest," as the dissent suggests. The improvements are assuredly "private

The Government argues that it would be unreasonable to compensate Almota for the value of the improvements measured over their useful life, since the Government could purchase the fee and wait until the expiration of the lease term to take possession of the land. Once it has purchased the fee, the argument goes, there is no further expectancy that the improvements will be used during their useful life since the Government will assuredly require their removal at the end of the term. But the taking for the dam was one act requiring proceedings against owners of two interests. At the time of that "taking" Almota had an expectancy of continued occupancy of its grain elevator facilities. The Government must pay just compensation for those interests "probably within the scope of the project from the time the Government was committed to it." It may not take advantage of any depreciation in the property taken that is attributable to the project itself. At the time of the taking in this case, there was an expectancy that the improvements would be used beyond the lease term. But the Government has sought to pay compensation on the theory that at that time there was no possibility that the lease would be renewed and the improvements used beyond the lease term. It has asked that the improvements be valued as though there were no possibility of continued use. That is not how the market would have valued such improvements; it is not what a private buyer would have paid Almota.

"The constitutional requirement of just compensation derives as much content from the basic equitable principles of fairness as it does from technical concepts of property law." United States v. Fuller. It is of course true that Almota should be in no better position than if it had sold its leasehold to a private buyer. But its position should surely be no worse.

The judgment before us is reversed and the judgment of the District Court reinstated.

Mr. Justice POWELL, with whom Mr. Justice DOUGLAS joins, concurring. . . . It is clear, first of all, that the market value of improvements placed on a leasehold interest will vary depending in major part upon the probable future conduct of the landlord. In this case, based on the experience of nearly half a century and the evident self-interest of the

---

property" that the Government has "taken" and for which it acknowledges it must pay compensation. The only dispute in this case is over how those improvements are to be valued, not over whether Almota is to receive additional compensation for business losses. Almota may well be unable to operate a grain elevator business elsewhere; it may well lose the profits and other values of a going business, but it seeks compensation for none of that. Mitchell v. United States, 267 U.S. 341, did hold that the Government was not obliged to pay for business losses caused by condemnation. But it assuredly did not hold that the Government could fail to provide fair compensation for business improvements that are taken — dismiss them as worth no more than scrap value — simply because it did not intend to use them. Indeed, in *Mitchell* the Government paid compensation both for the land, including its "adaptability for use in a particular business," and for the improvements thereon.

landlord railroad, this conduct could be predicted with considerable confidence. There was every expectation that the improvements would continue to have significant value beyond the term of the present lease. In a transaction between a willing buyer and a willing seller there can be no doubt that this value would have been accorded appropriate weight.

On different facts, the market value of Almota's interest might have been significantly lower. If, for example, the railroad had relocated its tracks before the Government entered the picture, the leasehold improvements would have been nearly valueless in the market. A risk which Almota took in erecting those improvements, the risk that the railroad would relocate its tracks, would have proven a poor one. The risk would have been substantially the same if, independently of the present navigation project, the Government had purchased the railroad with the intention of operating it, and thereafter had decided to relocate it or to discontinue operation. Under those circumstances, the Government could properly have acted as an ordinary landlord, and its lessees could have been expected to bear the risk that it would put its land to a new use.

Here, however, the Government held no interest in the land until its navigation project required the acquisition of both the fee and the leasehold interests. If, at that point, the Government had condemned both interests in a single proceeding, or in separate proceedings, Almota would have been entitled to compensation for the value of the improvements beyond the present lease term. Almota bore the risk that the railroad would change its plans, but should not be forced to bear the risk that the Government would condemn the fee and change its use. Where multiple properties or property interests are condemned for a particular public project, the Government must pay *pre-existing market value for each*. Neither the Government nor the condemnee may take advantage of "an alteration in market value attributable to the project itself." . . .

Mr. Justice Rehnquist, with whom The Chief Justice, Mr. Justice White and Mr. Justice Blackmun join, dissenting. . . . While the inquiry as to what property interest is taken by the condemnor and the inquiry as to how that property interest shall be valued are not identical ones, they cannot be divorced without seriously undermining a number of rules dealing with the law of eminent domain which this Court has evolved in a series of decisions through the years. The landowner, after all, is interested not in the legal terminology used to describe the property taken from him by the condemnor, but in the amount of money he is to be paid for that property. It will cause him little remorse to learn that his hope for a renewal of a lease for a term of years is not a property interest for which the government must pay, if in the same breath he is told that the lesser legal interest which he owns may be valued to include the hoped-for renewal. . . .

It is quite apparent that the property on which the owner operates a prosperous retail establishment would command more in an open market sale than the fair value of so much of the enterprise as was "private property" within the meaning of the Fifth Amendment. Yet Mitchell v. United States, 267 U.S. 341 (1925), stands squarely for the proposition that the value added to the property taken by the existence of a going business is no part of the just compensation for which the Government must pay for taking the property:

"No recovery therefor can be had now as for a taking of the business. There is no finding as a fact that the government took the business, or that what it did was intended as a taking. If the business was destroyed, the destruction was an unintended incident of the taking of land."

More recently, the Court generalized further:

That which is not "private property" within the meaning of the Fifth Amendment likewise may be a thing of value which is destroyed or impaired by the taking of lands by the United States. But like the business destroyed but not "taken" in the *Mitchell* case it need not be reflected in the award due the landowner unless Congress so provides. [United States ex rel. TVA v. Powelson, 319 U.S. 266, 283 (1943).]

The Court's conclusion gains no support from its citation of the recognized principle that the Government may not take advantage of any depreciation in the property taken that is attributable to the project itself. The value of petitioner's property taken could not be diminished by the fact that the river improvement and navigation for which the Government took its property might have had a depressing effect on pre-existing market value. But the Government makes no such contention here. While under existing principles of constitutional eminent domain law the value of petitioner's property was not subject to diminution resulting from the effect on market value of the improvement which the Government proposed to construct, it *was* subject to the hazard of nonrenewal of its leasehold interest. The fact that the Government had condemned the underlying fee for the same project, and has therefore made the risk of nonrenewal a certainty, undoubtedly diminishes the market value of petitioner's leasehold interest. But the diminution results not from any depressing effect of the improvement which the Government will construct after having taken the leasehold, but from a materialization of the risk of transfer of ownership of the underlying fee to which its value was always subject.

In at least partially cutting loose the notion of "just compensation" from the notion of "private property" which has developed under the Fifth Amendment, the Court departs from the settled doctrine of numerous prior cases which have quite rigorously adhered to the principle that destruction of value by itself affords no occasion for compensation. "[D]amage alone gives courts no power to require compensation where there is not an actual taking of property." United States v. Willow River Power Co., 324 U.S. 499, 510 (1945). "[T]he existence of value alone does not generate interests protected by the Constitution against diminution by the government. . . ." While the Court purports to follow this well-established principle by requiring the compensation paid to be determined on the basis of private property actually taken, its endorsement of valuation computed in part on an expectancy which is no part of the property taken represents a departure from this settled doctrine. I therefore dissent.

Note

The compensation formula proposed by the United States was to pay "the fair market value of the use of the land and buildings for the seven years plus remainder of the term of [Almota's] lease, less the agreed annual rent, plus the value of the buildings for removal or salvage purposes." Almota, on the contrary, wanted "the full fair market value of the use of the land and of the buildings in place as they stood at the time of the taking on May 26, 1967, without limitation of such use to the remainder of the term of the existing lease." The parties agreed that the U.S. formula would lead to an award of $130,000 while that of Almota would produce a payment of $272,625.

The taking was for an Army Corps of Engineers project called Little Goose Lock and Dam, on the Snake River in Idaho. Prior to this litigation, the United States had already settled with the railroad, and "neither party . . . urges that those terms would be relevant in this case." Almota had the remainder of a 20-year lease to .75 acre, on which it had a 522,500 bushel grain elevator and "flat house." But Almota had been leasing the parcel since 1919, and was presently paying as rent $114 per year. The facts are in the lower court opinion, United States v. 22.95 Acres of Land, 450 F.2d 125 (9th Cir. 1971).

◆ UNITED STATES v. FULLER
409 U.S. 488 (1973)

Mr. Justice REHNQUIST delivered the opinion of the Court. Respondents operated a large-scale "cow-calf" ranch near the confluence of the Big Sandy and Bill Williams Rivers in western Arizona. Their activities were conducted on lands consisting of 1,280 acres that they owned in fee simple (fee lands), 12,027 acres leased from the State of Arizona, and 31,461 acres of federal domain held under Taylor Grazing Act permits issued in accordance with §3 of the Act, 48 Stat. 1270, as amended, 43 U.S.C. §315b. The Taylor Grazing Act authorizes the Secretary of the

Interior to issue permits to livestock owners for grazing their stock on Federal Government lands. These permits are revocable by the Government. The Act provides, moreover, that its provisions "shall not create any right, title, interest, or estate in or to the lands."

The United States, petitioner here, condemned 920 acres of respondents' fee lands. At the trial in the District Court for the purpose of fixing just compensation for the lands taken, the parties disagreed as to whether the jury might consider value accruing to the fee lands as a result of their actual or potential use in combination with the Taylor Grazing Act "permit" lands. The Government contended that such element of incremental value to the fee lands could neither be taken into consideration by the appraisers who testified for the parties nor considered by the jury. Respondents conceded that their permit lands could not themselves be assigned any value in view of the quoted provisions of the Taylor Grazing Act. They contended, however, that if on the open market the value of their fee lands was enhanced because of their actual or potential use in conjunction with permit lands, that element of value of the fee lands could be testified to by appraisers and considered by the jury. . . .

United States v. Cors, 337 U.S. 325 (1949), held that the just compensation required to be paid to the owner of a tug requisitioned by the Government in October 1942, during the Second World War, could not include the appreciation in market value for tugs created by the Government's own increased wartime need for such vessels. The Court said: "That is a value which the government itself created and hence in fairness should not be required to pay." . . .

These cases go far toward establishing the general principle that the Government as condemnor may not be required to compensate a condemnee for elements of value that the Government has created, or that it might have destroyed under the exercise of governmental authority other than the power of eminent domain. If the Government need not pay for value that it could have acquired by exercise of a servitude arising under the commerce power, it would seem *a fortiori* that it need not compensate for value that it could remove by revocation of a permit for the use of lands that it owned outright.

We do not suggest that such a general principle can be pushed to its ultimate logical conclusion. In United States v. Miller [317 U.S. 369 (1943)], the Court held that "just compensation" did include the increment of value resulting from the completed project to neighboring lands originally outside the project limits, but later brought within them. Nor may the United States "be excused from paying just compensation measured by the value of the property at the time of the taking" because the State in which the property is located might, through the exercise of its lease power, have diminished that value without paying compensation.

"Courts have had to adopt working rules in order to do substantial justice in eminent domain proceedings." Seeking as best we may to extrapolate from these prior decisions such a "working rule," we believe that there is a significant difference between the value added to property by a completed public works project, for which the Government must pay, and the value added to fee lands by a revocable permit authorizing the use of neighboring lands that the Government owns. The Government may not demand that a jury be arbitrarily precluded from considering as an element of value the proximity of a parcel to a post office building, simply because the Government at one time built the post office. But here respondents rely on no mere proximity to a public building or to public lands dedicated to, and open to, the public at large. Their theory of valuation aggregates their parcel with land owned by the Government to form a privately controlled unit from which the public would be excluded. If a person may not do this with respect to property interests subject to the Government's navigational servitude, he surely may not do it with respect to property owned outright by the Government. The Court's statement in *Rands* respecting port site value is precisely applicable to respondents' contention here that they may aggregate their fee lands with permit lands owned by the Government for valuation purposes:

> [I]f the owner of the fast lands can demand port site value as part of his compensation, "he gets the value of a right that the Government in the exercise of its dominant servitude can grant or withhold as it chooses. . . . To require the United States to pay for this . . . value would be to create private claims in the public domain." [United States v. Rands, 389 US 121, 125 (1967).]

We hold that the Fifth Amendment does not require the Government to pay for that element of value based on the use of respondents' fee lands in combination with the Government's permit lands.

Mr. Justice POWELL, with whom Mr. Justice DOUGLAS, Mr. Justice BRENNAN, and Mr. Justice MARSHALL join, dissenting.

. . . The permits held by respondents on the public land accorded exclusive but revocable grazing rights to respondents. By the terms of the Act, the issuance of a permit does not "create any right, title, interest, or estate in or to the lands." Nonetheless, grazing permits are of considerable value to ranchers and serve a corresponding public interest in assuring the "most beneficial use" of range lands. Respondents' permits had not been revoked at the time of the taking, nor, so far as the record reveals, have they yet been revoked. The record also shows that only a small fraction of the public grazing land will be flooded in the dam and reservoir project. Thus, the public land which respondents assert gave added value to their fee land remains substantially intact and available for Taylor Grazing Act purposes. . . .

The water rights cases may be subject to varying interpretations, but it is important to remember when interpreting them that they cut sharply against the grain of the fundamental notion of just compensation, that a person from whom the Government takes land is entitled to the market value, including location value, of the land. They could well be confined to cases involving the Government's "unique position" with respect to "navigable waters."[3] At most, these cases establish a principle no broader than that the Government need not compensate for location value attributable to the proximity of Government property utilized in the same project. In *Rands* the river adjacent to the property condemned was the focal point of the development project which led to the condemnation. The Government simply decided to put the river to a new use and in connection with that new use condemned adjacent land. . . .

The Government's role here is not an ambiguous one — it is simply a condemnor of private land which happens to adjoin public land. If the Government need not pay location value in this case, what are the limits upon the principle today announced? Will the Government be relieved from paying location value whenever it condemns private property adjacent to or favorably located with respect to Government property? Does the principle apply, for example, to the taking of a gasoline station at an interchange of a federal highway, or to the taking of a farm which in private hands could continue to be irrigated with water from a federal reservoir? . . .

The Court can hardly be drawing a distinction between Government-owned "completed public works" and Government-owned parks and grazing lands in their natural state. The "working rule" as articulated can, therefore, only mean that the respondents' revocable permit to use the neighboring lands is regarded by the Court as the distinguishing element. This is an acceptance of the Government's argument that the added value derives from the permit and not from the favorable location with respect to the grazing land. The answer to this, not addressed either by the Government or the Court, is that the favorable location is the central fact. Even if no permit had been issued to these respondents, their three tracts of land — largely surrounded by the grazing land — were strategically located and logical beneficiaries of the Taylor Grazing Act. In determining the market value of respondents' land, surely this location — whether or not a permit had been issued —

---

3. Arguably, then, these are water rights cases and nothing more. Suitable sites for hydroelectric plants or port facilities are important natural resources, highly valuable but limited in number, over which the Government has peculiar historical and constitutional sway. On this view, while the Government has equal authority over Taylor Grazing Act land and other Government-owned property, proximity to such property may appropriately be treated differently from proximity to navigable water for the purpose of measuring just compensation. This was one of the bases on which the court below distinguished the water cases from the present case, and in my view is an alternative ground for affirming the judgment below.

would enter into any rational estimate of value. This is precisely the rationale of the District Court's jury instruction, which carefully distinguished between the revocable permits "not compensable as such" and the "availability and accessibility" of the grazing land. It is this distinction which the Court's opinion simply ignores.

Finally, I do not think the Court's deviation from the market-value rule can be justified by invocation of long-established "basic equitable principles of fairness." It hardly serves the principles of fairness as they have been understood in the law of just compensation to disregard what respondents could have obtained for their land on the open market in favor of its value artificially denuded of its surroundings.

Notes

1. In the late 1960s, the secretary of the interior began to increase the fees charges for Taylor Act permits. In a class action seeking to stop one of these increases, permit holders alleged that the fee increase was an unconstitutional taking. Pankey Land and Cattle Co. v. Hardin, 427 F.2d 43 (10th Cir. 1970), held that the permit holders had no protected property interest in the low fees, and hence no grounds for constitutional complaint. The increases were, however, suspended by executive order, and in 1976 Congress dropped the language in 43 U.S.C. §315b saying "in fixing the amount of such fees the Secretary of the Interior shall take into account the extent to which such district yields public benefits over and above those accruing to the users," and instead prescribed "reasonable fees in each case to be fixed or determined from time to time in accordance with governing law."

2. United States v. 564.54 Acres of Land, More or Less, 441 U.S. 506 (1979), held that when the U.S. condemns property, the Fifth Amendment is satisfied by payment of fair market value even when the land taken is owned by a private non-profit organization and used for a public purpose. The landowner in the case, the Southeastern Pennsylvania Synod of the Lutheran Church, operated summer camps along the Delaware River and had argued that replacement cost should be the standard of compensation. The jury awarded fair market value of $740,000. The church contended that its cost of building replacement facilities was $5.8 million, in part because the new facilities would be subjected to strict government regulations from which the old facility was "grandfathered."

3. The U.S. government condemned a 50-acre tract of land owned by the city of Duncanville, Texas, which the city had operated as a sanitary landfill. The U.S., relying on 564.54 Acres, offered fair market value as "just compensation" for the land, while the city demanded the cost of a "functionally equivalent facility." The court of appeals ruled in

favor of Duncanville. It distinguished *564.54 Acres* on the ground that, while the condemnee there was under no "legal or factual obligation to replace the camps [condemned by the government]," Duncanville, by law, must continue to collect and dispose of garbage, and thus is "required to spend certain monies to purchase a new landfill site and prepare that site for its purpose." The Supreme Court rejected the distinction and reversed. United States v. 50 Acres of Land, 706 F.2d 1356 (5th Cir. 1983), *rev'd*, 105 S. Ct. 451 (1984).

4. When a city announces its intention to undertake urban renewal in a neighborhood, property values often fall: owners postpone repairs and tenants depart. Foster v. City of Detroit, 254 F. Supp. 655 (E.D. Mich. 1966), *aff'd*, 405 F.2d 138 (6th Cir. 1968), held Detroit liable where it had filed an intention to take and renew plaintiff's property in 1950, had frozen improvements and use changes without municipal permission, had later required demolition because the buildings had become dilapidated, but in 1960 changed its mind and called off the project. However Woodland Market Realty Co. v. City of Cleveland, 426 F.2d 955 (6th Cir. 1970), refused compensation to an owner whose property declined in value because neighboring parcels were the subject of an urban renewal designation. Cf. Sayre v. City of Cleveland, 493 F.2d 64, 69 (6th Cir. 1974): "Absent the abuse of eminent domain found in *Foster*, including some action by the city indicating that *the particular piece of property at issue* is to be appropriated, economic loss caused by urban renewal does not constitute a taking within the meaning of the fifth and fourteenth amendments."

5. Private buyers often consider the likelihood that present zoning rules will be changed. The possibility may either increase or diminish value. Masheter v. Wood, 36 Ohio St. 2d 175, 305 N.E.2d 785 (1973), refused to permit an expert to testify that the eminent domain payment should be larger because favorable zoning changes were likely. "Such an opinion constitutes speculation upon the probability of future decisions of a zoning board or a legislative body."

6. The city took a portion of plaintiff's land to widen a street. On that portion it constructed a median strip, preventing some cars from turning onto plaintiff's remaining land. Should the city pay the value of the appropriated land before the median was built, or must it also pay for the diminution to plaintiff's remaining land inflicted by the median? The Ohio Supreme Court ruled for the city. Richley v. Jones, 38 Ohio St. 2d 64, 310 N.E.2d 236 (1974).

7. After President Kennedy's assassination, the United States took title to certain property that had been treated as evidence by the Warren Commission. The statute authorizing the taking, P.L. 318, 79 Stat. 1185 (1965), provided for a later determination of compensation. Marina Oswald Porter sued to obtain compensation for her former husband's gun, which had become her property through his intestate death. The issue:

Should she receive its value as a weapon, or its value as the weapon that allegedly killed the president? The difference was almost $15,000. The court of appeals decided for Ms. Porter, holding that the incremental element of value attributable to collectors' demand should be part of compensable value. Porter v. United States, 473 F.2d 1329 (5th Cir. 1973), reversing 335 F. Supp. 498 (N.D. Tex. 1971). See Note, Just Compensation and the Assassin's Bequest: A Utilitarian Approach, 122 U. Pa. L. Rev. 1012 (1974), applying to these facts the theory articulated in Michelman, Property, Utility, and Fairness: Comments on the Ethical Foundations of "Just Compensation" Law, 80 Harv. L. Rev. 1165 (1967).

8. M'Clenachan v. Curwin, 3 Yeates 362 (Pa. 1802), was

> an action of trespass brought against the superintendant of the artificial road, leading from Philadelphia to Lancaster, called the Turnpike Road, for entering on the cleared tilled and enclosed lands of the plaintiff . . . and digging up the said land for a certain distance, and overlaying the same along the route or track of the said road with stone and gravel, . . . without having made any compensation for the said land. . . .

The court held that each Pennsylvania landowner had been given "under the grant of the late proprietaries of Pennsylvania . . . beyond the quantity of land actually purchased and paid for, 6 percent for roads and highways." Therefore this undesignated portion of plaintiff's land was "not his separate property, for that he held it as a trustee for the public. . . ." And therefore construction of the Turnpike was not a compensable taking.

9. Metropolitan Sanitary District of Greater Chicago, a public body, built an interceptor sewer and permitted connection of lines from Village of Huffman Estates. Until that time, the village had disposed of its sewage through Citizen Utilities, a private utility, which had built and improved a treatment plant in expectation of the village's trade and had obtained certificates of convenience and necessity from the Illinois Commerce Commission for its construction activity. The utility, owner of a now worthless plant, sued the sanitary district, demanding $520,000 as compensation for the loss.

Held: No compensation. Damage "means some direct physical disturbance of a right which owners of the plant in question enjoyed in connection with their property." Citizens Utilities Co. v. Metropolitan Sanitary District, 25 Ill. App. 3d 252, 322 N.E.2d 857 (1974).

10. The Eagle Protection Act and the Migratory Bird Treaty Act prohibit commercial transactions involving parts of birds legally killed before the birds come under the protection of the acts. The Supreme Court held that the laws do not unconstitutionally take the property rights of the owners of the dead birds. Andrus v. Allard, 444 U.S. 51 (1979).

B.   THE TAKING OF AN "IDEA"

◆ WHEATON v. PETERS
33 U.S. (8 Pet.) 591 (1834)

Appeal from the Circuit Court for the Eastern District of Pennsylvania. The case, as stated in the opinion of the court, was as follows:

The complainants, in their bill, state, that Henry Wheaton is the author of twelve books or volumes of the reports of cases argued and adjudged in the supreme court of the United States, and commonly known as "Wheaton's Reports," which contain a connected and complete series of the decisions of said court, from the year 1816 until the year 1827. That before the first volume was published, the said Wheaton sold and transferred his copyright in the said volume to Matthew Carey, of Philadelphia; who, before the publication, deposited a printed copy of the title page of the volume in the clerk's office of the district court of the eastern district of Pennsylvania where he resided. That the same was recorded by the said clerk, according to law, and that a copy of the said record was caused by said Carey to be inserted at full length in the page immediately following the title of said book. And the complainants further state, that they have been informed and believe, that all things which are necessary and requisite to be done in and by the provisions of the acts of congress of the United States, passed the 31st day of May 1790, and the 29th day of April 1802, for the purpose of securing to authors and proprietors the copyrights of books, and for other purposes, in order to entitle the said Carey to the benefit of the said acts, have been done.

It is further stated, that said Carey afterwards conveyed the copyright in the said volume to Matthew Carey, Henry C. Carey and Isaac Lea, trading under the firm of Matthew Carey & Sons; and that said firm, in the year 1821, transferred the said copyright to the complainant, Robert Donaldson. That this purchase was made by an arrangement with the said Henry Wheaton, with the expectation of a renewal of the right of the said Henry Wheaton under the provisions of the said acts of congress; of which renewal he, the said Robert Donaldson, was to have the benefit, until the first and second editions of the said volume which he, the said Donaldson, was to publish, should be sold. That at the time the purchase was made from Carey & Sons, a purchase was also made of the residue of the first edition of the first volume, which they had on hand; and in the year 1827, he published another edition of said volume, a part of which still remains unsold.

The bill further states, that for the purpose of continuing to the said Henry Wheaton the exclusive right, under the provisions of the said acts of congress, to the copy of the said volume, for the further term of fourteen years, after the expiration of the term of fourteen years from the recording of the title of the said volume in the clerk's office as aforesaid, the said Robert Donaldson, as the agent of Wheaton, within six months before the expiration of the said first term of fourteen years, deposited a printed copy of the title of the said volume in the clerk's office of the district court of the southern district of New York, where the said Wheaton then resided; and caused the said title to be a second time recorded in the said clerk's office; and also caused a copy of the said record to be a second time published in a newspaper printed in the said city of New York, for the space of four weeks, and delivered a copy of the said book to the secretary of state of the United States; and that all things were done agreeably to the provisions of the said act of congress of May 31st, 1790, and within six months before the expiration of the said term of fourteen years.

The same allegations are made as to all the other volumes which have been published; that the entry was made in the clerk's office and notice given by publication in a newspaper, before the publication of each volume; and that a copy of each volume was deposited in the department of state.

The complainants charge, that the defendants have lately published and sold, or caused to be sold, a volume called "Condensed Reports of Cases in the Supreme Court of the United States," containing the whole series of the decisions of the court, from its organization to the commencement of Peters's reports, at January term 1827. That this volume contains, without any material abbreviation or alteration, all the reports of cases in the said first volume of Wheaton's reports, and that the publication and sale thereof is a direct violation of the complainants' rights; and an injunction, &c., is prayed.

The defendants in their answer deny that their publication was an infringement of the complainants' copyright, if any they had; and further deny that they had such right, they not having complied with all the requisites to the vesting of such right under the acts of congress.

The bill of the complainants was dismissed by the decree of the circuit court; and they appealed to this court.

The case was argued by *Paine* and *Webster*, for the appellants; and by *Ingersoll*, by a printed argument, and *Sergeant*, for the defendants. . . .

Webster, in reply. — There was at one period no regular series of reports of the decisions of this court. Mr. Cranch's reports had been published so far as the sixth volume; the rest of the matter, which afterwards formed the remaining volumes, was in manuscript. In this state of things, Mr. Wheaton proposed a regular annual publication of the decisions, with good type, and to be neatly printed. It was found necessary that there should be some patronage from the legislature, there being so few persons who would purchase the reports. Mr. Wheaton applied to congress, personally solicited its aid, and made a case which prevailed. Congress passed a temporary law which was renewed again and again. The successor of Mr. Wheaton has had the full benefit of the grant obtained by the personal exertions of Mr. Wheaton.

If the work of the appellee be an interference with the rights of the appellants, it is not a heedless one; it may not be an intentional interference, but the acts which constitute it are intentional. The defendant was well advised of the injury which the appellants foresaw; this is fully proved by the evidence. The publication of the defendant has materially injured the appellants. Many volumes of Wheaton's reports were on hand, unsold, at the time of the publication of the third volume of Condensed reports. The intention of the defendant was not to make an abridgement, but to make a substitute for the whole of the appellant's work. The reports of the appellant were the result of the joint action of congress and the reporter; they set the price. If congress had thought that the people should have them cheaper, they would have lowered the price. The defendant should not have run the risk in accommodating the public; they could judge for themselves.

The question before the court is one for the most enlarged and liberal consideration. Cases which are not in form, but are in substance, an infringement of the author's rights, are to be viewed, as respects the author, liberally. This spirit pervades all the adjudged cases. Has there been an indefensible use of the appellant's labors? In the Condensed reports there is the same matter as in the reports of the appellant, under the same names. Is this an abridgment? An abridgment, fairly done, is itself authorship, requires mind; and is not an infringement any more than another work on the same subject. In the English courts, there are frequently more reports than one of the same cases. These reports are distinct works. Abridgments are the efforts of different minds. The Condensed reports have none of the features of an abridgment, and the work is made up of the same cases, and no more than is contained in Wheaton's reports. . . .

McLean, Justice, delivered the opinion of the court. . . . Perhaps, no topic in England has excited more discussion, among literary and talented men, than that of the literary property of authors. So engrossing was the subject, for a long time, as to leave few neutrals, among those who were distinguished for their learning and ability. At length, the question, whether the copy of a book or literary composition belongs to the author at common law, was brought before the court of king's bench, in the great case of Millar v. Taylor, 4 Burr. 2303. This was a case of great expectation; and the four judges, in giving their opinions, *seriatim*, exhausted the argument on both sides. Two of the judges, and Lord Mansfield, held, that, by the common law, an author had a literary property in his works; and they sustained their opinion with very great ability. Mr. Justice Yates, in an opinion of great length, and with an ability, if equalled, certainly not surpassed, maintained the opposite ground. Previous to this case, injunctions had issued out of chancery to prevent the publication of certain works, at the instance of those who claimed a property in the copyright, but no decision had been given. And a case had been commenced, at law, between *Tonson* and *Collins*, on the same ground and was argued with great ability, more than once, and the court of king's bench was about to take the opinion of all the judges, when they discovered that the suit had been brought by collusion, to try the question, and it was dismissed. This question was brought before the house of lords, in the case of Donaldson v. Beckett and others, reported in 4 Burr. 2408. Lord Mansfield, being a peer, through feelings of delicacy, declined giving any opinion. The eleven judges gave their opinions on the following points.

1st. Whether, at common law, an author of any book or literary composition, had the sole right of first printing, and publishing the same for sale; and might bring an action against any person who printed, published and sold the same, without his consent? On this question, there were eight judges in the affirmative, and three in the negative.

2d. If the author had such right, originally, did the law take it away, upon his printing and publishing such book or literary composition; and might any person, afterwards, reprint and sell, for his own benefit, such book or literary composition, against the will of the author? This question was answered in the affirmative, by four judges, and in the negative by seven.

3d. If such action would have lain, at common law, it is taken away by the statute of 8 Anne; and is an author, by the said statute, precluded from every remedy, except on the foundation of the said statute, and on the terms of the conditions prescribed thereby? Six of the judges, to five, decided that the remedy must be under the statute. . . .

That an author, at common law, has a property in his manuscript, and may obtain redress against any one who deprives him of it, or by improperly obtaining a copy, endeavors to realize a profit by its publication, cannot be doubted; but this is a very different right from that which asserts a perpetual and exclusive property in the future publication of the work, after the author shall have published it to the world. The argument that a literary man is as much entitled to the product of his labor as any other member of society, cannot be controverted. And the answer is, that he realizes this product by the transfer of his manuscripts, or in the sale of his works, when first published. A book is valuable on account of the matter it contains, the ideas it communicates, the instruction or entertainment it affords. Does the author hold a perpetual property in these? Is there an implied contract by every purchaser of his book, that he may realize whatever instruction or entertainment which the reading of it shall give, but shall not write out or print its contents?

In what respect does the right of an author differ from that of an individual who has invented a most useful and valuable machine? In the production of this, his mind has been as intensely engaged, as long, and, perhaps, as usefully to the public, as any distinguished author in the composition of his book. The result of their labors may be equally beneficial to society, and in their respective spheres, they may be alike distinguished for mental vigor. Does the common law give a perpetual right to the author, and withhold it from the inventor? And yet it has never been pretended, that the latter could hold, by the common law, any property in his invention, after he shall have sold it publicly. It would seem, therefore, that the existence of a principle may well be doubted, which operates so unequally. This is not a characteristic of the common law. It is said to be founded on principles of justice, and that all its rules must conform to sound reason. Does not the man who imitates the machine profit as much by the labor of another, as he who imitates or republishes a book? Can there be a difference between the types and press with which one is formed, and the instruments used in the construction of the others? That every man is entitled to the fruits of his own labor, must be admitted; but he can enjoy them only, except by statutory provision, under the rules of property which regulate society, and which define the rights of things in general. . . .

The question respecting the literary property of authors, was not made a subject of judicial investigation in England until 1760; and no decision was given until the case of Millar v. Taylor was decided in 1769. Long before this time, the colony of Pennsylvania was settled. What part of the common law did Penn and his associates bring with them from England? The literary property of authors, as now asserted, was then unknown in that country. Laws had been passed, regulating the publication of new works, under license. And the king, as the head of the church and the state, claimed the exclusive right of publishing the acts of parliament, the book of common prayer, and a few other books. No such right at the common law had been recognized in England, when the colony of Penn was organized. Long afterwards, literary property became a subject of controversy, but the question was involved in great doubt and perplexity; and a little more than a century ago, it was decided by the highest judicial court in England, that the right of authors could not be asserted at common law, but under the statute. The statute of 8 Anne was passed in 1710. Can it be contended, that this common law right, so involved in doubt as to divide the most learned jurists of England, at a period in her history, as much distinguished by learning and talents as any other, was brought into the wilds of Pennsylvania by its first adventurers? Was it suited to their condition?

But there is another view, still more conclusive. In the eighth section of the first article of the constitution of the United States, it is declared, that congress shall have power "to promote the progress of science and useful arts, by securing, for limited times, to authors and inventors, the exclusive right to their respective writings and discoveries." And in pursuance of the power thus delegated, congress passed the act of the 30th of May 1790. This is entitled "an act for the encouragement of learning, by securing the copies of maps, charts and books, to the authors and proprietors of such copies, during the times therein mentioned." In the first section of this act, it is provided,

> that from and after its passage, the author and authors of any map, chart, book or books, already printed within these United States, being a citizen, &c., who hath or have not transferred to any other person the copyright of such map, chart, book or books, &c., shall have the sole right and liberty of printing, reprinting, publishing and vending such map, book or books, for fourteen years. . . .

From these considerations, it would seem, that if the right of the complainants can be sustained, it must be sustained under the acts of congress. Such was, probably, the opinion of the counsel who framed the bill, as the right is asserted under the statutes, and no particular reference is made to it as existing at common law. The claim, then, of the complainants, must be examined in reference to the statutes under which it is asserted. . . .

It will be observed, that a right accrues, under the act of 1790, from the time a copy of the title of the book is deposited in the clerk's office. But the act of 1802 adds another requisite to the accruing of the right, and that is, that the record made by the clerk, shall be published in the page next to the title page of the book. And it is argued with great earnestness and ability, that these are the only requisites to the perfection of the complainant's title. That the requisition of the third section, to give public notice in the newspapers, and that contained in the fourth, to deposit a copy in the department of state, are acts subsequent to the accruing of the right, and whether they are performed or not, cannot materially affect the title. The case is compared to a grant with conditions subsequent, which can never operate as a forfeiture of the title. It is said, also, that the object of the publication in the newspapers, and the deposit of the copy in the department of state was merely to give notice to the public; and that such acts, not being essential to the title, after so great a lapse of time, may well be presumed. That if neither act had been done, the right of the party having accrued, before either was required to be done, it must remain unshaken.

This right, as has been shown, does not exist at common law — it originated, if at all, under the acts of congress. No one can deny, that when the legislature are about to vest an exclusive right in an author or an inventor, they have the power to prescribe the conditions on which such right shall be enjoyed; and that no one can avail himself of such right who does not substantially comply with the requisitions of the law. This principle is familiar, as it regards patent-rights; and it is the same in relation to the copyright of a book. If any difference shall be made, as it respects a strict conformity to the law, it would seem to be more reasonable, to make the requirement of the author, rather than the inventor. The papers of the latter are examined in the department of state, and require the sanction of the attorney-general; but the author takes every step on his own responsibility, unchecked by the scrutiny of sanction of any public functionary. . . .

But we are told, they are unimportant acts. If they are, indeed, wholly unimportant, congress acted unwisely in requiring them to be done. But whether they are important or not, is not for the court to determine, but the legislature; and in what light they were considered by the legislature, we can learn only by their official acts. Judging then of these acts, by this rule, we are not at liberty to say they are unimportant, and may be dispensed with. They are acts which the law requires to be done, and may this court dispense with their performance?

But the inquiry is made, shall the non-performance of these subsequent conditions operate as a forfeiture of the right? The answer is, that this is not a technical grant on precedent and subsequent conditions. All the conditions are important; the law requires them to be performed; and, consequently, their performance is essential to a perfect title. On the performance of a part of them, the right vests; and this was essential to its protection under the statute; but other acts are to be done, unless congress have legislated in vain, to render the right perfect. The notice could not be published, until after the entry with the clerk, nor could the book be deposited with the secretary of state, until it was published. But these are acts not less important than those which are required to be done previously. They form a part of the title, and until they are performed, the title is not perfect. The deposit of the book in the department of state, may be important to identify it, at any future period, should the copyright be contested, or an unfounded claim of authorship asserted. . . .

The construction of the acts of congress being settled, in the further investigation of the case, it would become necessary to look into the evidence and ascertain whether the complainants have not shown a substantial compliance with every legal requisite. But on reading the evidence, we entertain doubts, which induce us to remand the cause to the circuit court, where the facts can be ascertained by a jury. And the case is accordingly remanded to the circuit court, with directions to that court to order an issue of facts to be examined and tried by a jury, at the bar of said court, upon this point, viz., whether the said Wheaton, as author, or any other person, as proprietor, had complied with the requisites prescribed by the third and fourth sections of the said act of congress, passed the 31st day of May 1790, in regard to the volumes of Wheaton's reports in the said bill mentioned, or in regard to one or more of them in the following particulars, viz., whether the said Wheaton, or proprietor, did, within two months from the date of the recording thereof in the clerk's office of the district court, cause a copy of said record to be published in one or more of the newspapers printed in the resident states, for the space of four weeks; and whether the said Wheaton, or proprietor, after the publishing thereof, did deliver or cause to be delivered to the secretary of state of the United States, a copy of the same, to be preserved in his office, according to the provisions of the said third and fourth sections of the said act. And if the said requisites have not been complied with in regard to all the said volumes, then the jury to find in particular in regard to what volumes they or either of them have been so complied with.

It may be proper to remark, that the court are unanimously of the opinion, that no reporter has or can have any copyright in the written opinions delivered by this court; and that the judges thereof cannot confer on any reporter any such right.

THOMPSON, Justice (dissenting) . . . The common law, says an eminent jurist, 2 Kent's Com. 471, includes those principles, usages and rules of action, applicable to the government and security of person and property which do not rest for their authority upon any express and positive declaration of the will of the legislature. A great proportion of the rules and maxims which constitute the immense code of the common law, grew into use by gradual adoption, and received, from time to time, the sanction of the courts of justice, without any legislative act or interference. It was the application of the dictates of natural justice, and of cultivated reason, to particular cases. In the just language of Sir Matthew Hale, the common law of England is not the product of the wisdom of some one man, or society of men, in any one age, but of the wisdom, counsel, experience and observation of many ages of wise and observing men. And, in accordance with these sound principles, and as applicable to the subject of copyright, are the remarks of Mr. Christian, in his notes to Blackstone's Commentaries. Nothing, says he, is more erroneous, than the practice of referring the origin of moral rights, and the system of natural equity, to the savage state, which is supposed to have preceded civilized establishments, in which literary composition, and, of consequence, the right to it, could have no existence. But the true mode of ascertaining a moral right, is to inquire whether it is such as the reason, the cultivated reason of mankind, must necessarily assent to. No proposition seems more conformable to that criterion, than that every one should enjoy the reward of his labor, the harvest where he has sown, or the fruit of the tree which he has planted. Whether literary property is *sui generis*, or under whatever denomination of rights it may be classed, it seems founded upon the same principle of general utility to society, which is the basis of all other moral rights and obligations. Thus considered, an author's copyright ought to be esteemed an invaluable right, established in sound reason and abstract morality. . . . The objections to the admission of the common-law right of authors, are generally admitted to be summed up, in all their force and strength, by Mr. Justice Yates, in the case of Millar v. Taylor. These objections may be classed under two heads: the one founded upon the nature of the property or subject-matter of the right claimed; and the other, on the presumed abandonment of the right by the author's publication.

The first appears to me to be too subtle and metaphysical to command the assent of any one, or to be adopted as the ground of deciding the question. It seems to be supposed, that the right claimed is to the ideas contained in the book. The claim, says Mr. Justice Yates, is to the style and ideas of the author's composition; and it is a well-established maxim, that nothing can be an object of property, which has not a corporal substance. The property claimed is all ideal; a set of ideas which have no bounds or marks whatever — nothing that is capable of a visible possession — nothing that can sustain any one of the qualities or incidents of property. Their whole existence is in the mind alone. Incapable of any other modes of acquisition and enjoyment than by mental possession or apprehension; safe and invulnerable from their own immateriality, no trespass can reach them, no tort affect them; no fraud or violence diminish or damage them. Yet these are the phantoms which the author would grasp and confine to himself; and these are what the defendant is charged with having robbed the plaintiff of. He asks, can sentiments themselves (apart from the paper on which they are contained) be taken in execution for a debt; or if the author commits treason or felony, or is outlawed, can the ideas be forfeited? Can sentiments be seized; or, by any act whatever, be vested in the crown? If they cannot be seized, the sole right of publishing them cannot be confined to the author. How strange and singular, says he, must this extraordinary kind of property be, which cannot be visibly possessed, forfeited or seized, nor is susceptible of any external injury, nor, consequently, of any specific or possible remedy. . . .

If, as Mr. Justice Yates admits, it is a question of *intention* whether the author meant to abandon his work to the public, and relinquish all private or individual caims to it, no possible doubt can exist as to the conclusion in the present case. Would a jury hesitate a moment upon the question, under the evidence before the court? The right set up and stamped upon the title page of the book, shuts the door against any inference, that the publication was intended to be a gift to the public. Mr. Justice Yates admits, that so long as a literary composition is in manuscript, and remains under the sole dominion of the author, it is his exclusive property. It would seem, therefore, that the idea, when once reduced to writing, is susceptible of identity, and becomes the subject of property. But property, without the right to use it, is empty sound, says Mr. Justice Aston, in Millar v. Taylor. And, indeed, it would seem a mere mockery for the law to recognise anything as property, which the owner could not use safely and securely for the purposes for which it was intended, unless interdicted by the principles of morality or public policy.

Notes

1. Article 1, section 8 of the U.S. Constitution grants Congress the power "to promote the Progress of Science and useful arts by securing for limited time to authors and inventors the exclusive right to their respective writings and discoveries." This protection of property interests in creative works is accomplished through patents and copyrights.

Patents are granted for processes, machines, and substances, but not for bare ideas. They are a grant "for the term of 17 years . . . of the right to exclude others from making, using, or selling an invention throughout the United States." 35 U.S.C. §154 (1970). To be patented, an invention must have social utility (almost any lawful effect is sufficient); must be novel, meaning that it must not have been previously described, used, invented, or patented by another (even independently); and must show "invention" — no patent is awarded when

> the differences between the subject matter sought to be patented and the prior art are such that the subject matter as a whole would have been obvious at the time the invention was made to a person having ordinary skill in the art to which said subject matter pertains. [35 U.S.C. §103.]

A copyright is conferred for the unique manner of expression of an idea — writings, photographs, sculpture, movies, textile patterns, computer programs. Unlike a patent, a copyright may be granted for any original work: If two authors by chance write the same book or take the same photograph, each may hold a copyright on it.

For the first time since 1909, the Copyright Act was substantially revised in 1976, and now deals with at least some modern technologies of "copying." The new law extends protection for the life of the author plus 50 years. For a detailed investigation of possible economic justifications for the monopoly property right called "copyright" see Breyer, The Uneasy Case for Copyright, 84 Harv. L. Rev. 281 (1970).

2. In 1970 New York's State Reporter awarded a five-year contract to Lawyers Co-operative Publishing Co. for publication of the state's official law reports. The Williams Press, Inc., publisher of the reports since 1898 and the unsuccessful bidder this time, refused to turn over the list of subscribers. The court of appeals held that "considering the State's substantial interest in official law reporting . . . , the claim to a property interest in the list of subscribers is without legal foundation

and is, as a matter of policy, simply untenable." Williams Press, Inc. v. Flavin, 35 N.Y.2d 499, 323 N.E.2d 693, 364 N.Y.S.2d 154 (1974).

3. Plaintiffs, "owners" of the Mickey Mouse March, sued defendants, who used the song in "The Life and Times of the Happy Hooker" as "background music while the female protagonist of the film appears to simultaneously gratify the sexual drive of the three other actors [wearing "Mouseketeer" hats] while the group of them is located on or near a billiard table." The district court said this was not "fair use" of the song as a parody, and enjoined showing of the film. But it recognized that the injunction "could be used improperly to publicize" the movie, and declared that "no such commercialization of this decision will be permitted under the penalty of contempt." Walt Disney Productions v. Mature Pictures Corp., 389 F. Supp. 1397 (S.D.N.Y. 1975).

4. Plaintiff complained that the publishers of Time, Esquire, Playboy, and the Ladies Home Journal, as well as the issuer of American Express credit cards, had sold subscription lists including his name to direct mail advertisers. The court found no infringement of plaintiff's privacy. It cited an Ohio law permitting sale of the names and addresses of motor vehicle registrants, and quoted a New York opinion on that subject: "The mailbox, however noxious its advertising contents often seem to judges as well as other people, is hardly the kind of enclave that requires constitutional defense. . . . The short, though regular, journey from mailbox to trash can . . . is an acceptable burden. . . ." Shibley v. Time, Inc. 45 Ohio App. 2d 69, 341 N.E.2d 337 (1975), quoting from Lamont v. Commissioner, 269 F. Supp. 880 (S.D.N.Y. 1967).

5. Plaintiff, "Human Cannonball," performs an act in which he is shot from a cannon into a net 200 feet away. While performing at the Geauga County Fair in Burton, Ohio, a freelance reporter for a local station took film, which was shown for 15 seconds on the local 11:00 P.M. news without plaintiff's permission.

Held: The U.S. Constitution does not require that the press have a privilege against state tort actions (for example, for privacy or loss of commercial opportunities — one state court had upheld actions for conversion and for infringement of a common law copyright) on these facts. The dissent called the events "a routine example of the press' fulfilling the informing function so vital to our system." Zacchini v. Scripps-Howard Broadcasting Co., 433 U.S. 562 (1977) (5-4).

6. Courts have disagreed over whether private property rights in Elvis Presley's name and likeness survived his death. See, e.g., Memphis Development Foundation v. Factors Etc., Inc., 616 F.2d 956 (6th Cir.), *cert. denied,* 449 U.S. 953 (1980); Factors Etc., Inc. v. Pro Arts, Inc., 579 F.2d 215 (2d Cir. 1978), *cert. denied,* 440 U.S. 908 (1979).

7. The California Resale Royalties Act, an American version of the French *droit de suite,* provides that when "a work of fine art" by a living

artist is sold in California or by a California resident for more than $1,000, the seller must pay the artist 5 percent of the sales price. The act survived assertions that it was preempted by the federal Copyright Act, that it effected an unconstitutional taking, and that it violated the Contracts Clause, Morseburg v. Balyon, 621 F.2d 972 (9th Cir.), *cert. denied*, 449 U.S. 983 (1980).

8. European law recognizes an author's and an artist's "moral right." The moral right includes the right to prevent distortion or destruction of the work as well as the right to credit, and protection against false attribution. In France, the moral right is perpetual; in Germany and many other countries, it expires a fixed number of years after the creator's death. The important fact about the moral right is that unlike the economic rights represented by a copyright, the moral right remains with the author or artist after sale of the work.

The United States has never recognized an author's or artist's moral right. However in Gilliam v. American Broadcasting Co., 538 F.2d 14 (2d Cir. 1976), "a group of British writers and performers known as 'Monty Python' " persuaded a court of appeals panel that ABC's editing of three television programs originally broadcast by the BBC destroyed their artistic integrity and misrepresented their work to the world, and thus might well constitute a trademark infringement in violation of the Lanham Act. *Gilliam* may merely require, however, that purchasers of rights to an artist's work obtain explicit acknowledgment in the contract of the authority to edit or alter the work. Under European "moral right" doctrines, no such waiver is permitted.

9. New York's Artists' Authorship Rights Act., N.Y. Arts & Cultural Affairs Law §§14.51-14.59 (McKinney 1984), provides:

> Public display, publication and reproduction of works of fine art. [N]o person other than the artist or a person acting with the artist's consent shall knowingly display in a place accessible to the public or publish a work of fine art of that artist or a reproduction thereof in an altered, defaced, mutilated or modified form if the work is displayed, published or reproduced as being the work of the artist, or under circumstances under which it would reasonably be regarded as being the work of the artist, and damage to the artist's reputation is reasonably likely to result therefrom.

Robert Newmann, an artist, began sandblasting a wall of the Palladium Theater in Manhattan in 1982 with the intention of creating a work of art on it. The theater's new tenant, the Muidallap Corp., halted Newmann's work, however, and announced plans for exterior modifications that included painting the wall black and possibly installing a new entrance in it. While Newmann claimed that the tenant's plan violated his rights as an artist under the act, Muidallap countered that "the statute protects artists against having their works altered or modified," but not against "outright destruction," and that painting over the wall in no way damaged Newmann's reputation. N.Y. Times, Mar. 3, 1984.

10. A patent is available to a person who invents or discovers any new or useful "manufacture" or "composition of matter." The Supreme Court has said that claims are not outside the scope of patentability merely because they are live organisms. Claimant, a microbiologist, asserted invention of "a bacterium from the genus *Pseudomonas*, containing therein at least two stable energy-generating plasmids." The bacterium is capable of breaking down components of crude oil, a property possessed by no naturally occurring bacteria. Chief Justice Burger quoted Thomas Jefferson's view that "ingenuity should receive a liberal encouragement," but he limited the holding: "Einstein could not patent his celebrated law that $E = mc^2$; nor could Newton have patented the law of gravity." Diamond v. Chakrabarty, 447 U.S. 303 (1980) (5-4).

11. For a good summary and analysis of the Copyright Act, see Gorman, An Overview of the Copyright Act of 1976, 126 U. Pa. L. Rev. 856 (1978).

◆ INTERNATIONAL NEWS SERVICE v. ASSOCIATED PRESS
248 U.S. 215 (1918)

Mr. Justice PITNEY delivered the opinion of the court. The parties are competitors in the gathering and distribution of news and its publication for profit in newspapers throughout the United States. The Associated Press, which was complainant in the District Court, is a cooperative organization, incorporated under the Membership Corporations Law of the State of New York, its members being individuals who are either proprietors or representatives of about 950 daily newspapers published in all parts of the United States. That a corporation may be organized under that act for the purpose of gathering news for the use and benefit of its members and for publication in newspapers owned or represented by them, is recognized by an amendment enacted in 1901. Complainant gathers in all parts of the world, by means of various instrumentalities of its own, by exchange with its members, and by other appropriate means, news and intelligence of current and recent events of interest to newspaper readers and distributes it daily to its members for publication in their newspapers. The cost of the service, amounting approximately to $3,500,000 per annum, is assessed upon the members and becomes a part of their costs of operation, to be recouped, presumably with profit, through the publication of their several newspapers. Under complainant's by-laws each member agrees upon assuming membership that news received through complainant's service is received exclusively for publication in a particular newspaper, language, and place specified in the certificate of membership, that no other use of it shall be permitted, and that no member shall furnish or permit anyone in his employ or connected with his newspaper to furnish any of complainant's news in advance of publication to any person not a member. And each member is required to gather the local news of his district and supply it to the Associated Press and to no one else.

Defendant is a corporation organized under the laws of the State of New Jersey, whose business is the gathering and selling of news to its customers and clients, consisting of newspapers published throughout the United States, under contracts by which they pay certain amounts at stated times for defendant's service. It has wide-spread news-gathering agencies; the cost of its operations amounts, it is said, to more than $2,000,000 per annum; and it serves about 400 newspapers located in the various cities of the United States and abroad, a few of which are represented, also, in the membership of the Associated Press.

The parties are in the keenest competition between themselves in the distribution of news throughout the United States; and so, as a rule, are the newspapers that they serve, in their several districts.

Complainant in its bill, defendant in its answer, have set forth in almost identical terms the rather obvious circumstances and conditions under which their business is conducted. The value of the service, and of the news furnished, depends upon the promptness of transmission, as well as upon the accuracy and impartiality of the news; it being essential that the news be transmitted to members or subscribers as early or earlier than similar information can be furnished to competing newspapers by other news services, and that the news furnished by each agency shall not be furnished to newspapers which do not contribute to the expense of gathering it. And further, to quote from the answer:

> Prompt knowledge and publication of world-wide news is essential to the conduct of a modern newspaper, and by reason of the enormous expense incident to the gathering and distribution of such news, the only practical way in which a proprietor of a newspaper can obtain the same is, either through coöperation with a considerable number of other newspaper proprietors in the work of collecting and distributing such news, and the equitable division with them of the expenses thereof, or by the purchase of such news from some existing agency engaged in that business.

The bill was filed to restrain the pirating of complainant's news by defendant in three ways: First, by bribing employees of newspapers published by complainant's members to furnish Associated Press news to defendant before publication, for transmission by telegraph and telephone to defendant's clients for publication by them; Second, by inducing Associated Press members to violate its by-laws and permit defendant to obtain news before publication; and Third, by copying news from bulletin boards and from early editions of complainant's newspapers and selling this, either bodily or after rewriting it, to defendant's customers. . . .

The only matter that has been argued before us is whether defendant may lawfully be restrained from appropriating news taken from bulletins issued by complainant or any of its members, or from newspapers published by them, for the purpose of selling it to defendant's clients. Complainant asserts that defendant's admitted course of conduct in this regard both violates complainant's property right in the news and constitutes unfair competition in business. And notwithstanding the case has proceeded only to the stage of a preliminary injunction, we have deemed it proper to consider the underlying questions, since they go to the very merits of the action and are presented upon facts that are not in dispute. As presented in argument, these questions are: 1. Whether there is any property in news; 2. Whether, if there be property in news collected for the purpose of being published, it survives the instant of its publication in the first newspaper to which it is communicated by the news-gatherer; and 3. Whether defendant's admitted course of conduct in appropriating for commercial use matter taken from bulletins of early editions of Associated Press publications constitutes unfair competition in trade.

The federal jurisdiction was invoked because of diversity of citizenship, not upon the ground that the suit arose under the copyright or other laws of the United States. Complainant's news matter is not copyrighted. It is said that it could not, in practice, be copyrighted, because of the large number of dispatches that are sent daily; and, according to complainant's contention, news is not within the operation of the copyright act. Defendant, while apparently conceding this, nevertheless invokes the analogies of the law of literary property and copyright, insisting as its principal contention that, assuming complainant has a right of property in its news, it can be maintained (unless the copyright act be complied with) only by being kept secret and confidential, and that upon the publication with complainant's consent of uncopyrighted news by any of complainant's members in a newspaper or upon a bulletin board, the right of property is lost, and the subsequent use of the news by the public or by defendant for any purpose whatever becomes lawful. . . .

In considering the general question of property in news matter, it is necessary to recognize its dual character, distinguishing between the substance of the information and the particular form of collocation of words in which the writer has communicated it.

No doubt news articles often possess a literary quality, and are the subject of literary property at the common law; nor do we question that such an article, as a literary production, is the subject of copyright by the terms of the act as it now stands. In an early case at the circuit Mr. Justice Thompson held in effect that a newspaper was not within the protection of the copyright acts of 1790 and 1802. But the present act is broader; it provides that the works for which copyright may be secured shall include "all the writings of an author," and specifically mentions "periodicals, including newspapers." Evidently this admits to copyright a contribution to a newspaper, notwithstanding it also may convey news; and such is the practice of the copyright office, as the newspapers of the day bear witness.

But the news element — the information respecting current events contained in the literary production — is not the creation of the writer, but is a report of matters that ordinarily are *publici juris;* it is the history of the day. It is not to be supposed that the framers of the Constitution, when they empowered Congress "to promote the progress of science and useful arts, by securing for limited times to authors and inventors the exclusive right to their respective writings and discoveries," intended to confer upon one who might happen to be the first to report a historic event the exclusive right for any period to spread the knowledge of it.

We need spend no time, however, upon the general question of property in news matter at common law, or the application of the copyright act, since it seems to us the case must turn upon the question of unfair competition of business. And, in our opinion, this does not depend upon any general right of property analogous to the common-law right of the proprietor of an unpublished work to prevent its publication without his consent; nor is it foreclosed by showing that the benefits of the copyright act have been waived. We are dealing here not with restrictions upon publication but with the very facilities and processes of publication. The peculiar value of news is in the spreading of it while it is fresh; and it is evident that a valuable property interest in the news, as news, cannot be maintained by keeping it secret. Besides, except for matters improperly disclosed, or published in breach of trust or confidence, or in violation of law, none of which is involved in this branch of the case, the news of current events may be regarded as common property. What we are concerned with is the business of making it known to the world, in which both parties to the present suit are engaged. That business consists in maintaining a prompt, sure, steady, and reliable service designed to place the daily events of the world at the breakfast table of the millions at a price that, while of trifling moment to each reader, is sufficient in the aggregate to afford compensation for the cost of gathering and distributing it, with the added profit so necessary as an incentive to effective action in the commercial world. The service thus performed for newspaper readers is not only innocent but extremely useful in itself, and indubitably constitutes a legitimate business. The parties are competitors in this field; and, on fundamental principles, applicable here as elsewhere, when the rights or privileges of the one are liable to conflict with those of the other, each party is under a duty so to conduct its own business as not necessarily or unfairly to injure that of the other.

Obviously, the question of what is unfair competition in business must be determined with particular reference to the character and circumstances of the business. The question here is not so much the rights of either party as against the public but their rights as between themselves. See Morison v. Moat, 9 Hare, 241, 258. And although we may and do assume that neither party has any remaining property interest as against the public in uncopyrighted news matter after the moment of its first publication, it by no means follows that there is no remaining property interest in it as between themselves. For, to both of them alike, news matter, however little susceptible of ownership or dominion in the absolute sense, is stock in trade, to be gathered at the cost of enterprise, organization, skill, labor, and money, and to be distributed and sold to those who will pay money for it, as for any other merchandise. Regarding the news, therefore, as but the material out of which both parties are seeking to make profits at the same time and in the same field, we hardly can fail to recognize that for this purpose, and as between them, it must be regarded as *quasi* property, irrespective of the rights of either as against the public. . . .

The peculiar features of the case arise from the fact that, while novelty and freshness form so important an element in the success of the business, the very processes of distribution and publication necessarily occupy a good deal of time. Complainant's service, as well as defendant's, is a daily service to daily newspapers; most of the foreign news reaches this country at the Atlantic seaboard, principally at the City of New York, and because of this, and of time differentials due to the earth's rotation, the distribution of news matter throughout the country is principally from east to west; and, since in speed the telegraph and telephone easily outstrip the rotation of the earth, it is a simple matter for defendant to take complainant's news from bulletins or early editions of complainant's members in the eastern cities and at the mere cost of telegraphic transmission cause it to be published in western papers issued at least as early as those served by complainant. Besides this, and irrespective of time differentials, irregularities in telegraphic transmission on different lines, and the normal consumption of time in printing and distributing the newspaper, result in permitting pirated news to be placed in the hands of defendant's readers sometimes simultaneously with the service of competing Associated Press papers, occasionally even earlier.

Defendant insists that when, with the sanction and approval of complainant, and as the result of the use of its news for the very purpose for which it is distributed, a portion of complainant's members communicate it to the general public by posting it upon bulletin boards so that all may read, or by issuing it to newspapers and distributing it indiscriminately, complainant no longer has the right to control the use to be made of it; that when it thus reaches the light of day it becomes the common possession of all to whom it is accessible; and that any purchaser of a newspaper has the right to communicate the intelligence which it contains to anybody and for any purpose, even for the purpose of selling it for profit to newspapers published for profit in competition with complainant's members.

The fault in the reasoning lies in applying as a test the right of the complainant as against the public, instead of considering the rights of complainant and defendant, competitors in business, as between themselves. The right of the purchaser of a single newspaper to spread knowledge of its contents gratuitously, for any legitimate purpose not unreasonably interfering with complainant's right to make merchandise of it, may be admitted; but to transmit that news for commercial use, in competition with complainant — which is what defendant has done and seeks to justify — is a very different matter. In doing this defendant, by its very act, admits that it is taking material that has been acquired by complainant as the result of organization and the expenditure of labor, skill, and money, and which is salable by complainant for money, and that defendant in appropriating it and selling it as its own is endeavoring to reap where it has not sown, and by disposing of it to newspapers that are competitors of complainant's members is appropriating to itself the harvest of those who have sown. Stripped of all disguises, the process amounts to an unauthorized interference with the normal operation of complainant's legitimate business precisely at the point where the profit is to be reaped, in order to divert a material portion of the profit from those who have earned it to those who have not; with special advantage to defendant in the competition because of the fact that it is not burdened with any part of the expense of gathering the news. The transaction speaks for itself, and a court of equity ought not to hesitate long in characterizing it as unfair competition in business. . . .

The decree of the Circuit Court of Appeals [enjoining defendant from bodily taking of the words or substance of complainant's news until its commercial value as news had passed away] will be affirmed.

Mr. Justice HOLMES. When an uncopyrighted combination of words is published there is no general right to forbid other people repeating them — in other words there is no property in the combination or in the thoughts or facts that the words express. Property, a creation of law, does not arise from value, although exchangeable — a matter of fact. Many exchangeable values may be destroyed intentionally without compensation. Property depends upon exclusion by law from interference, and a person is not excluded from using any combination of words merely because someone has used it before, even if it took labor and genius to make it. If a given person is to be prohibited from making the use of words that his neighbors are free to make some other ground must be found. One such ground is vaguely expressed in the phrase unfair trade. This means that the words are repeated by a competitor in business in such a way as to convey a misrepresentation that materially injures the person who first used them, by appropriating credit of some kind which the first user has earned. The ordinary case is a representation by device, appearance, or other indirection that the defendant's goods come from the plaintiff. But the only reason why it is actionable to make such a representation is that it tends to give the defendant an advantage in his competition with the plaintiff and that it is thought undesirable that an advantage should be gained in that way. Apart from that the defendant may use such unpatented devices and uncopyrighted combinations of words as he likes. The ordinary case, I say, is palming off the defendant's product as the plaintiff's, but the same evil may follow from the opposite falsehood — from saying, whether in words or by implication, that the plaintiff's product is the defendant's, and that, it seems to me, is what has happened here.

Fresh news is got only by enterprise and expense. To produce such news as it is produced by the defendant represents by implication that it has been acquired by the defendant's enterprise and at its expense. When it comes from one of the great news-collecting agencies like the Associated Press, the source generally is indicated, plainly importing that credit; and that such a representation is implied may be inferred with some confidence from the unwillingness of the defendant to give the credit and tell the truth. If the plaintiff produces the news at the same time that the defendant does, the defendant's presentation impliedly denies to the plaintiff the credit of collecting the facts and assumes that credit to the defendant. If the plaintiff is later in western cities it naturally will be supposed to have obtained its information from the defendant. The falsehood is a little more subtle, the injury a little more indirect, than in ordinary cases of unfair trade, but I think that the principle that condemns the one condemns the other. It is a question of how strong an infusion of fraud is necessary to turn a flavor into a poison. The dose seems to me strong enough here to need a remedy from the law. But as, in my view, the only ground of complaint that can be recognized without legislation is the implied misstatement, it can be corrected by stating the truth; and a suitable acknowledgment of the source is all that the plaintiff can require. I think that within the limits recognized by the decision of the Court the defendant should be enjoined from publishing news obtained from the Associated Press for   hours after publication by the plaintiff unless it gives express credit to the Associated Press; the number of hours and the form of acknowledgment to be settled by the District Court.

Mr. Justice BRANDEIS dissenting. . . . No question of statutory copy-right is involved. The sole question for our consideration is this: Was the International News Service properly enjoined from using, or causing to be used gainfully, news of which it acquired knowledge by lawful means (namely, by reading publicly posted bulletins or papers pur-chased by it in the open market) merely because the news had been originally gathered by the Associated Press and continued to be of value to some of its members, or because it did not reveal the source from which it was acquired? . . .

News is a report of recent occurrences. The business of the news agency is to gather systematically knowledge of such occurrences of interest and to distribute reports thereof. The Associated Press con-tended that knowledge so acquired is property, because it costs money and labor to produce and because it has value for which those who have it not are ready to pay; that it remains property and is entitled to protec-tion as long as it has commercial value as news; and that to protect it effectively the defendant must be enjoined from making, or causing to be made, any gainful use of it while it retains such value. An essential element of individual property is the legal right to exclude others from enjoying it. If the property is private, the right of exclusion may be absolute; if the property is affected with a public interest, the right of exclusion is qualified. But the fact that a product of the mind has cost its producer money and labor, and has a value for which others are willing to pay, is not sufficient to ensure to it this legal attribute of property. The general rule of law is, that the noblest of human productions — knowl-edge, truths ascertained, conceptions, and ideas — become, after volun-tary communication to others, free as the air to common use. Upon these incorporeal productions the attribute of property is continued after such communication only in certain classes of cases where public policy has seemed to demand it. . . . There are also many other cases in which courts interfere to prevent curtailment of plaintiff's enjoyment of incor-poreal productions; and in which the right to relief is often called a property right, but is such only in a special sense. In those cases, the plaintiff has no absolute right to the protection of his production; he has merely the qualified right to be protected as against the defendant's acts, because of the special relation in which the latter stands or the wrongful method or means employed in acquiring the knowledge or the manner in which it is used. Protection of this character is afforded where the suit is based upon breach of contract or of trust or upon unfair competi-tion. . . .

That competition is not unfair in a legal sense, merely because the profits gained are unearned, even if made at the expense of a rival, is shown by many cases besides those referred to above. He who follows the pioneer into a new market, or who engages in the manufacture of an article newly introduced by another, seeks profits due largely to the labor and expense of the first adventurer; but the law sanctions, indeed encourages, the pursuit. He who makes a city known through his product, must submit to sharing the resultant trade with others who, perhaps for that reason, locate there later. He who has made his name a guaranty of quality, protests in vain when another with the same name engages, perhaps for that reason, in the same lines of business; provided, precaution is taken to prevent the public from being deceived into the belief that what he is selling was made by his competitor. One bearing a name made famous by another is permitted to enjoy the unearned benefit which necessarily flows from such use, even though the use proves harmful to him who gave the name value.

The means by which the International News Service obtains news gathered by the Associated Press is also clearly unobjectionable. It is taken from papers bought in the open market or from bulletins publicly posted. No breach of contract or of trust, and neither fraud nor force, is involved. The manner of use is likewise unobjectionable. No reference is made by word or by act to the Associated Press, either in transmitting the news to subscribers or by them in publishing it in their papers. Neither the International News Service nor its subscribers is gaining or seeking to gain in its business a benefit from the reputation of the Associated Press. They are merely using its product without making compensation. That, they have a legal right to do; because the product is not property, and they do not stand in any relation to the Associated Press, either of contract or of trust, which otherwise precludes such use. The argument is not advanced by characterizing such taking and use a misappropriation. . . .

The great development of agencies now furnishing country-wide distribution of news, the vastness of our territory, and improvements in the means of transmitting intelligence, have made it possible for a news agency or newspapers to obtain, without paying compensation, the fruit of another's efforts and to use news so obtained gainfully in competition with the original collector. The injustice of such action is obvious. But to give relief against it would involve more than the application of existing rules of law to new facts. It would require the making of a new rule in analogy to existing ones. The unwritten law possesses capacity for growth; and has often satisfied new demands for justice by invoking analogies or by expanding a rule or principle. This process has been in the main wisely applied and should not be discontinued. Where the problem is relatively simple, as it is apt to be when private interests only are involved, it generally proves adequate. But with the increasing complexity of society, the public interest tends to become omnipresent; and the problems presented by new demands for justice cease to be simple. Then the creation or recognition by courts of a new private right may work serious injury to the general public, unless the boundaries of the right are definitely established and wisely guarded. In order to reconcile the new private right with the public interest, it may be necessary to prescribe limitations and rules for its enjoyment; and also to provide administrative machinery for enforcing the rules. It is largely for this reason that, in the effort to meet the many new demands for justice incident to a rapidly changing civilization, resort to legislation has latterly been had with increasing frequency. . . .

Courts are ill-equipped to make the investigations which should precede a determination of the limitations which should be set upon any property right in news or of the circumstances under which news gathered by a private agency should be deemed affected with a public interest. Courts would be powerless to prescribe the detailed regulations essential to full enjoyment of the rights conferred or to introduce the machinery required for enforcement of such regulations. Considerations such as these should lead us to decline to establish a new rule of law in the effort to redress a newly-disclosed wrong, although the propriety of some remedy appears to be clear.

Notes

1. Does International News Service v. Associated Press suggest that a cable television station unlawfully takes property when it erects an antenna, receives the signal of a disant broadcast station, and delivers the signal for a fee to its subscribers? The Supreme Court held that the action of the cable company was not a broadcast and so not a "performance" within the meaning of the 1909 Copyright Act. The court drew a simple line: Broadcasters perform; viewers do not. CATV systems fall "on the viewer's side of the line." Fortnightly Corp. v. United Artists Television, Inc., 392 U.S. 390 (1968).

Controversy ensued. The parties most concerned — cable owners, broadcasters, and the networks — recognized that the 1909 law could not deal adequately with the new technology. Attention turned to the FCC, which in 1972 adopted Cable Regulations, 36 FCC2d 143 (1972), protecting the property rights of over-the-air broadcasters in their (government granted) oligopoly industry, by restricting the rights of cable systems to compete. Limits were imposed on simultaneous duplication of local programming, on the number of distant signals that can be imported, and on when cable can present certain programs, especially movies and sports. The 1976 copyright law generally undergirds the 1972 FCC compromise and makes cable liable to copyright payments for non-network programming.

2. For a review of more recent cases similar to International News Service v. Associated Press, see Libling, Property in Intangibles, 94 Law Q.R. 103 (1978). Mr. Libling argues for this proposition:

Any expenditure of mental or physical effort, as a result of which there is created an entity, whether tangible or intangible, vests in the person who brought the entity into being, a proprietary right to the commercial exploitation of that entity, which right is separate and independent from the ownership of that entity.

◆ SONY CORP. OF AMERICA v. UNIVERSAL CITY STUDIOS, INC.
104 S. Ct. 774 (1984)

Justice STEVENS delivered the opinion of the Court.

Petitioners manufacture and sell home video tape recorders. Respondents own the copyrights on some of the television programs that are broadcast on the public airwaves. Some members of the general public use video tape recorders sold by petitioners to record some of these broadcasts, as well as a large number of other broadcasts. The question presented is whether the sale of petitioners' copying equipment to the general public violates any of the rights conferred upon respondents by the Copyright Act. . . .

[The findings of the District Court] reveal that the average member of the public uses a VTR principally to record a program he cannot view as it is being televised and then to watch it once at a later time. This practice, known as "time-shifting," enlarges the television viewing audience. For that reason, a significant amount of television programming may be used in this manner without objection from the owners of the copyrights on the programs. For the same reason, even the two respondents in this case, who do assert objections to time-shifting in this litigation, were unable to prove that the practice has impaired the commercial value of their copyrights or has created any likelihood of future harm. Given these findings, there is no basis in the Copyright Act upon which respondents can hold petitioners liable for distributing VTR's to the general public. The Court of Appeals' holding that respondents are entitled to enjoin the distribution of VTR's, to collect royalties on the sale of such equipment, or to obtain other relief, if affirmed, would enlarge the scope of respondents' statutory monopolies to encompass control over an article of commerce that is not the subject of copyright protection. Such an expansion of the copyright privilege is beyond the limits of the grants authorized by Congress.

The two respondents in this action, Universal Studios, Inc. and Walt Disney Productions, produce and hold the copyrights on a substantial number of motion pictures and other audiovisual works. In the current marketplace, they can exploit their rights in these works in a number of ways: by authorizing theatrical exhibitions, by licensing limited showings on cable and network television, by selling syndication rights for repeated airings on local television stations, and by marketing programs on prerecorded videotapes or videodiscs. Some works are suitable for exploitation through all of these avenues, while the market for other works is more limited.

Petitioner Sony manufactures millions of Betamax video tape recorders and markets these devices through numerous retail establishments, some of which are also petitioners in this action. Sony's Betamax VTR is a mechanism consisting of three basic components: (1) a tuner, which receives electromagnetic signals transmitted over the television band of the public airwaves and separates them into audio and visual signals; (2) a recorder, which records such signals on a magnetic tape; and (3) an adapter, which converts the audio and visual signals on the tape into a composite signal that can be received by a television set.

Several capabilities of the machine are noteworthy. The separate tuner in the Betamax enables it to record a broadcast off one station while the television set is tuned to another channel, permitting the viewer, for example, to watch two simultaneous news broadcasts by watching one "live" and recording the other for later viewing. Tapes may be reused, and programs that have been recorded may be erased either before or after viewing. A timer in the Betamax can be used to activate and deactivate the equipment at predetermined times, enabling an intended viewer to record programs that are transmitted when he or she is not at home. Thus a person may watch a program at home in the evening even though it was broadcast while the viewer was at work during the afternoon. The Betamax is also equipped with a pause button and a fast-forward control. The pause button, when depressed, deactivates the recorder until it is released, thus enabling a viewer to omit a commercial advertisement from the recording, provided, of course, that the viewer is present when the program is recorded. The fast forward control enables the viewer of a previously recorded program to run the tape rapidly when a segment he or she does not desire to see is being played back on the television screen.

The respondents and Sony both conducted surveys of the way the Betamax machine was used by several hundred owners during a sample period in 1978. Although there were some differences in the surveys, they both showed that the primary use of the machine for most owners was "time-shifting," — the practice of recording a program to view it once at a later time, and thereafter erasing it. Time-shifting enables viewers to see programs they otherwise would miss because they are not at home, are occupied with other tasks, or are viewing a program on another station at the time of a broadcast that they desire to watch. Both surveys also showed, however, that a substantial number of interviewees had accumulated libraries of tapes. Sony's survey indicated that over 80% of the interviewees watched at least as much regular television as they had before owning a Betamax. Respondents offered no evidence of decreased television viewing by Betamax owners.

Sony introduced considerable evidence describing television programs that could be copied without objection from any copyright holder, with special emphasis on sports, religious, and educational programming. For example, their survey indicated that 7.3% of all Betamax use is to record sports events, and representatives of professional baseball, football, basketball, and hockey testified that they had no objection to the recording of their televised events for home use.

Respondents offered opinion evidence concerning the future impact of the unrestricted sale of VTR's on the commercial value of their copyrights. The District Court found, however, that they had failed to prove any likelihood of future harm from the use of VTR's for time-shifting. . . .

Article I, Sec. 8 of the Constitution provides that: "The Congress shall have Power . . . to Promote the Progress of Science and useful Arts, by securing for limited Times to Authors and Inventors the exclusive Right to their respective Writings and Discoveries."

The monopoly privileges that Congress may authorize are neither unlimited nor primarily designed to provide a special private benefit. Rather, the limited grant is a means by which an important public purpose may be achieved. It is intended to motivate the creative activity of authors and inventors by the provision of a special reward, and to allow the public access to the products of their genius after the limited period of exclusive control has expired. . . .

If vicarious liability is to be imposed on petitioners in this case, it must rest on the fact that they have sold equipment with constructive knowledge of the fact that their customers may use that equipment to make unauthorized copies of copyrighted material. There is no precedent in the law of copyright for the imposition of vicarious liability on such a theory. . . .

The question is thus whether the Betamax is capable of commercially significant noninfringing uses. In order to resolve that question, we need not explore *all* the different potential uses of the machine and determine whether or not they would constitute infringement. Rather, we need only consider whether on the basis of the facts as found by the district court a significant number of them would be non-infringing. Moreover, in order to resolve this case we need not give precise content to the question of how much use is commercially significant. For one potential use of the Betamax plainly satisfies this standard, however it is understood: private, noncommercial time-shifting in the home. It does so both (A) because respondents have no right to prevent other copyright holders from authorizing it for their programs, and (B) because the District Court's factual findings reveal that even the unauthorized home time-shifting of respondents' programs is legitimate fair use. . . .

Second is the testimony of Fred Rogers, president of the corporation that produces and owns the copyright on *Mr. Rogers' Neighborhood*. The program is carried by more public television stations than any other program. Its audience numbers over 3,000,000 families a day. He testified that he had absolutely no objection to home taping for noncommercial use and expressed the opinion that it is a real service to families to be able to record children's programs and to show them at appropriate times.

If there are millions of owners of VTR's who make copies of televised sports events, religious broadcasts, and educational programs such as *Mister Rogers' Neighborhood,* and if the proprietors of those programs welcome the practice, the business of supplying the equipment that makes such copying feasible should not be stifled simply because the equipment is used by some individuals to make unauthorized reproductions of respondents' works. The respondents do not represent a class composed of all copyright holders. Yet a finding of contributory infringement would inevitably frustrate the interests of broadcasters in reaching the portion of their audience that is available only through time-shifting. . . .

The purpose of copyright is to create incentives for creative effort. Even copying for noncommercial purposes may impair the copyright holder's ability to obtain the rewards that Congress intended him to have. But a use that has no demonstrable effect upon the potential market for, or the value of, the copyrighted work need not be prohibited in order to protect the author's incentive to create. The prohibition of such noncommercial uses would merely inhibit access to ideas without any countervailing benefit.

Thus, although every commercial use of copyrighted material is presumptively an unfair exploitation of the monopoly privilege that belongs to the owner of the copyright, noncommercial uses are a different matter. A challenge to a noncommercial use of a copyrighted work requires proof either that the particular use is harmful, or that if it should become widespread, it would adversely affect the potential market for the copyrighted work. Actual present harm need not be shown; such a requirement would leave the copyright holder with no defense against predictable damage. Nor is it necessary to show with certainty that future harm will result. What is necessary is a showing by a preponderance of the evidence that *some* meaningful likelihood of future harm exists. If the intended use is for commercial gain, that likelihood may be presumed. But if it is for a noncommercial purpose, the likelihood must be demonstrated.

In this case, respondents failed to carry their burden with regard to home time-shifting. . . .

In summary, the record and findings of the District Court lead us to two conclusions. First, Sony demonstrated a significant likelihood that substantial numbers of copyright holders who license their works for broadcast on free television would not object to having their broadcasts time-shifted by private viewers. And second, respondents failed to demonstrate that time-shifting would cause any likelihood of nonminimal harm to the potential market for, or the value of, their copyrighted works. The Betamax is, therefore, capable of substantial noninfringing uses. Sony's sale of such equipment to the general public does not constitute contributory infringement of respondent's copyrights. . . .

One may search the Copyright Act in vain for any sign that the elected representatives of the millions of people who watch television every day have made it unlawful to copy a program for later viewing at home, or have enacted a flat prohibition against the sale of machines that make such copying possible.

It may well be that Congress will take a fresh look at this new technology, just as it so often has examined other innovations in the past. But it is not our job to apply laws that have not yet been written. Applying the copyright statute, as it now reads, to the facts as they have been developed in this case, the judgment of the Court of Appeals must be reversed.

Justice BLACKMUN, with whom Justice MARSHALL, Justice POWELL, and Justice REHNQUIST join, dissenting.

. . . I . . . conclude that, at least when the proposed use is an unproductive one, a copyright owner need prove only a *potential* for harm to the market for or the value of the copyrighted work. Proof of actual harm, or even probable harm, may be impossible in an area where the effect of a new technology is speculative, and requiring such proof would present the "real danger . . . of confining the scope of an author's rights on the basis of the present technology so that, as the years go by, his copyright loses much of its value because of unforeseen technical advances."

Infringement thus would be found if the copyright owner demonstrates a reasonable possibility that harm will result from the proposed use. When the use is one that creates no benefit to the public at large, copyright protection should not be denied on the basis that a new technology that may result in harm has not yet done so.

The Studios have identified a number of ways in which VTR recording could damage their copyrights. VTR recording could reduce their ability to market their works in movie theaters and through the rental or sale of pre-recorded videotapes or video-discs; it also could reduce their rerun audience, and consequently the license fees available to them for repeated showings. Moreover, advertisers may be willing to pay for only "live" viewing audiences, if they believe VTR viewers will delete commercials or if rating services are unable to measure VTR use; if this is the case, VTR recording could reduce the license fees the Studios are able to charge even for first-run showings. Library-building may raise the potential for each of the types of harm identified by the Studios, and time-shifting may raise the potential for substantial harm as well. . . .

From the Studios' perspective, the consequences of home VTR recording are the same as if a business had taped the Studios' works off the air, duplicated the tapes, and sold or rented them to members of the public for home viewing. The distinction is that home VTR users do not record for commercial advantage; the commercial benefit accrues to the manufacturer and distributors of the Betamax.

The District Court found that Sony has advertised the Betamax as suitable for off-the-air recording of "favorite shows," "novels for television," and "classic movies," with no visible warning that such recording could constitute copyright infringement. It is only with the aid of the Betamax or some other VTR, that it is possible today for home television viewers to infringe copyright by recording off-the-air. Off-the-air recording is not only a foreseeable use for the Betamax, but indeed is its intended use. Under the circumstances, I agree with the Court of Appeals that if off-the-air recording is an infringement of copyright, Sony has induced and materially contributed to the infringing conduct of Betamax owners. . . .

The Court of Appeals, having found Sony liable, remanded for the District Court to consider the propriety of injunctive or other relief. Because of my conclusion as to the issue of liability, I, too, would not decide here what remedy would be appropriate if liability were found. I concur, however, in the Court of Appeals' suggestion that an award of damages, or continuing royalties, or even some form of limited injunction, may well be an appropriate means of balancing the equities in this case. Although I express no view on the merits of any particular proposal, I am certain that, if Sony were found liable in this case, the District Court would be able to fashion appropriate relief. The District Court might conclude, of course, that a continuing royalty or other equitable relief is not feasible. The Studios then would be relegated to statutory damages for proved instances of infringement. But the difficulty of fashioning relief, and the possibility that complete relief may be unavailable, should not affect out interpretation of the statute.

Like so many other problems created by the interaction of copyright law with a new technology, "[t]here can be no really satisfactory solution to the problem presented here, until Congress acts." But in the absence of a congressional solution, courts cannot avoid difficult problems by refusing to apply the law. We must "take the Copyright Act . . . as we find it," and "do as little damage as possible to traditional copyright principles . . . until the Congress legislates."

23 ◆ NEW PROPERTY

A. PROPERTY AS PROCESS

1. *Deprivation of Possession*

◆ FUENTES v. SHEVIN
407 U.S. 67 (1972)

Mr. Justice STEWART delivered the opinion of the Court. We here review
the decisions of two three-judge federal District Courts that upheld the
constitutionality of Florida and Pennsylvania laws authorizing the summary seizure of goods or chattels in a person's possession under a writ
of replevin. Both statutes provide for the issuance of writs ordering state
agents to seize a person's possessions, simply upon the *ex parte* application of any other person who claims a right to them and posts a security
bond. Neither statute provides for notice to be given to the possessor of
the property, and neither statute gives the possessor an opportunity to
challenge the seizure at any kind of prior hearing. The question is
whether these statutory procedures violate the Fourteenth Amendment's guarantee that no State shall deprive any person of property
without due process of law.

. . . Margarita Fuentes is a resident of Florida. She purchased a gas
stove and service policy from the Firestone Tire and Rubber Co. (Firestone) under a conditional sales contract calling for monthly payments
over a period of time. A few months later, she purchased a stereophonic
phonograph from the same company under the same sort of contract.
The total cost of the stove and stereo was about $500, plus an additional
financing charge of over $100. Under the contracts, Firestone retained
title to the merchandise, but Mrs. Fuentes was entitled to possession
unless and until she should default on her installment payments.

For more than a year, Mrs. Fuentes made her installment payments.

But then, with only about $200 remaining to be paid, a dispute developed between her and Firestone over the servicing of the stove. Firestone instituted an action in a small-claims court for repossession of both the stove and the stereo, claiming that Mrs. Fuentes had refused to make her remaining payments. Simultaneously with the filing of that action and before Mrs. Fuentes had even received a summons to answer its complaint, Firestone obtained a writ of replevin ordering a sheriff to seize the disputed goods at once.

In conformance with Florida procedure, Firestone had only to fill in the blanks on the appropriate form documents and submit them to the clerk of the small-claims court. The clerk signed and stamped the documents and issued a writ of replevin. Later the same day, a local deputy sheriff and an agent of Firestone went to Mrs. Fuentes' home and seized the stove and stereo.

Shortly thereafter, Mrs. Fuentes instituted the present action in a federal district court, challenging the constitutionality of the Florida prejudgment replevin procedures under the Due Process Clause of the Fourteenth Amendment. She sought declaratory and injunctive relief against continued enforcement of the procedural provisions of the state statutes that authorize prejudgment replevin. . . .

Under the Florida statute challenged here, "[a]ny person whose goods or chattels are wrongfully detained by any other person . . . may have a writ of replevin to recover them. . . ." There is no requirement that the applicant make a convincing showing before the seizure that the goods are, in fact, "wrongfully detained." Rather, Florida law automatically relies on the bare assertion of the party seeking the writ that he is entitled to one and allows a court clerk to issue the writ summarily. It requires only that the applicant file a complaint, initiating a court action for repossession and reciting in conclusory fashion that he is "lawfully entitled to the possession" of the property, and that he file a security bond "in at least double the value of the property to be replevied conditioned that plaintiff will prosecute his action to effect and without delay and that if defendant recovers judgment against him in the action, he will return the property, if return thereof is adjudged, and will pay defendant all sums of money recovered against plaintiff by defendant in the action." On the sole basis of the complaint and bond, a writ is issued "command[ing] the officer to whom it may be directed to replevy the goods and chattels in possession of defendant . . . and to summon the defendant to answer the complaint." If the goods are "in any dwelling house or other building or enclosure," he shall cause such house, building or enclosure to be broken open and shall make replevin according to the writ. . . ." . . .

The constitutional right to be heard is a basic aspect of the duty of government to follow a fair process of decisionmaking when it acts to deprive a person of his possessions. The purpose of this requirement is not only to ensure abstract fair play to the individual. Its purpose, more particularly, is to protect his use and possession of property from arbitrary encroachment — to minimize substantively unfair or mistaken deprivations of property, a danger that is especially great when the State seizes goods simply upon the application of and for the benefit of a private party. So viewed, the prohibition against the deprivation of property without due process of law reflects the high value, embedded in our constitutional and political history, that we place on a person's right to enjoy what is his, free of governmental interference.

The requirement of notice and an opportunity to be heard raises no impenetrable barrier to the taking of a person's possessions. But the fair process of decisionmaking that it guarantees works, by itself, to protect against arbitrary deprivation of property. For when a person has an opportunity to speak up in his own defense, and when the State must listen to what he has to say, substantively unfair and simply mistaken deprivations of property interests can be prevented. It has long been recognized that "fairness can rarely be obtained by secret, one-sided determination of facts decisive of rights. . . . [And] no better instrument has been devised for arriving at truth than to give a person in jeopardy of serious loss notice of the case against him and opportunity to meet it." . . .

The right to a prior hearing, of course, attaches only to the deprivation of an interest encompassed within the Fourteenth Amendment's protection. In the present cases, the Florida and Pennsylvania statutes were applied to replevy chattels in the appellants' possession. The replevin was not cast as a final judgment; most, if not all, of the appellants lacked full title to the chattels; and their claim even to continued possession was a matter in dispute. Moreover, the chattels at stake were nothing more than an assortment of household goods. Nonetheless, it is clear that the appellants were deprived of possessory interests in those chattels that were within the protection of the Fourteenth Amendment. . . .

The appellants who signed conditional sales contracts lacked full legal title to the replevied goods. The Fourteenth Amendment's protection of "property," however, has never been interpreted to safeguard only the rights of undisputed ownership. Rather, it has been read broadly to extend protection to "any significant property interest," including statutory entitlements.

The appellants were deprived of such an interest in the replevied goods — the interest in continued possession and use of the goods. They had acquired this interest under the conditional sales contracts that entitled them to possession and use of the chattels before transfer of title. In exchange for immediate possession, the appellants had agreed to pay a major financing charge beyond the basic price of the merchandise. Moreover, by the time the goods were summarily repossessed, they had made substantial installment payments. Clearly, their possessory interest in the goods, dearly bought and protected by contract, was sufficient to invoke the protection of the Due Process Clause. . . .

Nevertheless, the District Courts rejected the appellants' constitutional claim on the ground that the goods seized from them — a stove, a stereo, a table, a bed, and so forth — were not deserving of due process protection, since they were not absolute necessities of life. The courts based this holding on a very narrow reading of Sniadach v. Family Finance Corp., 395 U.S. 337 (1969), and Goldberg v. Kelly, 397 U.S. 254 (1970), in which this Court held that the Constitution requires a hearing before prejudgment wage garnishment and before the termination of certain welfare benefits. They reasoned that *Sniadach* and *Goldberg*, as a matter of constitutional principle, established no more than that a prior hearing is required with respect to the deprivation of such basically "necessary" items as wages and welfare benefits.

This reading reflects the premise that those cases marked a radical departure from established principles of procedural due process. They did not. Both decisions were in the mainstream of past cases, having little or nothing to do with the absolute "necessities" of life but establishing that due process requires an opportunity for a hearing before a deprivation of property takes effect. . . .

Finally, we must consider the contention that the appellants who signed conditional sales contracts thereby waived their basic procedural due process rights. The contract signed by Mrs. Fuentes provided that "in the event of default of any payment or payments, Seller at its option may take back the merchandise. . . ." The contracts signed by the Pennsylvania appellants similarly provided that the seller "may retake" or "repossess" the merchandise in the event of a "default in any payment." These terms were parts of printed form contracts, appearing in relatively small type and unaccompanied by any explanations clarifying their meaning. . . .

The conditional sales contracts here simply provided that upon a default the seller "may take back," "may retake" or "may repossess" merchandise. The contracts included nothing about the waiver of a prior hearing. They did not indicate *how* or *through what process* — a final judgment, self-help, prejudgment replevin with a prior hearing, or prejudgment replevin without a prior hearing — the seller could take back the goods. Rather, the purported waiver provisions here are no more than a statement of the seller's right to repossession upon occurrence of certain events. The appellees do not suggest that these provisions waived the appellants' right to a full post-seizure hearing to determine whether those events had, in fact, occurred and to consider any other available defenses. By the same token, the language of the purported waiver provisions did not waive the appellants' constitutional right to a preseizure hearing of some kind.

For the foregoing reasons, the judgments of the District Courts are vacated. . . .

Mr. Justice White, with whom The Chief Justice and Mr. Justice Blackmun join, dissenting. . . . It goes without saying that in the typical installment sale of personal property both seller and buyer have interests in the property until the purchase price is fully paid, the seller early in the transaction often having more at stake than the buyer. Nor is it disputed that the buyer's right to possession is conditioned upon his making the stipulated payments and that upon default the seller is entitled to possession. Finally, there is no question in these cases that if default is disputed by the buyer he has the opportunity for a full hearing, and that if he prevails he may have the property or its full value as damages. . . .

The Court's rhetoric is seductive, but in end analysis, the result it reaches will have little impact and represents no more than ideological tinkering with state law. It would appear that creditors could withstand attack under today's opinion simply by making clear in the controlling credit instruments that they may retake possession without a hearing, or, for that matter, without resort to judicial process at all. Alternatively, they need only give a few days' notice of a hearing, take possession if hearing is waived or if there is default; and if hearing is necessary merely establish probable cause for asserting that default has occurred. It is very doubtful in my mind that such a hearing would in fact result in protections for the debtor substantially different from those the present laws provide. On the contrary, the availability of credit may well be diminished or, in any event, the expense of securing it increased.

None of this seems worth the candle to me. The procedure that the Court strikes down is not some barbaric hangover from bygone days. The respective rights of the parties in secured transactions have undergone the most intensive analysis in recent years. The Uniform Commercial Code, which now so pervasively governs the subject matter with which it deals, provides in Art. 9, §9-503, that:

"Unless otherwise agreed a secured party has on default the right to take possession of the collateral. In taking possession a secured party may proceed without judicial process if this can be done without breach of the peace or may proceed by action. . . ."

Recent studies have suggested no changes in Art. 9 in this respect. I am content to rest on the judgment of those who have wrestled with these problems so long and often and upon the judgment of the legislatures that have considered and so recently adopted provisions that contemplate precisely what has happened in these cases.

♦ MITCHELL v. W. T. GRANT CO.
   416 U.S. 600 (1974)

Mr. Justice WHITE delivered the opinion of the Court. In this case, a state trial judge in Louisiana ordered the sequestration of personal property on the application of a creditor who had made an installment sale of the goods to petitioner and whose affidavit asserted delinquency and prayed for sequestration to enforce a vendor's lien under state law. The issue is whether the sequestration violated the Due Process Clause of the Fourteenth Amendment because it was ordered *ex parte*, without prior notice or opportunity for a hearing.

On February 2, 1972, respondent W. T. Grant Co. filed in the First City Court of the City of New Orleans, Louisiana, against petitioner, Lawrence Mitchell. The petition alleged the sale by Grant to Mitchell of a refrigerator, range, stereo, and washing machine, and an overdue and unpaid balance of the purchase price for said items in the amount of $574.17. Judgment for that sum was demanded. It was further alleged that Grant had a vendor's lien on the goods and that a writ of sequestration should issue to sequester the merchandise pending the outcome of the suit. The accompanying affidavit of Grant's credit manager swore to the truth of the facts alleged in the complaint. It also asserted that Grant had reason to believe petitioner would "encumber, alienate or otherwise dispose of the merchandise described in the foregoing petition during the pendency of these proceedings, and that a writ of sequestration is necessary in the premises." Based on the foregoing petition and affidavit, and without prior notice to Mitchell or affording him opportunity for hearing, the judge of the First City Court, Arthur J. O'Keefe, then signed an order that "a writ of sequestration issue herein" and that "the Constable of this court sequester and take into his possession the articles of merchandise described in the foregoing petition, upon plaintiff furnishing bond in the amount of $1,125." Bond in that amount having been filed by the respondent, the writ of sequestration issued, along with citation to petitioner Mitchell, citing him to file a pleading or make appearance in the First City Court of the city of New Orleans within five days. The citation recited the filing of the writ of sequestration and the accompanying affidavit, order, and bond. On March 3 Mitchell filed a motion to dissolve the writ of sequestration issued on February 2. The motion asserted that the personal property at issue had been seized under the writ on February 7, 1972, and claimed, first, that the goods were exempt from seizure under state law and, second, that the seizure violated Due Process Clauses of the State and Federal constitutions in that it had occurred without prior notice and opportunity to defend petitioner's right to possession of the property. The motion came on for hearing on March 14. It was then stipulated that a vendor's lien existed on the items, arguments of counsel were heard, and on March 16 the motion to dissolve was denied. The goods were held not exempt from seizure under state law. The trial court also ruled that "the provisional seizure enforced through sequestration" was not a denial of due process of law. "To the contrary," the trial judge said, "plaintiff insured defendant's right to due process by proceeding in accordance with Louisiana Law as opposed to any type of self-help seizure which would have denied defendant possession of his property without due process." The appellate courts of Louisiana refused to disturb the rulings of the trial court, the Supreme Court of Louisiana expressly rejecting petitioner's due process claims pressed under the Federal Constitution.

Petitioner's basic proposition is that because he had possession of and a substantial interest in the sequestered property the Due Process Clause of the Fourteenth Amendment necessarily forbade the seizure without prior notice and opportunity for a hearing. In the circumstances presented here, we cannot agree.

Petitioner no doubt "owned" the goods he had purchased under an installment sales contract, but his title was heavily encumbered. The seller, W. T. Grant Co., also had an interest in the property, for state law provided it with a vendor's lien to secure the unpaid balance of the purchase price. Because of the lien, Mitchell's right to possession and his title were subject to defeasance in the event of default in paying the installments due from him. His interest in the property, until the purchase price was paid in full, was no greater than the surplus remaining, if any, after foreclosure and sale of the property in the event of his default and satisfaction of outstanding claims. The interest of Grant, as seller of the property and holder of a vendor's lien, was measured by the unpaid balance of the purchase price. The monetary value of that interest in the property diminished as payments were made, but the value of the property as security also steadily diminished over time as it was put to its intended use by the purchaser.

Plainly enough, this is not a case where the property sequestered by the court is exclusively the property of the defendant debtor. The question is not whether a debtor's property may be seized by his creditors, *pendente lite*, where they hold no present interest in the property sought to be seized. The reality is that both seller and buyer had current, real interests in the property, and the definition of property rights is a matter of state law. Resolution of the due process question must take account not only of the interests of the buyer of the property but those of the seller as well.

With this duality in mind, we are convinced that the Louisiana sequestration procedure is not invalid, either on its face or as applied. Sequestration under the Louisiana statutes is the modern counterpart of an ancient civil law device to resolve conflicting claims to property. Historically, the two principal concerns have been that, pending resolution of the dispute, the property would deteriorate or be wasted in the

1366 ♦ 23. New Property

hands of the possessor and that the latter might sell or otherwise dispose of the goods. A minor theme was that official intervention would forestall violent self-help and retaliation. . . .

In our view, this statutory procedure effects a constitutional accommodation of the conflicting interest of the parties. We cannot accept petitioner's broad assertion that the Due Process Clause of the United States Constitution guaranteed to him the use and possession of the goods until all issues in the case were judicially resolved after full adversary proceedings had been completed. It is certainly clear under this Court's precedents that issues can be limited in actions for possession. Lindsey v. Normet, 405 U.S. 56 (1972). Petitioner's claim must accordingly be narrowed to one for a hearing on the issues in the possessory action — default, the existence of a lien, and possession of the debtor — before property is taken.

As to this claim, the seller here, with a vendor's lien to secure payment of the unpaid balance of purchase price, had the right either to be paid in accordance with his contract or to have possession of the goods for the purpose of foreclosing his lien and recovering the unpaid balance. By complaint and affidavit, the seller swore to facts that would entitle him to immediate possession of the goods under his contract, undiminished in value by further deterioration through use of the property by the buyer. Wholly aside from whether the buyer, with possession and power over the property, will destroy or make away with the goods, the buyer in possession of consumer goods will undeniably put the property to its intended use, and the resale value of the merchandise will steadily decline as it is used over a period of time. Any installment seller anticipates as much, but he is normally protected because the buyer's installment payments keep pace with the deterioration in value of the security. Clearly, if payments cease and possession and use by the buyer continue, the seller's interest in the property as security is steadily and irretrievably eroded until the time at which the full hearing is held.

The State of Louisiana was entitled to recognize this reality and to provide somewhat more protection for the seller. This it did in Orleans Parish by authorizing the sequestration of property by a judge. At the same time, the buyer being deprived of possession, the seller was required to put up a bond to guarantee the buyer against damage or expense, including attorney's fees, in the event the sequestration is shown to be mistaken or otherwise improvident. The buyer is permitted to regain possession by putting up his own bond to protect the seller. Absent that bond, which petitioner did not file in this case, the seller would be unprotected against the inevitable deterioration in the value of his security if the buyer remained in possession pending trial on the merits. The debtor, unlike the creditor, does not stand ready to make the opposing party whole, if his possession, pending a prior hearing, turns out to be wrongful.

Second, there is the real risk that the buyer, with possession and power over the goods, will conceal or transfer the merchandise to the damage of the seller. . . .

Third, there is scant support in our cases for the proposition that there must be final judicial determination of the seller's entitlement before the buyer may be even temporarily deprived of possession of the purchased goods. On the contrary, it seems apparent that the seller with his own interest in the disputed merchandise would need to establish in any event only the probability that his case will succeed to warrant the bonded sequestration of the property pending outcome of the suit. The issue at this stage of the proceeding concerns possession pending trial and turns on the existence of the debt, the lien, and the delinquency. These are ordinarily uncomplicated matters that lend themselves to documentary proof; and we think it comports with due process to permit the initial seizure on sworn *ex parte* documents, followed by the early opportunity to put the creditor to his proof. The nature of the issues at stake minimizes the risk that the writ will be wrongfully issued by a judge. The potential damages award available, if there is a successful motion to dissolve the writ, as well as the creditor's own interest in avoiding interrupting the transaction, also contributes to minimizing this risk.

Fourth, we remain unconvinced that the impact on the debtor of deprivation of the household goods here in question overrides his inability to make the creditor whole for wrongful possession, the risk of destruction or alienation if notice and a prior hearing are supplied, and the low risk of a wrongful determination of possession through the procedures now employed.

Finally, the debtor may immediately have a full hearing on the matter of possession following the execution of the writ, thus cutting to a bare minimum the time of creditor- or court-supervised possession. The debtor in this case, who did not avail himself of this opportunity, can hardly expect that his argument on the severity of deprivation will carry much weight, and even assuming that there is real impact on the debtor from loss of these goods, pending the hearing on possession, his basic source of income is unimpaired.

The requirements of due process of law "are not technical, nor is any particular form of procedure necessary." Due process of law guarantees "no particular form of procedure; it protects substantial rights." "The very nature of due process negates any concept of inflexible procedures universally applicable to every imaginable situation." Considering the Louisiana procedure as a whole, we are convinced that the State has reached a constitutional accommodation of the respective interests of buyer and seller.

Mr. Justice POWELL, concurring. In sweeping language, Fuentes v. Shevin, 407 U.S. 67 (1972), enunciated the principle that the constitutional guarantee of procedural due process requires an adversary hearing before an individual may be temporarily deprived of any possessory interest in tangible personal property, however brief the dispossession and however slight his monetary interest in the property. The Court's decision today withdraws significantly from the full reach of that principle, and to this extent I think it fair to say that the *Fuentes* opinion is overruled.

I could have agreed that the Florida and Pennsylvania statutes in *Fuentes* were violative of due process because of their arbitrary and unreasonable provisions. It seems to me, however, that it was unnecessary for the *Fuentes* opinion to have adopted so broad and inflexible a rule, especially one that considerably altered settled law with respect to commercial transactions and basic creditor-debtor understandings. . . .

Mr. Justice STEWART, with whom Mr. Justice DOUGLAS and Mr. Justice MARSHALL concur, dissenting. . . . The deprivation of property in this case is identical to that at issue in *Fuentes*, and the Court does not say otherwise. Thus, under *Fuentes*, due process of law permits Louisiana to effect this deprivation only after notice to the possessor and opportunity for a hearing. Because I would adhere to the holding of *Fuentes*, I dissent from the Court's opinion and judgment upholding Louisiana's *ex parte* sequestration procedure, which provides that the possessor of the property shall never have advance notice or a hearing of any kind. . . .

I would add, however, a word of concern. It seems to me that unless we respect the constitutional decisions of this Court, we can hardly expect that others will do so. A substantial departure from precedent can only be justified, I had thought, in the light of an altered historic environment. Yet the Court today has unmistakably overruled a considered decision of this Court that is barely two years old, without pointing to any change in either societal perceptions or basic constitutional understandings that might justify this total disregard of *stare decisis*.

The *Fuentes* decision was in a direct line of recent cases in this Court that have applied the procedural due process commands of the Fourteenth Amendment to prohibit govermental action that deprives a person of a statutory or contractual property interest with no advance notice or opportunity to be heard. In the short time that has elapsed since the *Fuentes* case was decided, many state and federal courts have followed it in assessing the constitutional validity of state replevin statutes and other comparable state laws. No data have been brought to our attention to indicate that these decisions, granting to otherwise defenseless consumers the simple rudiments of due process of law, have worked any untoward change in the consumer credit market or in other commercial relationships. The only perceivable change that has occurred since *Fuentes* is in the makeup of this Court.

A basic change in the law upon a ground no firmer than a change in our membership invites the popular misconception that this institution is little different from the two political branches of the Government. No misconception could do more lasting injury to this Court and to the system of law which it is our abiding mission to serve.

Mr. Justice BRENNAN is in agreement that Fuentes v. Shevin, 407 U.S. 67 (1972), requires reversal of the judgment of the Supreme Court of Louisiana.

Notes

1. But reports of the decease of *Fuentes* were premature. North Georgia Finishing, Inc. v. Di-Chem, Inc., 419 U.S. 601 (1975), struck down Georgia arrangements permitting a creditor to garnish a bank account by alleging before "some officer" that money is due and that he "has reason to apprehend the loss of the same." Justice White, for the Court, distinguished *W. T. Grant* on the grounds that Georgia required merely conclusory allegations and did not assure the debtor a quick hearing.

2. Related issues are posed when government, as proprietor of the machinery of justice, imposes financial hurdles to the enforcement of claims that some are too poor to surmount. The current state of constitutional doctrine is chaotic: Due process is denied when an indigent person is unable to obtain a divorce because he or she does not have the court costs, Boddie v. Connecticut, 401 U.S. 371 (1971), but not when that person is refused discharge in bankruptcy because of inability to raise the filing fees, United States v. Kras, 409 U.S. 434 (1973), or is denied the chance to appeal reduction in state old-age assistance payments because of inability to pay the $25 appellate court fee, Ortwein v. Schwab, 410 U.S. 656 (1973). For an argument that the opportunity to assert or defend one's state-created rights (including public provision of counsel when necessary) should receive constitutional protection, see Michelman, The Supreme Court and Litigation Access Fees: The Right to Protect One's Rights, Part I: 1973 Duke L.J. 1153; Part II: 1974 Duke L.J. 527.

2. *Self-Help Repossession*

◆ WATSON v. BRANCH COUNTY BANK
380 F. Supp. 945 (W.D. Mich. 1974)

Fox, Chief Judge. This is a challenge to the constitutionality of the self-help repossession and disposition provisions of the Uniform Commercial Code, Sections 9-503 and 9-504. . . . The plaintiffs Edward and Shirley Ann Watson are joint owners of a 1966 Buick, subject to a security interest held by defendant Branch County Bank. The plaintiffs purchased the vehicle for about $700, made a substantial down payment, and borrowed $484.64 from the Branch County Bank. The security agreement between the Watsons and the Bank provided:

> In the event Buyer defaults in the payment of any amount due hereunder, or in the performance of any other obligations hereunder, or if a proceeding in bankruptcy, receivership or insolvency is instituted by or against Buyer, then Seller may declare the full amount hereunder immediately due and payable without notice or demand, and shall have all of the remedies of a secured party under the Michigan Uniform Commercial Code and any other applicable laws.

On August 3, 1972, plaintiffs' vehicle was peacefully repossessed from the driveway, in accordance with M.C.L.A. Sec 440.9503. The plaintiffs did not receive notice of a judicial hearing before repossession, but they did receive notice of repossession and notice of the proposed sale. At the time of repossession, the plaintiffs still owed $170.88 to the Bank. It appears from the affidavit filed by the plaintiffs that they have a child which has a chronic bronchial condition which requires visits to the doctor's office for care. The plaintiffs' residence is approximately ten blocks from the nearest bus line and during the time that the plaintiffs were without their automobile, Mrs. Watson had to use a taxi cab or make request of friends for transportation in order to get the child to the doctor. . . .

The primary issue in this case is whether any legal process is due the plaintiffs from the state, whether, that is, the plaintiffs are entitled under the circumstances to any legal process at all in conjunction with the repossession of their automobile, and if so, in what form and at what time.

The Due Process Clause of the Fourteenth Amendment guarantees several fundamental rights. Three specifically mentioned substantive rights are life, liberty, and property. Necessarily associated with these rights, and implicit in the Clause considered as a whole, is a right to the pursuit of happiness. See Decl. of Ind. Also fundamental is a right to legal process, a right ultimately necessary to secure the great substantive rights.

There is no doubt that the "repossession" of an automobile by a secured party deprives a person of a "property interest" within the meaning of the Due Process Clause. Board of Regents v. Roth, 408 U.S. 564; Mitchell v. W. T. Grant Co., 416 U.S. 600. At the very least, "repossession" in accordance with U.C.C. 9-503 deprives a person of the possession and use of his automobile, cf., Sniadach v. Family Finance

Corp., 395 U.S. 337; and the sale of the automobile in accordance with U.C.C. 9-504 would deprive the owner of title.

The constitutional obligation of government to provide regular judicial process for the settlement of private disputes is of ancient lineage. The Magna Carta, cap. 39, provided, "No free man shall be taken or imprisoned or disseised or outlawed or exiled or in any way ruined, nor will we go or send against him, except by the lawful judgment of his peers, or by the law of the land." This provision did not apply only to actions of the King for purposes of state, but extended to private disputes as well.

More important, cap. 40 of the Magna Carta provided, "To no one will we sell, to no one will we deny, or delay right or justice." This provision required that legal process be afforded and was intended to set a standard for the regular and impartial administration of royal justice in private as well as public actions. Private litigants were further aided by the requirement that the common pleas be held in a fixed place, which came to be Westminister, and that certain land cases be regularly held in the counties in which they arose.

Although the Magna Carta was not immediately and fully implemented, many came to assume that the document embodied immutable principles of just, limited, constitutional government. Blackstone, who wrote on the eve of the American Revolution, recognized the necessity of providing legal process to resolve disputes. He stated that there were three absolute rights of Englishmen, the rights of life, liberty, and property. He further noted that these substantive rights would have been declared in vain unless the constitution had provided a method to secure [their] actual enjoyment. This method was the establishment of "certain other auxiliary subordinate rights of the subject, . . . [to] serve principally as outworks or barriers, to protect and maintain inviolate the three great and primary rights. . . ." . . .

The Anglo-American legal tradition and recent cases have firmly established that due process is not an "entitlement" similar to those in the area of property which the state may originally withhold altogether in its uncontrolled discretion. Rather, the state is constitutionally required to provide process of law in accordance with the mandates of the Fourteenth Amendment. This is emphatically the case to the extent that there is no independent federal remedy for what is ordinarily recognized in state law as a civil wrong.

However, the constitutional duty of the state to provide process of law is not unlimited. Certainly the state need not, and, practically, could not, require resort to process for the resolution of every private dispute. . . .

This case involves the self-help repossession of secured tangible personal property on the debtor's alleged default. Is process due from the state under these circumstances?

A basic purpose of American constitutionalism, and the Due Process Clause in particular, is to replace violent anarchy with a just and orderly society. . . .

Historically, one of the great missions of the law has been to bring disputes concerning the possession of real and personal property under the control of legal institutions. Except for personal injury, nothing has been so productive of contention and violence as the dispossession of tangible property. The taking of goods from another's possession, without the latter's contemporaneous consent, necessarily involves the hostile physical invasion of the possessor's personal territory, and is a serious assault upon his dignity, privacy and self-esteem. Such an invasion naturally tends to excite emotions and to provoke violent retaliation.

In the Anglo-Saxon period of English history, the law recognized, indeed, was almost entirely based upon, the concept of the personal "peace," or *grith*. The *grith* was a person's psychological sphere of interest, marked, with regard to tangibles, by possession and control. The concern for the integrity of the *grith* was part of the common law's concern for the preservation of human dignity in the context of a stable social order. Where a person's "peace" was respected, there was an absence of violence, and the person's "peace", in its modern connotation, prevailed. In contrast, where the personal peace was breached or broken, there was contention and violence. . . .

The concept of the personal "peace" remained implicit in the Anglo-American law, and was apparently recognized in Michigan during the nineteenth century, for example, in cases involving stray or trespassing animals. Wandering animals were a constant problem in a society of small farmers, and the remedies were closely regulated by statute. When a farmer found a trespassing animal upon his lands, he could impound it and, if notice given according to the statute failed to produce the owner, he could sell it. An owner's self-help repossession of his impounded animal was referred to as a "rescue." When an impounded animal was rescued, the statute gave the farmer an action for damages and forfeiture of five to twenty dollars as against the animal's owner.

In one case, the owner rescued his impounded animal from the farmer's barn without violence or menacing or threatening words. The farmer sued for damages under the statute, but the owner claimed that the statute did not apply because the animal had been repossessed without violence. The Michigan Supreme Court, after observing that distraint had existed at common law, held that the statute applied because "such a taking is esteemed in law a violent taking." Hamlin v. Mack, 33 Mich. 103, 108 (1885). (Emphasis supplied.) The Michigan Supreme Court thus followed the wisdom of the common law in recognizing that the repossession of tangible personal property from another even under a claim of right is always a violent transaction.

With the modern concentration of giant national and international corporations, characterized, like modern government, by heavy layers of impersonal bureaucracy, we are slipping backwards into disorder and fundamentally uncivilized business practices. Uncontrolled private corporate power imposes unilateral conditions and requirements on individuals in the name of contracts. Such extreme impositions necessarily erode the personal "peace," or *grith*, which the old law struggled for centuries to protect.

The Uniform Commercial Code allows self-help repossession by creditors "if this can be done without breach of the peace," 9-503. Breach of the peace in this context usually means forcible entry into a building. By failing to establish a standard of conduct which takes into account the personal peace, the human self-esteem and dignity which surrounds an individual's personal possessions, the U.C.C. departs from the ancient common law conception of the self-help repossession as a "violent taking." To this extent, the U.C.C. withdraws the protection of the peace of the community from the personal peace which was the foundation of the old common law. The U.C.C. substitutes that licensed violence which even the Anglo-Saxons strove to replace with a rule of law. . . .

Implicit in the Due Process Clause is an additional set of values for defining and measuring the interests of debtors and creditors in this case. The debtors' class in this suit includes only natural persons, while each of the creditors is a corporation. The ultimate focus of the Anglo-American legal order is the individual human being who is created by the Creator, Dec. of Ind., in the image and likeness of God, Genesis 1:26. Its basic purpose is the protection and advancement of human dignity. To this end, the Due Process Clause contemplates that legal process shall be provided to protect life, liberty, property,[19] and the pursuit of happiness. Certainly life, liberty, and happiness are the supreme human values. Property, however, is important and essential insofar as it is essential for the protection of human life and liberty and for the advancement of happiness.[20] Accordingly, because property is a derivative right, where the property of natural persons is at stake, the Due Process Clause requires a special inquiry to determine the impact of the deprivation of the interest on the individual. *Sniadach, supra.* It does not make much sense to recognize the fundamental importance of mar-

---

19. John Locke defined "property" to include the sum of the individual's legally cognizable attributes, "that is, his Life, Liberty and Estate." The Second Treatise of Government, Sec. 87 (Laslett ed. 1960). When he wrote, "The great and chief end . . . of Mens uniting into Commonwealths, and putting themselves under Government, is the Preservation of their Property," Id. at Sec. 124, Locke was referring to this broad conception of property.

20. "For an individual man to lead a good life, two things are required. The first and most important is to act in a virtuous manner (for virtue is that by which one lives well); the second, *which is secondary and instrumental*, is a sufficiency of those bodily goods whose use is necessary for virtuous life." St. Thomas Aquinas, in The Pocket Aquinas, 244 (V. Bourke ed. 1960).

riage and the family, see United States v. Kras, 409 U.S. 434, 444 (1973), without also recognizing that families in modern industrial society require a certain level of material welfare in order to be successful institutions.

In our geographically decentralized suburban society, adequate transportation is essential for full access to work, goods, services, schools, and places of recreation. Transportation is very expensive, and it takes a substantial part of every active family's budget. Most families choose to meet their transportation needs by purchasing one or more automobiles, each of which represents a substantial commitment of funds. Given the notoriously low prices paid for repossessed goods at foreclosure sales, the repossession of an automobile means a substantial loss of investment for the individual. Most families cannot duplicate the expenditures made for an automobile without cutting back on essentials. Repossession of an automobile thus not only deprives the individual of a property interest, but also impinges directly upon his life and liberty interests and upon his pursuit of happiness. . . .

The cognizable interests of the corporate creditors in repossessing automobiles without resort to legal process are *de minimis*. Corporations are not creatures of God endowed with life and human attributes, but merely creations of the state, economic interests given separate legal status. The corporate defendants have no human rights or values at stake here, merely profit. Alteration of the present system might reduce somewhat the volume of credit, but this would not so disrupt the system as to harm any vital human interests. If banks could no longer repossess automobiles without resort to legal process, they would not cease to exist. The system of production and distribution would certainly remain intact.

The defendants have insisted that, as a practical matter, substituting judicial supervision for self-help creditors' remedies would increase the cost and decrease the availability of credit. Since legal process is expensive and would have to be taken into account, these results would probably follow, although no one can predict precise amounts.

An increase in the cost and a decrease in the availability of credit would no doubt adversely affect some individuals on the economic margins. However, the ultimate issue for anyone with the financial ability to make a down payment and secure credit is where to put his transportation dollar. Alternatives to owning a private car are available to most persons in urban areas. The annual cost to buy, fuel, maintain, and insure an automobile will buy a lot of bus and taxi rides. The family who invests in a private car and loses it through repossession is in a lot worse shape financially than the family which systematically exploits other means of transportation.

Although the Constitution does recognize rights to life, liberty, property, and due process of law, all of which are violated by self-help repossession, a diligent search has failed to reveal that the institutional availability of credit is a fundamental constitutional value.[21] In past years, automobile advertising has been aimed at convincing the individual that his personal worth and happiness depend upon his owning a snazzy car. Dealers offered a car for a modest down payment plus so much per week. The individual was given a title and all the liability. Upon default in payment, however, it turned out that the car really wasn't the purchaser's at all. This hustle, and the credit which supports it, does not find protection in the Constitution.

The court concludes that the processes established by U.C.C. 9-503 and 9-504 do not fairly and rationally protect the cognizable interests of the plaintiffs in this case. The system gives little or no protection to the debtors' interests in avoiding mistaken or wrongful seizures, and to the debtors' implicated life and liberty interests in security, privacy, a minimum standard of living, and the pursuit of happiness. To the extent that the present scheme does enhance the institutional availability of credit, and to the extent that either debtor or creditor can be said to have a cognizable interest in this availability, the court concludes that this interest is outweighed by the severe damage done by the present system to the plaintiff's human rights protected by the Due Process Clause.

Notes

1. Many cases disagree with *Watson*. See, e.g., Adams v. Southern California First National Bank, 492 F.2d 324 (9th Cir. 1973), *cert. denied*, 419 U.S. 1006 (1975), which arose when the Bank of La Jolla, pursuant to a security agreement negotiated when plaintiff borrowed $1,000, paid a repossessor licensed by the state of California to take possession of plaintiff's 1959 Volkswagen van. The court held that even though a pervasive statutory scheme regulated the transaction, state action did not occur, and so no *Fuentes-W. T. Grant* inquiry was required.

2. PPG Industries made a contract with Bay State Harness Horse Racing and Breeding Association to furnish labor and materials neces-

21. There is a distinction between the "institutional availability of credit" and the ability of an individual to secure that credit which is generally available. The former is a function of the state of the economy and the policies of institutions. The ability of an individual to obtain credit when it is generally available depends upon his personal "credit rating" as ascertained by lenders, often with the help of credit reporting agencies. Modern law recognizes that each individual has a legal interest in maintaining a good credit rating. This interest is not implicated in the present suit. The over-all availability of credit depends more upon the fiscal policies of the federal government and the monetary policies of the Federal Reserve than on the existence of self-help repossession. If the availability of credit is protected by the Constitution, then numerous persons who have been unable to secure credit at moderate prices in the recent past surely have good causes of action against the Federal Reserve for driving the prime interest rate as high (at this writing) as twelve percent.

sary to glass-enclose the clubhouse at Bay State Raceway. Subsequently, PPG brought an action against Bay State arising out of that contract. Based on the writ, PPG caused an attachment in the amount of $150,000 to be made of Bay State's real estate by deposit of a copy of the writ in the Registry of Deeds of Norfolk County.

Mass. Gen. Laws Ann. Ch. 223, §§42, 63 provide *inter alia*:

> All real . . . property liable to be taken on execution . . . may be attached upon the original writ in any action in which debt or damages are recoverable, and may be held as security to satisfy such judgment as the plaintiff may recover. . . .
>
> No attachment . . . shall be valid against a subsequent attaching creditor, or against a subsequent purchaser in good faith and for value, unless the officer deposits a certified copy of the original writ . . . in the registry of deeds . . . where the land lies.

The Court struck down the Massachusetts procedure, citing *Fuentes*. See Bay State Harness Horse Racing and Breeding Association v. PPG Industries, Inc., 365 F. Supp. 1299 (D. Mass. 1973). What result after *W. T. Grant* and *Di-Chem?*

3. Puerto Rico seized plaintiff's yacht and declared it forfeited after police found marijuana aboard. The Supreme Court held that in these circumstances postponement of notice and hearing was consistent even with *Fuentes*. The seizure was also attacked as an uncompensated taking, especially as to the interest of the lessor: he had included in the lease agreement a prohibition against unlawful use of the yacht; as the case arose there was no showing that more than one marijuana cigarette was found; the lessor could hardly control the lessees' conduct. But Justice Brennan responded with a historical essay on the antecedents of forfeiture — for example an inanimate object causing the accidental death of a King's subject was forfeited to the crown — and upheld the seizure. Calero-Toledo v. Pearson Yacht Leasing Co., 416 U.S. 663 (1974).

4. A footnote in *Fuentes* left open the question whether a defendant in a preseizure hearing has a right to raise both negative ("I'm not in default. Here's the cancelled check") and affirmative ("I'm in default, but you broke a promise or covenant that excuses me") defenses. Plaintiff leased a computer to defendant. Defendant withheld $16,000 in rent payments to cover repairs it said it had to make. Plaintiff sought replevin of the computer, pursuant to a lease clause that "in the event of the occurrence of default, lessor shall have the right to . . . take immediate possession of the leased equipment." Defendant sought to counterclaim for the repairs. The court held that the plaintiff was entitled to possession, though defendant might be able to recover money damages at trial. Computer Leasing Co. v. Computing & Software, Inc., 37 Ohio Misc. 19, 306 N.E.2d 191 (C.P. 1973).

3. State Action

◆ JACKSON v. METROPOLITAN EDISON CO.
419 U.S. 345 (1974)

Mr. Justice REHNQUIST delivered the opinion of the Court. Respondent Metropolitan Edison Company is a privately owned and operated Pennsylvania corporation which holds a certificate of public convenience issued by the Pennsylvania Public Utilities Commission empowering it to deliver electricity to a service area which includes the city of York, Pennsylvania. As a condition of holding its certificate, it is subject to extensive regulation by the Commission. Under a provision of its general tariff filed with the Commission, it has the right to discontinue service to any customer on reasonable notice of nonpayment of bills.

Petitioner Catherine Jackson is a resident of York, who has received electricity in the past from respondent. Until September 1970, petitioner received electric service to her home in York under an account with respondent in her own name. When her account was terminated because of asserted delinquency in payments due for service, a new account with respondent was opened in the name of one James Dodson, another occupant of the residence, and service to the residence was resumed. There is a dispute as to whether payments due under the Dodson account for services provided during this period were ever made. In August 1971, Dodson left the residence. Service continued thereafter but concededly no payments were made. Petitioner states that no bills were received during this period.

On October 6, 1971, employees of Metropolitan came to the residence and inquired as to Dodson's present address. Petitioner stated that it was unknown to her. On the following day, another employee visited the residence and informed petitioner that the meter had been tampered with so as not to register amounts used. She disclaimed knowledge of this and requested that the service account for her home be shifted from Dodson's name to that of one Robert Jackson, later identified as her 12-year-old son. Four days later on October 11, 1971, without further notice to petitioner, Metropolitan employees disconnected her service.

Petitioner then filed suit against Metropolitan in the United States District Court for the Middle District of Pennsylvania under the Civil Rights Act, 42 U.S.C. §1983, seeking damages for the termination and an injunction requiring Metropolitan to continue providing power to her residence until she had been afforded notice, hearing, and an opportunity to pay any amounts found due. She urged that under state law she had an entitlement to reasonably continuous electrical service to her home and that Metropolitan's termination of her service for alleged nonpayment, action allowed by a provision of its general tariff filed with the Commission, constituted "state action" depriving her of property in violation of the Fourteenth Amendment's guarantee of due process of law.

The District Court granted Metropolitan's motion to dismiss petitioner's complaint on the ground that the termination did not constitute state action and hence was not subject to judicial scrutiny under the Fourteenth Amendment. On appeal, the United States Court of Appeals for the Third Circuit affirmed, also finding an absence of state action. . . .

The Due Process Clause of the Fourteenth Amendment provides: "[N]or shall any State deprive any person of life, liberty, or property, without due process of law." In 1883, this Court in The Civil Rights Cases, 109 U.S. 3, affirmed the essential dichotomy set forth in that Amendment between deprivation by the State, subject to scrutiny under its provisions, and private conduct, "however discriminatory and wrongful," against which the Fourteenth Amendment offers no shield. Shelley v. Kraemer, 334 U.S. 1. . . .

Here the action complained of was taken by a utility company which is privately owned and operated, but which in many particulars of its business is subject to extensive state regulation. The mere fact that a business is subject to state regulation does not by itself convert its action into that of the State for purposes of the Fourteenth Amendment. Nor does the fact that the regulation is extensive and detailed, as in the case of most public utilities, do so. . . .

All of petitioner's arguments taken together show no more than that Metropolitan was a heavily regulated private utility, enjoying at least a partial monopoly in the providing of electrical service within its territory, and that it elected to terminate service to petitioner in a manner which the Pennsylvania Public Utilities Commission found permissible under state law. Under our decisions this is not sufficient to connect the State of Pennsylvania with respondent's action so as to make the latter's conduct attributable to the State for purposes of the Fourteenth Amendment.

We conclude that the State of Pennsylvania is not sufficiently connected with respondent's action in terminating petitioner's service so as to make respondent's conduct in so doing attributable to the State for purposes of the Fourteenth Amendment. We therefore have no occasion to decide whether petitioner's claim to continued service was "property" for purposes of that Amendment, or whether "due process of law" would require a State taking similar action to accord petitioner the procedural rights for which she contends. The judgment of the Court of Appeals for the Third Circuit is therefore affirmed.

Mr. Justice DOUGLAS, dissenting. I reach the opposite conclusion from that reached by the majority on the state action issue. . . .

In the aggregate, these factors depict a monopolist providing essential public services as a licensee of the State and within a framework of extensive state supervision and control. The particular regulations at issue, promulgated by the monopolist, were authorized by state law and were made enforceable by the weight and authority of the State. Moreover, the State retains the power of oversight to review and amend the regulations if the public interest so requires. Respondent's actions are sufficiently intertwined with those of the State, and its termination-of-service provisions are sufficiently buttressed by state law, to warrant a holding that respondent's actions in terminating this householder's service were "state action" for the purpose of giving federal jurisdiction over respondent under 42 U.S.C. §1983. . . .

Section 1983 was designed to give citizens a federal forum for civil rights complaints wherever, by direct or indirect actions, a State, acting in cahoots with a private group or through neglect or listless oversight, allows a private group to perpetrate an injury. The theory is that in those cozy situations, local politics and the pressure of economic overlords on subservient state agencies make recovery in state courts unlikely. I realize we are in an area where we witness a great retreat from the exercise of federal jurisdiction which the Congress has conferred on federal courts. The sentiment here is that state courts are as hospitable as federal courts to federal claims. That may well be true, in some instances. But it is for the Senate and the House to make that decision. We should not tolerate an erosion of the policy Congress expressed in drafting §1983.

Mr. Justice MARSHALL, dissenting. . . . Our state-action cases have repeatedly relied on several factors clearly presented by this case: a state-sanctioned monopoly; an extensive pattern of cooperation between the "private" entity and the State; and a service uniquely public in nature. Today the Court takes a major step in repudiating this line of authority and adopts a stance that is bound to lead to mischief when applied to problems beyond the narrow sphere of due process objections to utility terminations. . . .

The fact that the Metropolitan Edison Company supplies an essential public service that is in many communities supplied by the government weighs more heavily for me than for the majority. The Court concedes that state action might be present if the activity in question were "traditionally associated with sovereignty," but it then undercuts that point by suggesting that a particular service is not a public function if the State in question has not required that it be governmentally operated. This reads the "public function" argument too narrowly. The whole point of the "public function" cases is to look behind the State's decision to provide public services through private parties.

In my view, utility service is traditionally identified with the State through universal public regulation or ownership to a degree sufficient to render it a "public function."

I agree with the majority that it requires more than a finding that a particular business is "affected with the public interest" before constitutional burdens can be imposed on that business. But when the activity in question is of such public importance that the State invariably either provides the service itself or permits private companies to act as state surrogates in providing it, much more is involved than just a matter of public interest. In those cases, the State has determined that if private companies wish to enter the field, they will have to surrender many of the prerogatives normally associated with private enterprise and behave in many ways like a governmental body. And when the State's regulatory scheme has gone that far, it seems entirely consistent to impose on the public utility the constitutional burdens normally reserved for the State.

Private parties performing functions affecting the public interest can often make a persuasive claim to be free of the constitutional requirements applicable to governmental institutions because of the value of preserving a private sector in which the opportunity for individual choice is maximized. Maintaining the private status of parochial schools, cited by the majority, advances just this value. In the due process area, a similar value of diversity may often be furthered by allowing various private institutions the flexibility to select procedures that fit their particular needs. But it is hard to imagine any such interests that are furthered by protecting public utility companies from meeting the constitutional standards that would apply if the companies were state-owned. The values of pluralism and diversity are simply not relevant when the private company is the only electric company in town.

Notes

1. In Flagg Brothers, Inc. v. Brooks, 436 U.S. 149 (1978), the Supreme Court held that a warehouseman's private sale of goods entrusted to him for storage — an action permitted by self-help provisions of New York's version of the Uniform Commercial Code — was not "state action" and therefore did not call into play constitutional due process protections. Justice Marshall, dissenting, said that with such a decision "the Court demonstrates, not for the first time, an attitude of callous indifference to the realities of life for the poor." Justices Stevens and White also dissented.

2. In Lugar v. Edmondson Oil Co., 457 U.S. 922 (1982), the Court held that in attaching debtor's property before judgment, defendants had acted jointly with the state of Virginia to deny him due process, and thus debtor stated a cause of action under 42 U.S.C. §1983. This time, Chief Justice Burger and Justices Powell, Rehnquist, and O'Connor dissented.

B.   PROPERTY AS PROCESS AND LIBERTY

1.   No "Sound Analogy" between Social Security and Property

◆ FLEMMING v. NESTOR
363 U.S. 603 (1960)

Mr. Justice HARLAN delivered the opinion of the Court. From a decision of the District Court for the District of Columbia holding §202(n) of the Social Security Act unconstitutional, the Secretary of Health, Education, and Welfare takes this direct appeal. The challenged section provides for the termination of old age, survivor, and disability insurance benefits payable to, or in certain cases in respect of, an alien individual who after September 1, 1954 is deported under the Immigration and Nationality Act on any one of certain grounds specified in §202(n).

Appellee, an alien, immigrated to this country from Bulgaria in 1913, and became eligible for old-age benefits in November 1955. In July 1956 he was deported for having been a member of the Communist Party from 1933 to 1939. This being one of the benefit-termination deportation grounds specified in §202(n), appellee's benefits were terminated soon thereafter, and notice of the termination was given to his wife, who had remained in this country. . . .

We think that the District Court erred in holding that §202(n) deprived appellee of an "accrued property right." Appellee's right to Social Security benefits cannot properly be considered to have been of that order. . . .

The Social Security system may be accurately described as a form of social insurance, enacted pursuant to Congress' power to "spend money in aid of the 'general welfare,' " whereby persons gainfully employed, and those who employ them, are taxed to permit the payment of benefits to the retired and disabled, and their dependents. Plainly the expectation is that many members of the present productive work force will in turn become beneficiaries rather than supporters of the program. But each worker's benefits, though flowing from the contributions he made to the national economy while actively employed, are not dependent on the degree to which he was called upon to support the system by taxation. It is apparent that the noncontractual interest of an employee covered by the Act cannot be soundly analogized to that of the holder of an annuity, whose right to benefits is bottomed on his contractual premium payments. . . .

To engraft upon the Social Security system a concept of "accrued property rights" would deprive it of the flexibility and boldness in adjustment to ever-changing conditions which it demands. It was doubtless out of an awareness of the need for such flexibility that Congress included in the original Act, and has since retained, a clause expressly reserving to it "[t]he right to alter, amend, or repeal any provision" of the Act. 42 U.S.C. §1304. . . .

We must conclude that a person covered by the Act has not such a right in benefit payments as would make every defeasance of "accrued" interests violative of the Due Process Clause of the Fifth Amendment.

This is not to say, however, that Congress may exercise its power to modify the statutory scheme free of all constitutional restraint. The interest of a covered employee under the Act is of sufficient substance to fall within the protection from arbitrary governmental action afforded by the Due Process Clause. In judging the permissibility of the cut-off provisions of §202(n) from this standpoint, it is not within our authority to determine whether the congressional judgment expressed in that section is sound or equitable, or whether it comports well or ill with the purposes of the Act. . . . Particularly when we deal with a withholding of a noncontractual benefit under a social welfare program such as this, we must recognize that the Due Process Clause can be thought to interpose a bar only if the statute manifests a patently arbitrary classification, utterly lacking in rational justification.

Such is not the case here. The fact of a beneficiary's residence abroad — in the case of a deportee, a presumably permanent residence — can be of obvious relevance to the question of eligibility. One benefit which may be thought to accrue to the economy from the Social Security system is the increased over-all national purchasing power resulting from taxation of productive elements of the economy to provide payments to the retired and disabled, who might otherwise be destitute or nearly so, and who would generally spend a comparatively large percentage of their benefit payments. This advantage would be lost as to payments made to one residing abroad. For these purposes, it is, of course, constitutionally irrelevant whether this reasoning in fact underlay the legislative decision, as it is irrelevant that the section does not extend to all to whom the postulated rationale might in logic apply. . . .

We need go no further to find support for our conclusion that this provision of the Act cannot be condemned as so lacking in rational justification as to offend due process. . . . It is said that the termination of appellee's benefits amounts to punishing him without a judicial trial; that the termination of benefits constitutes the imposition of punishment by legislative act, rendering §202(n) a bill of attainder; and that the punishment exacted is imposed for past conduct not unlawful when engaged in, thereby violating the constitutional prohibition on *ex post facto* laws. Essential to the success of each of these contentions is the validity of characterizing as "punishment" in the constitutional sense the termination of benefits under §202(n). . . .

Turning, then, to the particular statutory provision before us, appellee cannot successfully contend that the language and structure of §202(n), or the nature of the deprivation, requires us to recognize a punitive design. Here the sanction is the mere denial of a noncontractual governmental benefit. No affirmative disability or restraint is imposed, and certainly nothing approaching the "infamous punishment" of imprisonment, as in Wong Wing v. United States, 163 U.S. 228, on which great reliance is mistakenly placed. . . .

Mr. Justice BLACK, dissenting. . . . I agree with the District Court that the United States is depriving appellee, Ephram Nestor, of his statutory right to old-age benefits in violation of the United States Constitution.

Nestor came to this country from Bulgaria in 1913 and lived here continuously for 43 years, until July 1956. He was then deported from this country for having been a Communist from 1933 to 1939. At that time membership in the Communist Party as such was not illegal and was not even a statutory ground for deportation. From December 1936 to January 1955 Nestor and his employers made regular payments to the Government under the Federal Insurance Contributions Act, 26 U.S.C. §§3101-3125. These funds went to a special federal old-age and survivors insurance trust fund under 49 Stat. 622, 53 Stat. 1362, as amended, 42 U.S.C. §401, in return for which Nestor, like millions of others, expected to receive payments when he reached the statutory age. In 1954, 15 years after Nestor had last been a Communist, and 18 years after he began to make payments into the old-age security fund, Congress passed a law providing, among other things, that any person who had been deported from this country because of past communist membership under 66 Stat. 205, 8 U.S.C. §1251(a)(6)(C) should be wholly cut off from any benefits of the fund to which he had contributed under the law. 68 Stat. 1083, 42 U.S.C. §402(n). After the Government deported Nestor in 1956 it notified his wife, who had remained in this country, that he was cut off and no further payments would be made to him. This action, it seems to me, takes Nestor's insurance without just compensation and in violation of the Due Process Clause of the Fifth Amendment. Moreover, it imposes an *ex post facto* law and bill of attainder by stamping him, without a court trial, as unworthy to receive that for which he has paid and which the Government promised to pay him. The fact that the Court is sustaining this action indicates the extent to which people are willing to go these days to overlook violation of the Constitution perpetrated against anyone who has ever even innocently belonged to the Communist Party.

In Lynch v. United States, 292 U.S. 571, this court unanimously held that Congress was without power to repudiate and abrogate in whole or in part its promises to pay amounts claimed by soldiers under the War Risk Insurance Act of 1917, §§400-405, 40 Stat. 409. This Court held that such a repudiation was inconsistent with the provision of the

Fifth Amendment that "No person shall be . . . deprived of life, liberty, or property, without due process of law; nor shall private property be taken for public use, without just compensation." The Court today puts the *Lynch* case aside on the ground that "It is hardly profitable to engage in conceptualizations regarding 'earned rights' and 'gratuities.' " From this sound premise the Court goes on to say that while "The 'right' to Social Security benefits is in one sense 'earned,' " yet the Government's insurance scheme now before us rests not on the idea of the contributors to the fund earning something, but simply provides that they may "justly call" upon the Government "in their later years, for protection from 'the rigors of the poor house as well as from the haunting fear that such a lot awaits them when journey's end is near.' " These are nice words but they cannot conceal the fact that they simply tell the contributors to this insurance fund that despite their own and their employers' payments the Government, in paying the beneficiaries out of the fund, is merely giving them something for nothing and can stop doing so when it pleases. This, in my judgment, reveals a complete misunderstanding of the purpose Congress and the country had in passing that law. It was then generally agreed, as it is today, that it is not desirable that aged people think of the Government as giving them something for nothing. . . . The people covered by this Act are now able to rely with complete assurance on the fact that they will be compelled to contribute regularly to this fund whenever each contribution falls due. I believe they are entitled to rely with the same assurance on getting the benefits they have paid for and have been promised, when their disability or age makes their insurance payable under the terms of the law. The Court did not permit the Government to break its plighted faith with the soldiers in the *Lynch* case; it said the Constitution forbade such governmental conduct. I would say precisely the same thing here.

The Court consoles those whose insurance is taken away today, and others who may suffer the same fate in the future, by saying that a decision requiring the Social Security system to keep faith "would deprive it of the flexibility and boldness in adjustment to ever-changing conditions which it demands." People who pay premiums for insurance usually think they are paying for insurance, not for "flexibility and boldness." I cannot believe that any private insurance company in America would be permitted to repudiate its matured contracts with its policyholders who have regularly paid all their premiums in reliance upon the good faith of the company. It is true, as the Court says, that the original Act contained a clause, still in force, that expressly reserves to Congress "[t]he right to alter, amend, or repeal any provision" of the Act. Congress, of course, properly retained that power. It could repeal the Act so as to cease to operate its old-age insurance activities for the future. This means that it could stop covering new people, and even stop increasing its obligations to its old contributors. But that is quite different from disappointing the just expectations of the contributors to the fund which the Government has compelled them and their employers to pay its Treasury. There is nothing "conceptualistic" about saying, as this court did in *Lynch*, that such a taking as this the Constitution forbids. . . .

◆ REICH, THE NEW PROPERTY
73 Yale L.J. 733, 768-774, 785 (1964)

THE NEW FEUDALISM

The characteristics of the public interest state are varied, but there is an underlying philosophy that unites them. This is the doctrine that the wealth that flows from government is held by its recipients condition-ally, subject to confiscation in the interest of the paramount state. This philosophy is epitomized in the most important of all judicial decisions concerning government largess, the case of Flemming v. Nestor. . . .

The implications of Flemming v. Nestor are profound. No form of government largess is more personal or individual than an old age pen-sion. No form is more clearly earned by the recipient, who, together with his employer, contributes to the Social Security fund during the years of his employment. No form is more obviously a compulsory substitute for private property; the tax on wage earner and employer might readily have gone to higher pay and higher private savings in-stead. No form is more relied on, and more often thought of as property. No form is more vital to the independence and dignity of the individual. Yet under the philosophy of Congress and the Court, a man or woman, after a lifetime of work, has no rights which may not be taken away to serve some public policy. The Court makes no effort to balance the interests at stake. The public policy that justifies cutting off benefits need not even be an important one or a wise one — so long as it is not utterly irrational, the Court will not interfere. In any clash between individual rights and public policy, the latter is automatically held to be superior.

The philosophy of Flemming v. Nestor resembles the philosophy of feudal tenure. Wealth is not "owned," or "vested" in the holders. In-stead, it is held conditionally, the conditions being ones which seek to ensure the fulfillment of obligations imposed by the state. Just as the feudal system linked lord and vassal through a system of mutual depen-dence, obligation, and loyalty, so government largess binds man to the state. And, it may be added, loyalty or fealty to the state is often one of the essential conditions of modern tenure. In the many decisions taking away government largess for refusal to sign loyalty oaths, belonging to "subversive" organizations, or other similar grounds, there is more than a suggestion of the condition of fealty demanded in older times.

The comparison to the general outlines of the feudal system may best be seen by recapitulating some of the chief features of government largess. (1) Increasingly we turn over wealth and rights to government, which reallocates and redistributes them in the many forms of largess; (2) there is a merging of public and private, in which lines of private ownership are blurred; (3) the administration of the system has given rise to special laws and special tribunals, outside the ordinary structure of government; (4) the right to possess and use government largess is bound up with the recipient's legal status; status is both the basis for receiving largess and a consequence of receiving it; hence the new wealth is not readily transferable; (5) individuals hold the wealth conditionally rather than absolutely; the conditions are usually obligations owed to the government or to the public, and may include the obligation of loyalty to the government; the obligations may be changed or increased at the will of the state; (6) for breach of condition the wealth may be forfeited or escheated back to the government; (7) the sovereign power is shared with large private interests; (8) the object of the whole system is to enforce "the public interest" — the interest of the state or society or the lord paramount — by means of the distribution and use of wealth in such a way as to create and maintain dependence. . . .

The public interest state is not with us yet. But we are left with large questions. If the day comes when most private ownership is supplanted by government largess, how then will governmental power over individuals be contained? What will dependence do to the American character? What will happen to the Constitution, and particularly the Bill of Rights, if their limits may be bypassed by purchase, and if people lack an independent base from which to assert their individuality and claim their rights? Without the security of the person which individual wealth provides and which largess fails to provide, what, indeed, will we become? . . .

The public interest state, as visualized above, represents in one sense the triumph of society over private property. This triumph is the end point of a great and necessary movement for reform. But somehow the result is different from what the reformers wanted. Somehow the idealistic concept of the public interest has summoned up a doctrine monstrous and oppressive. It is time to take another look at private property, and at the "public interest" philosophy that dominates its modern substitute, the largess of government.

Property and Liberty

Property is a legal institution the essence of which is the creation and protection of certain private rights in wealth of any kind. The institution performs many different functions. One of these functions is to draw a boundary between public and private power. Property draws a circle around the activities of each private individual or organization. Within that circle, the owner has a greater degree of freedom than without. Outside, he must justify or explain his actions, and show his authority. Within, he is master, and the state must explain and justify any interference. It is as if property shifted the burden of proof; outside, the individual has the burden; inside, the burden is on government to demonstrate that something the owner wishes to do should not be done.

Thus, property performs the function of maintaining independence, dignity and pluralism in society by creating zones within which the majority has to yield to the owner. Whim, caprice, irrationality and "antisocial" activities are given the protection of law; the owner may do what all or most of his neighbors decry. The Bill of Rights also serves this function, but while the Bill of Rights comes into play only at extraordinary moments of conflict or crisis, property affords day-to-day protection in the ordinary affairs of life. Indeed, in the final analysis the Bill of Rights depends upon the existence of private property. Political rights presuppose that individuals and private groups have the will and the means to act independently. But so long as individuals are motivated largely by self-interest, their well-being must first be independent. Civil liberties must have a basis in property, or bills of rights will not preserve them.

Property is not a natural right but a deliberate construction by society. If such an institution did not exist, it would be necessary to create it, in order to have the kind of society we wish. The majority cannot be expected, on specific issues, to yield its power to a minority. Only if the minority's will is established as a general principle can it keep the majority at bay in a given instance. Like the Bill of Rights, property represents a general, long range protection of individual and private interests, created by the majority for the ultimate good of all.

Today, however, it is widely thought that property and liberty are separable things; that there may, in fact, be conflicts between "property rights" and "personal rights." Why has this view been accepted? The explanation is found at least partly in the transformations which have taken place in property.

During the industrial revolution, when property was liberated from feudal restraints, philosophers hailed property as the basis of liberty, and argued that it must be free from the demands of government or society. But as private property grew, so did abuses resulting from its use. In a crowded world, a man's use of his property increasingly affected his neighbor, and one man's exercise of a right might seriously impair the rights of others. Property became power over others; the farm landowner, the city landlord, and the working man's boss were able to oppress their tenants or employees. Great aggregations of property resulted in private control of entire industries and basic services capable of affecting a whole area or even a nation. At the same time much private property lost its individuality and in effect became socialized. Multiple ownership of corporations helped to separate personality from property, and property from power. When the corporations began to stop competing, to merge, agree, and make mutual plans, they became private governments. Finally, they sought the aid and partnership of the state, and thus by their own volition became part of public government.

These changes led to a movement for reform, which sought to limit arbitrary private power and protect the common man. Property rights were considered more the enemy than the friend of liberty. The reformers argued that property must be separated from personality. . . .

The struggle between abuse and reform made it easy to forget the basic importance of individual private property. The defense of private property was almost entirely a defense of its abuses — an attempt to defend not individual property but arbitrary private power over other human beings. Since this defense was cloaked in a defense of private property, it was natural for the reformers to attack too broadly. Walter Lippmann saw this in 1934:

> But the issue between the giant corporation and the public should not be allowed to obscure the truth that the only dependable foundation of personal liberty is the economic security of private property. . . . For we must not expect to find in ordinary men the stuff of martyrs, and we must, therefore, secure their freedom by their normal motives. There is no surer way to give men the courage to be free than to insure them a competence upon which they can rely. [Lippmann, The Method of Freedom 101 (1934).]

The reform took away some of the power of the corporations and transferred it to government. In this transfer there was much good, for the power was made responsive to the majority rather than to the arbitrary and selfish few. But the reform did not restore the individual to his domain. What the corporation had taken from him, the reform simply handed on to government. And government carried further the powers formerly exercised by the corporation. Government as an employer, or as a dispenser of wealth, has used the theory that it was handing out gratuities to claim a managerial power as great as that which the capitalists claimed. Moreover, the corporations allied themselves with, or actually took over, part of government's system of power. Today it is the combined power of government and the corporations that presses against the individual.

From the individual's point of view, it is not any particular kind of power, but all kinds of power, that are to be feared. This is the lesson of the public interest state. The mere fact that power is derived from the majority does not necessarily make it less oppressive. Liberty is more than the right to do what the majority wants, or to do what is "reasonable." Liberty is the right to defy the majority, and to do what is unreasonable. The great error of the public interest state is that it assumes an identity between the public interest and the interest of the majority. . . .

LARGESS AND THE PUBLIC INTEREST

The fact that the reform tended to make much private wealth subject to "the public interest" has great significance, but it does not adequately explain the dependent position of the individual and the weakening of civil liberties in the public interest state. The reformers intended to enhance the values of democracy and liberty; their basic concern was the preservation of a free society. But after they established the primacy of "the public interest," what meaning was given to that phrase? In particular, what value does it embody as it has been employed to regulate government largess?

Reduced to simplest terms, "the public interest" has usually meant this: government largess may be denied or taken away if this will serve some legitimate public policy. The policy may be one directly related to the largess itself, or it may be some collateral objective of government. A contract may be denied if this will promote fair labor standards. A television license may be refused if this will promote the policies of the antitrust laws. Veterans benefits may be taken away to promote loyalty to the United States. A liquor license may be revoked to promote civil rights. A franchise for a barber's college may not be given out if it will hurt the local economy, nor a taxi franchise if it will seriously injure the earning capacity of other taxis.

Most of these objectives are laudable, and all are within the power of government. The great difficulty is that they are simplistic. Concentration on a single policy or value obscures other values that may be at stake. Some of these competing values are other public policies; for example, the policy of the best possible television service to the public may compete with observance of the antitrust laws. The legislature is the natural arbiter of such conflicts. But the conflicts may also be more fundamental. In the regulation of government largess, achievement of specific policy goals may undermine the independence of the individual. Where such conflicts exist, a simplistic notion of the public interest may unwittingly destroy some values. . . .

FROM LARGESS TO RIGHT

Eventually those forms of largess which are closely linked to status must be deemed to be held as of right. Like property, such largess could be governed by a system of regulation plus civil or criminal sanctions, rather than a system based upon denial, suspension and revocation. As things now stand, violations lead to forfeitures — outright confiscation of wealth and status. But there is surely no need for these drastic results. Confiscation, if used at all, should be the ultimate, not the most common and convenient penalty. The presumption should be that the professional man will keep his license, and the welfare recipient his pension. These interests should be "vested." If revocation is necessary, not by reason of the fault of the individual holder, but by reason of overriding demands of public policy, perhaps payment of just compensation would be appropriate. The individual should not bear the entire loss for a remedy primarily intended to benefit the community. . . .

At the very least, it is time to reconsider the theories under which new forms of wealth are regulated, and by which governmental power over them is measured. It is time to recognize that "the public interest" is all too often a reassuring platitude that covers up sharp clashes of conflicting values, and hides fundamental choices. It is time to see that the "privilege" or "gratuity" concept, as applied to wealth dispensed by government, is not much different from the absolute right of ownership that private capital once invoked to justify arbitrary power over employees and the public.

Above all, the time has come for us to remember what the framers of the Constitution knew so well — that "a power over a man's subsistence amounts to a power over his will." We cannot safely entrust our livelihoods and our rights to the discretion of authorities, examiners, boards of control, character committees, regents, or license commissioners. We cannot permit any official or agency to pretend to sole knowledge of the public good. We cannot put the independence of any man . . . wholly in the power of other men.

If the individual is to survive in a collective society, he must have protection against its ruthless pressures. There must be sanctuaries or enclaves where no majority can reach. To shelter the solitary human spirit does not merely make possible the fulfillment of individuals; it also gives society the power to change, to grow, and to regenerate, and hence to endure. These were the objects which property sought to achieve, and can no longer achieve. The challenge of the future will be to construct, for the society that is coming, institutions and laws to carry on this work. Just as the Homestead Act was a deliberate effort to foster individual values at an earlier time, so we must try to build an economic basis for liberty today — a Homestead Act for rootless twentieth century man. We must create a new property.

Notes

1. "Distributions of wealth are available less frequently than those of income, but occasional measurements have been made. In 1962 the Federal Reserve Board conducted a survey of the ownership of all pri-

vate assets. At that time, the wealthiest 20 percent of the population owned over 75 percent of all private assets while the poorest 25 percent of all families had no net worth (their debts equaled their assets). The wealthiest 8 percent of the population owned 60 percent of all private assets; the wealthiest 1 percent owned over 26 percent of all private assets." L. Thurow and R. Lucas, Study for the Joint Economic Committee, 92d Congress, 2d Sess., The American Distribution of Income: A Structural Problem 11-12 (Comm. Print 1972).

2. Neumann, The Concept of Political Freedom, 53 Colum. L. Rev. 901, 924-926 (1953):

It seems clear that [private property] is conceived, throughout the history of social and political thought, as an instrument for the realization of the good (or at least the tenable) life. This is clearly Aristotle's position, which is carried on in the whole medieval tradition. It is equally the position of the more modern political thinkers — of Bodin, Spinoza, Hobbes, Kant and Hegel — whether they believe property to be a natural right or a grant by positive law. The instrumentalist character of property is probably the strongest link among these varied political theories. The connection of property and liberty is, of course, most candidly stated in Locke's theory, where liberty appears as inherent in the overall concept of property. But property is defined as labor-property, and possessory theories of property are thus rejected, the legitimation of property resting in the transformation of external nature, particularly land, by the creative activity of man. It is precisely the labor theory of property which demonstrates its instrumentalist role and it is here a matter of indifference that Locke drew no consequences from his own theory, which he merely intended as a legitimation of capitalist property. But the recognition of the instrumentalist nature of property in regard to liberty makes it obviously necessary to redefine the social function of property in each historical stage, and thus to distinguish clearly between various types of property and of property-owners. If property is to serve freedom, and if freedom pertains to man only, then corporate property, while it may or may not be necessary socially, cannot claim to be a civil right of the same rank as freedom of religion and communications. Similarly, the substrata of the property right — land, consumption goods, production goods — may require different treatment.

Most of the continental civil rights catalogues thus make a clear distinction between property and other civil rights, the protection of the latter being far more stringent than that of the former. One very simple consideration will make clear the instrumentalist role of property: all constitutions permit the condemnation of private property with adequate compensation. Yet no civilized constitution could possibly permit the state to do away with a person's life or liberty for public purposes even with more than adequate compensation. The value of political freedom is absolute; that of property is merely relative to it. Thus the tasks of a political theory concerned with man's freedom are to analyze whether property fulfills its function as an efficient instrument of freedom, and to discover what institutional changes are necessary to maximize its effectiveness.

3. While Reich views property as a social creation, he implies that the needs and rights it protects are natural to individuals. But might it be true that the rights that Reich wants property to protect are themselves the creation of modes of production and the system of property?

It is not individuals but capital that establishes itself freely in free competition. So long as production founded on capital is necessary and therefore the most suitable form in which social productive forces can develop, the movement of individuals within the pure conditions of capital will seem to be free. . . .

Hence the absurdity of considering free competition as being the final development of human liberty, and the negation of free competition as being the negation of individual liberty and of social production founded on individual liberty. It is only free development on a limited foundation — that of the dominion of capital. This kind of individual liberty is thus at the same time the most complete suppression of all individual liberty and total subjugation of individuality to social conditions which take the form of material forces — and even of all-powerful objects that are independent of the individuals relating to them. The only rational answer to the deification of free competition by the middle-class prophets, or its diabolisation by the socialists, lies in its own development. If it is said that, within the limits of free competition, individuals by following their pure self-interest realise their social, or rather their general, interest, this means merely that they exert pressure upon one another under the conditions of capitalist production and that this clash between them can only give rise to the conditions under which their interaction took place. Moreover, once the illusion that competition is the supposedly absolute form of free individuality disappears, this proves that the conditions of competition, i.e. of production founded on capital, are already felt and thought of as a barrier, that they indeed already are such and will increasingly become so. The assertion that free competition is the final form of the development of productive forces, and thus of human freedom, means only that the domination of the middle class is the end of the world's history — of course quite a pleasant thought for yesterday's parvenus! [K. Marx, The Grundrisse 129-132 (1857-1858) (D. McLellan ed. 1971).]

4. What are the assumptions implicit in the view that the government is now the dispenser of wealth? Who is the government?

In the case of the nations which grew out of the Middle Ages, tribal property evolved through various stages — feudal landed property, corporative movable property, capital invested in manufacture — to modern capital, determined by big industry and universal competition, i.e., pure private property, which has cast off all semblance of a communal institution and has shut out the State from any influence on the development of property. To this modern private property corresponds the modern State, which, purchased gradually by the owners of property by means of taxation, has fallen entirely into their hands through the national debt, and its

existence has become wholly dependent on the commercial credit which
the owners of property, the bourgeois, extend to it, as reflected in the rise
and fall of State funds on the stock exchange. By the mere fact that it is a
class and no longer an estate, the bourgeoisie is forced to organise itself no
longer locally, but nationally, and to give a general form to its mean
average interest. Through the emancipation of private property from the
community, the State has become a separate entity, beside and outside
civil society; but it is nothing more than the form of organization which the
bourgeois necessarily adopt both for internal and external purposes, for
the mutual guarantee of their property and interests. The independence of
the State is only found nowadays in those countries where the estates
have not yet completely developed into classes, where the estates, done
away with in more advanced countries, still have a part to play, and where
there exists a mixture; countries, that is to say, in which no one section of
the population can achieve dominance over the others. This is the case
particularly in America. The modern French, English and American writers all express the opinion that the State exists only for the sake of private
property, so that this fact has penetrated into the consciousness of the
normal man.

Since the State is the form in which the individuals of a ruling class
assert their common interests, and in which the whole civil society of an
epoch is epitomised, it follows that the State mediates in the formation of
all common institutions and that the institutions receive a political form.
Hence the illusion that law is based on the will, and indeed on the will
divorced from its real basis — on free will. Similarly, justice is in its turn
reduced to the actual laws. [K. Marx & F. Engels, The German Ideology
(1845-1846), from The Marx-Engels Reader 150-152 (Tucher ed. 1972).]

2.   "A Matter of Statutory Entitlement"

◆ GOLDBERG v. KELLY
397 U.S. 254 (1970)

Mr. Justice BRENNAN delivered the opinion of the Court. This action was
brought in the District Court for the Southern District of New York by
residents of New York City receiving financial aid under the federally
assisted program of Aid to Families with Dependent Children (AFDC) or
under New York State's general Home Relief program. Their complaint
alleged that the New York State and New York City officials administering these programs terminated, or were about to terminate, such aid
without prior notice and hearing, thereby denying them due process of
law. At the time the suits were filed there was no requirement of prior
notice or hearing of any kind before termination of financial aid. However, the State and city adopted procedures for notice and hearing after
the suits were brought, and the plaintiffs, appellees here, then challenged the constitutional adequacy of those procedures. . . .

. . . A caseworker who has doubts about the recipient's continued eligibility must first discuss them with the recipient. If the caseworker concludes that the recipient is no longer eligible, he recommends termination of aid to a unit supervisor. If the latter concurs, he sends the recipient a letter stating the reasons for proposing to terminate aid and notifying him that within seven days he may request that a higher official review the record, and may support the request with a written statement prepared personally or with the aid of an attorney or other person. If the reviewing official affirms the determination of ineligibility, aid is stopped immediately and the recipient is informed by letter of the reasons for the action. Appellees' challenge to this procedure emphasizes the absence of any provisions for the personal appearance of the recipient before the reviewing official, for oral presentation of evidence, and for confrontation and cross-examination of adverse witnesses. However, the letter does inform the recipient that he may request a post-termination "fair hearing." This is a proceeding before an independent state hearing officer at which the recipient may appear personally, offer oral evidence, confront and cross-examine the witnesses against him, and have a record made of the hearing. If the recipient prevails at the "fair hearing" he is paid all funds erroneously withheld. A recipient whose aid is not restored by a "fair hearing" decision may have judicial review. . . .

The constitutional issue to be decided, therefore, is the narrow one whether the Due Process Clause requires that the recipient be afforded an evidentiary hearing *before* the termination of benefits. The District Court held that only a pre-termination evidentiary hearing would satisfy the constitutional command, and rejected the argument of the state and city officials that the combination of the post-termination "fair hearing" with the informal pre-termination review disposed of all due process claims. . . .

Appellant does not contend that procedural due process is not applicable to the termination of welfare benefits. Such benefits are a matter of statutory entitlement for persons qualified to receive them.[8] Their

8. It may be realistic today to regard welfare entitlements as more like "property" than a "gratuity." Much of the existing wealth in this country takes the form of rights that do not fall within traditional common-law concepts of property. It has been aptly noted that "[s]ociety today is built around entitlement. The automobile dealer has his franchise, the doctor and lawyer their professional licenses, the worker his union membership, contract, and pension rights, the executive his contract and stock options; all are devices to aid security and independence. Many of the most important of these entitlements now flow from government: subsidies to farmers and businessmen, routes for airlines and channels for television stations; long term contracts for defense, space, and education; social security pensions for individuals. Such sources of security, whether private or public, are no longer regarded as luxuries or gratuities; to the recipients they are essentials, fully deserved, and in no sense a form of charity. It is only the poor whose entitlements, although recognized by public policy, have not been effectively enforced." Reich, Individual Rights and Social Welfare: The Emerging Legal Issues, 74 Yale L.J. 1245, 1255 (1965).

termination involves state action that adjudicates important rights. The constitutional challenge cannot be answered by an argument that public assistance benefits are "a 'privilege' and not a 'right.' " Relevant constitutional restraints apply as much to the withdrawal of public assistance benefits as to disqualification for unemployment compensation; or to denial of a tax exemption; or to discharge from public employment. The extent to which procedural due process must be afforded the recipient is influenced by the extent to which he may be "condemned to suffer grievous loss," and depends upon whether the recipient's interest in avoiding that loss outweighs the governmental interest in summary adjudication. . . .

[W]e agree with the District Court that when welfare is discontinued, only a pre-termination evidentiary hearing provides the recipient with procedural due process. For qualified recipients, welfare provides the means to obtain essential food, clothing, housing, and medical care.

Thus the crucial factor in this context — a factor not present in the case of the blacklisted government contractor, the discharged government employee, the taxpayer denied a tax exemption, or virtually anyone else whose governmental entitlements are ended — is that termination of aid pending resolution of a controversy over eligibility may deprive an *eligible* recipient of the very means by which to live while he waits. Since he lacks independent resources, his situation becomes immediately desperate. His need to concentrate upon finding the means for daily subsistence, in turn, adversely affects his ability to seek redress from the welfare bureaucracy.

Moreover, important governmental interests are promoted by affording recipients a pre-termination evidentiary hearing. . . . We have come to recognize that forces not within the control of the poor contribute to their poverty. . . . Welfare, by meeting the basic demands of subsistence, can help bring within the reach of the poor the same opportunities that are available to others to participate meaningfully in the life of the community. . . .

Appellant does not challenge the force of these considerations but argues that they are outweighed by countervailing governmental interests in conserving fiscal and administrative resources. . . . Summary adjudication protects the public fisc by stopping payments promptly upon discovery of reason to believe that a recipient is no longer eligible. Since most terminations are accepted without challenge, summary adjudication also conserves both the fisc and administrative time and energy by reducing the number of evidentiary hearings actually held.

We agree with the District Court, however, that these governmental interests are not overriding in the welfare context. The requirement of a prior hearing doubtless involves some greater expense, and the benefits paid to ineligible recipients pending decision at the hearing probably cannot be recouped, since these recipients are likely to be judgment-proof. But the State is not without weapons to minimize these increased costs. Much of the drain on fiscal and administrative resources can be reduced by developing procedures for prompt pre-termination hearings and by skillful use of personnel and facilities. . . .

We also agree with the District Court, however, that the pre-termination hearing need not take the form of a judicial or quasi-judicial trial. We bear in mind that the statutory "fair hearing" will provide the recipient with a full administrative review. Accordingly, the pre-termination hearing has one function only: to produce an initial determination of the validity of the welfare department's grounds for discontinuance of payments in order to protect a recipient against an erroneous termination of his benefits. Thus, a complete record and a comprehensive opinion, which would serve primarily to facilitate judicial review and to guide future decisions, need not be provided at the pre-termination stage. We recognize, too, that both welfare authorities and recipients have an interest in relatively speedy resolution of questions of eligibility, that they are used to dealing with one another informally, and that some welfare departments have very burdensome caseloads. These considerations justify the limitation of the pre-termination hearing to minimum procedural safeguards, adapted to the particular characteristics of welfare recipients, and to the limited nature of the controversies to be resolved. We wish to add that we, no less than the dissenters, recognize the importance of not imposing upon the States or the Federal Government in this developing field of law any procedural requirements beyond those demanded by rudimentary due process. . . .

The opportunity to be heard must be tailored to the capacities and circumstances of those who are to be heard. It is not enough that a welfare recipient may present his position to the decision maker in writing or secondhand through his caseworker. Written submissions are an unrealistic option for most recipients, who lack the educational attainment necessary to write effectively and who cannot obtain professional assistance. Moreover, written submissions do not afford the flexibility of oral presentations; they do not permit the recipient to mold his argument to the issues the decision maker appears to regard as important. Particularly where credibility and veracity are at issue, as they must be in many termination proceedings, written submissions are a wholly unsatisfactory basis for decision. The secondhand presentation to the decision maker by the caseworker has its own deficiencies; since the caseworker usually gathers the facts upon which the charge of ineligibility rests, the presentation of the recipient's side of the controversy cannot safely be left to him. Therefore a recipient must be allowed to state his position orally. Informal procedures will suffice; in this context due process does not require a particular order of proof or mode of offering evidence. . . .

Finally, the decision maker's conclusion as to a recipient's eligibility must rest solely on the legal rules and evidence adduced at the hearing. To demonstrate compliance with this elementary requirement, the decision maker should state the reasons for his determination and indicate the evidence he relied on, though his statement need not amount to a full opinion or even formal findings of fact and conclusions of law. And, of course, an impartial decision maker is essential. We agree with the District Court that prior involvement in some aspects of a case will not necessarily bar a welfare official from acting as a decision maker. He should not, however, have participated in making the determination under review.

Affirmed.

Mr. Justice BLACK, dissenting. In the last half century the United States, along with many, perhaps most, other nations of the world, has moved far toward becoming a welfare state, that is, a nation that for one reason or another taxes its most affluent people to help support, feed, clothe, and shelter its less fortunate citizens. The result is that today more than nine million men, women, and children in the United States receive some kind of state or federally financed public assistance in the form of allowances or gratuities, generally paid them periodically, usually by the week, month, or quarter. Since these gratuities are paid on the basis of need, the list of recipients is not static, and some people go off the lists and others are added from time to time. These ever-changing lists put a constant administrative burden on government. . . .

The more than a million names on the relief rolls in New York . . . are there because state welfare officials believed that those people were eligible for assistance. Probably in the officials' haste to make out the lists many names were put there erroneously in order to alleviate immediate suffering. . . . Many of those who thus draw undeserved gratuities are without sufficient property to enable the government to collect back from them any money they wrongfully receive. But the Court today holds that it would violate the Due Process Clause of the Fourteenth Amendment to stop paying those people weekly or monthly allowances unless the government first affords them a full "evidentiary hearing" even though welfare officials are persuaded that the recipients are not rightfully entitled to receive a penny under the law. In other words, although some recipients might be on the lists for payment wholly because of deliberate fraud on their part, the Court holds that the government is helpless and must continue, until after an evidentiary hearing, to pay money that it does not owe, never has owed, and never could owe. I do not believe there is any provision in our Constitution that should thus paralyze the government's efforts to protect itself against making payments to people who are not entitled to them. . . .

The procedure required today as a matter of constitutional law finds no precedent in our legal system. Reduced to its simplest terms, the problem in this case is similar to that frequently encountered when two parties have an ongoing legal relationship that requires one party to make periodic payments to the other. Often the situation arises where the party "owing" the money stops paying it and justifies his conduct by arguing that the recipient is not legally entitled to payment. The recipient can, of course, disagree and go to court to compel payment. But I know of no situation in our legal system in which the person alleged to owe money to another is required by law to continue making payments to a judgment-proof claimant without the benefit of any security or bond to insure that these payments can be recovered if he wins his legal argument. . . .

The Court apparently feels that this decision will benefit the poor and needy. . . . [T]he end result of today's decision may well be that the government, once it decides to give welfare benefits, cannot reverse that decision until the recipient has had the benefits of full administrative and judicial review, including, of course, the opportunity to present his case to this Court. Since this process will usually entail a delay of several years, the inevitable result of such a constitutionally imposed burden will be that the government will not put a claimant on the rolls initially until it has made an exhaustive investigation to determine his eligibility. While this Court will perhaps have insured that no needy person will be taken off the rolls without a full "due process" proceeding, it will also have insured that many will never get on the rolls, or at least that they will remain destitute during the lengthy proceedings followed to determine initial eligibility.

For the foregoing reasons I dissent from the Court's holding. The operation of a welfare state is a new experiment for our Nation. For this reason, among others, I feel that new experiments in carrying out a welfare program should not be frozen into our constitutional structure. They should be left, as are other legislative determinations, to the Congress and the legislatures that the people elect to make our laws.

♦ DANDRIDGE v. WILLIAMS
397 U.S. 471 (1970)

Mr. Justice STEWART delivered the opinion of the Court. . . . By statute [Maryland] participates in the AFDC program. It computes the standard of need for each eligible family based on the number of children in the family and the circumstances under which the family lives. In general, the standard of need increases with each additional person in the household, but the increments become proportionately smaller. The regulation here in issue imposes upon the grant that any single family may receive an upper limit of $250 per month in certain counties and Baltimore City, and of $240 per month elsewhere in the State. The appellees all have large families, so that their standards of need as computed by the State substantially exceed the maximum grants that they actually receive under the regulation. The appellees urged in the District Court that the maximum grant limitation operates to discriminate against them merely because of the size of their families, in violation of the Equal Protection Clause of the Fourteenth Amendment. They claimed further that the regulation is incompatible with the purpose of the Social Security Act of 1935, as well as in conflict with its explicit provisions. . . .

It cannot be gainsaid that the effect of the Maryland maximum grant provision is to reduce the per capita benefits to the children in the largest families. . . . Given Maryland's finite resources, its choice is either to support some families adequately and others less adequately, or not to give sufficient support to any family. We see nothing in the federal statute that forbids a State to balance the stresses that uniform insufficiency of payments would impose on all families against the greater ability of large families — because of the inherent economies of scale — to accommodate their needs to diminished per capita payments. The strong policy of the statute in favor of preserving family units does not prevent a State from sustaining as many families as it can, and providing the largest families somewhat less than their ascertained per capita standard of need. . . .

Although a State may adopt a maximum grant system in allocating its funds available for AFDC payments without violating the Act, it may not, of course, impose a regime of invidious discrimination in violation of the Equal Protection Clause of the Fourteenth Amendment. Maryland says that its maximum grant regulation is wholly free of any invidiously discriminatory purpose or effect, and that the regulation is rationally supportable on at least four entirely valid grounds. The regulation can be clearly justified, Maryland argues, in terms of legitimate state interests in encouraging gainful employment, in maintaining an equitable balance in economic status as between welfare families and those supported by a wage-earner, in providing incentives for family planning, and in allocating available public funds in such a way as fully to meet the needs of the largest possible number of families. . . .

In the area of economics and social welfare, a State does not violate the Equal Protection Clause merely because the classifications made by its laws are imperfect. If the classification has some "reasonable basis," it does not offend the Constitution simply because the classification "is not made with mathematical nicety or because in practice it results in some inequality." . . .

To be sure, the cases cited, and many others enunciating this fundamental standard under the Equal Protection Clause, have in the main involved state regulation of business or industry. The administration of public welfare assistance, by contrast, involves the most basic economic needs of impoverished human beings. We recognize the dramatically real factual difference between the cited cases and this one, but we can find no basis for applying a different constitutional standard. It is a standard that has consistently been applied to state legislation restricting the availability of employment opportunities. And it is a standard that is true to the principle that the Fourteenth Amendment gives the federal courts no power to impose upon the States their views of what constitutes wise economic or social policy.

Under this long-established meaning of the Equal Protection Clause, it is clear that the Maryland maximum grant regulation is constitutionally valid. We need not explore all the reasons that the State advances in justification of the regulation. It is enough that a solid foundation for the regulation can be found in the State's legitimate interest in encouraging employment and in avoiding discrimination between welfare families and the families of the working poor. By combining a limit on the recipient's grant with permission to retain money earned, without reduction in the amount of the grant, Maryland provides an incentive to seek gainful employment. And by keying the maximum family AFDC grants to the minimum wage a steadily employed head of a household receives, the State maintains some semblance of an equitable balance between families on welfare and those supported by an employed breadwinner.

It is true that in some AFDC families there may be no person who is employable. It is also true that with respect to AFDC families whose determined standard of need is below the regulatory maximum, and who therefore receive grants equal to the determined standard, the employment incentive is absent. But the Equal Protection Clause does not require that a State must choose between attacking every aspect of the problem or not attacking the problem at all. It is enough that the State's action be rationally based and free from invidious discrimination. The regulation before us meets that test.

[Justices Douglas, Brennan, and Marshall dissented.]

3. "Interests That a Person Has Already Acquired"

◆ BOARD OF REGENTS OF STATE COLLEGES v. ROTH
408 U.S. 564 (1972)

Mr. Justice STEWART delivered the opinion of the Court. In 1968 the respondent, David Roth, was hired for his first teaching job as assistant professor of political science at Wisconsin State University-Oshkosh. He was hired for a fixed term of one academic year. The notice of his faculty appointment specified that his employment would begin on September

1, 1968, and would end on June 30, 1969.[1] The respondent completed that term. But he was informed that he would not be rehired for the next academic year.

The respondent had no tenure rights to continued employment. Under Wisconsin statutory law a state university teacher can acquire tenure as a "permanent" employee only after four years of year-to-year employment. Having acquired tenure, a teacher is entitled to continued employment "during efficiency and good behavior." A relatively new teacher without tenure, however, is under Wisconsin law entitled to nothing beyond his one-year appointment.[2] There are no statutory or administrative standards defining eligibility for re-employment. State law thus clearly leaves the decision whether to rehire a nontenured teacher for another year to the unfettered discretion of university officials.

The procedural protection afforded a Wisconsin State University teacher before he is separated from the University corresponds to his job security. As a matter of statutory law, a tenured teacher cannot be "discharged except for cause upon written charges" and pursuant to certain procedures.[3] A nontenured teacher, similarly, is protected to some extent *during* his one-year term. Rules promulgated by the Board of Regents provide that a nontenured teacher "dismissed" before the end of the year may have some opportunity for review of the "dismissal." But the Rules provide no real protection for a nontenured teacher who simply is not re-employed for the next year. He must be informed by February 1 "concerning retention or non-retention for the ensuing year." But "no reason for non-retention need be given. No review or appeal is provided in such case."

---

1. The respondent had no contract of employment. Rather, his formal notice of appointment was the equivalent of an employment contract.

The notice of his appointment provided that: *"David F. Roth* is hereby appointed to the faculty of the Wisconsin State University Position number 0262. (Location:) *Oshkosh* as (Rank:) *Assistant Professor* of (Department:) *Political Science* this (Date:) *first* day of (Month:) *September* (year:) *1968.*" The notice went on to specify that the respondent's "appointment basis" was for the "academic year." And it provided that "[r]egulations governing tenure are in accord with Chapter 37.31, Wisconsin Statutes. The employment of any staff member for an academic year shall not be for a term beyond June 30th of the fiscal year in which the appointment is made." . . .

2. Wis. Stat. §37.31(1) (1967), in force at the time, provided in pertinent part that: "All teachers in any state university shall initially be employed on probation. The employment shall be permanent, during efficiency and good behavior after 4 years of continuous service in the state university system as a teacher."

3. Wis. Stat. §37.31(1) further provided that:

No teacher who has become permanently employed as herein provided shall be discharged except for cause upon written charges. Within 30 days of receiving the written charges, such teacher may appeal the discharge by a written notice to the president of the board of regents of state colleges. The board shall cause the charges to be investigated, hear the case and provide such teacher with a written statement as to their decision.

1402 ◆ 23. New Property

In conformance with these Rules, the President of Wisconsin State University-Oshkosh informed the respondent before February 1, 1969, that he would not be rehired for the 1969-1970 academic year. He gave the respondent no reason for the decision and no opportunity to challenge it at any sort of hearing.

The respondent then brought this action in Federal District Court alleging that the decision not to rehire him for the next year infringed his Fourteenth Amendment rights. He attacked the decision both in substance and procedure. First, he alleged that the true reason for the decision was to punish him for certain statements critical of the University administration, and that it therefore violated his right to freedom of speech. Second, he alleged that the failure of University officials to give him notice of any reason for nonretention and an opportunity for a hearing violated his right to procedural due process of law.

The District Court granted summary judgment for the respondent on the procedural issue, ordering the University officials to provide him with reasons and a hearing. The Court of Appeals, with one judge dissenting, affirmed this partial summary judgment. The only question presented to us at this stage in the case is whether the respondent had a constitutional right to a statement of reasons and a hearing on the University's decision not to rehire him for another year. We hold that he did not.

The requirements of procedural due process apply only to the deprivation of interests encompassed by the Fourteenth Amendment's protection of liberty and property. When protected interests are implicated, the right to some kind of prior hearing is paramount. But the range of interests protected by procedural due process is not infinite.

The District Court decided that procedural due process guarantees apply in this case by assessing and balancing the weights of the particular interests involved. It concluded that the respondent's interest in re-employment at Wisconsin State University-Oshkosh outweighed the University's interest in denying him re-employment summarily. Undeniably, the respondent's re-employment prospects were of major concern to him — concern that we surely cannot say was insignificant. And a weighing process has long been a part of any determination of the *form* of hearing required in particular situations by procedural due process. But, to determine whether due process requirements apply in the first place, we must look not to the "weight" but to the *nature* of the interest at stake. . . .

"Liberty" and "property" are broad and majestic terms. They are among the "[g]reat [constitutional] concepts . . . purposely left to gather meaning from experience. . . . [T]hey relate to the whole domain of social and economic fact, and the statesmen who founded this Nation knew too well that only a stagnant society remains unchanged." For that reason, the Court has fully and finally rejected the wooden distinction between "rights" and "privileges" that once seemed to govern the applicability of procedural due process rights. The Court has also made clear that the property interests protected by procedural due process extend well beyond actual ownership of real estate, chattels, or money. By the same token, the Court has required due process protection for deprivations of liberty beyond the sort of formal constraints imposed by the criminal process.

Yet, while the Court has eschewed rigid or formalistic limitations on the protection of procedural due process, it has at the same time observed certain boundaries. For the words "liberty" and "property" in the Due Process Clause of the Fourteenth Amendment must be given some meaning. . . .

The State, in declining to rehire the respondent, did not make any charge against him that might seriously damage his standing and associations in his community. It did not base the nonrenewal of his contract on a charge, for example, that he had been guilty of dishonesty, or immorality. Had it done so, this would be a different case. . . .

Similarly, there is no suggestion that the State, in declining to reemploy the respondent, imposed on him a stigma or other disability that foreclosed his freedom to take advantage of other employment opportunities. The State, for example, did not invoke any regulations to bar the respondent from all other public employment in state universities. Had it done so, this, again, would be a different case. . . .

The Fourteenth Amendment's procedural protection of property is a safeguard of the security of interests that a person has already acquired in specific benefits. These interests — property interests — may take many forms. . . .

Certain attributes of "property" interests protected by procedural due process emerge from these decisions. To have a property interest in a benefit, a person clearly must have more than an abstract need or desire for it. He must have more than a unilateral expectation of it. He must, instead, have a legitimate claim of entitlement to it. It is a purpose of the ancient institution of property to protect those claims upon which people rely in their daily lives, reliance that must not be arbitrarily undermined. It is a purpose of the constitutional right to a hearing to provide an opportunity for a person to vindicate those claims.

Property interests, of course, are not created by the Constitution. Rather, they are created and their dimensions are defined by existing rules or understandings that stem from an independent source such as state law — rules or understandings that secure certain benefits and that support claims of entitlement to those benefits. Thus, the welfare recipients in Goldberg v. Kelly had a claim of entitlement to welfare payments that was grounded in the statute defining eligibility for them. The recipients had not yet shown that they were, in fact, within the statutory terms of eligibility. But we held that they had a right to a hearing at which they might attempt to do so.

Just as the welfare recipients' "property" interest in welfare payments was created and defined by statutory terms, so the respondent's "property" interest in employment at Wisconsin State University-Oshkosh was created and defined by the terms of his appointment. Those terms secured his interest in employment up to June 30, 1969. But the important fact in this case is that they specifically provided that the respondent's employment was to terminate on June 30. They did not provide for contract renewal absent "sufficient cause." Indeed, they made no provision for renewal whatsoever.

Thus, the terms of the respondent's appointment secured absolutely no interest in re-employment for the next year. They supported absolutely no possible claim of entitlement to re-employment. Nor, significantly, was there any state statute or University rule or policy that secured his interest in re-employment or that created any legitimate claim to it.[16] In these circumstances, the respondent surely had an abstract concern in being rehired, but he did not have a *property* interest sufficient to require the University authorities to give him a hearing when they declined to renew his contract of employment.

Mr. Justice DOUGLAS, dissenting. . . . No more direct assault on academic freedom can be imagined than for the school authorities to be allowed to discharge a teacher because of his or her philosophical, political, or ideological beliefs. The same may well be true of private schools, if through the device of financing or other umbilical cords they become instrumentalities of the State. . . .

When a violation of First Amendment rights is alleged, the reasons for dismissal or for nonrenewal of an employment contract must be examined to see if the reasons given are only a cloak for activity or attitudes protected by the Constitution. . . .

Moreover, where "important interests" of the citizen are implicated they are not to be denied or taken away without due process. [In one case we said that a driver's license was such an interest.] But also included are disqualification for unemployment compensation; discharge from public employment; denial of tax exemption; and withdrawal of welfare benefits. . . . We should now add that nonrenewal of a teacher's contract, whether or not he has tenure, is an entitlement of the same importance and dignity. . . .

16. To be sure, the respondent does suggest that most teachers hired on a year-to-year basis by Wisconsin State University-Oshkosh are, in fact, rehired. But the District Court has not found that there is anything approaching a "common law" of re-employment, see Perry v. Sindermann, *post*, so strong as to require University officials to give the respondent a statement of reasons and a hearing on their decision not to rehire him.

Mr. Justice MARSHALL, dissenting. . . . The prior decisions of this Court, discussed at length in the opinion of the Court, establish a principle that is as obvious as it is compelling — i.e., federal and state governments and governmental agencies are restrained by the Constitution from acting arbitrarily with respect to employment opportunities that they either offer or control. Hence, it is now firmly established that whether or not a private employer is free to act capriciously or unreasonably with respect to employment practices, at least absent statutory or contractual controls, a government employer is different. The government may only act fairly and reasonably. . . .

In my view, every citizen who applies for a government job is entitled to it unless the government can establish some reason for denying the employment. This is the "property" right that I believe is protected by the Fourteenth Amendment and that cannot be denied "without due process of law." And it is also liberty — liberty to work — which is the "very essence of the personal freedom and opportunity" secured by the Fourteenth Amendment. . . .

It may be argued that to provide procedural due process to all public employees or prospective employees would place an intolerable burden on the machinery of government. The short answer to that argument is that it is not burdensome to give reasons when reasons exist. Whenever an application for employment is denied, an employee is discharged, or a decision not to rehire an employee is made, there should be some reason for the decision. It can scarcely be argued that government would be crippled by a requirement that the reason be communicated to the person most directly affected by the government's action.

Where there are numerous applicants for jobs, it is likely that few will choose to demand reasons for not being hired. But, if the demand for reasons is exceptionally great, summary procedures can be devised that would provide fair and adequate information to all persons. As long as the government has a good reason for its actions it need not fear disclosure. It is only where the government acts improperly that procedural due process is truly burdensome. And that is precisely when it is most necessary. . . .

◆ PERRY v. SINDERMANN
408 U.S. 593 (1972)

Mr. Justice STEWART delivered the opinion of the Court. From 1959 to 1969 the respondent, Robert Sindermann, was a teacher in the state college system of the State of Texas. After teaching for two years at the University of Texas and for four years at San Antonio Junior College, he became a professor of Government and Social Science at Odessa Junior College in 1965. He was employed at the college for four successive years, under a series of one-year contracts. He was successful enough to be appointed, for a time, the cochairman of his department.

During the 1968-1969 academic year, however, controversy arose between the respondent and the college administration. The respondent was elected president of the Texas Junior College Teachers Association. In this capacity, he left his teaching duties on several occasions to testify before committees of the Texas Legislature, and he became involved in public disagreements with the policies of the college's Board of Regents. In particular, he aligned himself with a group advocating the elevation of the college to four-year status — a change opposed by the Regents. And, on one occasion, a newspaper advertisement appeared over his name that was highly critical of the Regents.

Finally, in May 1969, the respondent's one-year employment contract terminated and the Board of Regents voted not to offer him a new contract for the next academic year. The Regents issued a press release setting forth allegations of the respondent's insubordination. But they provided him no official statement of the reasons for the nonrenewal of his contract. And they allowed him no opportunity for a hearing to challenge the basis of the nonrenewal. . . .

The first question presented is whether the respondent's lack of a contractual or tenure right to re-employment, taken alone, defeats his claim that the nonrenewal of his contract violated the First and Fourteenth Amendments. We hold that it does not.

For at least a quarter century, this Court has made clear that even though a person has no "right" to a valuable governmental benefit and even though the government may deny him the benefit for any number of reasons, there are some reasons upon which the government may not act. It may not deny a benefit to a person on a basis that infringes his constitutionally protected interests — especially, his interest in freedom of speech. For if the government could deny a benefit to a person because of his constitutionally protected speech or associations, his exercise of those freedoms would in effect be penalized and inhibited. This would allow the government to "produce a result which [it] could not command directly." Such interference with constitutional rights is impermissible. . . .

In this case, of course, the respondent has yet to show that the decision not to renew his contract was, in fact, made in retaliation for his exercise of the constitutional right of free speech. The District Court foreclosed any opportunity to make this showing when it granted summary judgment. Hence, we cannot now hold that the Board of Regents' action was invalid.

But we agree with the Court of Appeals that there is a genuine dispute as to "whether the college refused to renew the teaching contract on an impermissible basis — as a reprisal for the exercise of constitutionally protected rights." 430 F.2d, at 943. The respondent has alleged that his nonretention was based on his testimony before legislative committees and his other public statements critical of the Regents' policies. And he has alleged that this public criticism was within the First and Fourteenth Amendments' protection of freedom of speech. Plainly, these allegations present a bona fide constitutional claim. For this Court has held that a teacher's public criticism of his superiors on matters of public concern may be constitutionally protected and may, therefore, be an impermissible basis for termination of his employment.

For this reason we hold that the grant of summary judgment against the respondent, without full exploration of this issue, was improper.

The respondent's lack of formal contractual or tenure security in continued employment at Odessa Junior College, though irrelevant to his free speech claim, is highly relevant to his procedural due process claim. But it may not be entirely dispositive.

We have held today in Board of Regents v. Roth that the Constitution does not require opportunity for a hearing before the nonrenewal of a nontenured teacher's contract, unless he can show that the decision not to rehire him somehow deprived him of an interest in "liberty" or that he had a "property" interest in continued employment, despite the lack of tenure or a formal contract. In Roth the teacher had not made a showing on either point to justify summary judgment in his favor.

Similarly, the respondent here has yet to show that he has been deprived of an interest that could invoke procedural due process protection. As in Roth, the mere showing that he was not rehired in one particular job, without more, did not amount to a showing of a loss of liberty. Nor did it amount to a showing of a loss of property.

But the respondent's allegations — which we must construe most favorably to the respondent at this stage of the litigation — do raise a genuine issue as to his interest in continued employment at Odessa Junior College. He alleged that this interest, though not secured by a formal contractual tenure provision, was secured by a no less binding understanding fostered by the college administration. In particular, the respondent alleged that the college had a de facto tenure program, and that he had tenure under that program. He claimed that he and others legitimately relied upon an unusual provision that had been in the college's official Faculty Guide for many years:

"Teacher Tenure: Odessa College has no tenure system. The Administration of the College wishes the faculty member to feel that he has permanent tenure as long as his teaching services are satisfactory and as long as he displays a cooperative attitude toward his co-workers and his superiors, and as long as he is happy in his work."

Moreover, the respondent claimed legitimate reliance upon guidelines promulgated by the Coordinating Board of the Texas College and University System that provided that a person, like himself, who had been employed as a teacher in the state college and university system for seven years or more has some form of job tenure. Thus the respondent offered to prove that a teacher with his long period of service at this particular State College had no less a "property" interest in continued employment than a formally tenured teacher at other colleges, and had no less a procedural due process right to a statement of reasons and a hearing before college officials upon their decision not to retain him. . . .

A written contract with an explicit tenure provision clearly is evidence of a formal understanding that supports a teacher's claim of entitlement to continued employment unless sufficient "cause" is shown. Yet absence of such an explicit contractual provision may not always foreclose the possibility that a teacher has a "property" interest in reemployment. For example, the law of contracts in most, if not all, jurisdictions long has employed a process by which agreements, though not formalized in writing, may be "implied." Explicit contractual provisions may be supplemented by other agreements implied from "the promisor's words and conduct in the light of the surrounding circumstances." 3 A. Corbin on Contracts §562 (1960). And, "[t]he meaning of [the promisor's] words and acts is found by relating them to the usage of the past." Ibid.

A teacher, like the respondent, who has held his position for a number of years, might be able to show from the circumstances of this service — and from other relevant facts — that he has a legitimate claim of entitlement to job tenure. Just as this Court has found there to be a "common law of a particular industry or of a particular plant" that may supplement a collective-bargaining agreement, so there may be an unwritten "common law" in a particular university that certain employees shall have the equivalent of tenure. This is particularly likely in a college or university, like Odessa Junior College, that has no explicit tenure system even for senior members of its faculty, but that nonetheless may have created such a system in practice.

In this case, the respondent has alleged the existence of rules and understandings, promulgated and fostered by state officials, that may justify his legitimate claim of entitlement to continued employment absent "sufficient cause." We disagree with the Court of Appeals insofar as it held that a mere subjective "expectancy" is protected by procedural due process, but we agree that the respondent must be given an opportunity to prove the legitimacy of his claim of such entitlement in light of "the policies and practices of the institution." Proof of such a property interest would not, of course, entitle him to reinstatement. But such proof would obligate college officials to grant a hearing at his request, where he could be informed of the grounds for his nonretention and challenge their sufficiency.

Therefore, while we do not wholly agree with the opinion of the Court of Appeals, its judgment remanding this case to the District Court is affirmed.

◆ ARNETT v. KENNEDY
416 U.S. 134 (1974)

Mr. Justice REHNQUIST announced the judgment of the Court in an opinion in which THE CHIEF JUSTICE and Mr. Justice STEWART join. Prior to the events leading to his discharge, appellee Wayne Kennedy was a nonprobationary federal employee in the competitive Civil Service. He was a field representative in the Chicago Regional Office of the Office of Economic Opportunity (OEO). In March 1972, he was removed from the federal service pursuant to the provisions of the Lloyd-La Follette Act, 5 U.S.C. §7501, after Wendell Verduin, the Regional Director of the OEO, upheld written administrative charges made in the form of a "Notification of Proposed Adverse Action" against appellee. The charges listed five events occurring in November and December 1971; the most serious of the charges was that appellee "without any proof whatsoever and in reckless disregard of the actual facts" known to him or reasonably discoverable by him had publicly stated that Verduin and his administrative assistant had attempted to bribe a representative of a community action organization with which the OEO had dealings. The alleged bribe consisted of an offer of a $100,000 grant of OEO funds if the representative would sign a statement against appellee and another OEO employee.

Appellee was advised of his right under regulations promulgated by the Civil Service Commission and the OEO to reply to the charges orally and in writing, and to submit affidavits to Verduin. He was also advised that the material on which the notice was based was available for his inspection in the Regional Office, and that a copy of the material was attached to the notice of proposed adverse action.

Appellee did not respond to the substance of the charges against him, but instead asserted that the charges were unlawful because he had a right to a trial-type hearing before an impartial hearing officer before he could be removed from his employment, and because statements made by him were protected by the First Amendment to the United States Constitution. On March 20, 1972, Verduin notified appellee in writing that he would be removed from his position at the close of business on March 27, 1972. Appellee was also notified of his right to appeal Verduin's decision either to the OEO or to the Civil Service Commission.

Appellee then instituted this suit in the United States District Court for the Northern District of Illinois on behalf of himself and others similarly situated, seeking both injunctive and declaratory relief. In his amended complaint, appellee contended that the standards and procedures established by and under the Lloyd-La Follette Act for the removal of nonprobationary employees from the federal service unwarrantedly interfere with those employees' freedom of expression and deny them procedural due process of law. The three-judge District Court, convened pursuant to 28 U.S.C. §§2282 and 2284, granted summary judgment for appellee. The court held that the discharge procedures authorized by the Act and attendant Civil Service Commission and OEO regulations denied appellee due process of law because they failed to provide for a trial-type hearing before an impartial agency official prior to removal; the court also held the Act and implementing regulations unconstitutionally vague because they failed to furnish sufficiently precise guidelines as to what kind of speech may be made the basis of a removal action. . . .

The numerous affidavits submitted to the District Court by both parties not unexpectedly portray two widely differing versions of the facts which gave rise to this lawsuit. Since the District Court granted summary judgment to appellee, it was required to resolve all genuine disputes as to any material facts in favor of appellants, and we therefore take as true for purposes of this opinion the material particulars of appellee's conduct which were set forth in the notification of proposed adverse action dated February 18, 1972. The District Court's holding necessarily embodies the legal conclusions that, even though all of these factual statements were true, the procedure which the Government proposed to follow in this case was constitutionally insufficient to accomplish appellee's discharge, and the standard by which his conduct was to be judged in the course of those procedures infringed his right of free speech protected by the First Amendment.

The statutory provisions which the District Court held invalid are found in 5 U.S.C. §7501. Subsection (a) of that section provides that "[a]n individual in the competitive service may be removed or suspended without pay only for such cause as will promote the efficiency of the service."

Subsection (b) establishes the administrative procedures by which an employee's rights under subsection (a) are to be determined, providing:

> (b) An individual in the competitive service whose removal or suspension without pay is sought is entitled to reasons in writing and to —
> (1) notice of the action sought and of any charges preferred against him;
> (2) a copy of the charges;
> (3) a reasonable time for filing a written answer to the charges, with affidavits; and
> (4) a written decision on the answer at the earliest practicable date.

Examination of witnesses, trial, or hearing is not required but may be provided in the discretion of the individual directing the removal or suspension without pay. Copies of the charges, the notice of hearing, the answer, the reasons for and the order of removal or suspension without pay, and also the reasons for reduction in grade or pay, shall be made a part of the records of the employing agency, and, on request, shall be furnished to the individual affected and to the Civil Service Commission.

This codification of the Lloyd-La Follette Act is now supplemented by the regulations of the Civil Service Commission, and, with respect to the OEO, by the regulations and instructions of that agency. Both the Commission and the OEO have by regulation given further specific content to the general removal standard in subsection (a) of the Act. The regulations of the Commission and the OEO, in nearly identical language, require that employees "avoid any action . . . which might result in, or create the appearance of . . . [a]ffecting adversely the confidence of the public in the integrity of [OEO and] the Government," and that employees not "engage in criminal, infamous, dishonest, immoral, or notoriously disgraceful or other conduct prejudicial to the Government." The OEO further provides by regulation that its Office of General Counsel is available to supply counseling on the interpretation of the laws and regulations relevant to the conduct of OEO employees. . . .

Here appellee did have a statutory expectancy that he not be removed other than for "such cause as will promote the efficiency of [the] service." But the very section of the statute which granted him that right, a right which had previously existed only by virtue of administrative regulation, expressly provided also for the procedure by which "cause" was to be determined, and expressly omitted the procedural guarantees which appellee insists are mandated by the Constitution. Only by bifurcating the very sentence of the Act of Congress which conferred upon appellee the right not to be removed save for cause could it be said that he had an expectancy of that substantive right without the procedural limitations which Congress attached to it. In the area of federal regulation of government employees, where in the absence of statutory limitation the governmental employer has had virtually uncontrolled latitude in decisions as to hiring and firing, we do not believe that a statutory enactment such as the Lloyd-La Follette Act may be parsed as discretely as appellee urges. Congress was obviously intent on according a measure of statutory job security to governmental employees which they had not previously enjoyed, but was likewise intent on excluding more elaborate procedural requirements which it felt would make the operation of the new scheme unnecessarily burdensome in practice. Where the focus of legislation was thus strongly on the procedural mechanism for enforcing the substantive right which was simultaneously conferred, we decline to conclude that the substantive right may be viewed wholly apart from the procedure provided for its enforcement. The employee's statutorily defined right is not a guarantee against removal without cause in the abstract, but such a guarantee as enforced by the procedures which Congress has designated for the determination of cause.

To conclude otherwise would require us to hold that although Congress chose to enact what was essentially a legislative compromise, and with unmistakable clarity granted governmental employees security against being dismissed without "cause," but refused to accord them a full adversary hearing for the determination of "cause," it was constitutionally disabled from making such a choice. We would be holding that federal employees had been granted, as a result of the enactment of the Lloyd-La Follette Act, not merely that which Congress had given them in the first part of a sentence, but that which Congress had expressly withheld from them in the latter part of the same sentence. Neither the language of the Due Process Clause of the Fifth Amendment nor our cases construing it require any such hobbling restrictions on legislative authority in this area. . . .

In sum, we hold that the Lloyd-La Follette Act, in at once conferring upon nonprobationary federal employees the right to be discharged except for "cause" and prescribing the procedural means by which that right was to be protected, did not create an expectancy of job retention in those employees requiring procedural protection under the Due Process Clause beyond that afforded here by the statute and related agency regulations. We also conclude that the post-termination hearing procedures provided by the Civil Service Commission and the OEO adequately protect those federal employees' liberty interest, recognized in *Roth*, *supra*, in not being wrongfully stigmatized by untrue and unsupported administrative charges. Finally, we hold that the standard of employment protection imposed by Congress in the Lloyd-La Follette Act, is not impermissibly vague or overbroad in its regulation of the speech of federal employees and therefore unconstitutional on its face. Accordingly, we reverse the decision of the District Court on both grounds on which it granted summary judgment and remand for further proceedings not inconsistent with this opinion.

Reversed and remanded.

Mr. Justice POWELL, with whom Mr. Justice BLACKMUN joins, concurring in part and concurring in the result in part. The applicability of the constitutional guarantee of procedural due process depends in the first instance on the presence of a legitimate "property" or "liberty" interest within the meaning of the Fifth or Fourteenth Amendment. Governmental deprivation of such an interest must be accompanied by minimum procedural safeguards, including some form of notice and a hearing. . . .

The plurality opinion evidently reasons that the nature of appellee's interest in continued federal employment is necessarily defined and limited by the statutory procedures for discharge and that the constitutional guarantee of procedural due process accords to appellee no procedural protections against arbitrary or erroneous discharge other than those expressly provided in the statute. The plurality would thus conclude that the statute governing federal employment determines not only the nature of appellee's property interest, but also the extent of the procedural protections to which he may lay claim. It seems to me that this approach is incompatible with the principles laid down in *Roth* and *Sindermann*. Indeed, it would lead directly to the conclusion that whatever the nature of an individual's statutorily created property interest, deprivation of that interest could be accomplished without notice of a hearing at any time. This view misconceives the origin of the right to procedural due process. That right is conferred, not by legislative grace, but by constitutional guarantee. While the legislature may elect not to confer a property interest in federal employment, it may not constitutionally authorize the deprivation of such an interest, once conferred, without appropriate procedural safeguards. As our cases have consistently recognized, the adequacy of statutory procedures for deprivation of a statutorily created property interest must be analyzed in constitutional terms.

Having determined that the constitutional guarantee of procedural due process applies to appellee's discharge from public employment, the question arises whether an evidentiary hearing, including the right to present favorable witnesses and to confront and examine adverse witnesses, must be accorded *before* removal. The resolution of this issue depends on a balancing process in which the Government's interest in expeditious removal of an unsatisfactory employee is weighed against the interest of the affected employee in continued public employment. . . .

On balance, I would conclude that a prior evidentiary hearing is not required and that the present statute and regulations comport with due process by providing a reasonable accommodation of the competing interests.

Mr. Justice WHITE, concurring in part and dissenting in part. . . . I differ basically with the plurality's view that "where the grant of a substantive right is inextricably intertwined with the limitations on the procedures which are to be employed in determining that right, a litigant in the position of appellee must take the bitter with the sweet," and that "the property interest which appellee had in his employment was itself conditioned by the procedural limitations which had accompanied the grant of that interest." *Ante*, at 153-154, 155. The rationale of this position quickly leads to the conclusion that even though the statute requires cause for discharge, the requisites of due process could equally have been satisfied had the law dispensed with any hearing at all, whether pretermination or post-termination.

The past cases of this Court uniformly indicate that some kind of hearing is required at some time before a person is finally deprived of his property interests. . . .

Since there is a need for some kind of hearing before a person is finally deprived of his property, the argument in the instant case, and that adopted in the plurality opinion, is that there is something different about a final taking from an individual of property rights which have their origin in the public rather than the private sector of the economy, and, as applied here, that there is no need for any hearing at any time when the Government discharges a person from his job, even though good cause for the discharge is required.

In cases involving employment by the Government, the earliest cases of this Court have distinguished between two situations, where the entitlement to the job is conditioned "at the pleasure" of the employer and where the job is to be held subject to certain requirements being met by the employee, as when discharge must be for "cause." . . .

. . . The Court has thus made clear that Congress may limit the total discretion of the Executive in firing an employee, by providing that terminations be for cause, and only for cause, and, if it does so, notice and a hearing are "essential."

Where Executive discretion is not limited, there is no need for a hearing. In the latter event, where the statute has provided that employment as a clerk was conditioned on " 'maintain[ing] the respect due to courts of justice and judicial officers,' " or was subject to no conditions at all, no hearing is required. . . .

Where the Congress has confined Executive discretion, notice and hearing have been required. . . .

To be sure, to determine the existence of the property interest, as for example, whether a teacher is tenured or not, one looks to the controlling law, in this case federal statutory law, the Lloyd-La Follette Act, which provides that a person can only be fired for cause. The fact that the origins of the property right are with the State makes no difference for the nature of the procedures required. While the State may define what is and what is not property, once having defined those rights the Constitution defines due process, and as I understand it six members of the Court are in agreement on this fundamental proposition.

I conclude, therefore, that as a matter of due process, a hearing must be held at some time before a competitive civil service employee may be finally terminated for misconduct. Here, the Constitution and the Lloyd-La Follette Act converge, because a full trial-type hearing is provided by statute before termination from the service becomes final, by way of appeal either through OEO, the Civil Service Commission, or both.

A different case might be put, of course, if the termination were for reasons of pure inefficiency, assuming such a general reason could be given, in which case it would be at least arguable that a hearing would serve no useful purpose and that judgments of this kind are best left to the discretion of administrative officials. This is not such a case, however, since Kennedy was terminated on specific charges of misconduct.

The second question which must be addressed is whether a hearing of some sort must be held *before* any "taking" of the employee's property interest in his job occurs, even if a full hearing is available before that taking becomes final. I must resolve this question because in my view a full hearing must be afforded at some juncture and the claim is that it must occur prior to termination. If the right to any hearing itself is a pure matter of property definition, as the plurality opinion suggests, then that question need not be faced, for any kind of hearing, or no hearing at all, would suffice. As I have suggested, the State may not dispense with the minimum procedures defined by due process, but different considerations come into play when deciding whether a pretermination hearing is required and, if it is, what kind of hearing must be had. . . .

Perhaps partly on the basis of some of these constitutional considerations, Congress has provided for pretermination hearings. Certainly the debate on the Lloyd-La Follette Act indicates that constitutional considerations were present in the minds of Congressmen speaking in favor of the legislation. In any event, I conclude that the statute and regulations, to the extent they require 30 days' advance notice and a right to make a written presentation, satisfy minimum constitutional requirements.

Appellee in this case not only asserts that he is entitled to a hearing at some time before his property interest is finally terminated, and to a pretermination hearing of some kind before his wages are provisionally cut off, which are currently provided to him, but also argues that he must be furnished certain procedures at this preliminary hearing not provided by Congress: an impartial hearing examiner, an opportunity to present witnesses, and the right to engage in cross-examination. In other words, his claim is not only to a pretermination hearing, but one in which full trial-type procedures are available.

The facts in this case show that the Regional Director, Verduin, who charged appellee Kennedy with making slanderous statements about him as to an alleged bribe offer, also ruled in the preliminary hearing that Kennedy should be terminated. . . .

Congress is silent on the matter [of an impartial hearing examiner]. We [should] assume, because of the constitutional problem in not so providing, that, if faced with the question . . . Congress would have so provided. . . .

Mr. Justice MARSHALL, with whom Mr. Justice DOUGLAS and Mr. Justice BRENNAN concur, dissenting. I would affirm the judgment of the District Court, both in its holding that a tenured Government employee must be afforded an evidentiary hearing prior to a dismissal for cause and in its decision that 5 U.S.C. §7501 is unconstitutionally vague and overbroad as a regulation of employees' speech. . . .

Courts once considered procedural due process protections inapplicable to welfare on much the same theory — that "in accepting charity, the appellant has consented to the provisions of the law under which charity is bestowed." Obviously, this Court rejected that reasoning in *Goldberg*, where we held that conditions under which public assistance was afforded, which did not include a pretermination hearing, were violative of due process. In *Sindermann*, the Court held that the Constitution required a hearing before dismissal even where the implicit grant of tenure did not encompass the right to such a hearing. . . .

Applying that analysis here requires us to find that although appellee's property interest arose from statute, the deprivation of his claim of entitlement to continued employment would have to meet minimum standards of procedural due process regardless of the discharge procedures provided by the statute. Accordingly, a majority of the Court rejects Mr. Justice Rehnquist's argument that because appellee's entitlement arose from statute, it could be conditioned on a statutory limitation of procedural due process protections, an approach which would render such protection inapplicable to the deprivation of any statutory benefit — any "privilege" extended by Government — where a statute prescribed a termination procedure, no matter how arbitrary or unfair. It would amount to nothing less than a return, albeit in somewhat different verbal garb, to the thoroughly discredited distinction between rights and privileges which once seemed to govern the applicability of procedural due process. . . .

The decisions of this Court compel the conclusion that a worker with a claim of entitlement to public employment absent specified cause has a property interest protected by the Due Process Clause and therefore the right to an evidentiary hearing before an impartial decision-maker prior to dismissal. Accordingly, I would affirm the decision of the court below that appellee had been discharged in violation of his procedural due process rights.

♦ BISHOP v. WOOD
426 U.S. 341 (1976)

Mr. Justice STEVENS delivered the opinion of the Court. . . . Petitioner was employed by the city of Marion as a probationary policeman on June 9, 1969. After six months he became a permanent employee. He was dismissed on March 31, 1972. He claims that he had either an express or an implied right to continued employment.

A city ordinance provides that a permanent employee may be discharged if he fails to perform work up to the standard of his classification, or if he is negligent, inefficient or unfit to perform his duties. Petitioner first contends that even though the ordinance does not expressly so provide, it should be read to prohibit discharge for any other reason, and therefore to confer tenure on all permanent employees. In addition, he contends that his period of service, together with his "permanent" classification, gave him a sufficient expectancy of continued employment to constitute a protected property interest.

A property interest in employment can, of course, be created by ordinance, or by an implied contract. In either case, however, the sufficiency of the claim of entitlement must be decided by reference to state law. The North Carolina Supreme Court has held that an enforceable expectation of continued public employment in that State can exist only if the employer, by statute or contract, has actually granted some form of guarantee. Whether such a guarantee has been given can be determined only by an examination of the particular statute or ordinance in question.

On its face the ordinance on which petitioner relies may fairly be read as conferring such a guarantee. However, such a reading is not the only possible interpretation; the ordinance may also be construed as granting no right to continued employment but merely conditioning an employees's removal on compliance with certain specified procedures.[8] We do not have any authoritative interpretation of this ordinance by a North Carolina state court. We do, however, have the opinion of the United States District Judge who, of course, sits in North Carolina and practiced law there for many years. Based on his understanding of state law, he concluded that petitioner "held his position at the will and pleasure of the city." This construction of North Carolina laws was upheld by the Court of Appeals for the Fourth Circuit, albeit by an equally divided Court. In comparable circumstances, this Court has accepted the interpretation of state law in which the District Court and the Court of Appeals have concurred even if an examination of the state law issue without such guidance might have justified a different conclusion.

In this case, as the District Court construed the ordinance, the City Manager's determination of the adequacy of the grounds for discharge is not subject to judicial review; the employee is merely given certain procedural rights which the District Court found not to have been violated in this case. The District Court's reading of the ordinance is tenable; it derives some support from a decision of the North Carolina Supreme Court, and it was accepted by the Court of Appeals for the Fourth Circuit. These reasons are sufficient to foreclose our independent examination of the state law issue.

Under that view of the law, petitioner's discharge did not deprive him of a property interest protected by the Fourteenth Amendment. . . .

Petitioner argues, however, that the reasons given for his discharge

8. This is not the construction which six Members of this Court placed on the federal regulations involved in Arnett v. Kennedy, 416 U.S. 134. In that case the Court concluded that because the employee could only be discharged for cause, he had a property interest which was entitled to constitutional protection. In this case, a holding that as a matter of state law the employee "held his position at the will and pleasure of the city" necessarily establishes that he had *no* property interest. The Court's evaluation of the federal regulations involved in *Arnett* sheds no light on the problem presented by this case.

were false. Even so, the reasons stated to him in private had no different impact on his reputation than if they had been true. And the answers to his interrogatories, whether true or false, did not cause the discharge. The truth or falsity of the City Manager's statement determines whether or not his decision to discharge the petitioner was correct or prudent, but neither enhances nor diminishes petitioner's claim that his constitutionally protected interest in liberty has been impaired. A contrary evaluation of his contention would enable every discharged employee to assert a constitutional claim merely by alleging that his former supervisor made a mistake.

The federal court is not the appropriate forum in which to review the multitude of personnel decisions that are made daily by public agencies.[14] We must accept the harsh fact that numerous individual mistakes are inevitable in the day-to-day administration of our affairs. The United States Constitution cannot feasibly be construed to require federal judicial review for every such error. In the absence of any claim that the public employer was motivated by a desire to curtail or to penalize the exercise of an employee's constitutionally protected rights, we must presume that official action was regular and, if erroneous, can best be corrected in other ways. The Due Process Clause of the Fourteenth Amendment is not a guarantee against incorrect or ill-advised personnel decisions.

The judgment is affirmed.

Mr. Justice BRENNAN, with whom Mr. Justice MARSHALL concurs, dissenting. . . . [T]he federal courts *are* the appropriate forum for ensuring that the constitutional mandates of due process are followed by those agencies of government making personnel decisions that pervasively influence the lives of those affected thereby; the fundamental premise of the Due Process Clause is that those procedural safeguards will help the government avoid the "harsh fact" of "incorrect or ill-advised personnel decisions." Petitioner seeks no more than that, and I believe that his "property" interest in continued employment and his "liberty" interest in his good name and reputation dictate that he be accorded procedural safeguards before those interests are deprived by arbitrary or capricious government action.

---

14. The cumulative impression created by the three dissenting opinions is that this holding represents a significant retreat from settled practice in the federal courts. The fact of the matter, however, is that the instances in which the federal judiciary has required a state agency to reinstate a discharged employee for failure to provide a pretermination hearing are extremely rare. The reason is clear. For unless we were to adopt Mr. Justice Brennan's remarkably innovative suggestion that we develop a federal common law of property rights, or his equally far reaching view that almost every discharge implicates a constitutionally protected liberty interest, the ultimate control of state personnel relationships is, and will remain, with the States; they may grant or withhold tenure at their unfettered discretion. In this case, whether we accept or reject the construction of the ordinance adopted by the two lower courts, the power to change or clarify that ordinance will remain in the hands of the City Council of the city of Marion.

Mr. Justice WHITE, with whom Mr. Justice BRENNAN, Mr. Justice MARSHALL, and Mr. Justice BLACKMUN join, dissenting. I dissent because the decision of the majority rests upon a proposition which was squarely addressed and in my view correctly rejected by six Members of this Court in Arnett v. Kennedy, 416 U.S. 134.

Petitioner Bishop was a permanent employee of the Police Department of the City of Marion, N.C. The city ordinance applicable to him provides:

> *Dismissal.* A permanent employee whose work is not satisfactory over a period of time shall be notified in what way his work is deficient and what he must do if his work is to be satisfactory. *If* a permanent employee fails to perform work up to the standard of the classification held, or continues to be negligent, inefficient, or unfit to perform his duties, he may be dismissed by the City Manager. Any discharged employee shall be given written notice of his discharge setting forth the effective date and reasons for his discharge if he shall request such a notice. [Emphasis added.]

The second sentence of this ordinance plainly conditions petitioner's dismissal on cause — i.e., failure to perform up to standard, negligence, inefficiency, or unfitness to perform the job. The District Court below did not otherwise construe this portion of the ordinance. In the only part of its opinion rejecting petitioner's claim that the ordinance gave him a property interest in his job, the District Court said, in an opinion predating this Court's decision in Arnett v. Kennedy, *supra*:

> It is clear from Article II, Section 6, of the City's Personnel Ordinance, that the dismissal of an employee does not require a notice or hearing. Upon request of the discharged employee, he shall be given written notice of his discharge setting forth the effective date and the reasons for the discharge. It thus appears that both the city ordinance and the state law have been complied with.

Thus in concluding that petitioner had no "property interest" in his job entitling him to a hearing on discharge and that he held his position "at the will and pleasure of the city," the District Court relied on the fact that the ordinance described its own *procedures* for determining cause which procedures did not include a hearing. The majority purports to read the District Court's opinion as construing the ordinance *not* to condition dismissal on cause, and, if this is what the majority means, its reading of the District Court's opinion is clearly erroneous for the reasons just stated. However, later in its opinion the majority appears to eschew this construction of the District Court's opinion and of the ordinance. In the concluding paragraph of its discussion of petitioner's property interest, the majority holds that since neither the ordinance nor state law provides for a hearing, or any kind of review of the City Manager's dismissal decision, petitioner had no enforceable property interest in his job. The majority concludes:

In this case, as the District Court construed the ordinance, the City Manager's *determination of the adequacy of the grounds for discharge* is not subject to judicial review; the employee is merely given certain procedural rights which the District Court found not to have been violated in the case. The District Court's reading of the ordinance is tenable. . . . [Emphasis added.]

The majority thus implicitly concedes that the ordinance supplies the "grounds" for discharge and that the City Manager must determine them to be "adequate" before he may fire an employee. The majority's holding that petitioner had no property interest in his job in spite of the unequivocal language in the city ordinance that he may be dismissed only for certain kinds of cause rests, then, on the fact that state law provides no *procedures* for assuring that the City Manager dismiss him only for cause. The right to his job apparently given by the first two sentences of the ordinance is thus redefined, according to the majority, by the procedures provided for in the third sentence and as redefined is infringed only if the procedures are not followed.

This is precisely the reasoning which was embraced by only three and expressly rejected by six Members of the Court in Arnett v. Kennedy. . . .

The views now expressed by the majority are thus squarely contrary to the views expressed by a majority of the Justices in *Arnett*. As Mr. Justice Powell suggested in *Arnett*, they are also "incompatible with the principles laid down in *Roth* and *Sindermann*." I would not so soon depart from these cases nor from the views expressed by a majority in *Arnett*. The ordinance plainly grants petitioner a right to his job unless there is cause to fire him. Having granted him such a right it is the Federal Constitution, not state law, which determines the process to be applied in connection with any state decision to deprive him of it.

The state of the law thus appears to be that courts must first decide whether an individual has a property or a liberty interest; and if so, what procedures are constitutionally sufficient for asserting or defending that interest. Four important Supreme Court decisions show the sorts of conclusions that have resulted from these inquiries:

a. In Goss v. Lopez, 419 U.S. 565 (1975), nine students who were suspended from public high schools in Columbus, Ohio, during a period of widespread student unrest in 1971 alleged violations of due process. The Court found that on the basis of Ohio law, the students had "legitimate claims of entitlement to public education," a property interest protected by the Due Process Clause. While the severity of the deprivation is a factor that should be taken into consideration in determining the type of hearing that is constitutionally compelled,

> as long as a property deprivation is not *de minimis*, its gravity is irrelevant to the question of whether account must be taken of the Due Process Clause. . . . At the very minimum, therefore, students facing suspension and the consequent interference with a protected property interest must be given *some* kind of notice and afforded *some* kind of hearing.

In the Columbus circumstances, the hearing should at least have included "explanation of the evidence the authorities have and an opportunity to present [the student's] side of the story."

Dissenting, Justice Powell argued that the students' right to education was defined in the same statute that outlined their rights in the suspension procedure, and that the rights extended no further. Justice Powell also queried whether the Court could declare a right to a hearing before suspension and not be logically compelled to extend such rights before a student receives a failing grade, is placed in a lower "track," or is subjected to some other administrative ruling having comparable "serious consequences."

b. Charlotte Horowitz had been put on probation and later had been dismissed from the University of Missouri Medical School. Her grades were high, but her clinical performance and personal hygiene were condemned by faculty members. Ms. Horowitz said the faculty did not like her sex, her religion, her outspokenness, and her politics. The Supreme Court assumed that there was "a liberty interest in pursuing a medical career, but said the school's internal procedures had afforded "at least as much due process as the Fourteenth Amendment requires." *Goss* was distinguished as having been a disciplinary proceeding; this was an academic evaluation, "by its nature more subjective and evaluative than the typical factual questions presented in the average disciplinary decision." Although there were concurring opinions, the Court was unanimous that the procedures to which Ms. Horowitz was subjected were constitutionally adequate. Board of Curators v. Horowitz, 435 U.S. 78 (1978).

c. In Paul v. Davis, 424 U.S. 693 (1976), two Kentucky police chiefs distributed to local businesses a flyer containing names and photos, each page headed: "NOVEMBER 1972 — CITY OF LOUISVILLE — JEFFERSON COUNTY — POLICE DEPARTMENTS — ACTIVE SHOPLIFTERS." Plaintiff had been arrested for shoplifting but never tried, and his name and photo were in the flyer. The Supreme Court, by a 5 to 3 vote, found no denial of due process:

> [I]nterests attain . . . constitutional status [as liberty or property] by virtue of the fact that they have been initially recognized and protected by state law. . . . Kentucky law does not extend to respondent any legal guarantee of present enjoyment of reputation which has been altered as a result of petitioners' actions. Rather his interest in reputation is simply one of a number which the State may protect against injury by virtue of its tort law, providing a forum for vindication of those interests by means of damages actions. And any harm or injury to that interest, even where as here inflicted by an officer of the State, does not result in a deprivation of any "liberty" or "property" recognized by state or federal law, nor has it worked any change of respondent's status as theretofore recognized under the State's laws.

Justice Brennan's dissent argued that "the court by mere fiat and with no analysis wholly excludes personal interest in reputation from the ambit of 'life, liberty, or property' under the Fifth and Fourteenth Amendments, thus rendering due process concerns *never* applicable to the official stigmatization, however arbitrary, of an individual." The dissent also criticized the majority's suggestion that "liberty" or "property" interests are protected only if they are recognized under state law or protected by one of the specific guarantees of the Bill of Rights. Justice Brennan contended instead that property interests

> are created and their dimensions are defined by existing rules or understandings that stem from an independent source such as state law — rules or understandings that secure certain benefits and that support claims of entitlement to those benefits. However, it should also be clear that if the Federal Government, for example, creates an entitlement to some benefit, the States cannot infringe a person's enjoyment of that "property" interest without compliance with the dictates of due process.

d. In Meachum v. Fano, 427 U.S. 215 (1976), the Massachusetts prison classification board had determined that certain inmates should be transferred from a medium-security to a maximum-security prison, where the living conditions were substantially less favorable. The prison's decision had been based on reports from informants of alleged criminal misconduct, conveyed to the board by the prison superintendent while the inmates were not in the hearing room, after which the inmates were told that evidence supported the allegations against them and were allowed to present exculpatory evidence. By a 6 to 3 vote, the Supreme Court refused to consider the adequacy of the transfer-determination procedure, because the transfer did not infringe or implicate "a 'liberty' interest of respondents within the meaning of the Due Process Clause." The Court denied that "any grievous loss visited upon a person by the State is sufficient to invoke the procedural protections of the Due Process Clause." Massachusetts law did not give a prisoner the right to remain in the prison to which he or she was originally assigned, absent proof of misconduct. Therefore, a valid conviction "has sufficiently extinguished the defendant's liberty interest to empower the State to confine him in any of its prisons."

In dissent, Justice Stevens rejected the idea that liberty interests must have their roots in state law or the Constitution: "I had thought it self-evident that all men were endowed by their Creator with liberty as one of the cardinal unalienable rights. It is that basic freedom which the Due Process Clause protects, rather than the particular rights or privileges conferred by specific laws or regulations." Justice Stevens also warned: "[I]f the inmate's protected liberty interests are no greater than the State chooses to allow, he is really little more than the slave described in the 19th century cases."

Constitutional protection for property — an insistence on process before deprivation, but also a requirement of compensation — requires a definitional fabric for identifying those hopes and claims that achieve the special status. The confused saga that has so far run from *Roth* to *Bishop* is, in one sense, no more than a replay of *Almota* versus *Fuller*, and of Wheaton v. Peters versus *International News Service* (Chapter 22): the question of whether constitutional property rights attach to a minimal, stated, legislative, or contractual fee, or rather apply (in Locke's sense) to an assemblage of legitimate expectations broadly derived from social practice and cultural context. With Bishop v. Wood, the Supreme Court is taking the Wheaton v. Peters view that one should not expect to achieve through the court, solely because it is fair and reasonable, more protection than has been specifically conferred by contract or statute.

But the *Roth* progeny also stand as something else: tentative judicial attempts at disciplining the welfare state, taking the form of an insistence — as a national constitutional matter, enforced by the federal courts — on the state's duty to assure efficiency and fairness by granting adequate process when it distributes benefits and burdens, in a society where such statemade statuses are central to place, opportunity, and security. In Perry v. Sindermann and in *Arnett*, a Supreme Court majority totally uninterested in recognizing a minimal standard of living or a right to a job as property rights was nevertheless ready to attach to a publicly created fee more procedural protection than the legislature had promised. By Bishop v. Wood, the tasks of choosing which statuses to protect and of deciding how much process each requires have seemed both overwhelming and intrusive. But if, as must be true, estates in employment, food, shelter, health, and income security are to remain a major determinant of status and well-being, as well as a major subject of social conflict, then the constitutional question of when the courts should give them protection beyond what their claimants can obtain by political struggle will remain important and difficult.

Notes

1. Potter v. School Directors, 17 Ill. App. 3d 781, 309 N.E.2d 58 (1974):

> Residents of a school district have no protectible interest invested in the integrity of the boundary lines separating district attendance centers; nor do they have any proprietary interest in the administrative determination concerning the location of attendance centers within a school district. [T]he plaintiffs have no discernible property right. . . ."

Why not?

2. Second- and third-year medical students at Northwestern University challenged a $2,505 tuition increase, saying "course of conduct" had led them to expect smaller increases.

Held: The students had no contractually binding expectations. Eisele v. Ayers, 63 Ill. App. 3d 1039, 381 N.E.2d 21 (1978).

3. The president of the State University of New York at Binghamton had banned from campus and declared *persona non grata* a person who had been an on-again-off-again student for ten years. When university police found the occasional student at the Campus Pub in the student union, they arrested him. The court of appeals reversed a conviction of the student, finding that the state had not met its burden of showing that the university president had acted lawfully and with a legitimate purpose in writing a letter that identified the student as a *persona non grata*. People v. Leonard, 62 N.Y.2d 404, 465 N.E.2d 831, 477 N.Y.S.2d 111 (1984).

4. *Whose Property?*

◆ O'BANNON v. TOWN COURT NURSING CENTER
447 U.S. 773 (1980)

Mr. Justice STEVENS delivered the opinion of the Court. The question presented is whether approximately 180 elderly residents of a nursing home operated by Town Court Nursing Center, Inc. have a constitutional right to a hearing before a state or federal agency may revoke the home's authority to provide them with nursing care at government expense. Although we recognize that such a revocation may be harmful to some patients, we hold that they have no constitutional right to participate in the revocation proceedings.

Town Court Nursing Center, Inc. (Town Court) operates a 198-bed nursing home in Philadelphia, Pa. In April 1976 it was certified by the Department of Health, Education, and Welfare (HEW) as a "skilled nursing facility," thereby becoming eligible to receive payments from HEW and from the Pennsylvania Department of Public Welfare (DPW), for providing nursing care services to aged, disabled, and poor persons in need of medical care. After receiving its certification, Town Court entered into formal "provider agreements" with both HEW and DPW. In those agreements HEW and DPW agreed to reimburse Town Court for a period of one year for care provided to persons eligible for Medicare or Medicaid benefits under the Social Security Act, on the condition that Town Court continue to qualify as a skilled nursing facility.

On May 17, 1977, HEW notified Town Court that it no longer met the statutory and regulatory standards for skilled nursing facilities and that, consequently, its Medicare provider agreement would not be renewed. The HEW notice stated that no payments would be made for services rendered after July 17, 1977, explained how Town Court might request reconsideration of the decertification decision, and directed it to notify Medicare beneficiaries that payments were being discontinued. Three days later DPW notified Town Court that its Medicaid provider agreement would also not be renewed.

Town Court requested HEW to reconsider its termination decision. While the request was pending, Town Court and six of its Medicaid patients filed a complaint in the United States District Court for the Eastern District of Pennsylvania alleging that both the nursing home and the patients were entitled to an evidentiary hearing on the merits of the decertification decision before the Medicaid payments were discontinued. The complaint alleged that termination of the payments would require Town Court to close and would cause the individual plaintiffs to suffer both a loss of benefits and "immediate and irreparable psychological and physical harm." . . .

[The patients] contend that the Medicaid provisions relied upon by the Court of Appeals give them a property right to remain in the home of their choice absent good cause for transfer and therefore entitle them to a hearing on whether such cause exists. Second, they argue that a transfer may have such severe physical or emotional side-effects that it is tantamount to a deprivation of life or liberty, which must be preceded by a due process hearing. We find both arguments unpersuasive.

Whether viewed singly or in combination, the Medicaid provisions relied upon by the Court of Appeals do not confer a right to continued residence in the home of one's choice. 42 U.S.C. §1396a(a)(23) gives recipients the right to choose among a range of *qualified* providers, without government interference. By implication, it also confers an absolute right to be free from government interference with the choice to remain in a home that continues to be qualified. But it clearly does not confer a right on a recipient to enter an unqualified home and demand a hearing to certify it, nor does it confer a right on a recipient to continue to receive benefits for care in a home that has been decertified. Second, although the regulations do protect patients by limiting the circumstances under which a *home* may transfer or discharge a Medicaid recipient, they do not purport to limit the Government's right to make a transfer necessary by decertifying a facility. Finally, since decertification does not reduce or terminate a patient's financial assistance, but merely requires him to use it for care at a different facility, regulations granting recipients the right to a hearing prior to a reduction in financial benefits are irrelevant.

In holding that these provisions create a substantive right to remain in the home of one's choice absent specific cause for transfer, the Court of Appeals failed to give proper weight to the contours of the right conferred by the statutes and regulations. As indicated above, while a patient has a right to continued benefits to pay for care in the qualified institution of his choice, he has no enforceable expectation of continued benefits to pay for care in an institution that has been determined to be unqualified.

The Court of Appeals also erred in treating the Government's decision to decertify Town Court as if it were equivalent in every respect to a decision to transfer an individual patient. Although decertification will inevitably necessitate the transfer of all those patients who remain dependent on Medicaid benefits, it is not the same for purposes of due process analysis as a decision to transfer a particular patient or to deny him financial benefits, based on his individual needs or financial situation.

In the Medicare and the Medicaid programs the Government has provided needy patients with both direct benefits and indirect benefits. The direct benefits are essentially financial in character; the Government pays for certain medical services and provides procedures to determine whether and how much money should be paid for patient care. The net effect of these direct benefits is to give the patients an opportunity to obtain medical services from providers of their choice that is comparable, if not exactly equal, to the opportunity available to persons who are financially independent. The Government cannot withdraw these direct benefits without giving the patients notice and an opportunity for a hearing on the issue of their eligibility for benefits.

This case does not involve the withdrawal of direct benefits. Rather, it involves the Government's attempt to confer an indirect benefit on Medicaid patients by imposing and enforcing minimum standards of care on facilities like Town Court. When enforcement of those standards requires decertification of a facility, there may be an immediate, adverse impact on some residents. But surely that impact, which is an indirect and incidental result of the Government's enforcement action, does not amount to a deprivation of any interest in life, liberty or property.

Medicaid patients who are forced to move because their nursing home has been decertified are in no different position for purposes of due process analysis than financially independent residents of a nursing home who are forced to move because the home's state license has been revoked. Both groups of patients are indirect beneficiaries of government programs designed to guarantee a minimum standard of care for patients as a class. Both may be injured by the closing of a home due to revocation of its state license or its decertification as a Medicaid provider. Thus, whether they are private patients or Medicaid patients, some may have difficulty locating other homes they consider suitable or may suffer both emotional and physical harm as a result of the disruption associated with their move. Yet none of these patients would lose the ability to finance his or her continued care in a properly licensed or certified institution. And, while they might have a claim against the nursing home for damages, none would have any claim against the responsible governmental authorities for the deprivation of an interest in life, liberty or property. Their position under these circumstances would be comparable to that of members of a family who have been dependent on an errant father; they may suffer serious trauma if he is deprived of his liberty or property as a consequence of criminal proceedings, but surely they have no constitutional right to participate in his trial or sentencing procedures. . . .

Whatever legal rights these patients may have against Town Court for failing to maintain its status as a qualified skilled nursing home — and we express no opinion on that subject — we hold that the enforcement by HEW and DPW of their valid regulations did not directly affect their legal rights or deprive them of any constitutionally protected interest in life, liberty or property.

Mr. Justice BLACKMUN, concurring in the judgment. . . .

In my view, there exists a more principled and sensible analysis of the patients' "property" claim. Given §1396(a)(23), I am forced to concede that the patients have some form of property interest in continued residence at Town Court. And past decisions compel me to observe that where, as here, a substantial restriction inhibits governmental removal of a presently enjoyed benefit, a property interest normally will be recognized. To state a general rule, however, is not to decide a specific case. The Court never has held that *any* substantive restriction upon removal of *any* governmental benefit gives rise to a generalized property interest in its continued enjoyment. Indeed, a majority of the Justices of this Court are already on record as concluding that the term "property" sometimes incorporates limiting characterizations of statutorily bestowed interests. Common sense and sound policy support this recognition of some measure of flexibility in defining "new property" expectancies. Public benefits are not held in fee simple. And even if we analogize the patients' claim to "continued residence" to holdings more familiar to the law of private property — even to interests in homes, such as life tenancies — we would find that those interests are regularly subject to easements, conditions subsequent, possibilities of reverter, and other similar limitations. In short, it does not suffice to say that a litigant holds property. The inquiry also must focus on the dimensions of that interest.

The determinative question is whether the litigant holds such a legitimate "claim of entitlement" that the Constitution, rather than the political branches, must define the procedures attending its removal. Claims of entitlement spring from expectations that are "justifiable," "protectable," "sufficient," or "proper." In contrast, the Constitution does not recognize expectancies that are "unilateral," or "too ephemeral and insubstantial."

To mouth these labels does not advance analysis far. We must look further to determine which set of labels applies to particular constellations of fact. . . .

In applying this analysis to this case, four distinct considerations convince me that — even though the statutes place a significant substantive restriction on transferring patients — their expectancy in remaining in their home is conditioned upon its status as a qualified provider.

(1) The lengthy process of deciding the disqualification question has intimately involved Town Court. The home has been afforded substantial procedural protections, and, throughout the process, has shared with the patients who wish to stay there an intense interest in keeping the facility certified. These facts are functionally important. Procedural due process seeks to ensure the accurate determination of decisional facts, and informed unbiased exercises of official discretion. To the extent procedural safeguards achieve these ends, they reduce the likelihood that persons will forfeit important interests without sufficient justification. In this case, since the home had the opportunity and incentive to make the very arguments the patients might make, their due process interest in accurate and informed decisionmaking already, in large measure, was satisfied. . . .

(2) Town Court is more than a *de facto* representative of the patients' interests; it is the underlying source of the benefit they seek to retain. Again, this fact is important, for the property of a recipient of public benefits must be limited, as a general rule, by the governmental power to remove, through prescribed procedures, the underlying source of those benefits. . . .

(3) That the asserted deprivation of property extends in a nondiscriminatory fashion to some 180 patients also figures in my calculus. . . .

(4) Finally I find it important that the patients' interest has been jeopardized not at all because of alleged shortcomings on their part. Frequently, significant interests are subjected to adverse action upon a contested finding of fault, impropriety, or incompetence. In these con-

texts the Court has seldom hesitated to require that a hearing be afforded the "accused." . . .

Citing articles and empirical studies, the patients argue that the trauma of transfer so substantially exacerbates mortality rates, disease, and psychological decline that decertification deprives them of life and liberty. Although the Court assumes that "transfer trauma" exists, it goes on to reject this argument. By focusing solely on the "indirectness" of resulting physical and psychological trauma, the Court implies that regardless of the degree of the demonstrated risk that widespread illness or even death attends decertification-induced transfers, it is of no moment. I cannot join such a heartless holding. . . .

The fact of the matter, however, is that the patients cannot establish that transfer trauma is so substantial a danger as to justify the conclusion that transfers deprive them of life or liberty. Substantial evidence suggests that "transfer trauma" does not exist, and many informed researchers have concluded at least that this danger is unproved. Recognition of a constitutional right plainly cannot rest on such an inconclusive body of research and opinion. It is for this reason, and not for that stated by the Court, that I would reject the patient's claim of a deprivation of life and liberty.

Few statements are more familiar to judges than Holmes' pithy observation that "hard cases make bad law." I fear that the Court's approach to this case may manifest the perhaps equally valid proposition that easy cases make bad law. Sometimes, I suspect the intuitively sensed obviousness of a case induces a rush to judgment, in which a convenient rationale is too readily embraced without full consideration of its internal coherence or future ramifications. With respect, I express my concern that that path has been followed here.

I concur in the judgment.

Mr. Justice BRENNAN, dissenting. Respondents chose a home which was, at the time, qualified. They moved into the home reasonably expecting that they would not be forced to move unless, for some sufficient reason, the home became unsuitable for them. The Government's disqualification of the home is, of course, one such reason. Respondents have no right to receive benefits if they choose to live in an unqualified home. That does not mean, however, that they have no right to be heard on the question whether the home is qualified — the answer to which will determine whether they must move to another home and suffer the allegedly great ills encompassed by the term "transfer trauma." The Government's action in withdrawing the home's certification deprives them of the expectation of continued residency created by the statutes and regulations. Under our precedents, they are certainly "entitled . . . to the benefits of appropriate procedures" in connection with the decertification.

C. PROPERTY AS CONTRACT

♦ OPINION OF THE JUSTICES
364 Mass. 847, 303 N.E.2d 320 (1973)

On October 30, 1973, the Justices submitted the following answers to questions propounded to them by the House of Representatives.

To the Honorable the House of Representatives of the Commonwealth of Massachusetts:

The Justices of the Supreme Judicial Court submit the following reply to the questions set forth in the order adopted by the House of Representatives on September 11, 1973, and transmitted on September 14, 1973.

1. *Summary of the order.* The present order relates to a bill, House No. 7409, as reported by the Committee on Ways and Means, and certain proposed amendments thereto, pending in the General Court. The subject matter is the contributory retirement system for employees of the Commonwealth or subdivisions delineated in G.L. c.32, §§1-28. The bill as reported has two distinct features. First, members of the retirement system who are veterans (as defined), having at least twenty years accumulative service in the government, could obtain "creditable" service up to four years military service performed — which would have the effect of enhancing their ultimate benefits — on making certain contributions for an equivalent number of years in addition to their regular contributions. §§1, 3. Second, §2 of the bill would increase from the present five per cent to seven per cent the rate of withholdings from the regular compensation of government employees who are or will hereafter become members of the retirement system. These withholdings represent the members' contributions to the funding of the system, the balance required being furnished by government appropriations.

The House makes no inquiry as to the provision for veterans, but as to the far-reaching §2 it asks whether that section, if enacted, would be constitutionally valid notwithstanding G.L. c.32, §25(5), establishing membership in the retirement system as a contractual relationship under which the rights of members from time to time retired for superannuation are guarded against impairment as there set forth.

The proposed amendments to House No. 7409, besides changing the title of the bill, would state that §2 shall apply only to persons entering government service after January 1, 1974 (§3A), and would declare that it was the intent of the General Court to provide funds to reduce appropriations required for the payment of contributory pensions (§5).

The House asks whether §2 would be constitutionally valid if given only the prospective operation just indicated. . . .

Section 25(5) of G.L. c.32 states:

The provisions of sections one to twenty-eight, inclusive, and of corresponding provisions of earlier laws shall be deemed to establish and to have established membership in the retirement system as a contractual relationship under which members who are or may be retired for superannuation are entitled to contractual rights and benefits, and no amendments or alterations shall be made that will deprive any such member or any group of such members of their pension rights or benefits provided for thereunder, if such member or members have paid the stipulated contributions specified in said sections or corresponding provisions of earlier laws. . . .

Administration of the retirement system is largely in the hands of over a hundred retirement boards severally covering groups of State employees or employees of particular counties, cities, towns, districts or authorities, with two boards — the State Board of Retirement and the State Teachers' Retirement Board — having by far the largest numbers of employee-members. With some variations, however, the system is uniform in its application to all these boards and their members. The system is predominantly "compulsory" and "contributory"; most employees join the system automatically as the governmental unit which they serve accepts it, and they contribute to it by means of deductions automatically made from their salaries. Since the revamping of the system in 1945 (St. 1945, c.658, §1), the rate of deductions has been fixed at five per cent of salary. The participating governmental units by annual appropriations, on a pay-as-you-go basis, furnish the rest of the wherewithal, that is, such amount as is required, over and above the contributions of members (augmented by investment), to meet the legal obligations of the system, the amount being determined yearly by the actuary in the Commonwealth's Department of Banking and Insurance.

The legal obligations of the system consist of liabilities for a spectrum of retirement and similar benefits upon retirement of members for superannuation or for ordinary or accidental disability, as well as benefits in the form of termination allowances in certain cases of resignation of members, failure of reelection or reappointment, removal, or discharge.

The arrangements concerning retirement for superannuation are central to the system and are digested here. During the period of his employment the member will have made his contributions through deductions from his salary at the five per cent rate and these contributions and those of other members will have been earning further sums through investment. When age, term-of-service, and other qualifications are met, the member retires with benefits. The normal yearly amount of his retirement allowance is computed on the basis of age at retirement, years of "creditable" service with the government-employer, job grouping, and average rate of compensation over a prescribed period, with certain stated additions, for example, for veterans' status and "cost of living" increases, and with certain maximum limits. The computation results in a dollar amount as the normal yearly allowance. It is worked out mathematically without reference to how much of the allowance so determined represents funding through the member's own contributions, and how much is to be supplied by government appropriations. . . .

The impact on the superannuation retirement category of a raise in salary deductions from five to seven per cent can now be appreciated. Considering option (a), the change would mean a forty per cent increase of the member contributions providing the annuity share of the yearly allowance, and a comparable decrease in the pension share furnished by government, for the pension share represents roughly the difference between what the member has created in the way of an annuity and the fixed yearly retirement allowance to which he is entitled. The member would pay more without enlargement of the benefits. In essence the same is true of the other options. The general effect of §2 of House No. 7409 is indeed plainly indicated in §5, proposed as an amendment to the bill: "It is the intent of the general court to provide funds to reduce appropriations required for the payment of contributory pensions." This is done by increasing the members' contributions without substantially altering the current benefits, i.e. the amounts being paid out to members. . . .

We add as a matter of common knowledge that the level of retirement allowances to members has risen over the years as the result not only of the higher salaries entering into the computation formulas but of favorable legislative decisions like that proposed for veterans in the present bill. Appropriations have correspondingly mounted.

4. *Nature of the "contractual relationship" of G.L. c.32, §25(5).* It is convenient to start with the view that this court has expressed in the past about the Legislature's power to change the terms of a retirement benefits scheme when no statutory provision such as §25(5) has been applicable.

In Foley v. Springfield, 328 Mass. 59, 102 N.E.2d 89 (1951), the court said that benefits under a noncontributory retirement scheme — one in which the government footed the entire cost — were merely "gratuities" or "expectancies" rather than "contractual obligations" and therefore the Legislature could abrogate them at will. The statute under attack, amending the existing scheme, cut down in certain events the stated pensions payable to members in case they accepted and had earnings from outside employment after their retirement; in the particular instance the member had already retired when the statute was passed. In Kinney v. Contributory Retirement Appeal Bd., 330 Mass. 302, 113 N.E.2d 59 (1953), the same attitude was taken toward a phase of a chapter 32 contributory retirement scheme: it was competent for the

Legislature to reduce benefits payable to a member, and this without regard to whether the member had already fulfilled the conditions upon which those benefits would become due at the time the amendatory law went into effect. The amendment — changing the provision in force when the member entered the system and when he made the relevant contributions — declared that time of service as an elected representative in the General Court should not count as "creditable" service. The court aligned itself with those decisions in other jurisdictions, taken by the court to represent the numerical weight of authority, which treated compulsory contributory plans as not different from noncontributory plans, and held that none was to be read as establishing a contractual relationship vesting rights that were constitutionally protected against subsequent destructive legislation. To say that a member "contributed" to a plan by salary deductions was merely another way of saying — so it was suggested — that his salary was less than the stated amount, and the retirement benefits under the plan were still State-granted gratuities. . . . [I]n McCarthy v. State Bd. of Retirement, 331 Mass. 41, 116 N.E.2d 852 (1954), the court held that it did not matter that the member was actually receiving his retirement benefits when the statute was passed denying him "creditable" service for his period in the General Court. . . .

As is suggested by the disagreement of the Justices on the *Kinney* problem, the law in this country defining the character of retirement plans for public employees was not settled at the time (indeed it remains unsettled today). There was growing realization that public employees look upon pension and similar benefits as in substance delayed compensation for their services, and rely on these benefits as a security against destitution in their old age and against catastrophe. Government, on the other hand, sees retirement plans as a necessary means of attracting able workers who will remain on the job for the long run. These practical understandings have been reflected in court decisions characterizing retirement benefits as earnings rather than gratuities, and the plans as "contractual." See annotation, 52 A.L.R.2d 437 (1957). The cases in the mid-1950s might thus have been expected to raise serious questions not only among government employees but their employers as well.

A Special Commission to Study and Revise the Laws Relating to Retirement Systems and Pensions had been created in 1951 and was at work when those cases were decided. The Final Report of the commission in 1955 reflects the dissatisfaction with the decisions. The commission, however, was divided on what to do. A majority was prepared to add contractual language to §25(4) (to be entitled "Guaranty of Allowance by Governmental Unit"), but not to alter materially §25(5) as it then stood. Section 25(5) then allowed alteration from time to time or repeal of the basic provisions of chapter 32, but not so far as to reduce the amount of any annuity, pension, or retirement allowance previously granted, or to affect adversely benefits accrued to members by reason of previous contributions and service. Thus for members on the job, benefits for the future could be reduced without limit. A minority of the commission was not content with this narrow assurance to members. The minority wanted a full acceptance of the contractual idea, and referred to a New York constitutional provision in that style. It proposed legislation which would establish membership as a contractual relationship and entitle a member to the benefits provided from time to time during the period of his service without diminution by subsequent alteration or repeal; but an employee becoming a member after such a change would take subject to it. This envisaged the progressive vesting from time to time during a member's service of increasing benefits as they might be provided by the Legislature.

A spate of bills was introduced by various hands in 1955-1956, from which emerged St. 1956, c.525, amending §25(5); there has been no change in the text since 1956. Amended §25(5) definitely leans toward the minority proposal, but detached from its background this provision is not altogether clear. . . .

An advisory opinion which does not follow full debate and is not addressed to concrete cases is hardly the occasion to attempt a complete elucidation of the statutory language, an elucidation which could not be authoritative in any event. Still we think the following can be fairly said. The first, and dominating, clause of §25(5), overcomes the "gratuity" thesis and imports a "contractual relationship." The minimal meaning of this change is that the "contract" is formed when a person becomes a member by entering the employment, and he is entitled to have the level of rights and benefits then in force preserved in substance in his favor without modification downwards. Anything short of this interpretation would result in an approximation of the pre-1956 version of §25(5), and render the 1956 amendment aimless and nugatory. When we speak of the level of rights and benefits protected by §25(5) we mean the practical effect of the whole complex of provisions not excluding the deductions, as an increase in deductions is little different from a diminution of the allowance. There is a further interpretive question harder to resolve: whether a member is protected in additional benefits that may be legislated from the date of his becoming a member to the time of his retirement — i.e. whether the viewpoint of the minority of the commission was fully adopted. To this matter we return below.

"Contract" (and related terms such as rights, benefits, protection) should be understood here in a special, somewhat relaxed sense. The label "gratuity" could never have been taken with sober literalness, and so also for "contract." It is not really feasible — nor would it be desirable — to fit so complex and dynamic a set of arrangements as a statutory retirement scheme into ordinary contract law which posits as its model a joining of the wills of mutually assenting individuals to form a specific bargain. As the commentators show, a retirement plan for public employees does not readily submit itself to analysis according to Professor Williston's canons. . . .

When, therefore, the characterization "contract" is used, it is best understood as meaning that the retirement scheme has generated material expectations on the part of employees and those expectations should in substance be respected. Such is the content of "contract."

It is true that a few cases that adopt the label of "contract" have approached the terms of a retirement plan as they would a bond indenture, but closer to the realities is the view that "contract" protects the member of a retirement plan in the core of his reasonable expectations, but not against subtractions which, although possibly exceeding the trivial, can claim certain practical justifications. Attention should then center on the nature of these justifications in the light of the problems of financing and administering these massive plans under changing conditions. . . .

5. *Validity of proposed increase of rate of deductions.* The contract so envisaged is under the shelter of the impairment-of-contract clause, or what amounts to much the same thing, the due process clause of the Federal Constitution and State constitutional provisions cognate to the latter. The Supreme Court of the United States early held that a retirement plan, if fairly interpreted as involving mere gratuities or expectancies, could be whittled away by the State, see Pennie v. Reis, 132 U.S. 464, 471-472 (1889), and this court took the same position in its 1951-1954 gratuity cases cited above. On the other hand, a retirement plan establishing a contractual relationship invites a different analysis and whether viewed strictly as contract or as property may be constitutionally guarded against impairment. But it is basic that the State reserves police powers that may in particular predicaments enable it to alter or abrogate even conventional contractual rights.

Legislation which would materially increase present members' contributions without any increase of the allowances finally payable to those members or any other adjustments carrying advantages to them, appears to be presumptively invalid — invalid, that is to say, unless saved by the reserved police powers. Whether a situation of stress exists here sufficiently serious to call those powers into play and save the legislation is a question grounded ultimately in fact, not to be resolved in an advisory opinion. It is, however, instructive in this connection to note that in Allen v. Long Beach, 45 Cal. 2d 128, 287 P.2d 765 (1955), a statute simply increasing the contributions of public employees to a retirement plan from two to ten per cent of salary was denied enforcement. . . . That the maintenance of a retirement plan is heavily burdening a governmental unit has not itself been permitted to serve as justification for a scaling down of benefits figuring in the "contract," although no case presenting proof of a catastrophic condition of the public finances has been put. It should be added that the Legislature's opinion that justification does in fact exist for the modification of a plan is entitled to judicial respect; especially so if that opinion is buttressed by prior formal investigation of the facts.

What has been said about the presumptive invalidity of the proposed increase in the rate of members' contributions applies most clearly to members who entered the retirement system at approximately its present level of benefits for them (and while §25[5] in its present form was on the statute book). But there may be other members who entered when the level was lower and who have been the recipients of step-by-step enlargements of retirement rights and benefits through favorable legislation over the years. We revert to the question whether they can claim impairment if the proposed change of the rate of contribution, while worsening their current situation, does not reduce them in net effect below the level at which they entered the system. If they can claim impairment, the question would remain whether, in considering the seriousness of the impairment as related to a claimed justification for it, the government is conceivably entitled to any credit (so to speak) for its past indulgences to those members. One sees in the decisions a tendency to compare the situation just before the proposed reduction of benefits with that which would exist afterwards, without much if any consideration of the significance of a progressive increase of benefits in the past: perhaps the courts implicitly assume that there are corresponding enhancements of the members' just expectations. But the problem has not been analyzed exhaustively, and we can do no more than advert to it in the absence of concrete states of fact. It may be noted that the Legislature has means of preventing a given increase of benefits from becoming vested if it takes due precautions at the time.

6. *Validity of proposed increase of rate with respect to prospective employees.* The House inquires about the constitutionality of legislation applying the increased rate of deductions from compensation not to present members but only to those persons who will become members after January 1, 1974. We see no constitutional difficulty with such a provision. The expectations of a member safeguarded by §25(5) have their origin in the terms of the plan as they apply to him when he enters upon employment and becomes a member, not in other terms not addressed to him. Nor does it seem that a distinction in the applicable terms between present and future members would be arbitrary or discriminatory in a constitutional sense. However, the §25(5) "contractual" regime would — nothing being legislated to the contrary — attach to the new member from the date he joins at the level made applicable to him.

October 30, 1973.

◆ SPINA v. CONSOLIDATED POLICE & FIREMEN'S
PENSION FUND COMMISSION
41 N.J. 391, 197 A.2d 169 (1964)

WEINTRAUB, C.J. Plaintiffs seek a judgment that they and other members of certain police and firemen's pension plans are entitled to retire at age 50 after 20 years of service under the terms of Chapter 160 of the Laws of 1920. That statute had originally so provided, but amendatory legislation now requires 25 years of service and a minimum age of 51.

Plaintiffs were appointed policemen or firemen between 1940 and 1944. As we understand the situation, membership in their pension funds was closed by Chapter 255 of Laws of 1944, which required policemen and firemen thereafter appointed to participate in a new retirement plan created by that chapter.

The complaint is that the amendatory legislation enlarging the requirements for retirement under the 1920 statute is constitutionally void as an impairment of a contract or a taking of property without due process. On cross motions for summary judgment the trial judge found that precedents in our State firmly rejected the assault and hence ordered judgment for defendants. We certified the appeal before it was heard in the Appellate Division.

The legal issues must be viewed realistically against the story of these pension plans. . . .

Between 1887 and 1917, 26 laws were passed relating to retirement of policemen and firemen. By 1918 there were 55 funds covering 3,000 of a total of 3,700 policemen and 2,150 of 2,300 paid firemen. The plans varied, with service requirements ranging from 20 to 25 years and retirement age from 50 to 60. Benefits too were not uniform. The members contributed to some funds but not to others. Member contributions, where required, were from 1 percent to 2 percent of salary, while municipalities contributed from 1 percent to 4 percent of salaries. In addition there were miscellaneous revenues from certain tax sources and even from social events sponsored by the funds.

All of these funds had in common the promise of inevitable doom. The reason was that the annual revenues were not related to the ultimate cost of pension benefits, so that while current income might suffice for the earlier pensioners, the day had to come when little or nothing would remain for others, even of their own contributions to the fund. Accordingly there were periodic crises, in connection with which long-range solutions were offered, only to be rejected in favor of something more palatable for the moment.

In fact the 1920 act to which plaintiffs would recur was itself a "solution" that merely delayed a true one. On January 31, 1918 the Pension and Retirement Fund Commission submitted its report to the Legislature. It estimated that to be solvent, a typical police pension fund should start with an annual contribution of 17.13 percent of salary which would gradually decrease to a normal contribution of 8.34 percent in the course of 60 years, whereas in fact nearly three-fourths of those funds started with total annual revenues of less than 5 percent and in nearly half the funds the revenues were 2 percent or less. The report noted that legislation had already been sought and obtained to permit municipalities to appropriate additional moneys to meet deficits, and that as to a number of the larger funds the annual outlay, already at 10 percent of payroll, eventually would reach 20 percent to 25 percent because of the absence of reserves.

The Commission recommended stern measures, but instead Chapter 160 of the Laws of 1920 was enacted. It constituted a uniform retirement law to which existing and subsequent funds had to conform. It provided benefits more liberal than under a majority of the existing local funds whereas the Commission had recommended raising age and service requirements. The statute made little change in the contributions required of members and municipalities whereas the Commission proposed the rates be increased to provide for the benefits on an actuarial reserve basis. Chapter 160 also contained in section 4 the following provision upon which plaintiffs lay great emphasis and to which we will later refer:

". . . In case there shall not be sufficient money in said pension fund created as aforesaid, the common council or other governing body shall include in any tax levy a sum sufficient to meet the requirements of said fund for the time being."

In 1930 the Legislature constituted a Pension Survey Commission. In its report (1932) the Commission found that in 1931 there were 108 local funds operating under the 1920 law and covering 11,153 out of 15,417 active paid police and fire personnel. At that time there were 2,116 pensioners, with an annual pension roll already in excess of the total annual contributions to the funds. The Commission found that the contributions to the funds averaged 7.17 percent of the members' salary of which the members supplied 2.17 percent of salary, whereas the annual contributions needed to support the benefits for a new employee were an average of 15.67 percent of salary. In dollars, the funds had assets of but $3,269,000 and a deficit of $99,500,000, the latter being the amount which, if added at once and invested at 5 percent interest, would permit liquidation of future pension obligations. The Commission's remedial recommendations were not enacted.

The 1952 report refers to a study in 1940 by the State Chamber of Commerce. That study showed that by 1940 the municipal deficiency appropriations already exceeded the fixed municipal contributions required by law, and the two represented a total municipal contribution of 9.6 percent of payroll. The study estimated "conservatively" that in the ensuing 35 years the 190 municipalities having these funds would pay $250,000,000 in deficiency appropriations alone.

Such was the situation when these plaintiffs became members of the funds. In 1940 annual deficiency appropriations to seven of the larger funds reached $1,167,000, and by 1944 the figure climbed to $1,729,000, with more than one million of that sum contributed in Newark and Jersey City, the two municipalities joined as defendants in this action. The situation was so grave that in 1944 representatives of employee groups, taxpayer groups, municipal officials, and State officials joined in search of an answer. There emerged a compromise, a major step toward improvement but still short of a solution. The highlights were these. Active (uniformed) personnel could retire at age 53 (other personnel at age 60) after 25 years of service. The pension was based on average salary of the member during his last five years of service. The members and the municipality were each required to contribute 5 percent of salary. The State agreed to contribute $1,000,000 annually. No new pension funds could be established under Chapter 160, Laws of 1920; instead a state-wide actuarially sound Police and Firemen's Retirement System was created by L.1944, c.255, covering all new employees.

As thus revised, these funds were still fiscally unsound. Further, some of the gains of the 1944 compromise were lost when amendments were made in 1947 and 1948, lowering the retirement age of uniformed members to 51 and increasing certain benefits.

In 1950 the State Department of Banking and Insurance issued a report on the 1920 funds. It was found that as of July 1, 1949 the funds, numbering some 200, had a combined deficit of $209,110,636, being the sum which, if immediately added, would, with earnings at 3 percent, permit fulfillment of the funds' obligations. As to Newark and Jersey City, the report revealed their funds respectively had assets of $95,089 and $137,283 with deficits of $40,383,290 and $31,487,523.

This brings us to Chapter 358 of the Laws of 1952 which was a response to the 1952 report. The statement annexed to the bill referred to the "combined unfunded deficit of over $209,000,000.00," noted the "very serious concern to municipal officials and taxpayers, as well as the police and firemen," and stated the purpose to fund the deficits through a 30-year annual amortization program. To that end the statute consolidated all of the 1920 pension funds. It continued the 5 percent rate of contribution on the part of both members and municipalities, and required municipalities to contribute annually for the ensuing 30 years sums equal to two-thirds of the amount needed to achieve actuarial solvency at the end of that period, the remaining one-third to be contributed by the State. This act withstood sundry attacks by a municipality in City of Passaic v. Consolidated Police & Firemen's Pension Fund Commn., 18 N.J. 137, 113 A.2d 22.

As we have said, plaintiffs seek the right to retire at age 50 upon 20 years of service as the 1920 act originally provided. It is clear from the foregoing review that it was the 1944 amendment that invaded that alleged right since it raised the required period of service to 25 years and the retirement age to 53, which age was later reduced to 51 and so remains today. . . . This case is a rerun of Emanual v. Sproat, 136 N.J.L. 154, 54 A.2d 765 (Super. Ct. 1947). There, too, a policeman sought retirement at age 50 after 20 years of service and assailed the 1944 act which, as we noted above, had enlarged the requirements of the 1920 law. In rejecting the claim the court said "It is settled beyond question that the prosecutor had no contractual or vested right under the Pension Act of 1920." Our cases have uniformly held that the Legislature may revise[1] pension plans which governmental employees are required to join. . . .

As we noted above, the 1952 statute provides for payment by the State of one-third of the deficit over a period of 30 years. In City of Passaic v. Consolidated Police & Firemen's Pension Fund Comm'n, *supra*, 18 N.J. at p.147, 113 A.2d at p.27, it was urged that the State thereby created a debt in violation of Art. VIII, §II, par. 3 of our Constitution. We answered that "No debt has been created here, but rather present legislation merely provides that the State shall annually contribute to the fund." So here, the provision quoted above was simply an expression of legislative policy which remained within the control of that and every subsequent Legislature.

This is in harmony with the general approach in our State that the terms and conditions of public service in office or employment rest in legislative policy rather than contractual obligation, and hence may be changed except of course insofar as the State Constitution specifically provides otherwise. . . .

Plaintiffs say the abundant case law rejecting their position emerged from the erroneous concept that pension benefits are a mere "gratuity," whereas today their compensatory quality is more plainly in view. If these benefits are compensation, then, the argument goes, it should follow that there is an immutable right to them.

We think there is no profit in dealing in labels such as "gratuity," "compensation," "contract," and "vested rights." None fits precisely, and it would be a mistake to choose one and be driven by that choice to some inevitable consequence.

Government's contribution to a pension fund has several facets. In

---

1. Upon the premise that a member of the fund acquired no fixed right, it was held that after he was dismissed for dishonorable conduct, he could not claim retirement benefits upon the theory that he acquired a right to them prior to dismissal because he had already served the required period and reached the required age. Plunkett v. Board of Pension Commrs., 113 N.J.L. 230 (Super. Ct. 1934). And in Salley v. Firemen's & Policemen's Pension Fund Commn. 124 N.J.L. 79 (Super. Ct. 1940), it was held the Legislature could provide that pension benefits shall not be paid during imprisonment of the pensioner even though the retirement occurred before the statute was enacted.

part it compensates for services already rendered. It is also a reward for services to be rendered over the required minimum number of years, but the employee has no right to be continued in employment for enough years to earn it. In both respects the contribution seems compensatory, at least as of the time of eligibility for retirement. Yet it can be viewed also as noncompensatory payment to further the public employer's own interests, i.e., to permit the employer to release an aged servant who cannot decently be let out if he is unable to meet the necessities of life. Indeed, public pension plans are strongly urged on that account, and to that end public employees are usually required to be members.

As to the employee's contribution, it seems to be a sum already earned. Yet it is earned with a string, for it must go into the fund and in fact is deducted from the ostensible total pay. Moreover, the Legislature need not provide that the contribution must be returned upon cessation of employment; it may direct that it be retained for the common benefit of all. Pension plans go both ways, and neither approach can be said to be palpably unfair. Thus the employee's contribution, even though taken from his pay, is something he never had in hand and could not insist upon receiving.

In these circumstances, it seems idle to sum up either the public's or the employee's contribution in one crisp word. We have no doubt that pension benefits are not a gratuity within the constitutional ban against the donation of public moneys. And we think the employee has a property interest in an existing fund which the State could not simply confiscate. Whether the interest thus secured from arbitrary action is limited to the employee's own contribution or extends to the entire fund and whether it becomes still more secure upon retirement, we need not say. The question is too academic to be pursued, for our Legislature would not think of making off with a fund. The usual situation, as in the case before us, is a fund that cannot meet all of the present and future demands upon it. And the question is whether the Legislature is free to rewrite the formula for the good of all who have contributed. . . .

[E]ven as to the disposition of the fund itself, the contract concept is cumbersome. What happens if the plan is unsound, so that little or nothing will remain for those presently contributing? May there be a judicial receivership and some equitable proration if all parties to the plan cannot agree upon a program of rehabilitation? As a practical matter, legislative intervention is the only sensible approach. . . . True the needed power in the Legislature to revise a plan without the consent of the parties to the "contract" could be said to be "implied," but it seems odd to say the State may unilaterally rewrite its own contract or rewrite contracts between its municipal agents and others. We think it more accurate to acknowledge the inadequacy of the contractual concept.

In any event, we think it is clear that even in the "contract" jurisdictions, there would be little doubt as to the power of the Legislature to deal with an insolvent fund in the way in which our Legislature has dealt with the funds before us.

This of course does not mean that the Legislature may not recognize a moral obligation to provide public funds in aid of an insolvent plan. Our Legislature has in fact accepted a considerable measure of responsibility for the errors of predecessors with respect to the pension funds here involved and other pension programs as well. But we are satisfied that we should not surprise the Legislature with a decision that it heretofore imposed immutable obligations upon some 200 municipalities to underwrite the solvency of plans with liabilities running into several hundred millions of dollars notwithstanding a long line of cases which assured it that its enactments would remain within its power to revise. The responsibility for creating public contracts is the Legislature's. A commitment of that kind should be so plainly expressed that one cannot doubt the individual legislator understood and intended it.

The judgment is affirmed.

Notes

1. When plaintiff became a Seattle policeman in 1925, a state law provided for retirement at one half the salary attached to the rank held for the year next preceding retirement. He made compulsory contributions from his salary. When plaintiff retired in 1950, his relevant salary was $370 per month, but a 1937 statutory change had fixed a maximum pension of $125 per month.

The court said that a public employee's pension "is not a gratuity but is deferred compensation for services rendered." But it held plaintiff constitutionally entitled only to his "reasonable expectation," and confirmed to the legislature "the freedom necessary to improve the pension system and adapt it to changing economic conditions. . . . [Plaintiff's] pension rights may be modified prior to retirement, but only for the purpose of keeping the pension system flexible and maintaining its integrity." Applying this test, the court found that the municipal defendants "have not shown wherein this arbitrary limitation was justified." The dissenting justice identified many pension changes favorable to plaintiff during his service, described plaintiff's theory as "Heads, I win, tails, the city loses"; and suggested plaintiff should have sought other employment after 1937 if he didn't like the statutory change. Bakenhus v. City of Seattle, 48 Wash. 2d 695, 296 P.2d 536 (1956).

2. State pensioners in Ohio have a "vested" right to their benefits: *Held:* That right was not infringed by enactment of a state income

tax that applied to income from such pensions, even though the income and the pension had previously been "exempt from any state tax":

> Admittedly the net bankable retirement income might be the same whether the rate of pension is reduced, or a tax is levied on such income. However, there is a definite legal distinction between reducing the rate of a pension and levying a tax upon the income received from that pension. The vesting statutes prohibit only a reduction in the rate of payment. They do not prohibit the imposition of a tax. [Herrick v. Lindly, 59 Ohio St. 2d 22, 391 N.E.2d 729 (1979).]

◆ BERNSTEIN v. RIBICOFF
299 F.2d 248 (3d Cir.), *cert. denied*, 369 U.S. 887 (1962)

McLAUGHLIN, Circuit Judge. The district court sustained administrative decision requiring refund of Social Security benefits by plaintiff and latter appeals.

Appellant was born on September 15, 1886. He worked as a law clerk in his brother's law office for a number of years. He was admitted to the bar himself in 1950 when he was sixty-four years old. He has practiced law as a self-employed lawyer in Philadelphia since September 1951. During that period he has been an investing partner in a knitting mill. In 1951 he was awarded Social Security benefits of $68.50 a month effective September 1951. By the 1954 amendments to the Act these were increased to $88.50 monthly, effective September 1, 1954. As of the latter date appellant's wife was awarded benefits in the sum of $44.30 a month. Both benefits were paid during 1955 and 1956. These were re-computed in 1957 to total $162.80 monthly, effective July 1956.

Thereafter the Bureau determined appellant had received income from a trade or business in which he had rendered substantial services in excess of $2,080 during each of the years 1955 and 1956 and that he was not entitled to benefits for any month of either of those taxable years except for August 1956 when he was on vacation. Appellant and his wife were found to have been overpaid the sum of $1,593.60 for 1955 and $1,430.80 for 1956. . . .

Prior to the 1954 amendments, income derived from "the performance of service by an individual in the exercise of his profession as a . . . lawyer . . ." was not applicable in determining earnings under the Act. In 1954, the Act was amended *inter alia* to make deductions applicable ". . . from *any* payment or payments under this title, to which an individual is en-entitled . . ." and charging such individual ". . . *with any earnings* under the provisions of subsection (e) of this section. . . ." And 403(e)(4)(B), outlining the method of determining an individual's net earnings from self-employment, was amended to specifically eliminate the application thereto of Section 211(c)(5) which, as above noted, had made earnings of lawyers self-employed in their profession, not applicable in determining earnings from which deductions should be made under the Act.

Appellant urges that the 1954 amendments were intended to operate prospectively. Disclaiming any attack on the constitutionality of the amendments, he contents himself with the assertion that the administrative retroactive interpretation of them is at fault.

As has been already seen, the 1954 amendments specifically apply the new deduction provisions to all future benefit payments irrespective of the date an individual became entitled to benefits. . . . House Report 1698 makes it very clear that the Congressional action was taken in order to end the unfairness of this portion of the Social Security Act which had enabled full benefits to be drawn by individuals working in non-covered employment and self-employment regardless of the amounts received from those sources. The amendment was remedial. It caused all income of an individual to be considered on the question of benefits. It thereby deliberately not only removed an unwitting source of favoritism from the Act respecting individuals qualifying for benefits after January 1, 1955 but stopped any further benefits of this type which emanated from earlier qualification. . . .

Appellant next argues that, what he describes as the administrative interpretation of the 1954 amendments, deprived him of vested property rights, contrary to the Fifth Amendment. He . . . quotes several portions of both the majority and dissenting opinions in Flemming v. Nestor, 363 U.S. 603 (1960), commenting thereon. He fails utterly to mention the opinion's controlling general language characterizing the interest of an employee covered by the Act as "noncontractual," stating that

> To engraft upon the Social Security system a concept of "accrued property rights" would deprive it of the flexibility and boldness in adjustment to ever-changing conditions which it demands. . . . It was doubtless out of an awareness of the need for such flexibility that Congress included in the original Act, and has since retained, a clause expressly reserving it "[t]he right to alter, amend, or repeal any provision" of the Act. That provision makes express what is implicit in the institutional needs of the program. It was pursuant to that provision that §202(n) was enacted. . . .

We said in Price v. Fleming, 280 F.2d 956, 958-959 (3rd Cir. 1960):

> It is the fact that Nestor, as stressed by both appellant and the *amicus curiae*, was not eligible for benefits under the Act until after the statute covering deportation because of past Communist membership became effective. Nestor, states appellant, therefore had no accrued property right. But the Supreme Court did not decide Nestor on that narrow ground. It expressly rejects the concept of accrued property rights as being

a part of the Social Security System. It describes in terms certain the identical benefit with which we are dealing as "a noncontractual benefit under a social welfare program." Its clear mandate leaves to us only the determination of whether the inclusion of practice of law income in deductions from Social Security benefits by the 1954 Amendments "manifests a patently arbitrary classification, utterly lacking in rational justification." And with the 1954 Amendment including all income [the reference here is of course to all income from "net earnings from self-employment"] without any exception in the deductions for benefits under the Act, it is not possible to reasonably suggest that the Congressional decision abolishing preferential treatment for lawyers in this statute is "a patently arbitrary classification, utterly lacking in rational justification."

We are satisfied that our above conclusion was and is sound and that it rightly controls our decision on the "vested rights" contention before us.

◆ UNITED STATES TRUST CO. v. NEW JERSEY
431 U.S. 1 (1977)

Mr. Justice Blackmun delivered the opinion of the Court.

This case presents a challenge to a New Jersey statute, Laws 1974, c.25, as violative of the Contract Clause[1] of the United States Constitution. That statute, together with a concurrent and parallel New York statute, Laws 1974, c.993, repealed a statutory covenant made by the two States in 1962 that had limited the ability of The Port Authority of New York and New Jersey to subsidize rail passenger transportation from revenues and reserves.

The suit, one for declaratory relief, was instituted by appellant United States Trust Company of New York in the Superior Court of New Jersey, Law Division, Bergen County. Named as defendants were the State of New Jersey, its Governor, and its Attorney General. Plaintiff-appellant sued as trustee for two series of Port Authority Consolidated Bonds, as a holder of Port Authority Consolidated Bonds, and on behalf of all holders of such bonds.[3] . . .

In 1960 the takeover of the Hudson & Manhattan Railroad by the Port Authority was proposed. This was a privately owned interstate electric commuter system then linking Manhattan, Newark, and Hoboken through the Hudson tubes. It had been in reorganization for many

1. "No State shall . . . pass any . . . Law impairing the Obligation of Contracts. . . ." U.S. Const., Art. I, §10, cl. 1.

3. Appellant is trustee for the Fortieth and Forty-first Series of Port Authority Consolidated Bonds, with an aggregate principal amount of $200 million. At the time the complaint was filed, appellant also held approximately $96 million of Consolidated Bonds in its own account, as custodian, and as fiduciary in several capacities. There were then over $1,600 million of Consolidated Bonds outstanding.

years, and in 1959 the Bankruptcy Court and the United States District
Court had approved a plan that left it with cash sufficient to continue
operations for two years but with no funds for capital expenditures. A
special committee of the New Jersey Senate was formed to determine
whether the Port Authority was "fulfilling its statutory duties and obligations." The committee concluded that the solution to bondholder concern was "[l]imiting by a constitutionally protected statutory covenant
with Port Authority bondholders the extent to which the Port Authority
revenues and reserves pledged to such bondholders can in the future be
applied to the deficits of possible future Port Authority passenger railroad facilities beyond the original Hudson & Manhattan Railroad system." And the trial court found that the 1962 New Jersey Legislature
"concluded it was necessary to place a limitation on mass transit deficit
operations to be undertaken by the Authority in the future so as to
promote continued investor confidence in the Authority."

The statutory covenant of 1962 was the result. The covenant itself
was part of the bistate legislation authorizing the Port Authority to acquire, construct and operate the Hudson & Manhattan Railroad and the
World Trade Center. The statute in relevant part read:

> The 2 States covenant and agree with each other and with the holders
> of any affected bonds, as hereinafter defined, that so long as any of such
> bonds remain outstanding and unpaid and the holders thereof shall not
> have given their consent as provided in their contract with the port author-
> ity, (a) . . . and (b) neither the States nor the port authority nor any
> subsidiary corporation incorporated for any of the purposes of this act will
> apply any of the rentals, tolls, fares, fees, charges, revenues or reserves,
> which have been or shall be pledged in whole or in part as security for
> such bonds, for any railroad purposes whatsoever other than permitted
> purposes hereinafter set forth.

The "permitted purposes" were defined to include (i) the Hudson &
Manhattan as then existing, (ii) railroad freight facilities, (iii) tracks and
related facilities on Port Authority vehicular bridges, and (iv) a passenger railroad facility if the Port Authority certified that it was "self-
supporting" or, if not, that at the end of the preceding calendar year the
general reserve fund contained the prescribed statutory amount, and
that all the Port Authority's passenger revenues, including the Hudson
& Manhattan, would not produce deficits in excess of "permitted
deficits."

A passenger railroad would be deemed "self-supporting" if the
amount estimated by the Authority as average annual net income
equaled or exceeded the average annual debt service for the following
decade. Though the covenant was not explicit on the point, the States,
the Port Authority, and its bond counsel have agreed that any state

subsidy might be included in the computation of average annual net income of the facility.

"Permitted deficits," the alternative method under permitted purpose (iv), was defined to mean that the annual estimated deficit, including debt service, of the Hudson tubes and any additional nonself-sustaining railroad facility could not exceed one-tenth of the general reserve fund, or 1% of the Port Authority's total bonded debt.

The terms of the covenant were self-evident. Within its conditions the covenant permitted, and perhaps even contemplated, additional Port Authority involvement in deficit rail mass transit as its financial position strengthened, since the limitation of the covenant was linked to, and would expand with, the general reserve fund.

A constitutional attack on the legislation containing the covenant was promptly launched. New Jersey and New York joined in the defense. The attack proved unsuccessful. Courtesy Sandwich Shop, Inc. v. Port of New York Authority, 12 N.Y.2d 379, 190 N.E.2d 402, *appeal dismissed*, 375 U.S. 78 (1963). See Kheel v. Port of New York Authority, 331 F. Supp. 118 (SDNY 1971), *aff'd*, 457 F.2d 46 (CA2), *cert. denied*, 409 U.S. 983 (1972).

With the legislation embracing the covenant thus effective, the Port Authority on September 1, 1962, assumed the ownership and operating responsibilities of the Hudson & Manhattan through a wholly owned subsidiary, Port Authority Trans-Hudson Corporation (PATH). Funds necessary for this were realized by the successful sale of bonds to private investors accompanied by the certification required by §7 of the Consolidated Bond Resolution: that the operation would not materially impair the credit standing of the Port Authority, the investment status of the Consolidated Bonds, or the ability of the Port Authority to fulfill its commitments to bondholders. This §7 certification was based on a projection that the annual net loss of the PATH system would level off at about $6.6 million from 1969 to 1991. At the time the certification was made the general reserve fund contained $69 million, and thus the projected PATH deficit was close to the level of "permitted deficits" under the 1962 covenant.

The PATH fare in 1962 was 30 cents and has remained at that figure despite recommendations for increase. As a result of the continuation of the low fare, PATH deficits have far exceeded the initial projection. Thus, although the general reserve fund had grown to $173 million by 1973, substantially increasing the level of permitted deficits to about $17 million, the PATH deficit had grown to $24.9 million. In accordance with a stipulation of the parties, the trial court found that the PATH deficit so exceeded the covenant's level of permitted deficits that the Port Authority was unable to issue bonds for any new passenger railroad facility that was not self-supporting.

Governor Cahill of New Jersey and Governor Rockefeller of New York in April 1970 jointly sought increased Port Authority participation in mass transit. In November 1972 they agreed upon a plan for expansion of the PATH system. This included the initiation of direct rail service to Kennedy Airport and the construction of a line to Plainfield, N.J., by way of Newark Airport. The plan anticipated a Port Authority investment of something less than $300 million out of a projected total cost of $650 million, with the difference to be supplied by federal and state grants. It also proposed to make the covenant inapplicable with respect to bonds issued *after* the legislation went into effect. This program was enacted, effective May 10, 1973, and the 1962 covenant was thereby rendered inapplicable, or in effect repealed, with respect to bonds issued subsequent to the effective date of the new legislation.

It soon developed that the proposed PATH expansion would not take place as contemplated in the Governors' 1972 plan. New Jersey was unwilling to increase its financial commitment in response to a sharp increase in the projected cost of constructing the Plainfield extension. As a result the anticipated federal grant was not approved.

New Jersey had previously prevented outright repeal of the 1962 covenant, but its attitude changed with the election of a new governor in 1973. In early 1974, when bills were pending in the two States' Legislatures to repeal the covenant retroactively, a national energy crisis was developing. On November 27, 1973, Congress had enacted the Emergency Petroleum Allocation Act, 87 Stat. 627. In that Act Congress found that the hardships caused by the oil shortage "jeopardize the normal flow of commerce and constitute a national energy crisis which is a threat to the public health, safety, and welfare." This time, proposals for retroactive repeal of the 1962 covenant were passed by the legislature and signed by the governor of each State.

On April 10, 1975, the Port Authority announced an increase in its basic bridge and tunnel tolls designed to raise an estimated $40 million annually. This went into effect May 5 and was, it was said, "[t]o increase [the Port Authority's] ability to finance vital mass transit improvements." . . .

The trial court concluded that repeal of the 1962 covenant was a valid exercise of New Jersey's police power because repeal served important public interests in mass transportation, energy conservation, and environmental protection. Yet the Contract Clause limits otherwise legitimate exercises of state legislative authority, and the existence of an important public interest is not always sufficient to overcome that limitation. "Undoubtedly, whatever is reserved of state power must be consistent with the fair intent of the constitutional limitation of that power." Home Bldg. & Loan Ass'n v. Blaisdell, 290 U.S. 398, 439 (1934). Moreover, the scope of the State's reserved power depends on the nature of the contractual relationship with which the challenged law conflicts. . . .

When a State impairs the obligation of its own contract, the reserved power doctrine has a different basis. The initial inquiry concerns the ability of the State to enter into an agreement that limits its power to act in the future. As early as Fletcher v. Peck, the Court considered the argument that "one legislature cannot abridge the powers of a succeeding legislature." 6 Cranch, at 135. It is often stated that "the legislature cannot bargain away the police power of a State." Stone v. Mississippi, 101 U.S. 814, 817 (1879).[20] This doctrine requires a determination of the State's power to create irrevocable contract rights in the first place, rather than an inquiry into the purpose or reasonableness of the subsequent impairment. In short, the Contract Clause does not require a State to adhere to a contract that surrenders an essential attribute of its sovereignty.

In deciding whether a State's contract was invalid *ab initio* under the reserved powers doctrine, earlier decisions relied on distinctions among the various powers of the State. Thus, the police power and the power of eminent domain were among those that could not be "contracted away," but the State could bind itself in the future exercise of the taxing and spending powers. Such formalistic distinctions perhaps cannot be dispositive, but they contain an important element of truth. Whatever the propriety of a State's binding itself to a future course of conduct in other contexts, the power to enter into effective financial contracts cannot be questioned. Any financial obligation could be regarded in theory as a relinquishment of the State's spending power, since money spent to repay debts is not available for other purposes. Similarly, the taxing power may have to be exercised if debts are to be repaid. Notwithstanding these effects, the Court has regularly held that the States are bound by their debt contracts.

The instant case involves a financial obligation and thus as a threshold matter may not be said automatically to fall within the reserved powers that cannot be contracted away. Not every security provision, however, is necessarily financial. For example, a revenue bond might be secured by the State's promise to continue operating the facility in question; yet such a promise surely could not validly be construed to bind the State never to close the facility for health or safety reasons. The security provision at issue here, however, is different: the States promised that revenues and reserves securing the bonds would not be depleted by the Port Authority's operation of deficit-producing passenger railroads beyond the level of "permitted deficits." Such a promise is purely financial and thus not necessarily a compromise of the State's reserved powers.

20. Stone v. Mississippi sustained the State's revocation of a 25-year charter to operate a lottery. Other cases similarly have held that a State is without power to enter into binding contracts not to exercise its police power in the future.

Of course, to say that the financial restrictions of the 1962 covenant were valid when adopted does not finally resolve this case. The Contract Clause is not an absolute bar to subsequent modification of a State's own financial obligations. As with laws impairing the obligations of private contracts, an impairment may be constitutional if it is reasonable and necessary to serve an important public purpose. In applying this standard, however, complete deference to a legislative assessment of reasonableness and necessity is not appropriate because the State's self-interest is at stake. A governmental entity can always find a use for extra money, especially when taxes do not have to be raised. If a State could reduce its financial obligations whenever it wanted to spend the money for what it regarded as an important public purpose, the Contract Clause would provide no protection at all. . . .

Mass transportation, energy conservation, and environmental protection are goals that are important and of legitimate public concern. Appellees contend that these goals are so important that any harm to bondholders from repeal of the 1962 covenant is greatly outweighed by the public benefit. We do not accept this invitation to engage in a utilitarian comparison of public benefit and private loss. Contrary to Mr. Justice Black's fear, expressed in sole dissent in El Paso v. Simmons, 379 U.S. 497, 517 (1965), the Court has not "balanced away" the limitation on state action imposed by the Contract Clause. Thus a State cannot refuse to meet its legitimate financial obligations simply because it would prefer to spend the money to promote the public good rather than the private welfare of its creditors. We can only sustain the repeal of the 1962 covenant if that impairment was both reasonable and necessary to serve the admittedly important purposes claimed by the State.

The more specific justification offered for the repeal of the 1962 covenant was the States' plan for encouraging users of private automobiles to shift to public transportation. The States intended to discourage private automobile use by raising bridge and tunnel tolls and to use the extra revenue from those tolls to subsidize improved commuter railroad service. Appellees contend that repeal of the 1962 covenant was necessary to implement this plan because the new mass transit facilities could not possibly be self-supporting and the covenant's "permitted deficits" level had already been exceeded. We reject this justification because the repeal was neither necessary to achievement of the plan nor reasonable in light of the circumstances.

The determination of necessity can be considered on two levels. First, it cannot be said that total repeal of the covenant was essential; a less drastic modification would have permitted the contemplated plan without entirely removing the covenant's limitations on the use of Port Authority revenues and reserves to subsidize commuter railroads. Second, without modifying the covenant at all, the States could have adopted alternative means of achieving their twin goals of discouraging automobile use and improving mass transit. Appellees contend, however, that choosing among these alternatives is a matter for legislative discretion. But a State is not completely free to consider impairing the obligations of its own contracts on a par with other policy alternatives. Similarly, a State is not free to impose a drastic impairment when an evident and more moderate course would serve its purposes equally well. In El Paso v. Simmons, *supra,* the imposition of a five-year statute of limitations on what was previously a perpetual right of redemption was regarded by this Court as "quite clearly necessary" to achieve the State's vital interest in the orderly administration of its school lands program. In the instant case the State has failed to demonstrate that repeal of the 1962 covenant was similarly necessary.

We also cannot conclude that repeal of the covenant was reasonable in light of the surrounding circumstances. In this regard a comparison with El Paso v. Simmons, *supra,* again is instructive. There a nineteenth century statute had effects that were unforeseen and unintended by the legislature when originally adopted. As a result speculators were placed in a position to obtain windfall benefits. The Court held that adoption of a statute of limitations was a reasonable means to "restrict a party to those gains reasonably to be expected from the contract" when it was adopted.

By contrast, in the instant case the need for mass transportation in the New York metropolitan area was not a new development, and the likelihood that publicly owned commuter railroads would produce substantial deficits was well known. As early as 1922, over a half century ago, there were pressures to involve the Port Authority in mass transit. It was with full knowledge of these concerns that the 1962 covenant was adopted. Indeed, the covenant was specifically intended to protect the pledged revenues and reserves against the possibility that such concerns would lead the Port Authority into greater involvement in deficit mass transit.

During the 12-year period between adoption of the covenant and its repeal, public perception of the importance of mass transit undoubtedly grew because of increased general concern with environmental protection and energy conservation. But these concerns were not unknown in 1962, and the subsequent changes were of degree and not of kind. We cannot say that these changes caused the covenant to have a substantially different impact in 1974 than when it was adopted in 1962. And we cannot conclude that the repeal was reasonable in the light of changed circumstances.

We therefore hold that the Contract Clause of the United States Constitution prohibits the retroactive repeal of the 1962 covenant. The judgment of the Supreme Court of New Jersey is reversed.

Mr. Justice BRENNAN, with whom Mr. Justice WHITE and Mr. Justice MARSHALL join, dissenting.

Decisions of this Court for at least a century have construed the

Contract Clause largely to be powerless in binding a State to contracts limiting the authority of successor legislatures to enact laws in furtherance of the health, safety, and similar collective interests of the polity. In short, those decisions established the principle that lawful exercises of a State's police powers stand paramount to private rights held under contract. Today's decision, in invalidating the New Jersey Legislature's 1974 repeal of its predecessor's 1962 covenant, rejects this previous understanding and remolds the Contract Clause into a potent instrument for overseeing important policy determinations of the state legislature. At the same time, by creating a constitutional safe haven for property rights embodied in a contract, the decision substantially distorts modern constitutional jurisprudence governing regulation of private economic interests. I might understand, though I could not accept, this revival of the Contract Clause were it in accordance with some coherent and constructive view of public policy. But elevation of the clause to the status of regulator of the municipal bond market at the heavy price of frustration of sound legislative policymaking is as demonstrably unwise as it is unnecessary. The justification for today's decision, therefore, remains a mystery to me, and I respectfully dissent. . . .

I would not want to be read as suggesting that the States should blithely proceed down the path of repudiating their obligations, financial or otherwise. Their credibility in the credit market obviously is highly dependent on exercising their vast lawmaking powers with self-restraint and discipline, and I, for one, have little doubt that few, if any, jurisdictions would choose to use their authority "so foolish[ly] as to kill a goose that lays golden eggs for them." But in the final analysis, there is no reason to doubt that appellant's financial welfare is being adequately policed by the political processes and the bond marketplace itself. The role to be played by the Constitution is at most a limited one. For this Court should have learned long ago that the Constitution — be it through the Contract or Due Process Clause — can actively intrude into such economic and policy matters only if my Brethren are prepared to bear enormous institutional and social costs. Because I consider the potential dangers of such judicial interference to be intolerable, I dissent.

Note

Minnesota enacted the Private Pension Benefits Protection Act imposing a "pension funding charge" on any employer with more than one hundred employees — at least one of whom is a resident of the state — that closed its Minnesota offices with the intention of carrying on its business elsewhere. The state law was quickly preempted by federal pension regulation (ERISA, see p.541 *supra*); however, before that happened, appellant, an Illinois company, closed its Minnesota office and the state tried to collect a pension funding charge of $185,000.

The Supreme Court said application of the act to appellant "grossly distorted the company's existing contractual relationship with its employees by superimposing retroactive obligations upon the company substantially beyond the terms of its employment contracts," and so unconstitutionally impaired the obligations of contract.

Justice Brennan, dissenting, said the act "simply creates an additional, supplemental duty of the employer, no different in kind from myriad duties created by a wide variety of legislative measures which defeat settled expectations but which have nonetheless been sustained by this court." Allied Structural Steel Co. v. Spannaus, 438 U.S. 234 (1978).

D. PROPERTY AS RIGHTS AND AS POLITICS

◆ R. v. LONDON BOROUGH OF HILLINGDON
[1974] 2 All E.R. 643 (Q.B.)

Lord WIDGERY C.J. In these proceedings counsel moves on behalf of Royco Homes Ltd for an order of *certiorari* to bring up into this court with a view to its being quashed a purported grant of planning permission by the London Borough of Hillingdon dated 12th December 1973 and permitting the development of a parcel of land in the borough of Hillingdon known as 'Buntings', Swakeleys Road, for residential development. The permission was subject to certain conditions to which I will refer in a great deal more detail later on. If counsel for the applicants succeeds in obtaining an order for *certiorari* and the quashing of the planning permission in question, he then moves for an order of *mandamus* to require the planning authority, the London Borough of Hillingdon, to reconsider the planning application on which the planning permission is based and to decide it afresh according to law.

The whole matter, as I have said, arises out of the future of a small parcel of land at Hillingdon by the name of Buntings. It is land which on any view of the matter is appropriate for development and appropriate for development by the building of residential homes. The issue between the parties is whether this land should be developed by the planning authority, the borough council, under its duties as a housing authority for the provision of homes for those for whom the housing authority is responsible, or in the alternative whether it should be developed for residential purposes by its present owners, who are the applicants in this case.

The matter began on 18th May 1973 when the applicants made an application for permission to develop the land for residential purposes. . . .

The form of the permission, which is dated 12th December 1973, is to —

"GRANT permission for . . . Erection of 7 blocks of 3 storey flats to provide 36 two bedroom flats with garaging and parking and estate road at The Buntings . . ." The permission is made subject to conditions, many of which are not controversial and raise no sort of issue before us, but within the ambit of the conditions are four which constitute the basis of counsel for the applicants' submission that this grant of permission is a nullity.

Condition 2:

> The dwellings hereby approved shall be so designed as to provide space and heating standards at least to the standards (a) defined in Appendix I to circular 36/67 dated 25th April, 1962 issued by the then Ministry of Housing and Local Government, and (b) which shall have been designated as mandatory requirements for local authority housing schemes qualifying for Government subsidy or loan sanction, and the detailed drawings required by condition No. 6 shall show compliance with such standards.

What that comes to is that the planning authority are insisting as a condition of the planning permission that the dwellings shall be designed so as to provide space and heating to the standards required for local authority housing. For myself I would not have thought this condition on its face was a departure from the functions and powers of the planning authority to which reference must later be made, but counsel for the applicants, apart from other arguments designed to show that this permission is invalid, says that it is outside the powers of a planning authority to lay down conditions as to the internal design of houses or flats the erection of which it authorises. He says, as is the fact, that once a house has been built in accordance with planning permission, its internal arrangements can be varied to any degree without further planning permission. He, therefore, contends that it would be wholly illogical if a planning authority when granting planning permission tried to dictate the internal arrangements in the detail which this condition contemplates. For my part I do not find it necessary to reach a conclusion on that argument of counsel for the applicants and I deliberately do not attempt to pursue the matter further on that particular point.

Condition 3:

> The dwellings hereby approved shall be constructed at a cost per dwelling which shall not exceed the relevant housing cost yardstick (as defined by Circular 36/67) . . .

The condition goes on to further detail but the essence of it is contained in the sentence which I have read. The effect of it, if it is valid, is that the houses to be erected pursuant to this planning permission must be erected to a maximum cost equivalent to that to which local authorities are subject if they seek to obtain normal housing subsidies for development which they have carried out. This is a condition then the effect of which is to restrict the maximum cost per dwelling and in fact the yardstick chosen is the yardstick appropriate to the local authorities who seek, as they naturally would, to obtain the appropriate government subsidies for the houses which they erect.

Condition 4:

> The dwellings hereby approved shall be first occupied by persons (together with their families and/or dependents) who on the qualifying date shall have been recorded on the Housing Waiting List of the Hillingdon London Borough Council (as distinct from the Council's statutory register of applications for accommodation) for a period of not less than 12 months immediately preceding the qualifying date. The qualifying date for any person shall be any date within the period of 6 months before the commencement of his occupation of one of the dwellings hereby approved.

Again cutting through the detail of the language, this is a requirement that if the houses are erected pursuant to the permission obtained by the applicants, the occupiers of those houses shall not be occupiers chosen by the developers themselves but shall be persons who are on the local authority's housing waiting list in the terms of the condition which I have read. That is on any view an extremely serious restriction on the character of the occupier who is to go into these houses if they are built pursuant to this permission.

Finally, condition 5:

> The dwellings hereby approved shall for a period of 10 years from the date of first occupation be occupied as the residence of a person who occupies by virtue of a tenure which would not be excluded from the protection of the Rent Act 1968 by any provision of Section 2 of that Act.

Again the provision with regard to the security of tenure to be enjoyed by the respective tenants is there restricted when compared with the freedom which a developer would normally have in choosing not only the tenants who occupy his property but the terms on which they should so occupy it.

The case for the applicants before us today is that those four conditions are as a matter of law *ultra vires* as being in excess of the power to impose conditions enjoyed by a planning authority when granting a planning permission. . . .

That the planning authority has wide power to impose conditions has been a common feature of this legislation ever since 1947, or indeed it may be before that. The power is presently contained in §29(1) of the 1971 Act which provides:

> Subject to the provisions of sections 26 to 28 of this Act, and to the following provisions of this Act, where an application is made to a local planning authority for planning permission, that authority, in dealing with the application, shall have regard to the provisions of the development plan, so far as material to the application, and to any other material considerations, and — (*a*) subject to sections 41, 42, 70 and 77 to 80 of this Act, may grant planning permission, either unconditionally or subject to such conditions as they think fit. . . .

Those wide words "subject to such conditions as they think fit" confer authority for a wide range of conditions to be attached to planning permissions. However those words are clearly too wide to be given their literal meaning and a number of years ago they were restricted by a dictum of Lord Denning, which is constantly quoted in these matters. The dictum appears in the decision of the Court of Appeal in Pyx Granit Co. Ltd. v. Ministry of Housing and Local Government, [1958] 1 All E.R. 625, 633, where Lord Denning said this:

> The principles to be applied are not, I think, in doubt. Although the planning authorities are given very wide powers to impose "such conditions as they think fit", nevertheless the law says that those conditions, to be valid, must fairly and reasonably relate to the permitted development. The planning authority are not at liberty to use their powers for an ulterior object, however desirable that object may seem to them to be in the public interest. . . .

There, of course, is counsel for the applicants' case in a sentence. He says that four conditions were imposed to suit an ulterior purpose, a purpose ulterior to the duty of the borough council as planning authority. He says their purpose was to ensure that if a private developer was allowed to develop this land, he should have to use it in such a way as to relieve the local authority of a significant part of its burden as housing authority to provide houses for the homeless, and whether it is put as being a condition which is unreasonable or one not related to the development, or for an ulterior purpose, the argument for the applicants is that, however you look at it, these conditions are *ultra vires* and that they bring the whole planning permission down. . . .

I find Hall & Co. Ltd. v. Shoreham-by-Sea District Council, [1964] 1 All E.R. 1, helpfully similar to the situation which is before us. In Hall's case the local authority, with the best of motives, wanted in effect a new extension to the public highway and thought it right to require the developer to provide it at his own expense as a condition of getting planning permission. That was rejected in the Court of Appeal because it was a fundamental departure from the rights of ownership and it was so unreasonable that no planning authority, appreciating its duty and properly applying itself to the facts, could have reached it. I think exactly the same can be said of the conditions in issue in this case.

Taking nos 4 and 5 first of all, they undoubtedly in my judgment are the equivalent of requiring the private developer to take on at his own expense a significant part of the duty of the local authority as housing authority. However well intentioned and however sensible such a desire on the part of the planning authority may have been, it seems to me that it is unreasonable in the sense in which Willmer LJ was using the word in *Hall's* case. I, therefore, have no doubt for myself that conditions 4 and 5 are clearly *ultra vires*, but I have for some time thought that conditions 2 and 3 might be saved. Conditions 2 and 3, however strange and perhaps oppressive, do not by themselves appear to me to have a clear badge of *ultra vires* on them, although I would expect the Secretary of State on an appeal to him to have something to say about them. By themselves, however, I doubt whether they would have justified the allegation that they were clearly in excess of jurisdiction and clearly *ultra vires*. But I am persuaded in the end that one must not sever conditions 2 and 3 from conditions 4 and 5 because they are all designed to the single purpose. Conditions 2 and 3 are designed to see that the houses physically should be suitable for local authority tenants and conditions 4 and 5 are designed to see that in fact they should be occupied by the local authority tenants. I think the four being different facets of the single purpose stand or fall together and with that approach they must unquestionably fall in my opinion.

On the authority of *Hall's* case, the conditions being fundamental to the planning permission, I think they bring the planning permission down with them and that means that the applicants are entitled to the order of *certiorari* which they seek.

What happens after this is a matter which I do not think this court can finally deal with today. In my view the position following the order that *certiorari* should go is that the planning authority will now be required to reconsider the second application for planning permission and reach a conclusion on it according to law. I have little doubt that the local authority will do what is required of it under those circumstances and, therefore, at the moment it would be, I think, wholly premature for this court to consider an order of *mandamus*. I would for myself say that *certiorari* should go but that the application for *mandamus* should be adjourned *sine die* with liberty to apply in case it proves necessary hereafter to achieve the proper solution to this problem.

◆ OTERO v. NEW YORK CITY HOUSING AUTHORITY
484 F.2d 1122 (2d Cir. 1973)

MANSFIELD, Circuit Judge: Upon this appeal we encounter a type of confrontation that sometimes occurs when a housing authority's use of low cost public housing to promote or maintain racial integration clashes with other demands or interests in the community. Usually the problem arises when an effort is made to introduce a non-white minority into a community that is populated almost entirely by white residents. Here, however, the context is one in which the community is presently integrated, with a racial balance that is almost equally divided between white and non-white residents, but the housing authority seeks to stem a steady decline in the percentage of the white population in the community.

The primary issue is whether the New York City Housing Authority ("the Authority" herein), in selecting tenants for a public housing project on the Lower East Side, was required to adhere to its regulation, which would give first priority to present and former occupants of the urban renewal site upon which the project was constructed, despite its contention that the effect of adherence to its regulation would be to create a non-white "pocket ghetto" that would operate as a racial "tipping factor" causing white residents to take flight and leading eventually to non-white ghettoization of the community. The district court held that, although the Authority was under a constitutional and statutory duty to foster and maintain racial integration, this duty could not as a matter of law be given effect where to do so would be to deprive a non-white minority of low cost public housing that would otherwise be assigned to it under the Authority's regulation. It therefore granted summary judgment in favor of the plaintiffs.

We disagree as to the district court's interpretation of the Authority's duty to integrate. We do not view that duty as a "one-way street" limited to introduction of non-white persons into a predominantly white community. The Authority is obligated to take affirmative steps to promote racial integration even though this may in some instances not operate to the immediate advantage of some non-white persons. It was entitled to show that adherence to its regulation would conflict with this duty. We further find that a genuine dispute exists as to various material facts, including certain facts relied upon by the district court as the basis for its finding that adherence to the regulation would not "result in further ghettoization of the Lower East Side." Accordingly we reverse and remand for further proceedings not inconsistent with this opinion. . . .

Two apartment buildings containing 360 apartments for low income tenants are the immediate subject of dispute in this case. They were designed by and built for the Housing Authority, with the assistance of federal funds, to be part of a larger complex of low and middle income housing to be constructed on the site of the Seward Park Extension Urban Renewal Area which covers approximately 14 square blocks located on the Lower East Side of Manhattan ("Urban Renewal Area" herein). Overall supervision of the Urban Renewal Area is the responsibility of New York City's Housing and Development Administration ("HDA" herein). In addition to the two low income buildings, construction of three buildings comprising 600 middle income units is in the process of being completed.

The City of New York obtained title to the Urban Renewal Area on November 1, 1967. HDA proceeded to relocate the 1,852 families who lived there to other housing, many of them to public housing on the Lower East Side. These families were told at the time of their relocation that they would have a first priority to return to the buildings to be built on the site they were leaving. Although only 55 of these 1,852 families moved from the actual portion of the site on which the Authority's two-building project was constructed, all the families were given the assurance of first priority to return. Again, when the two buildings were nearing completion in January, 1972, and the process of leasing the 360 apartments they contained was commenced, HDA wrote to the class of urban renewal site residents, not just the 55 families who were project site residents,[1] notifying them that "all present and former residential tenants of Seward Park Extension will be given first priority to return to *any* housing built *within this urban renewal area* provided they meet certain qualifications [of income, family size, etc.]." They were also notified that if they were already living in public housing, they would have to apply for a transfer at their present project and notify the field office at the Seward Park Extension project of their intention to transfer.

The response by former site occupants to the invitation to return to the Authority's buildings in the Urban Renewal Area was much larger than anticipated. Experience had indicated that normally only 4 percent of those relocated from such an area would apply for return to the new housing constructed on it. In this case, however, 27 percent applied for apartments in the Authority's two buildings. Of the 360 available apartments, 161 were leased to former site occupants (15 to project site residents and the balance of 146 to urban renewal site residents). Three hundred twenty-two more applications from former site occupants were not honored. Instead, the Authority proceeded to lease or commit 171 apartments to the defendants-intervenors, who were not former site occupants. Former site occupants who inquired were told that the apart-

---

1. We adopt the terminology used by Judge Lasker, which describes the 1,852 families relocated from the overall Urban Renewal Area as "urban renewal site residents," those 55 families relocated from the site of the Housing Authority's project as "project site residents," and both groups considered together as "former site occupants."

ments were filled, or given no response at all. Of these 171 families, 48 were allowed to transfer from other public housing because of the proximity of the Seward Park Extension buildings to an historic synagogue at which they worshipped.

When those former site occupants (mostly non-white) who had applied for but were denied apartments discovered that the 171 apartments had been committed to others (mostly white) in disregard of the Authority's representation that former site occupants would have first priority, they filed a complaint on April 27, 1972, against the Authority and the Department of Housing and Urban Development ("HUD" herein) on behalf of a purported class of non-whites seeking admission to the Seward Park Extension project, including not only those who were former site occupants but also those in emergency need or in overcrowded public housing elsewhere on the Lower East Side. The complaint sought to prevent the Authority from renting to persons other than former site occupants until all in that category who were eligible for public housing and for whom there were appropriate apartments had been accommodated. The complaint also sought to prevent the Authority from discriminating against non-white persons in the renting of any apartments which might be available after all former site occupants were housed, and to compel HUD to insure that the Authority would follow its regulation and would cease all discriminatory practices in renting apartments in the Seward Park Extension buildings. . . .

On June 6, 1972, the Authority raised for the first time the issue of the effect of Judge Frankel's decision on the racial balance in the project, claiming that the result of the decision might be to violate the Authority's duty to prevent segregation in public housing. The Authority also pointed out that those persons to whom it had made commitments for apartments but who were not former site occupants wanted to be heard on the question of whether their leases could be abrogated to meet the requirements of the decision. . . .

The parties did not dispute the following facts, which Judge Lasker accepted: (1) that 60 percent of the 1,852 urban renewal site residents who had been relocated were non-white, (2) that of the 161 leases granted to former site occupants 60 percent went to non-white families and 40 percent to white families, while the 171 leases granted or committed to intervenors were divided 12 percent non-white and 88 percent white, and (3) that if plaintiffs prevailed, the project would become 80 percent non-white to 20 percent white by family, whereas if defendants prevailed, the ratio would be 40 percent non-white to 60 percent white by family and closer to 50-50 by population. However, an issue is raised to certain facts stated in plaintiffs' reply memorandum and accepted by Judge Lasker. Plaintiffs stated that even if they should prevail and the *project* should be made up of 80 percent non-white families, the 14 square block Seward Park Extension Urban Renewal Area as a whole, when completed, would "in all probability" become 73 percent white by family in view of the large amount of moderate income housing and housing for the elderly that was planned for the remainder of the urban renewal site. Conversely, the memorandum asserted that if the defendants prevailed, the number of non-white families in the Urban Renewal Area, when finally constructed, would be reduced to 18 percent. On the basis of this factual prognostication plaintiffs argued that if the Authority honored its first priority regulation it would "assist in integrating what [would] otherwise be a heavily white neighborhood." . . .

We have little difficulty in concluding that, subject to such overriding constitutional or statutory mandates as may exist with respect to racial integration, the Authority's regulation GM 1810 (rather than GM 1282) applies to this case. GM 1810, which was issued effective August 14, 1968, provides in pertinent part that "[p]riority in assignment of apartments is given to eligible applicants in the following order:

"1. site residents of the site upon which the project was built, and if the project is within an urban renewal area, model city area, or other redevelopment area, site residents of sites acquired to effectuate the plan for such area; . . ."

Prior to this 1968 regulation, GM 1282 (first issued in 1962) governed priority of admission to public housing. It restricted the first priority to *project* site residents only. Since the City acquired title to the Seward Park Extension Urban Renewal Area in November, 1967, the Authority urges that the earlier regulation applies and that only those former site occupants who were relocated from the actual site of the present two-building project, rather than the larger group relocated from the entire Urban Renewal Area, are entitled to the first priority to return, and then only to the project built on the site of their former homes. We disagree.

The Authority was not required to adopt any regulation giving first priority for admission to a particular public housing project to families it had relocated from the site. It did so voluntarily, out of commendable desire to minimize the disruption inherent in urban renewal by enabling uprooted occupants to return to the site of their former homes. Nor was the Authority obligated to give former urban renewal site residents the benefit of GM 1810 in renting apartments in the Seward Park Extension project, since that project was planned and relocation was commenced prior to the issuance of GM 1810, at a time when only former project site residents were guaranteed by GM 1282 a first right of return. But, as Judge Lasker recognized, the Authority itself acted consistently as if the 1968 regulation, GM 1810, applied and treated it as controlling. Most of the former site occupants were relocated after the new, broader regulation had become effective. They all were assured by HDA representatives, who had coordinated with the Authority, that families displaced from the Urban Renewal Area would have the first right to return to housing constructed on the urban renewal site. Even more importantly, when the Authority in 1972 sent out invitations to former site occupants to return, reiterating their entitlement to the first priority for admission to the new apartments, the notice was sent to *all* urban renewal site residents, even though only project site residents were sent such notices under the earlier regulation. Finally, of the 161 former site occupants who were actually given leases in the project, only 15 had formerly lived on the project site, whereas 106 had lived in the area but not on the project site. On the other hand, 40 families in the plaintiff class who formerly lived on the project site were nevertheless denied apartments in the two buildings.

In view of the Authority's disregard for its earlier regulation in actual practice, we would be closing our eyes to reality if we were to accept the view that only project site residents under GM 1282 and not urban renewal site residents under GM 1810 were entitled to the first priority for the apartments in the Seward Park Extension project. The undeniable fact is that the Authority proceeded under GM 1810. It was logical for it to have taken this course in tenanting the project in 1972, for more than four years had passed since its adoption of GM 1810. Having bound itself to that course in statements to plaintiffs, having publicly held itself out as prepared to follow that course with respect to this project and having in fact acted accordingly, it could not switch back in midstream to its earlier policy, even though it might have done so *ab initio*. The Authority's failure to assert its current contention when it first began to process applications for the apartments, its advice to some inquiring former site occupants that the apartments were filled, and its failure to respond to other inquiries, all adds weight to the conclusion that plaintiffs were deprived of a governmental benefit, i.e., a priority to specific public housing in their old neighborhood, without notice, hearing, or other due process of law. Plaintiffs had a right to rely on the Authority's regulation and representations. Under the circumstances the Authority was not entitled to disregard its own adopted procedure for offering apartments in the project in the absence of some overriding constitutional or statutory duty obligating it to do so.

Were the applicability of GM 1810 the only consideration in the Authority's choice of tenants for the Seward Park Extension buildings, our task would be completed. The Authority, however, points out that even if it would otherwise be bound to follow the first priority regulation as to all former site occupants, to do so in this instance would result in a racial composition in the two buildings of 80 percent non-white and 20 percent white by family. This result, the Authority asserts, is barred by the Constitution and by Title VIII of the Civil Rights Act of 1968.

Plaintiffs do not deny that the Authority has a duty to integrate under the 1968 Act. However, they contend, as Judge Lasker held, that the duty cannot be employed to deny non-whites housing. They further suggest that integration is achieved, in any event, when non-whites occupy 80 percent of a given project as well as when 80 percent of the project is white, particularly when Judge Lasker found that the Urban Renewal Area would probably be predominantly white overall and the Authority itself admits that the Lower East Side as a whole is 48 percent white. That overall figure, plaintiffs assert, will not be affected by adherence to the priority regulation since the plaintiff class will merely be transferring within the Lower East Side community. Defendants rejoin that large concentrations of non-whites in one or more pockets within the community would act as a "tipping" factor which would precipitate an increase in the non-white population in the surrounding neighborhoods, leading to a steady loss of total white population over a given period of time. It argues that it is under an obligation to prevent the formation of such concentrations or pockets of non-whites rather than limit itself to consideration of the overall current community proportions of whites and non-whites.

We agree with the parties and with the district court that the Authority is under an obligation to act affirmatively to achieve integration in housing. The source of that duty is both constitutional and statutory. Various discriminatory housing practices have been outlawed by judicial decree as violative of the Equal Protection Clause. An authority may not, for instance, select sites for projects which will be occupied by non-whites only in areas already heavily concentrated with a high proportion of non-whites. A tenant assignment policy which assigns persons to a particular project because of the concentration of persons of his own race already residing at the project has been prohibited. An authority is barred from using assignment methods which seek to exclude, or have the evident effect of excluding, persons of minority races from residing in predominantly white areas or of restricting non-whites to areas already concentrated by non-white residents. Not only may such practices be enjoined, but affirmative action to erase the effects of past discrimination and desegregate housing patterns may be ordered. . . .

An additional source of the affirmative duty to integrate is found in the 1968 Fair Housing Act ("the Act" herein) which provides that "[i]t is the policy of the United States to provide, within constitutional limitations, for fair housing throughout the United States," 42 U.S.C. §3601, and, in §3608, that "(d) The Secretary of Housing and Urban Development shall . . . (5) administer the programs and activities relating to housing and urban development in a manner affirmatively to further the polices of this sub-chapter." It is true that the Act was designed primarily to prohibit discrimination in the sale, rental, financing, or brokerage of *private* housing and to provide federal enforcement procedures for remedying such discrimination so that members of minority races would not be condemned to remain in urban ghettos in dense concentrations where employment and educational opportunities were minimal. However, we are satisfied that the affirmative duty placed on the Secretary of

HUD by §3608(d)(5) and through him on other agencies administering federally-assisted housing programs also requires that consideration be given to the impact of proposed public housing programs on the racial concentration in the area in which the proposed housing is to be built. Action must be taken to fulfill, as much as possible, the goal of open, integrated residential housing patterns and to prevent the increase of segregation, in ghettos, of racial groups whose lack of opportunities the Act was designed to combat. . . .

Judge Lasker recognized these mandates. However, he further concluded that because the primary intention of the Act's sponsors was to benefit minority groups, the affirmative duty to integrate public housing should not be given effect where it would deprive such groups of available and desirable housing. We disagree. Such a rule of thumb gives too little weight to Congress' desire to prevent segregated housing patterns and the ills which attend them. To allow housing officials to make decisions having the long range effect of increasing or maintaining racially segregated housing patterns merely because minority groups will gain an immediate benefit would render such persons willing, and perhaps unwitting, partners in the trend toward ghettoization of our urban centers.

There may be some instances in which a housing decision will permissibly result in greater racial concentration because of the overriding importance of other imperative factors in furtherance of national housing goals. But Congress' desire in providing fair housing throughout the United States was to stem the spread of urban ghettos and to promote open, integrated housing, even though the effect in some instances might be to prevent some members of a racial minority from residing in publicly assisted housing in a particular location. The affirmative duty to consider the impact of publicly assisted housing programs on racial concentration and to act affirmatively to promote the policy of fair, integrated housing is not to be put aside whenever racial minorities are willing to accept segregated housing. The purpose of racial integration is to benefit the community as a whole, not just certain of its members. In the absence of a history of deliberate discrimination against non-white persons, which would necessitate undoing the harmful effects, that objective cannot be achieved by adoption of a double standard under which low cost housing would be available to poor whites rather than to poor non-whites, or vice versa. . . .

We turn to the question of what effect the Authority's regulation GM 1810 has on its duty to integrate. . . . To the extent that the regulation conflicts with the Authority's duty to integrate, the regulation must yield. On the other hand, absent a showing of such conflict, the Authority may not disregard its regulation where the effect would be to violate the due process rights of former site residents who relied upon it. . . .

Thus we are confronted with genuine issues between the parties as to material facts bearing on the ultimate question of whether the non-white concentration in the two project apartments would have a "tipping" effect which the Authority was entitled, in the exercise of its duty to integrate, to avoid by suspending the operation of its priority regulation. Judge Lasker found it unnecessary to reach these issues, partly because of his conclusion that as a matter of law plaintiffs, as a minority group, could not be deprived of their priority rights through application of GM 1810, and partly because of his acceptance, without taking proof, of plaintiffs' projection that if they prevailed the Urban Renewal Area would be 73 percent white. However, since we disagree with his interpretation of the Authority's duty to integrate and with his acceptance of the disputed 73 percent figure, we conclude that the existence of a genuine dispute as to material facts rendered summary judgment an inappropriate procedure. A trial, at which the parties may offer evidence with respect to the relevant issues, is required.

At such a trial the parties would be permitted to offer evidence as to the relevant community, the impact of adherence to the priority regulation, including the declining white population in that community, the effect of transfers from other locations in the community to the Seward Park Project, estimates as to the total racial composition of the Urban Renewal Area upon completion, and the racial composition of the available population that is eligible for public housing. Such evidence should permit the trial judge to make findings as to whether adherence to GM 1810 would tend to precipitate a racial imbalance which might ultimately prevent the Authority from exercising its duty to maintain racial integration in the community. . . .

Finally, we turn to the question of whether, if the Authority can succeed in establishing that it was necessary to grant leases in the Seward Park Extension buildings to at least some of the white intervenors in order to meets its affirmative responsibilities to foster integrated housing, it nevertheless would be barred from renting apartments in the project on a priority basis to some or all of the 48 Jewish families whom it would transfer from other housing projects so that they could live in close proximity to a particular landmark synagogue at which they worship. . . .

[W]e conclude that it would be impermissible for the Authority to prefer persons of a particular faith for admission to a housing project in a preferred location if admission would otherwise go to others. If, on the other hand, the transfers were made solely on the basis of non-religious criteria, such as the personal safety of the transferees and the need to protect them against physical and verbal abuse, the fact that the transferees happened to be Jewish should not invalidate the transfers any more than would be the case if they were red-headed, blue-eyed, white, black, of foreign extraction, or possessed other non-religious characteristics which subjected them to harassment. Of course it would be preferable to incorporate the standard of personal safety in a clearly defined regulation rather than leave it to ad hoc determination, particularly since it is not difficult to visualize situations where persons of certain religious persuasions could be granted preferences under the guise of vague safety criteria. However, since an issue of fact has been raised as to the grounds upon which the 48 transfers were made in the present case we conclude that the defendants should be afforded the opportunity, upon remand, to show that the purpose was to assure the safety of the transferees rather than to accommodate their religious preferences.

Note

A policy of distributing scarce subsidized housing units to performing artists, in a complex on West 42nd Street in Manhattan, was upheld against a challenge that the policy favored whites over blacks. Daubner v. Harris, 514 F. Supp. 856 (S.D.N.Y. 1981).

PHOTOGRAPH 23-1
Robert Rauschenberg, poster for the Environmental Defense Fund

◆ ACKNOWLEDGMENTS

The authors acknowledge the permissions kindly granted to reproduce the materials indicated below.

Aaron, Shelter and Subsidies: Who Benefits from Federal Housing Benefits from Federal Housing Policies. Copyright © 1972 by the Brookings Institution, Washington, D.C. Reprinted with permission.

Abbott, Housing Policy, Housing Codes and Tenant Remedies. Boston University Law Review. Reprinted with permission.

Ackerman, Regulating Slum Housing Markets on Behalf of the Poor: Of Housing Codes, Housing Subsidies and Income Redistribution Policy. Reprinted by permission of the Yale Law Journal Company and Fred B. Rothman from Yale Law Journal, Vol. 80, pp. 1102-1106, 1113-1116.

Agnello and Donnelly, Property Rights and Efficiency in the Oyster Industry. Journal of Law and Economics. Reprinted with permission.

American Law Institute, Model Land Development Code, copyright © 1975 by the American Law Institute. Reprinted with permission of the American Law Institute.

Berger, Unification of the Law of Servitudes. University of Southern California Law Review. Reprinted with permission.

Berger, A Policy Analysis of Promises Respecting the Use of Land. Minnesota Law Review. Reprinted with permission.

Berger, Condominium: Shelter on a Statutory Foundation. Columbia Law Review. Reprinted with permission.

Blumberg and Robbins, Beyond URLTA: a Program for Achieving Real Tenant Goals, copyright © 1976 by the Harvard Civil Rights-Civil Liberties Law Review. Reprinted with permission.

Bordwell, The Repeal of the Statute of Uses, copyright © 1926 by The Harvard Law Review Association. Reprinted with permission.

Calabresi and Melamed. One View of the Cathedral. Copyright © 1972 by The Harvard Law Review Association. Reprinted with permission.

Cardozo, The Growth of the Law. Copyright © 1924 by Yale University Press. Reprinted with permission.

Chandler, Farewell My Lovely. Copyright © Alfred A. Knopf, Inc. Reprinted with permission.

Christman, Tin Horns and Calico (Cornwallville, N.Y.: Hope Farm Press 1975). Reprinted with permission.

1469

Clark, Real Covenants and Other Interests which Run with the Land, Callaghan & Co. Reprinted with permission.

Cobbe, Conversion of Apartments to Condominiums and Cooperatives. Michigan Journal of Law Reform. Reprinted with permission.

Cohen, Dialogue on Private Property, 9 Rutgers Law Review 357 (1954). Copyright © Rutgers—the State University. Reprinted with permission.

Comment, Yes Virginia—There is a Torrens Act. Reprinted with the permission of the University of Richmond Law Review.

David, Urban Land Development, copyright © 1968 by the President and Fellows of Harvard College. Reprinted by permission.

Demsetz, Some Aspects of Property Rights. Journal of Law and Economics. Reprinted with permission.

Dunham, Land Parcel Identifiers and the Uniform Land Transactions Act. University of Cincinnati Law Review. Reprinted with permission.

Dunham, Promises Respecting the Use of Land. Journal of Law and Economics. Reprinted with permission.

Ellickson, Alternatives to Zoning. Copyright © 1973 by the University of Chicago Law Review. Reprinted with permission.

Ellickson, Cities and Homeowners Associations; Frug, A Reply. University of Pennsylvania Law Review. Reprinted with permission of University of Pennsylvania Law Review and the authors.

Friedman, Contract Law in America (Madison: The University of Wisconsin Press). Copyright © 1965 by the Regents of the University of Wisconsin. Reprinted with permission.

Glendon, Matrimonial Property. Tulane Law Review. Reprinted with permission.

Griffin, The About Turn. American Journal of Comparative Law. Reprinted with permission.

Hay, Albion's Fatal Tree. Reprinted with permission of Allen Lane Penguin Books, Ltd.

Hirsch, Social Limits to Growth. Reprinted by permission of Harvard University Press © 1976 Harvard University Press.

Holdsworth, An Historical Introduction to the Land Law. Reprinted by permission of the Oxford University Press.

Horwitz, The Transformation in the Conception of Property in American Law: 1780-1860. Copyright © 1973 by the University of Chicago. Reprinted with permission.

Hyatt, Condominium and Homeowner Associations. Reprinted by permission of the Emory Law Journal of the Emory School of Law. All rights reserved.

Johnston, Sex and Property. New York University Law Review. Reprinted with permission.

Jordahl, Conservation and Scenic Easements. 39 Journal of Land

Economics. Copyright © 1963 by the Board of Regents of the University of Wisconsin system. Reprinted with permission.

Kantowitz, Women and the Law. Copyright © 1969 by Leo Kantowitz. Reprinted by permission.

Kennedy, Legal Formality. Journal of Legal Studies. Reprinted with permission.

Kennedy, The Structure of Blackstone's Commentaries. 28 Buffalo Law Review 205, 210-211 (1979) © with Buffalo Law Review. Reprinted with permission.

Kennedy and Michelman, Are Property and Contract Efficient? 8 Hofstra Law Review 711 (1980). Reprinted with permission.

Kiralfy, "The English Law," in Comparative Law of Matrimonial Property (Leiden, Netherlands: International Publishing Co.). Reprinted with permission.

Kulzer, Law and the Housewife: Property, Divorce and Death. Copyright © 1975 by the University of Florida Law Review. Reprinted with permission.

Langbein, Substantial Compliance with the Wills Act. Copyright © 1975 by The Harvard Law Review Association. Reprinted with permission.

Lawson, Introduction to the Law of Property. Reprinted with permission of the Oxford University Press.

Levy, Exclusionary Zoning. Reprinted with permission from Planning, the magazine of the American Society of Planning Officials, Chicago.

McDougal, Title Registration and Land Law Reform: A Reply. Copyright © 1941 by the University of Chicago. Reprinted with permission.

Mandelker, Delegation of Power and Function in Zoning Administration. Washington University Law Quarterly. Reprinted with permission.

Llewellyn and Hoebel, The Cheyenne Way. University of Oklahoma Press. Reprinted with permission.

Markovits, Marriage and the State. Copyright © 1971 by the Board of Trustees of the Leland Stanford Junior University. Reprinted with permission.

Marx and Engels, The German Ideology, from the Marx-Engels Reader, edited by Robert C. Tucker. Copyright © 1972 by W. W. Norton & Company, Inc. Reprinted with permission.

Marx, The Grundrisse, edited and translated by David McLellan. Copyright © 1971 by David McLellan. Reprinted with permission of Harper and Row Publishers.

Meyers, The Covenant of Habitability and the American Law Institute. Copyright 1975 by the Board of Trustees of the Leland Stanford Junior University. Reprinted with permission.

Michelman, Property as a Constitutional Right. 38 Washington & Lee Law Review 1097 (1981). Reprinted with permission.

Mosier and Scobie, Modern Legislation, Metropolitan Court, Miniscule Results. University of Michigan Journal of Law Reform. Reprinted with permission.

Nader and Blackwell, You and Your Pension. Copyright © Grossman Publishers. Reprinted with permission.

Note, Condominium Regulation: Beyond Disclosure. Reprinted with permission of University of Pennsylvania Law Review and Fred B. Rothman, Co.

Note, Fiduciary Standards and the Prudent Man Rule. Copyright © 1975 by The Harvard Law Review Association. Reprinted with permission.

Note on Indian Views of Property. Reprinted with permission from Michigan Natural Resources Magazine, March-April 1974.

Note, Tenant Unions: Collective Bargaining and the Low Income Tenant. Reprinted by permission of the Yale Law Journal Co. and Fred B. Rothman from the Yale Law Journal, Vol. 77, pp. 1383-87, 1395-96.

Note, The Great Green Hope. Copyright © 1976 by the Board of Trustees of the Leland Stanford Junior University. Reprinted with permission.

Offer to Purchase Real Estate and Purchase and Sale Agreement, published by the Greater Boston Real Estate Board. Reprinted with permission. The forms may not be copied or otherwise reproduced without the express written permission of the Greater Boston Real Estate Board.

Pasley, book review. Minnesota Law Review. Reprinted with permission.

Perkins et al., Uniform Acts for Statutory Will. ABA Real Property, Probate & Trust Journal. Reprinted with permission.

Philbrick, Changing Conceptions of Property Law. Reprinted with permission of the Pennsylvania Law Review and Fred B. Rothman & Co.

Plucknett, A Concise History of The Common Law. Copyright © Little, Brown & Co. (Boston: 1956). Reprinted with permission.

Polinsky, Economic Analysis as a Defective Product. Harvard Law Review. Copyright © 1974 by the Harvard Law Review Association. Reprinted with permission.

Posner, Economic Analysis of Law, Little, Brown & Co. (Boston: 1973). Reprinted with permission.

Prucha, American Indian Policy in the Formative Years © 1962 Harvard University Press. Reprinted with permission of Harvard University Press.

Radin, Property and Personhood. Stanford Law Review. Reprinted with permission.

Rauschenberg, "Earth Day," 1970. Publisher: Gemini, G.E.L. Reprinted with permission.

Reichman, Unified Concept of Servitudes. Southern California Law Review. Reprinted with permission.

Reich, The New Property. Reprinted by permission of the Yale Law Journal Co. and Fred B. Rothman Co. from Yale Law Journal, Vol. 73, pp. 769-774, 785.

Reichman, Residential Private Governments. Copyright © 1976 by the University of Chicago. Reprinted with permission.

Reno, The Enforcement of Equitable Servitudes in Land. Reprinted with permission of Virginia Law Review and Fred B. Rothman & Co.

Sand, Socialist Response: Environmental Protection in the GDR. Reprinted by permission of the Ecology Law Quarterly.

Sax and Hiestend, Slumlordism as a Tort. Reprinted with the permission of the authors and the Michigan Law Review.

Sclar, From the Legislatures: Minnesota Simplifies Land Registration. Reprinted by permission from the Real Estate Law Journal (Winter 1983) Vol. 11, no. 3, copyright © 1983 Warren, Gorham & Lamont, Inc., 210 South Street, Boston, Mass. All rights reserved.

Seeley, Access to Sunlight. Harvard International Law Journal. Reprinted with permission.

Shupe, Waste in Western Water Law. Oregon Law Review. Reprinted with permission. Copyright © 1982 by University of Oregon.

Siegel, Is the Modern Lease a Contract or a Conveyance? Journal of Urban Law. Reprinted with permission.

Simes and Taylor, The Improvement of Conveyancing by Legislation. Copyright © University of Michigan. Reprinted with permission.

Simes, Public Policy and the Dead Hand. Copyright © University of Michigan. Reprinted by permission.

Simpson, An Introduction to the History of the Land Law. Reprinted with permission of the Oxford University Press.

Sternlieb, The Tenant Landlord. Reprinted with permission of the Center for Urban Policy Research, Rutgers—the State University of New Jersey.

Sternlieb and Burchell, Residential Abandonment. Reprinted with permission of the Center for Urban Policy Research, Rutgers—the State University of New Jersey.

Sutherland, Tenantry of New York Manors. Reprinted with permission from the Cornell Law Review and Fred B. Rothman & Co.

Swanberg, Pulitzer. Reprinted with permission from W. A. Swanberg. Published by Charles Scribner's Sons, 1967.

"Teamsters at End of Line." Reprinted with permission from Variety, March 31, 1976.

West, Penn's Treaty with the Indians. Courtesy of the Pennsylvania Academy of the Fine Arts. Reprinted with permission.

Wolf, Shared Appreciation Mortgages. Reprinted with permission of Lincoln Institute.

Wright, letter to Professor Rabin, 60 Cornell Law Review 549 (1984). Reprinted with permission of Judge Wright, Professor Rabin, Cornell Law Review, and Fred B. Rothman & Co.

Younger, Community Property. New York University Law Review. Reprinted with permission.

◆ TABLE OF CASES

Italics indicates principal cases.

◆ INDEX